The Handbook of Intellectual Disability and Clinical Psychology Practice

The Handbook of Intellectual Disability and Clinical Psychology Practice will equip clinical psychologists in training with the skills necessary to complete a clinical placement in the field of intellectual disability.

The book is divided into seven sections, which cover **conceptual frameworks, assessment frameworks** and **intervention frameworks**, and the specific problems that arise in **infancy and early childhood, middle childhood, adolescence** and **adulthood**. Chapters combine discussion of the theoretical and empirical issues with practical considerations. The authors incorporate detailed practice descriptions throughout, which will allow clinicians to use the book as a step-by-step guide to clinical work. Practice exercises are also included where relevant to aid skills development.

This comprehensive, evidence-based practice handbook will prove an invaluable resource for anyone undertaking postgraduate training in clinical psychology, as well as practising clinical psychologists, psychiatrists and psychotherapists.

The Handbook of Intellectual Disability and Clinical Psychology Practice is one of a set of three handbooks published by Routledge, which includes *The Handbook of Child and Adolescent Clinical Psychology* and *The Handbook of Adult Clinical Psychology* (edited by Alan Carr and Muireann McNulty).

Alan Carr is professor and director of the Doctoral Programme in Clinical Psychology at University College Dublin and Consultant Psychologist and Family Therapist at the Clanwilliam Institute Dublin.

Gary O'Reilly is deputy director of the Doctoral Programme in Clinical Psychology at University College Dublin. He is a principal clinical psychologist a the Children's University Hospital Temple Street.

Patricia Noonan Walsh is NDA Professor of Disability Studies and director of the Centre for Disability Studies at University College Dublin.

John McEvoy is lecturer in Psychology at the Dundalk Institute of Technology and Research Associate with the Centre for Disability Studies at University College Dublin.

The Handbook of Intellectual Disability and Clinical Psychology Practice

Edited by

Alan Carr, Gary O'Reilly, Patricia Noonan Walsh and John McEvoy

Routledge
Taylor & Francis Group

LONDON AND NEW YORK

First published 2007 by Routledge
27 Church Road, Hove, East Sussex BN3 2FA

Simultaneously published in the USA and Canada
by Routledge
270 Madison Ave, New York, NY 10016

Routledge is an imprint of the Taylor & Francis Group, an informa
business

Typeset in Times by RefineCatch Limited, Bungay, Suffolk
Printed and bound in Great Britain by
TJ International Ltd, Padstow, Cornwall
Paperback cover design by Sandra Heath

British Library Cataloguing-in-Publication Data
A catalogue record for this book is available from the British Library

Library of Congress Cataloging-in-Publication Data
The handbook of intellectual disability and clinical psychology
practice / edited by Alan Carr . . . [et al.].
    p. ; cm.
  Includes bibliographical references and index.
  ISBN-13: 978-1-58391-861-6 (hardback)
  ISBN-10: 1-58391-861-2 (hardback)
  ISBN-13: 978-1-58391-862-3 (pbk.)
  ISBN-10: 1-58391-862-0 (pbk.)
  1. Mental retardation—Handbooks, manuals, etc.   2. Clinical
psychology—Handbooks, manuals, etc.   I. Carr, Alan, Dr.
  [DNLM: 1. Mentally Disabled Persons—rehabilitation.   2. Mentally
Disabled Persons—psychology.   3. Psychology, Clinical—methods.
WM 300 H2356 2007]
  RC570.2.H365 2007
  616.89—dc22   2007000369

ISBN: 978-1-58391-861-6 (hbk)
ISBN: 978-1-58391-862-3 (pbk)

Contents

Figures

Tables

Preface

People with intellectual disability, as children and later as adults, are at significantly increased risk of facing discrimination, social exclusion, and abuse. Children with intellectual disability are much more likely than their non-disabled peers to experience child poverty. As adults, people with intellectual disabilities are significantly less likely than their non-disabled peers to move out of their family home, have long-term intimate relationships, be employed, have friends and participate in the life of their communities. They are also more likely to live in poor health, have poorer mental health and to die young. These inequalities transcend national boundaries.

Clinical psychology, as both an academic discipline and a profession, has an important role to play in addressing these inequalities. Support and intervention offer the possibility of improving health, well-being and social functioning, enhancing resilience and helping people overcome emotional and behavioural challenges.

To make a real and lasting difference, however, supports and interventions need to be based on robust evidence about the nature and distribution of need, and the effectiveness and efficiency of different approaches to meeting need. For far too long have interventions been based on fads, fashions and the interests of professionals.

This book does an excellent job of bringing together existing knowledge that is relevant to the practice of clinical psychology. It highlights how much we have learned over the past three decades about the *possibilities* of providing effective support to people with intellectual disabilities across the lifespan. We now have relatively robust evidence of the efficacy of particular approaches to intervention for a wide range of challenges (we know much about what *can* work). This evidence, of course, provides an effective guide to clinical practice.

However, the contributions also provide a salutary reminder about how much more we need to learn about the effectiveness (what *does* work in routine practice) and efficiency (which approaches offer the *best* cost–benefit ratio in routine practice) of our interventions and supports. Addressing this lack of this type of evidence will provide a significant challenge to both the profession and the discipline of clinical psychology over the next decade.

Eric Emerson
Professor of Disability and Health Research
Institute for Health Research, Lancaster University, UK

Foreword and acknowledgements

This *Handbook of Intellectual Disability and Clinical Psychology Practice* provides clinical psychologists in training with a comprehensive practice handbook to help build the skills necessary to complete a clinical placement in the field of adult mental health. While practical in orientation, the book is based solidly on empirical evidence. This book is one of a set of three which cover the lion's share of the curriculum for clinical psychologists in training in the UK and Ireland. The other two volumes are the *Handbook of Child and Adolescent Clinical Psychology Second Edition* (by Alan Carr) and the *Handbook of Adult Clinical Psychology* (edited by Alan Carr and Muireann McNulty). The book aims to provide clinical psychologists in training in the UK and Ireland with a comprehensive practice handbook to equip them with the skills necessary to complete a clinical placement in the field of disability. While practical in orientation, the book is based solidly on empirical evidence. That is, it is an evidence-based practice manual. The book is divided into seven sections. Section 1 covers general conceptual frameworks for practice including those for diagnosis and case formulation. Section 2 focuses on assessment of ability and quality of life, and the processes of interviewing and report writing. Section 3 covers intervention frameworks, specifically person-centred planning, applied behavioural analysis and cognitive behaviour therapy. Section 4 deals with preschool difficulties and problems initially evident in the first five years: feeding, sleeping and toileting problems; and challenges posed by specific syndromes and autism spectrum disorders. Section 5 covers challenges associated with intellectual disability first evident or prevalent in middle childhood, including meeting special educational needs and addressing challenging behaviour and communication difficulties. Section 6 deals with adolescent concerns including life skills training, relationships and sexuality. Section 7 focuses on vocational and residential challenges of adulthood and aging; managing mental health problems; and managing complex practice-related issues. Chapters cover theoretical and empirical issues on the one hand and practice issues on the other. Practice descriptions are given in sufficient detail to allow clinicians to use the book as a step-by-step guide to clinical work. Chapters close with a summary, and suggestions for further reading for practitioners and families containing a member with an intellectual disability. Where appropriate, in many chapters, practice exercises to aid skills development also have been included.

We are grateful to the American Psychiatric Association for permission to reproduce diagnostic criteria previously published in 2000 in the Text Revision of the Fourth Edition of the *Diagnostic and Statistical Manual of Mental Disorders* and to the World Health Organization for permission to reproduce diagnostic criteria previously published in 1992 in *The ICD-10 Classification of Mental and Behavioural Disorders: Clinical Descriptions and Diagnostic Guidelines*.

We are grateful to our many colleagues, friends and families for their support during the production of this volume. We owe a debt of gratitude to our clients and students for inviting us to articulate the ideas in this volume with increased clarity.

Alan Carr
(on behalf of the Editorial Team)
April 2006

Editors

Alan Carr, PhD is Professor and Director of the Doctoral Programme in Clinical Psychology at UCD and consultant clinical psychologist at the Clanwilliam Institute in Dublin. His publications include the *Handbook of Child and Adolescent Clinical Psychology* (second edition, Brunner Routledge, 2006), *Handbook of Adult Clinical Psychology* (with Muireann McNulty, Brunner-Routledge, 2006), and *Family Therapy: Concepts Process and Practice* (second edition, Wiley, 2006). Professor Carr has conducted clinical practice in the UK, Canada and Ireland.

Gary O'Reilly, PhD is Senior Lecturer and Deputy Director of the Doctoral Programme in Clinical Psychology at UCD and co-ordinator of the disability curriculum for this programme. He is a principal clinical psychologist at the Children's University Hospital. His publications include the *Handbook of Clinical Intervention with Juvenile Sexual Offenders* (Brunner-Routledge, 2004), *Clinical Psychology in Ireland Volume 5: Empirical Studies of Child Sexual Abuse* (Edwin Mellen Press, 2004) and *Understanding, Assessing, and Treating Juvenile and Adult Sex Offenders: A Special Issue of the Irish Journal of Psychology* (1998).

Patricia Noonan Walsh, PhD is NDA Professor of Disability Studies and Director of the Centre for Disability Studies UCD. She is a Fellow of the International Association for the Scientific Study of Intellectual Disability (IASSID) and a member of the Professional Advisory Board of Bancroft NeuroHealth, USA. She is also a member of the Reference Group for the Learning Disability Research Initiative led by the Department of Health in the UK. She serves on the editorial boards of the *Journal of Vocational Rehabilitation, Journal of Applied Research in Intellectual Disability, British Journal of Learning Disabilities* and *REACH – Journal of Special Education in Ireland.* Professor Walsh's books are *Health of Women with Intellectual Disabilities* (with Tamar Heller, Blackwell, 2002), *Lives and Times: Practice, Policy and People with Disabilities* (with Hugh Gash, Rathdown, 2004), and

Health of Women with Disabilities Aging Well: A Global View (with Barbara le Roy, Paul Brookes, 2004).

John McEvoy, PhD is Lecturer in Psychology at the Dundalk Institute of Technology, Research Associate with the Centre for Disability Studies at UCD and serves on the editorial board of *REACH – Journal of Special Education in Ireland*. He has held a variety of clinical, managerial and teaching posts in the field of Intellectual Disability and has conducted staff training and service-based research both within Ireland and the UK. He is a member and former chairperson of the Learning Disability Special Interest group of The Psychology Society of Ireland.

Contributors

Bruce L. Baker, PhD, Distinguished Professor; Senior Vice Chair, Department of Psychology, University of California, Los Angeles, USA.

Jan Blacher, PhD, Professor and Faculty Chair, Graduate School of Education, University of California, Riverside, California, USA.

Nick Bouras, FRCPsych, Professor of Psychiatry, Institute of Psychiatry, King's College London and the Estia Centre-York Clinic, Guy's Hospital, London, UK.

Helen Cannella, PhD, Assistant Professor, Department of Special Education, Ohio State University, USA.

Coral Choinski, MSSW, Ongoing Case Manager, La Causa, Inc., Bureau of Milwaukee Child Welfare, Milwaukee, USA.

Kevin Coyle, MEd., Senior Clinical Psychologist, Carmona Services, Hospitaller Order of St John of God, Dublin.

Dave Dagnan, PhD, Professor, Psychology Department, Cumbria Partnership NHS Trust, Community Learning Disabilities Services, Workington, Cumbria, UK.

Eric Emerson, PhD, Professor of Disability and Health Research, Institute for Health Research, Lancaster University, Lancaster, UK.

Kristin A. Feinfield, PhD, University of California, Los Angeles, USA.

Vanessa A. Green, PhD, Lecturer, Faculty of Education, The University of Tasmania, Australia.

Ian Grey, PhD, Senior Clinical Psychologist and KARE Lecturer in Intellectual Disabilities, Department of Psychology, Trinity College, Dublin, Ireland.

Anthony D. Harman, MSc, DD (Hons), Research Fellow, Centre for Developmental Disability Studies, The University of Sydney, Australia.

Geraldine Holt, FRCPsych, Consultant Psychiatrist and Senior Lecturer, Institute of Psychiatry, King's College London and the Estia Centre-York Clinic, Guy's Hospital, London, UK.

Andrew Jahoda, PhD, Department of Psychological Medicine, Gartnavel Royal Hospital, Glasgow, Scotland.

Rita Jordon, PhD, School of Education, University of Birmingham, Birmingham, UK.

Kenneth D. Keith, PhD, Professor and Chair, Department of Psychology, University of San Diego, San Diego, California, USA.

Bonnie R. Kraemer, PhD, Assistant Professor, San Diego State University, San Diego, California, USA.

Biza Stenfert Kroese, PhD, University of Birmingham, School of Psychology, Edgbaston, Birmingham, and Psychology Services for Adults with Learning Disabilities, Shropshire County PCT, UK.

Adam Kuczynski, DClinPsy, South London and Maudsley NHS Trust, Mary Sheridan Centre for Child Health, London, UK.

Giulio E. Lancioni, PhD, Professor and Chair, Department of Psychology, University of Bari, Italy.

Suk-Hyang Lee, PhD, Fulbright Scholar, University of Kansas, Kansas, USA.

Christine Linehan, MA, Senior Researcher, Centre for Disability Studies, UCD, Belfield, Dublin 4, Ireland.

Johnny L. Matson, PhD, Professor and Distinguished Research Master. Director of Clinical Training, Department of Psychology, Louisiana State University, Baton Rouge, USA.

Stephen B. Mayville, PhD, Clinical Psychologist and Board Certified Behavior Analyst, Department of Psychology, Louisiana State University, USA.

Philip McCallion, PhD, Professor and Director, Centre for Excellence in Aging Services, University at Albany, Albany, New York, USA.

Mary McCarron, PhD, Director of Research and Lecturer, School of Nursing and Midwifery, Trinity College Dublin, Ireland; Policy and Service Adviser on Dementia, Daughters of Charity Service.

Brian McClean, D. Psych, Principal Clinical Psychologist, Brothers of Charity, Lanesborough Road Roscommon, Ireland.

Brian McGuire, PhD, Director of the Doctoral Programme in Clinical Psychology, National University of Ireland, Galway, Ireland.

Glynis Murphy, PhD, Professor of Clinical Psychology, Tizard Centre, University of Kent, Canterbury, Kent, UK.

Melissa Olive, PhD, Assistant Professor, Department of Special Education, The University of Texas at Austin, USA.

Trevor R. Parmenter, PhD, Professor and Director of the Centre for Developmental Disability Studies, The University of Sydney, Australia.

Mark O'Reilly, PhD, Professor, Department of Special Education, University of Texas at Austin, USA.

Howie Reyer, PhD, Associate Psychologist, Queens College and The Graduate Centre, City University of New York, New York, USA.

Vivienne C. Riches, PhD, Senior Research Fellow, Centre for Developmental Disability Studies, The University of Sydney, Australia.

Jeff Sigafoos, PhD, Professor, Faculty of Education, The University of Tasmania, Australia.

Peter Sturmey, PhD, Professor, Queens College and The Graduate Centre, City University of New York, New York, USA.

Orlee Udwin, PhD, Child and Adolescent Mental Health, West London Mental Health Trust, London, UK.

Denise Valenti-Hein, PhD, Outgamie County Health and Human Services, and the University of Wisconsin, Oshkosh, Wisconsin, USA.

Michael L. Wehmeyer, PhD, Professor, Department of Special Education and Director of the Kansas University Centre on Developmental Disabilities, University of Kansas, Kansas, USA.

Luci Wiggs, DPhil, Senior Lecturer, Department of Psychology, Oxford Brookes University, Headington, Oxford, UK.

Marie Yazbeck, MA, Research Fellow, Centre for Developmental Disability Studies, The University of Sydney, Australia.

Shahid H. Zaman, MRCPsych, Specialist Registrar in Psychiatry, South London and Maudsley NHS Trust and the Estia Centre-York Clinic, Guy's Hospital, London, UK.

Section 1

Conceptual frameworks

Chapter 1

Diagnosis, classification and epidemiology

Alan Carr and Gary O'Reilly

Infants and children who show apparent developmental delays in achieving milestones, such as those in Table 1.1, may be referred to clinical psychologists for assessment. The main questions usually centre on whether the child's developmental delay is significant, the degree and range of disabilities, and the child's special educational and social needs. Later in childhood, adolescence and adulthood, referrals may be made to re-evaluate the nature and extent of such disabilities; the changing educational, vocational and social needs of the individual, and the requirement for appropriate supports and interventions. To address these sorts of clinical questions for individual cases, knowledge of the definitions, classification, course and outcome of intellectual disabilities is essential. To plan services for whole populations of people with disabilities, it is helpful to know the prevalence of intellectual disabilities, patterns of comorbidity, their course and outcome. In this chapter the diagnosis, classification, epidemiology, course and outcome of intellectual disabilities will be considered. Differential diagnosis in the field of intellectual disability will also be addressed. Throughout the chapter the term 'intellectual disability' will be used to refer to what is called 'mental retardation' in parts of the USA, 'learning difficulties' in the UK, and 'mental handicap' in parts of Ireland and elsewhere. A thorough discussion of the evolution of the term 'intellectual disability' is given in Parmenter (2001).

DEFINITION

Three definitions of intellectual disability are given in Table 1.2. These are taken from three widely used classification systems: ICD 10, DSM-IV-TR and AAMR 10. ICD 10 is the tenth edition of the World Health Organization's International Classification of Diseases (WHO, 1992; 1993; 1996). Chapter five of ICD 10 covers the classification of mental and behavioural disorders. DSM-IV-TR is the textual revision of the fourth edition of the American Psychiatric Association's *Diagnostic and Statistical Manual of the Mental Disorders* (APA, 2000). AAMR 10 is the tenth revision of the American

Table 1.1 Milestones in the first five years

Month	Gross motor	Fine sensorimotor	Language	Adaptive behaviour
1m	Partial head control Primitive reflexes	Clenches fists	Alert to sounds Makes sounds	Fixates objects and follows 90°
2m	Good head control Lifts chin when prone			Follows 180° Smiles responsively
3m	Lifts chest off bed Fewer primitive reflexes	Holds hands open Reaches towards objects Pulls at clothing	Coos	Follows 360° Recognizes mother
4m	Swimming movement	Hands come to midline	Laughs aloud Produces different sounds for different needs	Shakes rattle Anticipates food Belly laughs
5m	Rolls over stomach to back Holds head erect		Orients towards sound Blows raspberry	Frolics when played with
6m	Anterior propping response	Transfers objects Holds bottle Palmer grasp	Babbles Recognizes friendly and angry voices	Looks after lost toy Mirror play
7m	Bounces when standing Sits without support	Feeds self biscuit	Imitates noise Responds to name	Drinks from cup
8m	Lateral propping responses	Rings bell Radial raking grasp	Uses non-specific MAMA Understands NO	Shows separation anxiety Tries to gain attention
9m	Crawls		Recognizes familiar words	Mouths objects
10m	Stands with support	Plays with bell	Says specific MAMA and DADA	Waves BYE BYE Plays PAT A CAKE
11m	Cruises around objects	Uses pincer grasp	Follows gesture command	Puts on some clothes Takes turns

Age	Gross motor	Fine motor / manipulation	Language / speech	Social / self-care
1y	Makes first steps Can sit down without help	Throws objects Puts objects in containers Tries to build a tower out of 2 blocks Turns through pages of a book by flipping many at a time	Says two or three specific words Comprehends several words Tries to imitate animal sounds	Follows a fast-moving object Searches for objects that are hidden Develops attachment to security blanket
1y 3m	Climbs stairs	Marks with pencil	Speaks word-like sounds	Indicates when wet Spoon feeds Gives kisses Imitates household jobs
1y 6m	Runs stiffly Handedness is determined Able to jump in place Able to get onto chairs without assistance Walks up stairs with one hand held	Plays with toys constructively Scribbles Imitates lines Puts objects in form board Builds a tower of 3 to 4 blocks Turns pages two or three at a time	Speaks monologues with many word-like sounds Uses 10 words Points to 1 picture in a book Follows 2 step commands	Places objects in form board Parallel play Takes off shoes Does puzzles Frequently imitates Feeds self
2y	Walks up and down stairs with both feet on each step Can run with better co-ordination Kicks ball without losing balance Picks up objects while standing without losing balance	Imitates vertical lines Builds a tower of 6 blocks Turns pages one at a time Turns door knob	Vocabulary of about 300 words Uses I Says YES and NO Identifies 4 body parts Can form 3 word sentences	Puts on shoes Indicates toilet needs
3y	Can briefly balance on one foot Walks up the stairs with alternating feet	Builds a tower of more than 6 blocks Places small objects in a small opening	Vocabulary of hundreds of words Composes sentences of 3 to 4 words Frequently asks Who? What? When? Where? Why? and How? questions	Can put on all clothes Only requiring assistance with laces, buttons and fasteners in awkward places Plays imaginatively Reduction in separation anxiety Daytime control over bowel and bladder

(Continued overleaf)

Table 1.1 Continued

Month	Gross motor	Fine sensorimotor	Language	Adaptive behaviour
4y	Hops on one foot without losing balance	Throws a ball overhand Cuts out a picture using scissors	Vocabulary over 1500 words Composes sentences of 4 to 5 words Can use the past tense Uses words they do not understand Uses vulgar words	Can count to 4 Sings simple songs Increased aggressive behaviour Tells personal family matters to others Has imaginary playmates Distinguishes between two objects based on one criterion (such as size, weight, etc.) Believes that their thoughts and emotions can make things happen Lacks moral concepts of right and wrong
5y	Skips and jumps with good balance Stands on one foot with eyes closed	Ties shoelaces Draws a square	Vocabulary over 2100 words Uses sentences of 6 to 8 words Names coins Names primary colours	Can count to 10 Decreased aggressiveness Childhood fears weaken Accepts the validity of others' perspective Identifies with the parent of the same sex

Table 1.2 Diagnostic criteria and classification of intellectual disability

ICD 10 / ICF	DSM-IV-TR	AAMR 10
For a definite diagnosis of mental retardation there should be a (A) reduced level of intellectual functioning resulting in (B) diminished ability to adapt to the daily demands of the normal social environment. The assessment of intellectual level should be based on clinical observation, standardized ratings of adaptive behaviour and psychometric test performance.	Mental retardation A. Significantly subaverage mental functioning shown by an IQ of approximately 70 or below on an individually administered IQ test (for infants, a clinical judgement of significantly subaverage intellectual functioning).	Mental retardation is a disability characterized by significant limitations both in (A) intellectual functioning and in (B) adaptive behaviour as expressed in conceptual, social, and practical adaptive skills. (C) This disability originates before age 18.
Mild mental retardation • An IQ of between 50 and 69 • A mental age of 9 to 12 years in adults Children may have some learning difficulties in school • Many adults will be able to work, maintain good social relationships and contribute to society	B. Concurrent deficits or impairments in present adaptive functioning (i.e. the person's effectiveness in meeting the standards expected for his age or her age by his or her cultural group) in at least two of the following areas: • communication • self-care • home living • social – interpersonal skills • use of community resources • self-direction • functional academic skills • work • leisure • health and safety	For a diagnosis there must be • A standardized intelligence test score 2 standard deviations below the mean • A standardized rating of adaptive behaviour in one or more domains (conceptual social or practical) 2 standard deviations below the mean Five assumptions are entailed by this definition 1 Limitations in present functioning must be considered within the context of community environments typical of the individual's age peers and culture.
Moderate mental retardation • An IQ of between 35 and 49 • A mental age of 6 to 9 years in adults Most children will show marked developmental delays but most can learn to develop some degree of independence in self-care and acquire adequate communication and academic skills	C. The onset is before 18 years of age Code as Mild: IQ level 50–55 to 70 (approx) Moderate: IQ level 35–40 to 50–55 Severe: IQ level 20–25 to 35–40 Profound: IQ level below 20–25. Diagnosis coded on Axis II	2 Valid assessment considers cultural and linguistic diversity as well as differences in communication, sensory, motor and behavioural factors. 3 Within an individual, limitations often coexist with strengths.

(Continued overleaf)

Table 1.2 Continued

ICD 10 / ICF	DSM-IV-TR	AAMR 10

ICD 10 / ICF	DSM-IV-TR	AAMR 10
• Adults will need varying degrees of support to live in the community **Severe mental retardation** • An IQ of between 20 and 34 • A mental age of 3 to 6 years • Likely to result in continuous need for support **Profound mental retardation** • An IQ of below 20 • A mental age less than 3 in adults • Severe limitation in self-care, continence, communication and mobility **Model of intellectual disability** In ICF functioning and level of disability is determined by • Health status (disease of disorder) • Bodily functions and structures (impairments) • Activities (limitations) • Participation (restrictions) • Environmental factors (barriers and hindrances) • Personal factors (demographic profile) Diagnosis coded on Axis III for children Diagnosis coded on Axis I for adults		4 An important purpose of describing limitations is to develop a profile of needed supports. 5 With appropriate personalized supports over a sustained period, the life functioning of the person with mental retardation generally will improve. **Model of intellectual disability** The definition is based on a model in which level of individual functioning is defined by status on 5 factors. • Intellectual abilities • Adaptive behaviour • Participation, interactions and social roles • Health • Social context The impact of these 5 factors on functioning is mediated by supports

Note: Adapted from DSM-IV-TR (APA, 2000), ICD 10 (WHO, 1992; 1993; 1996) ICF (WHO, 2001) and AAMR 10 (Luckasson *et al.*, 2002).

Association for Mental Retardation's manual – *Mental Retardation: Definition, Classification and Systems of Support* (Luckasson, Borthwick-Duffy, Buntinx, Coulter *et al.*, 2002). Also included in the table in the column summarizing the ICD 10 definition of intellectual disability is reference to the disability model described in ICF. ICF is the World Health Organization's *International Classification of Functioning, Disability and Health* (WHO, 2001). This is included in the table under ICD 10 because it is the model the WHO uses to conceptualize disability arising from ICD 10 diagnoses including intellectual disability. The ICF model of intellectual disability is presented diagrammatically in Figure 1.1 and a diagram of the model on which the AAMR 10 definition is based is presented in Figure 1.2.

Deficits in both intellectual functioning and adaptive behaviour are central to the definitions of intellectual disability in all three systems included in Table 1.2. In addition to these deficits, the criterion that the diagnosis of

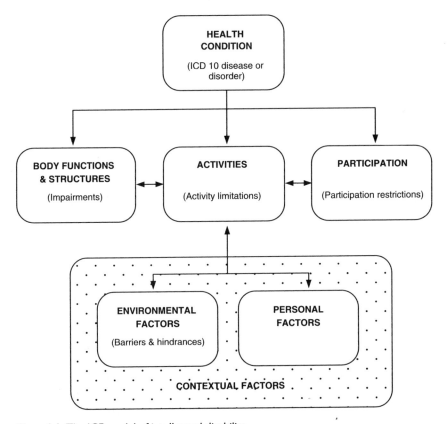

Figure 1.1 The ICF model of intellectual disability.

Note: Adapted from World Health Organization (2001). *The International Classification of Functioning, Disability and Health (ICF)*. Geneva: WHO p. 18.

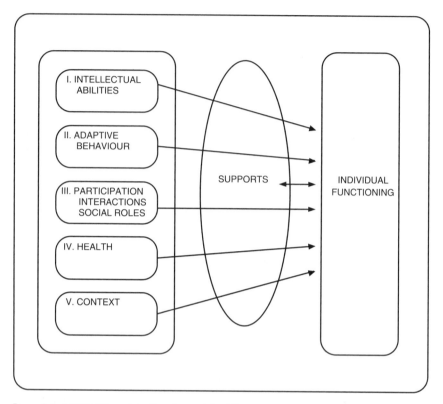

Figure 1.2 AAMR 10 model of intellectual disability.

Note: Adapted from Luckasson, R., Borthwick-Duffy, S., Buntinx, W., Coulter, D., Craig, E., Reeve, A., Schalock, R., Snell, M., Spitalnik, D., Spreat, S., and Tasse, M. (2002) *Mental Retardation: Definition, Classification, and Systems of Supports* (10th edn). Washington, DC: American Association on Mental Retardation, p. 10.

intellectual disability be made before the age of 18 is specified in DSM-IV-TR and AAMR 10, but not ICD 10, although it is probably implicit in the ICD system.

There is also an acceptance in the three systems that functional deficits are indicated by scores of 70 or below on reliable and valid appropriately standardized psychometric assessment instruments. A list of widely used intelligence tests for people of different ages is given in Table 1.3. In Table 1.4 a list of widely used adaptive behaviour scales is given. It is important for psychologists in clinical training to know the range of such instruments that are available and to become skilled in administering some of these. The psychometric assessment of cognitive functioning and adaptive behaviour are covered in detail in Chapters 2 and 3 respectively.

Table 1.3 Psychometric instruments for the assessment of intelligence

Age range where instrument is particularly useful	Instrument	Comments
Infancy	Bayley, N. (2005). *Bayley Scales of Infant Development – 3rd Edition (BAYLEY-III)*. San Antonio: Psychological Corporation	• It yields scores in cognitive, language, motor, social-emotional, and adaptive behaviour domains • Contains over 100 items and requires about an hour to administer • Standardized in the US on children age 1–42 months
	Huntley, M. (1996). *Griffiths Mental Development Scales from Birth to Two Years*. UK. Association for Research on Infant and Child Development Griffiths, R. (1970). *Griffiths Mental Development Scales* High Wycombe, Bucks: Test Agency	• Yields a general quotient and six subscale scores: locomotor; personal-social; hearing and speech; eye and hand co-ordination; performance; and practical reasoning • Contains over 100 items and takes about an hour to administer • Standardized in the UK on children aged 1 month to 8 years
Toddlers under 5	McCarthy, D. (1972). *McCarthy Scales of Children's Abilities*. San Antonio: Psychological Corporation	• Yields scores on a general scale and five subscales (verbal; perceptual-performance; quantitative; memory and motor). • Contains 18 tests and takes about an hour to administer. • Standardized in the US on children 2.5–8.5 years
	Kaufman, A. and Kaufman, N. (2004). *Kaufman Assessment Battery for Children. Second Edition (KABC-II)*. Circle Pines, MN: American Guidance Service	• Yields scores for components of both the Luria neuropsychological model and the Cattell-Horn-Carroll model • On the Luria model give an index of overall intelligence and non-verbal intelligence as well as four scale scores (sequential processing; simultaneous processing; planning ability; learning ability) *(Continued overleaf)*

Table 1.3 Continued

Age range where instrument is particularly useful	Instrument	Comments
		• OntheCattell-Horn-Carroll model gives an overall fluid crystallized index and a non-verbal index as well as five subscale scores (visual processing, short-term memory, fluid reasoning, long-term storage and retrieval and crystallized ability) • Contains many subtests and takes an hour to administer • Standardized in the US on children aged 2.5–18 years
	Wechsler, D. (2004). *Wechsler Preschool and Primary Scale of Intelligence – III UK (WPPSI-III[uk])*. San Antonio: Psychological Corporation	• Validated in the UK on 800 children aged 2:6–7:3 years reflecting 2001 census data • For children aged between 2:6–3:11, 4 core subtests and 1 supplemental subtest taking 25–35 minutes to administer yield a full-scale IQ, verbal IQ, and Performance IQ • For children aged between 4:0–7:3, 7 core subtests and 5 supplemental subtests taking 40–50 minutes to administer yield a full-scale IQ, verbal IQ, Performance IQ and a Processing Speed Quotient
Under 5s (but also over 5s and adolescents)	Elliott, C. (1996). *British Ability Scales. Second Edition. (BAS II)*. Windsor: NFER Nelson	• Yields index of intelligence, reading, spelling, arithmetic and various cognitive skills • Contains 21 subtests and brief or long versions may be administered • Standardized in the UK on children aged 2–18 years
	Roid, G. (2003). *Stanford-Binet Intelligence Scales, Fifth Edition (SB-V)*. Itasca, IL: Riverside Publishing.	• Yields a full-scale IQ, verbal and non-verbal IQ and scores on five factors – Fluid Reasoning,

	http://www. riverpub. com/products/clinical/ sbis/home. html	Knowledge, Quantitative Reasoning, Visual-Spatial Processing, and Working Memory • Contains 10 subtests • Normed on a stratified random sample of 4,800 individuals that matches the 2000 US Census
Children over 6 and adolescents	Wechsler, D. (1991). *Wechsler Intelligence Scale for Children. Third Edition (WISC-III)*. San Antonio: Psychological Corporation	• Yields a full-scale IQ and verbal and performance IQs • Also yields four factor scores (verbal comprehension; perceptual organization; freedom from distractibility and processing speed) • Contains 13 subtests and takes about an hour to administer • Standardized in the US on children 6–17 years and validated in the UK
	Wechsler, D. (2003). *Wechsler Intelligence Scale for Children. Fourth Edition (WISC-IV)*. San Antonio: Psychological Corporation	• Designed to incorporate advances in theoretical ideas on intelligence, the WISC-IV contains 11 core subtests and 5 supplemental subtests • Yields a full-scale IQ, a verbal comprehension index, a perceptual reasoning index, a working memory index, and a processing speed index • Standardized in the US on 2,200 children aged between 6:0 and 16:11 years matching the 2000 Census data. • UK validation study in progress
Adolescents and adults	Wechsler, D. (1999). *Wechsler Adult Intelligence Scale – Third Edition (WAIS-III)*. San Antonio, Texas: Psychological Corporation	• Yields a full-scale IQ and verbal and performance IQs • Contains 12 subtests and takes about an hour to administer • Standardized in the US on population 16–74 years of age

Table 1.4 Psychometric instruments for the assessment of adaptive behaviour

Instrument	Comments
Lambert, N., Nihira, K. and Leyland, H. (1993). *Adaptive Behaviour Scale-School Version Second Edition.* Washington, DC: AAMR Nihira, K., Leyland, H. and Lambert, N. (1993). *Adaptive Behaviour Scale-Residential and Community Version Second Edition.* Austin, TX: Pro-ed	• Yields scores in multiple adaptive behaviour domains (e.g. independent functioning, physical development, economic activity) and problem behaviour domains (e.g. violent or destructive behaviour) • Standardized in the US on large population of 3–69-year-olds. • Contains over 100 items and takes 30 minutes for a parent or caretaker to complete
Sparrow, S., Balla, D. and Cicchetti, D. (1984). *Vineland Adaptive Behaviour Scales.* Pine Circles, MN: American Guidance Service	• Yields scores in four domains: communication; daily living skills; socialization; and motor skills. The expanded version also includes a maladaptive behaviour domain • Standardized in the US on a population of 3,000 0–19 year olds • There are three versions: survey form; expanded form; and classroom edition • The expanded form contains over 500 items and takes an hour for a parent or caretaker to complete. The other two forms contain between 200 and 300 items and take about 30 minutes to complete
Bruininks, R., Woodcock, R., Weatherman, R. and Hill, B. (1996). *Scales of Independent Behaviour – Revised.* Ithica, IL: Riverside	• Yields scores on multiple adaptive behaviour subscales grouped into four domains (motor; social interaction; and communication; personal living; and community living) and 8 maladaptive behaviour subscales grouped into three domains (internalized behaviour problems; externalized behaviour problems; and social maladaptive behaviour) • Standardized in the US on children and adults • Contains over 300 items and takes an hour for a parent or caretaker to complete. There is a 32-item short form, which can be completed in 10 minutes. There is also an early development form • The scale is a component of the Woodcock Johnson Psychoeducational Battery
Adams, G. (1999). *Comprehensive Test of Adaptive Behaviour – Revised and Normative Adaptive Behaviour Checklist – Revised.* Seattle, WA: Educational Achievement Systems. www.edresearch.com	• Yields scores for self-help skills, home living skills, independent living, social skills, sensory and motor skills, language and academic skills • Normed on large USA sample of children and adults • Contains 495 male and 523 female items and yields scores on adaptive behaviour and problematic behaviour and can be completed using data from teachers and parents or carers

Harrison, P. and Oakland, T. (2000). *ABAS. Adaptive Behaviour Assessment System*. San Antonio, TX: Psychological Corporation.	• Yields scores for 10 DSM IV specified areas of adaptive behaviour: communication, functional academics, health and safety, self-care, social, community use, home living, leisure, self-direction and work • Normed on large USA sample of children and adults • Scores are linked to WISC III and WAIS III

From a statistical perspective, the diagnostic criteria of having scores of 70 or below on instruments that assess intelligence and adaptive behaviour, imply that scores must be more than two standard deviations below the mean on tests that yield standard scores with means of 100 and standard deviations of 15. All of the Wechsler tests, the fifth edition of the Stanford Binet and many other tests use such standard scores. Most widely used intelligence tests have a standard error of measurement of between 2 and 5 IQ points. This means that the boundaries of categories must span a range of about 5 points, since measurement errors of this magnitude are possible. In diagnosing and classifying individual cases it is important to take account of the standard error of measurement of the specific test used, which will be specified in the test's manual. There is latitude in the DSM-IV-TR to take account of measurement errors of up to 5 points. When classifying intellectual disability, the following IQ ranges are specified, with category boundaries having bandwidths of 5 points:

- Mild: IQ level 50–55 to 70 (approx)
- Moderate: IQ level 35–40 to 50–55
- Severe: IQ level 20–25 to 35–40
- Profound: IQ level below 20–25.

MODELS

Explicit models of key factors that affect functioning in people with intellectual disabilities have been offered by the World Health Organization in the ICF (WHO, 2001) and by the AAMR in the tenth revision of their diagnostic handbook (Luckasson *et al.*, 2002).

The WHO – ICF model

In the ICF model, which is reproduced in Figure 1.1 above, level of functioning and disability are conceptualized as being determined by multiple interrelated factors the first of which is the person's health status. This is defined in terms of the presence or absence of any ICD 10 disease of disorder.

Disability level is also influenced by impairments in physiological and psychological body functions (including intellectual functioning), and impairments in body structures such as those entailed by deafness, blindness and so forth. In the ICF model activity limitations also contribute to levels of disability, as do participation restrictions. Activity limitations are difficulties people may have in carrying out any activities or adaptive skills typically executed by non-disabled people with similar demographic profiles to the disabled person. Participation restrictions refer to problems fulfilling social roles typical for non-disabled people with similar demographic profiles arising from lack of access to important resources and services. Level of disability in this model is also influenced by both personal and environmental contextual factors. Personal factors in this model refer to age, gender, race, educational background, fitness, lifestyle, coping strategies, social background and other characteristics important for overall functioning. Environmental factors in this model refer to the physical and social aspects of the arenas in which people conduct their lives. Included here are home, school and workplaces; health, education, and social services; and broader aspects of society including systems of accommodation, transport, policies and legislation.

The AAMR 10 model

Within the AAMR 10 model, which is reproduced in Figure 1.2 above, a person's level of individual functioning is conceptualized as being affected by five factors. The first two of these are their level of intellectual ability and adaptive behaviour. In this context, intelligence refers to the theoretical construct 'g' which includes the capacity for reasoning, planning, problem-solving, abstract thinking, and learning from experience (Dreary, 2000). Adaptive behaviour refers to conceptual, social and practical skills, three domains repeatedly identified in factor analytic studies (Schalock, 2002). In the AAMR 10 model, level of functioning is also viewed as being influenced by degree of inclusion in mainstream society through participation in valued social activities, meaningful social interactions, and age-appropriate social roles (Schalock and Verdugo, 2002). For children with intellectual disabilities, attending a mainstream school, pursuing leisure activities and sports, and living in a family are examples of participation. For adults with intellectual disabilities, examples of participation include living relatively independently and working in employment settings in the community. Physical and mental health are also viewed as influencing level of individual functioning within the AAMR 10 model. Diseases and psychological disorders and the side-effects of medications used to treat these may impact on level of individual functioning. For example, sensory and motor disabilities may directly compromise the acquisition of adaptive behavioural skills and medications such as anticonvulsants or psychotropic medications can impair concentration and so reduce the capacity for skill acquisition and level of functioning. Within the AAMR 10 model, level of individual functioning is viewed as being influenced by the social context within which the individual lives. This includes the immediate family or microsystem; the community with its educational, social, and health services (the mesosystem); and the wider society with its cultural, socio-political, and economic aspects (the megasystem) (Bronfenbrenner, 1979). Contexts that offer opportunities to have a place in the community, to have choices about one's life, to have opportunities to develop competencies, to be offered respect, and to participate in a growing network of family and friends all foster well-being and promote better individual functioning. The impact of intelligence, adaptive behaviour, participation, health and context on functioning is conceptualized within the AAMR 10 model as being mediated by the availability of appropriate supports. Supports are resources that aim to promote development and enhance functioning. Supports will be discussed in more detail below in the section on the classification of intellectual disabilities by level of required supports.

CLASSIFICATION

The classification of intellectual disability into mild, moderate, severe and profound subcategories is used in both ICD 10 and DSM-IV-TR, but not explicitly in AAMR 10.

This approach to classification by level of disability, initially introduced in AAMR 5 in 1959 (Heber, 1959), was abandoned in AAMR 9 in 1992 (Luckasson *et al.*, 1992) in favour of a classification system based on level of required supports. So within AAMR 9, cases were classified into those requiring intermittent, limited, extensive or pervasive supports. The decision to move from level of disability to level of required supports was based on the recognition that one function of the classification of disabilities is to facilitate the appropriate allocation of funding for required supports, a function not well served by a classification system based on ability level only. For example, funding for supports required by infants with mild and severe intellectual disabilities may be quite similar. In contrast, funding for supports required by adolescents or adults with mild intellectual disabilities may be far greater than those with severe intellectual disabilities.

There has been a further change to the classification of intellectual disabilities in AAMR 10. In AAMR 10, a very flexible approach is taken within which it is possible to classify cases in a variety of ways depending upon the purpose or function of classification. For service funding it may be appropriate to classify by level of support required (intermittent, limited, extensive or pervasive). For service development and interprofessional communication it may be appropriate to classify by level of disability (mild, moderate, severe or profound). For placement within supported employment or residential care facilities, it may be appropriate to classify by level of adaptive behaviour. For research purposes it may be appropriate to classify cases by aetiology.

Classification by intellectual level

The classification of intellectual disabilities by level of intellectual ability currently relies heavily on IQ testing. While this is far from an ideal situation the use of appropriately standardized, valid and reliable tests to classify intellectual level remains best practice (Luckasson *et al.*, 2002). Extensive evidence from factor analytic studies of intelligence test scores show that general intellectual ability contains a unitary construct normally distributed within the population often referred to as 'g' (Dreary, 2000). Evidence from factor analytic studies also shows that intellectual abilities are best understood within a hierarchical model, with general intellectual ability (g) at the apex of a pyramid, with second-order abilities such as crystallized intelligence or broad visuospatial abilities at the next level, and highly specific third-order abilities, such as vocabulary skills, occupying a third and lower level of this hierarchy (Carrol, 1993). However, most widely used intelligence tests, such as the Wechsler scales listed in Table 1.3 above, yield scores which, when administered to individuals, do not offer pure measures of g, second- or third-order abilities. Instead they usually yield a global score, often called Full-Scale IQ or Composite Score. This offers a summary amalgam of g plus second-order abilities plus third-order abilities as exercised by a person as they complete the full test battery. Intelligence tests are often organized also to reflect more specific abilities such as Verbal, Performance, or Quantitative skills. However, while these are useful summaries that reflect aspects of the test that require the greater use of more specific intellectual abilities, they are not pure measures of the specific ability concerned, free from the influence of g or other specific abilities. A third level of analysis sometimes adopted in test interpretation is to think of individual subtests as very specific measures of an area of functioning. However, individual subtests are rarely designed to be used in this manner and caution is needed to ensure that a specific subtest is not confused and interpreted as a refined measure of a third-order intellectual ability. Nevertheless, statements about a person's overall intellectual level, and also their unique profile of strengths and weaknesses, can usefully be made based on those aspects of intelligence measured by commonly used IQ tests. When intellectual disabilities are classified by level of general intellectual ability, distinctions are made between mild, moderate, severe and profound levels of disability. What follows are brief accounts of the clinical features of each of these presentations at different stages of the lifecycle.

Clinical features of mild intellectual disability

People with mild intellectual disabilities have IQs below about 70 and above 50–55. They also have comparable levels of adaptive behaviour deficits. They are slower to develop communication and adaptive behavioural skills during their preschool years than children of normal ability. However, by five years of age they can interact socially with a degree of competence. They show little significant sensorimotor impairment. However, during their primary school years they show significant difficulties in acquiring academic skills such as those required for reading, writing and arithmetic. It is often because of these difficulties that they are referred for psychological assessment. Unlike children with specific learning disabilities, such as dyslexia, children with mild intellectual disabilities have pervasive rather than circumscribed academic difficulties and their overall IQ falls below 70. In contrast children with specific learning disabilities have IQs above 70 and circumscribed academic difficulties. With sufficient educational supports most children and adolescents with mild intellectual disabilities can develop some academic and vocational skills. As adults they can function well in semiskilled or unskilled regular or supported employment. With appropriate supports some attain the skills required for independent living or living in a setting with limited supervision. Additional supports are typically needed at lifecycle transitions such as the transition from primary to secondary school, from secondary school to regular or supported employment, and from one residential setting to another. Indeed, this is true for all levels of disability. With adequate supports, marriage and rearing a family are possible for some people with mild intellectual disabilities.

Clinical features of moderate intellectual disability

People with moderate intellectual disabilities have IQs above 35–40 and below 50–55. They also have comparable levels of adaptive behaviour deficits. They show a significant developmental delay in the acquisition of gross motor, fine sensorimotor, communication and adaptive behavioural skills during the preschool years, which often leads to a referral for psychological assessment. During their childhood years some develop skills to interact socially with adults and peers with a degree of competence, while others have great difficulty developing such skills throughout their lives. During their primary school years they show significant difficulties in acquiring basic academic skills. With sufficient educational supports and an appropriate curriculum, some children and adolescents with moderate intellectual disabilities can develop some academic and vocational skills. As adults, some can function well in supported or sheltered, unskilled employment. They can travel independently in familiar environments. Most or all require supervised accommodation, but with support can live active, socially meaningful lives.

Clinical features of severe intellectual disability

Children with severe intellectual disabilities have IQs above 20–25 and below 35–40. They also have comparable levels of adaptive behaviour deficits. They show a pronounced developmental delay in the acquisition of gross motor, fine sensorimotor, communication and adaptive behaviour skills during the preschool years. This often leads to a referral for psychological assessment prior to 3 years of age. During their primary school years some develop skills to interact socially with adults and peers, while others have great difficulty developing such skills throughout their lives. During their primary school years the focus is appropriately on acquiring adaptive behavioural skills rather than academic skills. With sufficient educational supports and an appropriate curriculum some adolescents with severe intellectual disabilities can develop a small reading vocabulary, which is useful for interpreting public signs or notices. As adults, some can function well in supported or sheltered, unskilled employment. All require supervised accommodation, but with adequate support can live active socially meaningful lives.

Clinical features of profound intellectual disability

People with profound intellectual disabilities have IQs below 20–25. They show a very marked developmental delay in the acquisition of gross motor, fine sensorimotor, communication and adaptive behavioural skills. This usually leads to a referral for psychological assessment prior to 3 years of age. Because of restricted mobility, incontinence and difficulty acquiring communication skills, as children, adolescents and adults, people with profound disabilities usually require intensive supports to maximize their quality of life. A highly structured environment with an individualized relationship with a caregiver is an appropriate level of support for people with severe intellectual disability. As adults, some can function in intensively supported or sheltered, unskilled employment. All require supervised accommodation.

Classification by adaptive behaviour

Factor analytic studies of the many skills that constitute adaptive behaviour indicate that such behaviour is best conceptualized as falling into three domains representing conceptual, social and practical skills (Schalock, 2002).

- **Conceptual skills.** These include language, literacy and numeracy skills, money skills, and self-direction.
- **Social skills.** The capacity to make and maintain relationships, accept responsibilities appropriate to one's age and ability level and the capacity to maintain an adequate level of self-esteem are important social skills. Social skills also include the capacity to understand and follow informal

rules for social interactions and formal societal laws as well as being able to interpret social situations accurately without being gullible, naïve or prone to victimization.

- **Practical skills.** These include those necessary for activities of daily living such as eating, toileting, washing, dressing, meal preparation, housekeeping, mobility, money management, using telephones, maintaining personal safety, and managing the occupational demands of work situations.

Psychometrically robust measures of adaptive behaviour are listed in Table 1.4 above. For placement within mainstream schools, residential care, supported employment, or other facilities it may be appropriate to classify people by their level of adaptive behaviour in conceptual, social and practical domains.

Classification by aetiology

Historically, in what has come to be termed the 'two group' approach, cases were classified into those whose intellectual disability was due to known organic causes such as Down syndrome, and those where it was assumed that social disadvantage was the primary aetiological factor (Kaski, 2000; Volkmar and Dykens, 2002). Within this system the 'organic' group tended to have more severe intellectual disabilities than the 'environmental' group. The former were typically classified as having moderate, severe or profound intellectual disabilities, and the latter as having mild disabilities. However, for many cases a range of aetiological factors may be identified. Also, there is now evidence that some cases of mild intellectual disability are associated with organic factors. For example, many females with fragile X syndrome and most people with Prader-Willi syndrome have mild intellectual disabilities (Volkmar and Dykens, 2002). This led in AAMR 9 to the introduction of a multifactorial system for classifying aetiological factors as biomedical social, behavioural and educational. The continued use of such a system has been recommended when classifying by aetiology in AAMR 10. Biomedical, social, behavioural and educational risk factors for intellectual disability which may occur during prenatal, perinatal and postnatal periods are summarized in Table 1.5.

Biomedical aetiological factors

During the prenatal period a variety of biomedical factors have been implicated in the aetiology of intellectual disability. Intellectual disability may be caused by genetically determined syndromes with behavioural phenotypes including Down, Angelman, Cornelia de Lange, fragile X, Lesch-Nyhan, Prader-Willi, Rett, Smith-Magenis, tuberous sclerosis complex, velocardiofacial, and Williams syndromes, all of which are described in detail in

Table 1.5 Risk factors for intellectual disability

Timing	Biomedical	Social	Behavioural	Educational
Prenatal	• Syndromes and behavioural phenotypes • Metabolic disorders • Maternal illness • Parental age	• Poverty • Maternal malnutrition • Lack of access to prenatal care	• Parental drug use • Parental alcohol use • Parental smoking • Domestic violence	• Parental intellectual disability without supports • Lack of preparation for parenthood
Perinatal	• Prematurity • Birth injury • Neonatal disorders	• Lack of access to birth care	• Parental rejection of caretaking • Parental abandonment of child	• Lack of medical referral for intervention services at discharge
Postnatal	• Traumatic brain injury • Malnutrition • Meningoencephalitis • Seizure disorders • Degenerative disorders	• Poverty • Institutional upbringing	• Lack of stimulation • Child abuse and neglect • Inadequate safety • Chronic parent–child conflict • Domestic violence	• Delayed diagnosis • Inadequate early intervention • Inadequate special educational services • Inadequate family support

Note: Adapted from Luckasson, R., Northwick-Duffy, S., Buntinx, W., Coulter, D., Craig, E., Reeve, A., Schalock, R., Snell, M., Spitalnik, D., Spreat, S., and Tasse, M. (2002) *Mental Retardation: Definition, Classification, and Systems of Supports* (10th edn). Washington, DC: American Association on Mental Retardation, p. 127.

Chapter 14. Down syndrome and fragile X syndrome are by far the most common of these behavioural phenotypes. Metabolic disorders may lead to intellectual disability. Of these phenylketonuria and congenital hypothyroidism are the most common. Fortunately both of these can be treated: hypothyroidism with thyroxine and PKU with a diet low in phenylalanine. Many countries routinely screen neonates for these conditions (Deb and Ahmed, 2000). Increasing maternal age (past thirty years) and maternal illness, particularly HIV infection, hepatitis, rubella, diabetes, cytomegalovirus (which causes inflammation of brain tissue), toxoplasmosis (which destroys brain tissue) and bacterial meningitis are risk factors for intellectual disability, as is maternal exposure to potential toxins such as lead or radiation. During the perinatal period, prematurity, low birth weight, birth injury, and neonatal disorders are all significant risk factors for delayed cognitive development (Kaski, 2000; Volkmar and Dykens, 2002). Important neonatal disorders include seizures, infections, respiratory distress or anoxia indicated by low Apgar scores, or brain haemorrhage. The infant's postnatal medical status is typically expressed as an Apgar score. Apgar scores range from 0–10, with scores below 4 reflecting sufficient difficulties to warrant intensive care. The score is based on an evaluation of the infant's skin colour (with blue suggesting anoxia), respiration, heart rate, muscle tone, and response to stimulation. After birth intellectual disability may be caused by many factors including traumatic brain injury, malnutrition, seizure disorders and by degenerative disorders (Goodman, 2002). Identifying specific aetiological biomedical factors is important for good clinical practice. In some instances, such as PKU or hypothyroidism, intellectual disability may be prevented. In cases where intellectual disability is associated with a particular syndrome or behavioural phenotype, then information on the course and outcome for the condition may be used in planning supports. Specific support needs associated with a number of syndromes associated with intellectual disability are discussed in Chapter 14. Genetic counselling may be given to families in instances where there is evidence for the role of genetic factors in the aetiology of intellectual disability. Also, families may benefit from membership of support groups formed specifically for parents of children with specific syndromes.

Social aetiological factors

During the prenatal, perinatal and postnatal periods a variety of social factors can have a negative impact on cognitive development. Poverty is chief among these and other social risk factors are a direct or indirect consequence of poverty (Friedman and Chase-Lansdale, 2002). Prenatal social risk factors include maternal malnutrition and lack of access to prenatal care. A lack of access to birth care is the principal perinatal risk factor. Institutional upbringing is an important social risk factor during the postnatal period.

Comprehensive family support which includes social welfare supports may modify the impact of these risk factors (Lange and Carr, 2002).

Behavioural aetiological factors

Disorganized parental behaviour during the prenatal, perinatal and postnatal periods may contribute directly or indirectly to impaired cognitive development (Friedman and Chase-Lansdale, 2002). During the prenatal period parental drug and alcohol use and smoking as well as domestic violence can increase the risk of intellectual disability. Alcohol use can lead to foetal alcohol syndrome, a condition characterized by microcephaly, mental handicap and craniofacial anomalies (Steinhausen, Williams and Spohr, 1994). During the perinatal period, rejection of the caretaking role or abandonment of the child may increase the risk of delayed cognitive development. In infancy and early childhood, the risk of intellectual disability is increased by lack of sensory and intellectual stimulation, child abuse and neglect, inadequate safety, chronic parent–child conflict and domestic violence. Pre-, peri- and postnatal family supports, therapy, and parent training may modify the impact of these risk factors (Lange and Carr, 2002).

Educational aetiological factors

Inadequate education and support, particularly for vulnerable parents and families, may be considered a risk factor for delayed cognitive development. During the prenatal period, where parents with intellectual disabilities have minimal support and lack preparation for parenthood, risks of cognitive delay in their children are increased. During the perinatal period, the risk of intellectual disability is increased where such families are not referred for intervention services before being discharged from the maternity hospital. During infancy and early childhood, delayed diagnosis of developmental delay and inadequate early intervention, special educational services and family support all contribute to the development of intellectual disability. Pre-, peri- and postnatal family supports, timely referral for diagnosis, and early intervention may modify the impact of these risk factors (Lange and Carr, 2002; O'Sullivan and Carr, 2002).

Classification by supports

It may be appropriate to classify cases by level of support required when the principal reason for classification is establishing appropriate levels of required funding. The AAMR 10 model for supports is given in Figure 1.3. Supports are resources that aim to promote development and enhance functioning. Such supports may be provided by service agencies or by a person's natural social network. Supports fall into nine areas: (1) human development; (2)

teaching and education; (3) home living; (4) community living; (5) employment; (6) health and safety; (7) behavioural; (8) social; (9) protection and advocacy. The nature and intensity of supports required in each of these areas depends upon the discrepancy between the requirements and demands of a person's social environment on the one hand and their intellectual capabilities, adaptive skills, and risk and protective factors on the other. The functions of supports are: (1) teaching; (2) befriending; (3) financial planning; (4) employee assistance; (5) behavioural support; (6) in-home living assistance; (7) community access and use; and (8) health assistance. The desired outcomes from using supports include enhanced independence, relationships, and contributions to society, school and community participation and personal well-being. The intensity of supports that any person with an intellectual disability needs will vary across situations and stages of the lifecycle. Distinctions are made in AAMR 10 between intermittent, limited, extensive or pervasive levels of support.

- **Intermittent supports.** A person requiring intermittent supports needs the support at specific times on an 'as needed' basis, such as during lifecycle transitions or crises, such as following job loss or during an episode of illness.
- **Limited supports.** A person requiring limited supports needs the support consistently rather than intermittently, but for a time-limited period, for example the need for employment training when entering the workforce.
- **Extensive supports.** A person requiring extensive supports needs regular, long-term support in at least some living environments. This includes daily supports at home, school or work.
- **Pervasive supports.** A person requiring pervasive supports needs constant, high-intensity support across all living environments and these supports are potentially life-sustaining, for example long-term residential care.

The AAMR 10 manual recommends that a systematic procedure be used to assess required supports and plan the delivery of these. First, identify areas in which supports may be required, with reference to the nine areas in Figure 1.3. The identification of areas should be family-centred in the case of very young children and person-centred in the case of older children and adults. Second, identify support activities for each relevant support area, giving priority to the client's interests and preferences, or those of the family in the case of very young children. Third, evaluate the intensity of support needed in each area, with reference to the four levels of support outlined above. The level of support required is that necessary to achieve outcomes and goals associated with the client living in a more inclusive, integrated and productive environment, not that required to maintain the status quo. Fourth, write an individualized supports plan which specifies how specific support activities will address the requirements for specific levels of support,

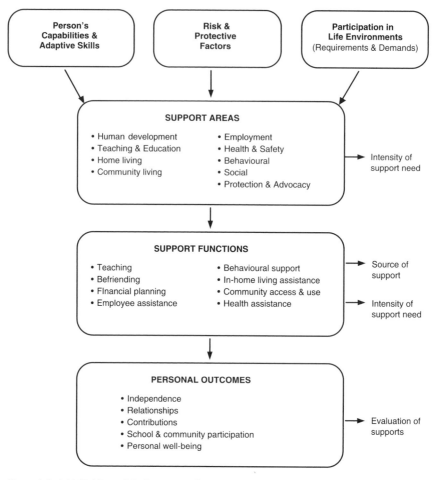

Figure 1.3 AAMR 10 model of supports for people with intellectual disability.

Note: Adapted from Luckasson, R., Borthwick-Duffy, S., Buntinx, W., Coulter, D., Craig, E., Reeve, A., Schalock, R., Snell, M., Spitalnik, D., Spreat, S., and Tasse, M. (2002) *Mental Retardation: Definition, Classification, and Systems of Supports* (10th edn). Washington, DC: American Association on Mental Retardation, p. 148.

and which prioritize the client's interests and preferences, or those of the family in the case of infants and young children. The plan should include clearly stated outcomes or goals and a system for monitoring goal attainment. The plan should favour supports in the client's natural social network. Finally the plan should specify the agencies and people responsible for finding and implementing the plan.

For preschool children, primary school children and adolescents, such individualized support plans will include individual educational plans (IEPs) and also requirements for family support. For adolescents, such plans should address requirements for supports necessary to make the transition from school to employment and to adult activities. Family service planning is covered in Chapter 9, individual educational plans are covered in Chapter 16, and person-centred planning is covered in detail in Chapter 6. Instruments that may be used for support planning for adults with intellectual disabilities are listed in Table 1.6. The Supports Intensity Scale was developed in the US to be compatible with AAMR 10. The Camberwell Assessment of Need for Adults with Developmental and Intellectual Disabilities was developed in the UK. Both instruments have adequate psychometric properties.

EPIDEMIOLOGY

Key findings from reviews of epidemiological literature of relevance to intellectual disabilities are given in Table 1.7. Conclusions drawn from these data

Table 1.6 Psychometric instruments for the assessment of needs and intensity of required supports

Instrument	Comments
Xenitidis, K., Slade, M., Thornicroft, G., and Bouras, N. (2003). *CANDID. Camberwell Assessment of Need for Adults with Developmental and Intellectual Disabilities.* London: Gaskell.	• Interview and rating scale yields a profile of service needs for adults with intellectual disabilities and mental health problems • Covers 25 areas in the domains of social needs (e.g. transport, budgeting), physical health needs, (seizures) and mental health needs (substance misuse, safety) • Standardized in the UK on a small sample of adults • Contains 25 items and takes 30 minutes for a clinician to complete by interviewing a service user or carer
Thompson, J., Bryant, B., Campbell, E., Craig, E., Hughes, C., Rotholz, D., Shalock, R., Silverman, W., Tasse, M., Wehmeyer, M. (2003). *Supports Intensity Scale.* Washington, DC: AAMR. www.aamr.org.	• Interview and rating scale yields a profile of required supports for adults with intellectual disabilities covering 57 activities in 7 areas: home living, community living, life-long learning, employment, health and safety, social interaction, and protection and advocacy • Yields a profile of supports required for 16 physical health and 13 behavioural or mental health problems • Standardized in the US on a sample of over 1000 adults 16–70+ years

Table 1.7 Epidemiology of intellectual disability

	Prevalence %	Source
INTELLECTUAL DISABILITY		
Prevalence of ID in community populations	1–3	DSM-IV
Proportion of all ID that have mild disabilities	85	DSM-IV
Proportion of all ID that have moderate disabilities	10	DSM-IV
Proportion of all ID that have severe disabilities	3–4	DSM-IV
Proportion of all ID that have profound disabilities	1	DSM-IV
ANY PSYCHOLOGICAL DISORDER		
Prevalence of psychological disorders in child community population	10–20	Fombonne (2002)
Prevalence of psychological disorders in children with ID	30–40	Volkmar and Dykens (2002)
Prevalence of psychological disorders in adults community population	20–30	Henderson (2000)
Prevalence of psychological disorders in adults with ID	30–40	Dosen and Day (2001)
AUTISM AND PERVASIVE DEVELOPMENTAL DISORDERS		
Prevalence of autism in the general population	0.2	Melville and Cameron (2003)
Prevalence of autism in people with all levels of ID	1–2	Volkmar and Dykens (2002)
Prevalence of autism in people with severe ID	5	Volkmar and Dykens (2002)
Prevalence of pervasive developmental disorders in people with severe ID	50	Volkmar and Dykens (2002)
Prevalence of learning disabilities in a population of people with autism	80	Howlin (2002)
Prevalence of IQ < 50 in a population of people with autism	50	Howlin (2002)
ADHD		
Prevalence of ADHD in child community population	1–2	Schachar and Tannock (2002)
Prevalence of ADHD in children with ID in the community	7–11	Volkmar and Dykens (2002)
SCHIZOPHRENIA		
Prevalence of schizophrenia in community population	0.4–0.7	Henderson (2000)
Prevalence of schizophrenia in community samples of people with ID	1–9	Volkmar and Dykens (2002)
CHALLENGING BEHAVIOUR		
Prevalence of challenging behaviour in people with ID	7–14	(Emerson, 2001)

Prevalence of challenging behaviour in people with mild ID	7	(Borthwick-Duffy, 1994)
Prevalence of challenging behaviour in people with moderate ID	14	(Borthwick-Duffy, 1994)
Prevalence of challenging behaviour in people with severe ID	22	(Borthwick-Duffy, 1994)
Prevalence of challenging behaviour in people with profound ID	33	(Borthwick-Duffy, 1994)
EPILEPSY		
Prevalence of epilepsy in people with ID	20–25	Iivanainen (2000)
Prevalence of epilepsy in people with mild ID	15–20	Iivanainen (2000)
Prevalence of epilepsy in people with moderate, severe and profound ID	30–50	Iivanainen (2000)
SENSORY IMPAIRMENTS		
Visual impairment in people with ID	10–30	Fryers and Russell (2001)
Auditory impairment in people with ID	5	Fryers and Russell (2001)
MOTOR IMPAIRMENTS	5–40	Fryers and Russell (2001)

are presented in this section. Using a criterion of an IQ below 70 and impaired adaptive behaviour, the overall prevalence of intellectual disability is between 1 per cent and 3 per cent (Fryers, 2000; Volkmar and Dykens, 2002). About 85 per cent of people with intellectual disability fall into the mild range, 10 per cent into the moderate range, 3–4 per cent into the severe range and 1–2 per cent into the profound range. These figures are based on epidemiological community surveys. Typically, administrative prevalence rates are lower than those from such surveys. For example, the national administrative prevalence of intellectual disability in Ireland in the year 2000 was 0.7 per cent and of these cases 41 per cent had mild disabilities, 36 per cent moderate, 15 per cent mild and 4 per cent profound (Mulvaney, 2000). Clearly, many cases of mild intellectual disability went undetected in Ireland in 2000.

Psychological disorders are more common among children and adults with intellectual disabilities than among people without intellectual disabilities in community populations. Autism and other pervasive developmental disorders, psychoses, disruptive behaviour disorders, especially attention deficit hyperactivity disorder (ADHD), challenging behaviour, epilepsy, and sensory and motor impairments are all far more common among people with intellectual disabilities.

Prevalence rates of 'pure' autism are as high as 5 per cent among people with severe intellectual disabilities. However, if all autistic-like pervasive developmental disorders are taken into account, 50% of people with severe intellectual disabilities have these comorbid disorders. The assessment of autism and other pervasive developmental disorders is discussed in Chapter 15.

Rates of ADHD are 3–5 times higher among people with intellectual disabilities than in the normal population. Behaviour problem rating scales that may be used to screen children for ADHD and other behaviour problems are listed in Table 1.8.

The prevalence of schizophrenia is about a half of one per cent in the normal population compared with prevalence rates from 1–9% for people with intellectual disabilities. The assessment and treatment of mental health problems in people with intellectual disabilities is covered in Chapter 22. Between 7 and 14 per cent of people with intellectual disabilities engage in challenging behaviour. This includes aggression, self-injury and damaging property. Rates of challenging behaviour are higher among people with more

Table 1.8 Psychometric instruments for the assessment of behaviour problems

Instrument	*Comments*
Achenbach, T. (2002). *Achenbach System of Empirically Based Assessment* (ASEBA) Burlington, VT, USA http://www.aseba.org/	• This is the most widely used – US-developed – behaviour problem rating scale for children • This suite of instruments includes checklists for completion by parents, teachers and adolescents, each of which contains about 100 items • There are versions of the checklists for $1\frac{1}{2}$–5-year-olds and 6–18-year-olds, and 18–59-year-olds • The instruments are well standardized in the USA and computer scoreable on a PC • Each checklist yields a social competence score, an overall behaviour problems score, broad-band internalizing and externalizing behaviour problem subscale scores and scores on a series of narrow-band subscales • The most widely used of this suite of instruments are called the Child Behaviour Checklist (CBCL), the Teacher Report Form (TRF) and the Youth Self-Report (YSR)
Goodman, R. (2002). *Strengths and Difficulties Questionnaire.* Institute of Psychiatry, London, UK. http://www.sdqinfo.com/	• This is the most widely used – UK-developed – behaviour problem rating scale for children • This suite of instruments includes checklists for completion by parents, teachers and adolescents, each of which contains about 25 items • There are versions of the checklists for 3-year-olds and 4–15-year-olds • The instruments are well standardized in the UK • Each checklist yields a prosocial behaviour score, an overall behaviour problems score and scores for scales that measure emotional symptoms, conduct problems, hyperactivity/inattention, and peer relationship problems

severe intellectual disabilities. The management of challenging behaviour is addressed in Chapter 18.

Seizure disorders occur in up to a quarter of people with intellectual disabilities and the prevalence of epilepsy is higher among people with moderate, severe and profound intellectual disabilities compared with people who have mild intellectual disabilities. Visual and auditory sensory impairments and motor impairments such as cerebral palsy affect more than a quarter of people with intellectual disabilities. Psychometric instruments appropriate for assessing children with sensory and motor deficits are listed in Table 1.9. Depression and substance abuse are less prevalent among people with intellectual disabilities (Volkmar and Dykens, 2002).

In assessment and planning supports it is critical to take account of service needs entailed by the sorts of comorbid mental and physical health problems highlighted in this section.

Table 1.9 Instruments for assessing children with motor and sensory impairments

Disability	Assessment instruments	Comments
Motor disability	Verbal subtests of WPPSI-III; WISC-III; WAIS-III and SB-V	• Gives verbal IQ or estimate of Full-Scale IQ
	Dunn, L. and Dunn, L. (1981). *Peabody Picture Vocabulary Test-Revised.* Circle Pines, MN: American Guidance Service	• Yields measure of receptive language
Hearing disability	Performance subtests of WPPSI-III; WISC-III; WAIS-III and SB-V	• Gives non-verbal IQ or estimate of Full-Scale IQ
	Roid, G. and Miller, L. (1997). *Leiter international Performance Scale – Revised.* Odessa, FL: Psychological Assessment Resources	• Give a measure of non-verbal ability • Standardized on over 2000 US normal and clinical children aged 2–20 • Requires 40 minutes for administration
Visual disability	Verbal subtests of WPPSI-III; WISC-III; WAIS-III and SB-V	• Gives verbal IQ or estimate of Full-Scale IQ
	Davis, C. (1980). *Perkins-Binet Tests of Intelligence for the Blind.* Watertown, MA: Perkins School for the Blind	• Gives Full-Scale IQ
	Newland, T. (1971). *Blind Learning Aptitude Test.* Champaign, IL: University of Illinois Press	• Gives index of overall ability

Dual diagnosis, comorbidity and multiaxial systems

Given the range of comorbid physical and mental health problems associated with intellectual disability, an important consideration is administratively how to code all of this diagnostic information. To address this issue a multiaxial version of ICD 10 (WHO, 1996) has been developed for use with children and the DSM-IV-TR includes a multiaxial system for use with adults and children. These two systems are summarized in Table 1.10. In both systems intellectual disability is not coded on the first axis, which is reserved for psychological disorders such as autism, ADHD or schizophrenia which are of primary concern for mental health services and professions for

Table 1.10 DSM-IV-TR and ICD 10 multiaxial classification systems

ICD 10	DSM-IV-TR
AXIS I CLINICAL PSYCHIATRIC SYNDROMES Pervasive developmental disorders (e.g. childhood autism, Rett's syndrome etc.) **Behavioural and emotional disorders with onset usually occurring in childhood and adolescence** Hyperkinetic disorders (e.g. disturbance of activity and attention) Conduct disorders Mixed disorders of conduct and emotion (e.g. depressive conduct disorder) Emotional disorders with onset specific to childhood (e.g. separation anxiety disorder) Disorders of social functioning with onset specific to childhood (e.g. elective mutism) Tic disorders (e.g. de la Tourette's syndrome) Other childhood disorders (e.g. encopresis and pica) **Organic mental disorders** **Mental and behavioural disorders due to psychoactive substance use** **Schizophrenia, schizotypal and delusional disorders** **Mood disorders** **Neurotic, stress-related and somatoform disorders** **Behavioural syndromes associated with physiological disturbances and physical factors** **Disorders of adult personality and behaviour**	**AXIS I CLINICAL DISORDERS** **Disorders usually first diagnosed in infancy, childhood or adolescence** Learning disorders (e.g. reading disorder) Motor skills development disorder Communication disorders (e.g. expressive language disorder) Pervasive developmental disorder (e.g. autistic disorder) Attention deficit and disruptive behaviour disorders (e.g. conduct disorder) Feeding and eating disorders of infancy and early childhood (e.g. pica) Tic disorders (e.g. Tourette's disorder) Elimination disorders (e.g. encopresis) Other childhood disorders **Delirium, dementia, amnesic and other cognitive disorders** **Mental disorders due to a general medical condition** **Substance-related disorders** **Schizophrenia and other psychotic disorders** **Mood disorders** **Anxiety disorders** **Somatoform disorders** **Factitious disorders** **Dissociative disorders** **Sexual and gender identity disorders** **Eating disorders** **Sleep disorders** **Impulse control disorders** **Adjustment disorders**

AXIS II SPECIFIC DELAYS IN DEVELOPMENT

Specific developmental disorders of speech and language (e.g. expressive language disorder)

Specific developmental disorders of scholastic skills (e.g. specific reading disorder)

Specific developmental disorder of motor function

AXIS III INTELLECTUAL LEVEL

Mild, moderate, severe and profound mental retardation

AXIS IV MEDICAL CONDITIONS

AXIS V ASSOCIATED ABNORMAL PSYCHOSOCIAL SITUATIONS

Abnormal intrafamilial relationships

Familial mental disorder deviance or handicap

Inadequate or distorted intrafamilial communication

Abnormal qualities of upbringing

Abnormal immediate environment

Acute life events

Societal stressors

Chronic interpersonal stress associated with school work

Stress resulting from the child's disorder

AXIS VI GLOBAL ASSESSMENT OF PSYCHOSOCIAL DISABILITY

A score between 0 and 8 is given, e.g.

8: Profound and pervasive social disability

5: Serious and pervasive social disability

2: Slight social disability

0: Superior social functioning

AXIS II MENTAL RETARDATION

(and personality disorders in adults)

AXIS III GENERAL MEDICAL CONDITIONS

AXIS IV PSYCHOSOCIAL AND ENVIRONMENTAL PROBLEMS

Problems with primary support group

Problems related to the social environment

Educational problems

Occupational problems

Housing problems

Economic problems

Problems with access to health care services

Problems related to interaction with the legal system

AXIS V GLOBAL ASSESSMENT OF FUNCTIONING

A score between 1 and 100 is given, e.g.

10: Danger to self and others

50: Serious symptoms and impairment of social functioning

75: Transient impairment of social functioning

100: Superior functioning

Note: Based on WHO (1996) and APA (2000).

which the coding systems were developed. In ICD 10 intellectual disability is coded on axis III and in DSM-IV-TR it is coded on axis II. Both systems have axes on which general medical conditions such as epilepsy or sensory and motor disorders can be coded. Both systems also have axes for coding psychosocial stresses and overall level of functioning, both of which have implications for planning supports. ICD 10 has an additional axis on which specific developmental delays in language, scholastic skills or motor development may be coded. This axis is of little relevance to intellectual disability cases, since specific developmental delays are rarely diagnosed where children show overall delays in cognitive development. For clinical psychologists in training it is important to know about the ICD 10 and DSM-IV TR multiaxial systems in case either is routinely used for coding diagnostic information at placement or internship sites.

DIFFERENTIAL DIAGNOSIS AND COMORBID CONDITIONS

The process of assessment and diagnosis is usually carried out by a multidisciplinary team which may include members of the following professions: paediatrics; nursing; clinical, educational or school psychology; speech and language therapy; teaching; psychiatry; neurology; social work; occupational therapy; and physiotherapy. The composition of the assessment team, the way clinical and administrative responsibilities are shared within teams, and the way people are referred for assessment will vary depending upon local practices; health, education and social service systems; and overall policies and legislation, all of which vary from one jurisdiction to another. For clinical psychologists in training, it is important when working on a disability placement or internship to find out how local guidelines are used to implement national policies. For qualified professionals it is vital to keep abreast of changes in policy, practices and funding systems for people with disabilities.

Early detection, metabolic disorders, syndromes and multiple disabilities

In some instances, the risk of intellectual disability will be detected through postnatal screening procedures and it may be possible to prevent the development of intellectual disability. For example, in Ireland, the UK and many other countries, a test for PKU is routinely conducted shortly after the child is born, since, as has been previously mentioned, early detection of this disorder permits the prevention of intellectual disability through dietary intervention.

In clinical practice the range of disorders to include in the differential diagnosis depends upon the degree of intellectual disability, the presence and extent of comorbid physical and mental health problems, the age of the client, and the observational skills and communication skills of the client's primary carers.

Children with specific syndromes that have distinctive clinical features, such as Down syndrome, associated with intellectual disability, and intellectually disabled children with low birth weight, distress at birth, or who have been exposed to any prenatal factors that may cause intellectual disability (listed in Table 1.5) will be detected early, usually by a paediatrics service.

Children with multiple sensory or motor disabilities who show a low level of alertness will, in most jurisdictions, be intensively monitored during the first months of life, usually by a paediatrics service. If severe intellectual disabilities are present, these will be detected early. In such cases, careful documentation over a number of months of the child's rate of attainment of the milestones listed in Table 1.1 will indicate the occurrence of a developmental delay.

Specific language delay

Once there is evidence of a developmental delay, to determine whether it is a specific language delay, or a general delay in cognitive development, formal psychological assessment of intellectual abilities and language development may be conducted and repeated at six-monthly or annual intervals coupled with direct observation of the child and interviews with parents. Where test scores, clinical observations and data from parental interviews consistently indicate an IQ below 70 and deficits in adaptive behaviour, then a diagnosis of intellectual disability may be made. Where children have sensory and motor deficits, psychometric instruments listed in Table 1.9 may be used. With developmental language delay or motor delay, the child shows delayed development in a circumscribed area but age-appropriate development in other areas. This may be indicated by a major discrepancy of 1–2 standard deviations between scores on a standardized language test such as the *Reynell Developmental Language Scales. III*, listed in Table 1.11, and scores which fall in the normal range on a non-verbal test of general intelligence such as the *Leiter International Performance Scale – Revised* listed in Table 1.9. The diagnostic criteria for developmental language delay are given in Table 1.12.

Table 1.11 Psychometric instruments for the assessment of specific language difficulties and specific learning disabilities

Instrument	Comments
Edwards, S., Fletcher, M., Garman, A., Hughes, A., Letts, C. and Sinka, I. (1997). *Reynell Developmental Language Scales. III.* Windsor: NFER-Nelson	• Measures children's expressive language and verbal comprehension • The Comprehension Scale comprises 62 items organized into 10 sections: single words, relating two named objects, agents and actions, clausal constituents, attributes, noun phrases, locative relations, verbs and thematic role assignment, vocabulary and complex grammar and inferencing • The Expressive Scale comprises 62 items organized into 6 main sections: simple words, verbs and phrases, inflections – plurals and third person and past tense, clausal elements, auxiliaries – negatives and questions and tags, complex structures – initiation and correction of errors and utterance completion • UK norms available for children aged 15 mths–7 yrs

(Continued overleaf)

Table 1.11 continued

Instrument	Comments
Rust, J. (1995). *Wechsler Individual Achievement Tests.* San Antonio, TX: Psychological Corporation	• Contains the Wechsler Objective Reading Test (WORD) which yields measures of Basic Reading, Reading Comprehension and Spelling • Contains the Wechsler Objective Language Dimension (WOLD) which yields measures of Listening Comprehension, Oral Expression and Written Expression • Contains the Wechsler Objective Numerical Dimensions (WOND) which yields measures of Mathematics Reasoning and Numerical Operations • Standardized in the US and UK on children 6–17
Wilkinson, G. (1993). *Wide Range Achievement Test – 3 (WRAT-3).* Wide Range Inc, 15 Ashley Place, Suite 1a, Wilminton, Delaware 19804–1314. Phone 302–652–4990	• For preschool and primary school children and adults aged 5 years to 75 years • Contains three subtests and takes about 30 minutes to administer. • Yields word recognition, spelling and arithmetic quotients • Standardized in the US

Table 1.12 Diagnostic criteria for developmental language delay

	ICD 10	DSM-IV-TR
Mixed receptive-expressive language disorder	A specific developmental disorder in which the child's understanding of language is below the appropriate level for his or her mental age. In almost all cases, expressive language is markedly disturbed and abnormalities in word-sound production are common Failure to respond to familiar names by the first birthday; inability to name a few objects by 18 months or failure to follow simple, routine instructions by the age of 2 years should be taken as significant signs of delay. Later difficulties include inability to understand	A. The scores obtained from a battery of standardized individually administered measures of both receptive and expressive language development is substantially below those obtained from standardized measures of non-verbal intellectual capacity. Symptoms include those for expressive language disorder as well as difficulty understanding words, sentences, or specific types of words such as spatial terms B. The difficulties with receptive and expressive language significantly interfere with academic or occupational achievement or with social communication C. Criteria are not met for a pervasive developmental disorder

grammatical structures (negatives, questions or comparatives) and lack of understanding if more subtle aspects of language (such as tone of voice)

D. If mental retardation, a speech-motor or sensory deficit or environmental deprivation is present, the language difficulties are in excess of those usually associated with these problems

Expressive language disorder

A specific developmental disorder in which the child's ability to use expressive spoken language is markedly below the appropriate level for his or her mental age, but in which language comprehension is within normal limits. There may or may not be abnormalities in articulation

The absence of single words (or word approximations) by 2 years and the failure to generate simple two-word phrases by 3 years should be taken as significant signs of delay. Later difficulties include restricted vocabulary development; overuse of a small set of general words; difficulties in selecting appropriate words; word substitutions; short utterances; immature sentence structure; syntactical errors especially omissions of word endings or prefixes; misuse or failure to use prepositions, pronouns, articles, and verb and noun inflections. Incorrect overgeneralizations of rules may occur as may lack of sentence fluency and difficulties in sequencing when recounting past events. There may also be delays or abnormalities in word-sound production

A. The scores obtained from a battery of standardized individually administered measures of expressive language development are substantially below those obtained from standardized measures of both non-verbal intellectual capacity and receptive language development. The disturbance may be manifest by symptoms that include having a markedly limited vocabulary, making errors in tense, or having difficulty recalling words or producing sentences with developmentally appropriate length or complexity

B. The difficulties with expressive language significantly interfere with academic or occupational achievement or with social communication

C. Criteria are not met for a mixed receptive-expressive language disorder or a pervasive developmental

D. If mental retardation, a speech-motor or sensory deficit or environmental deprivation is present, the language difficulties are in excess of those usually associated with these problems

Note: Adapted from ICD 10 (WHO, 1992; 1996) and DSM-IV-TR (APA, 2000).

The autistic spectrum and pervasive developmental disorders

With preschool children, particularly those who show moderate, severe or profound levels of intellectual disability, the possibility of comorbid pervasive developmental disorders (or autistic spectrum disorders as they are also known) should be borne in mind. These include autism, Rett's syndrome, childhood disintegrative disorder, and pervasive developmental disorder – not otherwise specified. Children with intellectual disability and comorbid pervasive developmental disorders show both delayed development as indicated by full-scale IQs below 70 and varying degrees and patterning of qualitative impairments in reciprocal social interaction and communication as well as restricted, stereotyped behaviour patterns. The diagnostic criteria for autism are given in Table 1.13. Assessment of these features is discussed in Chapter 15.

Table 1.13 Diagnostic criteria for autism in DSM-IV and ICD 10

ICD 10	DSM-IV-TR
A pervasive developmental disorder defined by the presence of abnormal and/or impaired development that is manifest before the age of 3 years, and by the characteristic type of abnormal functioning in three areas of social interaction, communication and restricted repetitive behaviour	A At least six of the following with at least two items from 1 and one each from 2 and 3 1. Qualitative impairment of social interaction as manifested by at least two of the following: (a) Marked impairments in the use of multiple non-verbal behaviours such as eye-to-eye gaze, facial expression, body postures, and gestures to regulate social interaction
Usually there is no prior period of unequivocally normal development but, if there is, abnormality become apparent before the age of 3 years. There are always qualitative impairments in reciprocal social interaction. These take the form of an inadequate appreciation of socio-emotional cues, as shown by a lack of responses to other peoples' emotions and/or a lack of modulation of behaviour according to social context; poor use of social signals and a weak integration of social, emotional, and communicative behaviours; and, especially, a lack of socio-emotional reciprocity	(b) Failure to develop peer relationships appropriate to developmental level (c) A lack of spontaneous seeking to share enjoyment, interests, or achievements with other people (d) Lack of social or emotional reciprocity 2. Qualitative impairments in communication as manifested by at least one of the following:
Similarly qualitative impairments in communication are universal. These take the form of a lack of social usage of whatever language skills are present; impairment of make-believe and social imitative play; poor synchrony and lack of reciprocity in conversational interchange; poor flexibility	(a) Delay in, or total lack of, the development of spoken language (b) In individuals with adequate speech, marked impairment in the ability to initiate or sustain a conversation with others

in language expression and a relative lack of creativity and fantasy in thought processes; lack of emotional response to other people's verbal and non-verbal overtures; impaired use of variations in cadence or emphasis to reflect communicative modulation; and a similar lack of accompanying gesture to provide emphasis or aid meaning in spoken communication

The condition is also characterized by restricted, repetitive and stereotyped patterns of behaviour, interests and activities. These take the form of a tendency to impose rigidity and routine on a wide range of aspects of day-to-day functioning; this usually applies to novel activities as well as to familiar habits and play patterns

In early childhood there may be attachment to unusual, typically non-soft objects. The children may insist on the performance of particular routines or rituals of a non-functional character; there may be stereotyped preoccupations with interests such as dates, routes or timetables; often there are motor stereotypes; a specific interest in non-functional elements of objects (such as their smell or feel) is common; and there may be resistance to changes in routine or details of the personal environment

(c) Stereotyped and repetitive use of language or idiosyncratic language
(d) Lack of varied, spontaneous make-believe play or social imitative play appropriate to developmental level

3. Restricted repetitive and stereotyped patterns of behaviour, interests, and activities as manifested by at least one of the following:
    (a) Encompassing preoccupation with one or more stereotyped and restricted patterns of interest that is abnormal either in intensity or focus
    (b) Apparently inflexible adherence to specific, non-functional routines or rituals
    (c) Stereotyped and repetitive motor mannerisms
    (d) Persistent preoccupation with parts of objects

B Delays or abnormal functioning in at least one of the following areas, with onset prior to age 3 years: (1) social interaction; (2) language as used in social communication; or (3) symbolic or imaginative play

C The disturbance is not better accounted for by Rett's Disorder or Childhood Disintegrative Disorder

Note: Adapted from ICD 10 (WH0, 1992; 1996) and DSM-IV-TR (APA, 2000).

Specific learning disabilities

School-aged children or adolescents, with mild or moderate intellectual disabilities that have gone undiagnosed during the preschool years, are typically referred to psychologists for assessment of scholastic attainment often coupled with either behaviour problems or daydreaming. The principal differential diagnosis in school-aged children is between a specific learning disability and a general intellectual disability. Diagnostic criteria for specific learning disabilities are given in Table 1.14. Children with specific learning disabilities obtain full-scale IQ scores above 70 and scores on standardized achievement tests, such as those listed in Table 1.11, that fall below the level expected, given their overall IQ. In the manual for the *Wechsler Individual Achievement Tests* (listed in Table 1.11), tabular systems are given for deciding

Table 1.14 Diagnostic criteria for specific learning disabilities

	ICD 10	DSM-IV-TR
Reading disorder	The child's reading performance should be significantly below the level expected on the basis of age, general intelligence, and school placement and not due to visual acuity problems Performance is best assessed by means of an individually administered, standardized test of reading accuracy and comprehension In early stages of learning there may be difficulties in reciting the alphabet, naming letters or rhyming Later there may be difficulties in oral reading such as omissions, substitutions, distortions, or additions. Slow reading speed, frequent loss of place, and reversals may also occur Comprehension problems, such as inability to recall facts read and inability to draw conclusions from material read, may also occur In later childhood and adulthood, spelling difficulties may predominate, with phonological errors being the most common	A Reading achievement as measured by individually administered standardized tests of reading accuracy or comprehension is substantially below that expected given the person's chronological age, measured intelligence and age-appropriate education B The disturbance significantly interferes with academic achievement or activities of daily living that require reading skills C If a sensory deficit is present, the reading difficulties are in excess of those usually associated with it
Mathematics disorder	The child's arithmetical performance should be significantly below the level expected on the basis of his or her age, general intelligence, and school placement, and is best assessed by means of an individually administered standardized test of arithmetic Reading and spelling should be within the normal range	A Mathematical ability as measured by individually administered standardized tests is substantially below that expected given the person's chronological age, measured intelligence and age-appropriate education B The disturbance significantly interferes with academic achievement or activities of daily living that require mathematical ability

The difficulties in arithmetic should not be due to grossly inadequate teaching, or to the direct effects of defects of visual, hearing, or neurological function and should not have been acquired as a result of any neurological, psychiatric or other disorder

The arithmetic difficulties that occur are various but may include failure to understand the concepts underlying particular arithmetic operations; lack of understanding of mathematical terms or signs; failure to recognize numerical symbols; difficulty in carrying out standard numerical manipulations; difficulties in understanding which numbers are relevant to the arithmetic problem being considered; difficulty in properly aligning numbers or in inserting decimal points or symbols during calculations; poor spatial organization of arithmetic calculations; and inability to learn multiplication tables

There may be impairment of visuospatial skills

C If a sensory deficit is present, the difficulties in mathematical ability are in excess of those usually associated with it

Note: Adapted from ICD 10 (WH0, 1992; 1996) and DSM-IV-TR (APA, 2000).

whether achievement test scores are significantly below the level expected for the child's IQ on a Wechsler intelligence test (all of which are listed in Table 1.3). Where a person's scores on tests of both intelligence and achievement fall below 70, and they show other adaptive behaviour deficits, then a diagnosis of intellectual disability may be made.

Attention deficit hyperactivity disorder

As has been mentioned, often when school-aged children with undetected learning disabilities are referred for assessment, in addition to scholastic problems, behavioural difficulties are also a concern. Screen for behavioural difficulties using the parent and teacher versions for *Strengths and Difficulties Questionnaire* (SDQ) or the Child Behaviour Checklist (CBCL) and Teacher Report Form (TRF), which are listed in Table 1.8 above. These instruments will indicate the extent of the behaviour problems and the degree to which these are coupled with attention problems suggestive of Attention Deficit Hyperactivity Disorder. Diagnostic criteria for ADHD are given in Table 1.15. Children who meet these criteria and who do not respond to behavioural management of challenging behaviour described in Chapter 18 may benefit from a multimodal treatment programme, which includes stimulant treatment (with methylphenidate) and behavioural management (Nolan and Carr,

Table 1.15 Diagnostic criteria for attention and hyperactivity syndromes

ICD 10 Hyperkinetic Disorders	DSM-IV-TR Attention Deficit Hyperactivity Disorder

The cardinal features are impaired attention and overactivity. Both are necessary for the diagnosis and should be evident in **more than one situation** (e.g. home or school)
Impaired attention is manifested by prematurely breaking off from tasks and leaving activities unfinished. The children change frequently from one activity to another, seemingly losing interest in one task because they become diverted to another. These deficits in persistence and attention should be diagnosed only if they are excessive for the child's age and IQ
Overactivity implies excessive restlessness, especially in situations requiring relative calm. It may, depending upon the situation, involve the child running and jumping around, getting up from a seat when he or she was supposed to remain seated, excessive talkativeness and noisiness, or fidgeting and wriggling. The standard for judgement should be that the activity is excessive in the context of what is expected in the situation and by comparison with other children of the same age and IQ. This behavioural feature is most evident in structured, organized situations that require a high degree of behavioural self-control
	A Either 1 or 2
	1. Six or more of the following symptoms of inattention have persisted for at least 6 months to a degree that is maladaptive and inconsistent with developmental level
	Inattention
	  a Often fails to give close attention to details or makes careless mistakes in schoolwork, work or other activities
	  b Often has difficulty sustaining attention in tasks or play activities
	  c Often does not seem to listen when spoken to directly
	  d Often does not follow through on instructions and fails to finish schoolwork, chores or work duties
	  e Often has difficulty organizing tasks and activities
	  f Often avoids or dislikes tasks that require sustained mental effort
	  g Often loses things necessary for tasks or activities
	  h Is often easily distracted by extraneous stimuli
	  i Is often forgetful in daily activities
	
	2 Six or more of the following symptoms of **hyperactivity-impulsivity** have persisted for at least 6 months to a degree that is

The characteristic behaviour problems should be of early onset (before the age of 6 years) and long duration

Associated features include disinhibition in social relationships, recklessness in situations involving some danger, impulsive flouting of social rules, learning disorders, and motor clumsiness

Specify:

Hyperkinetic disorder with disturbance of activity and attention when antisocial features of conduct disorder are absent

Hyperkinetic conduct disorder when criteria for both conduct disorder and hyperkinetic disorder are met

maladaptive and inconsistent with developmental level

Hyperactivity

  a Often fidgets with hands or feet or squirms in seat

  b Often leaves seat in classroom or in other situations in which remaining seated is expected

  c Often runs about or climbs excessively in situations in which it is inappropriate

  d Often has difficulty playing or engaging in leisure activities quietly

  e Is often on the go or acts as if driven by a motor

  f Often talks excessively

Impulsivity

  g Often blurts out answer before questions have been completed

  h Often has difficulty awaiting turn

  i Often interrupts or intrudes on others

B Some of these symptoms were present before the age of 7 years

C Some impairment from the symptoms is present in **two or more settings** (e.g. home and school)

D Clinically significant impairment in social, academic or occupational functioning

E Not due to another disorder

Specify:

Combined type if inattention and overactivity-impulsivity are present; *inattentive type* if overactivity is absent; *hyperactive-impulsive type* if inattentiveness is absent

Note: Adapted from ICD 10 (WHO, 1992; 1996) and DSM-IV-TR (APA, 2000).

2000). Clinical psychologists typically contribute to such multimodal programmes in collaboration with colleagues from paediatrics or psychiatry.

Seizure disorders – epilepsy

As has been mentioned, often when school-aged children with undetected learning disabilities are referred for assessment, in addition to scholastic problems, daydreaming is also a concern. Of course in some instances children with intellectual disabilities lose concentration and do not focus on their schoolwork. However, frequently what appear to be daydreaming are petite mal epileptic 'absences'. If children report 'losing time' or not being aware of what is happening during these episodes, a referral for neurological assessment and an EEG is appropriate to determine if a diagnosis of a seizure disorder is appropriate. As was noted in Table 1.7 above, more than a quarter of people with intellectual disabilities also have epilepsy, which can be controlled in most cases with anticonvulsant medication. Also, distress associated with the reactions of the child, parents and teachers to seizures may be greatly reduced if a definitive diagnosis is given, clear psychoeducation about epilepsy offered and an appropriate medication regime put in place.

COURSE AND OUTCOME

The outcome for intellectual disability depends on a range of factors including the level of disability; the level of adaptive behaviour; the presence of comorbid sensory and motor disabilities; the presence of comorbid psychological disorders; family stability; and level of supports available (Dosen and Day, 2001; Kaski, 2000; Volkmar and Dykens, 2002). The best prognosis occurs for people with mild disabilities and good adaptive behavioural skills who have few comorbid difficulties and come from stable families and contexts within which there is a good deal of support.

SUMMARY

Infants and children who do not achieve milestones at expected times and youngsters with scholastic attainment problems may be referred to clinical psychologists for assessment of suspected intellectual disability. Definitions of intellectual disability are given in ICD 10, DSM-IV-TR and AAMR 10. Deficits in both intellectual functioning and adaptive behaviour are central to the definitions of intellectual disability in all three systems. Multifactorial models of key factors that affect functioning in people with intellectual disabilities have been offered by the WHO in the ICF and by the AAMR in the tenth revision of their diagnostic handbook. The classification of intellectual disability into mild, moderate, severe and profound subcategories is used in both ICD 10 and DSM-IV-TR. In AAMR 10 it is possible to classify cases on the basis of level of disability, level of adaptive functioning, aetiology and level of support requirement depending upon the purpose of classification. When profiling cases on adaptive behaviour, an individual's status on measures of conceptual, social and practical skills should be given. When classifying cases aetiologically, account should be taken of the role of biomedical social, behavioural and educational risk factors present at prenatal, perinatal and postnatal periods. Cases may be classified as requiring intermittent, limited, extensive or pervasive supports. The AAMR 10 manual recommends that a systematic procedure be used to assess required supports and plan the delivery of these. The plan should specify the agencies and people responsible for funding and implementing the plan. The overall prevalence of intellectual disability is between 1 per cent and 3 per cent and the majority of cases have mild levels of intellectual disabilities. Autism and other pervasive developmental disorders, psychoses, disruptive behaviour disorders, especially attention deficit hyperactivity disorder (ADHD), challenging behaviour, epilepsy, and sensory and motor impairments are all far more common among people with intellectual disabilities than among people with normal levels of intellectual ability. In assessment and planning supports it is critical to take account of service needs entailed by such comorbid mental and physical health problems. ICD 10 and DSM-IV-TR multiaxial systems may be used to code these comorbid conditions. The process of assessment and diagnosis is usually carried out by a multidisciplinary team. In some instances, the risk of intellectual disability will be detected through postnatal screening. For children with specific syndromes that have distinctive clinical features associated with intellectual disability, and children with low birth weight, distress at birth, or who have been exposed to significant prenatal risk factors, intellectual disability will usually be detected in the early weeks of life. For children requiring assessment for suspected intellectual disability in infancy, the main differential diagnosis is between a specific language delay and general intellectual disability which is indexed by the absence of a major discrepancy between scores on standardized language and non-verbal intelligence tests. For preschool children, the possibility of comorbid pervasive developmental disorders or autistic spectrum disorders should be borne in mind. School-aged children or adolescents with mild or moderate intellectual disabilities who have gone undiagnosed during the preschool years are typically referred to psychologists for assessment of scholastic attainment often coupled with either behaviour problems or daydreaming. The principal differential diagnosis in school-aged children is between a specific learning disability and general intellectual disability, which is indexed by the absence of a major discrepancy between attainment and intelligence scores. Behaviour problems in school-aged children may reflect the presence of ADHD. Referrals for daydreaming may indicate the need for assessment of seizure disorders. The best outcome occurs for people with mild disabilities and good adaptive behavioural skills who have few comorbid difficulties and who come from stable families and contexts within which there is a good deal of support.

EXERCISE

Work in teams of 2–4 people. For each of the case vignettes below, list your main hypotheses about (1) Level of intellectual functioning; (2) Level of adaptive behaviour; (3) Overall level of intellectual disability; (4) Possible comorbid conditions or problems; (5) Possible aetiological factors; (6) Probable required supports. For each case, develop an assessment plan indicating the interviews, tests and other investigations that you think should be conducted. Also outline the professionals or disciplines on a disability assessment team that would need to make a contribution to the overall assessment process. Present your hypotheses and assessment plan to your class.

Sarah is a 2½-year-old girl who was referred to a disability assessment team by a community health nurse. Sarah was a premature low birth-weight child. At the end of her first year she began babbling. She sat up at 13 months, stood at 18 months and walked at 2, and shortly afterwards began to say 'MAMA'. She plays a little now. She feeds well. Her body is well developed but her face has always looked a bit peculiar. The proportions of her features are unusual. She lives with her mother and father both of whom are in their late thirties. They are both employed and are devoted to Sarah who is their only child.

Sam is a 9-year-old boy and was referred for psycho-educational assessment by his school principal. Sam is in the second class in a mainstream primary school. He is about a year older than the other children, having repeated a year to give him a chance to catch up with his peers academically. However, despite this extra year and some remedial tuition, his reading, spelling and arithmetic scores on standardized tests are all below the fifth percentile. Also his behaviour is very troublesome. He has difficulty sitting still, completing tasks, and following his teacher's instructions. He also has difficulty mixing with his peers. As far as the referring teacher knows, Sam's preschool development was fairly normal, but there is little information on his first five years. He lives with his unemployed mother in a rented apartment. His father, who lives in another town, visits him occasionally.

FURTHER READING AND RESOURCES FOR CLINICIANS

Luckasson, R., Borthwick-Duffy, S., Buntinx, W., Coulter, D., Craig, E., Reeve, A., Schalock, R., Snell, M., Spitalnik, D., Spreat, S. and Tasse, M. (2002). *Mental Retardation: Definition, Classification, and Systems of Supports* (10th edn, AAMR 10). Washington, DC: American Association on Mental Retardation.
Schalock, R. (2002). *Adaptive Behaviour and Its Measurements: Implications for the Field of Mental Retardation.* Washington, DC: American Association on Mental Retardation.
Learning Disabilities – Learning Abilities. 45-minute video that gives information on recognizing intellectual disabilities available at www.brookespublishing.com
British Institute of Learning Disabilities. http://www.bild.org.uk/

American Association for Mental Retardation. http://www.aamr.org
Brookes Publishers. www.brookespublishing.com
National Autistic Society. www.nas.@nas.org.uk

REFERENCES

American Psychiatric Association (APA) (2000). *Diagnostic and Statistical Manual of the Mental Disorders (Fourth Edition-Text Revision, DSM-IV-TR)*. Washington, DC: APA.

Borthwick-Duffy, S. (1994). Prevalence of destructive behaviours. In T. Thompson and D. Gray (eds), *Destructive Behaviour in Developmental Disabilities: Diagnosis and Treatment* (pp. 3–23). Thousand Oaks, CA: Sage.

Bronfenbrenner, U. (1979). *The Ecology of Human Development: Experiments by Nature and Design*. Cambridge, MA: Harvard University Press.

Carrol, J. B. (1993). *Human Cognitive Abilities: A Survey of Factor Analytic Abilities*. New York: Cambridge University Press.

Deb, S. and Ahmed, Z. (2000). Specific conditions leading to mental retardation. In. M. Gelder, J. Lopez-Ibor and N. Andreasen (eds), *New Oxford Textbook of Psychiatry* (vol. 2, section 10.4, pp. 1953–63). Oxford: Oxford University Press.

Dosen, A. and Day, K. (2001). Epidemiology, aetiology and presentation of mental illness and behaviour disorders in persons with mental retardation. In A. Dosen and K. Day (eds), *Treating Mental Illness and Behaviour Disorders in Children and Adults with Mental Retardation* (pp. 3–26). Washington, DC: American Psychiatric Association.

Dreary, I. (2000). *Looking Down on Human Intelligence*. Oxford. Oxford University Press.

Emerson, E. (2001). *Challenging Behaviour: Analysis and Intervention in People with Severe Intellectual Disabilities* (2nd edn). Cambridge: Cambridge University Press.

Fombonne, E. (2002). Case identification in an epidemiological context. In Rutter, M. and Taylor, E. (eds), *Child and Adolescent Psychiatry* (4th edn, pp. 52–69). Oxford: Blackwell.

Friedman, R. and Chase-Lansdale, P. (2002). Chronic adversities. In Rutter, M. and Taylor, E. (eds), *Child and Adolescent Psychiatry* (4th edn, pp. 261–76). Oxford: Blackwell.

Fryers, T. (2000). Epidemiology of mental retardation. In M. Gelder, J. Lopez-Ibor and N. Andreasen (eds), *New Oxford Textbook of Psychiatry* (vol. 2, section 10.2, pp. 1941–45). Oxford: Oxford University Press.

Fryers, T. and Russell, O. (2001). Applied epidemiology. In W. Fraser and M. Kerr (2003), *Seminars in the Psychiatry of Learning Disabilities* (2nd edn, pp. 16–48). London: Gaskell.

Goodman, R. (2002). Brain disorders. In M. Rutter and E. Taylor (eds), *Child and Adolescent Psychiatry* (4th edn, pp. 241–60). Oxford: Blackwell.

Heber, R. (1959). A manual on terminology and classification in mental retardation. *American Journal of Mental Deficiency*, 64, Monograph Supplement.

Henderson, S. (2000). The contribution of epidemiology to psychiatric aetiology.

In M. Gelder, J. Lopez-Ibor and N. Andreasen (eds), *New Oxford Textbook of Psychiatry* (vol. 1, pp. 308–19). Oxford: Oxford University Press.

Howlin, P. (2002). Autistic disorders. In P. Howlin and O. Udwin (eds), *Outcomes in Neurodevelopmental and Genetic Disorders* (pp. 136–68). Cambridge: Cambridge University Press.

Iivanainen, M. (2000). Epilepsy and epilepsy related behaviour disorders among people with mental retardation. In M. Gelder, J. Lopez-Ibor and N. Andreasen (eds), *New Oxford Textbook of Psychiatry* (vol. 2, section 10.5.3, pp. 1979–88). Oxford: Oxford University Press.

Kaski, M. (2000). Aetiology of mental retardation: General issues and prevention. In M. Gelder, J. Lopez-Ibor and N. Andreasen (eds), *New Oxford Textbook of Psychiatry* (vol. 2, section 10.3, pp. 1948–52). Oxford: Oxford University Press.

Lange, G. and Carr, A. (2002). Chapter 3. Prevention of cognitive delays in socially disadvantaged children. In A. Carr (ed.), *Prevention: What Works with Children and Adolescents? A Critical Review of Psychological Prevention Programmes for Children, Adolescents and their Families* (pp. 41–63). London: Routledge.

Luckasson, R., Borthwick-Duffy, S., Buntinx, W., Coulter, D., Craig, E., Reeve, A., Schalock, R., Snell, M., Spitalnik, D., Spreat, S. and Tasse, M. (2002). *Mental Retardation: Definition, Classification, and Systems of Supports* (10th edn). Washington, DC: American Association on Mental Retardation.

Luckasson, R., Coulter, D., Polloway, E., Reiss, S., Schalock, R. W., Snell, M., Spitalnik, D. and Stark, J. (1992). *Mental Retardation: Definition, Classification, and Systems of Supports* (9th edn). Washington, DC: American Association on Mental Retardation.

Melville, C. and Cameron, J. (2003). Autism. In W. Fraser and M. Kerr (eds), *Seminars in the Psychiatry of Learning Disabilities* (2nd edn, pp. 115–34). London: Gaskell.

Mulvaney, F. (2000). *Annual Report of the National Intellectual Disability Data Base Committee.* Dublin: Health Research Board.

Nolan, M. and Carr, A. (2000). Chapter 4. Attention deficit hyperactivity disorder. In A. Carr (ed.), *What Works with Children and Adolescents? A Critical Review of Psychological Interventions with Children, Adolescents and their Families* (pp. 65–102). London: Routledge.

O'Sullivan, A. and Carr, A. (2002). Chapter 2. Prevention of developmental delay in low birth weight infants. In A. Carr (ed.), *Prevention: What Works with Children and Adolescents? A Critical Review of Psychological Prevention Programmes for Children, Adolescents and their Families* (pp. 17–40). London: Routledge.

Parmenter, T. (2001). Intellectual disabilities – Quo Vadis? In G. Albrecht, K. Seelman and M. Bury (eds), *Handbook of Disability Studies* (pp. 267–96). Thousand Oaks, CA: Sage.

Schachar, R. and Tannock, R. (2002). Syndromes of hyperactivity and attention deficit. In M. Rutter and E. Taylor (eds), *Child and Adolescent Psychiatry* (4th edn, pp. 399–418). Oxford: Blackwell.

Schalock, R. (2002). *Adaptive Behaviour and its Measurements: Implications for the Field of Mental Retardation.* Washington, DC: American Association on Mental Retardation.

Schalock, R. L. and Verdugo, M. A. (2002). *Handbook on Quality of Life for Human*

Service Practitioners. Washington, DC: American Association on Mental Retardation.

Steinhausen, H., Williams, J. and Spohr, H. (1994). Correlates of psychopathology and intelligence in children with foetal alcohol syndrome. *Journal of Child Psychology and Psychiatry*, 35, 323–31.

Volkmar, F. and Dykens, E. (2002). Mental retardation. In M. Rutter and E. Taylor (eds), *Child and Adolescent Psychiatry* (4th edn, pp. 697–710). Oxford: Blackwell.

World Health Organization (WHO) (1992). *The ICD-10 Classification of Mental and Behavioural Disorders: Clinical Descriptions and Diagnostic Guidelines.* Geneva: WHO. Available at http://www.informatik.fh-luebeck.de/icd/welcome.html

World Health Organization (1993). *The ICD-10 Classification of Mental and Behavioural Disorders. Diagnostic Criteria for Research.* Geneva: WHO.

World Health Organization (1996). *Multiaxial Classification of Child and Adolescent Psychiatric Disorders: The ICD 10 Classification of Mental and Behavioural Disorders in Children and Adolescents.* Cambridge: Cambridge University Press.

World Health Organization (2001). *The International Classification of Functioning, Disability and Health (ICF).* Geneva: WHO.

Chapter 2

Lifespan development and the family lifecycle

Alan Carr and Gary O'Reilly

The development of people with intellectual disability is influenced by the balance of risk and protective factors in their lives. The growth of sensory, motor, cognitive, linguistic and social competencies over the lifespan occurs within the context of the family lifecycle. These issues are the focus of this chapter.

RISK AND PROTECTIVE FACTORS

Let us briefly recap risk factors for intellectual disability mentioned in Chapter 1 and then consider important protective factors.

Risk factors

Biomedical, social, behavioural and educational risk factors for intellectual disability which may occur during prenatal, perinatal and postnatal periods are summarized in Table 1.5 and detailed in Chapter 1 (Burack, Hodapp and Zigler, 1998; Friedman and Chase-Lansdale, 2002; Goodman, 2002; Kaski, 2000; Lange and Carr, 2002; O'Sullivan and Carr, 2002; Volkmar and Dykens, 2002).

Biological risk factors for intellectual disability include genetically determined syndromes such as Down syndrome (which are described in detail in Chapter 14) and metabolic disorders such as phenylketonuria. Other pre- and perinatal biological risk factors for intellectual disability include increasing maternal age, maternal illness, maternal exposure to toxins, prematurity, low birth weight, birth injury, and neonatal disorders. After birth, intellectual disability may be caused by many factors including traumatic brain injury, malnutrition, seizures and degenerative disorders.

During the prenatal, perinatal and postnatal periods social factors, notably poverty, maternal malnutrition, lack of access to medical services, and institutional upbringing, can have a negative impact on psychological development.

Disorganized parental behaviour during the prenatal, perinatal and post-natal periods may contribute directly or indirectly to impaired development.

During the prenatal period parental drug and alcohol use, which can lead to foetal alcohol syndrome, and smoking as well as domestic violence can increase the risk of intellectual disability. During the perinatal and postnatal periods, poor parenting may increase the risk of delayed development.

Inadequate education and support, particularly for vulnerable parents and families, may be considered a risk factor for delayed development.

Protective factors

A wide range of protective factors may impact on motor, cognitive, linguistic and social development at different stages of the individual lifecycle (Burack *et al.*, 1998; Carr, 2002; 2004; Luthar, 2003; Rolf, Masten, Cicchetti, *et al.*, 1990). Although not all of the research leading to the conclusions outlined below has been conducted with intellectually disabled populations, strong arguments may be made for generalizing findings from studies of other vulnerable populations to people with disabilities.

Good physical health is a protective factor. The absence of genetic vulner-abilities, an adequate intrauterine environment, an uncomplicated birth, no history of serious illnesses and injuries, adequate nutrition, regular exercise and a balanced diet all contribute to robust physical health.

Individuals are more likely to show good adjustment if they have an easy rather than a difficult temperament and a positively oriented belief sys-tem. Such belief systems involve a high level of self-esteem, an optimistic attributional style, a general belief in control over one's life and a specific belief that factors related to specific stresses may be controlled (high self-efficacy). These traits (easy temperament) and positive belief systems probably render individuals less vulnerable to becoming overly physiologically aroused and aggressive or demoralized and depressed when faced with life stresses.

Individuals are less adversely affected by life stresses if they have good planning skills, a sense of humour and the capacity to empathize with others.

Selecting or creating a positive social network (through positive peer group, school and vocational experiences, and developing trusting relation-ships with supportive mentors) can halt negative chain reactions or start positive chain reactions that facilitate personal development.

Better adjustment to intellectual disability occurs when individuals come from higher socio-economic groups, with few major life stresses, have good social support networks comprising family members and peers, and attend preschools and mainstream schools that provide a supportive yet moderately challenging educational environment. Such preschools and schools have a stable cohort of well-trained staff, adequate staff–student ratios, appropriate equipment and a participative management structure. Schools that promote resilience take a child-centred rather than a curriculum-centered approach;

nurture children's strengths to help compensate for their weaknesses; have a caring achievement-oriented ethos that values both academic and non-academic achievements; and offer opportunities for students to take age-appropriate responsibilities that contribute to the overall functioning of the school.

Secure attachment relationships to primary caregivers who adopt an authoritative parenting style and the involvement of both mothers and fathers in parenting are the major positive family factors associated with adjustment to life stress.

The absence of childhood separations, losses, bereavements, parental mental health problems, criminality and marital discord also characterize the families of individuals who are resilient in the face of stress.

People with disabilities are also more likely to benefit from involvement with disability services where there is good co-ordination among professionals on multidisciplinary teams or in interagency networks.

Clinical implications

The sensory, motor, cognitive, linguistic and social development of an individual with intellectual disability is influenced by the balance of risk and protective factors present in their lives. Thus, risk and protective factors should be routinely evaluated when assessing people with intellectual disabilities with a view to planning supports (Luckasson, Borthwick-Duffy, Buntinx, Coulter, et al., 2002). There is a strong evidence base which shows that multisystemic early intervention programmes for children biologically at risk through low birth weight, or environmentally at risk through social disadvantage can facilitate cognitive development (Lange and Carr, 2002; O'Sullivan and Carr, 2002). Families at risk should be engaged in such programmes immediately after the birth of the child. Effective programmes involve a comprehensive range of components delivered by a multidisciplinary team. Key components include child stimulation at home and in preschool settings; parent training and support; and conjoint parent–child sessions to promote secure attachment. Home visiting and the provision of transport to day centres are used in effective programmes to help parents stay engaged. Effective programmes are intensive with frequent, long-term contact. They involve children's families fully and build upon their cultural beliefs, traditions, and practices. Preschools in effective programmes have small child–teacher ratios and modify the curriculum to meet the unique needs of individual children. Effective programmes use manualized curricula to ensure that all staff involved in implementation provide the intervention as intended. Effective programmes also evaluate participants with appropriate assessment instruments before, during and after the intervention and at follow-up to monitor progress and respond to children who are having difficulties benefiting from participation. It is good practice to arrange for families to continue to be involved in early intervention programmes throughout the preschool and early school-going years until a comprehensive multidisciplinary assessment indicates that the child's development falls within normal limits.

SENSORY AND MOTOR DEVELOPMENT

The development of sensory and motor competencies in people with intellectual disabilities may be conceptualized in comparison to normal sensory and motor development. It should also be borne in mind that impairments in sensory and motor functioning, as was noted in Chapter 1, often accompany intellectual disability. At birth normally developing infants have certain sensory and motor competencies (Rutter and Rutter, 1993; Smith, Cowie and Blades 2003). They can distinguish good and bad smells and sweet, sour and salt flavours. Even before birth, babies can respond to tactile stimulation and recognize their mother's voice. The skill of localizing a sound is also present at birth. In the first weeks of life infants can only focus on objects about a foot away and show a particular interest in dark–light contrasts. By three months they have relatively well-developed peripheral vision and depth perception and a major interest in faces. Visual acuity is usually fully developed by 12 months.

When considering motor development a distinction is usually made between gross motor development including locomotion and postural development on the one hand, and fine motor development including prehension or manipulative skills on the other (Rutter and Rutter, 1993; Smith, *et al.*, 2003). The former concerns the development of control over the trunk, arms and legs for moving around. The latter refers to the ability to use the hands to manipulate objects. Some of the normal milestones of gross motor and fine motor development are set out in Table 1.1 in Chapter 1. The development of motor skills follow proximodistal (from trunk to extremities) and cephalocaudal (from head to tail) progressions. So infants first learn to control their arms before their fingers and their heads before their legs. After infancy motor development entails increased co-ordination of locomotion and manipulative skills. The development of effective motor skills in childhood, including those required for sports, gives the child a sense of mastery and engenders self-efficacy and self-esteem.

The rate at which sensory and motor skills develop in children with intellectual disabilities depends upon the child's level of intellectual disability and the degree of sensory and motor impairments. Children with more severe intellectual disabilities are slower to develop sensory and motor skills. Children with sensory or motor impairments also acquire sensory and motor skills at a slower rate or in some instances not at all. What follows is a brief account of key features of sensory and motor impairments which may occur as comorbid conditions with intellectual disability and have a significant impact on sensory and motor development.

Hearing impairment

Normal hearing refers to the ability to detect sounds of within 0 to 15–20 dB HL at a variety of frequencies (e.g. 500Hz, 1000Hz etc.) and hearing loss refers to deficits in this sensory ability, with such deficits being classified as mild (15–30dB HL), moderate (31–60dB HL), severe (61–90dB HL) and profound (90dB HL or greater) (American National Standards Institute, 1989; Bess and Humes, 1995). Distinctions are made between congenital deafness which is present from birth and deafness which occurs postnatally. Further distinction exists between the deterioration of hearing loss over time, termed progressive hearing loss, and acquired hearing loss which occurs following a period of normal development.

Aetiology

Sensorineural and conductive hearing loss constitute the main types of hearing loss (Carney and Moeller, 1998). The former is associated with defects of the auditory nerve, the cochlea, the organ of Corti, or the central nervous system and is indicative of more severe hearing loss than the conductive form which involves the middle ear. Both types of hearing loss can occur simultaneously. Heredity and meningitis are the main causes of hearing loss. Maternal rubella, birth trauma, complications of pregnancy, prematurity, Rh incompatibility, postnatal infections and viruses such as mumps and measles, high fever and ottis media are other potential precursors of hearing impairment.

Epidemiology

In every 1,000 children 1.2 is born with severe to profound hearing loss and the prevalence of deafness, if acquired cases are included, is about 4 per 1,000 (Hindley and vanGent, 2002). Hearing loss presents in the majority of these cases before the age of 3 and mostly during the first year of life. Eighty per cent of hearing loss involves sensorineural defects, 25 per cent of deaf children have multiple disabilities, while 90 per cent of deaf children have hearing parents (Strong, Clark, Barringer, Walden and Williams, 1992). In Chapter 1 it was noted that there are high rates of hearing impairment among people with intellectual disabilities.

Effects of deafness on development

Regardless of type, time of onset, severity or cause, language, cognitive, social and emotional development are invariably more problematic for the hearing-impaired child (Hindley and vanGent, 2002). Impoverished linguistic input associated with hearing impairment compromises the ability of the child with hearing loss to extract linguistic cues from the environment. This leads to delays in all aspects of language development. Since language is essential for reading and writing, literacy skills are also compromised. Children with moderate and severe degrees of hearing loss also have difficulties in discriminating and labelling speech sounds. These phonetic deficiencies make speech production difficult. With respect to social and emotional development, a higher level of impulsiveness, more limited problem-solving skills and greater difficulty in labelling and identifying emotions make deaf children vulnerable to developing psychological problems.

Visual impairment

Visual impairment refers to corrected visual acuity (in the better eye) of less than 6/18 metres and no more than 6/60 metres, or a central visual field of less than 10 degrees (World Health Organization, 1984). A distinction is made between severe visual impairment (corrected acuity of between 6/60 and 3/60 metres) and blindness (corrected visual acuity worse than 3/60 metres).

Aetiology

Central nervous system damage due to maternal infections during pregnancy, alterations of embryonic development, genetic factors and birth complications are the main pre- and perinatal factors associated with visual impairment (Menacker and Batshaw, 1997). Children rendered blind after birth are termed adventitiously blind. Adventitious blindness is rare and is usually caused by traumatic brain injury and neoplasms affecting the visual system.

Epidemiology

About 1 in every 3,000 children has severe visual impairment (Menacker and Batshaw, 1997). Hereditary retinopathy accounts for 25 per cent–50 per cent of cases. Congenital rubella accounts for a further 10 per cent of cases. Up to 50 per cent of children with blindness have additional disabilities including intellectual disability, cerebral palsy, epilepsy, and hearing impairment. In Chapter 1 it was noted that there are high rates of visual impairment among people with intellectual disabilities.

Impact of blindness on development

Blind children face a number of developmental challenges (Fraiberg, 1977; Norris, Spaulding and Brodie, 1957). The development of motor activities, particularly those which involve visual-motor integration, is delayed in blind children. Hearing becomes the dominant sense. The acquisition of object concept, object permanence, spatial conservation and understanding of causality is delayed as a result of blindness. Consequently, higher-order cognitive skills such as classification and conservation develop later in blind children. Language, symbolic play and non-verbal communication also develop more slowly. Lack of reciprocity in blind child–caregiver interactions interferes with the development of attachments. In later years, blind children may have difficulty initiating and maintaining peer relations due to their lack of awareness of non-verbal social cues and strategies which facilitate social relations, such as smiling, nodding and using eye contact.

Impairment of motor development – cerebral palsy

Cerebral palsy is the most common disorder of motor development, movement and posture. It results from an insult to, or anomaly of, the immature central nervous system in centres which govern motor activity (Capute and Shapiro, 1985; Pellegrino, 1997; Shapiro and Capute, 1999). Symptoms of cerebral palsy include extreme muscular tension and muscular rigidity with a partial paralysis or a loss of voluntary movement together with spasm of the affected muscles. Cerebral palsy may not become apparent until after 6 months when the infant develops to the stage where reflex action is largely replaced by purposive movements and motor skills for which an intact central nervous system is essential. Motor delay is the basis for diagnosis of cerebral palsy and may vary from minimal to severe-profound. Insults to, or anomalies of, the central nervous system which cause cerebral palsy in some cases may also cause other comorbid disabilities including intellectual disability, seizure disorders, visual and auditory impairments, learning difficulties and behaviour problems. The more profound the motor impairments and the more extensive the comorbid disabilities, the greater the adjustment difficulties youngsters with cerebral palsy face.

Aetiology

A range of aetiological factors can lead to cerebral palsy (Pellegrino, 1997; Shapiro and Capute, 1999). These include blood rhesus factor incompatibility, anoxia, cerebral vascular accident, trauma, bacterial or viral infection, and low birth weight. There are different subtypes of cerebral palsy and these are associated with different types of cerebral lesions. Cerebral palsy may be classified according to the type of motor impairment that predominates. Distinctions are made between spastic, dyskinetic and ataxic conditions. Spastic cerebral palsy is further subclassified according to the distribution of limbs involved. Distinctions are made between hemiplegia (affecting one side of the body), quadriplegia (affecting all four limbs), and diplegia (affecting the lower limbs). Spastic hemiplegia is associated with unilateral brain damage whereas diplegia and quadriplegia are associated with bilateral brain damage. Dyskinetic conditions include athetoid cerebral palsy involving fluctuating muscle tone and dystonic cerebral palsy involving rigid muscle tone. Ataxic cases are characterized by poor muscle tone, balance and co-ordination problems. Damage to the cortico-spinal tracts, basal ganglia, brainstem, and cerebellum is responsible for the differing types of motor symptoms. Cortico-spinal damage is associated with spasticity; basal ganglial damage with dyskinesia, and cerebellar damage with ataxia. Cases of cerebral palsy may be classified as mild, moderate or severe depending upon their level of overall motor functioning as indexed by motor development quotients-based observations and scales such as the Bayley Scales of Infant Development (Bayley, 1993; Capute and Shapiro, 1985; Coolman, Bennett, Sells, Sweanson et al., 1985).

Epidemiology

Cerebral palsy affects 2.3 per 1,000 live births or about 1 in 400 children (Pellegrino, 1997; Shapiro and Capute, 1999). Spastic cerebral palsy is the most common subtype accounting for 50 per cent–75 per cent of all cases. About 25 per cent of cases are athetoid, about 10 per cent are dystonic, and about 10 per cent are ataxic. Comorbid intellectual disability occurs in about 60 per cent of cases of cerebral palsy; comorbid seizure disorders occur in about 50 per cent of cases; comorbid behavioural and psychological problems occur in about 50 per cent of cases; comorbid hearing, speech and language impairments occur in 30 per cent of cases; and comorbid visual impairments in a proportion of cases. Feeding problems may also occur in cerebral palsy due to poor control of oral muscles.

Impact of cerebral palsy on development

About 50 per cent of people with cerebral palsy develop functional independence in the community in adulthood and about 25 per cent develop partial independence. Outcome in adulthood is dependent upon both the degree of initial disability and the quality of rehabilitative and preventive intervention during the preschool and school-going years.

Clinical implications

The evaluation of children with multiple disabilities including sensory and motor impairments should be conducted by a multidisciplinary team. Paediatric audiological assessment and assessment of visual acuity are required where there is clinical evidence of sensory impairment. A physiotherapist should be involved in the assessment of motor disorders. In assessing supports required by children with intellectual disabilities, to help them adapt despite delays in gross and fine motor development, take account of both their level of intellectual disability and the presence of other sensory and motor impairments such as deafness, blindness or cerebral palsy.

Sensory impairment

There is a strong evidence base to show that multisystemic family-based programmes are effective in preventing adjustment problems in children with sensory impairments (Fahey and Carr, 2002). Effective programmes include child-focused and parent-focused components which are offered flexibly on a home-visiting and outpatient basis. Child-centred interventions focus on promoting the use of all senses including the impaired sense, especially in the case of visually impaired children. In addition, child-centred interventions focus on training the child in communication skills including oral speech and sign language. Child-centred interventions may be taught by an adult with a sensory impairment who acts as mentor and role-model for the child, introducing them to the deaf and blind minority cultures. Parent-centred interventions should provide information on sensory impairment, and coaching in techniques that parents can use to help their children learn communication and social skills. Parent-centred interventions should also provide support and advice on how to access health, social and educational services. For school-aged children, effective school-based programmes follow on from home-based, child-centred programmes. In school-based programmes, systematic and intensive instruction, tailored to children's unique learning profiles, are used to promote language development. Social problem-solving skills should also be taught to promote social understanding and behavioural adjustment. Long-term parent-centred programmes should run in parallel with the child-centred school-based programmes, to provide a forum within which parents can address the various problems that occur as their sensorally impaired children make various lifecycle transitions, such as entering puberty and leaving high school.

Impairment of motor development

For children with cerebral palsy, best practice involves offering comprehensive multidisciplinary rehabilitative programmes of care specifically designed to minimize the impact of the constraints placed by cerebral palsy and comorbid conditions on the child's physical and psychosocial development (Waldron and Carr, 2002). Such programmes may include environmental alterations to manage the musculoskeletal complications of cerebral palsy; the use of carefully designed devices to aid posture and mobility; medication, nerve blocks and motor point blocks and neurosurgery to reduce spasticity; and orthopaedic surgery. In addition to these essentially physical interventions, a range of other interventions including neurodevelopmental therapy, infant stimulation, therapeutic electrical stimulation, special education and conductive education should be included in overall multidisciplinary care plans. To be effective neurodevelopmental therapy must be offered at a high level of intensity with clinic physiotherapy sessions once or twice a week and daily home practice. Such intensive programmes should not be offered until the infant is six months and the effectiveness of this type of treatment for infants is enhanced if it is preceded by an infant stimulation programme during the child's first six months. In toddlers and young children, when coupled with inhibitive limb-casting, neurodevelopmental therapy is particularly effective in improving the motor functioning of limbs for which inhibitive casts are worn for a set period of time each day. Therapeutic electrical stimulation may be offered as a parent-administered manualized home-based programme to improve gross motor functioning effectively in specific muscles or muscle groups. Special education and conductive education, when offered as day programmes, are equally effective in promoting cognitive, motor and social development to young children.

COGNITIVE DEVELOPMENT

Jean Piaget's theory of intellectual growth is the dominant developmental framework for conceptualizing cognitive development in children with and without intellectual disabilities (Inhelder and Piaget, 1958; Smith *et al.*, 2003). The Piagetian tradition and the psychometric testing tradition, mentioned in Chapter 1, have made different contributions to our understanding of intelligence. The psychometric tradition has yielded intelligence tests for measuring levels of cognitive ability and disability; hierarchical models of the structure of abilities; and evidence for the normal distribution of intelligence within populations. In contrast, the Piagetian movement has provided us with a map of the typical stages of cognitive growth. Two other important traditions of relevance to cognitive development deserve mention. Information processing models of problem-solving have thrown light on the sequence of cognitive events that underpin skilled performance. Social models of intelligence, particularly Vygotsky's, point to important contextual factors that may facilitate skill acquisition. Key insights and findings from the Piagetian, information processing and social approaches to intelligence that are of relevance to intellectual disability will be considered below.

Piaget's stages of cognitive development

Piaget viewed the growth of intelligence as dependent upon the child actively attempting to adapt to the world, assimilating new knowledge into available schemas or accommodating to new knowledge and experiences by altering schemas. He developed an elaborate theory of the stages of cognitive development which he tested through observations of children's performance on stage-specific tasks (Inhelder and Piaget, 1958; Smith *et al.*, 2003).

Piaget posited the existence of four main stages. In the first of these – the sensorimotor period – which extends from birth until about 2 years of age, the child's approach to problem-solving and knowledge acquisition is based upon manipulating objects and trial and error learning. The main achievements of this stage are the development of cause and effect sensorimotor schemas and the concept of object permanence, that is, the realization that objects have a permanent existence independent of our perception of them.

The second stage of development in Piagetian theory is the pre-operational period. During this stage the child moves from the use of sensorimotor schemas as the main problem-solving tool to the formation of internal representations of the external world. The ability to use internal representations of the world to solve problems underpins a number of important achievements readily observable in normal preschoolers. These include increasingly sophisticated language usage, engagement in make-believe or symbolic play, the ability to distinguish between appearance and reality and the ability to infer what other people are thinking. This ability to infer what others are thinking has been referred to as theory-of-mind and deficits in this ability typify children with autism. (Autism is discussed in Chapter 15.) Reasoning in the pre-operational period is largely intuitive, with the child linking one particular instance to another rather than reasoning from general to particular. For example, a pre-operational child will say, 'I'm tired so it must be night-time' rather than 'It's getting dark so it must be night-time.' The pre-operational child's attempts to solve problems are influenced to a marked degree by what is perceived rather than by what is remembered. The main limitations of the pre-operational period are an inability to take the visual perspective of another person, difficulty in retelling a story coherently (egocentric speech), a belief that inanimate objects can think and feel like people (animism), and an inability to focus on more than one dimension of a problem at a time. For example, if liquid is poured from a short, wide glass into a tall, narrow glass, the pre-operational child may say there is now more liquid because the level is higher, without making reference to the decreased width of the second glass. Piaget referred to the capacity to take account of two dimensions simultaneously as conservation of quantity.

Conservation of quantity is one of the primary achievements of the concrete operational period which extends from between 5 and 7 years up until about 12 years in normally developing children. The concrete operational period is the third of Piaget's developmental stages. During this period the child develops the ability to classify objects, place objects in series, engage in rule-governed games, adopt the geographic perspective of another person, and manipulate numbers using addition, subtraction, multiplication and division. These abilities involve the use of logic (rather than intuition) to solve concrete problems.

At about the age of 12 the normally developing child begins to use logic to solve abstract problems. That is, the child can develop hypotheses about what might be true and then make plans to test these hypotheses out. This is the primary characteristic of the formal operational period. This is Piaget's fourth and final developmental stage. There are many achievements which occur during this period. The adolescent can manipulate two or more logical categories, such as speed and distance, when planning a trip. Time-related changes can be projected, so the adolescent can predict that her relationship with her parents will be different in ten years. The logical consequences of actions can be predicted, so career options related to certain courses of study can be anticipated. The adolescent can detect logical inconsistencies, such as those that occur when parents do not practise what they preach. A final achievement of the formal operational period is the capacity for relativistic thought. Teenagers can see that their own behaviour and that of their parents is influenced by situational factors.

Piaget's theory has been partially supported and modified by subsequent independent research. Evidence from developmental studies suggests that the transition to concrete operations may occur earlier than Piaget suggested and the transition to formal operations may occur later. Also, performance on the wide variety of tasks Piaget used to demonstrate stage-specific competencies do not intercorrelate highly. Explanations as to why these deviations from traditional Piagetian theory occur, that invoke constructs from information processing theory and that take account of children's familiarity with the context within which they are asked to solve problems, have been offered by Neo-Piagetian researchers (Smith *et al.*, 2003). For example, younger children with less-well developed memories, who are given opportunities through extensive training to become familiar with Piagetian tasks, can show stage-specific competencies earlier than Piaget's theory predicts. Despite its limitations, Piaget's theory is a widely used conceptual framework and so the implications of it for intellectual disability deserve mention.

Progression through the Piagetian stages of cognitive development is slower for people with intellectual disabilities and the level of disability determines the highest stage reached (Inhelder, 1968). Using the mental ages achieved by adults with varying levels of intellectual disability specified in ICD 10 (WHO, 1993), hypotheses about the achievement of Piagetian stages may be made, some of which have been supported by empirical research (Burack *et al.*, 1998; Inhelder, 1968). Adults with mild intellectual disabilities achieve a mental age of between and 9 and 12 years, which means that from a Piagetian viewpoint it would be expected that most would achieve the level of concrete operations but few would achieve the level of formal operations. Adults with moderate intellectual disabilities achieve a mental age of between 6 and 9 so it would be expected that all would achieve the level of pre-operational cognition, and some would achieve the level of concrete operations. Adults with severe intellectual disabilities achieve a mental age of 3 to

6 years and so most would be expected to achieve a pre-operational level of cognition. Adults with profound intellectual disabilities achieve a mental age less than 3 and so most would be expected to achieve the sensorimotor level of cognitive development.

There is no evidence that the sequence of progression through Piagetian stages, as indexed by successful completion of tasks that test progression from one stage to the next, is any different for people with intellectual disabilities than for their non-disabled counterparts (Burack *et al.*, 1998; Inhelder, 1968).

Development of information processing

Information processing models of intelligence propose a sequence of cognitive events or components which intervene between encountering a problem and performing a solution (Flavell, Miller and Miller, 2002; Smith *et al.*, 2003). Most information processing models distinguish between: (1) sensory registers where images of visual and auditory stimuli are held for less than a second; (2) short-term memory where information is retained for a few seconds; (3) temporary working memory where information from the short-term memory is processed by using control strategies including rehearsal, organization and elaboration; (4) long-term memory; and (5) retrieval. Regardless of age or ability level, the individual's information processing capacity is limited. In normal adults the limits are 7 bits (+ or − 2). Effective strategies allow people to remember more material. Three commonly used strategies are rehearsal (repetition), organization (chunking or grouping) and elaboration (using a device such as imagery to link together items to be remembered). When people decide to use these strategies they do so in light of knowledge about the impact of these strategies on recall, recognition and reconstruction of material they wish to remember. This knowledge about memory is called metamemory. For example, if there are more than five items on a shopping list, some people will consciously use chunking to help them recall the list.

Automatization and strategy construction are two of the main processes by which cognitive change occurs. In the early stages of learning a new skill, much information processing capacity is taken up with attention to each component of the skill. With rehearsal, sequences of components become automatic and spare capacity becomes available for developing strategies for refining the skill or using it to develop further skills or expertise. For example, a child whose bicycle-riding skills have become automatic may use the available spare capacity to learn new cycle routes.

When we have little knowledge of a topic, we rely largely on recall memory. However, reconstructive memory is an alternative to recall. Here, we rebuild the material we have remembered on the basis of information coded as schemas and scripts. The greater the level of expertise (or knowledge base in a particular domain) the more effective is the use of reconstructive memory since there is a rich network of associations through which to reconstruct the newly learned material. Knowledge bases contain both schemas and scripts. Schemas are representations of the typical structure of familiar experiences, for example the way furniture is laid out in a dining room. Scripts are representations of typical sequences of events, for example the routine used to make a cup of tea. Schemas and scripts aid the learning of new material.

The information processing approach has demonstrated that short-term memory capacity, the amount of relevant information encoded in a problem-solving situation, the rate of automatization, the strategies employed, and the use of meta-cognitive skills evolve with age. Studies of people with intellectual disabilities show that the information processing components associated with efficient problem-solving, that improve with age in normal children, do not develop as quickly or to the same extent in people with intellectual disabilities. So, for people with intellectual disabilities, less rapid and extensive development occurs in short-term memory capacity; the amount of relevant information encoded in a problem-solving situation; rate of skills automatization; and the use of cognitive strategies and meta-cognitive skills (Detterman, Gabriel and Ruthsatz, 2000).

At a microlevel, there is no evidence that one specific information processing deficit accounts for all of the cognitive difficulties shown by people with intellectual disabilities. Nevertheless, specific deficits in larger cognitive competencies have been found to characterize people with conditions associated with intellectual disabilities. For example, children with autism have been shown to have poorly developed executive functioning (Russell, 1997) and theory-of-mind (Baron-Cohen, 1995), both of which are described in Chapter 15. Theory-of-mind refers to the capacity to infer what other people are experiencing in particular situations and understanding that these experiences may be different from one's own thoughts and feelings. Executive function is the capacity to solve problems in a systematic way and entails planning, selectively attending to relevant information, following through on plans and modifying these in light of feedback to ensure success without being distracted or unduly influenced by irrelevant stimuli or past unsuccessful attempted solutions.

A further finding from research conducted in the information processing tradition is that non-cognitive contextual factors can have a significant impact on information processing and problem-solving. For example, after repeated failure experiences on a particular problem-solving task, people with intellectual disabilities have been shown to fail tasks that they previously performed successfully. This finding points to the importance of keeping in mind the role of non-cognitive contextual factors when assessing people with intellectual disabilities. Many people with intellectual disabilities accumulate multiple failure experiences over the course of their development which may lead them to expect failure, to avoid learning new skills, to become over-dependent on others, and to lose skills that they have already acquired (Clements, 1987). It also suggests that a social conceptualization of intelligence may be particularly fruitful when working with people who have intellectual disabilities.

Vygotsky and the social context of intellectual development

Vygotsky conceptualized the development of intelligence in fundamentally social terms (Smith *et al.*, 2003; Vygotsky, 1962/34). He observed that children who displayed similar levels of individual problem-solving skills when operating in isolation often showed marked individual differences when coached by an adult or peer. This discrepancy between aided and unaided performance he referred to as the *zone of proximal development*. Within this zone optimal learning occurs if parents, teachers or peers adjusts their level of input to take account of the child's actual ability level. With this teaching method, which he called *scaffolding*, the teacher gives just enough help to ensure that the pupil has a mastery experience. Scaffolding involves: (1) engaging the person's interest; (2) simplifying the task into a predefined small number of steps; (3) providing external encouragement to complete the task until engagement in the task becomes intrinsically motivating; (4) giving feedback by highlighting correctly executed parts of the task; and (5) modelling correct performance of incorrectly completed aspects of the task. In clinical practice, helping carers and people with intellectual disabilities define the zone of proximal development and employ scaffolding may be useful in facilitating the development of adaptive behaviour. Indeed, many of the evidence-based approaches to special education and the provision of educational and behavioural supports are structured guidance on the provision of scaffolding in specific contexts (Kavale and Forness, 1999).

Clinical implications

In designing skills training programmes, take account not only of quantitative indices of cognitive functioning and adaptive behaviour, but also of the stage of cognitive development, related thinking style, and information processing capacity. Design programmes that include adequate scaffolding to allow the person to develop the required skills. Of particular relevance are applied behavioural analysis approaches to programme design which are addressed in Chapter 7, special educational programmes discussed in Chapter 16, and life skills programmes which are the focus of Chapter 19.

LANGUAGE DEVELOPMENT

The development of communication in people with intellectual disabilities may be conceptualized with respect to both normal language development and specific language delay (Smith *et al.*, 2003). The milestones of language development are presented in Table 1.1 in Chapter 1. *In utero*, the foetus can recognize the mother's voice and at birth infants orient to voices differently than to other sounds. Babbling begins at three to four months and at seven months is used for both social interaction and personal amusement. By six months babbling is affected by sensory input. Evidence for this comes from the fact that deaf children show a gradual cessation of babbling from this age. Children with language problems do not show the characteristic speech-like cadences which characterize babble at the end of the first year and do not show any signs of comprehension or communicative pointing in the way that normally developing children do. The use of single words begins between 12 and 18 months. By two years, most children know 300 words and before their third birthday the vast majority of children use two-word sentences and grammatical morphemes such as -ed and -ing. Between 3 and 5 years vocabulary, grammar and the accuracy with which words are used to denote concepts increase. Overextensions (e.g. calling a horse a dog) and underextensions (e.g. not calling a poodle a dog) of the meanings of words and the coining of new words, where the child has a vocabulary gap, are all common during this period. So too are grammatical inaccuracies such as over-regularization (e.g. house, houses; mouse, mouses).

The rapidity of language development and the creativity shown by children in their use of language suggests that the capacity to derive and apply linguistic rules is subserved by some set of genetically based mechanisms. Psycholinguistic theorists have focused their efforts on clarifying the characteristics of these mechanisms although they are more complex than originally proposed in Chomsky's original language acquisition device (LAD) (Rosenberg, 1993). However, the finding that severe environmental deprivation, such as being locked in an attic throughout infancy, can completely arrest language development while subsequent placement in a normal environment can lead to normal levels of linguistic development within a few years points to the importance of the environment in the development of language (Skuse, 1984).

Environmentalists have focused attention on the way in which parent–child interactions facilitate language development. During their first four months, babies cycle between states of attention and inattention. Mothers gradually learn to concentrate their emotional face-to-face interactions with their babies during the infants' periods of attention. This interactional synchrony gives way to turntaking, which may represent the infant's first conversations (Kaye, 1982). Infants of depressed mothers have difficulty establishing interactional synchrony and it may be this that compromises their later adjustment (Field, Healy, Goldstein and Guthertz, 1990).

A further finding which underpins the important role of environmental factors in language development is the observation that adults in all cultures speak to their children in a unique idiom which has been termed *motherese* (Snow and Ferguson, 1977). Motherese has the following attributes.

- It is simpler than adult speech
- Shorter sentences than adult speech are used
- It is more concrete than adult speech
- It involves repetition of what the child said
- The adult expands on what the child said
- The adult's voice is pitched at a higher frequency
- The adult's pattern of intonation is more meaningful.

A third important aspect of parent–child interaction in the development of language is the provision of a series of formats or structured social interactions in which verbal communication occurs. These include looking at books, naming things and playing word and action games and rhymes. Simplification, repetition and correction of errors characterize the parents' behaviour within these formatted interactions. Taken together, these formats comprise the language support system (LASS) (Bruner, 1983).

Language is used by children both to control their own behaviour and to engage in speech acts, intended to influence others in their social world. Vygotsky (1962/34) distinguished between private speech, internal speech and social speech. Private speech is used to control the child's own behaviour but is spoken aloud. For example saying 'up-down, up-down' when playing ball. Internal speech or self-talk is silent. It is used to guide and control the child's own behaviour and appears after the age of 7 in normally developing children. Social speech is used for controlling interactions with others and appears by 3 years. Social speech is made up of speech acts such as 'Daddy bobo' which is a request to Daddy for a bottle.

Specific language delay

When children show a delay in language development, a distinction may be made between secondary language delay due to intellectual disability, autism, hearing loss or some such condition and specific language delay (Bishop, 2002; Whitehurst and Fischel, 1994; Rapin, 1996). Specific language delays may be subclassified as expressive, which are the most common, and mixed receptive-expressive delays, which are the most debilitating. This distinction is the central organizing principle in the classification of language disorders in DSM-IV-TR (APA, 2000) and ICD 10 (WHO, 1993). Diagnostic criteria for specific language delays from DSM-IV-TR and ICD 10 are presented in Table 1.12 in Chapter 1. In addition to these distinctions, it is useful to describe language difficulties in terms of phonology, semantics, syntax, pragmatics and fluency.

Phonology

Phonological difficulties are manifested as inaccurate articulation of specific sounds, typically consonants rather than vowels. The following consonants tend to pose the most difficulties *r, l, f, v,* and *s*. For example, omissions such as *ee* for *sleep*; substitution such as *berry* for *very*; and cluster reduction such as *ream* for *cream*. Where these phonological problems reflect a preschooler's difficulty in the motor skills required for correct articulation, the prognosis for both language development and reading skills is good, and such children are indistinguishable from their peers by middle childhood. Phonological disorder and specific speech articulation disorder are the terms used to describe this condition in the DSM-IV-TR and the ICD 10 respectively. Where phonological difficulties reflect a lack of phonological awareness, such as an inability to use rhyme and alliteration, the prognosis for the development of reading skills is poor.

Semantics

With semantic difficulties the child has a restricted vocabulary and so understands the meaning of a limited number of words and can only use a limited number of words to communicate verbally with others.

Syntax

Problems with syntax or grammar include restricted length of utterance and restricted diversity of utterance types. By 2 years of age, most children should be using multiword utterances. Children with specific language delays, characterized by syntactical difficulties, are unable to use such multiword utterances at this stage. Later on, they are slow to use multiclausal sentences such as 'Where is the ball, that I was playing with yesterday?' They will be confined to using less complex utterances such as 'Where is the ball?' Syntactic difficulties are predictive of later reading and spelling problems.

Pragmatics

Problems with pragmatics occur where children are unable to use language and gestures within particular relationships or contexts to get their needs met or achieve certain communicational goals. Up to the age of 2 years, integrating gestures with speech is a key pragmatic skill. In preschoolers up to the age of 5, important pragmatic skills are used to tell coherent extended stories about events that have happened.

Fluency

Stuttering and cluttering are distinctive fluency problems with the latter involving a rapid rate of speech and consequent breakdown in fluency and the former involving repetitions, prolongations and pauses that disrupt the rhythmic flow of speech.

Epidemiology of specific language delay

Up to 17 per cent of 2-year-olds; 8 per cent of 3-year-olds; and 3 per cent of 5-year-olds have expressive language delay. The male–female ratio is between 3 and 5 : 1. The majority of children with specific language delay recover by 5 years of age and have few later adjustment problems (Whitehurst and Fischel, 1994). Two to three per cent of 6–7-year-olds have phonological disorders but most outgrow these problems and only 0.5 per cent of 17-year-olds present with this problem, which is more prevalent in boys than girls. The vast majority of children with phonological problems in the preschool years have no later academic or adjustment problems. The prevalence of stuttering among children is about 1 per cent and it is three times more common among boys than girls. Up to 60 per cent of cases recover spontaneously before the age of 16 years. Conduct problems occur in up to 95 per cent of cases of specific receptive-expressive language disorder; 45 per cent of cases of expressive language disorder; and 29 per cent of cases of articulation disorder (Baker and Cantwell, 1982). Of cases with persistent specific language disorders 35 per cent to 45 per cent develop dyslexia (Bishop and Adams, 1990).

Aetiology

Language delays are predominantly genetically determined, but environmental factors also play a role (Bishop, 2002; Whitehurst and Fischel, 1994). There is a hierarchy of vulnerability in the components of language that are affected in cases of language delay, and children who change symptoms over time during recovery move up this hierarchy. Moving from the most to the least vulnerable component, the hierarchy is as follows:

1   Expressive phonology
2   Expressive syntax and morphology
3   Expressive semantics
4   Receptive language.

Thus a child with expressive semantic problems, with maturation when these semantic problems resolve, will develop expressive syntax and morphology problems rather than receptive language problems. This hierarchy of vulnerability has led to the view that some aetiological factors must be common to all language disorders. However, there is no doubt that some factors are specific to particular disorders. All language delays are more common in boys than girls, so some gender-related biological factors are probably involved in the aetiology of all language problems. A delay in the development of speeded fine motor skills (but not general clumsiness) has been found to characterize most specific language delays. The language delay and motor delay may both reflect an underlying neurological immaturity which finds expression in slow and limited information processing capacity. Middle ear infection in the 12–18 month period has been shown to precede rapidly resolving specific expressive language delay at 2 years, and expressive language delay at 2 years is associated with problems in oral motor development. It is unlikely that psychosocial factors play a major aetiological role in specific developmental language delay but they may play a role in maintaining language problems. Low socio-economic status, large family size and problematic parent–child interaction patterns involving conduct problems characterize many cases of language disorder and the more severe the disorder, the worse the conduct problem. A variety of mechanisms may link these psychosocial factors to language problems. First, language problems may lead to frustration in the areas of communicating with others or achieving valued goals which finds expression in misconduct. Second, children with language problems may have difficulty controlling their conduct with inner speech. Third, parents with poor parenting skills and multiple stresses (such as large family size and low socio-economic status), may become trapped in coercive cycles of interaction with their children. These coercive interaction patterns may then prevent the children from developing language skills through engaging in positive verbal exchanges with their parents.

Clinical implications

Psychological assessment of language problems should ideally be conducted by a multidisciplinary team. A full paediatric assessment of the child should be conducted to detect the presence of problems such as middle ear infection and to outrule the presence of neurological and medical conditions. An audiological examination should be conducted to outrule hearing impairment.

In addition to routine interviewing, observation and completion of behaviour checklists and adaptive behaviour scales, assessment should involve the administration of standardized receptive and expressive language tests along with a measure of non-verbal intelligence as outlined in Chapter 1. Where measures of non-verbal intelligence, receptive and expressive language and adaptive behaviour all fall two standard deviations below the mean (or a standard score of 70), then the language problem is secondary to intellectual disability.

The patterning of the development of semantic, syntactic and pragmatic language skills varies among children with intellectual disabilities. This variability is associated with the level of disability, the presence of comorbid conditions, and the presence of specific syndromes. More rapid language development occurs among people with less severe disabilities. Children with autism (discussed in detail in Chapter 15) show more echolalia, pronominal reversal, stereotyped utterances, and lack of gesture than children with intellectual disabilities but without autism. Specific syndromes (discussed in Chapter 14) are associated with specific types of language difficulties. For example, children with fragile X syndrome show language delays that are more pronounced than their overall intellectual disability. The expressive language of children with Williams syndrome is fluent, complex and pseudomature. Language testing or careful interviewing usually reveals that their expressive language abilities far outstrip their comprehension. Speech articulation is often impeded in velocardiofacial syndrome by the palatal defects and children with this syndrome speak with a high-pitched, hypernasal voice. The management of communication problems in intellectual disability is discussed in Chapter 17 and the unique communication challenges associated with autism are addressed in Chapter 15.

Where the non-verbal intelligence score is within the normal range, and receptive or expressive language quotients fall 1.5–2 standard deviations below average, a diagnosis of specific language disorder may be made. Specific language delay may be distinguished from autism, Landau-Kleffner syndrome and selective mutism (Bishop, 2002). Autistic children (discussed in Chapter 15) show more echolalia, pronominal reversal, stereotyped utterances, lack of gesture, undue sensitivity to noise and lack of imaginative play. In Landau-Kleffner syndrome a normally developed child between the ages of 3 and 7 years loses expressive and receptive language skills, shows EEG bilateral temporal lobe abnormalities and seizures consistent with a diagnosis of epilepsy, while retaining normal intelligence. About a third of cases recover and two-thirds retain a severe mixed receptive-expressive language disorder. The disorder is presumed to be due to an inflammatory encephalitic process. With selective mutism children speak to family members and close friends privately in the home but not to teachers or to people in public. The condition may be managed like an anxiety disorder (Carr, 1999).

In cases of specific expressive language disorder, there is little evidence to suggest that preschool interventions add much to recovery rates which occur due to maturation (Bishop, 2002). In cases of specific receptive-expressive language disorders and secondary language disorders, referral for an individualized speech therapy programme; involvement of parents in implementing aspects of the programme in the home; and placement of the child in a therapeutic school environment (ideally in a mainstream school) are the principal types of treatments that, singly or in combination, have been shown to have positive short-term effects (Whitehurst and Fischel,

1994). Typically these speech and language programmes need to be conducted in conjunction with home and school-based behavioural management programmes (Carr, 1999).

DEVELOPMENT OF ADAPTIVE SOCIAL BEHAVIOUR

In Chapter 1 it was noted that adaptive social behaviour is currently conceptualized as falling into three domains representing conceptual, social and practical skills (Schalock, 2002). In this section the focus will be on social and practical skills. The developmental patterning of adaptive behaviour over the lifespan depends upon the aetiology of intellectual disability, the presence of comorbid conditions such as autism and the level of disability (Loveland and Tunali-Kotoski, 1998). People with more severe levels of intellectual disability show less improvement in adaptive behaviour over the course of the lifespan. For people with Down syndrome adaptive behaviour improves through childhood, adolescence and adulthood but may decline in later life, especially when depression or dementia occur. These conditions are particularly prevalent among people with Down syndrome. In contrast, the adaptive behaviour of people with autism or fragile X syndrome improves throughout childhood but reaches a plateau in late childhood or early adolescence and in both of these conditions daily living skills become better developed than social skills.

Emotional regulation and social skills

To place the development of emotions and social skills of people with intellectual disability in context, let us first consider emotional development in children of normal intelligence. The range of emotions that a child can display increases over the first few years of life (Malatesta, 1985). At birth, infants can express interest as indicated by sustained attention to novel stimuli, and disgust in response to foul tastes and odours. Smiling, reflecting a sense of pleasure, in response to the human voice appears at 4 weeks. Sadness and anger in response to removing a teething toy are first evident at 4 months. Facial expressions reflecting fear following separation become apparent at 9 months. The frequency of outbursts of anger (or temper tantrums) reaches a peak at 2 years. Hence the term 'the terrible twos'. Outbursts of anger and physical aggression which are used to elicit care or attention decrease from 2 to 7 years. Concurrently there is an increase in both verbal and physical aggression, the aim of which is retaliation rather than eliciting care. So a school-going child will typically respond to angry threats from peers or parents with retaliatory anger (unless inhibited by fear) whereas a preschooler is less likely to do so. At about the age of 9 children distinguish between intentional and accidental provocation and begin to attribute aggressive intentions to bullying peers who have reputations for intentional aggression.

While physical and cognitive capabilities place constraints on the range of emotions that a child may experience at each stage of development, reinforcement, modelling and the labelling of emotions by parents are the primary psychosocial processes through which the expressions of emotions are learned. Over the first year of life mothers tend to be more socially responsive to positive emotional displays and therefore to reinforce these, while extinguishing negative emotional displays (Malatesta, 1985). At about the end of the first year, in ambiguous social situations infants actively inspect their mothers' faces to see what the appropriate emotion is for the situation. This process of learning emotions through modelling is called social referencing (Feinman, 1992). From the second year until school entry there is a tendency for toddlers to imitate the emotions that others are displaying.

The experience and expression of emotional empathy requires the child to be able to see the world from another's perspective, an ability that Piagetians have shown does not begin to emerge until the concrete operational period at 5–7 years in children of normal ability. More complex emotions such as envy and embarrassment, like empathy, also require cognitive development to have progressed sufficiently for the child to be able to imagine how the world looks from another's perspective.

Emotion regulation skills evolve with age. Preschoolers know that they can change emotions by changing the situation. For example, a sad child may distract herself by watching a cartoon on the TV. By middle childhood, children regulate emotions not only by changing the situation but also by changing their thoughts. So older children may deal with sadness by thinking about their forthcoming birthday party. By 6 years children have learned what displays of emotions are socially acceptable and are capable of hiding socially unacceptable emotions. For example, boys learn to hide their sadness when they are hurt. While it is probable that preschoolers experience mixed feelings or ambivalence, insight into emotional ambivalence does not occur until middle childhood in children of normal ability.

Throughout middle childhood and up until adolescence, the awareness that actions may lead to approval or disapproval by parents and other important attachment figures leads to the internalization of standards of conduct (Kochanska, 1993). This process of internalizing standards permits the experience of complex emotions such as pride, shame and guilt. These emotions and the capacity to follow formal and informal rules governing social behaviour have particular implications for making and maintaining peer relationships (Dunn and McGuire, 1992; Malik and Furman, 1993; Williams and Gilmore, 1994). Emotionally expressive children who have developed secure attachments to their parents and whose parents adopt an authoritative parenting style are more likely to develop good peer friendships and to be rated as popular by their peers. Popular children are effective in joining in peer group activities. They hover on the edge, tune in to the group's activities and carefully select a time to become integrated into the group's activities. Unpopular children, particularly the aggressive type, do not tune in to group activities. They tend to criticize other children and talk about themselves rather than listening to others. Warmth, a sense of humour and sensitivity to social cues are important features of socially skilled children.

In contrast to normally developing children, those with intellectual disabilities are less proficient at recognizing, expressing and regulating emotions, responding to emotions in others, following formal and informal social rules and making and maintaining friendships (Kasari and Bauminger, 1998). Cognitive constraints make it more difficult for people with intellectual disabilities to recognize emotions in themselves and others, because emotions are complex stimuli to process. Cognitive constraints also make it difficult for people with intellectual disabilities to regulate their own emotional states by, for example, distracting themselves from unpleasant situations or sustaining social behaviour that will prolong pleasant social interactions. People with intellectual disabilities find it more difficult to respond in a socially skilled way to complex emotions in others. For example, showing sympathy when others are sad or frightened; or being assertive when others are inappropriately angry or bullying. The process of learning formal and informal rules that regulate social interactions and relationships is more difficult for people with intellectual disabilities, because learning these rules and internalizing them depends to some degree on the capacity to recognize, regulate or respond to emotions of the self and others. For example, people learn that generosity and expressions of joy elicit care and approval while aggression elicits disapproval or punishment. Over the long term difficulties in recognizing, regulating and responding to emotions in others and following social rules render the process of making and maintaining long-term relationships more difficult for people with intellectual disabilities.

Maintaining self-esteem is another important social skill, the development of which follows a distinct trajectory in people with intellectual disabilities (Evans, 1998). In children of normal ability, self-concept is relatively undifferentiated in early childhood and self-esteem is overinflated. Young children do not make distinctions between the way they conceive of themselves as people with distinctive physical, social and cognitive attributes, and they evaluate themselves in a predominantly positive way. In adolescence normal youngsters show differentiated self-concepts with physical, social and academic attributes being regarded as separate domains. They also show a gradually increasing gap between ideal and actual self-concepts, as their evaluation of themselves become more realistic and their aspirations become more lofty. Adolescents with intellectual disabilities have less differentiated self-concepts, with little distinction being made between self-evaluations in the physical, social or cognitive domains. They also show a smaller disparity between their actual and ideal self-concepts, but this is accounted for by the lower ideal images they report compared with normally developing youngsters.

Practical skills

As part of the socialization process, children of normal ability learn practical skills for self-care and activities of daily living. Research in a tradition initiated by Robert Hodapp and Edward Zigler has shown that a particular personality profile characterizes people with intellectual disabilities, and this profile compromises skill development by reducing motivation to learn new skills (Hodapp, Burack and Zigler, 1998). The profile involves five traits. The first of these is overdependence on adults in the immediate environment. This arises from routines in which caregivers, parents or older siblings have become accustomed to providing assistance. The second trait is wariness in initial interactions with unfamiliar adults. This is probably an overgeneralization of the learned safety skill of 'avoiding stranger danger'. Lower expectations of success in completing tasks is the third trait. This often arises from repeated failure experiences. Outerdirectedness, the fourth trait, involves an increased reliance on others for solutions to problems rather than relying on personal problem-solving skills. Normal children are outerdirected when they perceive tasks to be beyond their capabilities, but youngsters with intellectual disabilities are apt to be outerdirected regardless of task difficulty. Again, this may arise from repeated failure experiences and repeated injunctions of people with intellectual disabilities to base their actions on the directives of others. The fifth trait, effectance motivation, refers to diminished pleasure in solving problems and a preference for tangible rather than intangible rewards.

Clinical implications

For people with intellectual disability, across the lifespan but particularly at the transitions from preschool to school, childhood to adolescence and adolescence to adulthood, training in social and practical skills that will facilitate these transitions is essential for good adjustment. The skills curriculum and the style and pacing of teaching should take account of the clients' age and ability profile (Zetlin and Morrison, 1998). Social skills training programmes should aim to help clients recognize and regulate their own emotions; recognize and respond appropriately to emotions of others; and learn basic formal and informal rules that govern social interactions. Collectively these skills enhance clients' chances of making and maintaining long-term relationships. Managing emotions within relationships and sexuality is discussed in Chapter 20. Managing the emotion of anger associated with challenging behaviour is addressed in Chapter 18. Programmes to help clients develop practical skills for self-care, activities of daily living and vocational adjustment should take account of the way people with intellectual disabilities have often been socialized into a dependent, pessimistic, outer-directed way of dealing with challenges. Effective approaches to educating school-aged children with intellectual disabilities so they develop adequate repertoires of adaptive behavioural skills is addressed in Chapter 16, life skills in Chapter 19, and vocational development in Chapter 21.

THE FAMILY LIFECYCLE

The sensory, motor, cognitive, linguistic and social development of the individual occurs within the context of the developmental lifecycle of the family. Models of the family lifecycle are based upon the norm of the traditional nuclear family with other family forms being conceptualized as deviations from this norm (Carter and McGoldrick, 1999). One such model is presented in Table 2.1. This model delineates the main developmental tasks to be completed by the family at each stage of development, along with additional tasks entailed by having a child with an intellectual disability (Rolland, 1994; 2003). Before addressing these additional tasks, let us first look at the lifecycle of the traditional nuclear family.

Table 2.1 Lifecycle of families with a child who has an intellectual disability

Stage	Tasks
1 **Family of origin experiences**	• Maintaining relationships with parents, siblings and peers • Completing school
2 **Leaving home**	• Differentiation of self from family of origin and developing adult-to-adult relationship with parents • Developing intimate peer relationships • Beginning a career
3 **Premarriage stage**	• Selecting partners • Developing a relationship • Deciding to marry
4 **Childless couple stage**	• Developing a way to live together based on reality rather than mutual projection • Realigning relationships with families of origin and peers to include spouses
5 **Family with young children**	• Adjusting marital system to make space for children • **Adjusting to the birth of a child with an intellectual disability by going through the process of denial, emotional turmoil towards constructive adaptation** • Adopting parenting roles • Realigning relationships with families of origin to include parenting and grandparenting roles • Children developing peer relationships

(Continued overleaf)

Table 2.1 Continued

Stage	Tasks
	• **Adjusting to the extra care tasks entailed by a child having an intellectual disability** • **Involving other children in parenting tasks to care for the child with an intellectual disability** • **Working with health, education and social care disability service agencies**
6 **Family with adolescents**	• Adjusting parent–child relationships to allow adolescents more autonomy • **Arranging appropriate supports to allow the person with intellectual disability to move towards independence in the social and vocational areas** • Adjusting marital relationships to focus on mid-life marital and career issues • Taking on responsibility of caring for families of origin
7 **Launching children**	• **Dealing with premature launching of person with disability** • **Dealing with postponed launching of the person with disability** • Resolving mid-life issues • Negotiating adult-to-adult relationships with children **(or missing out on this)** • Adjusting to living as a couple again **(or missing out on this)** • Adjusting to including in-laws and grandchildren within the family circle • Dealing with disabilities and death in the family of origin
8 **Later life**	• **Planning for the child with intellectual disability following parental decline and death** • Coping with physiological decline • Adjusting to the children taking a more central role in family maintenance **(or missing out on this)** • Making room for the wisdom and experience of the elderly • Dealing with loss of spouse and peers • Preparation for death, life review and integration

Note: Nuclear family lifecycle tasks are based on Carter, B. and McGoldrick, M. (1999), *The Expanded Family Lifecycle: Individual, Family and Social Perspectives* (3rd edn), Boston: Allyn and Bacon, and additional tasks associated with intellectual disability have been added in bold type.

Normal family lifecycle

In the first two stages of family development, the principal concerns are with differentiating from the family of origin by completing school, developing relationships outside the family, completing one's education and beginning a career. In the third stage, the principal tasks are those associated with selecting a partner and deciding to marry. In the fourth stage, the childless couple must develop routines for living together which are based on a realistic appraisal of the other's strengths, weaknesses and idiosyncrasies rather than on the idealized views which formed the basis of their relationship during the initial period of infatuation.

In the fifth stage, the main task is for couples to adjust their roles as marital partners to make space for young children. This involves the development of parenting roles which entail routines for meeting children's needs for safety, care, control and intellectual stimulation. Routines for meeting children's needs for safety include protecting children from accidents by, for example, not leaving young children unsupervised and also developing skills for managing frustration and anger that the demands of parenting young children often elicit. Routines for providing children with food and shelter, attachment, empathy, understanding and emotional support must be developed to meet children's needs for care in these various areas. Failure to develop such routines may lead to a variety of emotional difficulties. Routines for setting clear rules and limits; for providing supervision to ensure that children conform to these expectations; and for offering appropriate rewards and sanctions for rule-following and rule-violations meet children's need for control. Conduct problems may occur if such routines are not developed. Parent–child play and communication routines for meeting children's needs for age-appropriate intellectual stimulation must also be developed, if the child is to avoid developmental delays. In addition to developing parental roles and routines for meeting children's needs, a further task of this stage is the development of grandparental roles and the realignment of family relationships that this entails.

In the sixth stage, which is marked by children's entry into adolescence, parent–child relationships require realignment to allow adolescents to develop more autonomy. However, parents who find their families at this stage of development must contend not only with changes in their relationships with their maturing children, but also with the increased dependency of the grandparents upon them and also with a mid-life re-evaluation of their marital relationship and career aspirations. The demands of grandparental dependency and mid-life re-evaluation may compromise parents' abilities to meet their adolescents' needs to negotiate increasing autonomy.

The seventh stage is concerned with the transition of young adult children out of the parental home. Ideally this transition entails the development of a less hierarchical relationship between parents and children. During this stage, the parents are faced with the task of adjusting to living as a couple again, to dealing with disabilities and death in their families of origin and of adjusting to the expansion of the family if their children marry and procreate. In the final stage of this lifecycle model, the family must cope with the parents' physiological decline, and approaching death, while at the same time developing routines for benefiting from the wisdom and experience of the elderly.

This lifecycle model draws attention to the ways in which the family meets the developing child's needs and also the way in which the family places demands upon children and other members at different stages of the lifecycle. For example, the parents of a teenager may meet her needs for increasing autonomy by allowing greater freedom and unsupervised travel, and she may meet her grandparents' needs for continued connectedness by visiting regularly. Family lifecycle models also focus attention on the transitions that the child and other family members must make as one stage is left behind and another stage is entered. Families require some degree of flexibility to adapt the way relationships are organized as each of these transitions is negotiated. They also require the capacity to maintain stable roles and routines during each of the stages. A third important requirement is the capacity to permit children movement from dependency towards autonomy as development progresses. This is as true for the transition into adolescence as it is for the launching stage where children are leaving home. A further feature of family lifecycle models is that they point to certain junctures where there may be a build-up of family stress with many individual transitions occurring simultaneously. For example, in the launching stage it is not uncommon for older children to be leaving home and having their first children while their grandparents may be succumbing to late-life illnesses or death.

Additional family lifecycle tasks associated with intellectual disability

When a family member has an intellectual disability, additional tasks must be completed at certain stages of the lifecycle and these have been incorporated into Table 2.1 in bold type (Blancher and Baker, 2002; Gath, 2000; Kraus and Seltzer, 1998; Marfo, Dedrick and Barbour, 1998; Minnes, 1998; Rolland, 1994; 2003; Shapiro, Blancher and Lopez, 1998; Stoneman, 1998). When a child is diagnosed with intellectual disability, parents and siblings typically respond initially with shock. The timing of the diagnosis will depend upon a range of factors including the level of intellectual disability; the presence of other comorbid disabilities and physical and mental health problems; and the sophistication of the diagnostic team. The more disabled the child, and the more sophisticated the diagnostic team, the earlier the diagnosis. Children with mild intellectual disability sometimes are not diagnosed until the school-going years. However, in western cultures, most children with intellectual disabilities are now identified in infancy or early childhood. The way the news of handicap is broken affects parents' satisfaction with the consultation service received. The following factors are particularly important: the approachableness of the clinician, and the degree to which the clinician understands the parent's concerns; the sympathy of the clinician; the directness and clarity of communication (Quine and Rutter, 1994).

The initial shock reaction to diagnosis is usually followed by a phase in which the processes of denial and emotional turmoil predominate. Denial may involve disbelieving the diagnosis, requesting second opinions from mainstream or alternative practitioners, attempting to discredit the diagnostic team, and so forth. Emotional turmoil may include anger and sadness about the loss of the non-disabled child that was expected, and anxiety about what the future may hold. Anger may be expressed as marital conflict; conflict between parents and other children within the family; conflict between family members and members of the disability services; or as anger at God for causing the disability. Sadness may range from occasional tearfulness to clinical depression or substance use. Anxiety may range from worrying about how the family will cope with accessing appropriate supports and caring for the child with intellectual disability, to the development of panic attacks. Cohesive families with strong marital and parent–child relationships; good problem-solving and communication skills; and a degree of social support from the extended family, friends, support groups and disability services manage this phase without parental separation or other crises. The duration of the phase of emotional turmoil is highly variable. For many families, this grief reaction recurs at transitional stages throughout the lifecycle. So when the child goes to school, enters adolescence or reaches adulthood the family is reminded of the non-disabled child they have lost and re-experiences some vestige of the original grief and emotional turmoil which occurred following initial diagnosis.

After the first phase of emotional turmoil, some degree of constructive adaptation occurs in almost all families. In this phase the family addresses the lifecycle tasks of adjusting to the extra responsibilities entailed by caring for a child with an intellectual disability and working with disability services to arrange appropriate supports to meet the child's needs. The major concerns for families of children with intellectual disabilities in this stage of the lifecycle are obtaining accurate information on their child's condition, and obtaining access to appropriate services including special education, respite care, and advice on behavioural management. Constructive adaptation therefore involves forming good collaborative relationships with disability services; obtaining accurate information about the child's profile of abilities, special educational needs, and probable prognosis; participating in the development, implementation and regular review of an individual family support plan; joining appropriate parent support groups; and developing effective childcare routines.

Children with disabilities place considerable demands on the family's coping resources. Caring for children with intellectual disabilities is very time-consuming and demanding. These children have greater difficulty forming secure attachments to caregivers, greater difficulty engaging in sustained interactions with caregivers, and are slow to develop basic self-care skills. A major sustained investment of time and energy is required for many caregiving tasks including feeding, dressing, toileting, supervision, intellectual simulation, control, arranging transport, dealing with professionals in disability services to obtain service entitlements, and arranging respite care, educational, and other placements. Children with disabilities also place significant constraints on families by reducing time and energy for the marriage, for sibling interaction with parents, for sibling activities outside the home, and opportunities for family holidays. This additional burden of care affects mothers more than fathers. Rates of depressive symptoms are higher among mothers of children with intellectual disabilities than mothers of normally developing children. However, on many indices of personal and social adjustment mothers of children with intellectual disabilities are indistinguishable from mothers of normal children. Siblings are typically involved in the care of people with intellectual disabilities. Over time, parents and siblings incorporate their specialized caregiving roles into their daily routines and so caring for the child with intellectual disability becomes an integral part of family life.

The level of stress experienced by parents and siblings in families with children who have intellectual disabilities depends upon the child's characteristics, including level of disability, temperament and comorbid physical and mental health problems on the one hand and the levels of adaptability, cohesion and communication within the family and availability of external social support on the other. Greater disability, difficult temperament and more physical and mental health problems, particularly autism, and sensory and motor disabilities, contribute to greater stress. However, high levels of adaptability associated with well-developed family problem-solving skills, good family communication skills, and emotional cohesion within the family are associated with good adjustment. Good adjustment is also associated with the availability of social support from the extended family, friends, support groups and professional agencies.

During childhood, in most western cultures, children with intellectual disabilities attend either mainstream schools with special educational support, special educational classes in mainstream schools, or special schools. It has become good practice for children with intellectual disabilities, their parents, teachers, carers, and involved professionals to develop individual educational plans for each child and review and modify these on a regular (annual) basis. The incorporation of this planning and review process into the family's routine is one aspect of the additional lifecycle task of working with disability service agencies to arrange supports to meet the disabled child's needs.

With the transition to adolescence, an important task is arranging appropriate supports to allow the person with intellectual disability to move towards independence in the social and vocational areas. Moving towards social independence involves learning social skills necessary for managing sexuality and intimate relationships. Skills training may be required for managing sexual urges, masturbation, contraception, personal safety and self-protection, as well as for communicating with heterosexual partners and maintaining long-standing relationships, all of which are discussed in Chapter 20. Some people with intellectual disabilities marry and have children, although this is not the norm. When this occurs, careful planning of intensive supports are required. The types of intensive multi-systemic early intervention programmes mentioned earlier in this chapter offer young families with parents who have intellectual disabilities an appropriate level of support (Lange and Carr, 2002; O'Sullivan and Carr, 2002).

With the transition to adulthood at the end of adolescence, a major task is taking steps towards vocational independence. This involves learning practical and vocational skills necessary for travelling to and from a workplace, carrying out work-related responsibilities in a reliable way, managing relationships with managers, colleagues and customers at work, and managing money received in payment for work. Supported employment programmes, discussed in Chapter 21, offer a context within which these skills may be learned.

The launching stage may occur prematurely in some families where children with intellectual disabilities are placed in residential centres well before adulthood. In other families the launching stage may be postponed or delayed and the person with the disability remains in the family home well into adulthood. Premature launching occurs (in western cultures committed to normalization and community-based care) when the demands of coping with the child's disability, comorbid mental and physical health problems, or challenging behaviour outstrip the parents' coping resources, while the person with the disability is still a minor. Postponed or delayed launching occurs where parents are initially reluctant to transfer the care of their adult offspring to community-based services, because they judge the quality of the services offered to be unsuited to meeting their children's needs, but then eventually find the home-based care of their adult offspring is unsustainable. Launching in late adulthood occurs when the burden of care becomes too great for aging, debilitated or ill parents. Sometimes a decrease in the parents' coping resources coincides with an increase in the demands their offspring place on them due to physical or mental health problems or increased challenging or dependent behaviour. For example, there is a high rate of dementia in adults with Down syndrome and the demands associated with caring for an adult offspring with Down syndrome and dementia may lead to late-life launching, an issue discussed in Chapter 25.

The prospect of developing adult-to-adult relationships with one's children or the opportunity to live as a couple after all children have left home may not occur for some couples who have adult offspring with intellectual disabilities. In this sense, the family lifecycle for them is different from the norm for most nuclear families. However, there are positive aspects to the continued residence of the person with an intellectual disability in their parent's home. As the parents age, their offspring can adopt a caretaking role, provided they are not overly constrained by their level of intellectual disability.

With the transition to later life, a major concern for aging parents whose adult offspring with intellectual disability still live with them, is planning what will happen when they are unable to care for their children or when they die. Siblings, the extended family and disability service agencies may collaborate in this planning process.

At the beginning of this section it was noted that shock, emotional turmoil and constructive adaptation were identifiable phases in family adjustment to intellectual disability. For some families, over time, a process of resolution gradually occurs, where the person with the disability is accepted as they are without comparison to the person they might have been had they been born without intellectual disability. However, throughout the lifecycle at each transition, families are reminded of the loss of the able-bodied child that was initially expected, and unresolved grief reactions, involving emotional turmoil, may recur, albeit in a progressively attenuated form (Goldberg, Magrill, Hale, *et al.*, 1995). Lifecycle transitions are particularly strong triggers for grief processes in families of children with intellectual disabilities because they herald threats to the child's well-being. The transition to primary school raises concern that the child will be rejected by peers; the transition to adolescence raises concern that the youngster will become involved in inappropriate sexual or risk-taking activities; the transition to adulthood raises concern that the young adult will not be able to obtain a job and living arrangements that permit an acceptable level of independence and inclusion in the community; the decline of parents in later life raises concern about who will care for the person with the intellectual disability in future. An important function of the clinical psychologist is to help families acknowledge this recurring unresolved grief process, but also to celebrate the achievements of their children with intellectual disabilities and help with planning supports that will address these very legitimate anxieties associated with lifecycle transitions.

Clinical implications

Families with children who have intellectual disabilities require multidisciplinary assessment and planning services and the provision of supports over the course of the family lifecycle. Early in the child's life, diagnosis and individual family support plans need to be established and regularly monitored throughout the preschool years. These may involve parent training and support, preschool programmes for children, and respite care. Throughout the school-going years, regular individual education plans need to be established and monitored. These involve intensive home–school liaison and respite care. If the child has multiple disabilities or additional physical or mental health problems or challenging behaviour, multidisciplinary assessment and provision of appropriate supports will be required to meet these needs. In adulthood individual personal plans need to be established and monitored to maximize vocational and residential opportunities for independence and inclusion. Clinical psychologists may play an important role in contributing to the design of such assessment and care-planning systems and to staff training. They may also contribute to role case management through assessment of abilities, adaptive behaviour and support needs, developing plans, provision of supports, and the ongoing review processes. Some instruments for assessing family strengths are given in Table 2.2.

Table 2.2 Psychometric instruments for the assessment of family functioning

Instrument	Comments
The McMaster Family Assessment Device (FAD) and the McMaster Clinical Rating Scale (MCRS) by I. Miller, N. Epstein, D. Bishop, and G. Keitner, are available from Ivan W. Miller, Ph.D, Department of Psychiatry and Human Behavior, Brown University, Potter 3, Rhode Island Hospital, 593 Eddy Street, Providence, R.I. 02903, USA and Ivan_Miller_III@postoffice.brown.edu	• The FAD and MCRS are based on the McMaster Model of Family Functioning • The FAD is a 60-item self-report inventory and the MCRS is a rating scale that can be completed by experienced clinicians following a family interview • The FAD and MCRS measure: (1) problem-solving; (2) communication; (3) roles; (4) affective responsiveness; (5) affective involvement; (6) behaviour control; and (7) general functioning
Home Observation for Measurement of the Environment (HOME) by B. Caldwell and R. Bradley Little of Rock, AR: University of Arkansas at Little Rock, USA is available at http://www.ualr.edu/crtldept/home4.htm	• The Infant/Toddler (IT) HOME is for children ages 0–3, contains 45 items and yields scores for: (1) Parental Responsivity; (2) Acceptance of Child; (3) Organization of the Environment; (4) Learning Materials; (5) Parental Involvement; and (6) Variety in Experience • The Early Childhood (EC) HOME is for use with 3–6-year-olds contains 55 items and yields scores for: (1) Learning Materials; (2) Language Stimulation; (3) Physical Environment; (4) Parental Responsivity; (5) Learning Stimulation; (6) Modelling of Social Maturity; (7) Variety in Experience; and (8) Acceptance of Child • The Middle Childhood (MC) HOME is for use with 6–10-year-olds. It contains 59 items and yields scores for: (1) Parental Responsivity; (2) Physical Environment; (3) Learning Materials; (4) Active Stimulation; (5) Encouraging Maturity; (6) Emotional Climate; (7) Parental Involvement; and (8) Family Participation • The Early Adolescent (EA) HOME is for 10–15-year-olds. It contains 60 items and yields scores for: (1) Physical Environment; (2) Learning Materials; (3) Modelling; (4) Instructional Activities; (5) Regulatory Activities; (6) Variety of Experience; and (7) Acceptance and Responsivity

DEVELOPMENTAL CASE FORMULATION

When developing individual family support plans in infancy, individual educational plans in childhood and adolescence and individual personal plans in adulthood, base these on a comprehensive case formulation. Construct each case formulation so it explains how risk and protective factors have impacted on the person's developmental status in the sensory, motor, cognitive, linguistic and social domains. These developmental achievements may also be stated in terms of level of intellectual ability and adaptive behaviour, as noted in Chapter 1. The formulation should also contextualize the person's development by pointing to the stage of the family lifecycle, the last family lifecycle transition just managed or the next significant lifecycle transition anticipated. Such formulations provide a useful backdrop, for goal setting, and stating supports required to achieve these goals.

SUMMARY

The sensory, motor, cognitive, linguistic and social development of people with intellectual disability is influenced by the balance of risk and protective factors present in their lives. Biomedical, social, behavioural and educational, risk and protective factors for intellectual disability which may occur during prenatal, perinatal and postnatal periods all impact on development. The rate of developing sensory and motor skills depends upon the child's level of intellectual disability and the degree of sensory and motor impairments. Progression through the Piagetian stages of cognitive development is slower for people with intellectual disabilities and the level of disability determines the highest stage reached. For people with intellectual disabilities, less rapid and extensive development occurs in information processing but no one specific information processing deficit accounts for all of the cognitive difficulties shown by people with intellectual disabilities. Non-cognitive contextual factors can have a significant impact on information processing and problem-solving. Repeated failure leads to deskilling, but the provision of *scaffolding* leads to mastery experiences and skill acquisition. When children show a delay in language development, a distinction may be made between specific language delay and secondary language delay due to intellectual disability, autism, hearing loss or some such condition. Where measures of non-verbal intelligence, receptive and expressive language and adaptive behaviour all fall two standard deviations below the mean (or a standard score of 70), then the language problem is secondary to intellectual disability. The developmental patterning of adaptive behaviour over the lifespan depends upon the aetiology of intellectual disability, the presence of comorbid conditions such as autism, and the level of disability. In contrast to normally developing children, those with intellectual disabilities are less proficient at recognizing, expressing and regulating emotions, responding to emotions in others, and following formal and informal social rules, and this renders the process of making and maintaining long-term relationships more difficult for people with intellectual disabilities. The motivation to learn adaptive skills is inhibited by a personality profile which characterized many people with intellectual disabilities. The profile involves over-dependence on familiar adults, wariness of unfamiliar adults, lower expectations of success, outerdirectedness, and reduced effectance motivation. Skills training programmes should take this profile into account. When a family member has an intellectual disability, additional tasks must be completed at various stages of the family lifecycle including addressing the diagnosis of intellectual disability, developing routines for caring with a child with intellectual disability, managing additional demands, particularly planning appropriate supports, associated with the transitions to adolescence, adulthood, and later life. When developing individual family support plans in infancy, individual educational plans in childhood and adolescence and individual personal plans in adulthood, these should be based on a comprehensive case formulation which takes account of the risk and protective factors present in the case, the person's developmental status in the sensory, motor, cognitive, linguistic and social domains, and the family's lifecycle stage and coping resources.

EXERCISE

Work in teams of 2–4 people. For each of the case vignettes below list your main hypotheses about key developmental issues for the person with intellectual disabilities and their families. Specify how you would investigate these hypotheses and the probable supports that might be required depending upon the outcome of your investigations. Present your views on these issues to your class.

Lucy is a 3½-year-old girl who was referred to a disability assessment team by a community health nurse. Lucy was a premature low birth-weight child. She has shown developmental delays in motor and speech development, and has a moderate intellectual disability. She lives with her mother who is in her forties and her three siblings who are all teenagers. Her father visits occasionally, but has had limited contact with the family since Lucy's parents' separation two years ago. The family are economically disadvantaged.

Brian is in his late teens and was referred for assessment by his school principal as he is due to leave next year. Sam has a mild-moderate intellectual disability and a history of challenging behaviour at the start of each new school year. He also has difficulty mixing with his peers. He lives with his parents, who both have demanding professional careers, and is an only child.

FURTHER READING FOR PARENTS

Miller, N. *et al.* (1994). *Nobody's Perfect: Living and Growing with Children who have Special Needs.* Baltimore, MD: Brookes. (A guide for parents.)

Naseef, R. (2001). *Special Children, Challenged Parents: The Struggles and Rewards of Raising a Child with a Disability* (rev. edn). Baltimore, MD: Brookes. (Psychologist/ father first-person account.)

FURTHER READING AND RESOURCES FOR CLINICIANS

Freeman, N.B.E. (1985). *The Deaf-Blind Baby: A Programme of Care.* London: William Heinemann Medical Books.

Kusche, C.A. and Greenberg, M.T. (1994). *The PATHS Curriculum.* Seattle, WA: Developmental Research and Programs.

Resnick, M. and Packer, A. (1990). *Infant Development Activities for Parents.* New York: St Martin's Press.

Sparling, J. and Lewis, I. (1979). *Learning Games for the First Three Years: A Program for Parent/Centre Partnership.* New York: Walker Educational Book Corp.

Sparling, J. and Lewis, I. (1984). *Partners for Learning.* Lewisville, NC: Kaplan Press.

Sparling, J. and Lewis, I. (1984). *Learning Games for Threes and Fours: A Guide to Parent–Child Play.* New York: Walker.

Sparling, J., Lewis, I. and Neuwirth, S. (1988). *Early Partners Curriculum Kit.* Lewisville, NC: Kaplan Press.

Wasik, B. (1984a). *Problem Solving for Parents.* Chapel Hill, NC: Frank Porter Graham Child Development Centre.

Wasik, B. (1984b). *Coping with Parenting through Effective Problem Solving: A Handbook for Professionals.* Chapel Hill, NC: Frank Porter Graham Child Development Centre.

Wasik, B., Bryant, D. and Lyons, D. (1990). *Home Visiting.* Newbury Park: Sage.

Watkins, S. and Clark, T.C. (1992). *The SKI*HI model: A Resource Manual for Family-Centred, Home-Based Programming for Infants, Toddlers, and Pre-school-Aged Children with Hearing Impairment.* Logan, UT: HOPE.

British Institute for Learning Disabilities. http://www.bild.org.uk/

American Association for Mental Retardation http://www.aamr.org/Bookstore/

Brookes Publishers www.brookespublishing.com

National Autistic Society www.nas.@nas.org.uk

Gaskell Press, Royal College of Psychiatry www.rcpsych.ac.uk/publications/gaskell/ Gaskell Press (Royal College of Psychiatry) has a lovely series of picture books for people with intellectual disabilities by Sheila Hollins on a wide variety of lifecycle challenges (*Speaking Up For Myself, George Gets Smart, Susan's Growing Up, Going Into Hospital, Michelle Finds A Voice*).

REFERENCES

American National Standards Institute (1989). *Specifications for Audiometers (ANSI)*. New York: Acoustical Society of America.

American Psychiatric Association (APA) (2000). *Diagnostic and Statistical Manual of the Mental Disorders (Fourth Edition-Text Revision, DSM-IV-TR)*. Washington, DC: APA.

Baker, L. and Cantwell, D. (1982). Psychiatric disorder in children with different types of communication disorder. *Journal of Communication Disorders*, 15, 113–26.

Baron-Cohen, S. (1995). *Mindblindness: An Essay on Autism and Theory of Mind*. Cambridge, MA: MIT Press.

Bayley, N. (1993). *Bayley Scales of Infant Development* (2nd edn). New York, NY: Psychological Corporation.

Bess, F.H. and Humes, L.E. (1995). *Audiology: The Fundamentals*. Baltimore: Williams and Wilkins.

Bishop, D. (2002). Speech and language difficulties. In M. Rutter and E. Taylor (eds), *Child and Adolescent Psychiatry* (4th edn, pp. 664–81). Oxford: Blackwell.

Bishop, D. and Adams, C. (1990). A prospective study of the relationship between specific language impairment, phonological disorders and reading retardation. *Journal of Child Psychology and Psychiatry*, 31, 1027–50.

Blancher, J. and Baker, B. (2002). *Families and Mental Retardation*. Washington, DC: AAMR.

Bruner, J. (1983). *Child's Talk: Learning to Use Language*. New York: Norton.

Burack, J., Hodapp, R. and Zigler, E. (1998). *Handbook of Mental Retardation and Development*. Cambridge: Cambridge University Press.

Capute, A. and Shapiro, B. (1985). The motor quotient: A method for the early detection of motor delay. *American Journal of Disability in Children*, 139, 940–1.

Carney, A.E. and Moeller, M.P. (1998). Treatment efficacy: Hearing loss in children. *Journal of Speech, Language and Hearing Research*, 41, 61–84.

Carr, A. (1999). *Handbook of Clinical Child and Adolescent Psychology: A Contextual Approach*. London: Routledge.

Carr, A. (2004). *Positive Clinical Psychology*. London: Brunner-Routledge.

Carr, A. (ed.) (2002). *Prevention: What Works with Children and Adolescents? A Critical Review of Psychological Prevention Programmes for Children, Adolescents and their Families*. London: Brunner-Routledge.

Carter, B. and McGoldrick, M. (1999). *The Expanded Family Lifecycle: Individual, Family and Social Perspectives* (3rd edn). Boston: Allyn and Bacon.

Clements, J. (1987). *Severe Learning Disability and Psychological Handicap*. Chichester: Wiley.

Coolman, R., Bennett, F., Sells, C., Sweanson, M., Andrews, M. and Robinson, N. (1985). Neuromotor development of graduates of the neonatal intensive care unit: Patterns encountered in the first two years of life. *Journal of Developmental and Behavioural Paediatrics*, 6, 327–33.

Detterman, D., Gabriel, L. and Ruthsatz, J. (2000). Intelligence and mental retardation. In R. Sternberg (ed.), *Handbook of Intelligence* (pp. 141–58). Cambridge, UK: Cambridge University Press.

Dunn, J. and McGuire, S. (1992). Sibling and peer relationships in childhood. *Journal of Child Psychology and Psychiatry*, 33, 67–105.

Evans, D. (1998). Development of the self concept in children with mental retardation: Organizmic and contextual factors. In J. Burack, R. Hodapp and E. Zigler (eds), *Handbook of Mental Retardation and Development* (pp. 462–80). Cambridge: Cambridge University Press.

Fahey, A. and Carr, A. (2002). Chapter 5. Prevention of adjustment problems in children with sensory disabilities. In A. Carr (ed.), *Prevention: What Works with Children and Adolescents? A Critical Review of Psychological Prevention Programmes for Children, Adolescents and their Families* (pp. 83–106). London: Routledge.

Feinman, S. (1992). *Social Referencing and the Social Construction of Reality in Infancy*. New York: Plenum.

Field, T., Healy, B., Goldstein, S. and Guthertz, M. (1990). Behaviour-state matching and synchrony in mother–infant interactions of nondepressed versus depressed dyads. *Developmental Psychology*, 26, 7–14.

Flavell, J., Miller, P. and Miller, S. (2002). *Cognitive Development* (4th edn). Englewood Cliffs, NJ: Prentice-Hall.

Fraiberg, S. (1977). *Insights from the Blind: Comparative Studies of Blind and Sighted Children*. New York: Basic Books.

Friedman, R. and Chase-Lansdale, P. (2002). Chronic adversities. In M. Rutter and E. Taylor (eds), *Child and Adolescent Psychiatry* (4th edn, pp. 261–76). Oxford: Blackwell.

Gath, A. (2000). Families with a mentally retarded member and their needs. In M. Gelder, J. Lopez-Ibor and N. Andreasen (eds.), *New Oxford Textbook of Psychiatry* (Vol. 2, Sec 10.8, pp. 2001–5). Oxford: Oxford University Press.

Goldberg, D., Magrill, L., Hale, J., Damaskinidou, Paul, J. and Tham, S. (1995). Protection and loss: Working with learning-disabled adults and their families. *Journal of Family Therapy*, 17, 263–80.

Goodman, R. (2002). Brain disorders. In M. Rutter and E. Taylor (eds), *Child and Adolescent Psychiatry* (4th edn, pp. 241–60). Oxford: Blackwell.

Hindley, P. and vanGent, T. (2002). Psychiatric aspects of specific sensory impairments. In M. Rutter and E. Taylor (eds), *Child and Adolescent Psychiatry* (4th edn, pp. 842–57). Oxford: Blackwell.

Hodapp, R., Burack, J. and Zigler, E. (1998). Developmental approaches to mental retardation: A short introduction. In J. Burack, R. Hodapp and E. Zigler (eds), *Handbook of Mental Retardation and Development* (pp. 3–19). Cambridge: Cambridge University Press.

Inhelder, B. (1968). *The Diagnosis of Reasoning in the Mentally Retarded*. New York: Chandler.

Inhelder, B. and Piaget, J. (1958). *The Growth of Logical Thinking from Childhood to Adolescence*. London: Routledge and Kegan Paul.

Kasari, C. and Bauminger, N. (1998). Social and emotional development in children with mental retardation. In J. Burack, R. Hodapp and E. Zigler (eds), *Handbook of Mental Retardation and Development* (pp. 411–33). Cambridge: Cambridge University Press.

Kaski, M. (2000). Aetiology of mental retardation: General issues and prevention. In M. Gelder, J. Lopez-Ibor and N. Andreasen (eds), *New Oxford Textbook of Psychiatry* (Vol. 2, Sec 10.3, pp. 1948–52). Oxford: Oxford University Press.

Kavale, K. and Forness, S. (1999). *Efficacy of Special Education*. Washington, DC: AAMR.

Kaye, K. (1982). *The Mental and Social Life of Babies*. Chicago: University of Chicago Press.

Kochanska, G. (1993). Towards a synthesis of parental socialization and child temperament in the early development of conscience. *Child Development*, 64, 325–47.

Kraus, M. and Seltzer, M. (1998). Lifecourse perspective in mental retardation research: The case of family caregiving. In J. Burack, R. Hodapp and E. Zigler (eds), *Handbook of Mental Retardation and Development* (pp. 504–20). Cambridge: Cambridge University Press.

Lange, G. and Carr, A. (2002). Chapter 3. Prevention of cognitive delays in socially disadvantaged children. In A. Carr (ed.), *Prevention: What Works with Children and Adolescents? A Critical Review of Psychological Prevention Programmes for Children, Adolescents and their Families* (pp. 41–63). London: Routledge.

Loveland, K. and Tunali-Kotoski, B. (1998). Development of adaptive behaviour in persons with mental retardation. In J. Burack, R. Hodapp and E. Zigler (eds), *Handbook of Mental Retardation and Development* (pp. 521–41). Cambridge: Cambridge University Press.

Luckasson, R., Borthwick-Duffy, S., Buntinx, W., Coulter, D., Craig, E., Reeve, A., Schalock, R., Snell, M., Spitalnik, D., Spreat, S. and Tasse, M. (2002). *Mental Retardation: Definition, Classification, and Systems of Supports* (10th edn). Washington, DC: American Association on Mental Retardation.

Luthar, R. (2003). *Resilience and Vulnerability*. Cambridge: Cambridge University Press.

Malatesta, D. (1985). Developmental course of emotional expression in the human infant. In G. Zivin (ed.), *The Development of Expressive Behaviour: Biology-Environment Interactions*. Orlando, FL: Academic Press.

Malik, N. and Furman, W. (1993). Practitioner review: Problem in children's peer relations: What can the clinician do. *Journal of Child Psychology and Psychiatry*, 34, 1303–26.

Marfo, K., Dedrick, C. and Barbour, N. (1998). Mother–child interactions and the development of children with mental retardation. In J. Burack, R. Hodapp and E. Zigler (eds), *Handbook of Mental Retardation and Development* (pp. 637–68). Cambridge: Cambridge University Press.

Menacker, S. and Batshaw, M. (1997). Vision: Our window on the world. In M. Batshaw (ed.), *Children with Disabilities* (4th edn, pp. 211–39). Baltimore, MD: Paul Brookes.

Minnes, P. (1998). Mental retardation: The impact on the family. In J. Burack, R. Hodapp and E. Zigler (eds), *Handbook of Mental Retardation and Development* (pp. 693–712). Cambridge: Cambridge University Press.

Norris, M., Spaulding, P. and Brodie, F. (1957). *Blindness in Children*. Chicago: University of Chicago Press.

O'Sullivan, A. and Carr, A. (2002). Prevention of developmental delay in low birth weight infants. In A. Carr (ed.), *Prevention: What Works with Children and Adolescents? A Critical Review of Psychological Prevention Programmes for Children, Adolescents and their Families* (pp. 17–40). London: Routledge.

Pellegrino, L. (1997). Cerebral palsy. In M. Batshaw (ed.), *Children with Disabilities* (4th edn, pp. 499–528). Baltimore, MD: Brookes.

Quine, L. and Rutter, D. (1994). First diagnosis of severe mental and physical disability. *Journal of Child Psychology and Psychiatry*, 35, 1273–89.

Rapin, I. (1996). Practitioner review: Developmental language disorders: A clinical update. *Journal of Child Psychology and Psychiatry*, 37, 643–55.

Rolf, J., Masten, A., Cicchetti, D., *et al.* (1990). *Risk and Protective Factors in the Development of Psychopathology*. New York: Cambridge University Press.

Rolland, J. (1994). *Families, Illness and Disability: An Integrative Treatment Model*. New York: Basic Books.

Rolland, J. (2003). Mastering family challenges in serious illness and disability. In F. Walsh (ed.), *Normal Family Process* (3rd edn, pp. 460–89). New York: Guilford.

Rosenberg, S. (1993). Chomsky's theory of language: Some recent observations. *Psychological Science*, 4, 15–19.

Russell, J. (1997). *Autism as an Executive Disorder*. Oxford: Oxford University Press.

Rutter, M. and Rutter, M. (1993). *Developing Minds: Challenge and Continuity across the Lifespan*. London: Penguin.

Schalock, R. (2002). *Adaptive Behaviour and its Measurements: Implications for the Field of Mental Retardation*. Washington, DC: American Association on Mental Retardation.

Shapiro, B. and Capute, A. (1999). Cerebral palsy. In J. McMillan, C. DeAngelis, R. Feigin and J. Warshaw (eds), *Oski's Pediatrics: Principles and Practice* (3rd edn, pp. 1910–17). Philadelphia, PA: Lippincott, Williams and Wilkins.

Shapiro, J., Blancher, J. and Lopez, S. (1998). Maternal reactions to children with mental retardation. In J. Burack, R. Hodapp and E. Zigler (eds), *Handbook of Mental Retardation and Development* (pp. 606–36). Cambridge: Cambridge University Press.

Skuse, D. (1984). Extreme deprivation in early childhood. II. Theoretical issues and a comparative review. *Journal of Child Psychology and Psychiatry*, 25, 543–72.

Smith, P., Cowie, H. and Blades, M. (2003). *Understanding Children's Development* (4th edn). Oxford: Blackwell.

Snow, C. and Ferguson, C. (1977). *Talking to Children: Language Input and Acquisition*. Cambridge: Cambridge University Press.

Stoneman, Z. (1998). Research on siblings of children with mental retardation: Contributions of developmental theory and aetiology. In J. Burack, R. Hodapp and E. Zigler (eds), *Handbook of Mental Retardation and Development* (pp. 669–92). Cambridge: Cambridge University Press.

Strong, C.J., Clark, T.C., Barringer, D.G., Walden, B. and Williams, S.A. (1992). *SKI*HI Home-Based Programming for Children with Hearing Impairments: Demographics, Child Identification and Programme Effectiveness, 1979–1990: Final Report to the US Department of Education, Office of Special Education and Rehabilitative Services*. Logan: Utah State University of Communication Disorders. SKI*HI Institute.

Volkmar, F. and Dykens, E. (2002). Mental retardation. In M. Rutter and E. Taylor (eds), *Child and Adolescent Psychiatry* (4th edn, pp. 697–710). Oxford: Blackwell.

Vygotsky, L. (1962/1934). *Thought and Language*. Cambridge, MA: MIT Press (originally published in 1934).

Waldron, B. and Carr, A. (2002). Chapter 4. Prevention of adjustment problems in children cerebral palsy. In A. Carr (ed.), *Prevention: What Works with Children and Adolescents? A Critical Review of Psychological Prevention Programmes for Children, Adolescents and their Families* (pp. 64–82). London: Routledge.

Whitehurst, G. and Fischel, J. (1994). Practitioner review: Early developmental language delay: What, if anything should the clinician do about it? *Journal of Child Psychology and Psychiatry*, 35, 613–48.

Williams, B. and Gilmore, J. (1994). Annotation: Sociometry and peer relationships. *Journal of Child Psychology and Psychiatry*, 35, 997–1013.

World Health Organization (WHO) (1984). *Strategies for the Prevention of Blindness in National Programmes*. Geneva, Switzerland: WHO.

World Health Organization (WHO) (1993). *The ICD-10 Classification of Mental and Behavioural Disorders: Diagnostic Criteria for Research*. Geneva: WHO.

Zetlin, A. and Morrison, G. (1998). Adaptation through the life span. In J. Burack, R. Hodapp and E. Zigler (eds), *Handbook of Mental Retardation and Development* (pp. 481–503). Cambridge: Cambridge University Press.

Assessment frameworks

Chapter 3

Evaluating intelligence across the life-span: integrating theory, research and measurement

Gary O'Reilly and Alan Carr

WHAT DOES THE TERM 'INTELLIGENCE' MEAN?

Charles Spearman (1927: 14) expressed the exasperated view of many when he said 'in truth, "intelligence" has become a mere vocal sound, a word with so many meanings that finally it has none'. In the intervening years many have added their voices to the chorus of potentially confusing definitions and opinions on what is intelligence. However, Deary (2000) has wisely observed that there are two types of definition of any term that may be offered. The first is to offer a precise statement of meaning. The second is broadly to outline the boundaries and limitations of what a term means. Deary comments that to attempt to offer a precise definition of intelligence is fruitlessly to offer a hostage to fortune; in contrast, to attempt to outline broadly what we mean when we use the word intelligence is certainly possible and indeed useful.

A practical insight into the areas of strong agreement and frayed edges of what is meant by the term 'intelligence' is offered by Snyderman and Rothman (1987) who surveyed 661 psychologists and educational experts, identified through their membership of professional associations, on various aspects of intelligence and intelligence testing. Table 3.1 outlines the degree

Table 3.1 Areas of agreement and disagreement on what constitutes intelligent behaviour among psychologists and educators with expertise in the area (adapted from Snyderman and Rothman, 1987)

Statement	Agreement %	Statement	Agreement %
Almost unanimous agreement			
1 Abstract thinking or reasoning	99.3	8 Mathematical competence	67.9
2 Problem-solving ability	97.7	9 General knowledge	62.4
3 Capacity to acquire knowledge	96.0	10 Creativity	59.6
Majority agreement		**Low-level agreement**	
4 Memory	80.5	11 Sensory acuity	24.4
5 Adaptation to one's environment	77.2	12 Goal-directedness	24.0
6 Mental speed	71.7	13 Achievement motivation	18.9
7 Linguistic competence	71.0		

to which respondents agreed that each of thirteen behavioural descriptors adequately reflected an important aspect of intelligence. Clear and almost unanimous agreement is apparent among the 'experts' that intelligence involves abstract thinking, problem solving, and acquiring knowledge. A majority agree that it includes features such as memory, adapting to one's environment, mental speed, linguistic and mathematical competence, general knowledge, and creativity. Finally, a minority feel that sensory acuity, goal-directedness, and motivation are features of intelligence.

From the perspective of those working with people who have an intellectual disability arguably the most important definition of intelligence is offered by the American Association on Mental Retardation (AAMR, 2002) which defines it as follows:

> Intelligence is a general mental capability. It includes reasoning, planning, solving problems, thinking abstractly, comprehending complex ideas, learning quickly, and learning from experience.
>
> (American Association on Mental Retardation, 2002: 14)

This definition offers guidance on what should be considered the core features of intelligence: reasoning; planning; solving problems; thinking abstractly; comprehending complex ideas; learning quickly; and learning from experience. The AAMR further highlights the importance of understanding that the expression of human intelligence depends on the context of an individual's life, their level of adaptive behaviour, their opportunities for participation in society, their interactions with others, the social roles available to them, and their health status. It also concludes that, despite many limitations, the best approach to the formal assessment of intelligence currently available to us is through the appropriate use of standardized psychometric tests (an issue we will return to later in this chapter).

MODELS OF INTELLIGENCE

After outlining a working definition of intelligence that is applicable in the context of working with people who have an intellectual disability, it is appropriate to consider some of the more influential theoretical models that have emerged in the literature. Broadly speaking these can be thought of in three categories: (a) those that stem from the psychometric approach to intelligence; (b) those that go beyond this approach by adopting non-psychometric evidence or a speculative consideration of intelligence; and (c) those that adopt a predominantly developmental perspective. In this chapter we will confine our discussion to selected theories in the first two categories. Developmental theories have already been described in Chapter 1.

THE PSYCHOMETRIC APPROACH

The psychometric approach to modelling intelligence is based on the administration of IQ-type tests to various populations and then through statistical analysis deducing from the data gathered a theoretical model of what happens when we engage in mental activity to solve intellectual problems. The American Psychological Association Task Force on Intelligence (Neisser, Boodoo, Bonchard, Boykin, *et al.*, 1996) described the psychometric approach as having the greatest research base and the widest application in practical settings. It might seem that this is an approach that would yield broad agreement on a model of intelligence. However, there has in fact been much debate on the best way to analyse and interpret the data yielded by the many intelligence tests and empirical studies that form the basis of research within this tradition.

Spearman and Thurstone's models

Charles Spearman (1904; 1923; 1927) is credited as the founding father of psychometric models of intelligence. Spearman's theory was initially based on data concerning a small number of English school-children collected from teacher-ratings of academic ability, peer-ratings of 'sharpness and common sense' outside school, and observed execution of sensory tasks involving pitch, hue and weight discrimination. Based on the correlations in this data, and those from another similar study, Spearman observed that there appears to be a general factor (which he termed 'g') substantially influencing an individual's performance on all types of mental tasks, in combination with more specific lower-level factors (which he referred to as 's') uniquely required for some tasks. That is, Spearman observed that people who tend to perform at a given level on one type of task (being clever at school) also tend to perform similarly on other tasks (using your common sense outside school or making a sensory judgement). He proposed that the general factor evident between ratings on these apparently different tasks might be explained by a real underlying psychological factor of general intelligence, which differs between individuals, is employed to some degree in all intellectual tasks, and has a physiological foundation which he speculatively considered to be a neurologically based mental energy.

Since the publication of Spearman's work, a significant debate within the psychometric tradition has concerned the impact on the structure of models of intelligence generated through factor analysis from using different statistical techniques to analyse the data gathered by researchers. For example, Thurstone (1938), using an equally valid statistical technique to that developed by Spearman but which favours the separation of abilities, thought his data were supportive not of a single 'g' factor but a number of Primary Mental Abilities (verbal ability, perceptual speed, inductive reasoning, numerical ability, memory, deductive reasoning, word fluency, and spatial visualization).

The Cattell–Horn model

Continuing in the Thurstonian tradition, Cattell (1943) and Horn (1986) developed a hierarchical model of intelligence which initially posited that g in fact reflects two distinct types of intelligence (*fluid ability*, known as Gf, which is reasoning that primarily draws upon underlying neurological resources; and *crystallized ability*, known as Gc, which is reasoning that largely draws upon knowledge individually accumulated by a person within their unique cultural context). Over time the Gf–Gc model has been extended to incorporate the implications from new psychometric evidence, combined to a lesser extent, with findings from developmental psychology, neuropsychology, behavioural-genetics, and research on school and occupational achievement. This has suggested not just two important subtypes of intelligence but eight or nine roughly equivalent but separable mental abilities which are described in detail in Table 3.2 (Horn, 1994; Horn and Blankson, 2005; McGrew and Flanagan, 1998). In turn these abilities rest upon at least eighty-seven primary mental skills which are in some ways independent but nevertheless combine to produce the eight or nine second-order parts of the model (see Table 3.2).

A very significant feature of the Cattell–Horn model is its rejection of psychometric g as a meaningful cognitive reality. Based on psychometric evidence, and studies of ageing and neurological functioning, Horn and Blankson (2005) argue that although a positive correlation is evident among second-order abilities, it is not best represented as a single higher-order factor (as in Spearman's g). Instead they tentatively suggest three distinct clusters of higher organization as follows. Fluid intelligence (Gf), short-term memory (Gsm), and processing speed (Gs) form the first unique hierarchically higher cluster of second-order abilities. These are termed '*Vulnerable Abilities*' reflecting their vulnerability to age-related decline in adulthood. The next cluster of second-order abilities are termed '*Expertise Abilities*' comprising crystallized intelligence (Gc), quantitative reasoning (Gq), and fluency of retrieval from long-term memory (Glm). Skills within this domain typically continue to develop throughout the life-span into older adulthood. A third and final cluster of '*Sensory-Perceptual Abilities*' are also described comprising visual thinking (Gv), and auditory thinking (Ga). Both of these abilities are intimately tied to sensory modalities. Their age-related development tends to fall between the trajectories evident for vulnerable and expertise abilities and decline is usually linked to injury or damage to relevant aspects of the sensory nervous system.

Cattell and Horn's extended Gf–Gc theory can be viewed as a work in progress as it accepts that the full range of mental abilities that underlie our

Table 3.2 Defining aspects of the Horn–Cattell model of intelligence (adapted from Horn 1994; Horn and Blankson, 2005; and McGrew and Flanagan, 1998)

Ability	Definition	Reflecting abilities that include . . .
'VULNERABLE ABILITIES'		
1 **Fluid intelligence (Gf)**	Various forms of reasoning typically applied to solve novel intellectual tasks. Thought to be largely reflective of underlying biological factors that influence intelligence and not reflective of problem solving that is reliant on previous learning. Gf is vulnerable to age-related decline in adulthood	• Inductive reasoning • Deductive reasoning • General sequential reasoning • Piagetian reasoning • Speed of reasoning
2 **Short-term memory (Gsm)**	Immediate awareness of information that allows it to be processed further or forgotten within about two seconds. Most people can retain seven chunks of unrelated information (plus or minus two chunks) in their short-term memory. Some aspects of Gsm are vulnerable to age-related decline in adulthood	• Immediate memory span • Immediate memory associational ability
3 **Processing speed (Gs)**	Mental speediness. The ability to concentrate and perform rudimentary cognitive tasks quickly. Intimately related to working memory or the limited processing capabilities that an individual has at their disposal for mental activity. Gs is vulnerable to age-related decline in adulthood	• Perceptual speed • Rate-of-test-taking • Facility with numbers
4 **Correct decision speed (CDS)**	Quickness of decision-making in response to intellectual tasks (as opposed to quickness of processing information)	• Simple reaction time • Choice reaction time • Semantic processing speed • Mental comparison speed

(Continued overleaf)

Table 3.2 Continued

Ability	Definition	Reflecting abilities that include . . .
'EXPERTISE ABILITIES'		
5 Crystallized intelligence (Gc)	Knowledge which has been acquired through experience within a cultural context that allows an individual to solve problems. This knowledge may take many forms and includes declarative (knowing that) and procedural (knowing how) knowledge. It is not synonymous with school attainment. On average Gc continues to increase during adulthood, possibly up to 70 or 80 years of age	• Language development • Lexical knowledge • Listening ability • General verbal information • Information about a culture • General science information • Geographical knowledge • Communication ability • Oral production and fluency • Grammatical sensitivity • Foreign language knowledge
6 Quantitative thinking	Ability to understand and apply the concepts and skills required for mathematical problem solving	• Facility with numbers • Estimation • Algebraic reasoning
7 Fluency of retrieval from long-term memory (Glr)	Ability to store, recall and associate information fluently in long-term memory. It should not be confused with crystallized ability (which in some ways includes the store of learnt information) as it is concerned with the fluency of storage, retrieval and association of information rather than content. Research suggests either no change or improvement in Glr during most of the adult phase of the lifecycle	• Associational fluency • Free recall fluency • Ideational fluency • Expressional fluency • Naming fluency • Word fluency • Figural fluency • Figural flexibility • Originality/Creativity
'SENSORY PERCEPTUAL ABILITIES'		
8 Visual thinking (Gv)	The ability to think visually, including the ability mentally to perceive and manipulate figural stimuli and spatial relations and orientations	• Visualization • Spatial relation thinking • Visual memory • Visual closure speed • Flexibility of closure • Spatial scanning ability

		• Perception and integration of serial visual stimuli
• Length estimation
• Perceptual illusion resistance
• Perceptual alternations
• Imagery
9 Auditory thinking (Ga)	The ability to think using auditory stimuli, including the ability to perceive, analyse, and discriminate patterns and subtle differences between sounds such as language and music. These abilities do not include language comprehension but do include the phonetic awareness that underpins verbal communication	• Phonetic coding
• Speech sound discrimination
• Resistance to auditory stimulus distortion
• Memory for sound patterns
• General sound discrimination
• Temporal tracking
• Musical discrimination and judgement
• Maintaining and judging rhythm
• Discriminating sound duration/discrimination
• Speech pitch discrimination
• Identifying sound localization

intelligence may as yet await full description. That is, gathering further experimental evidence may yield insight into other areas of intellectual functioning that usefully describe us. For example, Horn and Blankson (2005) argue that there may be an Expertise Wide-Span Memory (EWSM) which is distinct from short-term memory. It is speculated that EWSM has the capacity to hold relatively large amounts of information in awareness for several minutes in order to facilitate the expert solution of problems. Its inclusion as a separate second-order factor with the extended Gf–Gc model will require its substantiation through further research. Other potential candidates proposed for separate second-order ability status which await fuller confirmation or rejection include language-use, psychomotor, olfactory, tactile, kinaesthetic, and general knowledge abilities.

Carroll's model

In what is universally regarded as an epic contribution to the field that provided a unifying momentum, Carroll (1993) reviewed 467 data-sets from studies that adopted a psychometric approach to studying human intelligence published during the greater part of the twentieth century (1927–1987). Carroll's review included data-sets associated with the most widely known psychometric models encompassing those of Thurstone, Cattell and Horn among others. Carroll's objective was to apply what he judged to be the single most appropriate and comprehensive approach to factor-analysis to all of these data-sets in order to determine a coherent evidenced-based model of intelligence. The outcome of his endeavours (see Figure 3.1) outlined a model with three stratums or layers that make up the structure of human cognitive abilities. Stratum one comprised sixty-six quite specific and narrow aspects of cognitive functioning. These accounted for small amounts of variance in individual performance on IQ test tasks. Stratum two consisted of eight broader ability factors in which groups of the more specific stratum one abilities clustered. The eight factors identified were as follows: Fluid Intelligence, Crystallized Intelligence, General Memory and Learning, Broad Visual Perception, Broad Auditory Perception, Broad Retrieval Ability, Broad Cognitive Speediness, and Processing Speed. Carroll's definition of each of these factors is outlined in Table 3.3. Finally stratum three reflected a higher-order general intelligence factor or 'g', representing the correlation between stratum two abilities.

What is g?

At this point it seems appropriate to ask if we can be any more specific about what psychometric g represents? Proponents of g cite its enduring appearance throughout a century of intelligence testing, its ability to predict educational and vocational performance, its relative stability throughout the life-span, and its apparent heritable basis to establish the reality of its importance (Jensen, 1998; Nyborg, 2003; Sternberg and Grigorenko, 2002). Nevertheless, despite the significance given by many within the literature to psychometric g it remains difficult to give a clear, theoretically coherent definition of what it actually is. Consequently, Deary (2002) calls g a psychometric triumph and a cognitive enigma.

Despite the ambiguity about what g represents, many IQ test developers encourage the interpretation of the composite score yielded by their IQ tests as equivalent to g (see Table 3.10 below). They do so on the basis that the overlap between Full-Scale IQ (FSIQ) and g tends to be high. However, they do not help us to understand better what g is. Instead they usually refer to it with little effort to get beyond the surface, providing descriptive definitions that are low in explanation, such as 'the hierarchical g factor that exists among the scores of an intelligence battery' (Roid, 2003b: 135). Caution appears warranted here as we know that there are differences in the correlation across FSIQ scores from different instruments, thus establishing that these summary scores, although often similar, are not capturing a single

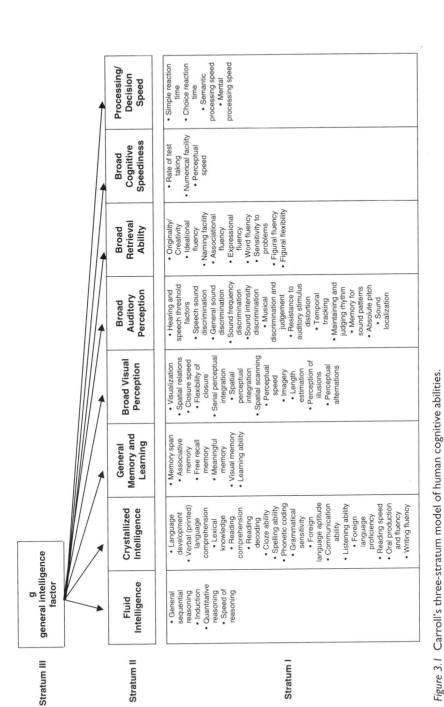

	Stratum III							
		g general intelligence factor						
	Stratum II	**Fluid Intelligence**	**Crystallized Intelligence**	**General Memory and Learning**	**Broad Visual Perception**	**Broad Auditory Perception**	**Broad Retrieval Ability**	**Broad Cognitive Speediness**	**Processing/ Decision Speed**
Stratum I		• General sequential reasoning • Induction • Quantitative reasoning • Speed of reasoning	• Language development • Verbal (printed) language comprehension • Lexical knowledge • Reading comprehension • Reading decoding • Cloze ability • Spelling ability • Phonetic coding • Grammatical sensitivity • Foreign language aptitude • Communication ability • Listening ability • Foreign language proficiency • Reading speed • Oral production and fluency • Writing fluency	• Memory span • Associative memory • Free recall memory • Meaningful memory • Visual memory • Learning ability	• Visualization • Spatial relations • Closure speed • Flexibility of closure • Serial perceptual integration • Spatial perceptual integration • Spatial scanning • Perceptual speed • Imagery • Length estimation • Perception of illusions • Perceptual alternations	• Hearing and speech threshold factors • Speech sound discrimination • General sound discrimination • Sound frequency discrimination • Sound intensity discrimination • Musical discrimination and judgement • Resistance to auditory stimulus distortion • Temporal tracking • Maintaining and judging rhythm • Memory for sound patterns • Absolute pitch • Sound localization	• Originality/ Creativity • Ideational fluency • Naming facility • Associational fluency • Expressional fluency • Word fluency • Sensitivity to problems • Figural fluency • Figural flexibility	• Rate of test taking • Numerical facility • Perceptual speed	• Simple reaction time • Choice reaction time • Semantic processing speed • Mental processing speed

Figure 3.1 Carroll's three-stratum model of human cognitive abilities.

Source: adapted from Carroll (1993: 626)

Table 3.3 Carroll's (1993) definition of his second-order cognitive abilities

Ability	Definition
1 **Fluid intelligence**	'Concerned with basic processes of reasoning and other mental activities that depend only minimally on learning and acculturation' (1993:624)
2 **Crystallized intelligence**	'Concerned with mental processes that reflect not only the operation of fluid intelligence but also the effects of experience, learning, and acculturation' (1993:624)
3 **General memory and learning**	'Probably involved in any task that calls for learning and memory of new content or responses. However, there may be several varieties of this factor; one variety is a higher-order memory span' (1993:624)
4 **Broad visual perception**	'Involved in any task that requires the perception of visual forms *as such*. (That is, it is involved only minimally, if at all, in the perception of printed language forms)' (1993:625)
5 **Broad auditory perception**	'Involved in any task or performance that requires the perception or discrimination of auditory patterns of sound or speech, particularly when such patterns present difficulties because of fine discriminations, auditory distortion, or complex musical structure' (1993:625)
6 **Broad retrieval ability**	'Involved in any task or performance that requires the ready retrieval of concepts or items from long-term memory. It is possible that there are several varieties of this factor, depending on the degree of "originality" required in the responses' (1993:625)
7 **Broad cognitive speediness**	'Involved in any task or performance that requires rapid cognitive processing of information. There appear to be several subvarieties of this ability including [one] governing speed of decision in various types of reaction-time tasks' (1993:625)
8 **Processing speed**	'Speed of psychomotor response performance . . . Has minimal cognitive content and should not be taken to be strictly a cognitive ability' (1993:625)

underlying general ability. Furthermore, FSIQ is a summary of all aspects of ability (from the most general to the most specific) as measured on any given test. In contrast, g is a distillate not a summary or an average (Jensen, 2002).

As yet there is no definitive reason to assume that despite the convincing emergence of g from the psychometric approach to intelligence it truly reflects some neurologically based aspect of what happens when we exercise our intellectual abilities. Even among psychometricians, whether or not g represents something real remains in dispute. Most notable is Horn's continued rejection of g as a cognitive reality. He challenges that its emergence in factor analysis does not provide convincing evidence of a real-world significance (Horn and Blankson, 2005). Nevertheless, there is presently much interest in the apparent very high correlation between g and working memory (Colom, Flores-Mendoza, Quiroga and Privado, 2005; Colom, Rebollo, Palacios, Juan-Espinosa and Kyllonen, 2004). This has prompted researchers to develop hypotheses designed to throw light on whether individual differences in g can be explained through understanding individual differences in cognitive processes such as working memory.

Conclusion

Despite the fundamental differences apparent in the various psychometric models reviewed, here a consensus view has emerged in the form of a combined Cattell–Horn–Carroll model (also known as the CHC model; McGrew, 2005) represented in Figure 3.2. Consequently, it seems fair to conclude that when we administer psychometric tests of intelligence to a population and analyse the results, the best representation of latent variables evident from the application of factor analytic techniques are reflected in the CHC model. The main point of divergence between Cattell–Horn and Carroll concerns whether or not g exists as a cognitive reality. The convergence in the CHC model is strongly evident in its description of about nine separate second-order cognitive abilities.

Although the proponents of the psychometric tradition would fervently disagree, a fundamental unresolved potential problem with this approach remains. It is arguable that we continue to be unclear about what exactly *all* of the latent variables reflected in these models actually are. Do they accurately reflect something of the cognitive processes of our brain as we tackle and solve intellectual problems, as the psychometricians claim? Or are they simply commonalities underlying the nature of the intelligence tests used which have large areas of similarity in format and content (which might explain something like the emergence of a g factor) as well as having areas of related specific content (stratum II), and very uniquely specific content (stratum I)? Or do they simply reflect the statistical approach utilized by researchers thus organizing data in a certain manner? Or do they reflect some other unknown entity? Disentangling these fundamental and potentially confounding influences has never been resolved in a truly satisfying manner, which in part explains the emergence of models of intelligence that have looked beyond the psychometric data.

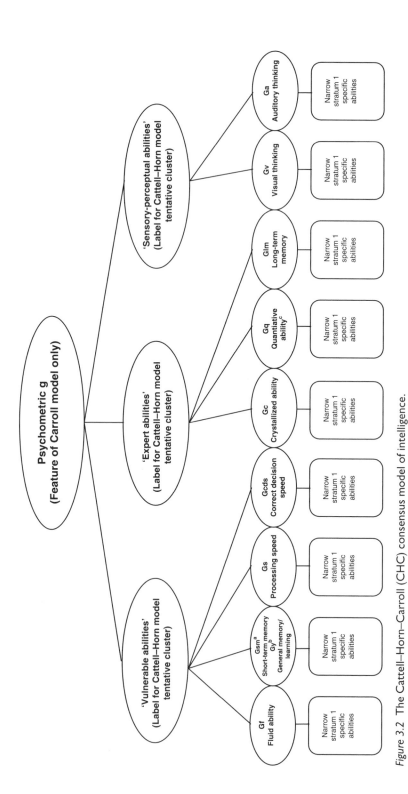

Figure 3.2 The Cattell–Horn–Carroll (CHC) consensus model of intelligence.

Notes: [a]Carroll model version of this stratum II ability; [b]Cattell–Horn model version of this stratum II ability; [c]Not in Carroll (1993) model.

MODELS OF INTELLIGENCE BEYOND THE PSYCHOMETRIC TRADITION

An alternative perspective on human intelligence is offered by those who set out either to challenge deliberately, or to supplement further, the psychometric approach. Two of the most influential models within this tradition that are highly critical of the limitations of psychometric theories are offered by Gardner (1983; 1993; 1999) and Sternberg (1994; 2002; 2005).

Gardner's multiple intelligences model

Gardner (1983; 1993; 1999) deliberately set out to challenge the prevailing psychometric approach to modelling human intelligence. He wished to broaden the range of abilities that we consider to be 'intelligent'. Instead of confining himself to the administration of IQ-type tests as the basis for model development, Gardner chose eight sources of evidence (which he termed criteria) that he argued could be instrumental in developing a fuller model of human intelligence that had a consequent greater utility. In fact the delineation of these criteria is regarded by Gardner (1999) as a substantial aspect of his contribution to the field.

The eight criteria he considered for each of his candidate intelligences are outlined below and are illustrated here with reference to 'Linguistic Intelligence'. The first two of the eight sources of evidence were drawn from the biological sciences. These were *Criteria 1*, that the candidate intelligence has the potential to be isolated through brain-damage. For example, there is clear evidence that human linguistic ability can either remain intact, or be damaged, depending on whether key areas of the neocortex have been subject to, or spared, liaison (Kolb and Wishaw, 2003). *Criteria 2* states that the candidate intelligence has an evolutionary history, or an evolutionary plausibility, supporting its selection as a unique cognitive ability that would aid the survival of our ancestors. For example, evolutionary psychologists such as Dunbar (2004) describe the importance of human language development as a social grooming technique which aided our survival through group-bonding as the size of hominid communities became so large that social relationships could no longer be adequately sustained through the mutual physical grooming used by our primate ancestors.

The second two sources of evidence used by Gardner came from logical analysis. These were *Criteria 3*, that the candidate intelligence concerned itself with an identifiable core operation, or set of core operations. In the case of language the set of core operations includes making phonetic discriminations, having a command of syntax, acquiring the meaning of words, and having a sensitivity to the pragmatic uses of language. *Criteria 4* states that the candidate intelligence has a susceptibility to encoding in a symbol system, for example spoken and written language.

The next two criteria were drawn from developmental psychology. *Criteria 5* considers whether the intelligence has a distinct developmental history along with a definable set of 'expert' end-state performances. Language has a clear developmental trajectory during childhood. *Criteria 6* examines whether there is evidence in the domain of a candidate intelligence of savants, prodigies, and other people with exceptional ability. Within the domain of linguistic intelligence in the cultural setting of Ireland, we value the work of literary creators and innovators such as James Joyce, Flann O'Brien, Patrick Kavanagh, and Seamus Heaney: men who vary greatly in their educational history but who excel in their use of language.

Gardner's final two criteria are drawn from traditional psychological research. *Criteria 7* considers support from experimental tasks. In the case of language Gardner refers to support from experimental evidence that the separateness of linguistic and spatial intelligences are supported by the fact that we can converse with someone as we find our way, but not solve crossword puzzles and converse at the same time. Finally, despite Gardner's overt criticism of the psychometric approach for *Criteria 8*, he draws on evidence from psychometric findings. He states that such evidence supports a linguistic or verbal intelligence.

Using these criteria Gardner argues that he achieves two fundamental things: first, a theory of human intelligence that offers a full description of our cognitive abilities; and second, a model that allows each individual's cognitive profile to be understood as a unique blend of separate intelligences. The eight separate cognitive abilities currently acknowledged by Gardner are linguistic, logical-mathematical, musical, bodily kinaesthetic, spatial, interpersonal, intrapersonal, and naturalistic intelligence (see Figure 3.3). These are defined more fully in Table 3.4.

Inevitably, there are aspects of Gardner's model that have invited criticism. This includes his deliberate rejection of psychometric g, and the absence within his model of a clear mechanism through which separate intelligences can seamlessly blend to work together. The application of Gardner's criteria for an intelligence are also problematic. The evidence under each criteria for the different intelligences is established through a retrospective review of the literature rather than through prospective research. In addition, the arbiter of whether or not a candidate intelligence sufficiently meets Gardner's criteria is Gardner. This results in some inconsistency in the application of the criteria, as understandably not all of his eight intelligences have strong evidence in each category. The difficulties that this raises is further evident in Gardner's (1999) recent re-formulation of his model where he accepted 'naturalistic intelligence' as an eighth ability but rejected 'existential ability' as a ninth intelligence. The evidence described for both of these candidate intelligences according to the eight criteria was arguably equally convincing. However, Gardner rejected existential intelligence with the sole explanation of 'despite the attractiveness of a ninth intelligence, however, I am not adding existential

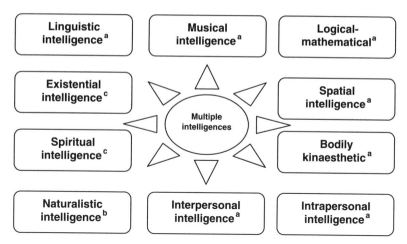

Figure 3.3 Gardner's (1983; 1993; 1999) model of multiple intelligences.

Notes: [a]Described as a separate intelligence as part of Gardner's original formulation of his model (1983; 1993); [b]Proposed and accepted as an additional separate intelligence by Gardner in a revised formulation of his model (1999); [c]Proposed and rejected as an additional separate intelligence by Gardner in a revised formulation of his model (1999).

Table 3.4 Gardner's (1999) definition of eight separate human intelligences

Intelligence	Definition
1 **Linguistic**	'involves sensitivity to spoken and written language, the ability to learn languages, and the capacity to use language to accomplish certain goals' (1999: 41). Described as highly used by lawyers, speakers, writers, and poets
2 **Logical-mathematical**	'involves the capacity to analyse problems logically, carry out mathematical operations, and investigate issues scientifically' (1999: 42). Described as highly used by mathematicians, logicians, and scientists
3 **Musical**	'entails skill in the performance, composition, and appreciation of musical patterns' (1999: 42). Described as highly used by musicians
4 **Bodily kinaesthetic**	'entails the potential of using one's whole body or parts of the body (like the hand or the mouth) to solve problems or fashion products' (1999: 42). Described as highly used by dancers, actors and athletes
5 **Spatial**	'features the potential to recognise and manipulate the patterns of wide space . . . as well as the patterns of more confined areas' (1999: 42). Described as highly used by navigators and pilots (wide space) as well as sculptors, surgeons, chess players, graphic artists, and architects (confined areas)

(Continued overleaf)

Table 3.4 Continued

Intelligence	Definition
6 Interpersonal	'denotes a person's capacity to understand the intentions, motivations, and desires of other people and, consequently to work effectively with others' (1999: 43). Described as highly used by salespeople, teachers, clinical psychologists, religious leaders, political leaders, and actors
7 Intrapersonal	'involves the capacity to understand oneself, to have an effective working model of oneself – including one's own desires, fears, and capacities – and to use such information effectively in regulating one's own life' (1999: 43)
8 Naturalistic	Includes 'the core capacities to recognise instances as members of a group (more formally a species); to distinguish among members of a species; to recognise the existence of other neighbouring species; and to chart out the relations, formally or informally, among the several species' (1999: 49). Described as highly used by naturalists and other people with extensive knowledge of the environment and its fauna and flora

intelligence to the list. I find the phenomenon perplexing enough and the distance from the other intelligences vast enough to dictate prudence – at least for now' (1999: 66). Such a situation is hardly the basis for the continued development of an objectively determined model.

Despite the shortcomings outlined above, Gardner's model has made many positive contributions to our understanding of human intelligence. In fact when his original model was published in 1983 it had a coherence that was completely absent from the psychometric literature at that time. Indeed, in some ways the psychometric approach has been catching up with Gardner. The current CHC model has considerable overlap at stratum II with the different abilities outlined in the multiple intelligences model (in fact the potential for synergy was noted by Carroll, 1993). Perhaps the most significant of Gardner's contributions is the way his influence brought other sources of evidence to centre-stage thus moving the field away from model development focused solely on psychometric testing. He also redressed some of psychology's cultural bias on what makes a person intelligent through the identification of other types of intelligence that are valued within our culture and beyond it. Finally, his model is respectful of varied profiles and unique blends of different intelligences. This has supported a fuller appreciation of individual strengths and has contributed to the development of broader, individually based educational curricula.

Sternberg's triarchic model of successful intelligence

Sternberg's (1994; 2002; 2005) triarchic theory describes three aspects of intelligence: (1) analytical; (2) creative; and (3) practical (defined in Table 3.5). He refers to his theory as 'successful' to denote his desire to explain how individuals utilize their strengths, or compensate for weaknesses, in each aspect of intelligence, to achieve positive accomplishments in life given their cultural and personal context. Underlying each aspect of intelligence Sternberg identifies three basic types of information processing that work together. These are (1) metacomponents, (2) performance components, and (3) knowledge acquisition components. These are also defined in Table 3.5. However, Sternberg's model is not simply concerned with the cognitive processes that he argues take place inside a person's head as they engage in

Table 3.5 Sternberg's (2005) definition of the three information processes underlying all aspects of intelligence and his (2002) definition of three aspects of intelligence according to his triarchic model

Construct	Definition
INFORMATION PROCESS COMPONENTS UNDERLYING ALL ASPECTS OF INTELLIGENCE	
A Metacomponents	'higher order, executive processes used to plan what one is going to do, to monitor it while one is doing it, and to evaluate it after it is done. These metacomponents include (1) recognising the existence of a problem; deciding on the nature of a problem; (3) selecting a set of lower-order lower processes to solve the problem; (4) selecting a strategy into which to combine these components; (5) selecting a mental representation upon which the components and strategy can act; (6) allocating one's mental resources; (7) monitoring one's problem solving as it is happening; and (8) evaluating one's problem solving after it is done' (2005: 105)
6 Performance Components	'lower-order processes that execute the instructions of the metacomponents. These lower-order components solve the problems according to the plans laid out by the metacomponents. Whereas the number of metacomponents used in the performance of various tasks is relatively limited, the number of performance components is probably quite large. Many of these performance components are relatively specific to narrow ranges of tasks' (2005: 107) *(continued overleaf)*

7 Knowledge-acquisition Components	'used *to learn how to do* what the metacomponents and performance components eventually do. Three knowledge-acquisition components appear to be central in intellectual functioning: (1) *selective encoding* [selecting relevant from irrelevant information]; (2) *selective combination* [combing the relevant information into a meaningful whole]; and (3) *selective comparison*' [seeing analogies to past experience] (2005: 108)
ASPECT OF INTELLIGENCE	
1 Analytical	'Analytical intelligence is involved when the components of intelligence are applied to analyze, evaluate, judge, or compare and contrast. It typically is involved when components are applied to relatively familiar kinds of problems where the judgements to be made are of an abstract nature' (2002: 233)
2 Creative	Creative intelligence is involved when an individual uses the components of intelligence to solve problems that are relatively novel
3 Practical	'Practical intelligence involves individuals' applying their abilities to the kinds of problems that confront them in daily life, such as on the job or in the home. Practical intelligence involves applying the components of intelligence to experience so as to (a) adapt to, (b) shape, and (c) select environments' (2002: 237)

intellectual activities, but also with how these processes find expression in a person's everyday environment, and what their experience of the expression of those internal abilities in the external world is like.

Sternberg (2005) supports the validity of his theory with reference to a series of what he acknowledges to be methodologically limited studies that suggest that interventions based on his model were found to be beneficial to children in educational settings and adults in real-life settings. One of the main contributions of Sternberg's ideas has been to encourage a theory of intelligence that recognizes that ideas such as those presented within the psychometric tradition at best only provide one part of the picture of what intelligence is (i.e. what goes on in a person's head). He advocates the need to consider how these processes are used by people to adapt to their environment, and the mediation between these internal and external aspects of intelligence. Furthermore, Sternberg's approach, like Gardner's, emphasizes that to be intelligent is not just to be analytically or academically smart but in reality is defined in a large variety of ways by different individuals in different contexts. Nevertheless, Sternberg's theory is not without its critics. Gottfredson (2003) challenges that Sternberg overstates the evidence that supports the practical intelligence part of his theory, while the AAMR (2002) remind us that to date multiple intelligence theorists such as Sternberg and Gardner have not yet generated convincing evidence to support the validity of their models.

INTELLIGENCE, GENES, AND ENVIRONMENT

Having outlined some of the main theoretical models, we now turn to what the psychological literature tells us about the influence of genes and environment on intelligence. In doing so we will focus first on a discussion of evidence from twin studies on the influence of genes on IQ. We will then describe in detail a phenomenon termed the Flynn effect which has had profound implications for our understanding of the influence of environmental factors on IQ, and for the psychometric assessment of intellectual disability.

EVIDENCE OF A GENETIC BASIS TO DIFFERENCES IN INTELLIGENCE?

Plomin, DeFries, McClearn and McGuffin (2000) provide a useful introduction to contemporary behavioural genetics and make a number of key points necessary for understanding the nature of heritability in psychological traits. Heritability refers to the contribution of genes to *individual variation* for a particular trait within a *specific population*. Consider height as an example. Imagine we found that the heritability for the height of all adults living in the Republic of Ireland is 90 per cent. This means that we can say that 90 per cent of the reason why adults living in Ireland differ in height is due to genetic factors. That is, heritability helps us to understand what makes individuals within a particular population differ from each other in height, as opposed to what makes a single individual a certain height.

The notion of heritability is intimately tied to understanding how it is influenced by defining features of environments and populations. Imagine an environment that is equally enriching for all. In such circumstances individual differences for a given trait would be highly heritable, as everyone is equally supported in their development by their environmental circumstances. Thus genetic factors are the reason why people within the population differ. However, were the same population to live in an environment that varied dramatically from person to person, providing optimal enrichment for some and extreme deprivation for others, then the heritability of the same trait would be lower if estimates were based on studies that were truly representative of the whole population. This is because some of the variation in the population now reflects the unequal environment. However, a biased sampling procedure that drew research participants predominantly from one section of the population (either deprived or privileged) would indicate high heritability for the same trait even though in reality this would not be a true reflection for the population as a whole. These examples also illustrate that we should not regard a heritability estimate as something universal and fixed.

Plomin, DeFries, McClearn, and McGuffin (2000) also point out that it is widely acknowledged that if the heritability for a certain trait is established to be high *within* a single population or *within* different social groups, genders, racial groups, or other groupings (say people with and without depression), then this offers no automatic genetic basis for an explanation of differences *between* groups. For example, US normative IQ data have shown average FSIQ score differences between some racial groupings. Demonstrating that there is a high heritability for IQ *within* racial group A and/or *within* racial group B offers no evidence of a genetic explanation for any observed difference *between* groups A and B.

Importantly, behavioural genetic studies not only inform us of the heritability of psychological traits but also provide research-based estimates of environmental influence (Plomin *et al.*, 2000). That is, allowing for measurement error, what is not attributable to genes is attributable to environment. High heritability for a trait does not carry implicit social or political implications. These are added by people who interpret research findings through a particular political lens. Finally, although a trait may be highly heritable within a particular population this does not mean that it cannot be potently influenced by environmental factors (and vice versa). Consider the height example from the start of this section. Height actually is estimated to be roughly 90 per cent heritable in western nations, and yet we have seen considerable rises in average height over the course of the twentieth century due to the entirely environmental influence of improved diet, again underlining that within a population high heritability (e.g. 1920s cohort, 1950s cohort, 1990s cohort) offers no automatic insight into the reasons for variation across populations. With these ideas in mind we now turn to research studies indicating that individual differences in IQ are highly heritable.

Identical twins reared apart

It is sometimes said that identical (monozygotic: MZ) and non-identical (dizygotic: DZ) twins are an experiment of nature that allow insight into the influence of genes on psychological factors, while adoption similarly provides an experiment of society. However, if so, both nature and society are remarkably sloppy methodologists. If we assume that all of the following factors have no confounding influence on results from studies of twins reared apart then we can say that there is indeed evidence for a genetic basis to individual differences in intelligence: (1) the effects of sharing a womb for nine months; (2) time spent together prior to separation; (3) similarities in the separate environments of each twin pair; (4) the psychological impact of being adopted; (5) the potential psychological adjustment to discovering the existence of having a twin sibling; (6) the effects of time spent together subsequent to reunion after separation; and (7) that standardized IQ tests (particularly the older editions used in twin studies) measure some meaningful aspect of intelligence. Proponents of twin-research claim that either these factors do not confound their results or that their attempts to measure their influence demonstrate that they do not affect their findings.

One of the most comprehensive and well-known studies of identical twins reared apart reported to date is that of Bouchard, Lykken, McGue, Segal, and Tellegen (1990). Referred to as the 'Minnesota Study of Twins Reared Apart (MISTRA)' it reports data on a variety of physiological and psychological factors on up to fifty-six sets of identical twins reared apart during childhood who were subsequently reunited in adulthood. The average age of the twins at the time of their participation in the study was 41.0 years (ranging from 19 to 68 years). The average amount of time spent together postnatally prior to separation was 5.1 months (ranging from 0 months to 4 years). The average amount of time spent separated was 30 years (ranging from half-a-year to 64 years). The average length of time spent reunited post-separation was just over 2 years (ranging from 1 week to 23 years). Bouchard *et al.* (1990) report data from what they describe as three independent measures of IQ: (i) The Weschler Adult Intelligence Scale (WAIS); (ii) a composite test combining the Raven's Progressive Matrices with the Mill-Hill Vocabulary Test; and (iii) the first principal component emergent from the administration of two ability batteries (fifteen subscales from the battery used in a previous study combined with thirteen subscales from the Comprehensive Ability Battery). Bouchard *et al.* (1990) argue that their study of identical twins reared apart gives us an insight into the influence of genes on an individual's IQ. That is, if genes exert a significant effect on IQ, then twins who are genetically identical should resemble each other on this aspect of intellectual functioning despite being raised in different family (environmental) contexts.

Table 3.6 indicates that Bouchard *et al.* (1990) found that among their sample of identical twins reared apart there were very high levels of correlation in their IQ scores, thus supporting the genetic hypothesis. Importantly, Bouchard *et al.* (1990) also investigated whether environmental factors, which may be similar across the separate rearing environments, may have confounded results. They recorded SES (socio-economic status) indicators from each twin's rearing environment (adoptive father education level, adoptive mother education level, adoptive father SES), physical features of each environment (material possessions, scientific/technical aspects, cultural aspects, and mechanical aspects), and psychological features of each environment (as measured by the Achievement and Intellectual Orientation

Table 3.6 Correlation in IQ scores among identical twins separated early in life and reared apart (Bouchard et al., 1990)

Measure of intellectual ability based on ...	Number of MZA twin-pairs	Correlation	Score range
WAIS Full-Scale IQ	48	0.69	79–133 ($\bar{x}$ = 108.1)
WAIS Verbal IQ	48	0.64	–
WAIS Performance IQ	48	0.71	–
Raven's/Mill-Hill Composite Score	42	0.78	–
First principal component of combined abilities tests	43	0.78	–
Mean of 15 Hawaii-battery subscales	45	0.45	–
Mean of 13 Comprehensive Ability Battery subscales	41	0.48	–

Note: MZA = Monozygotic Twins Reared Apart; – = Unreported.

subscales of the Moos Family Environment Scale: FES). Small to moderate similarities were found in variables across separated twin-pair environments with correlations ranging from $r = 0.11$ for FES Achievement to $r = 0.40$ for material possession. Only two variables had significant correlations with IQ scores (material possessions $r = 0.279$ and cultural aspects $r = -0.279$). However, when the contribution of each variable to the similarity in IQ between twin-pairs was estimated, no significant relationship was evident for any of the environmental factors measured in the study (r ranging from 0.001 to 0.03). Bouchard *et al.* conclude that their findings demonstrate that individual variation in IQ is strongly affected by our genes. Given the difficulties of conducting this kind of research Bouchard *et al.*'s study is a very significant contribution to knowledge. However, caution reminds us that the study (a) contains a relatively small sample of individuals; who (b) are drawn mostly from the US and the UK; and who (c) fall within a certain IQ range (79–133). When these individuals are separated and reared apart in childhood their genes appear to exert a significant effect on variation in IQ. However, researchers in the field of behavioural genetics strongly agree that Bouchard *et al.*'s study (1990), combined with the rest of the extended research literature in this area, leads to the conclusion that, within population, variation in IQ in western nations is highly heritable (Plomin *et al.*, 2000).

Identical and non-identical twins reared together

The majority of other twin studies published in the literature make comparisons between identical (MZ) and non-identical (DZ) twins who are not separated during childhood but who are reared together. The rationale underlying these studies is that if genes play a significant role in the variability found in a psychological factor such as IQ then we should expect to find a greater correlation in scores in identical twin-pairs compared to non-identical twins. An additional assumption is made within this research design, namely that if a greater correlation is found, it is attributable to identical twins having more genes in common, rather than the shared environmental influence of people treating them more similarly due to their identical rather than non-identical twin status. This is a controversial point and is referred to as the equal environment assumption (see Joseph, 2003; and Plomin *et al.*, 2000 for the two sides to this controversy).

The Louisville Twin Study (Wilson, 1983) reports IQ data on almost 500 pairs of twins and their non-twin siblings collected at three-month intervals from 3 to 12 months, at six-month intervals from 18 to 36 months, at one-year intervals from 4 to 9 years, and an additional assessment at 15 years. In addition Wilson collected data on some non-twin siblings of participants in his study. Non-twin siblings share the same amount of genes (roughly 50 per cent) as DZ twins, are raised in the same family, but lack the experience of being treated as a twin. The rationale behind this study was that variation in Q score in the same individual across the different data collection points would reflect growth spurts, plateaus and lags in their cognitive development. If the impetus for cognitive development across childhood is genetic in origin then the pacing of spurts, plateaus and lags in each individual should be more closely matched among MZ twins compared to the degree of concordance among DZ twins or non-twin siblings.

In order to analyse his data, Wilson (1983) clustered IQ scores into five data points as illustrated in Table 3.7. As evident from this table Wilson found that at data analysis point one (up to 12 months) MZ and DZ twins did not differ from each other in the relative within twin-pair correlation in IQ scores but both differed significantly from the IQ correlation with non-twin siblings. At data analysis point two (12–36 months) the IQ correlation for all three groups increased. However, the increase in the MZ twin correlation was greater than that found among DZ twins, making them significantly different from each other. At data analysis point three (ages 3, 4, 5 and 6 years) the MZ twin IQ correlation increased, the DZ twin IQ correlation decreased, and the non-twin sibling correlation increased. At data analysis point four (ages 6, 7 and 8 years) the MZ IQ correlation decreased, and the DZ twin IQ correlation remained stable. The nature of the non-twin sibling data in the study changed at this point (from younger siblings to a different group of older siblings) but appeared relatively stable. At the final data analysis point (ages 8 and 15) the MZ twin IQ correlation remained very high but relatively unchanged, while the DZ IQ correlation decreased further to a level similar to that found among older non-twin siblings of the same age.

At face value it is difficult to know what to make of these results. Initially MZ and DZ twin-pairs look the same in terms of IQ correlation. Over the course of childhood DZ twins increasingly diverge from MZ twins in IQ

Table 3.7 Correlation in IQ scores across childhood among identical and non-identical twins and their younger non-twin siblings (adapted from Wilson, 1983)

IQ data collected at each age within age-bands	N of twin pairs (MZ–DZ–SIB)	IQ Correlation			IQ test	Heritability estimate[b]	
		MZ	DZ	SIB		Genes[c]	Envir[d]
3, 6, 9 and 12 months	81-84-33	0.69	0.63	0.37	• Bayley Scales of Mental Development	0.12	0.57
12, 18, 24 and 36 months	66-69-28	0.80	0.72	0.46	• Bayley Scales of Mental Development; • Stanford-Binet Scale	0.16	0.64
3, 4, 5 and 6 years	75-87-19	0.87	0.65	0.55	• Stanford-Binet Scale; • Weschler Preschool and Primary Scale of Intelligence; • McCarthy Scales of Children's Abilities	0.44	0.43
6, 7 and 8 years	45[a] 95-85-126[a] 58[a]	0.81	0.66	0.54[a] 0.55[a] 0.44[a]	• Weschler Preschool and Primary Scale of Intelligence; • Weschler Intelligence Scale for Children; • Weschler Intelligence Scale for Children Revised	0.30	0.51
8 and 15 years	126[a] 76-63-70[a]	0.82	0.50	0.44[a] 0.51[a]	• Weschler Intelligence Scale for Children; • Weschler Intelligence Scale for Children Revised	0.64	0.18

Notes: MZ = Monozygotic Twins; DZ = Dizygotic Twins; SIB = Non-Twin Sibling
a Data at these points drawn from younger non-twin siblings and presented separately at each age rather than collapsed for analysis across ages as in the other participant groups.
b Based on comparison between MZ and DZ twins.
c Influence of shared genes on IQ using the formula described by Patrick (2000) where genetic contribution = 2(rMZ-rDZ).
d Influence of shared environment on IQ using the formula described by Patrick (2000) where environmental contribution = 2rDZ-rMZ.

a Data at these points assessed when they reached age-points indicated in the table.

correlation, eventually approaching the level found in non-twin siblings at age 15. Wilson interprets his data as clearly supporting his initial hypothesis. That is, comparing IQ data depending on MZ, DZ or non-twin sibling status reveals cognitive development to be determined by an underlying genetic ground-plan. However, this does not seem to resonate fully with the initial similarity between MZ and DZ twins, or address the considerable assumption that meas-uring IQ at different ages is a valid way to assess the course of cognitive development, or take account of the potentially confounding influence of the variety of IQ tests used within and across data analysis points (see Table 3.7).

We have presented Wilson's (1983) study data here as they are interesting in their own right but also because Patrick (2000) reviews data from the Louisville Twin Study and other similar sources to review whether the influ-ence of genes on individual differences in IQ declines, remains static, or increases with age. In doing so he utilizes a commonly used formula using MZ and DZ twin data to work out the relative contribution of genes and environment to a variable (Purcell, 2000). This is based on the idea that the relative difference in genetic contribution to a variable can be computed by utilizing the degree of genetic difference between MZ and DZ twins. MZ twins are genetically identical whereas DZ twins on average share 50 per cent of their genes. Thus if genes play a role in variation in IQ, MZ twins will differ in their degree of similarity on that variable compared to DZ twins. Doubling the difference will give us the proportion of the variation that we can attribute to genetic factors. Patrick applies this and another formula to Wilson's data at every age in which data were collected. In Table 3.7 we apply the formulae to the data given for the collapsed age-bands used by Wilson to compute the significance of difference in IQ correlations between MZ and DZ twins (as described above). Behavioural geneticists have found that apply-ing these formulae reveals a counter-intuitive finding. It appears that the influence of genes strengthens rather than declines as children get older and that the influence of the aspects of the environment that twins share (such as their family) becomes increasingly weaker. Importantly Wilson's data con-cern the same population over time and not different cohorts at the same time. Bearing various methodological limitations in mind Patrick (2000: 87) concludes this trend of strengthening genetic influence and weakening shared environmental influence on twin IQ scores during the course of childhood although counter-intuitive is a 'somewhat consistent' finding in the literature.

Further evidence of the very strong influence of genes on individual differ-ences in cognitive ability throughout the life-span is reported by McClearn *et al.* (1997). Their study utilized the Swedish Twin Registry to assess cogni-tive functioning in MZ (110 pairs) and DZ (130 pairs) twins who were 80 years of age or older and who maintained normal cognitive functioning. A mixed test-battery was utilized which yielded a general factor (first principal component), a short-form WAIS IQ estimate, a verbal index, a spatial index, a speed index, and a memory index. Table 3.8 reports the findings from their

Table 3.8 Influence of genes, shared environment, and non-shared environment on IQ and cognition based on McClearn *et al.*'s (1997) study of normally functioning reared together MZ and DZ twins aged 80 years or more

Variable	% variance attributed to genes	% of variance attributed to shared environmental factors	% of variance attributed to non-shared environmental factors
General factor	62	11	17
WAIS short-form IQ estimate	53	15	22
Verbal index	55	20	15
Spatial index	32	13	45
Speed index	62	0	28
Memory index	52	0	38

model fitting data analysis assigning variation in IQ scores to genetic, shared environmental, and non-shared environmental influences. The results reveal that even in older adulthood the influence of genes on general and specific cognitive functioning is pronounced. Environmental influence is also clearly evident. Interestingly the impact of non-shared rather than shared aspects of twins' environments appear to exert a greater influence on their general cognitive functioning by the time they reach older adulthood.

Based on the available evidence we can tentatively accept that in western nations within population individual differences in IQ appear to be strongly influenced by genes. With regard to variation in the non-intellectually disabled population it is hypothesized that this is mediated through a relatively large but unknown number of genes working together perhaps each contributing small amounts to the overall variance. This model (known as Quantitative Trait Loci or QTLs) is at present frustratingly difficult to support or disprove experimentally and so as yet there are no specific genes within our genome that are reliably associated with IQ. With regard to mild intellectual disability a significant role is attributed to environmental factors. At lower levels of functioning (moderate to profound) strong genetic factors are thought to be at work, reflecting the influence of non-inherited chromosomal abnormalities or single gene disorders rather than normal gene variation.

RISING IQ: THE FLYNN EFFECT

We turn now to research concerning evidence of a strong environmental effect on IQ, principally the work of James Flynn (1984; 1987; 1999, in press) who formalized observations that IQ scores have been increasing in successive generations since psychologists first began to standardize IQ tests. In doing so Flynn has risen to various methodological challenges to establish beyond reasonable doubt that IQ is rising. Flynn's work began with the observation of an apparent catch-up in IQ among African-Americans compared to 'white' Americans, based on evidence from US armed forces data. Flynn wondered about how much we could infer from this observation and looked to the literature to establish how well the IQ scales used by the US military correlated with 'genuine' tests of IQ used in more mainstream settings. Such IQ measures did not provide Flynn with the information for which he was looking. However, he did notice something else. Whenever a new test was compared with a previous older version of the same scale, or with an older version of a different IQ test, then the most recent generation always scored higher on the older test compared to the newer one. Flynn (1984) formalized this observation by collating an exhaustive review of studies which compared either two editions of the same test, or an older IQ test with a newer version of a different test, that allowed comparison of the IQ scores of one generation with where their ability placed them when compared with a test normed with a preceding generation. Without exception these studies revealed the same finding. Children who performed at a given level on the newer test (for example, WISC-R FSIQ = 100) out-performed children of the previous generation when assessed on the older test using its normative data (WISC IQ = 108). The key here is that the comparison of ability in each instance is made with either the child's current generation (newer test) or with a preceding generation (older test). As such, a child whose performance on the current test places him at average ability compared to his contemporaries, manages, with the same level of intellectual functioning at his disposal, to perform relatively better when the reference group is not his current peers but children from an earlier generation.

Although fascinating and consistent, these findings were not deemed conclusive proof that the average IQ was rising. Arthur Jensen suggested four criteria to Flynn that he thought would offer a stringent test to the apparent effect (Flynn, 1987). These were that Flynn should (a) remove the possibility that children were simply reaching cognitive maturity sooner, rather than becoming smarter, by using adult rather than child samples; (b) remove the possibility of sample bias by establishing the effect in larger samples (as collected in countries where all adult males were tested on entering compulsory national military service) than those reported in Flynn's (1984) paper; (c) use culturally reduced rather than culturally influenced tests (i.e. tests based on the Raven's Progressive Matrices rather than the Weschler or Binet scales); and (d) use raw scores rather than converted scores from tests which have not undergone modification from edition to edition but have remained unchanged over time (again this suggested IQ tests like the Ravens Progressive Matrices rather than those like the Weschler scales). In response Flynn has gathered data from twenty-five countries that, to varying degrees, meet the criteria suggested by Jensen. Remarkably, without exception all demonstrate gains in IQ scores over time. In many of these studies the nature of the gains is not simply significant but, as Flynn describes it, 'massive', typically ranging from 3 to 5 IQ points per decade or from 5 to 25 points per generation (see Table 3.9).

The best-quality data come from The Netherlands, Belgium, Israel, and Norway (see Table 3.9). These countries have tested national samples of young men entering military service on IQ measures based on Raven's Progressive Matrices often over long periods of time. Denmark and Sweden provide data which are almost as good in quality. After this comes data from nations with periodic re-norming of IQ tests using stratified, nationally representative samples. Data in this category comes from the US, New Zealand, Canada, Australia, and Spain. The combination of culture-reduced and more culturally influenced tests turns out to be very instructive. It appears that the most 'massive' gains in IQ scores are found on tests such as the Raven's or subscales such as Weschler's 'Similarities'. These are thought to measure fluid intelligence or 'on-the-spot problem solving'. While the

Table 3.9 Evidence for the Flynn Effect in countries with testing of young men entering the army on national service (Source: Flynn 1987)

Sample	Raven's Based Scores %	IQ Scores	IQ Point Gain
The Netherlands	% getting 24/40 items correct	Setting 1952 as anchor year*	Relative to 1952
1952	31.2	100	–
1962	46.4	106.2	+6.2
1972	63.2	112.4	+12.4
1981/82	82.2	121.1	+21.1
Belgium (French-speaking)	Total correct minus penalty	–	Relative to 1958
1958	32.74	–	–
1967	37.88	–	+6.47
Belgium (Dutch-speaking)	Total correct minus penalty	–	Relative to 1958
1958	30.98	–	–
1967	36.99	–	+7.82
Norway		Setting 1954 as anchor year*	Relative to 1954
1954	–	100	–
1961	–	105.8	+5.8
1965	–	107.1	+7.1
1968	–	109.3	+9.3
1974	–	110.0	+10.0
1977	–	109.7	+9.8

Note: * Anchor year = year at which raw scores are converted to reflect a distribution with a population mean score of 100 and standard deviation of 15.

smallest gains are found on subscales of IQ tests such as Arithmetic or Vocabulary which are thought to be more culturally based and influenced by environmental factors such as education.

Genes and environment paradox

This introduces one of many paradoxes raised by Flynn's work. As he points out the IQ gains are observed in at least twenty-five countries, appear across entire nations, are massive in size, and appear strongest on those aspects of IQ that are considered culture-reduced measures of fluid intelligence. Other evidence, such as the twin studies described above, are generally interpreted as indicating that individual differences in IQ (at least within western cohorts/ populations) are strongly influenced by genes rather than the environment. Yet no one would seriously suggest that the gains in IQ as documented by Flynn could be genetic in origin, that is they are too large, too widespread, have appeared too fast, and in the absence of a Eugenic-style breeding of people with higher IQs. Consequently, we are left with either explaining the potent influence of environmental factors on IQ-type scores (when other snapshot evidence points to a strong genetic influence), or the unravelling of the idea that IQ tests are adequately measuring intelligence.

At first Flynn (1987; 1999) appeared to interpret his work as potentially undermining the notion that IQ testing is a valid approach to assessing intelligence. Although the documentary evidence was clearly indicative of a rising IQ, Flynn himself was initially sceptical that the data he collated reflected a real-world rise in intelligence. He invited us to think through the implications of the Dutch data. It suggested that comparing Dutch men of 1982 with their fathers' generation tested in 1952, sons have gained on average 21 IQ points over their fathers. The magnitude of the rise implies that if we assume that the averagely scoring person of the 1952 generation was in fact of average intelligence, then over the time period 1952–1982 the number of young Dutch men who could be classified as 'gifted' (IQ = 130 or above) has risen from 2 per cent to 25 per cent! Conversely, if we define the averagely scoring person of the most recently tested generation as having average ability, then the observed rise in scores from the two time periods suggests that, relative to the 1982 generation, 25 per cent of those in the 1952 data-set had an IQ that placed them in the intellectually disabled range. Flynn pointed out that clearly such an implication underlines the fact that the rise in IQ is not a rise in real-world intelligence.

The Dickens–Flynn model

More recently Flynn has revised his position based on a model developed with William Dickens (Dickens and Flynn, 2001; Flynn, in press) which attempts to explain how a real-world rise in intelligence is plausible given:

(a) the implication of Flynn's work which suggests a strong influence of environmental factors on rising IQ scores; (b) the evidence that individual differences in IQ within western populations are strongly influenced by genetic factors; and (c) without resorting to ridiculous implications that large numbers of previous or current generations are either gifted or intellectually disabled. To do so Dickens and Flynn (2001) introduce two concepts: (1) Individual Multipliers which drive individual differences within a generation; and (2) Social Multipliers which drive differences between generations.

Individual multipliers concern the matching of individuals with a genetic advantage to superior environments that foster the development of their endowed potential. Dickens and Flynn explain their model through analogy. Imagine a child born with a slight genetic advantage over his peers in height and reflexes. He goes to school, plays basket-ball in the playground better than his peers, enjoys it more, joins a primary school team, benefits from coaching, and progresses to a second-level school where he also plays on a team and receives more professional coaching. His slight genetic advantage has been developed through a superior basket-ball environment to that enjoyed by his average peer. Now imagine that this basket-ball playing prodigy had an identical twin separated at birth. It is likely that his slight genetic advantage for height and speed of reflex would similarly elicit an environment that maximized his abilities. If reunited with his identical twin later in life and invited to take part in a prestigious international study assessing the genetic influence on basket-ball skills, it would appear that the striking similarity between the two reflected potent genetic and weak environmental influences. Individual multipliers take small genetic differences between individuals and tie their development to potent environmental factors. So, individual differences in ability when approached through twin studies appear strongly genetic and weakly environmental in origin. Dickens and Flynn argue what is plausible for basket-ball is also plausible for IQ and so twin studies indicating within cohort strong genetic and weak environmental influences potentially have an alternative explanation: that they have masked the effect of potent environmental factors.

According to Dickens and Flynn the social multiplier explains how the improved abilities of individuals form part of the environment that ultimately enriches the abilities of others. In this way they hope to explain how successive generations can gain in ability relative to one another. Again they use basket-ball to illustrate their argument. They invite us to consider the impact of the industrial revolution on basket-ball performance. With the advent of television basket-ball reached a wider audience. As more people played, the standard required for superior performance increased. More accuracy in shooting became required to excel. Some players developed the ability to shoot accurately with two hands; rather than a single-dominant hand; others followed. Exceptional players could pass with two hands which others then imitated. With each development, what was exceptional performance, over time becomes commonplace. Similarly with IQ, as some individuals enjoy the development of their IQ-type abilities they form part of the global environment of other individuals. This enriched environment drives a global improvement among the population as a whole.

At this point Dickens and Flynn (2001) have argued, but not proved, a model that makes the existence of a genuine rise in IQ driven by environmental factors plausible. Flynn (in press) argues that the social-multiplier factors responsible (at least in the USA) differ between the time periods 1900–1948 and post-1948–present. Prior to 1948 Flynn attributes the rise to factors driven by the industrial revolution. Principally he nominates an increased number of years spent by children in school, improved nutrition, and better child health-care. Post-1948, Flynn argues that the rise in IQ was driven by different factors. He still anchors these to the industrial revolution, which by the late 1940s had produced an affluent US society that shifted its attitude so that on-the-spot problem-solving skills (fluid abilities) were taken more seriously and a saturation point was reached in the emphasis given to basic literacy and numerical skill development (crystallized abilities). Flynn links these attitudinal shifts to what he sees as strong environmental factors acting as social multipliers, including changes in schools, teaching, leisure-time interests, family size, and job skill requirements.

But what of those Dutchmen? How do we reconcile Flynn's current view that rising IQ reflects a recent real increase in the average ability to successfully solve on-the-spot abstract problems, with his prior common-sense objection that the data were made ridiculous by implying previous generations had relatively higher levels of intellectual disability. Flynn (in press) argues that if we were to travel back in time we would find that the level of intellectual disability has remained constant at about 2 per cent. If we met our parents' generation (c. 1974) or our grandparents (c. 1944) and compared ourselves with people of a similar level of education we would find their intellectual abilities to be much the same as ours; except, however, in the area of on-the-spot problem solving, an ability in which we are relatively superior, not due to any brain or genetic difference between us, but due to our societies' shift towards valuing this capacity in educational, vocational, and leisure contexts, thus creating a social-multiplier effect. Were we to travel further back in time and compare ourselves to our great-grandparents' generation (c. 1914) we would find that not only did their society not promote abstract problem solving among all or most people, but it also lacked a globally enjoyed equality in basic education, nutrition, and child health-care. Thus from relative performance on an IQ test that measures crystallized (attained intelligence) and fluid ability (abstract problem solving) it would appear that on average our great-grandparents' generation were less able intellectually than us. However, if an alternative IQ test were used that adequately measured the expression of intelligence that the social context of our great-grandparents' generation valued, and controlled for nutrition, heath, educational and vocational opportunities, then we would in fact discover that our ancestors were relatively our equals or perhaps superiors (depending on whether these abilities were still valued within our society).

As the preceding account demonstrates, Flynn's work has been extremely challenging to the field of human intelligence and much more thinking, debating, and research remains to be done. Flynn's ideas have evolved over time with many theoretical and practical implications. He has gradually moved from: (a) overcoming initial scepticism that IQ scores were rising to clearly establishing the Flynn effect; (b) plausibly reconciling the paradoxical evidence of a strong genetic influence on intelligence with evidence for a strong environmental influence; and (c) suggesting that the rise in IQ called into question the validity of IQ testing, to arguing that in fact it demonstrates that IQ scores were affected by a real socially driven change that emphasized the development and expression of certain intellectual abilities, first promoted by a drive for basic educational attainment and then replaced with a drive for the development of abstract problem-solving skills.

Profound implications for the assessment of intellectual disability

Flynn's work has profound implications for psychologists using IQ tests for the diagnosis of intellectual disability (Flynn, 2000). First, Flynn reminds us that the accepted cut-off score of an IQ of 70 commonly used for the diagnosis for intellectual disability was chosen as it reflected two standard deviations below the mean score of 100 thus isolating the bottom 2.27 per cent of the population. This was seen as acceptable as it coincided with the estimate that between 2 per cent and 3 per cent of the population have an intellectual disability as reflected in their real-world behaviour. However, the validity of using a cut-off score of 70 (rather than another figure such as 65 or 75) has never been adequately supported by empirically demonstrating that it is *the* IQ cut-off figure that best distinguishes people whose adaptive behaviour identifies them as having an intellectual disability.

Second, Flynn (2000) points out that once psychologists open the lid of a newly published IQ test they begin to use assessment instruments with normative data that become increasingly confounded by the influence of IQ gains. Take the Weschler Intelligence Scales for Children (WISC) as an example. Between the time when the original WISC was normed in 1947/48 to the collection of normative data for the revised WISC-R in 1972, children in the US gained 8.25 IQ points. IQ gains apply to the whole distribution and not just those at certain points such as the average range or above. Consequently in 1947/48 an IQ of 70 was the cut-off score for the lowest scoring 2.27 per cent of the population. However, due to rising scores it was the cut-off score for only 0.54 per cent of the population by the time the scale was re-normed in 1972. Then overnight, with the publication of the revised WISC-R, an IQ score of 70 again was the correct cut-off score for 2.27 per cent of the population. By the time the revised WISC-III normative data were collected in 1989 it appears that US children had gained up to 9 IQ points. Thus the proportion of children below the IQ of 70 score on the WISC-R had fallen from 2.27 per cent in 1972 to 0.47 per cent of the population in 1989. With the publication of the WISC-III, an IQ of 70 was again returned overnight as the correct discriminator of the lower-scoring 2.27 per cent of US children. Flynn points out that the response of clinical psychologists, educational psychologists, and test publishers to this situation was one of deafening silence and inadequacy which arguably further establishes the arbitrary nature of using 70 as an IQ score that marks the threshold of intellectual disability.

The reality of Flynn's claim that IQ scores have been rising and falling above and below a score of 70 (thus influencing whether individual children are classified as intellectually disabled or borderline) reflecting changing normative data, rather than ability, has been confirmed. Through a large-scale review of US school psychologist data, Kanaya, Scullin and Ceci (2003) compared the IQ scores of children who were routinely assessed and then subsequently routinely reassessed for intellectual disability around the time the WISC-III was published in 1991 (see also Kanaya, Ceci and Scullin, 2003). Their review clearly demonstrates that when tested on the same test twice (WISC-R/WISC-R or WISC-III/WISC-III) there was little difference in IQ score for children whose abilities placed them in the intellectually disabled or borderline ranges (on average from 0–1 IQ point differences). However, children initially assessed on the WISC-R and then reassessed on the WISC-III had significant differences in scores. Those whose original WISC-R score placed them in the borderline range (IQ 71–85) had an average drop of 6 IQ points when reassessed on the WISC-III. Those whose WISC-R assessment placed them in the intellectually disabled range (55–70 in this study) had an average WISC-III reassessment drop of 5 IQ points. In real terms this means that some individuals who had a single assessment would have scored above or below an IQ of 70 depending on whether they were administered the WISC-R or the WISC-III. Correct classification of intellectual disability has implications for eligibility for educational, vocational, family, and financial support. In the USA it also has implications for whether or not an individual may face the death penalty (Kanaya, Scullin and Ceci, 2003).

Utilizing our current awareness of IQ gains does not appear to be a reliable solution to addressing the effect of shifting test scores (Flynn, 2000). That is, we cannot simply deduct an appropriate and increasing figure from an individual's observed IQ score depending on how much time has passed since the publication of a test's normative data to someone's assessment. This is because we cannot rely on past rates of gain to act as the standard used to adjust IQ scores for newly normed tests once they have come into use. Rates of gain have been variable over time even in the same country. Furthermore, prediction that assumes that gains in the future will be constant and continuous is unjustified. For example, recently published data demonstrate that in Norway and Denmark, where the Flynn Effect has been solidly evidenced in the past, the rise in IQ has halted or even declined slightly since the beginning of the 1990s (Sundet, Barlaug and Torjussen, 2004; Teasdale and Owen, 2005).

However, if we wish to continue to use a particular IQ score (such as 70) or range of scores (70–75) as a valid point at which to classify people with an intellectual disability then clearly supportive evidence tying that score or range of scores with deficits in adaptive behaviour is needed. If we wish to continue to use IQ tests as part of clinical assessments for people who may have an intellectual disability then it is vital that we use instruments that have normative data which are nationally representative for the country in which we work, and that provides us with a contemporaneous comparison. Using out-of-date tests for reasons of economy is clearly never acceptable practice. Finally, if Flynn is correct about the environmental factors driving real gains in fluid abilities in the latter half of the twentieth century, then we would do well to remember that intelligence as seen through the window of IQ tests, even when they are apparently culturally reduced, are never truly free from measuring ability without the strong contextual influence of what aptitudes are currently valued within our society. In other words, there is no such thing as a culture-free IQ test. Flynn's view is that we should abandon using IQ testing as part of assessments for people who may have an intellectual disability and concentrate instead on gaining an adequate understanding of how people function in the context of the everyday world in which they live and are engaged (Flynn, 2000).

IQ TESTING: FOLLY OR VALUABLE?

As outlined in Chapter 1, the American Association on Mental Retardation (AAMR, 2002) offers a suitably complex definition of intellectual disability which is about a great deal more than IQ. Accepting the various assumptions of their definition and the other aspects of assessment that are required for diagnosis, the AAMR adopts a pragmatic approach that suggests that when used with appropriate caution IQ tests, despite their many shortcomings, can contribute usefully to the diagnosis of intellectual disability. We will briefly review some of the cautions it suggests here. First, the AAMR reminds us that standardized IQ tests function at their best when they measure ability within the average range (that is, within two standard deviations either side of the mean). Extreme scores beyond this boundary, either within the gifted or intellectually disabled range, are less reliable and more subject to measurement error.

Second, the AAMR (2002) recommends that an observed IQ score must always be considered with reference to the IQ test's Standard Error of Measurement (SEM). The SEM allows for the fact that when an IQ test is administered, an individual's obtained score includes some measurement error reflecting factors other than their ability which affected their performance on the day of assessment. For most standardized IQ scales the SEM is estimated to be +/– 3 or 4 IQ points. Consequently, an individual's observed score is best interpreted when bounded by the SEM for the IQ test used. That is, an IQ score of 70 on a test that has an SEM of +/– 4 points indicates that, allowing for error of measurement, we can be 66 per cent confident that their 'true' IQ score lies between the range of scores from 66 to 74, and 95 per cent confident that it lies between 62 and 78 (+/– 2 SEMs). Consequently, given the importance of allowing for measurement error, the AAMR does not set a precise cut-off score for the identification of intellectual disability. Instead it recommends a cut-off point that allows for error of measurement and the appropriate use of clinical judgement where 'the criteria for diagnosis is approximately two standard deviations below the mean, considering the standard error of measurement for the specific assessment instruments used and the instruments strengths and limitations' (2002: 14).

Choosing an IQ test?

At this point we hope we have clearly introduced some of the theoretical and research-based knowledge that we feel is a prerequisite for critically judging the value of the most frequently used commercially available IQ assessment instruments. We suggest that the instruments described in Table 3.10 are judged with reference to: (a) the degree to which they measure the constructs identified by psychometric and other models; (b) the adequacy of the definitions provided of the constructs they do measure; (c) the adequacy of the normative data provided; and (d) their psychometric properties.

Almost all of the main commercially available IQ tests have undergone revision since the turn of the twenty-first century. The quality and user-friendly nature of tests continues to improve with each successive revision. In the current generation of IQ assessment instruments, test developers have made genuine attempts to address the shortcomings in many of the older instruments. Consequently, in current IQ assessment instruments a serious effort has been made to replace a-theoretical or loosely theoretical index scores with indices that have been refined so they reflect constructs that match current psychometric theories of intelligence. In particular most scales offer some form of separate measure of fluid ability and crystallized ability. The definition of constructs measured by IQ tests has also improved as a consequence of recent revisions. However, occasionally manuals still lapse into defining index scores by simply listing aspects of the skills required within some or all of the subtests that make up the index score rather than defining a

Table 3.10 Description of commercially available standardized IQ tests

Test feature	Comment

BAYLEY SCALES OF INFANT DEVELOPMENT 3ᴿᴰ EDITION (BSID-III) (Bayley, 2006)

Published by	• The Psychological Corporation, San Antonio, USA; www.psychologicalcorporation.com
Year of publication	• 2005
Age-range	• 1 mth–42 mths
Normative data	• Derived from a random stratified nationally representative sample of 1,700 children aged 1 mth–42 mths reflective of the Oct 2000 US census
	• No UK normative data
	• No Republic of Ireland normative data
Average testing time	• 30–60 minutes
Mean scores and SD	• Mean IQ/Factor Score = 100; SD = 15 points
Co-normed attainment test available	• Social-Emotional and Adaptive Behaviour Questionnaire

DEFINITION OF BSID-III SCALES

Cognitive domain (COG)	• Assesses aspects of infant cognition reflective of research and theory in developmental psychology. In particular the cognitive scale assesses play (solitary and social), attention to novelty, habituation (processing speed), memory, and problem solving
Language domain (LANG)	• Assesses Receptive and Expressive Communication. Assessment of Receptive Communication includes the ability to respond to a person's voice, to discriminate and respond to sounds in the environment, the ability to localize sound, and the ability to understand and respond to words and requests. The assessment of Expressive Communication includes the ability to vocalize, use consonant-vowel combinations, imitate sounds and words, name pictures objects and actions, express wants and needs, respond to questions, use one and multi-word expressions, and the ability to combine words and gestures
Motor domain (MOT)	• Assesses Fine Motor and Gross Motor skills, particularly basic milestones, quality of movement, sensory integration, and perceptual-motor integration
Social-emotional Domain (SE)	• Questionnaire completed by parents assessing children's attainment of age-related functional social-emotional milestones in the areas of self-regulation, engaging in relationships, using emotions in an interactive manner, communicating emotions, using symbols or ideas to express emotions, and creating logical connections between emotions and ideas
Adaptive behaviour Domain (ADAPT)	• Questionnaire assessing the attainment of functional adaptive behaviours in the areas of communication, community use, health and safety, leisure, self-care, self-direction, functional pre-academics, home living, social, and motor

Average reliability	• Cog = 0.91; Lang = 0.93; Mot = 0.92; SE = 0.90; Adapt = 0.97 (Bayley, 2006)
Average SEM	• Cog = 0.95; Lang = 4.47; Mot = 4.42; SE = 1.0; Adapt = 3.11 (Bayley, 2006)

STANFORD-BINET 5TH EDITION (SB5) (Roid, 2003a)

Published by	• Riverside Publishing, Illinois, USA; www.stanfordbinet.com
Year of publication	• 2003
Age-range	• 2–85 years
Normative data	• Derived from a US nationally representative sample of 4,800 individuals aged 2–85 years
	• No UK normative data
	• No Republic of Ireland normative data
Average testing time	• 45–75 minutes
Mean scores and SD	• Mean IQ/Factor Score = 100; SD = 15 points
Co-normed attainment test available	• None

DEFINITION OF SB5 IQ SCORES

Full-Scale IQ (FSIQ)
• 'The FSIQ is computed as a sum of all the tasks in the SB5; that is all subtests covering both the Verbal and Nonverbal domains of cognitive ability. Thus, the FSIQ is a global summary of the current level of intellectual functioning as measured by the SB5. Researchers such as Carroll (1993) or Gustafsson (1984) would describe the FSIQ as a measure of the hierarchical g factor that exists among the scores of an intelligence battery' (Roid, 2003b: 134–5)

Verbal IQ (VIQ)
• Not formally defined. A summary score based on the 5 verbal subtests of the SB5

Non-verbal IQ (NVIQ)
• Not formally defined. A summary score based on the 5 non-verbal subtests of the SB5. Verbal instructions are minimised but some receptive language is required on the part of the testee

DEFINITION OF SB5 FACTOR SCORES

Fluid reasoning (FR)
• 'is the ability to solve verbal and nonverbal problems using inductive and deductive reasoning' (Roid, 2003b: 136)

Knowledge (KN)
• 'is a person's accumulated fund of general information acquired at home, school, or work. In research this factor has been called crystallized ability, because it involves learned material, such as vocabulary, that has been acquired and stored in long-term memory' (Roid, 2003b: 136)

Quantitative reasoning (QR)
• 'is an individual's facility with numbers and numerical problem solving, whether with word problems or with pictured relationships. Activities in the SB5 emphasize applied problem solving more than specific mathematical knowledge acquired through school learning' (Roid, 2003b: 137)

Visual-spatial processing (VS)
• 'measures an individual's ability to see patterns, relationships, spatial orientations, or the gestalt whole among diverse pieces of a visual display' (Roid, 2003b: 137)

(Continued overleaf)

Table 3.10 Continued

Test feature	Comment
Working memory (WM)	• 'is a class of memory processes in which diverse information stored in short-term memory is inspected, sorted, or transformed . . . The concept of Working Memory is derived from theories such as Baddeley (1996)' (Roid, 2003b: 137)
Average reliability	• FSIQ = 0.98; VIQ = 0.96; NVIQ = 0.95; FR = 0.90; KN = 0.92; QR = 0.92; VS = 0.92; WM = 0.91 (Roid, 2003c)
Average SEM	• FSIQ = 2.30; VIQ = 3.05; NVIQ = 3.26; FR = 4.85; KN = 4.36; QR = 4.33; VS = 4.41; WM = 4.62 (Roid, 2003c)

BRITISH ABILITY SCALES 2ND EDITION (BAS-II) (Elliot, 1997)

Published by	• Nfer Nelson, London, UK. www.nfer-nelson.co.uk
Year of publication	• 1997
Age-range	• 2 yrs 6 mths–17 yrs 11 mths
Normative data	• Derived from a UK nationally representative sample of 1,689 individuals aged 2yrs 6 mths–17yrs 11mths collected in 1995
	• No Republic of Ireland normative data
	• No US normative data
Average testing time	• 25–90 minutes
Mean scores and SD	• Mean IQ/Factor Score = 100; SD = 15 points
Co-normed attainment test available	• Built into the BAS-II providing an assessment of Word Reading, Spelling, and Number Skills

DEFINITION OF BAS-II CORE SCALES

General conceptual ability (GCA)	• 'In contrast to the composite score of many other individually administered test batteries, which give equal weighting to all subtests, the GCA score of the BAS-II is derived only from those scales with high g-loadings. With this feature, a valid and focused measure of a central component of intellectual ability can be efficiently obtained' (Elliott, 1997: 16). 'the GCA score is primarily a well-saturated measure of psychometric-g, that is, it provides an assessment of the ability to perform the complex transformations on information that are involved in reasoning and the application of concepts' (Elliott, 1997: 19)
Verbal ability (VA)	• 'measures complex verbal mental processing including acquired verbal concepts, verbal knowledge and reasoning. In terms of the Horn–Cattell and Carroll factor theories, [it] is a measure of crystallized intelligence (Gc)' (Elliott, 1997: 91)
Non-verbal reasoning ability (NRA)	• 'This Cluster score measures non-verbal, inductive reasoning and requires complex mental processing. [It] represents the factor of fluid intelligence (Gf) in the Horn–Cattell and Carroll factor theories' (Elliot, 1997: 92)
Spatial ability (SA)	• 'is a measure of complex visuo-spatial processing. It represents the broad visualisation (Gv) factor in the Horn–Cattell and Carroll factor theories' (Elliott, 1997: 93)

| **Average reliability** | • GCA = 0.95; VA = 0.92; NRA = 0.92; SA = 0.87 |
| **Average SEM** | • GCA = 3.18; VA = 4.04; NRA = 4.36; SA = 5.23 |

KAUFMAN ASSESSMENT BATTERY FOR CHILDREN 2ND EDITION (KABC-II) (Kaufman and Kaufman, 2004)

Published by	• AGS Publishing, MN, USA. www.agsnet.com
Year of publication	• 2004
Age-range	• 3–18 yrs
Normative data	• Derived from a US nationally representative sample of 3,025 individuals aged 3–18 years collected from September 2001–January 2003
	• No UK normative data
	• No Republic of Ireland normative data
Average testing time	• 25–70 minutes
Mean scores and SD	• Mean IQ/Factor Score = 100; SD = 15 points
Co-normed attainment test available	• Kaufman Test of Educational Achievement, Comprehensive From 2ND Edition. KTEA-II

DEFINITION OF KABC-II SCALES

The KABC-II can be interpreted according to the Luria model (LM) or the Cattel–Horn–Carroll (CHC) model of cognitive ability. The test administrator chooses which model is appropriate for the assessment at hand in advance of assessing a child. Consequently the KABC-II scales are defined to reflect their underlying interpretive model

Luria model (LM): Mental processing Index (MPI)	A measure of general mental *processing* that de-emphasizes acquired knowledge. This global score based on the Luria model of interpreting the test is based upon learning ability, sequential processing, simultaneous processing, and planning ability
CHC Model: Fluid/ Crystallized Index (FCI)	A measure of general cognitive ability (g) as reflected in level III of the CHC model. In the KABC-II the FCI is derived from the following level II abilities: Long-Term Storage and Retrieval; Short-Term Memory; Visual Processing; Fluid Reasoning; and Crystallized Ability
LM: Learning;	Assesses the ability to learn and retain new information efficiently by integrating cognitive processes of attention-concentration, coding, storage, sensory integration, and strategy generation
LM: Sequential processing	Assesses cognitive processing that requires 'arranging input in sequential or serial order to solve a problem, where each idea is linearly and temporally related to the preceding one' (Kaufman and Kaufman, 2004: 16)
LM: Simultaneous;	Assesses cognitive processing that requires input 'to be integrated and synthesized simultaneously (holistically), usually spatially, to produce the appropriate solution' (Kaufman and Kaufman, 2004: 16)
LM: Planning;	Assesses cognition that 'measures high-level, decision making, executive processes' (Kaufman and Kaufman, 2004: 16)
CHC: Long-term storage and retrieval (Glr)	Assessing storage and efficient retrieval of new or previously learnt material

(Continued overleaf)

Table 3.10 Continued

Test feature	Comment
CHC: Short-term memory (Gsm)	Assessing ability to hold information and use it within a few seconds
CHC Visual processing (Gv)	Assessing visual perception, storage, manipulation and cognition
CHC: Fluid reasoning (Gf)	Assessing novel problem solving through the use of reasoning abilities
CHC Crystallized ability (Gc)	Assessing the body of knowledge acquired within one's particular cultural setting
Average reliability	• MPI = 0.95; FCI = 0.96; Non-Verbal Index (NVI) = 0.91; Learning/Glr = 0.93; Sequential/Gsm = 0.89; Simultaneous/Gv = 0.89; Planning/Gf = 0.96; Knowledge/Gc = 0.92
Average SEM	• MPI = 3.21; FCI = 2.79; NVI = 4.20; Learning/Glr = 4.00; Sequential/Gsm = 5.02; Simultaneous/Gv = 5.16; Planning/Gf = 5.31; Knowledge/Gc = 4.14

LEITER INTERNATIONAL PERFORMANCE SCALE REVISED (LIPS-R) (Roid and Miller, 1997)

Published by	• Stoelting, Illinois, USA. www.agsnet.com
Year of publication	• 1997
Age-range	• 2–20 yrs
Normative data	• Derived from a US nationally representative sample of 1,719 individuals aged 2–20 years collected in 1995
	• No UK normative data
	• No Republic of Ireland normative data
Average testing time	• 90 minutes
Mean scores and SD	• Mean IQ/Factor Score = 100; SD = 15 points
Co-normed attainment test available	• None, however an additional 10 subscale Attention and Memory Battery is built into the LIPS-R

DEFINITION OF LIPS-R VISUAL REASONING SCALES

Full-scale IQ (FSIQ)	• 'a measure of nonverbal intelligence which includes diverse aspects of cognition. Those subtests that correlate highly with the overall construct 'g' are included to obtain a single measure of intellectual ability' (Roid and Miller, 1997: 101)
Fluid reasoning (FR)	• 'Fluid reasoning is typically defined as the ability to solve novel problems which are not tied to "school learning" (crystallized) or culturally determined knowledge' (Roid and Miller, 1997: 110)
Fundamental visualization (FV)	• Ages 2–5 only – 'measures a basic level of visualization ability . . . requires attention to visual detail, but no memory or re-organization of visual stimuli appears to be involved' (Roid and Miller, 1997: 110)
Spatial visualization (SV)	• Ages 11–20 only – 'measures complex visual spatial processing abilities . . . This composite taps into inductive reasoning abilities related to synthesizing visual patterns (Elliott, 1990) and the ability to perceive and preserve space orientation and size and position of objects' (Roid and Miller, 1997: 110)

Attention and memory battery	• In addition the LIPS-R has an additional 10 subscale battery which yields 6 composite scores: Memory Screener; Recognition Memory; Associative Memory; Memory Span; Attention; and Memory Process
Average reliability	• FSIQ = 0.93; FR = 0.89; FV = 0.92; SV = 0.91 (Roid and Miller, 1997)
Average SEM	• FSIQ = 4.24; FR = 5.05; FV = 4.24; SV = 4.50 (Roid and Miller, 1997)

WESCHLER PRESCHOOL and PRIMARY SCALE OF INTELLIGENCE 3RD EDITION (WPPSI-III) (Weschler, 2002)

Published by	• The Psychological Corporation, San Antonio, USA. www.psychologicalcorporation.com
Year of publication	• 2002 (UK 2003)
Age-range	• 2yrs 6mths–7yrs 3mths
Normative data	• Derived from a US nationally representative sample of 1,700 children aged 2yrs 6mths–7yrs 3mths
	• UK normative data based on a nationally representative validation sample of 805 children
	• No Republic of Ireland normative data
Average testing time	• 30–50 minutes
Mean scores and SD	• Mean IQ/Factor Score = 100; SD = 15 points
Co-normed attainment test available	• WIAT-II co-normed with approximately 200 US children aged 4yrs–7 yrs 3mths

DEFINITION OF WAIS-III IQ SCORES

Full-scale IQ (FSIQ)	• 'The FSIQ is usually considered to be the score that is most representative of g, or general intellectual functioning' (Weschler, 2002: 135)
Verbal IQ (VIQ)	• 'is a measure of acquired knowledge, verbal reasoning and comprehension, and attention to verbal stimuli' (Weschler, 2002: 135)
Performance IQ (PIQ)	• 'is a measure of fluid reasoning, spatial processing, attentiveness to detail, and visual-motor integration. The performance tasks included in the WPPSI-III should be fairly novel to child' (Weschler, 2002: 136)
Processing speed quotient (PSQ)	• 'provides a measure of the child's ability to quickly and correctly scan, sequence, or discriminate simple visual information. This composite also measures short-term visual memory, attention, and visual-motor coordination' (Weschler, 2002: 136)
General language composite (GLC)	• 'is an indicator of the child's language development in two modalities: expressive and receptive' (Weschler, 2002: 137)
Average reliability	• FSIQ = 0.96; VIQ = 0.95; PIQ = 0.93; PSQ = 0.89; GLC = 0.93
Average SEM	• FSIQ = 2.92; VIQ = 3.35; PIQ = 4.15; PSQ = 4.94; GLC = 4.03

WESCHLER INTELLIGENCE SCALE FOR CHILDREN 4TH EDITION (WISC-IV) (Weschler, 2003)

Published by	• The Psychological Corporation, San Antonio, USA. www.psychologicalcorporation.com
Year of publication	• 2003 (UK 2004)

(Continued overleaf)

Table 3.10 Continued

Test feature	Comment
Age-range	• 6yrs 0mths–16yrs 11mths
Normative data	• Derived from a US nationally representative sample of 2002 children aged 6yrs 0 mths–16yrs 11 mths collected in 2002
	• UK normative data based on a nationally representative validation sample of 780 children collected in 2003
	• No Republic of Ireland normative data
Average testing time	• 60–90 minutes
Mean scores and SD	• Mean IQ/Factor Score = 100; SD = 15 points
Co-normed attainment test available	• Weschler Individual Achievement Test 2ND Edition (WIAT-II)

DEFINITION OF WISC-IV SCORES

Full-scale IQ (FSIQ)	• 'It is derived from the combined sums of scaled scores for the VCI, PRI, WMI, and PSI. The FSIQ is usually considered to be the score that is most representative of *g*, or general intellectual functioning' (Weschler, 2003: 103)
Verbal comprehension index (VCI)	• 'is a measure of verbal concept formation, verbal reasoning, and knowledge acquired from one's environment' (Weschler, 2003: 103)
Perceptual reasoning index (PRI)	• 'is a measure of perceptual and fluid reasoning, spatial processing, and visual-motor integration' (Weschler, 2003: 104)
Working memory index (WMI)	• 'provides a measure of the child's working memory abilities. Tasks that require working memory require the ability to temporarily retain information in memory, perform some operation or manipulation with it, and produce a result. Working memory involves attention, concentration, mental control, and reasoning' (Weschler, 2003: 104)
Processing speed index (PSI)	• 'The PSI provides a measure of the child's ability to quickly and correctly scan, sequence, or discriminate simple visual information. Faster processing of information may conserve working memory resources. This composite also measures short-term visual memory, attention, and visual motor co-ordination' (Weschler, 2003: 104)
Average reliability	• FSIQ = 0.97; VCI = 0.94; PRI = 0.92; WMI = 0.92; PSI = 0.88
Average SEM	• FSIQ = 2.68; VCI = 3.78; PRI = 4.15; WMI = 4.27; PSI = 5.21

WESCHLER ADULT INTELLIGENCE SCALE 3RD EDITION (WAIS-III) (Psychological Corporation, 1997a)

Published by	• The Psychological Corporation, San Antonio, USA. www.psychologicalcorporation.com
Year of publication	• 1997
Age-range	• 16–89 years
Normative data	• Derived from a US nationally representative sample of 2,450 individuals aged 16–89 years reflective of the 1995 US Census data

- UK normative data based on a nationally representative validation sample of 332 people
- No Republic of Ireland normative data

Average testing time	• 45–75 minutes
Mean scores and SD	• Mean IQ/Factor Score = 100; SD = 15 points
Co-normed attainment test available	• Weschler Test of Adult Reading (WTAR) and The Weschler Memory Scale 3ND Edition (WMS-II)

DEFINITION OF WAIS-III IQ SCORES

Full-scale IQ (FSIQ)	• 'is the overall summary score that estimates an individual's general level of intellectual functioning. It is the aggregate score of the VIQ and PIQ scores and is usually considered to be the score that is most representative of g, or global intellectual functioning' (The Psychological Corporation, 1997b: 186)
Verbal IQ (VIQ)	• 'is a measure of acquired knowledge, verbal reasoning, and attention to verbal materials' (The Psychological Corporation, 1997b: 185)
Performance IQ (PIQ)	• 'is a measure of fluid reasoning, spatial processing, attentiveness to detail, and visual-motor integration. The tasks should be fairly novel to the first-time examinee' (The Psychological Corporation, 1997b: 186)

DEFINITION OF WAIS-III FACTOR SCORES

Verbal comprehension index (VCI)	• 'is a measure of verbal acquired knowledge and verbal reasoning . . . [It] may be conceptualized as a more refined, "purer" measure of verbal comprehension [than VIQ]' (The Psychological Corporation, 1997b: 186)
Perceptual organization index (POI)	• 'is a measure of nonverbal, fluid reasoning, attentiveness to detail, and visual motor integration . . . The composition of the POI score makes it a more refined measure of fluid reasoning and visual-spatial problem solving than the PIQ score' (The Psychological Corporation, 1997b: 186)
Working memory index (WMI)	• Measures 'a range of tasks that require the examinee to attend to information, to hold briefly and process that information in memory, and then to formulate a response' (The Psychological Corporation, 1997b: 186)
Processing speed index (PSI)	• 'is a measure of the individual's ability to process visual information quickly (The Psychological Corporation, 1997b: 187)
Average reliability	• FSIQ = 0.98; VIQ = 0.97; PIQ = 0.94; VCI = 0.96; POI = 0.93; WMI = 0.94; PSI = 0.88
Average SEM	• FSIQ = 2.29; VIQ = 2.50; PIQ = 3.75; VCI = 3.03; POI = 3.79; WMI = 3.84; PSI = 5.36

coherent underlining ability (for example see the WPPSI-III definition of the processing speed quotient in Table 3.10). Test publishers have become increasingly better at providing guidelines and data that facilitate the interpretation of test results. This has prompted clearer presentation of IQ and index scores with their associated SEMs, confidence intervals, percentiles, and data that allow the magnitude of differences between index scores to be meaningfully interpreted. As most revisions of commercially available IQ tests are recent this means that their normative data too are relatively contemporaneous. All scales provide exceptionally high-quality data for assessments conducted in the USA. Some provide validation data that allow for test use in places like the UK. None of the tests provide data for the Republic of Ireland and so the status of the applicability of these tests within an Irish or similar smaller-nation context remains unclear.

CONCLUSION

In this chapter we have outlined a working definition of the term 'intelligence' suitable for use in the context of working with people with an intellectual disability which fits with the understanding of this term among researchers and experts in the field of intelligence. We have reviewed the main theoretical models of intelligence that stem from the psychometric approach and contrasted them with models that go beyond this tradition. We also reviewed a small section of the large body of research evidence that is usually interpreted as indicating that individual differences in intelligence as measured by IQ tests has a strong genetic basis. We have also introduced evidence concerning the Flynn Effect that offers the apparently contradictory conclusion that environmental factors have very considerable effects on IQ scores. We have described Flynn's resolution of this apparent paradox while signalling the profound implications of his work for the assessment of IQ and diagnosis of intellectual disability. Finally, the main commercially available IQ instruments covering assessment across the life-span have been described with an emphasis on highlighting the quality and recency of their normative data, the clarity of definition offered of the aspects of intelligence that they purport to measure, and the psychometric properties of the scales that are especially relevant for an assessment of a person with an intellectual disability. It is our hope that in doing so we have provided an introduction to some of the key ideas and debates that shape the current understanding of the term intelligence among psychologists. We anticipate that this may prove useful in understanding the contributions and limitations of IQ testing in the lives of people with intellectual disabilities, thus contributing to good decision-making about the appropriate use and selection of IQ instruments in clinical practice.

EXERCISE

In pairs, practise giving an intelligence test and then discuss the positive and negative aspects of having a test administered to you. Identify what you have learned from this that may be helpful to you in administering tests to clients and share these views with your class.

FURTHER READING FOR FAMILIES

Ian Deary (2001). *Intelligence: A Very Short Introduction.* Oxford: Oxford Paperbacks. This is an outstanding and accessible introduction to the field of mainstream intelligence theory and research.

FURTHER READING AND RESOURCES FOR CLINICIANS

Ian Deary (2000). *Looking Down on Human Intelligence: From Psychometrics to the Brain.* Oxford: Oxford University Press.

Flanagan, D. P. and Harrison, P. L. (eds) (2005). *Contemporary Intellectual Assessment: Theories, Tests and Issues* (2nd edn). New York: Guilford Press.

List Essentials Series (WILEY) for Test Interpretation for main IQ scales.

American Psychological Association's section on assessment in their code of ethics http://www.apa.org/ethics/code2002.html

BPS psychological testing centre: http://www.psychtesting.org.uk/

REFERENCES

American Association on Mental Retardation (AAMR) (2002). *Mental Retardation: Definition, Classification, and Systems of Support* (10th edn). Washington: AAMR.

Baddeley, A. (1996). *Working Memory.* New York: Oxford University Press.

Bayley, N. (2006). *Bayley Scales of Infant and Toddler Development Technical Manual* (3rd edn). San Antonio, TX: Psychological Corporation.

Bouchard, T. J., Lykken, D. T., McGue, M., Segal, N. L. and Tellegen, A. (1990). Sources of human psychological differences: The Minnesota study of twins reared apart. *Science,* 250, 223–50.

Carroll, J. B. (1993). *Human Cognitive Abilities: A Survey of Factor-Analytic Studies.* Cambridge: Cambridge University Press.

Cattell, R. B. (1943). The measurement of adult intelligence. *Psychological Bulletin,* 40, 153–93.

Colom, R., Flores-Mendoza, C., Quiroga, M. and Privado, J. (2005). Working memory and general intelligence: The role of short-term storage. *Personality and Individual Differences,* 39 (5), 1005–14.

Colom, R., Rebollo, I., Palcios, A., Juan-Espinosa, M. and Kyllonen, P. (2004). Working memory is (almost) perfectly predicted by g. *Intelligence,* 32, 277–96.

Deary, I. (2000). *Looking Down on Human Intelligence: From Psychometrics to the Brain.* Oxford: Oxford University Press.

Deary, I. (2002). g and cognitive elements of information processing: An agnostic view. In R. J. Sternberg and E. L. Grigorenko (eds), *The General Factor of Intelligence: How General Is It?* London: Lawrence Erlbaum Associates Publishers.

Dickens, W. T. and Flynn, J. R. (2001). Heritability estimates versus large environmental effects: The IQ paradox resolved. *Psychological Review,* 108 (2), 346–69.

Dunbar, R. (2004). *The Human Story: A New History of Mankind's Evolution.* London: Faber and Faber.

Elliott, C. D. (1990). *Differential Ability Scales: Introductory and Technical Handbook*. San Antonio, TX: The Psychological Corporation.

Elliot, C. D. (1997). *The British Ability Scales* (2nd edn). *Technical Manual*. London: Nfer Nelson.

Flynn, J. R. (1984). The mean IQ of Americans: Massive gains 1932 to 1978. *Psychological Bulletin*, 95 (1), 29–51.

Flynn, J. R. (1987). Massive IQ gains in 14 nations: What IQ tests really measure. *Psychological Bulletin*, 101 (2), 171–91.

Flynn, J. R. (1999). Searching for justice: The discovery of IQ gains over time. *American Psychologist*, 54 (1), 5–20.

Flynn, J. R. (2000). The hidden history of IQ and special education: Can the problems be solved? *Psychology, Public Policy and Law*, 6, 191–8.

Flynn, J. R. (in press). Efeito Flynn: respensando a inteligencia e seus efeitos [The Flynn effect: Rethinking intelligence and what effects it]. In C. Flores-Mendoza and R. Colom (eds), *Introducia a Psicologia das Diferencas Individuais [Introduction to the Psychology of Individual Differences]*. Porto: ArtMed. English translation of his chapter generously supplied by J. Flynn.

Gardner, H. (1983). *Frames of Mind: The Theory of Multiple Intelligences*. New York: Basic Books.

Gardner, H. (1993). *Frames of Mind: The Theory of Multiple Intelligences* (2nd edn). London: Fontana Press.

Gardner, H. (1999). *Intelligence Reframed: Multiple Intelligences for the 21st Century*. New York: Basic Books.

Gottfredson, L. S. (2003). Dissecting practical intelligence theory: Its claims and evidence. *Intelligence*, 21, 343–97.

Gustafsson, J. E. (1984). A unifying model for the structure of intelligence. *Intelligence*, 8, 179–203.

Horn, J. (1986). Intellectual ability concepts. In R. J. Sternberg (ed.), *Advances in the Psychology of Human Intelligence*. Hillsdale, NJ: Erlbaum.

Horn, J. (1994). Theory of fluid and crystallised intelligence. In R. J. Sternberg (ed.) *Encyclopaedia of Human Intelligence*. New York: Macmillan.

Horn, J. and Blankson, N. (2005). Foundations for better understanding of cognitive abilities. In D. P. Flanagan and P. L. Harrison (eds), *Contemporary Intellectual Assessment: Theories, Tests and Issues* (2nd edn). New York: Guilford Press.

Jensen, A. R. (1998). *The g Factor: The Science of Mental Ability*. Connecticut; London: Praeger.

Jensen, A. R. (2002). Psychometric g: definition and substantiation. In R. J. Sternberg and E. L. Grigorenko (eds), *The General Factor of Intelligence: How General Is It?* London: Lawrence Erlbaum Associates Publishers.

Joseph, J. (2003). *The Gene Illusion: Genetic Research in Psychiatry and Psychology Under the Microscope*. Herefordshire: PCCS Books.

Kanaya, T., Ceci, S. and Scullin, M. H. (2003). The rise and fall of IQ in special ed: Historical trends and their implications. *Journal of School Psychology*, 41, 453–65.

Kanaya, T., Scullin, M. H. and Ceci, S. (2003). The Flynn Effect and US policies: The impact of rising IQ scores on American society via mental retardation diagnoses. *American Psychologist*, 58 (10), 778–90.

Kaufman, A. S. and Kaufman, N. L. (2004). *Kaufman Assessment Battery for Children* (2nd edn). MN: AGS Publishing.

Kolb, B., and Wishaw, I. Q. (2003). *Fundamentals of Human Neuropsychology*, (5th edn). New York: Freeman.

McClearn, G. E., Johansson, B., Berg, S., Pedersen, N. L., Ahern, F., Petrill, S. A. and Plomin, R. (1997). Substantial genetic influence on cognitive abilities in twins 80 or more years old. *Science*, 276, 1560–3.

McGrew, K. S. (2005). The Cattell–Horn–Carroll theory of cognitive abilities: Past, present and future. In D. P. Flanagan and P. L. Harrison (eds), *Contemporary Intellectual Assessment: Theories, Tests and Issues* (2nd edn). New York: Guilford Press.

McGrew, K. S. and Flanagan, D. P. (1998). *The Intelligence Test Desk Reference: Gf–Gc Cross-Battery Assessment*. Boston: Allyn and Bacon.

Neisser, U., Boodoo, G., Bouchard, T. J., Boykin, A. W., Brody, N., Ceci, S. J., Halpern, D. F., Loehlin, J. C., Perloff, R., Sternberg, R. J. and Urbina, S. (1996). Intelligence: Knowns and unknowns. *American Psychologist*, 51 (2), 77–101.

Nyborg, H. (ed.) (2003). *The Scientific Study of General Intelligence: Tribute to Arthur R. Jensen*. New York: Pergamon.

Patrick, C. L. (2000). Genetic and environmental influences on the development of cognitive abilities: Evidence from the field of developmental behaviour genetics. *Journal of School Psychology*, 38 (1), 79–108.

Plomin, R., DeFries, J. C., McClearn, G. E. and McGuffin, P. (2000). *Behavioral Genetics 4th Edition*. New York: Worth Publishers.

Purcell, S. (2000). Statistical methods in behavioural genetics. In R. Plomin, J. C. DeFries, G. E. McClearn and P. McGuffin (2000). *Behavioural Genetics 4th Edition*. New York: Worth Publishers.

Roid, G. H. (2003a). *Stanford-Binet Intelligence Scales, Fifth Edition*. Itasca, IL: Riverside Publishing.

Roid, G. H. (2003b). *Stanford-Binet Intelligence Scales, Fifth Edition, Examiner's Manual*. Itasca, IL: Riverside Publishing.

Roid, G. H. (2003c). *Stanford-Binet Intelligence Scales, Fifth Edition, Technical Manual*. Itasca, IL: Riverside Publishing.

Roid, G. H. and Miller, L. J. (1997). *Leiter International Performance Scale—Revised: Examiner's Manual*. Illinois: Stoeling Co.

Psychological Corporation, The (1997a). *The Weschler Adult Intelligence Scale 3rd Edition*. San Antonio, TX: The Psychological Corporation.

Psychological Corporation, The (1997b). *The Weschler Adult Intelligence Scale 3rd Edition, Technical Manual*. San Antonio, TX: The Psychological Corporation.

Snyderman, M. and Rothman, S. (1987). Survey of expert opinion on intelligence and aptitude testing. *American Psychologist*, 42 (2), 137–44.

Spearman, C. (1904). General intelligence, objectively determined and measured. *American Journal of Psychology*, 15, 201–93.

Spearman, C. (1923). *The Nature of 'Intelligence' and the Principles of Cognition*. London: Macmillan and Co.

Spearman, C. (1927). *The Abilities of Man: Their Nature and Measurement*. London: Macmillan and Co.

Sternberg, R. J. (1994). Triarchic theory of human intelligence. In R. J. Sternberg (ed.), *Encyclopaedia of Human Intelligence*. New York: Macmillan.

Sternberg, R. J. (2002). Intelligence is not just inside the head: The theory of successful intelligence. In J. Aronson (ed.), *Improving Academic Achievement: Impact of Psychological Factors on Education*. New York: Academic Press.

Sternberg, R. J. (2005). The triarchic theory of successful intelligence. In D. P. Flanagan and P. L. Harrison (eds), *Contemporary Intellectual Assessment: Theories, Tests and Issues* (2nd edn). New York: The Guilford Press.

Sternberg, R. J. and Grigorenko, E. L. (eds) (2002). *The General Factor of Intelligence: How General Is It?* London: Lawrence Erlbaum Associates Publishers.

Sundet, J. M., Barlaug, D. G. and Torjussen, T. M. (2004). The end of the Flynn Effect? A study of secular trends in mean intelligence test scores of Norwegian conscripts during half a century. *Intelligence*, 32, 349–62.

Teasdale, T. W. and Owen, D. R. (2005). A long-term rise and recent decline in intelligence test performance: The Flynn Effect in reverse. *Personality and Individual Differences*, 39, 837–43.

Thurstone, L. L. (1938). Primary mental abilities. *Psychometric Mongraphics* No. 1.

Weschler, D. (2002). *Weschler Preschool and Primary Scale of Intelligence, 3rd Edition, Technical and Interpretive Manual*. San Antonio, TX: The Psychological Corporation.

Weschler, D. (2003). *Weschler Intelligence Scale for Children, 4th Edition, Technical and Interpretive Manual*. San Antonio, TX: The Psychological Corporation.

Wilson, R. S. (1983). The Louisville twin study: Developmental synchronies in behaviour. *Child Development*, 54, 298–316.

Chapter 4

Quality of life

Kenneth D. Keith

At the beginning of *We Can Speak For Ourselves*, their remarkable early book on self-advocacy, Williams and Shoultz (1982) quoted John Lennon's sentiment that we may be dreamers, but we're not the only ones. They went on to present the aims and activities of people with intellectual disabilities who were working to create a better life for themselves and their friends. Following their lead, one could argue that the *raison d'être* of services, supports, and organizations established on behalf of those with disabilities should be to improve quality of life. It was thus not long before researchers took seriously the challenge to develop approaches to defining, measuring, and understanding quality of life (Keith, Schalock and Hoffman, 1986; Landesman, 1986). Consequently, Schalock (1990) was right when he predicted that quality of life would be 'the issue' of the 1990s. Research on quality of life virtually exploded during that decade, leading Cummins (1995) to note the existence of more than 100 definitions of the concept. By the same year, more than 1,000 measures of quality of life had found their way into the research literature (Hughes, Hwang, Kim, Eisenman and Killian, 1995). And in the three-year period 1992–1995 researchers produced 1,400 publications on quality of life (Antaki and Rapley, 1996). Subsequently, Schalock and Verdugo (2002) reported that well over 20,000 articles were published in the years since 1985 with the term 'quality of life' in their titles. Despite (or perhaps because of) this wealth of work on the topic, at the dawn of the new millennium a singular definition of quality of life continued to elude investigators (Hensel, 2001).

My task in this chapter is to attempt to reduce this massive body of work to a workable definition that may prove useful for clinical work, to discuss some practical approaches to measuring quality of life, and to suggest meaningful ways to use the concept on behalf of individuals with intellectual disabilities. I will also offer references and recommendations for further reading about quality of life and quality-of-life measures that may be of interest to clinical practitioners and family members of people with an intellectual disability.

THE CONCEPT OF QUALITY OF LIFE

The rich, and sometimes bewildering, range of definitions and approaches to quality of life can present a complex picture that might, on its surface, seem to defy reasonable discussion. In fact, some writers have proposed that a unitary definition of quality of life may not be a good idea (Schalock, 1996). That is, it may be better to conceptualize quality of life as an organizing notion, comprising multiple dimensions, valuable for shaping the direction of services or planning. Thus, Schalock (1996) argued, the essential point may not be that quality of life is an entity possessed by an individual. Instead it might be better viewed as a range of multidimensional attributes and indicators. And researchers have conducted a good deal of work in an effort to identify and articulate the dimensions and indicators that might prove useful in this regard.

A multidimensional perspective

Hughes and Hwang (1996), in noting a wide range of definitions of quality of life, reported that aggregation of these definitions produced fifteen dimensions, ranging from well-being and satisfaction to personal competence, community integration, and civic responsibility. In a study spanning seven countries, Keith, Heal, and Schalock (1996) found fairly broad agreement on ten key quality-of-life concepts: rights; relationships; satisfaction; environment; economic security; social inclusion; individual control; privacy; health; and growth and development. At about the same time, Felce (1996) proposed six key aspects of life quality: physical well-being; material well-being; social well-being; productive well-being; emotional well-being; and (civic) rights well-being.

Eventually, a broad-based international research group (Schalock, Brown, Brown, Cummins *et al.*, 2002) reported consensus on eight dimensions or 'core domains' of quality of life: emotional well-being; interpersonal relations; material well-being; personal development; physical well-being; self-determination; social inclusion; and rights. Furthermore, as Keith (2001) noted, it is important that efforts to define the dimensions of quality of life take account not only of the conclusions of researchers, but also of individuals with disabilities and their advocates (Felce, 1996; Goode and Hogg, 1994; Keith, 1990; Renwick and Brown, 1996; Renwick, Brown and Raphael, 2000; Taylor and Bogdan, 1996); and serious efforts have been made to gather and use quality-of-life data from non-researchers (Amado, Conklin, and Wells, 1990; ARC of Nebraska, 1998; 1999; 2000; 2001; 2002; 2003; Bonham, Basehart and Marchand, 2000; Keith and Bonham, 2005). Ultimately, quality of life, multidimensional as it is, has come to imply, for individuals and researchers alike, the notion of pursuit of excellence in common human values, and is generally associated with feelings of well-being, positive social involvement, and opportunity to reach personal potential (Schalock *et al.*, 2002).

Underlying assumptions and themes

In addition to the idea of multiple dimensions or domains as key components of quality of life, this area is characterized by other assumptions and working principles. These assumptions (also designated by Schalock *et al.*, 2002 as 'core ideas') include: (1) the notion that individual personal contexts (the environments of life, work, and play) are critical to quality of life; (2) that life is experienced differently by different people, or by the same people at different times (thus leading to a life-span approach); (3) that quality of life is holistic, with various domains interacting and affecting others; (4) that personal choice, control, and empowerment are important to the experience of quality of life; and (5) to understand quality of life, we must appreciate the significant role of subjective perception – that quality of life is, in other words, in the eyes of the beholder.

Keith and Schalock (2000) have predicted that these notions of quality of life are likely to be played out in the lives of people with intellectual disabilities in the context of four central conceptual themes: community; self-advocacy; culture; and aesthetics.

Community

A growing body of research has consistently demonstrated higher quality of life among people whose lifestyles approximate those of the 'normal' community, and that people with disabilities have too often been isolated from their communities (Keith and Schalock, 2000; Rapley, 2000). Community integration is a powerful determinant of quality of life.

Self-advocacy

Individuals with intellectual disabilities, like other people, want their voices to be heard and taken seriously. The connection among self-advocacy, self-determination, and empowerment is well established. Wehmeyer and Schwartz (1998) and Lachapelle, Wehmeyer, Haelewyck, Courbois, *et al.* (2005) showed the relationship between self-determination and quality of life, thus affirming Ward's assertion that quality of life is related to personal empowerment (Ward, 2000; Ward and Keith, 1996).

Culture

Cultural experience influences individual worldview (Matsumoto and Juang, 2004), personal sense of self (Markus and Kitayama, 1991), levels of individuality-communality (Myers, 1992), and views of disability (Watson, Barreira and Watson, 2000). It should come as no surprise, then, that cultural experience must be taken into consideration in defining and understanding one's quality of life. Care must be exercised when transporting research conclusions, values, or programmatic imperatives from one culture to another (Keith, 1996).

Aesthetics

Kupfer (1983) has suggested that the ordinary activities of life – such as relationships, work, education, and decision making – should be seen as opportunities for aesthetic experience. If we take seriously the idea that quality of life is concerned with achievement of excellence in the values of everyday life, then it is evident that a life of quality is likely to be a life carried out with as much grace and dignity as possible – a lifelong dance, if you will. Our role, then, becomes one of supporting and assisting an individual to this end, attempting, in the words of poet William Kloefkorn, to 'let the dance begin' (1981: 5).

In the end, perhaps it is sufficient simply to say that quality of life is a human goal comprising success and satisfaction with the experience of life, including happiness and contentment in its physical, emotional, social, financial, and professional dimensions (Watson and Keith, 2002). A definition of this sort, simple as it may seem on its surface, nevertheless provides sufficient complexity seriously to challenge those who might attempt its measurement. And finally, I should say that, as Cummins (2005b) suggested, our conceptual approach is likely to mature into a model capable of developing testable theory – including identification of causal variables that would allow more confidence in our assertions about those factors leading to improved quality of life.

APPROACHES TO THE ASSESSMENT OF QUALITY OF LIFE

Although measuring quality of life has a reasonably long history (Campbell, Converse and Rodgers, 1976; Thorndike, 1939), unanimity in techniques has not been achieved, and perhaps, for a variety of reasons, should not be a goal of measurement efforts. Quality of life, after all, can be seen in the objective conditions under which people live, work, and play, as well as in the subjective individual perceptions through which they may interpret such objective conditions (Campbell et al., 1976; Keith, 2001). Furthermore, the relationship between objective and subjective measures of quality of life remains far from clear, and, especially for people with intellectual disabilities, presents some essential concerns (Edgerton, 1996; Hatton, 1998; Parmenter, 1992).

Most measurement techniques designed for use with individuals of all ages with intellectual disabilities are multidimensional scales or question-naires (Schalock and Verdugo, 2002). However, direct behavioural measures (McGill, Emerson and Mansell, 1994; Rawlings, 1985), ethnographic approaches (Edgerton, 1991; 1996), and analysis of person–environment fit (discrepancy analysis) (Heal, Borthwick-Duffy and Saunders, 1996) have also been reported in the research literature. I have briefly reviewed these approaches elsewhere (Keith, 2001), and will focus attention in this chapter primarily on the most commonly used (and most extensively studied) multi-dimensional scales. I do this, however, with the caveat that quality of life should never be assessed with total reliance upon a single scale or technique. Instead, any particular measurement tool should be complemented by other approaches: such as direct behavioural measures (Felce, 2000; McGill *et al.*, 1994), assessment of support services (Felce and Perry, 1996), in-depth study of individual lives (Edgerton and Gaston, 1991), analysis of goodness of fit between individual and environment (Heal *et al.*, 1996), and recognition of the importance of self-determination (Lachappelle *et al.*, 2005; McComb, 2003; Wehmeyer and Schwartz, 1998).

Some important measurement concerns

I present the most commonly used measurement techniques with the full understanding that others (Hatton, 1998) have questioned the foundations of standardized measurement of quality of life, particularly as it may be played out in the potential conflict between the intended aims of an individual approach to quality of life and the aims of standardized measurement. Earlier, Taylor (1994) expressed the fear that quality of life might be trans-formed to 'QOL', with the latter term connoting a standardized approach that risks losing sight of the individual in the push to impose a particular lifestyle. Edgerton (1990) warned against the tendency to oversimplify quality of life in subjecting it to measurement via typical scales. Throughout this chapter, I deliberately choose to use the full phrase, 'quality of life', in lieu of the common term 'QOL', in order to attempt to keep the emphasis on the role of quality of life as a broad, guiding concept, and not a psychometric 'buzz-word'. Beyond the broad question of our ability to measure quality of life meaningfully, however, there are additional significant questions about *how* we conduct measurement.

Subjective or objective?

Although objective, readily measurable indicators (e.g. economic status, size of home, presence or absence of pets) have traditionally been associated with quality of life, the relationship between objective factors and more per-sonal subjective perceptions has become widely accepted as an important issue for quality-of-life measurement (Campbell *et al.*, 1976; Keith, 1996).

However, there seems to be only a modest relationship between economic income and subject well-being (Myers, 1992; 2000), and a number of investigators have reported weak relationships between objective and subjective aspects of quality of life (Edgerton, 1996; Hensel, Rose, Stenfert Kroese and Banks-Smith, 2002; Parmenter, 1992). Further, there are significant problems measuring subjective quality of life. These include the difficulty of subjective assessment of people with limited communicative skills (Hatton, 1998) and the possibility that subjective perceptions of well-being may be associated with traits of the individual as much as with environmental conditions (Edgerton, 1990; 1996).

Thus, no clear objective standards exist for overall quality-of-life assessment, and numerous observers have noted that some people might live quite happily (subjectively) in circumstances that would be unacceptable to others. The result is a recognition that, because subjective and objective quality of life do frequently differ, both must be taken into account (Cummins, 1999). Commonly used instruments have tended to do this (Cummins, 1997; Schalock and Keith, 1993). However, this state of affairs has not precluded deliberate attempts to measure subjective quality of life and recent work has continued to explore the connection between subjective and objective factors (Bramston, Bruggerman and Petty, 2002; Perry and Felce, 2002).

The problem of proxies or informants

Many individuals with intellectual disabilities, of course, experience communicative deficits that complicate the effort to measure their views on their personal well-being and life-satisfaction. Numerous investigators have recognized this fact, and some have made attempts to deal with the resulting dilemma (Brown, Brown and Bayer, 1994; Campo, Sharpton, Thompson and Sexton, 1996; Felce and Perry, 1995; Keith and Schalock, 1995; Oulette-Kuntz and McCreary, 1996; Schalock and Keith, 1993). Of these investigators, some have reported agreement between individuals with intellectual disabilities and their proxy respondents (Keith and Schalock, 1995; Keith, Schalock and Hoffman, 1986; McVilly, Burton-Smith and Davidson, 2000; Schalock and Keith, 1993; Stancliffe, 1999). However, these agreements have often been obtained by comparing proxy responses with those of individuals who actually *can* respond for themselves, thus calling into question conclusions generalized to proxy responses made on behalf of those who *cannot* speak for themselves.

Furthermore, proxy responses are sometimes not well correlated with the responses of individuals themselves (Perry and Felce, 2002). In addition, agreement has been found to be better for objective rather than subjective aspects of quality of life (Patrick and Erickson, 1993; Perry and Felce, 2002; Schalock, Keith and Hoffman, 1990). Thus, there are legitimate concerns that the reports of proxies simply may not adequately capture the perceptions of individuals with disabilities (Goode and Hogg, 1994; Heal and Sigelman, 1990; Stancliffe, 1995). Even the authors of scales calibrated for use by proxies (Schalock and Keith, 1993), as well as their critics (Hatton, 1998), have recognized the inherent limitations of judgements made by informants in lieu of those made by individuals themselves. It is also likely that the adequacy of proxy reports may vary widely depending on who the proxy is. Schalock and Keith (1993) specify that informants should be a family member or other person who knows the individual well, while Perry and Felce (2002) suggest the need for more research to illuminate the role of the relationship between individual and proxy. Suffice it to say that a proxy or other informant should never be used as a primary source of quality-of-life data in any case in which the individual can speak for him- or herself, and proxy reports should always be considered in the context of other information concerning the person's life circumstances and well-being.

QUALITY-OF-LIFE SCALES – A BRIEF REVIEW

In the field of intellectual disabilities, one of the first multidimensional quality-of-life scales was The Lifestyle Satisfaction Scale (Heal and Chadsey-Rusch, 1985). Its four subscales included Community Satisfaction, Friends and Free Time Satisfaction, Satisfaction with Services, and General Satisfaction. In later revisions, job satisfaction, satisfaction with interpersonal interactions, and recreation and leisure were added (Harner and Heal, 1993; Heal, Rubin, and Park, 1995).

At about the same time, Keith, Schalock, and Hoffman (1986) produced the first edition of the Quality of Life Questionnaire (QOL.Q), initially encompassing three quality-of-life factors (Social Relations, Community Involvement, and Environmental Control). This instrument was later revised (Schalock, Keith and Hoffman, 1990; Schalock and Keith, 1993), and its accompanying manual was updated more recently (Schalock and Keith, 2004). In its current version, the QOL.Q measures quality of life in four scales – Satisfaction, Productivity, Empowerment, and Social Belonging – and encompasses several domains, including social inclusion, self-determination, material well-being, personal development, and emotional well-being (Schalock and Verdugo, 2002). Although it was originally developed for use with adults with intellectual disabilities, the QOL.Q has been used successfully with other adult populations, including the elderly (Keith, 2001; Keith and Olvera, 2004), people with type A behaviour (Kashfian and Keith, 2003), and optimists and pessimists (Keith and Sieber, 2004). The QOL.Q (Schalock and Keith, 1993) has been translated into numerous languages, including French, Spanish, Japanese, Polish, and Chinese, among others, and its factor structure has proven sufficiently robust for cross-cultural use (Caballo, Crespo, Jenaro, Verdugo and Martinez, 2005;

Kober and Eggleton, 2002; Rapley and Lobley, 1995). It is applicable to populations with and without intellectual disabilities, thus allowing comparison of quality-of-life scores across groups (Keith and Ferdinand, 2000). Finally, its forty items are easily administered in a fairly short period of time.

Cummins (1991; 1992; 1993; and 1997) developed another widely used quality of life scale in a research programme producing the *Comprehensive Quality of Life Scale – Intellectual Disability* (ComQol-ID). This measure assesses seven domains: material well-being; physical well-being; productivity; intimacy; safety; community; and emotional well-being. This scale was developed specifically for applications with people with intellectual disabilities. The ComQol-ID (Cummins, 1997) also provides for evaluation of respondent acquiescence, an issue of some concern in assessment of quality of life (Heal and Sigelman, 1995; Perry and Felce, 2002; Rapley, 2000), and for determination of discriminative competence. In developing the ComQol-ID, Cummins (1991) stressed the role of personal values in determining the importance of the various quality-of-life domains for each individual.

A third multidimensional instrument, developed to measure the quality of life of people with severe disabilities is the Quality of Life Interview Schedule (QUOLIS; Oullette-Kuntz and McCreary, 1996). It is designed to measure twelve domains (health services, family guardianship, income maintenance, education-employment, housing and safety, transportation, social-recreational, religious-cultural, case management, advocacy, counselling, and aesthetics), and uses proxies as informants to speak on behalf of individuals who cannot be independently interviewed.

Schalock and Verdugo (2002) reviewed measurement techniques reported in multiple empirical studies in various domains in the quality-of-life research literature. Their analysis suggested that the two most frequently employed scales in research on quality of life for people with intellectual disabilities are various editions of the QOL.Q and the ComQol-ID. The popularity of these two instruments is in part explained by the fact that they share the following characteristics: (1) they are both multidimensional measures (assessing most of the commonly agreed quality-of-life domains); (2) they contain items tapping into objective and subjective aspects of quality of life; (3) they have good psychometric properties; (4) they allow for proxy respondents to reply on behalf of people who cannot respond for themselves; and (5) both have been the subject of extensive research.

Although to date the quality-of-life concept has been studied only to a limited degree among school-age children (Schalock and Verdugo, 2002), and little is known about the quality of life of school-age children with intellectual disabilities (Watson and Keith, 2002), some instruments have been developed with particular attention to the quality-of-life issues of children and adolescents. Several of these instruments place an emphasis on health-related quality of life (Zekovic and Renwick, 2003). Some, such as the Quality of Life Profile: Adolescent Version (QOLPAV; Raphael, Rukholm,

Brown, Hill-Bailey and Donato, 1996), have yet to be widely applied outside 'mainstream' student groups. One such scale, the *Quality of Student Life Questionnaire* (QSLQ; Keith and Schalock, 1994; 1995), was developed using samples of children with and without intellectual disabilities, and has been subsequently applied in research with these groups (Watson and Keith, 2002). The QSLQ measures quality of life using four scales: Satisfaction, Well-Being, Social Belonging, and Empowerment/Control.

USING QUALITY-OF-LIFE ASSESSMENTS EFFECTIVELY

Schalock and Verdugo (2002) discussed the application of the quality-of-life concept at three levels: individual, organizational, and societal. I will organize this discussion in a similar way, because I do not believe it useful (or perhaps even possible) to use quality-of-life measures at the individual clinical level without placing them in the broader context of organizations and cultures.

Individual applications

I begin this discussion with a cautionary word of advice: measures of quality of life should *never* be used in a prescriptive way, directing an individual to a particular lifestyle on the basis of an inflexible, imposed approach to assessment. Such a tactic would surely produce what Taylor (1994) termed the 'tyranny of QOL', with an accompanying risk of restricted freedom and personal satisfaction. In other words, no specific scale or test should become the standard by which all lives are measured. We must recognize the wide range of circumstances and standards that might be seen as acceptable or desirable to various individuals (Edgerton, 1990). The values of the individual should remain central to assessment of quality of life at the level of the person (Keith, 2001; Raphael, 1996; Renwick and Brown, 1996).

Does this admonition against the imposition of a quality-of-life structure on the lives of people mean that quality-of-life assessment is not meaningful at the level of the individual? Of course not. However, we must use the concept of quality of life to enhance the ability of individuals to achieve their own aims in life. Thus, if we take seriously the finding that self-determination is critical to quality of life (Lachapelle *et al.*, 2005; Wehmeyer and Schalock, 2001), then measures such as the Empowerment/Independence scale of the QOL.Q become important in assessing well-being in order to support the aspirations of individuals. Intervention should be aimed towards enabling the person to act on his or her own behalf in moving towards those aspirations. The quality-of-life measure may help us to clarify the individual's goals, but it cannot impose those goals.

To the extent that measurement of quality of life may serve as a sensitizing notion (Keith and Schalock, 2000), it can raise consciousness and provide guidance about the individual's perspective, as long as we keep the focus on the person and his or her environment and needs. For example, let us assume the quality-of-life scale asks, 'Do you have a pet?' as one question among many. Perhaps the individual (or family) has never actually considered the possibility of having a pet. In this case, the assessment may serve to raise awareness of options, and it is possible the person may choose to pursue such an option. But raising the question is not the same as assuming that having a pet is a requisite (or even a good) thing. Ultimately, autonomy, self-regulation, psychological empowerment, and self-realization are the aims of self-determination in pursuit of quality of life (Schalock and Verdugo, 2002).

Just as assessment of quality of life may raise the awareness of individuals themselves, so may it also increase the consciousness of family members and other programme planners. Protective family members may give no thought to the fact that their son or brother does not have a key to his own flat; but if the question is posed in a quality-of-life interview, a new possibility arises, opening the door to increased autonomy and personal control and, perhaps, to enhanced quality of life. In the US state of Massachusetts, a programme called Tools for Tomorrow (ARC of Massachusetts, 2003) engages individuals and their family members in the process of 'envisioning the future', not to prescribe a *particular* future for any one individual, but to encourage all people to broaden their horizons and to play a role in considering the real possibilities they might want in their lives.

It is this spirit of possibility in which quality-of-life scales, questionnaires, tests, or interviews must be undertaken. This is critical for the good administration of such instruments because, as Rapley (2000) has made clear, there are real dangers in this process if the individuals interviewed come to believe that there are 'correct' responses, or that giving wrong answers might somehow affect their life situations. Rapley points out that the interview does not produce data 'belonging' solely to the interviewee, but that the exchange is one conducted jointly with the interviewer. It is therefore crucial that the interviewer realize that he or she has the power to include or exclude various aspects of the interviewee's responses, particularly if the format is highly structured or inflexible. The message to clinicians or others who conduct such interviews, then, is to respect the integrity of the individual's responses and to be certain that questions or other aspects of the questionnaire material are worded (or reworded) in such a way as to be clearly understandable (Schalock and Keith, 1993). One interesting approach to this problem has been undertaken in the US state of Maryland, where the *Ask Me!* project (Bonham *et al.*, 2000; Keith and Bonham, 2005; Schalock, Bonham and Marchand, 2000) of the ARC of Maryland has employed individuals with intellectual disabilities as interviewers in assessing the quality of life of their peers.

Organizational applications

It has long been recognized that human service organizations should work to maximize the dignity, development, and well-being of people with intellectual disabilities (Menolascino, 1977). Landesman (1986) proposed that the concept of quality of life should be helpful in the pursuit of innovative programmes and their evaluation. Quality of life has been proposed as an evaluative tool for students making the transition from school to adult life (Halpern, 1993), in aging (Brown, 1989), in rehabilitation (Fabian, 1991), and in residential services (Bellamy, Newton, LeBaron and Horner, 1990). And Felce (2000) has shown the role of such organizational features as staff training and engagement in activity as determinants of quality of life.

The use of quality-of-life measures as outcome indicators has shown differences among various organizational service delivery arrangements for both residential and employment settings (Harner and Heal, 1993; Heal and Chadsey-Rusch, 1985; Keith, Schalock and Hoffman, 1986; Otrębski, 2000; Schalock, Keith and Hoffman, 1990). Findings generally indicate that quality-of-life scores increase as service models become more like those of normal community life. Furthermore, in a large American sample, Gardner, Carran and Nudler (2001) found a number of differences, particularly in choice, autonomy, attainment, and affiliation, associated with organizational size (the largest organizations were associated with lower measured levels of these constructs).

In the US state of Nebraska, the ARC of Nebraska (1998; 1999; 2000; 2001; 2002; and 2003), working cooperatively with the state government, publishes an annual compendium of quality-of-life data from virtually all service delivery programmes in the state. This volume, known as the *Provider Profiles*, summarizes data on nine quality-of-life domains for the clientele of service providers in more than forty cities, as well as information on types of services provided, number of people served, staffing, staff training, quality-of-life enhancement activities, and quality assurance activities. Any individual can use this information to make decisions about choice of services, evaluate current services, or compare various aspects of organizations providing services. Likewise, in the state of Maryland, the state administration uses data collected annually, in the *Ask Me!* project, from statewide samples of people with intellectual disabilities to develop organizational goals and to monitor achievements (Keith and Bonham, 2005). These projects may change, in a real way, the relationship between individuals and service providers as they work to enhance quality of life.

In their discussion of organizational-level applications of the concept of quality of life, Schalock and Verdugo (2002) set forth a rather ambitious agenda for determination of organizational context, evaluation, and change, all based upon outcomes associated with quality of life. Their focus is the relationship between organizational characteristics and the opportunities (or impediments) they present for enhanced individual quality of life. This is an approach that is critical to development of programmes that are responsive to individual satisfaction and tied to personal quality of life. In addition to the Nebraska *Provider Profiles*, and the Maryland *Ask Me!* project, the Tools for Tomorrow approach of the ARC of Massachusetts (2003) illustrates another effort to make this connection.

Societal applications

Individuals and organizations exist within societies and cultures. Thus, personal well-being is inexorably linked to a wide range of societal policies, characteristics, and practices, resulting in quite different conditions and possibilities for citizens of different countries (Goel, 2000; McConkey and O'Toole, 2000; Walsh, 2000; Watson, 2000). Although this might suggest that quality of life is largely determined by social conditions and policy, some writers have proposed a significant role for individual quality-of-life outcome data in determining public policy (Gardner *et al.*, 2001; Turnbull and Brunk, 1997).

A wide range of quality-of-life issues both govern, and are governed by, societal-level factors (Schalock and Verdugo, 2002). Some of these are of direct relevance to the clinician interested in assessing individual quality of life. For example, cultural assumptions about the causes of disabilities or disorders may affect clinical views of the individual (Matsumoto and Juang, 2004), and the sense of self in relation to society may be significantly influenced by the cultural context (Keith, 1996). As a result, quality-of-life notions may sometimes be quite useful in setting programmatic direction within a culture, but more limited when compared with other cultures (Keith, 1996), whereas at other times (or in contrast to other ideas) they may transcend the boundaries of culture (Davies, 1986). For example, the value of work (or the so-called 'work ethic') may vary across cultures (Lobley, 1992) in contrast to the concept of human rights, which are the subject of a large number of international treaties and conventions concerning individuals with disabilities (Schalock and Verdugo, 2002).

The key issue in societal applications, as in organizational applications, is that assessment of quality of life for individuals is clearly related to the broader context. Those who would undertake measurement of quality of life must take stock of the cultural backdrop, social customs, and views of disability extant in the settings in which they work.

ADVICE FOR CLINICIANS WORKING WITH QUALITY OF LIFE

I will begin my advice to clinicians adopting a quality-of-life perspective by paraphrasing several principles offered by Edgerton (1996: 83): (1) quality of life, although it may be measured objectively, is always experienced subject-ively; (2) living standards alone do not determine individual feelings of well-being; (3) a single standard for quality of life cannot satisfy everyone; (4) personal choice should be the basis of action taken to enhance quality of life; and (5) people with intellectual disabilities must be encouraged to participate in planning that involves their own quality of life. Respecting these principles, and the dignity of people for whom we care, suggests, I believe, six clinical imperatives.

1. Any effort to evaluate quality of life must be multidimensional

This means not only choosing an instrument capable of sampling multiple quality-of-life domains, but also examining other key aspects of individual life: nature of life settings (home, work, community); personal control and voice in key settings; friends and family; and the rhythm and flow of daily life.

2. Assessment must be conducted in a comfortable, meaningful way that does not connote a 'testing' context

As Antaki and Rapley (1996) have suggested, it is far too easy for an inter-viewer or tester to direct or select individual responses in a manner that may lose sight of the voice and intent of the person whose quality of life is under scrutiny. Quality-of-life assessment is a conversation, jointly undertaken, intended to provide opportunity for the personal views and wishes of the individual to be articulated and respected.

3. The views of others, variously identified as proxies, informants, advocates, and so forth, should never be seen as an adequate substitute for the voice and the perspective of the individual him/herself

When resorting to these sources of information we must solicit a range of views, and we must collect other kinds of data (beyond interviews or scales) from the person (direct behavioural observation, assessment of program-matic activity, etc.). After all, although I have no doubt that my mother would have my best interests at heart, I also know that her wishes for me would not always coincide with my own, and so it is for many people with intellectual disabilities. I am reminded of a friend who once gave a talk titled 'Would You Like to Go to Church, or Would You Rather Watch *The Lone Ranger*?' My friend, wishing to respect the right of non-verbal individuals to participate in religious activities if they liked, but not wanting to impose such activities on those who might not want them, arranged to provide samples of both: church services and televised reruns of *The Lone Ranger* (a popular US television series, chosen because it was scheduled on local TV at the same time as Sunday morning religious services). The behaviour of individuals during the two activities was then taken as an indicator of their wishes. Some people appeared to enjoy the activities at the church. Others seemed more at home watching *The Lone Ranger*. The wishes of both groups were respected. This was not, however, an outcome that would have been possible if only a questionnaire or interview had been employed.

4. Individual quality-of-life data need not always be compared to the data of other people

The fact that quality of life is, in many ways, a subjective phenomenon, means that individuals need not always strive to be like others. On the other hand, there are times when it is clear that the data indicate an abridgement of rights, restriction of personal autonomy, or obviously dangerous or substandard living conditions, and good clinical judgement indicates the importance of assessing one's quality of life in relation to a reasonable community standard. Unfortunately, to date most investigations in which quality-of-life measures of people with intellectual disabilities have been compared to the broader community have shown those with disabilities to have a measured quality of life that is lower than the mainstream community (Keith and Bonham, 2005; Keith and Ferdinand, 2000; Kishi, Teelucksingh, Zollers, Park-Lee and Meyer, 1988; Sands and Kozleski, 1994). When these discrepancies are apparent, it is certainly appropriate to use individual quality-of-life data as a consciousness-raising tool for service providers or the community.

5. Care must be taken to get beyond superficial judgements of standard social values (such as community integration)

Research evidence suggests that simply living *in* the community is not the same as being a meaningful member *of* the community (Bramston, Bruggerman and Petty, 2002). Far too many people live in the community in isolation and loneliness. If we take the importance of meaningful interaction with others seriously, our assessments must not treat quality of life as nothing more than another individual attribute (Rapley, 2000), but must truly examine the interconnected role of the person in his or her context.

6. Living standards alone do not constitute quality of life

As Edgerton (1996) argued, individuals may differ in their sensitivity to environmental variables, and better places to live or better jobs do not necessarily produce lasting changes in personal perception of well-being.

Furthermore, Gardner, Carran and Nudler (2001) found that health and safety measures did not vary in concert with other quality-of-life indicators across types and sizes of service organizations. Thus, although no responsible person would want to see any individual living or working in substandard conditions, it is important to understand that improvement in these objective circumstances alone is not likely to produce long-range changes in quality of life.

CONCLUSION

Evaluating quality of life is at once fraught with dangers and frustrations and ripe with opportunity and potential. Is it, as Hermie observed, in the movie *Summer of '42*, a great idea if we can simply 'overlook the fact that it is impossible?' Or is it, as James Watson thought, upon grasping the double-helix structure of DNA, 'too pretty not to be true?' Assessing quality of life can be either, or both. If it is undertaken reasonably, in concert with the individual and with sensitivity to personal needs and wishes, the possibilities are great for improved lives and personal well-being. On the other hand, if approached as simply another way to test people or to gather data, quality of life may become, as Wolfensberger (1994: 285) argued, merely a 'hopeless term'.

The outcome depends, in large measure, upon the approach taken by those in clinical, programmatic, and advocacy roles. If we heed the voices of individuals with intellectual disabilities, who tell us 'people have to have a life of their own' (Williams and Schoultz, 1982: 194), the quality-of-life movement may prove revolutionary. For this to happen, those in evaluative roles must be flexible, open-minded, and committed to assessment aimed towards hearing and honouring the voices of the people. We could then all be dreamers, and none of us would be the only one.

EXERCISES

I should say at the outset of this section that I am reluctant to characterize assessment of quality of life as a *clinical* enterprise, *per se*, to the extent that the term clinical may suggest a grappling with abnormality, or something gone awry. I say this in recognition of the fact that we have come to accept that quality of life is, at least in large part, defined in the subjective view of the individual. It is thus risky, in dealing with any particular person, to assume the existence of a 'correct' or 'normal' state of affairs (although increasingly, evidence suggests the general possibility that satisfaction and a positive outlook may be the normal baseline for humans (Cummins, 2005a)). However, there are some ways in which a clinician can become better prepared to assist individuals in enhancement of their quality of life.

A   **How about your quality of life?** Ask yourself what factors are important to *you* in thinking about your own quality of life. These will not, of course, necessarily be the issues of greatest importance to someone else, but the exercise may help you to begin to conceptualize quality of life from the point of view of an individual. In particular, notice that you are likely to include dimensions that would be *nice*, or *pleasant* – not just those things you *need*. Human service workers have a long history of assessment based upon determining gaps between current status and perceived needs; it is important to realize that no one ever learned to play a musical instrument or a sport because an assessment identified it as a *need*. Quality of life often depends upon having the imagination to see what would be *good* to do, not what one *must* do.

B   **What about your community?** Think about your own community or city. Identify typical indicators of quality of life that might be meaningful to a person living there. We know that quality of life varies, not only across cultures, but from place to place within cultures. Although community standards should not dictate the aspirations of individual residents, they may be good indicators of the kinds of goals that might be important to one living there, and a clinician should have some awareness of this reality.

C   **Practise talking with individuals about quality of life.** As Rapley (2003) made clear in his discussion of conversation analysis, interviews about quality of life can be dramatically altered by the dynamics ensuing between the interviewer and the interviewee. In preparing to interview an individual about his or her quality of life, you must give careful thought to the words you will use, the tone you will use in asking questions, and above all, establishment of an environment that will allow the individual's thoughts, wishes, and aspirations to be heard as straightforwardly as possible.

FURTHER READING FOR PARENTS AND FAMILIES

The ARC of Massachusetts (2003). *Tools for Tomorrow*. Waltham, MA, 2003 USA: ARC Massachusetts.

The ARC of Nebraska (2003). *2003 Nebraska Developmental Disabilities Provider Profiles*. Lincoln, NE, USA: ARC Nebraska.

Bonham, G. S., Basehart, S. and Marchand, C. B. (2000). *Ask Me! FY 2000*. Annapolis, MD, USA: ARC of Maryland.

Keith, K. D. (1990). Quality of life: Issues in community integration. In R. L. Schalock (ed.), *Quality of life: Perspectives and Issues* (pp. 93–100). Washington, DC: American Association on Mental Retardation.

Keith, K. D. and Schalock, R. L. (1995). *Quality of Student Life Questionnaire*. Worthington, OH, USA: IDS.

McComb, D. (2003). If not self-determination, then what? *Mental Retardation*, 41, 290–8.

Myers, D. G. (1992). *The Pursuit of Happiness: Who is Happy – and Why*. New York: William Morrow.

Renwick, R., Brown, I. and Raphael, D. (2000). Person-centred quality of life: Contributions from Canada to an international understanding. In K. D. Keith and R. L. Schalock (eds), *Cross-Cultural Perspectives on Quality of Life* (pp. 5–21). Washington, DC: American Association on Mental Retardation.

Ward, N. (2000). The universal power of speaking for oneself. In K. D. Keith and R. L. Schalock (eds), *Cross-Cultural Perspectives on Quality of Life* (pp. 33–6). Washington, DC: American Association on Mental Retardation.

Ward, N. A. and Keith, K. D. (1996). Self-advocacy: Foundation for quality of life. In R. L. Schalock (ed.), *Quality of Life: Volume I. Conceptualization and Measurement* (pp. 5–10). Washington, DC: American Association on Mental Retardation.

Wehmeyer, M. L. and Schalock, R. L. (2001). Self-determination and quality of life: Implications for special education services and supports. *Focus on Exceptional Children*, 33(3), 1–16.

Zekovic, B. and Renwick, R. (2003). Quality of life for children and adolescents with developmental disabilities: Review of conceptual and methodological issues relevant to public policy. *Disability and Society*, 18, 19–34.

FURTHER READING FOR CLINICIANS

Antaki, C. and Rapley, M. (1996). 'Quality of life' talk: The liberal paradox of psychological testing. *Discourse and Society*, 7(3), 293–316.

The ARC of Nebraska (2003). *2003 Nebraska Developmental Disabilities Provider Profiles*. Lincoln, NE: ARC of Nebraska.

Bonham, G. S., Basehard, S. and Marchand, C. B. (2000). *Ask Me! FY 2000*. Annapolis, MD, USA: ARC of Maryland.

Cummins, R. A. (1997). *Comprehensive Quality of Life Scale – Intellectual Disability* (5th edn). Melbourne, Australia: Deakin University School of Psychology.

Cummins, R. A. (1999). A psychometric evaluation of the Comprehensive Quality of Life Scale (5th edn). In L. L. Yuan, B. Yuen and C. Low (eds), *Urban Quality of Life: Critical Issues and Options* (pp. 51–9). Singapore: University of Singapore Press.

Cummins, R. A. (2005). Caregivers as managers of subjective well-being: A homeostatic perspective. *Journal of Applied Research in Intellectual Disabilities*, 18, 335–44.

Felce, D. (2000). Engagement in activity as an indicator of quality of life in British research. In K. D. Keith and R. L. Schalock (eds), *Cross-Cultural Perspectives on Quality of Life* (pp. 173–90). Washington, DC: American Association on Mental Retardation.

Felce, D. and Perry, J. (1995). Quality of life: Its definition and measurement. *Research in Developmental Disabilities*, 16, 51–74.

Gardner, J., Carran, D. T. and Nudler, S. (2001). Measuring quality of life and quality of services through personal outcome measures: Implications for public policy. *International Review of Research in Mental Retardation*, 24, 75–100.

Heal, L. W. and Chadsey-Rusch, J. (1985). The Lifestyle Satisfaction Scale (LSS):

Assessing individuals' satisfaction with residence, community setting, and associated services. *Applied Research in Mental Retardation*, 6, 475–90.

Heal, L. and Sigelman, C. K. (1995). Response biases in interviews of individuals with limited mental ability. *Journal of Intellectual Disability Research*, 39, 331–40.

Hughes, C., Hwang, B., Kim, J., Eisenman, L. T. and Killian, D. J. (1995). Quality of life in applied research: A review and analysis of empirical measures. *American Journal on Mental Retardation*, 99, 623–41.

Keith, K. D. (2001). International quality of life: Current conceptual, measurement, and implementation issues. *International Review of Research in Mental Retardation*, 24, 49–74.

Keith, K. D. and Schalock, R. L. (1995). *Quality of Student Life Questionnaire.* Worthington, OH, USA: IDS.

Lachappelle, Y., Wehmeyer, M. L., Haelewyck, M.-C., Courbois, Y., Keith, K. D., Schalock, R. L., Verdugo, M. A. and Walsh, P. N. (2005). The relationship between quality of life and self-determination: An international study. *Journal of Intellectual Disability Research*, 49, 740–4.

McComb, D. (2003). If not self-determination, then what? *Mental Retardation*, 41, 290–8.

McVilly, K., Burton-Smith, R. and Davidson, J. (2000). Concurrence between subject and proxy ratings of quality of life for people with and without intellectual disabilities. *Journal of Intellectual Disability Research*, 44, 19–39.

Myers, D. G. (1992). *The Pursuit of Happiness: Who is Happy – and Why.* New York: William Morrow.

Oulette-Kuntz, H. and McCreary, B. (1996). Quality of life assessment for persons with severe developmental disabilities. In R. Renwick, I. Brown and M. Nagler (eds), *Quality of Life in Health Promotion and Rehabilitation: Conceptual Approaches, Issues, and Applications* (pp. 268–78). Thousand Oaks, CA, USA: Sage.

Perry, J. and Felce, D. (2002). Subjective and objective quality of life assessment: Responsiveness, response bias, and resident: proxy concurrence. *Mental Retardation*, 40, 445–56.

Rapley, M. (2000). The social construction of quality of life: The interpersonal production of well-being revisited. In K. D. Keith and R. L. Schalock (eds), *Cross-Cultural Perspectives on Quality of Life* (pp. 155–72). Washington, DC: American Association on Mental Retardation.

Renwick, R., Brown, I. and Raphael, D. (2000). Person-centred quality of life: Contributions from Canada to an international understanding. In K. D. Keith and R. L. Schalock (eds), *Cross-Cultural Perspectives on Quality of Life* (pp. 5–21). Washington, DC: American Association on Mental Retardation.

Schalock, R. L., Brown, I., Brown, R., Cummins, R. A., Felce, D., Matikka, L., Keith, K. D. and Parmenter, T. (2002). Conceptualization, measurement, and application of quality of life for persons with intellectual disabilities: Report of an international panel of experts. *Mental Retardation*, 40, 457–70.

Schalock, R. L. and Keith, K. D. (1993; 2004). *Quality of Life Questionnaire.* Worthington, OH, USA: IDS.

Schalock, R. L. and Verdugo, M. A. (2002). *Handbook on Quality of Life for Human Service Practitioners.* Washington, DC: American Association on Mental Retardation.

Taylor, S. J. and Bodgan, R. (1996). Quality of life and the individual's perspective. In R. L. Schalock (ed.), *Quality of Life: Volume I. Conceptualization and Measurement* (pp. 11–22). Washington, DC: American Association on Mental Retardation.

Walsh, P. N. (2000). Quality of life and social inclusion. In K. D. Keith and R. L. Schalock (eds), *Cross-Cultural Pespectives on Quality of Life* (pp. 315–26). Washington, DC: American Association on Mental Retardation.

Ward, N. (2000). The universal power of speaking for oneself. In K. D. Keith and R. L. Schalock (eds), *Cross-Cultural Perspectives on Quality of Life* (pp. 33–6). Washington, DC: American Association on Mental Retardation.

Williams, P. and Shoultz, B. (1982). *We Can Speak for Ourselves*. London: Souvenir Press.

WEBSITES

Australian Centre on Quality of Life: http://acqol.deakin.edu.au

Beach Centre on Disability of the University of Kansas: http://www.beachcentre.org

European Commission Community Research Page for Quality of Life and Management of Living Resources: http://www.cordis.lu/life

Finnish Association on Mental Retardation: www.kehitysvammaliitto.fi/frontpage

Quality of Life Research Unit of the University of Toronto: http://www.utoronto.ca/qol

Welsh Centre for Learning Disabilities: http://www.cardiff.ac.uk/medicine/psychological_medicine/research/welsh_centre_learning_disabilities/index.htm

World Health Organization Quality of Life Page: http://www.who.int/evidence/assessment-instruments/qol

REFERENCES

Amado, A. N., Conklin, F. and Wells, J. (1990). *Friends: A Manual for Connecting Persons with Disabilities and Community Members*. St. Paul, MN, USA: Human Services Research and Development Centre.

Antaki, C. and Rapley, M. (1996). 'Quality of life' talk: The liberal paradox of psychological testing. *Discourse and Society*, 7(3), 293–316.

ARC of Massachusetts (2003). *Tools for Tomorrow*. Waltham, MA, USA: ARC of Massachusetts.

ARC of Nebraska. (1998). *1998 Nebraska Developmental Disabilities Service Provider Profiles*. Lincoln, NE, USA: ARC of Nebraska.

ARC of Nebraska (1999). *1999 Nebraska Developmental Disabilities Provider Profiles*. Lincoln, NE, USA: ARC of Nebraska.

ARC of Nebraska (2000). *2000 Nebraska Developmental Disabilities Provider Profiles*. Lincoln, NE, USA: ARC of Nebraska.

ARC of Nebraska (2001). *2001 Nebraska Developmental Disabilities Provider Profiles*. Lincoln, NE, USA: ARC of Nebraska.

ARC of Nebraska (2002). *2002 Nebraska Developmental Disabilities Provider Profiles*. Lincoln, NE, USA: ARC of Nebraska.

ARC of Nebraska (2003). *2003 Nebraska Developmental Disabilities Provider Profiles.* Lincoln, NE, USA: ARC of Nebraska.

Bellamy, G. T., Newton, J. S., LeBaron, N. M. and Horner, R. H. (1990). Quality of life and lifestyle outcomes: A challenge for residential programs. In R. L. Schalock (ed.), *Quality of Life: Perspectives and Issues* (pp. 127–37). Washington, DC: American Association on Mental Retardation.

Bonham, G. S., Basehart, S. and Marchand, C. B. (2000). *Ask Me! FY 2000.* Annapolis, MD, USA: ARC of Maryland.

Bramston, P., Bruggerman, K. and Petty, G. (2002). Community perspectives and subjective quality of life. *International Journal of Disability, Development and Education*, 49, 385–97.

Brown, R. I. (1989). Aging, disability and quality of life: A challenge for society. *Canadian Psychology*, 30, 551–9.

Brown, R. I., Bayer, M. and McFarlane, C. (1989). *Rehabilitation Programmes: Performance and Quality of Life of Adults with Developmental Handicaps.* Toronto: Lugus Productions.

Brown, R. I., Brown, P. M. and Bayer, M. B. (1994). A quality of life model: New challenges arising from a six year study. In D. Goode (ed.), *Quality of Life for Persons with Disabilities: International Perspectives and Issues* (pp. 39–56). Cambridge, MA, USA: Brookline.

Caballo, C., Crespo, M., Janaro, C., Verdugo, M. A. and Martinez, J. L. (2005). Factor structure of the Schalock and Keith Quality of Life Questionnaire (QOL-Q): Validation on Mexican and Spanish samples. *Journal of Intellectual Disability Research*, 49, 773–6.

Campbell, A., Converse, P. and Rodgers, W. L. (1976). *The Quality of American Life: Perceptions, Evaluations, and Satisfactions.* New York: Russell Sage Foundation.

Campo, S. F., Sharpton, W. R., Thompson, B. and Sexton, D. (1996). Measurement Characteristics of the Quality of Life Index when used with adults with severe/profound disabilities. *American Journal on Mental Retardation*, 100, 546–50.

Cummins, R. A. (1991). The Comprehensive Quality of Life Scale – Intellectual Disability: An instrument under development. *Australia and New Zealand Journal of Developmental Disabilities*, 17, 259–64.

Cummins, R. A. (1992). *Comprehensive Quality of Life Scale – Intellectual Disability* (3rd edn). Melbourne, Australia: Deakin University Press.

Cummins, R. A. (1993). *Comprehensive Quality of Life Scale – Intellectual Disability* (4th edn). Melbourne, Australia: Deakin University Press.

Cummins, R. A. (1995). Assessing quality of life. In R. I. Brown (ed.), *Quality of Life for Handicapped People* (pp. 102–20). London: Chapman and Hall.

Cummins, R. A. (1997). *Comprehensive Quality of Life Scale – Intellectual Disability* (5th edn). Melbourne, Australia: Deakin University School of Psychology.

Cummins, R. A. (1999). A psychometric evaluation of the Comprehensive Quality of Life Scale (5th edn). In L. L. Yuan, B. Yuen and C. Low (eds), *Urban Quality of Life: Critical Issues and Options* (pp. 51–9). Singapore: University of Singapore Press.

Cummins, R. A. (2005a). Caregivers as managers of subjective well-being: A homeostatic perspective. *Journal of Applied Research in Intellectual Disabilities*, 18, 335–44.

Cummins, R. A. (2005b). Moving from the quality of life concept to a theory. *Journal of Intellectual Disability Research*, 49, 699–706.

Davies, N. (1986). *A Comparative Analysis of Services for the Mentally Handicapped in Nebraska and Britain.* Unpublished thesis, University of Birmingham, Birmingham, England.

Edgerton, R. B. (1990). Quality of life from a longitudinal research perspective. In R. L. Schalock (ed.), *Quality of Life: Perspectives and Issues* (pp. 149–60). Washington, DC: American Association on Mental Retardation.

Edgerton, R. B. (1991). Preface. In R. B. Edgerton and M. A. Gaston (eds), *'I've Seen It All!'* (pp. vii–x). Baltimore, MD, USA: Paul H. Brookes.

Edgerton, R. B. (1996). A longitudinal-ethnographic research perspective on quality of life. In R. L. Schalock (ed.), *Quality of Life: Volume I. Conceptualization and Measurement* (pp. 83–90). Washington, DC: American Association on Mental Retardation.

Edgerton, R. B. and Gaston, M. A. (eds). (1991). *'I've Seen It All!'* Baltimore, MD, USA: Paul H. Brookes.

Fabian, E. S. (1991). Using quality-of-life indicators in rehabilitation program evaluation. *Rehabilitation Counseling Bulletin,* 34, 344–56.

Felce, D. (1996). *Defining and Applying the Concept of Quality of Life.* Paper presented at the World Congress of the International Association for Scientific Study of Intellectual Disabilities, Helsinki, Finland, July.

Felce, D. (2000). Engagement in activity as an indicator of quality of life in British research. In K. D. Keith and R. L. Schalock (eds), *Cross-Cultural Perspectives on Quality of Life* (pp. 173–90). Washington, DC: American Association on Mental Retardation.

Felce, D., and Perry, J. (1995). Quality of life: Its definition and measurement. *Research in Developmental Disabilities,* 16, 51–74.

Felce, D. and Perry, J. (1996). Exploring current conceptions of quality of life. In R. Renwick, I. Brown and M. Nagler (eds), *Quality of Life in Health Promotion and Rehabilitation: Conceptual Approaches, Issues, and Applications* (pp. 51–62). Thousand Oaks, CA, USA: Sage.

Gardner, J., Carran, D. T. and Nudler, S. (2001). Measuring quality of life and quality of services through personal outcome measures: Implications for public policy. *International Review of Research in Mental Retardation,* 24, 75–100.

Goel, S. K. (2000). Improving quality of life in India: Challenges and emerging concerns. In K. D. Keith and R. L. Schalock (eds), *Cross-Cultural Perspectives on Quality of Life* (pp. 231–9). Washington, DC: American Association on Mental Retardation.

Goode, D. and Hogg, J. (1994). Towards an understanding of holistic quality of life in people with profound intellectual and multiple disabilities. In D. Goode (ed.), *Quality of Life for Persons with Disabilities: International Perspectives and Issues* (pp. 197–207). Cambridge, MA, USA: Brookline.

Halpern, A. S. (1993). Quality of life as a conceptual framework for evaluating transition outcomes. *Exceptional Children,* 59, 486–98.

Harner, C. J. and Heal, L. W. (1993). The Multifaceted Lifestyle Satisfaction Scale (MLSS): Psychometric properties of an interview schedule for assessing personal satisfaction of adults with limited intelligence. *Research in Developmental Disabilities,* 14, 221–36.

Hatton, C. (1998). Whose quality of life is it anyway? Some problems with the emerging quality of life consensus. *Mental Retardation,* 33, 295–303.

Heal, L. W., Borthwick-Duffy, S. A. and Saunders, R. R. (1996). Assessment of quality of life. In J. W. Jacobson and J. A. Mulick (eds), *Manual of Diagnosis and Professional Practices in Mental Retardation* (pp. 199–209). Washington, DC: American Psychological Association.

Heal, L. W. and Chadsey-Rusch, J. (1985). The Lifestyle Satisfaction Scale (LSS): Assessing individuals' satisfaction with residence, community setting, and associated services. *Applied Research in Mental Retardation*, 6, 475–90.

Heal, L. W., Rubin, S. S. and Park, W. (1995). *Lifestyle Satisfaction Scale.* Champaign-Urbana, IL, USA: Transition Research Institute, University of Illinois.

Heal, L. W. and Sigelman, C. K. (1990). Methodological issues in measuring the quality of life of individuals with mental retardation. In R. L. Schalock (ed.), *Quality of Life: Perspectives and Issues* (pp. 161–76). Washington, DC: American Association on Mental Retardation.

Heal, L. W. and Sigelman, C. K. (1995). Response biases in interviews of individuals with limited mental ability. *Journal of Intellectual Disability Research*, 39, 331–40.

Hensel, E. (2001). Is satisfaction a valid concept in the assessment of quality of life of people with intellectual disabilities? A review of the literature. *Journal of Applied Research in Intellectual Disabilities*, 14, 311–26.

Hensel, E., Rose, J., Stenfert Kroese, B. and Banks-Smith, J. (2002). Subjective judgements of quality of life: A comparison study between people with intellectual disability and those without disability. *Journal of Intellectual Disability Research*, 46, 95–107.

Hughes, C. and Hwang, B. (1996). Attempts to conceptualize and measure quality of life. In R. L. Schalock (ed.), *Quality of Life: Volume I. Conceptualization and Measurement.* (pp. 51–61). Washington, DC: American Association on Mental Retardation.

Hughes, C., Hwang, B., Kim, J., Eisenman, L. T. and Killian, D. J. (1995). Quality of life in applied research: A review and analysis of empirical measures. *American Journal on Mental Retardation*, 99, 623–41.

Kashfian, S. and Keith, K. D. (2003). *Is there a Correlation between Quality of Life and Type A Personality?* Poster presented at the annual meeting of the Western Psychological Association, Vancouver, BC, Canada, May.

Keith, K. D. (1990). Quality of life: Issues in community integration. In R. L. Schalock (ed.), *Quality of Life: Perspectives and Issues* (pp. 93–100). Washington, DC: American Association on Mental Retardation.

Keith, K. D. (1996). Measuring quality of life across cultures: Issues and challenges. In R. L. Schalock (ed.), *Quality of Life: Volume I. Conceptualization and Measurement* (pp. 73–82). Washington, DC: American Association on Mental Retardation.

Keith, K. D. (2001). International quality of life: Current conceptual, measurement, and implementation issues. *International Review of Research in Mental Retardation*, 24, 49–74.

Keith, K. D. and Bonham, G. S. (2005). The use of quality of life data at the organization and systems level. *Journal of Intellectual Disability Research*, 49, 799–805.

Keith, K. D. and Ferdinand, L. R. (2000). *Project to Compare Quality of Life of Nebraskans with Developmental Disabilities and Citizens without Disabilities.* Lincoln, NE, USA: Governor's Planning Council on Developmental Disabilities.

Keith, K. D., Heal, L. W. and Schalock, R. L. (1996). Cross-cultural measurement of critical quality of life concepts. *Journal of Intellectual and Developmental Disability*, 21, 273–93.

Keith, K. D. and Olvera, T. E. (2004). *Lives of Older People: Quality of Life Interviews and Narratives*. Poster presented at the annual meeting of the Western Psychological Association, Phoenix, AZ, USA, April.

Keith, K. D. and Schalock, R. L. (1994). The measurement of quality of life in adolescence: The Quality of Student Life Questionnaire. *The American Journal of Family Therapy*, 22(1), 83–7.

Keith, K. D. and Schalock, R. L. (1995). *Quality of Student Life Questionnaire*. Worthington, OH, USA: IDS.

Keith, K. D. and Schalock, R. L. (2000). Cross-cultural perspectives on quality of life: Trends and themes. In K. D. Keith and R. L. Schalock (eds), *Cross-Cultural Perspectives on Quality of Life* (pp. 363–80). Washington, DC: American Association on Mental Retardation.

Keith, K. D., Schalock, R. L. and Hoffman, K. (1986). *Quality of Life: Measurement and Programmatic Implications*. Lincoln, NE, USA: Region V Mental Retardation Services.

Keith, K. D. and Sieber, J. (2004). *Quality of Life and Explanatory Style: Optimism, Pessimism, and Satisfaction*. Poster presented at the annual meeting of the Western Psychological Association, Phoenix, AZ, USA, April.

Kishi, G., Teelucksingh, B., Zollers, N., Park-Lee, S. and Meyer, L. (1988). Daily decision-making in community residences: A social comparison of adults with and without mental retardation. *American Journal on Mental Retardation*, 92, 430–5.

Kloefkorn, W. (1981). *Let the Dance Begin*. Pittsford, NY, USA: State Street Press.

Kober, R. and Eggleton, I. R. C. (2002). Factor stability of the Schalock and Keith (1993) Quality of Life Questionnaire. *Mental Retardation*, 40, 157–65.

Kupfer, J. H. (1983). *Experience as Art: Aesthetics in Everyday Life*. Albany, NY, USA: State University of New York Press.

Lachappelle, Y., Wehmeyer, M. L., Haelewyck, M.-C., Courbois, Y., Keith, K. D., Schalock, R. L., Verdugo, M. A. and Walsh, P. N. (2005). The relationship between quality of life and self-determination: An international study. *Journal of Intellectual Disability Research*, 49, 740–4.

Landesman, S. (1986). Quality of life and personal life satisfaction: Definition and measurement issues. *Mental Retardation*, 24, 141–3.

Lobley, J. (1992). *Community Living for People with Learning Disabilities: Is Quality of Life a Useful Guiding Concept?* Unpublished thesis, Lancashire Polytechnic University, Preston, England.

Markus, H. and Kitayama, S. (1991). Culture and the self: Implications for cognition, emotion, and motivation. *Psychological Review*, 98, 224–53.

Matsumoto, D. and Juang, L. (2004). *Culture and Psychology* (3rd edn). Belmont, CA, USA: Wadsworth.

McComb, D. (2003). If not self-determination, then what? *Mental Retardation*, 41, 290–8.

McConkey, R. and O'Toole, B. (2000). Improving the quality of life of people with disabilities in least affluent countries: Insights from Guyana. In K. D. Keith and R. L. Schalock (eds), *Cross-Cultural Perspectives on Quality of Life* (pp. 281–9). Washington, DC: American Association on Mental Retardation.

McGill, P., Emerson, E. and Mansell, J. (1994). Individually designed residential provision for people with seriously challenging behaviours. In E. Emerson, P. McGill and J. Mansell (eds), *Severe Learning Disabilities and Challenging Behaviours* (pp. 119–56). London: Chapman and Hall.

McVilly, K., Burton-Smith, R. and Davidson, J. (2000). Concurrence between subject and proxy ratings of quality of life for people with and without intellectual disabilities. *Journal of Intellectual Disability Research*, 44, 19–39.

Menolascino, F. J. (1977). *Challenges in Mental Retardation: Progressive Ideology and Services*. New York: Human Sciences Press.

Myers, D. G. (1992). *The Pursuit of Happiness: Who is Happy – and Why*. New York: William Morrow.

Myers, D. G. (2000). The funds, friends, and faith of happy people. *American Psychologist*, 55, 56–67.

Otrębski, W. (2000). Quality of life of people with mental retardation living in two environments in Poland. In K. D. Keith and R. L. Schalock (eds), *Cross-Cultural Perspectives on Quality of Life* (pp. 83–92). Washington, DC: American Association on Mental Retardation.

Oulette-Kuntz, H. and McCreary, B. (1996). Quality of life assessment for persons with severe developmental disabilities. In R. Renwick, I. Brown and M. Nagler (eds), *Quality of Life in Health Promotion and Rehabilitation: Conceptual Approaches, Issues, and Applications* (pp. 268–78). Thousand Oaks, CA, USA: Sage.

Parmenter, T. R. (1992). Quality of life of people with developmental disabilities. *International Review of Research in Mental Retardation*, 18, 247–87.

Patrick, D. L. and Erickson, P. (1993). Assessing health-related quality of life for clinical decision-making. In S. R. Walker and R. M. Rosser (eds.), *Quality of Life Assessment: Key Issues in the 1990's* (pp. 11–63). London: Kluwer.

Perry, J. and Felce, D. (2002). Subjective and objective quality of life assessment: Responsiveness, response bias, and resident: proxy concordance. *Mental Retardation*, 40, 445–56.

Raphael, D. (1996). Defining quality of life: Eleven debates concerning its measurement. In R. Renwick, I. Brown and M. Nagler (eds), *Quality of Life in Health Promotion and Rehabilitation: Conceptual Approaches, Issues, and Applications* (pp. 146–65). Thousand Oaks, CA, USA: Sage.

Raphael, D., Rukholm, E., Brown, I., Hill-Bailey, P. and Donato, E. (1996). The quality of life profile – adolescent version: background, description, and initial validation. *Journal of Adolescent Health*, 19, 366–75.

Rapley, M. (2000). The social construction of quality of life: The interpersonal production of well-being revisited. In K. D. Keith and R. L. Schalock (eds), *Cross-Cultural Perspectives on Quality of Life* (pp. 155–72). Washington, DC: American Association on Mental Retardation.

Rapley, M. (2003). *Quality of Life Research: A Critical Introduction*. London: Sage Publications.

Rapley, M. and Lobley, J. (1995). Factor analysis of the Schalock and Keith (1993) Quality of Life Questionnaire: A replication. *Mental Handicap Research*, 8, 194–202.

Rawlings, S. (1985). Behaviour and skills of severely retarded adults in hospitals and small residential homes. *British Journal of Psychiatry*, 146, 358–66.

Renwick, R. and Brown, I. (1996). The Centre for Health Promotion's conceptual approach to quality of life: Being, belonging, and becoming. In R. Renwick, I. Brown and M. Nagler (eds), *Quality of Life in Health Promotion and Rehabilitation: Conceptual Approaches, Issues, and Applications* (pp. 75–86). Thousand Oaks, CA: Sage.

Renwick, R., Brown, I. and Raphael, D. (2000). Person-centred quality of life: Contributions from Canada to an international understanding. In K. D. Keith and R. L. Schalock (eds), *Cross-Cultural Perspectives on Quality of Life* (pp. 5–21). Washington, DC: American Association on Mental Retardation.

Sands, D. J. and Kozleski, E. B. (1994). Quality of life differences between adults with and without disabilities. *Education and Training in Mental Retardation and Developmental Disabilities*, 29, 90–101.

Schalock, R. L. (1990). Preface. In R. L. Schalock (ed.), *Quality of Life: Perspectives and Issues* (pp. ix–xii). Washington, DC: American Association on Mental Retardation.

Schalock, R. L. (1996). Reconsidering the conceptualization and measurement of quality of life. In R. L. Schalock (ed.), *Quality of life: Volume I. Conceptualization and Measurement* (pp. 123–39). Washington, DC: American Association on Mental Retardation.

Schalock, R. L., Bonham, G. and Marchand, C. (2000). Consumer-based quality of life assessment: A path model of perceived satisfaction. *Evaluation and Program Planning*, 23, 77–87.

Schalock, R. L., Brown, I., Brown, R., Cummins, R. A., Felce, D., Matikka, L., Keith, K. D. and Parmenter, T. (2002). Conceptualization, measurement, and application of quality of life for persons with intellectual disabilities: Report of an international panel of experts. *Mental Retardation*, 40, 457–70.

Schalock, R. L. and Keith, K. D. (1993). *Quality of Life Questionnaire*. Worthington, OH, USA: IDS.

Schalock, R. L. and Keith, K. D. (2004). *Quality of Life Questionnaire* (rev.). Worthington, OH, USA: IDS.

Schalock, R. L., Keith, K. D. and Hoffman, K. (1990). *1990 Quality of Life Questionnaire Standardization Manual*. Hastings, NE, USA: Mid-Nebraska Mental Retardation Services, Inc.

Schalock, R. L. and Verdugo, M. A. (2002). *Handbook on Quality of Life for Human Service Practitioners*. Washington, DC: American Association on Mental Retardation.

Stancliffe, R. J. (1995). Assessing opportunities for choice-making: A comparison of self- and staff reports. *American Journal on Mental Retardation*, 99, 418–29.

Stancliffe, R. J. (1999). Proxy respondents and the reliability of the Quality of Life Questionnaire Empowerment factor. *Journal of Intellectual Disability Research*, 43, 185–93.

Taylor, S. J. (1994). In support of research on quality of life, but against QOL. In D. Goode (ed.), *Quality of Life for Persons with Disabilities: International Perspectives and Issues* (pp. 260–5). Cambridge, MA, USA: Brookline.

Taylor, S. J. and Bogdan, R. (1996). Quality of life and the individual's perspective. In R. L. Schalock (ed.), *Quality of Life: Volume I. Conceptualization and Measurement* (pp. 11–22). Washington, DC: American Association on Mental Retardation.

Thorndike, E. L. (1939). *Your City*. New York: Harcourt Brace.

Turnbull, H. R., III and Brunk, G. L. (1997). Quality of life and public policy. In

R. L. Schalock (ed.), *Quality of Life: Volume II. Application to Persons with Disabilities* (pp. 201–9). Washington, DC: American Association on Mental Retardation.

Walsh, P. N. (2000). Quality of life and social inclusion. In K. D. Keith and R. L. Schalock (eds), *Cross-Cultural Perspectives on Quality of Life* (pp. 315–26). Washington, DC: American Association on Mental Retardation.

Ward, N. (2000). The universal power of speaking for oneself. In K. D. Keith and R. L. Schalock (eds), *Cross-Cultural Perspectives on Quality of Life* (pp. 33–6). Washington, DC: American Association on Mental Retardation.

Ward, N. A. and Keith, K. D. (1996). Self-advocacy: Foundation for quality of life. In R. L. Schalock (ed.), *Quality of Life: Volume I. Conceptualization and Measurement* (pp. 5–10). Washington, DC: American Association on Mental Retardation.

Watson, S. M. R. (2000). Themes affecting social inclusion of individuals with disabilities in Brazil. In K. D. Keith and R. L. Schalock (eds), *Cross-Cultural Perspectives on Quality of Life* (pp. 241–53). Washington, DC: American Association on Mental Retardation.

Watson, S. M. R., Barreira, A. M. and Watson, T. C. (2000). Perspectives on quality of life: The Brazilian experience. In K. D. Keith and R. L. Schalock (eds), *Cross-Cultural Perspectives on Quality of Life* (pp. 59–71). Washington, DC: American Association on Mental Retardation.

Watson. S. M. R. and Keith, K. D. (2002). Comparing the quality of life of school-age children with and without disabilities. *Mental Retardation*, 40, 304–12.

Wehmeyer. M. L. and Schalock, R. L. (2001). Self-determination and quality of life: Implications for special education services and supports. *Focus on Exceptional Children*, 33(8), 1–16.

Wehmeyer, M. and Schwartz, M. (1998). The relationship between self-determination and quality of life for adults with mental retardation. *Education and Training in Mental Retardation and Developmental Disabilities*, 33(1), 3–12.

Williams, P. and Shoultz, B. (1982). *We Can Speak for Ourselves*. London: Souvenir Press.

Wolfensberger, W. (1994). Let's hang up 'quality of life' as a hopeless term. In D. Goode (ed.), *Quality of Life for Persons with Disabilities: International Perspectives and Issues* (pp. 285–321). Cambridge, MA, USA: Brookline.

Zekovic, B. and Renwick, R. (2003). Quality of life for children and adolescents with developmental disabilities: Review of conceptual and methodological issues relevant to public policy. *Disability and Society*, 18, 19–34.

Chapter 5

Interviewing and report writing

Alan Carr and Gary O'Reilly

In the field of intellectual disability in Ireland, the UK and some other countries, clinical psychology services are offered to clients within the context of a chronic care model. That is to say, psychologists as part of multidisciplinary disability teams or agencies offer services to clients over the course of the lifespan. At critical points in the lifecycle intensive episodes of contact occur, for example at initial diagnosis; at transitional points in the lifecycle such as school entry or leaving home; and during crises, for example when challenging behaviour or mental health problems occur. Between these episodes of intensive contact, clients are attached to the service but have a low level of input from psychologists, perhaps in the form of annual reassessments or contributing to individual programme planning meetings. The framework in Figure 5.1 outlines the stages of consultation during an episode of intensive contact, from initially receiving a referral to the point where the episode of intensive contact with the case is ended. Many such episodes of contact occur over the course of a client's lifespan. In the first stage a plan for conducting an initial assessment is made. The second stage is concerned with the processes of engagement, alliance building, assessment and formulation. In the third stage, the focus is on case management, the therapeutic contract, and the management of resistance. In the final stage, disengagement or recontracting for further intervention occurs. After a period of disengagement, the process may recur at a later time in the client's life when further input from a clinical psychology service may be required. Interviews with clients, carers and other members of the client's network occur during all contacts, and it is vital that all contacts are appropriately recorded and documented. In this chapter a more detailed consideration of the stages of the consultation process will be given along with guidelines for interviewing and report writing.

STAGES OF THE CONSULTATION PROCESS

In clinical psychology, consultation is usefully conceptualized as a developmental and recursive process. At each developmental stage, key tasks must

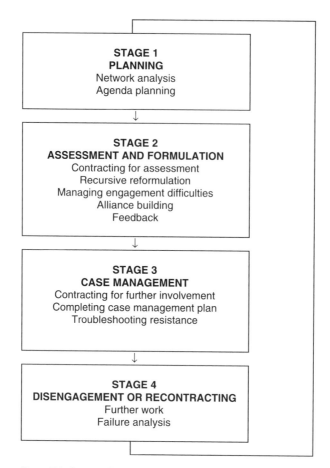

Figure 5.1 Stages of the consultation process.

be completed before progression to the next stage. Failure to complete the tasks of a given stage before progressing to the next stage may jeopardize the consultation process. For example, attempting to conduct an assessment without first contracting for assessment may lead to co-operation difficulties if the client or carers find the assessment procedures arduous. Consultation is a recursive process insofar as it is possible to move from the final stage of one episode of consultation to the first stage of the next. Usually there is a time lag between episodes of consultation. Episodes of consultation often occur at critical transitional periods in the lifecycle such as school entry, the transition from primary to secondary school, the transition from school to supported employment or adult services, and the transition from living at home to living outside the home. The lifecycle is covered in Chapter 2. Episodes of consultation may also occur during crises when clients present with challenging behaviour (covered in Chapter 18), mental health problems (covered in Chapter 22) or the need to learn new life skills such as how to deal with sexuality (covered in Chapter 20). What follows is a description of the stages of consultation and the tasks entailed by each.

STAGE 1: PLANNING

In the first stage of consultation the main tasks are to plan who to invite to the initial assessment session, or series of sessions, and what to ask them. To make this plan it is helpful to contact the referrer and obtain answers to these questions:

- Who is instigating the referral?
- Why is the referral being instigated by this member of the network at this time?
- What question needs to be answered or what problem needs to be solved?
- How will answering the question or solving the problem improve the client's quality of life?

The referral questions of concern to psychologists in the field of intellectual disability fall into four broad categories:

1 Has this client an intellectual disability?
2 What are this client's support and placement needs at this transitional point in the lifecycle?
3 How can this client's challenging behaviour be modified?
4 How can this client's skills be enhanced?

These apparently straightforward questions often are posed within a complex administrative and service-funding context. Referral questions posed by particular network members may occur against a backdrop of hidden agendas. These agendas may be about securing further resources for the referrer's agency or excluding clients from agencies or services in light of administrative regulations. Thus, psychologists must clarify referral questions, to make sure that the answers they may give have positive rather than negative implications for clients (Emerson, 1998). Let us look at each of the four categories of questions in turn.

Diagnostic questions

With infants and preschool children who are showing developmental delays, or school-going children who are not making expected levels of progress, the main referral question is usually 'Has this client an intellectual disability, and if so what supports need to be provided?' In some instances this question is overtly asked, but covertly there may be other agendas such as a mainstream school principal with minimal special educational resources asking, 'Can you demonstrate that this child who was previously shown to have a borderline IQ, really has an intellectual disability so we can access more resources for our school, and these resources will only be allocated if a definitive diagnosis of intellectual disability can be given?' Other times the overt question is phrased by distressed parents as: 'Has this child a language delay, dyslexia or an autism spectrum disorder?' and the covert agenda is to show that the client does not have a diagnosis of intellectual disability, because of the distress that parents suffer due to the stigma attached to the diagnosis of intellectual disability.

Transition and placement questions

With clients making a transition from one life stage to the next, such as preschool to school, primary to secondary school or from school to supported employment, the main problem may be how to place the client and provide appropriate supports. The overt referral question may be stated as: 'What is this client's diagnostic and skills profile, and what types of supports or placement will this client need at the next life stage?' However, sometimes when the referral is made by exhausted or under-resourced staff at an agency that is being asked to provide a potential future placement, the covert agenda is to establish that the client's level of disability, skills profile, or profile of comorbid conditions meet administrative criteria that will exclude the client from placement at the agency. So the agenda is to show that the client's disability is too mild or too severe, or the client shows complex comorbid difficulties such as an autism spectrum disorder in addition to intellectual disability, and these assessment findings mean that the client cannot be placed in the agency.

Challenging behaviour and mental health questions

When clients present with challenging behaviour such as aggression, self-injury or destructiveness, or mental health problems such as depression or dementia the overt referral question is usually 'How can this challenging behaviour or mental health problem be modified?' The covert agenda for exhausted staff in a poorly resourced unit may be to show that the client's challenging behaviour or mental health problems are so severe and unresponsive to psychological intervention that the client should be placed elsewhere or controlled with medication.

Skills building questions

When clients are involved in individual programme planning or where they present with adaptive behaviour skills deficits, the main question may be 'How can we help the client to learn this skill?' The skills may be in any area such as personal hygiene, self-care, communication, money management, using transport, and so forth. When there is a covert agenda associated with such questions, it may be for the psychologist who typically works in a consultative way, coaching carers or parents in how to implement programmes, to make a long-term commitment to working directly with the client.

Keep all of these hidden agenda themes in mind when clarifying referral problems and questions with referrers. When you have a clearer idea of what the referral question is, you need to decide who to invite to the initial assessment session and what to ask them. If there is confusion about who to invite to the first assessment meeting, a network analysis may be conducted. In planning an agenda for an initial assessment session, a routine intake interview and a core test battery may be supplemented by questions and tests which take account of the specific referral question or problem.

Network analysis

To make a plan about whom to invite to the sessions, find out from the referrer who is involved with the problem and tentatively establish what roles they play with respect to it. With some cases this will be straightforward. For example, where parents are concerned about a child's developmental progress, it may be sufficient to invite the child and the parents. In other cases, where group home staff or social services are most concerned about the case, the decision about whom to invite to the first interview is less straightforward. In complex cases it is particularly important to analyse network roles accurately before deciding whom to invite to the first session. Most network members fall into one or more of the following categories:

- The *referrer* to whom correspondence about the case should be sent
- The *customer* who is most concerned that the referral be made
- The *client* with the problem
- The legally responsible *guardians*, who are usually the parents but may be a social worker or other representative of the state
- The primary *carers*, who are usually the parents but may be house parents, residential care staff or nursing staff
- The client's main *teacher, instructor, or line-manager*
- The *social control agents* such as social workers

- *Other involved professionals* including the family doctor, the paediatrician, the public health nurse, area medical officer, etc.

Certain key network members constitute the minimum sufficient network necessary for effective case management. These include the customer, the legal guardians, the carers and the referred client. Ideally, all members of the minimum sufficient network should be invited to an intake meeting. If this is not possible, then individual meetings or telephone calls may be used to connect with these key members of the network.

Where psychologists are working as part of multidisciplinary teams, often the main customer for a psychological assessment is another team member. In such instances it is often useful to meet with the parents or carers and the referring team member briefly to clarify the reason for the referral and the implications of the psychologist's report for the services provided to the client once the assessment is completed.

Often the assessment process is conducted over a number of sessions. To develop a thorough understanding of the presenting problems and related issues, a number of different types of assessment meetings may be conducted. These may include some or all the following depending upon the case:

- Client-centred assessment interview and testing session
- Parental/Carer interviews
- School/workplace interviews
- Observations of client in home, placement, school or work settings
- Extended family interview
- Interviews with other involved professionals
- Clinical team meetings
- Professional network meetings
- Case conferences.

Following an intake interview, some combination of these various types of meetings will typically be planned to achieve certain assessment goals. It is important to distinguish between these different types of meetings and to keep records of which network members attended particular meetings; the reasons for their attendance; the information obtained; and the case management decisions made particularly in statutory cases.

In the intake information forms for children and adults in Tables 5.1 and 5.2, requests for information on involved professionals, and for consent to contact relevant involved professionals and obtain past reports, are included. These forms may be sent to literate parents or carers to complete before intake interviews or may be completed as part of routine intake assessment procedures.

Table 5.1 Intake information form for children and adolescents with developmental difficulties

---

INTAKE INFORMATION FORM FOR CHILDREN AND ADOLESCENTS WITH DEVELOPMENTAL DIFFICULTIES

Please read the information in this box and complete this form before talking to your psychologist. You may ask any questions about this during your first meeting.

Voluntary attendance. Our clinic offers help to young people and their families. Attendance at this clinic is voluntary. You may attend if you wish.

Both parents are invited. We find that it is most helpful if the young person and both parents attend the first appointment. Fathers have a particularly important contribution to make to our understanding of young people's problems and to their resolution.

First appointments. Your first appointment will last about 2 hours. During this meeting the young person and both parents may give their view of the problem, the things that you have tried to do in the past to solve it, and information about the young person's development. Sometimes, the young person is invited to complete some tests of ability and parents are invited to fill out some questionnaires.

Other appointments. At the end of the first appointment we will let you know if our service can offer you help with the problem of living that led you to visit us. We will offer you further appointments at times that are convenient to you at that point. If you cannot attend an appointment, please call us at least 2 days before the appointment so we can book in another person.

Confidentiality. In our clinic all staff work as part of a team. The team includes experienced senior psychologists, psychologists in training who work under the supervision of senior psychologists, and professionals in other disciplines such as speech and language therapy, paediatrics, social work, occupational therapy, and psychiatry. Everything that you say to your psychologist is confidential to our team.

The only circumstances under which we are obliged to give information to other people about your case is where a member of your family is at risk of serious harm.

We will not give information about your case to others, such as the young person's school, without your consent.

Anonymized case reports. As a routine part of psychologists' training they are required to write case reports for examination at the university where they are training. All identifying details of your child and family will be omitted from such reports.

Psychological reports. If you would like a psychological report sent to the young person's school, to your family doctor or to some other professional, discuss this with your psychologist.

Please sign the next line to indicate that you consent to the conditions of service outlined in this box.

Signature of parent_____

Please complete this form. The information you give here will be used to help us understand your child's difficulties. If there are any questions that you cannot answer or do not wish to answer for private reasons, please leave the answer boxes blank. Thank you.

Table 5.1 Continued

1	Please put your name and address and telephone number in the box opposite.			
2	What is your child's name?			
3	What is your child's age?			
4	What is your child's date of birth?			
5	What is your main concern about your child's behaviour and development?			
6	Please name anyone outside the family who is particularly concerned about your child's behaviour or school work, such as the public health nurse, area medical officer, teacher, social worker or family doctor.	1._____ 2._____ 3._____ 4._____ 5._____ Please write on the back of the page if you need to list more placements		
7	Who is your family doctor?			
8	May I contact your family doctor?	Yes	No	Please sign, if you give your consent. I_____consent for the psychologist to contact my family doctor.
9	What is your child's present preschool or school, and class and what is the name of your child's main teacher?			
10	May I contact your child's main teacher?	Yes	No	Please sign, if you give your consent. I_____consent for the psychologist to contact my child's teacher.
11	Can you please send me a recent preschool report or end-of-term school report?	Yes	No	If you have not given it to me already, please enclose this when returning the questionnaire.

12 Was your child assessed by a psychologist, social worker or doctor before?	Yes	No	Please give brief details.
13 If a report was prepared may I contact this person and ask them to send it to me?	Yes	No	Please sign, if you give your consent. I_____consent for the psychologist to contact_____
14 Has your child received early intervention, treatment, remedial tuition, or special education for his or her problems?	Yes	No	Please give brief details.
15 What input have you found most helpful?			

The following questions are about current behaviour problems

16 Has your child language problems?	Yes	No	Please give brief details.
17 Has your child problems with reading or other schoolwork?	Yes	No	Please give brief details.
18 Is your child very disobedient or disruptive at home?	Yes	No	Please give brief details.
19 Is your child very disobedient or disruptive at school?	Yes	No	Please give brief details.
20 Is your child sad, frightened, withdrawn or upset at home?	Yes	No	Please give brief details.
21 Is your child sad, frightened, withdrawn or upset at school?	Yes	No	Please give brief details.
22 Has your child sleeping or feeding problems?	Yes	No	Please give brief details.
23 Has your child toileting problems?	Yes	No	Please give brief details.

Table 5.1 Continued

24 Has your child a medical condition, such as one of these listed, that caused particular stress? • Head injury • Asthma • Diabetes • Head aches • Stomach aches • Other	Yes	No	Please give brief details.
25 Have any of the child's relatives (including yourself or the child's other parent) got language problems, reading problems, behaviour problems, mood problems or medical problems?	Yes	No	Please give brief details.

The following questions are about your child's developmental history

26 Was the pregnancy with this child normal?	Yes	No	Please give brief details.
27 Was the delivery normal?	Yes	No	Please give brief details.
28 Has your child had any major illnesses and if so please give details?	Yes	No	Please give brief details.
29 Has your child's hearing always been normal?	Yes	No	Please give brief details.
30 Does your child have problems with eyesight or wear glasses?	Yes	No	Please give brief details.
31 In your opinion was the development of your child's ability to walk, run, jump, and be physically co-ordinated and so forth normal?	Yes	No	Please give brief details.
32 Has your child, absences, daydreaming, fits, or a diagnosis of epilepsy	Yes	No	Please give brief details.
33 Is your child left-handed?	Yes	No	Please give brief details.

34 In your opinion, was your child's language development normal?	Yes	No	Please give brief details.
35 Has your child always been able to make friends?	Yes	No	Please give brief details.
36 Please list all the preschools and schools your child has attended giving the dates of attendance?	1. _____ 2. _____ 3. _____ 4. _____		

37 Is your child in the top third, the middle third or the bottom third of his or her class in terms of his or her overall marks?	Top third	Middle third	Bottom third

38 Does your child like going to school?	Yes	No	Please give brief details.
39 Does your child resist or refuse to do homework?	Yes	No	Please give brief details.

40 Please list your children's names and ages in order and indicate if any of them have learning problems or behaviour problems.	Name Age Learning or behavioural problem 1. _____ 2. _____ 3. _____ 4. _____ 5. _____ 6. _____ 7. _____		

41 Has your child been in a short- or long-term residential care placement?	Yes	No	Please give brief details.
42 Has your child been in a brief respite care placement?	Yes	No	Please give brief details.

Table 5.1 Continued

The following question is about recent life stresses and challenges			
43 Do you believe that any changes within your child's home or school such as the following are contributing to your child's current problems? • Changing school • Bullying at school • Moving house • Family member's illness • Parental unemployment • Birth of a sibling • Adoption of a child • Parental separation • Bereavement • Other major changes or conflicts at home or school	Yes	No	Please give brief details.

44 If you wish, please use this space to give your opinion about your child's difficulties and to provide any other relevant information.

Table 5.2 Intake information form for adults with intellectual disabilities

---

INTAKE INFORMATION FORM FOR ADULTS WITH INTELLECTUAL DISABILITIES OR LEARNING DIFFICULTIES

An adult in your family with an intellectual disability or learning difficulty has been referred to our service. From here on we will refer to that person as 'the client'. Please read the information in this box and complete this form before talking to your psychologist. You may ask any questions about this during your first meeting.

Voluntary attendance. Our clinic offers help to people with intellectual disabilities. Attendance at this clinic is voluntary. You and the client may attend the clinic if you wish. If other family members are involved in helping with the client's problems they are welcome to attend the first appointment also.

First appointments. Your first appointment will last about 2 hours. During this meeting you and the client will be invited to outline your current concerns and problems, the things that you have tried to do in the past to solve these, the client's developmental history, and family history. The client may also be invited to do some tests of ability and you may be asked to fill out some questionnaires about the client's strengths and weaknesses.

Other appointments. At the end of the first appointment we will let you know if our service can offer you help with the problems that led you to visit us. We will offer yourself and the client further appointments at times that are convenient to you at that point. If you cannot attend an appointment, please call us at least 2 days before the appointment so we can book in another person.

Confidentiality. In our clinic all staff work as part of a team. The team includes experienced senior psychologists, psychologists in training who work under the supervision of senior psychologists, and professionals in other disciplines such as social work, occupational therapy and psychiatry. Everything that you say to your psychologist is confidential to our team.

The only circumstances under which we are obliged to give information to other people about your case is where you or another person is at risk of serious harm because of your behaviour.

We will not give information about your case to others without your consent.

Anonymized case reports. As a routine part of psychologists' training they are required to write case reports for examination at the university where they are training. All your identifying details will be omitted from such reports.

Psychological reports. If you would like a psychological report sent to your family doctor or to some other professional, please discuss this with your psychologist.

Please sign the next line to indicate that you consent to the conditions of service outlined in this box.

Signature_____

(Continued overleaf)

Table 5.2 Continued

Please complete this form. The information you give here will be used to help us understand the client and family's current living situation, current concerns and problems, and the client's personal and family history. If there are any questions that you cannot answer or do not wish to answer for private reasons, please leave the answer boxes blank. Otherwise write your answers in the boxes on the right-hand side of the form or circle the answer that applies to the client. Please send this completed questionnaire to the clinic in the enclosed stamped addressed envelope if this has been posted to you. Thank you.

1	Please put the client's name and your name and address, telephone number and mobile number in the box opposite.		
2	What is the client's age?		
3	What is the client's gender?	Female	Male
4	What is the client's date of birth?		
5	Please name anyone outside the family who is particularly concerned about the client's behaviour, such as staff at his or her training, work, or residential placement, social worker or family doctor.	1. ———————————— 2. ———————————— 3. ———————————— 4. ———————————— 5. ———————————— Please write on the back of the page if you need to list more placements	
6	Who is your family doctor and what is his or her phone number or contact address?		
7	Please sign opposite if you give your consent for me to contact your family doctor and request a summary of the client's medical history.	Signature_____ Date_____	
8	Was the client assessed by a psychologist, social worker or doctor before?	Yes No	Please give brief details?

9 If reports were prepared may I contact these professionals and ask them to send them to me?	Yes	No	Please sign, if you give your consent. I_____ consent for the psychologist to contact these professionals 1. _____ 2. _____ 3. _____ 4. _____ 5. _____		
10 Has the client received special education or treatment for his or her problems?	Yes	No	Please give brief details.		
11 What input have you found most helpful?					
12 To the best of your knowledge what is the client's current level of intellectual disability?	Mild	Moderate	Severe	Profound	Don't know
13 Has the client any of these problems?	Deafness	Blindness	Cerebral palsy	Epilepsy	Other

The following questions are about the client's current living and working situation

14 Where does the client live now?	In the family home	In a group home	Other, specify
15 How long has the client lived in this situation?			
16 Who lives with the client?			
17 Does the client or others want new residential arrangements made?	No	Yes, specify	
18 How much access has the client to respite care?			

Table 5.2 Continued

19 Does the client or others want new respite care arrangements made?	No	Yes, specify
20 What is the client's current work or training situation?		
21 How long has the client been in this work or training situation?		
22 Does the client or others want new work or training arrangements made?	No	Yes, specify

The following questions are about current behaviour problems

23 Are you currently concerned about the client being aggressive to other people or harming others?	No	Yes
24 Are you currently concerned about the client injuring or harming him- or herself?	No	Yes
25 Are you currently concerned about the client damaging property?	No	Yes
26 Are you currently concerned about the client being socially withdrawn and not mixing with others?	No	Yes
27 Are you currently concerned about the client wandering, getting into the wrong company or being taken advantage of?	No	Yes
28 Are you currently concerned about the client being depressed, sad, having a low mood, or little energy?	No	Yes
29 Are you currently concerned about the client feeling anxious, frightened, panicky, or worrying too much?	No	Yes
30 Are you currently concerned about the client's sleep pattern?	No	Yes
31 Are you currently concerned about the client's eating and dieting habits?	No	Yes
32 Are you currently concerned about the client's use of alcohol or other drugs?	No	Yes
33 Are you currently concerned about the client's loss of memory or loss of ability to concentrate?	No	Yes

34 Are you currently concerned about medication the client is taking for the treatment of any of these problems?	No	Yes
35 Are you currently concerned about counselling or psychotherapy the client is receiving for any of these problems?	No	Yes
36 Are you currently concerned about the client's involvement with the police, the courts or the judicial system?	No	Yes

37 What are the current top 3 concerns about behaviour problems?	
38 How long have these been the main problems?	
39 What effects have these problems had on the client's life?	
40 What do you believe caused these problems?	
41 Is the client on medication for any of these problems at present?	If so please specify what medication he or she is taking
42 Is the client receiving behaviour therapy or counselling to help with these problems at present?	If so please specify what therapy is being received and for how long
43 For the 3 main problems that you listed in answer to question 37, what have you found most helpful?	

The following question is about recent life stresses and challenges

44 Circle any of the following events if they have happened to the client in the past 6 months:
- The client suffered a serious illness, injury or assault
- A serious illness, injury or assault happened to a close relative
- The client's parent, child or spouse died
- A close family friend or another relative (aunt, cousin, grandparent) died
- The client broke off a steady relationship
- The client had a serious problem with a close friend or relative
- The client became unemployed or was seeking work or placement unsuccessfully for more than one month
- The client had problems with the police and a court appearance
- Something the client valued was lost or stolen
- Another major life stress occurred (please specify)⎯⎯⎯⎯⎯⎯⎯⎯⎯

Table 5.2 Continued

The following questions are about the client's developmental history
45 List the places (home, residential placements, etc.) where the client has lived from birth until the present	1._____ 2._____ 3._____ 4._____ 5._____ 6._____ 7._____ 8._____ 9._____ 10._____ Please write on the back of the page if you need to list more placements
46 List the schools the client has attended, the training positions the client has held, and the work positions the client has held over the lifespan	1._____ 2._____ 3._____ 4._____ 5._____ 6._____ 7._____ 8._____ 9._____ 10._____ Please write on the back of the page if you need to list more placements

47 What are the major stresses or challenges that have occurred in these areas of the client's life since he or she was 18 years old: • Work or educational situation • Family life • Relationship with friends • Personal health?	
48 How has the client coped with these stresses or challenges?	
49 What are the main positive things that have occurred in these areas of the client's life since he or she was 18 years old: • Work or educational situation • Family life • Relationship with their friends • Personal health?	
50 In teenage years (11–18) did the client face any major stresses or challenges in these areas: • Educational situation • Family life • Relationships with friends • Personal health?	
51 How did the client cope with these stresses or challenges?	
52 In the client's teenage years (11–18) what were the main positive things that occurred in these areas: • Educational situation • Family life • Relationships with friends • Personal health?	

Table 5.2 Continued

53 In childhood years (0–10) did the client face any major stresses or challenges in these areas: • Educational situation • Family life • Relationships with friends • Personal health?	
54 How did the client cope with these challenges?	
55 In the client's childhood years (0–10) what were the main positive things that occurred in these areas: • Educational situation • Family life • Relationships with friends • Personal health?	

The following questions ask about the current family situation and family history

56 Currently who are the 3 main people in the family who support the client and make dealing with the demands of his or her life more manageable?	
57 Has anyone in the family (parents, grandparents, aunts, uncles, brothers, sisters, etc.) had difficulties like the client's?	
58 Has anyone in the family (parents, grandparents, aunts, uncles, brothers, sisters, etc.) had other stress-related difficulties or illnesses?	

59 Are there any other comments about your concerns and the client's situation that you wish to make?

Agenda planning

Planning what questions to ask or what investigative procedures to use in a preliminary consultation session and subsequent assessment sessions will depend upon the problem posed by the referrer, your preliminary hypotheses about these problems, and the routine assessment procedures you typically use in such cases.

Hypotheses

Different types of hypotheses or hunches are associated with different types of referral questions. For diagnostic questions, the hypotheses may centre on what profile of comorbid disorders the client may have and what potential aetiological factors are involved. For transitional questions, the hypotheses may centre on what the client's current diagnostic and skills profile is and the support requirements entailed by this profile. These types of hypotheses may be informed by material covered in Chapter 1 on diagnosis and Chapter 2 on lifespan development. For questions about challenging behaviour and mental health problems, hypotheses may focus on current maintaining factors, particularly inadvertent reinforcement, along with possible biological or psychosocial predisposing factors and precipitating life events or lifecycle transitions. These hypotheses may be informed by material in Chapter 18 on challenging behaviour and Chapter 22 on mental health problems. For skills-building questions, hypotheses may focus on appropriate ways to use task analysis to break big skills into smaller subskills and possible reinforcers to use in a behavioural programme. These hypotheses may be informed by a wide range of sources including material in Chapter 10 on parent training, Chapter 7 on applied behavioural analysis, Chapter 16 on special education or Chapter 19 on life skills.

Agendas for parent or carer interviews

An agenda for routine intake interviews with parents and areas is given in Table 5.3. The agenda moves from a description of the client's current life situation and living arrangements, to inquiries about multiagency input, and from there to parents and carers' current concerns and the history of how these concerns and other difficulties have been addressed in past episodes of treatment or problem solving. Against this backdrop, risk assessment is conducted. Risk assessment is covered in detail in Chapter 26. The client's developmental history and family history are then covered. A genogram may be constructed as part of the family history-taking process. Symbols for genogram construction are set out in Figure 5.2 and a sample genogram is given in Figure 5.3 (McGoldrick et al., 1999). Software

Table 5.3 Intake assessment for people with intellectual disabilities

The referral
- The *referrer*
- The *customer*
- The *child* and the reason for referral
- The legally responsible *guardians*
- The primary *caregivers*
- The child's main *teacher*
- The *social control agents*
- *Other involved professionals*

Types of meetings used for assessment
- Client-centred assessment
- Parental/carer interview
- School/workplace interview
- Observations of client in home, placement, school or work settings
- Extended family interview
- Interview with other involved professionals
- Professional network meeting
- Team meeting
- Case conference

Current life situation
- Current residential placement or family living arrangements
- Quality of living arrangements (safety, crowding, isolation, etc.)
- Current preschool, school, work or training placement
- Quality of school/work placement (suitability of placement, staff:pupil ratio, special programming, transport, etc.)
- Other current psychosocial supports (home visiting, respite care, behavioural support, community living, recreation, counselling, advocacy)
- Current financial supports (benefits, etc.)
- Current medical supports (neurology, psychiatry, etc.)

Multiagency input
- Current treatment network membership
- Family doctor and professionals in disability services (health, social services, education, etc.)
- Patterns of interaction with treatment network

Problems and treatment history
- Nature, frequency and intensity of current list of problems
- Fluctuations in recent episodes of chronic problems
- Previous episodes of problems, precipitating and maintaining factors
- Previous episodes of contact with professionals, assessment and intervention and helpful aspects of these
- Clients and carers' views of causes of problems and effective solutions
- Acceptance, ambivalence about or denial of disability
- Presence or absence of commitment to resolving problems

Current risk and challenging behaviour
- Suicide risk
- Risk of non-fatal self-injury
- Risk to children (impaired parenting capacity, neglect or abuse)
- Risk of harm to others
- Risk of damage to property

Developmental history
- Current living situation with family or placement elsewhere, recent changes and placement history
- Current preschool, school, work or training placement, recent changes and past history
- Pregnancy and birth complications (preterm, anoxia, low apgar, etc.)
- Physical health, disabilities, illnesses and injuries
- Birth weight (low or normal), feeding, sleeping, growth (normal or failure to thrive below third percentile), sports, current physical exercise
- Development of bowel and bladder control
- Sensory and motor development and past screening results
- Language and literacy development and past test results
- Cognitive development and past test results
- Development of adaptive social skills for regulating emotions including aggression and sexuality
- Development of adaptive social skills for making and maintaining relationships
- Development of practical adaptive skills for self-care and community living
- History of mental health problems (epilepsy, depression, anxiety, psychotic episodes, etc.)

Family history
- Current living arrangements and household membership
- Nuclear family membership and contact
- Father involvement in child-care (if nuclear family) and co-parenting arrangements (if reconstituted family)
- Parent's capacity to meet child's needs for safety (?neglect, abuse), care (physical and emotional), control (? challenging behaviour), intellectual stimulation (?neglect), autonomy (?overdependence)
- Extended family and network membership and contact
- Family strengths
- Family physical and mental health problems and disabilities
- Family lifecycle transitions
- Supportive family relationships
- Stressful family relationships
- Early family life experiences

Testing
- Cognitive abilities
- Adaptive behaviour
- Structured diagnostic interviews
- Support needs

Diagnoses and problem list
- Disabilities (intellectual, language, sensory, motor)
- Problem list

Formulation – predisposing factors
Biological predisposing factors
- Genetically determined syndromes
- Metabolic disorders
- Increasing maternal age
- Maternal illness
- Maternal exposure to toxins
- Prenatal and perinatal complications

Table 5.3 Continued

- Prematurity
- Birth injury
- Low birth weight
- Neonatal disorders
- Traumatic brain injury
- Malnutrition
- Seizures
- Degenerative disorders

Social predisposing factors
- Poverty
- Maternal malnutrition
- Maternal drug and alcohol use
- Parental psychopathology
- Disorganized parental behaviour
- Insecure attachment to parents
- Poor parenting (authoritarian, permissive, neglectful or inconsistent)
- Marital discord and domestic violence
- Parental criminality and deviant siblings
- Losses (bereavement and separation)
- Institutional upbringing
- Child abuse
- Lack of access to medical services
- Inadequate education and support

Formulation – precipitating factors
- Major stressful life events
- Build-up of minor stresses
- Illness and injury
- Victimization, abuse and neglect
- Family lifecycle transitions and changes

Formulation – maintaining factors

Biological factors
- Difficult temperament
- Physical disabilities, illnesses, injuries
- Medication (side-effects)

Problematic carer–client relationship
- Inadvertent reinforcement of problems
- Coercive interaction
- Insecure attachment
- Authoritarian, permissive, neglectful or inconsistent parenting style
- Neglect or abuse

Family disorganization
- Poor problem solving
- Poor communication
- Triangulation
- Enmeshment or disengagement
- Father absence
- Marital discord or violence

Carer or client cognitive factors
- Low self-esteem

- Pessimistic attributional style
- External locus of control
- Low self-efficacy
- Negative cognitive distortions
- Dysfunctional coping strategies (denial or avoidance)

Social network factors
- Poverty
- High stress
- Low support
- Lack of educational and occupational opportunities
- Lack of disability services and supports
- Problematic interaction patterns in the disability service network

Formulation – protective factors

Biological factors
- Good physical health
- Easy temperament
- Good premorbid adjustment

Positive carer–client relationship
- Supportive and respectful relationship that promotes autonomy
- Secure attachment
- Authoritative parenting style

Family support
- Good problem solving
- Good communication
- Joint parenting with father involvement in nuclear families and co-operative co-parenting in reconstituted families
- The absence of childhood separations, losses, bereavements, parental mental health problems, and marital discord

Carer or client cognitive factors
- High self-esteem
- Optimistic attributional style
- Internal locus of control
- High self-efficacy
- Good coping strategies (planning, problem solving, emotional self-regulation, seeking support)

Social network factors
- Adequate economic supports
- Low stress
- High social support
- Adequate educational and occupational opportunities
- Adequate disability services and supports
- Good co-operation in the disability service network

Current needs
- Immediate risk management
- Additional psychosocial supports (including specialist direct or indirect support from psychologist)
- Additional medical support
- Change in living arrangement or placement
- Change in work or training placement

Table 5.3 Continued

Case management options
- Refer back with no action
- Consultation with carers or key involved agency and periodic reassessment
- Refer within team
- Refer to outside team
- Conduct focal intervention and support plan
- Co-ordinate individual multimodal support plan

---

for genogram construction is listed in Table 5.4. Standardized questionnaires and scales (listed in Chapter 1) and structured interviews may be used routinely to assess parent and carer reports of adaptive behaviour, psychological problems and support needs. If appropriate the client's abilities may be assessed using standardized tests such as those listed in Chapter 1. In addition an individual interview with the client may be conducted.

Agendas for client-centred interviews and assessments

In addition to parental or family interviews it is good practice to conduct routinely a client-centred assessment. The following are key areas to include in client-centred assessments if the client is capable of giving views on these issues:

- The client's account of their current living situation
- The specific problems or difficulties with which they would like help
- Current coping strategies, their response to their carer's views of the problem
- Preferred placement arrangement
- Preferred educational and occupational arrangements
- Preferred leisure activities
- Accounts of situations requiring protective action (abuse or suicidal intent).

Agendas for school, vocational and residential placement interviews

What follows is a list of items which may form the agenda for an interview with staff at the client's school or vocational placements:

- Duration of current placement and history of how it was set up
- Client's daily routine at the placement

Table 5.4 Interviewing instruments

Instrument	Comments
Genogram-Maker Millennium based on work by Randy Gerson http://www.genogram.org/ Free genogram programme http://genogram.freeservers.com/index.html	• Both programmes produce genograms.
Moss, S. Psychiatric Assessment Schedules for Adults with Developmental Disabilities is available at http://web.onetel.com/~drplee/	• The PAS-ADD 10 produces research diagnoses, and involves present-state interviewing of the patient, followed by a similar interview with a key informant. Either interview can detect symptoms and produce diagnoses, so the PAS-ADD can also be used for the assessment of individuals whose linguistic ability does not permit a clinical interview. The ICD 10 version of PAS-ADD is derived from the Schedules for Clinical Assessment in Neuropsychiatry (SCAN) and uses a version of the SCAN's computer algorithms to produce ICD 10 diagnoses of psychotic disorders, hypomania, depression and anxiety disorders. • The Mini PAS-ADD is a structured interview that yields scores for depression, anxiety, expansive mood, obsessive compulsive disorder, psychosis, autism and unspecified disorder (including dementia). • The 25-item PAS-ADD Checklist yields scores for affective or neurotic disorder, possible organic condition (including dementia) and psychotic disorder.

- Client's current and past adaptive behaviour in conceptual, social and practical domains
- Current and past challenging behaviour or psychological problems
- Staff's beliefs about causes and possible solutions for client's problematic behaviour, support needs or placement needs
- Manager's opinions about the adequacy of funding and resourcing arrangements associated with offering a service to the client
- Arrangements for staff to work collaboratively with other members of the client's social and professional network.

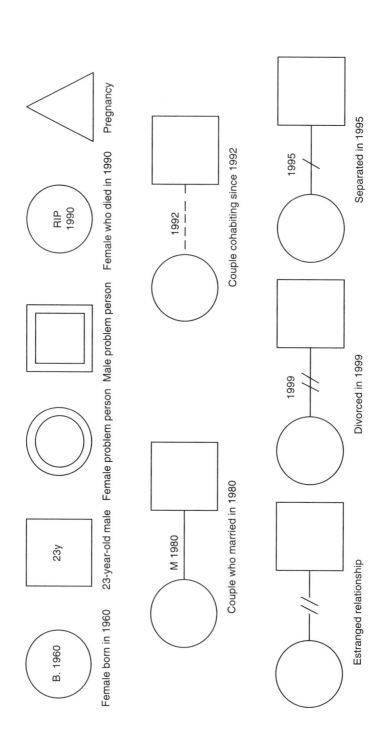

B. 1960 — Female born in 1960

23y — 23-year-old male

Female problem person

Male problem person

RIP 1990 — Female who died in 1990

Pregnancy

M 1980 — Couple who married in 1980

1992 — Couple cohabiting since 1992

Estranged relationship

1999 — Divorced in 1999

1995 — Separated in 1995

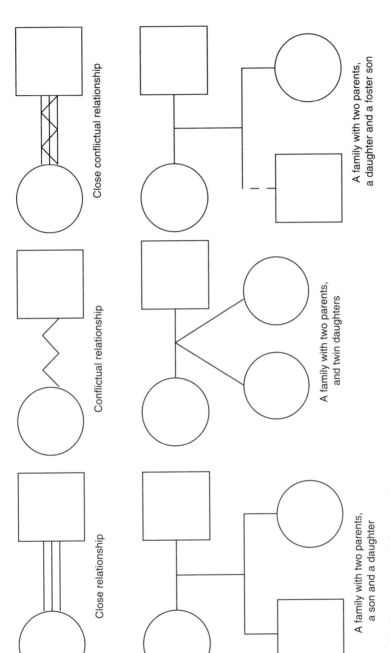

Close relationship

Conflictual relationship

Close conflictual relationship

A family with two parents, a son and a daughter

A family with two parents, and twin daughters

A family with two parents, a daughter and a foster son

Figure 5.2 Genogram symbols.

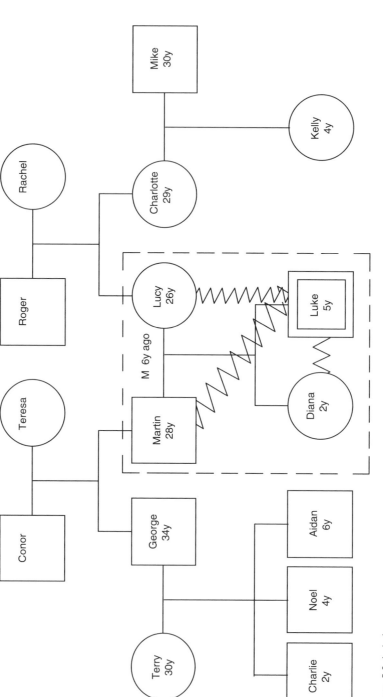

Figure 5.3 Luke's genogram.

STAGE 2: ASSESSMENT AND FORMULATION

Establishing a contract for assessment; working through the assessment agenda and recursively refining preliminary hypotheses in light of the information obtained; dealing with engagement problems; building a therapeutic alliance and giving feedback are the more important features of the assessment and formulation stage, which may span a number of sessions.

Contracting for assessment

The aim of contracting for assessment is to clarify expectations and reach agreement with carers and clients about completing an assessment which will point to a case management plan. The first task is to explain what assessment involves and to offer the carers, the client and each relevant member of the network a chance to accept or reject the opportunity to complete the assessment. For most carers, this will involve outlining the way in which the interviews and testing procedures will be conducted. Make it clear that the assessment will involve an interview with the carers, individual interviews and testing sessions with the client, observation sessions, and contacts with other involved professionals if appropriate. Inform carers and clients about the time commitment involved, the voluntary nature of the assessment, the limits of confidentiality, the possible outcomes of the assessment and the pros and cons of proceeding. Normally, the contents of sessions are confidential unless there is evidence that clients are a serious threat to themselves or to others or are in personal danger from others. For example, where there is evidence of suicidal intent, severe violence to others, or child abuse, confidentiality may be breached. When exploring the pros and cons of completing the assessment, mention that the downside of assessment is that it involves a significant commitment of time and energy and answering searching and potentially stressful questions. The benefits include reaching a clearer understanding of the client's difficulties and the possibility of finding solutions to the referral problems.

As part of contracting explore parents' willingness to accept preferred and non-preferred possible assessment outcomes. With diagnostic assessments, the possible outcomes may be that the client has a specific language delay, a specific learning disability, sensory and motor disabilities but normal intelligence, or intellectual disability with or without comorbid disabilities or disorders including autism spectrum disorder. Ask carers to consider carefully if they wish to find out their child's diagnosis and if they are prepared to accept a conclusion that is inconsistent with their wishes or expectations. With life transition and placement assessments, possible outcomes are that the child has or has not the profile that suits him or her to the carers' or client's preferred placement. With challenging behaviour or skills training assessment, the outcome may be that for the client to improve the carers are going to have to implement a programme which may involve making significant changes in their ways of interacting with the client and possibly major changes in their lifestyles.

With clients, correct any misconceptions they hold about the assessment process. For example, some clients fear that they will be involuntarily admitted to hospital, or that they may have to undergo painful medical procedures.

The contracting for assessment is complete when carers and clients have been adequately informed about the process and have agreed or declined (in an informed way) to complete the assessment.

Engagement difficulties

The process of contracting for assessment does not always run smoothly. Engagement problems are to be expected. In situations where carers are ambivalent about completing the assessment but a referring physician or social worker forcefully recommends attendance, convene a joint meeting which includes both the referrer and the carers to clarify the referral question. Non-attendance and inaccurate referral information are two of the more important obstacles to establishing a contract for assessment. When none of the people invited to the intake interview attend, phone the person that you have identified as the customer immediately and clarify why the family have not shown up. Non-attendance, in our experience, may be due either to practical difficulties or to a failure to identify the true customer for consultation. Non-attendance due to an inaccurate analysis of the problem system is best dealt with by arranging a meeting with the referrer to clarify who the customer for consultation is. Non-attendance due to practical problems occurs most frequently with chaotic families invited to attend a public clinic. In these instances, intake interviews may best be conducted in the clients' homes. Sometimes the information contained in the referral letter, or indeed through a referral phone call, is wildly inaccurate and clients indicate that the referral problem was only a red flag to mark a more profound difficulty. It is good practice to acknowledge the validity of clients using a small child-focused problem as a way of checking out the therapist's trustworthiness before mentioning more profound difficulties with which they want assistance.

Recursive reformulation

The assessment phase of the overall consultation process involves conducting the interviews, administering tests, and making behavioural observations to check out the accuracy of hypotheses made during the planning phase. It also involves modifying hypotheses in the light of the information gained in the interview, testing and observation sessions. In practice, the first round of interviewing, testing and observation may not only lead to a modification of the preliminary hypotheses but may raise further hypotheses that need to be checked out with further interviews, tests and observations. This recursive process, which characterizes the assessment and formulation stage, is diagrammed in Figure 5.4. The process comes to an end when a formulation has been constructed that fits with significant aspects of the client's presentation; with network members' experiences of the client; and with available knowledge about similar problems described in the literature. This formulation should point to one or more options for case management. Options for case management will be dealt with below.

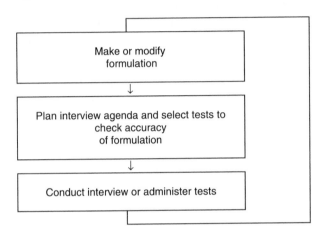

Figure 5.4 Process of recursive reformulation.

Alliance building

In addition to providing information, the process of assessment also serves as a way to build a working alliance. Building a strong working alliance is essential for valid assessment and effective intervention. All other features of the consultation process should be subordinate to the working alliance, since without it, carers and clients drop out or fail to make progress. The only exception to this rule is where the safety of a client or a member of the social network is at risk and in such cases protection takes priority over alliance building. Research on common factors that contribute to a positive outcome and ethical principles of good practice point to a number of guidelines which facilitate developing a strong working alliance (Hubble, Duncan and Miller, 1999; Norcross, 2002).

- **Genuine warmth and empathy.** Communicate with clients and carers in a warm, empathic and genuine way.
- **Collaboration.** Form a collaborative partnership in which clients and carers are experts on the specific features of their own life situations and you offer expertise on general scientific and clinical information relevant

to the broad class of problems of which the presenting problem is a specific instance.

- **Neutrality and acceptance.** Adopt a position of neutrality and acceptance. The client and carers must feel at the end of each session that you have understood, accepted and sympathized with each of their points of view. They must not feel judged or blamed. They should feel that you know they are each doing their best to manage a challenging situation.

- **Respectful curiosity.** Adopt a position of respectful curiosity. Continually uncover new information about the problem and potential solutions. Invite clients and carers to consider the implications of viewing their difficulties as determined by multiple factors and from multiple different perspectives. This positioning counters attempts to find the 'one cause', the 'person who is to blame', or 'the single right answer'.

- **Invitational approach.** Adopt an invitational approach in which clients and carers feel they are invited (not directed) to participate in assessment. Thus, if clients or carers cannot follow through on homework assignments or activities in sessions, they do not feel guilty or blamed for not doing as directed.

- **Strengths.** Hold a balanced focus on strengths and resilience on the one hand and on problems and constraints on the other. This positioning fosters optimism without colluding with denial.

- **Readiness to change.** Think about the change process as involving the stages of precontemplation, contemplation, planning, action and maintenance. Identify the stage at which the carers and clients are. Match the way the assessment is conducted and feedback is given to the clients' and carers' readiness to change. For example, if clients and carers are still in the contemplation stage, thinking about whether or not to invest time and energy in modifying challenging behaviour, then offer them assessment tasks in which they are exploring the pros and cons of change, rather than planning tasks such as monitoring behaviour rates and drawing up reinforcement menus.

- **Transference and counter-transference**. Acknowledge that clients, carers and psychologists inadvertently bring to the working alliance attitudes, expectations, emotional responses and interactional routines from early significant caregiving and care-receiving relationships. These transference and counter-transference reactions, if unrecognized, may compromise therapeutic progress.

Interviewing clients with intellectual disabilities

The following guidelines on how to interview clients with intellectual disabilities are based on research on the impact and effectiveness of different interviewing styles with children and people with intellectual disabilities (Angold, 2002; Jones, 2003; Prosser and Bromley, 1998).

Create a relaxed atmosphere

Put clients at their ease. Adopt a non-threatening accepting manner. If possible engage the person in informal conversation or joint non-threatening activity prior to the interview. Conduct the interview in a setting that is familiar to the client, rather than in an unfamiliar setting, since this last may be threatening or distracting. All of these strategies create a context that induces relaxation rather than anxiety. When clients are relaxed, they are more likely to offer reliable and valid answers in an interview. Anxiety interferes with the client's capacity to remember details accurately, to give valid accounts of their behaviours, beliefs and feelings, to solve problems and make judgements.

Explain what will happen

Open the interview by explaining its purpose, the sorts of questions that will be asked, the duration of the interview, and the limits of confidentiality. Let clients know that you are interested in their opinions, and that there are no right or wrong answers. When giving this explanation use simple, short sentences and check that you have been understood.

Give ground rules

Make it clear to the client that it's acceptable to say, 'I don't know'. Tell the client that it's acceptable to ask, 'What do you mean?' if the question is unclear. Tell clients that at any point if they say, 'I need a break', they can have one. These ground rules offer clients a sense of control over the interview. They limit the possibility of failure experiences, which can demoralize clients, cause anxiety, and so reduce clients' capacity to function effectively.

Progress from less to more demanding questions

Order the questions you ask so that they progress from the simple to the more complex, and from the emotionally neutral or positive to the emotionally negative. Begin by asking simple questions, to which clients know the answer and which address emotionally neutral or positive topics. This gives clients a sense of mastery. The sense of mastery makes it more likely that clients will be in a state of low anxiety when asked more complex and emotionally challenging questions.

Ask open questions first

When inquiring about a topic, ask open questions first and follow these up with closed questions about specific details. Here are some common open questions: 'Tell me about X? What happened when you were at Y? What did you see? How did you feel? What did you think? What was the best thing about Q? What was the worst thing about R? What would you like? What would you not like?' These sorts of open questions provide an opportunity for clients to give extended first-person accounts of their thoughts and feelings. Follow open questions with encouraging open probes like, 'Tell me more about that. What happened next? What did you think next? What did you feel then? Really? That sounds good/bad/hard/sad.'

Ask either/or questions next

Where clients lack the expressive language skills to answer open questions, ask either/or, forced-choice questions such as: 'Would you rather go swimming in the morning or after lunch?' Try not to use multiple-choice questions, such as: 'Would you rather live here or in the blue house or in the red house?' These questions can be confusing, especially where clients are unable to hold all the options in memory at one time. When you ask either/or questions, keep in mind that people with learning disabilities tend to choose the last of any two options. So if you ask, 'Was that on Monday or Tuesday?' the most likely answer clients will give is 'Tuesday'. To check whether an answer to an either/or question reflects this tendency to select the last option mentioned or the client's actual beliefs, rephrase each either/or question the other way and intersperse them through the interview. Then check whether responses to each pair of questions were consistent.

Ask closed questions to get specific details

To fill in details ask closed questions such as: 'Was that on Tuesday? Was X there? Did you see Y?' However, use closed questions cautiously. People with intellectual disabilities tend to acquiesce and answer 'Yes' when asked closed questions that require a 'Yes' or 'No' answer. This tendency is due to impaired cognitive development and a social desirability response set, which entails a wish to gain approval from the interviewer. This tendency to answer 'Yes' to most questions occurs even when two or more 'Yes' answers are inconsistent. This brief segment of an interview illustrates acquiescence to closed questions, leading to inconsistent responses.

Q 1 Are you happy? A1. Yes.
Q 2 Do you like this place? A2. Yes.
Q 3 Are you sad? A3. Yes.

To check whether an answer to a closed question reflects this tendency to acquiesce, or the client's actual beliefs, rephrase each closed question the other way and intersperse them through the interview. Then check whether responses to each pair of closed questions were consistent.

Use simple language

Phrase questions briefly in the present tense. Use single-clause questions with simple grammatical structures and short, commonly used words, for example: 'How are you today? What do you like most about this place? Where will you go tomorrow?' If you prepare a questionnaire or structured interview schedule for clients, apply the Flesch formula to the text, and edit the text so that the Flesch quotient is as low as possible (Flesch, 1948). Low Flesch quotients reflect easy readability.

Anchor questions to salient events

In questions about time, event frequency, or internal states use highly salient, memorable, concrete anchor events or comparative stimuli. If you are asking questions about a time of day, use mealtimes or bedtime as anchors, for example: 'Was that before lunch or after lunch?' If you are asking questions about the time of year, use birthdays or Christmas, Easter, or holidays as anchor points, for example: 'Was that near Christmas?' If you are asking questions about internal states, use responses to known events as anchors, for example: 'Does it make you sleepy, like when you drink hot milk before bed?'

Clearly indicate topic changes

When you have finished inquiring about one area and move on to another, make this very explicit, for example: 'You have told me about your home. Now let us talk about your school?'

Check seriation skills before asking questions about seriation

It is common practice when assessing mood states, preferences, and so forth in people of normal intellectual ability to ask them to rate specific behaviours, beliefs, moods and urges on paper and pencil scales from 1–3, 1–5, 1–7, 1–10, or 1–100, and to specify anchor points such as 1 = strongly agree to 5 = strongly disagree, 1 = rarely and 7 = frequently, 1 = very relaxed and 10 = very anxious, or 1 = no urge to drink and 100 = an exceptionally strong urge to drink. Visual analogue scales are also used where anchor points only are given, separated by a horizontal line on which the client places a mark to indicate the intensity of their behaviour, belief, mood or urge. These sorts of scales can all be used when interviewing people with intellectual disabilities, provided clients can show in the interview situation that they understand serration. This may be tested by asking them to arrange different-sized blocks or sticks in order from the smallest to the largest, and then to rate the size of the objects on 3,5,7,10,100 point scales or visual analogue scales. If clients can demonstrate this skill, then they may legitimately be asked to rate how strong their feelings of happiness or sadness are on numbered scales or visual analogue scales (Prosser and Bromley, 1998).

Avoid leading questions and complex language

Do not ask questions that suggest a particular answer, like 'You were very angry, weren't you?' Do not ask complex, multiclausal questions that involve abstract concepts and rarely used words. For example, try to avoid saying things like this all in one breath: 'Although you have been here since you were discharged from the Metropolitan Hospital, I'm wondering if you have settled in OK, yea? or if you are still a bit apprehensive about what the future might hold in store for you, yea? or maybe not? I don't know, what do you think, Charlie?'

Summarize periodically

Periodically give clients brief summaries of what has been covered so far in the interview. Give an overall summary at the end of the interview. When summarizing use simple language and short sentences. Check that the client understands the summary and that it is accurate. Modify the summary if it is inaccurate and check again with the client that you have understood what has been said correctly. Summarizing is important because people with intellectual disabilities have relatively short attention spans, and may lose track of the overall direction of the interview without such summaries.

Use augmentative and alternative communication systems

Where appropriate use augmentative and alternative communication (AAC) systems, including manual signs, voice-output communication aides (VOCAs), and the Picture-Exchange Communication System (PECS). These are described in Chapter 17.

Structured interviews

To assess mental health problems the Psychiatric Assessment Schedules for Adults with Developmental Disabilities listed in Table 5.4 is a well-validated structured interview.

Formulation and feedback

The assessment is complete when the presenting problem and related difficulties are clarified; related predisposing, precipitating, maintaining and protective factors have been identified; a formulation linking these has been constructed; possible goals have been identified; options for case management or treatment have been identified; and these have been discussed with the carers and client.

Formulation

A formulation is a mini-theory that explains why the presenting problems developed, why they persist, and what protective factors either prevent them from becoming worse or may be enlisted to solve the presenting problems. Common predisposing, precipitating, maintaining and protective factors used in formulations in cases of intellectual disability are listed in Table 5.3, and these are based on information reviewed in Chapters 1 and 2. To construct a formulation, first draw up a problem list which includes all the significant problems that have been identified during the assessment. Then, unless there is good reason to do otherwise, prioritize the problems central to the referring question. So, if the question concerned initial diagnosis or diagnostic profiling and placement needs at a lifecycle transition, then the core problem to be explained by the formulation is the main diagnosis or set of comorbid diagnoses that has arisen from the assessment. Predisposing, precipitating and maintaining factors associated with these diagnoses then need to be specified. If the referral question concerned challenging behaviour or skills deficits, then these problems are placed at the centre of the formulation, and relevant predisposing precipitating and maintaining factors are specified. Second, salient points from all of the assessment interviews, testing and observation sessions are abstracted, labelled and listed. These salient points are those which may have a role in causing the clients problems, such as stressful life events or problematic relationships. Third, salient points are then categorized as those which may play a role in maintaining one or more of the problems; those which either precipitated the onset of the problems or made the problems sufficiently severe to warrant referral; and those background factors which predisposed the client to developing his or her current difficulties. These predisposing, precipitating and maintaining factors may then be linked into the most useful and coherent mini-theory possible. In addition, protective factors that may have implications for treatment and the prognosis of the case should be listed. The importance of formulation cannot be overemphasized. The process of constructing a formulation is the process of linking academic knowledge of theory and research to clinical practice. If the working alliance is the engine that drives the therapeutic process, formulation is the map that provides guidance on what direction to take.

Feedback

Once a formulation has been constructed, give feedback to the carers, client and relevant members of the client's network. Begin by restating the referral question and offer the formulation as an answer to the referral question. During feedback, use all opportunities to label the clients' and carers' strengths, to build hope. Match the level of detail in giving feedback to the clients' and carers' cognitive ability to comprehend it and their emotional readiness to accept it. It is also important to empathize with each person's position when outlining the way in which the problem appears to have evolved. Usually carers and members of the client's network are well intentioned but under stress, and without adequate information they inadvertently contribute to problem development or maintenance. In the process of feeding back some or all of the formulation, in order to maintain a good working alliance, regularly check that they have understood and accepted the formulation so far.

Support needs

Once the carers and clients have understood and accepted the formulation, move on to exploring clients' current needs in light of the formulation. Immediate risk management should always be prioritized where the clients are a danger to themselves or others or at risk of abuse. This need often arises in cases of challenging behaviour. Other needs that may be identified in light of the formulation are additional psychosocial supports, medical supports, or changes in living residential, educational or vocational placements.

Case management options

The most common types of case management options to meet support needs are listed in Table 5.3. What follows are examples of these. In some cases, further input from a psychologist in a disability service may be unnecessary, for example where assessment reveals that a child is of normal intelligence with an expressive developmental language delay. In other cases, it is appropriate to offer consultation to carers or key involved agency and periodic reassessment. For example, where the primary concern is a skill deficit, the psychologist may develop a skills training programme and coach the carers and teachers in implementing this programme and periodically review progress. Sometimes, difficulties identified by a psychologist may require assessment or intervention from another team member. For example, a child with a major discrepancy between verbal and performance ability scores may be referred to a speech and language therapist for a specialist language assessment. In other cases, referrals to specialist services outside the team may be necessary. For example, where psychological assessment reveals clinical evidence of seizures, a referral to paediatric neurology may be appropriate in some localities. For a proportion of cases, the psychologist may design and implement a focal intervention and support plan. For example, parents of a newly diagnosed preschooler may be offered behavioural parent training, along with a concurrent placement for their child at the disability team's preschool for children with intellectual disabilities. In more complex cases, the psychologist may co-ordinate individual multimodal support plans. For example, arranging residential and vocational placements and life skills training for a young adult who is leaving secondary school and moving out of his parents' home. These case management options are listed in Table 5.3.

STAGE 3: CASE MANAGEMENT

When carers and clients have completed the assessment stage, have accepted the formulation, and are aware of the broad possibilities for case management, it is appropriate to progress to the stage of case management. The central tasks of this stage are contracting for further involvement to achieve specific goals; participating in the completion of the agreed case management plan; and troubleshooting resistance.

Contracting for case management and goal setting

The contracting process involves inviting carers, clients and, where relevant, members of the professional network (for example care workers, teachers, and nurses) to make a commitment to pursue a specific case management plan to reach specific goals. This plan may include one or more of the case management options discussed in the previous section. Where part of the plan includes either focal or multisystemic intervention, goal setting is particularly important. Clear, realistic, visualized goals that are fully accepted by all family members and that are perceived to be moderately challenging are crucial for effective therapy.

In this context it is important to give carers, clients and colleagues clear information about research on the costs and benefits of psychological interventions and the overall results of outcome studies (Carr, 2000; 2002; Emerson, 2001; Kavale and Forness, 1999; Nathan and Gorman, 2002). Broadly speaking, most evidence-based psychological interventions are effective in only 66–75 per cent of cases and about 10 per cent of cases deteriorate as a result of interventions. The more protective factors that are present in a given case, the more likely it is that therapy will be effective. If psychological interventions are going to be effective, most of the gains for most types are made in the first 6–10 sessions. Relapses are inevitable for many types of problems and periodic booster sessions may be necessary to help clients and carers handle relapse situations. With disabilities, further episodes of intervention are typically offered at life-stage transitions. This psychoeducational input is appropriate to give where intervention programmes constitute a significant part of the proposed case management programme. This information is not relevant to residential, educational or vocational placements.

The contracting session is complete when all involved members of the client's network necessary for implementing the case management plan agree to be involved in an episode of consultation to achieve specific goals. In these cost-conscious times, in public services or managed care services, therapeutic episodes should be time-limited.

Carers and colleagues may point out that they have been through unsuccessful intervention programmes in the past, and that it appears that the programme being offered is similar to that which failed before. Where programmes that have failed in the past are recommended as part of the approach described here, it may be that in the past they were tried for too short a time; inappropriately applied; or used alone rather than as part of an integrated multisystemic treatment plan.

Completing case management plans

Case management programmes for a range of problems across the lifespan are given in sections 4–7 of this volume. These diverse programmes have a number of common features. They assume that clients' problems are complex and require thorough assessment. This assessment may be multidisciplinary and takes into account the team's observations but also those of the parents and involved professionals. For each case, all of the information is integrated into a formulation. Various systematic approaches to formulation are offered by different contributors to this volume. All of these formulation models are multifactorial, and none attempt to pinpoint a single cause for any specific difficulty. Intervention plans are based on case formulations and on evidence about the types of programmes that have been shown to work in controlled outcome studies.

Troubleshooting resistance

It is one of the extraordinary paradoxes of clinical psychology that people go to considerable lengths to seek professional advice on how to manage their difficulties and often do not follow through on such advice or other responsibilities entailed by the treatment contract. This type of behaviour has traditionally been referred to as non-compliance or resistance. Accepting the inevitability of resistance and developing skills for managing it is central to the effective practice of clinical psychology (Anderson and Stewart, 1983). Resistance may take the form of not completing tasks between sessions, not attending sessions, or refusing to terminate the therapy process. It may also involve not co-operating during therapy sessions. For carers and placement staff to make progress with contributing to the resolution of client difficulties, the therapist must have some systematic way of dealing with resistance. First, describe the discrepancy between what the carer or staff member agreed to do and what they actually did. Second, ask about the difference between situations where they managed to follow through on an agreed course of action and those where they did not. Third, ask what they believed blocked them from making progress. Fourth, ask if these blocks can be overcome. Fifth, ask about strategies for getting around the blocks. Sixth, ask about the pros and cons of these courses of action. Seventh, frame a therapeutic dilemma which outlines the costs of maintaining the status quo and the costs of circumventing the blocks.

When resistance is questioned, factors that underpin it are uncovered. In some instances unforeseen events – Acts of God – hinder progress. In others, the problem is that carers or staff lack the skills and abilities that underpin resistance. Where a poor case management contract has been formed, resistance is usually due to a lack of commitment to the therapeutic process. Specific convictions which form part of culturally based belief systems may also contribute to resistance, where the clients' values prevent them from following through on specific intervention tasks, such as only offering positive regard to clients contingent upon acceptable or skilful behaviour. The wish to avoid emotional pain is a further factor that commonly underpins resistance.

Questioning resistance is only helpful if a good therapeutic alliance has been built. If carers or staff feel that they are being blamed for not making progress, then they will usually respond by pleading helplessness, blaming the psychologist or someone else for the resistance, or distracting the focus away from the problem of resistance into less painful areas. Blaming, distraction or pleading helplessness often elicit counter-transference reactions on the psychologist's part which compound rather than resolve the therapeutic *impasse*. The commonest of these is intense ambivalence.

Co-ordinating or contributing to individual programme plan meetings

Often psychologists' contributions to case management involves co-ordinating or contributing to individual multimodal programme plans (individual family support plans, individual education plans, individual programme plans, etc.). The aim of these plans is to provide a co-ordinated seamless service tailored to the clients' unique needs, and to modify this service plan in light of periodic feedback. When co-ordinating or key working individual support plans, follow a coherent case management system. Develop a clear system for monitoring and recording the progress of the plan and a system where members of the client's network regularly review progress and deal with co-ordination difficulties. A paper-based or computer-based system for keeping track of such programmes is vital. A front sheet should be placed in the file or on the database that specifies the following points:

- The name of each subcomponent of the programme (e.g. parent training; preschool placement; home-visiting support; speech therapy)
- A brief statement of the goal for each component
- The names of the professional responsible for implementing the subcomponents
- The number of sessions and dates of these (if that is feasible)
- The review dates for the overall programme
- The case manager or key worker responsible for convening review meetings.

With complex cases, review meetings for the network are particularly important since they provide a forum within which the client, carers and all involved professionals may share information and strive to retain a shared view of the case formulation, goals and management plan. Without a shared view, the opportunities for synergistic service provision may be lost.

When convening a review meeting, particularly where difficulties have developed in the co-ordination and delivery of the agreed programme, set clear goals. Such goals typically include agreeing a plan for providing appropriate supports in light of the overall case formulation and client needs, and agreeing on roles and responsibilities. Open review meetings with introductions if any team members have not met and set the agenda and the rules for participation clearly. Arrange for an advocate to sit with and support the client. Make sure that everyone gets a fair hearing by helping the reticent to elaborate their positions and the talkative to condense their contributions. Summarize periodically to help members maintain focus. Above all, retain neutrality by siding with no one, and curiously inquiring about each person's position. Use time-out, if necessary, to integrate contributions, and refine the supports plan. Once the meeting accepts the overall supports plan, request a commitment to implementing the plan. Then work towards that by examining options and agreeing on which team members are responsible for particular parts of the programme plan. Minute all agreements and agree on further review dates.

When contributing to a review meeting, prepare points on your involvement in the case, your formulation, your understanding of required supports and what your service can contribute to an individual programme plan. Use slack time at the beginning of the meeting or during the tea break to build good working alliances with team members. Always introduce yourself before making your first contribution, if you are new to the team. Outline your involvement first and formulation and possible contributions to a support plan later. Make your points briefly and summarize your points at the end of each major contribution. When you disagree, focus on clarifying the issue and not on attacking the person with whom you disagree. Keep notes on who attended the meeting, on the formulation, and the plan agreed. If you have unresolved ambivalent feelings after the meeting, discuss these in supervision.

STAGE 4: DISENGAGING OR RECONTRACTING

Disengagement follows different patterns depending upon the type of case management plan. Where cases are placed or referred elsewhere following assessment, then the process of placement or referral constitutes disengagement. In cases where the psychologist was involved in implementing a focal or multimodal programme or consulting with others implementing such a programme, begin the process of disengagement from an episode of intensive contact once the carers, client and others involved in the programme notice improvement. Review goals attainment. If goals have been achieved, ask the carers, client and other involved network members their beliefs about the permanence of this change. Help the carer, client and involved network members construct an understanding of the change process by reviewing with them the problem, the formulation, their progress through the treatment programme and the concurrent improvement in the problem. Then discuss relapse management (Marlatt and Gordon, 1985). Help carers, clients and involved network members to forecast the types of stressful situations in which relapses may occur; their probable negative reactions to relapses; and the ways in which they can use the lessons learned in the recent programme to cope with these relapses in a productive way. Talk about the process of disengagement as an episodic event rather than as the end of a relationship. Make it clear that psychology departments in disability services offer episodes of intensive contact during crises and at lifecycle transitions, to help clients and their carers manage these difficult patches. So the end of an episode of contact is not the end of a relationship, but the conclusion of one episode in a series of episodes.

Failure analysis

If goals are not reached, it is in the clients' best interests to avoid doing *more of the same* (Segal, 1991). Rather, analyse these therapeutic failures in a systematic way. The understanding that emerges from this is useful both for clients and for psychologists. From the clients' and carers' perspectives, they avoid becoming trapped in a consultation process that maintains rather than resolves the problem. From psychologists' viewpoints failure analysis provides a mechanism for coping with burn-out that occurs when multiple therapeutic failures occur. Failures may occur for a number of reasons. First, they may occur because of the engagement difficulties. The correct members of the client's network may not have been engaged. For example, where fathers are not engaged in the therapy process, drop-out is more likely. The construction of a formulation of the presenting problem which does not open up possibilities for change or which does not fit with the carers' belief systems is a second possible reason for failure. A third reason why failure occurs may be that the case management plan was not appropriately designed, the therapeutic alliance was poorly built, or the psychologist had difficulties in offering the client and carers invitations to complete the therapeutic tasks. Problems with handling clients' and carers' reservations about change, and the resistance that this may give rise to, is a fourth and further source of failure. Disengaging without empowering the clients and carers to handle relapses is a fifth possible factor contributing to therapeutic failure. A sixth factor is counter-transference. Where counter-transference reactions seriously compromise therapist neutrality and the capacity to join in an empathic way with clients and carers, therapeutic failure may occur. Finally, failure may occur because the goals set did not take account of the constraints under which clients and carers were operating. These constraints include biological factors such as illness, psychological factors such as multiple comorbid psychological disorders, economic factors such as poverty, social factors such as general life stress, and broader socio-cultural factors such as minority-group membership. The analysis of treatment failure is an important way to develop therapeutic skill, and an appropriate focus to address in supervision.

REPORT WRITING

Report writing is central to the practice of clinical psychology. The limitations of our memories require us to keep detailed accounts of complex information about our clients. An accurate account of information gained in interviews, testing, and observation sessions and meetings with other professionals is the basis on which a formulation is constructed and a treatment plan developed. Records also help us to keep track of progress with case management plans. At the end of an episode of consultation, a summary of the episode provides information that may be useful to ourselves or our colleagues in helping clients should they return for a further episode of consultation in the future. During the process of assessment and case management, other members of the client's network may require verbal or written reports. Carers and placement staff may also benefit from having written communication about how to implement specific programmes to help clients learn skills or modify challenging behaviour. In some cases it may be necessary to write specialized reports as assignments for clinical psychology training programmes. On an annual basis it may be necessary to write a service report. Guidelines for writing the following types of reports are given below:

- Progress notes
- Comprehensive assessment reports

- End of episode case summaries
- Verbal reports
- Correspondence with professionals
- Correspondence with carers and placement staff
- Case study reports
- Annual service reports.

Confidentiality and freedom of information

Psychologists have a duty to their clients to maintain confidentiality, and so all reports about clients should be written and managed with this as a central guiding principle. In all circumstances where psychologists wish to exchange information with other members of the client's professional or social network, the carer's or client's consent should be sought. Confidentiality may be broken only in circumstances where to maintain confidentiality would place the client or some other person in danger. Clients' reports should be written, stored and managed in a way that is consistent with, and takes full account of, freedom of information legislation. A guideline for all forms of reports is always to write in such a way that you would be prepared to give your case files or service reports to clients, their families and involved professionals to read.

Progress notes

In making progress notes about clinical cases, five categories of information should always be recorded. These are

- Time
- Attendance
- Review
- Agenda
- Plan.

The first letters of these category names form the acronym TARAP. The issues covered by each category will be expanded below.

- **Time.** This category includes the date, day, time and duration of the session. It may be useful also to include the number of the session, particularly if working within a time-limited contract for assessment or intervention. Often in clinical psychology, time-limited contracts of six, ten or twenty sessions are used.
- **Attendance.** The people who attended the session and those who were invited and did not attend may be noted in this category. In the case of total non-attendance (or DNAs as they are often called) it is important to

record what steps were taken to inquire about reasons for non-attendance, especially where there are risks of self-harm.

- **Review.** A review of significant events that may have occurred since the previous session are recorded here. Changes in the presenting problem and factors related to its resolution or maintenance should be reviewed. Inquiries should also routinely be made about completion of assessment tasks such as self-monitoring and treatment tasks. In the case of an initial session, changes that have occurred since the referral was made may be noted.
- **Agenda.** Information about the main *content* issues and the main *processes* which occurred may be recorded in this category. Content issues include the topics discussed and the tests administered. Process issues include the quality of the working alliance and the impact of this on the progress of assessment or treatment.
- **Plan.** Future action for clients, network members and the psychologist may be noted in this category. These include assessment or treatment tasks that clients have been invited to complete; assessment procedures or particular therapy-related themes for inclusion on the agenda for the next session; and clinical hypotheses requiring further exploration.

The TARAP format for making progress notes is appropriate for assessment and treatment sessions with clients and members of their social systems.

Comprehensive assessment report

A comprehensive assessment report is typically written at the end of the assessment stage and as the basis from which to conduct case management. This type of report represents a summary and integration of information obtained throughout the assessment process, which may have spanned a number of sessions and include a review of reports from other professionals. The comprehensive assessment report is written primarily for the psychologist and members of the psychologist's team. All other reports and correspondence are based on this document. Usually it should include the section on the issues listed below.

- **Demographic information.** The client's name, date of birth and address should be given here along with names, addresses and contact numbers for next of kin, and carers where relevant.
- **Referral information.** This section includes the referring agent's name, address and contact number, and the central problems that led to the referral or the principal referral question. It is also useful to include here details of significant members of the professional network, such as the name, address and contact numbers of other involved professionals including the family doctor, paediatrician, public health nurse,

educational psychologist, psychiatrist, social worker, hostel manager, and so forth.

- **Sources.** The sources of information on which the report is based should be listed. These sources include all assessment sessions with dates and a note of who attended the sessions. If previous reports by physicians, social workers or other professionals were used, these, too, should be noted.
- **History of the presenting problem and previous treatment.** This section should include an account of how the problem developed and previous episodes of treatment. Note any factors that precipitated the onset or exacerbation of the main problems and what was helpful in previous intervention episodes. The role of other involved professionals may be mentioned here. If medical, psychiatric or social work reports are available, salient points from these may be summarized in this section.
- **Developmental history.** Reference should be made to nature and timing of significant events or abnormalities in physical, cognitive and psychosocial development over the course of the lifecycle. Note possible personal predisposing factors that may have rendered the client vulnerable to their current difficulties and any personal strengths that may act as protective factors.
- **The family history.** Family membership; stresses and supports; relationship patterns; and significant achievements or difficulties in managing family transitions over the lifecycle should all be mentioned in this section. Note possible social predisposing factors that may have rendered the client vulnerable to their current disorder and any strengths in the client's social network that may act as protective factors.
- **Psychological testing.** If psychological testing has been conducted, it is appropriate to include a section where reference may be made to the results of psychometric assessments, cognitive abilities, adaptive behaviour, and specific presenting problems such as challenging behaviour. In presenting psychological test results include the following information:

  - The tests used
  - The number and duration of testing sessions
  - The impact of co-operation, medication, physical factors (noise, cold, crowding, etc.), extraneous psychosocial factors (e.g. exhaustion) on the validity of the results
  - A list of results and an interpretation of these.

Present the results and their interpretation in a logical, orderly way.

- **Differential diagnosis and diagnosis.** If there has been concern about the differential diagnosis, it is appropriate to include this section. State the main presenting problems, the diagnostic possibilities that were considered and the diagnosis that is best supported by the data gathered during the psychological assessment.

- **Formulation.** A brief restatement of the central problems should be given here, along with an explanation of how they developed based on salient points drawn from previous sections of the report. Reference should be made to predisposing, precipitating and maintaining factors. In addition, protective factors that have a bearing on the prognosis should be mentioned. It is important to emphasize the client's strengths and resources, as well as deficits and difficulties.
- **Recommended case management and supports plan.** A prioritized list of options for case management may be given here. Taking no further action; periodic reassessment; referral to another team member for consultation; referral elsewhere for consultation; focal psychological intervention; or an individualized multimodal intervention should all be considered. Where an individualized multimodal intervention programme is central to the management plan, details of the components of the programme and the professionals responsible should be indicated. A key worker responsible for reviewing progress at designated times should be specified.
- **Signature.** Most agencies have a policy about signing reports. Unless there are ethical reasons for not doing so, follow this policy, particularly if you are still in training. If there is no policy in your agency and you are in training, write your name and degrees on one line and underneath Clinical Psychologist in Training (in the UK) or Clinical Psychologist Intern, Extern of Practicum Student (in Canada and the US). In addition, the supervisor's name, degrees and appointment is also placed on the report and co-signed.

Comprehensive assessment reports are usually written up by the key worker for the case.

End of episode case summary

When clients conclude an episode of intervention or case management, an end of episode case summary (or discharge summary) may be written. This report summarizes progress made as a result of implementing the case management plan. An end of episode case summary should contain the following sections:

- The formulation
- The implementation of the case management and support plan
- The outcome.

The formulation outlined in the comprehensive assessment report may be restated in the first section of the end of episode case summary. In the second section, a summary of the case management plan that was implemented should be given. It is also useful to note here any co-operation or co-ordination difficulties that occurred and how various resistances within the client's network were managed. In cases that did not respond to treatment, a hypothesis about the reasons for treatment failure should be given. If any new information came to light that led to the original formulation being substantially revised, this should be noted. In the final section of an end of episode summary, the degree to which specific treatment goals were met should be noted along with other positive or negative changes. Follow-up plans for review sessions or relapse management should also be noted.

Verbal reports

During the consultation process it may be necessary to give verbal reports to carers, clients and colleagues in feedback sessions, team meetings and case conferences. In preparing verbal reports, first identify the audience to whom your report will be addressed. Is it a carer, client, social worker, physician or a mixed group of professionals? Then, clarify the sort of question to which you believe they require an answer. They may want to know if your assessment indicates a client has an intellectual disability; what the most appropriate placement or support plan is for the next stage of the lifecycle; how to manage challenging behaviour; or how to enhance the client's skills repertoire. From your progress notes or the comprehensive assessment report, abstract the points that you are confidently able to make to answer the question. If you are unable to answer the question on the basis of the available information, arrange interviews, testing or observation sessions to obtain such information if this is feasible and within the remit of your professional role.

Then prepare the list of points you wish to make in the meeting to answer the questions you know or guess are of central concern to your audience. Frame the points in language and at a level of technical sophistication that will be optimally intelligible to the audience. So, for example, it may be useful to give detailed psychometric information in a verbal report to a neuropsychologist but of little use to give such information to a surgeon or occupational therapist. In some instances, you will be unable to offer valid information to other professionals.

When making a verbal report to any audience state:

- The question you aimed to answer
- The source of your information and your confidence in its reliability and validity
- The key pieces of information that answer the question (and no more).

If you are presenting information in a team meeting or case conference and do not know all of the participants, it is important to identify yourself as a clinical psychologist (or a clinical psychologist in training working under the supervision of a senior staff member).

If information presented by other professionals in a team meeting or case conference is inconsistent with your findings, think through the possible reasons for the discrepancy between the two sets of information before offering your opinion on this to the team or conference. Discrepancies between professional reports are common. The important issue to resolve is why the discrepancy occurred, not which view is correct and which is incorrect. Discrepancies may be due to the time and place where the assessment was conducted; the assessment or treatment methods used; the informants; the level of co-operation between the client and the professional; and a wide range of other factors.

Correspondence with professionals

All correspondence should be written with the concerns of the recipient of the letter in mind. Before writing a letter, clarify what question the recipient would like answered or the request you would like to make. Common questions that other professionals would like psychologists to answer are:

• Has the client been placed on your waiting list and if so when will the client be offered an appointment?
• Has this client an intellectual disability?
• Has this client an autistic spectrum disorder, anxiety, depression or some other condition?
• What is the client's current profile and what are the client's future support and placement requirements?
• Why is the client behaving in an unusual or challenging way and what can be done about it?
• How can the client be helped to develop additional skills?

Common requests are:

• Can you assess this client's speech and language difficulties and advise on treatment or management?
• Can you assess this client's sensory difficulties and advise on management?
• Can you assess this client for a possible seizure disorder and advise on management?
• In view of the client's profile and support needs, can your agency offer this client a placement?

Decide what precise pieces of information the recipient would like abstracted from your case file to answer their question. Judge in what level of detail and what degree of technical sophistication they would like such information. Account should be taken of their knowledge of developmental psychology, psychometrics, psychotherapy, applied behaviour analysis, and so forth. If any action will be required on their part in response to your letter, decide exactly what it is that you are suggesting they do.

Routinely in most public service agencies, letters are written to referrers following the receipt of a referral to indicate that the referral has been placed on a waiting list. Letters are also written following a period of assessment to indicate the way the case has been formulated and the recommended case management and supports plan. Finally, letters are also written at the end of an episode of contact to inform the referrer of the outcome of any intervention programme.

From experience of talking with more than 1,000 professional recipients of psychologists' reports on both sides of the Atlantic over the past twenty-five years, one reasonably valid conclusion may be drawn. Clinical psychologists' reports are perceived by the referrer to be too long and often the key information required by the referrer is buried under a mountain of detail, deemed by the referrer to be unnecessary.

When a referral is received, it is sufficient to return a single sentence letter indicating that the case will be placed on a waiting list and seen within a specified time frame. Following a preliminary interview or series of assessment sessions, it is sufficient to write a brief letter specifying the referral question, the assessment methods used, the formulation and the case management plan. A common mistake here is to send referrers (particularly family doctors) unwanted comprehensive assessment reports. It may be useful to conclude letters summarizing preliminary assessments by noting that a comprehensive report is available on request. In closing letters to referrers, it is sufficient to restate the initial question; the formulation; the case management and supports plan; the degree to which it was implemented and the outcome. The text from an end of episode case summary may be used as a basis for writing a closing note to a referrer.

Asking other professionals to follow a particular course of action in a letter is more likely to lead to confusion than to co-ordinated action. It is better practice to outline your formulation in a letter and invite other professionals to join you in a meeting to discuss joint action than to ask them to implement a programme you have already designed.

Psychologists working on a disability team may sometimes have to write to other professionals requesting assessment and advice on management of speech and language difficulties, sensory disabilities and seizure disorders. In such reports it is good practice to specify the observations and test results that have led you to make the request along with a succinct summary of the formulation. Psychologists working on a disability team may sometimes have to write to other agencies requesting educational, vocational or residential placements for clients. In such instances, it is a good idea initially to phone the agency director and find out the level of detail required in a placement request letter and also ask for the admission criteria. Then write the placement request letter with the level of detail required, specifying the evidence for the client's suitability for the placement.

Correspondence with carers and placement staff

Letters may be used to help carers and residential, educational or vocational placement staff remember what was said during a consultation and to highlight key aspects of sessions. Case formulations, test results and instructions for implementing programmes may all be given in written form.

When writing a letter to a carer or placement staff member, first clarify what you want to achieve by writing the letter. Do you want to inform them or invite them to implement a particular programme? Second, guess what are the main concerns of the carer or staff member and how they will be likely to respond to the information or invitation that you offer. In some instances they will be likely to receive information positively and respond to invitations to implement programmes quite flexibly. In other situations, their ability level or qualifications, their fear or anger that they are being negatively labelled by the psychologist, or their belief that the invitation in the letter to view the problem differently or behave differently will lead to some negative outcome may prevent them from understanding information or following through on invitations contained in letters. The third step in writing letters to carers or placement staff is to decide how information or invitations should be framed so that they have the desired impact. Where carers have limited verbal or intellectual abilities, use simple language. Where there is a danger that carers or staff may feel blamed for failing to solve the presenting problem previously, acknowledge carers' and placement staffs' strengths and commitment to change. Where carers fear that looking at the problem differently or behaving differently will lead to negative outcomes, highlight the benefits of accepting the invitation but also the dangers of accepting the invitation without due consideration and deliberation.

Case study reports

In many clinical psychology training programmes conceptual clinical skills are assessed by case study. Case studies are an opportunity for candidates to demonstrate that they can bring their knowledge of relevant psychological literature to bear on the way in which they conceptualize and manage clinical problems. The precise requirements for writing a case study report vary from one clinical psychology training programme to another. The guidelines presented here are those used in our doctoral programme in clinical psychology at University College, Dublin.

Case studies should be based on clients with which the candidate has had clinical involvement as the key worker or as a co-worker with another clinician. The scientist-practitioner model should be used. That is, scientific knowledge and systematic investigative and intervention methods should be brought to bear on a specific clinical problem in an interpersonally sensitive way. A knowledge of the relevant literature must be demonstrated. A case study should highlight the candidate's ability to formulate and test clinical hypotheses. The ability to synthesize salient points from a range of investigative procedures into a comprehensive formulation should be clearly shown. A case study should indicate that the candidate can develop and implement treatment programmes and case management plans which follow logically from case formulations. Interpersonal sensitivity and an awareness of process and ethical issues should also be demonstrated in case study reports.

A case study may focus on describing how assessment procedures were used to resolve a diagnostic issue and arrive at a coherent integrative formulation. In other instances, case studies may show how assessment and formulation led to the development and implementation of a case management or treatment plan. Where candidates had primary responsibility for implementing one aspect of this plan, particular attention may be paid to that in the case report. Where clients with similar problems have received group treatment, an entire group may serve as the focus for the case study. In such instances, a generic formulation of the problem addressed by the group treatment programme may be presented.

A case study should follow the outline structure presented in Table 5.5 and contain no more than 4,000 words (excluding appendices and references). Copies of reports, correspondence and test forms may be included in appendices. Clients' names and other identifying information should be deleted from these documents to preserve confidentiality. Consent for writing case studies should be obtained at the outset of the assessment and treatment contract. This issue is covered in the intake form in Table 5.1. Where the case study format given in Table 5.5 is clearly unsuitable, candidates may order and organize case material and relevant information from the literature in a way which is most coherent. While psychologists in clinical training usually

Table 5.5 Framework for writing a case study

I **Demographic information about the case and the referral process**
   - Demographic information
   - Referral agent, instigator of the referral and reason for referral
   - History of the presenting problem
   - Relevant background individual and family psychosocial and medical history
   - Previous and current assessment and treatment

2 **Review of relevant literature**
   - Classification, epidemiology, clinical features, course, assessment, treatment and controversial issues
   - Reference to AAMR, ICD and DSM and other relevant classification systems
   - Reference to major clinical texts and recent relevant literature (particularly review papers, book chapters, assessment manuals, treatment manuals and handbooks)

(Continued overleaf)

Table 5.5 Continued

3 Preliminary hypotheses and preliminary formulation of problem
- Hypotheses and proposed plan for testing hypotheses
- Preliminary formulation of the problem from a theoretical perspective

4 Assessment
- Procedures used, e.g. interviews, psychometric tests, observation sessions
- Rationale for choice
- Developmental history with particular reference to salient features
- Family history and genogram with particular reference to salient features
- Current cognitive functioning (including a table of test results if cognitive tests were conducted)
- Current psychosocial adjustment (including results of behaviour checklists and personality tests)

5 Formulation
- Implications of data from assessment for preliminary formulation and hypotheses
- Integration of assessment data into a comprehensive formulation highlighting predisposing, precipitating, maintaining and protective factors or other relevant CBT, psychodynamic, systemic or biomedical formulation model

6 Case management
- Consider options for action in the light of formulation (taking no further action; periodic reassessment; referral to another team member for consultation; referral elsewhere for consultation; focal intervention; or multimodal intervention)
- Choice of option and reason for choice in light of formulation
- Description of programme plan and goals of programme
- Review of progress in the light of goals
- Evaluation of outcome specifying assessment instruments used (graph changes in problems or symptoms if appropriate; at a minimum pre- and post-treatment measures may be used. Single-case designs may be used if appropriate)

7 Process issues
- Impact of clinician–client relationship factors on the consultation process
- Impact of interprofessional and interagency relationships on the consultation process

8 Ethical issues
Ethical issues and the way they were managed should be addressed. Common issues include:
- The ability to give informed consent
- Confidentiality of reports
- Risk assessment (suicide, violence, impaired judgement, fitness to parent)
- Right of attorney

9 Summary and conclusions
- Reason for referral
- Summary of assessment and formulation
- Summary of treatment
- Recommendation or future management

10 References and appendices
- No more than 10 references most of which should be to key review articles, book chapters, manuals, and handbooks should be included as references and these should be in the format used in *Journal of Consulting and Clinical Psychology* or the *Irish Journal of Psychology* which follow the BPS or APA referencing styles
- All relevant test result forms; checklists; reports from other professionals; correspondence; client drawings, etc. should be included as appendices with identifying information deleted.

choose to write up cases where the work proceeded smoothly in accordance with a treatment manual, the client improved and was satisfied with services received, it may be more useful to write up work that is more representative of routine practice. Indeed, the purpose of the case study is to demonstrate learning, reflection and professional development, and it is often in difficult work with clients where things do not go smoothly, where clients are challenging or do not improve that we learn most. Such case studies may provide excellent opportunities for reflection and development.

Service reports

On an annual basis, it is useful for clinical psychology service departments to produce reports that describe their performance over the preceding twelve-month period. Such reports are useful for service planning and for keeping managers, service purchasers and funders abreast of departmental performance. Most psychology departments provide consultative and research services to colleagues as well as clinical services to clients. It is therefore important to include sections on both of these in annual reports. However, here the focus will be on producing that section of the annual report concerned with services to clients. Give a description of the types of services offered, the staff who offer these; the target population for whom the service is intended; and the avenues of referral. Then give a short statistical summary of the number and type of cases that received consultation, with a breakdown of the way they were referred; their demographic characteristics; their main diagnoses or presenting problems; and the amount of input made to cases in terms of the numbers of hours of clinical contact and the number of hours of administrative time. These data may be routinely recorded for each case using a simple database. It is useful also in annual reports to include data on clients' level of goal attainment. Attainment of goals in client case management and support plans may be routinely rated on 10-point scales and clients' average goal-attainment scores may be entered onto the data base for annual analysis. It is also valuable to include information on service-users' perspectives, as given by qualitative self-reports, and carers' satisfaction ratings may be assessed with psychometric instruments such as the Client Satisfaction with Treatment Scale (Larsen et al., 1979).

SUMMARY

In the field of intellectual disability, clinical psychology services may be offered to clients within the context of a chronic care model with episodes of intensive contact occurring at critical points in the lifecycle. These episodes may be conceptualized as involving a series of stages, the first of which involves planning whom to invite and what to ask at the first consultation.

The second stage is concerned with the processes of engagement, alliance building, assessment and formulation. In the third stage, the focus is on case management, the therapeutic contract, and the management of resistance. In the final stage, disengagement or recontracting for further intervention occurs. After a period of disengagement, the process may recur at a later time in the client's life when further input from a clinical psychology service may be required. Interviews with clients, carers and other members of the client's network occur during all contacts, and it is vital that all contacts are appropriately recorded and documented.

Intake interviews, test results, observations, formulations and case management plans are usually written up as comprehensive assessment reports and held on clients' clinical files. In routine progress notes, five categories of information may be recorded at the end of each session: Time, Attendance, Review, Agenda, and Plan (TARAP). Throughout case management, progress notes may be recorded following the TARAP system and at the end of an episode of contact, a case summary may be written containing the formulation, a summary of how the plan was implemented and the outcome to which it led. In case-related, verbal or written reports and letters to carers and professionals, identify the audience to whom the report or letter will be addressed, the main questions they have or requests you wish to make, and the main points that need to be made to address these questions and requests. Then frame the points in language and at a level of technical sophistication that will be optimally intelligible to the audience. Guidelines for case study reports and service development reports were also given in the chapter.

EXERCISE

Working in pairs, role play all or part of an intake interview in which one person takes the role of a parent with a 3-year-old child who has not developed language skills. The interviewer should follow the guide in Table 5.3. After the interview, write as brief a comprehensive report as possible and an even briefer letter to the referring family doctor indicating the initial formulation and treatment plan.

FURTHER READING FOR PRACTITIONERS

Emerson, E., Hatton, C., Bromley, J. and Caine, A. (1998). *Clinical Psychology and People with Intellectual Disabilities*. Chichester: Wiley.

REFERENCES

Anderson, C. and Stewart, S. (1983). *Mastering Resistance*. New York: Guilford.

Angold, A. (2002). Diagnostic interviews with parents and children. In M. Rutter and E. Taylor (eds), *Child and Adolescent Psychiatry* (4th edn, pp. 32–51). Oxford: Blackwell.

Carr, A. (2000). *What Works with Children and Adolescents? A Critical Review of Research on Psychological Interventions with Children, Adolescents and their Families*. London: Routledge.

Carr, A. (2002). *Prevention: What Works with Children and Adolescents? A Critical Review of Psychological Prevention Programmes for Children, Adolescents and their Families*. London: Brunner-Routledge.

Emerson, E. (1998). Assessment. In E. Emerson, C. Hatton, J. Bromley and A. Caine (eds), *Clinical Psychology and People with Intellectual Disabilities* (pp. 114–24). Chichester: Wiley.

Emerson, E. (2001). *Challenging Behaviour. Analysis and Intervention in People with Severe Intellectual Disabilities* (2nd edn). Cambridge: Cambridge University Press.

Flesch, R. (1948). A new readability yardstick. *Journal of Applied Psychology*, 32, 221–33.

Hubble, M., Duncan, B. and Miller, S. (1999). *The Heart and Soul of Change*. Washington, DC: APA.

Jones, D. (2003). *Communicating with Vulnerable Children*. London: Gaskell.

Kavale, K. and Forness, S. (1999). *Efficacy of Special Education*. Washington, DC: AAMR.

Larsen, D., Attkinson, C., Hargreaves, W. and Nguyen, T. (1979). Assessment of client/patient satisfaction: Development of a general scale. *Evaluation and Programme Planning*, 2, 197–207.

Marlatt, G. and Gordon, J. (1985). *Relapse Prevention*. New York: Guilford.

McGoldrick, M., Gerson, R. and Schellenberger, S. (1999). *Genograms: Assessment and Intervention*. New York: Norton.

Nathan, P. and Gorman, J. (2002). *A Guide to Treatments that Work* (2nd edn). New York: Oxford University Press.

Norcross, J. (2002). *Psychotherapy Relationships that Work: Therapist Contributions and Responsiveness to Patients*. New York: Oxford University Press.

Prosser, H. and Bromley, J. (1998). Interviewing people with intellectual disabilities. In E. Emerson, C. Hatton, J. Bromley and A. Caine (eds), *Clinical Psychology and People with Intellectual Disabilities* (pp. 99–113). Chichester: Wiley.

Segal, L. (1991). Brief therapy: The MRI approach. In A. Gurman and D. Kniskern (eds), *Handbook of Family Therapy* (vol. 2, pp. 17–199). New York: Brunner/Mazel.

Section 3

Intervention frameworks

Chapter 6

Person-centred planning

Kevin Coyle

A number of planning approaches in the area of disability, collectively known as person-centred planning, have been developed over the last fifteen years or so. These person-centred planning approaches have been seen as alternatives to traditional, service-based planning systems and are aimed at further enhancing the quality of the lives of people with intellectual disabilities (Department of Health, 2001; Emerson and Standcliffe, 2004; Holburn and Vietze, 2002; Mansell and Beadle-Brown, 2004). Person-centred planning, however, is a process with wider aspirations. It offers a challenge not only to individuals committed to support people with intellectual disabilities but also to service organizations, state and voluntary agencies and the wider community. Person-centred planning is concerned ultimately with supporting people with intellectual disabilities to choose and experience the lives of their choice and with social change that enables people with intellectual disabilities to take their place as full members of local communities.

Person-centred planning has become in recent times what Marrone, Hoff and Helm (1997) have termed the mantra of services for people with intellectual disabilities and has been adopted, at least in name, by many agencies, 'often by the very systems, such as special education and adult day services, that this approach was seen as rising above' (p. 285). Some authors (for example, O'Brien, O'Brien and Mount, 1997) are critical of what they consider a tendency for service organizations to misapply person-centred planning. Nonetheless, Holburn and Vietze (1999) argue that 'real' person-centred planning has not changed and is happening currently. This chapter aims to delineate the philosophy and processes of person-centred planning and to discuss those issues that impact on its application.

SELF-DETERMINATION: THE CONTEXT OF PERSON-CENTRED PLANNING

Person-centred planning is a process not a product to be consumed. Person-centred planning essentially arranges for a group of people who know and

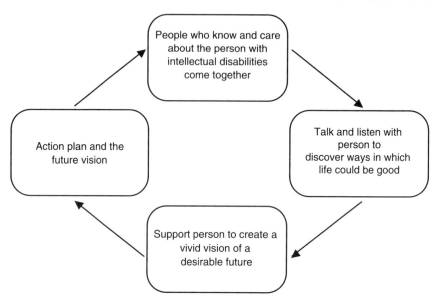

Figure 6.1 The person-centred planning cycle.

care about a person with an intellectual disability to come together with the person to talk and listen to him or her about how life could be good. These conversations lead to the development of a clear picture of a desirable future for the focus person that all involved are prepared to support and work towards. People then work together to implement this future vision, learning as they go by considering their successes and failures. The process continues with ongoing implementation of elements of the vision or with modifications which the focus person chooses based on learning and experience as illustrated in Figure 6.1.

Person-centred planning as a rubric covers a number of alternative processes for individual planning (Personal Futures Planning (Mount, 2000); MAPS (Vandercook, York and Forest, 1989); Essential Life-Style Planning (Smull and Lakin, 2002); Whole Life Planning (Butterworth *et al.*, 1993); PATH (Pearpoint, O'Brien and Forest, 1993)) but all share a common framework of values and principles that are located in the wider context of promoting the self-determination of people with intellectual disabilities.

Self-determination refers to the capacity to act as a causal agent in one's life and to make choices and decisions regarding one's quality of life free from undue external influence or interference (Wehmeyer 1992; Wehmeyer and Kelchner, 1995). Wehmeyer and allies consider self-determination, from the specific perspective of people with intellectual disabilities, to be based on four key principles:

1 **Freedom**: Traditionally, people with intellectual disabilities are funded to take part in a programme from service providers. The principle of freedom involves the capacity of individuals with intellectual disabilities with backup from freely chosen supporters, typically family and friends, to plan a life with requisite support rather than merely access a programme provided by a service organization.

2 **Authority**: Authority is the principle that acknowledges that the person with intellectual disability should control resources, again with backup from others of their choice, so that he or she can purchase the necessary supports to plan and make real the life of his or her choice.

3 **Responsibility**: People with intellectual disabilities are often seen as dependent. The principle of responsibility requires the acceptance that people with intellectual disabilities should assume responsibility to contribute in a variety of roles in their communities, for example as students, workers, members of clubs and associations.

4 **Support**: Support is the fourth principle underpinning all of the above. In this context, support involves the arrangement of both resources and personnel (paid staff and others) so that a person with an intellectual disability can choose and experience this life of his or her choice. This notion of support will be a central facet of person-centred planning.

It will be seen that self-determination is not person-centred planning. Self-determination encompasses a fundamental reform of current service system organization, delivery and its funding mechanisms. Person-centred planning, however, is a prerequisite for implementing the above principles and the implementation of person-centred planning will promote self-determination.

PERSON-CENTRED PLANNING: KEY VALUES

Person-centred planning approaches are deeply rooted in a strong set of values. The primary values are choice and inclusion. Authors may vary as to the relative importance of these values but choice and inclusion lie at the heart of all person-centred planning endeavours. The Five Accomplishments (O'Brien, 1987) are often used as a statement of the key values underpinning person-centred planning and these are listed in Figure 6.2. They include community presence, community participation, dignity, choice and supporting contributions. These values impact on the way one assesses, plans and supports individuals with intellectual disabilities. They may also be used to evaluate the process and outcomes of person-centred planning and wider service or programme outcomes.

1 **Community presence**: Inclusion in local communities involves creating opportunities for people with intellectual disabilities to be physically

```
1   Community presence

2   Community participation

3   Dignity

4   Choices

5   Supporting contributions
```

Figure 6.2 Person-centred planning: key values.

present where local community life takes place. Person-centred plans will enable a person with an intellectual disability to enjoy rich and varied opportunities to be physically present where citizens live, work and play. Inherent in this value is the notion that, while community life has much to offer people with intellectual disabilities, they in turn have much to offer wider society.

2   **Community participation**: Physical presence in community life alone is inadequate. Person-centred planning will also seek to create opportunities for the person with an intellectual disability to make, develop and maintain friendships and relationships with others.

3   **Dignity**: Respect is something that we all desire. We are valued in those places where we live, work and recreate because of who we are and because of our contributions to our world. Our social roles are the engines of how we are perceived as worthy of respect. Person-centred planning will emphasize those experiences and activities that support social roles for the person with intellectual disability that will promote respect and not merely focus on a person's deficits and his or her disability label.

4   **Choice**: Lack of choice is a common experience for many people with intellectual disabilities. Traditional planning approaches sometimes have limited choice because the function of assessment and planning was to decide to which programme to allocate an individual. Choices could be made but choices within the boundaries of a specific programme. Person-centred planning initiatives will deliberately seek to create maximum opportunities for the individual with intellectual disability to make choices about the important areas of life, where to live, work and recreate, and how he or she would like to be supported to make these choices happen. Person-centred planning will also promote opportunities for a person with an intellectual disability to engage in a wide variety of experiences so that these choices are informed choices.

5   **Supporting contributions**: This value acknowledges that people with intellectual disabilities will need backup from others to assume those roles

that they have not traditionally assumed or been allowed to assume in wider society. Person-centred planning, as we will see, actively seeks to identify the gifts and capacities of individuals with intellectual disabilities. The action-planning process will aim to discover ways that the person driving the planning can use these gifts and abilities in mainstream society. The process will also look to extend the range of a person's capacities through learning and instruction.

PERSON-CENTRED PLANNING: KEY PRINCIPLES

Person-centred planning approaches share a number of key, common principles. Different approaches may delineate different strategies and techniques but all have the following elements in common.

1   **Centrality of person with intellectual disability**. Person-centred planning affords a central place to the person with intellectual disability in directing the planning process and its outcomes. The person with intellectual disability is the driving force in the process. It is she or he who will assume the leadership role and who will be supported to assume this role. This means that the process and its outcomes will be determined by the individual central to the planning process and not by those methods and options available in a particular service agency. The service, then, needs to structure itself around the individual service-user rather than the service-user automatically fitting into service structures and programme options.
2   **Focus on the involvement of family members and friends in the process**. Person-centred planning emphasizes that personal, social relationships form the bedrock of that support required to produce the outcomes desired by individuals with disabilities. These relationships have been referred to in the literature on person-centred planning as natural supports and include those people that most of us use on a routine basis as part of living, working and recreating in our communities (Everson and Reid, 1999). This does not obviate the need for professional input or mean that individuals with intellectual disabilities will not require specialized services. Rather, this approach seeks for service organizations to identify and deliver specialized inputs in ways that allow natural supports to supplement their work so that service-users can live and function in mainstream society.
3   **Focus on an individual's gifts and abilities**. Service systems in the past have focused on an individual's needs and limitations. Person-centred planning encourages participants to identify an individual's preferences, talents and capacities so that learning and support can be focused on these. In many ways, this process is no different to career guidance or life planning

that happens for people without disabilities where the objective is to build on peoples' interests and strengths and where these interests and strengths determine career and life choices.

4   **The development of a clear vision of a desirable future**. Person-centred planning approaches support an individual with an intellectual disability to outline the future that she or he wishes. This future vision serves as the compass directing all activity and experience. Experiences, skills acquisition and support should deliver this future vision or even move the person towards its achievement. Older planning systems for people with intellectual disabilities tended to focus on a person's needs and limitations and then tried to eliminate these deficits via a range of programmes or specialized inputs.

5   **The requirement for change in traditional service systems**. Traditional service systems have been structured around programme delivery to groups of people with intellectual disabilities. Further, these programmes have largely been delivered in segregated settings. Service-users are assigned to a programme or range of programme options depending on their assessed suitability for one or more of these programmes. Assessment indeed has largely been focused on determining eligibility and suitability for pre-determined service options. Person-centred planning will challenge this approach by requiring service systems to move from a group to an individual focus, from assessment of deficits to a determination of a service-user's strengths and interests, from an emphasis on professional support to the development of strategies that engage networks of people to provide support, and to deliver inputs and supports in regular community settings and not in specialized environments.

It should be obvious from the above principles that a person-centred approach to planning and service delivery is different from what one might deem a traditional approach. Person-centred planning is (a) person-driven; (b) personal interests and capacity-focused; (c) directed by desirable outcomes determined by the individual with intellectual disability; and (d) marked by an emphasis on fostering and building networks of people around the person who are willing to engage and offer support. Traditional service planning is (a) service-driven; (b) focused on what needs to be learned; (c) driven by programmes; and (d) based on professional input and support. These distinctions are presented in Figure 6.3.

SOME APPROACHES TO IMPLEMENTING PERSON-CENTRED PLANNING

Person-centred planning in any of the forms detailed below seeks answers to three key questions: (a) who is this person with an intellectual disability

PERSON-CENTRED PLANNING	TRADITIONAL APPROACHES
• Person-driven • Focus on abilities and capacities • Focus on desirable outcomes • Aims to build networks	• Service-driven • Focus on what needs to be learnt • Focus on programmes • Emphasis on professional support

Figure 6.3 A comparison of person-centred planning and traditional systems.

whom we are charged and want to support; (b) what mainstream community opportunities will enable this person to achieve life options and personal interests in a positive way; and (c) what support and personal development will be required to make this happen? Each of the approaches differs in terms of its main intended purpose and the population of people with whom it is commonly used.

Personal Futures Planning

Personal Futures Planning (Mount, 2000; Mount and Zwernik, 1988) seems to have become the dominant method of person-centred planning in many settings. The system is presented in Figure 6.4. It is a well-delineated approach that emphasizes that individual quality of life is realized through the O'Brien accomplishments noted above. Personal Futures Planning is a group process that seeks the engagement of a range of people from a variety of backgrounds to work across what O'Brien and Lovett have termed the 'usual organizational and status boundaries' (O'Brien and Lovett, 1993: 13). This approach moves through a series of stages that ultimately ends in the action planning of a vision of a desirable future that has been developed by a person with intellectual disabilities with the support of others, usually called the person's circle of support.

Personal Futures Planning has evolved from two distinct contexts. The first context centred on the efforts of some parents, families and friends of people with disabilities to support the family member or friend with disability to achieve the lives of their choice but who were receiving limited, if any, support from service organizations. The second context centred on a number of professionals offering technical assistance to service organizations that sought to change their systems to be more responsive to the needs and wishes of their service-users. Personal Futures Planning was a development of this endeavour.

Personal Futures Planning may be described as a stage approach to planning. The first stage involves the construction of a personal profile of the

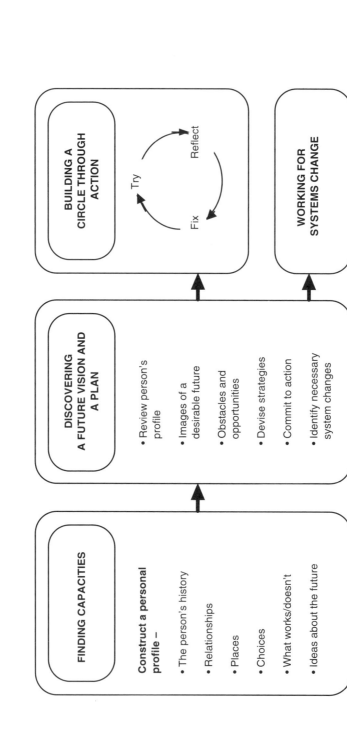

Figure 6.4 Personal Futures Planning.

individual with an intellectual disability. This profile includes information on the person's history, his or her relationships, the places where the person spends his or her time, a list of the person's choices, what approaches suit the person and what strategies are unsuitable. This personal profile forms the basis for the development of a vision of a desirable future and an action-plan for its implementation. Then ensues an action-learning cycle in which the future vision is implemented or modified based on experience. The process of planning and action will attempt to influence change in wider systems so that they are more responsive to the needs and wishes of the person with an intellectual disability. These wider systems include both service agencies and a society that may not yet be open to welcoming people with intellectual disabilities in new ways.

McGill Action Planning System (MAPS)

The McGill Action Planning System (MAPS) (Vandercook *et al.*, 1989) was devised as a planning system to support families to include their son or daughter with disabilities in regular schools. The system is diagrammed in Figure 6.5. Again, MAPS is a group system that brings together students, family members, the peers of a student with a disability, teachers and school staff who meet to create a shared understanding of the student with disabilities. This group of people are required to address seven questions that will guide the group to develop strategies designed to produce desirable

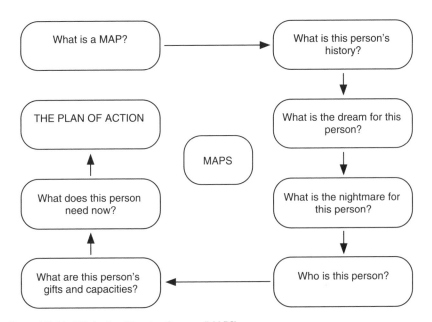

Figure 6.5 McGill Action Planning System (MAPS).

outcomes for the person who is the focus of planning and to maintain the person in the mainstream classroom. These strategies rely on the creation of a circle of support that assumes responsibility for dealing with the day-to-day issues that arise for the person or the school system.

Essential Life-Style Planning

Essential Life-Style Planning (Smull and Harrison, 1992; Smull and Lakin, 2002) focuses on supporting individuals with challenging behaviour and planning for the provision of system supports that take account of such an individual's preferences. The system is diagrammed in Figure 6.6. Essential Life-Style Planning was specifically developed to help the process of moving people with behavioural challenges from institutional settings to community-based services. This process differs slightly from other approaches with its 'emphasis on influencing formal services rather than broadly engaging family and community resources as sources of support, although family and others are involved as sources of information in the planning process' (Butterworth, Steere and Whitney-Thomas, 1997: 9). Essential Life-Style Planning seeks to identify a number of key pieces of information so that an individual with intellectual disability's preferences can be determined and a future vision for the person can be established which takes account of safety issues. An independent agent usually directs this process.

Whole Life Planning

Whole Life Planning (Butterworth, Hagner, Heikkinen, Faris, et al., 1993) is similar to Personal Futures Planning in that it seeks to create a powerful vision of a desirable future which is then action-planned. Like Personal Futures Planning, Whole Life Planning can involve a circle of support in the planning process but the process is flexible to allow for the choice of the appropriate format, which for some individuals with intellectual disability may not be a group process. The process further can be used not just for the purpose of supporting the planning of a desirable life but equally can have a more specific purpose of planning for one element of such a life, an employment or living arrangement, for example.

PATH

PATH (Pearpoint et al., 1993) is an approach designed to complement person-centred planning. The system is diagrammed in Figure 6.7. PATH recognizes that such planning approaches will encounter problems in implementation and thus offers a seven-step procedure for understanding and solving the complex, implementation problems that inevitably occur. It is, in

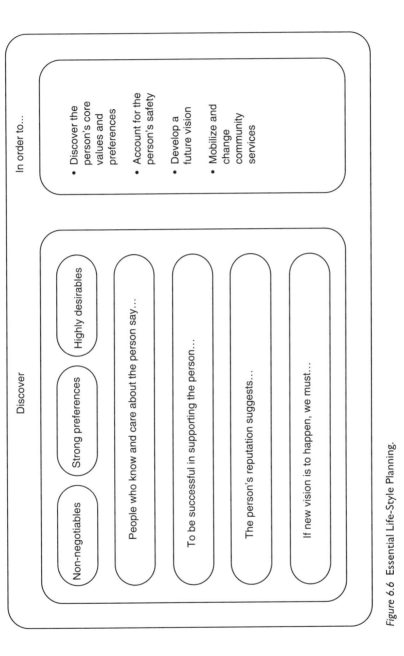

Figure 6.6 Essential Life-Style Planning.

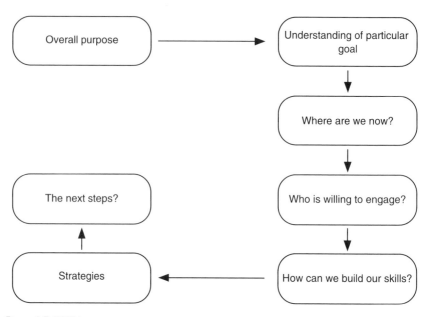

Figure 6.7 PATH.

effect, a problem-solving process to help those members of a circle of support to move from current realities towards the actualization of the desirable future that is the key purpose of our person-centred endeavours. PATH involves participants in the outline of a clear description or whatever specific goal is causing difficulty, in determining who is willing to work on its realization, in discovering how these forces can be best marshalled, in outlining a series of steps that will move towards the realization of the goal and in identifying a list of strategies to work through these steps.

PERSON-CENTRED PLANNING: COMMON ELEMENTS

Inadequate planning with people with intellectual disabilities has a number of key elements. Such planning is likely to be carried out by people who do not fully understand the person with disability and who are more likely to make decisions on behalf of the person. The person who is the focus of planning is unlikely to have chosen who is involved in the process or when and where the planning process will take place. The process has probably predetermined boundaries about what activities and experiences are possible either because of perceptions of people with intellectual disabilities or by the service structures and options that are current.

Good person-centred planning, however, is likely to stand in marked contrast to this. It will have a number of defining characteristics that differentiate it from the traditional approaches described above.

I Empowerment of the individual with intellectual disability

Person-centred planning will seek to empower the individual with an intellectual disability. This is enacted in many initiatives through the use of a facilitator whose major function is to ensure the active participation of the focus person. The facilitator will ensure that the process is conducted in a positive atmosphere aimed at producing those outcomes that are of importance to the person who is the focus of planning. The facilitator will support the person to invite only those people who she or he wishes to be involved. Others are not involved in person-centred planning as of right. They attend and are involved only at the behest of the individual who is the focus of planning. The facilitator ensures that the person is supported to develop their own future vision and is not restricted in so doing by resources or current service provision. The facilitator will help the person with intellectual disability to prepare for and to participate in planning meetings (Steere, Gregory, Heiny and Butterworth, 1995). The use of a facilitator should promote processes that are not just person-centred, that is, not just ensuring that planning efforts best meet an individual with intellectual disability's needs, but are processes that are person-driven and person-controlled, 'whereby the individual being helped, not the helper, sets the agenda and where that person's aspirations are equated with his or her needs' (Marrone, Hoff and Helm, 1997: 286).

2 The use of a facilitator

'The facilitator conducts the meeting on behalf of the individual with the disability. In this sense, it is the person with the disability who directs and propels the meeting' (Smull and Harrison, 1992: 22). The use of a facilitator has become a feature of person-centred planning initiatives. The facilitator is an independent person who carries out the role outlined above. It can be seen that their independence is essential so that the process is driven by the demands and requirements of the person with disability which are not subordinate to service system procedures.

3 New roles for professionals

Person-centred planning emphasizes the primary role of a circle of support, that is a network of people who know and care about an individual with an intellectual disability. The circle of support involves people who are prepared to come together over a significant period of time to help the person establish and to support a personal vision for him- or herself and to harness community backup and action on behalf of the person with disability. A circle of support is motivated by a sense of voluntary commitment from a range of people who are interested in helping someone for whom they care. Professionals involved in person-centred planning initiatives do come as service providers but with new perspectives, those of facilitators and consultants. This will mean that professionals are required to cede their traditional dominant role in planning and to develop partnerships with individuals with intellectual disabilities, families and wider communities. 'In the area of employment, for example, these changes include employment specialists supporting co-workers as they train a worker with a disability rather than providing training directly, or involving personal and family social networks in the job search' (Butterworth et al., 1997: 10).

4 Creative brainstorming

The group processes of most person-centred planning are designed to encourage getting multiple perspectives so that creative brainstorming can take place. The circle of support ensures that people from a variety of backgrounds are present and are likely to come with different understandings and solutions to the issues that will inevitably arise. Holburn and Pfadt (1998) note that the composition of a person-centred planning team is critical. Where such teams have only included service professionals and those people who form part of regular multidisciplinary teams, these authors claim that planning processes and their results are unlikely to be different from those evident in traditional planning systems. Inviting the voluntary contributions of both the person who is the focus of planning and others promotes discussions and problem-solving that leads to outcomes more akin to the focus person's own vision for his or her life.

5 Action towards life-style change

It is often assumed that planning will automatically lead to action but this need not always be the case. Planning for the sake of planning that does not lead to action can cause frustration and disappointment. Person-centred planning has been accused of raising the expectations and hopes of individuals with intellectual disabilities, which indeed it does. But proper person-centred planning demands action and change in a person's immediate life circumstances. Person-centred plans are long-range but they also include a series of intermediate steps to move towards the long-term goals, steps that can and should happen immediately. The action-planning process requires that people sign up to specific actions and these actions are time-lined. The continuous nature of the process means that commitments to action are followed up on, problems identified and solutions found. Person-centred planning requires action but it recognizes that setbacks will occur and that there may be some false starts.

PERSON-CENTRED PLANNING: STAFF TRAINING

A key factor in transforming agencies providing services for people with intellectual disabilities is staff training. Staff training on its own, however, will be insufficient to generate the necessary system change required to transform agencies from traditional philosophies and practices to methodologies that are person-driven and person-controlled. Staff training needs to be located in a wider organizational context where management endorses person-centred planning modalities and agency systems and structures support such modalities. Otherwise, person-centred planning will be adopted by agencies that do not embrace significant change, required as a standard process, attended by people who do not know the person well, done in the absence of crucial players, and evaluated quantitatively and inappropriately for its effectiveness (Holburn and Vietze, 1999; 2002).

Everson and Reid (1999) note this need for a comprehensive plan for staff development embedded in a wider process of organizational change. This staff training process, these authors suggest, should move from introductory, exploratory staff training inputs to a more general agency decision to design a whole-personnel development package with concomitant structural change. The initial introductory training typically involves a short planning meeting between the trainer and key agency personnel with the aim of increasing agency interest in person-centred planning. This initial contact may have originated in the expressed interest of identified agency staff in such initiatives. But equally, the initiative may have been provoked by the dissatisfaction of individuals with intellectual disabilities or of their families with service options currently on offer. A more formal development package can then be outlined should the service organization decide to proceed with the person-centred planning initiative.

Everson and Reid propose that such a development package should include the following elements:

- a series of training sessions to introduce person-centred values, strategies and various methodologies to key agency staff who will embark on person-centred planning with a pilot group of service-users;
- follow-up technical assistance to identify outstanding training needs, more general issues and to detail the next steps in the process once the initial planning with the pilot group is in train;
- once a number of person-centred plans have been delineated, the agency will need to look from a broader perspective at service-user outcomes and how staff should be organized and work to support these outcomes;

- the final stage involves follow-up technical assistance to the service organization so that agency staff and agency structures do actually change to support person-centred planning.

Everson and Reid (1999: 49) give an example of an introductory training package on person-centred planning which is presented in Figure 6.8.

Coyle and Moloney (1999), in a study based on an Irish agency, surveyed staff who had been trained to facilitate person-centred planning for people with a range of levels of intellectual disability. Staff were clear from their perspective about the types of training they consider essential. Staff in this agency (59 per cent of those surveyed) said that they would prefer to learn about person-centred planning from others who are directly involved in facilitating the process. Staff, further, are clear that person-centred planning is a process and therefore training might be best delivered using a coaching or mentoring strategy. These staff, then, were proposing development for those expected to facilitate person-centred planning as follows:

- initial information about person-centred planning, its processes and strategies;
- the provision of a detailed information pack or literature;

DAY 1

Goals of workshop
Icebreaker activity
Definition of person-centred planning
Discussion of values and practices inherent in all person-centred planning models
Overview of common models, tools and strategies
Examples of person-centred plans
Practice using person-centred tools and strategies
Discussion of practice activity

DAY 2

Review of day one
Roles and responsibilities of person-centred planning facilitators
Discussion of current support staff and managerial roles and responsibilities
Developing and implementing individualized service plans in a more person-centred manner
Management implications of adopting a person-centred way of doing business
Closing activity
Homework assignment/ date of follow-up training
Discussion of next steps

Figure 6.8 Sample training agenda.

- access to 'expert' training inputs;
- ongoing coaching or mentoring;
- in-house information exchange about what works and what does not.

These agency staff, in later contacts, emphasized that staff development should also encompass other inputs particularly in the areas of group facilitation, negotiation and conflict resolution. Interestingly, 30 per cent of staff surveyed felt that not all agency staff would be suited to facilitate person-centred planning.

PERSON-CENTRED PLANNING: IMPLEMENTATION ISSUES

Person-centred planning has been applied to a number of specific areas, for example in transition from school to adulthood (Everson, 1996), for determining employment options (Everson and Reid, 1997; Powell, Pancsofar, Steere, Butterworth, *et al.*, 1991), as part of the process of positive behavioural support (Lucyshyn, Olson and Horner, 1995), for assessing supported community living options (Racino, Walker, O'Connor and Taylor, 1993) and to promote local community presence and participation (Pancsofar, 1998). Nonetheless, the implementation of person-centred planning has raised issues and concerns, some amongst those who are its strongest supporters.

The problems and issues that arise with person-centred planning are either system or process ones. There is a general concern, already alluded to, that service systems in adopting person-centred planning will debase the process so that the process termed person-centred becomes in reality a travesty of real person-driven, person-controlled planning. Service systems tend to be bureaucratic in nature and thus by definition, difficult to change or adapt to change. Such agencies take on person-centred planning as the mantra of which Marrone *et al.* (1997) have written. The person-centred planning process becomes rigid and codified. It turns into a technique that is systematically applied to large numbers of service-users rather than the flexible, open process that takes whatever time it takes and which can be difficult for administrators and managers to come to terms with. It is unsurprising, then, that many service-initiated person-centred planning attempts do not match their promise. O'Brien and O'Brien (2000) have argued that implementations of person-centred planning will be disappointing if staff rigorously apply a procedure without sufficient sensitivity to the context of relationships and agreements necessary for the process to achieve its aims. When person-centred planning is viewed only as a tool or technique, poor results will generate efforts to modify the technique rather than lead to a search for new categories, further information, the articulation of other perspectives, and the strengthening of important relationships in client networks. A misunderstanding of person-centred planning as an isolated technique, without due regard to context, runs the risk of transforming person-centred planning from a useful idea into another fad which contributes little to the quality of clients' lives.

Agencies are under pressure from those who fund them to detail their planning methods and programme activity. Funding agencies are happier with a systematized approach to service planning and delivery. They usually monitor service organizations in terms of how they comply with regulations rather than in terms of the outcomes provided to individual service-users. In this context, managers and administrators may feel coerced into requiring those person-centred planning initiatives in their agencies to become systematized and timetabled according to deadlines not of the service-users' choosing. It is difficult to promote approaches that are based on developing different sorts of relationships with service-users, their supporters and the wider community.

It should be noted that implementing person-centred planning in service agencies poses a dilemma for practitioners. The process seeks to impact on service systems and produce organizational change. This process of organizational change, almost by default, seems to require some level of systematization which is anathema to real person-centred planning.

The facilitators of most service-initiated person-centred planning are generally staff employed by the agency promoting the planning. In such contexts, person-centred planning has not always engineered the community engagement at the heart of the process. There needs to be some thought given to developing facilitators from outside the particular agency providing services to the individual with an intellectual disability as we have already seen (Holburn and Pfadt, 1998) that involvement of service-workers alone tends to produce the outcomes that are typical of the old strategies.

Process issues and problems also exist. It can sometimes be difficult to ascertain the gifts and capacities of some individuals with disabilities. This can often be the case for persons with more significant disabilities and with whom we have difficulties communicating. Equally, some participants with intellectual disabilities are unclear about a vision of a desirable future, looking to rely on others, parents and staff, for example, for decisions. Some participants may even choose to remain in segregated settings, which seems to fly in the face of our person-centred planning value system. Participants come to the person-centred planning process with histories which some may find hard to ignore. People with disabilities may come to a circle-of-support meeting feeling uncomfortable about discussing certain matters in front of a parent. Parents may come to such a meeting well entrenched in a parent–child mode which they cannot leave despite best efforts. Clinicians accustomed to positions of authority and certain power or professional relationships may experience issues in changing to new ways to relate to people with intellectual disability and their families. Person-centred planning demands nothing short of a paradigm shift in how a broad range of people relate to one another, which is a process that can only happen over time.

Controversy and debate also exists among those engaged in person-centred planning. There is a difference of opinion about the extent to which the individual with an intellectual disability should actually control how the process evolves. People with intellectual disabilities have often had limited opportunities to engage in the broad range of experiences that are natural for their non-disabled peers. Services have traditionally been delivered in ways that have meant that most people with intellectual disabilities have been educated and work apart from their non-disabled peers significantly reducing occasions where friendships and relationships can be formed, developed and maintained. In this context, one school of thought thinks that person-centred planning should actively encourage the person who is the focus of planning to try out new experiences. Others disagree and argue that the circle of support should respond only to the specific requests of the person with an intellectual disability. As a development of this debate, some advocates of person-centred planning would not support a person with intellectual disability to live, work and recreate in segregated circumstances while others would be happy to action-plan such requests.

There is a clear difference of opinion among protagonists about the advisability of staff from an individual's service agency facilitating that person's planning process for the reasons outlined above. Further, some proponents of person-centred planning would prefer not to work within the context of service organizations as they believe such organizations can only pervert real person-centred planning.

Finally, there is an ongoing debate about exactly how much one can and should expect from the families of people with disabilities. While some will argue that natural supports should be sufficient and efforts should be made to increase and skill such supports, others believe that input from service providers is desirable and essential.

CONCLUDING REMARKS

The rubric of person-centred planning, then, covers a number of approaches to the provision of support to persons with intellectual disabilities to maximize their quality of life. It attempts to do this by focusing very specifically on their preferences and wishes and seeks to build on their strengths and capacities much as we, their non-disabled peers, plan our own lives. Person-centred planning enlists others who know and care for the person to work together with willing service agencies to help the person with an intellectual disability to realize his or her own personal vision of a future and to discover his or her place in the wider community that may not yet be open to welcoming him or her in new ways.

Person-centred planning is certainly a non-traditional process of planning with people with intellectual disabilities but more, it can be a process for wider societal change even if many current attempts at person-centred planning tend to use the process as merely a tool. The best measure of person-centred planning effectiveness, then, may be wider social action. People who are working for real change will find themselves embroiled in political conflict. Their civic action will produce the single most reliable indicator that person-centred planning is really happening in a service system. Agency and system administrators will find themselves perturbed as they deal with the uncertainties, anxieties and conflicts of fitting their organization better to the lives of the people they serve (O'Brien and Lyle-O'Brien, 1998).

FURTHER READING AND RESOURCES

Butterworth, J. (1994). *More Like a Dance: An Introduction to Whole Life Planning.* Videotape available from the Institute for Community Inclusion, Children's Hospital, 300 Longwood Avenue, Boston, MA 02115.

Department of Health (2001). *Valuing People: A New Strategy for Learning Disability for the 21st Century – Planning with People – Towards Person Centred Approaches.* London: HMSO. http://www.doh.gov.uk/learningdisabilities/personcentredapproach.htm

Holburn, S. and Vietze, P. (2002). *Person-Centred Planning: Research, Practice and Future Directions.* Baltimore, ML: Paul Brookes.

ASSESSMENT INSTRUMENTS

Holburn, S., Jacobson, J., Vietze, P., Schwartz, A. and Sersen, E. (2000). Quantifying the process and outcomes of person-centred planning. *American Journal on Mental Retardation*, 105, 5, 402–16.

Stancliffe, R. and Parmenter, T. (1999). The Choice Questionnaire: A scale to assess choices exercised by adults with intellectual disability. *Journal of Intellectual and Developmental Disability*, 24, 2, 107–32.

WEBSITES

Inclusion. http://www.inclusion.com/ – A place where you can buy some of the very best person-centred resources.

Inclusion. http://www.inclusiononline.co.uk/index.html – A UK-based distributor for person-centred materials.

A Resource List on Person-Centred Planning. http://allenshea.com/resource.html

REFERENCES

Butterworth, J., Hagner, D., Heikkinen, B., Faris, S., DeMello, S. and McDonough, K. (1993). *Whole Life Planning. A Guide for Organizers.* Washington, DC: Office of the Assistant Secretary for Planning and Evaluation (DHHS).

Butterworth, J., Steere, D. E. and Whitney-Thomas, J. (1997). Using person-centred planning to address personal quality of life. In R. Schalock (ed.), *Quality of Life: Application to Persons with Disabilities II* (pp. 5–23). Washington, DC: American Association on Mental Retardation.

Coyle, K. and Moloney, K. (1999). The introduction of a person centred planning in an Irish agency for people with intellectual disabilities. *Journal of Vocational Rehabilitation*, 12, 175–80.

Department of Health (2001). *Valuing People: A New Strategy for Learning Disability for the 21st Century – Planning with People – Towards Person Centred Approaches.* London: HMSO. http://www.doh.gov.uk/learningdisabilities/ personcentredapproach.htm

Emerson, E. and Standcliffe, R. (2004). Planning and action: Comments on Mansell and Beadle-Brown. *Journal of Applied Research in Intellectual Disabilities*, 17, 23–6.

Everson, J. (1996). Using person-centred planning concepts to enhance school-to-adult life transition planning. *Journal of Vocational Rehabilitation*, 6, 7–13.

Everson, J. M. and Reid, D. H. (1997). Using person centred planning to determine employment preferences among people with the most severe developmental disabilities. *Journal of Vocational Rehabilitation*, 9, 99–108.

Everson, J. M. and Reid, D. H. (1999). *Person-Centred Planning and Outcome Management: Maximizing Quality Lifestyles among People with Disabilities.* Morganton, NC: Habilitative Management Consultants.

Holburn, C. S. and Pfadt, A. (1998). Clinicians on person-centred planning teams: New roles, fidelity of planning, and outcome assessment. *Mental Health Aspects of Developmental Disabilities*, 1, 82–8.

Holburn, S. and Vietze, P. (1999). Acknowledging barriers in adopting person-centred planning. *Mental Retardation*, 37, 117–24.

Holburn, S. and Vietze, P. (2002). *Person-Centred Planning: Research, Practice and Future Directions.* Baltimore, ML: Paul Brookes.

Lucyshyn, J. M., Olson, D. and Horner, R. H. (1995). Building an ecology of support: a case study of one young woman with severe problem behaviours living in the community. *Journal of the Association for Persons with Severe Handicaps*, 20, 16–30.

Mansell, J. and Beadle-Brown, J. (2004). Person centred planning or person centred action? Policy and practice in intellectual disability services. *Journal of Applied Research in Intellectual Disabilities*, 17, 1–9.

Marrone, J., Hoff, D. and Helm, D. T. (1997). Person-centred planning for the millennium: We're old enough to remember when PCP was just a drug. *Journal of Vocational Rehabilitation*, 8(3): 285–97.

Mount, B. (2000). *Person-Centred Planning: Finding Directions for Change Using Personal Futures Planning.* New York: Graphic Futures.

Mount, B. and Zwernik, K. (1988). *It's Never too Early, It's Never too Late: A Booklet about Personal Futures Planning.* Mears Park Centre, MN: Metropolitan Council. (Available from: Metropolitan Council, Mears Park Centre, 230 East Fifth St, St Paul, MN 55101.)

O'Brien, C. L. and O'Brien J. (2000). *The Origins of Person-Centred Planning: A Community of Practice Perspective.* Atlanta: Responsive Systems Associates, Inc.

O'Brien, C. L., O'Brien, J. and Mount, B. (1997). Person-centred planning has arrived . . . or has it? *Mental Retardation,* 35, 480–3.

O'Brien, J. (1987). A guide to lifestyle planning: Using the activities catalogue to integrate services and natural support systems. In B. Wilcox and G. T. Bellamy (eds), *The Activities Catalogue: An Alternative Curriculum Design for Youth and Adults with Severe Disabilities* (pp. 104–10). Baltimore: Brookes.

O'Brien, J. and Lovett, H. (1993). *Finding a Way toward Everyday Lives: The Contribution of Person-Centred Planning.* Harrisburg, PA: Pennsylvania Office of Mental Retardation.

O'Brien, J. and Lyle-O'Brien, C. (1998). The politics of person centered planning. In C. Griffin, M. Flaherty, D. Hammis, R. Shelley, N. Maxson and D. Spas (eds), *Knowing the Ropes: Reaching New Heights in Rural Community Employment* (pp. 26–30). Missoula, MT: The Rural Institute, University of Montana.

Pancsofar, E. L. (1998). *Building Community Together: Developing Positive Profiles.* St Augustine, FL: Training Resource Network, Inc.

Pearpoint, J., O'Brien, J., and Forest, M. (1993). *PATH: A Workbook for Planning Positive, Possible Futures and Planning Alternative Tomorrows with Hope for Schools, Organizations, Businesses and Families.* Toronto: Inclusion Press.

Powell, T. H., Pancsofar, E. L., Steere, D. E., Butterworth, J., Itzkowitz, J. S. and Rainforth, B. (1991). Co-workers and supervisors. In T. Powell, E. Pancofar, D. Steere, J. Butterworth, J. Itzkowitz and B. Rainforth, (eds), *Supported Employment: Providing Integrated Employment Opportunities for Persons with Disabilities* (pp. 116–26). New York: Longman.

Racino, J. A., Walker, P., O'Connor, S. and Taylor, S. J. (1993). *Housing Support and Community: Choices and Strategies for Adults with Disabilities*: Baltimore: Paul H. Brookes.

Smull, M. and Harrison, S. B. (1992). *Supporting People with Severe Reputations in the Community.* Alexandria, VA: NASMRPD. (NASMRPD, 113 Oronoco Street, Alexandria, VA 22314.)

Smull, M., and Lakin, C. (2002). Public policy and person-centred planning. In S. Holburn and P. Vietze (eds), *Person-Centred Planning: Research, Practice and Future Directions* (pp. 100–20). Baltimore: Paul H. Brookes.

Steere, D. E., Gregory, S. P., Heiny, R. W. and Butterworth, J. (1995). Lifestyle planning: Considerations for use with people with disabilities. *Rehabilitation Counselling Bulletin,* 38, 207–23.

Vandercook, T., York, J. and Forest, M. (1989). The McGill Action Planning System (MAPS): A strategy for building the future. *Journal of the Association for Persons with Severe Handicaps,* 14(3), 205–15.

Wehmeyer, M. L. (1992). Self-determination and the education of students with mental retardation. *Education and Training in Mental Retardation and Developmental Disabilities,* 27, 302–14.

Weymeyer, M. and Kelchner, K. (1995). *Whose Future is it, Anyway? A Student-Directed Transition Planning Process.* Arlington, TX: The ARC.

Chapter 7

Applied behaviour analysis

*Mark O'Reilly, Jeff Sigafoos, Giulio E. Lancioni,
Vanessa A. Green, Melissa Olive and
Helen Cannella*

OVERVIEW

In this chapter we will describe some of the most important technologies that
have been developed within the discipline of applied behaviour analysis
(ABA) to support individuals with developmental disabilities. We will begin
with a brief background description of ABA to familiarize the audience with
this discipline. We will then describe ABA technologies to teach new skills to
individuals. Finally, we will describe the use of ABA technology to assess and
support individuals with challenging behaviour.

ABA has made significant contributions in terms of developing instructional strategies for people with developmental disabilities. First, instructional objectives (e.g. self-care skills, or communication skills) must be
broken down, or task analysed, into teachable units in order to facilitate their
acquisition. We will describe the process of developing task analyses illustrating our discussion with examples from self-care, domestic, and community
skills. Once a task has been broken down into teachable units, the next step is
to select an appropriate teaching strategy to facilitate the acquisition of these
skills. A variety of effective teaching strategies have been developed and
evaluated and include a least-to-most prompt strategy, most-to-least prompt
strategy, and time delay strategy. We will describe each of these instructional
strategies with examples of using them to teach individuals with developmental disabilities. In order to maximize the acquisition of new skills during
the teaching situation, it is important to acknowledge accurate performance
with positive/pleasant consequences. It may not always be obvious what types
of consequences might reinforce new behaviours. Prior to teaching new
skills it is therefore important to conduct a preference assessment to identify
items/events that might act as positive consequences during the teaching
process. Examples of preference assessment strategies will be described.
Individuals with developmental disabilities often display difficulties spontaneously generalizing newly acquired skills to different persons, places, or
events. This difficulty can be overcome by incorporating strategies to promote

generalization of responding as teaching occurs. We will describe several of the strategies to promote generalization.

ABA technologies also provide the clinician with some of the most effective methods to assess and develop support plans for individuals with developmental disabilities who engage in challenging behaviour. We will describe some of the most frequently used methods to assess challenging behaviour. These assessment methods can be indirect (e.g. interviewing significant others) or direct (i.e. directly observing the person under contexts in which the challenging behaviour is most likely to occur). We will then describe how the results of such assessments can be translated into interventions that maximize adaptive behaviour and minimize challenging behaviour.

In this chapter we will focus on the 'how' or the technology of instruction and intervention for individuals with developmental disabilities. We will focus to a lesser extent on the 'what', such as the selection of curricular objectives. Of course it is very important to develop instructional or teaching objectives and behaviour support plans which maximize the overall quality of life, independence, and inclusion of these individuals. These latter issues are discussed in great detail in other chapters of this text.

WHAT IS APPLIED BEHAVIOUR ANALYSIS?

Applied behaviour analysis is a natural science approach to the study of the behaviour of humans. The fundamental premise of a natural science approach to psychology is that all behaviour is caused, and that the cause of our behaviour is physical and external to us (Leslie and O'Reilly, 1999). Behaviour is defined as everything that we do. Our behaviour can be observable to others or it can be private (thoughts, feelings) and only directly observable to ourselves. Whether behaviour is public or private it is still subject to, or a function of, external physical causes. To say that behaviour is otherwise is to say that it is not caused, or that it is caused by something other than the physical world. These latter explanations are unscientific. External physical causes can include such phenomena as our biological make-up and our learning history (at individual, familial, cultural, and anthropological levels). This is in stark contradiction to conventional perceptions, and indeed the position of much of mainstream psychology, with regard to cause and human behaviour. In conventional thought we typically see ourselves as being the originators of our own behaviour. That we possess the ability to act freely, independent of our history. Additionally, a mental (non-physical) world is the central subject matter of mainstream psychology. While we cannot discuss these positions in detail it is important to be aware of them as we believe that much of the antagonism against behaviourism can be distilled into arguments for and against a natural science approach to the study of humans.

There are two sub-disciplines within the behavioural field – the experimental analysis of behaviour (EAB) and ABA. EAB involves the study of the fundamental principles that govern behaviour. This research is usually conducted under highly controlled laboratory conditions with human and non-human organisms. The goal of such research is to determine environmental conditions that control (cause) behaviour in organisms. ABA is primarily interested in the application of the principles of behaviour, which are derived from laboratory research, to issues of human interest.

Some of the pioneers of ABA proposed a number of defining features of the field that are still useful today (Baer, Wolf and Risley, 1968). It is *applied* in that the problems studied are those that are important to society rather than those that are crucial to theory development. It is *behavioural* in that it asks how it is possible to get an individual to do something effectively. And it involves *analysis*, and thus requires a demonstration of the events that can be responsible for the occurrence of the behaviour in question. Other features include that it must be *effective*, in that substantial behaviour change should be produced, and the behaviour change should show *generality*. That is, it endures over time and is seen in a range of situations.

TEACHING INDIVIDUALS WITH DEVELOPMENTAL DISABILITIES

One of the major contributions of ABA to the field of developmental disability has been within the area of instruction. In the early-to-mid 1970s several researchers began to demonstrate that people with developmental disabilities were capable of performing community, vocational, and domestic tasks traditionally thought to be beyond their capabilities (Gold, 1976). Complex skills such as preparing meals, self-grooming, and grocery shopping could be taught if they were broken down into small discrete steps that were then taught systematically using instructional prompts and positive reinforcement. In the following sections we will discuss the core components of these teaching strategies.

Task analysis

Many independent living skills involve complex sequences of behaviours. In order to teach such independent living skills to persons with developmental disabilities we must first break them down into their component parts. The process by which a complex sequence of behaviours is broken down and the resulting set of behaviours is called a task analysis. To illustrate, we have included examples of task analyses for self-care (tooth brushing), domestic (making a sandwich), and community (grocery shopping) skills in Table 7.1. Each of these skills has been broken down into a discrete set of observable behaviours.

Table 7.1 Task analysis for brushing teeth (Horner and Keilitz, 1975); making a sandwich (Schuster, Gast, Wolery and Guiltinan, 1988); and supermarket shopping (Taylor and O'Reilly, 1997), with permission from the Journal of Behaviour Analysis

Step	Description

Task analysis for brushing teeth

1 Pick up and hold the toothbrush
2 Wet the toothbrush
3 Remove the cap from the toothpaste
4 Apply the toothpaste to the brush
5 Replace the cap on the toothpaste
6 Brush the outside surfaces of the teeth
7 Brush the biting surfaces of the teeth
8 Brush the inside surfaces of the teeth
9 Fill the cup with water
10 Rinse the mouth
11 Wipe the mouth
12 Rinse the toothbrush
13 Rinse the sink
14 Put the equipment away

Task analysis for making a sandwich

1 Take bread from cabinet
2 Carry cold-cut container from refrigerator
3 Pick up knife from drawer
4 Select mayonnaise from refrigerator
5 Open bread
6 Remove two pieces of bread; lay flat on counter
7 Close bread and return to cabinet
8 Open jar of mayonnaise
9 Pick up knife and dip into mayonnaise
10 Spread mayonnaise with knife on top of both slices
11 Close mayonnaise and return to refrigerator
12 Open cold-cut container
13 Place one slice of meat on one slice of bread
14 Place one cheese slice on top of meat
15 Place lettuce on top of cheese
16 Place remaining bread slice on top, mayonnaise side down
17 Close cold-cut container and return to refrigerator
18 Get a plate from the cabinet
19 Place sandwich on plate
20 Cut sandwich in half diagonally
21 Place knife in sink

Task analysis for supermarket shopping

1 Walks from car to supermarket
2 Enters supermarket through correct door
3 Lifts a basket
4 Looks at shopping list
5 Looks on shelves for item
6 Puts item in basket
7 Looks at list for next item

8   Looks on shelves for item
9   Puts item in basket
10   Checks list and basket to see that all items are correct
11   Goes to correct checkout (i.e. express checkout)
12   Takes place in line
13   Behaves appropriately in line
14   Puts contents of basket on counter
15   Replaces basket
16   Pays for items using next dollar strategy
17   Waits for change
18   Packs sack
19   Picks up sack
20   Exits store through correct door
21   Returns to car

Developing a task analysis can be a complex affair. The first step consists of identifying the essential behaviours involved in performing the task sequence. This can be achieved by observing and recording the behaviours of individuals who are skilled in performing the task. For example, Cuvo, Leaf, and Borakove (1978) taught janitorial skills (sweep and mop the floor, clean the stool, and clean the mirror) to individuals with developmental disabilities. The task analyses were developed by observing janitors perform these tasks. In other circumstances, specialist texts might be consulted such as cookbooks, or medical dictionaries. For example, O'Reilly, Green, and Braunling-McMorrow (1990) consulted the National Safety Council Guidelines when developing task analyses to teach individuals to remediate safety hazards in the home.

Once the essential behaviours of a task are identified, they must then be broken down into a series of discrete and trainable behaviours. The size and number of behaviours in each step of the task analysis must be determined by the skill level of the person to be taught. Individuals with low levels of functioning will require a task to be broken into small component behaviours. A summarized series of generic behaviours may be required for individuals with higher levels of functioning. Once the task has been tailored to the person then instruction is initiated to teach each component behaviour until the entire task sequence is taught. The teaching strategies used are described in the next sections.

Instructional strategies

In this section we will first describe a number of instructional prompting techniques that can be used to teach new behaviour such as those described in the task analyses of the previous section. We will then describe methods used systematically to remove these prompts as the person acquires the skills.

Finally, we will describe a number of options with regard to presenting the task during instructional trials.

Instructional prompts are cues used to evoke a desired response. They are supplementary stimuli that will be removed once the person can perform the targeted behaviours at the desired level of independence. Prompts are of two general types: response prompts and stimulus prompts. Response prompts are cues that describe or demonstrate the new desired response. Stimulus prompts are cues that highlight the natural discriminative stimuli in the environment and therefore increase the probability of correct responding. There are several types of response prompts including verbal, model, picture, and physical prompts.

Verbal response prompts

These are the most commonly used instructional prompts in applied and instructional settings. These prompts can be oral or written. Verbal prompts are often classified as direct or indirect. An indirect verbal prompt is used to cue the person that some behaviour needs to be performed, but it does not describe what the behaviour is. For example, 'What do you need to do next?' is an example of an indirect verbal prompt for it indicates that the person needs to perform, but it does not indicate what the person needs to do. A direct verbal prompt specifies what the person needs to perform. For example, 'Open your book' clearly describes what needs to be performed. Written instructions can also be used to prompt performance. For example, Cuvo, Davis, O'Reilly, Mooney, and Crowley (1992) taught individuals with mild intellectual disability to use written descriptions of domestic tasks (cleaning household appliances) as prompts. These written descriptions of how to perform the tasks, combined with positive and corrective feedback from the therapist, resulted in rapid acquisition of the skills. Performance was maintained once the written prompts were removed.

Model response prompts

These involve the teacher demonstrating the desired behaviour so that it can be imitated by the person. In other words the teacher shows the person what they are to perform. For example, O'Reilly and Glynn (1995) used a modelling protocol to teach social skills to two students with mild intellectual disabilities who were socially withdrawn. Target social skills were selected through interviews with the teacher, and observation of the students during class. These social skills were then taught to the students in a room removed from the classroom. During intervention the therapist first modelled the social skills, for example appropriately demonstrating how to ask the teacher a question. The participants then imitated the modelled social skills and received feedback on their performance from the therapist. This intervention produced an increase in appropriate social skills for the participants across school settings.

Picture response prompts

These are visual representations of the behaviours to be performed. Behaviours can be illustrated using drawings, photographs, or paintings. Picture prompts can be used to illustrate single behaviours, or many pictures can be used to illustrate complete sequences of behaviours. Picture prompt systems have been used to teach complex community and vocational skills to people with intellectual disabilities. Connis (1979) used picture sequences to teach people with moderate intellectual disabilities to change work tasks independently. The workers were first taught to use photographs to sequence daily work tasks, and then to change work tasks independently throughout the work day. Similarly, Sowers, Rusch, Connis, and Cummins (1980) taught individuals with intellectual disabilities to use picture cues of clock faces to leave and return from lunch and work breaks. Johnson and Cuvo (1981) taught meal preparation skills to rehabilitation clients using picture prompt sequences.

Physical response prompts

These produce correct responding by manually guiding the person through the appropriate response. Physical prompting is obviously a very intrusive way to teach somebody to respond correctly. However, in cases where the response is very difficult to perform it may be the only option. Physical prompting can consist of manually guiding the person through the entire sequence of steps of a task. For example, in teaching tooth brushing to a child with severe disabilities (see Table 7.1) the therapist may place her hands on top of the child's and guide the child to: open the toothpaste; reach for the toothbrush; place toothpaste on the toothbrush; and so on. However, in many cases of physical prompting reported in the literature the manual guidance is only partial. This form of partial physical guidance is often referred to as shadowing. When shadowing, the teacher guides the student's movements by keeping her hands a few inches away from the student, and physically guiding the student only when necessary.

Stimulus prompts

These are additional stimuli that are used to highlight important stimuli in the environment and enhance the evocative effectiveness of natural stimuli. Stimulus prompts can be used in conjunction with response prompts when teaching new skills. For example, a salient component of a complex stimulus might be highlighted. When teaching cooking skills to people, the teacher may attach a cue to the temperature dial of the oven that indicates the appropriate oven temperature for the meal. The student can then attend to the artificial cue, and not to the range of temperatures on the dial, when setting the oven. Another example of a stimulus cue is a point prompt. The teacher may point to the relevant stimulus during training. In teaching time an instructor may ask, 'What time is it?' (response prompt) and then point to the hour hand and minute hand on the clock (stimulus prompt).

Response and stimulus prompts are instructional protocol that must eventually be partially or totally removed. The goal of any instructional programme is that the student will eventually be able to perform the skills as independently as possible. The natural stimuli in the everyday environment should eventually control responding. Once the student performs the skill at an appropriate level for a predetermined period of time, the prompting conditions are gradually removed. Prompts should be removed in a manner that minimizes the possibility of errors in performance. The fading of prompts is therefore sometimes called 'errorless learning' (Terrace, 1963). Minimizing error responses during instruction is highly desirable for a number of reasons. First, if an incorrect response occurs, it tends to be repeated and must be unlearned. This can substantially delay the overall goals of a teaching programme. Second, the student may lose interest or begin to find the task to be aversive if they continue to make mistakes. This may result in challenging behaviour in an attempt to escape the teaching situation. The fading of stimulus prompts is a relatively straightforward task which involves the gradual removal of the highlighted stimulus. On many occasions it may be more appropriate to leave the highlighted stimulus (e.g. temperature cue on the oven dial), as it will not interfere with independent responding.

On the other hand, fading response prompts is a more complex matter. Response prompts are not usually used individually but are incorporated within a sequence of response prompts during instruction (but see time delay instructional protocol below for an exception to this). Response prompts differ in their capacity to evoke correct responding. Physical prompts are the most effective as they virtually ensure responding. Modelling and picture prompts would be the next most effective because they involve demonstrations of the behaviour to be performed. Verbal prompts would be the least effective as they require the student to be able to perform the skill when verbally requested. Response prompts can be presented, and then faded, in a least-to-most effective or most-to-least effective sequence when teaching new skills.

Least-to-most prompting

This is a prompt fading sequence that has been used to teach a large variety of skills to persons with developmental disabilities. The student is given the opportunity to perform a response with a minimum amount of assistance during each training trial. If the student does not respond appropriately with minimal assistance, then more intrusive response prompts are systematically introduced. Typically, the natural cue for the response is first presented. The student is given a predetermined period of time (usually a number of seconds) to perform the response. If the response does not occur, or the student begins to make an incorrect response during this time period, then the least intrusive response prompt is implemented (e.g. a direct verbal prompt). Again, the student is given the predetermined time to respond correctly. If the student does not respond, or begins to respond incorrectly, then the next most intrusive prompt is given (e.g. model). The least intrusive prompt (e.g. verbal) is always paired with the more intrusive prompts during instruction (e.g. physical prompt). This is done to pair the least intrusive prompt with correct responding and reinforcement, so that it will eventually come to control the targeted response.

Richman, Reiss, Bauman, and Bailey (1984) used a least-to-most instructional strategy to teach menstrual care to women with moderate to severe developmental disability. Each step of the task analysis was taught using a least-to-most prompt sequence. The prompt hierarchy consisted of direct verbal, model, and physical guidance. For instance, a direct verbal prompt would consist of the therapist stating that particular step of the task analysis (e.g. 'Pull down your underwear and sit on the toilet'). A latency of five seconds was used between the presentation of the natural stimulus of each step of the task analysis and the first response prompt. The authors noted that participants responded appropriately with direct verbal prompts throughout the study. Model or physical prompts were not necessary to evoke behaviour. The results of this research indicated that the training package was successful in teaching these women menstrual care, and the women continued to perform the skills during naturally occurring menses for up to five months following termination of the intervention.

Most-to-least

These prompt sequences employ the alternative logic to the least-to-most strategy. With most-to-least prompts the most intrusive prompt is employed initially, gradually faded to the least intrusive prompt, and eventually to the natural stimulus. Many most-to-least procedures that have been reported begin with a full physical prompt. The student is physically guided through the response sequence for a predetermined number of trials. The natural stimuli (i.e. those stimuli that should eventually control responding) are always present during training trials. Following the physical prompt stage the student may be shadowed (i.e. the next most intrusive response prompt) by the teacher through the response sequence. If the participant begins to err, or does not respond for a predetermined time period on a particular response (i.e. step of the task analysis), then the therapist can intervene with the previous prompt level (i.e. physical prompt) and complete that component of the task. Once the student has performed the task without error under the current level of prompt for a predetermined number of trials then the next level of less intrusive prompt is initiated. This process continues until the student performs the targeted responses under the control of the natural stimuli.

Sisson, Kilwein, and Van Hasselt (1988) used a most-to-least prompt strategy to teach two students with multiple disabilities to dress in tube socks, shorts, t-shirts, sweatshirts, and sweatpants. The teacher physically guided (hand over hand) the students through all steps of these tasks, provided verbal instructions, and reinforced all completed steps of the task analyses. The teacher then faded physical instruction to a milder form of physical guidance (she used two fingers and a thumb gently to guide performance). Physical guidance was then faded to one finger and a thumb, and so on. Eventually the students learned to perform the task with only verbal prompts.

The time delay

This instructional protocol differs from the least-to-most and most-to-least instructional protocol in that the response prompt remains the same throughout teaching, but the delay between the natural stimulus and the response prompt is gradually increased over time. First, a response prompt that is capable of evoking the desired behaviour is selected. At the beginning of training the natural stimulus and the response prompt are often delivered simultaneously (called a zero-second time delay). This gives the student the opportunity to respond without error. This format is continued for a pre-determined number of trials. Trials are then introduced in which the prompt is delayed. This gives the student the opportunity to respond independently in the presence of the natural stimulus. If the student does not respond or begins to err during the delay then the therapist uses the original response prompt to evoke correct responding.

Halle, Baer, and Spradlin (1981) used a time delay protocol to teach language skills to students with severe disabilities in classroom settings. Prior to the intervention the authors observed classroom activities to identify natural situations across the day where appropriate verbal requests could be taught to these children. Teachers were then taught to delay activities/items systematically (e.g. help during gross motor play, or while drinking juice during snack time) for five seconds during these classroom activities. If the child requested the activity/item during the five seconds then it was delivered. If the child did not request the item/activity during the five seconds then the teacher modelled the appropriate request (e.g. 'Push, please' or 'Juice please'). The child then repeated the request and was given the activity/item. This intervention produced substantial increases in the students' use of requests.

How much of a task analysis should you teach during each training trial?

What components of a task analysis should be taught during a training trial? While the terminal goal of instruction is to teach the person to perform all steps of the task in the appropriate sequence and with accuracy, it may not be possible or advisable to teach all steps of the task analysis during each training trial. There are a number of suggested ways of introducing a task analysis during training.

Forward chaining

This involves initially teaching the person on the first step of the task analysis, while the therapist completes all subsequent steps. Training continues on the first step until a predetermined criterion of responding is reached. At this point the participant is trained on the first *and* second steps of the task until criterion is reached. Then the third step is added and so on. During training, the therapist completes all remaining untrained steps herself. Each successive step trained involves cumulative practice on all previous steps. One advantage of forward chaining is that it involves cumulative practice of the earlier steps of the task analysis. The earlier steps of the task analysis are usually the first steps to begin to deteriorate following training. This occurs because the earlier steps are furthest removed from the reinforcement contingencies at the end of the chain.

Backward chaining

This involves training the last step of the task analysis initially. When the student achieves criterion responding on the last step then the second to last step of the task is added to the training. Once the last two steps are completed to criterion then the third to last step is added to training and so on. All previously learned steps are cumulatively practised during each training trial. Those steps that are not currently targeted for training are completed by the therapist prior to the training trial.

   Backward chaining protocols may be particularly useful for teaching skills to individuals who have difficulty maintaining extended periods of on-task behaviour. Initial backward training trials are brief and end with completion of the task. This allows the participant to escape the task and access the reinforcer almost immediately. As subsequent steps of the task are gradually added, increased on-task behaviour is shaped for the student. O'Reilly (1995) used a backward chaining procedure as part of an intervention strategy to teach vocational skills to an individual with severe developmental disabilities who exhibited high rates of escape-maintained aggression (as determined by a prior functional analysis – see functional assessment section later in the chapter). For example, when teaching floor sweeping, the therapist removed the brush and dust pan from the closet, swept the entire floor area, swept the materials into the dust pan, brought the dust pan to the trash can and emptied it. The therapist then taught the participant to complete the last step of the floor-sweeping task, which was putting the sweeping materials back into the closet, using a least-to-most prompting procedure. When the participant successfully completed that step of the task, he was allowed access to the reinforcer, which was to sit and listen to music for a brief period of time. Once criterion was reached for the last step of the task, the participant was taught to carry out the last two steps of the task, which were to empty the trash into the trash can and replace the cleaning materials. He then received his reinforcer. This intervention resulted in increased levels of participation while aggression was virtually eliminated.

Total task presentation

This involves giving the student the opportunity to perform all steps of the task analysis during each training trial. The task is presented in the natural sequence in which the behaviours occur. Training continues until the student is able to perform all steps of the task to a predetermined criterion. One of the major advantages of this protocol is that the student has the opportunity to practise the entire sequence of responding during each training trial, which may promote more efficient mastery of the task. One of the disadvantages of this procedure is that training trials may be more extended than with forward or backward chaining, as the student must perform all steps of the task during each trial. This may be particularly true during early training trials when the student may not be competent in the majority of steps of the chain or task. This becomes less of a problem as the student's mastery increases over training trials.

Reinforcing correct responses

Another very important component of the teaching process is to reinforce new behaviour as it occurs. Reinforcement describes a process whereby behaviours increase in probability when they are followed by certain consequences (Leslie and O'Reilly, 1999). When establishing new behaviours, such as each step of a task analysis, it is important to reinforce these new behaviours each time they occur, no matter what level of prompt was used to occasion the behaviours. In layperson's terms, the student receives a pleasant consequence, such as verbal praise (e.g. 'Very nice job putting the toothpaste on the toothbrush!'), each time they perform the behaviour correctly. Once new behaviour becomes established or learned, then reinforcement can become less frequent. That is, not every instance of the behaviour will be reinforced.

Selecting the appropriate reinforcer or pleasant consequence for a teaching programme may not be a simple matter. Certain consequences may act as reinforcers for some individuals but not for others. For example, some individuals may find social praise to be a pleasant consequence whereas other students may not like to be praised at all. It may therefore be prudent to select reinforcers systematically for a student when developing a teaching programme.

There are several tactics that can be used to select reinforcers. First, one can ask parents, family members, and others who know the student what they believe to be most desirable or favoured by the student. Second, the student could be observed over time to determine what objects he or she seeks, holds, or manipulates for periods of time. If a student seeks out specific items or activities then it can be inferred that such items/activities could act as reinforcers. Finally, when working with students with more severe disabilities we suggest that the clinician use a preference assessment procedure to identify reinforcers (Cannella, O'Reilly and Lancioni, 2005). It is often very difficult to identify preferred items for these students clearly without conducting a formal preference assessment.

A preference assessment consists of systematically presenting items and events to a person and measuring their reaction. Preferred items generally will be identifiable, because the student will exert more effort to acquire them, exhibit longer periods of interaction with an item, or show expressions of happiness, indicating that the item is desirable (Lancioni, O'Reilly, Campodonico and Mantini, 1998a; 1998b). There are several different ways of conducting a preference assessment. For example, the teacher can present each stimulus individually and record the student's reaction. Stimuli can also be presented in pairs and the student is allowed to choose one. In this paired assessment the student's choice is used as an indicator of preference. For a detailed description of preference assessment formats the reader should consult Cannella *et al.* (2005). The items identified as preferred during the assessment can subsequently be used to reinforce new behaviours during teaching.

Enhancing the generalization of new skills

Thus far, we have described the instructional and reinforcement strategies used to teach new skills. Increasing or establishing new skills is a pyrrhic victory if these gains are not maintained following the removal of the intervention or do not occur in settings other than those in which they are taught. An effective behavioural intervention must therefore do more than change behaviour; it must produce behaviour that occurs in a variety of appropriate environments. Stokes and Baer (1977) outlined a series of intervention strategies that could be incorporated into instructional interventions to promote generalization of newly established behaviours across settings, persons, behaviours, and time. Some of these strategies include: introducing natural maintaining contingencies; programming of common stimuli; and training sufficient exemplars.

Introducing natural maintaining contingencies

When you are selecting a new behaviour to teach, it is important that this new behaviour will produce positive consequences for the person in the post-intervention environment. Behaviours that do not produce positive consequences for the person will not be maintained outside of the teaching setting. In a sense, we are again emphasizing the importance of selecting skills for instruction that are important for that person and that enhance their independence. Baer and Wolf (1970) define the maintenance and generalization of such behaviours in terms of 'trapping'. Once the behaviour is taught in the classroom setting and subsequently exposed to natural maintaining contingencies, it becomes trapped by those contingencies. In some situations, reinforcement may currently be unavailable or dormant in the post-intervention environment. In such situations the clinician may teach the student to recruit reinforcement in this environment when they have performed the new behaviour. For example, Stokes, Fowler, and Baer (1978) taught preschool children appropriate classroom skills such as working consistently and quietly. In addition, the therapists taught the children to evaluate the quality of their work and to cue their teacher to deliver positive consequences for quality performance ('How is this work? Have I been working carefully?'). Selecting a skill that will result in reinforcement when instruction is removed is of fundamental importance when developing any applied intervention programme to teach new behaviour.

Programme common stimuli

Generalization to other settings is more likely to occur if salient stimuli that are present in the teaching setting are also present in the generalization settings. This can be accomplished by incorporating stimuli from the criterion environments (where generalization is expected to occur) into the training environment. For example, O'Reilly and Glynn (1995) used peer confederates to train social skills to students with mild disabilities who were diagnosed as socially withdrawn. Students were taught such classroom social skills as: to ask for help when unable to complete written exercises; and to indicate to their teacher when they had completed exercises. Social skills training was conducted in a room removed from the classroom setting. Peer confederates were selected from the same classroom as the participants. These peer confederates role-played the appropriate social skills with the participants during training. Peers were subsequently present in the classroom where participants were required to generalize the social skills. The peers therefore acted as a common stimulus between training and classroom generalization settings.

Train sufficient exemplars

Another strategy to enhance generalization is to train several examples of the new skill during the training phase. For successful generalization to occur, the topographies of new responses must vary as a function of changes in the environment across settings. For example, laundry machines, microwaves, and bathrooms incorporate a wide variety of different stimulus parameters in the natural environment. These differing stimulus parameters will require different responses to achieve success. The instructor must therefore include a sufficient number of training examples during the training phase in order to expose the student to the relevant response and stimulus parameters that will be encountered in the natural environment. Prior to selection of training examples, the instructor must first identify those environments in which the target response will be expected to occur. The instructor will then identify the significant variations in the topography of the response that will need to be performed across these different settings. The instructor should then select a sub-group of teaching examples for training the variety of response and stimulus variations in the natural environment. Teaching on this sub-group of examples should produce generalized responding to all untrained examples. This protocol for identifying the sufficient number of training examples to be used is described as general case programming (Horner, Sprague and Wilcox, 1982) and has been used to successfully produce generalized responding for persons with severe disabilities.

The strategies discussed in this section provide examples of instructional protocols that can be incorporated during training in order to maximize generalization of responding. It is important to note that it is probably preferable to include as many strategies as possible during training to maximize the probability of generalization. Research findings suggest that the more generalization strategies are included in training the greater the chances are of achieving generalized responding (Chandler, Lubeck and Fowler, 1992).

ASSESSMENT AND SUPPORT OF INDIVIDUALS WITH CHALLENGING BEHAVIOUR

As many as 15 per cent–17 per cent of individuals with developmental disabilities exhibit challenging behaviour (Sigafoos, Arthur and O'Reilly, 2003). Challenging behaviour is a broad description of behaviours that can be dangerous to self or others and tend to limit the participation of the person in regular life settings. Types of challenging behaviour can include stereotypic, self-injurious, and aggressive behaviours. Stereotypic behaviours are repetitive cycles of behaviour that consist of idiosyncratic rhythmic movements of the body. Such behaviours become problematic when they occur to such an extent that the individual is unable to participate in other activities.

Examples include hand-weaving, hand-mouthing, finger-flicking, and body-rocking. Self-injury is a repetitive behaviour that causes tissue damage to the person. It is more prevalent in individuals with more severe levels of developmental disability. Types of self-injury can include head-hitting, head-banging (hitting the head on a solid object like a floor), face-slapping, and eye-poking. Aggressive and disruptive behaviour results in injury or damage to others or their property. These behaviours often occur in combination as part of a general tantrum that may also include screaming and crying (O'Reilly, Lancioni and Lacey, 2001).

Practitioners in the field of ABA have conducted research into the assessment and treatment of challenging behaviour for over thirty years. In fact, ABA has produced the most influential and clinically significant body of research in this area of developmental disability (Sigafoos et al., 2003). We can make several general deductions about challenging behaviour in the population based on this body of research. Challenging behaviour, for the most part, is controlled by the consequences that it produces. In other words, the person engages in challenging behaviour to access certain consequences and avoid or escape other consequences (Iwata, Pace, Dorsey, Zarcone et al., 1994). This has led several researchers to propose that challenging behaviour might best be conceptualized as a form of communication (Carr, 1977; Durand, 1990). Other variables such as permanent biological conditions (e.g. genetic syndromes), transient physical or health conditions (e.g. menses, sleep difficulties, illness) or environmental conditions (e.g. general quality of services provided to the person) can influence the severity and type of challenging behaviour (Carr, Levin, McConnachie, Carlson, Kemp and Smith, 1994; McGill, 1999; O'Reilly, 1995; 1997; O'Reilly, Lacey and Lancioni, 2000).

In order to treat challenging behaviour clinically we must first identify the context in which it occurs. This is done through a functional assessment. This term describes a variety of systematic procedures used to isolate environmental events that occasion and maintain challenging behaviour. Functional assessment typically involves a process whereby challenging behaviours are clarified by interviewing significant others, and these behaviours are subsequently observed in naturalistic contexts (environments where the behaviour is described as being problematic). This form of assessment reveals correlational information regarding contexts that might be influencing challenging behaviour. Assessment procedures may also involve the systematic examination of contexts that potentially control challenging behaviour in order to demonstrate a causal relationship between specific contexts and challenging behaviour. This latter technique is typically referred to as a functional analysis (Iwata, Dorsey, Slifer, Bauman and Richman, 1982/1994).

Information derived from such assessment techniques can allow the clinician to select effective treatment procedures in at least two ways. First, the assessment results may indicate that the challenging behaviour is primarily maintained by the consequences it produces (e.g. to access attention from others). In such situations the clinician may opt to teach the person more appropriate skills to access attention from others. We discuss interventions based on manipulation of consequences in greater detail in a later section of this chapter. Second, the assessment may identify motivational conditions that influence challenging behaviour. The influence of such motivational variables might be reduced or eliminated. For example, if sleep deprivation leads to inappropriate aggression, the aggression can be eliminated by ensuring that sufficient sleep takes place (O'Reilly, 1995). The fundamental issue here is that interventions are derived from the results of these assessments.

Functional assessment protocol

In this section we provide some examples of functional assessment instruments. This overview is by no means exhaustive. For a more comprehensive overview the reader should consult Carr *et al.* (1994).

There are a number of interviews available that are easy to administer and provide valuable information to the clinician. Interviews are indirect measures in the sense that they do not require direct observation of the person who engages in challenging behaviour. Interviews rely on subjective verbal reports by a third party. Those who are interviewed should be in daily contact with the person and therefore be in a position to describe events they have witnessed and draw conclusions about the causes of the individual's behaviour. One interview that can be helpful in identifying motivational conditions is the Setting Event Checklist (Gardner, Cole, Davidson and Karan, 1986). This checklist contains questions about the person's physical condition, mood, and possible precipitating social interactions. It also queries how recently such conditions/interactions occurred. Examples of items from the Setting Event Checklist include: was the person (a) informed of something unusual or disappointing?; (b) excessively tired/lethargic?; and (c) under the care of someone new?

There are also a number of commercially available interviews that clinicians can use to identify consequences potentially maintaining challenging behaviour. These include the Motivation Assessment Scale (MAS; Durand and Crimmins, 1988), the Questions about Behavioural Function (Paclawskyj, Matson, Rush, Smalls and Vollmer, 2000) and a Behavioural Diagnostic form (Bailey and Pyles, 1989). The MAS for example, has sixteen questions that may help a clinician decide whether the person's behaviour is related to attention, escape, access to tangible items, or is sensory in nature (reinforced by some form of internal sensory consequence).

Because these rating scales and questionnaires are relatively inexpensive, readily available, and easy to use, it is highly recommended that clinicians use these as the first step in a functional assessment. At a minimum, clinicians should try to get answers to four main questions that need to be asked about the person's challenging behaviour: (1) are there any conditions under which this behaviour frequently or always occurs?; (2) are there any conditions under which this behaviour rarely or never occurs?; (3) what types of events or interactions are typically occurring when the behaviour starts?; and, (4) once the behaviour starts, what can you do to get the behaviour to stop? For example, will the behaviour stop if the person is given attention or left alone?

Interviews are typically followed by some direct observation of the person over a period of time. These should be conducted continuously for several days. Observations should certainly be conducted in contexts identified from prior interviews as associated with challenging behaviour. There are a number of direct observation protocols from which to choose. The Scatterplot Assessment (Touchette, MacDonald and Langer, 1985) is one of the most frequently used observational tools. The scatterplot is used to identify periods of time when behaviour occurs, which may in turn allow for a more detailed assessment of challenging behaviour during those time periods.

The first step in conducting a scatterplot assessment is to design a grid with equal time segments on the vertical axis and days on the horizontal axis. The time segments should suit the particular situation (e.g. 15 minutes, 30 minutes, 1 hour). An example of a scatterplot grid is given in Figure 7.1. It divides the time period from 9 a.m. to 2:30 p.m. into equal cells, each representing 30 minutes. A decision about how to record challenging behaviour during each of these 30-minute time segments needs to be made. A scatterplot does not require the observer to record the exact frequency of occurrence of challenging behaviour during each 30-minute period (i.e. there is no need to record every instance of the behaviour). Instead, a more general recording procedure can be used. In Figure 7.1, we used a light grey shading in the cell if there was one occurrence of the challenging behaviour during the 30-minute period, a darker shading in the cell if there were two occurrences, and filled in the square with black shading if there were three or more occurrences during a 30-minute period.

The scatterplot depicted in Figure 7.1 was used by day care staff to identify the temporal distribution of 'hitting other clients' by a woman with severe developmental disabilities in a day care setting. The scatterplot was conducted over five days. It indicates that the challenging behaviour occurred most frequently between 9:30 a.m. and 10:30 a.m. and between 11:30 a.m. and 12:30 p.m. These time periods correspond to when the woman was engaged in vocational training. Further assessment is now needed to clarify the reasons for why she might be engaging in challenging behaviour during vocational training. It is also interesting to note that her challenging behaviour is more severe on days one and three of the assessment. Interviews with staff indicated that this young woman had less than five hours' sleep the nights prior to days one and three of the assessment. This implies that poor sleep patterns may be influencing the severity of this person's challenging behaviour.

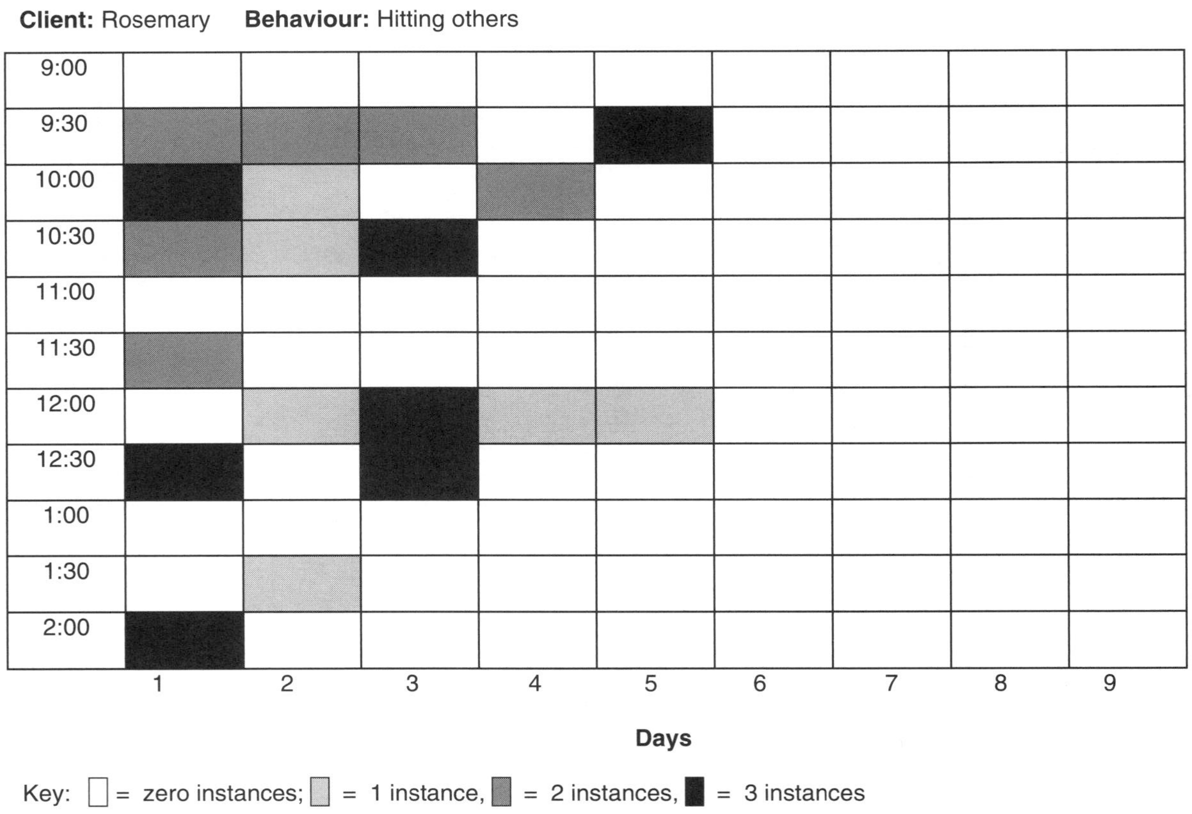

Client: Rosemary **Behaviour:** Hitting others

Key: ☐ = zero instances; ☐ = 1 instance, ☐ = 2 instances, ■ = 3 instances

Figure 7.1 Example of a scatterplot grid covering five days of observations.

The final assessment that we will describe is the experimental functional analysis methodology pioneered by Brian Iwata and his colleagues (Iwata *et al.*, 1982/1994). An experimental functional analysis involves a systematic examination of the person's challenging behaviour under a number of pre-determined social conditions. These social conditions are constructed in a manner designed to identify the specific consequences that are maintaining challenging behaviour. Generally, a functional analysis consists of exposing the person to at least four social conditions (social attention; academic demand; alone; and play). The specific contents of these conditions will be determined on an individual basis based on prior interviews and observations.

The initial report on this procedure (Iwata *et al.*, 1982/1994) described an assessment in an inpatient unit at the Kennedy Krieger Center of Johns Hopkins University School of Medicine. The authors were working with nine children with severe intellectual disability who were referred to this inpatient unit due to chronic self-injury. Each child was systematically and repeatedly exposed (with each session lasting 15 minutes) to four social conditions. The child's challenging behaviour was continuously measured during all sessions. Sessions were terminated if self-injury became severe.

Social attention

In the social attention condition the child was placed in a room with a therapist. The therapist directed the child to play with toys available in the room and then ignored the child by proceeding to do some paperwork at a table. If the child began to engage in self-injury the therapist immediately attended to the child with statements such as, 'Don't hit yourself' while giving the child brief and gentle physical contact (e.g. placing hand on shoulder). The therapist then went back to work and ignored the child until the child again engaged in self-injury. This condition was designed to assess whether self-injury was maintained by attention from others (i.e. positively reinforced by attention). Several 15-minute sessions of this condition were conducted during the functional analysis.

Academic demand

During the demand condition the therapist worked with the child on educational tasks that the child had difficulty completing. The therapist used a three-step instructional protocol (i.e. verbal prompt, model plus verbal prompt, and physical guidance) to complete the task. If the child engaged in self-injury the therapist removed the task and turned away from the child for 30 seconds. The task was removed in this manner when the child engaged in self-injury throughout each of the 15-minute sessions. This condition was designed to assess whether self-injury was maintained by escape from tasks (i.e. negatively reinforced by escape).

Alone

In the alone condition the child was placed in a therapy room on his or her own without access to toys or other materials that might act as sources of external stimulation. This condition was designed to assess whether self-injury was maintained by internal sources of stimulation (i.e. automatically reinforced). If some forms of self-injury are maintained by consequences of a sensory nature then we would expect higher levels of self-injury in situations where there is little external stimulation.

Play

In the play condition the therapist maintained close contact with the child and allowed her to engage in isolated or cooperative play. The therapist praised the child and gave brief physical contact approximately every 30 seconds. Self-injury was ignored by the therapist during sessions. This condition served as a control for the other conditions in that the therapist and materials were present, attention was delivered for appropriate behaviour, withheld for self-injury, and no demands were presented.

The results from these functional analyses showed that self-injury varied between and within individuals. For some children, self-injury occurred most frequently in the academic demand condition, suggesting that the behaviour was maintained by escape from aversive tasks. In other cases, self-injury did not seem to be sensitive to changes in social conditions, suggesting that the behaviour was maintained by some form of sensory consequences (i.e. automatic reinforcement). In still other cases, self-injury seemed to be maintained by multiple consequences in that high rates of self-injury might be observed in the academic demand and the social attention conditions. Such results imply that the child has learned to use their self-injury to access attention and to escape from aversive situations.

Results of these functional analyses indicate that the same behaviour (i.e. self-injury) can serve different functions for different individuals. These findings emphasize the importance of conducting assessments to identify factors maintaining challenging behaviour on a case-by-case basis. In other words, interventions need to be tailored to the individual needs of a person. Conducting a functional analysis as described above can take a considerable amount of time, effort, and training. Such assessments may not be practical in many settings (e.g. classrooms). However, this does not mean that persons could not be referred to a specialist therapeutic setting for such assessments when warranted. In fact, much research has now demonstrated that a variety of functional analysis techniques can be successfully conducted across multiple applied settings such as outpatient clinics, homes and schools (Northup, Wacker, Sasso, Steege et al., 1991; O'Reilly, Peck, Webster, Baird et al., 1999; O'Reilly, Lancioni, Sigafoos and Lacey, 2004).

Intervention guidelines based on functional analysis results

In the previous section we proposed that challenging behaviour, for the most part, is maintained by the consequences that it produces. In a recent epidemiological analysis of 152 cases that were assessed using functional analysis techniques Iwata *et al.* (1994) showed that self-injury seemed to be maintained by consequences such as access to attention and escape from demanding tasks for 145 of these individuals. In this section we make general suggestions for interventions based on the function of challenging behaviour in these two areas. (For a more detailed description of these interventions and interventions designed for challenging behaviour maintained by other consequences please consult Sigafoos *et al.*, 2003.) Obviously, interventions will be more comprehensive than those suggested below. Nevertheless, in our experience, the simpler the intervention, the greater the likelihood that those who have to implement them will do so in the long term. While clinicians are usually competent at conducting functional assessments and analyses they often have difficulty translating the results into effective intervention strategies.

Interventions for attention-maintained challenging behaviour

Challenging behaviour can be an effective means of gaining the attention of others. Thus the maintaining consequence is attention from others. Attention-maintained challenging behaviour can occur for individuals who have few, if any, alternative responses that are effective in recruiting attention. If attention is identified as a reinforcer then the clinician can use attention (the reinforcing consequence) to increase appropriate behaviour and reduce challenging behaviour. There are four main strategies for reducing attention-motivated challenging behaviour. It is preferable to combine as many of these strategies as possible when conducting an intervention.

1   **Increase the overall level of attention.** This involves increasing the overall amount of attention that the person receives. For example, the clinician may set a timer for varying intervals (e.g. 3-minutes, 1-minute, 5-minutes) and when the timer goes off the individual receives 10–20 seconds of positive attention. Technically, this procedure is known as non-contingent reinforcement because attention is delivered on a fixed-time schedule irrespective of the person's behaviour (Tucker, Sigafoos and Bushell, 1998). As the person starts to receive more attention than usual under this fixed-time schedule, there is likely to be less need for them to engage in attention-motivated challenging behaviour (O'Reilly, Lancioni, King, Matthews and Nic Dhomhnaill, 2000).

2   **Provide attention for appropriate behaviour.** A variation on the use of

non-contingent attention is to provide positive attention to the individual contingent upon the absence of challenging behaviour. The idea is to catch the person when they are not engaging in the behaviour and then deliver the reinforcer (Durand, 1990). As the person learns that attention is available without having to resort to challenging behaviour, it should decrease in frequency. Technically, this procedure is known as differential reinforcement of other behaviour. As with non-contingent reinforcement, the reinforcer takes the form of positive attention from others. This could be a kind word, a hug, smiles, as well as spending some time conversing with the person about something that interests her. The key point is to provide attention for the absence of challenging behaviour.

3   **Extinction.** Along with attention for appropriate behaviour the clinician (or whoever is implementing the support plan) should ignore challenging behaviour as much as possible. If the behaviour needs attention then it should be brief and as matter-of-fact as possible. Even negative attention in the form of reprimand can be reinforcing for attention-motivated challenging behaviour. In general, attention should no longer be available for challenging behaviour, but rather attention will be given only for appropriate behaviour (Durand, 1990).

4   **Teach attention-gaining skills.** In many cases challenging behaviour is the most efficient method of gaining attention for the individual. They may not have other effective communication skills in their repertoire that facilitate access to attention from others. To overcome this it may be appropriate to teach the person communication skills (Carr *et al.*, 1994). The person might be taught to seek attention ('Will you sit with me?') so that others will spend time with them. When teaching new communication behaviours it is important frequently to prompt the person to use the new form of communication in daily settings before they begin to engage in challenging behaviour.

Interventions for escape-maintained challenging behaviour

Many individuals engage in challenging behaviour to escape or avoid tasks that they find unpleasant. A number of strategies can be used to support them in such circumstances. Again, it is preferable to use as many of these strategies as possible when conducting an intervention (Durand, 1990).

1   **Reinforce participation.** If challenging behaviour is reinforced by escape from non-preferred activities, then intervention should focus on delivering reinforcement based on increases in participation. Initially the person might be reinforced for engaging appropriately for short durations (e.g. complete one step of the task analysis) and then receive reinforcement. Potential reinforcement might include brief periods away from the

task, access to desired items, or verbal praise. Over time the person is required to spend longer periods on the task in order to receive reinforcement (O'Reilly, 1995).

2   **Escape extinction.** Another important strategy is to ensure that challenging behaviour no longer produces escape (reinforcement). In other words the person is no longer allowed to escape from the task when they engage in challenging behaviour (Lalli, Casey and Kates, 1995). To use this procedure effectively the clinician must be prepared to persist with instruction even if the challenging behaviour escalates.

3   **Reduce task difficulty.** In some instances challenging behaviour may occur because the task is too difficult for the person to perform. For example, the task analysis may not be specified appropriately and therefore the person may have difficulty following and performing the steps of the task. In such cases the clinician may wish to re-evaluate the task analysis, or use a different instructional strategy (e.g. physical prompt with 0-second time delay) in order to increase success for the participant. In other cases, the clinician might teach the person to ask for help with the difficult task (Lalli *et al.*, 1995).

4   **Task preference.** In other situations challenging behaviour may occur because the current task is less preferred to alternative available activities. In such cases the clinician might simply decide to eliminate the difficult task, introduce reinforcement for participation, or provide the person with choices about activities. For example, the person might be given the choice to do the task now or later. Related to this, some individuals have difficulty moving from one task to another. This can be understood as a form of avoidance behaviour (i.e. they are moving from a more highly preferred to a less highly preferred task). One possible solution to such challenging behaviour is to present the person with a picture schedule of activities to occur during the day and ensure that the person can understand the sequence of the schedule. Making the activities predictable using a schedule can reduce challenging behaviour that occurs during the transition between tasks (Mesibov, Browder and Kirkland, 2002).

5   **Task duration.** Sometimes a person will participate in a task for a period of time and then engage in challenging behaviour to make it known that he or she has had enough. In such circumstances interventions should consist of providing more frequent breaks and gradually increasing the length of the task (Lalli, Casey and Kates, 1995).

SUMMARY

Applied behaviour analysis technology has made a tremendous contribution to the field of developmental disability. In this chapter we have described two of the central contributions of ABA – strategies to teach new skills, and strategies to assess and support individuals who engage in challenging behaviour. Behaviour analysts have shown that people with even the most severe disabilities are capable of learning new skills and are capable of participating in, and exerting control over, their environment. Teaching individuals with developmental disabilities involves a number of steps. Complex skills must first be broken down into discrete units of behaviour. These discrete units of behaviour are taught using a selection of response and stimulus prompts. Successful performance of new skills is reinforced using preferred items or events during instruction. Generalized performance of new skills across settings and time is actively programmed during instruction. Challenging behaviour such as self-injury and aggression is prevalent among this population and tends to limit participation in regular life settings. Behaviour analysts have demonstrated that much of this behaviour seems to be learned and may serve a communicative function. Assessment strategies such as interviews, systematic observations, and experimental functional analyses, can be used to isolate the consequences maintaining challenging behaviour. The information derived from such assessments can then be used to develop a behavioural support plan to make challenging behaviour unnecessary for the person.

EXERCISE

Work in groups of four. Select a large task such as 'dressing'. Break it down into a series of smaller tasks and design an instructional programme using principles in the chapter. Share the plan with the class.

FURTHER READING

Cooper, J., Heron, T. and Heward, W. (2006). *Applied Behaviour Analysis* (2nd edn). New York: Prentice-Hall.

REFERENCES

Baer, D. M. and Wolf, M. M. (1970). The entry into natural communities of reinforcement. In R. Ulrich, T. Stachnik and J. Mabry (eds), *Control of Human Behaviour* (vol. 2, pp. 319–24). Glenview, IL: Scott Foresman.

Baer, D. M., Wolf, M. M. and Risley, T. R. (1968). Some current dimensions of applied behaviour analysis. *Journal of Applied Behaviour Analysis*, 1, 91–7.

Bailey, J. and Pyles, A. M. (1989). Behavioural diagnostics. In E. Cipani (ed.), *The Treatment of Severe Behaviour Disorders: Behaviour Analysis Approaches*. Monographs of the American Association on Mental Retardation, No. 12 (pp. 85–107). Washington DC: American Association on Mental Retardation.

Cannella, H. I., O'Reilly, M. F. and Lancioni, G. E. (2005). Choice and preference assessment research with people with severe to profound developmental disabilities: A review of the literature. *Research in Developmental Disabilities*, 26 (1), 1–15.

Carr, E. G. (1977). The motivation of self-injurious behaviour: A review of some hypotheses. *Psychological Bulletin*, 84, 800–16.

Carr, E. G., Levin, L., McConnachie, G., Carlson, J., Kemp, D. and Smith, C. (1994). *Communication-Based Intervention for Problem Behaviour: A User's Guide for Producing Positive Change*. Baltimore: Paul H. Brookes.

Chandler, L. K., Lubeck, R. C. and Fowler, S. (1992). Generalization and maintenance of preschool children's social skills: A critical review and analysis. *Journal of Applied Behaviour Analysis*, 25, 415–28.

Connis, R. (1979). The effects of sequential pictorial cues, self-recording, and praise on the job task sequencing of retarded adults. *Journal of Applied Behaviour Analysis*, 12, 355–61.

Cuvo, A. J., Davis, P. K., O'Reilly, M. F., Mooney, B. and Crowley, R. (1992). Promoting stimulus control with textual prompts and performance feedback for persons with mild disabilities. *Journal of Applied Behaviour Analysis*, 25, 477–89.

Cuvo, A. J., Leaf, R. and Borakove, L. (1978). Teaching janitorial skills to the mentally retarded: Acquisition, generalization, and maintenance. *Journal of Applied Behaviour Analysis*, 11, 345–55.

Durand, M. (1990). *Severe Behaviour Problems: A Functional Communication Training Approach*. New York: The Guilford Press.

Durand, M. and Crimmins, D. (1988). Identifying the variables maintaining self-injurious behaviour. *Journal of Autism and Developmental Disorders*, 18, 99–117.

Gardner, W., Cole, C., Davidson, D. and Karan, O. (1986). Reducing aggression in individuals with developmental disabilities: An expanded stimulus control assessment and intervention model. *Education and Training of the Mentally Retarded*, 21, 3–12.

Gold, M. (1976). Task analysis of a complex assembly task by the retarded blind. *Exceptional Children*, 43, 78–84.

Halle, J., Baer, D. and Spradlin, J. (1981). Teacher's generalized use of delay as a stimulus control procedure to increase language use in handicapped children. *Journal of Applied Behaviour Analysis*, 14, 389–409.

Horner, R. D. and Keilitz, I. (1975). Training mentally retarded adolescents to brush their teeth. *Journal of Applied Behaviour Analysis*, 8, 301–9.

Horner, R. H., Sprague, J. R. and Wilcox, B. (1982). Conducting general case programs for community activities. In B. Wilcox and T. Bellamy (eds), *Design of High School for Severely Handicapped Students*. Baltimore: Paul H. Brookes.

Iwata, B., Dorsey, M., Slifer, K., Bauman, K. and Richman, G. (1982/1994). Toward a functional analysis of self-injury. *Journal of Applied Behaviour Analysis*, 27, 197–209. (Reprinted from: *Analysis and Intervention in Developmental Disabilities*, 2, 1–20.)

Iwata, B., Pace, G., Dorsey, M., Zarcone, J., Vollmer, T., Smith, R., Rodgers, T., Lerman, D., Shore, B., Mazaleski, J., Goh, H., Cowdery, G., Kalsher, M., McCosh, K. and Willis, K. (1994). The functions of self-injurious behaviour: An experimental-epidemiological analysis. *Journal of Applied Behaviour Analysis*, 27, 215–40.

Johnson, B. F. and Cuvo, A. J. (1981). Teaching mentally retarded adults to cook. *Behaviour Modification*, 5, 187–202.

Lalli, J., Casey, S. and Kates, K. (1995). Reducing escape behaviour and increasing task completion with functional communication training, extinction, and response chaining. *Journal of Applied Behaviour Analysis*, 28, 261–8.

Lancioni, G. E., O'Reilly, M. F., Campodonico, F. and Mantini, M. (1998a). Mobility versus sedentariness in task arrangements for people with multiple disabilities: An assessment of preferences. *Research in Developmental Disabilities*, 19, 465–75.

Lancioni, G. E., O'Reilly, M. F., Campodonico, F. and Mantini, M. (1998b). Task variation versus task repetition for people with profound developmental disabilities: An assessment of preferences. *Research in Developmental Disabilities*, 19, 189–99.

Leslie, J. C. and O'Reilly, M. F. (1999). *Behaviour Analysis: Foundations and Applications to Psychology*. Amsterdam: Harwood Academic Publishers.

Mesibov, G., Browder, D. and Kirkland, C. (2002). Using individualized schedules as a component of positive behavioural support for students with developmental disabilities. *Journal of Positive Behavioural Support*, 4, 73–9.

McGill, P. (1999). Establishing operations: Implications for the assessment, treatment, and prevention of problem behaviour. *Journal of Applied Behaviour Analysis*, 32, 393–418.

Northup, J., Wacker, D., Sasso, G., Steege, M., Cigrand, K., Cook, J. and DeRaad, A. (1991). A brief functional analysis of aggressive and alternative behaviour in an outclinic setting. *Journal of Applied Behaviour Analysis*, 24, 509–22.

O'Reilly, M. F. (1995). Functional analysis and treatment of escape-maintained aggression correlated with sleep deprivation. *Journal of Applied Behaviour Analysis*, 28, 225–6.

O'Reilly, M. F. (1997). Functional analysis of episodic self-injury correlated with recurrent otitis media. *Journal of Applied Behaviour Analysis*, 30, 165–7.

O'Reilly, M. F. and Glynn, D. (1995). Using a process social skills training approach with adolescents with mild intellectual disabilities in a high school setting. *Education and Training in Mental Retardation and Developmental Disabilities*, 30, 187–98.

O'Reilly, M. F, Green, G. and Braunling-McMorrow, D. (1990). Self-administered written prompts to teach home accident prevention skills to adults with brain injuries. *Journal of Applied Behaviour Analysis*, 23, 431–46.

O'Reilly, M. F., Lacey, C. and Lancioni, G. E. (2000). Assessment of the influence of background noise on escape-maintained problem behaviour and pain behaviour in a child with Williams Syndrome. *Journal of Applied Behaviour Analysis*, 33, 511–14.

O'Reilly, M. F., Lancioni, G., King, L., Matthews, G. and Nic Dhomhnaill, O. (2000). Using brief assessments to evaluate aberrant behaviour maintained by attention. *Journal of Applied Behaviour Analysis*, 33, 109–12.

O'Reilly, M. F., Lancioni, G. E. and Lacey, C. (2001). A preliminary investigation of the assessment and treatment of tantrums with two post-institutionalized Romanian adoptees. *Scandinavian Journal of Behaviour Therapy*, 30, 179–87.

O'Reilly, M. F., Lancioni, G. E., Sigafoos, J. and Lacey, C. (2004). Using paired-choice assessment to identify variables maintaining sleep problems in a child with severe disabilities. *Journal of Applied Behaviour Analysis*, 37, 209–12.

O'Reilly, M. F., Peck, S. M., Webster, J., Baird, S. J., Plowman, K., Lancioni, G. E., Tiernan, R., Gardiner, M. and Cummins, O. (1999). Using functional analysis techniques to develop educational support plans for students with high support needs. *Australasian Journal of Special Education*, 23, 5–14.

Paclawskyj, T., Matson, J. L., Rush, K., Smalls, Y. and Vollmer, T. (2000). Questions about behavioural function (QABF): A behavioural checklist for functional assessment of aberrant behaviour. *Research in Developmental Disabilities*, 21, 223–9.

Richman, G. S., Reiss, M. L., Bauman, K. E. and Bailey, J. S. (1984). Teaching menstrual care to mentally retarded women: Acquisition, generalization, and maintenance. *Journal of Applied Behaviour Analysis*, 17, 441–51.

Schuster, J., Gast, D., Wolery, M. and Guiltinan, S. (1988). The effectiveness of a constant time delay procedure to teach chained responses to adolescents with mental retardation. *Journal of Applied Behaviour Analysis*, 21, 169–78.

Sigafoos, J., Arthur, M. and O'Reilly, M. (2003). *Challenging Behaviour and Developmental Disability*. London: Whurr Publishers.

Sisson, L., Kilwein, M. and Van Hasselt, V. (1988). A graduated guidance procedure for teaching self-dressing skills to multihandicapped children. *Research in Developmental Disabilities*, 9, 419–32.

Sowers, J., Rusch, F., Connis, R. T. and Cummins, L. (1980). Teaching mentally retarded adults to time manage in a vocational setting. *Journal of Applied Behaviour Analysis*, 13, 119–28.

Stokes, T. and Baer, D. (1977). An implicit technology of generalization. *Journal of Applied Behaviour Analysis*, 10, 349–67.

Stokes, T., Fowler, S. and Baer, D. M. (1978). Training preschool children to recruit natural communities of reinforcement. *Journal of Applied Behaviour Analysis*, 11, 285–303.

Taylor, I. and O'Reilly, M. F. (1997). Toward a functional analysis of private verbal self-regulation. *Journal of Applied Behaviour Analysis*, 30, 43–58.

Terrace, H. S. (1963). Errorless transfer of a discrimination across two continua. *Journal of the Experimental Analysis of Behaviour*, 6, 223–32.

Touchette, P., MacDonald, R. and Langer, S. (1985). A scatterplot for identifying stimulus control of problem behaviour. *Journal of Applied Behaviour Analysis*, 18, 343–51.

Tucker, M., Sigafoos, J. and Bushell, H. (1998). Use of noncontingent reinforcement in the treatment of challenging behaviour: A review and clinical guide. *Behaviour Modification*, 22, 529–47.

Chapter 8

Cognitive behaviour therapy

Dave Dagnan, Andrew Jahoda and Biza Stenfert Kroese

More than 20 per cent of the general population living in the community have a 'psychiatric disorder' of some kind (Jenkins, Lewis, Bebbington, Brugha, Farrell *et al.*, 1997; Kessler, 1995). However, reported prevalence rates for people with intellectual disability differ widely. For example, Sturmey, Reed and Corbett (1991) reported rates that vary between 10 per cent and 39 per cent. Such variation is due to a variety of factors such as sample selection, the type of diagnostic methods (self-report, carers' reports, observation), and definitions of psychiatric disorder and learning disability used. The usefulness of psychiatric diagnosis has been queried both for the general population (Boyle, 2002) and for people with intellectual disability (Slade and Bentall, 1988). An alternative way of assessing the causative and maintaining factors of psychological distress is to adopt a formulation approach (Persons, Davidson and Tompkins, 2000). Individualized case formulation is at the core of cognitive behavioural therapy (CBT) and consists of an idiographic (individualized) theory that is linked to a nomothetic (general) cognitive behavioural theory (Tarrier, 2006).

There are a number of different approaches included under the cognitive umbrella (e.g. Beck, Rush, Shaw and Emery, 1979; Ellis, 2004; Kanfer and Gaelick, 1986; Meichenbaum, 1977). Cognitive therapy can be viewed as suggesting either a deficit or distortion model of psychological distress (Stenfert Kroese, Dagnan and Loumidis, 1997). Deficit models involve consideration of issues of language, memory, attention and other meta-cognitive processes. However, the cognitive therapeutic approaches that take a deficit approach are associated with assumed absence of self-talk (Whitman, 1990) or with poorly developed skills in self-talk such as social problem solving (Loumidis and Hill, 1997). Most of the cognitive therapy research with people with intellectual disability is concerned with deficit approaches. Such approaches include self-instruction and self-monitoring. For example, Harchick, Sherman and Sheldon (1992) reviewed fifty-nine studies that used self-management techniques for people with intellectual disability. Nine of these studies addressed the decrease of challenging behaviour and fifty aimed to increase social skills or performance in academic or work settings. Few of these studies discuss collaborative relationships between clients and therapists, and the psychological well-being of the client was rarely mentioned or measured.

Distortion models suggest a form of cognitive therapy that assumes that a person's reaction to an event is influenced by the meaning she or he attaches to the event. Emotional and behavioural responses are assumed to be a function of how an event is perceived and recalled, the attributions that are made about its causes, and the way in which the event effects self-perception (Reinecke, Dattilio and Freeman, 1996). Cognitive formulation may include an analysis of how early experiences induce core beliefs about self, others, and the world in general and assumptions or rules for living. For example, Beck (1976) used the term 'schemata' which he defined as cognitive structures which organize and process incoming information. Ellis (2004) identified the central importance of core self-evaluations and demands of the world. These structures can be seen as generalized ways of seeing the self and the world that are acquired early on in life or during later periods of extended traumatic experience. Certain critical incidents, often those which are similar to those earlier experiences that have shaped core beliefs, may activate these beliefs which will influence the interpretations of the incidents. These interpretations have emotional, physiological and behavioural consequences.

The difference between the deficit and distortion models is reflected in a continuing debate about the use of CBT with people who have intellectual disability (Allen, 2000; Whitaker, 2001). This may reflect, in part, many authors' and clinicians' continuing scepticism that the cognitive components of clinical interventions are effective. Their view could be reinforced by the fact that a number of approaches described as being 'cognitive' focus on skill acquisition or the development of self-regulation. For example, Meichenbaum's (1977) stress inoculation is at the heart of anger management work (Jahoda, Trower and Pert, 2001). The aim is to give people a variety of behavioural and cognitive skills to enable them to manage situations that they have previously found difficult. Yet there is increasing evidence that psychological distress is mediated by the meanings that people with intellectual disability attach to events. For example, Nezu, Nezu, Rothenburg, DelliCarpini and Groag (1995) have shown how a higher frequency of negative automatic thoughts and feelings of helplessness are significantly related to depression. Similarly the role of cognitive factors has been demonstrated in the field of anger and aggression. Jahoda, Pert and Trower (2006b) found that aggressive individuals made similar attributions of hostile intent to those of their non-aggressive peers when observing others facing provocation. However, when they were asked to imagine themselves facing provocation the pattern changed. In this self-referent condition the aggressive individuals attributed higher levels of hostile intent to the provocateur than their non-aggressive peers did. If the participants' problems of aggression had simply been due to a lack of socio-emotional understanding or deficient rule-governed behaviour, then they would have been expected to perceive a higher level of hostile intent irrespective of whether they were observing others or imagining that they were facing threat themselves. Instead, the meaning of the events for individuals appears to be crucial to how they interpret particular situations and to their feelings and actions. This highlights the potential value of adopting cognitive interventions that move beyond an educational or self-regulatory approach, and that investigate and aim to modify individual thoughts and beliefs.

A CLINICAL ILLUSTRATION OF THE DIFFERENCE BETWEEN DEFICIT AND MEANING-BASED APPROACHES

In order to examine the difference between deficit-based and distortion approaches further, it may be helpful to use a fictitious case example. Jean is a woman who has lost several residential placements due to seriously aggressive outbursts, generally when she feels that she is being watched carrying out household tasks. She has a tremor, and says that she becomes anxious when she is being watched and that her tremor becomes worse and her temper deteriorates. This is one of the main triggers for her aggression. When asked to reflect upon how she is treated in these situations she insists that the support worker was deliberately trying to make her uptight and lose her temper. This was her **primary appraisal** of the situation. Her **secondary appraisal**, or how she thinks that she should react, is to become aggressive. A deficit approach might try to teach her the necessary social skills or increase her assertiveness skills in order to deal with these situations without becoming aggressive. Alternatively, one might give her simple self-statements or other techniques to remain calm when facing perceived provocation. Either of these approaches might prove effective, but in neither instance is there an attempt to deal with her perceptions of the event.

The cognitive element of a CBT intervention could start by tackling the primary appraisals Jean makes regarding these anger-provoking events. Thus, one might examine the evidence for the member of staff deliberately trying to upset her, and guide her to consider alternatives, such as the likelihood that the member of staff wanted to help her with her work. This moves beyond self-regulation to address the meaning that she attaches to the anger-provoking event. She may accept that if she believed the staff member was trying to help her she would probably remain calm. It is possible that this attempt to change her primary appraisal will not work, and she will maintain her view that the staff member was being deliberately nasty. If this happens one might want to explore the beliefs or core self-schema underlying her negative primary appraisals. For example, she could believe that to fail in other people's eyes leads to a complete sense of incompetence or worthlessness.

Such beliefs might have been born out of real experiences of failure in her life, and her fear of being regarded as incompetent might lead to a heightened sensitivity to this kind of interpersonal threat.

There are a number of ways of working with Jean's core self-schema that might prove helpful. One can feed back the information to her as a formulation. In other words, describe how these beliefs may have developed and how they influence her perception of events. This feedback may be insufficient for change, but establishes a shared understanding between the therapist and client as a platform for this. The social position of people with intellectual disability means that they can often find themselves in situations where they feel powerless, excluded, or treated in a variety of ways that are threatening. Thus, Jean's attributions or primary appraisals of threat might be reasonable while the resulting self-evaluations are harmful. An act that she perceives as potentially undermining her sense of worth is perceived as hostile and results in aggression. Therefore, reducing the salience of these perceived threats for her sense of competence might lessen the emotional hurt and the likelihood of responding aggressively.

One of the concerns about challenging Jean's core beliefs about herself as incompetent might be that it is a rather abstract intellectual exercise that someone with a learning disability might struggle with. However, it is not merely through reflection that people learn about themselves, it is also through action (Markova, 1987). For example, by creating opportunities for her to experience success or giving her social roles with some status attached, an increased sense of worth could reduce the perceived everyday threats to her sense of self, and thus the number of aggressive outbursts.

In summary, cognitive behavioural therapy consists of a package of interventions that includes both behavioural and cognitive elements. Given the fact that people with intellectual disability have cognitive deficits, there may be a tendency to focus on skills training and self-regulation. Yet controlled studies and a rich anthropological literature indicates that a 'social-cognitive' deficit is only one factor to be considered in the genesis and maintenance of emotional difficulties (Edgerton, 1967; Jahoda *et al.*, 2006a; 2006b).

Skills-based work or training in more effective self-management or rule-governed behaviour fails to address explicitly the meaning that people attach to events. The cognitive component dealing with how and what people think, and the implications of this for their feelings and actions, is the least developed aspect of CBT for people with intellectual disability. To tackle and change people's perceptions about themselves and their world is not just an abstract reflective process, but is active and practical. This chapter will go on to consider in more detail how cognitive therapy can work for people with intellectual disability.

ADAPTING COGNITIVE THERAPY FOR PEOPLE WITH INTELLECTUAL DISABILITY

Cognitive therapy in outpatient settings is ordinarily carried out on an individual basis. Clients are expected to absorb the lessons of therapy gained in the clinic and generalize them to their everyday lives. While this model might be appropriate for some individuals with intellectual disability, it does not take account of the communicative or intellectual difficulties some can face. Nor does a focus on individual cognitions give sufficient weight to the social factors that influence and provide context for people's perceptions of themselves and their worlds (Smail, 2005). This chapter will consider how aspects of the therapeutic process can be adapted to make cognitive therapy accessible and meaningful for people with intellectual disability. First, we will consider assessment of skills associated with aspects of cognitive therapy, and the structure of sessions. We will then look at broader issues concerning interventions used during work with emotions and cognitions. Educating the client into the cognitive model and the process of assessment and formulation are closely tied to the development of interventions. Rather than identify a 'toolkit' of interventions, this chapter will emphasize the dynamic nature of the therapy process. Grounding the therapeutic process in the real lives of people with intellectual disability makes the assessment and educative process an essential part of the intervention, linking the cognitive model and the clients' own experience. The chapter will conclude by highlighting the importance of process issues in cognitive therapy for people with intellectual disability.

Adapting therapy: assessment issues

When conducting cogntive therapy with people who have intellectual disabilities, certain adaptations are essential that take account of the constraints entailed by intellectual disability (Dagnan and Lindsey, 2004). Central to these are the constraints that make understanding links between emotion, cognition and behaviour, particularly challenging. Safran, Vallis, Segal and Shaw (1986) describe an approach to accessing cognition in therapy. They suggest that the starting point is the behavioural or emotional consequence. The therapist and client then identify the activating event associated with the behaviour and/or the emotion. Finally they identify the mediating cognition. Dagnan and Chadwick (1997) describe a method for assessing the core skills associated with cognitive therapy that takes this process as its starting point. Thus the assessment has three components. These are the assessment of the ability to identify emotions; the ability to make links between activating events and subsequent emotions; and the ability to identify mediating cognitions.

Identifying emotions

To assess the person's ability to identify emotions and use emotional language we use a simple set of facial expressions (Dagnan and Proudlove, 1997). This material is standardized in that we know how people with mild and moderate intellectual disability tend to respond to the materials. We then use a range of less standardized methods to assess emotion recognition (see later in this chapter). At times, this type of assessment will suggest that a person's difficulties in understanding their social world might contribute to their emotional or interpersonal problems.

Making links between events and emotions

We then assess the person's ability to make links between activating events and subsequent emotions. We use as a starting point a simple standardized assessment described by Reed and Clements (1989). This assessment presents six simple scenarios and asks the person to indicate how they would feel in that situation by pointing at either a happy or a sad face. Each scenario has an expected response. For example, 'You take your dog for a walk, it runs away, you've lost your dog', is expected to generate a response of 'sad'. However, if people respond 'incorrectly' it is always worth asking why they would feel in this way, as some people may have idiosyncratic reasons for their response. For example, the scenario 'It is a hot day, you want an ice cream, but the ice cream shop is closed, which face is your face?' is expected to generate a 'sad' response. However, for someone who wishes not to spoil their diet, 'happy' might be an appropriate response.

Identifying cognitions

To assess the ability to identify mediating cognitions a simple scenario is presented along with an associated emotion and the person is asked to suggest what they would be 'thinking or saying to themselves' in that situation (Dagnan and Chadwick, 1997; Dagnan, Chadwick and Proudlove, 2000). The same scenario is then presented at a later stage with a different emotion associated with it. The degree to which the person is able to alter their response in order to accommodate the different emotion is an indication of how well the person is able to use a cognitive model. The task is a clinical method and as yet there is no standardized method for judging the appropriateness of any response from a client. However, the advantage of this is that it can be used with scenarios incorporating the issues facing the individual client.

Although the initial scenarios given for these assessments (Dagnan and Chadwick, 1997; Reed and Clements, 1989) are not specific to any individual client, it is a simple matter to adjust them to represent real-life experiences.

We might first use standardized scenarios to allow comparison with published data or accumulated clinical experience, and then start to introduce the same task using examples from the person's life. Thus it is possible from this initial assessment to begin to understand the emotional and cognitive responses of the client.

This assessment process is intended to offer the opportunity for the therapist to adjust therapy to match their clients' cognitive and emotional skills. The information gained can also provide a profile of particular strengths and weaknesses in the core skills and thus identify areas in which teaching may be required.

Adapting therapy: session structure

A collaborative and active structure for cognitive therapy thus needs to be maintained throughout the therapeutic process. Thus, it is particularly important to plan the structure of therapy sessions when using cognitive interventions with people with intellectual disability (Dagnan and Lindsey, 2004). Judith Beck (1995) suggests that the structural components which are common and important for cognitive therapy are: agenda setting, teaching the cognitive model, socializing clients into the cognitive model, identifying problems, setting goals, setting homework, eliciting feedback, providing a summary and reviewing sessions. In general the clinical literature suggests that each of these aspects can be applied to people with intellectual disability. For example, Lindsey, Neilson and Lawrenson (1997) describe approaches to helping people to cope with anxiety and depression that follow a standard cognitive therapy structure (Beck *et al.*, 1979). Whilst session structure can be organized according to these principles, other aspects of sessions can be flexible, such as the frequency, length and location. Sessions can take place more than once a week and can be relatively short but frequent. Sessions can take place within standard therapeutic settings, but can also take place within settings that are closer to the context that tends to produce the distress or discomfort, as concrete links to eliciting events and stimuli will often enable clients to access 'hot' cognitions and emotions more easily (Dryden, 1987). We will now consider each of the structural elements described above in turn.

Identifying problems

The routes into therapy taken by people with intellectual disability complicate the identification of problems. People without intellectual disability have multiple opportunities to choose whether or not to take up an offer of appointment with a therapist. For example, they may choose whether or not to consult with a General Practitioner. They may or may not agree to the General Practitioner making a referral to the therapist. They may choose whether or not to attend the appointment offered by the therapist. However, many people with intellectual disability are referred by carers and are taken to see the therapist without sufficient explanation of the therapeutic process. We have developed a video information pack that presents a brief description of what is involved in seeing a psychologist in order to provide potential clients with accessible information which allows them to make an informed choice about whether to see a psychologist or not.

However, there is little evidence or consensus available as to the preferred process for inviting a client to therapy when they have a learning disability. A standard appointment letter for non-disabled people may include details such as the difficulties identified in the referral letter, and other aspects of therapy process. In fact, therapists often see such letters as part of the therapeutic process. However, many people with intellectual disability will not be aware of the nature or even the fact of referral. Thus, it is important for therapists to share their knowledge and perception of the identified problem with the client in the early stages of therapy.

Agenda setting

Identifying the activities and work planned within each session is also important. Therapists may use flipcharts or whiteboards to make this accessible and available throughout the session. This will enable the structure of the session to be maintained, the completed agenda to be reviewed and the work remaining to be identified. Simple and agreed pictorial representations will aid understanding and engagement in this process. It is important that the agenda is not over-elaborate. A session could have three components. The first part might consist of a review of the previous session, and any lessons learned or practised from then. Secondly, there may be set activities or areas for discussion. Some issues will arise in the course of therapy, and other areas of activity will be planned from the initial assessment. For example, there may be a need to work on emotions and their recognition (Ludwig and Hingsburger, 1989). In the final part of the session, there will be an opportunity to discuss general issues, including gains and difficulties currently experienced. This component could also be used to make positive plans for the time between sessions.

When people come in with their own agenda the therapist needs to be able to listen properly to the client, but also be able to shift back to the topic in hand. Being too authoritarian goes against the collaborative spirit of therapy. Being too lax means that the session loses focus. This requires the therapist to maintain a sensitive balance.

Teaching the cognitive model

An earlier section of this chapter described an approach to assessing clients' understanding of the cognitive mediation model. The principles underpinning this approach can be used to help people grasp how it works. Kushlick, Trower and Dagnan (1997) describe a method for introducing the cognitive model, which can be used with people with intellectual disability. The core elements in this process are to illustrate that each time we experience the same event we do not necessarily experience the same emotions, and that what we think about the event is important in shaping our emotional and behavioural responses. This is illustrated by exploring how we can think 'happy' and 'sad' thoughts in response to the same event (Kushlick recommends using a neutral event such as 'It's your birthday'). When we think sad or bad thoughts we end up with sad or bad emotions and when we think happy thoughts we experience happy emotions. There will be many opportunities to illustrate the importance of cognitive mediation within therapy. People will talk about events that happen on a recurring basis ('I often argue with my mum', 'people always ignore me'). Identifying the different emotions that arise on different occasions and examining why the emotions are not always the same will be a useful way of reinforcing the cognitive model. Such approaches are particularly helpful as they are rooted in people's real experience rather than in abstract examples. When the events under discussion concern thoughts and emotions from the clients' everyday lives, the therapist can start exploring the meaning that clients attach to these events. This process should be active and engaging, for example using role-play with flip-charts showing cartoon bubbles. The cartoon bubbles can then be filled with the different beliefs people generate about a particular situation, along with their thoughts and feelings.

Eliciting feedback

When new information is being introduced to clients in therapy it is important to elicit feedback. In this context feedback serves two purposes. First, it ensures that the content and nature of the therapeutic endeavour has been understood. Secondly, it helps to maintain a collaborative relationship between the therapist and client. If the therapist fails to engage the interest of the client, or to make themselves understood, then the therapeutic relationship may break down. One way clients might display their sense of alienation from the process would simply be to disengage from therapy. Therefore it is important that feedback is both sought and heard by the therapist.

Providing a summary

Summarizing and illustrating points made in therapy are particularly important for people with intellectual disability, to ensure that information is remembered and understood. This should be continuous, and reviewing the same material on more than one occasion is essential. Summaries can be produced on a whiteboard or a flipchart. We are beginning to experiment with digital cameras to provide the client with a record of the whiteboard. Other therapists have reported using taped summaries to allow the client to listen to them again at a later time (Dryden, 1987). Therapists' understanding of the individual clients' strengths and needs, such as their ability to recall verbal and visual information, will allow the session structure and content to be appropriately adapted.

Setting homework

A number of people with intellectual disability will be able to carry out homework tasks, while others will not. Psychotherapists often view the failure to carry out such tasks as a sign of resistance, to be explored within the therapeutic environment. Yet for people with intellectual disability this may not be the most likely explanation. Both individual cognitive factors such as memory and motivation, and social factors such as lack of environmental control can prevent homework from being carried out. A number of steps can be taken to increase the likelihood of engagement in tasks between sessions. For example, it is important to take care to establish the clients' literacy skills before handing out charts and diaries, as otherwise there is a danger of making people feel incompetent and alienating them. Other efforts can be made to simplify homework tasks, like asking a client to tick a single box each day after a frequently watched TV programme such as *Eastenders* to illustrate how they are feeling or thinking at the time. It may also prove helpful or necessary to engage carers in prompting and enabling homework activities. The issues of boundaries and confidentiality raised by this last point deserve considerable discussion. If homework is to be completed with the help of someone else, then care should be taken to ensure that there is a trusting relationship.

Adapting therapy: working with emotions

We have already noted that the most commonly reported cognitive interventions used with people who have intellectual disability are based on a skill deficit model. These interventions are often concerned with the development and maintenance of behavioural skills, with little attention paid to the role of emotions in causing psychological distress or as a route for interventions (Harchik *et al.*, 1992). Deficit models have been used to develop interventions for emotional difficulties such as anger and anxiety (Lindsey *et al.*, 1997). These emotional difficulties have largely been identified as problems with information processing. Consequently, a skill-based approach involving management of arousal though the use of problem solving, positive self-statements and social skills development, has been applied with some success (Lindsey *et al.*, 1997). In fact, the few randomized control trials for cognitive interventions for people with intellectual disability have been in the area of anger (Taylor, 2002). However, cognitive therapy as described by Ellis (2004) and Beck *et al.* (1979) require a focus on emotions. Judith Beck (1995) identifies three activities which are the defining components of cognitive therapy applied to emotions. These include identifying and distinguishing emotions; labelling emotions; and the rating degree of emotion being experienced.

Identifying and distinguishing emotions

The simple discrimination of emotions from cognition or behaviour is addressed in a number of reports on the wider use of cognitive therapy (Quakley, Coker, Palmer and Reynolds, 2003). Discrimination may be taught using simple exercises that are easily adapted for people with intellectual disability. There is a considerable literature on the abilities of people with intellectual disability to identify emotions. It is hypothesized that people with intellectual disability have particular problems in the identification of emotions, although it is possible that these are a result of the language-based assessments used (Moore, 2001). In working clinically it may be necessary for people to be able to distinguish emotions such as sadness, happiness, anger, anxiety and fear. Cognitive therapy has developed emotion-specific interventions and in some cases interventions specific to different presentations of the same emotion. Some ability in differentiating emotions is important to enable people to take advantage of these approaches. There are a number of materials available for use in therapeutic settings, some of which have been standardized (e.g. Dagnan and Proudlove, 1997). Using standardized materials will allow comparison of the types of error and levels of ability for each client that will help inform the therapist's interventions and adaptations. However, the use of non-standardized materials will also be important in engaging the client. For example, the person who is interested in football might be engaged by examining photographs of people such as David Beckham and interpreting their facial expressions; other people might respond to video material from television soaps or familiar programmes.

Labelling emotions

It is important to understand the language that the person uses to describe their own and others emotions. There has been little work on the emotional vocabulary of people with intellectual disability. Mellor and Dagnan (2005) asked forty people with mild to moderate intellectual disability to give multiple exemplars for the emotions happy, sad, angry and frightened. Their performance on this task was compared with their ability to name multiple exemplars for three non-emotion concepts: animals; flowers; and colours. The numbers of words given for the emotion and non-emotion task were summed. Twenty-one participants (52.5 per cent) did not identify any additional words for the emotions presented. The average number of emotional words generated by those able to name at least one alternative emotion was 1.8. This compared with 100 per cent of participants being able to give additional words for the non-emotion word task. On average 19.1 alternative words were identified for this task. These findings suggest that people with intellectual disability may experience particular difficulties expressing their emotions verbally. This might not be simply related to language ability. However, it is important to distinguish between the ability to express and the ability to experience and recognize emotions.

Rating degree of emotion

The aim of intervention within cognitive therapy is often not to extinguish a particular emotion but to alter its degree. The ability of people to recognize and label degrees of anger, sadness and fear is important in this endeavour. There is little literature on the ability of people with intellectual disability in this area.

Adapting therapy: working with cognition

Identifying cognitions with people with intellectual disability can be a complex and challenging task. People may or may not understand the concept of cognition or thought. However, people do describe themselves and their behaviour in their everyday accounts, and it is possible to help them identify mediating thoughts and beliefs using a number of methods.

Using structured assessments

The assessments described above, used to identify core competencies for therapy, might help to identify distressing cognitions or thoughts in some clients (Dagnan and Chadwick, 1997). Presenting people with scenarios that are comparable to situations known to be distressing for them, and asking them what they think to themselves in those situations, can identify important primary appraisals. Moreover, introducing this approach in the assessment phase could make it easier for clients to discuss their thoughts about distressing events at a later stage.

Listening to the language

People with intellectual disability describe their world using language that illustrates their cognitive content and processes. They may talk about events that are important to them in a way that will expose their evaluations of these situations. This means that the therapist should pay close attention to the clients' comments, which can be difficult in the course of a dialogue.

Reviewing taped sessions allows the therapist to identify important state-ments that they missed during the encounter.

The dialogue given in Dagnan and Chadwick (1997) demonstrates the benefit of listening carefully to the client. In this discussion with the therapist, AA (the client) is saying that the people who are laughing at him 'shouldn't treat him like dirt'. This is an evaluation and one that would be related either to anger, anxiety or depression. We could explore further with this man by asking him what he thinks the other people are thinking about him when they do not say 'hello'. We could further ask him what he thinks he should do in the situation or what he would like to do (see Jahoda, Pert, Squire and Trower, 1998, for examples of such assessment). These interpersonal problem-solving questions will reveal a range of inferential and behavioural responses.

Follow the emotion

Cognitions that are functionally related to emotions will be most easily accessed when 'hot' emotions are present. Thus when people are experiencing or expressing emotions it will be easier to identify the associated cognitions. Dryden (1987) discusses the use of vivid methods in rational emotive therapy. They are used to generate emotional responses that will allow cognition to be accessed. The following are some of these methods:

- Ask the person to imagine the situation.
- Use vivid language to create a full picture of the situation the person finds themselves in when they experience behavioural or emotional difficulties.
- Use photographs of significant others and significant events or times to help access the person's core evaluations and views of their personal history.

In addition to the methods identified by Dryden we would add further methods for generating vivid scenarios that are likely to access 'hot' cogni-tions. These include:

- Use video of people and places known to the person. Carers and the person themselves can be asked to make a video and to bring it to a session as a focus for discussion.
- Use role-play as a method of accessing cognitions and emotions perti-nent to the person. In some cases we have first been directed by the client through an incident that raised particular emotions. We have explored the thoughts behind the person's feelings at the time. Often the use of role-play will make it easier to access cognitions and feelings. We have then redirected the situation and asked the person how they might think

and feel in variations of the previous situation. This can both demonstrate the cognitive model (i.e. how we think can determine how we behave and feel) and illustrate the value of alternative behavioural responses.

• Take the person into the situations and settings that cause behavioural and emotional difficulties. For example, holding some sessions at home or in other settings where the person actually experiences emotional responses can help access cognitions and provide immediate opportunities to test out alternative cognitions and behaviours.

• Ask the person to draw themselves and/or situations which trigger strong emotions and ask them to describe these drawings. The descriptions will often include specific terms which reveal primary appraisals and idiosyncratic use of language. For example, 'Sometimes my problems rain down on me'. Noting these comments, checking their meaning and then incorporating them into one's own vocabulary can enable the therapist to generate a collaborative and symmetrical therapeutic relationship.

Using deductive approaches

It is sometimes the case that cognitive therapists are not as good at accessing core schema or evaluative cognitions as they are at accessing automatic and inferential thoughts in their clients (Young, Klosko and Weishaar, 2003). Beck *et al.*'s (1979) approach to Cognitive Therapy is to apply an inductive approach. Thus, through noting the repeated themes in automatic thoughts the person can start to identify their own schema and cognitive biases. Ellis's (2004) approach to Rational Emotive Therapy uses a deductive method that allows us to assume or pursue evaluative thoughts in a more direct way. If the client (AA) referred to earlier was unable to reveal any more evaluative comments we could probably start to suggest to him, from evidence of repeated themes and statements, the following interpretations: (a) he believes that 'other people should not ignore him'; (b) 'if people think he is dirt then he is dirt'; and (c) the possibility that he is beginning to believe that 'he is dirt'. If such interpretations are offered carefully and sensitively, we can begin to observe whether the suggestions provoke the emotions and potential behaviours that are related to the presenting problems. The 'vivid' methods described above, aiming to produce an emotional trace to distressing thoughts, might help to draw out and explore the relevance of the therapist's interpretations. This can be an uncomfortable process for the therapist. However, in the context of a strong relationship people will usually tell you, either directly or with a variety of behavioural and emotional responses, whether your interpretations are in the right area.

Other ways of eliciting 'personal meaning' are to use sentence completion and/or multiple choice tasks. For example, 'I get angry when mum uses the phone because':

- It costs too much money
- I want her to talk to *me*
- She's telling tales about me
- The colour of the phone doesn't suit her
- None of these.

When multiple choice tasks are used, it is useful to include one or two humorous/strange options to assess whether the client understands the options and is not making random choices. Using multiple methods to access beliefs allows for reliability testing.

CONCLUSIONS AND DEVELOPMENTS

This chapter has considered ways of adapting the therapeutic process in CBT for people with intellectual disability. We suggest that developing a greater understanding of the process of CBT is essential for facilitating its sensitive use to meet the emotional needs of individuals. For this reason, assessment and implications for treatment have been integrated in this chapter. Moreover, it is hoped that process research will lead to the development of key interventions that contain essential features, which may used in manualized treatments amenable to outcome research.

Greenberg (1986) points to three levels of analysis for the therapy process: the individual speech act, which might entail a detailed analysis of the interactions between client and therapist (Stiles, Shapiro and Firth-Cozens, 1988); the identification of change episodes which involve key events within therapy that the therapist or client sees as important in contributing to change (Stiles and Shapiro, 1994); and an exploration of how therapeutic relationships are developed and the factors that enable them to support real change in people's lives (Lambert,1983). His structure highlights the core assumptions that need to be addressed in the use of CBT with people with intellectual disability. First of all, it is necessary to examine the nature of communication between the therapist and client, and ways of overcoming barriers to communication and understanding. At a second level of analysis, there must be an examination of how people with intellectual disability understand what happens in therapy. The question here is: what are the salient features of sessions for these clients? Finally, attention may focus on the nature of the therapeutic relationship. The questions here are: do therapists form truly collaborative relationships with their clients? Are such relationships essential for therapeutic progress? It is likely that many of the answers to these questions posed within the context of intellectual disability will be similar to those for non-disabled individuals. However, being forced to examine the basic assumptions of therapy will also have a more general relevance to other marginalized groups, regarded as difficult to engage in psychological work.

Another key element in working with people who have intellectual disability that has only been touched upon in this chapter is the fact that they often have limited control over many aspects of their lives. This brings particular challenges, and is an important area for investigation. It is clear that people's lives continue when they leave the therapy session. Further involvement by the psychologist or therapist is often expected by carers and clients to ensure that people achieve real change in their lives. Once again, this is a component of work with people with intellectual disability that will resonate with other marginalized groups who face social or personal barriers to effecting positive change in their lives. In addition to engaging with clients' networks and support systems, there has also been work concerning the inclusion of significant others in therapy for interpersonal problems such as anger and aggression. However, it is clear that subtle decisions have to be made about when this is helpful and when it may be counter-therapeutic to involve significant others in sessions. This perhaps relates to another lesson to be learned from process research, that the presence of important therapeutic 'ingredients' and their relationship to change is not linear. Stiles and Shapiro (1994) point out that simply because a therapy process or event is positive does not mean that it will be helpful in terms of leading to better long-term outcome. Instead, the right component at the right time will produce change while at other times the same component will be ineffective. For example, a careful reflection made to the client regarding an issue that has been the focus of a session might, if presented at a time that they are emotionally involved in what they are saying, help the client assimilate new ways of thinking about that issue. However, at other times reflection might be experienced as obvious or might break the flow of the client's engagement in the issues they are discussing. The key is to match the therapeutic intervention and the adaptation of therapy to client need at relevant times. Research in this area is needed to help therapists make these decisions with greater confidence.

EXERCISE

Work in groups of two and plan an intake interview for Martin, aged 26, who has a mild intellectual disability and has been referred for treatment of depression. Over the past six months he has become increasingly tearful and inactive since his work placement finished. Martin lives with his mother and older brother. Both are employed, so Martin spends much time alone in the house. Share your plan with the class.

FURTHER READING

Stenfert Kroese, B., Dagnan, D. and Loumidis, K. (1997). *Cognitive-Behaviour Therapy with People with Learning Disabilities*. London: Routledge.

REFERENCES

Allen, D. (2000). Recent research on physical aggression in persons with intellectual disability: An overview. *Journal of Intellectual and Developmental Disability*, 25, 41–57.

Beck, A. (1976). *Cognitive Therapy and the Emotional Disorders*. New York: International Universities Press.

Beck, A. T., Rush, A. J., Shaw, B. F. and Emery, G. (1979). *Cognitive Therapy of Depression*. New York: John Wiley.

Beck, J. (1995). *Cognitive Therapy: Basics and Beyond*. New York: Guilford.

Boyle, M. (2002). *Schizophrenia: A Scientific Delusion* (2nd edn). London: Routledge.

Dagnan, D. and Chadwick P. (1997). Cognitive-behaviour therapy for people with learning disabilities: assessment and intervention. In B. Stenfert Kroese, D. Dagnan and K. Loumidis (eds), *Cognitive Behaviour Therapy for People with Learning Disabilities* (pp. 110–23). London: Routledge.

Dagnan, D. and Lindsey, W. R. (2004). Cognitive therapy with people with learning disabilities. In E. Emerson, C. Hatton, T. Thompson and T. Parmenter (eds), *International Handbook of Applied Research in Intellectual Disabilities* (pp. 517–30). Chichester: Wiley.

Dagnan, D. and Proudlove, J. (1997). Using Makaton drawings to assess the ability to recognise facial expression of emotion in people with learning disabilities. *Clinical Psychology Forum*, 195, 3–5.

Dagnan, D., Chadwick, P. and Proudlove, J. (2000). Towards and assessment of suitability of people with mental retardation for cognitive therapy. *Cognitive Therapy and Research*, 24, 627–36.

Dryden, W. (1987). *Counselling Individuals: The Rational-Emotive Approach*. London: Taylor and Francis.

Edgerton, R. B. (1967). *The Cloak of Competence*. Berkeley: University of California Press.

Ellis, A. (2004). *Rational Emotive Behaviour Therapy: It Works for Me It can Work for You*. New York: Prometheus.

Greenberg, L. S. (1986). Change process research. *Journal of Consulting and Clinical Psychology*, 54, 4–9.

Harchik, A. E., Sherman, J. A. and Sheldon, J. B. (1992). The use of self-management procedures by people with developmental disabilities: A brief review. *Research in Developmental Disabilities*, 13, 211–27.

Jahoda, A., Pert, C. and Trower, P. (2006a). Frequent aggression and attribution of hostile intent in people with mild to moderate mental retardation: An empirical investigation. *American Journal on Mental Retardation*, 111(2), 90–9.

Jahoda, A., Pert, C. and Trower, P. (2006b). Socioemotional understanding and frequent aggression in people with mild to moderate intellectual disabilities. *American Journal on Mental Retardation*, 111(2), 77–89.

Jahoda, A., Pert, C., Squire, J. and Trower, P. (1998). Facing stress and conflict: A comparison of the predicted response and self-concept of aggressive and non-aggressive people with learning disabilities. *Journal of Intellectual Disability Research*, 42, 360–9.

Jahoda, A., Trower, P. and Pert, C. (2001). Contingent reinforcement or defending the self? A review of evolving models of aggression in people with mild learning disabilities. *British Journal of Medical Psychology*, 74, 305–21.

Jenkins, R., Lewis, G., Bebbington, P., Brugha, T., Farrell, M. and Gill, B. *et al.* (1997). The national psychiatric morbidity surveys of Great Britain – Initial findings from the household survey. *Psychological Medicine*, 27(4), 775–89.

Kanfer, F. H. and Gaelick, L. (1986). Self-management methods. In F. H. Kanfer and A. P. Goldstein (eds), *Helping People Change: A Text Book of Methods* (3rd edn). New York: Pergamon Press.

Kessler, R. (1995). Epidemiology of psychiatric comorbidity. In M. Tsuang, M. Tohen and G. Zahner (eds), *Textbook in Psychiatric Epidemiology* (pp. 179–98). New York: Wiley.

Kushlick, A., Trower, P. and Dagnan, D. (1997). Applying cognitive behavioural approaches to the carers of people with learning disabilities who display challenging behaviour. In B. Stenfert Kroese, D. Dagnan and K. Loumidis (eds), *Cognitive Behaviour Therapy for People with Learning Disabilities* (pp. 141–61). London: Routledge.

Lambert, M. (1983). *Psychotherapy and Patient Relationship*. New York: Dorsey Press.

Lindsey, W. R., Neilson, C. and Lawrenson, H. (1997). Cognitive-behaviour therapy for anxiety in people with learning disabilities. In B. Stenfert Kroese, D. Dagnan and K. Loumidis (eds), *Cognitive Behaviour Therapy for People with Learning Disabilities* (pp. 124–40). London: Routledge.

Loumidis, K. and Hill, A. (1997). Social problem solving groups for adults with learning disabilities. In B. Stenfert Kroese, D. Dagnan and K. Loumidis (eds), *Cognitive Behaviour Therapy for People with Learning Disabilities* (pp. 86–109). London: Routledge.

Ludwig, S. and Hingsburger, D. (1989). Preparation for counseling and psychotherapy: teaching about feelings. *Psychiatric Aspects of Mental Retardation Reviews*, 8, 1–7.

Markova, I. (1987). *Human Awareness*. London: Hutchison Educational.

Meichenbaum, D. (1977). *Cognitive Behaviour Modification: An Integrative Approach*. New York: Plenum.

Mellor, K. and Dagnan, D. (2005). Exploring the concept of alexithymia in the lives of people with learning disabilities. *Journal of Intellectual Disabilities*, 9, 3, 229–39.

Moore, D. (2001). Reassessing emotion recognition performance in people with mental retardation: A review. *American Journal on Mental Retardation*, 106(6), 481–502.

Nezu, C. M., Nezu, A. M., Rothenburg, J. L., DelliCarpini, L. and Groag, I. (1995). Depression in adults with mild mental retardation: Are cognitive variables involved? *Cognitive Therapy and Research*, 19, 227–39.

Persons, J. B., Davidson, J. and Tompkins, M. A. (2000). *Essential Components of*

Cognitive-Behavior Therapy for Depression. Washington, DC: American Psychological Association.

Quakley, S., Coker, S., Palmer, K. and Reynolds, S. (2003). Can children distinguish between thoughts and behaviours? *Behavioural and Cognitive Psychotherapy*, 31, 159–68.

Reed, J. and Clements, J. (1989). Assessing the understanding of emotional states in a population of adolescents and young adults with mental handicaps. *Journal of Mental Deficiency Research*, 33, 229–33.

Reinecke, M., Dattilio, F. and Freeman, A. (1996). *Cognitive Therapy with Children and Adolescents: A Casebook of Clinical Practice*. New York: Guilford.

Safran, J. D., Vallis, T. M., Segal, Z. V. and Shaw, B. F. (1986). Assessment of core cognitive processes in cognitive therapy. *Cognitive Therapy and Research*, 10, 509–26.

Slade, P. D. and Bentall, R. P. (1988). *Sensory Deception: A Scientific Analysis of Hallucination*. London: Croom Helm.

Smail, D. (2005). *Power, Interest and Psychology: Elements of a Social Materialist Understanding of Distress*. London: PCCS Books.

Stenfert Kroese, B., Dagnan, D. and Loumidis, K. (1997). *Cognitive-Behaviour Therapy with People with Learning Disabilities*. London: Routledge.

Stiles, W. and Shapiro, D. (1994). Disabuse of the drug metaphor: Psychotherapy process-outcome correlations. *Journal of Consulting and Clinical Psychology*, 62 (5), 942–59.

Stiles, W. B., Shapiro, D. A. and Firth-Cozens, J. A. (1988). Verbal response mode use in contrasting psychotherapies: A within subjects comparison. *Journal of Consulting and Clinical Psychology*, 56, 727–33.

Sturmey, P., Reed, J. and Corbett, J. (1991). Psychometric assessment of psychiatric disorders in people with learning difficulties (mental handicap) – A review of measures. *Psychological Medicine*, 21, 143–55.

Tarrier, N. (2006). *Formulation in Cognitive Behaviour Therapy*. London: Routledge.

Taylor, J. L. (2002). A review of assessment and treatment of anger and aggression in offenders with intellectual disability. *Journal of Intellectual Disability Research*, 46 (Suppl. 1), 57–73.

Whitaker, S. (2001). Anger control for people with learning disabilities: A critical review. *Behavioural and Cognitive Psychotherapy*, 29, 277–93.

Whitman, T. L. (1990). Self-regulation and mental retardation. *American Journal on Mental Retardation*, 94, 347–62.

Young, J., Klosko, J. and Weishaar, M. (2003). *Schema Therapy: A Practitioner's Guide*. New York: Guilford.

Section 4

Infancy and early childhood

Chapter 9

Supporting families who have children with disabilities

Jan Blacher, Kristin A. Feinfield and Bonnie R. Kraemer

Whether an act of God or fate, chance mutation, or the inevitability of a genetic blueprint, having a child with an intellectual disability is rarely a welcome event. To further complicate matters, such children do not come with instructions. Parents are often rushed through a crash-course in their child's disorder and disability, and they are prepared neither for the behavioural and emotional challenges that their children might bring, nor for the family stresses that often ensue.

Research and practice have shown, though, that supporting families may be key to their adjustment and coping. Too, the provision of support can allow families to actually enjoy their child and to recognize the positive contributions that their child makes to family life. There are many types of supports or care-giver needs that can alleviate stress for parents, and the specific types of supports may evolve or even change over the course of the lifecycle. This chapter is about *supporting families* who have a child with an intellectual disability. The focus is on the relationship of support to the overall care-giving experience, and on what types of support have been most effective. Care-giving needs of minority families will be addressed, as well as the supportive roles that can be provided by siblings and grandparents. The chapter concludes with suggestions for training strategies to be used with clinicians or other professionals.

PARENTAL RESPONSE TO DISABILITY

Throughout the first half of the twentieth century, having a child with intellectual disability was viewed as a 'tragedy' of mammoth proportions. This sentiment comes through clearly in the research of the period, as documented by Blacher and Baker (2002) in their analysis of research involving parents and families across 100 years. From the early 1900s through the 1960s, professionals portrayed nothing but a negative impact of intellectual disability on the family. Some professionals assumed that parents needed as much 'fixing' as their children: 'Thus, the problem becomes, not one of the individual subnormal child, but of the whole family unit' (Schonell and Watts, 1956: 219). It was no wonder, then, that supports were not available to families. Indeed, the only consistent service offered was that of out-of-home placement, whereby parents were actually advised to place their child out-of-home, to be raised by paid care-providers (Blacher and Baker, 2002).

Not so today. Now we know that residential placement is but one of many options available to families. Also, placement after high school or as a young adult is now considered 'normative', and consistent with the moving-out and moving-on process experienced by many 'typical' young adults. While parents do experience an adjustment process after the birth of a child with disabilities, professionals are less likely to stereotype parents as being fully negatively affected, and more likely to offer both tangible and emotional forms of support (Blacher, 1984). Here, we briefly review parental responses to disability.

Stage of adjustment: obsolete or here to stay?

The idea that parents of children with disabilities pass through a series of 'stages of adjustment' or adaptation has been around for nearly half a century (Kubler-Ross, 1969; Solnit and Stark, 1961), though researchers continually question the validity of these stages (Blacher, 1984; Eden-Piercy, Blacher and Eyman, 1986; Ho and Keiley, 2003; Roll-Pettersson, 2001). There are many versions of 'stages' in the literature, but they essentially include the following three: (1) a period of shock and denial; (2) some form of emotional disorganization (such as guilt, blame, shame, anger); and (3) emotional organization (such as acceptance or adaptation). Some authors claim that these are invariant stages, some that parents may go through one or two but not all stages. Others suggest that parents may re-cycle through these stages as they (and their child with an intellectual disability) enter different periods of the life-span (Blacher, 1984).

Many investigators and writers have bemoaned the negativity embedded within this stage concept (Roll-Pettersson, 2001). The stage of denial in particular, has received much criticism and comment. For example, Ho and Keiley (2003) reviewed all of the different ways that denial was conceptualized in the literature. Interestingly, they did find one positive interpretation of denial proposed by Marshak and Seligman (1993) who suggested that it can serve as a coping mechanism giving parents time to adjust to their child's disability. However, these authors do note that prolonged denial can prevent parents from ultimately adapting to their child's intellectual disability.

Whether or not parents endorse a stage model of adjustment may depend on the causal attributions parents make about the disability itself. Furthermore, some attributions may be more or less beneficial to a parent's adjustment. Mickelson, Wroble and Helgeson (1999) found that parents of children with Down syndrome made different causal attributions from those of the parents of children with autism or undifferentiated developmental delay. Even definitive causal explanations, such as a genetic origin of the child's disability, can bring about difficulty in parents' adjustment. In a unique study of experiences and expectations following genetic counselling, Barr and Millar (2003) found that parents had a number of broader concerns once information was provided. Some expressed anxieties about sharing the news with siblings or family members. Others had 'guilt' about having passed the condition onto the child.

Many models that incorporate one or more stages of adjustment view parents and families from a deficit-perspective. That is, they focus on skill deficits in the child and parents' lack of resources. The latter are usually attributed to deficits in parents' ingenuity or motivation, rather than inefficiencies or deficits in the service delivery system. A number of authors have argued for a more collaborative-resource perspective that would more appropriately, positively, and efficiently move parents toward advocacy for, and acceptance of, their child (Ho and Keiley, 2003). Continuing their emphasis on the positive, Marshak and Seligman (1993) encourage parents to form positive definitions of disability (although, ironically, parents who do so early on may be accused of being in 'denial' by professionals).

When developing strategies for moving parents more readily toward acceptance of intellectual disability, it is also important that professionals respect differences between the majority culture and parents' own beliefs, values, and expectations for their child (Arcia, Reyes-Blanes and Vazquez-Montilla, 2000; Mary, 1990; Wolman, Garwick, Kohrman and Blum, 2001; Zea, Quezada and Belgrave, 1994). In the United States of America, for example, where Latinos are the fastest-growing minority group, prevailing social policies about the transitions of children with intellectual disabilities (such as in or out of school) may clash with the cultural context of these children (Blacher, 2001).

In sum, there has been an evolution in theories about parental adjustment to intellectual and other types of disabilities. This evolution pertains to *how* parents react or adjust to having a child with an intellectual disability; *when* these reactions are assessed; and *what* kinds of supports will be most beneficial. As to how parents react to their child, many investigators now recognize that although parents may encounter daily strains and care-giving burdens, there are also positive contributions that the child makes to the family (Turnbull, Patterson, Behr, Murphy, Marquis and Blue-Banning, 1993). There are instruments available to researchers that directly assess the positive impact of a child on the family and researchers have been making a conscious effort to take this perspective into account (Donenberg and Baker, 1993). For example, parents may view the child as a source of personal growth, maturity, happiness, fulfilment, or family closeness (Hastings, Allen, McDermott and Still, 2002a). Indeed, some parents express positive perceptions for their family's future (Taunt and Hastings, 2002). Thus, assessing strengths or positive perspectives in families is now *de rigueur*.

Another change in assessing parental adjustment has to do with when one examines parents' coping, especially if the goal is to influence the types of resources or supports that will be offered. It is critical that both researchers and clinicians consider the stage of the family lifecycle in making such determinations. What families need when their child with an intellectual disability is an infant or young child will differ considerably from what will be needed as the child grows older. So, too, will the needs of the parents change, as they themselves age.

Finally, it is critical that professionals determine what kinds of resources and supports will best meet the needs of families of children with an intellectual disability. Regardless of the 'stage of adjustment' of parents, they will require services and support. Furthermore, as the remainder of this chapter will indicate, the provision of supports to families is probably the biggest single influence on enhancing the positive impact of having a child with an intellectual disability and better adaptation or coping among family members.

RELATIONSHIP OF SUPPORT NEEDS TO THE CARE-GIVING EXPERIENCE

There are some significant challenges, concerns, and needs faced by parents of children with intellectual disabilities. First, parents of children with physical or intellectual disabilities have worse physical and mental health than parents of non-disabled children (Singhi, Goyal, Pershad, Singhi and Walia, 1990). Care-givers of children with special needs report experiencing fatigue, feelings of being overwhelmed, financial distress, and depression (Blacher, Lopez, Shapiro and Fusco, 1997; Heiman, 2002; Helitzer, Cunningham-Sabo, VanLeit and Crowe, 2002; Singhi *et al.*, 1990). Second, parents also report experiencing interpersonal distress ranging from social isolation and poor social interactions to family stress (Baker, McIntyre, Blacher, Crnic, Edelbrock and Low, 2003; Heiman, 2002; Helitzer *et al.*, 2002; Singhi *et al.*, 1990). Relative to parents of typically developing children, research suggests that parents of children with intellectual disabilities experience frequent disruptions in family routines and more marital adjustment problems (Bristol, Schopler and Gallagher, 1988; Singhi *et al.* 1990). In fact, Singhi *et al.* (1990) reported that 62 percent of their sample wished that they had never married. Third, mothers of children with intellectual disabilities may experience a variety of role adjustments including lower career expectations, a sense of losing their own identity, and a feeling that they lack freedom (Heiman, 2002; Helitzer *et al.* 2002). Based on a study of children with intellectual disabilities living in a section of North Wales, Grant and McGrath (1990) found that nearly half of the care-givers reported that they could not leave their child alone either at all or for more than ten minutes.

Some parents of children with intellectual disabilities have reported that the three most anxiety-provoking areas are surveillance, long-term support, and behaviour (Grant and McGrath, 1990). Others worried about their children's abilities to function independently in the future, expressing concerns about the need for ongoing care throughout adulthood (Floyd and Gallagher, 1997). In a Latino sample, Blue-Banning, Turnbull, and Pereira (2002) reported similar future-oriented concerns, including worries about residential options, employment, and skill proficiency.

In addition to concerns about their children's future, many parents struggle with their children's ongoing psychiatric or behavioural challenges. According to Hoare, Harris, Jackson, and Kerley (1998), 38 percent of children with severe intellectual disabilities have significant psychiatric morbidity. In a sample of children with intellectual disabilities, 75 percent of the care-givers reported problem behaviours, and more than one third reported at least three areas of difficulty (Grant and McGrath, 1990). Among families who have children with intellectual disabilities, challenging behaviour is a common predictor of parenting stress and burden, and is a better predictor than type of disorder or cognitive level (Baker *et al.*, 2003; Floyd and Gallagher, 1997; Heller, Markwardt, Rowitz and Farber, 1994; McIntyre, Blacher and Baker, 2002). Likewise, challenging behaviours are generally more important than level of physical dependency in predicting parent needs. Behaviour difficulties were predictive of a need for respite and moral support (Grant and McGrath, 1990).

COPING STYLES AND ADJUSTMENT

Given the multitude of challenges faced by the parents of children with intellectual disabilities it is not surprising that researchers have explored which aspects of coping effectively improve personal and family adjustment. Information seeking, problem solving, or seeking social support are considered active coping strategies for parents and relate to a more positive attitude toward their child's disability and a decrease in psychological stress (Frey, Greenberg and Fewell, 1989; Shapiro and Tittle, 1990). Likewise, reframing has been associated with positive family adjustment, and a more positive perception of child, family, and self (Hastings *et al.*, 2002a; Lustig, 2002). On the other hand, passive coping styles, such as avoidance, self-blame, and wishful thinking, show a variety of poor outcomes ranging from increased psychological distress to low family adjustment and increased parenting stress (Frey *et al.*, 1989). There is also some evidence that there are ethnic differences in coping, with Caucasian mothers reporting more burden or conflict than African-American mothers (Valentine, McDermott and Anderson, 1998).

NEED FOR SUPPORT SYSTEMS

Informal social support

Based on a sample of families with children who had intellectual disabilities, Bristol et al. (1988) reported on the importance of spousal support (both instrumental and expressive) in mothers' level of personal, marital, and parental adaptation. In a sample of Latina mothers of children with intellectual disability, spousal support was low. Forty percent were single and many of the married women felt that they were rejected because of their child's disability (Blacher et al., 1997). This group of women experienced higher levels of depression than both Latina women with typically developing children, and Caucasian women with children who had intellectual disabilities. In a Latino sample of families with children who had physical handicaps, Shapiro and Tittle (1990) found that emotional support from informal networks related to a decrease in maternal depression.

Salisbury (1990) reported a negative correlation between the size of mothers' social support networks and their stress levels. However, a number of researchers have found that the actual amount of support may be less important than one's perception of support. Shin (2002) found that mothers' perceived quality of support (i.e. helpfulness) mediated the relationship between the amount of informal support and maternal stress. In other words, mothers' perception of being cared for, rather than the degree of the service, was directly related to their level of stress. Likewise, in predicting mothers' adaptation, Bristol et al. (1988) found that disharmony between mothers' current and expected level of spousal support was more important than the actual level of spousal support. These studies underscore the importance of including social support measures that go beyond evaluating availability and include quality of, or satisfaction with, support.

Formal support: respite

The need for respite is common among care-givers of children with intellectual disabilities. Parents request respite care for a variety of reasons, including increasing community integration, developing their children's interests, and preparing their children for other living environments. However, the most common reason is providing the care-givers with a break (Grant and McGrath, 1990). Salisbury (1990) collected data on parents who had expressed interest in receiving respite services and found that only 30 percent ultimately used these services despite their expressed need. The top three reasons for non-use were: (1) ultimately they did not need it; (2) they used family members instead; and (3) they were not able to obtain it when needed. This discrepancy between expressed need and actual utilization may be explained by problems with the service system.

In order to better understand discrepancies between respite needs and utilization rates, Chadwick, Beecham, Piroth, Bernard, and Taylor (2002) addressed three questions. First, who wants respite services? They found that only 30 percent of families were receiving respite services, even though 68 percent wanted them. Care-givers who wanted respite but did not receive it were told that no place was available (34 percent), were unwilling to take an over-night placement (9 percent), or were unaware of available respite services (19 percent). Relative to those who did not want respite care, those that did were more likely to speak English, experienced more stress and distress, and had children with more severe disabilities and behaviour problems. However, these distinctive characteristics of those who desired respite care were not relevant to who actually received it. The second question addressed by Chadwick *et al.* (2002) asked, who receives respite services? Among families who wanted respite care, those who actually received it were more likely to have larger families, with an older target child, and have a target child with epilepsy. Chadwick *et al.*'s (2002) third question asked, who wants more respite services? The majority of care-givers (67 percent) who received respite care would like to receive even more. Grant and McGrath (1990) reported that the need for more respite care was related to challenging behaviours but not to level of physical dependency. Interestingly, although larger family size was a factor associated with expressed need for respite care in the first place, larger families were not among those requesting more respite care (Chadwick *et al.*, 2002). In fact, Salisbury (1990) found that one of three reasons cited for not needing respite services was that family members were available to care for the child.

According to Chadwick *et al.* (2002), families who did not speak English at home were less likely to express a need for respite. This may be due, in part, to the fact that Latina mothers have been characterized by themes of self-sacrifice and duty (Mary, 1990; Shapiro, Monzo, Rueda, Gomez and Blacher, 2004). Too, they may have a low level of English proficiency, which has been shown to relate to higher need for, and use of, family and social support (Bailey, Skinner, Correa, Arcia, *et al.*, 1999). Although these factors may suggest that Spanish-speaking families are less likely to need respite, it is possible that they are less likely to express a need for formal services due to cultural issues (e.g. discrimination, personal duty toward child, issues of privacy) but could still benefit from formal services presented in a culturally appropriate fashion (Blacher and Widaman, 2003). Perhaps these families are more likely to turn inward for increased family support, rather than seeking external formal support systems which may seem cold and impersonal.

NEEDS AND SERVICE UTILIZATION

One of the most commonly cited needs for families with children who have intellectual disabilities is the need for information about services and developmental issues (Bailey et al., 1999; Ellis, Luiselli, Amirault, Byrne, O'Malley-Cannon, Taras et al., 2002; Haveman, van Berkum, Reijnders and Heller, 1997; Herman, 1994; Holland and Hattersley, 1980; Romer, Richardson, Nahom, Aigbe and Porter, 2002). In particular, families need information about respite services, life planning, and strategies for interacting with and teaching their children (Bailey et al., 1999; Grant and McGrath, 1990; Herman, 1994; McCarthy and Boyd, 2002; Nicks, Villa, Reeves and Nichols, 1999). Given that 38 percent of children with severe intellectual disabilities have significant psychiatric morbidity it is not surprising that parents express needs for respite and help dealing with their children (Hoare et al., 1998). In a study of needs and services, Floyd and Gallagher (1997) studied five groups: (1) families of children with intellectual delays with behaviour problems; (2) families of children with intellectual delays without behaviour problems; (3) families of children with chronic illnesses with behaviour problems; (4) families of children with chronic illnesses without behaviour problems; and (5) families of regular children with behaviour problems. Although families of children with intellectual disabilities and behaviour problems were more likely than the other groups to use family therapy, the utilization rate was low. Floyd and Gallagher (1997) reported high stress levels in families of children with intellectual disabilities and behaviour problems, yet they found no relationship between stress/caregiving demands and mental health service use (i.e. high need was not related to increased service use). Additionally, they reported that the group of children with intellectual disabilities and behaviour problems were not more likely than the other groups to use non-mental health services (e.g. community support services such as respite or after school programmes). They suggested that these services may not be supportive of, or utilized by, those families who need them the most (i.e. stressed parents who need relief or instruction in behaviour management strategies, and children who need opportunities to develop social competence).

BARRIERS TO SERVICE UTILIZATION

General barriers

It is important to understand the specific obstacles that may impede the availability and accessibility of family services. Two of the greatest barriers include the lack of co-ordination between agencies and parents' limited knowledge about how to navigate through complex service systems (Castellani, Downey, Tausig and Bird, 1986; Downey, Castellani and Tausig, 1985; Freedman and Boyer, 2000). Based on a survey of 133 public and private service providers for people with intellectual disabilities, Downey et al. (1985) reported that the majority of agencies (87 percent) provided information and referral services, but 84 percent did not co-ordinate with other agencies (e.g. lacked co-ordination in planning, referring, or joining). Agencies themselves were quite limited in that they lacked knowledge about other agencies and referrals generally took place within one's own agency. Furthermore, the majority of agencies (72 percent) reported that consumers were unaware of their service. Other barriers include restrictive eligibility criteria or lengthy assessment periods, crisis-driven systems, shortage of qualified staff, and lack of funding (Ayer, 1984; Castellani *et al.*, 1986; Downey *et al.* 1985; Freedman and Boyer, 2000; Herman and Hazel, 1991; McCarthy and Boyd, 2002).

Herman and Hazel (1991) conducted a survey of agencies in the US state of Michigan prior to and following new policy and funding for family support services (during 1984 and 1985 Michigan provided 4.65 million dollars to the fifty-five county-based mental health boards that serve its eighty-three counties). Ninety-eight percent of the boards responded to the survey. Despite this increased funding, there continued to be problems with availability and accessibility of services. Although there was a significant increase in five of nine policy recommended services, the availability differed between mental health boards, with decreases in number of services available occurring in boards with the least funding. Accessibility was also poor (only 41 percent supported family empowerment via parent advisory committees), and access to services was unchanged (there were lengthy waiting times for family services).

Cultural diversity and service utilization

Latinos are the fastest growing minority group in the United States, show high overall service need and low service use, yet only a handful of researchers have explored variables that may put Latino families at risk for limited access to services (Bailey *et al.*, 1999; McCallion, Janicki and Grant-Griffin, 1997). Latino families have been characterized as having more problems with the service delivery system (including poor access to and under-utilization of services); have reduced participation in the planning and co-ordination of services; have difficulty participating in parent groups; and may lack service information (Bailey *et al.*, 1999; Heller *et al.*, 1994).

There may be a clash between the Latino culture and the current service delivery system. An appreciation of certain Latino values may be important in understanding this clash, such as *personalismo* (interpersonal relationships based on trust) and *familism* (family unity). Bailey *et al.* (1999) suggest that there is a distrust of the professional service system, with its history of an out-of-home emphasis and individual focus, as opposed to a more culturally appropriate family-oriented emphasis. Based on a variety of focus groups, Latina mothers have reported feeling patronized by workers who ignored parent expertise and were cold, untrustworthy, and too busy (McCallion *et al.*, 1997; Shapiro, Monzo, Rueda, Gomez and Blacher, 2004). Language issues and limited knowledge of systems have also been described as problematic. There is a lack of outreach to minority cultures, written materials are generally not in Spanish, and there is often an assumed level of education (Bailey et al., 1999; McCallion et al., 1997; Shapiro et al., 2004). There may also be an experience of discrimination. Parents have reported feeling stereotyped as being less involved or knowledgeable, and feel there is a lack of effort by the service providers in areas such as co-ordination, follow-up, consistency, continuity, and service provision (Bailey et al., 1999; Shapiro et al., 2004). Additionally, Latina mothers have been disgruntled by the system's history of emphasizing failure and deficits, rather than individual and family strengths (McCallion et al., 1997; Shapiro et al., 2004). In contrast, one study showed that Latina mothers emphasized the 'positive transformations' in their lives brought about by having a young child with disabilities (Skinner, Bailey, Correa and Rodriguez, 1999).

In order to better understand and address the needs of minority families, we need to appreciate how culture impacts on service needs and utilization. McCallion et al. (1997) recommend two major cultural themes for understanding the care-giving experience and service use. First, service providers need a clear picture of how the family perceives the disability (i.e. what is disability? Who constitutes the family? What cultural values are important?). Second, agencies need to understand how an individual family operates (i.e. who provides the care? How does the family make decisions? What are members' expectations for each other? What supports are received from friends and the community?). Providers should also consider intra-group variability including, but not limited to, level of acculturation, place of origin, social class, education, and migration history. For example, McCallion et al. (1997) suggested that parents who were younger and more distant from their country of origin showed more diversity in their level of adherence to their own group norms. Based on parents' input during focus groups, McCallion et al. (1997) recommended that workers should seek to understand key values around aging, disability, and care-giving common to the culture with which the family identifies. They should then explore the family's level of adherence to those cultural values, and the conflicts and disappointments caused by variation in adherence among family members and key community members. These remarks could easily apply to those working with parents of young children with intellectual disability as well.

SERVICE EFFECTIVENESS AND SATISFACTION

In the early 1990s, family-centred services began to receive increasing support (Yuan, Baker-McCue and Witkin, 1996). These programmes aim to identify individual family needs and current resources, as well as to assist families in locating and utilizing formal and informal support systems (Romer et al.,

2002). Family support may include services such as flexible funding, home care, respite services, support groups, family education, and family service co-ordinators. Yuan *et al.* (1996) evaluated the impact of two flexible funding programmes in one US state, Vermont. Families were pleased with the concept of requesting money for services tailored to their individual needs, rather than being told how to spend the money. Although they found the money to be quite helpful, they continued to express the importance of having family support guides.

In order to meet the range of needs experienced by families with children who have disabilities, service delivery systems need to do more than simply provide money without guidance, such as flexible funding programmes, and they need to go beyond just creating isolated, generic services. Based on a series of focus groups, Freedman and Boyer (2000) reported that families appreciated the empowerment of flexible funding, yet continued to experience a lack of education, advocacy, adequately trained staff, and service co-ordination. Public policy needs to place greater emphasis on inter-agency collaboration, thorough staff training, and family support.

One effort to increase the effectiveness of family support involved the use of community members or 'guides'. Romer *et al.* (2002) reported on the impact of a Community Guide Initiative in the state of Washington. This initiative was one of five components of the Families Support Opportunities Programme, and involved the use of community guides to assist families in linking up with community resources. Families tended to rate their experience with their guides as being either very dissatisfying (26 percent) or very satisfying (44 percent). Highly rated community guides tended to be persistent, clear about their roles, knowledgeable, and receptive to individual families' needs. Interestingly, satisfaction with the overall five-component programme was lower for families with poor guides than for those with no guides at all. This finding underscores the importance of comprehensive screening and training of community guides. Unfortunately, the results of this study are limited in that the overall response rate was less than 30 percent.

One way to evaluate the effectiveness of family support programmes is to determine collateral benefits associated with them. Reduction in care-giver stress would certainly be a benefit and provide a reason for satisfaction. Shu, Lung, and Huang (2002) evaluated care-givers' mental health following a home care programme which included guidance in accessing and utilizing community services and social support. Care-givers' mental health improved after nine months of receiving home care services. However, these results are limited by the lack of control or non-English speaking groups.

OTHER FAMILY MEMBERS AS CARE-GIVERS

Siblings

Although research with families of children with intellectual disability has an overwhelming focus on mothers, understanding the impact on siblings is a growing area of concern. Most investigators have viewed siblings to be at heightened risk for experiencing psychological problems due to the stress, increased responsibility, and decreased parental support associated with having a sibling with a disability (Hannah and Midlarsky, 1985). However, although some research in this area has indicated psychological and behavioural adjustment difficulties in siblings of children with intellectual disability (Breslau and Prabucki, 1987; Colby, 1995; Lobato, Barbour, Hall and Miller, 1987; McHale and Gamble, 1989) other investigations have not supported these findings (Dyson, 1999; Eisenberg, Baker and Blacher, 1998; Ferrari, 1984; Hannah and Midlarsky, 1999; Wilson, Blacher and Baker, 1989). Indeed, the research is equivocal, with results varying according to family, child, sibling and environmental variables.

In a review of the literature on the effects of intellectual disability on typically developing siblings, Hannah and Midlarsky (1985) identified emerging themes regarding the psychopathology evidenced by siblings. Brothers and sisters of children with intellectual disability have been reported to evidence anxiety, withdrawal or depression, aggression, and poor peer relations (Carver and Carver, 1972; Lloyd-Bostock, 1976; Lonsdale, 1978; McAndrew, 1976; Tew and Laurence, 1975). Unfortunately, many of these early studies failed to utilize a control group in their research design; thus, comparisons to children with siblings without disabilities are tenuous at best.

In an effort to remedy this methodological flaw in sibling research Summers, White, and Summers (1994) reviewed the literature on the psychological impact on children with siblings with intellectual disability, only including those studies that utilized a control group in their analyses. Thirteen studies met the review's criteria. Summers *et al.* (1994) concluded that although there was a higher incidence of negative findings compared to positive findings (25 percent and 9 percent respectively) across the studies as a whole, these results were attenuated somewhat when only studies of the highest quality were examined. Thus, although it appears that in general siblings of children with intellectual disability show an increased susceptibility toward anxiety, withdrawal and aggression, they also demonstrate an increased tendency toward more positive behaviours, particularly pro-social behaviour.

Evidently a more positive and less pathological focus on families of individuals with ID is emerging. Stoneman and Brody (1993) reported that investigators have only recently examined the potential benefits of having a brother or sister with a disability. To this end, in a comparison of siblings of children with autism, Down syndrome and no known disability, Kaminsky and Dewey (2002) found that siblings of children with autism and Down syndrome were well adjusted and reported low levels of loneliness. They also received high levels of social support. In a three-group study involving siblings who had a brother or sister with severe intellectual disability living at home, siblings whose brother or sister lived out-of-home (e.g. in a residential placement) and a control group of typical brothers and sisters, no solid evidence of psychopathology was found in any group (Eisenberg *et al.*, 1998). In a similar positive vein, Grissom and Borkowski (2002) found no differences in the level of self-efficacy or peer competence among adolescents who had a sibling with a disability and those who did not.

Several variables come into play when examining the well-being of siblings of children with intellectual disability. In a recent study, Williams, Williams, Graff, Hanson, Stanton, Hafeman, *et al.* (2002) examined the relationships between variables affecting well-being in siblings and mothers in families of children with a chronic illness or disability. They found that socio-economic status (SES), family cohesion, age of the sibling, support felt by the sibling, and knowledge about the disability/illness were directly related to the parent's rating of the behaviour of the non-affected sibling. Higher SES and greater family cohesion were associated with fewer behaviour problems in siblings of children with a disability or illness. Additionally, being older, having increased social support, and having more knowledge about the illness related to fewer behaviour problems in the well sibling. This has implications for practitioners, in that while SES and age cannot be altered by psychosocial interventions, family cohesion, sibling social support, and knowledge of the disability are variables that are more amenable to intervention.

Undoubtedly, parental response to having a child with a disability will impact on the response of other children in the family (Cuskelly, 1999; Lynch, Fay, Funk and Nagel, 1993). Dyson, Edgar, and Crnic (1989) found that family stress, and some dimensions of the family social environment, were related to adjustment on measures of self-concept and behaviour problems in the siblings of children with intellectual disability. Sibling self-concept was particularly influenced by family and parent problems related to the care needs of the child with the disability. Additionally, fewer behaviour problems in siblings of children with intellectual disability were reported in families that were supportive and had little interpersonal conflict. Indeed, the dynamic aspects of family functioning can also affect sibling outcomes. For example, when another study statistically controlled for differences in parenting stress between groups, differences in behavioural adjustment between siblings with disabilities and siblings with typical brothers and sisters were mitigated (Fisman, Wolf, Ellison, Gillis, Freeman and Szatmari, 1996).

The differential impact on non-disabled siblings as a function of their brother or sister's diagnosis is a growing area of study. Many researchers have begun to compare various disability groups to determine if type of diagnosis or phenotype is related to psychological adjustment in well siblings. The most common comparisons involve siblings of children with autism/pervasive developmental disorder, siblings of children with Down syndrome, and a normal control group. Although the findings are mixed, several studies have shown that siblings of children with autism-spectrum disorder are at an increased risk of negative outcomes such as internalizing, externalizing, and poor pro-social behaviours (Gold, 1993; Hastings, 2003; Rodrigue, Geffken and Morgan, 1993; Wolf, Fisman, Ellison and Freeman, 1998). As an example, Hastings (2003) examined adjustment in twenty-two siblings of children with autism and found that they had more peer problems, lower levels of pro-social behaviour, and more overall adjustment problems than a normative sample of children. As noted previously, however, the study by Kaminsky and Dewey (2002) did not find dramatic differential effects on siblings of children with Down syndrome as opposed to autism. Although other studies of siblings of children with Down syndrome reveal mixed findings, more recent research indicates no differences in behavioural adjustment between the siblings of children with Down syndrome and typical controls (Cuskelly, Chant and Hayes, 1998; Fisman et al., 1996; Rodrigue et al., 1993).

Siblings in the role of care-giver is another topic that has received attention in the family disability literature. It has been presumed that the siblings of children with intellectual disability, particularly older females, have increased care-giving responsibilities when there is a child with a disability in the family. However, when empirical studies specifically investigating the relationship between care-giving and psychological adjustment are examined, it is evident that a positive relationship between family responsibility and problems in psychological adjustment has not been firmly established (Damiani, 1999). Girls do appear to have more home and child-care responsibility than boys, but not necessarily as a result of having a sibling with an intellectual disability (Damiani, 1999). The socio-economic status of families appears to play a significant role in the level of home and child-care responsibility for the siblings of children with intellectual disabilities, with typical siblings in lower-income and lower-education families having higher levels of responsibility (Gold, 1993; Stoneman, Brody, Davis and Crapps, 1988; Wilson et al., 1989).

As individuals with intellectual disability age, siblings often take on an increased care-giving role and express realistic concerns about their brother's or sister's future (Eisenberg et al., 1998). Greenberg, Seltzer, Orsmond, and Krauss (1999) found that almost 60 percent of a sample of adult siblings (whose brother or sister had an intellectual disability) were expected to assume primary care-giving responsibility in the future. Females in particular were more likely to take on future care-giving roles. Additionally, those siblings who reported a closer relationships in adolescence were more likely to report being the future care-giver of their intellectually disabled brother or sister. More daily involvement in a disabled sibling's life was related to the residential proximity, and to a lower number of competing family responsibilities.

Increased involvement of adult siblings of people with intellectual disability has also been associated with increased family well-being. Seltzer, Begun, Seltzer, and Krauss (1991) found that mothers whose non-disabled adult children were involved in their sibling's life had better health and life satisfaction. These mothers also reported less burden and stress associated with care-giving. Thus, siblings occupy a pivotal position within the family and need to be actively involved in the development and implementation of long-term care-plans for their brother or sister with an intellectual disability.

Grandparents

Grandparents are important sources of support for parents of children with intellectual disability, yet they have received little attention in the family disability literature. Studies which have been published have focused on two primary areas: (1) the type of support provided by grandparents to their adult children, as well as to their grandchildren with disabilities; and (2) the impact of grandparent support or involvement on parental stress and well-being (Hastings, Thomas and Delwiche, 2002b).

Grandparent support to parents of children with disabilities has been classified as one of two main types: (a) instrumental support; and (b) emotional support (Hastings, 1997). Instrumental support involves more practical or direct aspects of care-giving, while emotional support includes more affective or non-tangible aspects of support (Baranowski and Schilmoeller, 1999; Hastings et al., 2002b; Seligman, Goodwin, Paschal, Applegate and Lehman, 1997). Frequently cited types of instrumental support include baby-sitting, helping with household tasks, and providing financial assistance (Gardner, Scherman, Mobley, Brown and Schutter, 1994; Sandler, Warren and Raver, 1995; Vadasy, Fewell and Meyer, 1986). In fact, Green (2001) found that grandparents are a significantly more common source of weekly assistance for parents of children with disabilities than other relatives or friends. In addition, Green found that in families where grandparents provide instrumental support, the number of other informal (unpaid) sources of support was also higher.

Commonly cited types of emotional support include providing encouragement to an adult son or daughter, being someone to talk to, and being a good listener (Baranowski and Schilmoeller, 1999; Schilmoeller and Baranowski, 1998). In general, it has been found that maternal grandparents provide more emotional support than paternal grandparents, and grandmothers provide more emotional support than grandfathers (Seligman et al., 1997). Other variables related to higher levels of instrumental and emotional support include the residential proximity of the grandparent to their son or daughter, and how affectionate (affectional solidarity) they are toward their son or daughter (Baranowski and Schilmoeller, 1999). Green (2001) also found greater levels of grandparent involvement in low-income families with young, unmarried heads of household.

Although in its infancy, researchers have begun to examine the relationship between grandparent involvement and parental well-being. Green (2001) found that grandparent participation contributed to parental well-being over and above other sources of support. Sandler *et al.* (1995) found a positive relationship between paternal adjustment and grandparent support, but no association was found between maternal adjustment and grandparent support. On the other hand, Hastings *et al.* (2002b) found the opposite, with grandparent support relating to mothers' but not fathers' ratings of stress. Not surprisingly, higher levels of support were related to lower levels of maternal stress. Interestingly, Hastings *et al.* (2002b) also found grandparent conflict, or disagreement with parents over the care of the grandchild, to be related to maternal stress, with higher levels of conflict associated with increased levels of stress. It has been hypothesized that a possible reason for conflict between grandparents and their adult daughters and sons is the difference between their perceptions of the child (Hastings, 1997). Indeed, Vadasy *et al.* (1986) found that grandparents frequently report a desire for more information regarding their grandchild's disability. These findings demonstrate that one cannot simply classify grandparents as supportive or burdensome. They are likely to both facilitate, as well as create difficulties for, the parents of children with intellectual disabilities.

Finally, studies that have investigated grandparent perceptions of having a grandchild with a disability have revealed the importance of the intergenerational relationships between grandparents and their adult sons and daughters. In a qualitative study of twelve parent–grandparent pairs Mirfin-Veitch, Bray, and Watson (1997) found that having a positive relationship history was critical in maintaining positive family interactions and directly related to the quantity and nature of support provided by grandparents to parents. They found that neither the type nor severity of disability was related to grandparent involvement and support.

Several implications for professionals can be drawn from the extant literature on the grandparents of children with intellectual disability. First, there is growing evidence that grandparents are an important source of support for families of children with intellectual disabilities. They need to be recognized as a valuable resource, particularly in times where formal supports are scarce (Hastings *et al.*, 2002b). Grandparents often request more information regarding their grandchild's disability. This is often in addition to information provided by their adult son or daughter (Schilmoeller and Baranowski, 1998). Thus, they need to be included in training and family support groups. Professionals working with families should plan intervention to support and encourage grandparents to be more involved in the care of the child with disabilities. Finally, those working with families need to be aware of the nature of the intergenerational relationship that exists within the family. This information ensures that professionals encourage a level of involvement by grandparents that is acceptable and useful to parents.

NEED FOR SUPPORT FROM CLINICIANS AND PRACTITIONERS

In order to provide effective support to families, clinicians need to be sensitive to a number of issues. McCollum (2002) provided a helpful developmental-systems model for providing early intervention in the area of intellectual disabilities. Based on current research and practice recommendations, this intervention model emphasized two interrelated themes: (1) development occurs within a context; and (2) intervention consists of a system of services. We refer the reader to Perez, Peifer, and Newman (2002) for an example of a comprehensive systems assessment/prevention model that emphasizes the above themes. Additionally, Fox, Benito, and Dunlap (2002) used a detailed case example of a child with autism to illustrate vividly a family-centred intervention with a collaborative parent–professional approach. In order to fully address the needs of families who have children with intellectual dis-abilities, clinical psychologists should be fully versed in the goals and chal-lenges associated with the practical application of McCollum's intervention model.

Development in context

1 Family and other child-care environments

Effective intervention goes beyond a focus on the individual child with an intellectual disability and should include the family and other child-care environments. Clinicians need to be knowledgeable about early childhood development, milestones, and transitions that may both impact, and be impacted by, family adjustment. Additionally, clinical psychologists require training and experience working with parents, teachers and other child-care providers around a variety of issues (such as personal, parenting, and family strengths and vulnerabilities).

2 Parent training

Parent training can provide a number of important functions including teaching parenting skills and behaviour management strategies, as well as addressing a range of factors that may impact on family adjustment. Two of the most commonly cited needs of parents who have children with intellectual disabilities include: (1) a need for information about developmental issues;

and (2) a need for strategies for interacting with and teaching children (Bailey *et al.*, 1999; Baker, 1989; Haveman *et al.*, 1997; Herman, 1994; Holland and Hattersley, 1980; Romer *et al.*, 2002). Parent training is one forum in which clinicians can address these needs in a sensitive and professional manner.

Many parents of children with developmental disabilities struggle with their child's ongoing psychiatric or behavioural challenges. One of the most anxiety-provoking areas for parents relates to their children's behaviour (Grant and McGrath, 1990). In a sample of children with intellectual disabilities, 75 percent of care-givers reported problem behaviours, and more than one third reported at least three areas of difficulty (Grant and McGrath, 1990). Among families who have children with intellectual disabilities, challenging behaviour is a common predictor of parenting stress or burden (Heller *et al.*, 1994; McIntyre *et al.*, 2002). Behavioural parent-training has been effective in reducing child problem behaviours and family-related stress, as well as improving child and family quality of life (Feldman and Werner, 2002).

Within a parent training context, clinicians can also sensitively address obstacles that may interfere with family adjustment and with consistent implementation of parenting skills. First, parents of children with intellectual disabilities are at risk for depression (Blacher *et al.*, 1997). In addition to the obvious negative impact of depression on family adjustment, depression may also serve as a risk factor in the success of early intervention programmes (Stormshak, Kaminski and Goodman, 2002). Second, the parents of children with special needs report interpersonal distress including social isolation and poor social interactions (Heiman, 2002; Helitzer *et al.*, 2002; Singhi *et al.*, 1990). Relative to parents of typically developing children, parents of children with intellectual disabilities experience frequent disruptions in family routines and more marital adjustment problems (Bristol *et al.*, 1988; Singhi *et al.*, 1990). In fact, Singhi *et al.* reported that 62 percent of the sample wished that they had never married. Third, parents of children with intellectual disabilities experienced higher stress than parents of non-delayed children (high parenting stress contributes to increased child behaviour problems over time, and high child behaviour problems contributes to increased parenting stress; Baker *et al.*, 2003). Clinicians need to evaluate these potential areas of vulnerability so that they can create a comprehensive, contextually sensitive intervention plan. Additionally, clinicians will be most effective if they have a comprehensive understanding of the complex relationships between parent and child behaviours.

3 Parent–child relationships

A number of experiences may put strain on parent–child relationships. Parents of children with physical or intellectual disabilities report worse physical and mental health than parents of typical children (Singhi *et al.*, 1990). Care-givers of children with special needs experience fatigue, feelings of being over-whelmed, financial distress, and depression (Blacher *et al.*, 1997; Heiman, 2002; Helitzer *et al.*, 2002; Singhi *et al.*, 1990). Clinicians need to be sensitive to the care-giver experience, and to be familiar with strategies that help foster parent–child relationships. In order to help develop the parent–child connection, clinicians should start with a thorough evaluation of the parents' beliefs and attitudes in relation to the child (e.g. attributions for the child's behaviour toward parent; understanding of the child's needs and ways of expressing them; perceptions of the child's strengths; hopes, expectations, and disappointments regarding child's behaviours and abilities; parents' sense of control, competence, and coping style). Based on this assessment, clinicians can enhance the parents' ability to be sensitive and responsive to the child's needs, educate the parents about appropriate developmental expectations, encourage increased acknowledgement of the child's positive behaviours as well as praise for selves, and target the specific beliefs and attitudes that may be interfering with the parent–child relationship.

4 Communication with teachers and other service providers

Clinicians will benefit from training in how to empower parents to be assertive communicators and strong advocates for their children. Parents may need help in communicating effectively with other care-givers about their children's needs, strengths, and vulnerabilities. They may also need guidance on how to collaborate with others in order to adapt behaviour management programmes across care-givers and environments so as to maintain as much consistency as possible. Additionally, parents need to be informed about what services exist and how to obtain them. Clinicians should be educated about the potential cognitive, emotional, cultural, and practical obstacles that may interfere with parents' active pursuit of services for their child and family. Staff training could include role-plays in which clinicians identify obstacles for parents, facilitate problem solving, and explore their own anger, defensiveness, or feelings of inadequacy in the face of parental resistance to advocacy training.

5 Collaboration with professionals

Interventions will be most effective when they are comprehensive and focused around natural environments. Families with children who have an intellectual disability require a variety of services which may include speech and language therapy, occupational therapy, physical therapy, medical treatment, respite care, psychological services, and special education. Clinicians should be adept at collaborating with professionals from a range of fields. Weaving interventions into everyday contexts requires co-ordination and communication between families and professionals in diverse settings.

6 Focus on individual families

In order to provide effective support to families who have children with intellectual disabilities, clinicians must be sensitive to needs that these families tend to have in common (e.g. behaviour management skills; respite care; social support; information about services, and information about development), as well as the specific needs of each individual family. Clinician training should include practice in developing a comprehensive intervention programme based on a thorough, individualized needs assessment. In establishing needs, goals, and obstacles, clinicians need to be responsive to each family's beliefs, values, culture, and religious background.

SYSTEMS OF SERVICE

1 Systems perspective

In order to meet the range of families' needs, clinicians must work with professionals from different disciplines and with a variety of agencies. Family support may include services such as flexible funding, home care, respite services, support groups, family education, and family service co-ordinators. Effective family support is comprehensive, integrated, and collaborative.

2 Comprehensive services

Families who have children with intellectual disabilities require a variety of services that target different people, settings, and skills. Professionals need to learn how to facilitate effective communication between service providers both within and between agencies. Professionals who are serving in the role of case manager need to have a thorough understanding of the families' needs and priorities, as well as familiarity with the range of services available. This knowledge will enable professionals to make appropriate matches between family needs and community resources, while avoiding unwanted or duplicated services.

3 Co-ordinated, integrated services

Clinicians require training in how to work as a member of a collaborative, multidisciplinary team where they will need effectively to integrate ideas, techniques, and goals. It is not uncommon for clinicians to develop and oversee programmes that go beyond their areas of speciality. Thus, professional staff training should include the development of skills such as communicating effectively, balancing assertiveness with being open-minded and flexible, group brain storming and problem solving, and integrating diverse ideas around a common goal.

4 Parent–professional partnerships

A family-centred approach focuses on family strengths, needs, and vulnerabilities. In a collaborative manner, clinicians can facilitate a discussion of strengths and empower parents to mobilize these current resources. Additionally, clinicians can sensitively explore vulnerabilities, needed resources, and potential obstacles (e.g. practical, emotional, financial) that may interfere with families meeting their goals. Families may need help in breaking down goals into smaller, more manageable tasks.

Clinicians need to be aware of the community resources available to families in order to support their pursuit of services. A major barrier to families accessing services is their limited knowledge about how to navigate through complex service systems (Downey et al., 1985; Freedman and Boyer, 2000). Finally, in order really to combine efforts with parents, clinicians should explore and be sensitive to families' frustrations and reservations about their current and past experiences with agencies, systems, and professionals.

SUMMARY

Parents of children with disabilities, intellectual and otherwise, have a variety of reactions to their child's birth. How they react, and what resources and supports they receive during the early years, will likely determine the course of their own adjustment. Families will have different needs and require different supports to help them cope, depending on a number of demographic factors, such as age, ethnicity, education, income, and marital status. Yet, the experience of supporting families during the early years suggests more similarities than differences. The literature reviewed in this chapter suggests that the more 'tuned-in' that professionals are to parents' emotional and service needs, and the more successful they are in accessing and providing specific supports, the better the parent and family outcome. Supporting parents might also require the involvement of other family members, such as siblings and grandparents, whenever possible. In short, there are positive contributions to be made by all.

EXERCISES

Effective clinical psychology training programmes should aim to develop or enhance the following qualities in clinicians: (1) ability to communicate, collaborate, and apply a developmental, systems approach to intervention effectively; (2) awareness of resources, cultural issues, current research recommendations, and of one's own limitations; and (3) ability to be non-judgemental, persistent, non-defensive, flexible, and consistent. Trainees should be provided with a forum in which they can express their frustrations, concerns, challenges, and successes in their experiences with families. Constructive evaluations and feedback, as well as ongoing supervision, should be a priority. The following are some recommended training goals and exercises.

Training goal

Enhance awareness of parenting experience and improve relationship-building skills.

Exercises

1   Attend a focus group centred on the needs of parents who have children with intellectual disabilities.
2   Engage in some open-ended, informal interviews with parents focused on their hopes, expectations, fears, frustrations, challenges, and strengths in relation to their families and their experiences with the service delivery system.
3   Read about the latest research on challenges, concerns, and needs expressed by parents of children with intellectual disabilities.
4   In class engage in 'establishing rapport' role-plays in which one trainee interviews another about a fictional personal area of difficulty. The interviewer can ask questions following an ineffective script (e.g. asking closed questions, being judgemental, providing too much or too little direction, showing poor eye contact and responsiveness, being defensive, providing minimal reflections, focusing on negatives, being in a hurry). Following the role-play, the interviewee can discuss what feelings were elicited, his/her comfort level, and his/her likelihood of opening up and trusting the interviewer. The group can engage in a discussion of how to improve the interaction and then role-play a more effective approach.

Training goal

Improve assessment skills and ability to develop comprehensive, family-centred treatment programmes.

Exercises

1   Review the list of key assessment instruments on p. 327 below for working with this population of parents with children with intellectual disability.
2   Using case studies, role-play interviews to model the process of identifying and eliciting: (a) client strengths and current resources; (b) challenges and needs; and (c) obstacles (e.g. cognitive, financial, emotional, practical). Use these to develop meaningful and feasible goals for clients.

3   Review case studies and then brainstorm concrete ways of applying a developmental, systems model of intervention.

Training goal

Develop effective communication skills and enhance ability to collaborate with others.

Exercises

1   Observe a team meeting at a psychiatric hospital and evaluate team members' ability to integrate input from various disciplines into a comprehensive treatment plan.
2   Observe an educational programme planning meeting and discuss the ways in which teachers, therapists, and parents agree and differ on strategies, priorities, and goals.
3   Engage in role-plays in which small groups of trainees are 'assigned' to different disciplines (e.g. physical therapist, child behaviour management therapist, parent trainer, occupational therapist, physician, special education teacher). After reading a case study, each representative must identify goals and strategies within their field and then practise communicating, collaborating, and integrating ideas with the representatives from the other disciplines.

Training goal

Increase knowledge base on available services and how to access them.

Exercise

Contact representatives from local agencies and request information about their available services, how to access them, and the key contact numbers for parent and staff use.

Training goal

Develop a sensitive and professional approach to issues of confidentiality, child abuse, and different cultures.

Exercises

1   Engage in small group discussions about your own cultural upbringing and how it has influenced your relationships with others, help-seeking behaviours, coping styles, values, and approach to challenges.

2   The following exercise is designed to promote awareness of stereotypes and discrimination. Each participant sticks a label on his/her forehead (e.g. snobby, athletic, shy, wealthy, stupid), but each is not aware of his/her own label. Participants interact with one another as though the label is representative of that person. Then, they can discuss how it felt to be treated in such a way and how it impacted their subsequent behaviours and style of interacting.

FURTHER READING FOR PARENTS AND FAMILIES

Baker, B. L. and Brightman, A. J. (2004). *Steps to Independence Series: Teaching Everyday Skills to Children with Special Needs* (4th edn). Baltimore, MD: Paul H. Brookes.

Batshaw, M. L. (ed.) (2001). *When Your Child Has a Disability: The Complete Sourcebook of Daily and Medical Care* (rev. edn). Baltimore, MD: Paul H. Brookes.

Blacher, J. and Baker, B. L. (2002). *The Best of AAMR. Families and Mental Retardation: A Collection of Notable AAMR Journal Articles across the 20ᵗʰ Century*. Washington, DC: American Association on Mental Retardation.

Hogenboom, M. (2001). *Living with Genetic Syndromes Associated with Intellectual Disability*. London: Jessica Kingsley Publishers.

McHugh, M. (2002). *Special Siblings: Growing up with Someone with a Disability* (rev. edn). Baltimore, MD: Paul H. Brookes.

Miller, N. B. (1994). *Nobody's Perfect: Living and Growing with Children who have Special Needs*. Baltimore, MD: Paul H. Brookes.

Naseef, R. A. (ed.) (2001). *Special Children, Challenged Parents: The Struggles and Rewards of Raising a Child with a Disability* (rev. edn). Baltimore, MD: Paul H. Brookes.

Santelli, B., Poyadue, F. P. and Young, J. (2001). *The Parent to Parent Handbook: Connecting Families of Children with Special Needs*. Baltimore, MD: Paul H. Brookes.

FURTHER READING FOR CLINICIANS

Baker, B. L. (1989). *Parent Training and Developmental Disabilities*. Washington, DC: American Association on Mental Retardation.

Blacher, J. and Baker, B. L. (2002). *The Best of AAMR. Families and Mental Retardation: A Collection of Notable AAMR Journal Articles across the 20ᵗʰ Century*. Washington, DC: American Association on Mental Retardation.

Fox, L., Benito, N. and Dunlap, G. (2002). Families and positive behaviour support addressing problem behaviour in family contexts. In J. M. Lucyshyn, G. Dunlap and R. W. Albin (eds), *Early Interventions with Families of Young Children with Autism and Behaviour Problems* (pp. 251–69). London: Paul H. Brookes Publishing Company.

Hogenboom, M. (2001). *Living with Genetic Syndromes Associated with Intellectual Disability*. London: Jessica Kingsley Publishers.

Leal, L. (1999). *A Family Centred Approach to People with Mental Retardation.* Washington, DC: American Association on Mental Retardation.

McCollum, J. A. (2002). Influencing the development of young children with disabilities: Current themes in early intervention. *Child and Adolescent Mental Health,* 7, 4–9.

McHugh, M. (2002). *Special Siblings: Growing Up with Someone with a Disability* (rev. edn). Baltimore, MD: Paul H. Brookes.

Naseef, R. A. (ed.) (2001). *Special Children, Challenged Parents: The Struggles and Rewards of Raising a Child with a Disability* (rev. edn). Baltimore, MD: Paul H. Brookes.

Perez, L. M., Peifer, K. L. and Newman, M. C. (2002). A strength-based and early relationship approach to infant mental health assessment. *Community Mental Health Journal,* 38, 375–90.

ASSESSMENT INSTRUMENTS

Family needs or family adjustment

Corcoran, K. and Fischer, J. (1994). *Measures for Clinical Practice: A Sourcebook, 2nd Edition* (vol. 1). New York: Free Press. Provides information on a large number of measures that could be adopted for use with the families of people with intellectual disabilities.

McGrew, K. S., Gilman, C. J. and Johnson, S. (1992). A review of scales to assess family needs. *Journal of Psychoeducational Assessment,* 10, 4–25. This article sources, reviews and evaluates fifteen instruments used for assessing family needs. Each instrument is evaluated according to its administration procedure, content validity, and psychometric properties. The authors identify how these instruments could be used in the assessment of family needs related to developing an individual family service plan for young children with disabilities. The fifteen scales are:

Family Information Preference Inventory. Turnbull, A. P. and Turnbull, H. R. (1986). *Families, Professionals, and Exceptionality: A Special Partnership.* Columbus, OH: Merrill.

Family Needs Scale. Dunst, C. J., Trivette, C. M. and Deal, A. G. (1988). *Enabling and Empowering Families: Principles and Guidelines for Practice.* Cambridge, MA: Brookline Brooks.

Family Needs Survey. Bailey, D. B., Blasco, P. M. and Simeonsson, R. J. (1992). Needs expressed by mothers and fathers of young children with disabilities. *American Journal on Mental Retardation,* 97, 1–10.

Family Resource Scale. Dunst, C. J., Trivette, C. M. and Deal, A. G. (1988). *Enabling and Empowering Families: Principles and Guidelines for Practice.* Cambridge, MA: Brookline Brooks.

FISC Family Needs Survey. McGrew, K. S., Gilman, C. J. and Johnson, S. D. (1989). *Family Needs Survey Results: Responses from Parents of Young Children with Disabilities.* Minneapolis: University of Minnesota, Institute on Community Integration.

How can we help? Child Development Resources. (1989). How can we help? In B. H. Johnson, M. J. McGonigel and R. K. Kaufmann (eds), *Guidelines and*

Recommended Practices for the Individualized Family Service Plan (pp. E11–E13). Washington, DC: Association for the Care of Children's Health.

Parent Needs Inventory. Fewell, R., Meyer, D. J. and Schell, G. (1981). *Parent Needs Inventory.* Unpublished scale, University of Washington, Seattle.

Parent Needs Survey. Seligman, M. and Benjamin-Darling, R. (1989). *Ordinary Families, Special Children: A Systems Approach to Childhood Disability.* New York: Guilford Press.

Parenting Stress Index. Abidin, R. R. (1986). *Parenting Stress Index.* Charlottesville, VA: Pediatric Psychology Press.

Prioritizing Family Needs Scale. Finn, D. M. and Vadasy, P. F. (1988). *Prioritizing Family Needs Scale.* Seattle: University of Washington.

Quality of Life-Parent Form. Olson, D. H. and Barnes, H. L. (1985). Quality of Life (Parent Form). In D. H. Olson, H. I. McCubbin, H. Barnes, A. Larsen, M. Muxen and M. Wilson (eds), *Family Inventories* (pp. 93–105). St Paul: University of Minnesota, Department of Family and Social Sciences.

Questionnaire on Resources and Stress-Short Form. Friedrich, W. N., Greenberg, M. T. and Crnic, K. (1983). A short form of the Questionnaire on Resources and Stress. *American Journal of Mental Deficiency,* 88, 41–8.

Resource Scale for Teenage Mothers. Dunst, C. J., Trivette, C. M. and Deal, A. G. (1988). *Enabling and Empowering Families: Principles and Guidelines for Practice.* Cambridge, MA: Brookline Brooks.

Support Functions Scale. Dunst, C. J., Trivette, C. M. and Deal, A. G. (1988). *Enabling and Empowering Families: Principles and Guidelines for Practice.* Cambridge, MA: Brookline Brooks.

Survey for Parents of Children with Handicapping Conditions. Moore, J. A., Hamerlynck, L. A., Barsh, E. T., Spicker, S. and Jones, R. R. (1982). *Extending Family Resources.* Unpublished scale, Children's Clinic and Preschool, Seattle, WA.

Other measures that are useful in the assessment of families include the following:

Family Impact Questionnaire. Donenberg, G. and Baker, B. L. (1993). The impact of young children with externalizing behaviours on their families. *Journal of Abnormal Child Psychology,* 21, 179–98.

Life Experiences Survey. Sarason, I. G., Johnson, J. H. and Siegel, J. M. (1978). Assessing the impact of life changes: Development of the Life Experiences Survey. *Journal of Consulting and Clinical Psychology,* 46, 932–46.

Parenting Daily Hassles. Crnic, K. A. and Greenberg, M. T. (1990). Minor parenting stresses in young children. *Child Development,* 61, 1628–37.

Daily Hassles Scale Revised. Belsky, J., Crnic, K. and Woodworth, S. (1995). Personality and parenting: Exploring the mediating role of transient mood and daily hassles. *Journal of Personality,* 63, 905–29.

Dyadic Adjustment Scale. Baker, B. L. and Heller, T. L. (1996). Preschool children with externalizing behaviours: Experience of fathers and mothers. *Journal of Abnormal Child Psychology,* 24, 513–42.

Spousal Agreement and Support Scale. Spanier, G. B. (1976). Measuring dyadic adjustment: New scales for assessing quality of marriage and similar dyads. *Journal of Marriage and Family Therapy,* 38, 15–28.

Family Expressiveness Questionnaire. Halberstadt, A. G. (1986). Family socialization of emotional expression and non-verbal communication styles and skills. *Journal of Personality and Social Psychology*, 51, 827–36.

Family Environment Scale. Moos, R. H. and Moos, B. S. (1986). *Family Environment Scale Manual* (2nd edn). Palo Alto, CA: Consulting Psychologists Press.

Life Orientation Test. Scheirer, M. R. and Carver, C. S. (1985). Optimism, coping, and health: Assessment and implications of generalized outcome expectancies. *Health Psychology*, 4, 219–47.

REFERENCES

Arcia, E., Reyes-Blanes, M. and Vazquez-Montilla, E. (2000). Constructions and reconstructions: Latino parents' values for children. *Journal of Child and Family Studies*, 9 (3), 333–50.

Ayer, S. (1984). Community care: Failure of professionals to meet family needs. *Child: Care, Health and Development*, 10, 127–40.

Bailey, D. B., Skinner, D., Correa, V., Arcia, E., Reyes-Blanes, M. E., Rodriguez, P., Vazquez-Montilla, E. and Skinner, M. (1999). Needs and supports reported by Latino families of young children with developmental disabilities. *American Journal on Mental Retardation*, 104, 437–51.

Baker, B. L. (1989). *Parent Training and Developmental Disabilities*. Washington, DC: American Association on Mental Retardation.

Baker, B. L., McIntyre, L. L., Blacher, J., Crnic, K., Edelbrock, C. and Low, C. (2003). Pre-school children with and without developmental delay: Behaviour problems and parenting stress over time. *Journal of Intellectual Disability Research*, 47 (4/5), 217–30.

Baranowski, M. D. and Schilmoeller, G. L. (1999). Grandparents in the lives of grandchildren with disabilities: Mother's perceptions. *Education and Treatment of Children*, 24 (4), 427–46.

Barr, O. and Millar, R. (2003). Parents of children with intellectual disabilities: Their expectations and experience of genetic counselling. *Journal of Applied Research in Intellectual Disabilities*, 16, 189–204.

Blacher, J. (1984). Sequential stages of parental adjustment to the birth of a child with handicaps: Fact or artifact? *Mental Retardation*, 22 (2), 55–68.

Blacher, J. (2001). The transition to adulthood: Mental retardation, families, and culture. *American Journal of Mental Retardation*, 106, 173–88.

Blacher, J. and Baker, B. L. (2002). *The Best of AAMR. Families and Mental Retardation: A Collection of Notable AAMR Journal Articles across the 20th Century*. Washington, DC: American Association on Mental Retardation.

Blacher, J., Lopez, S., Shapiro, J. and Fusco, J. (1997). Contributions to depression in Latina mothers with and without children with retardation: Implications for caregiving. *Family Relations*, 46 (4), 325–34.

Blacher, J. and Widaman, K. F. (2003). *Purchase of Services Study II. Final Report 2*. Sacramento, CA: Department of Developmental Services.

Blue-Banning, M. J., Turnbull, A. P. and Pereira, L. (2002). Hispanic youth/young adults with disabilities: Parents' visions for the future. *Research and Practice for Persons with Severe Disabilities*, 27(3), 204–19.

Breslau, N. and Prabucki, K. (1987). Siblings of disabled children: Effect of chronic stress in the family. *Archive of General Psychiatry*, 44, 1040–6.

Bristol, M. M., Schopler, E. and Gallagher, J. J. (1988). Mothers and fathers of young developmentally disabled and nondisabled boys: Adaptation and spousal support. *Developmental Psychology*, 24 (3), 441–51.

Castellani, P. J., Downey, N. A., Tausig, M. B. and Bird, W. A. (1986). Availability and accessibility of family support services. *Mental Retardation*, 24, 71–9.

Carver, J. N. and Carver, N. E. (1972). *The Family of the Retarded Child.* Syracuse, NY: Syracuse University Press.

Chadwick, O., Beecham, J., Piroth, N, Bernard, S. and Taylor, E. (2002). Respite care for children with severe intellectual disability and their families: Who needs it? Who receives it? *Child and Adolescent Mental Health*, 7 (2), 66–72.

Colby, M. (1995). The school-aged siblings of children with disabilities. *Developmental Medicine and Child Neurology*, 37, 415–26.

Cuskelly, M. (1999). Adjustment of siblings of children with a disability: Method-ological issues. *International Journal for the Advancement of Counselling*, 21, 111–24.

Cuskelly, M., Chant, D. and Hayes, A. (1998). Behaviour problems in the siblings of children with Down syndrome: Associations with family responsibilities and par-ental stress. *International Journal of Disability, Development and Education*, 45, 295–311.

Damiani, V. B. (1999). Responsibility and adjustment in siblings of children with disabilities: Update and review. *Family in Society*, 80, 34–40.

Donenberg, G. and Baker, B. L. (1993). The impact of young children with external-izing behaviours on their families. *Journal of Abnormal Child Psychology*, 21, 179–98.

Downey, N. A., Castellani, P. J. and Tausig, M. B. (1985). The provision of information and referral services in the community. *Mental Retardation*, 23, 21–5.

Dyson, L. (1999). The psychological functioning of school-age children who have siblings with developmental disabilities: Change and stability over time. *Journal of Applied Developmental Psychology*, 20, 253–71.

Dyson, L., Edgar, E. and Crnic, K. (1989). Psychological predictors of adjustment by siblings of developmentally disabled children. *American Journal on Mental Retardation*, 94, 292–302.

Eden-Piercy, G., Blacher, J. and Eyman, R. (1986). Exploring parents' reactions to their young child with severe handicaps. *Mental Retardation*, 24, 285–91.

Eisenberg, L., Baker, B. L. and Blacher, J. (1998). Siblings of children with mental retardation living at home or in residential placement. *Journal of Child Psychology and Psychiatry*, 39, 355–63.

Ellis, J. T., Luiselli, J. K., Amirault, D., Byrne, S., O'Malley-Cannon, B., Taras, M. *et al.* (2002). Families of children with developmental disabilities: Assessment and comparison of self-report needs in relation to situational variable. *Journal of Developmental and Physical Disabilities*, 14 (2), 191–202.

Feldman, M. A. and Werner, S. E. (2002). Collateral effects of behavioural parent training on families of children with developmental disabilities and behaviour disorders. *Behavioural Intervention*, 17, 75–83.

Ferrari, M. (1984). Chronic illness: Psychological effects on siblings – I. Chronically ill boys. *Journal of Child Psychology and Psychiatry*, 25, 459–6.

Fisman, S., Wolf, L., Ellison, D., Gillis, B., Freeman, T. and Szatmari, P. (1996). Risk and protective factors affecting the adjustment of siblings of children with chronic disabilities. *Journal of the American Academy of Child and Adolescent Psychiatry*, 35, 1532–41.

Floyd, F. J. and Gallagher, E. M. (1997). Parental stress, care demands, and use of support services for school-age children with disabilities and behaviour problems. *Family Relations*, 46, 359–71.

Fox, L. Benito, N. and Dunlap, G. (2002). Families and positive behaviour support addressing problem behaviour in family contexts. In J. M. Lucyshyn, G. Dunlap and R. W. Albin (eds), *Early Interventions with Families of Young Children with Autism and Behaviour Problems* (pp. 251–69). London: Paul H. Brookes Publishing Company.

Freedman, R. I. and Boyer, N. C. (2000). The power to choose: Supports for families caring for individuals with developmental disabilities. *Health and Social Work*, 25, 59–68.

Frey, K. S., Greenberg, M. T. and Fewell, R. R. (1989). Stress and coping among parents of handicapped children: A multidimensional approach. *American Journal on Mental Retardation*, 94, 240–9.

Gardner, J. E., Scherman, A., Mobley, D., Brown, P. and Shutter, A. (1994). Grandparents beliefs regarding their role and relationship with special needs grandchildren. *Education and Treatment of Children*, 17 (2), 185–96.

Gold, N. (1993). Depression and social adjustment in siblings of boys with autism. *Journal of Autism and Developmental Disorders*, 23, 147–63.

Grant, G. and McGrath, M. (1990). Need for respite-care services for caregivers of persons with mental retardation. *American Journal on Mental Retardation*, 94, 638–48.

Green, S. E. (2001). Grandma's hands: Parental perceptions of the importance of grandparents as secondary caregivers in families of children with disabilities. *International Journal of Aging and Human Development*, 53 (1), 11–33.

Greenberg, J. S., Seltzer, M., Orsmond, G. I. and Krauss, M. (1999). Siblings of adults with mental illness or mental retardation: Current involvement and expectation of future caregiving. *Psychiatric Services*, 50, 1214–19.

Grissom, M. O. and Borkowski, J. G. (2002). Self-efficacy in adolescents who have siblings with or without disabilities. *American Journal on Mental Retardation*, 107, 79–90.

Hannah, M. E. and Midlarsky, E. (1985). Siblings of the handicapped: A literature review for school psychologists. *School Psychology Review*, 14, 510–20.

Hannah, M. E. and Midlarsky, E. (1999). Competence and adjustment of siblings of children with mental retardation. *American Journal on Mental Retardation*, 104, 22–37.

Hastings, R. P. (1997). Grandparents of children with disabilities: A review. *Journal of Disability, Development and Education*, 44 (4), 329–40.

Hastings, R. P. (2003). Brief report: Behavioural adjustment of siblings of children with autism. *Journal of Autism and Developmental Disorders*, 33, 99–104.

Hastings, R. P., Allen, R., McDermott, K. and Still, D. (2002a). Factors related to positive perceptions in mothers of children with intellectual disabilities. *Journal of Applied Research in Intellectual Disabilities*, 15, 269–75.

Hastings, R. P., Thomas, H. and Delwiche, N. (2002b). Grandparent support for children with Down's syndrome. *Journal of Applied Social Research in Intellectual Disabilities*, 15 (1), 97–104.

Haveman, M., van Berkum, G., Reijnders, R. and Heller, T. (1997). Differences in service needs, time demands, and caregiving burden among parents of persons with mental retardation across the life cycle. *Family Relations*, 46, 417–25.

Heiman, T. (2002). Parents of children with disabilities: Resilience, coping, and future expectations. *Journal of Developmental and Physical Disabilities*, 14 (2), 159–71.

Helitzer, D. L., Cunningham-Sabo, L.D., VanLeit, B. and Crowe, T. K. (2002). Perceived changes in self-image and coping strategies of mothers of children with disabilities. *The Occupational Therapy Journal of Research*, 22, 25–33.

Heller, T., Markwardt, R., Rowitz, L. and Farber, B. (1994). Adaptation of Hispanic families to a member with mental retardation. *American Journal of Mental Retardation*, 99, 289–300.

Herman, S. E. (1994). Cash subsidy program: Family satisfaction and need. *Mental Retardation*, 32, 416–21.

Herman, S. E. and Hazel, K. L. (1991). Evaluation of family support services: Changes in availability and accessibility. *Mental Retardation*, 29, 351–7.

Ho, K. M. and Keiley, M. (2003). Dealing with denial: A systems approach for family professionals working with parents of individuals with multiple disabilities. *The Family Journal: Counselling and Therapy for Couples and Families*, 11 (3), 239–347.

Hoare, P., Harris, M., Jackson, P. and Kerley, S. (1998). A community survey of children with severe intellectual disability and their families: Psychological adjustment, carer distress and the effect of respite care. *Journal of Intellectual Disability Research*, 42 (3), 218–27.

Holland, J. M. and Hattersley, J. (1980). Parent support groups for the families of mentally handicapped children. *Child Care, Health and Development*, 6, 165–73.

Kaminsky, L. and Dewey, D. (2002). Psychosocial adjustment in siblings of children with autism. *Journal of Child Psychology and Psychiatry*, 43, 225–32.

Kastner, T. A., Walsh, K. K. and Criscione, T. (1997). Overview and implications of Medicaid managed care for people with developmental disabilities. *Mental Retardation*, 35, 257–69.

Kubler-Ross, E. (1969). *On Death and Dying*. New York: Macmillan.

Lloyd-Bostock, S. (1976). Parents' experiences of official help and guidance in caring for a mentally handicapped child. *Child: Care, Health and Development*, 2, 325–38.

Lobato, D., Barbour, L., Hall, L. J. and Miller, C. T. (1987). Psychosocial characteristics of preschool siblings of handicapped and nonhandicapped children. *Journal of Abnormal Child Psychology*, 15, 329–38.

Lonsdale, C. (1978). Family life with a handicapped child: The parents speak. *Child: Care, Health and Development*, 4, 99–120.

Lustig, D. C. (2002). Family coping in families with a child with a disability. *Education and Training in Mental Retardation and Developmental Disabilities*, 37, 14–22.

Lynch, D. J., Fay, L., Funk. J. and Nagel, R. (1993). Siblings of children with mental retardation: Family characteristics and adjustment. *Journal of Child and Family Studies*, 2 (2), 87–96.

Marshak, L. and Seligman, M. (1993). *Counselling Persons with Physical Disabilities: Theoretical and Clinical Perspectives*. Austin, TX: Pro-Ed.

Mary, N. L. (1990). Reactions of Black, Hispanic, and White mothers to having a child with handicaps. *Mental Retardation*, 28, 1–5.

McAndrew, I. (1976). Children with a handicap and their families. *Child: Care, Health and Development*, 2, 213–37.

McCallion, P., Janicki, M. and Grant-Griffin, L. (1997). Exploring the impact of culture and acculturation on older families caregiving for persons with developmental disabilities. *Family Relations: Interdisciplinary Journal of Applied Family Studies. Special Issue: Family Caregiving for Persons with Disabilities*, 46 (4), 347–57.

McCarthy, J. and Boyd, J. (2002). Mental health services and young people with intellectual disability: Is it time to do better? *Journal of Intellectual Disability Research*, 46 (3), 250–6.

McCollum, J. A. (2002). Influencing the development of young children with disabilities: Current themes in early intervention. *Child and Adolescent Mental Health*, 7, 4–9.

McHale, S. M. and Gamble, W. C. (1989). Sibling relationships of children with disabled and nondisabled brothers and sister. *Developmental Psychology*, 25, 421–9.

McIntyre, L. L., Blacher, J. and Baker, B. L. (2002). Behaviour/mental health problems in young adults with intellectual disability: The impact on families. *Journal of Intellectual Disability Research*, 46 (3), 239–49.

Mickelson, K. D., Wroble, M. and Helgeson, V. S. (1999). 'Why my child?': Parental attributes for children's special needs. *Journal of Applied Social Psychology*, 29, 1263–92.

Mirfin-Veitch, B., Bray, A. and Watson, M. (1997). 'We're just that sort of family': Intergenerational relationships in families including children with disabilities. *Family Relations: Interdisciplinary Journal of Applied Family Studies*, 46, 305–11.

Nicks, S. D., Villa, A. Y., Reeves, A. M. and Nichols, K. J. (1999). Family perceptions of future programming needs in a sample of individuals with mental retardation. *Psychological Reports*, 84, 837–9.

Perez, L. M., Peifer, K. L. and Newman, M. C. (2002). A strength-based and early relationship approach to infant mental health assessment. *Community Mental Health Journal*, 38, 375–90.

Rodrigue, J. R., Geffken, G. R. and Morgan, S. B. (1993). Perceived competence and behavioural adjustment of siblings of children with autism. *Journal of Autism and Developmental Disorders*, 23, 665–74.

Roll-Pettersson, L. (2001). Parents talk about how it feels to have a child with a cognitive disability. *European Journal of Special Education*, 16 (1), 1–14.

Romer, L. T., Richardson, M. L., Nahom, D., Aigbe, E. and Porter, A. (2002). Providing family support through community guides. *Mental Retardation*, 40, 191–200.

Salisbury, C. L. (1990). Characteristics of users and nonusers of respite care. *Mental Retardation*, 28, 291–7.

Sandler, A. G., Warren, S. H. and Raver, S. A. (1995). Grandparents as a source of support for parents of children with disabilities: A brief report. *Mental Retardation*, 33 (4), 248–50.

Schilmoeller, G. L. and Baranowski, M. D. (1998). Intergenerational support in families with disabilities: Grandparents' perspectives. *Families in Society*, 79, 465–76.

Schonell, F. J. and Watts, B. H. (1956). A first survey of the effects of a subnormal child on the family unit. *American Journal of Mental Deficiency*, 61, 210–19.

Seligman, M., Goodwin, G., Paschal, K., Applegate, A. and Lehman, L. (1997). Grandparents of children with disabilities: Perceived levels of support. *Education and Training in Mental Retardation and Developmental Disabilities*, 32 (4), 293–303.

Seltzer, G. B., Begun, A., Seltzer, M. M. and Krauss, M. W. (1991). Adults with mental retardation and their aging mothers: Impacts of siblings. *Family Relations*, 40, 310–17.

Shapiro, J., Monzo, L. D., Rueda, R., Gomez, J. A. and Blacher, J. (2004). Alienated advocacy: The perspective of Latina mothers of young adults with developmental disabilities on service systems. *Mental Retardation*, 42, 37–54.

Shapiro, J. and Tittle, K. (1990). Maternal adaptation to child disability in a Hispanic population. *Family Relations*, 39, 179–85.

Shin, J. Y. (2002). Social support for families of children with mental retardation: Comparison between Korea and the United States. *Mental Retardation*, 40, 103–18.

Shu, B. C., Lung, F. W. and Huang, C. (2002). Mental health of primary family caregivers with children with intellectual disability who receive a home care programme. *Journal of Intellectual Disability Research*, 46 (3), 257–63.

Singhi, P. D., Goyal, L., Pershad, D., Singhi, S. and Walia, B. N. S. (1990). Psychosocial problems in families of disabled children. *British Journal of Medical Psychology*, 63, 173–82.

Skinner, D., Bailey, D. B., Correra, V. and Rodriguez, P. (1999). Narrating self and disability: Latino mother's construction of identities vis-a-vis their child with special needs. *Exceptional Children*, 65 (4), 481–95.

Solnit, A. J. and Stark, M. H. (1961). Mourning and the birth of the defective child. *Psychoanalytic Study of the Child*, 16, 523–37.

Stoneman, Z. and Brody, G. H. (1993). Sibling relations in the family context. In Z. Stoneman and P. W. Berman (eds), *The Effects of Mental Retardation, Disability and Illness on Sibling Relationships* (pp. 3–30). Baltimore: Brookes.

Stoneman, Z., Brody, G. H., Davis, C. H. and Crapps, J. M. (1988). Child care responsibilities, peer relations and sibling conflict: Older siblings of mentally retarded children. *American Journal on Mental Retardation*, 93, 174–83.

Stormshak, E. A., Kaminski, R. A. and Goodman, M. R. (2002). Enhancing the parenting skills of Head Start families during the transition to kindergarten. *Prevention Science*, 3 (3), 223–34.

Summers, C. R., White, K. R. and Summers, M. (1994). Siblings of children with a disability: A review and analysis of the empirical literature. *Journal of Social Behaviour and Personality*, 9 (5), 169–84.

Taunt, H. M. and Hastings, R. P. (2002). Positive impact of children with development disabilities on their families: A preliminary study. *Education and Training in Mental Retardation*, 37 (4), 410–20.

Tew, B. and Laurence, K. (1975). Mothers, brothers and sisters of patients with spina bifida. *Developmental Medicine and Child Neurology*, 15, 69–76.

Turnbull, A. P., Patterson, J. M., Behr, S. K., Murphy, D. L., Marquis, J. G. and Blue-Banning, M. J. (1993). *Cognitive Coping, Families, and Disability*. Baltimore, MD: Paul H. Brookes.

Vadasy, P., Fewell, R. and Meyer, D. (1986). Grandparents of children with special needs: Insights into their experiences and concerns. *Journal of the Division for Early Childhood*, 10, 36–44.

Valentine, K. P., McDermott, S. and Anderson, D. (1998). Mothers of adults with mental retardation: Is race a factor in perceptions of burden and gratifications? *Families in Society: The Journal of Contemporary Human Services* (November–December), 577–84.

Williams, P. D., Williams, A. R., Graff, J. C., Hanson, S., Stanton, A., Hafeman, C. *et al.* (2002). Interrelationships among variables affecting well siblings and mothers in families of children with a chronic illness or disability. *Journal of Behavioural Medicine*, 25, 411–24.

Wilson, J., Blacher, J. and Baker, B. L. (1989). Siblings of children with severe handicaps. *Mental Retardation*, 27, 167–73.

Wolf, L., Fisman, S., Ellison, D. and Freeman, T. (1998). Effect of sibling perception of differential parental treatment in sibling dyads with one disabled child. *Journal of the American Academy of Child and Adolescent Psychiatry*, 37, 1317–25.

Wolman, C., Garwick, A., Kohrman, C. and Blum, R. (2001). Parent's wishes and expectations for children with chronic conditions. *Journal of Developmental and Physical Disabilities*, 13, 261–77.

Yuan, S., Baker-McCue, T. and Witkin, K. (1996). Coalitions for family support and the creation of two flexible funding programs. In G. H. S. Singer, L. E. Powers and A. L. Olson (eds), *Redefining Family Support – Innovations in Public-Private Partnerships* (pp. 357–88). Baltimore, MD: Paul H. Brookes Publishing.

Zea, M. C., Quezada, T. and Belgrave, F. Z. (1994). Latino cultural values: Their role in adjustment to disability. *Journal of Social Behaviour and Personality*, 9 (5), 185–200.

ACKNOWLEDGEMENT

The preparation of this chapter was supported in part by NICHD Grant # 21324 (J. Blacher, Principal Investigator) and NICHD Grant # 34879–1459 (K. Crnic, B. L. Baker, J. Blacher and C. Edelbrock, Co-Principal Investigators). Portions of this chapter appear in adapted form in Appendix A, Final Report 2, of the 'Purchase of Services II Study', Department of Developmental Services, State of California (J. Blacher and K. F. Widaman, Co-Principal Investigators).

Chapter 10

Early intervention and parent education

Bruce L. Baker and Kristin A. Feinfield

CASE

Terrance got off to a bad start. *In utero* he was exposed to crack cocaine, alcohol, and what else his mom couldn't remember from the fog of drug abuse. If he'd known that he would never see his dad, that his world would be all-encompassing poverty, that he'd struggle so to learn – if he'd known these things he might have resisted birth. But he came early, and his low birth weight and Apgar score of 4 concerned the doctors. Paula, his mother, had never held a job for much income or for long. But this time she was trying seriously to be clean and sober, with the help of the residential program that was to be Terrance's first home. Now a year old, with sad eyes but an occasional flash of a smile, Terrance was not meeting the milestones of walking or talking, and the nurse's screening pointed to developmental delay. She talked to Paula about an early intervention program.

EARLY INTERVENTION

Early intervention is undertaken to influence the development and learning of children from birth to 5 years who have a developmental delay or disability, or who are at risk due to biological and/or environmental factors (Baker and Feinfield, 2003; McCollum, 2002). Early intervention includes systems, services, and supports designed to promote the development of young children, minimize the potential for developmental delay and need for special education services, and enhance the capacity of families as caregivers (Guralnick, 1997; 2005; Oser and Ayankoya, 2000; Ramey and Ramey, 1998a; 1998b). McCollum (2002), discussing themes in early intervention, noted that there is considerable diversity in early intervention populations, purposes, approaches, and indicators of success. We can as easily find examples of failures as of triumphs in the broad array of programs that fall under the early intervention umbrella. We were guided in our focus within this enormous literature by McCollum's (2002) further observation: the evidence supports the conclusion that high-quality, comprehensive intervention programs, do, indeed, work.

Persistent themes in this literature are that early intervention programs must be comprehensive and that they should be supported by well-conducted evaluation. What is comprehensive? Craig Ramey and his co-authors drew on the well-known Abecedarian Project, a replication (Project CARE), and an extension (Infant Health and Development Program – IHDP), to suggest five primary components in successful comprehensive interventions (Ramey, Ramey, Lanzi and Cotton, 2002). These programs are: (1) multidisciplinary, focused both on child and parent needs; (2) individualized; (3) embedded within local service delivery systems; and (4) research-based with randomized control designs. Moreover, (5) early intervention outcomes of interest go beyond the child's cognitive functioning also to include child developmental gains in emotional, behavioural, communication, and social spheres, as well as parent/family benefits in improved well-being, parenting, and health care.

This chapter will consider early intervention programs broadly and also one specific approach to early intervention: parent-mediated intervention. Although early intervention programs all aim at enhancing child development, they differ widely in the extent to which they work directly with parents, to increase their capacity as caregivers and teachers. This approach, variously termed 'parent training' or 'parent education', has a strong empirical base. However, a 'family-centred' philosophy of service provision in the developmental disability field has represented a sort of paradigm shift during the past two decades, leading many professionals to eschew parenting education programs as too directive and incompatible with being attentive to family needs and offering support. Thus parent-mediated intervention has been de-emphasized. We will explore this current professional controversy about how best to serve families in some detail further on. In this first part of the chapter, however, we will consider issues in early intervention more generally and introduce some of the most influential programs.

EVIDENCE-BASED TREATMENTS

A major influence on early intervention programs over the past decade has been the broader emphasis, especially in psychology, on evidence-based treatments. Psychologists, who have research as well as clinical training, are well prepared to help move the early intervention field in this more empirical direction. Following several American Psychological Association task-force recommendations, there has been a substantial movement in the US toward developing and implementing evidence-based services (Chambless and Hollon, 1998). Randomized clinical trials are central to establishing efficacy (Harrington, Cartwright-Hatton and Stein, 2002). The essential components are that participants represent a true clinical population, that they are assigned at random to the active intervention and at least one alternative intervention or no treatment, and that outcome be objectively assessed with reliable and valid measures.

Within this framework, early intervention programs do not typically stand up very well. Consider, for example, early intervention programs for children with autism – clearly the major target of early intervention (EI) in developmental disabilities over the past decade. Chorpita and colleagues (Chorpita, Yim and Donkervoet, 2002) reported the conclusions concerning autism from a state-established panel in Hawaii to examine child treatments for efficacy (i.e. how well an intervention brings about change in clinical research) and effectiveness (i.e. how well an intervention performs in the real world). The Task Force on Psychological Intervention Guidelines (2002) defined two levels of efficacy: (1) well-established treatments; and (2) probably efficacious treatments. Within this framework, no comprehensive treatment for autism was found yet to meet criteria for efficacy. However, Functional Communication Training and Applied Behaviour Analysis (similar focal approaches to communication training) were deemed 'possibly efficacious' (a third category). We'll consider these in a later section. We should acknowledge here that while the aim of developing evidence-based treatments is a worthy one, the guidelines may not fit developmental disorders well. McConachie (2002) argues that using random clinical trials is a medically derived approach to evaluation and that it does not fit well with a disorder like autism, which presents with relatively low frequency and requires multiple and long-term interventions.

MODEL PROGRAMS AND ISSUES

Overall, early intervention programs for at-risk children and children with delays have been effective (Shonkoff and Meisels, 2000). High-quality pre-school interventions have continued to demonstrate academic, social, and economic advantages (e.g. $30,000 to $100,000 per child in savings to society) (Dunkle and Vismara, 2003). However, within the field of early intervention, it is difficult to make cross-study comparisons because there is such diversity in the populations, goals, settings, and approaches studied.

One important distinction is between programs that are aimed at children who are at high risk for developmental delay due to biological or environmental factors (e.g. prematurity, low birth weight, maternal drug use during pregnancy, poverty), and those aimed at children already diagnosed with developmental disability. We have organized our consideration of model programs under the two broad categories of high risk vs. developmental disability.

Beyond this risk-disability distinction, programs vary in many other respects. The age that the child enters the program varies, from before birth through preschool. Timing and duration are often confounded making it difficult to tease apart the effect of targeting a child at or before birth from the effect of program length. Program settings vary, and there is still no consensus as to whether a home-visit program is more or less effective than a centre-based one (cf. Olds, 2002; Ramey *et al.*, 2002). Programs differ in the extent to which environmental factors are addressed, ranging from a basic focus on parenting skills to the inclusion of paediatric visits, nutritional supplements, job training for mothers, and full-time cognitively stimulating day care for the child. Additionally, goals may be client-driven (i.e. based on individual families' needs) or program-driven. Outcome goals may be narrow (e.g. improving IQ) or expanded to include socio-emotional variables and family measures. It is difficult to compare varying models, then, as outcome measures differ, and model approaches are often confounded with treatment intensity.

There have been several recent and excellent reviews of early intervention programs specifically directed towards autism, which have raised methodological shortcomings and/or suggestions for the future (Baranek, 2002; Bryson, Rogers and Fombonne, 2003; Chorpita *et al.*, 2002; Goldstein, 2002; Kasari, 2002; McConnell, 2002). These are relevant, as well, to early intervention programs generally. Among the most often-cited program needs were these: (1) a need for better basic research designs that reduce threats to internal validity (e.g. random assignment, alternate intervention controls, avoiding observer bias); (2) a need for clearly described interventions, with treatment manuals, so the intervention can be replicated; (3) a need for more thorough description of child and family characteristics, so that these can be studied in an effort to understand the variability in program outcomes; (4) a need to dismantle interventions to determine active ingredients (e.g. treatment frequency, intensity); and (5) a need to evaluate generalization and long-term intervention effects. For early intervention programs generally we might just add: (6) a need to do program evaluation, as the great majority of programs have not been evaluated systematically.

Effectively trained psychologists should be able to convey an in-depth understanding of the complex issues associated with designing, delivering, and evaluating comprehensive early intervention programs. In the last two decades, there has been a shift away from focusing on the individual child to providing the family with more comprehensive, systems-oriented services that are continuous and collaborative (Halpern, 2000). Along with this movement, there has been an expansion of outcome measures, including the addition of non-cognitive measures for the child (e.g. socio-emotional development, life indicators), and more generalized family measures (e.g. stress, sense of competence). However, researchers continue to struggle with answering more sophisticated questions than whether or not the program works, or what Guralnick (1997) has called second-generation questions (i.e. for whom, in what areas, and which treatment components are responsible for which improvements?).

We describe four evidence-based programs in some detail. These have multiple publications and provide the reader with examples of some of the best early intervention efforts. They serve children who are at high developmental risk (three programs) or already developmentally delayed (one program).

HIGH-RISK CHILDREN

Early interventions targeting high-risk families can play a critical role in preventing the development of cognitive and behavioural difficulties in children. The target children are at risk due to biological (e.g. low birth weight) and/or environmental factors (e.g. poverty). While there are numerous program reports, researchers are still struggling to clarify the best combinations of timing, duration, intensity, and service delivery models to achieve a range of successful outcomes across a variety of high-risk groups. We highlight three service delivery models. These comprehensive, well-researched programs address several second-generation questions, utilize developmentally appropriate curricula and a range of outcome measures, and include long-term follow-up results.

Abecedarian Project

The Abecedarian Project is a well-known centre-based program developed in the 1970s in North Carolina by Craig Ramey and colleagues (Campbell and Ramey, 1995; Ramey and Campbell, 1984; Ramey and Ramey, 2004). The originators were interested in the specific effects of a five-year, high-quality, early childhood education program with an emphasis on language and cognitive development. The sample consisted of four cohorts ($N = 111$) of at-risk children from very low-income and undereducated families living in and around a southern college town; most parents were single and unemployed. Children were defined as 'at-risk' based on thirteen family demographic and psychological factors, with factors related to education and income given heavier weight in the calculation of the high-risk index score. Although ethnicity was not a selection criterion, the majority of the sample was African-American.

Program

One of the program's strengths was the random assignment of participants to either (1) a control group consisting of paediatric support, other treatment or referral, nutritional supplements, and family support services or (2) a treatment group, with these same services, but also with a full-day educational program, five days a week, fifty weeks a year; children attended from 6 months of age until entering kindergarten. Families who met inclusion criteria enrolled their infants at birth. The child curriculum (Sparling and Lewis, 1984; Sparling, Lewis and Ramey, 1995) focused on activities in cognition, fine and gross motor development, social and self-development, and language. As the children developed, emphasis was placed on language and pre-literacy skills. Parent support and involvement was encouraged via parenting programs (based on a survey of parents' interests), parent-based advisory boards, and social events at the centre.

Staff received both pre-service and in-service training in how to create individualized learning experiences within a natural preschool context. Interestingly, the child-care staff ranged from adults with advanced degrees in early childhood education to non-college graduates with similar backgrounds to the sample. Teacher-to-child ratios were low (1:3 for infants and 1:6 for 5-year-olds) and teacher turnover was minimal. A good description of the curriculum can be found in Ramey and Campbell (1984).

Evidence

The Abecedarian Project has been evaluated for child ages from 3 months through 21 years (Ramey and Ramey, 2004). Figure 10.1 shows cognitive outcomes across the preschool years. The treatment and control groups had similar IQ scores over the first nine months of life, and while by eighteen months the treatment group had not declined, the control group had shown marked decline. Throughout the remainder of the preschool period the treatment group averaged 14 IQ points higher than the control group. By 48 months, 95 percent of treatment group children remained in the normal range of intelligence (>=85 IQ), compared with only 45 percent of control

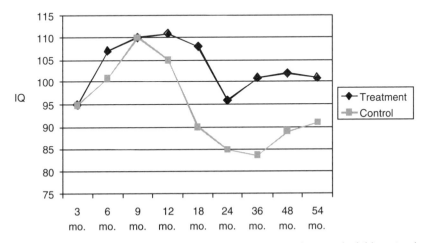

Figure 10.1 Mean IQ for high-risk preschool treatment and control children in the Abecadarian Project at nine preschool measurement occasions (adapted from Ramey et al., 2000).

group children (Ramey and Ramey, 2004). At age 8 years, the treatment group still scored significantly higher than the control group on intelligence tests, and also on academic tests of reading and math.

By age 15 years, the IQ superiority of the treated over control groups had dropped to 4.6 points; the treatment group maintained its superiority on math and reading achievement tests (Campbell and Ramey, 1995). Additionally, relative to the control group, the treatment group had fewer grade retentions (30 percent versus 55 percent) and fewer special education assignments (12 percent versus 48 percent) (Ramey, Campbell, Burchinal, Skinner et al., 2000). The program also had a positive impact on the mothers. By child age 15, the younger treatment group mothers (who were 17 or younger when the child was born) were more likely than younger control mothers to have obtained a post-high school education (80 percent vs. 28 percent) and to be employed (92 percent vs. 66 percent) (Ramey et al., 2000).

At age 21, almost all of the young adults took part in a follow-up assessment (104 of the original 111 in the study). Compared to controls, those who had been in the treatment program during preschool were doing better on a range of cognitive and social indicators: they had higher scores on intellectual and academic measures, more years of total education, fewer teen pregnancies, less self-reported marijuana use, and a greater likelihood of working at skilled jobs (70 percent vs. 40 percent) (Campbell, Ramey, Pungello, Sparling and Miller-Johnson, 2002).

Infant Health and Development Program (IHDP)

The Abecedarian Project was replicated and extended in the Infant Health and Development Program, at first a randomized, controlled study of 985 low birth weight, premature infants in eight sites (Ramey, Bryant, Wasik, Sparling, et al., 1992). IHDP is a broad-based, early intervention program designed to improve the cognitive and behavioural status of high-risk infants. However, IHDP differed from the Abecedarian Project on a number of factors: (1) focus of intervention during the first year (i.e. weekly home visits as opposed to centre-based program during the first year); (2) size of study (i.e. IHDP consisted of an eight-site randomized trial); and (3) selection criteria ('high-risk' infants were selected on the basis of low birth weight and prematurity rather than low socio-economic status (SES)). Qualifying infants had to weigh LE 2,500 g and be younger than 37 weeks' gestational age. Nine hundred and eighty-five infants were accepted with an average birth weight of 1,800 g and an average gestational age of 33 weeks.

Program

From birth to age 3, treatment families were provided with weekly (and later biweekly) home visits consisting of social support, developmental information, parenting, and problem solving. Unlike the Abecedarian Project, children entered the intensive early childhood education program later (i.e. age 1) and completed the program earlier (i.e. at age 3). Although shorter in duration, this centre-based program also focused on developing cognitive/fine motor, social/self, motor, and language skills within adult–child transactions. During this same period of time, parents attended bimonthly parent meetings in addition to home visits. A fuller description of the curriculum can be found in Sparling *et al.* (1995).

Evidence

Immediately following treatment, children in the treatment group showed behavioural and cognitive improvements relative to the control group (Brooks-Gunn, Klebanov, Liaw and Spiker, 1993), demonstrated significant but small improved parent–child interactions (Spiker, Ferguson and Brooks-Gunn, 1993), and had parents who reported reduced maternal distress relative to the control group (Klebanov, Brooks-Gunn and McCormick, 2001). Positive IQ effects and reductions in maternal distress were greatest for those children who had mothers with lower education levels (Ramey and Ramey, 1998a; Klebanov *et al.*, 2001). However, by age 5, the cognitive and behavioural differences between children in the treatment and control groups no longer existed (Brooks-Gunn, McCarton, Casey, Bauer *et al.*, 1994). At age 8 follow-up, the treatment group did not differ from the control group on a number of factors, including cognition, behaviour, and school progress (McCarton, Brooks-Gunn, Wallace, Bauer *et al.*, 1997).

A number of researchers have explored factors influencing IHDP treatment outcome. In a unique study of IHDP long-term effects, Hill, Brooks-Gunn, and Waldfogel (2003) examined differential dosage effects across two categories of low birth weight (LBW) groups. They reported that more intense treatment led to the most positive results (i.e. larger and longer duration of cognitive improvement). Additionally, more intensive treatment seemed particularly important for maintenance of change in the lower LBW group. In one of the first studies of temperament and later development in LBW infants, Blair (2002) reported that the positive changes in behaviour and intelligence at 36 months was greatest for those children with difficult temperaments as infants.

Nurse–Family Partnership

David Olds and his collaborators at the University of Colorado have conducted the longest and best-researched demonstration of early intervention through home visitation. Now called the Nurse–Family Partnership, this twenty-five-year-old program has focused on low-income mothers and children, from pregnancy to child age 2 years (Olds, Hill, O'Brien, Racine and Moritz, 2003).

The premise is that many of the most pervasive and intractable problems faced by young children and families are a consequence of harmful maternal health behaviours, dysfunctional infant caregiving, and adverse environmental conditions (Olds, Henderson, Kitzman *et al.*, 1998b). The aims include improving early health and development and also future life trajectories.

Program

This program is most notable for having conducted randomized trials in three US cities, Elmira, New York ($N=400$), Memphis, Tennessee ($N=1135$) and Denver, Colorado ($N=735$). Despite some program variations, the concentration has been on prenatal and early childhood home visitation, enrolling women with no previous live births; each replication focused recruitment on women who were low income, unmarried, and/or adolescents (Olds, 2002). Olds views selecting nurses as home visitors to be critical to the program's success, because of both their formal training and their credibility.

The core intervention is home visits over a long period by the same nurse. In the Elmira program, for example, there were an average of nine prenatal visits and twenty-three visits during the first two years. In these, the nurses promoted three areas of maternal functioning: '(1) positive health-related behaviours during pregnancy and the early years of the child's life, (2) competent care of their children, and (3) maternal personal development (family planning, educational achievement, and participation in the workforce)' (Olds, Henderson, Cole, Eckenrode *et al.*, 1998a: 1239). Interventions are based on research related to poor child outcomes. For example, as prenatal exposure to tobacco, alcohol, and illegal drugs are established risk factors for a range of adverse outcomes, home visitors seek to reduce mothers' use of these substances, while also focusing on a range of other health-related practices. The program focuses on first pregnancies because these women may be most receptive to home-visitation services, would then be better able to care for subsequent children, and, could be helped to plan pregnancies to make it easier to finish their education and find work (Olds, 2002).

Evidence

This home visiting program has been conducted within a research framework, reporting immediate and long-term outcomes and utilizing random assignment to three primary conditions: (a) routine prenatal care (control); (b) routine care plus nurse home visits during pregnancy only; or (c) routine care plus nurse home visits during pregnancy and through the child's second birthday (Olds, 2002). One striking finding was that the benefits of the full program (c above) were greatest for families at highest risk – low income, unmarried women and their children. Relative to families receiving routine prenatal care, these home-visited families showed improved parental care of the child (e.g. fewer injuries/injections; fewer reports of child abuse and neglect) and greater improvement in the home's developmental appropriateness (Olds *et al.*, 1998a), although the program did not reduce maltreatment reports in families with very high domestic violence (Eckenrode, Ganzel, Henderson, Smith *et al.*, 2000). At a fifteen-year follow-up, mothers' life course improved most in these high-risk families (e.g. fewer pregnancies, greater workforce participation, and reduced use of public assistance). The adolescents in these families were also functioning better on a range of indicators (e.g. fewer incidents of running away, arrests, sex partners, days of alcohol use) (Olds *et al.*, 1998a; Olds *et al.*, 1998b).

Olds has recently developed the National Centre for Children, Families, and Communities (www.nccfc.org), with the primary aim of further disseminating the Nurse–Family Partnership program into new organizations and communities. To date, the programme is being replicated in over 150 communities. Over forty programme staff are helping organizations conduct and sustain the program, training nurses and providing them with structured guidelines, and continuing to conduct research aimed at sustaining and improving the quality of it.

Evaluation outcomes

Each of the three highlighted programs has utilized randomized clinical trials and has demonstrated significant outcomes effects. Many questions remain, however, about the most successful program design and delivery for different at-risk groups. A recent meta-analysis of nineteen studies of early intervention program effectiveness is enlightening (Blok, Fukkink, Gebhardt and Leseman, 2005). The authors report an overall moderate effect size in the cognitive domain, with larger effect sizes associated with centre-based interventions and those that combined centre and home delivery, compared with programs that were entirely home-based. The inclusion of coaching of parenting skills was also positively related to cognitive outcomes. In the socio-emotional domain, however, the authors did not find a significant effect size. There is clearly a need for further controlled assessments, examining a wide range of socially valid outcomes.

CHILDREN WITH DEVELOPMENTAL DISABILITIES

In the US, early intervention services are now mandated for children with disabilities. At present these rights are codified in, among others, The Individuals with Disabilities Education Act (IDEA) of 1987, reauthorized in 1997. Public school systems are mandated to serve children starting at age 3, with the option for states to provide services to children from birth to age 3.

All infants and toddlers diagnosed with developmental disabilities are thus eligible for early intervention, and a large early intervention system has developed across the fifty states (Guralnick, 2005; Ramey and Ramey, 1998a). Now states have the option to extend early intervention to children considered at risk, such as those we have considered earlier in this chapter.

UCLA Young Autism Project (YAP)

This widely disseminated program, developed by Ivar Lovaas and his co-workers at UCLA, provides a comprehensive intervention for young children diagnosed with autism or pervasive developmental disorder (Lovaas, 2003). When families enter the program, their child is not yet 4 years of age; the average is 2 years, 10 months (Lovaas and Smith, 2003). The focus of intervention is to optimize the child's functioning in all areas of development.

Program

Intervention typically continues for three years, beginning with forty hours each week of one-to-one intervention in the child's home. Children younger than age 3, or near the end of intervention, may receive fewer hours. Intervention follows the principles of applied behaviour analysis, and is delivered in 'discrete trials'. Over time the training builds from foundational skills (e.g. imitation, receptive language, toy play) to communication and peer interactions. The program includes not only discrete trials but also naturalistic interventions, and the locus shifts from home to a preschool classroom for typically developing children (Lovaas, 2003; Lovaas and Smith, 2003).

The staffing of the YAP draws on its relationship with the university. Student therapists, who provide most of the intervention, must first complete a course in behaviour modification with a high grade and then work alongside experienced therapists; at this point they join a team (usually five student therapists to a case), provide a minimum of five hours/week of therapy, and attend weekly clinic meetings. In attendance are the child's parents, a senior therapist, and the case supervisor. Senior therapists are full-time employees, who supervise one or two treatment teams and conduct intervention. Case supervisors are selected from among senior therapists who have a minimum of 1,500 supervised hours of intervention, high ratings by parents and student therapists, and successful completion of objective tests. Overall supervision is provided by Program directors, who are doctoral-level mental health specialists (usually psychologists) with years of experience. Parents are involved in all meetings, for sharing of information; moreover, during the early months of training they are asked to work with the therapist for five hours a week. Thus they are able subsequently to do incidental teaching by incorporating what the child has learned into daily routines and activities (e.g. encouraging the use of newly learned communication skills during the day). A fuller description of the curriculum can be found in Lovaas (2003) as well as Lovaas and Smith (2003).

Evidence

The 'classic' outcome study (Lovaas, 1987) involved children with autism in: (1) intensive treatment as described above (*n*=19); (2) minimal behavioural treatment of ten hours per week (*n*=19); and (3) a comparison group of children in a special education class (*n*=21). Assignment to the intensive or minimal treatment conditions was not random; it was based on availability of therapists at the time of intake. However, the three groups did not differ on any of a wide range of measures at intake. Nine of the nineteen intensive treatment children (47 percent) were designated as 'best outcome', because, by the end of intervention, their IQs had risen to the average range and they were performing satisfactorily in typical school classrooms for 7-year-olds; one child from among the other groups had best outcome. A follow-up at age 12, conducted by psychologists who were kept blind to the child's previous history, found that these best-outcome children had maintained their gains (McEachin, Smith and Lovaas, 1993).

Evaluation of the Young Autism Project has been extended to community agencies (Anderson *et al.*,1987), to programs with as few as 25 hours per week (Eikeseth *et al.*, 2002); to somewhat older children, aged 4–7 (Eikeseth *et al.*, 2002), and to children with greater intellectual deficiency (Smith, Goren and Wynn, 2000). Outcomes have favoured children receiving the YAP program, although gains typically have been about half as great as in the initial intensive program. A successful replication has now been reported (Sallows and Graupner, 2005), and efforts are now under way to conduct a multi-site clinical trial with random assignment (Lovaas and Smith, 2003).

An interesting perspective on Early Intensive Behavioural Intervention (EIBI) programs such as the Young Autism Project involves cost–benefit estimates. One analysis projected a range of outcomes, with some children ultimately participating in regular education without supports, some in special education, and others in intensive special education (Jacobson, Mulick and Green, 1998). This model estimated that cost savings in 1998 dollars would range from $656,000 to $1,082,000 per child, from ages 3 to 55 years. While high initial costs ($33,000 to $50,000 per year) prevent many children with autism from receiving EIBI during the critical early years, these costs would be greatly outweighed by the estimated long-term savings.

ISSUES IN EARLY INTERVENTION

One issue that arises with the programs we have described and other early intervention programs is the question of a *critical period for intervention*. In most programs, entry points are determined by funding mandates or intervention focus. However, there is little evidence to support the starting point – and particularly the termination point – for programs (Blok *et al.*, 2005). Intervention for autism highlights this issue, as the diagnosis is often not made until the child is aged 3 or older, but it is generally held that treatment that begins early, preferably before age 4, has better outcomes (Green, Brennan and Fein, 2002; Harris and Handleman, 2000), putting pressure on families and providers for early assessment and intervention. It would be a breakthrough if diagnosis could be made earlier or treatment begun later. Recent research speaks to this issue of extending the limits of assessment and intervention. Regarding earlier diagnosis, Osterling and co-authors (2002) demonstrated that autism can be detected even at 1 year of age, and differentiated from intellectual disability. These authors analyzed home videotapes of first birthday parties from twenty infants later diagnosed with autism-spectrum disorders. These infants differed from twenty typically developing infants in a number of ways, but also differed from fourteen infants later diagnosed with intellectual disability (without autism); the 'autism' infants looked at others and oriented to their names less frequently than infants with intellectual disability.

Regarding later treatment, Eikeseth and colleagues (2002) reported an evaluation of an intensive behavioural treatment (after Lovaas, 1987) compared to an eclectic intervention of the same intensity, for children aged 4 to 7 years. The behavioural treatment group gained an average of 17 IQ points (vs. 4 for the eclectic intervention) and also showed significantly more gains in language and adaptive behaviour. It is encouraging that these positive outcomes were found despite several other program adaptations from the original; the children were treated in a school rather than home setting, and they received an average of twenty-eight hours of therapy per week for one year (compared with forty hours a week for two years).

Another issue is the need for readily available early intervention programs that focus on *building self-regulation and social skills and reducing behaviour problems*. Recent research with children with intellectual disabilities is providing increased rationale for early intervention programs with broader goals than cognitive development. Sparked by the high rates of mental disorder in adults with intellectual disability, recent epidemiological studies have found rates of behaviour problems in children with ID ranged from 30 percent to over 40 percent (Einfeld and Tonge, 1996 in Australia; Molteno, Molteno, Finchilescu and Dawes, 2001 in South Africa). Stromme and Diseth (2000), examining all children aged 8–13 born during a five-year period in a county in Norway, found that 37 percent of those with ID met ICD-10 criteria for psychiatric disorder. Linna, Moilanen, Ebeling, Piha *et al.* (1999), studying 6,000 8-year-olds in Finland, found psychiatric disorder in three times as many children with ID as in typically developing children. This same ratio was found in children as young as 3 years of age in a US sample, where Child

Behaviour Checklist scores were in the clinical range for 26.1 percent of children with developmental delays compared with 8.3 percent in typically developing children (Baker, Blacher, Crnic and Edelbrock, 2002). Behaviour problems in young children with developmental delays were found to be stable across preschool years (Baker, McIntyre, Blacher, Crnic, Edelbrock and Low, 2003) and were predictive of a range of adverse outcomes, including poorer relationships with teachers and peers (Eisenhower, Baker and Blacher, in press; McIntyre, Blacher and Baker, 2006). Of particular interest, the increased stress experienced by parents raising a child with disability was primarily accounted for not by the fact of disability but by the extent of behaviour problems, and higher parenting stress is a risk factor for further behaviour problem development (Baker *et al.*, 2003). There is a clear need to intervene early to break this cycle, and one successful approach has been through parent education.

PARENT EDUCATION

Case (continued)

Terrance, now 2, seems healthy and happy in his day care. Paula says she will be eternally thankful to Avi, her home visitor in the early intervention program. Avi was there to provide support and advice through many rough spots, and it meant so much to have her help with 'the big moves' to Paula's own apartment and job. She really misses Avi, as the intervention program ended when Terrance turned two. Paula feels she learned so much about parenting from Avi when Terrance was an infant and toddler – the home safety tips, the doctor and dentist checkups, the healthy meals, and, above all, how to talk and play with him. The whole idea that you should talk, and even read, to a baby was so new – no one in her world had ever done those things. But Terrance, as suspected, was delayed developmentally. There was so much to teach him, and Paula didn't really know where to start, how to proceed. To make matters worse, the day care teacher had told her last week, and then again today, that she was concerned about Terrance's behaviour with the other children, especially the hitting. Paula was experiencing increased stress around her parenting, both from the daily hassles exacerbated by behaviour problems and by the nagging feeling that she was not being as good a parent as she wished to be. She called Avi, who suggested a parent education program that would help her become a better 'teacher', in areas of development (e.g. self-help skills, social skills, communication) and behaviour management.

The terms parent training, or parent education, refer generally to interventions with caregivers that are designed to influence their children (Baker, 1996). Mahoney, Kaiser, Girolametto, MacDonald *et al.* (1999) note that although almost any early intervention activity that parents become involved with could be construed as 'educational', the term parent education 'typically refers to systematic activities implemented by professionals to assist parents in accomplishing specific goals or outcomes with their children' (p. 131). Parents of children with ID often have wide-ranging and long-lasting needs for assistance, and educational programs directed toward meeting specific parenting challenges should be viewed as one component within the panoply of services and supports. These include information, diagnostic and referral services, needs assessment, emotional supports, financial supports, respite care, parent self-help groups, self-instructional books, counselling, and family therapy.

Professional views of parents, their needs, roles, and how best to serve them, have evolved over time. Blacher and Baker (2002), in their review of families and intellectual disability across the twentieth century, noted that parents were first viewed as invisible; a consideration of parents and families was absent from the professional literature up until the 1940s. In discovering parents, the professional community focused on the presumed devastating effects of raising a child with disabilities, and for decades primarily approached parents as patients, themselves in need of counselling and therapy. The view of parents as teachers, who were key to maximizing their children's learning, emerged in the 1960s, inspiring professionals to develop parent training programs. A further paradigm shift over the past two decades, a 'family-centred' orientation, has focused more on how services should be conceived and delivered, with an emphasis on professionals working in partnership with parents to be supportive and responsive to their unique needs. While these two perspectives, of parents as teachers and partners, come together in the best parent education programs, they are distinct views of the professional role and often clash.

> Parent education differs from support in that its primary purpose is instructing the parent rather than encouraging or socially supporting the parent. Parent education may in fact provide encouragement and support to the parent, but that is not its primary purpose.
>
> (Mahoney et al., 1999: 131)

A provocative paper by leading special educators noted a de-emphasis on parent education as a key component in early intervention and called for a renewed focus (Mahoney et al., 1999). They note two reasons for this, to which we will add a third. First, they argued that some professionals perceive that explicit instruction of parents is incompatible with the family-centred philosophy that emphasizes collaboration. They note, though, the twin paradox that many early interventionists, in fact, report that parent education is a major part of their job responsibilities (Filer and Mahoney, 1996), but that their actual practice may not support this. McBride and Peterson (1997) conducted observations of 160 home-based early intervention sessions, finding that the interventionists spent over half of their time directly teaching the child. These observations described a model in which the professional 'functions as the key agent of change, with little emphasis on working collaboratively with parents to implement strategies or activities to promote the development of their child' (Mahoney *et al.*, 1999: 132). Mahoney *et al.* (1999) cite several compelling studies that support their contention that parent involvement is *the* key to intervention effectiveness. Moreover, in large-scale studies, mothers receiving early intervention completed surveys of the types of family services they would like to receive. Their highest preferences were for parent education activities (Mahoney *et al.*, 1999).

Second, Mahoney and his co-authors noted a number of criticisms that have been raised about hypothetical ill-effects of parent education programs, such as additional stress that is imposed on the family (Gallagher, Beckman and Cross, 1983), implicit blaming of parents (Turnbull and Turnbull, 1990), role conflict for parents (Vincent and Beckett, 1993), and potential cultural bias of parent education (Hanson and Lynch, 1995). We say 'hypothetical', because, as Mahoney *et al.* note, despite the frequency of these concerns there are few empirical studies examining whether parents indeed experience these adverse effects. To the contrary, in addressing this issue of generalized effects previously, we noted a number of studies that have found positive generalized effects on parents and families of children with developmental disabilities; these included less depression and stress, greater satisfaction with the family, and more time for recreation (Baker, 1996). We concluded at that time that:

> Intellectual disability is, in part, a social construct, and as such, this field is particularly apt to be influenced by changing social, philosophical, and institutional pressures. Professionals with an empirical orientation are often taken aback at how the practices promoted at any given time may be more the result of what policy makers think should be done than those indicated by systematic study. This leaves the field particularly vulnerable to overlooking validated practices while advocating for unproven ones.
>
> (Baker, 1996: 299)

Our added third reason why interventionists might de-emphasize parent education is an obvious one: it's difficult. To be a good parent educator requires considerable training, expertise, preparation, and effort. It requires that the interventionist understand the behavioural model, be well-read in the relevant literature, be personally comfortable teaching young children and good at it, know how to implement and assess outcomes of teaching programs, and have the clinical skills to listen to, and collaborate with parents in a way that speaks to their needs. This also means adapting intervention strategies to the family's current parenting practices, cultural beliefs, and resources. There is an appeal to the 'family-centred' model, as many well-intentioned people can form a friendly, respectful, collaborative, and support-ive relationship with parents, even if they do not have the above-mentioned expertise. This is not a contrasting model, however. We would see an equal and supportive professional–parent relationship as being a necessary condi-tion of service provision, not the service *per se*. Jeanette McCollum writes:

> It may be that, in our efforts to learn and implement the meaning of being family centred, we have lost sight of the meaning of the family's most direct roles in children's early development and learning – those that occur through direct interactions with the child. We may also have lost sight of what we as professional bring to the partnership with families – namely, our own knowledge and skills about how children develop and learn.
>
> (McCollum, 1999: 148)

She goes on to say that: 'Although professionals speak of providing ser-vices in natural environments, they conveniently forget that home is the most natural and powerful of all environments for young children, and that interactions with family members are a major reason for this' (McCollum, 1999: 148).

MODEL PARENT EDUCATION PROGRAMS AND ISSUES

This section contains detailed descriptions of two early intervention pro-grams for children with ID that have parent education as the primary or sole approach. Both the Portage Project and Pivotal Response Training utilize a behavioural model, as we have described in the Lovaas program. However, as both view parents as the critical change agents, they each pay considerable attention to the family context. Also, both programs work individually with parents, and both work in natural environments, primarily the home. Group parent education is also effective (and cost-effective), although it is, of neces-sity, somewhat less individualized and leading groups requires some addi-tional skills and preparation from the interventionist; we will consider group programs separately in a later section.

Portage Project

The Portage Project is a home-visiting educational service for parents of young children (birth to five) with special needs. It was first implemented in Portage, Wisconsin, in 1969, by Shearer and Shearer (1972); it was sub-sequently adapted and implemented in the UK and throughout the world and translated into over thirty languages. The program, quite simply, recognized parents as the first teachers of their children and the aim, then and now, is to help parents become more effective teachers (Cameron, 1986).

Program

In the Portage Home Teaching Program, teachers visit the homes of preschool-aged children with intellectual disabilities once a week, to consult with parents (typically mothers) who teach the child daily. The program begins with a skill assessment from a behavioural model, and is aimed almost exclusively at progressive skill development, using behavioural teaching principles. During each visit the teacher reviews progress for the previous week, determines new skills to teach, writes down the activities for the following week, demonstrates them to the parent and establishes baselines, and then watches the parent carry out the program, giving feedback. Over time the conceptualization of the program has evolved, embracing the family-centred values while maintaining the focus on parents as teachers and the behavioural model. At present it is characterized by the four core values: (1) relationship-based (the home visitor's relationship with the parent and the parent's with the child); (2) family-centred (parents determine intervention goals); (3) ecological approach (teaching skills in a functional manner, and including family rituals, play, and daily routines as opportunities for intervention), and; (4) strength-based (finding family strengths and building on them).

Central to the program is the three-part *New Portage Guide*, available in an Infant/Toddler and a Preschool form. The Portage Tool for Observation and Planning (TOP) assesses the child's functioning level on over 600 items based on normal development of children from birth to 6 years; these include self-help, motor, language, social, and cognitive development. The Activity/Interaction Cards accompany the checklist, with one card per item that details steps to teaching the skill, along with alternative procedures and suggestions. The Weekly Planning Form summarizes the teaching plan and is used to evaluate progress. Each activity chart includes a learning objective designed to be achieved in a week, along with instructions for how to teach the skill, how often to teach each day, and a record for recording trial-by-trial progress.

Home visitors participate in one or several weeks of training, followed by weekly half-day supervision and group training. Home visitors have included, among others, teachers, health visitors, nurses, social workers, therapists, paraprofessionals, and lay volunteers.

Evidence

A clear strength of the Portage model is the ease with which home visitors can be trained, in large part due to the support materials. Similarly, the program has enjoyed widespread dissemination, with adoptions and adaptations to different populations and cultures. Portage sites include over sixty countries, throughout Europe and in countries as widespread as Japan, China, Taiwan, India, Samoa, Kuwait, Equador, Peru, Canada, Mexico, and Jamaica (Cameron, 1997). Ironically, the flexibility of the model that has made it popular and easy to disseminate has also made it difficult to evaluate.

The support materials provide a build-in system for monitoring progress. In their original report, Shearer and Shearer (1972) found that parents could observe, and accurately record change and that children with handicaps progressed above their expected developmental rate. Brue and Oakland (2001) did a thorough search of the literature, and identified only five empirical studies of program outcome, with four showing evidence of effectiveness. Examples were an 18-point IQ increase following eight months of intervention in a US sample (Cochran and Shearer, 1984) and significant gains in five areas of development after eight to sixteen months of intervention in an Indian sample (Kohli, 1990). A large study of Palestinian children from the Gaza Strip found no significant gains (Oakland, 1997). There is clearly a need for further, and better-controlled, study of this widely used intervention. Current information about the Portage Project can be found on their website, at <www.portageproject.org/npg>, and in the Brue and Oakland (2001) article.

Pivotal Response Treatment

Pivotal Response Treatment (PRT) is a parent-mediated intervention for individuals with autism. This approach was developed by Robert and Lynn Koegel and their collaborators at the University of California, Santa Barbara Autism Research and Training Clinic. The program serves a wide age range, from 1 through adulthood, primarily through one-to-one training programs in behaviour management for their parents (Koegel, Koegel and Brookman, 2003).

Program

PRT is grounded in well-established principles of behaviour modification and shares much in common with the Lovaas intervention that we considered above. However, there are important differences. First, the primary interventionists are the child's parents, so the Koegels' program is in the tradition of parent training programs. Second, pivotal response treatment focuses on several specific areas of functioning for intervention – these areas are considered pivotal, in that when developed further one would anticipate widespread collateral changes in numerous other behaviours. Two pivotal areas that are deemed especially important in producing generalized change are the child's motivation and self-initiations. Thus, while intervention goals and activities are developed based on the individual child's needs, there is a continuing focus on motivation and self-initiation. Third, PRT is functional training, in that it utilizes elements in the child's environment and takes place in the community as well as home. There is typically a focus on communication skills and appropriate social communication interactions, and these are taught using items in the child's everyday settings.

Parents are typically instructed in an individual format, although some families who live outside of the area attend for a full week of training that may involve a group format as well (Koegel, Symon and Koegel, 2002). Parents are introduced to the basics of behavioural intervention and given a training manual to read (Koegel, Schreibman, Good, Cerniglia, *et al.* 1989). Intervention begins with teaching parents the basics of the behavioural approach through one-on-one training, with immediate and specific feedback as the parent works with the child. A primary aim in developing program objectives is to make them consistent with the family's goals, values, and cultural identity (Santarelli, Koegel, Casas and Koegel, 2001).

Evidence

One study illustrates how program evaluation efforts can further program development. The authors examined six children who had completed their program, three with high success and three with low success (Koegel, Koegel, Shoshan and McNerney, 1999). The high and low success was documented by a range of post-intervention data in language, social, and community functioning. At follow-up, the three high-success children were all in regular education school programs, with average or above grades, and social activities with typically developing peers. The three low-success children did not remain in regular education programs; all three exhibited considerable inappropriate behaviour and had no interactions with typically developing peers. These two groups of children did not differ on pre-intervention language or adaptive behaviour, but they did differ considerably on the key variable: number of spontaneous initiations. In Phase 2, four additional children who were equally low in self-initiation began an intervention program similar to the earlier one, except that it was focused on teaching verbal child initiations. Children learned these, and subsequently showed good outcomes comparable to the high-success children in Phase I.

Another evaluation randomly assigned seventeen young children (average age = 6) to two intervention conditions: (a) PRT, and (b) ITB, a more traditional approach that serially taught individual target behaviours (Koegel, Bimbela and Schreibman, 1996). The aim was to assess collateral effects of treatment; the outcomes of interest were family interactions, coded from videotapes of dinnertime together. The interactions in the ITB group did not change, but in the PRT families all four domains that were coded showed positive change. Families increased in greater expressed happiness, interest in the interaction, lower stress, and improved communication style.

ISSUES IN PARENT EDUCATION

Although there are a great many issues to consider in choosing, or developing, and then conducting and evaluating a parent education program, we will consider two broad ones: (1) the generalized impact of parent education on the family; and (2) implementing a parent education program within an agency.

Family generalization

Griest and Forehand (1982) introduced the term 'family generalization' to refer to changes in parents' personal and marital adjustment or family activities when the focus of treatment has been on parent teaching rather than these broader family issues. Parents who teach their children more effectively may experience positive changes in themselves (e.g. in their stress levels, attitudes about the child, sense of competence as parents, communication with partners and teachers). We noted above that while some authors have been concerned about possible negative generalized effects on the family from the time, frustration, and role demands of an education program (Gallagher, Beckman and Cross, 1983; Turnbull and Turnbull, 1990; Vincent and Beckett, 1993), the thrust of the research evidence is that parent education programs either produce no measurable family generalization or trigger a benign cycle, where other areas of family functioning improve as well (Anastopoulos, Shelton, DuPaul, Guevremont, 1993; Baker, 1996; Feinfield and Baker, 2004; Pisterman, McGrath, Firestone, Goodman *et al.*, 1992). A study of parents of children with autism who participated in an individual format clinic and home-based program found that they reported greater time teaching, less time in caretaking, and more family recreation relative to an untrained control group. A study of parents of children with intellectual disability who participated in group training assessed changes on adjustment variables that previous researchers had found were affected by disability in the family: depression, stress, and satisfaction with the family. On all three dimensions there was significant improvement following training (Baker, Landen and Kashima, 1991). A study of families of young children with externalizing behaviour problems not only found a reduction in parenting stress but also demonstrated that this was fully mediated by reductions in child behaviour problems (Feinfield and Baker, 2004). Program developers should consider including a measure of consumer satisfaction, in order to detect dissatisfaction with aspects of the program, and also consider including measures of parent well-being to assess family generalization.

Agency implementation

The two exemplary parent education programs that we described each use an individual format, which continues to be the most commonly employed. There is evidence, however, that group parent education programs also can be quite effective; indeed, in most comparison studies, individual and group outcomes were indistinguishable (Brightman, Baker, Clark and Ambrose, 1982; Salzinger, Feldman and Portnoy, 1970) and in some studies groups were superior (Cunningham, Bremner and Boyle, 1995). Parent education groups can be much less costly in staff time than individual consultation. One drawback to the individual parent education model, especially when it is open-ended and crisis-driven, is that a small number of clients can occupy considerable agency resources. Perhaps a wiser allocation of resources would be to provide group prevention and early intervention programs, making these services available to families when children are quite young and following an established curriculum (e.g. Baker, 1989; Feinfield and Baker, 2004; Webster-Stratton and Reid, 2003).

Despite the apparent simplicity of parent education, it takes many good decisions to make a program truly successful. While limitations in space, and the reader's indulgence, preclude a lengthy discussion of strategies for success, our own research and experiences do underscore a smaller number of points at which a program can practically ensure its *failure*. Table 10.1 lists suggestions for failure – thirteen in all (for bad luck)! If you seek to develop a successful program, use this list as a guide to make sure that you are not following any of our suggestions. While these pertain especially to group programs, there are many good ways here to make programs following an individual format fail as well.

Table 10.1 How to make a parent training program fail

1   *Assign just one staff member to parent training.* A staff member working alone, without the social support and collaboration of a colleague, is much less likely to actually implement parent training
2   *Create role conflict.* Select staff whose other roles within the agency are quite different from the role of parent trainer. It also helps not to give staff sufficient preparation time; this way, they will feel ill-prepared when they begin the program
3   *Select inexperienced leaders.* It is particularly important to select those who do not have good behaviour modification problem-solving skills. They will be less likely to implement the program at all; if they do implement it, they will do so less well. Some programs also have ensured failure by selecting staff who are sceptical about the aims and strategies involved
4   *Select leaders who cannot teach children.* This is a common strategy for failure, for as soon as parents see that the leader cannot get down on the floor with a child and put teachings into practice, they may lose faith

(Continued overleaf)

Table 10.1 Continued

5   Tie parent training to a poor school program. Schools must in some way involve
    parents. In a school where children are not taught very well, however, a parent
    training program may be a formula for failure, for it will not have legitimacy.
    Moreover, parents who complete the program may become sophisticated critics
    of the school
6   Recruit impersonally. You may be able to avoid ever having to start the program if you
    recruit through mail or through notices sent home with children. If you do not make
    personal contact with parents, especially if you are working with low-income, ethnic
    minority parents, they will be much less likely to join
7   Make participation required. This will not always insure failure; if parents are desperate
    enough for their children to be enrolled in a special program, they will participate
    successfully
8   Make access difficult. Schedule the meetings only during the day, when it is
    convenient for staff but inconvenient for working parents. Also, do not provide child
    care, bilingual staff when needed, telephone reminders, and make-up sessions to
    facilitate involvement
9   Follow too tight a curriculum. Go into each session with such a strict game plan that
    there is no room to address individual parent concerns. Take the position that you
    know just what parents need. Follow a tight time schedule – if a topic requires more
    time to be really helpful, cut it short in the interest of time. Don't consider adapting
    your plan. Some parents will feel they are not benefiting and will drop out
10 Follow too loose a curriculum. Go into each session with only a vague sense of what
    you want to accomplish. In a group, be receptive to any parent who would like to
    use up most of the meeting time discussing his or her child's problem. Better still, let
    the discussion drift to other topics. Some parents will feel they are not benefiting
    and will drop out
11 Go over parents' heads. Failure can be assured by being overly didactic, giving long
    lectures at a high level of abstraction, or insisting on tiresome recordkeeping. Failure
    will be more certain with parents whose education is limited, and who would
    benefit more from action-oriented approaches
12 Focus on behaviour problems. Begin with behaviour-problem management and
    make this the main focus of your consultation. Do not begin with skill building,
    where parents can get a better understanding of their child's learning needs and
    become comfortable teachers before they tackle the more emotionally charged
    area of behaviour problems
13 Select measures that are too general. If you get to the end of the program and the
    parents have participated and liked it, you can still seize failure from the jaws of
    success. Evaluate the program's success with broad developmental scales rather
    than measures that specifically tap the skills targeted. In this way, the children,
    especially if they have severe handicaps, will seem not to have benefited

STAFF TRAINING

There is a strong need for a coordinated system of catalogued training
materials and better dissemination of information to facilitate staff training
(McConnell, 2002; Roberts, Wasik, Casto and Ramey, 1991). Additionally,
we need to develop staff training models further and to evaluate training

models, so that we can assess the relationship between specific training programs and level of staff preparedness. Klein and Gilkerson (2000) recommend the development of an extensive empirical database to guide staff training practices. We need a better understanding of the types of training techniques, processes, specific content areas, and staff and trainer characteristics that relate to effective personnel preparation.

What should staff be trained to do? As noted, there has been a shift in the field of early intervention from focusing on the child, to mother–child interactions, to a more expansive family-centred approach. In a family-centred philosophy, as we have noted, families are viewed as partners and there is a focus on families' strengths and range of needs. Despite the generally positive buzz over family-centred practices, the implementation of these concepts has been slow. Krauss (2000) raises the concern that we may be spending too much time defining this concept and embracing its principles, rather than empirically evaluating it and then providing specific training, if appropriate. Although training programs acknowledge this shift in conceptualization, very few have adapted their staff orientation to reflect the goals and methods associated with a family-centred assessment and intervention approach (Krauss, 2000). According to Klein and Gilkerson (2000), this approach would include: (1) developing respectful and collaborative family relationships; (2) focusing on family strengths; (3) developing a systems perspective; (4) improving one's ability for reflection and self-knowledge; (5) understanding atypical and typical children's development; (6) practicing interdisciplinary/collaborative teaching and learning; and (7) engaging in more applied teaching/learning environments.

Many of the evidence-based parent training or education programs, including our two exemplary programs above, are behavioural in their orientation. Behavioural psychologists traditionally have been trained as 'experts' in specific areas (e.g. behaviour management). They typically educate parents about developmental issues and teach behavioural techniques and strategies for improving child skills and decreasing behaviour problems. Staff training generally does not include practice collaboration with other disciplines or with family members around various needs, goals, strengths, and resources. Forehand and Kotchick (2002) provide a helpful discussion of challenges and creative solutions to providing behavioural parent training that is more comprehensive and expansive. They emphasize the importance of clinicians understanding the individual family processes (e.g. marital discord, psychological distress) that may interfere with effective implementation of parenting strategies.

Forehand and Kotchick (2002) also point out the importance of addressing the broader social context (e.g. poverty, low education, minimal social support). Thus staff training needs to incorporate more practical considerations, such as how best to provide on-site child care, transportation help, community-centred locations such as schools or churches, enhanced social supports, and possible social service agency involvement. In a group parent training program, Feinfield and Baker (2004) incorporated a number of strategies to accommodate individual families' diverse needs and stressors, and to improve attendance. These included: a sliding scale fee, transportation assistance, child care for siblings, information conveyed in a range of formats, manuals and handouts, child social skills group, interspersed individual sessions, sessions designed to go beyond child behaviour management (e.g. enhance the parent–child relationship, reduce stress, and improve problem solving), social support development (e.g. members were encouraged to bring a supportive person to groups; homework assignments involving pairs of group members), and follow-up phone calls. This program for parents of children aged 4–7 years with externalizing behaviour problems served diverse families with excellent attendance and significant child improvements, mediated by changes in parenting behaviours.

The success of interventions may rest as much on the quality of the relationship established as on the content. In a study of families participating in the Head Start program, Stormshak, Kaminski, and Goodman (2002) reported higher caregiver involvement when families were assigned the same staff member to provide both in-home services and parenting groups, as opposed to two different leaders. In addition to being open to parent-identified needs (Llewellyn, McConnell, Russo, Mayes and Honey, 2002), staff need to invest time in establishing a trusting relationship with families; the quality of this partnership impacts parent compliance or resistance (Forehand and Kotchick, 2002). However, professionals may feel inadequately trained to step out of their limited role as 'child experts'; the literature suggests that staff are likely to lack knowledge of community resources, worry about offending families, and feel uncomfortable addressing sensitive family issues (Harbin, McWilliam and Gallagher, 2000). Staff training might be more successful if expanded to include practice in (1) establishing trusting partnerships with parents; (2) coordinating systems of care; and (3) exploring counter-transference issues so that staff's personal issues do not lead to misinterpretations or denial of family needs and concerns.

In order for interventionists to learn to clearly convey reasonable expectations, roles, and goals to families and the surrounding systems, staff training programs, too, should be structured 'with a clear philosophy and clear goals, well-articulated role definitions, and job descriptions [which will provide] a "holding environment" – a guiding structure for staff at all levels' (Musick and Stott, 2000). McCollum (2002) notes that successful interventionists have developed skills for effective communication and integration with multiple services and families. Table 10.2 provides one summary of training goals based on nine principles recommended by Knitzer (2000) for creating an effective early childhood mental health system. In addition to educating their staff in how to meet these goals, program planners need to train them in how to take on a supportive supervisor position so that they can eventually

Table 10.2 Nine training goals

---

1 Ability to assess staff and family needs
2 Ability to develop and promote supportive nurturing relationships
     Establishing partnership with parents
     Providing emotional support and knowledge to promote caring relationships
     between parent and child, as well as among other family members
3 Ability to provide services within natural environments
     Understanding developmental processes
     Exploring resources in flexible manner based on individual families' needs
4 Ability to be sensitive to cultural, community, and ethnic values of families
5 Ability to access mental health program consultation, case consultation, and
     backup support to help both families and staff
6 Ability to understand when more intensive services are needed (e.g. substance abuse,
     mental illness, child maltreatment
7 Ability to promote emotional development and understanding of child behavioural cues
     Utilizing available support for burnout, cultural, and workplace conflicts
     Providing outreach and/or crisis intervention as necessary
8 Ability to develop partnerships and effective communication between systems of care:
     Coordinating goals and strategies, and mapping resources
9 Ability to assess effectiveness of training

---

oversee their own group of trainees. Few programs provide adequate training for supervisor roles (Roberts *et al.*, 1991). Llewellyn *et al.* (2002) developed some useful parent educator guidelines that could be adapted and included in staff training programs for educating both parent trainers and supervisors.

MANUALS, MEDIA, AND THE INTERNET: REDEFINING PROFESSIONAL ROLES

The behaviour modification orientation upon which most parent training programs were based relied on parents to carry out teaching programs with their children. Thus parents became part of the 'team', and parents and professionals worked together. Nonetheless, parent training initially was based on a model of professional as teacher, parent as learner. To be sure, individual parent training, and to some extent group programs, were much less didactic and unidirectional than the model and literature implied. Effective professionals collaborated with parents – they understood the child and family's needs as well as resources and extant parenting practices. Indeed, the success of interventions had much to do with how they were perceived and how they meshed with the family's child-rearing conventions. Yet, as we have noted, the family-directed paradigm of today puts such considerations first and foremost, and moves professionals from the lectern to just another chair at the table.

The paradigm shift was inevitable. Legislated child rights to education, parent rights and responsibilities to have a voice in that process, the self-advocacy movement, the decline of institutions, and greater inclusiveness in society in general all came together with professionals' own changing views of helping services. Technology came to play an important part too. On the 'low tech' side, consider manuals and visual media. From the beginning of parent education programs, professionals wrote instructional manuals as 'how to' resources that would supplement, or even substitute for, professional consultation (Lovaas, Ackerman, Alexander, Firestone *et al.*, 1980; Patterson, 1977; Patterson and Gullion, 1976). Our own *Steps to Independence* series, which was first published in 1975 and has been continuously in print for thirty years (Baker, Brightman *et al.*, 2004), has accompanied thousands of children as they throw balls, pull on sweaters, sit on the toilet, or ponder their misdeeds in time-out. Initially published as manuals, and then as a book (available in English, Spanish, German, Chinese, and Russian), the *Steps* series, like many other instructional manuals, has been a valuable guide to parents and an essential tool for many parent educators. Likewise, videos produced to accompany parent education programs have become very popular with leaders and participants alike.

The greatest impact on the role of professionals, however, will likely come from the 'high tech' side, from the internet. Computers are already in more than half of American homes, with information (and misinformation) about disabilities now just clicks away. Blacher and Baker (2002) have noted three ways in which the internet is affecting families and redefining roles. First, with exponentially increasing knowledge about causes of intellectual disability, it is unlikely that any one professional will know as much about a particular rare syndrome as the parent who has searched out information from websites. Therefore, the professional's 'expert' role evolves into that of a collaborator, helping parents to sift through the information and supporting their efforts to problem solve. Second, parents are finding emotional and functional support through the internet, as they hear from, and talk to, other parents with similar experiences. Third, and related, many parents will feel more supported as they keep in touch with their own family members, friends, and service providers through email. This increased access to information and support, rather than diminish the need for early intervention services, in fact increases the ability of families to derive benefits from such services. Yet, the internet isn't equally available to families. One US survey (Kaye, 2000) found that internet usage increases with education (33.1 percent of high school graduates but 63.9 percent of college graduates) and is three times as high for Whites and Asian/Pacific Islanders as for African-Americans and Hispanics, although these figures are likely to change dramatically in the coming years.

CONCLUDING COMMENTS

We concluded a review of the early intervention literature (Baker and Feinfield, 2003) by noting that there is no shortage of young children and families at risk who could benefit from comprehensive early intervention. There is ample evidence that childhood disability covaries with poverty, and in 1997, 16 percent of families with children in the US were living below the poverty level, up from 10.8 percent 25 years earlier. Thus we welcome the increased mandate for early intervention services. We also welcome the increasing emphasis on evaluating the effectiveness of programs and putting resources into disseminating programs that are evidence-based. A word of caution, however. As professionals working to understand and to serve families, we need to distinguish between an 'awareness of the complexity of family needs and an inflated belief that we have, or should have, something to offer that meets them all. We must maintain our concentration on developing focused services that have a sound empirical basis. It is more honest to be clear about what a professional and an agency can do for families – and then do it well' (Baker, 1989: 195). The field of early intervention provides a fine opportunity for psychologists to bring their expertise in assessment, research, and program evaluation to a collaboration with service providers.

EXERCISE

Work in teams of four. Develop a preliminary plan for setting up a parent training programme for parents of children aged 3–6 with intellectual disabilities in a typical catchment area or district. In developing your plan, consider space, resources, transport, staffing, links to preschools, the parenting curriculum, programme evaluation, specialist input for complex cases and other key issues. Write a summary of your plan and read the summary to your class.

FURTHER READING FOR PARENTS

Baker, B. L. and Brightman, A. J., with Blacher, J., Hinshaw, S. P., Heifetz, L. J. and Murphy, D. M. (2004). *Steps to Independence: Teaching Everyday Skills to Children with Special Needs* (4th edn). Baltimore: Paul H. Brookes Publishing Co.

FURTHER READING

Baker, B. L. (1989). *Parent Training and Developmental Disabilities*. Washington, DC: American Association on Mental Retardation.

Baker, B. L. and Brightman, A. J., with Blacher, J., Hinshaw, S. P., Heifetz, L. J. and Murphy, D. M. (2004). *Steps to Independence: Teaching Everyday Skills to Children with Special Needs* (4th edn). Baltimore: Paul H. Brookes Publishing Co.

REFERENCES

Anastopoulos, A. D., Shelton, T. L., DuPaul, G. J. and Guevremont, D. C. (1993). Parent training for attention-deficit hyperactivity disorder: Its impact on parent functioning. *Journal of Abnormal Child Psychology*, 21, 581–96.

Anderson, S. R., DiPietro, E. K., Edwards, G. L. and Christian, W. P. (1987). Intensive home-based early intervention with autistic children. *Education and Treatment of Children*, 10, 352–66.

Baker, B. L. (1989). *Parent Training and Developmental Disabilities*. Washington, DC: American Association on Mental Retardation.

Baker, B. L. (1996). Parent training. In J. W. Jacobson and J. A. Mulick (eds), *Manual of Diagnosis and Professional Practice in Mental Retardation* (pp. 289–99). Washington, DC: American Psychological Association.

Baker, B. L., Blacher, J., Crnic, K. A. and Edelbrock, C. (2002). Behaviour problems and parenting stress in families of three-year-old children with and without developmental delays. *American Journal on Mental Retardation*, 107, 433–44.

Baker, B. L. and Brightman, A. J., with Blacher, J., Hinshaw, S. P., Heifetz, L. J. and Murphy, D. M. (2004). *Steps to Independence: Teaching Everyday Skills to Children with Special Needs* (4th edn). Baltimore, MD: Paul H. Brookes.

Baker, B. L. and Feinfield, K. A. (2003). Early intervention. *Current Opinion in Psychiatry*, 16, 503–9.

Baker, B. L., Landen, S. J. and Kashima, K. J. (1991). Effects of parent training on families with mentally retarded children: Increased burden or generalized benefit? *American Journal on Mental Retardation*, 96, 127–36.

Baker, B. L., McIntyre, L. L., Blacher, J., Crnic, K. A., Edelbrock, C. and Low C. (2003). Preschool children with and without developmental delay: Behaviour problems and parenting stress over time. *Journal of Intellectual Disability Research*, 47, 217–30.

Baranek, G. T. (2002). Efficacy of sensory motor interventions for children with autism. *Journal of Autism and Developmental Disorders*, 32, 397–422.

Blacher, J. and Baker, B. L. (2002). *The Best of AAMR: Families and Mental Retardation: A Collection of Notable AAMR Journal Articles across the 20th Century* (382pp). Washington, DC: American Association on Mental Retardation.

Blair, C. (2002). Early intervention for low birth weight, preterm infants: The role of negative emotionality in the specification of effects. *Developmental Psychopathology*, 14, 311–32.

Blok, H., Fukkink, R. G., Gebhardt, E. C. and Leseman, P. P. M. (2005). The relevance of delivery mode and other programme characteristics for the effectiveness of early childhood intervention. *International Journal of Behavioural Development*, 29, 35–47.

Brightman, R. P., Baker, B. L., Clark, D. B. and Ambrose, S. A. (1982). Effectiveness of alternative parent training formats. *Journal of Behaviour Therapy and Experimental Psychiatry*, 13, 113–17.

Brooks-Gunn, J., Klebanov, P. K., Liaw, F. and Spiker, D. (1993). Enhancing the development of low birthweight premature infants: Changes in cognition and behaviour over the first three years. *Child Development*, 64, 736–53.

Brooks-Gunn, J., McCarton, C., Casey, P., Bauer, C., Berman, J., Tyson, J., Swanson, M., Bennett, F., Scott, D., Tonascia, J. and Meinert, C. (1994). Early intervention in low-birth-weight premature infants. *Journal of the American Medical Association*, 272, 1257–62.

Brue, A. W. and Oakland, R. (2001). The Portage Guide to Early Intervention: An evaluation of published evidence. *School Psychology International*, 22, 243–52.

Bryson, S. E., Rogers, S. J. and Fombonne, E. (2003). Autism spectrum disorders: Early detection, intervention, education, and psychopharmacological management. *Canadian Journal of Psychiatry*, 48, 506–16.

Cameron, R. J. (1986). Portage: Pre-schoolers, parents and professionals. In R. J. Cameron (ed.), *Portage: Pre-schoolers, Parents and Professionals: Ten Years of Achievement in the UK* (pp. 1–12). England: NFER-NELSON.

Cameron, R. J. (1997). Early intervention for young children with developmental delay: The Portage approach. *Child: Care, Health and Development*, 23, 11–27.

Campbell, F. A. and Ramey, C. T. (1995). Cognitive and school outcomes for high-risk African-American students at middle adolescence: Positive effects of early intervention. *American Educational Research Journal*, 32(4), 743–72.

Campbell, F. A., Ramey, C. T., Pungello, E., Sparling, J. and Miller-Johnson, S. (2002). Early childhood education: Young adult outcomes from the Abecedarian Project. *Applied Developmental Science*, 6, 42–57.

Chambless D. L. and Hollon, S. D. (1998). Defining empirically supported therapies. *Journal of Consulting and Clinical Psychology*, 66, 7–18.

Chorpita, B. F., Yim, L. M., Donkervoet, J. C., *et al.* (2002). Toward large-scale implementation of empirically supported treatments for children: A review and observations by the Hawaii empirical basis to services task force. *Clinical Psychology: Science and Practice*, 9, 165–90.

Cochran, D. C. and Shearer, D. E. (1984). The Portage Model for home teaching. In S. C. Paine, G. T. Bellamy and B. Wilcox (eds), *Human Services that Work* (pp. 93–115). Baltimore, MD: Brookes.

Cunningham, C. D., Bremner, R. and Boyle, M. (1995). Large group community-based parenting programs for families of preschoolers at risk for disruptive behaviour disorders: Utilization, cost effectiveness, and outcome. *Journal of Child Psychology and Psychiatry*, 36, 1141–59.

Dunkle, M. and Vismara, L. (2003). A different kind of test. *Education Week*, 23(4), 38–9.

Eckenrode, J., Ganzel, B., Henderson, C. R., Smith, E., Olds, D. L., Powers, J., Cole, R., Kitzman, H. and Sidora, K. (2000). Preventing child abuse and neglect with a program of nurse home visitation: The limiting effects of domestic violence. *Journal of the American Medical Association*, 284, 1385–91.

Eikeseth, S., Smith, T., Jahr, E. and Eldevik, S. (2002). Intensive behavioural treatment at school for 4 to 7-year-old children with autism: A 1-year comparison controlled study. *Behaviour Modification*, 26, 49–68.

Einfeld, S. L. and Tonge, B. J. (1996). Population prevalence of psychopathology in children and adolescents with intellectual disability: II. Epidemiological findings. *Journal of Intellectual Disability Research*, 40, 99–109.

Eisenhower, A. S., Baker, B. L. and Blacher, J. (In press). Early student–teacher relationships of children with and without intellectual disability: Contributions of behavioral, social, and self-regulatory competence. *Journal of School Psychology*.

Feinfield, K. A. and Baker, B. L. (2004). Empirical support for a treatment program for families of young children with externalizing problems. *Journal of Clinical Child and Adolescent Psychology*, 33, 182–95.

Filer, J. and Mahoney, G. (1996). Collaboration between families and early intervention service providers. *Infants and Young Children*, 9, 22–30.

Forehand, R. and Kotchick, B. A. (2002). Behavioural parent training: Current challenges and potential solutions. *Journal of Child and Family Studies*, 11(4), 377–84.

Gallagher, J. J., Beckman, P. and Cross, A. H. (1983). Families of handicapped children: Sources of stress and its amelioration. *Exceptional Children*, 50, 10–19.

Goldstein, H. (2002). Communication intervention for children with autism: A review of treatment efficacy. *Journal of Autism and Developmental Disorders*, 32, 373–96.

Green, G., Brennan, L. C. and Fein, D. (2002). Intensive behavioural treatment for a toddler at high risk for autism. *Behaviour Modification*, 26, 69–102.

Griest, D. L. and Forehand, R. (1982). How can I get any parent training done with all these other problems going on? The role of family variables in child behaviour therapy. *Child and Family Behaviour Therapy*, 4, 73–80.

Guralnick, M. J. (1997). *The Effectiveness of Early Intervention: Second Generation Research*. Baltimore, MD: PH Brookes.

Guralnick, M. J. (2005). Early intervention for children with intellectual disabilities: current knowledge and future prospect. *Journal of Applied Research in Intellectual Disabilities*, 18, 313–23.

Halpern, R. (2000). Early childhood intervention for low-income children and families. In J. P. Shonkoff and S. J. Meisels (eds), *Handbook of Early Childhood Intervention* (pp. 361–86). New York: Cambridge University Press.

Hanson, M. J. and Lynch, E. W. (1995). *Early Intervention: Implementing Child and Family Services for Infants and Toddlers Who Are at Risk or Disabled* (2nd edn). Austin, TX: PRO-ED.

Harbin, G. L., McWilliam, R. A. and Gallagher, J. J. (2000). Services for young children with disabilities and their families. In J. P. Shonkoff and S. J. Meisels (eds), *Handbook of Early Childhood Intervention* (pp. 387–415). New York: Cambridge University Press.

Harrington, R., Cartwright-Hatton, S. and Stein, A. (2002). Annotation: Randomised trials. *Journal of Child Psychology and Psychiatry*, 43, 695–704.

Harris, S. and Handleman, J. (2000). Age and IQ at intake as predictors of placement for young children with autism: A four-to six-year follow-up. *Journal of Autism and Developmental Disorders*, 30, 137–42.

Hill, J. L., Brooks-Gunn, J. and Waldfogel, J. (2003). Sustained effects of high participation in an early intervention for low-birth-weight premature infants. *Developmental Psychology*, 39(4), 730–44.

Jacobson, J. W., Mulick, J. A. and Green, G. (1998). Cost-benefit estimates for early intensive behavioural intervention for young children with autism – general model and single state case. *Behavioural Interventions*, 13, 201–26.

Kasari, C. (2002). Assessing change in early intervention programs for children with autism. *Journal of Autism and Developmental Disorders*, 32, 447–61.

Kaye, H. S. (2000). *Computer and Internet Use among People with Disabilities: Disability Statistics Report (13)*. Washington DC: US Department of Education, National Institute on Disability and Rehabilitation Research.

Klebanov, P. K., Brooks-Gunn, J. and McCormick, M. C. (2001). Maternal coping strategies and emotional distress: Results of an early intervention program for low birth weight young children. *Developmental Psychology*, 37(5), 654–67.

Klein, N. K. and Gilkerson, L. (2000). Personnel preparation for early childhood intervention programs. In J. P. Shonkoff and S. J. Meisels (eds), *Handbook of Early Childhood Intervention* (pp. 454–86). New York: Cambridge University Press.

Knitzer, J. (2000). Early childhood mental health services: A policy and systems development perspective. In J. P. Shonkoff and S. J. Meisels (eds), *Handbook of Early Childhood Intervention* (pp. 416–38). New York: Cambridge University Press.

Koegel, L. K., Koegel, R. L., Shoshan, Y. and McNerney, E. (1999). Pivotal response intervention II: Preliminary long-term outcome data. *The Journal of the Association for Persons with Severe Handicaps*, 24, 186–98.

Koegel, R. L., Bimbela, A. and Schreibman, L. (1996). Collateral effects of parent training on family interactions. *Journal of Autism and Developmental Disorders*, 26, 347–59.

Koegel, R. L., Koegel, L. K. and Brookman, L. I. (2003). Empirically supported pivotal response interventions for children with autism. In A. Kazdin and J. Weisz (eds), *Evidence-Based Psychotherapies for Children and Adolescents* (pp. 325–40). New York: The Guilford Press.

Koegel, R. L., Schreibman, L., Good, A., Cerniglia, L., Murphy, C. and Koegel, L. K. (1989). *How to Teach Pivotal Behaviours to Children with Autism: A Training Manual*. Santa Barbara, CA: University of California Press.

Koegel, R. L., Symon, J. B. and Koegel, L. K. (2002). Parent education for families of children with autism living in geographically distant areas. *Journal of Positive Behavioural Interventions*, 4, 88–103.

Kohli, T. (1990). The Portage Project: history and promise. In M. White and R. J. Camerson (eds), *Portage: Progress, Problems, and Possibilities* (pp. 107–16). London: NFER-NELSON.

Krauss, M. W. (2000). Family assessment within early intervention programs. In J. P Shonkoff and S. J. Meisels (eds), *Handbook of Early Childhood Intervention* (pp. 290–308). New York: Cambridge University Press.

Linna, S. L., Moilanen, I., Ebeling, H., Piha, J., Kumpulainen, K., Tamminen, T. and Almqvist, F. (1999). Psychiatric symptoms in children with intellectual disability. *European Child and Adolescent Psychiatry*, 8, Suppl 4, IV/77–82.

Llewellyn, G., McConnell, D., Russo, D., Mayes, R. and Honey, A. (2002). Home-based programmes for parents with intellectual disabilities: Lessons from practice. *Journal of Applied Research in Intellectual Disabilities*, 15, 341–53.

Lovaas, O. I. (1987). Behavioural treatment and normal educational and intellectual functioning in young autistic children. *Journal of Consulting and Clinical Psychology*, 55, 3–9.

Lovaas, O. I. (2003). *Teaching Individuals with Developmental Delays: Basic Intervention Techniques*. Austin, TX: PRO-ED, Inc (www.proedinc.com).

Lovaas, O. I. and Smith, T. (2003). Early and intensive behavioural intervention in autism. In A. Kazdin and J. Weisz (eds) *Evidence-Based Psychotherapies for Children and Adolescents* (pp. 325–40). New York: The Guilford Press.

Lovaas, O. I., Ackerman, A. B., Alexander, D., Firestone, P., Perkins, J. and Young, D. (1980). *Teaching Developmentally Disabled Children: The Me Book*. Austin, TX: Pro-Ed.

Mahoney, G., Kaiser, A., Girolametto, L., MacDonald, J., Robinson, C., Safford, P. and Spiker, D. (1999). Parent education in early intervention: A call for a renewed focus. *Topics in Early Childhood Special Education*, 19, 131–40.

McBride, S. L. and Peterson, C. (1997). Home-based intervention with families of children with disabilities: who is doing what? *Topics in Early Childhood Special Education*, 17, 209–33.

McCarton, C., Brooks-Gunn, J., Wallace, I., Bauer, C., Bennett, F., Bernbaum, J., Broyles, S., Casey, P., McCormick, M., Scott, D., Tyson, J., Tonascia, J. and Meinert, C. (1997). Results at age 8 years of early intervention for low-birth-weight premature infants: The Infant Health and Development Program. *Journal of the American Medical Association*, 277(2), 126–32.

McCollum, J. A. (1999). Parent education: What we mean and what that means. *Topics in Early Childhood Special Education*, 19, 147–9.

McCollum, J. A. (2002). Influencing the development of young children with disabilities: Current themes in early intervention. *Child and Adolescent Mental Health*, 7, 4–9.

McConachie, H. (2002). Appropriate research design in evaluating interventions for children with disabilities. *Child, Care, Health and Development*, 28, 195–7.

McConnell, S. R. (2002). Interventions to facilitate social interaction for young children with autism: Review of available research and recommendations for educational intervention and future research. *Journal of Autism and Developmental Disorders*, 32(5), 351–72.

McEachin, J. J., Smith, T. and Lovaas, O. I. (1993). Long-term outcome for children with autism who received early intensive behavioural treatment. *American Journal on Mental Retardation*, 97, 359–72.

McIntyre, L. L., Blacher, J. and Baker, B. L. (2006). The transition to school: Adaptation in young children with and without intellectual disability. *Journal of Intellectual Disability Research*, 50, 349–61.

Molteno, G., Molteno, C. D., Finchilescu, G. and Dawes, A. R. L. (2001). Behavioural and emotional problems in children with intellectual disability attending special schools in Cape Town, South Africa. *Journal of Intellectual Disability Research*, 45, 515–20.

Musick, J. and Stott, F. (2000). Paraprofessionals revisited and reconsidered. In J. P. Shonkoff and S. J. Meisels (eds), *Handbook of Early Childhood Intervention* (pp. 439–53). New York: Cambridge University Press.

Oakland, T. (1997). A multi-year home-based program to promote development of young Palestinian children who exhibit developmental delays. *School Psychology International*, 18, 23–39.

Olds, D. L. (2002). Prenatal and infancy home visiting by nurses: From randomized trials to community replication. *Prevention Science*, 3, 153–72.

Olds, D. L., Hill, P. L., O'Brien, R., Racine, D. and Moritz, P. (2003). Taking preventive intervention to scale: The nurse-family partnership. *Cognitive and Behavioural Practice*, 10, 278–90.

Olds, D., Henderson, C. R., Cole, R., Eckenrode, J., Kitzman, H., Luckey, D., Pettitt, L., Sidora, K., Morris, P. and Powers, J. (1998a). Long-term effects of nurse home visitation on children's criminal and antisocial behaviour: 15-year follow-up of a randomized controlled trial. *Journal of the American Medical Association*, 280, 1238–44.

Olds, D., Henderson, C., Kitzman, H., Eckenrode, J., Cole, R. and Tatelbaum, R. (1998b). The promise of home visitation: Results of two randomized trials. *Journal of Community Psychology*, 26, 5–21.

Oser, C. and Ayankoya, B. (2000). The early interventionist. *Zero to Three*, 21: 24–31.

Osterling, J. A., Dawson, G. and Munson, J. A. (2002). Early recognition of 1-year-old infants with autism spectrum disorder versus mental retardation. *Developmental Psychopathology*, 14, 239–52.

Patterson, G. R. (1977). *Families: Applications of Social Learning to Family Life* (rev. edn). Champaign, IL: Research Press.

Patterson, G. R. and Gullion, M. E. (1976). *Living with Children: New Methods for Parents and Teachers* (rev. edn). Champaign, IL: Research Press.

Pisterman, S., McGrath, P., Firestone, P., Goodman, J., Webster, I., Mallory, R. and Goffin, B. (1992). The effects of parent training on parenting stress and sense of competence. *Canadian Journal of Behavioural Science*, 24, 41–58.

Ramey, C. T. and Campbell, F. A. (1984). Preventive education for high-risk children: cognitive consequences of the Carolina Abecedarian Project. *American Journal of Mental Deficiency*, 88, 515–23.

Ramey, C. T. and Ramey, S. L. (1998a). Early intervention and early experience. *American Psychologist*, 53, 109–20.

Ramey, C. T. and Ramey, S. L. (1998b). Prevention of intellectual disabilities: Early interventions to improve cognitive development. *Preventive Medicine*, 27, 224–32.

Ramey, C. T. and Ramey, S. L. (2004). Early learning and school readiness: Can early intervention make a difference? *Merrill-Palmer Quarterly*, 50, 471–91.

Ramey, C. T., Bryant, D. M., Wasik, B. H., Sparling, J. J., Fendt, K. H. and Lavange, L. M. (1992). Infant Health and Development Program for low birth weight, premature infants: Program elements, family participation, and child intelligence. *Paediatrics*, 89, 454–65.

Ramey, C. T., Campbell, F. A., Burchinal, M., Skinner, M. L., Gardner, D. M. and Ramey, S. L. (2000). Persistent effects of early childhood education on high-risk children and their mothers. *Applied Developmental Science*, 4(1), 2–14.

Ramey, C.T., Ramey, S. L., Lanzi, R. G. and Cotton, J. N. (2002). Early educational interventions for high-risk children: How centre-based treatment can augment and improve parenting effectiveness. In J. G. Borkowski, S. L. Ramey, and M. Bristol-Power (eds), *Parenting and the Child's World: Influences on Academic, Intellectual and Social-Emotional Development* (pp. 125–40). London: Lawrence Erlbaum Associates.

Roberts, R. N., Wasik, B. H., Casto, G. and Ramey, C. T. (1991). Family support in the home: programs, policy, and social change. *American Psychologist*, 46(2), 131–7.

Sallows, G. O. and Graupner, T. D. (2005). Intensive behavioral treatment for children with autism: Four-year outcome and predictors. *American Journal on Mental Retardation*, 110, 417–38.

Salzinger, K., Feldman, R. S. and Portnoy, S. (1970). Training parents of brain injured children in the use of operant conditioning procedures. *Behaviour Therapy*, 1, 4–32.

Santarelli, G., Koegel, R. L., Casas, J. M. and Koegel, L. K. (2001). Culturally diverse families participating in behaviour therapy parent education programs for children with developmental disabilities. *Journal of Positive Behaviour Interventions*, 3, 120–3.

Shearer, M. S. and Shearer, D. E. (1972). The Portage Project: A model for early childhood education. *Exceptional Children*, 39, 210–17.

Shonkoff, J. P. and Meisels, S. J. (2000). *Handbook of Early Childhood Intervention* (2nd ed). New York: Cambridge University Press.

Smith, T., Goren, A. and Wynn, J. W. (2000). Randomized trial of intensive early intervention for children with pervasive developmental disorder. *American Journal on Mental Retardation*, 104, 269–85.

Sparling, J. and Lewis, I. (1984). *Learning Games for Threes and Fours: A Guide To Parent-Child Play*. New York: Walker.

Sparling, J. J., Lewis, I. and Ramey, C. T. (1995). *Partners for Learning: Birth to 36 Months*. Lewisville, NC: Kaplan Press.

Spiker, D., Ferguson, J. and Brooks-Gunn, J. (1993). Enhancing maternal interactive behaviour and child social competence in low birth-weight premature infants. *Child Development*, 64, 754–68.

Stormshak, E. A., Kaminski, R. A. and Goodman, M. R. (2002). Enhancing the parenting skills of head start families during the transition to kindergarten. *Prevention Science*, 3(3), 223–34.

Stromme, P. and Diseth, T. H. (2000). Prevalence of psychiatric diagnoses in children with mental retardation: Data from a population-based study. *Developmental Medicine and Child Neurology*, 42, 266–70.

Task Force on Psychological Intervention Guidelines (2002). *Template for Developing Guidelines: Interventions for Mental Disorders and Psychosocial Aspects of Physical Disorders*. Washington, DC: American Psychological Association.

Turnbull, A. P. and Turnbull, H. R. (1990). *Families, Professionals, and Exceptionality: A Special Partnership* (2nd edn). Columbus, OH: Merrill.

Vincent, L. J. and Beckett, J. A. (1993). Family participation. In *DEC Recommended Practices: Indicators of Quality in Program for Infants and Young Children with Special Needs and their Families* (pp. 19–29). Reston, VA: Council for Exceptional Children, Division for Early Childhood, Task Force on Recommended Practices.

Webster-Stratton, C. and Reid, M. J. (2003). The Incredible Years parents, teachers, and children training series: A multifaceted treatment approach for young children with conduct problems. In A. Kazdin and J. Weisz (eds), *Evidence-Based Psychotherapies for Children and Adolescents* (pp. 224–40). New York: The Guilford Press.

ACKNOWLEDGEMENT

Preparation of this chapter was supported in part by NICHD Grant #34879–1459 (Dr Keith Crnic, PI: Drs Bruce Baker, Jan Blacher, and Craig Edelbrock, Co-PIs).

Chapter 11

Sleep disorders

Luci Wiggs

'What hath night to do with sleep?' wrote Milton (1608–1674). It has taken the scientific and therapeutic community many centuries to appreciate and understand the significance of that sentence. Sleep disorders are widespread amongst the general adult and child population but there are a number of special populations who are particularly prone to have sleep disturbance. These include people with intellectual disabilities (ID).

It is well documented that persistent sleep disruption is associated with diminished cognitive abilities, emotional and behavioural difficulties and also physical impairments. Carers and parents of young people with sleep disorders are also prone to suffer similar effects, if their own sleep is disturbed. Fortunately, many of these effects are rapidly reversed by successful treatment of the sleep disorder but early identification and intervention are clearly important, especially so in young people; some cognitive impairments associated with sleep disorders may be less easily reversed, if at all, if they occur at critical stages of development.

For people with ID, who are already prone to cognitive, emotional and behavioural difficulties, ensuring that sleep disruption is not playing a causal role in such problems is imperative as it may be one of the most easily treatable aspects of their condition.

This chapter will focus primarily on sleep disorders in children; however, it should not be assumed that the rate of sleep disorders decreases dramatically as the young people become adults. The limited literature on adults with intellectual disabilities strongly suggests that high rates of sleep problems persist although their nature and cause may change.

NORMAL SLEEP

It is beyond the scope of this chapter to provide a detailed account of normal sleep physiology and readers are referred to Kryger, Roth and Dement (2005) and Sheldon, Ferber and Kryger (2005) for further information, including developmental aspects. Key elements include the following:

- Sleep can be defined both behaviourally and physiologically.
- Behavioural indicators include periods of quiet inactivity, increased arousal threshold, reversibility with moderate stimulation, species specific body postures and regular occurrence.
- Physiologically, sleep is divided into different sleep stages, defined by the electrophysiological parameters of electroencephalogram (EEG), electro-oculogram (EOG) and electromyogram (EMG). Together, recording of these parameters, by means of electrodes attached to the scalp and face is called 'polysomnography' (PSG).
- There are two distinct types of sleep; Rapid eye movement (REM) sleep and Non-rapid eye movement (NREM) sleep.
- NREM sleep is further divided into stages 1, 2, 3 and 4 indicating increasing depth of sleep. Stages 3 and 4 are often referred to as 'deep', 'delta' or 'slow wave' sleep. The stages of NREM sleep are primarily differentiated from each other by way of the EEG changes associated with the different sleep stages. Heart and breathing rates are generally reduced and regular. There are no eye movements and skeletal muscle tone is preserved, as in the waking state.
- REM sleep EEG resembles that of wakefulness or the lighter stages of NREM sleep. However, this stage is characterized by higher and more variable heart and breathing rates, bursts of rapid eye movements and a loss of postural muscle tone (which prevents large movements although twitching is common). Most dreaming occurs during REM sleep.
- These sleep stages alternate throughout the night in several 'sleep cycles' (a period of sleep encompassing NREM and REM sleep) as shown in the hypnogram in Figure 11.1. There is most deep NREM sleep in the first third of the night and most REM sleep in the last third of the night. The pattern of the different sleep stages is referred to as 'sleep architecture'.
- Typically, a sleep cycle in adults takes about 90 minutes and in children about 50 minutes. Brief periods of wake at the end of a sleep cycle are normal and usually so brief that they go undetected by the individual. Typically these 'normal' wakes are from light NREM sleep or REM sleep and thus are more prevalent towards the end of the sleep period when these sleep stages predominate.
- Other briefer, sub-clinical arousals, known as 'microarousals', are also a feature of normal sleep.
- An individual's pattern of sleep and wake follows a circadian ('about a day') rhythm, governed by a 'biological clock' primarily controlled by the suprachiasmatic nucleus of the hypothalamus. There are a number of physiological processes which follow a circadian pattern (temperature, hormone release, levels of blood and urine constituents) and many of these processes are 'synchronized' so that typically, for example, we fall asleep as temperature is dropping and wake as it rises. The endogenous body clock is also affected by external environmental cues or 'zeitgebers'

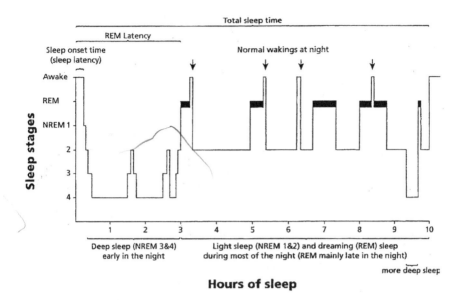

Figure 11.1 A hypnogram.

Note: Reproduced from G. Stores and L. Wiggs (eds) (2001) with kind permission from the publishers.

(German for 'time givers'). The light/dark cycle is a major synchronizer of circadian rhythms but social/environmental cues such as knowledge of the clock time, timing of meals and the behaviour of other people are also important. Jet lag is an example of what happens when circadian rhythms get desynchronized and one is trying to sleep at times when one's biological clock is not set at the same hour as the 'real' clock time. That it can be relatively quickly overcome is also an indication of how our biological clock can adapt and be re-set to a new clock time by external zeitgebers.

CLASSIFICATION OF SLEEP DISORDERS

There are three basic types of sleep problem which are likely to present:

- Difficulty getting to sleep or staying asleep
- Sleeping too much
- Disturbed episodes that interfere with sleep.

However, there are over eighty different underlying sleep disorders listed in the International Classification of Sleep Disorders (ICSD) (American Sleep Disorders Association, 2005) which can cause these symptoms. Identifying the sleep disorder rather than describing the presenting sleep problem is an important distinction with implications for management. For example, 'difficulty getting off to sleep' is a presenting sleep problem which might be caused by a number of sleep disorders including those relating to anxiety, poor limit-setting on the part of carers, an inappropriate sleep environment or disruption to the child's body clock. Very different treatment approaches would be required for each of these examples.

The ICSD divides sleep disorders into the following categories:

- **Insomnia** (difficulty with sleep initiation, duration, consolidation or quality and resulting in daytime impairment) (e.g. *behavioural insomnia of childhood, inadequate sleep hygiene*)
- **Sleep related breathing disorders** (disordered respiration during sleep) (e.g. *obstructive sleep apnoea, central sleep apnoea*)
- **Hypersomnias of central origin** (primary complaint of daytime sleepiness not due to disturbed nocturnal sleep or a circadian rhythm sleep disorder) (e.g. *narcolepsy, Kleine-Levin syndrome*)
- **Circadian rhythm sleep disorders** (misalignment between the individual's circadian clock and the clock time or alteration of the circadian timing system) (e.g. *delayed sleep phase syndrome, irregular sleep phase syndrome*)
- **Parasomnias** (disorders that intrude into the sleep process. Usually manifestations of central nervous system activity). These are subdivided according to the stage of sleep with which they are associated

  - Disorders of arousal (arising from NREM sleep) (e.g. *sleep terrors, sleep walking*)
  - Parasomnias usually associated with REM sleep (e.g. *nightmares*)
  - Other parasomnias which can be associated with various stages of sleep (e.g. *nocturnal enuresis*)

- **Sleep related movement disorders** (primarily characterized by relatively simple, often stereotyped movements that disturb or are associated with sleep resulting in daytime sleepiness/impairments) (e.g. *restless legs syndrome, periodic limb movement disorder, rhythmic movement disorder*)
- **Isolated symptoms/normal variants/unresolved issues** (disorders lying on the borderline or continuum of normal/abnormal sleep or symptoms which, in the absence of further information, cannot be considered to be definite pathologies) (e.g. *short sleeper/long sleeper, sleep talking*)
- **Other** (e.g. sleep disorders which overlap several of the above categories).

ICSD summarizes each sleep disorder including its main characteristics, associated features and possible complications, course, predisposing factors, prevalence, age at onset, sex ratio, familial patterns, polysomnographic and other laboratory features, and differential diagnosis.

In addition to a glossary of basic terms and concepts, two appendices are also included which described some medical and psychiatric disorders with which sleep disorders are commonly associated.

This recently revised classification system has addressed many of the shortcomings of earlier versions although it remains biased towards adults and the particular issues for children and people with ID are often not adequately addressed.

For practical purposes, it can be diagnostically helpful, initially at least, to think of sleep problems in terms of presenting symptoms. These fall under the broad headings of sleeplessness, excessive daytime sleepiness, and parasomnias (in the remainder of this chapter the term 'parasomnia' is used to include sleep-related movement disorders).

SLEEPLESSNESS

Sleeplessness can present as difficulty falling asleep, nightwaking or early morning waking.

Difficulty falling asleep

Common causes of difficulty falling asleep in children with ID include the following:

- **Sleep onset association disorder** – where the child requires a particular set of circumstances in order to initiate sleep (presence of parent, to be in parents' bed, etc.).
- **Limit setting sleep disorder** – consistent rules for settling to sleep are not implemented by parents and bedtime (including the period leading up to it) can be chaotic and prolonged by child's behaviour/requests.
- **Over-arousal at bedtime** – often due to night-time fears, over-stimulating sleep environment or bedtime routine, worry about family/daytime activities, bedtime too early.
- **Conditioned insomnia** – where the habit of lying awake for extended periods has become learned behaviour and persists beyond the presence of the original cause, for example, once a source of stress has passed.
- **Delayed sleep phase syndrome** – a circadian rhythm disorder where the child's body clock is set at the wrong time and the child's sleep phase has become displaced so that they fall asleep later than desired and, in order to meet their sleep needs, would ideally sleep-in later than desired in the morning. These children generally have to be woken in the morning for school (with difficulty) and can experience daytime sleepiness. Often weekend patterns of sleeping at their preferred sleep times can maintain the problem.

- **Inappropriate daytime nap schedules** – prolonged or ill-timed (e.g. too late in the afternoon or too early in the morning) daytime napping may contribute to night-time sleeping difficulties. Many children with IDs have taxi or bus transport provided to and from school, and the journey home, which can be long, is frequently a time when inappropriate naps take place.
- **Short sleep requirements** – everyone has different individual sleep needs and some children will require less sleep than others. This explanation can only be attributed after excluding all other possibilities AND when the child shows no ill-effects of the reduced sleep period (which is rarely the case).

Nightwaking

Common causes of nightwaking include the following:

- **Sleep onset association disorder** – normal nocturnal brief wakings become prolonged because the child becomes distressed when they find the set of circumstances during the night is not the same as when they fell asleep in the evening (e.g. the child is settled with the mother present and wakes to find her gone, to her bed, in the middle of the night).
- **Limit-setting sleep disorder** – parents fail to set limits or inadvertently reinforce nocturnal disturbance.
- **Irregular sleep phase syndrome** – a circadian rhythm disorder where the child's sleep-wake schedule shows no discernible pattern. Several brief sleep periods occur over each 24-hour period, varying in number, timing and duration from day to day.
- **Various parasomnias** – which are described below.

Early waking

Common causes of early waking include:

- **Sleep onset association disorder** – again, what might have been a brief, normal night waking followed by re-entry into sleep becomes the 'final waking' when a child arouses, for reasons described above, at a time when their sleep-drive is low (e.g. because they are nearing the end of their sleep period).
- **Limit-setting sleep disorder** – failing to set limits or inappropriately rewarding early waking by allowing children to get up or get into the parents' bed or watch TV or do otherwise 'rewarding' activities can encourage the early waking to continue. If early waking continues it is likely eventually to evolve into advanced sleep phase syndrome.

- **Advanced sleep phase syndrome** – a circadian rhythm disorder where the child's body clock is set at the wrong time and the child's sleep phase has become displaced so that they fall asleep earlier than desired and therefore have met their sleep needs earlier than is desirable and present with 'early waking'.
- **Short sleep requirements** – again, this explanation can only be attributed after excluding all other possibilities AND when the child shows no ill-effects of the reduced sleep period (which is rarely the case). Treatment may still be required in order to alter the timing (if not the duration) of the child's sleep pattern, to achieve a pattern which is compatible with family life. A later bedtime and later rising time can often be sustained better than a 'suitable' bedtime which is associated with an exceptionally early waking time.
- **Environmental factors** – when the sleep-drive is lower (which it is in the morning hours of sleep), typically after a long period of sleep, environmental factors such as bright sunlight, environmental noise, etc. can be particularly disruptive.

EXCESSIVE DAYTIME SLEEPINESS

Excessive daytime sleepiness (EDS) is usually the result of either insufficient sleep, poor-quality overnight sleep or conditions where an increased sleep need is present.

Clinicians need to be aware that EDS in children may not present as 'sleepiness' but rather as over-activity or behavioural difficulties. It should also be noted that 'sleepiness' should be distinguished from, for example, extended time in bed, periods of inactivity, chronic medical conditions associated with physical fatigue or factors related to epilepsy such as post-ictal sleepiness or non-convulsive status epilepticus.

Insufficient sleep

The most common causes of insufficient sleep have been described above in the section titled 'Sleeplessness'.

Poor-quality overnight sleep

Poor-quality overnight sleep may be suspected where sleep duration and timing appears normal but EDS presents.

Sleep disordered breathing (SDB) due to upper airway obstruction of varying degrees, with or without apnoeic episodes, or apnoeas of central origin is a prominent complication in many developmental disorders. This is a common cause of EDS (or associated behavioural disturbance, in children). In typically developing children the main cause of obstruction is enlarged tonsils and adenoids. In many children with ID the cause can be more complicated. For example in Down syndrome it may be due to craniofacial abnormalities, macroglossia, hypotonia and narrowing of airways. In adults obesity and use of alcohol may be contributory factors. Obesity is rarely a cause of SDB in children. Indeed, often, children with SDB 'fail to thrive' and have low body weight.

Periodic limb movements in sleep (PLMs) are brief, often very subtle, stereotyped contractions of limbs (usually toes, knees and hips) which may be associated with arousal sufficient to disturb sleep quality. PLMs may be accompanied by restless legs syndrome (RLS) where discomfort in the legs, and an urge to move the legs to dissipate the sensation, prevents sleep onset.

Increased sleep need

Narcolepsy may be associated with an increased need for sleep. It is a life-long condition, which is characterized by 'sleep attacks', cataplexy (sudden loss of muscle tone, usually in response to strong emotions such as amusement or anger), vivid dream-like experiences on falling asleep or waking up (hypnagogic or hypnopompic hallucinations respectively) and sleep paralysis (inability to move when going off to sleep or waking up). Other common causes include **medication effects**, **chronic medical conditions**, **organic brain abnormalities** or as a **post-infection feature**. Intermittent excessive sleepiness may be related to recurrent **depression**, **non-convulsive status epilepticus**, the **menstrual cycle** or the **Kleine-Levin syndrome**. This syndrome is characterized by a normal sleep pattern punctuated by periods of hypersomnia (sometimes up to 20 hours' sleep per 24 hours) lasting for hours or weeks which, in classic form, may be associated with overeating, hypersexual behaviour, mood disorder and other behavioural disturbance during wakeful periods.

Case example of sleep apnoea

Jessica was a 6-year-old girl with Down syndrome referred because of her challenging and hyperactive daytime behaviour. As part of routine history taking, preliminary screening questions about her sleep patterns were asked. She went to sleep without undue problems, at a normal time and no night-wakes were reported. She didn't appear to be excessively sleepy during the day but her mother reported that she was often difficult to wake in the morning and had to be 'dragged from bed' at 7.45 am in order to be up in time to catch the school taxi. This difficulty waking, especially combined with day-time behavioural difficulties, suggested that although sleep quantity appeared to be normal, sleep quality might be compromised and more detailed assessment was indicated. Screening questionnaires completed by her parents indicated that a number of features of sleep-related breathing problems were common. These included noisy breathing during sleep, snoring and sleeping with her neck extended. This pattern of daytime and nocturnal symptoms, especially in a child with Down syndrome, indicated that referral to a sleep centre for polysomnography with respiratory measures would be appropriate. Obstructive sleep apnoea was confirmed.

PARASOMNIAS

Many parasomnias can be dramatic but they are not necessarily indicative of underlying physical or psychological problems, nor do they necessarily need 'treatment'. Some parasomnias are common in childhood (e.g. nightmares, arousal disorders, rhythmic movement disorders) and are typically outgrown with no adverse effects. Intervention may be required if they are frequent, severe (in terms of the behaviour during episodes being injurious or distressing), recur after having previously stopped (suggestive of a stressor inducing them) or occur following trauma. In typically developing children one might also consider further exceptions to be those parasomnias which start later or persist longer than might be expected. Speculatively, atypical age of onset or course of parasomnias may be less indicative of 'abnormality' in children with ID where chronological age may be less significant.

That said, even if treatment is not required, it is important to identify and diagnose any 'episodes' associated with sleep in view of the fact that diagnostic confusion is common; it may involve misdiagnosing one form of parasomnia with another or misdiagnosing parasomnias with other 'episodic' conditions, notably epilepsy.

As indicated earlier, parasomnias are classified according to the stage of sleep from which they originate. This can be helpful diagnostically when trying to differentiate between parasomnias because typically one has most deep NREM sleep in the first third of the night and most REM sleep in the last third of the night (although young children may also have a brief period of deep NREM shortly before waking in the morning). Of course, for children with severe or profound ID whose basic sleep architecture is not typical these generalizations may not apply.

Descriptions of some common parasomnias are given below.

Sleep-wake transition disorders

Sleep starts are benign single brief bodily jerks when falling asleep. They can occur repeatedly, perhaps explaining why they have been confused with myoclonic seizures. Sometimes they take the form of a brief sensory experience (e.g. hearing a loud noise).

Rhythmic movement disorders are stereotyped, repetitive behaviours including head banging, head rolling and body rocking. The child may make rhythmic noises during the episode. They are generally thought to be 'self-soothing' behaviours which help the child to induce sleep and, as such, can occur at evening sleep onset, at nap times and during the night following a waking but may also present during sleep. They can last for a few minutes or several hours. Rhythmic movement disorders are very common in typically developing infants and young children. Perhaps they are even more common in children with developmental disorders, where the problem can be more intense and frequent and may also be apparent during daytime wakefulness.

Parasomnias arising from deep NREM sleep

These are collectively known as 'partial arousal disorders' because they involve incomplete arousal from deep NREM sleep and include sleepwalking, confusional arousals and sleep terrors. Because they occur from deep NREM sleep they typically occur within an hour or two after falling asleep (when NREM sleep is most abundant). The individual remains asleep during the episode, and therefore is generally non-responsive and has little, if any, recall of the event the following morning (unless they woke at the end of it). It is difficult (and ill-advisable) to wake someone from a partial arousal disorder. If they can be woken they are usually agitated and confused. Episodes can last from a few minutes up to, in extreme cases, an hour. There is often a family history for partial arousal disorders.

Specific behaviours during the episodes are variable but **confusional arousals** usually involve sitting up in bed, appearing confused and agitated; **sleepwalking** typically involves semi-purposeful wandering (this can be calm or agitated) and can involve complicated behavioural-action sequences (e.g. people have driven cars!); **sleep terrors** present as sudden-onset 'fear' (both behavioural and autonomic manifestations), often with screaming, vocalizations and accompanied by agitated sleepwalking. Individuals will quite often display 'escape' behaviour during partial arousal disorders (e.g. trying to leave rooms through windows or doors, moving about the house, even downstairs or outside) and as such the likelihood of accidental injury can be high.

Parasomnias usually associated with REM sleep

As with the partial arousal disorders, a child experiencing a **nightmare** may also appear fearful, confused and agitated but in contrast they will be awake at this time. A nightmare is a frightening dream and the fear has been sufficient to wake the individual (generally from REM sleep when most dreaming occurs and thus typically they occur during the last part of the sleep period when there is most REM sleep). If verbal, the child can usually recall and recount the narrative or content of the dream that scared them and is generally comforted by the presence of parents. Because there can be

Table 11.1 Comparison of features of arousal disorders, nightmares and seizures

	Partial arousals	Nightmares	Nocturnal seizures
Time of occurrence	First third	Last third	Variable
Stage of sleep	Deep NREM	REM	Variable
Distress/ autonomic arousal	Low/mild with sleepwalking; high/very high with sleep terrors	Mild to high	Variable
Motor behaviour	Variable (complex behaviours possible)	Little motor behaviour	Repetitive, stereotypical
Arousal threshold	High; distressed/ confused if awoken	Low; distressed and awake after episode	High; confused and awake after episode
Memory of event	None or patchy	Vivid	Variable
Family history	Common	None	Variable
Potential for injury	Moderate	Low	Moderate
Daytime sleepiness	Uncommon	Uncommon	Common
Prevalence	Common	Very common	Much less common

diagnostic confusion surrounding nightmares, partial arousal disorders and seizures, some pertinent defining features are summarized in Table 11.1. If a child has daytime seizures it should not be *assumed* that nocturnal episodes are also epileptic in origin. Similarly, a lack of daytime seizures does not preclude the possibility of nocturnal episodes being epileptic.

Parasomnias associated with any stage of sleep

Teeth grinding (bruxism) may occur at elevated rates in children with ID. Usually, family members, rather than the bruxist, have their sleep disturbed by the noise of the grinding. Problems for the bruxist are more typically jaw pain and dental erosion, if severe and persistent.

Nocturnal enuresis (involuntary bedwetting) is very common in typically developing children and even more common in children with ID. It is important to distinguish between primary enuresis (when a child has never achieved bladder control at night) and secondary enuresis (when a child who has been dry at night for at least six months begins to wet the bed again). Secondary enuresis is generally associated with physical problems such as urinary infections, diabetes, and epilepsy, or with emotional stress.

EPIDEMIOLOGY

Good epidemiological data concerning sleep disturbance in people with an ID are lacking. Interpretation of research results is often limited by the heterogeneous nature of the groups studied in terms of their intellectual impairment being of mixed aetiology and severity and the presence of associated medical and psychological factors. This is particularly relevant since, for example, high rates of epilepsy, psychiatric disorder and other conditions which can be associated with sleep disturbance, such as sensory impairments and discomfort due to muscle spasms, are generally present at elevated rates in ID samples. Limitations aside, there have been several accounts documenting abnormalities of sleep physiology and reports of persistent and severe sleep disturbance, mostly taking the form of sleeplessness. As in typically developing children, the presence of sleep disturbance has been seen to be associated with adverse effects on sufferers and their carers.

Physiology of sleep in children with an intellectual impairment

In children with profound ID it can be difficult to distinguish physiologically between waking and sleeping states ('monostage sleep'). Where sleep physiology can be discerned, the most consistent non-specific finding in intellectual impairment of various aetiologies has related to REM sleep abnormalities, specifically, a relative overall deficiency in amount, fewer and/or shorter REM sleep periods and fewer eye movements ('low REM density'). Such findings have been generally more pronounced in individuals with lower levels of intelligence. Within this context it is noteworthy that in typical development, the proportion of REM sleep is high in neonates and decreases as the infant matures and that this supports other data which also suggest that this stage of sleep is particularly involved in information processing and other aspects of the learning process.

In children with ID, sleep spindle activity (normally an EEG feature of Stage 2 NREM sleep) may be abnormal. Spindles may be absent or unusually frequent, high voltage and continuous ('extreme spindles') and their pattern of development may be abnormal.

The pattern of developmental changes seen in children of typical ability which involves a decrease in total sleep time and in the proportion of REM sleep is preserved, even in severely intellectually impaired children.

Sleep problems and intellectual disability

Although there have only been a limited number of studies looking at sleep problems in intellectual disability, the evidence suggests that the prevalence of these problems is alarmingly high (about 80 per cent even up to age 16) with sleeplessness difficulties of settling, nightwaking and early waking problems affecting about 50 per cent of children. These types of problems frequently co-exist.

Contrary to the commonly held belief that sleeplessness will be 'outgrown' a three-year follow-up study suggested that sleeplessness is persistent, with over half of the children with settling and nightwaking difficulties still having such problems. In addition, about a quarter of children had developed sleep problems which were not present three years previously.

SLEEP PROBLEMS ASSOCIATED WITH SPECIFIC SYNDROMES AND CONDITIONS

Increasingly patterns of sleep disturbance associated with particular syndromes or conditions associated with ID are being recognized. Current knowledge regarding the nature of the sleep patterns, likely aetiology and special considerations for assessment and treatment have recently been described in relation to specific syndromes and conditions (Stores and Wiggs, 2001). Readers are referred to this text for detailed information. Summary information concerning presenting sleep disorders and problems is provided in Table 11.2. Syndromes not listed in the table may still have associated sleep disturbance. Their omission from the list indicates that this has yet to be investigated and documented.

As well as sleep disorders and patterns which may be associated with particular ID syndromes, many of the medical and psychiatric conditions which occur with ID may predispose to sleep disturbance of various sorts. For example, in cerebral palsy, SDB, circadian rhythm disorders and sleeplessness have all been reported; in neuromuscular disease, reports of SDB and sleeplessness may occur and the latter may perhaps be mainly due to discomfort; with visual impairment, circadian rhythm disorders are common due to the effects of compromised light perception and possibly social or environmental cues; in autism, circadian rhythm disorders, sleeplessness and parasomnias may occur; SDB, PLMs and sleeplessness can occur in Attention Deficit Hyperactivity Disorder (ADHD). It has been suggested that for some children with ADHD, their daytime symptoms of attentional difficulties and hyperactive behaviour are *caused* by a primary sleep disorder; in depression, sleeplessness or hypersomnia can present; gastro-oesophageal reflux may be associated with a variety of sleep difficulties.

It should be particularly noted that epilepsy can be associated with sleep in a number of ways, depending on the type of epilepsy. Sleep may induce (or suppress) seizure activity, sleep loss may lead to increased seizure frequency, seizures can occur predominantly (or exclusively) during sleep. Also, there can be diagnostic confusion between epilepsy and sleep disorders,

Table 11.2 Sleep disorders/problems reported in the literature to be associated with specific syndromes

	SDB	Sleeplessness	CRD	PLMs	EDS	BD	PA disord	Sleep disturbance
Angelman syndrome			*			*		
Cornelia de Lange syndrome								*
Craniofacial syndromes	*							
Down syndrome	*	*						
Fragile X	*	*						
Joubert syndrome	*							
Lesch-nyhan syndrome		*		*		*		
Mucopolysaccharidosis	*	*				*		
Neurofibromatosis	*	*					*	
Phenylketonuria					*			
Prader-Willi syndrome								*
Rett syndrome			*			*		
Rubenstein-Taybi syndrome	*							

Syndrome	SDB	Sleeplessness	CRD	PLMs	EDS	BD	PA disord	Sleep disturbance
Smith-Lemli Opitz syndrome								*
Smith-Magenis syndrome	*	*						
Sotos syndrome								*
Tuberous sclerosis	*							
Williams syndrome	*		*	*	*			

Legend
SDB – sleep disordered breathing
Sleeplessness – problems with settling, nightwaking and/or early waking
CRD – circadian rhythm disorder
PLMs – periodic limb movements during sleep
EDS – excessive daytime sleepiness
BD – behavioural disturbance during sleep periods (including laughing, destructive behaviour and self-mutilation)
PA disord – partial arousal disorders
Sleep disturbance – unspecified sleep disturbance

particularly parasomnias involving disturbed behaviour at night or, less commonly, daytime sleepiness.

A further consideration is that medications for co-existing conditions may in themselves have a disruptive effect on sleep.

PREDISPOSING, PRECIPITATING AND MAINTAINING FACTORS

The reasons for high rates of disturbed sleep amongst children with an ID are likely to be due to a combination of physical and psycho-social factors. Some of the more important factors to consider are listed below.

Physiological/organic abnormalities

Atypical functioning of the structures and processes involved with the control of sleep and wake states may be associated with severe and extensive neurodevelopmental problems and related brain abnormalities or damage.

Medical conditions

These include craniofacial abnormalities, obesity, seizure disorders, muscle disease, and medication use for these and other conditions.

Sensory impairments

Sensory impairments, which are associated with sleep problems, are more common in children with ID. Sleep problems associated with visual impairment may be due to the effects of impaired light perception on melatonin production and reduced social and environmental cues for sleeping and waking. Sleep problems associated with hearing impairment include reduced social and environmental cues, in addition to the possible effects of tinnitus, and anxiety associated with hearing-aid removal at night.

Impaired learning

Teaching good sleep habits to an intellectually impaired child may be difficult. A link between the presence of communication difficulties and sleep problems in children with ID has been consistently noted.

Parental limit-setting

Out of compassion for their child and perhaps because of guilt feelings or safety concerns for the child, parental discipline may be compromised.

Parents may feel unable to impart discipline in the way that is usually needed to avoid bedtime problems and to avoid the child's overdependence on parents when settling to sleep or on waking during the night.

Emotional or behavioural disturbance

These sorts of problems, which are more common in children with ID, can impede the process of establishing good sleep habits. Associated parental difficulties may also contribute to sleep problems in children. These include parental demoralization, parental psychological problems and parent disharmony about managing their child's problems.

Mistaken beliefs

Parents of ID children, and some professionals involved with their care, may hold the mistaken belief that sleep problems are an inevitable part of the child's basic condition. Unless told otherwise, they may well not realize that with appropriate early advice it may be possible to prevent or minimize such problems, or to treat them effectively even when the sleep problem is severe or of long-standing and also despite the child's behaviour being severely disturbed (or 'challenging').

ASSESSMENT

The foremost aim of an assessment is to diagnose the underlying cause of the problem, i.e. the *sleep disorder*, and not to document the *sleep problem or complaint*. As mentioned already, this distinction is often not made but it is essential for adequate diagnosis and choice of treatment.

Many families of children with ID and sleep disorders do not seek help. Reasons for this appear to be wide-ranging but can include habituating to the difficulties if they are long-standing, viewing them as inevitable, or unawareness of the problem (the latter perhaps particularly likely with sleep-related breathing disorders). It is therefore important to screen routinely for the presence of sleeping difficulties with some simple questions in order to avoid the harmful effects of sleep disorders on the child and their family:

- Does the child have difficulty getting off to sleep or staying asleep?
- Is the child excessively sleepy or overactive during the day?
- Does the child have any disturbing episodes at night?

If there is a positive answer to any of these questions further assessment is required.

Sleep history

Information is usually primarily provided by parents but children themselves, siblings and teachers may also need to be consulted for a full account. Important aspects to be covered are:

- the precise nature of the current sleep complaint and its development;
- associated medical or other factors, including triggering factors or other patterns of occurrence;
- effects on the child and others;
- past and present treatments and their effectiveness (the details are important as treatment may have been inappropriate or inadequately carried out).

The child's 24-hour *sleep-wake schedule* should be described (see Table 11.3).

Table 11.3 Review of child's 24-hour sleep/wake pattern (which may be modified according to age/as appropriate)

Evening
What time is the child's last meal?
What activities typically take place between then and getting ready for bed?
Does the child take any sleep/other medicine?

Going to bed
Who gets the child ready for bed and how? Is it always the same person and done in the same way?
Is there a bedtime routine? If so, what is the sequence of events? Does it include a wind-down period?
What time does he go to bed?
Is he put to bed awake or asleep?
Where and how does he fall asleep (own bed, parent's bed, downstairs, being rocked, nursed or fed, with or without a parent present)?
Does he need a bottle, dummy or special object to fall asleep or want someone else to sleep with?
Does he express fears about going to bed?
Does he have his own room?
Is the bedroom conducive to sleep or is it a place for entertainment or other arousing experiences?
Does he have any unusual experiences when going off to sleep?
Exactly what happens if the child will not go to bed or does not go to sleep readily? Who deals with the problem and how consistently?

Night time
Does the child wake during the night? If so, when and how often? Does he get up in the night to go to the toilet or to have a drink? Is he able to return to sleep easily or does he need his parents or join them in their bed? If so, what precisely happens, who is involved and what is the result?
Is the child's sleep disturbed in other ways, e.g. restlessness, sleep talking, sleepwalking, banging head or rocking, teeth grinding, nightmares or terrified episodes, jerking or

convulsive movements or other episodes of disturbed behaviour? How often do these things occur, what time of night, how long do they last and does he seem awake at the time? What do the parents do?
Does the child snore or have any difficulty breathing when asleep?
Does he wet the bed?
What is the child's usual period of continuous sleep?

Waking
What time does the child wake up? For how long has he slept?
Does he wake up spontaneously or have to be woken? Is it very difficult to wake him up?
Does he look tired? Is he irritable and in a bad mood?
Does he have any unusual experiences and how does he feel between waking up and getting out of bed?

Daytime
Is the child drowsy or does he sleep during the day? If he sleeps, can he resist doing so and does he fall asleep when engaged in activities?
What is the number, duration and timing of naps?
Do his muscles become weak when he laughs or is upset or surprised?
Does he find it difficult to concentrate?
Has his performance at school deteriorated?
Is he overactive, irritable or depressed?
Are there any unusual episodes during the day?
What is the total time spent asleep each 24 hours?

Note: Reproduced from G. Stores and L. Wiggs (eds) (2001) *Sleep Disturbance in Children and Adolescents with Disorders of Development: Its Significance and Management*. London: MacKeith Press, with kind permission from the publishers.

It is important to explore possible inconsistencies from night to night, or from weekday to weekend or during holiday periods which can be associated with circadian rhythm disorders. Events of particular diagnostic significance may come to light (e.g. chronic noisy breathing). The child's *sleep rhythm* (timing and duration of overnight sleep and daytime naps) and *overall amount of sleep* (including naps) each 24 hours should be established. The child's *sleep onset associations* both at sleep onset in the evening and during nightwakes is often of significance. Although a child may settle readily in the evening is this because certain factors (e.g. parents' presence) facilitate sleep and the absence of these factors during the night are fuelling nightwaking episodes? *Parental handling* during any 'problematic' episodes should be described in detail. Enquiries about *sleep hygiene* should also be made, i.e. whether the sleeping environment and the child's general activities are conducive to sleep (see Table 11.4).

As part of the history-taking process, a review of the child's developmental, medical and psychiatric history should be made. Special attention should be paid to conditions which might affect sleep or predispose to sleep disorders (e.g. obesity, craniofacial abnormalities, depression, etc.). If the child's underlying syndrome has been identified, the presenting sleep complaint should be considered in the context of what is known about the

Table 11.4 Principles of sleep hygiene

Sleeping environment should be conducive to sleep
Familiar setting (child should always go to sleep in the same place)
Comfortable bed
Correct temperature (not too cold or hot)
Darkened, quiet room (a nightlight is fine if children are scared of the dark; blackout-material blinds can help prevent unwanted sunlight in evening or morning)
Non-stimulating (store toys out of sight/turn off stimulating mobiles/light sources)
No negative associations (don't use the child's room for punishment)

Encourage
Bedtime routines (the same every night: 20–30 minutes of calm activities with a definite end-point)
Consistent bedtime and waking up times (weekdays, weekends, holidays)
Consistent daytime timing of all meals
Thinking about problems and plans before going to bed
Falling asleep without parents (children)
Regular daily exercise, exposure to sunlight (especially in the morning), and general fitness
Positively reinforce good sleep behaviour with praise/rewards

Avoid
Overexcitement near bedtime (avoid boisterous play and mentally stimulating activities such as computer games)
Late evening exercise
Caffeine-containing drinks late in the day (that includes cola and most chocolate drinks)
Large meals late at night (a light snack is good if it prevents hunger)
Excessive or late napping during the day
Too much time awake in bed (especially if distressed)

sleep patterns of such children. Family history should also be reviewed as the genetic component of some sleep disorders is prominent (e.g. arousal disorders, narcolepsy).

Sleep questionnaires

Ideally, these clinical enquiries should be supplemented by means of a general screening *sleep-wake questionnaire* (e.g. Bruni, Ottavanio, Guidetti, Romoli *et al.*, 1996; Owens, Spirito and McGuinn 2000) which may reveal further aspects of importance. There are also questionnaires directed at specific aspects of sleep if they are thought likely to be particularly relevant (e.g. sleep disordered breathing (Chervin, Hedger, Dillon and Pituch, 2000)). Sleepiness is typically screened for by using The Epworth Sleepiness Scale (ESS) (Johns, 1991), a well-established brief measure of the tendency to fall asleep in various everyday situations. The adult form can be adapted for use with children. However, its validity and reliability with paediatric populations remains unknown. Sleepiness in young people does not usually manifest itself as lethargy and a tendency to fall asleep. Indeed, quite the reverse, and over-active daytime behaviour may be a significant indication that the child's sleep quantity or quality is impaired. References for a selection of assessment questionnaires are provided at the end of the chapter.

Sleep diaries

For the assessment of most sleep disorders a *sleep diary* kept over at least a two-week period is often very revealing compared with retrospective general impressions given by parents. Diaries can indicate aspects of (a) timing (e.g. bed, sleep, wake, episodes during sleep), (b) frequency of problems, (c) behaviour (of parents and child) and (d) patterns (e.g. connections between sleep and daytime activities). They are also useful as a general indication of motivation on the part of those keeping the diary and as a method of monitoring treatment compliance and efficacy. Typical information that might be gathered is shown in Figure 11.2, although of course diaries can be tailored to enquire about any pertinent aspects.

For many of the most common sleep disorders, information gathered from a detailed history, questionnaire and diary can be sufficient to guide management decisions or suggest appropriate referral or further investigations that are required. Further investigations of sleep are likely to include one or more of the following 'objective' assessment procedures: actigraphy, video and PSG.

Actigraphy

Actigraphy is a method of objectively assessing sleep/wake patterns by means of a watch-like movement sensor worn (most typically) on the wrist. Validated scoring algorithms allow one to detect periods of sleep and wake although more detailed staging of sleep is not possible. It is useful for obtaining objective data on children who are unable to tolerate PSG or, in other circumstances, where parents are unable to provide reliable information by means of a diary. A particular advantage of this technique compared to PSG is that recordings can be made over an extended period (e.g. up to a month or so at a time). Basic sleep-wake patterns (i.e. timing, continuity, duration) are the main variables it generates although it has also been validated for the detection of period limb movements in sleep (PLMs). A further advantage of this technique, especially for children with ID, is that it can be used as an outpatient procedure. As such, where objective information about basic sleep-wake patterns is required, it may be the assessment method of choice.

Date	Thursday March 22nd
*Time woke/woken?*_____	Woken by Mum at 7.30am
Time got up?	Dragged out of bed at 7.30am
Any problems on waking? Please describe	She was very tired and difficult to wake. Didn't want to get out of bed.
Did your child seem tired or actually sleep at any time today? When, for how long and what was he/she doing at the time?	She had a sleep in the taxi on the way home from school (3.30 until 4.00pm). Teacher reported that she seemed sleepy at school until mid-morning.
What did your child do in the hour before bed?	Watched TV, had a bath, changed into nightwear, had a story read to her.
Time to bed?	7.15pm
Time to sleep?	8.30pm
Any difficulty going to bed/falling asleep? Why (if known)? What did you do, what did your child do and how did they eventually fall asleep?	Got out of bed as soon as we said goodnight and came downstairs asking for a drink. Gave her a drink and put her back into bed. Came downstairs again at 7.45pm saying she was scared. Dad took her back to bed and stayed with her (lying on her bed) until she fell asleep at 8.30pm
Time and length of any wakes during the night? Why did your child wake (if known)? What did you do, what did your child do and how did he/she eventually fall asleep?	2.30am woke and came into parents' room saying she was scared. She got into our bed and spent the rest of the night there. Fell asleep within about 10 minutes.
Please describe anything else that happened during sleep/the night (snoring, nightmares etc.)	She was snoring very noisily most of the night.
Time of breakfast, lunch and dinner	Breakfast - 7.45am; Lunch - 12.30pm; Tea – 5.30pm.
Anything else unusual/significant, day or night?	She wasn't very well today. I think she may be getting a cold.

Figure 11.2 An example sleep diary extract.

Video

Audiovisual recordings, including amateur home recordings made with the family's own video equipment, can be a useful assessment tool. Video has been used to score sleep-wake patterns and snoring reliably but perhaps its greatest application is in providing information about night-time 'episodes' which can otherwise only be described 'second-hand'. Of importance is that, diagnostically, the nature of onset of nocturnal episodes (e.g. sudden/gradual, vocalizations, level of awareness, stereotypic posturing, etc.) can be significant and thus ensuring that the whole episode (and not just part of it) are captured on tape should be emphasized.

Polysomnography (PSG)

As already described, standard PSG involves recording EEG, EOG and EMG from which basic measures of NREM sleep, REM sleep and sleep continuity can be made. Additional parameters can also be included (e.g. respiratory measures (for sleep-related breathing problems), EEG channels (for the detection of epilepsy), or anterior tibialis EMG recording for assessment of PLMs. PSG is typically performed in an inpatient setting and for two nights, data from the first night having to be discarded since there are significant first-night effects of the procedure itself. Even after a night of adaptation, a child's sleep in a laboratory setting is unlikely to be truly representative in all respects. Home PSG is possible using portable systems and may overcome some of these issues although the potential for recording failure may be increased, especially in ID populations, where individuals may be less likely to tolerate the equipment throughout the full recording period.

In the UK and Ireland, clinical services able to offer PSG are limited and for this and other reasons PSG should not be viewed as essential for the accurate diagnosis of most sleep disorders. The main indications for PSG are the differential diagnosis of parasomnias (where careful clinical enquiry has not been helpful) and the investigation of excessive daytime sleepiness. For excessive daytime sleepiness, PSG is especially indicated where other investigations suggest that sleep quantity and continuity appear normal. PSG evaluation of detailed sleep structure and arousals should be conducted to investigate these subtle aspects of sleep quality. PSG may be used for the objective assessment of daytime sleepiness by means of the 'gold standard' Multiple Sleep Latency Test (MSLT). The MSLT measures the time the individual takes to fall asleep during five opportunities (at two-hourly intervals) to do so in standardized conditions during the day. However, the validity of this procedure, for children, has been questioned. Finally, PSG can serve as an objective check on the accuracy of a reported sleep complaint or to establish response to treatment.

Other special investigations

Depending on the outcome of other enquiries, further investigations may be appropriate. These include haematological, biochemical or endocrine tests, urinalysis, drug toxicity screening, ENT evaluation, and more detailed EEG studies for further consideration of epilepsy.

TREATMENT OF SLEEP DISORDERS

There are a wide variety of treatments from which to choose depending on the nature of the sleep disorder (see Table 11.5.) and careful assessment of the child, their family and particular circumstances. An individualized approach may be particularly appropriate for children with ID, all of whom have different abilities and needs. The same types of treatments for sleep disorders that are used with children from the general population are increasingly being found to be of use for children with ID. The presence of ID and co-existing problems, including physical conditions and severe behaviour problems, should not be viewed as inevitable obstacles to successful resolution of sleep problems.

With over eighty different sleep disorders listed in the International Classification it is not possible to provide detailed information about intervention strategies for all sleep disorders in a brief chapter. Rather, emphasis will be placed on the most common sleep disorders of childhood and highlighting those management approaches, applicable to psychologists, for which there is evidence of their efficacy (ideally in ID populations, although in the absence of such research the literature relating to typically developing children will be drawn upon). It should also be emphasized that some sleep disorders, particularly many of the common sleeplessness problems, could perhaps be discouraged from developing in the first place, or becoming long-standing,

Table 11.5 Overview of treatment approaches for management of sleep disorders

- Preliminary steps
    - Reassurance/explanation
    - Sleep hygiene
    - Safety measures
    - (Treatment of any underlying medical/psychiatric condition)
- Psychological
    - Behavioural
    - Cognitive
- Chronotherapy (altering sleep timing)
- Medication
    - Hypnotics
    - Stimulants
    - Melatonin
    - Others
- Physical measures
    - Nasal CPAP/BiPAP
    - Light therapy
- Surgery
    - e.g. Tonsillectomy/adenoidectomy

if a preventive approach was adopted and parents were routinely advised about principles of good sleep hygiene (see Table 11.4 above) and behavioural methods for preventing undesirable sleep patterns from becoming established.

A basic preliminary aim of intervention is likely to be *explanation and education*. Recognizing that the problem is not unique by explaining the nature and cause of the sleep disorder can be comforting. Sometimes, this stage might involve *adjusting expectations* if they are unrealistic. As well as the timing of sleep, *reassurance* about the benign nature, common occurrence or developmental occurrence of some sleep disorders may be appropriate.

Another practical first step may be to take *precautionary safety measures* to ensure that no one comes to any harm during the sleep period (e.g. fitting locks to windows, removing objects from the bedroom that could be dangerous, attaching furniture to the walls so that they can't be pulled over, etc.). This may be particularly appropriate for children with arousal disorders such as sleepwalking or sleep terrors (where self-injury can be severe), and for children with sleeplessness if they are agitated during the wakeful period.

An important accompaniment to most treatments is explanation of basic *sleep hygiene* principles (practices which help promote good sleep), as outlined in Table 11.4 above. Identification, and modification, of any practices which may be contributing to the sleep disorder should be a priority before embarking upon other specific interventions and may sometimes be effective in isolation.

INTERVENTIONS FOR SLEEPLESSNESS

Behavioural treatments for sleeplessness are perhaps the most researched intervention approach for sleep difficulties in people with ID and there is general support for the efficacy of all the approaches described below, based upon controlled studies, although more research is needed to evaluate the relative (and combined) efficacy of different approaches with particular groups of children. Of note is that there is also some evidence that these techniques can be used successfully for dealing with the sleeplessness problems of children with ID when provided in a simple booklet form. This, potentially, could greatly increase the number of families who could access the information.

Settling and nightwaking problems commonly co-exist and the same types of treatments for changing child behaviour can be used for both these problems. Quite often, successful treatment of settling difficulties will lead to an improvement or resolution of nightwaking problems. If a child has learnt to settle off to sleep appropriately, and in their own bed, without parents or the TV or other supports, they will be able to resettle themselves when they wake in the night. It may therefore be recommended that parents start by tackling settling difficulties and later, if required, implement a similar strategy for re-settling the child after any nightwakes. However, if preferred, parents can deal with the two problems contemporaneously.

In addition to adhering to sleep hygiene principles, particular behaviour strategies may be effective in managing sleeplessness. These include stimulus control, extinction procedures, positive reinforcement and chronotherapy.

Stimulus control

Stimulus control relies on the ability of an antecedent stimulus to act as a signal for the performance of a specific behaviour. The bedtime routine should be the antecedent stimulus; many parents find the use of a key-phrase, such as 'Goodnight it's time for sleep now' as a definite end-point to the routine, helpful for both reminding children what's expected for them and as a means of attempting to resettle the child, if necessary, later in the evening or during the night. The sequence of activities in the bedtime routine can also be presented visually to the child to help them learn the routine and that sleep will follow (e.g. pictures of a bath, pyjamas, toothbrush, book, light switched off and child asleep in bed). The timing of the bedtime routine is as important as its content in terms of its efficacy as a means of stimulus control training. Sleep scheduling should be used so that appropriate and consistently timed sleep periods are aimed for. For children with bedtime resistance this may be achieved by setting a bedtime that coincides with (or is even a little later than) the child's current sleep onset time (this may be very different from the desired sleep onset time!). Start the routine 20–30 minutes before this late bedtime. This will ensure that the child is sleepy when put to bed (encouraging the child to associate the end of the bedtime routine with sleep onset) and eliminate or reduce the time period available for bedtime struggles and thus hopefully the tension or anger surrounding bedtime. Once the child is falling asleep rapidly, 'bedtime fading' can be implemented. This involves gradually bringing the child's bedtime (and bedtime routine) forward in 15-minute increments every few nights until the desired bedtime is reached. If at any point the period between going to bed and going to sleep becomes prolonged one can revert to a later bedtime for a few more nights. Bedtime fading has been used successfully with a 'response cost' element (e.g. removing a pre-specified amount of a valued item following undesired behaviour). In this context it has meant removing the child from bed if not asleep within about 20 minutes of being put to bed.

Stimulus control: case example

Tom, an 8-year-old with severe intellectual disabilities, had a long-standing difficulty settling to sleep at night. His parents would try and start to get him ready for bed about 8pm, although if he didn't look tired they might leave it until later. Once in his pyjamas he would usually come downstairs and watch a video, or play, and they would try taking him upstairs to brush his teeth and putting him up to bed when he began to look sleepy. Once in bed they would leave the room, which he accepted, but he usually got out of bed and either came downstairs again or played in his room. If he got too noisy in his bedroom they would bring him downstairs again to try and prevent him from waking his sleeping sister. Typically he would fall asleep anywhere between 10.30pm and midnight, sometimes in his bedroom and sometimes downstairs. He woke spontaneously in the morning although his parents reported that he often seemed sleepy during the daytime.

Treatment involved three components. The first was establishing an appropriate bedtime routine – all the component parts were already there, they just needed to be linked together into a chain of behaviour. The routine involved telling him it was bedtime, going upstairs for a bath, changing into pyjamas and nappy, brushing his teeth and going into his bedroom where his parents looked at a book with him. Once the book was finished they said 'goodnight', turned out the light and left the room. Second, sleep scheduling was used to try and teach Tom to associate the wind-down routine with falling asleep. His current bedtime of 8pm was too far away in time from his actual 'falling asleep time'. The information in the sleep diary his parents completed showed that he fell asleep, on average, about 11pm. Therefore, the bedtime routine was started about 10.30pm, allowing them 30 minutes to perform the routine in an attempt to make his 'bedtime' coincide with his 'sleep time'. Before 10.30pm Tom was encouraged to stay downstairs, to help him see a clear difference between 'daytime' and 'night-time' behaviours, although exciting and stimulating activities after about 9.30pm were discouraged. Starting the bedtime routine later and setting a later bedtime instantly made the whole family's evenings less fraught since the evening battles to try and get him into bed and/or be quiet were eliminated. Also, setting a firm bedtime relieved Tom's parents of the guesswork involved as to when might be a good bedtime for him on that particular night. Because Tom was tired when put to bed he fell asleep rapidly. His parents were told to wake him every morning (including weekends) at the time he would usually have to get up to attend school (7.30am). After a week or so of doing this every night his parents began to introduce the third component of treatment – bedtime fading. Now that Tom associated the routine with falling asleep it was possible gradually to bring his bedtime forward so they started the routine at 10.15pm (bedtime 10.45pm), then 10pm (bedtime 10.30pm), etc., changing the bedtime every three or four days once he had adjusted to the new time and was settling quickly. They continued to wake him at 7.30am every morning. Three attempts to change from starting the routine at 8.15pm (bedtime 8.45pm) to 8pm (bedtime 8.30pm) resulted in his having trouble getting to sleep quickly so they reverted to the 8.45pm bedtime and stuck to this every night from then on.

Tom's parents also reported that having a firmly established bedtime routine made it much easier when his grandparents babysat and also when they went on holiday as he adjusted to these changes more easily.

Extinction techniques

Extinction involves withholding reinforcement of an unwanted behaviour. In treating sleep disorders, extinction or modifications of it, such as the removal of reinforcement gradually, in discrete steps may be used to treat sleeplessness. In the context of sleeplessness, the reinforcing stimulus must first be identified. Usually it is parental presence or attention (even parental anger can be reinforcing) or achieving a particular set of circumstances (e.g. watching television, playing with toys or getting into parental bed). Whatever the technique used, an important rule for parents is that after they have settled the child to sleep during any dealings with the child they should be as 'unrewarding' and boring as possible. In practice this means no conversation, no cuddles, no acceding to the child's requests and, ideally, no eye contact.

Extinction techniques involve removing the stimulus (e.g. once the child is put in bed parents are to ignore the child, other than to return the child to the bedroom if they come out). This 'cold turkey' approach has been shown to be effective, and more rapidly so than graduated approaches, but may not be practical for children who may injure themselves (intentionally or otherwise) if not attended to during wakeful periods, for example, if a child has a co-existing physical condition (such as epilepsy, breathing disorder or difficulty changing his position in bed) which may require his parents' attention during the night or if the child's behaviour during wakeful periods is potentially self-injurious. Understandably, parents find extinction techniques unacceptable in these circumstances and more gradual treatment approaches are preferable. Extinction may also not be viewed as psychologically acceptable to the families and can be difficult to implement consistently if parents have any doubts about their ability to ignore for an extended time period. Parents can be reassured, however, that there is no evidence of long-term psychological distress associated with the use of this technique. Indeed, psychological benefits are more likely if the procedure eliminates the sleep problem. When using this technique parents need to be warned about a likely post-extinction burst (e.g. the problem becoming more severe for a few nights before any improvements are seen) so that they persist with the treatment through this period. They also need to know that extinction, if performed incorrectly, may exacerbate a problem as illustrated in the case example below.

Extinction: case example

Phoebe had never settled well as a baby and toddler and in order to ensure that they got some sleep her parents had got into the habit of taking her into their bed when she woke in the night. Over time, this had become a well-established pattern so that now, aged 12, whilst she settled off to sleep in her own bed every night, she would always come into her parents' bed at some point during the night and they would wake to find her there in the morning. As she got bigger this was becoming increasingly uncomfortable and she showed no signs of stopping this habit, as they had hoped she would as she got older! Phoebe's parents decided to use an extinction technique and as soon as she came out of her bed were to take her back to her own bed. Since they often were not aware of her actually entering their bed during the night, the first thing they did was to attach a large string of jangly bells to her bedroom door so that these would make a noise when she opened the door and alert them to the fact that she was up. As soon as they heard the bells and awoke they took her straight back to her own bedroom, told her to go to sleep and left the room. On the first night she came straight out again and attempted to get into their bedroom. They repeated taking her back and had to do so another nine times before finally, on her tenth attempt that night, they were so exhausted they could take no more and let her come into their bed, effectively teaching her that persistence pays! A similar pattern continued for the next few nights and the problem showed no sign of reducing. Telephone discussion and support was vital to detect the reason why the treatment was not resulting in any improvements and to encourage them that things were likely to get worse before they got better. Having stressed the need to return her to her bed every time she came into their room, that night they had to take her back fifteen times and a further three times when she made a second attempt later in the night. Over the next few nights she gradually came in less and less until on the tenth night she came in once and they were able simply to tell her to return to her bed and she took herself back to her own bed. On the eleventh night she did not come out of her room and spent the whole night in her own bed. This pattern has continued since.

Graduated extinction

Techniques which gradually reduce reinforcement of waking behaviour may be the more acceptable solution for many families of children with ID. Specific techniques include checking and graduated withdrawal.

Checking

With checking, the child is placed in bed and the parents (i.e. reinforcement) remove themselves from the room for a pre-agreed time interval (this can be as small as the parents feel able to tolerate, e.g. anything from 1 minute to start with but ideally perhaps 5 minutes). At the end of that time period, if the child is still upset the parent should re-enter the room, check that the child

Day	1	2	3	4	5	6
First check	5	10	15	20	25	30
Second check	10	15	20	25	30	35
Third check	15	20	25	30	35	40
Subsequent checks	15	20	25	30	35	40

Figure 11.3 Example of timings (in minutes) used for a checking procedure.

Note: These times can be changed according to parents' preferences although the general pattern of gradual increase should remain whatever the absolute times involved.

is OK, repeat the key end-phase of the bedtime routine and leave the room again, not returning until the next agreed time check. Figure 11.3 provides an example of a pattern of time checks. The gradually increasing time between checks serves to teach the child that increasingly greater effort is required for very little reward.

Graduated withdrawal

Graduated withdrawal may be more suitable for parents who would find it difficult to tolerate even a short duration of distress in their child, either for emotional reasons or more practical ones (e.g. the crying disturbing siblings, etc.). Here, parents gradually increase the physical distance between themselves and their child. The rate of change can be as small or as large as the parents feel comfortable with. For example, for children who will not settle without the presence of a parent in the bed one might start by lying in the bed but not touching the child, then sitting on the bed not touching the child, then sitting beside the bed on a chair, then moving the chair a little away from the bed and continuing to move it away until one reaches the door, then placing the chair outside the door, etc. If parents have tended to sleep all night in the child's room they can use a small mattress rather than a chair. These changes can be made over many days or weeks, not moving onto the next step until the child has happily accepted the previous stage. The benefit of such a technique is that it minimizes the upset for the child (and possibly parents) but the potential drawback is that it can take a long time (maybe months) to achieve success and parents will therefore need a lot of ongoing support to sustain their motivation and to ensure that they don't get 'stuck' at a particular stage. Telephone support has proved sufficient in many studies.

Graduated withdrawal: case example

Freddy's parents came to the clinic because of his frequent nightwaking. He would wake, be upset and only resettle to sleep if his parents stayed in his bed until he fell asleep. There was nothing about the description of the wakes, nor his behaviour during the wakes, to indicate that they were anything other than a common childhood-nightwaking problem. Further support for this idea was that in the course of reviewing his sleep-wake pattern his parents told us that when Freddy fell asleep in the evening it was always on the sofa downstairs with them and, once he had fallen asleep, they later carried him to his own bed still asleep. It was explained to them that Freddy's nightwakes were likely due to the fact that he was falling asleep with one set of circumstances (downstairs on the sofa with his parents, noise of TV, light on, etc.) and then waking in the night – the brief waking being itself normal – to find another set of circumstances (upstairs in a bed, alone, in a quiet, dark, room, etc.) and that this change of circumstances was likely anxiety-producing for him, or at the least sufficiently strange to induce a full awakening. If he could be taught to settle himself to sleep in the evening, alone and in his own bed he would be more likely to be able to do this when he woke during the night. His parents already had a bedtime routine – it just ended with him in the wrong setting! So, to begin with they transferred the routine upstairs, ending it with him being put in his own bed but they stayed with him, lying down beside him on his bed, as they would have been on the sofa downstairs. Freddy readily accepted this change and adjusted to the new venue for his bedtime routine. After a week or so his parents began gradually to reduce the physical contact they had with him when settling to sleep. For the first few nights they sat on his bed. Then, when he had accepted this, they put a chair beside his bed and sat on that. Every three or four nights they moved the chair a little further away from his bed towards the door. During this time, when Freddy woke in the night they resettled him in the same way as they had settled him in the evening. For example, if they'd settled him to sleep in the evening on a chair a metre from his bed, then when he woke in the night they reassured him, told him it was time for sleep then sat down on the chair a metre from his bed. After several weeks Freddy's parents were able to move the chair out of his bedroom and place it in the hallway, out of his sight. At this stage Freddy's dependence on their presence as a means of getting to sleep was almost non-existent. They were able to put him to bed, leave the room and go downstairs and he stopped waking in the night (or at least if he did wake he was able to soothe himself back to sleep without alerting them).

Positive reinforcement

Positive reinforcement may be used in conjunction with extinction techniques for treating sleeplessness. Positive reinforcement may take the form of praise but can also be the use of sticker charts, certain foods or anything else that the child might find rewarding. Some key features of the successful use of positive reinforcement include:

- Making sure that the reward is actually rewarding for the child.
- Rewarding as soon as possible after the behaviour, for example first thing in the morning.
- Starting with easily achievable rewards so that the child understands the concept of a behaviour leading to a reward (behaviours necessary to achieve a reward can be gradually changed).
- Giving larger rewards such as a trip out, purchase of a particular desired toy for sustained positive behaviour; for example, if the child achieves a set number of stickers (over whatever time period) they can have a larger reward. For children with ID this can be conveyed by placing a picture of the larger reward on the sticker chart.

Positive reinforcement: case example

John, with severe ID and autism, took part in one of our research projects. He went to sleep without a problem and didn't wake in the night. However, he usually woke up about 4.30am and was fully alert and ready to start his day! Once awake, his parents didn't like to leave him 'up' whilst they slept, fearful that he might injure himself or do something dangerous. Equally, they didn't want his morning noisiness to wake his brother so, upon hearing him wake, his mother would get up with him and together they would go downstairs and he would watch videos or play with toys whilst she lay on the sofa, attempting to stay awake. It was felt that such behaviour might well be reinforcing his early waking because he enjoyed coming down and having his choice of the videos and his mother's sole attention! To treat this, his parents waited until the school holidays when they were less worried about his brother's sleep being disturbed as a result of the treatment. They introduced a picture hung in his room showing a moon on one side and a sun on the other (visual reminders of the difference between day and night). Once he got into bed they turned it to show the moon and when he woke in the morning, his mother went in, as usual, and turned the picture around to show the sun, to tell him that it was time to get up. Once he had learnt this, his mother began to introduce a small delay (two minutes to start with) between hearing him wake and going in to turn the picture to show the sun. This helped to put her in control of when 'the day' had begun. If he had stayed in bed until she came in he earned a sticker of a train (his particular passion!) for his sticker chart. After he had earned a few stickers in this way he only got a sticker if he'd stayed in bed *and* been quiet. Over the ensuing weeks she gradually extended the amount of time that he had to stay in bed to 5 minutes, then 10, then 15, then 20, etc. If, on any morning, he failed to earn a sticker he still had to wait that time period before they got up to come downstairs to watch a video. When he had earned five stickers he was awarded a special, pre-agreed 'treat'; a picture of the treat he was working towards was stuck on his sticker chart as a visual reminder. John found the reward chart very motivating and over the following weeks he stopped associating 'waking up' with 'getting up to play with his toys' and quite often, whilst lying there quietly trying to earn a sticker, he would return to sleep, not waking again until sometime after 6.30am, a time which his family found much more manageable.

Practice guidelines for behavioural treatment of sleep problems

When implementing any behavioural approach, preparing for the intervention is an important phase. This includes being sure of the details of the approach which will be used and how any likely problems will be overcome and dealt with. It also involves choosing a time that is suitable when no one in the family is under any particular stress and there are no imminent changes such as going on holiday, or the child changing school. If appropriate, neighbours may be warned about the possibility of increased noise for a while.

The consistency with which the programme is implemented influences how effective the programme will be. If the programme is implemented consistently, this makes it easier for the child to learn any new behaviours. In this context consistency is required in both a night-to-night basis and also in the behaviour of the various family members. It can be helpful to have a clear, concise written 'plan' of what to do that can be followed by anyone involved with the child's night-time behaviour, including parents, respite carers, grandparents, etc.

If the child becomes ill the behavioural intervention should be temporarily suspended and can be re-implemented, with little lost, once the child is well again.

In addition to these general principles there are, however, special considerations for certain aspects of behavioural management in children with ID. As mentioned earlier, extinction techniques, which involve 'ignoring' the child, may not be appropriate in certain circumstances.

A further consideration is that research suggests that most parents of children with ID and a sleep problem will have had little positive experience of successful treatment for the sleep problem. Clinicians need to be sensitive to the possibility that parents may doubt the likely efficacy of a further course of treatment. Where possible, clinicians should be optimistic, identify why any previous attempts at behavioural intervention were unsuccessful and explain this to parents. It should also be stressed to parents that sometimes what was unsuccessful at one time period may be highly successful at a later date for a variety of reasons. For example, the child's understanding may have increased; the family may be in a different set of environmental and psychological circumstances; or the cause of presenting sleep problem may have changed.

One aspect of management that may be easier with children with an ID than for typically developing children is the practical support from the child's school and teachers. The exchange of information about the child's behaviour, sleepiness, and nap schedules between parents and teachers of children with ID is usually frequent and more complete than for other children. Daily diaries, notebooks or charts are often standard. Further, teachers at special schools are often particularly familiar with behavioural approaches and willing to reinforce any home-based interventions in any way they can. The use of morning 'reward' ink stamps on the child's hand or stickers stuck on their clothes, that can be seen and commented upon by teachers, can be used successfully to increase reinforcement.

Chronotherapy

Chronotherapeutic treatments for circadian rhythm disorders involve gradually altering sleep times. Treatment for delayed sleep phase syndrome (DSPS) begins by letting the individual sleep (and wake) at their desired times for a few days. One then begins to wake them up about 15 minutes earlier every day, whilst keeping their bedtime the same (effectively restricting the amount of sleep that they get each night so that they become increasingly likely to feel sleepy even before bedtime). Once the desired wake-up time has been reached one begins bringing their bedtime forward in 15-minute increments each day until the desired bedtime, that enables the individual to fit in their sleep needs, is reached. This approach is outlined in the case example below.

If the phase delay (i.e. the difference between the actual sleep onset and desired sleep onset) is more than three hours it may be easier to successively delay bedtimes and wake-up times around the clock. This again involves starting by letting the individual sleep and wake at their desired sleep times and then to delay bedtime (and wake-up time) by two to three hours every night, continuing until the desired sleep phase is reached. An example of shifting sleep times in this way is shown in Figure 11.4.

Advanced sleep phase syndrome (ASPS) is treated similarly (sleep times are gradually delayed) although the increment of the shift will be smaller (perhaps half an hour each night) and strategies for keeping the child awake or engaged during the evening period to prevent them falling asleep too early need to be planned in advance with the family to increase the likelihood of success.

	Bedtime	Waketime
Baseline	3.30am	1.30pm
Treatment night one	6.30am	4.30pm
Treatment night two	9.30am	7.30pm
Treatment night three	12.30pm	10.30pm
Treatment night four	3.30pm	1.30am
Treatment night five	6.30pm	4.30am
Desired sleep phase	9.00pm	7.00am

Figure 11.4 Round-the-clock time schedule for treating severe delayed sleep phase syndrome.

Chronotherapy: case example

Florence was a 15-year-old with mild ID of indeterminate origin. Her mother and her teachers were worried about her inability to get up to attend school and her mother was being threatened with legal action if she continued to fail to get Florence to attend school. She often only made it into school after lunchtime because her parents frequently could not wake her, despite very vigorous attempts. Although she went to bed without any resistance, about 9.45pm, it was often not until 1am that she actually fell asleep. In between, she lay in bed and was no trouble to anyone. At weekends her parents let her sleep in, in order that she should make up some of the sleep that she had lost during the week and she tended to wake spontaneously about 11am. Florence's sleep pattern was a classic example of the delayed sleep phase syndrome. Just getting a diagnosis significantly helped the family (and reassured the school). She was treated by initially letting her sleep at her 'natural' sleep times (10 hours in total from about 1am to 11am, based upon the sleep diary her parents kept) and not letting her go to bed until 1am. Then over two weeks, every day she was woken about 15 minutes earlier (10.45am, then 10.30am, 10.15am, 10am, 9.45am, 9.30am, 9.15am, 9am, 8.45am, 8.30am, 8.15am, 8am, 7.45am, 7.30am), whilst still going to bed at 1am. Because she was effectively being increasingly sleep deprived she became progressively more sleepy during the day (and evening) over this period. Once the desired wake-up time of 7.30am was reached, this wake-up time was adhered to every day and her bedtime was gradually brought forward in similar 15 minute increments until a bedtime which allowed her to meet her sleep requirement of 10 hours was reached (12.45am, 12.30am, 12.15am, 12midnight, 11.45pm, 11.30pm, 11.15pm, 11pm, 10.45, 10.30, 10.15, 10pm, 9.45pm). Once this bedtime was reached it was firmly adhered to every night, as were her mealtimes and wake-up time. On the occasion of Florence having a late night her parents tried to prevent the problem from escalating by ensuring that they woke her at 7.30am the next morning anyway and didn't allow 'catch-up' sleeps.

Chronotherapy: practice guidelines

Common factors for all these approaches are that:

- they require considerable motivation on the part of the parents (and child where appropriate) both to implement the treatment and to ensure that any benefits are maintained. Any purpose that the circadian rhythm disorder served (e.g. inability to get up in the morning due to the phase delay enabled the child to avoid school in the mornings) needs to be addressed as part of the treatment;
- sleep habits and hygiene will need to be reviewed and possibly altered as part of treatment;
- when sleep times are being moved so too should the timing of other salient daytime zeitgebers (mealtimes, time of bedtime routine, timing of periods of activity);
- decisions about how quickly to alter sleep times (daily or every few days) and the magnitude of that time change (how many minutes to shift by) should be determined by practical considerations and personal preference (within reason);
- once the desired sleep schedule is achieved, the schedule (sleep and wake times and mealtimes) must be maintained consistently (every day, including weekends and holidays). In time, it may be possible to relax this rule but even then, altering sleep times by more than an hour are discouraged. The maintenance phase may be difficult to sustain and families need to be highly motivated to succeed;
- although the active treatment phases of chronotherapy are generally quite short, the treatment can be very disruptive (especially if going 'around the clock' to treat DSPS) and thus should be undertaken at a time which suits the whole family;
- exposure to appropriately timed bright light can help to re-set the sleep-wake rhythm. In patients with DSPS, exposure should be in the morning and bright light should be avoided in the afternoon and evening. Patients with ASPS should avoid light in the morning and get exposure in the afternoon and evening. Simple strategies such as spending time outside in the morning, being in sunny rooms of the house when getting up and eating breakfast, walking to school rather than going in the car, etc. may all be helpful but exposure to high lux levels via commercially available lightboxes may be indicated in more difficult cases. Minimizing light levels at certain times can be achieved simply by wearing sunglasses.

Pharmacological approaches

Hypnotics and melatonin are widely used for sleeplessness in children with ID and so deserve mention here.

Hypnotic-sedatives

In general, there is still undue reliance on hypnotic medication (mainly anti-histamines) for sleeplessness despite the evidence that it is rarely helpful, especially long term. Also, improvements are clinically slight and can be associated with unwanted side-effects including withdrawal problems, hangover-daytime sleepiness and the paradoxical effect of over-arousal. Studies of the efficacy of hypnotic medication in people with ID are lacking. Pharmacological intervention of this sort, if helpful, may have a role as a short-term crisis treatment in order to facilitate a few restful nights for carers before embarking upon more suitable treatments but should not be viewed as a long-term solution.

Melatonin

Endogenous melatonin is a hormone secreted mainly by the pineal gland in response to darkness and suppressed by light. It acts on the suprachiasmatic nucleus which influences circadian rhythms. As such, exogenous melatonin has been used in the treatment of sleep disorders (notably jet-lag) typically, being administered about 30 minutes before desired sleep-onset. Slow-release preparations are also available. Stores (2003) thoughtfully considers the clinical use of melatonin in view of the available literature. It has been used for the treatment of sleeplessness with ID populations. Some enthusiastic claims about its efficacy have been made although these should be treated with caution for a number of reasons. In many studies there were problems with various important aspects of study-design, and variability of the administration of the melatonin itself. Most studies have used melatonin in conjunction with behavioural approaches. There is also a lack of information about possible side-effects. In the short term it is unclear what effect melatonin has on seizure frequency. In the long term it is not clear what effects melatonin has on reproductive function, puberty, or immune function. Melatonin should not be viewed as a panacea but rather as a possibly useful treatment for *some* sleep disorders, especially circadian rhythm disorders, in *some* populations. Good results have been achieved in children with Angelman syndrome. Children with Smith-Magenis syndrome may benefit as their melatonin profiles can be inverted. More research is needed before melatonin's usefulness can be estimated and its use encouraged. When melatonin is used, the client and their family need to be made aware of these significant limitations in scientific and clinical knowledge.

EXCESSIVE DAYTIME SLEEPINESS

If insufficient sleep is the cause of the EDS, the procedures outlined above in the section titled 'sleeplessness' are likely to be the treatment approaches of choice.

Diagnosis and treatment of aspects of poor-quality overnight sleep or increased sleep need are typically undertaken in specialized settings. In children, treatment for SDB often involves removal of enlarged tonsils and adenoids. In many children with ID, the cause can be more complicated. However, adenoid-tonsillectomy may still be indicated as a first-line surgical procedure. In some instances, further surgical procedures may be necessary. These include tongue reduction, reconstructive surgery, and tracheostomy. Nasal Continuous Positive Airways Pressure (CPAP) or Bilevel Positive Airways Pressure (BiPAP) may be required. CPAP and BiPAP involve wearing a face mask through which air can be 'pumped' all night to splint-open the airways. Non-compliance may be a problem requiring psychological intervention when people with ID are treated with CPAP or BiPAP. In adults obesity and use of alcohol may contribute to SDB. Psychological intervention to promote lifestyle changes may be helpful in such cases.

Treatment of periodic limb movements in sleep (PLMs) is pharmacological, typically with dopaminergic medication. Clonazepam has been used successfully in children with Williams syndrome with PLMs.

Narcolepsy is treated symptomatically with stimulant medication to control the daytime sleepiness and tricyclic antidepressants or SSRIs to suppress REM sleep and address cataplexy, hypnogogic hallucinations or sleep paralysis. Psychological input does play a large role in the life-long management of this condition. Particular features of management include: patient and family education (and support); sleep hygiene; planned naps (prescribed short naps at set times); and behavioural change such as avoiding dangerous activities, increasing physical activity and adhering to strict sleep-wake schedules.

PARASOMNIAS

The parasomnias have not been the focus of much research in ID populations (or indeed in the general population). As said earlier, before deciding to 'treat' a parasomnia one needs first to be sure that the disorder is severe, frequent or developmentally atypical such that it warrants more than parental reassurance, explanation and the implementing of practical measures to ensure the child's safety during an episode.

Rhythmic movement disorders

A behavioural approach employing omission training (positively reinforcing the non-occurrence of a behaviour) has been used successfully to completely resolve rhythmic movement disorder (day and night-time) in ID. In practice this involved providing small amounts of reward (food) if no head banging occurred for progressively extending time periods. Other aspects of treatment involve:

- Removing reinforcement of the behaviour (parents to ignore it – even attempts to prevent the child from head banging may be reinforcing because of the attention involved)
- Parents may feel more comfortable doing this (and able to) if appropriate safety and practical measures are in place (bed structure is secure – tighten nuts and bolts; move bed away from the wall; oil squeaky bedframes to reduce noise; fit padding as appropriate; put child's mattress on the floor)
- Paying attention to sleep hygiene and treating any co-existing sleep or medical disorders with a view to increasing the sleep that the child achieves
- Encouraging rhythmic daytime activities (music and swings) has been reported as helpful
- Generally, attempts to prevent the child from injuring themselves (use of padding and pillows) is not helpful, because the child simply seeks out a new hard surface, nor necessary because injury is actually rare. However, in some children with ID where the severity/frequency of the rhythmic movement disorder is such that injury may be a possibility, such measures (even the use of helmets) may be appropriate
- In such severe cases medication (benzodiazepines or tricyclic antidepressants) has been used and temporary pharmacological suppression of the behaviour may 'break the habit' so that remission continues after the medication is withdrawn.

Head banging: case example

Belinda was aged 3 when she was referred to the clinic. Her parents were worried by her repetitive head banging both when she was put to bed and also sometimes during the night (the noise of her banging her head on the bed woke them because the bed frame creaked and knocked against the wall each time she hit her head and she also made strange noises as she banged). They had gone to their GP worried that she might have epilepsy, even though she had never had any other episodes which had been diagnosed as epileptic. She had been doing this for a few months by the time she came to the clinic and her parents brought a video of the episodes that they had taken with their family recorder. The episodes on the video, and her parents' description of them, were typical of a rhythmic movement disorder. The episodes usually lasted for only a few minutes because as soon as her parents heard her banging they would go into her room and tell her to stop and she would generally comply. Her parents tended to offer her a drink at this time to try and divert her from the activity. Sometimes, once stopped, she might re-start the behaviour after a few minutes but, again, could be stopped with verbal prompting and more diversion. Explaining the essentially benign nature of the episodes was very reassuring to her parents. Thinking of the behaviour as something she did to soothe herself to sleep (both in the evening and at night) helped them to feel more comfortable with it. It was also explained to them that it was possible that their intervening might be encouraging the head banging to occur as their presence, and the offer of drinks, might be pleasant for Belinda. They were not convinced of the likely usefulness of our suggestion that they try to ignore the head banging, as they feared she would just continue to bang until she injured herself, but were willing to experiment with this approach with encouragement. We suggested that they try to minimize the noise of her banging by letting her sleep on a mattress on the floor so that the noisy bed wouldn't creak or bang against the wall. They were also advised that the episodes might go on for much longer than usual when they started this treatment. To begin with, ignoring Belinda's head banging did result in her banging for up to 45 minutes on the third night. Her parents found it very difficult to ignore her completely and did go in to check that she was OK every 10 minutes or so but, as instructed, they did not say anything, nor touch her nor offer any drinks. Reassured by this checking on the fourth night they did not go in at all, and the banging at sleep-onset went on for just over an hour. However, over the next few nights the duration of the head banging began to reduce and two weeks after treatment began she was head banging for only about five minutes before falling asleep and the night-time episodes were occurring less frequently (or at least her parents reported this since they were less disturbed because the removal of the bed had reduced the associated noise). When they returned to clinic four weeks later they reported that the episodes were happening only a few nights a week, and continued to be brief. A continued reduction in frequency and severity was seen over the ensuing weeks.

Sleep-terrors and sleepwalking

Apart from reassurance, explanation and taking practical safety measures (which may include fitting a bell or alarm to the child's door so that parents are alerted if the child tries to leave the bedroom), specific management advice is:

- Ensure child gets adequate sleep. Attend to sleep hygiene and treat any other sleep disorders which may be compromising sleep quality or quantity. Treatment of SDB and various problems of sleeplessness have been reported as leading to a complete resolution of co-existing partial arousal disorders. Sleep deprivation increases the amount of deep NREM sleep on subsequent nights and since partial arousal disorders originate from this stage of sleep they are therefore more likely to occur.

- Do not attempt to wake the child. This will generally increase distress and prolong the episode.
- Do not attempt to comfort the child. This too may increase agitation and prolong the event. Further, since the child is asleep anyway there is no benefit.
- Let the episode subside naturally, meanwhile making sure that the child is guided away from potentially harmful situations, and encourage the child to settle back to sleep in bed at the end of the episode.
- If the individual has no recall of the episode even occurring then discussing or acknowledging the episode the next day is not helpful and can induce anxiety associated with sleep which can make the situation worse.
- If the partial arousal disorder occurs most nights and, as is often the case, the timing of the episode is predictable (best assessed by using a sleep diary for a few weeks) 'scheduled wakings' may be helpful. This involves 'waking' (to the point when the child arouses sufficient to mumble, open eyes or roll over) the child about 15 minutes before the episode typically occurs, then letting them return to sleep. This induced arousal appears to suppress the anticipated 'partial arousal'. This strategy can be used for a few weeks and then discontinued if the partial arousals have stopped. Parents may need temporarily to re-use scheduled waking from time to time, especially at times of stress or illness, both of which can fuel partial arousal disorders in predisposed children.
- Use of medication (benzodiazepines) for a few months to suppress deep NREM sleep is an option for children with frequent, severe episodes.

Sleep-terrors: case example

The case of Milly raises some important diagnostic issues. Age 9, she was referred to the clinic with what were described as 'night-time disturbances', which had been going on for about a year. Her mother had mentioned these episodes to a variety of clinicians involved with her daughter's overall care but emphasis had instead been placed on management of her daytime challenging behaviour until this point. The clinical description of these episodes were consistent with some sort of arousal disorder. Milly aroused every night, about 60 minutes after she had fallen asleep, and appeared very distressed, screaming, crying and sometimes getting out of her bed and moving around her room in a fearful and agitated state. She appeared to have no awareness of her mother during the episode and nothing they said or did seemed to help. After a few minutes she would get back into bed and lie down and return to sleep. Her mother also suffered from sleep-terrors as a child. As part of Milly's routine assessment in the clinic her mother filled out a general screening sleep questionnaire and indicated that there were a number of features of Milly's sleep which were suggestive of the presence of a sleep-related breathing disorder. She was reported as snoring, choking, stopping breathing during sleep for a few seconds, mouth breathing and sweating every night. Her mother had not mentioned these features to any-one until being explicitly asked about them in the questionnaire. Daytime behavioural difficulties can, of course, also be associated with the presence of sleep-related breathing difficulties, as can arousal disorders. It seemed likely that Milly's arousal disorders could be being fuelled by any sleep-related breathing difficulty which was impairing her sleep quality. Extended polysomnography was performed both to confirm the diagnosis of the arousal disorder and to assess her respiratory function during sleep. Treatment of the obstructive sleep apnoea (by adenoid-tonsillectomy) improved her sleep quality (and quantity) and as a result her sleep-terrors stopped, without any specific intervention. It should be noted that with Milly's predisposition to arousal disorder she might be expected to have further episodes if her sleep quantity or quality were compromised in the future, for example if stressed or ill.

Nightmares

Nightmares are frightening dreams. They are more frequent and intense at times of change and stress and when the quantity or quality of sleep is impaired. Indeed, an increase in nightmare frequency or severity may alert parents to the presence of a stressor. The occurrence of nightmares may be prompted by such things as frightening TV programmes or stories prior to bedtime. Such things should be avoided as part of general sleep hygiene principles. Management strategies for nightmares include:

- Removing stressors, ensuring adequate sleep is obtained and having calming bedtime routines.
- Most importantly, comforting the child when they wake to reduce anxiety and facilitate a return to sleep. This can be physically and/or verbally and parents should try and remain calm themselves and not get upset by their child's distress. Some children respond well to distraction at this time (e.g. having a drink).
- Use of comforting sleep aids (such as night lights and established security objects) can be reassuring both at sleep onset and at the time of the episode.

- If appropriate, depending on the child's verbal skills, discussing the nightmare (and proposing alternative positive endings to the nightmare) the next morning may help to 'normalize' the episode and increase the child's feeling of self-control.
- For less verbal children, use of symbolic aids such as drawing pictures of the nightmare content and then throwing them away or using 'dream catchers' hung above the bed can be useful.
- Parents and children should be reassured that occasional nightmares are normal and common. If nightmares occur in the context of more widespread anxiety, treatment for the latter may be indicated.

SLEEP PROBLEMS IN ADULTS WITH ID

Although this chapter appears in the section of this book concerned with infants and children, the limited scientific literature addressing sleep problems in adults with ID suggests that high rates of sleep problems persist into adulthood, that a similar range of presenting sleep complaints may feature and that there are similar successful treatment possibilities. Adults in both residential and home settings appear to be equally likely to suffer although differences in the nature, cause and practicalities of treatment of sleep difficulties may exist. Factors which have been noted to be associated with the presence of sleep problems include high evening caffeine intake, antiepileptic medication, poor communication skills and inappropriate sleep schedules. High rates of sleep disturbance in the elderly and in individuals with conditions associated with dementia are also of note although beyond the scope of this chapter. There is also a suggestion that some sleep problems (frequent nightwaking, difficulty with sleep onset, excessive sleepiness), even if severe, are not always considered as problematic by carers although they may well be problematic for the individual. As such, it is again important to stress that routine screening enquiries about sleep should be made of adults with ID and that relying on sleep disorders to 'present' is likely to lead to many potentially treatable disorders being overlooked.

STAFF TRAINING

The low number of clinical services able adequately to assess and treat sleep disorders (especially with inpatient facilities) is no reflection of clinical need but perhaps rather that formal professional education about sleep and sleep disorders is severely limited. UK medical students receive, on average, 5 minutes' teaching time on the topic, with similar statistics reported at postgraduate level and for trainee clinical psychologists and nurses, in both Europe and the USA.

Given that primary sleep disorders are common, that they frequently co-exist with many medical and psychiatric conditions, that a number of special populations with which psychologists are concerned (e.g. children, elderly, people with ID) have elevated rates of sleep disorders and that sleep disturbance can present primarily as a problem with daytime functioning, it is imperative that psychologists have an awareness of the pertinence of this topic. At the very least they should be familiar with the range of sleep disorders and the effects of sleep loss so that potentially treatable, significant problems are recognized and not overlooked. Ideally, they would also be familiar with basic assessment procedures and approaches to management since many of the most successful treatments for common sleep disorders are best suited to being implemented by psychologists.

Many common sleep disorders could be treated at the primary care level with referral to secondary services or specialized sleep centres as appropriate. Sleep disorders cut across many different specialties (e.g. psychology, psychiatry, paediatrics, neurology, otorhinolaryngology) and, as such, a multidisciplinary approach to their assessment and treatment is desirable.

SUMMARY

Sleep disorders in children, adolescents and adults with ID are widespread and often neglected, with likely adverse effects on both the individual and their carers. There are a range of treatment approaches from which to select, depending on the nature of the sleep disorder and individual needs. Efforts should be made to use a few simple questions to enquire routinely about the sleep patterns of people with ID, with a view to identifying individuals who need further, more detailed assessment. Psychologists, at every level of service delivery, have a role to play in the recognition, assessment, diagnosis and management of sleep disorders.

EXERCISE

Divide the class into three groups (one to work on sleeplessness problems; the second to work on sleepiness problems; and the third to work on parasomnias). Each group is invited to a) read the italicized questions in Box 11.1 and to discuss why these are important questions to ask of a client presenting with this problem and b) answer the other questions in Box 11.1 by listing possible causes of presenting symptoms; and approaches to management. Having done this, check the accuracy of answers by referring to Boxes 11.2, 11.3 and 11.4 where common examples are given. One member from each group may then tell the class the three most significant things their group learned from doing this exercise.

Box 11.1 Questions about sleep problems

1 Faced with a client presenting with SLEEPLESSNESS . . .

What is the nature and timing of the sleeplessness?
What conditions might cause sleep-onset problems and how might they be treated?
What conditions might cause nightwaking and how might they be treated?
What conditions might cause early waking and how might they be treated?

2 Faced with a client presenting with SLEEPINESS . . .

Is it really sleepiness or actually physical fatigue/lethargy?
NB Different causes of fatigue:
- *Physical illness esp. anaemia, endocrine disorder*
- *Chronic fatigue syndrome*

Is the sleepiness genuine?
NB Simulated excessive sleepiness can occur for psychological reasons.

If sleepiness is established, what is causing the sleepiness?
What conditions might cause insufficient sleep (short duration sleep) and how might they be treated?
What conditions might cause disturbed sleep and how might they be treated?
What conditions might cause increased sleep need and how might they be treated?

3 Faced with a client presenting with a PARASOMNIA

What are the precise characteristics including
- *timing*
- *nature of behaviour*
- *awareness during episode*
- *daytime attacks*
- *family history?*

What disorders might present at sleep onset and how might they be treated?
What disorders might present early in night (during deep NREM sleep) and how might they be treated?
What disorders might present late in night (i.e. during REM sleep) and how might they be treated?
What disorders might present with various timing and how might they be treated?

Box 11.2 Solutions to sleeplessness problems

SLEEPLESSNESS

Sleep-onset problems

• Won't go to bed/ misbehaviour	Set limits/don't reinforce Bedtime routine Alter lifestyle factors motivating staying up
• Afraid to go to bed	Emotional support Create positive sleep-onset associations Explore negative sleep-onset associations (abuse)
• Can't go to sleep (although wants to)	Delayed sleep phase Undo conditioned insomnia Exclude caffeine/overstimulation
• Ritualistic behaviour	Emotional support Avoid over-excitement at bedtime Psychiatric investigation

Nightwaking

• Demands parents' attention/crying	Correct poor sleep-onset association Train to go to sleep by self
• Frightened by nightmares or night-terrors	See 'Parasomnias' below
• Physical symptoms (pain, headache, breathing, scratching, seizure)	Treat medical condition

Early morning waking

• Going to bed too early	Correct advanced sleep phase
• Inappropriate napping	Change pattern
• Short sleep requirements	Provide amusements/occupations (reschedule sleep times)
• Reinforced early waking	Remove reinforcers

Box 11.3 Solutions to sleepiness problems

SLEEPINESS

Insufficient sleep

• Really true? (Compare with norms)	Parental reassurance
• Earlier causes of sleeplessness	See above
• Delayed sleep phase	Chronotherapy

Disturbed sleep

• Earlier causes of nightwaking	
• Obstructive sleep apnoea	Removal of tonsils and adenoids CPAP
• Periodic limb movements	Medication

Increased sleep requirements

• Narcolepsy	Medication, behavioural approaches
• Idiopathic hypersomnia	Medication
• Depression	Conventional treatment

• Drug abuse (may have widespread effects on sleep inc. withdrawal effects)/medication effects

---

Box 11.4 Treatment of parasomnias

PARASOMNIAS

Sleep onset

• Head banging/other rhythmic movements	Reassurance/behavioural treatment
• Hypnagogic hallucinations	Common in isolation and far less often a feature of narcolepsy (provide reassurance)
• Sleep paralysis	Common in isolation and far less often a feature of narcolepsy (provide reassurance)

| • Sleep starts | Reassurance/explanation |

Early in night (deep NREM sleep)
• Arousal disorders	Reassurance/explanation
(confusional arousals,	Scheduled waking
sleepwalking, sleep terrors)	Avoid waking up

Late in night (REM sleep)
| • Nightmares | Comfort |
| | Explore reason if severe |

Various timing
| • Epileptic seizures | Antiepileptic medication |

FURTHER READING FOR PARENTS

Daymond, K. (2001). *The ParentTalk Guide to Sleep*. London: Hodder and Stoughton.
Durand, M.V. (1998). *Sleep Better: A Guide to Improving Sleep for Children with Special Needs*. Baltimore: Paul H Brookes Publishing Co.
Ferber, R. (1986). *Solve your Child's Sleep Problems*. London: Dorling Kindersley.
Quine, L. (1997). *Solving Children's Sleep Problems: A Step by Step Guide for Parents*. Huntingdon, UK: Beckett Karlson.

FURTHER READING FOR PRACTITIONERS

American Sleep Disorders Association (2005). *International Classification of Sleep Disorders*, 2nd edn, *Diagnostic and Coding Manual*. Westchester, IL: American Sleep Disorders Association.
Ancoli-Israel, I., Poceta, S., Stepnowsky, C., Martin, J. and Gehrman, P. (1997). Identification and treatment of sleep problems in the elderly. *Sleep Medicine Reviews*, 1, 3–17.
Benca, R., Okawa, M., Uchiyama, M., Ozaki, S., Nakajima, T., Shibui, K. and Obermeyer, W. (1997). Review article: Sleep and mood disorders. *Sleep Medicine Reviews*, 1, 45–56.
Dahl, R. (1992). The pharmacologic treatment of sleep disorders. *Psychiatric Clinics of North America*, 15, 161–78.
Espie, C. (1991). *The Psychological Treatment of Insomnia*. Chichester: Wiley.
Ferber, R. and Kryger, M. (1995). *Principles and Practice of Sleep Medicine in the Child*. Philadelphia, PA: Saunders.
Horne, J. (1988). *Why We Sleep*. New York: Oxford University Press.
Kales, A., Soldatos, C. and Kales, J. (1980). Taking a sleep history. *American Family Physician*, (August), 100–7.
Kryger, M., Roth, T. and Dement, W. (2005). *Principles and Practice of Sleep Medicine* (4th edn). Philadelphia, PA: Elsevier Saunders.

Lancioni, G., O'Reilly, M. and Basili, G. (1999). Review of strategies for treating sleep problems in persons with severe or profound mental retardation or multiple handicaps. *American Journal of Mental Retardation*, 104, 170–86.

Mindell, J. and Owens, J. (2003). *A Clinical Guide to Paediatric Sleep: Diagnosis and Management of Sleep Problems*. Philadelphia, PA: Lippincott Williams and Wilkins.

Morin, C. (1993). *Insomnia: Psychological Assessment and Management*. New York: Guilford Press.

Morin, C. and Espie, C. (2003). *Insomnia: A Clinical Guide to Assessment and Treatment of Insomnia*. New York: Kluwer Academic – Plenum.

Pressman, M. and Orr, W. (1997). *Understanding Sleep: The Evaluation and Treatment of Sleep Disorders*. Washington, DC: American Psychological Association.

Reite, M., Ruddy, J. and Nagel, K. (1997). *Concise Guide to Evaluation and Management of Sleep Disorders* (2nd edn). Washington, DC: American Psychiatric Press.

Richdale, A. and Wiggs, L. (2005). Behavioral approaches to the treatment of sleep problems in children with developmental disorders. What is the state of the art? *International Journal of Behavioral and Consultation Therapy*, 1, 165–89.

Sheldon, S. H., Ferber, R. and Kryger, M. (2005). *Principles and Practice of Pediatric Sleep Medicine*. Philadelphia, PA: Elsevier Saunders.

Stores, G. (1996). Practitioner review: Assessment and treatment of sleep disorders in children and adolescents. *Journal of Child Psychology and Psychiatry*, 37, 907–25.

Stores, G. (2001). *A Clinical Guide to Sleep Disorders in Children and Adolescents*. Cambridge: Cambridge University Press.

Stores, G. (2003). Medication for sleep-wake disorders. *Archives of Disease in Childhood*, 88, 899–903.

Stores, G. and Wiggs, L. (2001). *Sleep Disturbance in Children and Adolescence with Disorders of Development: Its Significance and Management*. London: MacKeith Press.

Thorpy, M. (1990). *Handbook of Sleep Disorders*. New York: Marcel Dekker.

Wiggs, L. and France, K. (2000). Behavioural treatments for sleep problems in children and adolescents with physical illness, psychological problems or intellectual disabilities. *Sleep Medicine Reviews*, 4, 299–314.

ASSESSMENT INSTRUMENTS

Questionnaires which screen for a range of sleep disorders

Bruni, O., Ottaviano, S., Guidetti, V., Romoli, M., Innocenzi, M., Cortesi, F. and Giannotti, F. (1996). The Sleep Disturbance Scale for Children (SDSC): Construction and validation of an instrument to evaluate sleep disturbances in childhood and adolescence. *Journal of Sleep Research*, 5, 251–61.

Owens, J., Spirito, A. and McGuinn, M. (2000). The Children's Sleep Habits Questionnaire (CSHQ): Psychometric properties of a survey instrument for school-aged children. *Sleep*, 23, 1043–51.

Roth, T., Zammit, G., Kushida, C., Doghramji, K., Mathias, S., Wong, J. and Buysse, D. (2002). A new questionnaire to detect sleep disorders. *Sleep Medicine*, 3, 99–108.

Simonds, J. and Parraga, H. (1982). Prevalence of sleep disorders and sleep behaviours in children and adolescents. *Journal of the American Academy of Child Psychiatry*, 21, 383–8.

Questionnaires to evaluate specific aspects of sleep/sleep disorders

Buysse, D., Reynolds, C., Monk, T. and Berman, S. (1989). The Pittsburgh Sleep Quality Index: A new instrument for psychiatric practice and research. *Psychiatry Research*, 28, 193–213.

Chervin, R., Hedger, K., Dillon, J. and Pituch, K. (2000). Paediatric Sleep Questionnaire (PSQ): Validity and reliability of scales for sleep-disordered breathing, snoring, sleepiness and behavioural problems. *Sleep Medicine*, 1, 21–32.

Espie, C., Inglis, S., Harvey, L. and Tessier, S. (2000). Insomniacs' attributions: Psychometric properties of the Dysfunctional Beliefs and Attitudes about Sleep Scale and the Sleep Disturbance Questionnaire. *Journal of Psychosomatic Research*, 48, 141–8.

Johns, M. (1991). A new method for measuring daytime sleepiness: The Epworth sleepiness scale. *Sleep*, 14, 540–5.

Maislin, G., Pack, A., Kribbs, N., Smith, P., Schwartz, A., Kline, L., Schwab, R. and Dinges, D. (1995). A survey screen for prediction of apnea. *Sleep*, 18, 158–66.

REFERENCES

American Sleep Disorders Association (2005). *International Classification of Sleep Disorders*, 2nd edn, *Diagnostic and Coding Manual*. Westchester, IL: American Sleep Disorders Association:

Bruni, O., Ottaviano, S., Guidetti, V., Romoli, M., Innocenzi, M., Cortesi, F. and Giannotti, F. (1996). The Sleep Disturbance Scale for Children (SDSC): Construction and validation of an instrument to evaluate sleep disturbances in childhood and adolescence. *Journal of Sleep Research*, 5, 251–61.

Chervin, R., Hedger, K., Dillon, J. and Pituch, K. (2000). Paediatric Sleep Questionnaire (PSQ): Validity and reliability of scales for sleep-disordered breathing, snoring, sleepiness and behavioural problems. *Sleep Medicine*, 1, 21–32.

Johns, M. (1991). A new method for measuring daytime sleepiness: The Epworth sleepiness scale. *Sleep*, 14, 540–5.

Kryger, M., Roth, T. and Dement, W. (2005). *Principles and Practice of Sleep Medicine* (4th edn). Philadelphia, PA: Saunders.

Owens, J., Spirito, A. and McGuinn, M. (2000). The Children's Sleep Habits Questionnaire (CSHQ): Psychometric properties of a survey instrument for school-aged children. *Sleep*, 23, 1043–51.

Sheldon, S. H., Ferber, R. and Kryger, M. (2005). *Principles and Practice of Pediatric Sleep Medicine*. Philadelphia, PA: Elsevier Saunders.

Stores, G. (2003). Medication for sleep-wake disorders. *Archives of Disease in Child-hood*, 88, 899–903.

Stores, G. and Wiggs, L. (2001). *Sleep Disturbance in Children and Adolescence with Disorders of Development: Its Significance and Management*. London: MacKeith Press.

Chapter 12

Toileting problems

Ian Grey and Brian McClean

Faecal and urinary incontinence are relatively common conditions in typically developing children referred to general practitioners, clinical psychologists and psychiatrists (Procter and Loader, 2003) with referral rates of up to 10 percent of caseloads (Buchanan, 1992). Just as the attainment of bowel and bladder control is important for such children, it is equally important for children with intellectual disability if not more so considering the frequent barriers they experience with respect to inclusion. The purpose of this chapter is to provide the practitioner with sufficient information regarding the origin and maintenance of toileting problems and identify the factors that need to be taken into consideration during the course of an assessment. Descriptions and evaluations of the main interventions are also presented along with practical considerations surrounding treatment implementation.

TOILETING ISSUES IN BEHAVIOURAL ASSESSMENT

In recent years constipation has taken on an increasing importance in comprehensive behavioural assessment. Functional analysis seeks to identify the variables that may be associated with the occurrence and non-occurrence of challenging behaviour. Many serious challenging behaviours, including self-injury and aggression, can co-vary with the pain or discomfort which may be associated with intermittent constipation. Consider the following.

Andy is a 19-year-old man with a long history of three major challenges: severe physical aggression, severe grand mal epilepsy with drop attacks occurring as often as ten seizures per hour; and severe faecal impaction with overflow incontinence. For years, the efforts of the multi-disciplinary team had been directed to what were perceived to be the priority problems, Andy's severe aggression and his epilepsy, both of which necessitated a 2:1 staff-client ratio. After years of intervention and little change in the rate of Andy's aggression or epilepsy, the team agreed to tackle the comparatively less serious problem of overflow incontinence. On investigation, Andy was found to have severe faecal impaction in the upper bowel – quite difficult to detect through external physical examination. It took nine days to achieve clearance within his bowel. To the amazement of the team, Andy's epilepsy immediately disappeared, never to return, and the level of physical aggression reduced significantly, with episodes of severe aggression also disappearing. The lesson for the team was very simple; aggressive behaviour had an organic basis and was functional. Andy's behaviour seemed to communicate the message 'I feel awful.' This message was not attention-seeking (e.g. I feel awful, do something about it), but escape-motivated (e.g. I feel awful . . . don't ask me to get on the bus, leave me alone). In this example, constipation acted as a setting event for Andy's behaviour.

Increasingly, clinicians are alert to constipation as a sign of chronic bowel infection, which is implicated in some theories of the aetiology of autism, fragile X, attention-deficit disorder and many other serious conditions. For example, a number of researchers now hypothesize that autism is the consequence of the action of peptides which derive principally from casein and gluten. Because of low levels of sulphates there is an increase in the permeability of the upper intestinal wall of many children and adults with autism (Waring, 1993). This permeability leads to an excess of opioids, which break down from casein and gluten peptides. Research is still at an exploratory stage, but Knivsberg, Reichlet, Nodland and Hoien (1995) and Shattock and Savery (1999) have reported substantial reductions in challenging behaviours when gluten and milk were eliminated from the diets of children and adults with autism.

CLASSIFICATION AND PREVALENCE

Enuresis and encopresis constitute two clinical problems that may be referred to professionals working with children with intellectual disability. Diagnosis and classification of these two broad disorders in children with an intellectual disability must take account of two general factors. First, the diagnosis of both disorders is typically based upon the upper age limit at which bladder and bowel control are generally acquired amongst typically developing children at ages 4 and 5 years for bowel and bladder control respectively. Bowel control typically develops first and the median age of staying bowel movement-free overnight is twenty-three months and bladder movement-free is approximately thirty-five months for non-intellectually disabled children (Schum, Kilb and McAuliffe, 2002). With typically developing children, a diagnosis below ages 4 and 5 for the respective disorders is considered premature (McGrath, Mellon and Murphy, 2000). However, the DSM-IV stipulates that a diagnosis of either disorder may be premature in children below an equivalent developmental level or mental age equivalent. One difficulty with this caveat is that a child with a mental age equivalent of less than 4 or 5 years may not receive appropriate intervention despite a substantially older chronological age. Second, sub-classifications are generally made in respect of both disorders (see Table 12.1). In relation to enuresis a distinction is typically made between primary and secondary enuresis (failure to acquire urinary continence versus acquired continence which is subsequently lost after a period of time). With encopresis, aside from primary and secondary, a further distinction is generally made between soiling with constipation (retentive encopresis) and soiling without constipation (non-retentive encopresis).

Within the general population, it is estimated that 1 percent of 5-year-old children have encopresis, with a higher frequency for boys. With respect to enuresis, the prevalence at age 5 is approximately 7 percent for boys and 3 percent for girls (Nield and Kamat, 2004). This figure reduces by approximately 15 percent with each chronological year to 1 percent for both genders by age 18. Few reliable prevalence figures are available for elimination disorders in those with an intellectual disability. However, both level of intellectual disability and the presence of specific syndromes have been associated with higher rates of both enuresis and encopresis. Specifically, both are more common among those with a severe intellectual disability (Duker and Dekkers, 1992). Nocturnal enuresis (defined as at least two incidents per week) was noted in one study as having a prevalence rate of 6 percent amongst those with a moderate disability, 16 percent among those with a severe intellectual disability and 45 percent of those with a profound disability (Saloviita, 2002). With respect to syndromes, one study (Buntinx,

Table 12.1 Basic classification of toileting difficulties

Enuresis	Encopresis
• Child must have a developmental age of 5 (DSM-IV)	• Child must have a developmental age of 4 (DSM-IV)
• Primary enuresis is wetting in an individual who has never been dry for at least 6 months	• Primary encopresis is soiling in an individual who has never acquired bowel control
• Secondary enuresis is wetting that begins after at least 6 months of dryness	• Secondary enuresis is soiling that begins after at least 6 months of bowel control
• Nocturnal enuresis is wetting that usually occurs during sleep (night-time incontinence)	• Retentive encopresis is the failure of faecal control in cases with constipation
• Diurnal enuresis is wetting when awake (daytime incontinence)	• Non-retentive encopresis is the failure of faecal control in cases without constipation
• Approximate frequency of 2–3 times per week	• Approximate frequency of 2–3 times per week

Hennekam, Brouwer, Strink *et al.*, 1995) reported that in a sample of forty-seven children and adults with Angelman syndrome, approximately 62 percent were incontinent during the day. Despite the identified numbers of children in the severe and profound ranges of intellectual disability, anecdotal evidence suggests that relatively few referrals are made for the treatment of enuresis and encopresis. Possible factors for this may include diagnostic over-shadowing where such disorders are attributed to the intellectual disability itself and that other disorders such as challenging behaviours take referral priority for parents and staff.

CONSEQUENCES OF INCONTINENCE

The consequences of incontinence are both physical and social. Among the physical consequences are skin irritation and urinary tract infections. In the social domain, a child's access to community-based activities, school and transport may be restricted. Social relationships may also suffer too with caretakers and others possibly avoiding the child. It is possible that a child with incontinence may be viewed as having less-developed social and personal health care skills in general than a child without. For families, the burden may contribute significantly to experienced stress (Landgraf, Abidari, Cilento, Cooper *et al.*, 2004).

BIOLOGICAL FACTORS INVOLVED IN ENURESIS AND ENCOPRESIS

Approximately 70 percent of typically developing children with enuresis have a first-degree relative with the condition and the condition is more prevalent amongst monozygotic than dizygotic twins (Carr, 1999). However, these figures are established with the general population and not for those with an intellectual disability and consequently the role of genetics in this population remains unclear. However, other biological variables have been identified in enuresis and encopresis including urinary tract infections, urinary tract abnormalities, low functional bladder volume, diet, medication, diabetes mellitus, diabetes insipidus, sleep apnoea, hyperthyroidism, polydispsia, renal disease and constipation (Nield and Kamat, 2004; Robson and Leung, 2000).

Physical abnormalities typically occur at a higher level in those with an intellectual disability than those without and to date a number of such abnormalities have been identified in both enuresis and encopresis. However, while urinary tract abnormalities may be involved in enuresis, surgical inter-vention is typically ineffective in the treatment of enuresis as is antibiotic treatment for urinary tract infections. With respect to encopresis, abnormalities in anorectal sensory and motor function, the presence of megacolon,

Hirschsprungs disease, spina bifida and cerebral palsy are all associated with encopresis. With poor anorectal motor functioning, the child may recognize signals for the need to defecate but may be unable to do so. In some cases, this may be due to internal sphincter hypertrophy (Carr, 1999). Anatomic abnormalities, however, are rarely causal factors in cases of encopresis. Far more common as a causal factor is constipation.

BEHAVIOURAL THEORY

Behavioural theories of primary enuresis and encopresis focus on three broad factors. First, bladder filling and rectal distension have not become discriminative stimuli for appropriate toileting habits. Second, appropriate toileting may not have been properly reinforced. Third, avoidance of pain may be an important factor in the maintenance of toileting difficulties. In normal populations, behavioural theories focus on sensitizing children to bodily sensations that precede urination and defecation so that they operate as discriminative stimuli (Carr, 1999). These premises lead to a number of treatment goals. Treatment may focus on: (1) sensitizing children to bodily sensations that precede urination and defecation so that these operate as discriminative stimuli for toileting; (2) providing a rich schedule of reinforcement for toileting, for example using a structured toileting routine; and (3) removing pain, for example by providing a fibre-rich diet or eliminating food intolerances. In the cases of avoidance of toileting, removal of pain, desensitization to toileting and reinforcement of successive approximations of toileting are generally included in a multi-component treatment plan.

TREATMENT OF ENURESIS

Traditional toileting programmes are generally reported as being seldom effective in the treatment of enuresis in children with an intellectual disability (Didden, Sikkema, Bosman, Duker and Curfs, 2001) and as a result many children fail to acquire continence skills and often remain incontinent throughout their life, though again stability data on this issue is sparse. Parents typically report bringing their child with a developmental disability repeatedly to the toilet, often on the hour, yet the child fails to connect going to the toilet with actually urinating or eliminating faeces. In the face of ongoing incontinence difficulties, additional management approaches may include unsystematic reprimands and fluid restriction. However, these may contribute to an aversion to the toilet and consolidate rather than alleviate the problem.

Medication

The treatment of nocturnal enuresis is associated with abnormal vasopressin circadian rhythm. The pharmacologic treatment of nocturnal enuresis is primarily limited to two drugs that have been studied extensively: desmopressin acetate (DDAVP) and imipramine hydrochloride. A third, oxybutynin chloride, is now receiving interest as a treatment. Desmopressin acts by increasing water retention in the kidneys and urine concentration in the distal tubes of the kidney. A review of eighteen controlled studies in typically developing children demonstrated that only about 24 percent of children were completely dry on the medication and that 94 percent relapsed after medication was discontinued. No studies are available with respect to intellectual disability (Aman, Collier-Crespin and Lindsay, 2000). Impramine has higher rates of suppression with a range of between 10 percent and 60 percent. However, relapse is also very high with a figure in excess of 90 percent. Existing data suggests that children with intellectual disability have a less favourable response to imipramine (Aman *et al.*, 2000) and that relapse rates on withdrawal are similar to those reported above. Treatment of constipation may lead to a resolution of enuresis but is probably most effective in cases where enuresis has resulted from reduced bladder capacity owing to faecal mass (O'Regan and Yazbeck, 1987).

Behavioural treatment of enuresis

Like other adaptive behaviours, operant and classical processes are considered to be involved in toileting. Several types of instructional procedures have been developed in order to establish day- and night-time continence in children with intellectual disability. These include the scheduled toileting, the Azrin and Foxx procedure, discrimination training, dry bed training, generic habit training and response restriction. Several of these treatments have evolved over the years and this will be reflected in discussion of the various approaches. The goal of the majority of interventions are skills-oriented and aim to establish self-initiated toileting or gesturing to parents or staff that assistance is needed to go to the toilet.

Scheduled toileting

Perhaps the most common response by parents and staff when confronted by a child or adolescent with an intellectual disability displaying incontinence is to schedule toilet trips regularly across relatively short durations. In the event that the child does not void on these occasions, the typical response is to increase the frequency of trips. A typical schedule involves hourly trips to the toilet, with frequency increasing to half hour and then quarter hour if the child does not void. On its own typically this approach does not lead to independent self-initiated toileting or to the child communicating to a carer the need to use the toilet (cf. Lancioni, Duker, Klaase and Goossens, 1994). However, it will avoid the child being wet and others having a more unpleasant task in changing the child depending on whether the child actually voids while being brought to the toilet. This is probably the default intervention with parents and staff.

The Azrin and Foxx procedure

One of the most commonly used and cited toileting programs is that developed by Azrin and Foxx (1971). Originally developed with adults with intellectual disability, the procedure has been subsequently modified for use with children (e.g. Didden *et al.*, 2001). The goal of the program is typically to achieve self-initiated toileting or gesturing to parents or staff that the individual wants to go to the toilet. Initial success is identified as having no accidents for three consecutive days and at least three correct visits to the toilet and that voiding always occurred within ten minutes (Didden *et al.*, 2001).The original procedure involves the child drinking fluids every 30 minutes, with scheduled toileting also every 30 minutes. The child is given edible reinforcers for every five minutes for remaining dry and after every elimination on the toilet bowel. Toileting and undressing occurs with least-to-most prompting, to teach independent toilet use. However, the procedure contains at least six potentially aversive elements witch seem out of place with the current ethos of Positive Behavioural Support (Donnellan, LaVigna, Negri-Shoultz and Fassbinder, 1988) and with modern parenting practice (e.g. Leach, 1997). For example, it is prescribed that the child remains on the toilet bowel for 20 minutes or until elimination occurs. If an accident does occur, the procedure prescribes that the child feels their wet clothing while being verbally reprimanded, a practice that most children would find humiliating (not to say unhygienic!) and might lead to escape behaviours rather than successful toileting. The child also must clean the soiled area as part of an over-correction procedure for 15 minutes. Finally, all toys are removed from the bathroom and the child is placed in time-out from positive reinforcement for one hour. (It is not clear how the recommendation to maintain the child in time-out for positive reinforcement for one hour fits with the 30 minutes of scheduled toileting and drink breaks, quite apart from any other familial or educational schedule that may obtain.) The procedure as described above is also time-consuming and involves staffing considerations. The original procedure recommends the allocation of one or two staff members as full-time trainers and recommends that supervisors be identified and appointed to oversee programme implementation and that the dietary personnel in the service cooperate when adjusting meal schedules when necessary. Instead of the above, we propose the standard toileting procedure set out in Table 12.2.

One concern that has been posed is that the procedure requires a large

Table 12.2 Standard toileting procedure

Training phase

1   Child drinks fluid (water or natural fruit juice) every 30 minutes
2   Scheduled toileting occurs every 60 minutes using least-to-most prompting, either in the lavatory, or on a portable pot, or both
3   Toileting also occurs if the child shows gestural or behavioural precursors of elimination
4   Child remains on the toilet bowl or pot for 3 minutes or until elimination occurs
5   Scheduled toileting increases to 30 minutes if no elimination occurs
6   Child is given edible and social reinforcers for every 15 minutes for remaining dry and for elimination when on pot or toilet bowl. In cases of toilet refusal, reinforcement is given for successive approximations to toilet or pot use (e.g. visits the toilet, sits, sits for 30 seconds, sits for 3 minutes)
7   If an accident occurs, the parent gives a matter-of-fact response (e.g. 'hard luck, you left it a bit late, didn't you? Let's mop up . . .'). Some care is taken not to allow the subsequent dressing and mopping activities to be too enjoyable for the child
8   Child undresses him/herself with least-to-most prompting

Post-training phase

9   Pants checked at 0800, 1000, 1200, 1400, 1600, 1800, 2000 hr and bedtime
10   Continued use of reinforcers
11   Continued least-to-most prompting

degree of induction, in other words that the relationship between stimulus (i.e. bladder pressure) and the response (i.e. approaching and voiding in the toilet) remains relatively obscure. Further modifications may be made to the procedure, one of which incorporates the use of urine alarms (described subsequently) to help establish discrimination of bladder distension (Lancioni, Duker, Klasse and Goosens, 1994).

Aiding discriminative stimulus control: urine-alarm triggers

Drawn from the research of Van Wagenen, Meyerson, Kerr and Mahoney (1969) and originating with the work of Mowrer and Mowrer (1938), the method in its simplest form relies on the utilization of an alarm that sounds on contact with urine and the child is prompted to go rapidly to the toilet and sit on the toilet. The procedure works on the basis that 'prompting in relation to the alarm signal would probably become redundant as the behaviour of going to the toilet and urinating there is consolidated through reinforcement' (Lancioni and Markus, 1999: 262).

Urine alarms are most often used in the treatment of nocturnal enuresis for typically developing children and initial success varies around an average of 78 percent for children without an intellectual disability. The use of urine alarms in the context of psychological intervention is considered more effective than those without in the general treatment (Houts, Berman and Abramson, 1994). The procedure is simple and the goal of treatment typically involves familiarization with the required responding (i.e. going to the toilet or gesturing to others the need to go). Lancioni and Markus (1999) report on its implementation with a 9-year-old boy with a moderate level of intellectual disability. Visits to the toilet were scheduled two to three times per day in baseline. Intervention consisted of one day of familiarization with the device and the required responding. On subsequent days, the boy would go to the toilet on activation of the alarm. He was praised during urination and provided with access to favourite play materials immediately after urination. Self-initiated toileting appeared during intervention and the number of large urinary accidents decreased to zero levels. Small accidents continued to occur but at a much lower rate.

These devices are more practical in that they require minimal time to put them on and do not impose restrictions in respect of daytime activities. Additional advantages of the techniques include that the signal can be auditory or visual and can be invidualized for the child. One recent example by Lancioni, O'Reilly, Sernelli, and Campodonico (2000) had an LED mounted on the eye-glasses of a 31-year-old enuretic woman with a profound intellectual disability which was to function as a discriminative stimulus for cueing self-initiated toileting. Urination in the toilet was reinforced by delivery of the woman's favourite food item. At the start of the study she had a mean large urinary accident occurrence approximately once every two days. This was to function as a discriminative stimulus for going to the toilet. Following intervention, which lasted approximately eighty days, the rate of large urinary accidents was reduced to approximately one every twenty days.

Implementation guidelines suggest reducing the amount of scheduled toileting to approximately half that typically occurring prior to programme implementation for an initial period of time (depending upon the individual). This increases the number of alarm signals to provide the individual with increased opportunities to learn and to promote familiarization with the sequence of events (e.g. alarm, physical guidance or prompting to go to the toilet and reinforcer delivery). Effects on withdrawal of the device have not typically been examined but high relapse rates are postulated (Nawaz, Griffiths and Tappin, 2002).

Response restriction

Approaches to toileting based on response restriction theory operate on the basis that several studies have indicated that restricted access to one or more responses may have an effect on one or more other responses, independent of any contingent relationship. Response restriction, also called response deprivation, is the restriction of a child's opportunity to emit a particular behaviour (McEntee and Saunders, 1997). It is normally created when a contingency is established between two responses: the instrumental response and a second, usually more probable response, the contingent response. Limited research has examined response restriction as a method of establishing diurnal bladder control in children with intellectual disability. One of the most recent is that by Duker, Averink and Melein (2001). In the study, eight children ranging in age from approximately 5 years of age to 14 years of age with moderate and severe intellectual disability participated. With the exception of one child, all lived at home and all attended a day centre. During baseline conditions, all nappies were removed and scheduled toileting took place between 90 and 120 minutes for each child on a daily basis. If voiding occurred, the child was reinforced. If a urinary accident took place before scheduled toileting, no consequences were instigated. Training took place for six hours per day between 9am and 3pm over a five-day week whilst attending the day centre. During training, interventions took place in the bathroom and this area was devoid of any distracting stimuli but a table, two chairs, some toys and cups and bottles with favourite drinks were present. Fluids presented were given (1) at the beginning of each training day, (2) following each correct urination, (3) following each urinary accident, and (4) following each thirty-minute period without any liquid intake but not exceeding quantitative limits (Thompson and Hanson, 1983). The procedure involves the following basic steps:

1 Trainer brings trainee to a standing position next to the toilet. All other responses but approaching the toilet, lowering his or her pants and sitting on the toilet are physically prevented. If the child sat on the toilet prior to removal of clothing, the trainer assisted the removal of same.
2 If sitting occurred, the trainee was required to stay there for five minutes or until urination had occurred.
3 If urination occurred, he or she was praised and allowed to sit at the table in the bathroom and given access to toys for ten minutes.
4 If urination occurred while standing, walking or sitting at the table the following positive practice steps were initiated: (a) physically guided to the toilet; (b) lowered pants; (c) remained seated on toilet for three seconds; (d) raised pants and was guided to another area in the toilet. This sequence of steps was repeated four times.
5 Training now conducted in regular setting. Extra liquids discontinued and instructions to go to the toilet were given with increasing intervals from one hour up to 2.5 hours.

Follow-up occurred at one month and ten months over six-hour periods for four to five consecutive days. The training procedure resulted in a decrease of urinary accidents for seven of the eight children. Though the amount of time involved in the study to achieve continence by the children was not directly assessed, the authors report an average of 25 hours' training time. This is in contrast to the 250 hours reported by Smith (1979) for children with similar characteristics. At the second follow-up four of the trainees showed reliable self-initiated toileting. The decline from seven children to four indicates that some failure in maintenance occurred. A very practical problem response restriction is that it requires staff to be physically present in the toilet blocking responses and waiting for urination. This procedure takes staff out of the environment where other clients are, which may pose logistical problems for them.

Dry bed training (DBT)

One of the most frequently implemented interventions for nocturnal enuresis is that of Dry Bed Training. This is an intensive programme using urine alarms which occurs on the first night condensing many trials of rehearsal, retention and control training (see Table 12.3; for a more detailed description of the procedure see Saloviita, 2002). Dry bed training is a multi-component behavioural programme originally devised to treat nocturnal enuresis in children with a general intellectual disability (Azrin, Sneed and Foxx, 1973). The procedure has been identified as being more effective than urine alarms alone and as overcoming some of the shortcomings such as high relapse rates on withdrawal of the device (Nawaz, Griffiths and Tappin, 2002). While this claim is well supported by group comparisons across treatments for enuresis, efficacy of dry bed training over urine trigger alarm has not been established. Dry bed training teaches not only night-time arousal to bladder propriception but also sphincter strengthening, increased bladder capacity

Table 12.3 Dry bed training protocol from Saloviita (2002)

Phase 1	Phase 2
• Intensive Training	• Urine alarm placed under bedsheet/placed in underwear
• Urine alarm placed under bedsheet/placed in underwear	• No hourly awakenings, no fluids
• Child drinks 2 glasses of fluid 30 minutes before bed	• When accident – awaken and disconnect device
• Hourly wakenings with minimal prompting	• Changes wet bed clothing and own clothes
• Urination within 5 mins: reinforce and 2 glasses of fluid	• Positive practice in use of toilet for 45 minutes
• No urination within 5 mins: 2 glasses of fluid	• Back to phase 1 if more than 1 accident per night
• Praise for dry bed. Tactile feelings of dry sheets	• After 7 nights with no accident remove urine alarm and no awakenings
• Move to phase 2 when no more than one accident per night and uses toilet correctly 50% of visits to toilet	• Bed inspection in morning. If 2 more accidents in 7 nights return to start of phase 2

and rapid movement from bed to toilet. This procedure applied the traditional bell and pad apparatus but added to it five other features: (1) intensive training for night-time use; (2) an increase in learning opportunities through increased intake of drinking water; (3) abundant use of positive reinforcement; (4) use of punishment including over-correction and verbal reprimand; and (5) fading of prompts.

Efficacy of the procedure has been established in a number of studies. In the original 1973 paper, Azrin *et al.* reported that in a group of twelve adult enuretics, the rate of enuresis was reduced by about 85 percent during the first week and almost entirely (95 percent) during the fifth week of training. A later study by Smith (1981) used a shortened version of the DBT procedure and implemented it with five residents with severe or profound levels of intellectual disability. Despite considerable success and the fact that no relapse was reported between nine months and two years, this must be balanced against the fact that the mean duration of treatment was forty-eight weeks. Additional studies support the efficacy of DBT up to six years without relapse (van Son, van Heesch, Mulder and van Londen, 1995). A more recent study by Saloviita (2002) with two female clients reported that bed wetting was almost completely eliminated over a period of two months and that one participant remained dry at night with less than one incident per night over the next nine years. It is interesting to note also that the procedure in this study was described as cumbersome by staff and monitoring of one individual was discontinued owing to the amount of work involved.

Generic habit-training program

The focus of a generic habit training procedure is considerably different from the procedures described earlier. Parents may often attempt an hourly toileting procedure with little success. Such failure is conceptualized in the habit training as contributing to the maintenance of the problem as repeated trials may have taught the child to learn an association between the toilet and other activities such as playing or interacting. In a version of the procedure by Wilson (1995) nine steps are involved.

1   Identify the time that the child is most likely to urinate and bring them to the bathroom. The child typically waits until they urinate.
2   Once a time has been identified deliver 2 to 4 fl.oz of fluid approximately thirty minutes earlier. Fluids are not to be given if the child urinates inappropriately before getting started.
3   Removal of distractions: bathroom toys, toilet paper, toiletries. If child is dry, sit them on the toilet. If they need to get up and stretch legs then this is fine but they are not to leave the bathroom. Saturation reinforcement can be implemented but this may present a practical problem and a potential negative learning situation.

4   If the child does not urinate within 5 to 10 minutes, offer another 8 to 10 fl.oz of fluid. When the child first starts to urinate say nothing so as not to distract the child before their bladder is empty. Once they have completed urinating, reinforcers should be provided. If urination occurs in the bathroom but not in the urinal (in the case of boys) then shaping should be applied.

5   Continue process until the child is urinating within two to three minutes of being seated on the toilet. Once this is occurring regularly, add a second toileting time repeating the same steps.

6   Habit training: when the child sits on the toilet at any point and urinates within a minute or two. A connection has been made between sitting and urination. However, the child is not actually toilet trained at this point. The child is now ready for a toileting schedule. As many children have difficulties sensing when their bladders are full they have difficulty at this point.

7   When the child is physiologically ready to start monitoring bladder sensations, begin thinning prompts and schedule-based toileting. Introduce pictures into communication system for non-verbal children

8   Contingency shift: shift the emphasis away from reinforcement for urination in bathroom towards rewarding them for remaining dry. This generally will require frequent checking of the child to ensure dryness. This is to coincide with the existing toileting schedule so if the child is currently on a schedule of once per hour then checks could take place at a higher frequency at perhaps thirty-minute intervals.

9   Night-time incontinence: similar pattern as before but no fluids are given in the bathroom as the child is familiar with the procedure at this point and specific rewards are not implemented. If urination occurs just prior to getting up, get the child up earlier than usual to coincide with this event.

Time-out is recommended in the original procedure though only for younger children. To date, limited research is available that supports the use of generic habit training.

ASSESSMENT AND TREATMENT OF ENCOPRESIS

The review thus far has focused on the treatment of enuresis. Encopresis tends to occur at a lower frequency than enuresis and presents its own challenges to successful treatment. As stated at the outset of this chapter, a distinction is typically made with respect to 'retentive' and 'non-retentive' soiling. Retentive encopresis refers to the failure of faecal control in cases with constipation while non-retentive encopresis refers to failure in individuals without constipation (Lancioni, O'Reilly and Basili, 2001). Encopresis with constipation is reported as occurring more frequently than encopresis without (Huntley and Smith, 1999; McGrath *et al.*, 2000). Perhaps as a consequence of this, the majority of published treatment outcomes with individuals with intellectual disability are in relation to non-retentive encopresis. In a review of twenty-one treatment studies on encopresis and intellectual disability, Lancioni *et al.* (2001) identified thirteen studies addressing non-retentive encopresis, eleven of which implemented behavioural treatments while the remaining two used medical and behavioural interventions.

Biological factors in non-retentive encopresis

There is no standard definition for constipation but one generally accepted is that of bowel movements less than three times a week (Bohmer, Taminiau, Klinkenberg-Knol and Meuwissen, 2001; Clayden, 1992). Constipation is a frequent physical complaint among those with an intellectual disability. One review has identified that almost 70 percent of a population of individuals with severe and profound intellectual disability were constipated (having bowel movements less than three times a week or using laxatives more than three times a week; Bohmer *et al.*, 2001). Constipation in the same sample was significantly correlated with non-ambulancy, cerebral palsy, the use of anti-convulsive medication or benzodiazepines, H2 receptor antagonists, food refusal and a profound intellectual disability. In addition, the rate of challenging behaviour was twice that in the individuals experiencing constipation than those without. Other studies have identified additional factors such as low fluid intake, dietary habits and low fibre intake (Fischer, Adkins, Hall, Scaman, His and Marlett, 1985). Neuroleptic medication has also been identified as a contributing factor (Towers, Burgio, Locher, Merkel, Safaeian and Wald, 1994). A similar relationship between encopresis and constipation has been observed with children in the general population. For instance, Levine (1975) reported that 79 percent of his encopretic paediatric patients were constipated.

Biological factors interacting with operant factors have also been identified as important considerations in the assessment and treatment of constipation. Several studies have established that children with severe chronic constipation habitually withhold stools in an attempt to keep faecal matter out of contact with sensitive parts of the bowel wall. During withholding, contraction of the external anal sphincter and nearby muscles eject the faeces back into the recto sigmoid, where the faecal matter dries, hardens and enlarges, which then predisposes to additional withholding (Issenman, Filmer and Gorski, 1999). In most children, the problem begins with passing painful very large stools leading to the onset of 'holding-in'. As more stool collects in the child's lower intestine, the colon slowly stretches (called megacolon). Over time, looser partly formed stool from higher up the intestinal tract leaks around the large collection of harder more formed stool at the bottom of the colon (rectum). Initially, this leaking may lead to smears on underwear. Sometimes mistaken for diarrhoea, this phenomonon is known as overflow incontinence. Eventually, however, the child passes whole stools. Over time, the child with encopresis may also develop in-coordination of the muscles used to pass stools. In many children, the anal sphincter contracts rather than relaxes when they are trying to push out bowel movements. This disturbed coordination of muscle function, which causes faecal retention, is a key to the diagnosis and is also called anismus or paradoxic contraction of the pelvic floor to defecation.

Medical intervention

The most common laxatives used in medical management of constipation are bisacodyl or magnesium oxide and lactulose. Phosphate enemas are also used and, in a minority of cases, manual evacuation. However, evidence suggests that while laxatives are frequently prescribed, the results are often disappointing (Bohmer, Niezen-de Boer et al., 1999; Bohmer et al., 2001) perhaps in part owing to a failure to address aetiological and maintaining factors but also diffuse colon motility and diffuse transit problems. Several studies report the use of initial evacuation of the colon being conducted prior to behavioural interventions (O'Brien, Ross and Christophersen, 1986). Dietary recommendations include increasing roughage foods, decreasing dairy foods and increasing fluid intake (O'Brien et al., 1986). Substantial attention should be devoted to the medical assessment of constipation prior to any behavioural intervention. With regard to encopresis, the research has focused primarily on pathophysiological factors related to the colon and anal sphincter.

Behavioural treatment

Behavioural treatments have been identified as critical in the treatment of both retentive and non-retentive encopresis (Buttross, 1999; Lancioni et al., 2001). The majority of published studies on non-retentive faecal soiling have relied on behavioural treatments with only a minority examining adjunctive medical strategies (e.g. enema, laxative, dietary accommodations). O'Brien et al. (1986) report a relatively standard programme used in the home-based treatment of non-retentive encopresis for nine boys aged between 4 and 5 years. Components include: (1) an initial evacuation of the colon through enemas; (2) a morning routine of five minutes' toileting followed by suppository if the child had not produced enough faeces, defined as less than a quarter cup; (3) an afternoon five-minute toileting session; (4) pants checks; (5) simple correction involving washing own underwear quickly; (6) reinforcement for bowel movement involving fifteen minutes of child-preferred activity; (7) increase in bulk and roughage foods and a decrease in dairy and bland foods. In this case, encopresis in the children was eliminated after approximately eight weeks and suppositories were subsequently faded out and positive behaviour was maintained at twelve months. A variation by Smith (1996) incorporated scheduled toileting after each meal, pleasant events to occupy child while in toilet, adoption of squat position and reinforcement for appropriate activity. One additional implementation guideline is the use of scheduled toileting after meals to exploit the gastro-colic reflex (i.e. the colonic motor response elicited by feeding). The child should sit on the toilet for 5–10 minutes after breakfast and again after dinner every day. Some families may have to alter their daily routines to accomplish this, but it is a critical step, particularly for school-aged children.

Studies involving individuals with severe and profound intellectual disability typically include both behavioural and medical components: scheduled toileting, laxatives, reinforcement and positive practice components (Dalrymple and Angrist, 1988; Piazza, Fisher, Chinn and Bowman, 1991; Smith, 1994). For children with mild to moderate intellectual disability, back-up reinforcers tend to be used more frequently than primary reinforcers such as edibles to reinforce appropriate toileting (Ayllon, Simon and Wildman, 1975; Lyon, 1984; Steege and Harper, 1989). Many also involve the use of positive/simple practice or restitutional overcorrection (Lancioni *et al.*, 2001). The treatment of noctural non-retentive encopresis typically involves a variation of the dry bed training procedure described earlier.

Assessment issues

It is important that prior to implementation of any toileting programme that a comprehensive assessment occur. First, biological factors need to be examined including a urological examination to rule out any possible biological cause for incontinence particularly around urinary infections and urinary tract abnormalities. Gastrointestinal difficulties have also been identified in the development and maintenance of incontinence and consequently also need to be ruled out (Issenman *et al.*, 1999). Curiously, such difficulties have not been implicated in one recent study of children with intellectual disability (Bohmer *et al.*, 2001). The role of uncontrollable seizures if present should also be determined. As self-report is often compromised in children with intellectual disability, particularly those with severe and profound levels of intellectual disability, accurate observation and recording of objective information is important. Aside from a comprehensive behavioural assessment covering cognitive abilities, communication abilities, environmental and ecological analysis it should be ensured that the specific factors presented in Table 12.4 are also incorporated into the assessment process.

Table 12.4 Toileting problems assessment issues

• Enuresis or encopresis or both	• Degree of ambulation/exercise
• Diurnal or nocturnal or both	• Presence/absence of cerebral palsy
• Primary or secondary	• Medication (type and quantity)
• Encopresis with or without constipation	• Food/fluid refusal
	• Dietary habits
• Medical condition/physical abnormality (e.g. megacolon)	• Laxative use
	• Fear of bathroom/toilet
• Previous management approaches	
• Stool/urine characteristics	

Effectiveness of toileting procedures

The majority of published studies involving teaching self-initiated toileting report successful outcomes and in many cases outcome data suggest that gains are maintained long term. Some exceptions do exist, however. The results of a ten-year follow-up by Hyams, McCoull, Smith and Tyrer (1992) involving fourteen children indicated that self-initiated toileting with children with severe intellectual disability is hard to maintain. In contrast, however, Didden *et al.* (2001) report complete maintenance of prompted toileting 2.5 years after implementation of a modified Azrin–Foxx training procedure. However, it is possible that the environments of these children placed restrictions on self-toileting and the withdrawal of reinforcement may have been a factor also. There is some evidence to suggest that toileting procedures are more effective with children than with adults (Smith and Smith, 1977).

There are caveats, however, with respect to overall effectiveness. First, the majority of published literature relates to enuresis with relatively little published work relating to the treatment of encopresis (Lancioni *et al.*, 2001). Second, few studies explicitly state whether primary or secondary enuresis/ encopresis was present and most appear limited to primary disorders. Third, the majority of published studies involve children with an IQ of less than 35 (in the severe and profound range). Children with IQs above 60 are relatively rare in published behavioural studies. Fourth, procedural details are often omitted from published studies. For instance, few studies indicate whether scheduled toileting was reduced or discontinued following termination of formal interventions.

Effectiveness must also be balanced against a consideration of the use of punishment procedures. In recent years a protracted debate on the role of punishment as a technique of reducing the frequency of target behaviours has taken place. Much of this debate has taken place in the context of challenging behaviour and little if any has taken place in the domain of toileting. Several of the procedures described here involve the use of restitutional overcorrection/positive practice and/or time-out, which are technically punishment procedures and the use of such may be disputed. Parents have been found to consider the use of such procedures in the establishment of toileting as undesirable (Dalrymple and Ruble, 1992). Several studies report the use of restitutional overcorrection or positive practice such as that by Didden *et al.* (2001). Studies report anything between five minutes and one hour for restitution (Lyon, 1984; Scott, 1977). In busy service settings with constant demands on staff, the implementation of time-consuming procedures may be impractical for staff to implement. Furthermore, the collateral effects of punishment procedures are often under-reported and rarely examined. For instance, non-compliance with positive practice and overcorrection is not uncommon but is not reported. One exception is the study by Saloviita (2002) where the therapist was slapped several times at night as she attempted to implement a positive practice at night-time after waking up a client who experienced noctural enuresis. Finally, increased efficacy of interventions using punishment procedures over those that do not has not been established and available studies would not suggest that their use results in shorter interventions.

Practical aspects of programme implementation

While generic treatment studies have been described in some detail above, they often give the impression that the implementation of an off-the-shelf programme will provide a remedy. Few studies relate day-to-day difficulties that may emerge with programme implementation. This is perhaps due to two factors. Studies that are not successful are rarely published and second, attention is rarely devoted to the nuances of implementation in journal articles. Difficulties that may emerge with children include fear of the bathroom, fear of sitting, negative reactions to the removal of nappies, smearing, resistance to use of toilet paper, resistance to washing hands, resistance to using unfamiliar facilities particularly if they have an autistic-spectrum disorder (Wheeler, 1998). Behavioural procedures can be applied to these factors though early identification is important as failure to do so may impact on programme implementation and reduce motivation of parents or staff. General preparation guidelines include having a sufficient number of additional training pants and underwear on hand, having easy-to-manipulate clothing that the child can use, such as trousers with elastic waist bands, using a child-size toilet seat on a regular toilet with a block for the child's feet, or a potty chair, using the child's favourite beverage to ensure sufficient fluid intake and correct identification of reinforcers in advance (see Table 12.4 above).

In trying to promote bladder tension awareness and in using urine alarms, the elimination of especially distracting events in the environment may be important. The use of urine trigger alarms also cannot be used during the menstrual cycle and traditional methods during these times should be identified if necessary. The amount of fluid given to treat enuresis will generally depend on the age and weight of the child. However, Wilson (1995) recommends 2 to 4 fl.oz of a favourite liquid 20 to 30 minutes prior to a predetermined time.

Staff demands and preparation

The demands on staff charged with the implementation of a toileting programme can be quite high. The majority of interventions occur throughout the day and the amount of time involved in individual sessions can be considerable depending upon the individual components of the intervention. During baseline session, sessions are typically one hour in duration with checks occurring at the end of one-hour intervals and coincide with 'clock hours'. It is recommended that a given staff team identify busy times of day when scheduled checks and prompt times may compete with other tasks such as meal preparation, external activities, etc. The use of staff prompts such as kitchen timers can assist staff in maintaining the schedule. Despite the presence of incontinence it is not uncommon that such semblance of a pattern is evident with children and these should be identified if possible. The delivery of a high rate of reinforcement can also prove difficult for staff. Didden *et al.* (2001) report the implementation of reinforcement every five minutes using edible and social reinforcers. This is a high rate of reinforcement and ensuring a supply of reinforcers is crucial. Edible reinforcers or back-up reinforcers tend to be more practical for staff than social reinforcers as work schedules may restrict time availability which may be required for a play activity. Therefore, stimuli should be selected based upon their effectiveness as reinforcers and their practicality. Thinning of reinforcement schedule also needs to be considered in advance. Clear communication with staff around the length of time a programme may take and practical implementation is important from the outset. A mediator analysis, such as that developed by LaVigna and Willis (1992), should also be conducted to identify current capacity of a staff team to implement a toileting intervention. Only one child should be allocated to a trainer until the trainer is proficient.

Levels of disability

Adaptations to any toileting programme will have to be made depending upon the individual concerned and their level of disability. However, what is perhaps more important than the diagnosis of disability itself is the person's functional abilities and a clear identification of any sensory deficits. While the majority of interventions aim to establish discriminative stimulus control for self-initiated toileting to take place, the particular discriminative stimulus will depend upon the individual. Examples of discriminative stimuli include LEDs, buzzers and even wrist timers that can vibrate after a specified length of time. For the visually or hearing impaired, the use of a vibrating wristband can be of use though this should be combined with some visual cue so staff or parents know to bring the individual to the toilet. During training, for a stimulus to become established as a discriminative stimulus it is important that the correct behaviour occurs and is reinforced and therefore consistent staff responding is critical. Combining object cueing with this form of discriminative stimulus control can also be of use. Examples might include placing toilet paper in the individual's hand following presentation of the discriminative stimulus. For instance, Lancioni et al. (1994) report on three children with severe intellectual disabilities. Two of three children were either deaf or had significant hearing difficulties. The third child had no expressive language. Pictures of the toilet were used for the two children with hearing impairments and a piece of red cloth used for the third child. Immediately prior to scheduled toileting every thirty minutes, the hand was physically prompted to reach for one of the toileting cues, then the child was walked to the toilet with the cue, and reinforcement followed urination. This lasted until the children showed self-initiated toileting on six consecutive programme days. Liquids were subsequently reduced. Assisted toileting was totally eliminated with all children within the first ten days. As a result, the authors recommend that natural environments provide appropriate toileting cues. An earlier study indicated that children started to show self-initiated toileting by taking the cues. This could signal staff that would have to be responsive to such communication (Lancioni and Ceccarani, 1981).

CONCLUSIONS

Behaviourally based toileting interventions for children with intellectual disability have been shown to be effective in the treatment of enuresis and encopresis but should occur in the context of a thorough medical assessment. Any behavioural intervention must be balanced against the resources available for implementation and the assessment procedure should involve a close consideration of factors affecting implementation. Caution must be exercised with respect to taking a 'cookbook' approach to intervention and interventions will almost certainly require adaptations; in this respect comprehensive assessment of the child should guide both intervention selection and adaptation. Close consideration should be given to the role of punishment procedures. Though the majority of interventions involve the use of punishment, other studies without such components report equally effective results thereby questioning the use of such components (e.g. Lancioni and Markus, 1999). Specifically, urine trigger alarms in conjunction with positive reinforcement are effective as is response restriction though to date no component analysis studies have been conducted in this area.

EXERCISE

Work in groups of four. Brainstorm the ten main obstacles you think you would encounter in helping parents and teachers implement an enuresis or encopresis management programme. Organize these from the most to the least important, in terms of their impact on treatment effectiveness. For the top three most important obstacles, develop plans for overcoming them, so that probability of parents and teachers effectively implementing the programme is maximized. Read your plans to the class.

FURTHER READING AND RESOURCES FOR CLINICIANS

Buchanan, A. (1992). *Children who Soil: Assessment and Treatment*. Chichester: Wiley.

Foxx, R. M. and Azrin, N. H. (1973). *Toilet Training the Retarded: A Rapid Program for Day and Night Time Independent Toileting*. Champaign, IL: Research Press.

ERIC (Education and Resources for Improving Childhood Continence) (2005). *Promoting Continence in Children with Disabilities: Minimum Standards for Treatment and Service Delivery*.

ERIC (Education and Resources for Improving Childhood Continence) (2005). *Helping Children who Have Learning Disabilities with Bowel and Bladder Management: A Helpful Guide for Parents*.

Enuresis Alarms, Malem Bedwetting Alarms, Malem Medical, Nottingham, England, UK, www.malem.co.uk.

REFERENCES

Aman, M. G., Collier-Crespin, A. and Lindsay, R. L. (2000). Pharmacotherapy of disorders in mental retardation. *European Child and Adolescent Psychiatry*, 9, 1, 98–107.

Ayllon, T., Simon, S. J. and Wildman, R. W. (1975). Instructions and reinforcement in the elimination of encopresis: A case study. *Journal of Behaviour Therapy and Experimental Psychiatry*, 6, 3, 235–8.

Azrin, N. H. and Foxx, R. M. (1971). A method of toilet training the institutionally retarded. *Journal of Applied Behaviour Analysis*, 4, 89–99.

Azrin, N. H., Sneed, T. J. and Foxx, R. M. (1973). Dry bed training: A rapid method of eliminating bedwetting of the retarded. *Behaviour Research and Therapy*, 11, 427–34.

Bohmer, C. J., Niezen-de Boer, M. C., Klinkenberg-Knol, E. C., Deville, W. L., Nadorp, J. H. and Meuwissen, S. G. (1999). The prevalence of gastroesophagael reflux disease in intellectually disabled children. *American Journal of Gastroenterology*, 94, 804–10.

Bohmer, C. L., Taminau, J. A. J. M., Klinkenberg-Knol, E. C. and Meiwissen, S. G. M.

(2001). The prevalence of constipation in institutionalised people with intellectual disability. *Journal of Intellectual Disability Research*, 45, 3, 212–18.

Buchanan, A. (1992). *Children who Soil: Assessment and Treatment*. Chichester: Wiley.

Buntinx, I. M., Hennekam, R. C., Brouwer, O., Strink, H., Beuten, J., Mangelschots, K. and Fryns, J. P. (1995). Clinical profile of Angelman syndrome at different ages. *American Journal of Medical Genetics*, 56, 176–83.

Buttross, S. (1999). Encopresis in the child with a behaviour disorder: When initial treatment does not work. *Paediatric Annals*, 28, 317–21.

Carr, A. (1999). *The Handbook of Child and Adolescent Clinical Psychology*. London: Routledge.

Clayden, G. (1992). Personal practice: Management of chronic constipation. *Archives of Diseases of Childhood*, 67, 340–64.

Dalrymple, N. J. and Angrist, M. H. (1988). Toilet training a sixteen year old with autism in a natural setting. *British Journal of Mental Subnormality*, 34, 117–29.

Dalrymple, N. J. and Ruble, L. A. (1992). Toilet training and behaviours of people with autism: Parent views. *Journal of Autism and Developmental Disabilities*, 22, 265–75.

Didden, R., Sikkema, S. P. E., Bosman, L. T. M., Duker, P. C. and Curfs, L. M. G. (2001). Use of a modified Azrin-Foxx toilet training procedure with individuals with Angelman syndrome. *Journal of Applied Research in Intellectual Disabilities*, 14, 64–70.

Donnellan, A. M., LaVigna, G. W., Negri-Shoultz, N. and Fassbender, L. L. (1988). *Progress without Punishment: Effective Approaches for Learners with Behaviour Problems*. New York: Teachers College Press.

Duker, P. C., Averink, M. and Melein, L. (2001). Response restriction as a method to establish diurnal bladder control. *American Journal on Mental Retardation*, 106, 209–15.

Duker, P. C. and Dekkers, M. (1992). Development of diurnal bladder control in severely and profoundly mentally handicapped residents. *Journal of Intellectual Disability Research*, 36, 177–81.

Fischer, M., Adkins, W., Hall, L., Scaman, P., His, S. and Marlett, J. (1985). The effects of dietary fibres in a liquid diet on bowel function of mentally retarded children. *Journal of Mental Deficiency Research*, 29, 373–81.

Houts, A. C., Berman, J. S. and Abramson, H. (1994). Effectiveness of psychological and pharmacological treatments for nocturnal enuresis. *Journal of Consulting and Clinical Psychology*, 62, 4, 737–45.

Huntley, E. and Smith, L. (1999). Long term follow up of behavioural treatment for primary encopresis in people with intellectual disability in the community. *Journal of Intellectual Disability Research*, 43, 484–8.

Hyams, G., McCoull, K., Smith, P. S. and Tyrer, S. P. (1992). Behavioural continence training in mental handicap: A 10-year follow-up study. *Journal of Intellectual Disability Research*, 36, 551–8.

Issenman, R. M., Filmer, R. B. and Gorski, P. A. (1999). A review of bowel and bladder control development in children: How gastrointestinal and urologic conditions relate to problems in toilet training. *Paediatrics*, 103, 6, 1346–97.

Knivsberg, A. M., Reichlet, K. L., Nodland, M. and Hoien, T. (1995). Autistic syndromes and diet: A follow-up. *Scandanavian Journal of Educational Research*, 39, 223–36.

Lancioni, G. E. and Ceccarini, P. S. (1981). Teaching independent toileting within the normal daily program: Two studies with profoundly retarded children. *Behaviour Research of Severe Developmental Disabilities*, 2, 79–96.

Lancioni, G. E. and Markus, S. (1999). Urine triggered alarm signals and prompts to promote daytime urinary continence in a boy with severe intellectual disability. *Behavioural and Cognitive Psychotherapy*, 27, 261–5.

Lancioni, G. E., Duker, P. C., Klasse, M. and Goossens, A. (1994). Promoting self-initiated toileting in children with severe developmental disabilities. *Scandinavian Journal of Behaviour Therapy*, 23, 113–19.

Lancioni, G. E., O'Reilly, M. F. and Basili, G. (2001). Treating encopresis in people with intellectual disabilities: A literature review. *Journal of Applied Research in Intellectual Disabilities*, 14, 1, 47–63.

Lancioni, G. E., O'Reilly, M. F., Sernelli, S. and Campodonico, F. (2000). Alarm signals and prompts to eliminate large urinary accidents in a woman with multiple disabilities. *Scandinavian Journal of Behaviour Therapy*, 29, 3–4, 152–5.

Landgraf, J. M., Abidari, J., Cilento, G. C., Cooper, C. S., Schulman, S. L. and Ortenberg, J. (2004). Coping, commitment, and attitude: Quantifying the everyday burden of enuresis on children and their families. *Paediatrics*, 113, 2, 334–44.

LaVigna, G. W., and Willis, T. J. (1992). A model for multi-element treatment planning and outcome measurement. In D. Berkel (ed.), *Autism: Identification, Education, and Treatment* (pp. 135–49). Hillsdale, NJ: Lawrence Erlbaum.

Leach, P. (1997). Infant care from infants' viewpoint: The views of some professionals. *Early Development and Parenting*, 6, 2, 47–58.

Levine, M. D. (1975). Children with encopresis: A descriptive analysis. *Paediatrics*, 56, 412–16.

Lyon, M. A. (1984). Positive reinforcement and logical consequences in the treatment of classroom encopresis. *School Psychology Review*, 13, 238–43.

McEntee, J. E. and Saunders, R. R. (1997). A response-restriction analysis of stereotypy in adolescents with mental retardation: Implications for applied behaviour analysts. *Journal of Applied Behaviour Analysis*, 30, 485–506.

McGrath, M. L.., Mellon, M. W. and Murphy, L. (2000). Empirically supported treatments in paediatric psychology: Constipation and encopresis. *Journal of Paediatric Psychology*, 25, 225–54.

Mowrer, O. H. and Mowrer, W. M. (1938). Enuresis – a method for its study and treatment. *American Journal of Orthopsychiatry*, 8, 436–59.

Nawaz, S., Griffiths, P. and Tappin, D. (2002). Parent administered modified dry bed training for childhood nocturnal enuresis: Evidence for superiority over urine alarm conditioning when delivery factors are controlled. *Behavioural Interventions*, 17, 247–60.

Nield, L. S. and Kamat, D. (2004). Enuresis: How to evaluate and treat. *Clinical Paediatrics*, 43, 409–15.

O'Brien, S. Ross, L. V., and Christophersen, E. R. (1986). Primary encopresis: Evaluation and treatment. *Journal of Applied Behaviour Analysis*, 19, 137–45.

O'Regan, S. and Yazbeck, S. (1987). Constipation: A cause of enuresis, urinary tract infection and vesico-ureteral reflux in children. *Medical Hypotheses*, 17, 409–13.

Piazza, C. C., Fisher, W., Chinn, S. and Bowman, L. (1991). Reinforcement of Incontinent Stools in the Treatment of Encopresis. *Clinical Pediatrics*, 30, 28–32.

Proctor, E. and Loader, P. (2003). A six year follow up study of chronic constipation and soiling in a specialist paediatric service. *Child: Care, Health and Development*, 29, 2, 103–9.

Robson, W. L. M. and Leung, A. K. C. (2000). Secondary nocturnal enuresis. *Clinical Paediatrics*, 39, 379–85.

Saloviita, T. (2002). Dry bed training method in the elimination of bed wetting in two adults with autism and severe mental retardation. *Cognitive Behaviour Therapy*, 31, 3, 135–40.

Schum, T. R., Kilb, T. M. and McAuliffe, T. L. (2002). Sequential acquisition of toileting training skills: A descriptive study of gender and age differences in normal children. *Paediatrics*, 109, 48.

Scott, E. A. (1977). Treatment of encopresis in a classroom setting: A case study. *British Journal of Educational Psychology*, 47, 199–202.

Shattock, P. and Savery, D. (1999) *Autism as a Metabolic Disorder*. Autism Research Unit: University of Sunderland.

Smith, L. J. (1981). Training severely and profoundly mentally handicapped nocturnal enuretics. *Behaviour Research and Therapy*, 19, 67–74.

Smith, L. J. (1994). A behavioural approach to the treatment of non-retentive nocturnal encopresis in an adult with a severe learning disability. *Journal of Behaviour Therapy and Experimental Psychiatry*, 25, 81–6.

Smith, L. J. (1996). A behavioural approach to the treatment of non-retentive encopresis in adults with learning disabilities. *Journal of Intellectual Disability Research*, 40, 130–9.

Smith, P. and Smith, L. (1977). Chronological age and social age as factors in intensive daytime toilet training of institutionally mentally retarded children. *Journal of Behaviour Therapy and Experimental Psychiatry*, 8, 269–73.

Smith, P. S. (1979). A comparison of different methods of toilet training the mentally handicapped. *Behaviour Research and Therapy*, 17, 33–43.

Steege, M. W. and Harper, D. C. (1989). Enhancing the management of secondary encopresis by assessing acceptability of treatment: A case study. *Journal of Behaviour Therapy and Experimental Psychiatry*, 20, 333–41.

Thompson, T. and Hanson, R. (1983). Overhydration: Precautions when treating urinary incontinence. *Mental Retardation*, 21, 139–43.

Towers, A. L., Burgio, K. L., Locher, J. L., Merkel, I. S., Safaeian, M. and Wald, A. (1994). Constipation in the elderly. *Journal of the American Geriatric Society*, 42, 701–6.

Van Son, M., van Heesch, N., Mulder, G. and van Londen, A. (1995). The effectiveness of dry bed training for nocturnal enuresis in adults: A 3, 5, 6, years follow-up. *Behaviour Research and Therapy*, 33, 5, 557–9.

Van Wagenen, R. K., Meyerson, L., Kerr, N. J. and Mahoney, K. E. (1969). Field trials of a new procedure in toilet training. *Journal of Experimental Child Psychology*, 8, 147–59.

Waring, R. (1993) cited in Shattock, P. and Savery, D. (1999). *Autism as a Metabolic Disorder*. Autism Research Unit: University of Sunderland.

Wheeler, M. B.-W. (1998). *Toilet Training for Individuals with Autism and Related Disorders*. Arlington: Future Horizons.

Wilson, M. (1995). Generic habit-training program. *Focus on Autistic Behaviour*, 10, 2.

Chapter 13

Feeding difficulties and eating disorders

Peter Sturmey, Howie Reyer, Stephen B. Mayville and Johnny L. Matson

Case study: rumination in a man with ID

Mr Esperanza was a 29-year-old non-ambulatory Caucasian man diagnosed with profound intellectual disability. Immediately following meals, staff noticed that he would regurgitate and chew his food before re-swallowing. Given the serious health-risks associated with this behaviour, this problem was brought to the attention of the staff psychologist. A subsequent assessment battery of the Screening Tool of Feeding Problems (STEP), the Questions About Behavioural Function (QABF), and Maladaptive Behaviour Record (MBR) cards (i.e. cards that document antecedents, behaviours and consequences associated with a problem behaviour) were administered in conjunction with a barium swallow study. The results of the STEP indicated the problem was frequent in occurrence and severe in nature. Results of the QABF indicated that the behaviour served a non-social function. The MBR cards revealed that the behaviour was occurring at almost every meal. It did not appear to be socially maintained, because the behaviour took place whether or not other staff or clients were present. Staff observation also revealed that there was a greater tendency for Mr Esperanza to engage in rumination when there were sweet foods in his meal. The images obtained from the barium swallow study revealed that much of the food was not making it down into his stomach before it was brought back up to his oral cavity through constriction of his oesophagus. Medical staff did not find any structural anomalies that may better account for regurgitation, and the higher frequency of this behaviour with meals accompanied by specific types of food indicated that a diagnosis of rumination was appropriate.

From the results of the assessment it was determined the function of rumination was non-social. Therefore, it was decided that his treatment would consist of a nutritional intervention. His caloric intake would be increased and a thickening agent would be added to the liquids in his diet to make it more difficult to regurgitate his food. Mr Esperanza's leisure activities were also scheduled shortly after mealtime to keep him occupied during the digestion process.

Rumination decreased rapidly following introduction of the plan. There were only two occurrences of rumination over the first two weeks of intervention. Following the first two weeks, no further episodes of rumination were noted. The thickening agent was subsequently faded from John's mealtime liquids by progressively increasing the quantity of thickening agent in his liquids. He was maintained on a satiation diet with no adverse effect on his body weight.

DIAGNOSIS AND CLASSIFICATION OF EATING PROBLEMS

The text revision of the fourth edition of the Diagnostic and Statistical Manual of Mental Disorders (American Psychiatric Association; 2000) identifies both anorexia and bulimia under the category of *Eating Disorders*. The manual also identifies pica and rumination disorder under the category of *Feeding and Eating Disorders of Early Infancy and Childhood*. Anorexia and bulimia as well as pica and rumination disorder will be described in further detail within this chapter. Additional eating disorders that are described in the literature, but are not separate diagnostic categories, are overeating and obesity, polydipsia, food grabbing, food fads, challenging behaviour during meals, improper pacing, self-feeding deficits, and food refusal and selectivity. These disorders will be described in further detail within this chapter. However, overeating and obesity will be described only in reference to individuals with Down syndrome or Prader-Willi syndrome, because people whose ID is secondary to these conditions often have particularly pronounced problems in these areas, and an important body of research on the management of these conditions is now available.

The Royal College of Psychiatrists has published a set of diagnostic criteria modified specifically for people with intellectual disabilities (DC-LD: Cooper, Melville and Einfield, 2003), including criteria for eating disorders (Gravestock, 2003). These disorders include prototypical eating disorders, such as anorexia nervosa, bulimia nervosa, binge-eating disorder, as well as psychogenic overeating episode, psychogenic vomiting, psychogenic loss of appetite, food faddiness/refusal disorder, food ruination/regurgitation disorder, pica, and excessive chewing and spitting out food disorder. Gravestock (2003) noted that previous conceptions of eating disorders were too narrow and did not include a wide range of abnormal eating behaviours, many of which are commonly seen in people with intellectual disabilities. Thus, DC-LD represents a broadening of psychiatric classification of unusual patterns of eating in people with intellectual disabilities.

Despite diagnostic and methodological difficulties with epidemiological research in this area, available data suggests that 3 percent to 42 percent of adults with intellectual disabilities who reside in residential settings, and 1 percent to 19 percent of adults with intellectual disabilities who reside in the community have diagnosable eating disorders (Gravestock, 2000). Moreover, it is estimated that as many as 80 percent of individuals with severe or profound intellectual disability exhibit feeding problems (Munk and Repp, 1994). Individuals with developmental disabilities who develop feeding disorders are at an increased risk for malnutrition and respiratory problems (Stevenson, 1995). It is imperative that such disorders are diagnosed correctly as diagnosis-specific treatment results in significantly improved energy consumption and nutritional status (Schwarz, Corredor, Fisher-Medina, Cohen and Rabinowitz, 2001). Subsequently, successful management of feeding problems can result in lower hospitalization rates. Nevertheless, identifying eating disorders in individuals with intellectual disabilities can be difficult.

To address the lack of standardized methods for identifying individuals with intellectual disabilities who may have feeding problems, Matson and Kuhn (2001) developed a screening tool referred to as the Screening Tool of Feeding Problems, or STEP. The STEP screens for feeding problems early so that they can be targeted for assessment and treatment. Twenty-three items included in the STEP target five general categories, including the risk of aspiration (e.g. rumination), food selectivity (e.g. selective by texture), feeding skills deficits (e.g. eats too quickly), food refusal and associated behaviour problems (e.g. spits food out), and nutrition-related behaviour problems (e.g. pica).

Of course, one has to ensure that eating disorders are not secondary to medical or physical difficulties (Gedye, 1998). For example, individuals taking the mood stabilizer, Lithium, might experience excessive thirst. Excessive drinking to relieve the thirst could be mistaken for polydipsia. Moreover, excessive thirst could also be a symptom of either diabetes or renal dysfunction. Weight gain or overeating could be a side-effect of medication that increases appetite, a hypothalamic dysfunction, or even pregnancy. Individuals who ruminate or who exhibit a preference for either certain foods or textures might actually have difficulties swallowing. Pica could result from a nutritional or mineral deficit, such as zinc (Lofts, Schroeder and Maier, 1990). Food refusal could be due to allergies, dental pain, gastrointestinal dysfunction, or medication that either suppresses appetite (e.g. Prozac) or causes nausea (e.g. Tegretol). A case study on a man with Down syndrome (Holt, Bouras and Watson, 1988) revealed that refusal to eat was not due to his 'willingness' to lose weight (i.e. anorexia). Rather, the onset of food refusal occurred subsequent to a throat infection as well as being admitted to a hospital for many months – away from familiar surroundings.

PREDISPOSING, PRECIPITATING, AND MAINTAINING FACTORS

Eating and feeding disorders among people with intellectual disabilities occur throughout the lifespan and the aetiology of these conditions is often complex involving multiple factors. Luiselli (1989) made the distinction between organic and non-organic aetiologies. Organic refers to medical and physical variables resulting in slow growth or weight gain, especially in infants and children. Non-organic influences refer to psychosocial causes, such as parental neglect and familial stress, as well as positive and negative reinforcing contingencies that maintain problem behaviour. Both variables can also interact and maintain feeding disorders making mealtime and, subsequently, meals aversive. Gisel, Birnbaum, and Schwartz (1998) identified three behavioural expressions of underlying feeding disorders in children. These were resistance to accepting food orally, an apparent lack of energy or endurance to engage in the tasks that make up the operational definition of eating, and oral-motor disabilities resulting in an inability to produce the necessary motor skills for ingestion. Although feeding development is dependent upon structural integrity and neurological maturation, eating is a learned progression of behaviour influenced by sensory-motor development and experience (Stevenson, 1995). In the case of food refusal Kerwin, Ahearn, Eicher, and Bured (1995) suggested that a long association between eating and gastrointestinal distress, disruption of oral-motor skill development because of illness, and escape and/or avoidance of meals might all contribute to the development of food refusal. What research there has been into this question has focused on maintaining factors, rather than predisposing and precipitating factors.

Piazza, Fisher, Brown, Shore *et al.* (2003) conducted functional analyses of a wide variety of inappropriate mealtime behaviours in fifteen children aged 1 to 6 years. Several of these children had established intellectual disabilities or appeared to be at risk for intellectual disabilities and many had complicating neurological, medical, and physical disabilities. Inappropriate behaviours included batting, head turning, negative vocalizations, aggression, and self-injury. There were two parts to the study. First, the families were observed feeding their children in a quiet room. The parents were instructed to feed their children in the usual way that they did at home and to bring any objects that they typically used during mealtimes. The patterns of observed consequences were quite different from child to child. The children were then exposed to functional analysis conditions (Iwata, Dorsey, Slifer, Bauman and Richman, 1982/1994) to determine the environmental variables that influenced these behaviours. Inappropriate mealtime behaviours were systematically consequated with attention, tangibles, or removal of spoon and food. Of the fifteen children, ten displayed a clear relationship between environmental variables and behaviour. Nine showed escape behaviour, eight showed attention-related behaviour and two showed tangible-related behaviour. One child demonstrated different functions for different topographies of mealtime-inappropriate behaviours. Thus, current environmental events mediated through the behaviour of the parents were key determinants of the rate of inappropriate mealtime behaviours.

Piazza *et al.*'s analysis focused primarily on consequences and, by implication, the possible role of deprivation and satiation. Kerwin *et al.* (1995) presented an analysis of food refusal in terms of behavioural economics that emphasized the *costs* of eating. Behavioural economics quantifies the relationship between cost, measured as the number or rate of a response, and the quantity of a commodity, such as food, drugs, or both. The relationships between costs and commodities are known as demand functions. Thus, in the example of food refusal, the cost of acceptance of food may be influenced by the number of responses required as determined by the quantity of food and its texture. Kerwin *et al.* demonstrated that there was a lawful relationship between the likelihood of accepting a spoon of food and the quantity of food on the spoon. Based on this analysis, Kerwin *et al.* used physical guidance or non-removal of the spoon at a spoon volume at which some acceptance of food was likely. They observed, following this intervention, that food acceptance increased across several non-targeted food volumes, including less and more food than was targeted for the intervention. Thus, behavioural economics can act as a second behavioural model to explain food refusal and to develop effective interventions for this problem.

Piazza and Kerwin's work illustrate how psychological factors can be central to the maintenance of eating disorders.

EATING DISORDERS IN ADULTS: ASSESSMENT AND INTERVENTION

In this section a brief account of each of the following feeding problems in adults with ID will be given, along with guidance on assessment and intervention:

- polydipsia
- self-feeding deficits
- improper pacing
- food refusal and selectivity
- overeating in Prader-Willi syndrome
- problem behaviour during meals.

Polydipsia

Excessive water drinking, also known as polydipsia, is a potentially dangerous, yet underdiagnosed problem in individuals with intellectual disabilities. It has been defined as drinking more than three to five liters (Bremner and Regan, 1991; Deb, Bramble, Drybala, Boyle and Bruce, 1994) of non-alcoholic beverages over a 24-hour period. The behaviour can be reliably identified by caregivers in screening questionnaires (Hayfron-Benjamin, Peters and

Woodhouse, 1996b). Depending on the population, prevalence rates range from 3.5 percent to 6.2 percent (Bremner and Regan, 1991; Deb *et al.*, 1994; Hayfron-Benjamin, Peters and Woodhouse, 1996a) and possibly higher. Even though most individuals identified as polydipsic are schizophrenic, it has been identified in individuals with intellectual disabilities.

Terai, Munesue, and Hiratani (1999) found that children with autism were significantly more likely to display polydipsia than children with mental intellectual disabilities without concomitant autism regardless of the context. Further, the majority of the children with autism were not taking psychotropic medication. These authors concluded that some property of drinking water might be self-reinforcing; however, being diagnosed as having autism appears to be neither a necessary nor sufficient variable for developing polydipsia (Deb *et al.*, 1994).

Behavioural treatment of polydipsia

Many of these treatments have been used with individuals with schizophrenia. However, the underlying behavioural principles that make up these programs could be modified and implemented with individuals with intellectual disabilities, including tokens for daily weight loss and restricted fluid intake (Bowen, Glynn, Marshall, Kurth and Hayden, 1990; Pavalonis, Shutty, Hundley, Leadbetter *et al.*, 1992), and punishment following significant weight gain (Bowen, Glynn, Marshall, Kurth and Hayden, 1990). In settings where fluid restriction is not practical or ethical, serum sodium concentration levels could be measured (Pavalonis *et al.*, 1992; Waller, Hyde and Thomas, 1993) (there is an inverse relation between fluid intake and blood serum levels).

In a woman with severe intellectual disabilities and autism, polydipsia was addressed by reinforcing with edibles and reducing activity demands to reward water refusal (McNally, Calamari, Hansen and Kaliher, 1988). The authors presented the woman with a choice of either drinking or refusing water every 30 minutes throughout the day. Drinking water was followed by activity demands and consumption of water via a narrow straw, whereas edible reinforcers and a reduction in demands were provided for water refusal. Water consumption declined from 2.84 liters per day prior to treatment to less than 0.3 liters per day, twenty-nine weeks after the start of treatment. Unfortunately, experimental control was not demonstrated. Therefore, treatment effects could have been influenced by other factors.

Obesity in individuals with Down syndrome

One focus of eating disorders that is overlooked is individuals with Down syndrome who are overweight. Prevalence rates have been found to range from 31 percent to 71 percent for males, and 22 percent to a whopping

96 percent for females (Bell and Bhate, 1992; Prasher, 1995). Compared to rates found within the general population (i.e. 33 percent to 40 percent for males, and 32 percent to 36 percent for females) (Bell and Bhate, 1992; Rubin, Rimmer, Chicoine, Braddock and McGuire, 1998), obesity is a major health concern for individuals with Down syndrome. Individuals with Down syndrome who are overweight tend to live at home as opposed to residential settings and this difference appears to be significant (Prasher, 1995; Rubin et al., 1998). Height also appears to be a significant factor that predisposes individuals with Down syndrome to become overweight (Chad, Jobling and Frail, 1990; Luke, Sutton, Schoeller and Roizen, 1996). Shorter individuals tend to have lower resting metabolic rates than taller individuals with Down syndrome (Chad et al., 1990). Further, individuals with Down syndrome tend to have lower energy and micronutrient (e.g. thiamin) intake than healthy matched controls (Luke et al., 1996). Moreover, Fujiura, Fitzsimons, and Marks (1997) found that lifestyle variables, such as the pattern of friendship and access to recreation and social opportunities, covaried with body mass index. Taken together, it is believed that individuals with Down syndrome may have an inherent metabolic risk factor for expending less total energy because of their lower resting metabolic rate. Luke et al. (1996) as well as Chad et al. (1990) suggested that treating obesity in individuals with Down syndrome consists of a balanced diet *without* energy restriction, vitamin and mineral supplementation, and increased physical activity that would increase energy expenditure without decreasing energy intake.

Self-feeding deficits

Individuals who exhibited self-feeding deficits are unable or refuse to place food into their mouth independently. Other individuals may be able to feed themselves, but cannot use utensils or they exhibit considerable spillage. Such individuals either do not consume most of their food or must be fed by others. Luiselli (1989) reasoned that individuals who do not self-feed came from a meal format whereby food was presented rapidly with minimal social interaction, and where encouragement to display appropriate eating behaviour was nonexistent.

Operant conditioning techniques, such as shaping and chaining, are commonly used to teach new skills. Physical guidance is superior over modelling when teaching mealtime skills in individuals with disabilities (Nelson, Cone and Hanson, 1975), and follow-ups subsequent to training are necessary to ensure that learned skills are maintained (O'Brien, Bugle and Azrin, 1972). Teaching self-feeding skills also decreases the rate of inappropriate behaviour, such as eating with one's hands. Azrin and Armstrong (1973) described the 'Mini-Meal' program where regular meals were divided into quiet, hourly, smaller meals throughout the day. Individuals were taught to use utensils appropriately using graduated guidance, shaping, implementing correction for errors, and blocking inappropriate responses. They taught twenty-two individuals with profound intellectual disabilities within twelve days ($M = 5$ days) to eat appropriately with napkins, drinking from a glass, using a fork and spoon, as well as buttering and cutting with a knife. Barton, Guess, Garcia, and Baer (1970) distinguished inappropriate eating behaviour, such as eating with fingers and inappropriate use of utensils by implementing either time-out from meals or a 15 s tray removal time-out contingent on the display of inappropriate behaviour. The multiple-baseline design across behaviours was implemented for sixteen participants with severe and profound retardation. Rates of inappropriate behaviour decreased and appropriate behaviour increased as successive behaviours were addressed.

Although no data were provided, Rosen (1974) claimed that one or two teaching trials were needed (with response generalization) to train sipping through a straw, using a plastic squeeze bottle with a straw. The individuals learn to squeeze the bottle and thereafter to make the sucking response to avoid choking or spilling the liquid while squeezing the bottle. Petersen and Ottenbacher (1986) used successive approximations and a device called a vacuum cup to train lip closure in three boys with severe intellectual disabilities. Failure to close one's lips while eating contributes to abnormal feeding responses, including spillage, choking, and atypical chewing and swallowing patterns. The participants were unable to drink from a glass normally, but were physically able to close their lips. The vacuum cup contained a pressurized flow-control device that, when pressed, allowed a pump-like action that precisely released preferred liquid coinciding with the breathing cycle. Treatment efficacy was demonstrated using a multiple-baseline design across subjects. All subjects achieved 10 s of lip closure in less than eight trials. Anecdotal observations suggested that all of the participants drank from a glass, stimulus generalization occurred as improved lip closure was demonstrated when food from a spoon was presented, and two of the participants sucked liquid using straws.

Cipani (1981) reduced food spillage in a girl with severe intellectual disabilities. Tokens were presented contingent upon a certain amount of responses without spillage. If spillage occurred, a brief time-out from the meal was implemented and the participant was verbally instructed by the therapist on how to avoid spilling food. Treatment efficacy was evaluated in a multiple-baseline-across-meals reversal design. Spillage decreased, from a mean of 68 percent during dinner and 71 percent during lunch prior to treatment, to a mean of 10 percent during dinner and 21 percent during lunch three months later.

Improper pacing

Individuals with pacing problems eat either too fast or too slow. They usually do not demonstrate self-feeding problems or food aversion (Luiselli, 1989).

The problems with eating too fast include the risk of aspiration, choking, and vomiting. Individuals who eat too slowly do not complete their meals if time limits are imposed. This limits the amount of food that is consumed. Without time limitations, meals are completed long after others have finished.

Lennox, Miltenberger, and Donnelly (1987) modified high rates of eating in three individuals with profound intellectual disabilities. They compared several schedules. These included a fixed interval (FI) – 15 s schedule (i.e. placing food into one's mouth was not allowed until 15 s had elapsed), a spaced-responding, differential reinforcement of low rates of behaviour (DRL) – 15 s schedule (i.e. the interval was reset contingent on attempts to place food into one's mouth prior to completion of 15 s); and, the addition of a verbal prompt 'down' (i.e. the participant was physically guided to put the utensil on the table and their hand on their lap) to the DRL schedule. They found that the addition of the prompts to the DRL schedule was the most effective way of reducing high rates of eating. Treatment efficacy was demonstrated in a multiple-baseline design across two subjects and a reversal design for one subject.

Wright and Vollmer (2002) replicated the study by Lennox *et al.* (1987) by implementing an adjusting-DRL schedule rather than a fixed-DRL schedule in a 17-year-old girl with profound intellectual disabilities who exhibited high rates of rapid eating. She was initially allowed to consume a bite of food once every 15 s, which was signalled by a timer. If an attempt was made to eat the food prior to 15 s elapsing, the therapist blocked the response and physically guided her utensil to the table and her hand to her lap. Since she made many attempts and exhibited few bites, the DRL schedule was adjusted whereby the average inter-response time (IRT) was calculated for the previous five sessions, but was never greater than 15 s. At the completion of treatment, few attempts were made to consume food prior to the sound of the timer. Experimental control was demonstrated via a reversal design. Shore, LeBlanc, and Simmons (1999) reported similar results to reduce rapid eating using prompting and reinforcement.

Though studies in the literature addressing low rates of eating are sparse, Luiselli (1988) described his own study on treating a 13-year-old girl with intellectual disabilities, who took more than one hour to complete a meal. A differential reinforcement of high rates of behaviour (DRH) schedule was implemented where bites were reinforced if she did not take longer than 40 s to place food into her mouth; otherwise she was physically guided to complete a feeding response. This pacing strategy increased rates of independent feeding.

Food refusal and selectivity

Individuals who display *food selectivity* eat only certain foods, textures, or classes of food. Such individuals may also eat only under certain conditions, such as when the food is cold or when specific individuals are present. Typically, preferred foods are used as reinforcers contingent on the consumption of refused food. Individuals who exhibit *food refusal* either do not eat or reject most edible food, and are at risk for malnourishment. Any food that is consumed usually occurs only under tight stimulus control (Luiselli, 1989). Munk and Repp (1994) conducted a functional assessment to determine the relationship between a person's acceptance of food and the texture of that food. They hypothesized that setting events, such as food characteristics, might trigger problem behaviour. Five participants were assessed using ten to twelve foods. Each food was presented in any one of up to four possible textures (e.g. refined, ground, and chopped). Each texture determined whether food rejection was specific enough to show individual types of problems (e.g. if all foods were refused, if only certain foods at all textures were accepted, or if all foods at only one texture were accepted). Subjects fell into one of four categories: total refusal, type selectivity, texture selectivity, or type and texture selectivity. Since each problem was found to be different for each subject, treatments might be developed based upon assessments that show the relation between food type, or texture, and refusal.

Reinforcers must be selected carefully and with ingenuity, as edibles are usually not reinforcing for individuals who display chronic food refusal. Further, individuals who refuse most food and do not respond to social stimuli pose the greatest challenge to treatment. Luiselli and Gleason (1987) overcame this problem by using sensory stimulation, such as lights, as both a setting event and reinforcer contingent on the acceptance of food. They also gradually thickened the texture of foods, presented a greater variety of food types, and added more items at meals. Shore, Babbitt, Williams, Coe, and Snyder (1998) extended this study by treating food selectivity in four children with disabilities by probing coarser textures while reinforcing acceptance of smoother textures in a procedure referred to as *texture fading*. The children were initially presented with food at a texture that they regularly consumed. Treatment consisted of praise and access to preferred toys contingent on food acceptance. They also used escape-extinction (discussed below) as well as extinction for the display of behaviours incompatible with the acceptance of food. Successful consumption at a trained texture resulted in probe meals to determine the next texture for fading. The first probe was always the coarsest texture. If the probe meal did not meet acceptance criteria, the next higher texture was probed. All of the children consumed their target food texture at age-appropriate portions at the end of treatment. Although treatment efficacy was demonstrated using a multiple-baseline design across subjects, it is unknown to what extent the fading procedure contributed to the study. It is also unknown to what extent reinforcement and extinction alone, while providing the target texture, would have produced similar results.

Escape-extinction appears to be an integral component within procedures developed to treat food refusal. That is, the individual is not allowed to terminate, or escape from, the session when food is presented, regardless of the inappropriate behaviour that is displayed. Patel, Piazza, Martinez, Volkert, and Santana (2002) and Dawson, Piazza, Sevin, Gulotta *et al.* (2003), found that escape-extinction, combined with other components, such as differential positive reinforcement of accepting food as well as keeping one's mouth clean (Patel *et al.*, 2001), increased rates of food acceptance more than if these components were provided without escape-extinction. Although the combination of components systematically affected the behaviour, the efficacy of escape-extinction alone has yet to be investigated.

Since the behaviour of food refusal is traditionally believed to be maintained by negative reinforcement, positive reinforcement and response cost was found systematically to increase the rate of food acceptance and it decreased the rate of problem behaviour (e.g. aggression and property destruction) in a 5-year-old boy with intellectual disabilities. Using a reversal design, Kahng, Tarbox, and Wilke (2001) removed preferred items contingent on food refusal and returned them once food was accepted. Rates of food acceptance increased and problem behaviour decreased. Further, these results generalized to other family members.

To increase the consumption of food variety in children with food selectivity, Piazza *et al.* (2002) and Kern and Marder (1996) compared presenting food either simultaneously (i.e. both preferred and non-preferred food are presented at the same time) or sequentially (i.e. preferred foods are presented contingent on the consumption of non-preferred food). In both studies, they found that for most of the participants, the simultaneous method was the most effective in increasing rates of food acceptance. Riordan, Iwata, Finney, Wohl, and Stanley (1984) delivered either highly preferred food or toys contingent on consumption of target food items in four children with various disabilities. For two participants, the reinforcer was initially delivered simultaneously with the target food and, after a delay, thereafter. A multiple-baseline design across food groups as well as a reversal design, depending on the participant, was used to demonstrate treatment efficacy. For all participants, rates of food acceptance and consumption increased while rates of inappropriate eating behaviour decreased. One reason the sequential method might not be as effective is that the opportunity to contact the reinforcer is limited if food acceptance levels are almost zero (Piazza *et al.*, 2002).

Finally, food refusal is not just limited to solid food. Hagopian, Farrell, and Amari (1996) used backward chaining to shape drinking from a cup in a boy with autism and intellectual disabilities who displayed total liquid refusal. He was first reinforced for swallowing (a pre-existing response); then, for accepting water into his mouth (from a syringe), the amount of which was increased in subsequent phases; and, finally, for bringing a cup of water to his mouth. Functional control was demonstrated using a reversal design. Generalization data showed that the boy successfully consumed 90 cc of water and juice in a cup for 100 percent of trials.

Prader-Willi syndrome

Prader-Willi syndrome (PWS) is a congenital multisystem disorder character-ized by intellectual disabilities, infantile hypotonia, hypogonadism, short stature, and resultant morbid obesity (Butler, 1990; Kohn, Weizman and Apter, 2001). Further details about PWS will be discussed in Chapter 14. Individuals with PWS often engage in covert food stealing behaviour, are intensely preoccupied with food, and continually seek food (Dimitropoulos, Feurer, Roof, Stone, Butler *et al.*, 2000). Such behaviour can result in signifi-cant injury and death. Individuals with PWS usually show well-developed notions about the necessity for food to survive; however, they have an incomplete understanding about abstract concepts, such as germs and residue (Dykens, 2000). For example, they tended to endorse eating contaminated food even when such contaminants were removed and no longer visible. They also endorsed consuming highly unusual edible as well as inedible food com-binations (Dykens, 2000). It has been suggested that an impaired satiety response might be responsible for the excessive eating observed in this popu-lation (Holland, Treasure, Coskeran and Dallow, 1995). That is, compared to a control group, individuals with PWS reported subjective feelings of fullness only after consuming a greater amount of food. Moreover, they also reported subjective feelings of hunger, sooner.

Behavioural treatment of overeating in individuals with PWS

Traditional interventions to control overeating in individuals with PWS were either dietary restrictions or surgery. This trend has changed since the late 1970s. In one of the earliest studies that treated obesity in individuals with PWS without the use of these methods, Altman, Bondy, and Hirsch (1978) used a combination of self-monitoring and contingency contracting between two participants with PWS and their parents while punishing instances of food stealing. Using a multiple-baseline design across subjects, the parti-cipants were reinforced for reducing daily caloric intake, weekly weight loss and exercising. Both participants lost weight, modified their eating habits by reducing caloric intake, and either sustained or increased exercise rates. Lastly, weight loss was maintained for one year following the cessation of treatment.

At present, a multifaceted approach appears to be the best intervention for obesity in individuals with PWS. Hoffman, Aultman, and Pipes (1992) recommended the following for those individuals with PWS who live in group homes: a weight-loss programme, the input of the interdisciplinary team to maintain environmental consistency and control, weekly weighing to monitor progress, daily exercises to enhance fitness, and the inclusion of a nutritional component to control food-seeking behaviour and excessive weight gain. This component should actively involve the individual in menu planning since food is incredibly reinforcing. Finally, home visits should be brief as dietary non-compliance and rapid weight gain is often poor outside the group home.

Contrary to popular belief, individuals with PWS do have definitive and consistent food preferences. For example, individuals with PWS prefer foods high in carbohydrates to foods high in fat (Fieldstone, Zipf, Schwartz and Berntson, 1997). However, such preferences are also guided by quantity (Caldwell and Taylor, 1983; Glover, Maltzman and Williams, 1996; Joseph, Egli, Koppekin and Thompson, 2002). When presented with preferred, less-preferred, and non-preferred food (determined by preference assessments), individuals with PWS tended to select a larger quantity of less-preferred food, but not when the food was non-preferred, over a smaller quantity of preferred food (Glover et al., 1996). Further, when presented with a choice between a larger magnitude of food delivered after a delay of 15 s, 30 s, or 60 s, or a smaller magnitude of food delivered immediately, individuals with PWS tended to select the larger magnitude of food. This was true even if such food was less preferred (Joseph et al., 2002). Hence, it could be said that such individuals exhibited 'self-control', in contrast to individuals who were over-weight and did not have PWS. Therefore, perceived differences in food magni-tude and food preference might be an important determinant of food choice in individuals with PWS. This may also explain why such individuals eat indiscriminately in the absence of preferred food or if there is no indication that a larger quantity of food may soon become available. They might select large quantities of whatever is available, even if such food is slightly less preferred (Glover et al., 1996). Given these findings, behavioural interven-tions for this population could be developed using large magnitude, low-fat, low-calorie preferred or slightly less-preferred food as effective reinforcers for increased activity and exercise (Caldwell, Taylor and Bloom, 1986).

Problem behaviour during meals

Disruptive mealtime behaviour, such as food-grabbing, rumination and pica, are common and major problems among individuals with developmental disabilities (Barton et al., 1970; Groves and Carroccio, 1971). The display of such behaviour is usually secondary to the presence of feeding disorders (Luiselli, 1989). While the list of problem behaviour is extensive, and the literature is full of successful interventions, only a few will be discussed here.

Food-grabbing and food stealing

Food-grabbing during meals is a disruptive response. Aggression between individuals, the spread of bacteria, the ingestion of food that might result in either an allergic or fatal reaction, and dietary contraindications are prob-lems associated with food-grabbing (Smith, Piersel, Filbeck and Gross, 1983). Several studies have attempted to address food-grabbing using restrictive methods. Barton *et al.* (1970) used time-out to decrease the rate of food-grabbing as well as other undesirable mealtime behaviour in sixteen men with severe and profound intellectual disabilities. Contingent on food-grabbing, the participants were placed in a time-out room for the remainder of the meal. The rate of food-grabbing systematically decreased with the implementation of time-out. Henriksen and Doughty (1967) used physical restraint to decrease the rate of mealtime misbehaviour that included food-grabbing in four boys with severe and profound intellectual disabilities. Contingent on food-grabbing, the participants were verbally corrected and their physical response blocked. The participants were also verbally reinforced contingent on the display of appropriate behaviour. As training progressed, the participants responded more quickly to the verbal correction and misbehaviour as a class systematically decreased. Unfortunately, data only on food-grabbing were not provided. Azrin and Wesolowski (1974) used overcorrection to decrease the frequency of food-grabbing in thirty-four adults with severe and profound intellectual disabilities. The participants chose a snack from a display and ate it in close proximity to others. For the first five days of the procedure, simple correction was used where the participant returned the item to the owner contingent upon grabbing. Overcorrection was implemented on the sixth day where the participant not only returned the item but also procured another item and handed that over to the owner, as well. The frequency of food-grabbing systematically decreased to zero for the entire group by the tenth day. Unfortunately, experimental control was not demonstrated and individual data were not provided.

Only a few studies have used non-restrictive procedures to address food-grabbing. For example, to decrease the frequency of food-grabbing in a woman with severe intellectual disabilities, Smith *et al.* (1983) used discriminative stimuli, positive reinforcement, and response cost. During meals, a green bowl filled with candy was placed directly across from the participant, and the participant was provided with an empty red bowl. Candy was removed from the green bowl and placed into the red bowl for consumption every 60 s that she did not grab from others. If she grabbed from others, then all of the remaining candy was removed from the red bowl and placed back into the green bowl. Following intervention, the frequency of food-grabbing decreased to nearly zero. Unfortunately, this was only a case study and experimental control was not demonstrated. Doss (Sigafoos, Doss and Reichle, 1989) taught participants to request more food and to discriminate between '*yes*' and '*no*' following such a request. The rate of requesting additional food increased, and the frequency of taking items following 'no', as well as stealing, decreased. Unfortunately, communication instruction did not generalize from training to mealtime. Hence, food-grabbing continued during meals. Lastly, Reyer and Sturmey (2003) could not demonstrate that food-grabbing was a function of short-term food deprivation. They varied the magnitude of a preload 30 minutes prior to lunch and measured incidents of food-grabbing as well as the frequency of placing food into one's mouth during the initial 30 minutes of lunch. For all three participants, the preload did not systematically affect the frequency of food-grabbing. Further, the frequency of hand-to-mouth behaviour was systematically lower during lunch when a preload was provided for only one participant.

Food-grabbing and food-stealing among individuals with PWS

Since many individuals with PWS engage in covert food-stealing, interventions to address this problem have been designed specifically for this population. The data from these studies to decrease the rate of food-stealing appears promising. For example, in a multiple-baseline design across settings, Page, Stanley, Richman, Deal, and Iwata (1983) delivered tokens to a woman with PWS contingent on periods whereby food-stealing did not occur. A response-cost procedure was utilized wherein incidents of food-stealing resulted in the removal of earned tokens. The rate of food-stealing systematically decreased with the implementation of the token economy. Further, after two years, her weight dropped from 115 kg to 37 kg, although tokens were also delivered contingent on weight loss and exercising. In another study, Maglieri, DeLeon, Rodriguez-Catter, and Sevin (2000) used stimulus control combined with verbal reprimands to decrease the rate of food-stealing by a girl with PWS. She stole only when unsupervised, but from appropriate places (e.g. the refrigerator). She was instructed that if an orange sticker was placed on any item, then it was prohibited from being consumed. A brief verbal reprimand was delivered contingent on the consumption of prohibited foods. Although the combination of punishment and stimulus control was effective enough to decrease the rate of food-stealing systematically, the study did not demonstrate which component was responsible for the behaviour change.

FEEDING DISORDERS IN CHILDREN: ASSESSMENT AND INTERVENTION

In this section a brief account of each the following feeding problems in children and adolescents with ID will be given, along with guidance on assessment and intervention.

- pica
- rumination disorder
- food refusal
- obesity
- anorexia
- bulimia.

Before addressing these specific problems, an overview of feeding disorders in children with ID and general assessment and intervention considerations will be given.

Feeding disorder of infancy or early childhood

DSM-IV-TR (APA, 1994) defines Feeding Disorder of Infancy or Early Childhood as persistent failure to eat adequately with a failure to gain weight or a loss of weight for at least one month. It must not be better accounted for by general medical or other mental disorders. It must begin before the age of 6 years. Relatively little is known about this feeding disorder in infants and children with intellectual disability, although some case studies have been reported (Durand, 1975). Feeding Disorder of Infancy or Early Childhood presents a number of diagnostic challenges. For example, many infants and children with feeding problems also have co-existing medical disorders. These might more readily explain the observed feeding problem. In other cases the presumption that an observed feeding problem is psychogenic in nature may be due to an undiagnosed medical disorder. No empirical studies of differential diagnosis were found with infants and children with intellectual disabilities to answer this question directly. Failure to thrive may be associated with a number of factors that are also associated with the aetiology of intellectual disabilities. For example, lead exposure (Bithony, 1986), parental neglect, lack of parental stimulation and counter-habilitative patterns of interaction have all been implicated in the aetiology of both conditions. The web of interrelationships between these variables has yet to be clearly untangled. However, Boddy, Skuse, and Andrews (2000) found that only failure to thrive was associated with subsequent growth delay, whereas only maternal IQ was predictive of later intellectual delay.

Assessment of children with ID and feeding problems

Carefully identifying the precise target behaviours in food refusal is an essential element in assessment. Patel, Piazza, Martinez, Volkert and Santana (2001) described food refusal as a chain of behaviours consisting of accepting, swallowing and retaining food. They demonstrated that targeting the earlier responses in the chain was unlikely to result in overall decrease in food refusal, whereas targeting the terminal response in the chain was very likely to result in reduction in food refusal. Thus, it is necessary to describe carefully the adaptive behaviours that increase, but also to consider their relationship to one another when designing an intervention for food refusal. A variety of challenging behaviours that might compete with consuming food is described in Piazza, Fisher, Brown, Shore, Patel *et al.* (2003).

Identifying the function of food refusal is an essential element in assessment.

Descriptive functional assessments of feeding problems using the STEP can be found in Matson and Kuhn (2001). Piazza, Patel, Gulotta, Sevin and Layer (2003) described observational methods of conducting functional assessments of food refusal. Experimental analyses of inappropriate mealtime behaviours can be found in Piazza, Fisher, Brown, Shore, Patel et al. (2003) and Kerwin et al. (1995) (see above).

Intervention for children with ID and feeding problems

There have been a significant number of interventions for food refusal, including some participants with intellectual disability. Several studies have evaluated escape-extinction for food refusal. This is achieved by holding the spoon at the child's lips until the child consumes the food and removing the spoon only when food is consumed. This is an effective treatment for food refusal (Dawson et al., 2003; Kerwin et al., 1995; Patel et al., 2002; Sevin et al., 2002), even when positive reinforcement is ineffective (Coe et al., 1997; Cooper, Wacker, McComas, Brown et al., 1995; Piazza, Patel, Gulotta, Sevin and Layer, 2003), although the inclusion of positive reinforcement was associated with reduced maladaptive behaviours in one study (Coe et al., 1997). Other interventions have included stimulus fading by gradually introducing non-preferred textures (Patel, Piazza, Kelly, Ochsner and Santana, 2001). Others have used complex packages of both antecedents and consequences (Lamm and Greer, 1988). Modelling has been found to be of only modest effectiveness (Greer, Donrow, Wiliams, McCorkle and Asnes, 1991).

Pica

Pica is a feeding disorder characterized by the repeated consumption of inedible objects (APA, 1994). DSM-IV-TR criteria specify that the behaviour is part of a persistent pattern that has been occurring for at least one month in duration. In addition, the behaviour must be inappropriate to developmental level, and not part of a culturally sanctioned practice (APA, 1994). Common examples of pica include ingestion of cigarette butts, paint chips, fecal material, paper, and dirt (APA, 1994; Matson, and Bamburg, 1999). Others have extended the definition of pica to take in to account various aspects of this phenomenon (McLoughlin, 1987). For example, pica may be classified as non-food pica, food pica (e.g. consumption of rotten or frozen food), non-ingestion pica (e.g. mouthing, licking, or sucking inedible objects), or a combination of these pica subtypes. Pica may also be limited to a single substance (Specific pica) or may occur across a variety of substances (Generalized pica). Lastly, pica may vary in aetiology. Cultural factors, addiction, nutritional deficiency, and mental illness have all been implicated in the development of pica (McLoughlin, 1987). Currently, pica is one of the most thoroughly studied feeding disorders, and also one of the most dangerous. Ingestion of inedible objects may lead to physical consequences such as gastrointestinal obstruction, nutritional deficiency, disease, lead intoxication, and death (Dandford and Huber, 1982; McLoughlin, 1987). Prevalence estimates for Pica range from 4 percent–26 percent (Dandford and Huber, 1981; Dudley, Ahlgrim-Delzell and Calhoun, 1999). It is believed that the prevalence of pica tends to increase with the severity of intellectual disability (Dudley *et al.*, 1999; McAlpine and Singh, 1986). In addition to the previously mentioned methodological issues that result in a wide range of prevalence estimates, the way in which researchers have defined pica (e.g. including rotten food or hand mouthing) has likely contributed to inconsistent prevalence rates (Gravestock, 2000).

Assessment of pica

An assessment of pica should include a functional assessment of the behaviour, a reinforcer assessment, and a survey of the physical environment to determine if the environment can be arranged in a manner to make pica less likely to occur. A functional assessment of pica should consider whether the behaviour is initiated and/or maintained by social or non-social consequences. This may be facilitated by use of indirect measures of assessment and descriptive assessments that document the antecedents, the behaviour, and the consequences following the occurrence of each behaviour (see special references list for feeding problems). If the results of these assessments are unclear, an analogue assessment may be useful as long as the pica is not life-threatening.

Assessment should also take into account any circumstances surrounding the onset of pica that may not be readily identified in a functional assessment. For instance, did the onset coincide with the onset of a mood or psychotic disorder? Are there any nutritional deficiencies? Although the treatment implications of these factors have not been sufficiently investigated, the temporal relationship between the pica and other psychiatric and medical problems should be explored.

Intervention with pica

Behavioural interventions for pica that have resulted in the decrease or elimination of the behaviour include reinforcement and punishment procedures along with alternative sensory stimulation. Many of these procedures have also been investigated together as combination treatments and the results have been favorable. Thus far, none of these interventions appears to be particularly more efficacious than the others (Gravestock, 2000).

Punishment procedures for pica have been well studied. Aversives such as lemon juice, water mist, verbal reprimands, overcorrection procedures, negative practice, facial screening, and physical restraint have been used alone and in combination to reduce the occurrence of pica effectively (Bogart, Piersel and Gross, 1995; Bucher, Reykdal and Albin, 1976; Duker and Nielen, 1993; Kalfus, Fisher-Gross, Marvullo and Nau, 1987; Matson, Stephens and Smith, 1978; Paisey and Whitney, 1989; Paniagua, Braverman and Capriotti, 1986). Nevertheless, fading of punishment procedures may result in reoccurrence of pica (e.g. Paisey and Whitney, 1989), and may have a negative impact on quality of life that could otherwise be avoided through the use of non-aversive procedures (LeBlanc, Piazza and Krug, 1997).

Like punishment procedures, non-aversive interventions have been found effective for reducing or altogether eliminating the occurrence of pica. Differential reinforcement of alternative or incompatible behaviour has been found effective for the reduction of cigarette pica (Donnelly and Olczak, 1990; Goh, Iwata and Kahng, 1999), and other inedible objects (Datlow-Smith, 1987). Given mixed results for continued abstinence at follow-up, further evaluation of the maintenance of these procedures is needed.

Environmental enrichment procedures and the provision of competing reinforcers have also been found effective. For instance, Mace and Knight (1986) found that frequent staff interaction resulted in a significant reduction of pica for a 19-year-old with profound intellectual disability. Piazza, Fisher, Hanley, LeBlanc et al. (1998) reduced the occurrence of pica among three participants in part by identifying stimuli that could effectively compete with pica, and Rapp, Dozier, and Carr (2001) were able to suppress pica through use of contingent auditory stimulation. Piazza et al. (1998) demonstrates the utility of functional analysis in assisting in the development of appropriate intervention for pica.

Outside behavioural interventions, vitamin supplements and medications used to treat comorbid depression may hold promise for some individuals. Examples include Pace and Toyer (2000) who reported the reduction of pica for a young girl treated with a multiple vitamin, and Jawed, Krishnan, Prasher, and Corbett (1993) who observed a reduction in pica following the administration of a medication used to treat comorbid depression. Although alternatives to behavioural intervention may be promising, further research is needed to determine the efficacy of such an approach.

Rumination disorder

Rumination refers to the voluntary regurgitation of food during mealtime, where food is usually chewed and re-swallowed as part of a repetitive cycle (APA, 1994). According to DSM-IV-TR diagnostic criteria, this pattern is recurrent for at least one month following a period of normal functioning. Rumination is thought to occur more often in males than females (APA, 1994), yet little is known about the course of the disorder and prevalence among persons with intellectual disability. Regurgitation is facilitated by the individual through various means. Stimulation of the gag reflex and various body movements conducive to regurgitation (e.g. movements of the head and neck) are common, yet not all individuals who ruminate will display overt behaviour indicative of rumination (Johnston, 1993). The rate of ruminative behaviour also varies across individuals. Specific food characteristics have also been found to influence the likelihood of rumination (Johnston, Greene, Vazin, Winston and Rawal, 1990). For example, Johnston *et al.* (1990) found that rumination tended to increase when foods were of a pureed consistency. Ingestion of foods with high caloric density (Greene, Johnston, Rossi, Rawal, Winston and Barron, 1991; Rast, Johnston, Ellinger-Allen and Drum, 1985), favorable hedonic qualities of food (Johnston, 1993), and low rates of oropharyngeal stimulation (Rast *et al.*, 1985) have also been associated with increased rates of rumination. In addition, Kuhn, Matson, Mayville, and Matson (2001) found that social skills deficits are associated with rumination. Although the findings of this study are correlational, this relationship may hold implications for assessment and treatment of rumination.

Much like pica, rumination poses a significant health risk (APA, 1994). Adverse consequences such as weight loss, esophageal irritation, tooth decay, decreased resistance to disease, aspiration, and death have been linked to rumination (Johnston, 1993; Jones, 1982). Given the potential severity of consequences associated with rumination, the problem should be a treatment priority when it occurs.

Assessment of rumination disorder

Rumination must be differentiated from physiological problems that may result in involuntary regurgitation during or after a meal. To arrive at a differential diagnosis between physiological problems and rumination, pH testing, endoscopy, or a barium esophogram using imaging technology may be helpful (Kuruvilla and Trewby, 1989; Rogers, Stratton, Victor, Kennedy and Andres, 1992). While pH testing or endoscopy can detect high acid levels, or the effects of high acid levels within the esophagus, a swallow study allows for a detailed picture of the individual's oral cavity and esophagus during feeding. Furthermore, a medication review should be conducted as neuroleptics and benzodiazepines may also interfere with swallowing and be confused with rumination (Rogers *et al.*, 1992).

A thorough behavioural assessment of rumination is also of great importance (Fredericks, Carr and Williams, 1998). This includes the time of day/ meal during which rumination occurs, the social consequences of rumination (i.e. caregiver response), the type of food consumed that precedes rumination, and behaviours such as pitching one's body forth to initiate rumination. By gathering such information, progress towards identifying the role of behavioural and/or medical intervention for rumination may be facilitated.

Intervention with rumination disorder

Numerous interventions have been described for rumination. Key elements of these interventions have included differential reinforcement for the absence of rumination, punishment for the occurrence of rumination, and dietary intervention. Many of the early studies conducted on the treatment of rumination detailed the use of punishment procedures such as the use of electric shock and application of lemon juice contingent upon the occurrence of rumination (Fredericks et al., 1998). Additional behavioural interventions include the use of contingent exercise, differential reinforcement contingent upon the absence of rumination, and controlled eating strategies (Daniel, 1982; Foxx, Synder and Schroeder, 1979; McKeegan, Estill and Campbell, 1987).

Lastly, numerous reports have surfaced demonstrating the efficacy of nutritional intervention for rumination (Dunn, Lockwood, Williams and Peacock, 1997; Foxx et al., 1979; Rast et al., 1985; Rast and Johnston, 1986). In particular, dietary satiation has proven to be an effective means for reducing rumination. Research that has been conducted to determine whether or not the size of the meal is responsible for reduction of rumination for satiation versus the caloric density indicates the frequency of rumination varies as a function of caloric intake (Greene et al., 1991; Rast et al., 1985). Although dietary satiation appears to be effective, degree of weight gain and difficulty fading out the intervention may be problematic for some individuals.

Food selectivity and food refusal

Food selectivity and food refusal have been described as common among individuals with intellectual disability (Riordan, Iwata, Finney, Wohl and Stanley, 1984). Food selectivity refers to an individual's preference for certain foods, such as the types of foods, foods of a certain texture, etc. (Babbitt, Hoch, Coe, Cataldo et al., 1994). Food refusal is a common consequence of food selectivity where non-preferred foods are refused during mealtime (Babbitt et al., 1994). Complete food refusal is thought to be less prevalent than refusal occurring with food selectivity (Gravestock, 2000). The prevalence of food refusal appears to be quite high. In a sample of children with intellectual disability, Thomessen, Heiberg, Kase, Larsen, and Riis (1991) found that 30 percent displayed behaviour indicative of food selectivity/refusal. Moreover, 19 percent presented with a decrease in appetite. Given the high prevalence and serious nature of these problems, the need for further research in this area is underscored.

Various case studies detailing food selectivity/food refusal behaviour have illustrated a varied pattern of problematic eating behaviour. Included in the literature are reports of selectivity specific to food type (Leibowitz and Holcer, 1974; Shore, Babbitt, Williams, Coe and Snyder, 1998) and foods of a particular texture (Johnson and Babbitt, 1993; Luiselli and Gleason, 1987). Complete food refusal has also been reported (Kerwin *et al.* 1995), although it is thought to be less common than food selectivity (Gravestock, 2000).

Various organic and environmental factors have been implicated in the development and maintenance of food selectivity/food refusal (Jones, 1982; Riordan, Iwata, Wohl and Finney, 1980). Organic problems include physical obstructions and abnormalities that interfere with food intake. This includes deformities in oral musculature, food allergies, cleft palate, muscular dystrophy, and paralysis (Jones, 1982). Common environmental factors described in the onset of food selectivity/food refusal include a lack of opportunities for skill development, and aversive feeding experiences (Siegel, 1982). Following the onset of food selectivity/food refusal, reinforcement contingencies have been found responsible for maintenance of this problem behaviour (Cooper *et al.*, 1995; Jones, 1982; Riordan *et al.*, 1984).

Assessment of food refusal

Assessment of food refusal should include a detailed informant-based interview. Questions should pertain to the course of the feeding problem, prior treatment strategies, the amount of food consumed, meal duration, the client's daily feeding routine, home structure, and environmental-behaviour relationships (Babbitt *et al.*, 1994). Such an interview should also consider types of food consumed/not consumed, the texture of these foods, and the overall variety of foods included in the individual's diet. Furthermore, a thorough assessment should insure that an inadequate intake of food is not related to a physical problem.

Informant-based measures may also be helpful for identifying specific problems related to food refusal. For adults with intellectual disability, the Screening Tool of Feeding Problems (STEP; Matson and Kuhn, 2001) may be helpful for identifying the topography of refusal-related behaviours (e.g. refusal related to food type, food texture, etc.). For children, informant-based assessment counterparts include the Childhood Eating Behaviour Inventory (CEBI; Archer, Rosenbaum and Streiner, 1991) along with the Behavioural Paediatrics Feeding Assessment Scale (Crist and Napier-Phillips, 2001).

Intervention with food refusal

There are numerous interventions for food selectivity/food refusal described in the literature with demonstrated effectiveness. Early studies on the treatment of food refusal demonstrated the effectiveness of access to preferred foods contingent upon consumption of non-preferred foods (Bernal, 1972; Riordan *et al.*, 1980; Thompson and Palmer, 1974), and 'forced feeding' (e.g. Ives, Harris and Wolchik, 1978). However, researchers have been somewhat critical of forced feeding (e.g. placing pressure on the chin of the individual to encourage opening of the mouth) outside truly life-threatening cases. This is because of the potential health and maintenance problems associated with forced feedings, and the availability of less aversive treatment alternatives (Riordan *et al.*, 1980).

More recent research has demonstrated the utility of contingent attention for acceptance of non-preferred foods (Werle, Murphy and Budd, 1993). Kern and Marder (1996) found that for interventions utilizing both simultaneous and delayed reinforcement for food acceptance, both were effective, yet simultaneous reinforcement appeared to produce greater and more rapid change. Additional research has demonstrated that differential reinforcement and escape-extinction (i.e. not allowing the individual to leave the dining area without eating) are highly effective for increasing intake of non-preferred foods when presented as a packaged treatment (Kerwin *et al.*, 1995). In a component analysis of escape-extinction, positive reinforcement, and non-contingent play, Cooper *et al.* (1995) found that escape-extinction was always identified as an active treatment component with the four participants in the study. With two of the four children treated, positive reinforcement and non-contingent play were also found to be active treatment components.

An additional method of food acceptance, 'contingency contacting', has been described as an effective treatment for food refusal (Hoch, Babbitt, Coe, Krell and Hackbert, 1994). It has been presented as an alternative to positive reinforcement procedures that are not always effective for initiating feeding, as well as 'forced feeding' procedures that may result in untoward consequences. In essence, contingency contacting involves the placement of the feeding utensil touching the lips of the individual until the food is accepted. Following acceptance, positive reinforcement is administered in accordance with prior reinforcer assessments. All other behaviours are either ignored or blocked. Although both parents involved in the study reported disliking the procedure, they still endorsed its use as an effective treatment option.

Fading procedures have also been described as effective for food refusal. Shore *et al.* (1998) found that selectivity for food texture could be altered through gradually changing the texture of the food in combination with positive reinforcement and escape-extinction. Johnson and Babbitt (1993) used a fading procedure to transfer control from a bottle and pureed food, to consumption of more solid food from a spoon.

Overweight, obesity, and associated behaviours

Obesity is one of the most common and vexing health problems among the population-at-large of developed countries (Bray, 1998; Flegal, Carrol, Ogden and Johnson, 2002). Among many adverse associated features, individuals in the overweight (Body Mass Index ≥ 25) and obese (Body Mass Index ≥ 30) ranges of body composition are at an increased risk for numerous health complications (Bray, 1998). This includes an increased risk of morbidity and mortality (Allison, Fontaine, Manson, Stevens and VanItallie, 1999), and a negative effect on health-related quality of life (Fontaine and Barofsky, 2001).

Although much of the literature on obesity has been focused on the population-at-large, researchers estimating the occurrence of weight problems among those with intellectual disability have found that a large percentage of individuals are overweight (Burkart, Fox and Rotatori, 1985; Wood, 1994). Prevalence estimates have reached as high as 35 percent (Wood, 1994). Given that individuals with intellectual disability already experience health problems at a rate beyond the population at large, the study of weight problems among those with intellectual disability appears all the more urgent.

Unfortunately, eating behaviours that may be associated with overweight and obesity have not been thoroughly investigated among those with intellectual disability. For example, literature related to food-stealing is scarce outside a handful of notable studies (Maglieri *et al.*, 2000; Matson, Gardner, Coe and Sovner, 1991; Page, Stanley, Richman, Deal and Iwata, 1983; Reid, Ballinger and Heather, 1978). Likewise, research related to binge eating behaviour and binge eating disorder has largely neglected intellectual disability, yet behaviours characteristic of binge eating have been described. This includes excessive food-seeking behaviour, rapid consumption of food, and continuous food consumption (Matson *et al.*, 1991; O'Brien and Whitehouse, 1990; Smith, Branford, Collacott, Cooper and McGrother, 1996).

Assessment of obesity

The assessment of obesity and related problem behaviours consists primarily of a medical and functional assessment. Calculating Body Mass Index (BMI $= kg/m^2$) provides the clinician with an idea about the level of health risks that may be conferred by a certain body weight (e.g. BMI ≥ 30 is classified in the obese range of body composition). A physical exam conducted by a physician will also help determine if there are any physical problems that may preclude an individual from participating in an exercise programme.

With regard to behavioural assessment, self-monitoring is often a vital part of a behavioural weight-loss programme assessment and intervention. Monitoring by direct-care staff may help with accurately assessing problematic eating patterns. Self-monitoring and monitoring by caregivers should take into account type of meal (i.e. specific food and caloric content), time of meal, and relevant antecedents for eating such as emotional state prior to eating. Lastly, the individual should be weighed on a weekly basis to more accurately assess patterns of weight loss.

Intervention with obesity

Research on the intervention for obesity and related behaviours among individuals with intellectual disability has demonstrated the utility of behaviour modification techniques. Maglieri *et al.* (2000) treated food-stealing among a female with diagnosed with Prader-Willi syndrome with systematically delivered verbal reprimands. Warning labels were placed on food containers in refrigerators, and these labels apparently aided the individual in abstaining from further stealing. Along the same lines, Page *et al.* (1983) reduced food-stealing in an adult female with Prader-Willi syndrome through use of differential reinforcement of other behaviour, whereby reinforcement was provided through a token economy. A response-cost component was also added to the token economy where food-stealing resulted in token loss. The intervention was continued in the individual's group home following discharge from a hospital setting, and weight loss continued over a two year period totaling 80lb.

Similar to the population-at-large, studies examining the efficacy of behavioural weight-loss therapy among individuals with intellectual disability were conducted primarily in the 1970s and 80s. Significant weight loss can be achieved through use of social reinforcement (Foxx, 1972), therapist contact and self-monitoring (Joachim, 1975). Packaged treatments involving components such as stimulus control strategies (e.g. eating three meals at the same time and place each day), self- and social reinforcement for weight loss, self-monitoring, and exercise have also been shown to be effective (Fisher, 1986; Fox, 1984; Fox, 1985; Jackson and Thorbecke, 1982; Norvell and Ahern, 1987). Behavioural weight loss may aid in the prevention of Type II diabetes (Diabetes Prevention Program Research Group, 2002) and reduce the risk of other weight-related problems (Bray, 1998). However, it appears that behavioural weight-loss therapy among individuals with intellectual disability may encounter the same long-term maintenance difficulties seen among the population-at-large. Given the high rate of obesity among this population, further research examining the effectiveness of pharmacotherapy for weight loss in combination with additional applications of behavioural weight loss appears warranted.

Bulimia and anorexia nervosa

According to DSM-IV criteria, bulimia nervosa is characterized by recurrent episodes of binge eating that are followed by compensatory behaviour in order to prevent weight gain (e.g. vomiting, excessive exercise, use of diuretics, or laxatives). The frequency of bingeing/purging must occur at least two times per week for at least three months, and those affected with the disorder are invariably preoccupied with a fear of fatness (APA, 1994). Like bulimia, individuals diagnosed with anorexia nervosa face a preoccupation with weight, yet the hallmark feature of anorexia is body weight that is less than 85 percent of what would be expected (APA, 1994).

Eating disorders such as bulimia and anorexia nervosa are primarily phenomena of Western culture where thinness has become a symbol of physical attractiveness (Wilfley and Rodin, 1995). Among the population-at-large, the prevalence of bulimia is estimated to affect 1–3 percent of adolescent girls (APA, 1994) with an additional 2–3 percent suffering from symptoms of bulimia that do not meet DSM criteria for a diagnosis of bulimia nervosa (i.e. Eating Disorder Not Otherwise Specified) (Stunkard, 1993). For anorexia nervosa, the numbers are slightly less with estimates placed at approximately 1 percent (APA, 1994).

Among individuals with intellectual disability, case studies of anorexia nervosa have been reported (Clark and Yapa, 1991; Dymek and le Grange, 2002; Hurley and Sovner, 1979; Raitasuo, Virtanen and Raitasuo, 1998; Thomas, 1994). However, there should be more research regarding the prevalence and appropriateness of current diagnostic criteria for anorexia and bulimia nervosa among individuals with intellectual disability. Factors associated with anorexia among individuals with intellectual disability include a history of dieting, bereavement, and family problems, and issues with sexuality (Gravestock, 2000). Of the cases of anorexia nervosa that have been reported, individuals are almost invariably classified in the mild range of intellectual disability.

Assessment of anorexia and bulimia

Assessment of anorexia and bulimia should consist of both an assessment of potential medical complications as well as a behavioural assessment. Body Mass Index of the individual should be assessed, and a body weight less than 85 percent of that expected meets the cut-off criterion for a clinically significant low weight (APA, 1994). This figure generally corresponds to a BMI of 17.5. Collateral reports from caregivers and/or family members should be gathered in conjunction with self-report to assess the amount of food consumed, environmental factors involved in the onset and maintenance of problematic eating behaviour, purgative methods, and comorbid disorders such as clinically significant depression and/or anxiety. There are numerous self-report measures developed for the assessment of body image disturbance and problematic eating behaviours (Crowther and Sherwood, 1997), however, there are problems inherent with self-report assessment for individuals with eating disorders, as well as for individuals with intellectual disability. Given that individuals with eating disorders are frequently unwilling to comply with the treatment process, information gathered through self-report may be unreliable (Vitousek, Daly and Heiser, 1991). Furthermore, individuals with intellectual disability are frequently susceptible to response biases on measures of self-report that may invalidate the assessment (e.g. Sigelman, 1982). Sovner and Hurley (1983) also stated that individuals with intellectual disability may lack the ability to describe body image disturbance or have a fear of fatness, the hallmarks of both disorders. Consequently, they suggest that other observable behaviours such as food avoidance, hoarding of food, or other behaviours such as crumbling food may be more accurate indications of the presence of an eating disorder.

Intervention with anorexia and bulimia

Descriptions of intervention for bulimia are lacking for individuals with intellectual disability. However, the success of cognitive-behavioural therapy (CBT) for bulimia among the population-at-large has been well documented (Craighead and Agras, 1991). Main components of CBT include self-monitoring of antecedents, behaviours, and consequences associated with binge eating, stimulus control strategies (e.g. eating three meals a day), distraction strategies for avoiding binge eating, problem solving, reintroduction of feared foods into the diet, and relapse-prevention strategies (Fairburn, 1995). Given that CBT for bulimia has not been systematically evaluated among individuals with intellectual disability, the effectiveness of this form of intervention among this population remains to be seen.

A handful of studies have reported the treatment of anorexia nervosa among individuals with intellectual disability (e.g. Clark and Yapa, 1991; Dymek and le Grange, 2002; Hurley and Sovner, 1979; Raitasuo et al., 1998; Thomas, 1994). These studies have suggested that psychoeducation for eating disorders and access to social activities or token economies may be helpful for encouraging weight gain. Furthermore, like the population-at-large, a high level of staff/caregiver support appears warranted to ensure adequate weight gain and normalization of eating behaviour. However, given the relatively rare occurrence of anorexia and bulimia among individuals with intellectual disability, adequate evaluations of behavioural treatments for population are lacking.

SPECIAL ISSUES IN DEALING WITH FEEDING DIFFICULTIES AND EATING DISORDERS

Interventions for feeding difficulties and eating disorders often require untangling both medical and behavioural aspects of a presenting problem. Whereas these problems are often accompanied by medical problems, disentangling which are causes and which are consequences of a presenting behavioural problem is not easy. Sometimes the co-existing medical problems may be severe, and result in extreme measures to protect the client's health, or even life. Feeding problems and eating disorders also often involve multidisciplinary work which involve differing perspectives and beliefs concerning the nature of the presenting problem and whether treatments are seen as legitimate or likely to result in effective treatment. Some feeding problems and eating disorders also involve special ethical concerns. The client's prognosis may in some cases involve the possibility of serious health problems and even death.

Hence, unevaluated treatments and treatments with no empirical support should be avoided. Some treatments, such as extinction, may involve modest or significant client discomfort; in these cases measures should be taken to reduce this where possible while ensuring effective treatment where possible. Medical treatments, such as surgery for reflux, involve a significant risk of death. Hence, vigorous pursuit of behavioural alternatives, even when involving client discomfort or somewhat unusual treatments, such as food satiation, may be the ethical alternative (Dunn, Lockwood, Williams and Peacock, 1997).

STAFF AND PARENT TRAINING

Almost all behavioural interventions for feeding problems and eating disorders are mediated by the behaviours of family members, peers and various kinds of staff; they often inadvertently deliver the consequences maintaining the target behaviour (Piazza, Fisher, Brown, Shore et al., 2003) or request excessively large effort from the client (Kerwin et al., 1995). Hence, effective, efficient and acceptable training of third parties is an essential component of interventions for these problems. Parents and direct-care staff are also the gatekeepers to medical services and must identify and take prompt and appropriate actions when medical problems arise. Likewise, professional and paraprofessional staff must have sufficient skills to diagnose, identify target and competing behaviours, identify the function of the target behaviour, write an effective treatment plan, train third parties and then troubleshoot problems. Behavioural procedures for feeding problems have been successfully taught to trainers, nurses and mothers (Lamm and Greer, 1988) and simple behavioural skills have been taught to mothers with mild intellectual disabilities whose children might be at risk from these problems (Feldman, Case, Rincover, Towns and Betal, 1989).

How should these skills be taught? There is now robust evidence that traditional methods based on verbal and written instructions, lectures, classes, and other forms of verbally based interventions are ineffective in changing staff behaviour (Green, Rollyson, Passante and Reid, 2002; Iwata et al., 2000; Lavie and Sturmey, 2002; Sarakoff and Sturmey, 2004). Behavioural skills training (BST) is an alternative approach which involves careful operationalization and task analysis of staff performance, brief written or verbal instruction, modelling, rehearsal either in vivo or as role play, performance feedback and rehearsal to mastery. Use of multiple exemplars can be used to promote generalization to untrained tasks and situations (Ducharme, Williams, Cummings, Murray and Spencer, 2001). Maintenance must be planned, rather than hoped for, but can be successful over long periods of time (Sturmey, 1995). There is a strong evidence base for these approaches to staff and parents' training (Reid, 1998; Sturmey, 1999).

SUMMARY

Feeding problems and eating disorders represent a significant and preventable form of additional disability in people with intellectual disabilities. Behavioural interventions based on functional assessment and analysis and behavioural approaches to staff and parent training and support can be highly effective. There is currently little evidence for the effectiveness of other approaches. Psychologists should develop competency and skills in these areas as their primary approach to this class of problems.

EXERCISES

Work in groups of 2–4 to address the following four study questions. When you have completed the questions, tell your answers to the class.

Mr Kelly was a 27-year-old man with profound intellectual disabilities living in a group home. He was referred to you, a psychologist, who is a member of an interdisciplinary community team, because of weight loss, meal refusals and challenging behaviours at mealtimes. He is 5 foot 8 inches tall and weighed 145 pounds at referral. He has lost 25 pounds over the previous three months. Staff and parents report that he refuses to eat many of his meals. His person-centred plan indicates that he would like to feel more healthy, to enjoy his meals and to eat preferred foods.

Study question 1. Describe how your initial screening assessment should proceed based on this information. Suppose his treatment team and parents now agree that the problem has two aspects: eating slowly and eating only certain food groups, such as potatoes, milk products, and sweet items, but not vegetables or fried food. Unstructured direct observation also shows that when asked to eat more quickly, to eat a non-preferred food or to eat a complete meal he turns his head away, pushes away from the table, pushes the staff away and begins to whine and cry.

Study question 2. Describe how you would take baseline data and conduct a functional assessment of these problems. Baseline data reveal that he takes an average of 0.5 bites per minute (range 0.1 to 2.0 bites per minute) and he refused carrots, beans, and cauliflower 50 percent, 90 percent, and 95 percent of times they were offered to him. Your functional assessment shows that the consequences of maintaining food refusal are removal of the spoon and plate and staff offering bites of potato or a sip of milk.

Study question 3. Design an intervention based on positive behavioural support to increase Mr Kelly's rate of eating to four bites per minute and to eat all three vegetable groups. Your plan should incorporate the results of the functional assessment and the evidence base described earlier in this chapter.

What behaviours do you want to increase?

How does your intervention relate to the functions of the target behaviours?

Describe how your plan reflects the evidence base for effective treatment of these problems.

What ethical issues can you identify in the implementation of the plan?

Describe how you would train staff to implement this plan. How would you evaluate the effectiveness of this plan?

Study question 4. After three months of implementation the plan has been successfully implemented. Mr Kelly now enjoys his meals, his weight is 155 pounds, he eats about as quickly as his housemates do and he eats almost all foods offered to him. You reduce your support gradually from one visit per week to one per month over a six-month period. On your next visit you observe Mr Kelly refusing to eat and note that he has lost weight. The home manager asks you to review the plan, which is obviously no longer working. The home manager recommends that the plan should be revised so that Mr Kelly should lose his radio and go to his room after thirty minutes of having access to his meal, since he can eat if he wants to. The house manager tells you that Mr Kelly's parents and the nurses have agreed with this plan.

What are the ethical issues in this problem?

What are the behaviour analytic issues not addressed by this proposal?

In the light of the answers to the previous questions, describe your preferred course of action.

FURTHER READING FOR PRACTITIONERS

Gedye, A. (1998). *Behavioural Diagnostic Guide for Developmental Disabilities: Eating Disturbances* (pp. 99–124). Vancouver: Diagnostic Books.

Kedesdy, J. and Budd, K. (1998). *Childhood Feeding Disorders: Behavioural Assessment and Intervention*. Baltimore, MD: Brookes.

Luiselli, J. K. (1989). Behavioural assessment and treatment of paediatric feeding disorders in developmental disabilities. *Progress in Behaviour Modification*, 24, 91–131.

Matson, J. L. and Kuhn, D. E. (2001). Identifying feeding problems in mentally retarded persons: Development and reliability of the screening tool of feeding problems (STEP). *Research in Developmental Disabilities*, 22, 165–72.

ASSESSMENT INSTRUMENTS

Adults

Kuhn, D. E. and Matson, J. L. (2002). A validity study of the Screening Tool of Feeding Problems (STEP). *Journal of Intellectual and Developmental Disability*, 27, 161–7.

Matson, J. L. and Kuhn, D. E. (2001). Identifying feeding problems in mentally retarded persons: Development and reliability of the Screening Tool of Feeding Problems (STEP). *Research in Developmental Disabilities*, 22, 165–72.

Children

Archer, L. A., Rosenbaum, P. L. and Streiner, D. L. (1991). The Children's Eating Behaviour Inventory: Reliability and validity results. *Journal of Paediatric Psychology*, 16, 629–42.

Crist, W. and Napier-Phillips, A. (2001). Mealtime behaviours of young children: A comparison of normative and clinical data. *Journal of Developmental and Behavioural Paediatrics*, 22, 279–86. Contains the Behavioural Paediatrics Feeding Assessment Scale.

Durand, V. M. (1990). *Severe Behaviour Problems*. New York: Guilford Press.

Paclawskyj, T. R., Matson, J. L. and Rush, K. S. (2000). Questions About Behavioural Function (QABF): A behavioural checklist for functional assessment of aberrant behaviour. *Research in Developmental Disabilities*, 21, 223–9.

Paclawskyj, T. R., Matson, J. L. and Rush, K. S. (2001). Assessment of the convergent validity of the Questions About Behavioural Function scale with analogue functional analysis and the Motivation Assessment Scale. *Journal of Intellectual Disability Research*, 45, 484–94.

REFERENCES

Allison, D. B., Fontaine, K. R., Manson, J. E., Stevens, J. and VanItallie, T. B. (1999). How many deaths are attributable to obesity? *Journal of the American Medical Association*, 282, 1530–8.

Altman, K., Bondy, A. and Hirsch, G. (1978). Behavioural treatment of obesity in patients with Prader-Willi syndrome. *Journal of Behavioural Medicine*, 1, 403–12.

American Psychiatric Association (APA) (1994). *Diagnostic and Statistical Manual of Mental Disorders* (4th edn). Washington, DC: APA.

Archer, L. A., Rosenbaum, P. L. and Streiner, D. L. (1991). The Children's Eating Behaviour Inventory: Reliability and validity results. *Journal of Paediatric Psychology*, 16, 629–42.

Azrin, N. H. and Armstrong, P. M. (1973). The 'mini-meal' – A method for teaching eating skills to the profoundly retarded. *Mental Retardation*, 11, 9–13.

Azrin, N. H. and Wesolowski, M. D. (1974). Theft reversal: An overcorrection procedure for eliminating stealing by retarded persons. *Journal of Applied Behaviour Analysis*, 7, 577–81.

Babbitt, R. A., Hoch, T. A., Coe, D. A., Cataldo, M. F., Kelly, K. J., Stackhouse, C. and Perman, J. A. (1994). Behavioural assessment and treatment of paediatric feeding disorders. *Developmental and Behavioural Paediatrics*, 15, 278–91.

Barton, E. S., Guess, D., Garcia, E. and Baer, D. M. (1970). Improvement of retardates mealtime behaviours by timeout procedures using multiple baseline techniques. *Journal of Applied Behaviour Analysis*, 3, 77–84.

Bell, A. J. and Bhate, M. S. (1992). Prevalence of overweight and obesity in Down's syndrome and other mentally handicapped adults living in the community. *Journal of Intellectual Disability Research*, 36, 359–64.

Bernal, M. E. (1972). Behavioural treatment of a child's eating problem. *Behaviour Therapy*, 3, 43–50.

Bithony, W. G. (1986). Elevated lead levels in children with nonorganic failure to thrive. *Paediatrics*, 78, 891–5.

Boddy, J., Skuse, D. and Andrews, B. (2000). The development of sequelae of non-organic failure to thrive. *Journal of Child Psychology and Psychiatry*, 41, 1003–14.

Bogart, L. C., Peirsel, W. C. and Gross, E. J. (1995). The long-term treatment of life-threatening pica: A case study of a woman with profound mental retardation living in an applied setting. *Journal of Developmental and Physical Disabilities*, 7, 39–50.

Bowen, L., Glynn, S. M., Marshall, Jr., B. D., Kurth, C. L. and Hayden, J. L. (1990). Successful behavioural treatment of polydipsia in a schizophrenic patient. *Journal of Behaviour Therapy and Experimental Psychiatry*, 21, 53–61.

Bray, G. A. (1998). *Contemporary Diagnosis and Management of Obesity*. Pennsylvania: Handbooks in Health Care Co.

Bremner, A. J. and Regan, A. (1991). Intoxicated by water: Polydipsia and water intoxication in a mental handicap hospital. *British Journal of Psychiatry*, 158, 244–50.

Bucher, B., Reykdal, B. and Albin, J. (1976). Brief physical restraint to control pica in retarded children. *Journal of Behaviour Therapy and Experimental Psychiatry*, 7, 137–40.

Burkart, J. E., Fox, R. A. and Rotatori, A. F. (1985). Obesity of mentally retarded individuals: Prevalence, characteristics, and intervention. *American Journal of Mental Retardation*, 90, 303–12.

Butler, M. G. (1990). Prader-WIlli syndrome: Current understanding of cause and diagnosis. *American Journal of Medicine and Genetics*, 35, 319–32.

Caldwell, M. L. and Taylor, R. L. (1983). A clinical note on food preferences of individuals with Prader-Willi syndrome: The need for empirical research. *Journal of Mental Deficiency Research*, 27, 45–9.

Caldwell, M. L., Taylor, R. L. and Bloom, S. R. (1986). An investigation of the use of high- and low-preference food as a reinforcer for increased activity of individuals with Prader-Willi syndrome. *Journal of Mental Deficiency Research*, 30, 347–54.

Chad, K., Jobling, A. and Frail, H. (1990). Metabolic rate: A factor in developing obesity in children with Down syndrome? *American Journal on Mental Retardation*, 95, 228–35.

Cipani, E. (1981). Modifying food spillage behaviour in an institutionalized retarded client. *Journal of Behaviour Therapy and Experimental Psychiatry*, 12, 261–5.

Clark, D. J. and Yapa, P. (1991). Phenylketonuria and anorexia nervosa. *Journal of Mental Deficiency Research*, 35, 165–70.

Coe, D. A., Babbitt, R. L., Williams, K. E., Hajimihalis, C., Snyder, A. M., Ballard, C. and Efron, L. A. (1997). Use of extinction and reinforcement to increase food consumption and reduce expulsion. *Journal of Applied Behaviour Analysis*, 30, 581–3.

Cooper, L. J., Wacker, D. P., McComas, J. J., Brown, K., Peck, S. M., Richman, D., Drew, J., Frischmeyer, P. and Millard, T. (1995). Use of component analyses to identify active variables in treatment packages for children with feeding disorders. *Journal of Applied Behaviour Analysis*, 28, 139–53.

Cooper, S. A., Melville, C. A. and Einfield, S. I. (2003). Psychiatric disagnosis, intellectual disabilities and Diagnostic Criteria for Psychiatric Disorders for use with adults with learning disabilities / mental retardation (DC-LD). *Journal of Intellectual Disabilities Research*, 47, 3–15.

Craighead, L. W. and Agras, W. S. (1991). Mechanisms of action in cognitive-behavioural and pharmacological interventions for obesity and bulimia nervosa. *Journal of Consulting and Clinical Psychology*, 59, 115–25.

Crist, W. and Napier-Phillips, A. (2001). Mealtime behaviours of young children: A comparison of normative and clinical data. *Journal of Developmental and Behavioural Paediatrics*, 22, 279–86.

Crowther, J. H. and Sherwood, N. E. (1997). Assessment. In Garner, D. M. and Garfinkel, P. E. (eds) *Handbook of Treatment for Eating Disorders* (pp. 34–49). New York: Guilford Press.

Dandford, D. E. and Huber, A. M. (1981). Eating dysfunctions in an institutionalized mentally retarded population. *Appetite: Journal for Intake Research*, 2, 281–92.

Daniel, W. H. (1982). Management of chronic rumination with a contingent exercise procedure employing topographically dissimilar behaviour. *Journal of Behaviour Therapy and Experimental Psychiatry*, 13, 149–52.

Datlow-Smith, M. (1987) Treatment of pica in an adult disabled by autism by differential reinforcement of incompatible behaviour. *Journal of Behaviour Therapy and Experimental Psychiatry*, 18, 285–8.

Dawson, J. E., Piazza, C. C., Sevin, B. M., Gulotta, C. S., Lerman, D. and Kelley, M. L. (2003). Use of the high-probability instructional sequence and escape extinction in a child with food refusal. *Journal of Applied Behaviour Analysis*, 36, 105–8.

Deb, S., Bramble, D., Drybala, G., Boyle, A. and Bruce, J. (1994). Polydipsia amongst adults with a learning disability in an institution. *Journal of Intellectual Disability Research*, 38, 359–67.

Diabetes Prevention Program Research Group (2002). Reduction in the incidence of type 2 diabetes with lifestyle intervention or metformin. *New England Journal of Medicine*, 346, 393–403.

Dimitropoulos, A., Feurer, I. D., Roof, E., Stone, W., Butler, M. G., Sutcliffe, J. and Thompson, T. (2000). Appetitive behaviour, compulsivity, and neurochemistry in Prader-Willi syndrome. *Mental Retardation and Developmental Disabilities Research Reviews*, 6, 125–30.

Donnelly, D. R. and Olczak, P. V. (1990). The effect of differential reinforcement of incompatible behaviours (DRI) on pica for cigarettes in persons with intellectual disability. *Behaviour Modification*, 14, 81–96.

Ducharme, J. M., Williams, L., Cummings, A., Murray, P. and Spencer, T. (2001). General case quasi-pyramidal staff training to promote generalization of teaching skills in supervisory and direct-care staff. *Behaviour Modification*, 25, 233–54.

Dudley, J. R., Ahlgrim-Delzell, L. and Calhoun, M. L. (1999). Diverse diagnostic and behavioural patterns amongst people with a dual diagnosis. *Journal of Intellectual Disability Research*, 43, 70–9.

Duker P. C. and Nielen, M. (1993). The use of negative practice for the control of pica behaviour. *Journal of Behaviour Therapy and Experimental Psychiatry*, 24, 249–53.

Dunn, J., Lockwood, K., Williams, D. E. and Peacock, S. (1997). A seven year follow-up of treating rumination with dietary satiation. *Behavioural Interventions*, 12, 163–72.

Durand, B. (1975). A clinical nursing study: Failure to thrive in a child with Down syndrome. *Nursing Research*, 24, 272–86.

Dykens, E. M. (2000). Contaminated and unusual food combinations: What do people with Prader-Willi syndrome choose? *Mental Retardation*, 38, 163–71.

Dymek, M. and le Grange, D. (2002). Anorexia nervosa with comorbid psychosis and borderline mental retardation: A case report. *International Journal of Eating Disorders*, 31, 478–82.

Fairburn, C. (1995). *Overcoming Binge Eating*. New York: Guilford Press.

Feldman, M. A., Case, L., Rincover, A., Towns, F. and Betal, J. (1989). Parent education project III: Increasing affection and responsively in developmentally handicapped mothers: Component analysis, generalization, and effects on child language. *Journal of Applied Behaviour Analysis*, 22, 211–22.

Fieldstone, A., Zipf, W. B., Schwartz, H. C. and Berntson, G. G. (1997). Food preferences in Prader-Willi syndrome, normal weight and obese controls. *International Journal of Obesity and Related Metabolic Disorders*, 21, 1046–52.

Fisher, E. (1986). Behavioural weight reduction program for mentally retarded adult females. *Perceptual and Motor Skills*, 62, 359–62.

Flegal, K. M., Carrol, M. D., Ogden, C. L. and Johnson, C. L. (2002). Prevalence and trends in obesity among US adults, 1999–2000. *Journal of the American Medical Association*, 288, 1728–32.

Fontaine, K. R. and Barofsky, I. (2001). Obesity and health-related quality of life. *Obesity Reviews*, 2, 173–82.

Fox, R. A. (1984). A streamlined weight loss program for moderately retarded adults in a sheltered workshop setting. *Applied Research in Mental Retardation*, 5, 69–79.

Fox, R. A. (1985). Parent involvement in a treatment program for obese retarded adults. *Journal of Behaviour Therapy and Experimental Psychiatry*, 16, 45–8.

Foxx, R. M. (1972). Social reinforcement of weight reduction: A case report on an obese retarded adolescent. *Mental Retardation*, 10, 21–3.

Foxx, R. M., Snyder, M. S. and Schroeder, F. (1979). Food satiation and oral hygiene punishment program to suppress chronic rumination by retarded persons. *Journal of Autism and Developmental Disorders*, 9, 399–411.

Fredericks, D. W., Carr, J. E. and Williams, W. L. (1998). Overview of the treatment of rumination disorder for adults in a residential setting. *Journal of Behaviour Therapy*, 29, 31–40.

Fujiura, G. T., Fitzsimons, N. and Marks, B. (1997). Predictors of BMI among adults with Down Syndrome: The social context of health promotion. *Research in Developmental Disabilities*, 18, 261–74.

Gedye, A. (1998). *Behavioural Diagnostic Guide for Developmental Disabilities: Eating Disturbances* (pp. 99–124). Vancouver: Diagnostic Books.

Gisel, E. G., Birnbaum, R. and Schwartz, S. (1998). Feeding impairments in children: Diagnosis and effective intervention. *International Journal of Orofacial Myology*, 24, 27–33.

Glover, D., Maltzman, I. and Williams, C. (1996). Food preferences among individuals with and without Prader-Willi syndrome. *American Journal on Mental Retardation*, 101, 195–205.

Gravestock, S. (2000). Eating disorders in adults with intellectual disability. *Journal of Intellectual Disability Research*, 44, 625–37.

Gravestock, S. (2003). Diagnosis and classification of eating disorders in adults with intellectual disability: The diagnostic Criteria for Psychiatric Disorders for use with Adults with Learning disabilities / Mental Retardation (DC-LD). *Journal of Intellectual Disabilities Research*, 47, 72–83.

Green, C., Rollyson, J., Passante, S. and Reid, D. (2002). Maintaining proficient supervisor performance with direct support personnel: An analysis of two management approaches. *Journal of Applied Behaviour Analysis*, 35, 205–8.

Greene, K. S., Johnston, J. M., Rossi, M., Rawal, A., Winston, M. and Barron, S. (1991). Effects of peanut butter on ruminating. *American Journal on Mental Retardation*, 95, 631–45.

Greer, R. D., Donrow, L., Wiliams, G., McCorkle, N. and Asnes, R. (1991). Peer-mediated procedures to induce swallowing and food acceptance in young children. *Journal of Applied Behaviour Analysis*, 24, 783–90.

Goh, Han-Leong, Iwata, B. A. and Kahng, S. W. (1999). Multicomponent assessment and treatment of cigarette pica. *Journal of Applied Behaviour Analysis*, 32, 297–316.

Groves, I. D. and Carroccio, D. F. (1971). A self-feeding program for the severely and profoundly retarded. *Mental Retardation*, 9, 10–12.

Hagopian, L. P., Farrell, D. A. and Amari, A. (1996). Treating total liquid refusal with backward chaining and fading. *Journal of Applied Behaviour Analysis*, 29, 573–5.

Hayfron-Benjamin, J., Peters, C. A. and Woodhouse, R. A. (1996a). A demographic study of polydipsia in an institution for the intellectually disabled. *Canadian Journal of Psychiatry*, 41, 519–22.

Hayfron-Benjamin, J., Peters, C. A. and Woodhouse, R. A. (1996b). Screening patients with mental retardation for polydipsia. *Canadian Journal of Psychiatry*, 41, 523–7.

Henriksen, K. and Doughty, R. (1967). Decelerating undesired mealtime behaviour in a group of profoundly retarded boys. *American Journal of Mental Deficiency*, 72, 40–4.

Hoch, T. A., Babbitt, R. L., Coe, D. A., Krell, D. M. and Hackbert, L. (1994). Contingency contacting: Combining positive reinforcement and escape extinction procedures to treat persistent food refusal. *Behavior Modification*, 18, 106–28.

Hoffman, C. J., Aultman, D. and Pipes, P. (1992). A nutritional survey of and recommendations for individuals with Prader-Willi syndrome who live in group homes. *Journal of the American Dietetic Association*, 92, 823–30, 833.

Holland, A. J., Treasure, J., Coskeran, P. and Dallow, J. (1995). Characteristics of the eating disorder in Prader-Willi syndrome: Implications for treatment. *Journal of Intellectual Disability Research*, 39, 373–81.

Holt, G. M., Bouras, N. and Watson, G. P. (1988). Down's syndrome and eating disorders: A case study. *British Journal of Psychiatry*, 52, 847–8.

Hurley, A. D. and Sovner, R. (1979). Anorexia nervosa and mental retardation: A case report. *Journal of Clinical Psychiatry*, 40, 480–1.

Ives, C. C., Harris, S. L. and Wolchik, S. A. (1978). Food refusal in an autistic-type child treated by a multi-component forced feeding procedure. *Journal of Behavior Therapy and Experimental Psychatry*, 9, 61–4.

Iwata, B. A., Dorsey, M. F., Slifer, K. J., Bauman, K. and Richman, G. S. (1982/1994). Toward a functional analysis of self-injurious behaviour. *Journal of Applied Behaviour Analysis*, 27, 197–209. (Reprinted from *Analysis and Intervention in Developmental Disabilities*, 2, 3–20).

Iwata, B. A., Wallace, M. D., Kahng, S., Lindberg, J. S., Roscoe, E. M., Conners, J., Hanley, P., Thompson, R. H., and Worsdell, A. S. (2000). Skill acquisition in the implementation of functional analysis methodology. *Journal of Applied Behaviour Analysis*, 33, 181–94.

Jackson, H. J. and Thorbecke, P. J. (1982). Treating obesity of mentally retarded adolescents and adults: An exploratory program. *American Journal of Mental Deficiency*, 87, 302–8.

Jawed, S. H., Krishnan, V. H., Prasher, V. P. and Corbett, J. A. (1993). Worsening of pica as a symptom of depressive illness in a person with severe mental handicap. *British Journal of Psychiatry*, 162, 835–7.

Joachim, R. (1975). Experimenter contact and self-monitoring of weight with the mentally retarded. *Australian Journal of Mental Retardation*, 3, 222–5.

Johnson, C. R. and Babbitt, R. L. (1993). Antecedent manipulation in the treatment of primary solid food refusal. *Behaviour Modification*, 17, 510–21.

Johnston, J. M. (1993). Phenomenology and treatment of rumination. *Eating and Growth Disorders*, 2, 93–107.

Johnston, J. M., Greene, K. S., Vazin, T., Winston, M. and Rawal, A. (1990). Effects of food consistency on ruminating. *The Psychological Record*, 40, 609–18.

Jones, T. W. (1982). Treatment of behaviour-related eating problems in retarded student: A review of the literature. In Hollis, J. H. and Meyers, C. E. (eds), *Life Threatening Behaviour, Analysis and Intervention*. Washington, DC: American Association on Mental Deficiency.

Joseph, B., Egli, M., Koppekin, A. and Thompson, T. (2002). Food choice in people with Prader-Willi syndrome: Quantity and relative preference. *American Journal on Mental Retardation*, 107, 128–35.

Kalfus, G. R., Fisher-Gross, S., Marvullo, M. A. and Nau, P. A. (1987). Outpatient treatment of pica in a developmentally delayed child. *Child and Family Behaviour Therapy*, 9, 49–63.

Kern, L. and Marder, T. J. (1996). A comparison of simultaneous and delayed reinforcement as treatments for food selectivity. *Journal of Applied Behaviour Analysis*, 29, 243–6.

Kerwin, M. E., Ahearn, W. H., Eicher, P. S. and Bured, D. M. (1995). The costs of eating: A behavioural economic analysis of food refusal. *Journal of Applied Behaviour Analysis*, 28, 245–60.

Khang, S., Tarbox, J. and Wilke, A. E. (2001). Use of a multicomponent treatment for food refusal. *Journal of Applied Behaviour Analysis*, 34, 93–6.

Kohn, Y., Weizman, A. and Apter, A. (2001). Aggravation of food-related behaviour in an adolescent with Prader-Willi syndrome treated with fluvoxamine and fluoxetine. *International Journal of Eating Disorders*, 30, 113–17.

Kuhn, D. E., Matson, J. L., Mayville, E. A. and Matson, M. L. (2001). The relationship of social skills as measured by the MESSIER to rumination in persons with profound mental retardation. *Research in Developmental Disabilities*, 22, 503–10.

Kuruvilla, J. and Trewby, P. N. (1989). Gastro-oesophageal disorders in adults with severe mental impairment. *British Medical Journal*, 299, 95–6.

Lamm, N. and Greer, R. D. (1988). Induction and maintenance of swallowing responses in infants with dysphagia. *Journal of Applied Behaviour Analysis*, 21, 143–56.

Lavie, T. and Sturmey, P. (2002). Training staff to conduct a paired-stimulus preference assessment. *Journal of Applied Behaviour Analysis*, 35, 209–11.

LeBlanc, L. A., Piazza, C. C., and Krug, M. A. (1997). Comparing methods for maintaining the safety of a child with pica. *Research in Developmental Disabilities*, 18, 215–20.

Leibowitz, J. M. and Holcer, P. (1974) Building and maintaining self-feeding skills in a retarded child. *American Journal of Occupational Therapy*, 28, 545–8.

Lennox, D. B., Miltenberger, R. G. and Donnelly, D. R. (1987). Response interruption and DRL for the reduction of rapid eating. *Journal of Applied Behaviour Analysis*, 20, 279–84.

Lofts, R. H., Schroeder, S. R. and Maier, R. H. (1990). Effects of serum zinc supplementation on pica behaviour of persons with mental retardation. *American Journal on Mental Retardation*, 95, 103–9.

Luiselli, J. K. (1988). Improvement of feeding skills in multihandicapped children through paced-prompting interventions. *Journal of the Multihandicapped Person*, 1, 17–30. Cited in Luiselli, J. K. (1989). Behavioural assessment and treatment of paediatric feeding disorders in developmental disabilities. *Progress in Behaviour Modification*, 24, pp. 117–18.

Luiselli, J. K. (1989). Behavioural assessment and treatment of paediatric feeding disorders in developmental disabilities. *Progress in Behaviour Modification*, 24, 91–131.

Luiselli, J. K. and Gleason, D. J. (1987). Combining sensory reinforcement and texture-fading procedures to overcome chronic food refusal. *Journal of Behaviour Therapy and Experimental Psychiatry*, 18, 149–55.

Luke, A., Sutton, M., Schoeller, D. A. and Roizen, N. J. (1996). Nutrient intake and obesity in prepubescent children with Down syndrome. *Journal of the American Dietetic Association*, 96, 1262–7.

Mace, F. C. and Knight, D. (1986). Functional analysis and treatment of severe pica. *Journal of Applied Behaviour Analysis*, 19, 411–16.

Maglieri, K. A., DeLeon, I. G., Rodriguez-Catter, V. and Sevin, B. (2000). Treatment of covert food stealing in an individual with Prader-Willi syndrome. *Journal of Applied Behaviour Analysis*, 33, 615–18.

Matson, J. L. and Bamburg, J. W. (1999). A descriptive study of pica behaviour in persons with mental retardation. *Journal of Developmental and Physical Disabilities*, 11, 353–61.

Matson, J. L., Gardner, W. I., Coe, D. A. and Sovner, R. (1991). A scale for evaluating emotional disorders in severely and profoundly mentally retarded persons. *British Journal of Psychiatry*, 159, 404–9.

Matson, J. L. and Kuhn, D. E. (2001). Identifying feeding problems in mentally retarded persons: Development and reliability of the Screening Tool of Feeding Problems (STEP). *Research in Developmental Disabilities*, 22, 165–72.

Matson, J. L., Stephens, R. M. and Smith, C. (1978). Treatment of self-injurious behaviour with overcorrection. *Journal of Mental Deficiency Research*, 22, 175–8.

McAlpine, C. and Singh, N. N. (1986). Pica in institutionalized mentally retarded persons. *Journal of Mental Deficiency Research*, 30, 171–8.

McKeegan, G. F., Estill, K. and Campbell, B. (1987). Elimination of rumination by controlled eating and differential reinforcement. *Journal of Behaviour Therapy and Experimental Psychiatry*, 18, 143–8.

McLoughlin, I. J. (1987). The picas. *British Journal of Hospital Medicine*, 37, 286–90.

McNally, R. J., Calamari, J. E., Hansen, P. M. and Kaliher, C. (1988). Behavioural treatment of psychogenic polydipsia. *Journal of Behaviour Therapy and Experimental Psychiatry*, 19, 57–61.

Munk, D. D. and Repp, A. C. (1994). Behavioural assessment of feeding problems of individuals with severe disabilities. *Journal of Applied Behaviour Analysis*, 27, 241–50.

Nelson, G. L., Cone, J. D. and Hanson, C. R. (1975). Training correct utensil use in retarded children: Modelling vs. physical guidance. *American Journal of Mental Deficiency*, 1, 114–22.

Norvell, N. K. and Ahern, D. K. (1987). Worksite weight-loss intervention for individuals with mental retardation: A pilot study. *Education and Training in Mental Retardation*, 22, 85–90.

O'Brien, F., Bugle, C. and Azrin, N. H. (1972). Training and maintaining a retarded child's proper eating. *Journal of Applied Behaviour Analysis*, 5, 67–72.

O'Brien, G. and Whitehouse, A. M. (1990). A psychiatric study of deviant eating behaviour among mentally handicapped adults. *British Journal of Psychiatry*, 157, 281–4.

Pace, G. M. and Toyer, E. A. (2000). The effects of a vitamin supplement on the pica of a child with severe mental retardation. *Journal of Applied Behaviour Analysis*, 33, 619–22.

Page, T. J., Stanley, A. E., Richman, G. S., Deal, R. M. and Iwata, B. A. (1983). Reduction of food theft and long-term maintenance of weight loss in a Prader-Willi adult. *Behaviour Therapy and Experimental Psychiatry*, 14, 261–8.

Paisey, T. J. and Whitney, R. B. (1989). A long-term case study of analysis, response suppression, and treatment maintenance involving life-threatening pica. *Behavioural Residential Treatment*, 4, 191–211.

Paniagua, F. A., Braverman, C. and Capriotti, R. M. (1986). Use of a treatment package in the management of a profoundly mentally retarded girl's pica and self-stimulation. *American Journal of Mental Deficiency*, 90, 550–7.

Patel, M. R., Piazza, C. C., Kelly, M. L., Ochsner, C. A. and Santana, C. M. (2001). Using a fading procedures to increase fluid consumption in a child with feeding problems. *Journal of Applied Behaviour Analysis*, 34, 357–60.

Patel, M. R., Piazza, C. C., Martinez, C. J., Volkert, V. M. and Santana, C. M. (2002). An evaluation of two differential reinforcement procedures with escape extinction to treat food refusal. *Journal of Applied Behaviour Analysis*, 35, 363–74.

Patel, M. R., Piazza, C. C., Santana, C. M. and Volkert, V. M. (2002). An evaluation of food type and texture in the treatment of a feeding problem. *Journal of Applied Behaviour Analysis*, 35, 183–6.

Pavalonis, D., Shutty, M., Hundley, P., Leadbetter, R., Viewig, V. and Downs, M. (1992). Behavioural intervention to reduce water intake in the syndrome of psychosis, intermittent hyponatremia, and polydipsia. *Journal of Behaviour Therapy and Experimental Psychiatry*, 23, 51–7.

Petersen, P. and Ottenbacher, K. (1986). Use of applied behavioural techniques and an adaptive device to teach lip closure to severely handicapped children. *American Journal of Mental Deficiency*, 90, 535–9.

Piazza, C. C., Fisher, W. W., Brown, K. A., Shore, B., Patel, M. R., Katz, R. M., Sevin, B., Gulotta, C. S. and Blakey-Smith, A. (2003). Functional analysis of inappropriate mealtime behaviours. *Journal of Applied Behaviour Analysis*, 36, 187–204.

Piazza, C. C., Fisher, W. W., Hanley, G. P., LeBlanc, L. A., Worsdell, A. S., Lindauer, S. E. and Keeney, K. M. (1998). Treatment of pica through multiple analyses of its reinforcing functions. *Journal of Applied Behaviour Analysis*, 31, 165–89.

Piazza, C. C., Patel, M. R., Gulotta, C. S., Sevin, B. M. and Layer, S. A. (2003). On the relative contributions of positive reinforcement and escape extinction in the treatment of food refusal. *Journal of Applied Behaviour Analysis*, 36, 309–24.

Piazza, C. C., Patel, M. R., Santana, C. M., Goh, H. L., Delia, M. D. and Lancaster, B. M. (2002). An evaluation of simultaneous and sequential presentation of pre-ferred and nonpreferred food to treat food selectivity. *Journal of Applied Behaviour Analysis*, 35, 259–70.

Prasher, V. P. (1995). Overweight and obesity amongst Down's syndrome adults. *Journal of Intellectual Disability Research*, 39, 437–41.

Raitasuo, S., Virtanen, H. and Raitasuo, J. (1998). Anorexia, nervosa, major depression, and obsessive-compulsive disorder in a Down's syndrome patient. *International Journal of Eating Disorders*, 23, 107–9.

Rapp, J. T., Dozier, C. L. and Carr, J. E. (2001). Functional assessment and treatment of pica: A single-case experiment. *Behavioral Interventions*, 16, 111–25.

Rast, J. and Johnston, J. M. (1986). Social versus dietary control of ruminating by mentally retarded persons. *American Journal of Mental Deficiency*, 90, 464–7.

Rast, J., Johnston, J. M., Ellinger-Allen, J. and Drum, C. (1985). Effects of nutri-tional and mechanical properties of food on ruminative behaviour. *Journal of Experimental Analysis of Behaviour*, 44, 195–206.

Reid, A. H., Ballinger, B. R. and Heather, B. B. (1978). Behavioural syndromes identi-fied by cluster analysis in a sample of 100 severely and profoundly retarded adults. *Psychological Medicine*, 8, 399–412.

Reid, D. H. (ed.) (1998). *Organizational Behaviour Management and Developmental Disabilities Services: Accomplishments and Future Directions* (pp. 7–31). New York: Haworth Press.

Reyer, H. and Sturmey, P. (2003). *The effects of preloading on food grabbing and hand-to mouth behaviour in adults with developmental disabilities.* Manuscript submitted for publication.

Riordan, M. M., Iwata, B. A., Finney, J. W., Wohl, M. K. and Stanley, A. E. (1984). Behavioural assessment and treatment of chronic food refusal in handicapped children. *Journal of Applied Behaviour Analysis*, 17, 327–41.

Riordan, M. M., Iwata, B. A., Wohl, M. K. and Finney, J. W. (1980). Behavioural treat-ment of food refusal and selectivity in developmentally disabled children. *Applied Research in Mental Retardation*, 1, 95–112.

Rogers, B., Stratton, P., Victor, J., Kennedy, B. and Andres, M. (1992). Chronic regurgitation among persons with mental retardation: A need for combined medical and interdisciplinary strategies. *American Journal on Mental Retardation*, 96, 522–7.

Rosen, M. (1974). Teaching the mentally retarded to sip through a straw. *Journal of Applied Behaviour Analysis*, 7, 355.

Rubin, S. S., Rimmer, J. H., Chicoine, B., Braddock, D. and McGuire, D. E. (1998). Overweight prevalence in persons with Down syndrome. *Mental Retardation*, 36, 175–81.

Sarakoff, R. A. and Sturmey, P. (2004). The effects of behavioral skills training on staff implementation of discrete-trial teaching. *Journal of Applied Behavior Analysis*, 37, 535–8.

Schwarz, S. M., Corredor, J., Fisher-Medina, J., Cohen, J. and Rabinowitz, S. (2001). Diagnosis and treatment of feeding disorders in children with developmental disabilities. *Paediatrics*, 108, 671–6.

Sevin, B. M., Gulotta, C. S., Sierp, B. J. and Miller, L. J. (2002). Analysis of response covariation among multiple topographies of food refusal. *Journal of Applied Behaviour Analysis*, 35, 65–8.

Shore, B. A., Babbitt, R. L., Williams, K. E., Coe, D. A. and Snyder, A. (1998). Use of texture fading in the treatment of food selectivity. *Journal of Applied Behaviour Analysis*, 31, 621–33.

Shore, B. A., LeBlanc, D. and Simmons, J. (1999). Reduction of unsafe eating in a patient with esophageal stricture. *Journal of Applied Behaviour Analysis*, 32, 225–8.

Siegel, L. J. (1982). Classical and operant procedures in the treatment of a case of food aversion in a young child. *Journal of Clinical Child Psychology*, 11, 167–72.

Sigafoos, J., Doss, S. and Reichle, J. (1989). Developing mand and tact repertoires in persons with severe developmental disabilities using graphic symbols. *Research in Developmental Disabilities*, 10, 183–200.

Sigelman, C. K. (1982). Evaluating alternative techniques of questioning mentally retarded persons. *American Journal of Mental Deficiency*, 86, 511–18.

Smith, A. L., Piersel, W. C., Filbeck, R. W. and Gross, E. J. (1983). The elimination of mealtime food stealing and scavenging behaviour in an institutionalized severely mentally retarded adult. *Mental Retardation*, 21, 255–9.

Smith, S., Branford, D., Collacott, R. A., Cooper, S. A. and McGrother, C. (1996). Prevalence and cluster typology of maladaptive behaviours in a geographically defined population of adults with learning disabilities. *British Journal of Psychiatry*, 169, 219–27.

Sovner, R. and Hurley, A. D. (1983). Anorexia nervosa. *Psychiatric Aspects of Mental Retardation Newsletter*, 2, 1–4.

Stevenson, R. D. (1995). Feeding and nutrition in children with developmental disabilities. *Paediatric Annals*, 24, 255–60.

Stunkard, A. J. (1993). A history of binge eating. In C. G. Fairburn and G. T. Wilson (eds), *Binge Eating: Nature, Assessment, and Treatment* (pp.15–34). New York: Guilford Press.

Sturmey, P. (1995). Evaluating and improving group residential treatment during group leisure situations: An independent replication. *Behavioural Interventions: Theory and Practice in Residential and Community-Based Clinical Programs*, 10, 59–67.

Sturmey, P. (1999). History and contribution of organizational behaviour management to services for persons with developmental disabilities. In D. H. Reid, (ed.), *Organizational Behaviour Management and Developmental Disabilities Services: Accomplishments and Future Directions* (pp. 7–31). New York: Haworth Press.

Terai, K., Munesue, T. and Hiratani, M. (1999). Excessive water drinking behaviour in autism. *Brain and Development*, 21, 103–6.

Thomas, P. R. (1994). Anorexia nervosa in people with learning disabilities. *British Journal of Learning Disabilities*, 22, 25–6.

Thommessen, M., Heiberg, A., Kase, B. F., Larsen, S. and Riis, G. (1991). Feeding problems, height and weight in different groups of disabled children. *Acta Paediatrica Scandinavica*, 80, 527–33.

Thompson, R. J. and Palmer, S. (1974). Treatment of feeding problems: A behavioural approach. *Journal of Nutrition Education*, 6, 63–6.

Vitousek, K. B., Daly, J. and Heiser, C. (1991). Reconstructing the world of the eating disordered individual: Overcoming denial and distortion in self-report. *International Journal of Eating Disorders*, 10, 647–66.

Waller, G., Hyde, C. E. and Thomas, C. S. (1993). A 'biofeedback' approach to the treatment of chronic polydipsia. *Journal of Behaviour Therapy and Experimental Psychiatry*, 24, 255–9.

Werle, M. A., Murphy, T. B. and Budd, K. S. (1993). Treating chronic food refusal in young children: Home-based parent training. *Journal of Applied Behaviour Analysis*, 26, 421–33.

Wilfley, D. E. and Rodin, J. (1995). Cultural influences on eating disorders. In Brownell, K. D. and Fairburn, C. G. (eds), *Eating Disorders and Obesity: A Comprehensive Handbook* (pp. 79–82). New York: Guilford Press.

Wood, T. (1994). Weight status of a group of adults with learning disabilities. *British Journal of Learning Disabilities*, 22, 97–9.

Wright, C. S. and Vollmer, T. R. (2002). Evaluation of a treatment package to reduce rapid eating. *Journal of Applied Behaviour Analysis*, 35, 89–93.

Chapter 14

Behavioural phenotypes in genetic syndromes associated with intellectual disability

Orlee Udwin and Adam Kuczynski

With recent advances in molecular genetics, clinical geneticists, paediatricians and other health professionals are increasingly identifying specific genetic conditions in children who, until now, were usually characterized only in a very general way as having global or specific intellectual disability, often with accompanying behavioural and emotional difficulties. Many individuals who come to the attention of health and mental health professionals as having special learning needs can now be described much more precisely in terms of a genetic condition or syndrome. In this chapter, we hope to demonstrate the value of the process of syndrome identification or diagnosis for understanding the adjustment difficulties and needs of particular groups of people with intellectual disability, and for informing assessment and intervention work with them.

The syndromes we will cover are all known to have a genetic basis. Each is associated with a distinct pattern of physical and neurological characteristics that are unique to that syndrome, often including a typical facial appearance which may give the first clue to the diagnosis. Knowledge of the clinical features and natural history of a given syndrome means that medical problems can be anticipated, allowing for early intervention and even prevention of future morbidity.

More recently, as paediatricians, geneticists, psychologists and psychiatrists with an interest in this field have become involved in supporting and advising parent self-help groups for these rare syndromes, and as they – and the parents – have begun to see affected children and adults together with others with the same syndrome, it has become apparent that they not only share similar physical characteristics, but also behave in remarkably similar ways. Over the last 15–20 years, distinct cognitive profiles and patterns of intellectual disability, as well as characteristic patterns of behaviour and behavioural difficulties, have been identified in a range of genetic conditions (Howlin and Udwin, 2002; O'Brien and Yule, 1995). Indeed, for some syndromes it was the presence of distinctive behaviours which led to their demarcation, and these in turn now have biological markers.

The study of behavioural phenotypes has been defined by Flint (1996) as the study of 'behaviours, including cognitive processes and social interaction style, that [are] consistently associated with, and specific to, a syndrome which has a chromosomal or a genetic aetiology', and 'where there is little doubt that the phenotype is a consequence of the underlying anomaly'. However, most workers in the field view this definition as too limited and prefer Dykens and Cassidy's (1995) definition of behavioural phenotypes as reflecting a 'heightened probability [that] people with a given syndrome will exhibit certain behavioural sequelae relative to those without the syndrome'. It should be noted that rarely, if ever, are the particular behaviours or cognitive features identified unique to a given syndrome. Rather, there are characteristic *patterns* of behaviours and learning abilities linked to a particular syndrome which differentiate that syndrome from others. While it is assumed that the behavioural characteristics are causally linked with the genetic anomalies, understanding of the mechanisms by which these behavioural phenotypes arise is still limited.

Syndrome diagnosis has important implications for the subsequent care and support of the affected individual, and his or her family. Once an individual has been diagnosed, the family, school and others can be given information about the natural history of the condition, they can be forewarned of likely difficulties that may arise and can benefit from the knowledge and experience of other parents and professionals about medical, psychological and educational interventions that have proved effective with others with the same condition. This can help generate a sense of control and confidence in parents and teachers, and facilitate the process of adjustment and realistic planning for the future (Turk and Sales, 1996). Clinicians need to remember that parents differ in the amount of information they want following diagnosis. Some want to know all there is to know immediately; others may take longer to accept their child's difficulties and will not be ready for detailed information straightaway. It is important to be sensitive to parents' changing needs in this regard, and to facilitate access for them to the information that is available when they are ready. Access to the Internet means that some parents are extremely well informed about their child's condition. It is important that professionals should respect parents' expertise and work in close collaboration with families.

Turk and Sales (1996) identify other benefits of diagnosis, and the accompanying recognition of behavioural phenotypes. It can encourage a focus on areas of strength as well as need in the affected individual. It can also facilitate access to syndrome-specific support groups. These are usually run by parents, often with input from professionals with specialist knowledge of the particular syndromes, and provide information about the condition and its management, access to the research literature, local and national conferences and telephone advice networks. Syndrome diagnosis is further likely to relieve parents from guilt and uncertainty and help facilitate grief resolution. Too often professionals blame parents for the difficult and often bizarre behaviours shown by individuals with these syndromes. The growing recognition that many of these behaviours are not due to poor handling or lack of care from parents, nor to the child's wilfulness or intellectual disability, but are bound up with specific genetic factors, should correct inappropriate attribution of blame to parents. Finally, where a condition is familial, diagnosis has critical implications for future pregnancies in a family, and genetic counselling for the family, including the extended family, is required.

Whereas in the past, syndrome diagnosis or 'labelling' was viewed negatively by many professionals, it is now recognized that clinicians and educators are unlikely to provide optimal care if they do not take the individual's diagnosis into account. This is not to say that all children and adults with the same genetic anomaly have identical educational and emotional needs, or that they will all show all of the features that characterize the syndrome to the same extent. It is vital to appreciate that phenotypic behaviours are open to developmental and environmental influences like all behaviours are, resulting in enormous variability between individuals, even those diagnosed with the same genetic condition (Dyer-Friedman, Glaser, Hessl, Johnston, *et al.*, 2002). It is therefore important to undertake detailed assessment of each person's strengths and deficits, notwithstanding all that is known about the syndrome in question. Moreover, the fact that particular behaviours are associated with a given genetic condition does not mean that they are not amenable to modification and amelioration via psychological and educational approaches. Experience has shown that appropriate educational provision and standard behaviour management strategies can be very effective in many cases and should be the first line of intervention. Given sufficiently early and appropriate interventions, some of these behaviours may even be preventable. For many syndromes, research into effective interventions is still in its infancy. However, findings on behavioural phenotypes are already proving valuable for parents, teachers and clinicians, by facilitating information sharing about effective educational and behaviour management approaches.

Clinical psychologists have a valuable and varied contribution to make in supporting families of children and adults with rare genetic syndromes. This can include:

- supporting families through the process of diagnosis and helping them work through the resulting feelings of shock, loss and grief;
- when they are ready, providing families with information about the syndrome, its associated difficulties and long-term outcome, and helping them to think and plan realistically for the future;
- undertaking assessments of cognitive abilities, strengths and deficits, and advising on appropriate educational settings and strategies;
- working with families on management of the child's behavioural, social and emotional difficulties;

- educating teachers, health visitors, social workers and others about the medical, behavioural and cognitive features associated with particular syndromes, and the implications of these for managing and teaching the affected individual.

In the following pages we review a number of conditions which clinical psychologists may encounter when working in Child and Adolescent Mental Health Services, intellectual disability services or hospital settings, because of cognitive, behavioural, social and emotional difficulties that may arise as a result of the behavioural phenotype. We also describe treatment approaches that are recognized as being effective in managing these conditions.

CRI-DU-CHAT SYNDROME (5p-S)

Aetiology and epidemiology

The most common causal genetic anomaly of 5p- syndrome (5p-S; '5p minus') is a deletion on the short arm of chromosome 5 at 5p15. Most often, the deletion occurs *de novo* (85 per cent) and is paternal in origin. The majority of remaining cases arise from familial and sporadic translocations. The phenotype associated with translocations tends to be more severe than that associated with deletions. 5p-S affects between 1 in 50,000 and 1 in 37,000 live births, in a female:male ratio of 4:3.

Physical features

Low birthweight is usual in 5p-S, and almost all infants display hypotonia. Poor sucking, regurgitation, and severe constipation are common (Carlin, 1990). In some cases, underlying gastrointestinal anomalies and cardiac abnormalities have also been found. These may contribute to feeding problems and an early failure to thrive. Lasting signs of abnormal growth include short stature, microcephaly, and small hands and feet. Movement difficulties are widespread and the most severely affected individuals never learn to walk. Respiratory and ear infections are common.

The faces of individuals with 5p-S are usually round with wide-set features, epicanthal folds, slanting eyelid fissures, low-set ears, broad nose, and a small jaw.

Abnormalities in size or form of the larynx are common but not universal, leading to uncertainty about the extent to which these can account for the distinctive vocal abnormalities associated with the syndrome. Central nervous system dysfunction may also be a contributory factor.

Cognitive and behavioural features

The salient, defining behavioural marker of the syndrome in infancy is a qualitatively abnormal high-pitched cry resembling a cat's miaow (hence the still current alternative name 'Cri-du-Chat syndrome'). The cry persists into childhood and other vocalizations are also high-pitched and monotonous, including speech if present.

Individuals with 5p-S are usually friendly and sociable, orienting to family members and peers, imitating others, and responding to praise. Their amiable and socially responsive character and their ability to make progress in daily living skills are important strengths. The prognosis may be more favourable than initial descriptions suggested, although learning is slow and gradual. The presence of an autistic-like withdrawal may be linked to cases with translocations rather than deletions.

Young children with 5p-S show few object-directed behaviours in play, which may be related to elevated levels of distractibility and hyperactivity compared with some other groups with intellectual disability. Many individuals fulfil diagnostic criteria for ADHD.

Cognitive ability is usually in the severe intellectual disability range, with no reliable discrepancy between estimates of verbal and non-verbal IQs. Although some speech is acquired in most cases, there is a marked discrepancy between expressive and receptive language (Cornish, Bramble, Munir and Pigram, 1999). Expressive language development is severely delayed and appears to plateau by 10 years of age. Speech articulation is often impaired. Receptive language seems to be less affected, although still impaired. In addition, most individuals with 5p-S use preverbal communication skills, gestures, or standard signs to direct attention and express their needs.

Many exhibit motor stereotypies including rhythmic rocking of the head, body and limbs. These are linked to the prevalence of some forms of self-injurious behaviour, especially hitting the head with the hand or an object (Ross Collins and Cornish, 2002). Vomiting and rumination of food from the stomach can be classed as self-injurious behaviour. Individuals may also show aggression towards others, for example hitting and hair-pulling. The association between stereotypies and self-injurious behaviour is suggestive of a neurological substrate to both. Given their language difficulties, it is plausible that self-injurious and aggressive behaviours acquire a communicative function for individuals with 5p-S. The aggression often decreases with age, perhaps as communication skills improve.

Implications for assessment and management

There is little reliable information on the most appropriate interventions for individuals with 5p-S, although there are some recommendations for management (Cornish and Bramble, 2002). Early identification ought to enable timely medical and surgical interventions for the physical complications of the syndrome. Early establishment of routines is likely to promote adaptive behavioural habits.

The inverse relationship between aggressive behaviours and communicative competence in 5p-S underlines the importance of interventions aimed at enhancing verbal and non-verbal communication, including the use of signing and augmentative techniques, such as picture boards. Given the apparent plateau in expressive language development, early intervention, including increased stimulation and the introduction and reinforcement of signing, is especially appropriate. There is also anecdotal evidence that behaviour modification may be effective in reducing aggression.

One interesting question concerns the influence of the communicative function of the cat-cry in the developing parent–child interaction. Experimental research suggests that adults tend to be less responsive to the high-pitched cry compared to lower-pitched cries, but the significance of this finding for families is not known.

ANGELMAN SYNDROME

Aetiology and epidemiology

Angelman syndrome (AS) is caused by the absence of an active gene · (UB3EA) or genes from the maternal copy of chromosome 15 at 15q11–q13. Most often, this is because of a *de novo* maternal deletion, but it may result from paternal uniparental disomy (where both copies of chromosome 15 are inherited from the father), or maternal mutations. The paternally derived genes are normally silenced or 'imprinted' and therefore cannot compensate for failure of expression of the defective maternal genes. The risk of recurrence is low in cases of deletions and uniparental disomy, but may be as high as 50 per cent for some mutations.

Presentation of the classical syndrome tends to be associated with the deletion. The phenotype associated with other genetic abnormalities may be comparatively mild but still severely disabling.

Estimates of the incidence of AS vary between 1 in 25,000 and 1 in 12,000 live births, and males and females are presumed to be equally affected.

Physical features

Neonates with AS typically have normal birth weight, head circumference, and appearance, apart from hypotonia and abnormal skin pigmentation. However, outward signs of abnormal brain development gradually become apparent such as microcephaly and a flat occiput (Williams, Angelman, Clayton-Smith *et al.*, 1995). An emerging characteristic facial appearance features deep-set eyes and a wide mouth with widely spaced teeth above a long, prominent jaw. The mouth is habitually open allowing the tongue to protrude.

The syndrome always comprises a movement disorder, manifesting as a jerky ataxic gait. In addition, there may be feeding problems in infancy related to impaired sucking and swallowing.

Characteristic abnormalities on electroencephalography (EEG) are almost ubiquitous in infancy, and onset of epilepsy is common after 2–3 years of age. EEG abnormalities and seizure severity may diminish over time but only a minority of individuals become seizure-free in adulthood, and there is a risk of recurrence and loss of seizure-control.

Children with AS suffer frequent upper respiratory tract infections and otitis media, but physical health is otherwise thought to be good. However, the incidence of scoliosis and joint contractures increases with age, exacerbating the characteristic movement disorder.

Cognitive and behavioural features

AS is characterized by severe intellectual disability, marked inattention and a paucity of spoken language (Williams *et al.*, 1995). Language problems are particularly pronounced. Individuals with AS rarely acquire an expressive vocabulary of more than three words, and approximately one third do not speak at all. Most use communicative gestures to some extent. Receptive skills may be better than expressive skills.

A typically happy and excitable disposition includes frequent smiling, episodes of paroxysmal giggling or laughter, and hand-flapping, which, although often contingent on environmental events, may be deemed inappropriate. Interestingly, individuals with AS may be less prone to tantrums, irritability, and social withdrawal than others with comparable general developmental difficulties.

Hyperactivity is common especially in childhood, as are difficulties in initiating and maintaining sleep. Children with AS often nap and sleep for only five or six hours a night, and protest vehemently when put to bed. Both overactivity and sleep problems may spontaneously decrease with age. An attraction to water and activities such as bathing, as well as fascinations with mirrors and other reflective surfaces, and music, have also been described.

Implications for assessment and management

The qualities of individuals with AS, including their sociable manner, constitute important strengths, enabling them to interact with others and participate in a range of recreational activities.

Carers and professionals may also be encouraged by a decrease in hyperactivity and sleep disorder with age. Both behavioural methods and medication can be helpful in improving sleep. These changes, as well as improvements in attention, facilitate interventions aimed at the acquisition of functional skills (Clayton-Smith, 2001). Behavioural methods for training individuals with severe intellectual disability may be applicable to those with AS, with only minor modifications to accommodate movement difficulties. In due course, many individuals are able to perform some basic self-care and household tasks under appropriate supervision.

Speech and language therapy is important. While communication skills are limited, especially expressive language, gesture is common, and a sizeable minority of individuals are able to learn to use signing (e.g. Makaton). Other forms of augmentative communication, such as picture boards, may also be beneficial. Constant reinforcement may be necessary to maintain and extend any gains.

The combination of reduced activity, scoliosis, and joint contractures, in the context of an underlying movement disorder, contributes to immobility and predisposes adults with AS to obesity. Where possible, these difficulties should be anticipated and treated early, either by physiotherapy or surgery. Routine dietary control and regular exercise to maintain joint mobility are helpful.

CORNELIA DE LANGE SYNDROME

Aetiology and epidemiology

The genetic causes of Cornelia de Lange syndrome (CdLS) are thought to be heterogeneous, with genetic abnormalities on the third, fifth and the X chromosomes having been recently identified. The absence of biological markers in the past, as well as significant phenotypic heterogeneity, have complicated understanding of its epidemiology.

Estimates of the birth prevalence vary but a figure of 1 in 50,000 is widely cited. It is assumed that males and females are equally affected.

Physical features

The physical phenotype of CdLS is characterized by signs of growth failure, including short stature and microcephaly, reduction and other anomalies of the limbs, hands, and feet, and distinctive facial features (Ireland, Donnai and Burn, 1993). Overt growth abnormalities may be accompanied by peripheral sensory neuropathy. Lower birthweight is predictive of a more severe physical and behavioural phenotype.

Young affected individuals typically have small upturned noses with anteverted nostrils, well-defined arched eyebrows meeting in the middle, and a crescent-shaped mouth with a high arched palate above a small jaw.

Numerous other physical anomalies have been reported in CdLS. Sensory deficits concern both hearing loss and defects of the eye and optic nerve. Tears may be absent or reduced. Several anomalies related to the gastrointestinal system may contribute to regurgitation and vomiting. These, coupled with difficulties in chewing and swallowing, may result in life-threatening failure to thrive. Severe feeding problems often persist. Also, reflux interacts with thin dental enamel in CdLS, accelerating the development of cavities. Heart abnormalities have also been reported.

Cognitive and behavioural features

Most affected individuals have moderate to severe intellectual disability, although individuals of higher ability have been assessed. Depending on age, approximately half are able to complete daily activities such as self-feeding and dressing. Visuospatial and fine motor skills are areas of relative strength. In contrast, expressive language skills are often severely impaired and about a third of individuals develop no more than one or two words. In these cases, communicative competence may be further limited by a relative paucity of intentional communication. Receptive communication skills tend to be better than expressive skills.

Some individuals with CdLS are calm and good-natured, but overactivity, distractibility, irritability and stereotyped behaviours are common. Some also display an autistic-like lack of social relatedness and impassivity (Berney, Ireland and Burn, 1999).

High levels of self-injurious behaviour, including head-slapping, scratching and biting, are seen, particularly in more severely affected individuals. Optic defects may lead to self-stimulatory eye pressing and poking. It has been suggested that self-injurious behaviour may be a means of managing pain caused by medical complications of the syndrome. Peripheral neuropathy may mean that normally painful stimuli are perceived in a different way. Given a restricted ability to communicate by other means, self-injurious behaviour may assume a communicative function. On the other hand, it can have a compulsive quality, reflected in attempts at self-restraint and a preference for restrictive devices (Hyman, Oliver and Hall, 2002). The extent of injury is often relatively mild, although tissue damage can sometimes be caused.

It is important to note that self-injurious behaviour may not be any more common in CdLS than in other groups of individuals with severe developmental disorders, and that aggression towards others may actually be less common.

Implications for assessment and management

A number of individuals with CdLS develop basic self-care skills and continue to acquire new skills into early adulthood. Others require more intensive support throughout their lives.

Some of the medical conditions associated with CdLS are life-threatening and most are likely to cause significant pain or discomfort and need intervention. The possibility of such complications must be considered as a causal factor in self-injurious behaviour and treated as appropriate. Other factors maintaining self-injurious behaviour should be assessed by functional analysis, using standard methods such as questionnaires, record charts, natural observations, and analogue conditions, before intervention. Psychopharmacology may also play a role in the management of self-injurious behaviour.

Functional communication training plays an important part both in reducing self-injurious behaviour and in enhancing adaptive skills in everyday life. Typically, this builds on existing behaviours in the individual's behavioural repertoire that immediately precede an episode of self-injurious behaviour. These precursors can be reinforced and shaped into more effective and adaptive means of communication (Oliver, Moss, Petty *et al.*, 2003).

As noted above, intentional communications may be infrequent in prelinguistic individuals with CdLS. This suggests that intervention may need to focus on increasing their frequency (Sarimski, 2002). In these cases, responsive facilitating strategies may be applicable. These approaches systematically employ environmental conditions (e.g. interrupted play routines) to elicit and then reinforce self-initiated communication. Speech and language therapy is also invaluable for more able individuals with CdLS to enhance both verbal and non-verbal skills.

Individuals with CdLS may benefit from interactive computerized methods of teaching. In this way, their strengths in visuospatial memory and fine motor ability can be used to learn other skills.

DOWN SYNDROME

Aetiology and epidemiology

Down syndrome (DS) is caused by the possession of a third copy of chromosome 21 (trisomy 21). In more than 92 per cent of cases, the triplet form is present in all the individual's cells; mosaicism is found in 2–3 per cent, while translocation of material from chromosome 21 accounts for most of the remaining 3–5 per cent of cases. The phenotypes of the various forms appear to be essentially indistinguishable at an individual level, although those with mosaicism tend to be less severely affected.

The standard trisomy and mosaic forms are not familial, but the risk of occurence is closely related to increasing maternal age. In contrast, the translocation form can be inherited, and there is a much increased risk of a mother having a second child with DS, irrespective of her age.

DS is the most common known congenital condition associated with intellectual disability, with an incidence of between 1 in 700 and 1 in 1,000 live births. It is more prevalent in males than females, perhaps because of different survival rates in infancy.

Physical features

DS is characterized by a distinctive and widely recognized physiognomy, including short stature, a 'flat' face with epicanthal folds at the inner corners of the eyes and a protruding tongue, and single palmar crease in each hand. These features are often sufficient for the syndrome to be reliably diagnosed in infancy (Roizen and Patterson, 2003).

Congenital heart defects occur in half of individuals with DS. Hearing impairments, visual difficulties, hypothyroidism, and dental problems are found in the majority of cases. In addition, they are more liable to other medical disorders, including arthritis, diabetes mellitus, and gastrointestinal and dermatological conditions, than the general population. Late onset epilepsy, commencing in middle age in about 3 per cent of cases, may be a harbinger of Alzheimer's disease associated with premature ageing. Obesity is also common, in part a consequence of low resting metabolism.

Cognitive and behavioural features

Individuals with DS are often said to have pleasant and friendly personalities. The concept of a 'DS personality' has been questioned but the characteristics of appropriate social interest and positive affect in children have been commonly described.

Cognitive development follows a decelerating trajectory so that the highest estimates of ability are obtained in infancy and early childhood, and IQs tend to fall as the rate of progress declines in comparison to typically developing peers. From childhood onwards, DS is associated with moderate to severe intellectual disability (Carr, 2003; Hodapp, Evans and Gray, 1999). Evidence for poor persistence is equivocal, and it is important to note that the acquisition of academic, motor, and language skills continues at least into early adulthood.

Performance of visuospatial, perceptual and reasoning tasks is better than that of verbally mediated tasks. Similarly, visuospatial memory is superior to auditory memory. Consistent with this, non-verbal communication is an area of strength, including effective learning and use of natural gesture or signs. In contrast, individuals have marked difficulties in acquiring some aspects of linguistic function, most pronounced in expressive language and in grammar. Intelligibility may be impaired by poor articulation, which might also limit the use of relatively long, grammatically complex utterances.

It has been argued that the characteristic physiognomy of affected individuals, their stereotypically friendly and sociable personality, early diagnosis and the availability of support, may afford significant protection against psychopathology when compared to other conditions associated with intellectual disability (Dykens and Kasari, 1997). That said, the stereotype, as well as 'diagnostic overshadowing', may lead to neglect of psychological and psychiatric disorders in some cases. Younger and less able children tend to exhibit relatively frequent repetitive behaviours. Behavioural difficulties related to 'stubbornness' and oppositionality are also commonly described, and psychiatric conditions like ADHD and anxiety disorders may be diagnosed in as many as 15 per cent of children. The risk of affective disorders including anxiety and depression increases as the child grows into adolescence and adulthood, and comorbidity between DS and autism may be as high as 7 per cent.

Individuals with DS over 40 years of age are prone to Alzheimer's disease. Many show some signs of neuropathology although fewer than 45 per cent show clinical signs of dementia. The diagnosis can only be confirmed postmortem, but its course is marked by behavioural changes typical of dementia, including apathy, tearfulness, deterioration in self-care skills, and cognitive decline (Oliver and Holland, 1986). Lower-functioning individuals may be especially susceptible to the most severe deterioration.

Implications for assessment and management

DS is the most recognized genetic condition associated with intellectual disability, and, in contrast to the other syndromes reviewed in this chapter, there is a degree of public understanding of its distinctive phenotype. Research in DS has progressed to the extent that generalizations or stereotypes, including some mentioned here, are increasingly challenged in favour of greater awareness of individual differences. Nonetheless, there is some support for retaining the friendly and lovable stereotype, both because it reflects the nature of many people with DS and for the positive influence it may exert on the attributions and behaviours of others.

The potential medical complications of DS entail assessment and, if necessary, correction of cardiac, hearing, and ophthalmological conditions. In addition, monitoring for other disorders is necessary, including thyroid disease. Prevention of obesity may involve adherence to a selective diet and participation in physical and social activities, supported by behavioural interventions.

Evidence regarding the efficacy of intensive early intervention programmes on cognitive development is disappointing. However, as noted above, individuals with DS have the potential to make lasting gains in all aspects of development including academic and vocational skills. The cognitive profile of visuospatial relative strengths but significant speech and language difficulties has implications for longer-term intervention and educational strategies.

Signing and visual methods of teaching reading may enable children to access and use language in ways that circumvent auditory and verbal limitations. However, reading development in DS is thought to rely primarily on language skills. It is also important to address difficulties in phonological processing directly using the same analytic methods as in the teaching of typically developing children (Hodapp and Freeman, 2003). Generally, a social interactive approach to education is recommended, integrating various modalities and tasks (e.g. combining manual signs with speech; embedding learning in game formats) as part of a holistic approach. Social skills training groups and drama therapy may also be beneficial.

Monitoring of emotional well-being is necessary from adolescence, particularly with regard to mood disorders. Activities to build self-esteem may be important preventive interventions, while depression and anxiety can be treated using standard psychopharmacological and psychological interventions, including cognitive behaviour therapy for older and higher-functioning individuals. Assessment of affective disorders in middle-aged individuals should include the possibility of changes related to the onset of dementia. In this regard it should be remembered that mild declines in cognitive ability may simply be part of normal ageing.

FRAGILE X SYNDROME

Aetiology and epidemiology

Fragile X syndrome (FXS) is the second most common known genetic cause of intellectual disability and the most common inherited cause.

The syndrome arises from an expansion in the number of repeats of the trinucleotide CGG in the so-called *FMR1* (Fragile X Mental Retardation 1) gene on the X chromosome. Typically, this sequence contains between 5 and 50 repeats, but in 'carriers' it may include between 50 to 200 repeats. This intermediate degree of expansion is termed the premutation. The premutation appears to have only limited developmental effects on the carrier, but it is passed on to their children. The premutation in females is regarded as unstable and liable to expand further in offspring into the full mutation, where the critical sequence of DNA includes more than 200 repeats. The full mutation effectively inactivates *FMR1*, causing the FXS.

This mechanism contributes to considerable variability in the degree of expression of the FXS phenotype. Because the condition is X-linked, the syndrome tends to be more pronounced in males. In females, the expression of a full mutation on one X chromosome may be partially mitigated by the normal functioning of the other, and, depending on the X activation ratio, some individuals may be only mildly affected.

It is possible that epidemiological studies of individuals with recognized intellectual disability underestimate the prevalence of the FXS full mutation, as mildly affected females may go unidentified. That said, current data suggest an incidence of approximately 1 in 4,000 live births.

Given the relatively complex inheritance pattern of FXS, genetic counselling for the extended family is essential.

Physical features

Underlying connective tissue abnormalities in FXS result in 'velvet-like' skin, prominent ears, and joint laxity (Hagerman, 2002). Hypotonia is also common in infancy. Other signs of growth abnormality may only become conspicuous after the onset of puberty. These include an elongated face, prominent ears, an enlarged head circumference and, in males, macroorchidism.

Some medical complications of FXS reflect risks associated with the connective tissue disorder, such as inguinal or umbilical hernias, joint dislocation, and mitral valve prolapse. Recurrent otitis media is frequent. There may also be ophthalmological defects. Epilepsy occurs in perhaps 20 per cent of children, but tends to resolve in adolescence.

Cognitive and behavioural features

FXS is closely associated with moderate cognitive impairment, with 80 per cent of males obtaining IQs in the intellectual disability range. Visuoperceptual skills, visual working memory and visuospatial constructional skills are particularly impaired. There is a trend towards decreasing IQ with age. This reflects difficulties in acquiring skills in sequential processing and abstract reasoning, which are increasingly emphasized in cognitive assessments from late childhood onwards. Rote memory of meaningful information, imitation, and environmental or experiential learning are often relative strengths.

Language delay is typical in infancy and early childhood, although simple phrased speech is usually acquired late. Inattention, related to executive dysfunction (Wilding, Cornish and Munir, 2002) and overactivity are common features (Turk, 1998). These often persist, leading to diagnosis of ADHD in a high proportion of boys.

Contrary to earlier speculation, FXS is not a common genetic cause of autism, nor is autism exceptionally common in FXS, although the genetic anomaly may confer an additional risk over and above that associated with intellectual disability (Dykens and Volkmar, 1997). Perhaps 15 per cent of older children and adults with FXS meet diagnostic criteria for autism, but many others show some behaviours that are reminiscent of the autistic triad. The restricted and repetitive aspects of behaviour are especially salient. These may be seen in stereotypical hand gestures, such as flapping, hand-biting, perseveration of vocal automatisms and stock verbal phrases, and other mannerisms. There may also be intense circumscribed interests in objects or activities (e.g. reviewing of videos, etc.). In adolescence, the focus of interest may turn on to another person.

Rather than arising from an 'autistic-like' lack of social interest, these behaviours may be understood in terms of a pronounced shyness or social anxiety linked to sensory hyperarousal (Cohen, 1995). In physiological terms, children with FXS initially 'overreact' and habituate slowly to many visual, tactile, auditory, and olfactory stimuli, including social cues. Thus, eye contact with strangers may be avoided at first but gradually increases with familiarity. Social avoidance may diminish with age but mild social withdrawal in adulthood is common.

Females with the full mutation are usually less affected than males, but an approximation to a milder form of the same phenotype has been described. There may be specific weaknesses in visuospatial attention and executive functions, impulsivity and subtle social impairments. The relationship between these cognitive features and a vulnerability to social anxiety, sometimes including selective mutism, and other behavioural or emotional difficulties related to mood lability, perseveration, and unusual thinking remains unclear (Sobesky, Pennington, Porter, Hull and Hagerman, 1994).

Implications for assessment and management

Most individuals with FXS have a friendly disposition and a good sense of humour. These traits combined with strengths in rote and experiential learning enable many to attain greater skills than one might predict on the basis of IQ alone.

Early measures should focus on enhancing language and motor development and social experience. Sensory integration therapy may reduce the effects of hyperarousal. In cases of recurrent ear infections and hearing loss, medication and insertion of grommets may help.

Timely intervention may contribute to a significant reduction in autistic features in the early years. Nonetheless, educators should avoid unnecessary social stimulation, such as eye contact, during teaching and use calming techniques. Education should also draw on relative strengths in learning from familiar concrete experience, and avoid placing an undue load on visuospatial working memory and sustained attention. Computer-based instruction is valuable in teaching to the strengths of individuals with FXS, while minimizing the confrontational aspect of face-to-face instruction. Specific remediation of mathematical skills may be required. Rote memory skills enable many older individuals to succeed in vocational training.

Behavioural strategies are often effective in managing overactivity and ADHD. These include seating arranged close to the teacher with limited sources of distraction, 'packaging' of tasks into small blocks of time, well-structured and visually cued timetables, and frequent opportunities for movement. Psychostimulant medication may also be considered.

Hyperarousal, social anxiety, and impulsivity may contribute to low mood, agitation, and obsessive-compulsive behaviours across the lifespan. Again, there may be a role for medication in the treatment of these conditions. Higher-functioning individuals may benefit from cognitive behaviour therapy and counselling regarding anxiety and interpersonal issues. Planning and encouragement to participate in social activities as well as relevant training are needed to help develop social skills.

Some women with FXS have children of their own, who may also be affected. It is important to consider the effects of the syndrome in different generations of a family, including the possibility of maternal intellectual disability, anxiety, and impulsivity. High levels of support should be provided to these families, including advice on parenting skills, behavioural management, and problem-solving.

LESCH-NYHAN SYNDROME

Aetiology and epidemiology

Lesch-Nyhan syndrome (LNS) is the consequence of various mutations of the *HPRT* gene at Xq26–Xq27.2. The mutant alleles are recessive, so can be carried over generations without symptoms. Mendelian recessive inheritance accounts for most cases, although there are sporadic *de novo* mutations.

The condition is almost invariably found in males amongst whom the incidence is no more than 1 in 10,000 births and may be considerably lower. Cases of females with LNS are extremely rare.

Expression of the mutation disrupts purine metabolism leading to the overproduction of uric acid into the blood and the accumulation of other compounds in the central nervous system. Hyperuricaemia accounts for many of the somatic features of LNS. The biochemical mechanisms underlying the characteristic behaviours in LNS described below are poorly understood, but are presumed to arise from abnormal neurotransmitter metabolism (Nyhan, 2002).

Physical features

No distinctive morphological features associated with LNS have been described at birth. The first indication may be the appearance of orange crystals in the neonate's nappies. These are a product of hyperuricaemia and a sign of renal insufficiency. Other emerging and persistent signs of hyperuricaemia include urinary tract infections, gout, and renal disease. Renal failure may cause death by early adulthood.

Cognitive and behavioural features

Non-specific neurological signs become apparent in LNS after about the first three months of life, including hypotonia, motor delay, and feeding difficulties.

Towards the end of the first year, the muscles become hypertonic and spastic. This, the appearance of involuntary slow irregular, writhing, athetoid movements, and opisthotonic spasms of the back and rear neck muscles, signify a worsening motor condition. Feeding and digestion remain difficult, leading to abnormal maturation of the skeleton. Many individuals with LNS are unable to walk, sit, or hold up their head unsupported, and communication is impeded by poor speech articulation, all because of poor muscle control. Self-care skills are very limited, and assistance is required in most activities of daily living.

Formal assessment of cognitive functioning is complicated by the severe movement disorder. Most estimates indicate intellectual ability in the mild to severe intellectual disability range, but low average quotients have also been obtained. Scaled assessment scores fall by early adolescence; this represents a failure to progress relative to peers rather than an actual deterioration in ability (Matthews, Solan, Barabas and Robey, 1999). Affected individuals have a relative strength in the ability to orient to and learn about the environment, and in vocabulary, but marked difficulties in working memory and simultaneous processing.

All individuals with LNS display intermittent bouts of severe self-injurious behaviour, with an onset before 4 years of age and a characteristic topography and course. Typically, it begins with lip and cheek biting, extending to finger biting, eye poking, head banging, scratching, and to other self-injurious behaviour, such as trapping fingers in doors. Earlier onset is associated with greater later severity, sometimes leading to tissue loss and amputation. These behaviours appear to be involuntary; individuals seem to anticipate the behaviour but are unable to control it, show pain, accept protective restraints and are distressed by their removal. In time, they may resort to self-restraint (e.g. sitting on their hands).

In addition to self-injurious behaviour, many individuals show uncontrollable verbal and physical aggression towards others, so that a person might apologize even as he is swearing, spitting, hitting or biting. Observations suggest significant levels of fear, anxiety, and distress regarding these behaviours.

Despite the involuntary nature of self-injurious behaviour and aggression, its frequency is influenced by a variety of settings, events and environmental factors (Hall, Oliver and Murphy, 2001). Self-injurious behaviour increases in frequency during times of stress or emotional upset. Also, self-injurious behaviour may be more likely during periods of low social interaction.

Implications for assessment and management

The sociable and good-humoured personalities of individuals with LNS make them engaging companions when calm, and they are often well liked. This is an invaluable quality, particularly given the high level of dependence on others entailed by the syndrome.

Early diagnosis and medical treatment may significantly redress the effects of the accumulation of uric acid and renal disease. Unfortunately, neither these nor other pharmacological interventions reliably affect the signs of central nervous system dysfunction, including the movement disorder, self-injurious behaviour, and aggression.

The benefits of behavioural modification of self-injurious behaviour are at best inconsistent. There may be a role for differential reinforcement of incompatible or other behaviours, perhaps especially in the reduction of aggression to others. Aversive interventions are not appropriate and may even intensify the behaviours in question. Stress reduction measures may be more useful. Evidence for the influence of environmental contingencies suggests the need for functional analysis to identify maintaining factors for these behaviours, which can inform intervention. For example, teaching of effective verbal or signed communication might obviate any social function of self-injurious behaviour.

The most effective treatment for self-injurious behaviour in LNS is the application of restraints, such as tooth guards, gloves, masks, and splints. Any negative connotations of these measures need to be considered in the light of their willing acceptance by the person with LNS and the relief from distress they afford. Use of a 'least restrictive' method may enable the individual to engage in more constructive behaviour (Olson and Houlihan, 2000). Physical restraint may even be necessary during sleep. Failure to proffer this support and reassurance may add to the individual's distress and precipitate self-injurious behaviour.

PRADER-WILLI SYNDROME

Aetiology and epidemiology

As discussed above, the genetic bases of Prader-Willi syndrome (PWS) and Angelman syndrome (AS) are similar; both involve anomalies of chromosome 15. The distinct phenotypes result from parent-of-origin effects. Prader-Willi syndrome (PWS) is caused by the lack of several contiguous genes in the paternal 15q11–q13 region and the normal failure of expression of those maternally imprinted genes. Typically, this arises from paternal deletions (70 per cent), maternal uniparental disomy (20–25 per cent), or other structural abnormalities (5 per cent). Only in the few remaining cases, involving a microdeletion disrupting imprinting, is there a significant risk of recurrence in a family.

As in AS, the phenotype is generally more pronounced in cases of deletion than uniparental disomy. However, some symptoms, including psychosis, are more closely associated with uniparental disomy and may not be attributable to genes outside the typical critical region.

Incidence estimates vary between 1 in 10,000 and 1 in 15,000. Males and females are equally affected.

Physical features

A dysmorphic facies is apparent in infancy but becomes more obvious with age. Features include a narrow flat face, almond-shaped eyes, and a triangular mouth with down-turned corners.

Two stages in the physical development of PWS have been described, roughly corresponding to the periods before and after 3 years of age. In the first stage, there is a severe hypotonia, often detectable in the foetus, and evident in the baby's floppiness and passivity. Infantile feeding problems, related to weak sucking, and early failure to thrive constitute a major diagnostic criterion.

Between 1 and 4 years, there is an insidious but striking transition to the second stage, which is marked by hyperphagia, thought to reflect the failure of the normal satiety mechanisms (Holland, Treasure, Coskeran, Dallow, Milton and Hillhouse, 1993). Weight gain is exacerbated by a reluctance to exercise linked to hypotonia, and exaggerated by the absence of the normal pubertal growth spurt and short stature. Body weight often exceeds twice the ideal. This degree of obesity results in medical complications, including hypertension, cardiovascular and respiratory illness, and diabetes mellitus, and may be life-threatening. If weight is well controlled, lifespan can approach normal.

Other physical signs include hypopigmentation, hypogonadism, viscous saliva, visual defects, high thresholds for vomiting and pain, and a tendency to bruise easily.

Cognitive and behavioural features

The two-stage nature of PWS is also evident in its psychological features. Infants with PWS present with developmental delay including delayed passage of motor and language milestones, a weak cry, feeding problems and failure to thrive.

Alertness and mobility improve with age, the children are good-natured and cooperative for much of the time, and cognitive development progresses relatively well. Most children and adults with PWS obtain stable IQs in the borderline to moderate intellectual disability range, but low average scores are not unusual (Curfs, 1992). Cognitive profiles show a specific strength in visuospatial constructional tasks, which may also be displayed in a liking for jigsaw puzzles. In contrast, there are significant weaknesses in auditory working memory and sequential processing skills and specific intellectual disability.

Speech articulation can be impeded by oral motor dysfunction, facial and pharyngeal abnormalities, and the viscosity of saliva, giving the voice a high-pitched nasal quality, and speech fluency errors are widespread. That apart, assessments of language function have not found a particular pattern of expressive or receptive skills.

Regarding feeding, early failure to thrive resolves into the persistent hyperphagia mentioned above. Consistent with a failure to satiate, individuals with PWS eat continuously without slowing long into the course of a meal, and soon feel hungry again. They prefer a sweet and carbohydrate-rich diet, but may consume unusual or inappropriate foodstuffs and non-foods. Hyperphagia occurs in the context of a wider preoccupation with food, including questioning, foraging, stealing, hoarding, binge-eating, and rules and rituals around the order of eating different food types (Dykens and Cassidy, 1995; Dykens, Leckman and Cassidy, 1996).

This obsessional or compulsive quality may extend beyond food and feeding, to include repetitive questioning about other subjects, hoarding and ordering of objects, and other stereotypical activities. Self-injurious skin-picking is common. Sleep problems have also been reported, including early waking and excessive daytime sleepiness. These are not simply secondary to obesity, although obesity may contribute to obstructive sleep apnoea.

There may be links from obsessionality and disturbed sleep to other problems including irritability, tantrums, aggression, and depression. Young adults with PWS have an elevated risk of atypical depressive psychosis. If, as suggested earlier, this is an effect of maternal uniparental disomy, deleted cases may not be especially vulnerable in this respect.

Implications for assessment and management

The two developmental stages of PWS have different implications for assessment and management. In infancy, the focus is on treatment of the failure to thrive, and may include tube feeding and other special feeding methods. As feeding improves and the child moves into the second stage, other issues emerge.

Cognitive development in PWS represents a key area of strength, and implies a good outcome compared to other syndromes more closely associated with intellectual disability. Daily living skills are also often an asset.

Unfortunately, behavioural problems limit the opportunities available to children and adults with PWS, and, although substantial accomplishments are possible, few achieve full independence. The significance of these problems is reiterated by evidence that parents tend to experience higher levels of stress and negative affect towards their child with PWS than parents of children with other conditions, including Fragile X and Williams syndromes (van Lieshout, de Meyer, Curfs and Fryns, 1998).

Interestingly, intellectual ability is not a significant protective factor against hyperphagia or other maladaptive behaviours, with the possible exception of obsessionality. Indeed, it is possible that this ability entails a sensitivity about physical features, such as obesity, thereby adding to psychological complications.

Management of hyperphagia is vital to the well-being of individuals with PWS. Early diagnosis and prevention through limited food intake is ideal but later dietary interventions are equally important. Other measures, such as appetite-suppressant medication or surgery, have proved unsuccessful and it is unclear at present whether growth hormone treatments are beneficial in this respect. Clear early limit-setting, self-monitoring, regular exercise, and physiotherapy and occupational therapy may all be helpful, but long-term prevention or correction of obesity relies on restricting access to food, even if these restrictions aggravate other behavioural problems such as tantrums. Parents and carers may assume responsibility for children with PWS by intensive supervision and environmental modifications. However, similar 'compulsory dieting' in adulthood raises ethical and legal issues.

Obsessional behaviours may be limited to certain settings instead of suppressing them altogether. Some may be shaped into more adaptive and creative forms, suggesting directions for viable vocations.

Judicious and timely preparation for unexpected events and transitions may help avoid tantrums. Standard behavioural management techniques such as distraction and ignoring may also be effective.

Thorough preparation for the transition into adulthood, including the prospect of employment, is essential for individuals with PWS. This is not only because the change may precipitate problems, but also because their intellectual ability may temporarily mask the need for ongoing supervision and support that is essential for them to fulfil their potential.

RETT SYNDROME

Aetiology and epidemiology

Rett syndrome (RS) is caused by an abnormality of the *MeCP2* gene at Xq28. The majority of cases are thought to result from spontaneous mutations, although there are rare reports of RS in pairs of sisters and cousins, and in both a mother and her daughter.

RS typically occurs in females. Given that the syndrome is X-linked, this is thought to be because males with the anomaly often die *in utero*. Females may survive to term by virtue of their second X chromosome. Because of X inactivation, these effects are varied, and can be relatively mild. The present account emphasizes the 'classic' more severe RS. The estimated incidence is 1 in 10,000–15,000 females. The incidence in males is not known.

Physical features

An infant with RS is normal in appearance, and growth and development during the first months may appear unremarkable, although there may be subtle neurological signs, including hypotonia.

As early as 3 months of age, there is a dramatic deceleration in the rate of head growth, sometimes resulting in acquired microcephaly. This deceleration is thought to represent an underlying defect in late development of the infantile cortex. There is a gradual onset of pervasive growth failure, with the rate of weight gain falling away from the norm from the end of the first year and height declining soon after. However, growth usually recovers to some extent following a period of developmental regression.

Seizures are common after regression, although there does not appear to be a specific pattern of changes on electroencephalograpy (EEG).

After regression, the hypotonia of infancy is often replaced by increased muscle tone, predisposing the individual to a dystonic posture, scoliosis and contractures.

Cognitive and behavioural features

RS is unique among the syndromes described here in that its behavioural phenotype is included in the current major psychiatric nosologies as one of the Pervasive Developmental Disorders (as Rett's Disorder [APA, 1994]; Rett's Syndrome [World Health Organization, 1996]). Arguably, this recognition reflects the apparent consistency of the phenotype, at least within the 'classic' presentation.

In common with physical development, there is an initial period of apparently typical development in early infancy according to accepted milestones. Skills such as transferring objects between hands and self-feeding are acquired, and infants may be weaned onto solid foods, although they may be thought placid or unresponsive, as well as hypotonic.

The developmental trajectory plateaus at the 9–12 month level, so that, for example, language skills rarely exceed single word use. In addition, qualitative abnormalities, such as impaired mobility and an absence of imaginative activities, may contribute to parental and professional concerns.

The developmental plateau may last for up to three years. In parallel with the deceleration in physical development, it is followed by the abrupt onset of a period of rapid regression before the age of 4 years with no obvious antecedent. Regression may be sustained for months or years, with a pervasive loss of acquired skills including expressive and receptive language and purposeful hand use, sleep disturbance and distress, and a transient 'autistic-like' social withdrawal (Kerr, 2002).

An important diagnostic criterion refers to seemingly involuntary hand stereotypies including wringing, clapping, patting, and mouthing. These disrupt any more functional gestures and may cause self-injury through skin breakdown or dental damage. There are also disorders of voluntary movement, and severe or profound intellectual disability. Other common signs include irregular breathing, which may lead to hypoxia and fainting, air-swallowing and bloating, feeding difficulties, constipation, and agitation.

After regression, usually by 5 years, there may be limited recovery of skills. In particular mood and non-verbal social communication may improve, including 'eye pointing', although functional language often remains absent. There may be greater cooperation with activities such as feeding, dressing, and toileting, but these activities remain complicated by persistent cognitive and sometimes worsening motor difficulties (Cass, Reilly, Owen et al., 2003). Many individuals with RS remain unable to walk. Given the movement and communication problems, formal assessment of cognitive function is problematic, but the degree of impairment is at least severe. Interestingly, response latencies to instructions may be exceptionally long.

Affected individuals may express emotional distress as hyperventilation, screaming, and self-injury, typically to the hand or wrist, often in response to unexpected noise or other environmental change. Sleep problems are also very common, including night waking associated with laughter.

Most individuals with RS of all ages are reported to enjoy music and many show preferences for particular pieces or styles.

Implications for assessment and management

The course of RS, including the regression, presents many challenges for parents and other carers. In this context, the recovery of social interest and communication after regression, an increasingly happy demeanour, and a tendency to warm laughter, are very positive signs, and carers may comment on the child's openness to new experiences.

The love of music is also an asset and may be an important medium for communication-focused music therapy. Music may also comfort someone in distress. Singing, gentle holding, and quiet settings are all calming. Although tantrums and sleep disturbances tend to improve spontaneously with age, there may be a need for behaviour modification and the simple sleep management measures recommended for other children.

In general, it is inappropriate to interrupt or attempt to suppress the involuntary hand stereotypies displayed by individuals with RS, unless there is self-injury. Then, temporary light restraints may be applied to aid healing. That said, restraint may also be justified to facilitate the teaching of alternative and incompatible adaptive voluntary behaviours. Skills, such as self-feeding either with fingers or a spoon, may be taught through strategies including shaping, guidance, and hand regulation. Regular exercise, physiotherapy, and, in particular, hydrotherapy, are invaluable in avoiding complications such as scoliosis, and in the maintenance or recovery of skills, including walking in some cases. Occasional spontaneous functional movements may be a basis for developing motor abilities. Speech and language therapists can address issues regarding chewing and swallowing as much as language and communication.

Carers need to be sensitive to the often subtle means by which individuals with RS communicate their needs, for example eye-pointing. Computer touch screens, sometimes combined with voice synthesis, have also been used effectively to enable affected individuals to choose between alternatives such as foods. However, it is important to recognize that the rate of change and skill acquisition tends to be very slow and limited.

SMITH-MAGENIS SYNDROME

Aetiology and epidemiology

Smith-Magenis Syndrome (SMS) is a sporadic condition caused by an interstitial deletion of chromosome 17p11.2. Several candidate genes have been identified in the deletion region, but their significance still needs to be clarified (Chen, Potocki and Lupski, 1996). SMS is believed to have an incidence of at least 1 in 25,000 births, with an equal sex ratio (Greenberg, Lewis, Potocki et al., 1996).

Physical features

Infantile hypotonia, early feeding difficulties, failure to thrive and frequent ear infections are common, the latter often resulting in hearing loss. Dysmorphic features reported in over two-thirds of cases include a flat, broad head and prominent forehead, epicanthal folds, a broad nasal bridge, flat mid-face, down-turned mouth with cupid's bow, short stature and a hoarse, deep voice (Greenberg et al., 1996). With age there is a coarsening of the facial features. Clinical signs of peripheral neuropathy have been found in approximately 75 per cent of cases, including decreased sensitivity to pain and temperature, gait disturbances and muscle weakness. Individuals are also prone to retinal detachment, possibly as a result of the combination of high myopia, self-injurious head banging, aggression and hyperactivity. Less consistent features include cardiac defects, epilepsy, renal and thyroid abnormalities and scoliosis. Several individuals in their 60s and 70s have been reported, suggesting that life expectancy in this condition may be normal.

Cognitive and behavioural features

Most affected individuals have mild to severe intellectual disability, with the majority in the moderate range (Udwin, Webber and Horn, 2001). Most attend special schools, though a few are supported in mainstream settings. In terms of their cognitive profile, speech delay tends to be more pronounced than motor delay, and expressive language abilities are more impaired than receptive language skills. There are also relative weaknesses in sequential processing and short-term memory, and relative strengths in long-term memory, alertness to the environment and attention to meaningful visual detail (Dykens, Finucane and Gayley, 1997; Udwin et al., 2001).

Between 50 per cent and 100 per cent of children with SMS are described as hyperactive, restless, impulsive and distractible, and 70 per cent to 100 per cent show temper outbursts and aggression (Dykens et al., 1997; Dykens and Smith, 1998). These are often very severe, and may be triggered by tiredness, frustration, changes in routine, inability to get one's own way, or they may have no identifiable triggers. Self-injurious behaviours are reported in between 67 per cent and 100 per cent of samples (Dykens and Smith, 1998; Greenberg et al., 1996) and typically include hand-biting, self-pinching/scratching, picking at sores, hitting the head or body and tearing or picking fingernails or the skin around the nails. The self-injury may be a response to frustration, boredom or anger, and can be extreme, possibly due to the characteristic decreased sensation in the extremities and relative insensitivity to pain. Autistic-type behaviours are also common in SMS, and include resistance to change, repetitive questioning, and preoccupations with particular topics. A spasmodic upper-body squeeze has been reported in 90–100 per cent of affected individuals. In addition, severe sleep disturbance has been reported in all cases of SMS (Smith, Dykens and Greenberg, 1998), and includes difficulties falling asleep, shortened sleep cycles, frequent and prolonged night waking and early morning waking. These abnormalities, and a phase shift of the circadian rhythm of melatonin, with a paradoxical diurnal secretion of the hormone (De Leersnyder, de Blois, Vekemans, Sidi et al., 2001), are suggestive of an underlying biological clock problem in the syndrome.

On the positive side, children with SMS are frequently described as loving and caring, eager to please and with a good sense of humour. They like adult attention and enjoy interacting with adults.

Adults with SMS are more dependent on carers than might be expected from their level of intellectual functioning. They tend to have limited daily living skills and most attend day centres or college courses, some with work placements – but these need to be closely supervised (Udwin et al., 2001). In general, the severe behaviour difficulties described in children with the syndrome persist into adulthood. Some individuals show improved behaviour with age, but others show a worsening of the aggression and self-injury, or no change (Dykens et al., 1997). The aggressive behaviours can be very violent and alarming, and there are a few reports of individuals with SMS being hospitalized in secure units under the Mental Health Act.

Implications for assessment and management

Support for oral motor and feeding skills is important in the early years, and speech and language therapy using a total communication approach is likely to be helpful in promoting speech development and comprehension. Occupational therapy is recommended for difficulties with visuo-motor skills, sequencing and co-ordination. Regular medical checks are needed, including eye examinations and hearing checks. In school, teaching strategies that recognize the children's weakness in sequential processing and take advantage of their strengths in visual reasoning and other non-verbal areas are recommended. Their particular interest in computers and love of adult attention can serve as useful reinforcers for desired behaviour and attention to tasks.

Given their severe behaviour difficulties, children and adults with SMS can pose severe management problems for their carers, and in most cases support and input from health and social services is vital. Children with SMS do best in home and school environments that are highly structured and consistent, with regular routines. Attempts to anticipate and avoid situations that are likely to trigger aggressive and self-injurious behaviours are recommended, for example by preparing the child for any change in routine well ahead of time, using clear instructions, rewards and distraction techniques. If these do not diffuse the situation, then ignoring aggressive behaviours or removing the child to another room and letting the outburst run its course may be the only remaining course of action. Given the range of possible triggers, functional analysis may help identify appropriate interventions. In view of the prevalence of autistic-type behaviours in this group, it is recommended that multidisciplinary assessment for autistic-spectrum disorders is also undertaken. This would facilitate access to appropriate educational and mental health services and result in a better understanding of the individual's difficulties and needs.

The sleep difficulties of individuals with SMS may be responsive to behavioural strategies, including a firm and consistent approach; though this is by no means the case for all children. Parents' interventions have focused on keeping their children safe at night and attempting to minimize the disruption caused by night waking, for example by removing small objects and breakables from the bedroom, locking the bedroom door, and using blackout curtains to minimize light. In some cases medication has resulted in improvement in sleep patterns. Various medications have been tried in an attempt to reduce the characteristic aggressive outbursts, though with variable results. There is an urgent need for controlled trials of the effectiveness of these medications, and of behavioural approaches to guide intervention efforts.

Finally, it is worth noting that there have been a number of reports of parents being accused of physical abuse towards their children with SMS, when in fact the child's injuries were a result of self-injury. In other cases parents have been blamed by teachers or social workers for their children's aggressive outbursts and daytime sleepiness. It is crucial that teachers and health and social services staff are made aware of the severe behavioural and sleeping difficulties that are characteristic of the syndrome; and the implications of these for management.

TUBEROUS SCLEROSIS COMPLEX

Aetiology and epidemiology

The tuberous sclerosis complex (TSC) has been linked to two genes; *TSC1* on the long arm of chromosome 9 (9q34) and *TSC2* on the short arm of chromosome 16 (16p13.3). In two-thirds of cases, abnormalities of these genes occur by spontaneous mutations. In the remainder, the anomalies are inherited.

Presence of the genetic anomaly is not sufficient for expression of TSC. Cells contain two copies of each gene, called alleles. It is thought that a 'second hit' is necessary to knock out an individual's normal copy of the TSC alleles for effects to be evident. This happens in cell division, causing abnormal proliferation of cells in different regions of the body depending on which progenitors sustained the 'second hit'. Thus the manifestations of TSC are highly variable, even within families, but typically multisystemic. There are few clear differences between the effects of *TSC1* and *TSC2*, but it has been suggested that *TSC1* anomalies are less likely to cause intellectual disability.

Population prevalence is approximately 1 in 6,000.

Physical features

The main physical features of TSC are a panoply of internal and external lesions arising from the abnormal proliferation of cells. These may affect almost any part of the body, including the skin, other visceral organs, the eyes, and the central nervous system.

Amongst numerous dermatological signs, facial angiofibroma, a bilateral and symmetrical 'butterfly-shaped' rash on the cheeks, is found in 80 per cent of cases, becoming more visible in late childhood and adolescence. White hypomelanotic 'ashleaf' macules may occur on the torso, especially visible under ultraviolet light. Soft fibromas or skin tags may grow on the neck or trunk, although these are not diagnostic of TSC. There may be other, often benign, growths in the kidneys, heart, lungs, spleen, liver, digestive tract, endocrine organs, and skeleton. These may have significant medical complications. Serious renal conditions may present in adolescence and lung conditions occasionally emerge in middle adulthood.

Most consistent and clinically relevant are the nodules found in the central nervous system (Harrison and Bolton, 1997). These include cortical tubers and subependymal nodules in the walls of the brain ventricles. Occasionally, these nodules turn into subependymal giant cell astrocytomas (SEGA). These may obstruct the flow of cerebrospinal fluid, increasing intracranial pressure, leading to nausea, vomiting, hypersensitivity to light, and, if severe, coma, and death. The development of SEGA may also trigger the onset or worsening of epilepsy, and changes in behaviour.

The lifetime prevalence of seizures in TSC is around 84 per cent. Although infantile spasms and partial seizures predominate at first, seizures of any type may occur, often evolving and sometimes in combinations. Onset is typically before 5 years of age.

Cognitive and behavioural features

Estimates of the cognitive abilities of individuals with TSC span the entire range. IQ may be bimodally distributed. In the more than 50 per cent who have an intellectual disability, it is often severe or profound. Those with IQs in the normal range may exhibit specific difficulties in working memory and attentional control and have specific intellectual disability.

Individuals with TSC have elevated rates of various behavioural and neuropsychiatric disorders, including ADHD, aggressive and destructive behaviours, anxiety, communication disorders, and autism (Bolton, Park, Higgins, Griffiths and Pickles, 2002). These may be detected in children as young as 2 years old. Sleep disorders are also common, including late onset and subsequent sleep fragmentation.

In late childhood and adolescence, more able individuals with TSC may become increasingly aware of the nature of their condition, including physical stigmata like a facial angiofibroma and its uncertain prognosis. This may precipitate anxiety and depression, which are widespread in adults with TSC.

Implications for assessment and management

The extraordinary variability and unpredictability of TSC confounds general recommendations for management, and suggests the need for thorough assessment of the strengths and needs of the individual and his/her family.

Treatment of epilepsy is of primary importance. If epilepsy is a cause of intellectual disability and neuropsychiatric disorders, rather than an independent sign of a shared structural neurological abnormality, early intervention might significantly improve outcome. That said, serious developmental difficulties occur and persist in the context of otherwise acceptable seizure control.

Medical, psychological, and educational interventions may all contribute to the multidisciplinary management of the physical and neurodevelopmental aspects of TSC, including intellectual disability, ADHD, communication disorders including autism, sleep problems, and emotional and behavioural problems, as well as issues raised by hospitalization.

VELOCARDIOFACIAL SYNDROME

Aetiology and epidemiology

Velocardiofacial syndrome (VCFS) is caused by a microdeletion on chromosome 22 at 22q11.2, affecting 20–30 contiguous genes. In the majority of cases, the microdeletion is sporadic, but there is an autosomal dominant pattern of inheritance in the small proportion of familial cases. Sporadic cases may be less affected than familial cases. In addition, there may be a parent-of-origin effect, such that microdeletions on the maternally derived chromosome may have more severe effects on neurodevelopment, suggesting the involvement of imprinted genes.

VCFS is the most common known microdeletion syndrome, occurring in around 1 in 4,500 people.

Physical features

The salient physical features of the syndrome are a cleft palate or velopharyngeal insufficiency, various cardiac malformations, and a distinctive facies, which includes a long unexpressive face, a prominent nose, 'squinting' eyes with narrow palpebral fissures, small ears with thick helices, and a small down-turned mouth. In addition, there are numerous other possible features, such as immunodeficiency, susceptibility to otitis media, kidney anomalies, hypocalcaemia, etc., giving rise to substantial variability in the physical phenotype.

There may be early feeding difficulties linked in some cases to the cleft palate or to hypotonia. Growth rates tend to be below average, with resultant short stature. This may be especially pronounced if cardiac abnormalities are severe, but there may also be some 'catch up' if these are corrected.

Cognitive and behavioural features

Speech is often impeded by the palatal defects, manifest as a high-pitched, hypernasal voice, and articulation errors. It is also impaired by dysarthria, significant delay in the acquisition of first words, the immature syntax and brevity of subsequent utterance, and receptive language difficulties.

Approximately 50 per cent of individuals obtain IQs in the mild to moderate intellectual disability range. Severe intellectual disability is rare and many individuals function in the low average range. Evidence of language impairment notwithstanding, there is usually an advantage of verbal over non-verbal abilities, significantly higher verbal than visuospatial short-term memory, and a correspondingly higher attainment of literacy compared to numeracy skills, as well as abstract and social reasoning difficulties (Wang, Woodin, Kreps-Falk and Moss, 2000). This pattern appears to be stable over the course of development from childhood to adulthood, in that although the verbal–non-verbal discrepancy may become less pronounced, specific deficits in visuospatial perception and reasoning remain (Henry, van Amelsvoort, Morris, Owen, Murphy and Murphy, 2002).

Descriptions of the behaviour of children with VCFS range from shyness, blunted affect, and social withdrawal to concentration difficulties and disinhibition, encompassing significant anxiety and lability of mood. ADHD may be present in as many as a quarter of cases, and there is an increased risk of other neuropsychiatric disorders, including early onset schizophrenia and bipolar spectrum disorders. Rates of affective disorders and psychosis, particularly chronic paranoid schizophrenia, are elevated amongst adolescents and young adults with VCFS. It has been estimated that 20 per cent of adults with VCFS have a major psychiatric disorder. These findings have generated interest in VCFS as a potential genetic model of the pathogenesis of psychosis.

Implications for assessment and management

The clarity and quality of speech in VCFS may be improved significantly by surgical correction of the underlying abnormality of the palate in the preschool years, followed by speech and language therapy. Speech and language therapy may also be necessary to support progress in other areas of expressive and receptive language function.

The profile of cognitive strengths and weaknesses indicates significant educational needs. Children with VCFS may benefit from educational approaches recommended for children with non-verbal intellectual disability. These include early occupational therapy to enhance sensory-motor integration, the use of structured and 'concrete' teaching aids including computers, and compensatory verbal skills, and the explicit teaching of social skills and problem-solving strategies across home, school, and other settings.

The uncertain prospect of major psychiatric disorder is likely to be a cause of concern for families with a young member with VCFS. Reliable behavioural or neurobiological precursors have not yet been identified, and it is not possible to predict which individuals will develop such a condition with any precision. Regular clinical monitoring of the evolving behaviour in individual cases may be necessary to detect prodromal signs and symptoms and enable early intervention. That said, the optimal pharmacological and psychological approaches to the management of psychosis in VCFS remain unclear.

WILLIAMS SYNDROME

Aetiology and epidemiology

Williams Syndrome (WS) is a contiguous gene deletion syndrome, involving a microdeletion on chromosome 7 at 7q11.23. Most cases are the result of a new mutation, although the condition can be inherited as an autosomal dominant disorder. WS has an equal sex ratio and an incidence of at least 1 in 25,000 live births.

Physical features

Low birth weight and cardiac murmurs are often noted at birth, and difficulties with feeding, vomiting and constipation commonly lead to failure to thrive. Some children have raised levels of blood calcium, and treatment with a low-calcium and vitamin D-restricted diet usually improves feeding and normalizes serum calcium levels. Affected individuals have a distinctive facial appearance, with full prominent cheeks, a wide mouth, long philtrum and a retroussé nose with a flat nasal bridge. They also have renal and cardiovascular abnormalities, most commonly supravalvular aortic stenosis and peripheral pulmonary artery stenosis (Morris, Demsey, Leonard, Dilts and Blackburn, 1988), which vary in severity and may change over time. Joint contractures and laxity and gait abnormalities are also common, with early hypotonia giving way to hypertonia in older individuals. Growth retardation, short stature and a hoarse voice are further frequent findings.

Puberty tends to start early and progress rapidly. Many affected adults appear to age prematurely and at least some develop progressive multisystem medical problems, which can lead to premature death. These may include cardiovascular complications, hypertension, gastrointestinal problems, urinary tract abnormalities, and progressive joint limitations (Morris *et al.*, 1988).

Cognitive and behavioural features

Almost all individuals with WS have mild to severe intellectual disability and require special educational support. They have a distinctive cognitive profile with relative strengths in verbal abilities but poor visuospatial and gross and fine motor skills (Udwin, Yule and Martin, 1987). Comprehension is usually far more limited than expressive language, which tends to be verbose, superficially fluent and pseudo-mature. Vocabulary, verbal processing and social use of language are particularly well developed. At the same time the children show various syntactic, semantic and pragmatic deficits, and problems with turn taking and topic maintenance (Karmiloff-Smith, Grant, Berthoud, Davies *et al.*, 1996). The pattern of cognitive functioning reported in affected adults is similar to that described in children (Howlin, Davies and Udwin, 1998). Although general cognitive abilities appear to be well maintained in adulthood, there is little progress in literacy and numeracy beyond the early teenage years. In line with this, most adults require substantial amounts of supervision and support in self-care and daily living activities, and very few are capable of independent/semi-independent living or work, even in sheltered employment (Davies, Howlin and Udwin, 1997).

The behavioural characteristics of people with WS are particularly striking. They tend to be over-friendly and socially disinhibited towards adults, including strangers, yet have difficulty making and keeping friends. Their relatively good verbal abilities, engaging personalities and excessive sociability can be deceptive and result in an overestimate of other abilities, as well as making them vulnerable to exploitation and abuse. Davies, Udwin and Howlin (1998) found that at least 20 per cent of a sample of adults with WS had reportedly been victims of sexual abuse. Other characteristics commonly noted in both children and adults include poor concentration, distractibility, overactivity, attention-seeking behaviours, aggressive outbursts, phobias and generalized anxiety. They worry excessively about a range of anticipated or imagined situations and constantly seek reassurance from others. Severe anxiety and depression have been reported in some cases in response to particular life events, for example a move to a residential placement or death of a parent. Many also show intense pre-occupations and obsessions with particular activities or topics, for example collecting things or developing extreme attachments to a familiar of even unfamiliar person. Most of the children are hypersensitive to particular sounds, including electrical noises like vacuum cleaners and thunder. The basis for this hyperacusis is not understood, but it tends to diminish in adulthood. The behavioural characteristics described above understandably limit the levels of independence, self-care and educational and occupational attainments of individuals with WS (Davies *et al.*, 1998; Udwin *et al.*, 1987).

Implications for assessment and management

The behavioural phenotype in WS carries important implications for management.

In the early years speech therapists, occupational therapists and physiotherapists need to support the development of motor, pre-linguistic and feeding skills, with an emphasis on developing sucking, swallowing and chewing, turn taking and communication skills, gross and fine motor activities and visuospatial skills, as well as self-help skills such as dressing and eating. Regular examinations for possible heart, renal and gastrointestinal problems for both children and adults are important.

In the preschool and school years, as behaviour difficulties become more prominent, standard behaviour management approaches should be introduced. Carers and teachers should be advised on teaching the children and adults appropriate social skills such as greeting behaviours and sharing, from the start setting clear boundaries and firmly discouraging disinhibited behaviour towards others and excessive and inappropriate verbalizations. At the same time considerable supervision will continue to be needed for many individuals into adulthood to ensure their safety. Temper outbursts and aggressive behaviours are also best addressed behaviourally, for example by identifying and avoiding triggers for such behaviours, or teaching the person more appropriate ways of responding, as well as removing adult attention when the child displays unacceptable behaviours. People with WS do best in structured environments and with predictable routines. Additional psychological support to prepare individuals for changes or help them cope with unforeseen events may prevent longer-term difficulties. At the same time parents and teachers should be aware that too much reassurance and attention may serve to exacerbate anxiety. Obsessions and preoccupations should, where possible, be nipped in the bud by diverting the child's attention onto another activity. Where preoccupations are entrenched, carers should try to limit the amount of time spent on the obsession, and gradually reduce the time further. Alternatively, time spent engaged in the preoccupation could be used as a reward for desired behaviours in other areas.

Treatments for hyperacusis have not been systematically evaluated. Judicious use of filtered ear protectors may be helpful, as well as reassurance and an explanation about the source of the noise. A warning before predictable noises can help prepare the individual. Repeated, gentle exposure to the sounds, pre-recorded and played back on a tape recorder, may also help to desensitize the person, especially if s/he is able to control the source of the sound.

Since the good spoken language and outgoing personalities of people with WS can give a false expectation of their functioning in other areas, assessment of their cognitive abilities is essential in order to provide an accurate picture of their educational needs. Some will require special schooling, while others may be best placed in a mainstream school with additional support. In general, highly structured small group teaching is likely to be most effective, with standard behavioural approaches to address overactivity, impulsivity and poor concentration. These could include positive reinforcement for remaining seated and on task for increasing lengths of time, as well as self-instructional training for older children. Medication for ADHD may be helpful in some cases (Bawden, MacDonald and Shea, 1987). Strategies which harness the children's superior spoken language abilities in training perceptual and motor skills are also useful, for example encouraging the children to talk themselves through each step of a task, and phonetic approaches are most appropriate for teaching reading.

In adulthood, too, thorough assessment of cognitive abilities, mood and behaviour is important to ensure that living and occupational environments are sufficiently supportive and stimulating, but also appropriate to the individuals' interests and levels of ability. Occupational and residential settings which place excessive demands on individuals with WS, for example by providing too little support, may result in a deterioration in mood and/or behaviour. Individual and group work with adolescents and adults with WS themselves is recommended to address issues such as diagnosis, sexuality, reproductive issues and career counselling, and to foster independence.

CONCLUSION

Recognition of the coincidence of multi-systemic medical and psychological complications in genetic syndromes associated with intellectual disability emphasizes the need for effective continuous multidisciplinary assessment, management, and follow-up of individual cases.

Clinical geneticists are needed to confirm the diagnosis and are often sources of clinical expertise. Genetic counsellors should be available to discuss the implications of diagnosis of one individual for members of their extended family, including implications for future pregnancies. There may be physical complications that necessitate one-off or ongoing medical intervention. Characteristic patterns of abnormal electrical activity on electroencephalography or EEG may be of diagnostic utility, especially in infants when the overt physical and behavioural phenotypes may still be subtle, and optimal management of epileptic seizures is essential. Decreased or abnormal growth, failure to thrive, and infantile hypotonia are also very common and are associated with numerous sequelae, including poor feeding, motor disorders, and gradual emergence of disabling conditions such as scoliosis and joint contractures. Occupational therapists and physiotherapists have key contributions to make in this regard, and there may be a role for a speech and language therapist in treating oromotor problems. Language and communication problems are almost ubiquitous, again calling for the expertise of a speech and language therapist, whether in enhancing speech or in implementing non-verbal and augmentative means of communication.

Long-term development and acquisition of skills also depend on the appropriateness of educational provision. Although teachers are the obvious lead professionals here, psychologists may contribute to decisions regarding

educational placements and the details of individualized education programmes, through cognitive and behavioural assessments. The trajectory
of cognitive and behavioural development in some syndromes is not typical
(e.g. sometimes plateauing in late childhood) and it would be unwise to make
assumptions about the stability of estimates such as IQ scores or cognitive
profiles. It is important to remember that parents often have specific and
insightful views on their own child's educational needs (e.g. Fidler, Lawson
and Hodapp, 2003).

Assessment and intervention for behavioural and emotional problems may
also need to be multidisciplinary. Clinical psychologists must remain alert to
the interactions between physical and psychological factors and consult other
professionals as appropriate. For example, physical causes of pain should be
either excluded or, if need be, treated as a cause of behavioural change, before
a purely psychological intervention is proposed. Recognition of a genetic
cause does not exclude diagnosis of a comorbid neuropsychiatric disorder,
such as autism or attention deficit/hyperactivity disorder (ADHD). Medication may be appropriate, as well as behavioural interventions, but it would
need to be monitored with particular care in view of altered sensitivity to
medications in many individuals with developmental difficulties. The evidence base for interventions to address the behavioural difficulties described
above is still sparse, and research to evaluate the efficacy of treatments with
these populations is urgently needed.

Finally, comparisons between syndromes have found different levels of
family stress and need associated with different conditions (Dykens, Hodapp
and Finucane, 2000). The challenging behaviours and medical complications
of many individuals with rare genetic syndromes such as those described in
this chapter highlight the need of families for comprehensive psychosocial
support, including financial benefits, emotional support, physical assistance,
temporary respite and, in some cases, long-term residential care. The needs of
unaffected siblings should also not be forgotten. Most siblings are poorly
informed about the syndrome affecting their brother or sister, and they may
harbour unnecessary worries about their own risk of developing the same
condition or of having a child with the condition. Feelings of guilt about the
difficulties experienced by the affected sibling are commonly reported by
unaffected siblings. Siblings need information about the condition, its cause
and long-term course, which should help to allay unnecessary fears and
worries, and increase understanding of their brother's or sister's difficulties
and needs.

FURTHER READING FOR CLINICIANS

Howlin, P. and Udwin, O. (2002). *Outcomes in Neurodevelopmental and Genetic Disorders*. Cambridge: Cambridge University Press.

FURTHER READING AND RESOURCES FOR PARENTS

Hogenboom, M. (2001). *Living with Genetic Syndromes Associated with Intellectual Disability*. London: Jessica Kingsley.

Cri-du-chat syndrome (5p-S)

Cornish, K.M., Bramble, D. and Collins, M. (1998). *Cri-du-Chat Syndrome: Handbook for Parents and Professionals*. Earl Shilton: Cri-du-Chat Syndrome Support Group.

Cri du Chat Syndrome Support Group. 7 Penny Lane, Barwell, Leicester, LE9 8HJ, Tel: 01455 841680, Fax: 01455 842054, e-mail: cdcssg@yahoo.co.uk, Web site: http://www.cridchat.u-net.com

Angelman syndrome

Angelman Syndrome Support Education and Research Trust(ASSERT), PO Box 13694, Musselburgh, EH21 6XH, Tel/Fax: 01268 415940, e-mail: assert@angelmanuk.org, Web site http://www.angelmanuk.org

Cornelia de Lange syndrome

CDLS Foundation UK, 'Tall Trees', 106 Lodge Lane, Grays, RM16 2UL, Tel: 01375 376439, Fax: 020 7536 8998, e-mail: info@cdls.org.uk, Web site: http://www.cdls.org.uk

Oliver, C., Moss, J., Petty, J., Arron, K., Sloneem, J. and Hall, S. (2003). *Self-injurious Behaviour in Cornelia de Lange Syndrome: A Guide for Parents and Carers*. Coventry: Trident.

Down syndrome

Down's Syndrome Association, 155 Mitcham Road, Tooting, London, W17 9PG, Tel: 020 8682 4001, Fax: 020 8682 4012, e-mail: info@downs-syndrome.org.uk, Web site: http://www.downs-syndrome.org.uk

Rutter, S. (1996). *Down's Syndrome – Information for Teachers*. London: Down's Syndrome Association.

Seyman, S. (1995). *People with Down's Syndrome: Your Questions Answered*. London: Down's Syndrome Association.

Fragile X syndrome

Dew-Hughes, D. (2003). *Educating Children with Fragile X*. Hastings: Fragile X Society.

Fragile X Society (2002). *Fragile X Syndrome: An Introduction*. Hastings: Fragile X Society.

Fragile X Society, Rood End House, 6 Stortford Road, Dunmow, CM6 1DA,

Tel: 01424 813147 Helpline, Tel: 01371 875100 Office, e-mail: info@fragilex.org.uk, Web site: http://www.fragilex.org.uk

Lesch-Nyhan syndrome

Purine Metabolic Patients Association (PUMPA), c/o Contact a Family, 209–211 City Road, London EC1V 1JN, Tel: 020 7608 8700, Fax: 020 7608 8701, e-mail: info@cafamily.org.uk

Prader-Willi syndrome

Prader-Willi Syndrome Association (UK), 125a London Road, Derby DE1 2QQ, Tel: 01332 360400 Careline, Tel: 01332 365676, Fax: 01332 360401, e-mail: office@pwsa-uk.demon.co.uk, Web site: http://www.pwsa.co.uk

Rett syndrome

Rett Syndrome Association UK, 113 Friern Barnet Road, London, N11 3EU, Tel: 0870 770 3266, Fax: 0870 770 3265, e-mail: info@rettsyndrome.org.uk, Web site http://www.rettsyndrome.org.uk

Smith-Magenis syndrome

Smith-Magenis Syndrome Foundation, PO Box 1490, Dungannon, N. Ireland BT71 4YE, Tel. 02887750050, e-mail: sms@yolger.fsnet.co.uk
Webber, C. and Udwin, O. (2003). *Smith-Magenis Syndrome: Guidelines for Parents and Teachers.* Dungannon, N. Ireland: SMS Foundation.

Tuberous Sclerosis complex

Tuberous Sclerosis Association, Little Barnsley Farm, Catshill, Bromsgrove, B61 0NQ, Tel: 01527 871898, Fax: 01527 579452, e-mail: secretary@tuberous-sclerosis.org, Web site: http://www.tuberous-sclerosis.org
Tuberous Sclerosis Association. *Understanding Tuberous Sclerosis CD-ROM.* Bromsgrove: Tuberous Sclerosis Association

Velocardiofacial syndrome

Max Appeal, Lansdowne House, 13 Meriden Avenue, Stourbridge, DY8 4QN, Tel: 0800 389 1049 Freephone Helpline, Tel: 01384 821227, e-mail: info@maxappeal.org.uk, Web site: http://www.maxappeal.org.uk

Williams syndrome

Udwin, O. and Yule, W. (1998). *Williams Syndrome: Guidelines for Parents.* Tonbridge, Kent: WSF.

Udwin, O. and Yule, W. (1998). *Williams Syndrome: Guidelines for Teachers.* Tonbridge, Kent: WSF.

Udwin, O., Howlin, P. and Davies, M. (1996). *Adults with Williams Syndrome: Guidelines for Families and Professionals.* Tonbridge, Kent: WSF.

Udwin, O., Howlin, P. and Davies, M. (1996). *Adults with Williams Syndrome: Guidelines for Employers.* Tonbridge, Kent: WSF.

Williams Syndrome Foundation, 161 High Street, Tonbridge TN9 1BX, Tel. 0173236515, e-mail: John.nelson-wsfoundation@btinternet.com, Web site: http://www.williams-syndrome.org.uk

REFERENCES

American Psychiatric Association (APA) (1994). *Diagnostic and Statistical Manual of Mental Disorders* (4th edn). Washington, DC: American Psychiatric Association.

Bawden, H.N., MacDonald, G.W. and Shea, S. (1987). Treatment of children with Williams syndrome with methylphenidate. *Journal of Child Neurology*, 12, 248–52.

Berney, T.P., Ireland, M. and Burn, J. (1999). Behavioural phenotype of Cornelia de Lange Syndrome. *Archives of Disease in Childhood*, 81, 333–6.

Bolton, P.F., Park, R.J., Higgins, J.N.P., Griffiths, P.D. and Pickles, A. (2002). Neuro-epileptic determinants of autism spectrum disorders in tuberous sclerosis complex. *Brain*, 125, 1247–55.

Carlin, M.E. (1990). The improved prognosis in cri du chat (5p-) syndrome. In W.I. Fraser (ed.), *Key Issues in Mental Retardation Research* (pp. 64–73). London: Routledge.

Carr, J. (2003). Patterns of ageing in 30–35-year-olds with Down's syndrome. *Journal of Applied Research in Intellectual Disabilities*, 16, 29–40.

Cass, H., Reilly, S., Owen, L., Wisbeach, A., Weekes, L., Slonims, V., Wigram, T. and Charman, T. (2003). Findings from a multidisciplinary clinical case series of females with Rett syndrome. *Developmental Medicine and Child Neurology*, 45, 325–37.

Chen, R.S., Potocki, L. and Lupski, J.R. (1996). The Smith-Magenis syndrome [del(17)p.11.2]: Clinical review and molecular advances. *Mental Retardation and Developmental Disability Research Review*, 2, 122–9.

Clayton-Smith, J. (2001). Angelman syndrome: Evolution of the phenotype in adolescents and adults. *Developmental Medicine and Child Neurology*, 43, 476–80.

Cohen, I.L. (1995). A theoretical analysis of the role of hyperarousal in the learning and behaviour of fragile X males. *Mental Retardation and Developmental Disabilities Research Reviews*, 1, 286–91.

Cornish, K. and Bramble, D. (2002). Cri du chat syndrome: Genotype-phenotype correlations and recommendations for clinical management. *Developmental Medicine and Child Neurology*, 44, 494–7.

Cornish, K.M., Bramble, D., Munir, F. and Pigram, J. (1999). Cognitive functioning in children with typical cri du chat (5p-) syndrome. *Developmental Medicine and Child Neurology*, 41, 263–6.

Curfs, L.M.G. (1992). Psychological profile and behavioural characteristics in

Prader-Willi syndrome. In S.B. Cassidy (ed.), *Prader-Willi Syndrome and other 15q Deletion Disorders* (pp. 211–22). Berlin: Springer.

Davies, M., Howlin, P. and Udwin, O. (1997). Independence and adaptive behaviour in adults with Williams syndrome. *American Journal of Medical Genetics*, 70, 188–95.

Davies, M., Udwin, O. and Howlin, P. (1998). Adults with Williams syndrome: Preliminary study of social, emotional and behavioural difficulties. *British Journal of Psychiatry*, 172, 273–6.

De Leersnyder, H., de Blois, M.C., Vekemans, M., Sidi, D., Villain, E., Kindermans, C. and Munnich, A. (2001). Beta-adrenergic antagonists improve sleep and behavioural disturbances in a circadian disorder, Smith-Magenis syndrome. *Journal of Medical Genetics*, 38, 586–90.

Dyer-Friedman, J., Glaser, B., Hessl, D., Johnston, C., Huffman, L.C., Taylor, A., Wisbeck, J. and Reiss, A.L. (2002). Genetic and environmental influences on the cognitive outcomes of children with fragile X syndrome. *Journal of the American Academy of Child and Adolescent Psychiatry*, 41, 237–44.

Dykens, E.M. and Cassidy, S.B. (1995). Correlates of maladaptive behaviour in children and adults with Prader-Willi Syndrome. *American Journal of Medical Genetics*, 60, 546–9.

Dykens, E.M. and Kasari, C. (1997). Maladaptive behaviour in children with Prader-Willi syndrome, Down syndrome, and non-specific mental retardation. *American Journal on Mental Retardation*, 102, 228–37.

Dykens, E.M. and Smith, A.C.M. (1998). Distinctiveness and correlates of maladaptive behaviour in children and adolescents with Smith-Magenis syndrome. *Journal of Intellectual Disability Research*, 42, 481–9.

Dykens, E.M. and Volkmar, F.R. (1997). Medical conditions associated with autism. In D.J. Cohen and F.R. Volkmar (eds), *Handbook of Autism and Pervasive Developmental Disorders* (2nd edn) (pp. 388–407). New York: Wiley.

Dykens, E.M., Finucane, B.M. and Gayley, C (1997). Cognitive and behavioural profiles in persons with Smith-Magenis syndrome. *Journal of Autism and Developmental Disorders*, 27, 203–11.

Dykens, E.M., Hodapp, R.M. and Finucane, B.M. (2000). *Genetics and Mental Retardation Syndromes: A New Look at Behavioural Interventions*. Baltimore: Paul H. Brookes Publishing.

Dykens, E.M., Leckman, J.F. and Cassidy, S.B. (1996). Obsessions and compulsions in Prader-Willi syndrome. *Journal of Child Psychology and Psychiatry and Allied Disciplines*, 37, 995–1002.

Fidler, D.J., Lawson, J.E. and Hodapp, R.M. (2003). What do parents want? An analysis of education-related comments made by parents of children with different genetic syndromes. *Journal of Intellectual and Developmental Disability*, 28, 196–204.

Flint, J. (1996). Annotation: Behavioural phenotypes – a window onto the biology of behaviour. *Journal of Child Psychology and Psychiatry*, 37, 355–67.

Greenberg, F., Lewis, R.A., Potocki, L. *et al.* (1996). Multi-disciplinary clinical study of Smith-Magenis syndrome (deletion 17p11.2). *American Journal of Medical Genetics*, 62, 247–54.

Hagerman, R.J. (2002). The physical and behavioural phenotype. In R.J. Hagerman and P.J. Hagerman, *Fragile X Syndrome: Diagnosis, Treatment, and Research* (3rd edn) (pp. 3–109). Baltimore: Johns Hopkins.

Hall, S., Oliver, C. and Murphy, G. (2001). Self-injurious behaviour in young children with Lesch-Nyhan syndrome. *Developmental Medicine and Child Neurology*, 43, 745–9.

Harrison, J.E. and Bolton, P.F. (1997). Annotation: Tuberous sclerosis. *Journal of Child Psychology and Psychiatry*, 38, 603–14.

Henry, J., van Amelsvoort, T., Morris, R.G., Owen, M.J., Murphy, D.G.M. and Murphy, K.C. (2002). An investigation of the neuropsychological profile in adults with velo-cardiofacial syndrome (VCFS). *Neuropsychologia*, 40, 471–8.

Hodapp, R., Evans, D. and Gray, F.L. (1999). Intellectual development in children with Down syndrome. In J. Rondal, J. Perera and L. Nadel (eds), *Down Syndrome: A Review of Current Knowledge* (pp. 124–32). London: Whurr.

Hodapp, R.M. and Freeman, S.F.N. (2003). Advances in educational strategies for children with Down syndrome. *Current Opinion in Psychiatry*, 16, 511–16.

Holland, A.J., Treasure, J., Coskeran, P., Dallow, J., Milton, N. and Hillhouse, E. (1993). Measurement of excessive appetite and metabolic changes in Prader-Willi syndrome. *International Journal of Obesity*, 17, 527–32.

Howlin, P. and Udwin, O. (2002). *Outcomes in Neurodevelopmental and Genetic Disorders*. Cambridge: Cambridge University Press.

Howlin, P., Davies, M. and Udwin, O. (1998). Cognitive functioning in adults with Williams syndrome. *Journal of Clinical Psychology and Psychiatry*, 39, 183–9.

Hyman, P., Oliver, C. and Hall, S. (2002). Self-injurious behaviour, self-restraint, and compulsive behaviours in Cornelia de Lange Syndrome. *American Journal on Mental Retardation*, 107, 146–54.

Ireland, M., Donnai, D. and Burn, J. (1993). Brachmann-de Lange syndrome: Delineation of the clinical phenotype. *American Journal of Medical Genetics*, 20, 959–64.

Karmiloff-Smith, A., Grant, J., Berthoud, I., Davies, M., Howlin, P. and Udwin, O. (1996). Language and Williams syndrome: How intact is 'intact'? *Child Development*, 68, 274–90.

Kerr, A. (2002). Annotation: Rett syndrome: Recent progress and implications for research and clinical practice. *Journal of Child Psychology and Psychiatry and Allied Disciplines*, 43, 277–87.

Matthews, W., Solan, A., Barabas, G. and Robey, K. (1999). Cognitive functioning in Lesch-Nyhan syndrome: A 4-year follow-up study. *Developmental Medicine and Child Neurology*, 41, 260–2.

Morris, C.A., Demsey, S.A., Leonard, C.O., Dilts, C. and Blackburn, B.L. (1988). The Natural history of Williams syndrome: Physical characteristics. *Journal of Paediatrics*, 113, 318–26.

Nyhan, W.L. (2002). Lessons from Lesch-Nyhan syndrome. In S.R. Schroeder, M.L. Oster-Granite and T. Thompson (eds), *Self-Injurious Behaviour: Gene-Brain-Behaviour Relationships* (pp. 251–67). Washington, DC: American Psychological Association.

O'Brien, G. and Yule, W. (eds) (1995). *Behavioural Phenotypes*. London: MacKeith Press.

Oliver, C. and Holland, A.J. (1986). Down's syndrome and Alzheimer's disease: A review. *Psychological Medicine*, 16, 307–22.

Oliver, C., Moss, J., Petty, J., Arron, K., Sloneem, J. and Hall, S. (2003). *Self-Injurious Behaviour in Cornelia de Lange Syndrome: A Guide for Parents and Carers.* Coventry: Trident.

Olson, L. and Houlihan, D. (2000). A review of behavioural treatments used for Lesch-Nyhan syndrome. *Behaviour Modification*, 24, 202–22.

Roizen, N.J. and Patterson, D. (2003). Down's syndrome. *Lancet*, 361, 1281–9.

Ross Collins, M.S. and Cornish, K. (2002). A survey of the prevalence of stereotypy, self-injury and aggression in children and young adults with Cri du Chat syndrome. *Journal of Intellectual Disability Research*, 46, 133–40.

Sarimski, K. (2002). Analysis of intentional communication in severely handicapped children with Cornelia-de-Lange syndrome. *Journal of Communication Disorders*, 35, 483–500.

Smith, A.C.M., Dykens, E. and Greenberg, F. (1998). Sleep disturbance in Smith-Magenis syndrome (deletion 17p11.2). *American Journal of Medical Genetics*, 81, 186–91.

Sobesky, W.E., Pennington, B.F., Porter, D., Hull, C.E. and Hagerman, R.J. (1994). Emotional and neurocognitive deficits in fragile X. *American Journal of Medical Genetics*, 51, 378–85.

Turk, J. (1998). Fragile X syndrome and attentional deficits. *Journal of Applied Research in Intellectual Disabilities*, 11, 175–91.

Turk, J. and Sales, J. (1996). Behavioural phenotypes and their relevance to child mental health professionals. *Child Psychiatry and Psychology Review*, 1, 4–11.

Udwin, O., Webber, C. and Horn, I. (2001). Abilities and attainment in Smith-Magenis syndrome. *Developmental Medicine and Child Neurology*, 43, 823–8.

Udwin, O., Yule, W. and Martin, N. (1987). Cognitive abilities and behavioural characteristics of children with idiopathic infantile hypercalcaemia. *Journal of Child Psychology and Psychiatry*, 28, 297–309.

van Lieshout, C.F.M., de Meyer, R.E., Curfs, L.M.G. and Fryns, J.P. (1998). Family contexts, parental behaviour, and personality profiles of children and adolescents with Prader-Willi, fragile X, or Williams syndrome. *Journal of Child Psychology and Psychiatry and Allied Disciplines*, 39, 699–710.

Wang, P.P., Woodin, M.F., Kreps-Falk, R. and Moss, E.M. (2000). Research on behavioural phenotypes: velocardiofacial syndrome (deletion 22q11.2). *Developmental Medicine and Child Neurology*, 42, 422–7.

Wilding, J., Cornish, K. and Munir, F. (2002). Further delineation of the executive deficit in males with fragile-X syndrome. *Neuropsychologia*, 40, 1343–9.

Williams, C.A., Angelman, H., Clayton-Smith, J., Driscoll, D.J., Hendrickson, J.E., Knoll, J.H.M., Magenis, R.E., Schinzel, A., Wagstaff, J., Whidden, E.M. and Zori, R.T. (1995). Angelman Syndrome: Consensus for diagnostic criteria. *American Journal of Medical Genetics*, 56, 237–8.

World Health Organization (1996). *Multiaxial Classification of Child and Adolescent Psychiatric Disorders: The ICD-10 Classification of Mental and Behavioural Disorders in Children and Adolescents.* Cambridge: Cambridge University Press.

Chapter 15

Autistic spectrum disorders

Rita Jordan

The term 'autistic spectrum disorders' (ASD) covers pervasive developmental disorders that share common symptoms, including autism and Asperger's syndrome. Both international classification systems – the DSM-IV-TR (APA, 2000) and ICD 10 (WHO, 1992; 1996) – have features by which autism and Asperger's syndrome may be recognized, referring to areas of development rather than specific behaviours. Behaviours themselves vary across individuals and within an individual over time and all the behaviours may be seen in children with a range of other disorders or none. 'Missing' behaviours are more indicative of ASD, given the child's general level of development, but there may be other reasons for those gaps. There may be sensory problems, for example, or extreme deprivation and abuse. Diagnostic tests are reliable, but only if used and interpreted by trained professionals. The bases of both diagnostic systems are differences in three areas of development known as the 'triad of impairments'. These can be characterized as difficulties in:

- Emotional and social understanding
- All aspects of communication
- Flexibility in thinking and behaviour.

Emotional and social understanding

There are difficulties in developing social skills and in interacting, especially with peers, but the fundamental problem is understanding. There may be other reasons for lacking social skills or failing to interact, but ASD means lacking the inbuilt intuitive routes to processing and understanding emotional and social signals. If the dedicated systems in the brain for processing such information is disturbed in ASD, it will affect not just social interaction but also the ability to make cultural and social sense of the world. For example, a failure to use social referencing when reacting to new stimuli may lead to no sense of danger or, alternatively, extreme fear of every new experience. Understanding the world comes through other people and being denied that means children with ASD are literally 'on their own' in making sense of their experiences.

All aspects of communication

Language may be affected but communication difficulties are always present. Communication usually comes first in development and aids the acquisition of language but in ASD language and communication develop differently. Children with ASD may develop good speech (in form, vocabulary and articulation) yet still have difficulties in interpreting speech and in using language either for thinking or communication. All communication systems are affected. There is no intuitive understanding of social timing, communicative gestures, facial expressions, appropriate social distances, relevance to a particular topic or situation, and how meaning is conveyed through intonation. There may also be problems with idiosyncratic meanings (from no shared reference) and not adjusting what is said to the listener. Where there are additional language impairments, the autism will make it harder to acquire language or to acquire alternative forms of communication.

Flexibility in thinking and behaviour

This is not necessarily a lack of imagination or creativity. Difficulties in imagination in ASD are usually to do with distinguishing the real from the imagined. The ability to 'reality test' normally develops from social tutoring in situations such as experiencing nightmares and learning from the consequent comforting and labelling by parents. Difficulties come from being unable to signal distress effectively, accept comfort or understand verbal explanations. More pervasive difficulties in flexibility of thinking and behaviour include all the executive functions of planning, monitoring, reflecting on and inhibiting actions, and consequent reliance on set routines and rote or cued learning. It also involves attention direction, switching and sharing. People with ASD may succeed extraordinarily well at certain (usually narrow) tasks, when compared to their general level of functioning, but a 'savant skill' (a skill that is remarkable in the general population and not just in comparison with other areas of functioning within the individual) is only apparent in around 10 per cent.

ASD are diagnosed by impairments in all three areas of development. Thus, the impairments interact in development and it is this that leads to the characteristically complex and varied patterns of behaviour. Attempts to separate some sub-groups have been problematic, with difficulties in reaching a principled and agreed differential diagnosis. Two levels of analysis are needed in assessing and treating children with ASD: the broad diagnostic category of ASD enables the behaviour to be seen through the right interpretative lens and the individual level is needed to determine the special and unique difficulties, strengths and experiences of each individual.

DIAGNOSIS AND ASSESSMENT

The diagnostic systems are medical and categorical in nature but what diagnosis attempts to do is delineate those for whom differences in the developmental triad are such that they constitute a barrier to effective functioning and future development – those who need (additional) input and support. For some children, their autism will be so severe and/or there will be additional problems such that it is obvious that the child falls into that category. For others, the diagnosis is less clear. The situation is distorted because diagnoses have become 'gateways' to resources but the basis in functionality should be recognized. An able child with good support may function well without a diagnosis. A less able child in a less optimum environment (for his or her particular difficulties) may need that diagnosis. Thus, the diagnosis describes extremes of functioning on three dimensions (sociability and empathy; communicativeness; and flexibility), which vary across, and between, all individuals, but cannot be made simply on 'within child' factors. It is a clinical judgement, following the grading of the individual along those dimensions, which includes an assessment (from observation and interview) of how the individual is functioning in his or her everyday environment.

A medical professional should be involved in diagnosis to check aetiological factors and comorbid conditions, but other professional (and parental) views are also needed. The clinical psychologist has a role in applying diagnostic tools (based on analogues of the diagnostic systems, e.g. ADI-R (Lord, Rutter and LeCouteur, 1994), DISCO (Wing, Leekham, Libby, Gould and Larcombe, 2002) and in observation and interviewing (and using schedules, e.g. ADOS), to assess functional ability. The National Plan for Autism in the UK recognizes the importance of multidisciplinary assessment in the diagnostic process and suggests levels of diagnostic services that are needed.

At present there are no effective screens for ASD. The Checklist for Autism in Toddlers (CHAT; Baron-Cohen, Allen and Gillberg, 1992) has good specificity (few false positives) but poor sensitivity (many false negatives). This test is designed for 18-month olds, to be given by primary health professionals who (through questioning parents and direct tests) pick out failures to respond in three key areas: monitoring eye-gaze, indicative pointing and showing, and engaging in pretend play acts. CHAT is useful in training key health professionals to be aware of ASD, and helping them respond more sensitively to parental concerns, leading to earlier follow-up for diagnosis. More recently a screen for older children has also been piloted (CAST; Scott, Baron-Cohen, Bolton and Brayne, 2002).

In the UK the National Plan balances the need for early diagnosis (a locally based system available soon after the first concerns are raised) with the need for a thorough system for unequivocal diagnoses in which there are no (or few) false positives or negatives. It suggests a three-tier model. The first tier is ready access to local professionals within a few weeks of concerns.

This should lead to a speedy diagnosis for clear-cut cases, based on clinical experience and judgement, following observation and reports from the parents and other relevant professionals. If an ASD is suspected, whether or not a clear diagnosis can be made at this stage, help and support should be offered to the parents and the child, pending further investigation, or on the basis of the diagnosis made. This follows the principle of the 'least damaging assumption': that it will do children no harm to be supported as if they had ASD (providing the possibility that they do not, is remembered) whereas it will do harm to make children with ASD wait for appropriate help until the diagnostic process is complete.

The second tier involves regional specialist centres where there will be staff, trained to administer the longer diagnostic instruments and with greater expertise in differential diagnosis, to deal with more problematic cases. Here the process will take longer, but freeing such centres from the more obvious cases should enable them to concentrate their expertise where it is needed. The third tier involves a few national centres, which might see some of the most puzzling cases but whose prime role would be training and research.

Parents are usually pleased to have a 'label' for what are otherwise puzzling behaviours yet, even when they have suspected autism, it can be a shock to have their fears confirmed. Family adjustment after diagnosis depends partly on how parents are told, so it is important that positive messages are given, of what can be done and the importance of the parental contribution. The truth is that most individuals with ASD improve considerably over time and that prospects are continually improving as our knowledge of the condition and of effective education and support grows. People with ASDs also deserve to be respected and valued for who they are and not made to feel that the only way to gain acceptance is to become 'someone else'.

Clinical psychologists may also be involved in broader assessments of children's strengths and weaknesses to help plan treatment and educational programmes. It is a clinical judgement as to which assessments are necessary for each individual, but there are some general guidelines. The following areas should be explored. In some cases they can be discounted immediately. In others there may need to be in-depth testing (perhaps involving other professionals).

- Receptive and expressive language ability (expressive ability alone may mislead)
- Communicative level (number and use of communicative functions, forms used and understood)
- Social development (appropriate to age and context)
- Cognitive level (verbal and non-verbal)
- Visual versus verbal processing preference
- Sensory sensitivities (defensiveness or abnormal reactions to pain, light, sounds, pressure, touch, taste, texture)

- Sensory disabilities (hearing difficulties are often wrongfully suspected but need to be ruled out; visual problems are often overlooked)
- Sleep patterns
- Hyperactivity
- Attention (directing, changing, monitoring, sustaining, joint)
- Physical problems (including ataxia, dyspraxia, hypotonia, hypertonia, over-flexible joints, gait and posture difficulties)
- Behavioural difficulties (bearing in mind that treatment will be different once their origin in autism is established)
- Problems in eating, swallowing, restricted diet, pica, gastrointestinal problems.
- Family and related supports and/or problems (including parental understanding of the condition and treatments already undertaken)
- Social cognition – understanding of emotions and mental state terms as applied to self and others.

There may be other assessments, dictated by the treatment or educational environment in which the child is to be placed. For example, it may be important to know whether a child can participate in a group, has dyslexia, or needs one-to-one instruction to learn new skills. When involved in setting up a treatment programme, the psychologist will also want to know about the parents' priorities as a factor in choosing initial behaviours to target. The TEACCH programme has developed practical ways of incorporating parental priorities in goal planning.

EPIDEMIOLOGY

It is difficult to determine incidence (the number of new cases each year) because ASD are not discernible at birth and we have to rely on prevalence (the number of new cases identified each year), which has increased dramatically over the last two decades. But prevalence depends not only on incidence but also on the availability of good diagnostic services and public awareness of the signs, both of which have also increased dramatically over the same period. A third factor is that the category of ASD is far wider than the original one of autism, and many more children are included in an ASD diagnosis who would have been given other diagnoses (learning difficulty/ disability, or conduct disorder perhaps) before. However, what was once seen as a 'low incidence disorder' can no longer be so regarded. Planning for services is far from recognizing the rate of 1 per 160 that is currently the best estimate of prevalence.

AETIOLOGY

In 1943 Kanner originally saw autism as a biological disorder, but was influenced by the psychogenic theorists until evidence of its biological origin began to emerge. ASD are now regarded as the most genetically based of all the developmental disorders, although the actual genes involved are still unknown. All the chromosomes bar three have been identified as possible sites by at least one study, and work is concentrating on those that have been implicated by multiple studies. There is unlikely to be a single genetic cause and between three and ten genes are probably involved. There may also be environmental triggers necessary to 'turn on' genes. Most research is concentrating on genes thought to influence brain development directly, but a genetic cause could mean a more indirect route where the genetic effect is to make the person vulnerable to certain environmental influences.

Biological risk factors

There are some medical conditions that are high-risk factors for developing ASD. These include phenylketonuria, tuberous sclerosis and Fragile X. Epilepsy (especially late-onset epilepsy) is a common comorbid condition in autism, So also is intellectual disability. In adolescents and adults with ASD, depression and bipolar disorder are relatively common. There is nothing in ASD that protects from developing any other disorder or mental health problem and so people with ASD may also have sensory disabilities, physical disabilities, Down syndrome, intellectual disability, language disorders, and so on. It has been suggested that Asperger's syndrome rather than autism should be considered the core disorder, and that classic autism is Asperger's syndrome plus a language disorder. That may better reflect reality but there are social and political reasons why such a change is unlikely.

Psychological theories of ASD

Following the demise of psychogenic theories of autism, cognitive theories have dominated. The seminal work of Frith's (1989; updated, 2003) put forward the Theory of Mind Theory (TOMT), as well as introducing a supplementary theory of Weak Central Coherence. That latter theory has been developed further (Happé, 1994) and Baron-Cohen (1995) has extended TOMT to include pre-cursors. The other important cognitive theory in autism is that of a failure in executive functions (Russell, 1997). There is also a theory of ASD as rooted in fundamental failure in inter-subjectivity (Hobson, 2002) with cognitive problems as secondary consequences of this. New theories are also emerging, related to particular aspects of cognitive functioning such as attention or conceptual processing.

The value of theoretical accounts has been primarily to stimulate thinking about the nature of ASD and to better understand how behavioural manifestations might be interpreted. The original hopes that a theory would offer a total explanation, and a bridge to neurological correlates, have not been fulfilled. Seeking single theoretical accounts may prove fruitless, and the future may be greater delineation of ASD and firmer links between disturbances in psychological processes and their behavioural outcomes.

INTERVENTIONS FOR ASD

Intervention programmes for children with ASD involve working with the children themselves, but also working with parents and members of the child's educational system to equip them with the skills to interact in a therapeutic way with the child.

Working with parents

Parents are no longer held responsible for their child's condition, but knowledge of the genetic base produces its own problems. Parents may feel responsible for their genes, plus there is the additional worry of risks to siblings (or potential siblings) and future generations. Understanding the complexity of parental emotions will enable psychologists to be more sensitive to the needs of the family. It is never too early to help parents relate to their child, but parents will differ greatly in the time taken to accept the situation and take a more active role. The contribution of parents is vital, not only as one of the best teaching resources, but also because parents invariably react to their child, and helping them do so more productively benefits everyone. EarlyBird (Shields, 2001) is one eclectic programme for enabling parents to take an active role in their child's development. It provides the essential elements for a parent-training initiative in

- providing knowledge through eight weekly training sessions plus a manual to keep and refer to, especially on understanding the condition
- access to a support group of other parents in the workshops and then beyond
- training in working with their child, modelled, videoed and commented on in two home-visits
- early expressive communication training (PECS; Bondy and Frost, 1994)
- receptive communication and learning how to set up a structured environment (TEACCH; Schopler, Mesibov and Hearsey, 1995)
- early interaction development through HANEN (Sussman, 1999), where the parents are taught to OWL (Observe, Wait and Listen) to increase their child's capacity to interact.

It can be improved by adding contact with a local specialist support teacher, since this provides knowledge and access to the local educational opportunities. There should also be play training, and schemes to involve siblings or other children in integrated structured play-groups.

Child-focused intervention: psychological issues

ASD can be considered at different levels. Behaviour is necessary for the assessment of needs and strengths, as well as for diagnosis. Yet, ASD do not lie in the behaviours themselves, nor in the biology – given that different biological factors may be involved in different cases. Children with ASD need to be understood at the psychological level. Two children may each have a communication disorder but it is what lies behind that at the psychological level that will determine effective treatment. If the difficulties stem from a hearing impairment, that will require some very particular treatments (digital hearing aids, perhaps) as well as some more generally useful strategies (written language and/or symbols). If, however, the difficulties stem from ASD, the second general strategy will help but the first will be pointless, and in addition the child will need some very specific teaching to understand the nature of communication, and to develop different communicative functions. Working at the psychological level means trying to understand how the child is perceiving, attending, learning, memorizing, feeling, and so on.

Perception

Problems in processing sensory information are a dominant part of the experience of having an ASD, but it is not clear whether these appear as sensory problems because of difficulties in attributing meaning to the sensations (i.e. a perceptual problem) or whether there is a sensory problem *per se*. Inability to engage effectively in initial 'dialogues' with a caregiver means the child misses vital opportunities for cultural and social learning, including how to 'mean' in a culturally relevant way. Without that basis, the child develops idiosyncratic meanings and may miss the most relevant focus in any situation. The child has no way of knowing whether what she or he is thinking or 'seeing' is the same as others or whether it is so idiosyncratic that no one would guess what was being thought unless specifically told. It is rare for children to say what they are thinking, so these misperceptions go unchecked, often leading to bizarre behaviour.

Intervention

Help parents and staff provide specific and targeted ongoing descriptions of the world around them (in short phrases) and how it is to be interpreted – geared to the level and interest of the child. This is just how parents behave with infants but in ASD one needs to continue such tutoring well beyond early childhood. Also help the child develop joint attention by getting carers to imitate the child and progress the 'game' until the child is imitating them.

Attention

In ASD, children are not alert to the normal attention-grabbing stimuli of human voices, one's own name, eye-gaze, and facial expressions. Joint attention is slow to develop, if at all. In many teaching situations such attention is assumed, and misunderstandings then abound. Individuals with ASD can follow the direction of other people's eyes or points, but need training since they do not do so spontaneously. Above all, people with ASD appear to be 'monotropic' – only able to attend to one thing or dimension at a time.

Intervention

Children with ASD have to be taught specifically to respond to social signals, but then adults need training to use them as signals. Saying 'Sit down, Johnny!' seems the same as saying 'Johnny' (with time for him to orientate) 'Sit down!', but for Johnny (if he has ASD) it may mean the difference between being able to comply with the second request and being completely bemused by the first (where, once he attends to his name, no further instruction is given). Children with ASD need teaching specifically, and in many contexts, that holding up, pointing or eye-pointing to something, all mean that that is the object referred to. They need training to disengage from tasks and switch their attention, being given warning and time to do so. Sharing attention should be tackled initially by understanding the difficulties as the child tries to monopolize the attention of one adult when two are present, or becomes disruptive in social groups. Then the child should be taught to divide attention, very deliberately.

Learning style

Most individuals with ASD are visual learners, so visual rather than oral instructions are helpful. Visual instructions are more explicit, less dependent on social interpretation, more permanent and allow longer processing time. Language processing problems interfere with the understanding of all but the shortest and simplest of oral instructions and attention problems also interfere with processing. Visual instructions appear less 'personal', so many children with ASD, who have problems submitting to control, find it easier and more comfortable to obey a visual than a spoken instruction. Whether or not individuals with ASD always see details rather than the whole, they do have problems in keeping a goal in mind, understanding the meaning of activities and producing fluent integrated skills.

Intervention

Providing at least a visual back-up of a spoken command helps keep the instruction in the child's attention and available when she or he is ready to respond. Problems may be avoided simply by teaching children to follow their own visual schedules for the sequence of tasks. Teaching the child to be more flexible and to consider alternatives can be done through diagrams, maps, and flow charts, all showing how different actions can lead to the same end or that the same actions can have different consequences dependent on the context. In challenging behaviour children can be helped to perceive the step in the process where they have a choice and what the consequences of each course of action will be. Using visual means to emphasize goals, and teaching children to check their own actions against the goal, helps develop their understanding, whereas relying on prompted chains of actions may not.

Memory

Some aspects of memory appear exceptionally good in ASD, whilst others are poorly developed. What develops well, often as the only strategy available, is cued, rote, and procedural memory. Thus, the child may forget nothing, and memories can be cued months or years later. Aspects of memory that involve reconstruction, however, so that the gist is recalled and the rest is reconstructed, do not develop well. An individual may be able to repeat word for word the whole script of a movie and recognize many obscure details from stills of the film, yet have no idea of the plot or the motivations of characters. If interrupted when recounting the script, they have to restart at the beginning. They need each step to trigger the next and the memory is not able to be modified or used in any way other than its original form; thus it is hard to build on these apparently 'savant' memory skills.

It is also hard for them to establish and use personal episodic memory. They can develop semantic autobiographical memory in that they can know about themselves in the way one knows about someone else – a catalogue of life events and characteristics. Yet it is hard to develop aspects of memory that require a subjective experience of the self, knowing (without seeing or being told) what has happened to oneself, how one felt and so on, and using that sense to search memory (without external cues) to retrieve those personal episodes.

Intervention

Children can benefit from developing more meaningful and adaptable memory strategies, by being trained to recognize and pick out the salient points of a short (personal) event and use these later in recall. They can be helped also by drawing their attention to cues that can be reactivated in other environments.

Consolidating materials, through rehearsal at the point where the cues are available, helps to establish those cues to be used later in recall. One way is to use miniature symbols to sequence a task just undertaken, and then to fix those in the home–school book for parents to reactivate the memories and further consolidate them at home.

Emotional understanding and social cognition

People with ASD experience difficulties in understanding the emotions of themselves and others. Without this understanding, individuals are not able to control their own reactions to their emotional states (which are not processed consciously) nor to understand others (or the mental states that may underlie their actions). The core difficulty in ASD may not be an impairment in empathy as such, but in the emotional and social understanding underlying it. Able people with ASD develop an understanding of their own emotions, and then of other people's, but often not until adulthood; even then, it can be disrupted by information overload or high levels of stress.

Intervention

Attempts to teach social cognition (understanding mental states in others) through cognitive means (through examples in workbooks or on a computer) can have an effect on the mental state being taught. However, results show a limited capacity to generalize to real-life situations. Attempts to teach social and emotional engagement from the start have the ambition of helping the child build that sense of him- or herself and others through which this understanding emerges, but no long-term success has yet been reported. Providing a clear structure, which helps the child direct attention appropriately, and involves situations in which the child is already emotionally involved, seems the most promising approach.

Language and communication

Structural aspects of language (syntax, phonology, vocabulary acquisition and articulation) can be intact, although they frequently are not. Intonation and pausing may be heard (and mimicked exactly in echolalia) but often the individual is unable to attribute meaning to the intonation pattern or the pauses. Their own speech may appear wooden or with highly inflected phrases but reproduced in inappropriate circumstances, unadapted to new contexts. People with ASD report that it is easier to listen to computerized than human speech because the intonation is unvaried and it is not accompanied by all the other (for them) distractions from meaning: facial expressions, body postures, gestures, levels of proximity.

Receptive speech is often poorer than expressive, and the child's failures to understand may then be attributed to behavioural difficulties or non-compliance. The person with an ASD will not be monitoring the environment for social signals such as speech, in the way others do, so they may miss the start of utterances and, so often, the topic. Once they attend, they take longer to process speech and the effect of falling progressively behind is to make the speech appear louder, faster and less meaningful. Another major difficulty is that speech is full of metaphors, similes, puns, jokes, irony, sarcasm, idioms, inaccuracies, circumlocutions: we hardly ever say what we mean and certainly not precisely. Communication is about 'going beyond the information given' and that is exactly what is difficult in ASD. Depending on their language ability, they may understand what the words mean, but that is only a poor guide to what the speaker means.

Intervention

Train carers and teachers to speak in short phrases and to allow time to process between each phrase. Written language is often easier than spoken, and the child may learn to speak through learning to read. Written language is less ephemeral and tends to be more explicit and accurate. As far as other non-literal aspects of language are concerned, it is best to teach about them explicitly, rather than attempting to eliminate them from the child's environment, although in the early stages of acquiring a language it may be sensible to concentrate on unequivocal meanings. The priority is to teach a form of communication, which will help language develop and aid many other aspects of development, including behaviour control.

Where there is additional intellectual disability, there will need to be assessment of the child's semantic understanding before deciding on the method of communication. The child may need to be helped to move from relating to objects at purely a sensory level (just perceiving the cup, for example, as something to be twiddled and tapped), to associating particular objects with particular events – the level of presentation (a particular cup comes to mean a drink in a particular situation). COMFOR is a teaching pack developed specifically to aid this teaching step (Noens and Van Berckelaer-Onnes, 2002). The next stage is teaching the child to respond to 'objects of reference', where an object comes to 'stand for' or represent an event or activity. At that stage the child may be ready to move to pictorial symbols. Photographs or detailed realistic pictures may not be easier than more schematic ones; the level of detail and realism may cause the child to focus on the particular event or activity depicted and find it harder to perceive the symbol as representing a class of events or activities.

PECS can be useful for teaching basic communicative functions in a structured way that is easy for parents and teachers to adopt (Bondy and Frost, 1994). It involves two important principles: the first is that the child should learn to request spontaneously and not just in response to a particular prompt, e.g. 'What do you want!'; the second is that the child should learn that choice is always limited and any request has to take account of what might be available in that situation, i.e. there needs to be a 'menu'. The first principle is easiest to follow at home because parents are more likely to know what the child wants at any point, and find it easier to guide the child into selecting a symbol to place in the hand of the second adult, without using verbal prompts. In school situations, practical considerations mean the child often has to be prompted to request something by being offered it, e.g. one adult holds up a crisp while the other physically prompts the child to choose a symbol and give it to the first adult in exchange, or place it on a communication strip. From a pragmatic perspective, it is bizarre to ask for what one is offered (one either accepts or declines the offer, or it appears that one doubts the identity of the item) and it seems unfortunate actually to teach bizarre behaviour.

A menu is important in both home and school but again it is easier to illustrate it clearly in a home context, where there are no other menus from which to steal. For example, a child who always wants the same video on return from school can be helped to make alternative choices, extend his or her repertoire and prevent family discord, by being shown a menu without that video symbol. Of course, a child who is used to having it each day will not accept that, unless it is combined with a TEACCH strategy of showing the child a sequence of menus where the desired video appears in the next menu along (Schopler, Mesibov and Hearsey, 1995). As long as the child already understands how to use the TEACCH schedule, he or she will usually accept waiting for the next menu, especially if the choices on the first are also attractive and do not last very long.

While a system of communication is the priority, it is also necessary to foster speech specifically in those who do not develop it naturally. Children with ASD are able to appreciate musical structure, even when they cannot understand linguistic structure, so sung phrases can be used as instructions. Emphasized pauses in songs to accompany daily routines can gradually be introduced, to encourage the child to complete the phrase. Functional language is important rather than meaningless repetition of speech sounds, but songs allow the needed repetition and emphasis without being boring or bizarre.

Echolalia is now recognized as a first step in learning to communicate and use language. Immediate echolalia can be tackled by assuming it indicates recognition of the imperative to take a turn but inability to understand (or process) the language being used. Build up the child's understanding and try to minimize processing demands (using visual cues). Allowing the child more time to respond and initiate interaction will help reduce immediate echolalia and produce more spontaneity in speech. Delayed echolalia can be built on by prompting it in more appropriate situations and using sections to recombine with other sections to form new phrases and meanings. For example, the boy using 'Time to get your coat now' to mean he would like to go outside, may be taught 'Time to get your x now' to request many other items. Pronoun reversal comes from having a poor sense of the self-assertiveness that enables typical youngsters to resolve this difficulty, and from not noticing that the second- and third-person pronouns are used to indicate others, according to speech role. Games in which these understandings are specifically addressed, and ways of reinforcing that in daily life, can help resolve the problem.

More verbally able children will need to develop their conversational skills. They need to be taught specifically to turn take, listen actively and pick out the topic of conversations. They then need training, in maintaining, extending, developing, and changing that topic. They need to be taught (by labelling actual experience) what it means to be boring and then ways in which they can negotiate opportunities with friends for each to talk about what interests them, but never for too long. It helps if one can find a 'friend' with a shared interest but even then turn taking has to be structured. There are programmes that help with the social aspects of language (SULP). Narrative skills need to be developed and this is often best done through simple drama scripts, building from familiar stories or real events.

RATIONALE AND EVIDENCE BASE FOR SPECIFIC INTERVENTIONS

People with ASD are characterized by high levels of stress. The first principle for any intervention programme is that it should aim to reduce that stress, by teaching understanding and coping skills, enabling supportive prosthetic environments, and teaching techniques for stress reduction (exercise and/or relaxation). The second principle is that it should address understanding as well as compensatory skills, respecting the child and his or her difficulties and accepting him or her as an individual. The third is that the educational process should offer dignity and choice and enable the child to learn and develop through all aspects of learning – skill-based, cognitive, emotional, aesthetic, spiritual and social.

Choosing a particular intervention is problematic in a situation where uncertain aetiology and varied developmental patterns make it possible for proponents of particular approaches to make extravagant claims. The growth of the internet, and a failure to provide early and appropriate intervention for all, has meant that parents are vulnerable to such claims. The entitlement to a broad and relevant education changes the picture once a child reaches statutory school age, where the issue is one of access: how can the child be supported (and the systems adapted) to enable the child to gain the most from what is available to others? Very few specific treatments have addressed the broader issues of educational access in ASD, although the TEACCH programme sees this as an important aspect of its approach.

There is also the issue of how the autism itself can be addressed: what treatments can be used both prior to, and alongside, schooling, to help children manage their ASD or to reduce the symptoms? Specific treatments vary in the scope of their approach and in the extent of their claims. Interventions based on behaviourism (Applied Behaviour Analysis: ABA; Cooper, Heron and Heward, 2006) claim universal application across all children (and adults), for all aspects of development, by defining autism as excess or deficit in certain behaviours. Thus, by targeting those behaviours, it is claimed that the autism can be 'cured' and the child be said to have 'recovered'. A single (methodologically flawed) study showed 47 per cent to have 'recovered' but this has never been replicated. The claims continue, even though current treatments differ considerably from those used in the original study (Smith, 1999).

Behavioural methods undoubtedly offer a programme which can be implemented without knowledge of autism or professional expertise in education or therapy. The popularity of such programmes among parents does not just lie in the advertisements and the lack of effective alternatives (although these are important factors), since there is nearly always some success in teaching early skills and habits and in increasing parental confidence. Problems come when parents are told that it is the *only* proven approach or that it can work for all aspects of development. It is not just a matter of finding an approach to fit a child, but one that is appropriate to the skill or area of development. ABA is very useful for teaching behavioural conformity and that has a place in education. However, it is not all of education and trying to make it so raises both ethical and educational concerns. Children need experience of making choices and decisions and of problem solving and they need to learn through social and emotional routes as well as through behavioural control.

A good use of behavioural methods was in the original Lovaas study (1987; Lovaas and Smith, 2003) where local mainstream nurseries were targeted and the children taught just those skills that would enable them access (and to avoid just those behaviours that would deny them access). Using behavioural methods, for the narrow purpose of getting the child into a richer educational environment, may be one source of any success and requires replication. Recent comparative research shows that other approaches can be just as, or more, cost effective as ABA and it is likely that in future ABA will occupy a more realistic place as one among many useful strategies that have a place in the education of children with ASD.

Most interventions for children with ASD are not evaluated even at the level of a well-described case study. Some programmes, such as TEACCH (Schopler, 1997), do not make claims in relation to reducing autism and do not, therefore, provide output evaluations on those criteria, but that should not prevent the development of their own evaluation criteria (increased participation in learning opportunities, more time spent in independent activities, reduced stress levels, reduced challenging behaviour are all possibilities). TEACCH stresses its development from scientific research on the way individuals with ASD think and learn, yet relies on parental and professional endorsement rather than evaluation of how children are progressing in TEACCH classrooms and for what aspects of learning TEACCH is best suited.

Interactive approaches are based on adapted early dyadic routines, but also have not been effectively evaluated. These include both 'total' interventions and ones meant to form part of the child's programme (Child Talk [Aldred, 2002]; Framework for Communication [Chandler, Christie, Newson and Prevezer, 2002]; Floor-time [Wieder and Greenspan, 2003]; Hanen [Sussman, 1999]; Intensive Interaction [Nind and Hewett,1994]: Communicative gestures [Potter and Whittaker, 2000]; Son Rise Program [Kaufman, 1994]. Framework for Communication uses techniques (including music-supported interactions) between a key worker (or parent) and child in set sessions, to establish patterns of interaction that can be built on throughout the day and provide other opportunities for emotional and social learning. It differs from traditional music or other play therapies, for example, in that the role of the 'therapist' is to develop the relationship between the child and someone who can use that relationship at other times; a traditional therapist has no other contact with the child so the benefits may be difficult to generalize outside the therapeutic session. Daily Life Therapy (DLT; Kitahara, 1984) still lacks any clear rationale for its approach (based on Japanese primary education) but it now has schools in the UK, Boston and Tokyo.

There is not space to describe all the other therapies and approaches that are available. There are a few for which there is overwhelming evidence of a lack of efficacy, although even here it is difficult to be definite. Individuals with ASD represent a very heterogeneous group and group studies showing an overall lack of effectiveness do not preclude the possibility that a particular approach may work for a particular individual for a particular end. However, where there is no good evidence of any beneficial effect, it behoves the practitioner to justify the time and resources spent on such treatments. In this category are auditory integration therapy (no better than just listening to music through headphones) and facilitated communication, where most studies show authorship to lie with the facilitator.

The notion of 'evidence-based' practice is a new one in education and few typical educational approaches have been subject to any but the most crude of evaluations, in measures of general school effectiveness. There is certainly a need for evaluation of certain key educational policies in relation to pupils with ASD, such as the experience, degree, and outcomes of 'inclusion'. Individuals with ASD and their parents are often assumed to share the same goals and expectations with respect to inclusion as other disability groups but that assumption needs to be tested.

There are other treatments in which clinical psychologists may be involved, that are directed at targeted behaviours or temporary states. Challenging behaviour is dealt with below. Dealing with phobias, anxiety states, obsessive-compulsive disorder (OCD), depression and even bipolar disorder are somewhat different. Just as in the non-autistic population, there may be drug treatments that can help the individual over a crisis, but the psychologist should have a role in evaluating the effectiveness (and side-effects) of any such medication and (nearly always) in developing behavioural or counselling approaches to assist, and eventually replace, the medication. There may also be a role in identifying the problem, since many carers fail to distinguish the effects of autism from secondary mental health problems. For example, it can be difficult to judge when a pattern of behaviour represents an obsessional interest (as found in ASD) and when it has become an OCD. A good ontological history of the behaviour is the best guide, but as a rough measure, if the child is still getting pleasure from, and calming during, the performance of the activity, then it is probably still an ASD interest; OCD results in driven behaviour from which the sufferer receives no respite by performing the act. As outside the world of ASD, cognitive behavioural therapy (CBT) has been shown to be effective in ASD both with adults and children.

Psychologists may also be involved in running social skills groups (Howlin and Yates, 1999) or helping develop Social Stories (Gray, 1994) for individuals with ASD. Neither approach is supported by scientific evidence of efficacy, although each is valued by participants and practitioners. Social skills groups have the danger that individuals learn to perform within the group but cannot generalize to real-life situations. Social skills are probably best taught in the context of their use but the groups may provide a general source of mutual support. Circles of Friends in schools, involving their peers, are also valuable in providing joint problem-solving opportunities, minimizing bullying and in actualizing support for free time, sometimes leading to genuine friendships (Whitaker, Barratt, Joy, Potter and Thomas, 1998). Social stories provide set scripts for how to behave in certain problematic situations and have more limited goals in dealing with particular social or behavioural issues; they are nevertheless a useful tool for the psychologist him/herself or to train others to use.

CHALLENGING BEHAVIOUR

This is the area with which clinical psychologists are often most involved in a multidisciplinary service, either in working directly with a child or in training and supporting those who are. A functional analysis is essential since teaching a functional alternative is the best form of treatment, given that children with ASD find it difficult to inhibit their own behaviour. However, especially when dealing with individuals with a limited behavioural repertoire, any behaviour may serve more than one function, each of which may need to be tackled and replaced with an acceptable alternative. There may be particular triggers for challenging behaviour (pain caused by certain noises, fear caused by a particular phobic object or event) but there also may not. Many children with ASD live with a high degree of stress and if that builds to a high enough level, then the next stimulus (in itself innocuous) may lead to a challenging outburst. Analysis of the situation, therefore, should include the total experience of the child, as far as possible, and be alert for the more systemic forms of stress in the child's life and ways of reducing these.

Whether dealing with challenging behaviour itself, or helping others to do so, it is important to take account of the autism, when applying behavioural techniques. Try to look at the situation from the child's perspective and understand the real cause of the behaviour. Children with ASD, for example, are often said to be aggressive, although what is usually meant is 'violent' or 'destructive'. Using accurate descriptors helps those involved to see that the child is not targeting them or someone else (unless they are doing so to re-create a predicted pattern of behaviour) and that calling it 'aggression' does not help prevent or manage it. Recognizing that the child is behaving like that because:

- the child lacks alternatives to get his or her needs met
- the child wasn't expecting something and it has caused her or him to panic
- the child was expecting something that has not arrived and so is frustrated
- the child likes the effects on the environment or others
- the child always does this here or now
- the child has misunderstood or misperceived something and thinks this is appropriate
- the child is feeling out of control
- a strong emotion has directly triggered behaviour without her or him being aware of the emotion
- the child likes the consequent predictable attention

will all lead to somewhat different courses of action to help the child (and others) through the situation. Short-term strategies may be needed to keep the child and others safe, but a challenging event should trigger a longer-term view and an attempt to deal with the real causes in the situation. High degrees of stress may cause the child to 'forget' skills at least for a time and they may even lose speech; acting as if this is some deliberate act that the child can be coaxed or even bullied out of is not helpful.

ADOLESCENCE AND LIFE-SPAN ISSUES

The manifestation of ASD changes over time according to experience, treatment, and personal characteristics.

Emotional and sexual development

Work with children from an early age, helping them recognize and deal with their emotions in situations that are real and important to them. However, with adolescence, emotional lability is likely to increase and young people may find it increasingly hard to understand and recognize their emotional states, even if they could before. Adolescents may show wild swings of mood and need to be helped to relax and develop calming activities. Physical exercise regimes are useful, and having an emotionally and physically engaging task to perform can help the individual weather both depressive and more manic moods. People with ASD need sex education but care is needed to ensure aspects have not been misinterpreted and safe ways of meeting needs have been sought, sometimes involving outlets that may differ from the expressed 'norm'. Many will need help to make sure they understand how to masturbate and can achieve orgasm (perhaps with the aid of fetishes) in privacy, without causing themselves or others harm. They need to know how to keep themselves safe and should have been taught about assertiveness, privacy, and intimacy circles from an early age. Questions about marriage and relationships need to be treated with respect. It is not justified to suggest such goals are inappropriate, but often a discussion about what needs to be achieved (sharing space and interests, for example) is enough for some to prefer the single lifestyles, which we should make clear are open to them.

Play and leisure

Play is important throughout life for both social and cognitive development. Helping children, and later young people, develop play and leisure pastimes can relieve the burden of unstructured time on individuals and their families. Some young people with ASD do not have a problem in developing interests so much as in limiting an obsessive one, but the approach is much the same. The goal is to develop new interests either to replace boredom and restless behaviour or to limit an all-consuming obsession. When introducing a new activity, it should be presented as an activity that is going to take place for a set number of occasions (between five and ten) before there will be a review for the person to 'say' if they wish to continue or not. No one can tell from one or two occasions whether or not the person will like the new activity, because initially its newness will overwhelm the experience. Equally, if the person does not know how many times it will happen, and when (or if) it will 'end', the activity is likely to be resisted from the beginning. By having a time-limited commitment, the person gets a chance to 'get used to' the activity and consider his or her own reactions to it. It is important at that point to respect that decision.

Life skills

The difference from providing life-skill training to people with intellectual disability to those with ASD lies primarily in motivation and social understanding. Even those with high levels of intelligence will often need training and monitoring to check that they have understood the full safety or social consequences of their behaviour and one cannot rely on group identification, pleasing others, or conforming, to make sure daily personal and domestic hygiene rituals are maintained. The greatest asset is the willingness to follow rules (rather than personal instructions) and to stick to routines and habits, once these have been established. Sometimes, even with the most able, it may be best to make certain rigid rules about domestic chores, rather than rely on the person having to make a judgement about when to empty the contents of the rubbish bin and so on – all of which may lead to considerable stress.

TRAINING PROFESSIONALS AND ADDITIONAL RESOURCES

Increasingly, there are training programmes in ASD for all levels of staff engaged in their support and care, some of which may be suitable for clinical psychologists who intend to become specialists. Not every professional need be an expert in ASD, but each profession should have access to a specialist to provide extra support for colleagues and multidisciplinary teams, and to be involved in the training programmes for other staff and/or parents. In spite of the tremendous strides in knowledge and understanding of ASD, especially in psychology, it is a fast-developing field, and there is a need for continued professional development to ensure that the models we are working with are up to date.

SUMMARY

Autistic Spectrum Disorders (ASD) are defined and diagnosed as categorical pervasive developmental disorders at the behavioural level. In spite of clear evidence for their biological (largely genetic) base, they are best understood and addressed at the psychological level – the way initial problems in recognizing and processing social and emotional information lead to later cognitive, social and behavioural problems. The best current estimates of prevalence are

1 in 160, which makes them relatively common developmental problems. Psychological theories have been influential in aiding understanding of the conditions, but not in providing a single explanatory model.

Working with parents is essential in that early intervention is crucial, as are daily life aspects of interaction, not just specific training packages. There are specific issues to address in perception, attention, learning style, memory, emotional understanding, social cognition, language and communication. There is no clear comparative evidence for the superiority of any specific intervention, but the choice should be on the basis of particular developmental goals and using the proven strengths of several, in a principled mix. Challenging behaviours arise as a result of stress and lack of understanding, and should be dealt with by teaching functional alternatives. Issues in educational access still need research, as do ways of enabling emotional, sexual and play development. Social and leisure opportunities need to be provided. All professionals need awareness training and access to specialist colleagues.

EXERCISE

Actual assessments undertaken and tools used will depend on the purpose of the assessment (diagnosis? intervention? educational placement? behaviour management?), the age of the child and constraints of time and resources. Tools given in the table below are simply examples. Assuming, the child has already received a diagnosis of an ASD and assessment is needed for planning an intervention, carry out the following assessments and interpret the results in relation to choosing priorities and methods of intervention. Aim at as precise a description as possible under the following headings:

Area of development	Tools used for evidence	Date of data	Functioning age	Problems and deviances
Severity of autism	CARS			
Sociability	White (2002)			
Communication **a) Skills** **b) Meaning level**	CCC or PVC COMFOR			
Language **a) Receptive** **b) Expressive**	a) BPVS and TROG b) MLU			
Mental state **understanding**	Observation/ interviews/ Howlin et al. (1999)			

(Continued overleaf)

Area of development	Tools used for evidence	Date of data	Functioning age	Problems and deviances
Cognitive flexibility	Tower of Hanoi Wisconsin Card Test			
Cognitive ability	Non-verbal IQ Verbal IQ			
Learning style	Cognitive style analysis Observations/ interviews			
Strengths and interests	Observation and interviews			

FURTHER READING FOR PARENTS AND PRACTITIONERS

Baron-Cohen, S. (1995). *Mindblindness: An Essay on Autism and Theory of Mind.* Cambridge, MA: MIT Press.

Clements, J. and Zarkowska, E. (2000). *Behavioural Concerns and Autistic Spectrum Disorders.* London: Jessica Kingsley.

Cumine, V., Stephenson, G. and Leach, J. (1997). *Asperger Syndrome in the Mainstream School.* London: David Fulton.

De Clerque, H. (2003). *Is It a Man or a Beast?* London: Whurr Publications.

Fombonne, E. (2002). Epidemiological trends in rates of autism. *Molecular Psychiatry*, 7, Supplement 2, S4–S6.

Frith, U. (2003). *Autism: Explaining the Enigma* (2nd edn). Oxford: Blackwells.

Gerland, G. (1997). *A Real Person.* London: Souvenir Press.

Grandin, T. (1995). How people with autism think. In E. Schopler and G.B. Mesibov (eds), *Learning and Cognition in Autism.* New York: Plenum Press.

Hobson, R.P. (2002). *The Cradle of Thought.* Oxford: Macmillan.

Howlin, P. (1998). Practitioner review: Psychological and educational treatment for autism. *Journal of Child Psychology and Psychiatry*, 39, 307–22.

Jordan, R. (1999). *Autistic Spectrum Disorders: An Introductory Handbook for Practitioners.* London: David Fulton.

Jordan, R. (1999). Evaluating practice: Problems and possibilities. *Autism: The International Journal of Research and Practice*, 3, 411–34.

Jordan, R. (2001). *Autism with Severe Learning Difficulties.* London: Souvenir Press.

Jordan, R. (2001). Multidisciplinary work for children with autism. *Educational and Child Psychology*, 18, 2, 5–14.

Jordan, R. (2002). *Autistic Spectrum Disorders in the Early Years.* Lichfield: QED.

Jordan, R. and Powell, S. (1995). *Understanding and Teaching Children with Autism.* Chichester: Wiley.

Jordan, R., Jones, G. and Murray, D. (1998). *Educational Interventions for Children with ASDs: A Review of Recent and Current Research.* Nottingham: Department of Education and Employment, UK.

Kanner, L. (1943). Autistic disturbances of affective contact. *Nervous Child*, 2, 217–50.

National Initiative for Assessment, Screening and Education in Autism (2003). *National Plan for Autism.* London: National Autistic Society.

Powell, S.D. and Jordan, R.R. (1994). Developing a cognitive curriculum for individuals with autism. *REACH – Journal of Special Needs Education in Ireland*, 8, 9–18.

Prior, M. (ed.) (2003). *Learning and Behaviour Problems in Asperger Syndrome.* New York: Guilford Press.

Russell, J. (ed.) (1997). *Autism as an Executive Disorder.* Oxford: Oxford University Press.

Rutter, M. (1999). Autism: Two way interplay between research and clinical work. *Journal of Child Psychology and Psychiatry*, 40, 169–88.

Volkmar, F., Rhea, P., Klin, A. and Cohen, D. (2005). *Handbook of Autism and Pervasive Developmental Disorders. Volume 1. Diagnosis, Development Neurobiology and Behaviour. Volume 2. Assessment Interventions and Policy.* New York: Wiley.

Watson, L., Lord, C., Schaffer, B. and Schopler, E. (1989). *Teaching Spontaneous Communication to Autistic and Developmentally Handicapped Children.* New York: Irvington.

Williams, D. (1996). *Autism: An Inside Out Approach.* London: Jessica Kingsley.

Wing, L. (1996). *Autistic Spectrum Disorders.* London: Constable.

ASSESSMENT TOOLS AND INTERVENTION PROGRAMMES

ABA: Lovaas, O.I. (1981). *Teaching Developmentally Disabled Children – the ME Book.* Baltimore, MD: University Park Press.

ADI-R: Lord, C., Rutter, M. and LeCouteur, A. (1994). Autistic Diagnostic Interview-Revised: A revised version of a diagnostic interview for caregivers of individuals with possible pervasive developmental disorder. *Journal of Autism and Developmental Disorders*, 24, 659–85.

ADOS: Lord, C., Rutter, M. and DiLavore, P. (1997). *Autism Diagnostic Observation Schedule – Generic (ADOS-G).* New York: The Psychological Corporation.

BPVS: Dunn, L.M. *et al.* (1982). *British Picture Vocabulary Test.* Windsor, UK: NFER.

CARS: Schopler, E. *et al.* (1988). *The Childhood Autism Rating Scale.* Los Angeles, CA: Western Psychological Services.

CAST: Scott, F.J., Baron-Cohen, S., Bolton, P. and Brayne, C. (2002). The CAST (Childhood Asperger Syndrome Test): Preliminary development of a UK screen for mainstream primary-aged children. *Autism: the International Journal of Research and Practice*, 6, 9–31.

CBT: Hare, D.J. (1997). The use of cognitive behavioural therapy with people with Asperger syndrome: A case study. *Autism: The International Journal of Research and Practice*, 1, 215–25.

CCC: Bishop, D.V.M. (1989). *Checklist of Communicative Competence.* Cambridge, UK: Applied Psychology Unit.

CHAT: Baron-Cohen, S., Allen, J. and Gillberg, C. (1992). Can autism be detected at

18 months? The needle, the haystack and the CHAT. *British Journal of Psychiatry*, 161, 839–43.

Child talk: Aldred, C. (2002). Child's Talk: Early communication intervention for children with autism and pervasive developmental disorders. *Good Autism Practice*, 3, 1, 44–57.

Circles of friends: Whitaker, P., Barratt, P., Joy, H., Potter, M. and Thomas, G. (1998). Children with autism and peer group support: Using 'Circles of Friends'. *British Journal of Special Education*, 25, 60–4.

COMFOR: Noens, I. and Van Berckelaer-Onnes, I. (2002). In OTHER words: Augmentative communication for people with learning difficulties. Video and brochure. Leiden, NL: University of Leiden.

Communicative gestures: Potter, C. and Whittaker, C. (2000). *Enabling Communication in Children with Autism*. London: Jessica Kingsley.

CSA: Riding, R.J. (1991). *Cognitive Styles Analysis*. Birmingham, UK: Learning and Training Technology.

Diagnostic criteria – DSM-IV-TR: American Psychiatric Association (APA) (2000). *Diagnostic and Statistical Manual of Mental Disorders (DSM IV-TR)*. Washington, DC: American Psychiatric Press.

Diagnostic criteria – ICD 10. World Health Organization (1992). *International Classification of Diseases*, 10, Geneva: WHO.

DISCO: Wing, L., Leekham, S.R., Libby, S.J., Gould, J. and Larcombe, M. (2002). The diagnostic interview for social and communication disorders: Background, inter-rater reliability and clinical use. *Journal of Child Psychology and Psychiatry*, 43, 307–25.

DLT (Higashi): Kitahara, K. (1984). *Daily Life Therapy*, vols 1, 2 and 3. Boston, MA: Nimrod Press.

EarlyBird: Shields, J. (2001). NAS EarlyBird programme: Partnership with parents in early intervention. *Autism: The International Journal of Research and Practice*, 5, 1, 49–56.

Floor-time: Wieder, S. and Greenspan, S.I. (2003). Climbing the symbolic ladder in the DIR model through floor time/ interactive play. *Autism: The International Journal of Research and Practice*, 7, 425–35.

Frameworks for communication: Chandler, S., Christie, P., Newson, E. and Prevezer, W. (2002). Developing a diagnostic and intervention package for 2 to 3-year-olds with autism: outcomes of the Frameworks for Communication approach. *Autism: The International Journal of Research and Practice*, 6, 47–70.

HANEN: Sussman, F (1999) *More than Words: A Revised HANEN Programme*. New Brunswick: The Hanen Centre.

Intensive interacton: Nind, M. and Hewett, D. (1994). *Access to Communication*. London: David Fulton.

Mindreading: Howlin, P., Baron-Cohen, S. and Hadwin, J. (1999). *Teaching Children with Autism to Mind-Read: A Practical Guide*. Chichester: Wiley.

MLU: Mean Length of Utterance.

PECS: Bondy, A. S. and Frost, L. A. (1994). The Picture Exchange Communication System. *Focus on Autistic Behaviour*, 9, 1–19.

Play and drama: Sherratt, D. and Peter, M. (2002). *Developing Play and Drama in Children with Autistic Spectrum Disorders*. London: David Fulton.

PVC: Kiernan, C.C. and Reid, B. (1987). *Pre-verbal Communication Schedule.* Windsor: NFER.

Sociability scale: White, C. (2002). The Social Play Record: The development and evaluation of a new instrument for assessing and guiding the social interaction of children with autistic spectrum disorders. *Good Autism Practice,* 3, 1, 63–78.

Social skills groups: Howlin, P. and Yates, P. (1999). The potential effectiveness of social skills groups for adults with autism. *Autism: the International Journal of Research and Practice* 3, 299–307.

Social stories: Gray, C.A. (1994). *The Social Stories Book.* Arlington, TX: Future Horizons.

Son-Rise (Option): Kaufman, B. (1994). *Son-Rise: The Miracle Continues.* Tiburon, CA: Kramer.

SULP: Rinaldi, W. (2000). *Language Difficulties in an Educational Context.* London: Whurr Publications.

TEACCH: Schopler, E., Mesibov, G. and Hearsey, K. (1995). Structured teaching in the TEACCH approach. In E. Schopler and G. Mesibov (eds), *Learning and Cognition in Autism.* New York: Plenum Press.

TROG: Bishop, D.V.M. (1989b). *Test of Reception of Grammar.* Cambridge, UK: Applied Psychology Unit.

REFERENCES

Aldred, C. (2002). Child's talk: Early communication intervention for children with autism and pervasive developmental disorders. *Good Autism Practice,* 3, 1, 44–57.

American Psychiatric Association (APA) (2000). *Diagnostic and Statistical Manual of the Mental Disorders (Fourth Edition-Text Revision, DSM-IV-TR).* Washington, DC: APA.

Baron-Cohen, S. (1995). *Mindblindness: An Essay on Autism and Theory of Mind.* Cambridge, MA: MIT Press.

Baron-Cohen, S., Allen, J. and Gillberg, C. (1992). Can autism be detected at 18 months? The needle, the haystack and the CHAT. *British Journal of Psychiatry,* 161, 839–43.

Bondy, A.S. and Frost, L.A. (1994). The Picture Exchange Communication System. *Focus on Autistic Behaviour,* 9, 1–19.

Chandler, S., Christie, P., Newson, E. and Prevezer, W. (2002). Developing a diagnostic and intervention package for 2 to 3 year olds with autism: Outcomes of the Frameworks for Communication approach. *Autism: The International Journal of Research and Practice,* 6, 47–70.

Cooper, J., Heron, T. and Heward, W. (2006). *Applied Behaviour Analysis* (2nd edn). New York: Prentice-Hall.

Frith, U. (2003). *Autism: Explaining the Enigma* (2nd edn). Oxford: Blackwells.

Gray, C.A. (1994). *The Social Stories Book.* Arlington, TX: Future Horizons.

Happé, F. (1994). *Autism: An Introduction to Psychological Theory.* London: UCL Press.

Hobson, R.P. (2002). *The Cradle of Thought.* Oxford: Macmillan.

Howlin, P. and Yates, P. (1999). The potential effectiveness of social skills groups for adults with autism. *Autism: The International Journal of Research and Practice*, 3, 299–307.

Kanner, L. (1943). Autistic disturbances of affective contact. *Nervous Child*, 2, 217–50.

Kaufman, B. (1994). *Son-Rise: The Miracle Continues*. Tiburon, CA: Kramer.

Kitahara, K. (1984). *Daily Life Therapy: A method of educating autistic children. Record of Actual Education at Musashino Higashi Gakuen School, Japan* (3 vols). Boston, MA: Nimrod Press.

Lord, C., Rutter, M. and LeCouteur, A. (1994). Autistic Diagnostic Interview-Revised: A revised version of a diagnostic interview for caregivers of individuals with possible pervasive developmental disorder. *Journal of Autism and Developmental Disorders*, 24, 659–85.

Lovaas, O. (1987). Behavioural treatment and normal educational and intellectual functioning in young autistic children. *Journal of Consulting and Clinical Psychology*, 55, 3–9.

Lovaas, O. and Smith, T. (2003). Early and intensive behavioural intervention for autism. In A. Kazdin, and J. Weisz (eds), *Evidence Based Psychotherapies for Children and Adolescents* (pp. 325–40). New York: Guilford.

Nind, M. and Hewett, D. (1994). *Access to Communication*. London: David Fulton.

Noens, I. and Van Berckelaer-Onnes, I. (2002). In OTHER words: augmentative communication for people with learning difficulties. Video and brochure Leiden, NL: University of Leiden.

Potter, C. and Whittaker, C. (2000). *Enabling Communication in Children with Autism*. London: Jessica Kingsley.

Russell, J. (ed.) (1997). *Autism as an Executive Disorder*. Oxford: Oxford University Press.

Schopler, E. (1997). Implementation of TEACCH philosophy. In D. Cohen and F. Volkmar (eds.), *Handbook of Autism and Pervasive Developmental Disorders* (2nd edn, pp. 767–95). New York: Wiley.

Schopler, E., Mesibov, G. and Hearsey, K. (1995). Structured teaching in the TEACCH approach. In E. Schopler and G. Mesibov (eds). *Learning and Cognition in Autism*. New York: Plenum Press.

Scott, F.J., Baron-Cohen, S., Bolton, P. and Brayne, C. (2002). The CAST (Childhood Asperger Syndrome Test): Preliminary development of a UK screen for mainstream primary-aged children. *Autism: the International Journal of Research and Practice*, 6, 9–31.

Shields, J. (2001). NAS EarlyBird programme: Partnership with parents in early intervention. *Autism: the International Journal of Research and Practice*, 5, 1, 49–56.

Smith, T. (1999). Outcome of early intervention for children with autism. *Clinical Psychology: Science and Practice*, 6, 33–49.

Sussman, F. (1999). *More than Words: A Revised HANEN Programme*. New Brunswick: The Hanen Centre.

Whitaker, P., Baratt, P., Joy, H., Potter, M. and Thomas, G. (1998). Children with autism and peer group support: Using 'Circles of Friends'. *British Journal of Special Education*, 25, 60–4.

Wieder, S. and Greenspan, S.I. (2003). Climbing the symbolic ladder in the DIR model through floor time/ interactive play. *Autism: The International Journal of Research and Practice*, 7, 425–35.

Wing, L., Leekham, S.R., Libby, S.J., Gould, J. and Larcombe, M. (2002). The diagnostic interview for social and communication disorders: background, inter-rater reliability and clinical use. *Journal of Child Psychology and Psychiatry*, 43, 307–25.

World Health Organization (WHO) (1992). *Tenth Revision of the International Classification of Diseases and Related Health Problems* (ICD–10). Geneva: WHO.

World Health Organization (WHO) (1996). *Multiaxial Classification of Child and Adolescent Psychiatric Disorders: The ICD–10 Classification of Mental and Behavioural Disorders in Children and Adolescents.* Cambridge: Cambridge University Press.

Middle childhood

Chapter 16

Educating children with intellectual disability and autism-spectrum disorders

Michael L. Wehmeyer and Suk-Hyang Lee

That children with intellectual disability (ID) and autism-spectrum disorders have a right to educational services has become an internationally acknowledged standard for practice. For example, participants representing ninety-two governments at the 1994 UNESCO World Conference on Special Needs Education at Salamanca, Spain passed *The Salamanca Statement and Framework for Action on Special Needs Education*, espousing the beliefs that:

- Every child has a fundamental right to education, and must be given the opportunity to achieve and maintain an acceptable level of learning;
- Every child has unique characteristics, interests, abilities and learning needs;
- Education systems should be designed and educational programmes implemented to take into account the wide diversity of these characteristics and needs;
- Those with special educational needs (SEN) must have access to regular schools which should accommodate them within a child-centred pedagogy capable of meeting these needs; and
- Regular schools with this inclusive orientation are the most effective means of combating discriminatory attitudes, creating welcoming communities, building an inclusive society and achieving education for all; moreover, they provide an effective education to the majority of children and improve the efficiency and ultimately the cost-effectiveness of the entire education system (pp. viii–ix).

The Salamanca Statement provides a succinct summary of the ideal to which most countries strive with regard to the education of children with SEN and a description of what is considered 'best practice' in the education of children with ID or autism-spectrum disorders. This chapter focuses on how best to meet the educational needs of students with ID and autism spectrum disorders, particularly during elementary and middle-school years, within the framework outlined in the Salamanca Statement. The chapter overviews historical models of education for children with ID and autism-spectrum disorders, examines the evidence base for and benefits of inclusive educational practices, and overviews high-quality curricular and instructional methods, materials, and strategies that support the progress of students with ID within inclusive settings. The chapter concludes with recommendations to clinical psychologists regarding how best to work with teachers, parents, and other persons involved in the education of students with ID.

EFFECTIVE SPECIAL EDUCATION PRACTICES I

Where should students with intellectual disability and autism-spectrum disorders be taught?

The compulsory education of children with ID or autism-spectrum disorders is, historically, a contemporary idea. Indeed, the notion that children with ID could be educated at all is a fairly recent phenomenon. Prior to the nineteenth century, people with ID were seen as uneducable. This began to change with the 1801 publication of French physician Jean-Marc Gaspard Itard's *De l'éducation de l'homme sauvage* (published in English in 1802). The story of Itard's attempts to teach 'Victor, the wild boy of Aveyron' is, by now, well known. Those efforts are viewed as the first attempts to educate a person with ID. His pupil, Edouard Seguin, is generally recognized as implementing the first systematic approach to educating persons with ID, the 'Physiological Method', described in the publication of *Traitement moral, hygiène et education des idiots* in 1846. Seguin's methods were influential, first on the continent and then in the UK with the English translation of his 1846 text, and later in the US with the 1866 publication of a revised version of the text.

Both Itard and Seguin worked in the context of institutions. As the movement toward educating individuals with ID gained momentum through the efforts of physicians such as J. J. Guggenbuhl (Switzerland), William Wetherspoon Ireland (Scotland), John Langdon Down (England), and Hervey Backus Wilbur (US) and social reformers like Samuel Gridley Howe (US), it remained firmly entrenched in institutional settings. With the advent of the nineteenth century, institutions that previously had an educative mission became larger and primarily custodial (Trent, 1994). With the growth of the eugenics movement in the first half of the twentieth century, most of the early institutional emphasis on education disappeared entirely.

It is worth documenting this historical bias toward segregated settings and the education of people with ID because when an educative focus reemerged for students with ID in the second half of the twentieth century and compulsory education became an international standard, the starting point to address the question of where students with intellectual and other developmental disabilities should be educated was in segregated, congregate settings. Although most developed countries began serving students with SEN in publicly supported school settings by the early twentieth century, an outcome of compulsory school attendance laws enacted in England in the 1870s and the US in the early 1900s (Florian and Pullin, 2000), most children with ID were not included, instead being primarily served in increasingly larger custodial institutions, if served at all.

Not surprisingly, then, the earliest post-World War II models for educating students with ID involved the establishment of separate schools. In most developed countries, the deinstitutionalization movement (e.g. movement of people with ID from large institutions to community-based settings) preceded or paralleled the establishment of compulsory education, and thus children who were previously living in institutions were being moved into the community. As such, the post-war emphasis on education did not occur in the context of institutions, by and large, but in separate schools and, later, separate classrooms in typical schools.

From segregated schools to mainstreaming

In theory, one can describe a progression of models to serve the SEN of students with ID and autism-spectrum disorders as beginning with the above-mentioned separate schools and progressing to inclusive practices. For reasons described subsequently, the efficacy of separate schools and, eventually, self-contained classrooms in typical schools began to be questioned, with a particular focus on the social benefits of children with ID interacting with children without disabilities. It should be emphasized that the separate school or classroom model was not based on empirical evidence of its efficacy compared with other models, but instead on assumptions about the potential benefits, often financial, of serving students in homogeneous groups and bringing services and personnel to them (Gartner and Lipsky, 1987) and on the historical precedence of institutional settings for this population.

The most evident drawback of a model based on homogenous grouping is that students with ID have only other students with intellectual or other disabilities as role models. Increasingly, advocates for students with severe disabilities, who were more likely to be served in segregated settings, began to question the wisdom and efficacy of models based on homogeneous grouping. The initial response to these concerns involved the establishment of 'mainstreaming' efforts. The initial goal of the mainstreaming movement was to provide 'every student who is exceptional, regardless of type and severity of disability, with an appropriate education, as much as possible, alongside normally developing peers' (Winzer, 2000). As it was most frequently implemented, mainstreaming resulted in programmes in which children with ID continued to be grouped homogeneously, typically by level of cognitive impairment and age, but were 'integrated' into classes other than core academic areas. This typically involved students with ID going to physical education, art, and music classes with their non-disabled peers (Stainback, Stainback and Forest, 1989; Turnbull and Schultz, 1979). In many cases, students with the most severe disabilities were not involved even in this level of integration.

The increasing dissatisfaction with the progress of the mainstreaming movement led to the emergence of the inclusion movement. Gartner and Lipsky (1987) spoke for many, noting:

> While special education programmes of the past decade have been successful in bringing unserved students into public education and have established their right to education, these programmes have failed both to overcome the separation between general and special education and to make the separate system significant in terms of student benefits.
>
> (1987: 368)

The Green Paper *Excellence for All Children: Meeting Special Educational Needs*, issued in 1998 by the Department for Education and Skills, included language concerning the importance of inclusive practices, stating:

> The ultimate purpose of SEN provision is to enable young people to flourish in adult life. There are therefore strong educational, as well as social and moral, grounds for educating children with SEN with their peers. We aim to increase the level and quality of inclusion within mainstream schools, while protecting and enhancing specialist provision for those who need it.

As illustrated by the Salamanca Statement and the Green Paper, it is clear that inclusion has become the standard against which other models of educational provision are measured (Bergsson, Wood and Quirk, 2003; Harris, 2002). In fact, there is now a sizeable body of literature examining the efficacy of inclusive practices on multiple outcomes relevant to SEN populations. The following section defines inclusion, overviews two generations of the inclusion movement, and synthesizes the literature pertaining to the efficacy of inclusive practices.

From mainstreaming to inclusion

One frequently reads that 'inclusion' as a construct is not well defined. That may be, although it is usually the case that statements to that end are made by proponents of other models of service delivery who embrace some aspects of inclusion, but seek to retain aspects of what is referred to as 'the pull-out' model. This is where students with SEN receive some of their supports in the general education classroom and receive specialized supports outside that classroom based on unique needs of a given population, including students with specific intellectual disability (Kauffman and Hallahan, 1995) or students who are deaf (Winzer, 2000). In fact, it was the impact of children coming and going from mainstream educational classrooms that, in many ways, precipitated the call for 'full inclusion' and moved best practices away from a mainstreaming model (Schnorr, 1990).

It may be more accurate to state that there has been no single definition of inclusion that has been widely adopted. Most such definitions, however, resonate around common themes and vary primarily in their breadth or focus. For example, Lipsky and Gartner (1997) defined inclusion as:

> the provision of services to students with disabilities, including those with severe impairments, in the neighbourhood school, in age appropriate general education classes, with the necessary support services and supplementary aides (for the child and teacher) both to assure the child's success – academic, behavioural and social – and to prepare the child to participate as a full and contributing member of society.
>
> (1997: 763)

Zionts (1997) defined inclusion as referring to a:

> commitment to educate children and youth with disabilities in general education classrooms, to the maximum extent possible. Inclusion involves transporting support services to students in general classrooms, as opposed to pulling students out for services. Moreover, unlike mainstreaming, inclusion requires only that students profit from being in a general education classroom.
>
> (1997: 16)

Finally, Stainback and Stainback (1990) defined an inclusive school as one in which:

> Everyone belongs, is accepted, supports, and is supported by his or her peers and other members of the school community in the course of having his or her educational needs met.
>
> (1990: 3)

As illustrated above, definitions of inclusion range from specific supports in classrooms to statements of civil rights. Turnbull, Turnbull, Shank, Smith, and Leal (2002) provided a useful means to conceptualize the inclusion movement by describing two generations of inclusion.

Two generations of inclusion

According to Turnbull and colleagues (2002), the inclusion movement can best be described as two generations of related, though distinct, activities. According to these authors, first-generation inclusion focused on the basics of integrating students with disabilities into the general education classroom, and efforts during this time period were instrumental in changing prevailing educational settings for students with disabilities from primarily separate, self-contained settings to integration in the regular or mainstream education classroom. These basics of integration could be summarized in three 'key components of first-generation inclusion':

- All students receive education in the school they would attend if they had no disability.
- School and general education placements are age- and grade-appropriate.
- Special education supports exist within the general education class (p. 80).

The first-generation inclusion was characterized by Turnbull *et al.* (2002) as additive in nature. That is, resources and students were 'added' to the general education classroom. The second generation of inclusive practices was more generative in nature, in that instead of focusing on moving students from separate settings to regular classroom settings, efforts focused on improving practice in the general education classroom. Research and practice during this phase emphasized aspects of instructional practices that promoted inclusion, such as differentiated instruction and cooperative learning, several of which are described subsequently.

Efficacy of inclusive practices

Over the 1990s there emerged a convincing database with regard to the impact of first- and second-generation inclusive practices on educational outcomes (Farrell, 2000; McGregor and Vogelsberg, 1998). McGregor and Vogelsberg (1998) conducted an extensive review of the literature on pedagogical and research foundations for inclusive practices, examining the outcomes of inclusive practices on students with disabilities, their parents, and students without disabilities.

The outcomes of this review are synthesized in Table 16.1. As illustrated by this table, there is now sufficient evidence that students with disabilities who receive their education in inclusive settings have more positive educational outcomes than peers who do not, including enhanced opportunities to interact socially with peers, enhanced task engagement, improved skills acquisition, and enhanced social competence. This is achieved without cost to students without disabilities, who realize socially valued outcomes related to greater tolerance for diversity.

Table 16.1 Outcomes of inclusive schooling practices

Theme	Indicators	Key References
Skills acquisition for students with disabilities	• Students with disabilities demonstrate high levels of social interaction in settings with their typical peers, but placement alone does not guarantee positive social outcomes	Fryxell and Kennedy, 1995; Guralnick and Groom, 1988; Kennedy, Shukla and Fryxell, 1997; McDonnell, Hardman, Hightower and Kiefer-O'Donnell, 1991; Sale and Carey, 1995
	• Social competence and communication skills improve when students with disabilities are educated in inclusive settings	Cole and Meyer, 1991; Hunt, Alwell, Farron-Davis and Goetz, 1996; Jenkins, Odom and Speltz, 1989
	• Students with disabilities have demonstrated gains in other areas of development when they are educated in inclusive settings	Hunt, Farron-Davis, Beckstead, Curtis and Goetz, 1994; McDougall and Brady, 1998; Wang and Birch, 1984
	• Interactive, small group contexts facilitate skill acquisition and social acceptance for students with disabilities in general education classrooms	Hunt, Staub, Alwell and Goetz, 1994; Johnson, Johnson and Anderson, 1983; Wang and Birch, 1984
Social outcomes for students with disabilities	• Friendships do develop between students with disabilities and their typical peers in inclusive settings	Kennedy, Shukla and Fryxell, 1997; Meyer et al., 1998; Staub, Schwartz, Gallucci and Peck, 1994
	• Teachers play a critical role in facilitating friendships between students with disabilities and their typical peers	Janney and Snell, 1996; Kozleski and Jackson, 1993
	• Friendship and membership is facilitated by longitudinal involvement in the classroom and routine activities of the school	Hanline, 1993; Schnorr, 1990; Schnorr, 1997
Impact on students without disabilities	• The performance of typically developing students is not compromised by the presence of students with disabilities in their classrooms	Dugan, Kamps, Leonard, Watkins, Rheinberger and Stackhaus, 1995; Hollowood, Salisbury, Rainforth and Palombaro, 1994/1995; Hunt, Staub, Alwell and Goetz, 1994; McDonnell, Thorson, McQuivey and Kiefer-O'Donnell, 1997
	• Typically developing students derive benefits from their involvement and relationship with students with disabilities	Giangreco, Edelman, Cloninger and Dennis, 1993; Helmstetter, Peck and Giangreco, 1994; Peck, Donaldson and Pezzoli, 1990
	• The presence of students with disabilities in the general education classroom provides a catalyst for learning opportunities and experiences that might not otherwise be part of the curriculum	Evans, Salisbury, Palombaro and Goldberg, 1994; York and Tundidor, 1995

(Continued overleaf)

Table 16.1 Continued

Theme	Indicators	Key References
Impact on parents	• Parent support for inclusion is positively impacted by actual experience with this approach to education, although experience alone does not shape attitudes	Green and Shinn, 1994; Green and Stoneman, 1989; Palmer, Borthwick-Duffy and Widaman, 1998
	• Parents of students with disabilities are looking for positive attitudes, good educational opportunities, and acceptance of their child among educators	Giangreco, Cloninger, Mueller, Yuan and Ashworth, 1991; Green and Shinn, 1994
Impact on teachers	• Although many teachers are initially reluctant about inclusion, they become confident in their abilities with support and experience	Bennett, DeLuca and Bruns, 1997; Giangreco, Dennis, Cloninger, Edelman and Schattman, 1993b; Salend, Johansen, Mumper, Chase, Pike and Dorney, 1997
	• Support from other teachers is a powerful and necessary resource to empower teachers to problem-solve new instructional challenges	Pugach and Johnson, 1995; Salend, Johansen, Mumper, Chase, Pike and Dorney, 1997; Wood, 1998
	• Facilitating the inclusion of students with disabilities requires the sensitivity to make on-the-spot judgements about the type and amount of support to encourage participation while not interfering with student interactions	Ferguson, Meyer, Janchild, Juniper and Zingo, 1992; Olson, Chalmers and Hoover, 1997
Programme related outcomes	• These is some evidence to suggest that while start-up costs may initially increase the cost of inclusive services, the costs over time decrease, and are likely to be less than segregated forms of service delivery	McLaughlin and Warren, 1994; Pugach and Johnson, 1995

There are several caveats to these generally positive findings. Among them is the finding that proximity alone does not guarantee positive outcomes (Nakken and Pijl, 2002). Student presence in the general education classroom is a necessary but not sufficient step towards student success in the classroom. A characteristic of the first two generations of inclusive practices was that they focused primarily on 'where' the student received his or her education, with the concomitant development of strategies to ensure that students were supported in such environments. There was, however, less focus on what it was that students were learning. Additionally, the preponderance of studies focused on the social benefits of inclusion. There is evidence that students with disabilities benefit academically from inclusion, but the knowledge base to substantiate that is only just emerging. These caveats form the starting point for a third generation of inclusive practices (see below) which describes what should be expected with regard to high-quality educational services for students with ID and autism-spectrum disorders.

The efficacy of special education

Having described the historical models of service delivery for students with ID or autism-spectrum disorders and establishing the efficacy of inclusive practices, it is important to take a step back to examine the broader question of the efficacy of special needs education (SNE). That is, SNE is premised on the hypothesis that students with disabilities benefit from specially designed instruction. There is, by now, a large body of evidence that people with ID can acquire new knowledge and skills across multiple domains (Kavale and Forness, 1999). Saying that students with ID can learn is, however, not the same as saying that special educational services are effective.

There are, however, several meta-analytic studies that have examined the efficacy of special education. Kavale and Forness (1999) conducted a meta-analysis of meta-analytic studies examining special education interventions for students with intellectual disability. This review found moderate effects for most interventions that are, typically, found only in special needs education (e.g. social skills training), but strategies found in inclusive settings, including direct instruction, peer tutoring, computer-assisted instruction, behaviour management, and early intervention all were found to produce positive effects for this population of students.

Summary

The basic message from this section is that SNE services are effective and students with ID benefit more when receiving high-quality instruction with empirically validated methods in the general education classroom. The description of models addressing the question of where students with intellectual disability or autism-spectrum disorders receive their education began with the qualified statement that: 'In theory' one could describe a progression of models to serve students with ID and autism-spectrum disorders, beginning with separate schools and progressing to inclusive models. It will not take long for clinical psychologists who interact with schools to recognize that what is theoretically a progression from one model to the next has become, in essence, a continuum. In fact, versions of all of the above-mentioned models can be found in practice. The existence of such a continuum should not, however, be interpreted to mean that a continuum of service delivery models is best practice. Optimally, students with ID or autism-spectrum disorders should be educated in the general education classroom, along the lines of the principles described as representing first-generation inclusion, and using support methods identified through the second generation of inclusion programmes.

EFFECTIVE SPECIAL EDUCATION PRACTICES II

What and how should students with intellectual disability and autism-spectrum disorders be taught?

If the first two generations of the inclusion movement focused on where a student should receive his or her educational programme and ways to support students in that setting, the third generation takes as its foundation the assumptions of previous generations and turns attention to what students with ID are taught and how best to support learning. Nothing about the first or second generations of inclusion is either obsolete or unimportant. Both remain critical to ensure high-quality educational programmes for students with ID. The need to consider issues pertaining to third-generation inclusion is, in fact, an outcome of the success of these first two generations' efforts. That is, as more students with ID are successfully educated in the general education classroom, expectations for students has become higher, such that the field is at a point in the evolution of inclusive practices where there is a need to consider not only how to maximize participation in the general classroom but also how to maximize participation and progress in the general curriculum (Hanko, 2003; Wehmeyer, Sands *et al.*, 2002).

The earliest 'special education' curricula were, largely, watered-down versions of the regular curriculum for students with mild cognitive disabilities and life skills curricula for students with more severe disabilities. The implementation of curriculum modifications, particularly curriculum adaptations, became more commonplace for students with mild cognitive impairments, including students with specific intellectual disability and mild levels of ID. For students whose intellectual disability posed more barriers to learning, curriculum decisions became, largely, associated with their educational placement. That is, schools continued to provide services that placed students with ID in classrooms based on the level of their intellectual impairment (mild, moderate, or severe/profound). Changes in the way in which ID is conceptualized along with the impetus to move beyond first- and second-generation inclusion practices have laid the groundwork for a third generation of inclusive practices. This section overviews key elements of that third generation of practices, beginning with a brief examination of how changing views of disability impact educational practices.

Defining intellectual disabilities and education

Historically, the ways in which intellectual disability has been conceptualized and defined has had limited impact on educational programming, with the exception that a student's educational programme has tended to be based on the student's level of functioning. Increasingly, the field is moving away from deficits models of classifications towards functional models of disability, a move that has direct impact on educational programming for students with ID. Perhaps the most visible of these 'functional' models is the World Health Organization's *International Classification of Functioning, Disability, and Health* (ICF) (WHO, 2001). The ICF and similar frameworks are 'functional' classification systems because disability is seen as an outcome of the inter-action between a person's limitations and the environmental context in which that person must function (Luckasson, Borthwick-Duffy, Buntinx, Coulter *et al.*, 2002). Disability, within ICF-like models, is not something a person has or something that is a *characteristic of the person*, but is instead a *state of functioning* in which limitations in functional capacity and adaptive skills must be considered *within the context* of environments and supports. In 1992, the American Association on Mental Retardation introduced a definition and classification system aligned with the ICF functional model that, accord-ing to the manual's authors, 'reflects a changing paradigm [in the field of intellectual disability], a more *functional* [italics added] definition, and a focus on the interaction between the person, the environment, and the intensities and patterns of needed supports' (Luckasson, Coulter, Polloway, Reiss *et al.*, 1992: x).

The impact of the shift to a functional model on educational programming involves an increased emphasis on the design of supports to enable a student to function within his or her context, and a de-emphasis on trying to fix the student. The 1992 system eliminated classification of students into levels of ID, and identified four intensities of needed supports upon which to base instructional or support design. These intensities are categorized as:

- **Intermittent:** High- or low-intensity supports on an 'as needed' basis, episodic, or short-term supports needed during life-span transition.
- **Limited:** Time-limited but not of an intermittent nature, requiring fewer staff members and less cost than more intense levels of support.
- **Extensive:** Supports characterized by regular involvement (e.g. daily) in at least some environments (such as work or home) and not time-limited (e.g. long-term support and long-term home living support).
- **Pervasive:** Supports characterized by their constancy, high intensity; pro-vided across environments; potential life-sustaining nature. Pervasive supports typically involve more staff members and intrusiveness than do extensive or time-limited supports. (Luckasson *et al.*, 1992: 26)

Defining supports

The 1992 AAMR manual defined supports as:

Resources and strategies that promote the interests and causes of indi-viduals with or without disabilities; that enable them to access resources, information and relationships inherent within integrated work and living

environments; and that result in their enhanced interdependence, productivity, community integration, and satisfaction.

(Luckasson *et al.*, 1992: 101)

Luckasson and Spitalnik (1994) suggested that 'supports refer to an array,
not a continuum, of services, individuals, and settings that match the person's
needs' (p. 88). There are several aspects of a supports model that differentiate
it from previous models. First, as identified in the AAMR manual, supports:
(1) pertain to resources and strategies; (2) enable individuals to access other
resources, information, and relationships within integrated environments;
and (3) their use results in increased integration and enhanced personal
growth and development (Luckasson *et al.*, 1992: 102). In other words, supports have the unambiguous intent to enhance community integration and
inclusion by enabling people to access a wide array of resources, information,
and relationships. Second, supports are individually designed and determined
with the active involvement of key stakeholders in the process, particularly
the person benefiting from that support. Third, a supports model requires an
active and ongoing evaluation of the ecological aspects of the 'disability'
(because the 'disability' can only be defined within the context of the functional limitation and the social context) and efforts to design supports focus
heavily on changing aspects of the environment or social context or providing
individuals with additional skills or strategies to overcome barriers in those
environments.

Education's use of definitions

Historically, the definition and classification process was relevant primarily in
the process of diagnosis (usually the responsibility of psychologists, not educators) and placement decisions. Typical SNE services created 'programmes'
for students with mild, moderate, or severe/profound ID, and students were
placed in those programmes based on their diagnosis. By and large, there
was little impact of the definition and classification system on the *ways* in
which teachers taught students with ID, although one could argue that the
placement decision in essence determined the instructional programme.

Functional definitions of ID require, however, that educators attend to
constitutive aspects of the definition, with particular emphasis on the functional relationship between environment and social context and the person's
functional limitations. While such models make the diagnostic process more
complex, an issue clinical psychologists will certainly encounter, it is worth
keeping in mind that such models make the definition and classification process *more relevant* to instruction and the educational process, particularly in
the context of promoting access to the general curriculum and achieving a
third generation of inclusive practices.

Characteristics of third-generation inclusive practices

Third-generation inclusive practices have several features distinguishing them from first- and second-generation practices. In particular, third-generation practices embody overarching principles that extend the focus of inclusion from 'where' a student receives his or her education to 'what' is the content of that educational programme. Third-generation practices incorporate principles and practices from first- and second-generation inclusive practices to enable students with disabilities to progress in the general curriculum (e.g. the school's curriculum for all students) within the context of the general education classroom through the implementation of school-wide interventions based on the principles of universal design for learning.

More specifically, third-generation practices discard as obsolete the notion that educational programming is in any way derived from diagnostic features associated with levels of ID and, instead, focus on identifying support needs and designing supports and curriculum modifications to design individually appropriate educational programmes drawing on both the general curriculum and unique student learning needs. This section introduces issues of access to the general curriculum, universal design for learning, and school-wide interventions as overarching characteristics of third-generation inclusive practices. A subsequent section provides descriptions of classroom and individual instructional strategies, methods, and materials that support inclusion and progress in the general curriculum.

Access to the general curriculum

School reform efforts in both the UK and North America have emphasized the goal that students with SEN have the opportunity to receive instruction in the general curriculum (McLaughlin and Tilstone, 2000; Sebba, Thurlow and Goertz, 2000). This is, variously, to ensure that students with SEN are not left out of mechanisms to ensure accountability for educational outcomes, to raise expectations for students with SEN, and to counter the trend towards student curriculum as derived from disability labels. Such reform efforts provide a unique opportunity to focus attention on the content of the educational programmes of students with ID instead of just where students receive their education. The emphasis on instruction in the general curriculum is propelled by research in first- and second-generation inclusive practices that students with ID and other disabilities can achieve more positive academic outcomes in the context of the general education classroom.

Third-generation inclusive practices presume students with ID are educated in the general education classroom. This presumption is based both on findings from research in previous generations of inclusive practices and on emerging research showing that the 'place' in which students with ID receive access to the general curriculum is, in fact, in the general education classroom, not in segregated settings (Wehmeyer, Lattin, Lapp-Rincker and Agran, 2003).

Wehmeyer, Sands, Knowlton, and Kozleski (2002) identified five steps (Table 16.2) to ensure students with ID gain access to the general curriculum. Issues of educational planning, curriculum modification, universal design, and school-wide, group, and individually designed interventions are addressed subsequently. First, however, if students with widely varying skills, backgrounds, knowledge, and customs are to progress in the general curriculum, the standards upon which the curriculum is based, as well as the curriculum itself, must embody the principles of universal design, discussed subsequently, and be written to be open-ended and inclusive, not close-ended. The terms open- and close-ended refer to 'the amount of specificity and direction provided by curriculum standards, benchmarks, goals or objectives at both the building and classroom levels' (Wehmeyer, Sands et al., 2002). Close-ended standards are specific and require narrowly defined outcomes or performance indicators. Open-ended standards do not restrict the ways in which students exhibit knowledge or skills and focus more on the expectations that students will interact with the content, ask questions, manipulate materials, make observations, and then communicate their knowledge in a variety of ways. Research suggests that open-ended designs allow for greater flexibility as to what, when, and how topics will be addressed in the classroom (Stainback, Stainback, Stefanich, and Alper, 1996).

Table 16.2 Steps to gaining access to the general curriculum for students with intellectual disability

Action Step	Description
Standard setting and curriculum design	Standards are written as open-ended and the curriculum is planned and designed using principles of universal design that ensure that all students can show progress
Individualized educational planning	The individualized planning process ensures that a student's educational programme design is based on the general curriculum, taking into account unique student learning needs
School-wide materials and instruction	There is school-wide use of universally designed curricular materials and high-quality instructional methods and strategies that challenge all students
Partial school and group instruction	Groups of students who need more intensive instruction are targeted, and building and classroom instructional decision-making activities focus at the lesson, unit, and classroom level to ensure students can progress in the curriculum
Individualized interventions	Additional curricular content and instructional strategies are designed and implemented to ensure progress for students with learning needs not met by school-wide efforts or partial school efforts

Universal design for learning

The principle of universal design emerged initially from architecture. As applied to the built environment, the principle of universal design suggests that all buildings/environments should be accessible to all people (Moon, Hart, Komissar and Friedlander, 1995). This principle was, subsequently, applied to the design and development of consumer products and assistive devices with the same intent; that such products and devices should be accessible to all people. Universal design for learning, similarly, suggests that all 'learning' should be accessible to all students. Orkwis and McLane (1998) defined 'universal design for learning' as 'the design of instructional materials and activities that allows learning goals to be achievable by individuals with wide differences in their abilities to see, hear, speak, move, read, write, understand English, attend, organize, engage, and remember' (p. 9). Researchers at the Centre for Applied Special Technology (CAST, 1998–1999) suggested three essential *qualities* of universal design for learning. These qualities are that the curriculum is designed to: (1) provide *multiple representations* of content; (2) provide *multiple options for expression* and control; and (3) provide *multiple options for engagement* and motivation. These qualities are described in Table 16.3.

Most people think of universal design only as captioning videos, offering documents so students can change the font face, size and colour, or providing texts on computer disks so students can listen to them through screen-reading software. Providing flexible materials is certainly an important part of universal design for learning. However, for students with ID to succeed in accessing the general curriculum, educators must apply the principles of universal design to other aspects of the learning experience, including their teaching routines. Based on Bowe's (2000) examination of the principles of universal design as they applied to education, Wehmeyer, Lance, and Bashinski (2002) developed a list of universal design principles as they would apply to the curriculum for students with ID (see Table 16.4).

School-wide interventions

The implementation of school-wide interventions is both one of the distinguishing features of third-generation inclusive practices (compared to a focus primarily or exclusively on individualized interventions in the prior generations) and the third step in the process described in Table 16.2. School-wide interventions are those implemented throughout the school campus and which benefit all students (Morris and Parker, 1997). With regard to students with ID gaining access to the general curriculum, there are three school-wide interventions that warrant consideration, the first of which is the school-wide implementation of universally designed instructional materials and methods, described previously. The other two involve school-wide

Table 16.3 Features of universally designed curriculum (from CAST 1998–1999)

Feature	Description	Example
Curriculum provides multiple means of representation	Universally designed curricula accommodate diversity through alternative representations of key information. Students with different preferences and needs can either select the representational medium most suitable for them, or gather information from a variety of representational media simultaneously	World Wide Web pages: One of the benefits of the WWW over traditional mediums is the capacity to use graphic images in a variety of ways, from icons to hyperlinked pictures to streamed video. However, for a person who is blind or visually impaired who is using a text-reader to access the site, graphic depictions may make the site and the information contained therein inaccessible. As an alternative, accessible web sites include text descriptions of images and pictures. Similarly, the design of curricular materials should include multiple representations of important topics, features or points. Such multiple representations include a variety of methods of presentation of the material based on learner needs and characteristics. Students with ID, for example, need print-based information presented with graphic depictions, free from unnecessary clutter and with key information repeated or highlighted
Curriculum provides multiple means of presentation	Universally designed curricula modify the way information is conveyed or imparted to the student	Presentation of information has, historically, been through written formats (textbooks, student workbooks, etc.) or verbally (lectures). These primary means of presentation have drawbacks for many students who read ineffectively (or don't read at all) or who have difficulty attending to or understanding lecture-formats. There are a variety of ways of changing the presentation mode, from using film or video sources, to reading (or playing an audiotape of) written materials, to web-based information that can be read through text-reader programs or provided through digitized audio or video transmissions that accompany whatever representation means is used
Curriculum provides multiple means of student engagement	Curriculum adaptations that modify the student's engagement with the curriculum impact the ways in which students respond to the curriculum and show knowledge and skills	Typical means of student engagement within the curriculum involves written responses or, perhaps less frequently, oral responses. However, there are multiple other ways for students to respond to or engage in the curriculum, including artwork, photography, drama, music, animation, and video that would enable students to express their ideas and demonstrate their knowledge

Table 16.4 Principles of universal design applied to education

Principle	Explanation
Equitable use	Standards, curriculum, instructional interventions and educational materials should be 'designed' so they can be used by students with diverse linguistic, cognitive, communication, motor, and other abilities. One feature of equitable use is that to the largest degree possible designs should incorporate features that are necessary for people with disabilities, but which benefit everyone
Flexible use	The design of the curriculum should appeal to a wide range of user preferences and abilities. Materials should provide multiple means of representation, presentation and student expression
Simple and intuitive use	Materials are easy to use and avoid unnecessary complexity, directions clear and concise, examples provided
Perceptible information	Materials communicate needed information to user independent of ambient conditions or user's sensory abilities, essential information highlighted and redundancy included
Tolerance for error	Students have ample time to respond, are provided feedback, can undo previous responses, can monitor progress, and are provided with adequate practice time
Low physical and cognitive effort	Materials present information in chunks that can be completed in a reasonable time frame

implementation of high-quality instructional strategies and implementation of positive behaviour supports.

School-wide implementation of high-quality instructional strategies

The implementation of high-quality, empirically validated instructional strategies campus-wide is a critical feature of ensuring access for students with ID. Generally, it is important to remember that just as alignment of curriculum, instruction, and assessment practices is central to a high-quality educational programme for students who do not have a disability (English, 1992), the same is true for students who do have a disability – including ID. Instructional strategies that nurture the development of problem solving and critical thinking skills, as well as those that provide for active learning opportunities, are important for all students. Conversely, the fact that many instructional strategies developed for the purpose of individualizing instruction for students who have a disability, including ID, might well be of benefit to all students should not be overlooked. For example, there is considerable evidence that promoting the self-determination of children and youth with disabilities is an important instructional area if students are to become independent adults (Robertson, Emerson, Hatton, Gregeory, Kessissoglou, Hallam and Walsh, 2001; Wehmeyer, 2001; Wehmeyer, Abery, Mithaug and Stancliffe, 2003). It is almost always the case that school standards for all students include a focus on component elements of self-determined behaviour (e.g. goal setting, problem solving, decision-making, self-advocacy, self-management, etc.) and when such instruction is available school-wide, all students can benefit (Palmer, Wehmeyer, Gibson and Agran, 2004; Wehmeyer, Field, Doren, Jones and Mason, 2004).

Such implementation will include a wide array of interventions, including instructional strategies and classroom ecological interventions (Avramidis, Bayliss and Burden, 2002). For example, during the course of a school day, a teacher will utilize a variety of instructional groupings or arrangements (e.g. whole-class instruction, teacher-directed small-group instruction, cooperative learning groups, peer-directed instructional activities, independent seat work) through which to present lesson content. For students with ID (indeed students with disabilities in general), 'whole-class and independent seat work arrangements often pose the most problems' (Udvari-Solner, 1993: 4). Large-group instruction and independent seat work require all students to maintain attention over extended periods of time, interact only passively with the information to be learned, and self-reliantly to receive and process information that is presented in the same manner. To increase the likelihood that students who have ID will have access to the general curriculum, teachers should diversify their selection of instructional arrangements and not rely solely on these grouping strategies.

A critical school-wide strategy to ensure opportunities for all students to be actively involved in work tasks to the greatest extent possible is differentiated instruction. Differentiated instruction involves a teacher implementing a wider range of learning methodologies, increasing students' accessibility to instructional materials in a variety of formats, expanding test-taking parameters, and varying the complexity and nature of content presented during the course of a unit of study.

Research has demonstrated that teachers can effectively differentiate curricular content, the instructional process, product requirements, and/or assessment practices to facilitate students' access to, and success within, the general curriculum (Kronberg, 1999). Examples of curricular content differentiation include reducing the number of math problems assigned to certain students or giving students the option of taking a weekly spelling pre-test to opt out of spelling for that week.

Differentiating the instructional process can be accomplished through a myriad of techniques that, themselves, should be implemented school-wide to the benefit of all students, including providing visual or graphic organizers to accompany oral presentations; incorporating the use of models, demonstrations, or role play; utilizing teacher presentation cues (e.g. gestural, visual, or verbal) to emphasize key points; scaffolding key concepts to be learned; and getting students more actively involved in the learning process through the implementation of every pupil response techniques (e.g. lecture response cards, thumbs up / thumbs down) or the incorporation of manipulatives for student use (Janney and Snell, 2000).

In addition to the efficacy of these school-wide instructional strategies, research has empirically validated several ecological or environmental modifications to the physical conditions in which learning is to take place that should be implemented school-wide. It is commonly accepted that the environmental context of the school and classroom affects students' abilities to acquire information and demonstrate what they have learned. Adaptation of environmental conditions for students with ID enables them to better attend to and cope with the multiple demands that typify classroom instruction (Ault, Guy, Guess, Bashinski and Roberts, 1995; Siegel-Causey and Bashinski, 1997). The most obvious ecological modifications are those made for students who have sensory impairments, including modifications to lighting, glare, noise level, and providing visual cues to facilitate movement.

Positive behaviour supports

A final school-wide emphasis in third-generation inclusive practices is the implementation of positive behaviour supports (PBS). McClean (this volume) provides a comprehensive overview of PBS, and readers are referred to Chapter 18 for further information. However, it is important to note that research in PBS has addressed problem behaviours in school settings (Horner, Albin, Sprague and Todd, 2000; Sugai and Horner, 1994) by providing interventions at an individual, classroom, or whole-school level. PBS has been demonstrated to reduce office referrals in schools, create classroom environments more conducive to learning, and assist students with behaviour problems to improve their behaviour. PBS involves application of behaviourally based approaches to enhance the capacity of schools, families, and communities to design environments that improve the fit or link between students and the environments in which teaching and learning occurs. Attention is focused on creating and sustaining school environments that improve lifestyle results (personal, health, social, family, work, recreation, etc.) by making problem behaviour less effective, efficient, and relevant, and desired behaviour more functional. Additionally, such school-wide efforts create a climate in which all children have the opportunity to learn.

Instructional strategies that promote inclusion and student progress

The previous section overviewed the key elements of third-generation inclusive practices. This section provides an overview of specific practices that should be in place to promote inclusion and student progress in the general curriculum.

Educational planning

High-quality education for students with ID begins with educational planning that takes into account unique student needs and the demands of the general curriculum. Figure 16.1 provides a flow-chart for such a process (Wehmeyer, Lattin and Agran, 2001). The intent of this process is to support planning teams, which often include psychologists, to make decisions about a student's formal curriculum that includes input from both the general curriculum and individual student needs.

The model emphasizes three levels of curricular modifications:

1   **Curriculum adaptations:** modification to the presentation and representation of, and the ways in which students engage in and with, the curriculum;
2   **Curriculum augmentations:** enhancing or expanding the curriculum to teach students strategies or methods to impact and improve their capacity to succeed within the curriculum; and,
3   **Curriculum alterations:** changing the general curriculum in some way so as to address unique or more functional knowledge and skill content areas.

Historically, as described earlier, differences in curricular emphasis for students with ID was primarily a function of level of disability. This model assumes that students will vary according to the degree to which curriculum modifications need to be made even when they have similar levels of impairment. Most students with ID need, at least, curriculum adaptations to progress, while others will need additional augmentations and yet others will require a combination of all levels of curriculum modifications to succeed. When making decisions about adaptations, augmentations, and alterations, there needs to be a consideration of both the content and demands of the curriculum and needs and strengths of the student. The process ensures that planning-team members consider the use of assistive technology (AT) for students with ID to remove barriers introduced by a disabling condition that, in turn, might negate the need to modify the curriculum. Typical assistive technologies include augmentative and alternative communication devices, computer-based instruction, and mobility or sensory (vision, hearing) devices. Once AT is considered, the team should examine what curriculum modifications are necessary to ensure that the student with ID succeed. Each level is discussed briefly.

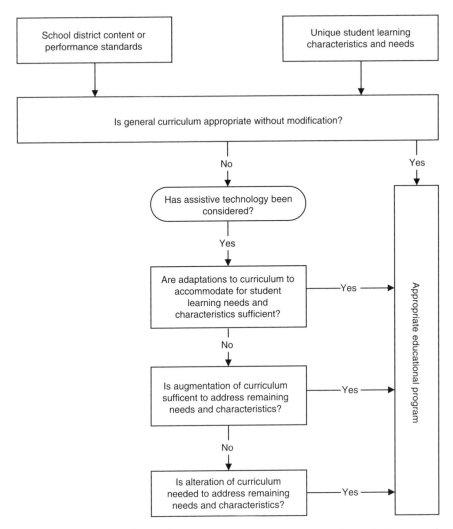

Figure 16.1 An individualized education planning process incorporating both the general curriculum and unique student needs (from Wehmeyer, Lattin, and Agran, 2001).

Curriculum adaptations

Curricular adaptations are those modifications that impact, through the implementation of principles of universal design for learning (as discussed previously and in Table 16.3), the presentation and representation of content information to students and the ways in which students engage with the curriculum to show evidence of knowledge and performance gains. There are numerous curriculum adaptations available, some of which are described in Table 16.3. As mentioned previously, the use of digitized and multimedia materials can provide multiple levels of adaptations that provide access. In addition, Table 16.5 provides examples of non-technology-based curriculum adaptations that modify the way that curriculum content is presented or represented, and which can promote progress in the general curriculum for students with ID. Importantly, nothing in the curriculum adaptation process changes the content of the general curriculum in any way. Some form of curriculum adaptations will enable most learners to gain access to some components of the general curriculum that they may not have been able to access before.

Curriculum augmentations

Curriculum augmentation involves enhancing the standard curriculum with 'meta-cognitive or executive processing strategies for acquiring and

Table 16.5 Examples of curriculum adaptations for modifying content presentation and representation (from Bulgren and Lenz, 1996)

	Presentation or representation mode	
Strategy	**Verbal**	**Visual**
Organize	Summarization	Outline
	Chunking	Web
	Advance organizer	Hierarchical graphic organizer
	Post organizer	Table
	Verbal cues about	Grid
	organization	Flowchart
Promote understanding	Analogy	Symbol
	Synonym	Concrete object
	Antonym	Picture
	Example	Model
	Comparison	Diagram
	Metaphor	
	Simile	
Describe	Current events	Film
	Past events	Filmstrip
	Fictional story	Video
	Hypothetical scenario	
	Personal story	
Demonstrate	Role-play	Physical gesture or movement
	Dramatic portrayal	Moveable objects
		Demonstration
Promote recall	Acronyms	Visual images
	Keywords	Sketches

generalizing standard curriculum' (Knowlton, 1998: 100). The augmentation process doesn't change the curriculum, but adds to or expands it to teach or provide students with strategies to succeed within the curriculum. For example, providing information in an outline format rather than a narrative format is a type of curriculum adaptation that changes the way information is represented. However, teaching the student to start from one source (narrative or text) and create an outline to aid in comprehension is an example of curriculum augmentation. That is, the curriculum is expanded to teach not only the content area of concern, but also the strategy of outlining that can be applied by the student to learn the content more effectively.

There are a variety of methods for augmenting the curriculum. Rosenthal-Malek and Bloom (1998) identified a number of such strategies that benefit students with ID (Table 16.6). The use of strategies to promote self-regulation and student-directed learning (described subsequently) provides other means of augmenting the curriculum.

Table 16.6 Cognitive or learning strategies appropriate for students with intellectual disabilities (from Rosenthal-Malek and Bloom, 1998)

Strategy domain	Specific strategy	Definition
Rehearsal strategies	Shadowing	Teaching students repeatedly to read aloud a written section, vocalize thinking (think aloud) or repeat information presented orally verbatim
	Verbatim notes	Teaching students to copy sections of text to rehearse information
Encoding and retrieval strategies	Organization and elaboration	Teaching students to organize information to facilitate learning or form additional links with information
	Graphic organizers	Teaching students to use visual representations of concepts or topics
	Semantic mapping	Teaching students to 'brainstorm' about words related to specific vocabulary words
	Question–answer relationships	Teaching students how to ask questions in order to understand a specific text better
	Mnemonics	Teaching students to form associations between content areas
	Key word method	Teaching students to associate specific images with particular words or constructs
	Rhymes	Teaching students to create rhymes to enhance memorization

Curriculum alterations

For many students with intermittent or limited support needs, providing curriculum adaptations and augmentations will be sufficient for them to succeed. As these students get older, however, or if their support needs are more intensive (e.g. moderate to severe intellectual disabilities), it is likely there will be a need to provide some alternative curricular and learning experiences. That is, planning teams must decide if there is a need to add content to the student's formal curriculum that is not found in the general curriculum. This step, curriculum alterations, provides the means to address unique student needs, often related to more functional or life skills concerns. Such alterations become particularly relevant for older students, and often focus on transition-related outcomes such as employment, independent living, community integration, recreation and leisure skills, and other life skills areas (see Parmenter, this volume, Chapter 19).

What works with students with intellectual disability and autism-spectrum disorders?

The educational planning and decision-making process described previously provides the types of modifications and supports necessary to ensure that students with ID can progress in the general curriculum and that the educational programmes of students with ID address both the general curriculum and unique student learning needs. This section overviews effective instructional practices at the classroom and individual student level.

Classroom curriculum and instructional practices

While the types of instructional practices described subsequently are important to ensure high-quality educational experiences for students with ID and autism-spectrum disorders, their efficacy is diminished when implemented without attention to certain classroom-wide activities that begin with establishing a 'learning community'. This is one in which students have a voice in rule setting, where diversity is valued, and which includes student assessment and unit and lesson-planning processes that take into account student differences across variables impacting learning, such as language and cognitive ability, previous experience with educational opportunities, and attention and memory capacity.

Assessment

When designing classroom curriculum, assessment is inseparable from instruction. Teachers need to assess first for the purposes of knowing their students. What do they know? What do they want to know? What is important for them to know? How do they learn best? What are their strengths and needs in the cognitive, affective, communicative, and physical domains? What are the cultural expectations and values that this group of students and their families bring to the classroom? What are their strengths and preferences? Data regarding students with ID can be derived from classroom observation, structured task analyses, student-report measures, and other means of assessing student strengths. Synthesizing this data provides a 'class map' of students' strengths, preferences, and needs and will be invaluable in making instructional decisions such as how to differentiate instruction, what particular instructional strategy to use or what adaptations to the curriculum would be beneficial (Wehmeyer, Sands *et al.*, 2002).

Designing units of study

Units of study are the 'maps' that teachers create to organize and plan how they are going to support students to learn and demonstrate their understanding of the content, skills, processes and knowledge required to achieve grade-level and broader school outcomes. Broadly, unit planning models tend to be organized by subject area, discipline structure, integrated designs, learner-centred designs, experience-centred designs, problem-centred designs, and life-situations designs (Wehmeyer, Sands *et al.*, 2002). Such units of study identify what needs to be accomplished by the end of the school year, district standards and benchmarks, and student knowledge and instructional needs. Once teachers understand the 'big picture' for the school year, they must 'backwards-map' to determine what students will need to know and do by the middle of the year, and then plan for more manageable instructional units. When a teacher has an overall idea of what needs to be accomplished by the end of the school year and has 'chunked' that content, skills, and knowledge into mid-year and quarterly components, he/she is ready to plan units of instruction (Wehmeyer, Sands *et al.*, 2002).

Lesson planning

Once learning targets have been identified, information needed to plan day-to-day activities that will support students to achieve unit outcomes is available. Generally, this planning leads to lesson plans, which serve as a tool for breaking large units of study into smaller, manageable increments. The amount of time needed for a particular lesson will vary according to the complexity of the learning targets and the number of tasks needed to scaffold students' readiness levels to meet those targets. Generally, lesson plans set forth the topic or theme of the lesson, clear expectations as to the purpose of the lesson (rationale), how the lesson will be conducted (activities), what students are expected to accomplish (objective), and how those accomplishments will be measured and accounted for (evaluation).

Importantly to the success of students with ID, the lesson plan should also describe the cognitive, affective, communicative and physical/health demands required of each learning target, and identify where various students will enter the learning sequence and what each student will need to succeed. Three lesson-planning tools: task analysis, cognitive taxonomies, and learning taxonomies, are important to ensure the success of students with ID.

TASK ANALYSIS

The use of task analysis enables teachers to break down the component parts of skills or knowledge sets to understand the demands to be made of students, and to match those demands with the 'class map'. Task analysis is a process that can be applied to help make decisions about the requisite skills that need to be taught as well as, in some cases, the order in which skills or knowledge should be taught. The steps in task analysis include defining instructional objectives, breaking the desired outcomes down into component parts, and sequencing steps for teaching purposes.

COGNITIVE TAXONOMIES

Cognitive taxonomies are used to classify the cognitive demands of learning targets (Biehler and Snowman, 1993). Perhaps the most familiar cognitive taxonomy is the one developed by Bloom and associates (1956). Bloom's taxonomy is a means of categorizing the cognitive skills students use when achieving learning targets. As one ascends Bloom's taxonomy, the cognitive demands from students are more complex.

As cognitive taxonomies are applied in lesson-planning activities, teachers track whether they are introducing students to increasingly complex skills and content. When learning objectives are set, students are expected to demonstrate their competence across levels of higher-ordered thinking skills and content types. Teachers should not automatically assume that students with ID can perform only at lower levels of cognitive taxonomies. Instead, they should apply what they understand about a student's cognitive abilities and create materials and supports that allow them to achieve at multiple levels. Clinical psychologists, who have more training in cognitive psychology and the psychology of learning, can assist teachers in thinking through how to vary the cognitive demands of a task.

LEARNING TAXONOMIES

Once a learning target has been specified, curriculum decision-makers also must consider the previous experiences of the learner with a skill or topic. Haring, Liberty, and White (1980) categorized learning into five phases: (1) acquisition; (2) fluency; (3) generalization; (4) adaptation; and

(5) maintenance. This hierarchy helps teachers to distinguish between those curriculum activities they might use if learners had no prior experience with a task or skill to be learned versus those that might be used to make sure that students continue to maintain their accuracy with a well-learned skill, and provides the basis for further differentiation.

Using information derived from unit and lesson planning, teachers can begin to match learning targets with the learning needs of students, and can make decisions about materials and instructional strategies they will incorporate into instruction. Finally, when this level of detail has been applied to unit and lesson plans, teachers will be able to identify those students who may not benefit from planned instruction and who may require additional adaptations, augmentations or alternative curricular activities.

Instructional strategies

Instructional strategies that work with students with ID in inclusive settings can be clustered in several ways. The following summary of such strategies has been grouped according to who delivers the instruction (teacher-mediated, student-mediated, peer-mediated, and technology-mediated instruction).

Teacher-mediated instructional strategies

Teacher-mediated instructional approaches require the leadership of a teacher to introduce, pace, and coach student performance. The most effective of such strategies for students with ID and autism-spectrum disorders include: direct instruction, modelling, match to sample, discrimination training, discrete trial, prompting and fading, and generalization training. For teachers who work with students with ID, these are fundamental teaching strategies because they do not rely on the learner's skill in generalizing, building patterns for learning new information, or problem solving in unfamiliar situations with unfamiliar tasks (Wehmeyer, Sands et al., 2002).

DIRECT INSTRUCTION

Direct instruction is typically conceptualized as having six elements: (1) focused instruction, (2) mastery learning, (3) error correction, (4) practice, (5) discrimination training, and (6) cumulative review (Gersten, Woodward and Carnine, 1987). Direct instruction approaches focus on the activities of the teacher in assuring that learning occurs and, typically using scripts, prescribe what teachers should do before, during, and after the instructional session. This part-to-whole instructional approach is most helpful when students are learning a new, foundational skill rather than practising a relatively intact skill in a novel or unfamiliar setting or content area (Rivera and Smith, 1997). Direct instruction has been demonstrated to result in successful learning outcomes for teaching math, reading, strategy skills, academic learning problems (Carnine, Silbert and Kameenui, 1990; Harris and Graham, 1996; Kameenui and Simmons, 1990) as well as skills in daily living (i.e. bathing, brushing teeth), oral communication (i.e. greeting others, requesting help), and transportation in the community such as bus riding (Snell and Brown, 1994). Briefly, the steps in direct instruction involve:

- **Focused instruction.** Teachers using direct instruction state the goals of instruction so students can narrow their focus on the learning targets.
- **Mastery learning.** In mastery learning *time*, not individual ability, is the key variable in assuring students achieve mastery. A teacher using direct instruction techniques will plan on spending more time coaching and supporting some students and providing more opportunities for independent practice for others. Sometimes, these steps in direct instruction are referred to as scaffolding, referring to the forms of temporary and adjustable supports teachers give students that help them move from their current abilities to the intended goal (Monda-Amaya and Pearson, 1996). Forms of supports can include the provision of prompts, cues, questions, error analyses, metaphors, elaboration, or cognitive modelling.
- **Error correction and practice.** Teachers using this model are encouraged to provide specific and frequent verbal comments that describe and affirm student effort, practice and correct performance. Further, correcting errors is a critical component of teaching. By correcting an error in a performance, students get better at identifying the elements of successful performance and learn to self-assess as they perform with more and more skill. Generally, practice is guided first and then done independently. Finally, students should be asked to complete successfully variations of a task or procedure.
- **Discrimination training.** Discrimination training creates the opportunity for students to recognize exemplars and non-exemplars of the performances and tasks they have been learning. The ability to apply newly acquired rules to unfamiliar examples and non-examples is a way of assessing the depth and stability of learning. When learners can approach a problem, apply their knowledge to understand and act upon new situations, they are said to be in the fluency stage of learning.
- **Cumulative review.** Finally, in cumulative practice, a student is asked to put together all the steps of a particular skill and produce a competent performance or product.

APPLIED BEHAVIOUR ANALYSIS

Applied behaviour analytic techniques have been found to be highly effective in increasing adaptive behaviours and promoting learning for students with ID across academic content and life skills areas of instruction (Schloss and Smith, 1998). Readers are referred to O'Reilly (Chapter 7) for a more detailed examination of instructional strategies derived from this approach. Of particular importance for educators with regard to increasing adaptive behaviours are techniques such as the above-mentioned task analysis, backward and forward chaining, prompting procedures, stimulus shaping and fading, errorless learning procedures, and discrete trial training.

GENERALIZED CASE INSTRUCTION

Generalized case instruction is an instructional procedure related to direct instruction that has been developed for and implemented with students with more severe disabilities in which teachers: (1) define the instructional universe; (2) define the range of relevant stimulus and response variations; (3) select examples for teaching and probe testing; (4) sequence teaching examples; (5) teach the sequence; and (6) test using non-trained probe examples (Horner, Sprague and Wilcox, 1982; Steere, Pancsofar, Powell and Buttersworth, 1989).

Peer-mediated instruction

While teacher-mediated instructional approaches focus on the relationship between the learner and the teacher, peer-mediated instructional strategies capitalize on relationships among peers. Like teacher-mediated strategies, peer-mediated strategies are useful for teaching in the content areas as well as teaching the basic tools for learning: literacy, numeracy, and technology. While peer-mediated strategies can be used with large groups, they require organizing the whole into smaller groups to engage in purposeful reflection, inquiry, and experimentation. Peer-mediated instruction is typically done in dyads or small groups. Grouping can and should be flexible, alternating use of heterogeneous and homogeneous grouping to meet different curriculum targets. Approaches to peer-mediated instruction include peer-tutoring, reciprocal teaching, cooperative learning, and role-play and simulations.

Peer-to-peer tutoring

PAIRED TUTORING

There are a variety of approaches to peer-tutoring, some of which are successful with young children in preschool programmes and others that are used successfully in elementary and secondary classrooms (Utley, Mortweet and Greenwood, 1997). A simple, yet effective peer-tutoring strategy involves organizing students into pairs for brief periods of time to discuss their reactions or connections to content presented in class. In another version of paired tutoring, students work together to solve problems. One student acts as the problem solver while the other student acts as a monitor for the problem-solving process. The focus of this method is on helping students make their thinking visible so they can track their thought patterns. The method requires intense, guided practice for effective partner work, but is worthwhile because of its power to adapt to many subjects and to emphasize the self-reflective aspects of cognition, affect and communication (Mortweet, Utley, Walker, Dawson *et al.*, 1999).

CLASS-WIDE PEER-TUTORING

Class-wide peer-tutoring pairs students for brief, but frequent, periods of drill and practice of factual material (Delquadri, Greenwood, Whorton, Carta, and Hall, 1986). It helps focus the student's attention for an intense practice period. While there is great variation in how pairs of students can work together to support and coach each others' learning, research demonstrates the efficacy of peer-tutoring in multiple settings with many kinds of students.

RECIPROCAL TEACHING

Reciprocal teaching is another form of peer-tutoring developed to support the teaching of reading comprehension. Palinscar (1986) described reciprocal teaching as ongoing interaction between two students about a particular reading passage they are working on. Pairs of students read a text passage either silently or orally. After the passage is read, a dialogue leader (a student or a teacher) asks questions about the content. The other member of the pair discusses these questions, raises additional questions, and in the case of disagreements rereads the text to find evidence to support their perspective. Once the basic elements of the passage are agreed upon, the discussion leader attempts to summarize and synthesize the passage. The pair clarifies and defines vocabulary as needed. Finally, the pair predicts what will happen next in the text.

Cooperative learning

Implementing cooperative learning groups is an essential feature of successful inclusion. Cooperative learning groups are distinguished by five components: positive interdependence, face-to-face interaction, individual accountability, interpersonal and small-group skills, and group processing (Johnson and Johnson, 1991). Plans for cooperative lessons must attend to each of these five elements as well as to specific academic and social objectives. There are many variations on these approaches including informal and formal cooperative learning techniques. Informal cooperative groups are temporary, ad hoc groups that last from a few minutes to an entire class period. In contrast, formal cooperative learning groups last longer – from one class period to several weeks of instruction focused on one specific task or project.

Role-play and simulation

Role-play involves students dramatizing a situation. The purpose of role-play varies. Role-play can be used to evaluate students' conceptual understandings of events, phenomena, and problem-solving strategies in a variety of subject areas. Role-play can be used to teach routines and procedures. For example, teachers can use role-play to provide guided practice to students so that they can be coached to perform accurate classroom attendance procedures. Finally, role-play is also frequently used to develop and practise interpersonal skills (Goldstein, 1988).

Student-mediated learning strategies

Student-directed learning strategies involve teaching students strategies that enable them to modify and regulate their own behaviour (Agran, 1997; Agran, King-Sears, Wehmeyer and Copeland, 2003). The emphasis is shifted from teacher-directed instruction to enabling the student to regulate his or her own behaviour. A variety of strategies have been used to teach students, including students with ID, how to manage their own behaviour. Among the most commonly used strategies are permanent prompts, self-instruction, self-monitoring, and self-reinforcement, each described briefly (from Agran *et al.*, 2003).

- **Picture cues and antecedent cue regulation** *strategies* involve the use of visual or audio cues that students use to guide their behaviour. Visual cues typically involve photographs, illustrations, or line drawings of steps in a task that support students to complete a sequence of tasks. Audio cues include pre-recorded, taped directions or instructions that the student can listen to as they perform a task.
- **Self-instruction** involves teaching students to provide their own verbal cues prior to the execution of target behaviours. Self-instruction allows a person to provide herself or himself with sufficient verbal information to cue a response, information that might otherwise not be provided or be provided by an adult. Students and adults with ID have been taught to use self-instruction to achieve academic content and life skills goals.
- **Self-monitoring** involves teaching students to observe whether they have

performed a targeted behaviour and whether the response met whatever existing criteria present.

* **Self-evaluation** involves teaching the student to compare his or her performance (as tracked through self-monitoring) and comparing that performance with a desired goal or outcome.

Technology-mediated instruction

Technology-mediated instruction can be supported through a variety of low- and high-technology systems. Low-tech systems include the use of tools such as calculators, audio recorders/players, and low-tech (e.g. battery-operated) switching systems that allow students with ID and autism-spectrum disorders to operate electrical equipment or toys. Higher-tech systems include computers, networks, digital-based systems or complex communication systems, such as those using voice-activated technology. Technology-mediated instruction can be implemented across all instructional grouping formats, and for introducing models and concepts and supporting the development of problem-solving skills, as well as to provide drills, practice, and feedback as students develop automaticity of basic skills. Technology-mediated instruction provides for flexibility needed for student access to and demonstration of their achievement of the curriculum. Information can be communicated, translated (e.g. text to speech) and received through text-based, auditory-based and graphics-based mediums. This allows teachers and students to use a variety of materials that range from auditory prompts and cues, graphics, organizers, outlines, video demonstrations, digitally recorded readings, and audio recordings to scaffold instruction and assess curriculum outcomes.

Summary

This section has provided an overview of how students with ID and autism-spectrum disorders can be supported in general education classrooms, and identified the features and instructional tools associated with what we've referred to as the third generation of inclusive practices. Because other chapters, particularly Parmenter (Chapter 19 this volume), describe issues pertaining to life skills instruction for students with ID in detail, we did not comprehensively address issues such as life skills instruction, social skills training, communication training, and community-based instruction. That does not mean, however, that these issues are not critical to the success of students with ID or, indeed, that students at elementary and middle-school ages cannot benefit from such a focus. The chapter concludes with a discussion of issues pertaining to collaborating with parents and other educational personnel, a topic that clinical psychologists may find directly relevant to their interaction with schools. However, although the instructional strategies, methods, and materials pertaining to third-generation inclusive practices fall largely under the professional domain of educators, if clinical psychologists are well informed of what is possible for students with ID, they can both assist educators in designing educational programmes and become an advocate for implementation of such high-quality practices.

COLLABORATING WITH TEACHERS, PARENTS AND OTHER EDUCATIONAL PERSONNEL

As students with ID and autism-spectrum disorders have been included in general education, the roles of psychologists have changed and been extended to include support both for students with disabilities and the people who work with them (Galloway, 1998; Stoker, Gersch, Fox, Lown and Morris, 2001). This section addresses how psychologists can support teachers, parents and other personnel involved in the education of children with ID, especially in three areas: (a) psychological consultancy with teachers; (b) contribution to an effective individual education programme; and (c) management of conflicts and resistance within school–home–hospital.

Psychological consultancy with teachers

From individual diagnosis of disability to support of classroom instruction

As discussed previously, the main focus within education for psychologists in the past was on diagnosis and the assessment of eligibility for SNE (Schulte, Osborne and Erchul, 1998). However, several problems emerged from this role, including an overemphasis on standardized testing and their negative impact, including problems with a focus on labelling rather than designing effective interventions, and the lack of support for the mental health needs of children with ID and their programmes (Habel and Bernard, 1999). In response to these issues and to the changing models of educational supports described previously, the role of psychologists has shifted to improving students' outcomes by supporting classroom instruction and promoting effective instruction practices (Schulte *et al.*, 1998). That is, the role of psychologists is changing from one of referral to a consultative problem-solving approach (DfEE, 2000a).

The consultative problem solver

The role of psychologists as consultative problem solvers has expanded to include assessment of and interventions for persons and factors beyond individual children so that students with disabilities can interact with wider school environments (Galloway, 1998; Habel and Bernard, 1999). For general education teachers in particular, psychologists can offer consultancy to increase their capacity to provide appropriate programmes for children with disabilities. Consultancy can be provided in the following areas:

Learning and cognitive development

Historically, as discussed previously, educational models focused on student deficits and a readiness to learn orientation (Gartner and Lipsky, 1987; Habel and Bernard, 1999). However, the application of knowledge about learning and cognitive development to educational practices like those described earlier provide the opportunity for psychologists to provide information on child development, cognitive and learning taxonomies, emotional development, and so forth.

Cooperative learning in the classroom

Educational psychologists also can support teachers to create cooperative groups, like those discussed above.

Behavioural consultation. Many educators, particularly general educators, are unaware of and have not received training in functional behaviour analysis (FBA) (Nelson, Roberts, Mathur and Aaroe, 1999) and other aspects of positive behaviour supports. As such, psychologists can play a key role in supporting use of FBA and, in general, with regard to creating positive learning communities and climates.

Contribution to an effective educational planning

As the focus of psychologists shifts increasingly to supporting classroom instruction, their roles have been extended to direct intervention, beyond indirect consultation (Habel and Bernard, 1999). As such, the role of psychologists in the process of educational planning has expanded.

Elements of effective educational planning

A planning process to ensure student access to the general curriculum was described earlier. More broadly, elements of effective planning can be summarized as follows. First, accurate information about students' needs and strengths is needed. Second, such planning should accurately describe peer interaction opportunities for students with disabilities. Unfortunately, instructional practices to facilitate peer interactions are often inappropriate (Gelzheiser, McLane, Meyers and Pruzek, 1998). Third, ensuring accountability through appropriate monitoring and evaluation is also important for effective educational planning (Cheney, 2000). Fourth, educational programmes should be designed for students' full or partial involvement in all aspects of the general curriculum, as discussed earlier. Fifth, effective planning can foster collaboration by promoting student involvement (Zickel and Arnold, 2001), family and school partnership (Lytle and Bordin, 2001; Muhlenhaupt, 2002), and general education teacher involvement (Weishaar, 2001). Finally, the planning process is most likely to be effective when it is consistent with school and family cultural values (Pearson, 2000).

How to contribute to effective educational planning

When considering elements for effective planning, psychologists can contribute as follows:

Providing accurate information and monitoring progress through authentic assessment

Psychologists can play an important role in providing teachers or other staff with accurate information on students' needs and strengths through authentic assessment focusing on performance and production, rather than exclusively on testing (Wiggins, 1993). They also can participate in evaluating and monitoring the progress of students and assist in designing interventions that will enable students to transfer learning to other situations. In addition, psychologists can provide appropriate information about the function of students' behaviour problems (Bugaj, 2000).

Supporting peer interaction and school culture through ecological assessment

Psychologists can analyse how students with disabilities interact with the wider school environment and how they make sense of that environment. Through such ecological assessments, they can help teachers deal with peer interactions and student integration and help children access the general curriculum by enabling them to engage in problem solving related to their environment (Habel and Bernard, 1999).

Promoting student involvement

In both the UK and US, there has been increased emphasis on student involvement in educational planning. Despite this, it is often the case that the wishes and feelings of children are not likely to be considered in educational plans (Galloway, 1998). Therefore, psychologists can support students to express opinions and engage in collaborative problem solving and decision-making (Thomson, Bachor and Thomson, 2002).

Conflict management within school–home–hospital

Collaboration as a key to manage conflicts

Planning is a collaborative process and it is likely that psychologists will, as such, be faced with conflicts over allocation of resources and complex inter-actions between children, parents, teachers, and others in the child's life (Galloway, 1998). The Department for Education and Employment (DfEE, 2000a) described the aim of psychological service delivery as: 'to promote child development and learning through application of psychology by work-ing with individual and groups of children, teachers and other adults in schools, families, other LEA officers, health and social services, and other agencies' (p. 5). That is, inter-professional and inter-agency collaboration is a key to inclusive education for students with disabilities (Farmakopoulou, 2002; Graham and Wright, 1999; Stanovich, 1996). Given the importance of collaboration, psychologists need to be familiar with current types of col-laboration and be aware of elements for effective collaboration to manage conflicts within school–home–hospital settings.

Types of collaboration

As the school-wide focus has expanded in education and services for special needs students, inter-professional and inter-agency collaboration is becoming more important. Inter-professional and inter-agency collaboration in the process of service delivery can be divided into three types: (a) collaboration between home and school (Deslandes, Royer, Potvin and Leclerc, 1999); (b) school (education) and health service (Law, Lindsay, Peacey et al., 2001; McConkey, 2002); and (c) practice (teacher) and research (researcher) (Forbes, 2003; Rose, 2002; Wilson, 2002). In terms of collaboration between home and school, various people can be involved such as: teacher, speech and language therapist, special needs assistants (SNAs), psychologists, and other professionals (Band, Lindsay, Law et al., 2002; Bruce and Schultz, 2002; Jerwood, 1999; Wright and Graham, 1997). A home visiting project is a good example of collaboration between home and school (Feiler, 2003). According to Galloway (1998), psychologists can collaborate, especially with parents, by forming multiple relationships based on varying roles, such as doctor–patient, advocacy, consultancy, child protection and resource management.

Elements for effective collaboration: beyond conflict, toward empowerment

Psychologists should recognize their roles for effective collaboration by being aware of its elements. Effective inter-personal and inter-agency collaboration includes four elements: (a) goals; (b) resources; (c) opportunities; and (d) relationship skills, as seen in Figure 16.2. Ironically, pursuing one's own personal goal along with a common goal is necessary in the process of collaboration, given that conflicts often occur when the goals and needs of an individual or group clash with those of others (Habel and Bernard, 1999). In this respect, 'voice and collaboration are interdependent processes' (Sailor, 1996: 170). For achieving the personal goal of the individual or the common goal of the group, resources such as information and experiences should be shared with others. Resources can be shared through various opportunities to interact with families and other professionals at appropriate times and places, such as communicating with other staff members, meeting families' basic needs, and extending learning at home and in the community (Turnbull and Turnbull, 2001). For maximizing the benefit from these opportunities for collaboration, skills for relationships are necessary, such as trust, respect, communication, commitment, and equality (Blue-Banning, Summers, Frankland, Nelson and Beegle, 2004; Bruce and Schultz, 2002). Most of all, effective collaboration can empower each family member, teacher, and other staff members, as well as resolve conflicts in relationships. In this

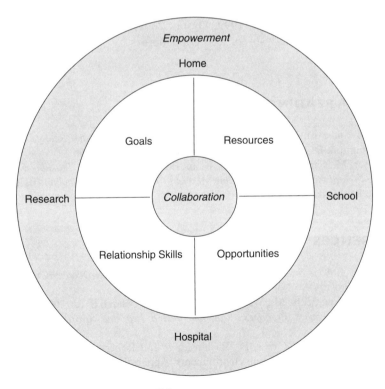

Figure 16.2 Elements for effective collaboration.

respect, psychologists should try to develop their own resources for pursing individual or common goals of the group, and create opportunities to interact with families, teachers, and other staff members based on relationship skills. Through such an effective collaboration, psychologists can empower others and themselves as well as manage conflicts in the relationships.

CONCLUSION

As clinical psychologists interact with children with special needs and their families, it is important to be able to identify what constitutes best practice in education. As described in this chapter, there is abundant evidence that students with ID and autism-spectrum disorders can and should be educated in the context of the general education classroom. By employing the types of school-wide practices and high-quality instructional strategies described in this chapter, and by creating individualized curriculum modifications and considering assistive technology needs, students with special needs can succeed within the general curriculum in that context. While it is frequently the case that this is not the status quo for students and it is certainly true that such changes are complex and often difficult (Clark, Dyson, Millward and Robson, 1999; Clough, 1999; Dyson, 2001), clinical psychologists can become important catalysts for and contributors to the implementation of these practices.

FURTHER READING FOR CLINICIANS

Kavale, K. and Forness, S. (1999). *Efficacy of Special Education and Related Services.* Washington, DC: American Association on Mental Retardation.
Wehmeyer, M., Sands, D., Knowlton, E. and Kozleski, E. (2002). *Teaching Students with Mental Retardation: Providing Access to the General Curriculum.* Baltimore, MD: Paul Brooks.

REFERENCES

Agran, M. (1997). *Student-Directed Learning: Teaching Self-Determination Skills.* Pacific Grove, CA: Brooks/Cole.
Agran, M., King-Sears, M., Wehmeyer, M. L. and Copeland, S. R. (2003). *Teachers' Guides to Inclusive Practices: Student-Directed Learning Strategies.* Baltimore: Paul H. Brookes.
Ault, M. M., Guy, B., Guess, D., Bashinski, S. and Roberts, S. (1995). Analyzing behaviour state and learning environments: Application in instructional settings. *Intellectual Disability*, 33, 304–16.
Avramidis, E., Bayliss, P. and Burden, R. (2002). Inclusion in action: An in-depth case

study of an effective inclusive secondary school in the south-west of England. *International Journal of Inclusive Education*, 6(2), 143–63.

Band, S., Lindsay, G., Law, J., Soloff, N., Peacey, N., Gascoigne, M. and Radford, J. (2002). Are health and education talking to each other? Perceptions of parents of children with speech and language needs. *European Journal of Special Needs Education*, 17(3), 211–27.

Bennett, T., DeLuca, D. and Bruns, D. (1997). Putting inclusion into practices: Perspectives of teachers and parents. *Exceptional Children*, 64(1), 115–31.

Bergsson, M., Wood, M. M. and Quirk, C. (2003). An emerging European model for educational inclusion of troubled children. *International Education*, 32(2), 5–26.

Biehler, R. F. and Snowman, J. (1993). *Psychology Applied to Teaching* (7th edn). Boston: Houghton Mifflin.

Bloom, B. S., Englehart, M. B., Furst, E. J., Hill, W. H. and Krathwohl, D. R. (eds) (1956). *Taxonomy of Educational Objectives: The Classification of Educational Goals. Handbook I: Cognitive Domain*. New York: McKay.

Blue-Banning, M., Summers, J. A., Frankland, H. C., Nelson, L. L. and Beegle, G. P. (2004). Dimensions of family and professional partnerships: Constructive guidelines for collaboration. *Exceptional Children*, 70, 167–84.

Bulgren, J. and Lenz, K. (1996). Strategic instruction in the content areas. In D. D. Deshler, E. S. Ellis and B. K. Lenz (eds), *Teaching Adolescents with Intellectual Disability: Strategies and Methods* (2nd edn, pp. 409–73). Denver, CO: Love Publishing Company.

Bowe, F. G. (2000). *Universal Design in Education: Teaching Nontraditional Students*. Westport, CT: Bergin and Garvey.

Bruce, E. and Schultz, C. (2002). Non-finite loss and challenges to communication between parents and professionals. *British Journal of Special Education*, 29(1), 9–13.

Bugaj, S. J. (2000). Avoiding the pitfalls of failing to implement an IEP: Tips for secondary school principals and guidance counsellors. *NASSP Bulletin*, 84(613), 41–6.

Carnine, D. W., Silbert, J. and Kameenui, E. J. (1990). *Direct instruction reading* (2nd edn). Columbus, OH: Merrill.

Centre for Applied Special Technology (CAST) (1998–1999). The National Centre on Accessing the General Curriculum [On-line]. Available: http://www.cast.org/initiatives/national_centre.html

Cheney, C. O. (2000). Ensuring IEP accountability in inclusive settings. *Intervention in School and Clinic*, 35(3), 185–9.

Clark, C., Dyson, A., Millward, A. and Robson, S. (1999). Inclusive education and schools as organizations. *International Journal of Inclusive Education*, 3(1), 37–51.

Clough, P. (1999). Exclusive tendencies: Concepts, consciousness, and curriculum in the project of inclusion. *International Journal of Inclusive Education*, 3(1), 63–73.

Cole, D. A. and Meyer, L. H. (1991). Social integration and severe disabilities: A longitudinal analysis of child outcomes. *Journal of Special Education*, 25, 340–51.

Delquadri, J., Greenwood, C. R., Whorton, D., Carta, J. J. and Hall, R. V. (1986). Class wide peer tutoring. *Exceptional Children*, 52, 535–42.

Department for Education and Skills (DfEE) (1998). *Excellence for All Children: Meeting Special Educational Needs*. London: DfEE.

Department for Education and Skills (DfEE) (2000a). *Educational Psychology Services (England): Current Role, Good Practice and Future Directions: Report of the Working Group*. London: DfEE.

Deslandes, R., Royer, E., Potvin, P. and Leclerc, D. (1999). Patterns of home and school partnership for general and special education students at the secondary level. *Exceptional Children*, 65(4), 496–506.

Dugan, E., Kamps, D., Leonard, B., Watkins, N., Rheinberger, A. and Stackhaus, J. (1995). Effects of cooperative learning groups during social studies for students with autism and fourth-grade peers. *Journal of Applied Behaviour Analysis*, 28, 175–88.

Dyson, A. (2001). Special needs in the twenty-first century: Where we've been and where we're going. *British Journal of Special Education*, 28, 24–9.

English, F. (1992). *Successful Schools Series: Vol. 4. Deciding What to Teach and Test: Developing, Aligning, and Auditing the Curriculum*. Newbury Park, CA: Corwin Press.

Evans, I. M., Salisbury, C., Palombaro, M. and Goldberg, J. S. (1994). Children's perception of fairness in classroom and interpersonal situations involving peers with severe disabilities. *Journal of the Association for Persons with Severe Handicaps*, 19(4), 326–32.

Farmakopulou, N. (2002). Using an integrated theoretical framework for understanding inter-agency collaboration in the special-educational needs field. *European Journal of Special Needs Education*, 17(1), 49–59.

Farrell, P. (2000). The impact of research on developments in inclusive education. *International Journal of Inclusive Education*, 4(2), 153–62.

Feiler, A. (2003). A home visiting project for reception children predicted to experience literacy difficulties. *British Journal of Special Education*, 30(3), 156–62.

Ferguson, D., Meyer, G., Janchild, L., Juniper, L. and Zingo, J. (1992). Figuring out what to do with the grownups: How teachers make inclusion 'work' for students with disabilities. *Journal of the Association for Persons with Severe Handicaps*, 17(4), 218–26.

Florian, L. and Pullin, D. (2000). Defining difference: A comparative perspective on legal and policy issues in education reform and special education needs. In M. J. McLaughlin and M. Rouse (eds), *Special Education and School Reform in the United States and Britain* (pp. 11–37). London: Routledge.

Forbes, J. (2003). Grappling with collaboration: Would opening up the research 'base' help? *British Journal of Special Education*, 30(3), 150–5.

Fryxell, D. and Kennedy, C. H. (1995). Placement along the continuum of services and its impact on students' social relationships. *Journal of the Association for Persons with Severe Handicaps*, 20, 259–69.

Galloway, D. (1998). Special education in the United Kingdom: Educational psychologists and the effectiveness of special education. *The School Psychology Review*, 27(1), 77–83.

Gartner, A. and Lipsky, D. K. (1987). Beyond special education: Toward a quality system for all students. *Harvard Educational Review*, 57, 367–95.

Gelzheiser, L. M., McLane, M., Meyers, J. and Pruzek, R. M. (1998). IEP-Specified peer interaction needs: Accurate but ignored. *Exceptional Children*, 65(1), 51–65.

Gersten, R., Woodward, J. and Carnine, D. W. (1987). Direct instruction research: The third decade. *Remedial and Special Education*, 8, 48–56.

Giangreco, M., Cloninger, C., Mueller, P., Yuan, S. and Ashworth, S. (1991). Perspectives of parents whose children have dual sensory impairments. *Journal of the Association for Persons with Severe Handicaps*, 16, 14–24.

Giangreco, M., Dennis, R., Cloninger, C., Edelman, S. and Schattman, R. (1993b). 'I've counted Jon': Transformational experiences of teachers educating students with disabilities. *Exceptional Children*, 59(4), 359–73.

Giangreco, M., Edelman, S. W., Cloninger, C. and Dennis, R. (1993). My child has a classmate with severe disabilities: What parents of nondisabled children think about full inclusion. *Developmental Disabilities Bulletin*, 21(1), 77–91.

Goldstein, A. P. (1988). *The PREPARE Curriculum: Teaching Prosocial Competencies*. Champaign, IL: Research Press.

Graham, J. and Wright, J. A. (1999). What does 'inter-professional collaboration' mean to professional working with pupils with physical disabilities? *British Journal of Special Education*, 26(1), 37–41.

Green, A. and Stoneman, Z. (1989). Attitudes of mothers and fathers of nonhandicapped children. *Journal of Early Intervention*, 13(4), 292–304.

Green, S. K. and Shinn, M. R. (1994). Parent attitudes about special education and reintegration: What is the role of student outcomes? *Exceptional Children*, 61(3), 269–81.

Guralnick, M. and Groom, J. M. (1988). Peer interactions in mainstreamed and specialized classrooms: A comparative analysis, *Exceptional Children*, 54(5), 415–25.

Habel, J. C. and Bernard, J. A. (1999). School and educational psychologists: Creating new service models. *Intervention in School and Clinic*, 34(3), 156–62.

Hanko, G. (2003). Towards an inclusive school culture – but what happened to Elton's 'affective curriculum'? *British Journal of Special Education*, 30, 125–31.

Hanline, M. F. (1993). Inclusion of preschoolers with profound disabilities: An analysis of children's interactions. *Journal of the Association for Persons with Severe Handicaps*, 18(1), 28–35.

Haring, N. G., Liberty, K. A. and White, O. R. (1980). Rules for data-based strategy decisions in instructional programs: Current research and instructional implications. In W. Sailor, B. Wilcox and L. Brown (eds), *Methods of Instruction for Severely Handicapped Students* (pp. 159–92). Baltimore, MD: Brookes.

Harris, K. R. and Graham, S. (1996). Memo to constructivists: Skills count, too. *Educational Leadership*, 53, 26–210.

Harris, N. (2002). England and Wales: Regulating school education for social inclusion. *The Yearbook of Education Law* (vol. 2002, pp. 302–25). Dayton, OH: ELA Publishers.

Helmstetter, E., Peck, C. A. and Giangreco, M. F. (1994). Outcomes of interactions with peers with moderate or severe disabilities: A statewide survey of high school students. *Journal of the Association for Persons with Severe Handicaps*, 19(4), 263–76.

Hollowood, T. M., Salisbury, C. L., Rainforth, B. and Palombaro, M. M. (1994/1995). Use of instructional time in classrooms serving students with and without severe disabilities. *Exceptional Children*, 61(3), 242–53.

Horner, R. H., Albin, R. W., Sprague, J. R. and Todd, A. W. (2000). Positive behaviour support. In M. E. Snell and F. Brown (eds), *Instruction of Students with Severe Disabilities* (5th edn, pp. 207–44). Upper Saddle River, NJ: Merrill Publishing.

Horner, R., Sprague, J. and Wilcox, B. (1982). General case programming for community activities. In B. Wilcox and G. Bellamy (eds), *Design of High School Programs for Severely Handicapped Persons* (pp. 61–98). Baltimore: Paul H. Brookes.

Hunt, P., Alwell, M., Farron-Davis, F. and Goetz, L. (1996). Creating socially supportive environments for fully included students who experience multiple disabilities. *Journal of the Association for Persons with Severe Handicaps*, 21(2), 53–71.

Hunt, P., Farron-Davis, F., Beckstead, S., Curtis, D. and Goetz, L. (1994). Evaluating the effects of placement of students with severe disabilities in general education versus special classes. *Journal of the Association for Persons with Severe Handicaps*, 19(3), 3–29.

Hunt, P., Staub, D., Alwell, M. and Goetz, L. (1994). Achievement by all students within the context of cooperative learning groups. *Journal of the Association for Persons with Severe Handicaps*, 19(4), 290–301.

Itard, J. M. G. (1802). *An Historical Account of the Discovery and Education of a Savage Man, or of the First Developments, Physical and Moral, of the Young Savage, Caught in the Woods near Aveyron, in the Year 1798*. London: Richard Phillips.

Janney, R. E. and Snell, M. E. (1996). How teachers use peer interactions to include students with moderate severe disabilities in elementary general education classes. *Journal of the Association for Persons with Severe Handicaps*, 21(2), 72–80.

Janney, R. and Snell, M. E. (2000). *Teachers' Guides to Inclusive Practices: Modifying Schoolwork*. Baltimore: Paul H. Brookes.

Jenkins, J. R., Odom, S. L. and Speltz, M. L. (1989). Effects of social integration on preschool children with handicaps. *Exceptional Children*, 55(5), 420–8.

Jerwood, L. (1999). Using special needs assistants effectively. *British Journal of Special Education*, 26(3), 127–9.

Johnson, D. W. and Johnson, R. T. (1991). *Cooperation and Competition: Theory and Research*. Edina, MN: Interaction Books.

Johnson, D. W., Johnson, R. T. and Anderson, D. (1983). Social interdependence and classroom climate. *Journal of Psychology*, 114, 135–42.

Kameenui, E. J. and Simmons, D. C. (1990). *Designing Instructional Strategies: The Prevention of Academic Learning Problems*. Columbus, OH: Merrill.

Kauffman, J. M. and Hallahan, D. P. (1995). *The Illusion of Full Inclusion. A Comprehensive Critique of a Current Special Education Bandwagon*. Austin, TX: Pro-Ed.

Kavale, K. A. and Forness, S. R. (1999). *Efficacy of Special Education and Related Services*. Washington, DC: American Association on Intellectual Disability.

Kennedy, C. H., Shukla, S. and Fryxell, D. (1997). Comparing the effects of educational placement on the social relationships of intermediate school students with severe disabilities. *Exceptional Children*, 64(1), 31–48.

Knowlton, E. (1998). Considerations in the design of personalized curricular supports for students with developmental disabilities. *Education and Training in Intellectual Disability and Developmental Disabilities*, 33, 95–107.

Kozleski, E. B. and Jackson, L. (1993). Taylor's story: Full inclusion in her neighborhood elementary school. *Exceptionality*, 4(3), 153–75.

Kronberg, R. (1999, March). *Creating and nurturing inclusive school communities*. Paper presented at the 5th Mid-West Regional Conference on Inclusive Education, Omaha, NE.

Law, J., Lindsay, G., Peacey, N., Gascoigne, M., Soloff, N., Radford, J. and Band, S. (2001). Facilitating communication between education and health services: the provision for children with speech and language needs. *British Journal of Special Education*, 28(3), 133–7.

Lipsky, D. K. and Gartner, A. (1997). *Inclusion and School Reform*. Baltimore, MD: Paul H. Brookes.

Luckasson, R., Borthwick-Duffy, S., Buntinx, W. H. E., Coulter, D. L., Craig, E. M., Reeve, A., Schalock, R. L., Snell, M. E., Spitalnick, D. M., Spreat, S. and Tasse, M. J. (2002). *Intellectual Disability: Definition, Classification, and Systems of Supports* (10th edn). Washington DC: American Association on Intellectual Disability.

Luckasson, R., Coulter, D. L., Polloway, E. A., Reiss, S., Schalock, R. L., Snell, M. E., Spitalnick, D. M. and Stark, J. A. (1992). *Intellectual Disability: Definition, Classification, and Systems of Supports*. Washington, DC: American Association on Intellectual Disability.

Luckasson, R. and Spitalnick, D. M. (1994). Political and programmatic shifts of the 1992 AAMR definition of intellectual disability. In V. Bradley, J. W. Ashbaugh and B. C. Blaney (eds), *Creating Individual Supports for People with Developmental Disabilities: A Mandate for Change at Many Levels* (pp. 81–96). Baltimore: Paul H. Brookes.

Lytle, R. K. and Bordin, J. A. (2001). Enhancing the IEP team. *Teaching Exceptional Children*, 33(5), 40–4.

McConkey, R. (2002). Reciprocal working by education, health and social services: lessons for a less-travelled road. *British Journal of Special Education*, 29(1), 3–8.

McDonnell, J., Hardman, M., Hightower, J. and Kiefer-O'Donnell, R. (1991). Variables associated with in-school and after-school integration of secondary students with severe disabilities. *Education and Training in Intellectual Disability*, 26, 243–57.

McDonnell, J., Thorson, N., McQuivey, C. and Kiefer-O'Donnell, R. (1997). Academic engaged time of students with low-incidence disabilities in general education classes. *Intellectual Disability*, 35(1), 18–26.

McDougall, D. and Brady, M. P. (1998). Initiating and fading self-management interventions to increase math fluency in general education classes. *Exceptional Children*, 64(2), 151–66.

McGregor, G. and Vogelsberg, R. T. (1998). *Inclusive Schooling Practices: Pedagogical and Research Foundations*. Baltimore, MD: Paul H. Brookes.

McLaughlin, M. J. and Tilstone, C. (2000). Standards and curriculum: The core of educational reform. In M. J. McLaughlin and M. Rouse (eds), *Special Education and School Reform in the United States and Britain* (pp. 38–65). London: Routledge.

McLaughlin, M. W. and Warren, S. H. (1994, November). The costs of inclusion: Reallocating financial and human resources to include students with disabilities. *The School Administrator*, 51, 8–18.

Meyer, L. H., Minondo, S., Fisher, M., Larson, M. J., Dunmore, S., Black, J. W. and D'Aquanni, M. (1998). Frames of friendships. Social relationships among adolescents with diverse abilities. In L. H. Meyer, H. Park, M. Grenot-Scheyer, I. S. Schwartz and B. Harry (eds), *Making Friends: The Influences of Culture and Development* (pp. 189–218). Baltimore: Paul H. Brookes.

Monda-Amaya, L. E. and Pearson, P. D. (1996). Toward a responsible pedagogy for teaching and literacy. In M. Pugach and C. Warger, *Curriculum Trends, Special Education, and Reform: Refocusing the Conversation* (pp. 143–68). New York: Teachers College Press.

Moon, M. S., Hart, D., Komissar, C. and Friedlander, R. (1995). Making sports and recreation activities accessible: Assistive technology and other accommodation strategies. In K. F. Flippo, K. J. Inge and M. Barcus (eds), *Assistive Technology: A Resource for School, Work, and Community* (pp. 223–44). Baltimore: Paul H. Brookes.

Morris, N. and Parker, P. (1997). Reviewing the teaching and learning of children with special educational needs: Enabling whole school responsibility. *British Journal of Special Education*, 24(4), 163–6.

Mortweet, S. L., Utley, C. A., Walker, D. Dawson, H. L., Delquadri, J. C., Reddy, S. S., Greenwood, C. R., Hamilton, S. and Ledford, D. (1999). Classwide peer tutoring: Teaching students with mild intellectual disability in inclusive classrooms. *Exceptional Children*, 65, 524–36.

Muhlenhaupt, M. (2002). Family and school partnerships for IEP development. *Journal of Visual Impairment and Blindness*, 96(3), 175–8.

Nakken, H. and Pijl, S.J. (2002). Getting along with classmates in regular schools: A review of the effects of integration on the development of social relationships. *International Journal of Inclusive Education*, 6(1), 47–61.

Nelson, J. R., Roberts, M. L., Mathur, S. R. and Aaroe, L. A. (1999). A statewide survey of special education administrators and school psychologists regarding functional behavioural assessment. *Education and Treatment of Children*, 22(3), 267–79.

Olson, M. R., Chalmers, L. and Hoover, J. H. (1997). Attitudes and attributes of general education teachers identified as effective inclusionists. *Remedial and Special Education*, 18(1), 28–35.

Orkwis, R. and McLane, K. (1998). *A Curriculum Every Student Can Use: Design Principles for Student Access.* ERIC/OSEP Topical Brief, Fall, 1998. Reston, VA: Council for Exceptional Children.

Palinscar, A. S. (1986). Metacognitive strategy instruction. *Exceptional Children*, 53, 118–24.

Palmer, D. S., Borthwick-Duffy, S. A. and Widaman, K. (1988). Parent perceptions of inclusive practices for their children with significant cognitive disabilities. *Exceptional Children*, 64(1), 271–82.

Palmer, S. B., Wehmeyer, M. L., Gibson, K. and Agran, M. (2004). Promoting access to the general curriculum by teaching self-determination skills. *Exceptional Children*, 70, 427–39.

Pearson, S. (2000). The relationship between school culture and IEPs. *British Journal of Special Education*, 27(3), 145–9.

Peck, C. A., Donaldson, J. and Pezzoli, M. (1990). Some benefits adolescents perceive for themselves from their social relationships with peers who have severe disabilities. *Journal of the Association for Persons with Severe Handicaps*, 15(4), 241–9.

Pugach, M. C. and Johnson, L. J. (1995). Unlocking expertise among classroom teachers through structured dialogue: Extending research on peer collaboration. *Exceptional Children*, 62(2), 101–10.

Rivera, D. P. and Smith, D. D. (1997). *Teaching Students with Learning and Behaviour Problems* (3rd edn). Boston: Allyn and Bacon.

Robertson, J., Emerson, E., Hatton, C., Gregory, N., Kessissoglou, S., Hallam, A. and Walsh, P. N. (2001). Environmental opportunities and supports for exercising self-determination in community-based residential settings. *Research in Developmental Disabilities*, 22, 487–502.

Rose, R. (2002). Teaching as a 'research-based profession': Encouraging practitioner research in special education. *British Journal of Special Education*, 29(1), 44–8.

Rosenthal-Malek, A. and Bloom, A. (1998). Beyond acquisition: Teaching generalization for students with developmental disabilities. In A. Hilton and R. Ringlaben (eds), *Best and Promising Practices in Developmental Disabilities* (pp. 139–55). Austin, TX: PRO-ED.

Sailor, W. (1996). New Structures and systems change for comprehensive positive behaviour support. In L. K. Koegel, R. L. Koegel and G. Dunlap, *Positive Behavioural Support: Including People with Difficult Behaviour in the Community*. Baltimore: Brookes.

Sale, P. and Carey, D. M. (1995). The sociometric status of students with disabilities in a full-inclusion school. *Exceptional Children*, 62, 6–19.

Salend, S. J., Johansen, M., Mumper, J., Chase, A. S., Pike, K. M. and Dorney, J. A. (1997). Cooperative teaching: The voices of two teachers. *Remedial and Special Education*, 18(1), 3–11.

Schloss, P. J. and Smith, M. A. (1998). *Applied Behaviour Analaysis in the Classroom* (2nd edn). Boston: Allyn and Bacon.

Schnorr, R. F. (1990). 'Peter? He comes and goes . . .': First graders' perspectives on a part-time mainstream student. *Journal of the Association for Persons with Severe Handicaps*, 15, 231–40.

Schnorr, R. F. (1997). From enrollment to membership: 'Belonging' in middle and high school classes. *Journal of the Association for Persons with Severe Handicaps*, 22(1), 1–15.

Schulte, A. C., Osborne, S. S. and Erchul, W. P. (1998). Effective special education: A United States dilemma. *The School Psychology Review*, 27(1), 66–76.

Sebba, J., Thurlow, M. L. and Goertz, M. (2000). Educational accountability and students with disabilities in the United States and in England and Wales. In M. J. McLaughlin and M. Rouse (eds), *Special Education and School Reform in the United States and Britain* (pp. 98–125). London: Routledge.

Seguin, E. (1846). *Traitement moral, hygiène et éducation des idiots et des autres enfants arrières*. Paris: J. B. Bailliere.

Siegel-Causey, E. and Bashinski, S. M. (1997). Enhancing initial communication and responsiveness of learners with multiple disabilities: A tri-focus framework for partners. *Focus on Autism and Other Developmental Disabilities*, 12, 105–20.

Snell, M. and Brown, F. (ed). (1994). *Instruction of Students with Severe Disabilities* (4th edn). New York: Merrill.

Stainback, S., Stainback, W. and Forest, M. (1989). *Educating All Students in the Mainstream of Regular Education*. Baltimore, MD: Paul H. Brookes.

Stainback, W. and Stainback, S. (1990). *Support Networks for Inclusive Schooling: Interdependent Integrated Education*. Baltimore, MD: Paul H. Brookes.

Stainback, W., Stainback, S., Stefanich, G. and Alper, S. (1996). Learning in inclusive classrooms: What about the curriculum? In S. Stainback and W. Stainback (eds), *Inclusion: A Guide for Educators* (pp. 209–19). Baltimore: Brookes.

Stanovich, P. J. (1996). Collaboration: The key to successful instruction in today's inclusive schools. *Intervention in School and Clinic*, 32, 39–42.

Staub, D., Schwartz, I. S., Gallucci, C. and Peck, C. A. (1994). Four portraits of friendship at an inclusive school. *Journal of the Association for Persons with Severe Handicaps*, 19, 314–25.

Steere, D. E., Pancsofar, E. L., Powell, T. H. and Buttersworth, J. (1989). Enhancing instruction through general case programming. *Teaching Exceptional Children*, 21, 22–4.

Stoker, R., Gersch, I., Fox, G., Lown, J. and Morris, S. (2001). Educational psychology services and their futures-some responses to the DfEE Working Group Report. *British Journal of Special Education*, 28(2), 86–8.

Sugai, G. and Horner, R. H. (1994). Including students with severe behaviour problems in general education settings: Assumptions, challenges, and solutions. In J. Marr, G. Sugai and G. Tindal (eds), *The Oregon Conference Monograph 6* (pp. 102–20). Eugene: University of Oregon.

Thomson, K., Bachor, D., and Thomson, G. (2002). The development of individualized educational programmes using decision-making model. *British Journal of Special Education*, 29(1), 37–43.

Trent, J. (1994). *Inventing the Feeble Mind: A History of Intellectual Disability in the United States*. Berkeley: University of California Press.

Turnbull, A. P. and Schultz, J. B. (1979). *Mainstreaming Handicapped Students: A Guide for the Classroom Teacher*. Boston: Allyn and Bacon.

Turnbull, A. P. and Turnbull, H. R. (2001). *Families, Professionals, and Exceptionality: Collaborating for Empowerment* (4th edn). Upper Saddle River, NJ: Merrill/Prentice Hall.

Turnbull, R., Turnbull, A., Shank, M., Smith, S. and Leal, D. (2002). *Exceptional Lives: Special Education in Today's Schools*. Columbus, OH: Merrill Prentice-Hall.

Udvari-Solner, A. (1993). *Curricular Adaptations: Accommodating the Instructional Needs of Diverse Learners in the Context of General Education*. Topeka, KS: Kansas State Board of Education.

United Nations Educational, Scientific, and Cultural Organization (UNESCO) (1994). *The Salamanca Statement and Framework for Action on Special Needs Education*. New York: UNESCO. http//www.unesco.org/education/pdf/SALAMA_E.PDF

Utley, C. A., Mortweet, S. L. and Greenwood, C. R. (1997). Peer-mediated instruction and interventions. *Focus on Exceptional Children*, 29, 1–23.

Wang, M. C. and Birch, J. W. (1984). Comparison of a full-time mainstreaming program and a resource room approach. *Exceptional Children*, 51(1), 33–40.

Wehmeyer, M. L. (2001). Self-determination and intellectual disability. In L. M. Glidden (ed.), *International Review of Research in Intellectual Disability* (vol. 24, pp. 1–48). Englewood Cliffs, NJ: Academic Press.

Wehmeyer, M. L., Abery, B., Mithaug, D. E. and Stancliffe, R. (2003). *Self-Determination: Theoretical Foundations for Education*. Springfield, IL: Charles C. Thomas.

Wehmeyer, M. L., Field, S., Doren, B., Jones, B. and Mason, C. (2004). Self-determination and student involvement in standards-based reform. *Exceptional Children*, 70, 413–25.

Wehmeyer, M. L., Lance, G. D. and Bashinski, S. (2002). Promoting access to the general curriculum for students with intellectual disability: A multi-level model.

Education and Training in Intellectual Disability and Developmental Disabilities, 37, 223–34.

Wehmeyer, M. L., Lattin, D. and Agran, M. (2001). Promoting access to the general curriculum for students with intellectual disability: A decision-making model. *Education and Training in Intellectual Disability and Developmental Disabilities*, 36, 329–44.

Wehmeyer, M. L., Lattin, D., Lapp-Rincker, G. and Agran, M. (2003). Access to the general curriculum of middle-school students with intellectual disability: An observational study. *Remedial and Special Education*, 24, 262–72.

Wehmeyer, M. L., Sands, D. J., Knowlton, H. E. and Kozleski, E. B. (2002). *Teaching Students with Mental Retardation: Accessing the General Curriculum*. Baltimore: Paul H. Brookes.

Weishaar, M. K. (2001). The regular educator's role in the individual education plan process. *The Clearing House*, 75(2), 96–8.

Wiggins, G. (1993). Assessment, authenticity, context, and validity, *Phi Delta Kappan*, 75, 200–14.

Wilson, J. (2002). Researching special needs. *British Journal of Special Education*, 29(3), 141–3.

Winzer, M. A. (2000). The inclusion movement: Review and reflections on reform in special education. In M. A Winzer and K. Mazurek (eds), *Special Education in the 21st Century: Issues of Inclusion and Reform* (pp. 5–26). Washington, DC: Gaullaudet University Press.

Wood, M. (1998). Whose job is it anyway? Educational roles in inclusion. *Exceptional Children*, 64(1), 181–96.

World Health Organization (WHO) (2001). *International Classification of Functioning, Disability, and Health*. Geneva: WHO.

Wright, J. A. and Graham, J. (1997). Where and when do speech and language therapists work with teachers? *British Journal of Special Education*, 24(4), 171–4.

York, J. and Tundidor, H. (1995). Issues raised in the name of inclusion: Perspectives of educators, parents, and students. *Journal of the Association for Persons with Severe Handicaps*, 20, 31–44.

Zickel, J. P. and Arnold, E. (2001). Putting the I in the IEP. *Educational Leadership*, 59(3), 71–3.

Zionts, P. (1997). Inclusion: Chasing the impossible dream? Maybe. In P. Zionts (ed.), *Inclusion Strategies for Students with Learning and Behaviour Problems: Perspectives, Experiences, and Best Practices* (pp. 3–26). Austin, TX: Pro-Ed.

Chapter 17

Communication difficulties and the promotion of communication skills

Jeff Sigafoos, Mark O'Reilly and Vanessa A. Green

This chapter begins with a brief description of speech, language, and communication. A case study is then presented to illustrate a clinical model for communication assessment and intervention for individuals with developmental disability. Following the case study, we summarize key findings on language delay in people with mild/moderate and severe/profound disabilities. Communication intervention issues for individuals with developmental disabilities are then considered from a lifespan perspective. Provided are descriptions of effective methods for enhancing communication skills and practical guidelines for managing cases where clients are non-verbal or have very limited language skills. Reference will be made to augmentative and alternative communication (AAC) systems that are commonly used with individuals who have developmental disabilities, including manual signs, voice-output communication aides (VOCAs), and the Picture-Exchange Communication System (PECS). The aim of this chapter is to provide clinicians with the necessary background knowledge to use these methods in practice and to offer guidance to psychologists in the role of training parents, teachers, and staff to enhance the communication skills of individuals with developmental disability, which encompasses intellectual and physical disabilities and/or autism-spectrum disorder.

SPEECH, LANGUAGE, AND COMMUNICATION

For our purposes, speech refers to the use of spoken words and sentences for functional communication with others, whereas language refers to a complex rule-based system that makes use of arbitrary symbols (e.g. spoken or signed words and sentences) to convey meaning (Lefrancois, 1995). The complexity of language stems in part from the fact that words or signs can be arranged in many different combinations – but not any combination – to convey meaning. There are of course other ways a speaker could communicate with the listener that do not involve speech or language. For example, a young girl might effectively communicate to her mother that she wants a toy by pointing to it while also vocalizing and at the same time shifting her gaze from the parent to the object. This example highlights the distinction between form (i.e. what the individual does to communicate) and function (i.e. the purpose of the communicative act). The following case study illustrates the importance of identifying the communicative forms and functions in the repertoires of individuals with developmental disabilities.

Case study

This case study involved Lauren, a 19-year-old woman with Rett syndrome. Rett syndrome is a developmental disorder associated with profound intellectual and physical impairments. Lauren was referred to a multidisciplinary clinic and subsequently recruited into an intervention program focused on enhancing the communication skills of children with intellectual and physical disabilities. Prior to enrolling her into the program, we arranged an initial in-take and referral meeting with the parents to determine whether Lauren was a suitable candidate for the program. During this meeting, we learned that, despite her age, Lauren had no formal means of communication. She did not speak, but instead used a number of informal and idiosyncratic gestures (e.g. reaching for objects, body movements, vocalizations) that were interpreted by others as communicative. As a result, we decided that Lauren was a suitable candidate who might benefit from our intervention program.

The program involved a number of steps representing best clinical practice when beginning a communication intervention for individuals with severe/profound intellectual and physical disabilities (Sigafoos, Drasgow and Schlosser, 2003). Table 17.1 summarizes the steps of the program.

Step 1: standardized assessments

We first obtained an objective description of Lauren's language and adaptive behaviours. Information on language and adaptive behaviour functioning is necessary for preparing clinical reports and for planning intervention. We administered two standardized rating scales to assess language development and adaptive behaviours. Intellectual functioning was not assessed because Lauren was considered untestable on standardized IQ measures.

Language development was assessed using the second edition of the Receptive-Expressive Emergent Language Scale (REEL-2) (Bzoch and League, 1991). The REEL-2 is a developmental checklist. This device yields expressive and receptive language ages based on the development of typical children up to 3 years of age. It was considered appropriate for Lauren because of the severe nature of her communication impairment. Lauren's receptive language age was estimated at 6 months and her expressive language age was estimated at 1 month.

Table 17.1 Steps of the communication assessment and intervention program

Step	Description
1 Standardized assessments	Standardized assessments are completed to obtain an objective description of the client's language development and adaptive behaviour functioning.
2 Structured observations	Structured observations are completed to identify existing behaviours that the child uses to indicate basic communicative functions, such as request object and recruit attention.
3 Brief intervention trial	Systematic instruction is implemented to teach an initial communication skill, such as requesting access to a preferred object. Results from a brief intervention trial may enable clinicians to determine if the individual appears interested in and capable of learning to use the alternative mode of communication that has been identified as a replacement for behaviour indication.
4 Follow-up	The results from the brief intervention trial are used to develop a follow-up plan in consultation with parents and teachers. The plan includes procedures for implementing and maintaining the intervention at home and school, expanding vocabulary, and teaching additional communication functions.

Adaptive behaviour was assessed with the TARC Assessment System (Sailor and Mix, 1975). The TARC assesses adaptive behaviour functioning across four domains: self-help, motor, communication, and social skills. It yields standard scores with a mean of 50 and a standard deviation of 20. A score of 50 means that the child's adaptive behaviour functioning is considered average when compared to the standardization sample, which consisted of 238 children (3–16 years of age) with severe intellectual and physical disabilities. Although Lauren, at 19 years of age, fell outside of this age range, the TARC was considered appropriate for descriptive purposes because it was developed specifically for children with severe intellectual and physical disabilities. On the TARC, Lauren achieved a standard score of 20, placing her 1.5 standard deviations below the norm when compared to other severely handicapped children.

Overall, the results from these two standardized assessments provide objective confirmation that Lauren had substantial deficits in language development and adaptive behaviour functioning consistent with her diagnosis of Rett syndrome. More specifically, her extremely low expressive language

age (1 month) provided a compelling rationale for intervention focused on developing early expressive communicative behaviours.

Step 2: structured observation

Although the REEL-2 indicated that Lauren had limited expressive language skills, it is often the case that such individuals will use behaviour indication to communicate basic wants and needs (Wetherby and Prizant, 1992). Behaviour indication refers to the use of prelinguistic forms (e.g. reaching, leading, vocalizations, facial expressions, body movements) to achieve basic communication functions such as gaining attention or requesting access to preferred objects (Drasgow, Halle and Sigafoos, 1999). Direct observations under structured conditions are often helpful in identifying how behaviour indication is used for communicative purposes. Once identified, intervention can begin by teaching more conventional forms (e.g. manual signs, VOCA use, PECS) to replace existing prelinguistic behaviours (Keen, Sigafoos and Woodyatt, 2001). Conventional forms are preferred because prelinguistic behaviours often fail to recruit an appropriate response from listeners (Houghton, Bronicki and Guess, 1987) and, as the child gets older, prelinguistic forms may become socially stigmatizing (Drasgow et al., 1999).

Table 17.2 outlines the direct observation assessment protocol implemented with Lauren. This assessment was completed in a single 90-minute session. The session was conducted in a clinical room with Lauren seated in her wheelchair at a table. During the session, Lauren was exposed to four conditions, each designed to assess a different aspect of communication functioning. Conditions were repeated in a within-subject ABCD-DCBA design. The session was videotaped and later analyzed to identify the percentage of 10-second intervals with behaviour indication, which in this instance was defined as reaching for a person or object.

Results from the structured observation are shown in Figure 17.1. Each data point represents the percentage of 10-second intervals with behaviour indication for that condition. These data show that over the course of the assessment, Lauren did not show behaviour indication during either of the two Diverted Attention conditions. This result suggests that Lauren was not using behaviour indication to gain the attention of an adult at least under these structured assessment conditions. In contrast, behaviour indication occurred in approximately one third of the intervals during the two choice-making conditions, suggesting that Lauren was using behaviour indication to gain access to preferred objects. Intermediate amounts of behaviour indication were observed during the Attend and Attend + Objects conditions, suggesting some level of responsivity to social interaction and perhaps some attempt by Lauren to direct her parents' attention to preferred objects.

Results from the structured observation shown in Figure 17.1 suggested a beginning point for intervention. Because these data showed that Lauren

Table 17.2 Direct observation protocol to identify prelinguistic behaviours related to recruiting attention, maintaining social interaction, gaining access to preferred objects, and choice making

Condition/Time	Description
Diverted attention (0–3 min)	Child and parent sit next to each other. Parent talks to clinician and ignores the child. This condition is designed to determine if the child uses behaviour indication to recruit parental attention.
Attend (4–6 min)	Parent gives the child undivided attention by directing positive conversational statements to the child every 10 seconds. This condition is designed to determine if child uses behaviour indication to respond to and maintain social interaction.
Attend + objects (7–9 min)	Three preferred items are placed in view, but out of reach. The parent gives the child undivided attention and makes positive conversational statements every 10 seconds. This condition is designed to assess whether the child uses behaviour indication to the parent to gain access to preferred objects.
Choice making (10–12 min)	Pairs of preferred items are placed on the table within reach. The parent points to the objects and asks, 'Which one do you want?' The child is allowed 30 seconds to respond. This condition is designed to assess if behaviour indication is used to make choices.

would consistently reach for a preferred object, we decided to begin intervention by teaching Lauren to request access to preferred objects using a more symbolic form of communication. The feasibility of this approach was evaluated in the next step of the program.

Step 3: brief intervention trial

The initial goal of this phase was to replace reaching by teaching Lauren to operate a BIGmack™ switch (AbleNet, Inc.). The BIGmack™ is a single-switch VOCA that measures 12.7 cm in diameter. It is operated by pressing down on the top of the switch to generate a pre-recorded message of up to 20 seconds in length. Her initial vocabulary consisted of a black and white line drawing representing *WANT* (Mayer-Johnson Co., 1994) that was affixed to the top of the switch. When this symbol was touched, the pre-recorded message 'I want more' was produced from the VOCA. Because Lauren could

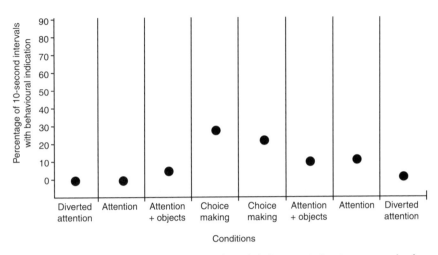

Figure 17.1 Percentage of 10-second intervals with behaviour indication across the four assessment conditions.

reach out and place her hand on objects, we anticipated that she would be able to operate this device. Manual signs or PECS were not appropriate for Lauren because of her severe physical impairments.

As with the structured observation, this brief intervention trial was also completed in a single 90-minute session. The session was scheduled a few weeks after her structured observation had been completed and after the results from that assessment had been analyzed. The session was conducted in the same clinical room as before with Lauren seated in her wheelchair at a table. The session began with a baseline phase followed by acquisition training, contingent reinforcement, and generalization. The procedures in effect during each of these phases are described in Table 17.3.

The results of the brief intervention trial are shown in Figure 17.2. Filled circles represent the cumulative number of VOCA responses for each phase, whereas open circles show the cumulative number of times Lauren reached for the object. During baseline, acquisition training and contingent reinforcement, food and drinks were used as reinforcers. During the generalization phase, generalized use of the requesting responses was assessed by replacing food and drink reinforcers with access to a musical toy. Lauren's mother implemented all but the final phase, when a new trainer was brought in to assess generalization across communicative partners.

During baseline, when a preferred object (e.g. a food item or a beverage) was placed on the table out of reach, Lauren would consistently reach toward the item within 30 s. We decided to use a 30-s constant time delay because Lauren seemed to require this amount of time to initiate a response. At no time during baseline did Lauren press the VOCA, even though it was within

Table 17.3 Procedures implemented during each phase of the brief intervention trial

Phase – Steps

Baseline
1 Place a preferred food, drink, or toy on the table just out of child's reach.
2 Wait up to 30 s for the child to reach for the object.
3 When the child reaches, give the item to the child.
4 If the child does not reach within 30 s, remove the item and place a different preferred object on the table.
5 Repeat (5–10 times) until the child is consistently reaching for the item.

Acquisition training
1 Place a preferred food, drink, or toy on the table just out of child's reach.
2 Wait up to 30 s for the child to reach for the object.
3 When the child reaches, physically guide the child's hand to press the BIGmack™ switch and then give the child the item.
4 Repeat until child consistently and independently presses the switch ten times instead of reaching for the object.
5 To promote independent switch pressing, use the least amount of physical guidance that is necessary to prompt a switch press.

Contingent reinforcement
1 Place a preferred food, drink, or toy on the table just out of child's reach.
2 Wait for the child to press the BIGmack™ switch.
3 Access to preferred items is contingent upon switch pressing.
4 Each time the child presses the switch, give her access to the object.
5 Physical guidance is no longer used at any time.
6 Reaching is ignored.
7 To build fluency this phase should continue until the child shows a steady rate of requesting using the BIGmack™ switch.

Generalization
1 Place additional preferred objects, not used in previous phases, on the table just out of child's reach.
2 A new trainer unfamiliar to the child should conduct some of the sessions.
3 The trainer waits for the child to press the BIGmack™ switch.
4 Access to preferred items is contingent upon switch pressing.
5 Each time the child presses the switch, give her access to the object (e.g. 30 seconds of music).
6 Physical guidance is not used because the aim is to determine whether the response will generalize to other objects and people without further training.
7 Reaching is ignored.

her reach at all times. Results from this phase confirm that Lauren used behaviour indication to request and did not use the VOCA.

Once this was confirmed, acquisition training was implemented until Lauren made ten independent requests using the VOCA and without first reaching for the object. Acquisition training was completed in less than 20 minutes. Contingent reinforcement was implemented for a further 10 minutes following acquisition to build fluency. As shown, Lauren used the VOCA

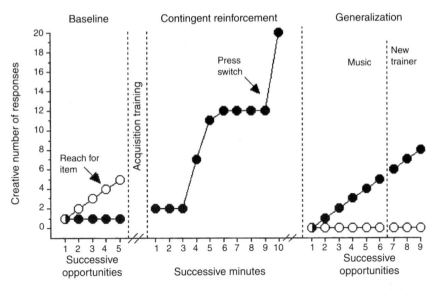

Figure 17.2 Percentage of 10-second intervals with behaviour indication and VOCA use during baseline, contingent reinforcement and generalization conditions.

approximately once every 30 s (i.e. twenty cumulative requests over 10 min) during this contingent reinforcement phase of the trial. The next phase showed that Lauren generalized her use of the VOCA to another object and to a new trainer.

Overall the results from the brief intervention trial were positive. The data suggested that Lauren learnt to use the VOCA to request access to preferred foods and beverages. In addition, she gained fluency in using the VOCA and her new requesting response generalized to another preferred object and to another communicative partner. This brief intervention trial therefore provided sufficient evidence to conclude that a VOCA-based system was a viable mode of communication for Lauren. Of course this was only a start and the next step of the clinical process requires collaborating with parents, teachers, and front-line staff to further develop the individual's communication system.

Step 4: follow-up

When a viable mode of communication has been identified, follow-up is needed to maintain and expand the intervention. For Lauren we consulted with the parents to identify activities at home where Lauren would continue to use her VOCA to request access to preferred objects. We also developed new procedures for teaching Lauren to use her VOCA to recruit her parents' attention, when they were not attending to her directly. This procedure involved teaching her to use two commands ('I want more' and 'Come here please'). Follow-up reports from parents suggested that the VOCA program we started in the clinic had readily transferred to the home setting and that Lauren continued to use her VOCA to request preferred objects. She also learnt to use her VOCA to recruit attention.

As illustrated with Lauren, in the follow-up phase of a clinical program, the emphasis shifts from piloting a beginning intervention to increasing vocabulary and expanding the individual's communication skills. Throughout this process, there remains the need to collect data so the intervention can be modified and expanded in light of the individual's progress. Even when the data show that a particular intervention approach is promising, parents, teachers, and staff may require support to implement the procedures and maintain the intervention in the home, school, workplace, and community. For many individuals in need of communication intervention, the process of supporting parents, teachers, and staff will require frequent consultation by clinicians rather than merely arranging one or two clinical sessions. While brief clinical sessions can be extremely useful during the beginning stages of the assessment and intervention process, maintaining and expanding the intervention beyond the initial stages will typically require continued follow-up and consideration of communication and language development across the lifespan.

KEY FINDINGS ON COMMUNICATION DEFICIT AND LANGUAGE DELAY

Impairment of speech and language is commonly associated with intellectual disability and autism-spectrum disorders (McQueen, Spence, Garner, Pereira and Winsor, 1987; Schopler and Mesibov, 1985). Impairments can be manifest as delayed, deficit, or abnormal speech and language development or by the complete absence of speech altogether. Among individuals with developmental disabilities, communication impairment and language delay typically affect more than one aspect of their speech and language development, including problems with the articulation of speech, acquisition of vocabulary, and disorders of syntax, semantics, and pragmatics.

The nature, extent, and circumstances of communication deficits and language delay among individuals with developmental disabilities have long been of considerable interest. This interest is no doubt fueled by necessity in that individuals with developmental disabilities almost always have delay or deficits in their speech, language, and communication development.

Historically, speech and language deficits indicated the lack of thought and hence lack of need or motivation to communicate. Esquirol (1845/1965) wrote that: 'Having no ideas, and thinking not, they have nothing to desire; therefore, they have no need of signs, or of speech' (1965: 467). Such pessimism did not deter others, such as Itard and Seguin, from attempting communication intervention with individuals who today would be diagnosed with developmental disability (Sheerenberger, 1983). Despite the fact that there was almost no empirical data on the nature of speech and language development or impairment at that time, these pioneers had some limited successes in their clinical work.

Fortunately, much has been learned since this early work. Numerous studies have investigated the nature, extent, and circumstances of speech, language, and communication impairment amongst individuals with developmental disabilities. One exemplary study examined the prevalence of intellectual disability and associated disabilities in the Canadian Maritime Provinces. In this study, McQueen *et al.* (1987) identified a cohort of 307 (7–10-year-old) children with severe intellectual disability (IQ < 55). Their case ascertainment methods ensured that this represented nearly the total population of children with major intellectual disability across the three provinces (New Brunswick, Nova Scotia, and Prince Edward Island). They found that speech disorder was the most common associated condition among this sample of children with intellectual disability. Specifically, 65.5 percent of the children were identified as having speech disorders of varying types and degrees. With respect to autism, evidence suggests that approximately 30–50 percent of individuals with autism do not have speech (National Research Council, 2001). Even when present, the speech of individuals with autism is often echolalic and nonfunctional. Given these high prevalence rates, it is understandable that communication intervention is a major priority for individuals with developmental disabilities.

However, it is important for clinicians to note that individuals with developmental disabilities do not constitute a homogeneous group. The type and extent of communication impairments, and hence the type of intervention that would be most appropriate, will vary depending on the etiology and severity of the person's disability. Intervention foci also change with age and lifestyle. The next two sections outline the types of communication and language delays and impairments that characterize individuals with different etiologies and degrees of developmental disability. Intervention needs are outlined in relation to the etiology and degree of disability.

Communication profiles of individuals with mild and moderate disability

Individuals with mild to moderate intellectual disability will typically experience delays in the emergence of speech and aspects of language use, such as multi-word utterances, syntax, and some aspects of pragmatic functioning, such as developing conversational turn-taking skills. There has been controversy as to whether the development of individuals with intellectual disabilities is best described as different or delayed (Zigler and Balla, 1982). The answer no doubt depends on the etiology and severity of the disability. From a clinical perspective, this debate would seem less relevant because, whether delayed or different, clinical best practice focuses on developing functional communication skills using evidence-based practices grounded in empirically validated principles of intervention (Schlosser, 2003).

Still, whether delayed or different, it is important to understand the nature of the individual's communication impairment as this will greatly assist in selecting the appropriate intervention path. Delayed speech and language development, for example, can indicate a variety of potential problems, such as possible hearing impairment, recurrent otitis media, or developmental disability. The appropriate intervention would be vastly different for a child with hearing impairment as compared to the child with moderate intellectual disability or autism-spectrum disorder. Similarly, delayed onset of two-word utterances may signal a less severe disability in comparison to the total absence of speech at 30 months of age. Loss of speech following a period of apparently normal development could indicate either the presence of a regressive disorder, such as Rett syndrome, or the effects of extinction of the child's early and initial communicative attempts.

Clinicians must therefore be familiar with typical development so that delays can be identified early. Table 17.4 lists the major language developmental

Table 17.4 Language milestones from birth to 4 years of age

Age	Description of receptive and expressive language
0–3 months	Attends to voices, appears to recognize familiar voices, makes frequent vocalizations, has different cries for different functions (hunger v. pain).
4–6 months	Respond to certain words (e.g. no) and intonations, frequent speech-like babbling, including p, b, and m sounds, makes simple requests using sounds and gestures.
7–12 months	Listens when spoken to, responds to name, recognizes names of familiar objects, responds to requests (e.g. Give it to daddy) and questions (More juice?), sounds used to recruit attention, first words appear.
1–2 years	Points to pictures and body parts named by others, follows simple commands (e.g. Shut the door) and understands simple questions (Where is your hat?), listens to stories, vocabulary of spoken words expands rapidly, will ask two-word questions.
2–3 years	Understands two-step commands (e.g. Get your hat and put it in the case), understands concepts such as hot/cold, stop/go, continued and rapid vocabulary growth, two- and three-word utterances emerge.
3–4 years	Understands who, what and where questions, hearing difficulties may become evident, sentences become longer as child combines four or more words, initiates conversations, speech is fluent and clear.

milestones for receptive and expressive language development. Early identification of delayed receptive and expressive language development is critical to ensure the child receives appropriate intervention as soon as problems are recognized. Evidence suggests that early intervention focused on developing communication skills and adaptive behaviours can be highly effective in closing the gap between children with developmental delays and their typically developing peers (Lovaas, 1987).

As with developmental disability in general, the type and extent of communication impairments associated with autism-spectrum disorder varies with the severity of the disability. While language problems are defining characteristics of autism at all levels of severity (American Psychiatric Association, 1994), Scheuermann and Webber (2002) noted that the extent of the individual's presenting language problems is often used to classify the severity of autism and to distinguish autism from other conditions, such as Asperger's syndrome. For example, when the individual is mute, their autism is considered more severe than if speech is present. Scheuermann and Webber also noted that even when a high level of speech and language has developed, the communication of individuals with autism-spectrum disorders is often characterized by certain odd and unusual features, including: (a) unusual voice tone and inflection; (b) pronoun reversals; (c) lack of variety in sentence structure; and (d) immature grammar (e.g. simple noun-verb formats).

It is unclear if the speech and language characteristics listed above represent a unique behavioural phenotype for autism, but this possibility is consistent with recent research suggesting that there may be distinct communication profiles for individuals with developmental disabilities of differing etiologies. To investigate this issue, Duker, van Driel, and van der Bercken (2002) compared the communication profiles of individuals with Down syndrome, Angelman syndrome, and Pervasive Developmental Disorder (PDD). The participants consisted of seventy-seven individuals from across the lifespan (ranging from 3.2 to 52.2 years of age). The sample consisted of nearly equal numbers of individuals with Down syndrome ($n = 26$), Angelman syndrome ($n = 26$), and PDD ($n = 25$). Communication profiles were obtained by interviewing parents, teachers, and front-line staff using the Verbal Behaviour Assessment Scale (VerBAS). This device consists of fifteen items rated for frequency on a 0 to 4 scale. Items were derived from Skinner's (1957) analysis of verbal behaviour to assess communication skills related to mands (i.e. requesting/rejecting), tacts (i.e. naming/commenting), and echoics (i.e. imitation) across a variety of modes (i.e. vocal, gesture, graphic). To assess rejecting, for example, one item asks, 'If s/he does not want the offered food, drink, or toy(s) any longer, does s/he say this, make the appropriate sign, or push it away?'

From this study, Duker et al. (2002) discovered that individuals with Down syndrome tended to have deficits in their mand repertoires relative to tacting and echoic behaviour. Participants with Angelman syndrome, in contrast, performed better on manding relative to tacting and had considerable deficits in their echoic repertoire. The communicative profiles of individuals with PDD did not differ from those with Down syndrome and there was also a considerable amount of within-syndrome variability. Still, the results suggest that there may be distinct communicative phenotypes associated with developmental disability syndromes and such results could have important implications for intervention. Duker *et al.* (2002) suggested, for example, that children with Down syndrome and PDD would benefit from intervention focused initially on teaching mands; whereas a focus on tacting may be the more appropriate initial training objective for individuals with Angelman syndrome. Furthermore, individuals with PDD may require interventions that compensate for their tendency to avoid social interaction and their general deficits in joint attention.

It may be important to consider that the results from Duker *et al.* (2002), while suggestive of syndrome-specific communication profiles, are based on group differences. Because there was individual variability within each diagnostic group, their data could also be used to argue that syndromes do not tell the whole story. Rather it may be the case that syndromes act indirectly and in interaction with environmental and developmental variables to shape the individual's communicative profile.

Abbeduto, Evans, and Dolan (2001) proposed an emergentism theory of language development and language problems that fits in well with the notion of indirect effects. In this account, 'language is seen to emerge as the result of the interaction between the child's biological abilities . . . and the characteristics of the child's language learning environment itself' (2001: 53). In this account, certain conditions or syndromes could act to constrain the child's biological abilities, thus requiring changes in the language-learning environment so as to compensate for any specific biological constraints. The clinician may therefore need to understand how biological factors interact with environmental factors so as to engineer a language-learning environment that is optimal for the individual given his or her biological abilities. What may be optimal for a child with Down syndrome may not necessarily be optimal for the child with Angelman syndrome.

Communication goals for individuals with mild and moderate disability

The goals of communication intervention for individuals with mild and moderate disabilities will vary across individuals and perhaps in relation to specific syndromes. Still, given what is currently known about the nature of communication disorders in mild and moderate disabilities, there is likely to be a number of commonly indicated intervention targets for individuals within this group. For example, regardless of their specific condition, most individuals with mild to moderate disabilities will be late talkers and require early intervention to accelerate their rate of speech and language acquisition. Clinicians will thus need to train parents to establish an effective speech and language-learning environment in the home.

Delays in learning to speak are usually more obvious than delays in receptive language abilities. This can be attributed to the fact that it is more difficult to assess receptive language and that many individuals learn to rely on environmental context to compensate for their lack of comprehension. Interventionists thus need to consider treatments to strengthen both expressive and receptive communication. In the expressive domain, training may be necessary to establish communicative functions that are absent or deficit and this may vary across different disability conditions as demonstrated by Duker *et al.* (2002). Articulation training may be indicated for individuals with mild disabilities or oral-motor problems. For those with moderate disabilities, development of speech and language is still a priority, but their delays and impairments will typically be more pronounced than for individuals with mild disabilities. However, both groups might nonetheless benefit from gesture or graphic mode communication systems to augment delayed speech and language.

Using AAC to augment the delayed or impaired speech of individuals with mild and moderate disabilities has met with some resistance. Some parents, teachers, front-line staff and even some speech pathologists may express concern that AAC might inhibit speech and language development. These concerns are unfounded. In fact, evidence suggests that AAC interventions facilitate speech and language development (Mirenda, 2003; Romski and Sevcik, 1996). For example, numerous studies (e.g. Barrera and Sulzer-Azaroff, 1983; Remington and Clarke, 1983; Yoder and Layton, 1988) have shown that a total communication approach involving simultaneous speech and manual sign training results in faster acquisition of expressive and receptive language skills than speech training alone.

With respect to AAC systems involving graphic symbols rather than manual signs, it has been shown that training to use PECS or VOCAs has also resulted in increased speech in some children with developmental disabilities (Bondy and Frost, 2001; Sigafoos, Didden and O'Reilly, 2003). However, the effects of AAC, especially aided AAC systems, on speech and language development should be interpreted with caution because few controlled studies have been conducted (cf. Romski and Sevcik, 1996). Still it would appear that AAC, while primarily indicated for individuals with severe and profound disabilities, may also be a promising supplement to orally based communication interventions for individuals with mild to moderate disabilities.

Communication profiles of individuals with severe to profound disability

Nearly all individuals with severe to profound disabilities also have a severe communication impairment (Matas, Mathy-Laikko, Beukelman and Legresley, 1985). The term severe communication impairment refers to situations where speech is either completely absent or so limited that it cannot meet the individual's communication needs. Many such individuals appear unlikely to acquire any appreciable amount of speech and are therefore obvious candidates for AAC. Until AAC is developed, however, these individuals typically have to rely on prelinguistic behaviours to communicate. Their prelinguistic forms might consist of informal gestures, undifferentiated vocalizations, eye contact, facial expressions, reaching and leading, and other body movements. In addition, some beginning communicators may use problem behaviour (e.g. aggression, self-injury, tantrums) to communicate. Reliance on prelinguistic forms is problematic because these acts are difficult to interpret and often socially inappropriate, or socially stigmatizing.

Given the above-listed characteristics, individuals with severe to profound disabilities are often considered to be at the very beginning stages of communication. When our case study with Lauren began, she would certainly have fit the characteristics of a beginning communicator. Beukelman and Mirenda (1998) considered beginning communicators to be individuals from across the lifespan with severe communication impairment associated with severe to profound levels of developmental, physical, and/or sensory disabilities such as cerebral palsy, intellectual disability, autism, or deaf/blindness.

Communication goals for individuals with severe to profound disability

The goal of communication intervention for individuals with severe to profound disabilities will differ from those for individuals with mild to moderate disabilities, although the underlying principles of intervention may be similar. Ferguson (1994) and Light and Binger (1998) argued that the overall aim of intervention for individuals with severe disabilities is to provide a system of communication that will lead to increased communicative competence. With increased communicative competence should come improved social interactions and increased participation in society.

To achieve this overall aim, individuals with severe to profound disabilities will need to acquire behaviours that will enable them to communicate efficiently. To be efficient, others must be able readily to interpret their communication responses. Once an efficient response mode is identified, the initial goal of intervention is to replace prelinguistic forms of requesting and rejecting with the new alternative response form. Our case study provided an example of how clinicians might set about to achieve this initial goal in an individual with profound disabilities.

This emphasis on teaching new forms to achieve requesting or rejecting functions is consistent with evidence from studies of communication development in typical children. Requesting and rejecting appear to be the first communicative functions to emerge in typically developing children (Carpenter, Mastergeorge and Coggins, 1983). This provides another rationale for beginning communication intervention by teaching appropriate forms of requesting and rejecting. In addition, the available evidence suggests that outcomes are enhanced when one focuses on teaching new AAC forms (e.g. manual signs, pointing to line drawings on a VOCA) to achieve the same communicative functions already expressed by existing prelinguistic acts (Wetherby, Warren and Reichle, 1998). Because requesting and rejecting are the functions most likely and most frequently expressed by beginning communicators using prelinguistic behaviour (Ogletree, Pierce, Harn and Fisher, 2002), it makes sense to begin intervention by replacing existing prelinguistic behaviours with AAC forms to achieve requesting and rejecting. Of course, this is only a beginning. Once this goal is achieved, intervention must expand to address the new communicative needs that arise as the individual develops across the lifespan.

COMMUNICATION INTERVENTION ACROSS THE LIFESPAN

Lifespan development can be viewed as a series of stages separated by shorter periods of transition (Marchetti and Matson, 1988). As illustrated in Table 17.4, the major milestones of typical speech and language development are associated with different age ranges or stages. Initial stages of communication development are characterized by increasing complexity in the child's communication. Bates and her colleagues (Bates, Camaioni and Volterra, 1975) described four initial stages that illustrate the increasing complexity of the child's communication development from unintentional responses to formal linguistic acts involving speech or manual signs (see Table 17.5).

As indicated by the descriptions in Table 17.5, communication development begins soon after birth with parents interpreting the child's crying as a form of communication. At first crying occurs for physiological reasons, but parental responses to the child's crying quickly establishes operant functions for the child's cry. Over a fairly brief period of time, 0–3 months for example, children learn to cry to get parents to meet their needs and they appear to emit different intonations and intensities of cries to achieve different functions. A similar process may occur in the next (perlocutionary) stage. During this stage, infants gain the ability to move their body, make facial expressions, and produce vocalizations. While these acts are not initially communicative in any formal sense, parents typically respond to such acts as

Table 17.5 Stages of communication development

Stage	Description
Birth cry	From 0–3 months, infants cry in response to physiological states (hunger, discomfort). Parents react to crying in ways that tend to address the presumed physiological state (e.g. by feeding or changing the child's diaper). Over time, because of contingent parental responsiveness, crying develops operant functions in that the child cries to get parents to meet his or her needs.
Perlocutionary	Between 4 and 10 months of age, children engage in a variety of prelinguistic acts (facial expression, body movements, vocalizations) that are interpreted by parents as forms of communication. While these acts may begin as simply respondent or orienting responses, parents often over-interpret the acts and assign a communicative function to these acts. As with crying, this over-interpretation may in fact shape prelinguistic behaviours into functional communicative responses.
Illocutionary	At this stage, which occurs between 9–18 months, children have acquired a range of prelinguistic behaviours and conventional gestures (e.g., headshake gestures, pointing) to communicate to request, reject, and comment.
Locutionary	During this stage (12 months and beyond), prelinguistic acts are supplemented by formal linguistic forms (words, manual signs). This final stage is characterized by rapid growth of vocabulary, emergence of two-word utterances, and complete sentences.

if they were intentional communication on the part of the child. With consistent over-interpretation on the part of the parent, these acts are thought to develop into functional communication responses related to requesting, rejecting, and commenting, which characterizes the subsequent, illocutionary, stage. Here prelinguistic acts continue and conventional gestures emerge that are clearly communicative. The child's prelinguistic acts and gestures are supplemented by more formal linguistic communication responses in the final (locutionary) stage of communication development.

Individuals with mild to moderate disabilities will typically make the transition from the perlocutionary stage to the locutionary stage, but they may do so at a delayed rate. As a result, intervention may be important to promote more rapid transition – especially from the illocutionary to the locutionary stage – because the child may have difficulty moving from the use of prelinguistic acts and conventional gestures to speech. Along these lines, the use of total communication involving manual signs and speech may be helpful in promoting the transition from the illocutionary to the locutionary stage. In addition, once the individual has entered the locutionary stage, their development beyond single words may be delayed. Incidental teaching procedures have been applied with good effects to establish more elaborate speech and language once the child has entered the locutionary stage of development (Hart and Risley, 1982). Incidental teaching involves waiting for the individual to initiate speech and then prompting an expansion. For example, an adult may ask for 'coffee' to which the trainer responds by prompting an expansion (say you want it with milk and sugar).

In the absence of explicit intervention, individuals with severe to profound disabilities, such as Lauren, may remain at the perlocutionary stage of communication development. While these individuals may produce a variety of prelinguistic behaviours (e.g. body movements, facial expressions, reaching/ leading) that are interpreted as communication it is often difficult to determine if the behaviours are in fact communicative. It is also often difficult to determine whether or not these behaviours have a communicative function because they are often subtle and idiosyncratic. Sigafoos, Woodyatt, Keen, Tait, Tucker *et al.* (2000) referred to prelinguistic behaviours that may or may not be communicative as 'Potential Communicative Acts' (PCA). The term PCA acknowledges:

> the possibility that existing informal and idiosyncratic behaviours could be, or might become, effective forms of communication if others consistently recognized and responded to particular actions as if they were indeed the child's way of expressing a specific message.
>
> (2000: 78)

It is critical to identify existing PCAs, so that parents, teachers, and front-line staff will recognize and react to these consistently. In identifying PCAs, it will often be difficult to determine if these represent intentional forms of communication and, if so, what communicative function the behaviours are serving. If existing PCAs are merely interpreted as communicative (perlocutionary), then a program of structured over-interpretation is indicated (von Tetzchner, 1997). This strategy involves recognizing the occurrence of PCAs, providing a consistent interpretation of the act (e.g. 'When Janet looks towards an item, we will interpret this as if she were requesting the item'), and then reacting in a manner that is consistent with the interpretation (e.g. giving Jane the item she looks at). Over time, this strategy may facilitate the transition from the perlocutionary to the illocutionary stage of development.

When existing PCAs are determined to represent intentional communication (illocutionary behaviour), intervention should focus on facilitating the transition to more symbolic forms of communication in line with the progression from the illocutionary to the locutionary stage of development. As in the case with Lauren, this will typically require explicit and deliberate instruction to map new and more symbolic forms onto existing functions.

A lifespan perspective considers the individual's current stage of communication development. However, clinicians should be alert to the possibility that a person's current level of communicative functioning can cut across stages and their progression from one stage to another may not be orderly or sequential. For example, an individual with autism might readily transition from the illocutionary to the locutionary stage through a program of instruction that leads to rapid acquisition of manual sign requests. And yet, despite the acquisition of symbolic requesting forms, the individual could well remain in the illocutionary stage in terms of other communicative functions, such as commenting and initiating conversation with peers. Thus, in addition to considering the individual's current stage of communication development, clinicians should also consider the ecological context in which the individual functions. There will be differing communicative demands at each life stage.

Early childhood (birth to 6 years of age)

In this stage, parents may first suspect that something is amiss in terms of their child's development. In fact it is often delayed speech and language development that alert parents to a potential problem. The diagnostic process is typically initiated in the early childhood years. Comprehensive assessments associated with diagnosis may help identify and clarify the nature of the child's communication problems.

An ecological inventory process will help to identify communicative demands of the early childhood environment. Reichle, York, and Sigafoos (1991) described the use of ecological inventories for selecting communication objectives. The process involves a number of steps:

1   First, identify the environments in which the individual is expected to function. In the early childhood stage, this is likely to be the family home, the preschool, and the general community (e.g. family outings to the park, grocery store, restaurants).
2   Second, for each environment, identify the sub-environments. For example, a child's home consists of several sub-environments, such as kitchen, bedroom, bathroom, family room, and yard.
3   Third, identify the activities that occur in each sub-environment. In the family room, for example, one major activity is for the child to play appropriately with siblings.
4   Forth, identify communication skills relevant to each activity. While playing with siblings in the family room after dinner, for example, it may be crucial for the child to learn how to request a turn, comply with instructions, and comment on aspects of the game.

An ecological inventory process of this type can be applied to any stage of development from early childhood to older adulthood. Once relevant communication skills are identified, specific age-appropriate vocabulary to represent the targeted communication skills can be selected. Along these lines, Banajee, Dicarlo, and Stricklin (2003) developed a core vocabulary list based on fifty 2–3-year-old children. The children were audiotaped across three days in two different activities (play and snack time). The result was a list of frequently used words (e.g. I, no, yes, want, mine, all done, etc.). Clinicians can make use of such lists in selecting vocabulary for toddlers with developmental disabilities.

Later childhood (6 to 12 years of age)

Even with effective early intervention during the period birth to 6 years, children with developmental disabilities will likely continue to experience communication problems as they enter school. In fact, as the academic demands increase, the gap in communicative competence between children with and without developmental disabilities is likely to become more apparent. Promoting communication at this life stage will require emphasis on developing skills that will enable the child to participate in academic activities and social interactions with peers. Depending on the severity of the disability, the child's academic program is likely to emphasize academic and pre-academic skills (matching, sorting, sight-word reading) and/or more basic self-care instruction. Vocabulary relevant to these tasks will need to be taught. Comprehensive skills that enable the child to follow more complex instructions will also assume greater importance at this stage. Visual supports such as picture schedules that illustrate the classroom routine may prove valuable. Communication skills related to initiating and maintaining social interaction with peers will also becoming increasingly important during later childhood. Children at this life stage will more likely be involved in a wider range of community activities than was the case in early childhood. Not only will they be exposed to a wider range of community settings, but they will also be expected to participate more fully in community activities. This will require selection of communication skills and vocabulary that are age-appropriate and relevant to the child's expected level of participation.

Adolescents (13 to 22 years of age)

Communication skills related to functional academic and social skills remain vitally important during adolescence. This will mean expanding vocabulary to suit the peer group. Community-based and pre-vocational instruction will become major components in the educational programs of adolescents with developmental disabilities. With these emphases comes the necessity to teach additional communication skills and vocabulary. In training job skills, for example, individuals will need to know how to communicate effectively with customers, co-workers, and supervisors. Specific job-relevant vocabulary will need to be taught. Teaching appropriate social skills for the job setting is of major importance because the lack of social skills contributes to job loss among workers with developmental disabilities (Siegel, Park, Gumpel, Ford, *et al.*, 1990).

Adulthood (22 to 65 years of age)

In adulthood, individuals with developmental disabilities exit formal school and enter supported employment services. Promoting communication skills necessary to retain employment will be of continuing importance at this life stage. The work environment provides opportunities to develop friendships, but taking advantage of such opportunities requires appropriate communication and social skills (Riches and Green, 2003). In areas where supported employment options are less developed, sheltered employment or day habilitation programs may occupy a good portion of the adult's weekday. Balandin and Iacono (1999) obtained conversation samples from thirty-four nondisabled workers across four worksites (restaurant, betting shop, health service, and cafeteria). Fifteen-minute conversation samples were obtained across three consecutive days, yielding a list of core vocabulary and conversational topics that could become targets for communication intervention. By teaching conversational skills that match that of their co-workers, individuals with developmental disabilities may be better assisted to interact socially in the job setting. Outside of work hours, efforts should be undertaken to develop a lifestyle for the individual that includes opportunities for social and recreational activities. The communication skills needed to participate in these types of lifestyle decisions will need to be developed. This may also be the time when parents seek out-of-home placement for their adult child. Many individuals with developmental disabilities will be placed in small community-based group homes. The habilitative programs in community-based homes should include an emphasis on promoting autonomy, independence, and self-determination (Wehmeyer and Bolding, 2001). In line with increased autonomy, community-based activities will constitute a major portion of the adult's life. Communication interventions will therefore need to be developed and implemented that will enable increased autonomy and assumption of adult roles.

Adults 65 years and older

Communication needs of older persons with developmental disabilities are beginning to receive increased attention. This is not surprising given that advances in medical care and related services have resulted in more individuals with developmental disabilities surviving into old age (Janicki and Walsh, 2002). While there is increased recognition of the needs of older persons with developmental disabilities, there has been little research on promoting communication skills in this population. One might anticipate, however, that the elderly will have different communication needs related to changing life circumstances and possible deterioration in vision and hearing acuity. Many individuals may transition to nursing facilities as they age and will therefore require communication systems that will be effective in those settings. Ashman and colleagues (e.g. Ashman, Hulme and Suttie, 1990; Ashman and Suttie, 1996) argued for a need to develop effective training programs for aged people with an intellectual disability. While programs specific to the promotion of communication skills in elderly people are lacking, a review of key findings from research on communication enhancement may offer useful principles that could be applied to this population.

KEY FINDINGS AND TRENDS FROM RESEARCH ON COMMUNICATION ENHANCEMENT

Given the ubiquity of deficits in communication development among individuals with developmental disabilities, it is not surprising that a considerable amount of research has focused on enhancing the communication and language skills of such individuals. Since the 1960s, a reliable body of knowledge has emerged on how to teach communication skills to individuals with developmental disabilities. This reliable body of knowledge stems from hundreds of intervention studies involving children, adolescents, and adults with varying types and degrees of disabilities. Overall, this research has consistently demonstrated the effectiveness of operant training procedures for teaching a variety of communication skills to individuals with developmental disabilities. This section reviews key findings and trends from the vast literature on teaching communication skills to individuals with developmental disabilities.

In one of the first controlled studies in this area, Lovaas and his colleagues (Lovaas, Berberich, Perloff and Schaeffer, 1966) demonstrated the effectiveness of a four-step procedure for developing speech in mute autistic children. Initially, the child is given food as reinforcement for any type of vocalization and for looking at the trainer's mouth. This produces an increase in the frequency of child vocalizations and attention to the trainer. Next, the child is reinforced only if they produce a vocalization following speech from the trainer. For example, the trainer says a word (e.g. 'baby') and the child is reinforced for any vocalization that occurs within 6 seconds. When the child's vocal behaviour occurs consistently in response to the trainer model, the third step involves withholding reinforcement unless the child's vocalization matches that of the trainer. In this way, speech sounds and words are shaped from the child's undifferentiated, yet contingent pattern of vocalization. The final step then involves adding new words while recycling previously mastered words.

Teaching imitation as the initial communicative goal was based in part on the assumption that modelling and imitation were essential to speech and language acquisition. Once the person could reliably imitate, additional studies showed that vocabulary could then be brought under stimulus control by reinforcing spoken responses (e.g. cup, ball) in the presence of a specific stimulus (e.g. an actual cup or ball) (Lovaas, 1977). Responses were prompted by providing a model that the individual would reliably imitate (e.g. 'Say cup', 'Say ball') while gradually fading the imitative model over successive opportunities.

In the 1970s, an increasing number of intervention studies demonstrated that – in addition to imitative speech – a variety of complex speech and language skills could also be taught using operant techniques. The basic operant techniques for training included response and stimulus prompting and fading, discrimination training, and differential reinforcement. Skills taught included expressive and receptive labelling (i.e. naming objects and pointing to objects named by the trainer), use of grammatical endings (s and ed), prepositions, and comparative relations (e.g. bigg*er* v. bigg*est* and small*er* v. small*est*) (Baer and Guess, 1971; Lovaas, 1977; Wheeler and Sulzer, 1970).

While the comprehensive intervention programs developed in the 1970s made use of operant techniques, their content was mainly derived from psycholinguistic theory and emphasized the training of syntactic and semantic structures. Less emphasis was placed on developing functional or pragmatic aspects of communication (Sigafoos, 1997). The 1980s, in contrast, brought increased attention to the acquisition of functional communication skills, such as requesting access to preferred objects and activities. This shift in emphasis was based in part on problems that arose in trying to teach commu-nication skills to learners who were not imitative. These problems included failure to acquire speech, lack of generalization, maintenance, and spon-taneity, and recognition of communicative function in prelinguistic and problematic forms of behaviour.

Developing alternatives to speech

While many individuals with developmental disabilities benefited from inter-ventions to teach speech, others failed to make progress. To address this issue, researchers investigated communicative alternatives to speech. Carr and his colleagues (Carr, Binkoff, Kologinsky and Eddy, 1978), for example, provided the first controlled study of teaching manual signs to children with autism. In this study, four children (10–15 years of age) with autism were taught to name objects by producing the corresponding manual sign when shown an object by the trainer. The training procedures consisted of prompting, fading, and reinforcement. Discriminations between objects were taught by rotating the objects presented. Since that time, numerous studies have replicated the effectiveness of using operant procedures for teaching manual signs to individuals with developmental disabilities who failed to acquire speech (Duker and Jutten, 1997). Because manual signs are ineffective with listeners who do not know sign language, investigators also showed the applicability of operant methods for teaching learners to use picture-based communication systems including VOCA and PECS (Sigafoos and Mirenda, 2002).

Generalization and maintenance

Researchers found that communication responses were not always maintained once training ended. In addition, responses often failed to generalize to other trainers, settings, or materials. Promoting the maintenance and generalized use of newly acquired communication responses was facilitated by a landmark review published in 1977 by Stokes and Baer. In this review, maintenance and generalization were re-conceptualized as active, rather than passive processes. Maintenance refers to the continued use of newly acquired responses after training is completed. Generalization can be viewed as establishing control over responding by a range of relevant stimuli; an outcome that is built up through explicit training rather than merely hoping for it to occur. Several procedures for promoting maintenance and generalization during communication intervention have been empirically validated. Duker, Didden, and Sigafoos (2004) provide a detailed description of tactics that have been used to promote maintenance and generalization of communication responses over time and across settings, trainings, and materials. Tactics include using existing functional contingencies, reducing instructional control, using multiple and sufficient exemplars, intermittent reinforcement, and programming common stimuli.

Spontaneity

In addition to maintenance and generalization problems, researchers noted that newly acquired vocabulary frequently did not occur spontaneously. Part of the problem stemmed from the fact that individuals were often taught to name objects, whereas spontaneous use involved requesting. It soon became apparent that naming and requesting were in fact separate communication skills (Lamarre and Holland, 1985). Thus teaching a word as an object name did not automatically enable the individual to use that word to make a request and vice versa. As with maintenance and generalization, efforts to address spontaneity were advanced by an influential conceptual paper (Halle, 1987). In this paper, Halle argued that spontaneity could be viewed along a continuum of cues that set the occasion for communication. Responses that require physical, gesture, or verbal prompting are less spontaneous than responses controlled by the presence of an object or a particular state of deprivation (e.g. requesting a drink when thirsty). Promotion of more spontaneous communication can therefore be seen as a process of transferring stimulus control from instructional prompts to natural contextual cues.

Prelinguistic interventions

As mentioned before, many individuals with developmental disabilities typically enter communication programs exhibiting a range of prelinguistic behaviours. Their prelinguistic behaviours most typically function as indicators of basic wants and needs, likes and dislikes. Growing recognition of the communicative potential of these types of prelinguistic acts has led to the development of new intervention approaches that focus on replacing the prelinguistic behaviours with more symbolic and appropriate forms of communication (Sigafoos, Arthur-Kelly and Butterfield, 2006; Sigafoos, Drasgow and Schlosser, 2003). For example, if a child tantrums to escape from a difficult task, one potentially effective intervention option would be to teach the individual to request help with the task. Instead of tantrums, the individual might request help using a manual sign or a VOCA. This approach, known as functional communication training, has been widely used in the treatment of severe behaviour problems in individuals with developmental disabilities (Durand, 1990; Sigafoos, Arthur and O'Reilly, 2003).

Keen et al. (2001) extended the logic of functional communication training to map new forms onto the existing functions of prelinguistic behaviours. In the study, the researchers taught teachers to use prompting and differential reinforcement to replace prelinguistic behaviours in four children with autism. Initially, three existing communicative functions were selected for each child. Next, the existing prelinguistic behaviours that the children used to achieve these functions were identified. Replacement forms that were considered more recognizable and symbolic were defined to achieve these same functions. After a baseline phase, teachers received inservice training, consultation, and feedback on how to prompt and reinforce the replacement forms. During intervention, replacement forms increased and prelinguistic behaviours decreased, suggesting that the teacher-implemented intervention was effective in replacing prelinguistic behaviours with alternative and more advanced forms of functional communication. The results from Keen et al. provide support for the applicability of basic operant training procedures in facilitating the transition from the illocutionary to locutionary stages of development.

PRACTICE GUIDELINES FOR ENHANCING COMMUNICATION

Our review of key findings and trends in communication intervention studies suggests that effective practice requires an understanding of the basic principles that underlie the treatment procedures. Clinicians should therefore have an understanding of the basic operant principles (e.g. reinforcement, prompting, shaping, fading) that underlie effective communication intervention for persons with developmental disabilities. In addition, clinicians should adopt an evidence-based approach to intervention.

Sigafoos, Drasgow and Schlosser (2003) outlined three essential components of evidence-based practice in communication intervention. First, evidence-based practice makes use of empirically validated procedures that have demonstrated effectiveness for teaching communication skills to individuals with developmental disabilities. Use of procedures that lack empirical support (e.g. facilitated communication) cannot be justified.

Second, clinicians must understand the basic operant mechanisms that underlie effective practice so that they can modify intervention procedures to suit the individual's unique circumstances and attributes. Various attributes and characteristics (e.g. visual acuity, degree of motor control, levels of alertness, impulsiveness, motivation, and preferences) will influence the course of intervention. For example, manual signs are contraindicated for individuals with physical disabilities and poor motor control. Clinicians must therefore work directly with the individual and collaborate with key stakeholders in undertaking comprehensive assessments to identify individual characteristics that will influence communication intervention.

The third part of evidence-based practice requires data-based instruction. This consists of using learner-generated performance data to evaluate the effects of intervention. Because even careful implementation of an empirically validated strategy is no guarantee that that strategy will be effective, clinicians must collect individual performance data to monitor the effects of the strategy on a daily or weekly basis.

More specific practice guidelines can be derived from an analysis of the program components that contribute to improved treatment outcomes for individuals with developmental disabilities. Lovaas (2002) identified a number of critical components that appear to be associated with more positive treatment outcomes for individuals with developmental disabilities. In what follows, we have adapted these guidelines for clinicians involved in organizing communication intervention:

1   **Focus on measurable and observable behaviours:** Goals should reference specific communication behaviours. These behaviours should be operationally defined and include a description of how the occurrence of the behaviour will be measured, so that progress toward goal attainment can be monitored.

2   **Evidence-based:** Training procedures should be based on empirically validated principles of learning. This requires an understanding of the basic operant and respondent conditioning principles that underlie effective instruction, as well as an understanding of how to create the motivation and need for communication. Effective instruction involves skilled application of shaping, prompting, and fading, and differential reinforcement techniques.

3   **Comprehensive emphasis:** Intervention should include goals to teach a wide range of communication skills using a variety of communicative modes appropriate to the individual (e.g. vocalizations and speech, gestures and manual signs, writing and picture-based communication systems). Additional training procedures may be needed to ensure spontaneous and functional communication that will generalize and maintain. The overall intervention effort should therefore aim to build a range of communicative behaviours that will facilitate participation in meaningful communicative exchanges with a variety of listeners and across a range of typical home, school, vocational, and community settings.

4   **Family, teacher, and staff involvement:** Parents, siblings, teachers, peers, and front-line staff should be involved in developing and maintaining the communication intervention. Including these individuals will help to ensure the skills acquired will be functional for the individual. In many cases, clinicians will need to provide training to parents, teachers, peers, and front-line staff on how to be effective communicative partners to individuals with developmental disabilities.

STAFF TRAINING

An important role for clinicians working in the field of developmental disabilities involves training parents, teachers, peers, and front-line staff. These individuals often require explicit training on how to be effective communicative partners for their children, students, and clients with developmental disabilities. Effective training for communicative partners is important because their responsivity appears to be one of the major variables affecting the communication performances of individuals with developmental disabilities (Harwood, Warren and Yoder, 2002). Partners must be able to respond in ways that will maintain and extend the learner's communicative repertoire. Becoming a responsive partner to individuals with communication difficulties may require explicit training.

This need for partner training stems, in part, from the fact that the communicative acts of individuals with developmental disabilities are often imprecise and subtle and hence listeners may not know how to respond when the individual initiates a communicative exchange (Sigafoos *et al.*, 2000). It also stems from the fact that, unlike typically developing children, individuals with developmental disabilities often require systematic instruction to develop their communicative potential. Providing systematic instruction is complex. Parents, teachers, and staff often need considerable support to learn and make use of systematic instructional procedures for promoting the communication development of individuals with developmental disabilities.

Complicating the issue is the fact that individuals with developmental disabilities often fail to initiate communication or initiate infrequently. In this situation, there will be little for partners to respond to and hence little opportunity to strengthen the individual's communicative repertoire by being responsive. Consequently, partners must learn how to: (a) motivate the individual to communicate; (b) set the occasion for communication; and (c) prompt and reinforce appropriate forms of communication.

Ferster (1961) explained that communication behaviour is likely to be weak in individuals with developmental disabilities due to inconsistent reinforcement from listeners. Compared to other kinds of behaviour (e.g. spinning, flapping), which have direct effects on the environment, communication is effective only indirectly through the mediation of a listener. To be effective in communication thus requires a listener who is both attentive and cognizant of the function or purpose of the learner's communicative attempt. As noted above, it may be difficult for listeners to determine when and what the individual is attempting to communicate, because of the nature of the person's communicative impairment, and so the partner's ability to reinforce the individual's communication acts is compromised. If subtle communicative acts fail to recruit reinforcement, the individual may escalate to tantrums in an attempt to repair the communicative breakdown. In addition to inconsistent reinforcement, Sundberg (1981) also implicated punishment as a potential inhibiting factor for language learning. Training should therefore focus on teaching parents, teachers, peers, and staff to: (a) recognize and reinforce appropriate forms of communication; (b) prevent escalation to problematic forms; and (c) refrain from punishing early and potential communicative acts that could be shaped into more symbolic forms of communication.

The quality and quantity of linguistic input and feedback received by beginning communicators is of critical importance in shaping more advanced and effective forms of communication (Abbeduto, Evans and Dolan, 2001; Hart and Risley, 1999). Hart and Risley (1999), for example, noted differences in parental reactions to child talk and these differences appeared to influence the child's language development. More and better reactions from parents lead to more and better child talk. The implications for communication intervention are obvious: communication partners who provide frequent and effective input and feedback will enhance the individual's communication development. Given the significant communication needs of individuals with developmental disabilities, quality input and output includes not only providing effective models and being responsive with feedback, but also creating frequent opportunities for teaching communication behaviour.

Along these lines, several studies have demonstrated effective procedures for training staff to be effective communicative partners to individuals with developmental disabilities. Duker and Moonen (1985) described a program for training staff and teachers to increase the use of manual signs among three students with severe/profound intellectual disability. Training was provided to one teacher and twelve residential staff (21–32 years of age). The training package was multifaceted and included: (a) written instructions describing the procedures; (b), live and video demonstrations of the teaching procedures; (c) cueing and feedback; and (d) group discussions. After staff received this training, they provided increased opportunities for sign use and the students showed increased use of manual signs to make requests. Their training package included a number of components that appeared to be useful (e.g. written descriptions, modelling, feedback, group discussions). However, although the study demonstrated the effectiveness of this package for training staff, it remained unclear if all components of the package were necessary.

Sigafoos, Kerr, Roberts, and Couzens (1994) evaluated a consultative approach for training teachers to provide communicative opportunities in classrooms for children with developmental disabilities. Teachers received a 1-hour inservice training during which the trainer described strategies that could be used to create opportunities for requesting (e.g. missing-item format, blocked response, and delayed assistance) (see Table 17.6 for examples of these and other strategies). Teachers also received a one-page description of each strategy. The innovative aspect of this training program was that the teachers then generated their own ideas on how to incorporate these strategies into classroom routines. The trainer facilitated the discussion by asking questions, such as 'How might the missing-item format be used at lunch-time?' and

Table 17.6 Strategies for creating opportunities for communication

Strategy	Description
Time delay	Preferred items/activities are present, but access is delayed until a request occurs. For example, a toy is placed on the table, but access to it is delayed for 10 seconds.
Missing item	An item that is needed for a preferred activity is missing. For example, a child may be given a colouring book but not the crayons.
Blocked response	Momentarily blocking a response or interrupting an ongoing activity. For example, the child is blocked from reaching for a toy, creating a need for the child to request.
Incomplete presentation	Initial request is followed by incomplete presentation of the requested item. For example, after requesting a toy that has several parts, the child is given only half of the parts.
Delayed assistance	Required assistance is delayed until a request occurs. For example, if the person needs help to open a jar of ketchup, the communicative partner would wait for the person to ask for help.
Wrong item format	Individual is given a non-matching referent. For example, the individual requests water, but is given a pencil. This creates a need for the person to clarify the initial request.

Note: From Sigafoos, J. and Mirenda, P. (2002). Strengthening communicative behaviours for gaining access to desired items and activities. In J. Reichle, D. R. Beukelman and J. C. Light (eds), *Exemplary Practices for Beginning Communicators: Implications for AAC* (p. 133). Baltimore: Paul H. Brookes Publishing Co.; reprinted by permission.

'Do you think the delayed assistance strategy could be used with Robert?' Subsequent classroom observations revealed that the teachers incorporated these strategies into a variety of typical classroom routines, resulting in more communication learning opportunities for their students.

Carter and Maxwell (1998) taught peers to be effective communicative partners to four children with cerebral palsy who relied on AAC. Their evaluation of the peer-training package was undertaken in a primary school that included children with and without disabilities. To promote communicative interactions, children without disabilities were taught to follow four steps: (a) establish eye contact; (b) ask questions; (c) wait for a response; and (d) respond to communicative overtures. After receiving training on these steps, the quantity and quality of the social-communicative interactions increased. As with the Duker and Moonen (1985) study, however, it is not clear if all four steps were critical for effective peer-to-peer communication. From a clinical perspective, however, it would seem unnecessary to be concerned with this issue because the 'package' was simple and easy for the non-disabled peers to learn.

Larger-scale programs to train staff have been attempted. Arthur, Butterfield, and McKinnon (1998) described a professional development program for training professionals and paraprofessionals to be more effective communicative partners for individuals with severe disabilities. Their program focused on developing knowledge and skills related to communication assessment, program development, and systematic instruction. Participants were taught how to create opportunities for meaningful communicative exchanges throughout the day. A total of 179 of the original 301 participants completed the pre- and post-inservice evaluations, consisting of 133 teachers, 37 teacher assistants, and 9 speech pathologists. From the inservice, participants reportedly gained new knowledge related to being a responsive communicative partner to people with severe disabilities, although the 41 percent attrition rate may have produced a biased sample. Inservice training is an economical approach to staff training and Arthur *et al.*'s evaluation suggested that inservice training can lead to increased knowledge. However, it is unclear if this new knowledge would translate into improved outcomes for individuals with developmental disabilities. While inservice training may be efficient for increasing knowledge, effective application of skills to promote the communication development of individuals with developmental disabilities may require a more competency-based approach to staff training.

Schepis and Reid (2003) outlined a competency-based model for training staff to enhance the communication skills of individuals with developmental disabilities. Although their model was specifically geared towards staff who were teaching children with severe disabilities to use VOCAs, their approach could be applied more generally. Table 17.7 summarizes the Schepis and Reid model, and includes an illustrative example.

Table 17.7 Steps for training parents, teachers, and front-line staff

Step	Description of Step	Example
1	The consultant collaborates with staff to identify behavioural objectives that reference observable and measurable behaviours.	Sign HELP when assistance is needed to complete daily living tasks.
2	The consultant develops procedures for teaching the specified objective. This includes a literature search to identify empirically validated procedures (e.g. Reichle, Drager and Davis, 2002), adjusting procedures to suit individual circumstances, and a written description of the procedures.	Procedures include: (1) wait 10 seconds for client to request help when needed: (2) if request does not occur, use least-to-most prompting: (3) give help after request.
3	Consultant explains procedures to staff, making sure they understand each step of the procedure.	'At this point, wait 10 seconds. This will motivate the person to request help.'
4	After explaining the written plan, the clinician shows the staff how to implement the plan while simultaneously describing each step of the procedure.	'Now I will have to use a physical prompt because the client did not respond to the model.'
5	Staff practise implementing the procedure, while the consultant watches and gives feedback. This continues until staff demonstrate proficiency.	'Good! You waited 10 s. Now because he has not requested, you need to deliver the verbal prompt.'

Note: Based on Schepis, M. M. and Reid, D. H. (2003). Issues affecting staff enhancement of speech generating device use among people with severe cognitive disabilities. *Augmentative and Alternative Communication*, 19, 59–65.

SUMMARY

Communication intervention is a major priority for individuals with developmental disabilities. The nature and extent of communication problems vary with type and severity of disability. Individuals with mild/moderate disabilities typically experience delayed speech and language development. In addition, emerging evidence suggests there may be differing patterns of delay depending on etiology. Incidental teaching procedures are often indicated to develop more elaborate speech in individuals with mild and moderate disabilities. Incidental procedures are generally less effective for individuals with severe/profound disability, who lack speech and rely on prelinguistic behaviours. Intervention for these individuals requires systematic instruction to map new and more symbolic communicative forms onto existing functions with the goal to replace prelinguistic behaviour with augmentative and alternative communication. Communication intervention for individuals with developmental disability must be comprehensive and ongoing, focusing on developing a wide range of communicative structures and functions, with specific vocabulary goals needing to change as the individual progresses through various life stages. A major role for clinicians in providing comprehensive support is to ensure that family, teachers, and staff receive adequate training in facilitating the communication development of individuals with developmental disabilities.

EXERCISES

1   Read the article by Sosne, Handleman, and Harris (1979). Based on the examples given in this article, brainstorm a list of strategies that could be used to create the need for communication in children, adolescents, and adults with intellectual disabilities or autism-spectrum disorders.
2   Study the procedural flow-charts in Duker, Didden, and Sigafoos (2004). Practise implementing Phases 1–3 of training when teaching a child, adolescent, and an adult to request access to preferred objects using manual signs.
3   Read the article by Mirenda (2003). Outline the advantages and disadvantages of selection-based versus topography-based communication modes.

FURTHER READING FOR FAMILIES

Carr, E. G., Levin, L., McConnachie, G., Carlson, J. I., Kemp, D. C. and Smith, C. E. (1994). *Communication-Based Intervention for Problem Behaviour: A User's Guide for Producing Positive Change*. Baltimore: Paul H. Brookes Publishing Co.

Frost, L. and Bondy, A. (2003). *The Picture Exchange Communication System Training Manual*. Newark, DE: Pyramid Educational Products.

Lovaas, O. I. (2003). *Teaching Individuals with Developmental Delays: Basic Intervention Techniques*. Austin, TX: Pro-Ed.

FURTHER READING FOR CLINICIANS

Reichle, J., Beukelman, D. R. and Light, J. C. (eds) (2002). *Exemplary Practices for Beginning Communicators: Implications for AAC*. Baltimore: Paul H. Brookes Publishing Co.

Rondal, J. A. and Edwards, S. (1996). *Language in Mental Retardation*. London: Whurr Publishers.

Schlosser, R. W. (ed.) (2003). *The Efficacy of Augmentative and Alternative Communication: Toward Evidence-Based Practice*. New York: Academic Press.

ASSESSMENT INSTRUMENTS

Bzoch, K. R. and League, R. (1991). *Receptive-Expressive Emergent Language Test* (2nd edn). Austin, TX: Pro-Ed.

Sparrow, S. S., Balla, D. A. and Cicchetti, D. V. (1984). *Vineland Adaptive Behaviour Scales: Expanded Form*. Circle Pines, MN: American Guidance Service.

Wetherby, A. M. and Prizant, B. M. (1993). *Communication and Symbolic Behaviour Scales*. Baltimore: Paul H. Brookes Publishing Co.

REFERENCES

Abbeduto, L., Evans, J. and Dolan, T. (2001). Theoretical perspectives on language and communication problems in mental retardation and developmental disabilities. *Mental Retardation and Developmental Disabilities Research Reviews*, 7, 45–55.

American Psychiatric Association (1994). *Diagnostic and Statistical Manual of Mental Disorders* (4th edn). Washington, DC: APA.

Arthur, M., Butterfield, N. and McKinnon, D. H. (1998). Communication intervention for students with severe disability: Results of a partner training program. *International Journal of Disability, Development and Education*, 45, 97–115.

Ashman, A. F., Hulme, P. and Suttie, J. (1990). The life circumstances of aged people with an intellectual disability. *Australia and New Zealand Journal of Developmental Disabilities*, 16, 335–47.

Ashman, A. F. and Suttie, J. (1996). The medical and health status of older people with mental retardation in Australia. *Journal of Applied Gerontology*, 15, 57–72.

Baer, D. M. and Guess, D. (1971). Receptive training of adjectival inflections in mental retardates. *Journal of Applied Behaviour Analysis*, 4, 129–39.

Balandin, S. and Iacono, T. (1999). Crews, wusses, and whoppas: Core and range vocabularies of Australian meal-break conversations in the workplace. *Augmentative and Alternative Communication*, 15, 95–109.

Banajee, M., Dicarlo, C. and Stricklin, S. B. (2003). Core vocabulary determination for toddlers. *Augmentative and Alternative Communication*, 19, 67–73.

Barrera, R. and Sulzer-Azaroff, B. (1983). An alternating treatment comparison of oral and total communication training programs for echolalic autistic children. *Journal of Applied Behaviour Analysis*, 16, 379–94.

Bates, E., Camaioni, L. and Volterra, V. (1975). The acquisition of performatives prior to speech. *Merrill-Palmer Quarterly*, 21, 205–26.

Beukelman, D. and Mirenda, P. (1998). *Augmentative and Alternative Communication: Management of Severe Communication Disorders in Children and Adults* (2nd edn). Baltimore: Paul H. Brookes Publishing Co.

Bondy, A. and Frost, L. (2001). The picture exchange communication system. *Behaviour Modification*, 25, 725–44.

Bzoch, K. and League, R. (1991). *Receptive-Expressive Emergent Language Scale* (2nd edn). Austin, TX: Pro-Ed.

Carpenter, R. L., Mastergeorge, A. M. and Coggins, T. E. (1983). The acquisition of communicative intentions in infants eight to fifteen months of age. *Language and Speech*, 26, 101–16.

Carr, E. G., Binkoff, J. A., Kologinsky, E. and Eddy, M. (1978). Acquisition of sign language by autistic children: I. Expressive labeling. *Journal of Applied Behaviour Analysis*, 11, 489–501.

Carter, M. and Maxwell, K. (1998). Promoting interaction with children using augmentative communication through a peer-directed intervention. *International Journal of Disability, Development and Education*, 45, 75–96.

Drasgow, E., Halle, J. and Sigafoos, J. (1999). Teaching communication to learners with severe disabilities: Motivation, response competition, and generalization. *Australasian Journal of Special Education*, 23, 47–63.

Duker, P. C., Didden, R. and Sigafoos, J. (2004). *One-to-One Training: Instructional Procedures for Individuals with Developmental Disabilities*. Austin, TX: Pro-Ed.

Duker, P. C. and Jutten, W. (1997). Establishing gestural yes-no responding with individuals with profound mental retardation. *Education and Training in Mental Retardation and Developmental Disabilities*, 32, 59–67.

Duker, P. C. and Moonen, X. M. (1985). A program to increase manual signs with severely/profoundly mentally retarded students in natural environments. *Applied Research in Mental Retardation*, 6, 147–58.

Duker, P. C., van Driel, S. and van de Bercken, J. (2002). Communication profiles of individuals with Down's syndrome, Angelman syndrome and pervasive developmental disorder. *Journal of Intellectual Disability Research*, 46, 35–40.

Durand, V. M. (1990). *Severe Behaviour Problems: A Functional Communication Training Approach*. New York: Guilford Press.

Esquirol, J. E. (1965). *Mental Maladies: A Treatise on Insanity. Fascimile of the English Edition of 1845*. New York: Hafner.

Ferguson, D. L. (1994). Is communication really the point? Some thoughts on interventions and membership. *Mental Retardation*, 32, 7–18.

Ferster, C. B. (1961). Positive reinforcement and behavioural deficits of autistic children. *Child Development*, 32, 437–56.

Halle, J. W. (1987). Teaching language in the natural environment: An analysis of spontaneity. *Journal of the Association for Persons with Severe Handicaps*, 12, 28–37.

Hart, B. and Risley, T. R. (1982). *How to Use Incidental Teaching for Elaborating Language*. Lawrence, KS: H and H Enterprises.

Hart, B. and Risley, T. R. (1999). *The Social World of Children Learning to Talk*. Baltimore: Paul H. Brookes Publishing Co.

Harwood, K., Warren, S. and Yoder, P. (2002). The importance of responsivity in developing contingent exchanges with beginning communicators. In J. Reichle, D. R. Beukelman, and J. C. Light (eds), *Exemplary Practices for Beginning Communicators* (pp. 59–95). Baltimore: Paul H. Brookes Publishing Co.

Houghton, J., Broniki, G. J. and Guess, D. (1987). Opportunities to express preferences and make choices among students with severe disabilities in classroom settings. *Journal of the Association for Persons with Severe Handicaps*, 12, 18–27.

Janicki, M. and Walsh, P. N. (2002). Editorial: An ageing world: New issues, more questions. *Journal of Intellectual and Developmental Disability*, 27, 229–30.

Keen, D., Sigafoos, J. and Woodyatt, G. (2001). Replacing prelinguistic behaviours with functional communication. *Journal of Autism and Developmental Disorders*, 31, 385–98.

Lamarre, J. and Holland, P. C. (1985). The functional independence of mands and tacts. *Journal of the Experimental Analysis of Behaviour*, 43, 5–19.

Lefrancois, G. R. (1995). *On Children: An Introduction to Child Development* (8th edn). Belmont, CA: Wadsworth.

Light, J. C. and Binger, C. (1998). *Building Communicative Competence with Individuals who Use Augmentative and Alternative Communication*. Baltimore: Paul H. Brookes Publishing Co.

Lovaas, O. I. (1977). *The Autistic Child: Language Development through Behaviour Modification*. New York: Irvington Publishers.

Lovaas, O. I. (1987). Behavioural treatment and normal educational and intellectual functioning in young autistic children. *Journal of Consulting and Clinical Psychology*, 55, 3–9.

Lovaas, O. I. (2002). *Teaching Individuals with Developmental Delays: Basic Intervention Techniques*. Austin, TX: Pro-Ed.

Lovaas, O. I., Berberich, J. P., Perloff, B. F. and Schaeffer, B. (1966). Acquisition of imitative speech by schizophrenic children. *Science*, 151, 705–7.

Marchetti, A. and Matson, J. L. (1988). An introduction to developmental disabilities: A life-span perspective. In J. L. Matson and A. Marchetti (eds), *Developmental Disabilities: A Life-Span Perspective* (pp. 1–30). Philadelphia, PA: Grune and Stratton.

Matas, J., Mathy-Laikko, P., Beukelman, D. and Legresley, K. (1985). Identifying the nonspeaking population: A demographic study. *Augmentative and Alternative Communication*, 1, 17–31.

McQueen, P. C., Spence, M. W., Garner, J. B., Pereira, L. H. and Winsor, E. J. T. (1987). Prevalence of major mental retardation and associated disabilities in the Canadian Maritime provinces. *American Journal of Mental Deficiency*, 91, 460–6.

Miranda, P. (2003). Toward functional augmentative and alternative communication for students with autism: Manual signs, graphic symbols, and voice output communication aids. *Language, Speech, and Hearing Services in Schools*, 34, 203–16.

National Research Council (2001). *Educating Children with Autism*. Washington, DC: National Academy Press.

Ogletree, B. T., Pierce, K., Harn, W. E. and Fisher, M. A. (2002). Assessment of communication and language in classical autism: Issues and practices. *Assessment for Effective Intervention*, 27, 61–71.

Reichle, J., Drager, K. and Davis, C. (2002). Using requests for assistance to obtain desired items and to gain release from nonpreferred activities: Implications for assessment and intervention. *Education and Treatment of Children*, 25, 47–66.

Reichle, J., York, J. and Sigafoos, J. (1991). *Implementing Augmentative and Alternative Communication: Strategies for Learners with Severe Disabilities*. Baltimore: Paul H. Brookes Publishing Co.

Remington, B. and Clarke, S. (1983). Acquisition of expressive signing by autistic children: An evaluation of the relative effects of simultaneous communication and sign-alone training. *Journal of Applied Behaviour Analysis*, 16, 315–27.

Riches, V. C. and Green, V. A. (2003). Social integration in the workplace for people with disabilities: An Australian perspective. *Journal of Vocational Rehabilitation*, 19, 127–42.

Romski, M. A. and Sevcik, R. A. (1996). *Breaking the Speech Barrier: Language Development through Augmented Means*. Baltimore: Paul H. Brookes Publishing Co.

Sailor, W. and Mix. B. (1975). *The Topeka Association for Retarded Citizens Assessment System*. Austin, TX: Pro-Ed.

Scheerenberger, R. C. (1983). *A History of Mental Retardation*. Baltimore: Paul H. Brookes Publishing Co.

Schepis, M. M. and Reid, D. H. (2003). Issues affecting staff enhancement of speech generating device use among people with severe cognitive disabilities. *Augmentative and Alternative Communication*, 19, 59–65.

Scheuermann, B. and Webber, J. (2002). *Autism: Teaching Does Make a Difference*. Belmont, CA: Wadsworth/Thomson Learning.

Schloper, E. and Mesibov, G. B. (eds) (1985). *Communication Problems in Autism*. New York: Plenum Press.

Schlosser, R. W. (ed.) (2003). *The Efficacy of Augmentative and Alternative Communication: Toward Evidence-Based Practice*. Boston, MA: Academic Press.

Siegel, S., Park, H., Gumpel, T., Ford, J., Tappe, P. and Gaylord-Ross, R. (1990). Research on vocational special education. In R. Gaylord-Ross (ed.), *Issues and Research in Special Education* (vol. 1, pp. 173–242).

Sigafoos, J. (1997). A review of communication intervention programs for people with developmental disabilities. *Behaviour Change*, 14, 125–38.

Sigafoos, J., Arthur, M. and O'Reilly, M. (2003). *Challenging Behaviour and Developmental Disability*. London: Whurr.

Sigafoos, J., Arthur-Velly, M. and Butterfield, N. (2006). *Enhancing Everyday Communication for Children with Disabilities*. Baltimore: Paul H. Brookes Publishing Co.

Sigafoos, J., Didden, R and O'Reilly, M. (2003). Effects of speech output on maintenance of requesting and frequency of vocalizations in three children with developmental disabilities. *Augmentative and Alternative Communication*, 19, 37–47.

Sigafoos, J., Drasgow, E. and Schlosser, R. W. (2003). Strategies for beginning communicators. In R. W. Schlosser (ed.), *The Efficacy of Augmentative and Alternative Communication: Toward Evidence-Based Practice* (pp. 323–46). New York: Academic Press.

Sigafoos, J., Kerr, M., Roberts, D. and Couzens, D. (1994). Increasing opportunities for requesting in classrooms serving children with developmental disabilities. *Journal of Autism and Developmental Disorders*, 24, 631–45.

Sigafoos, J. and Mirenda, P. (2002). Strengthening communicative behaviour for gaining and maintaining access to desired items and activities. In J. Reichle, D. R. Beukelman and J. C. Light (eds), *Exemplary Practices for Beginning Communicators: Implications for AAC* (pp. 123–56). Baltimore: Paul H. Brookes Publishing Co.

Sigafoos, J., Woodyatt, G., Keen, D., Tait, K., Tucker, M., Roberts-Pennell, D. and Pittendreigh, N. (2000). Identifying potential communicative acts in children with developmental and physical disabilities. *Communication Disorders Quarterly*, 21, 77–86.

Skinner, B. F. (1957). *Verbal Behaviour*. Englewood Cliffs, NJ: Prentice-Hall.

Sosne, J. B., Handleman, J. S. and Harris, S. L. (1979). Teaching spontaneous-functional speech to autistic-type children. *Mental Retardation*, 17, 241–5.

Stokes, T. F. and Baer, D. M. (1977). An implicit technology of generalization. *Journal of Applied Behaviour Analysis*, 10, 349–67.

Sundberg, M. L. (1981). *Developing a Verbal Repertoire Using Sign Language and*

Skinner's Analysis of Verbal Behaviour. Dissertation Abstracts International, 41 (10-B), 3922–3.

Von Tetzchner, S. (1997). Communication skills among females with Rett syndrome. *European Child and Adolescent Psychiatry*, 6 (Suppl. 1), 33–7.

Wehmeyer, M. and Bolding, N. (2001). Enhanced self-determination of adults with intellectual disability as an outcome of moving to community-based work or living environments. *Journal of Intellectual Disability Research*, 45, 371–83.

Wetherby, A. M. and Prizant, B. M. (1992). Profiling young children's communicative competence. In S. Warren and J. Reichle (eds), *Causes and Effects in Communication and Language Intervention* (vol. 1, pp. 217–53). Baltimore: Paul H. Brookes Publishing Co.

Wetherby, A. M., Warren, S. F. and Reichle, J. (1998). *Transitions in Prelinguistic Communication*. Baltimore: Paul H. Brookes Publishing Co.

Wheeler, A. J. and Sulzer, B. (1970). Operant training and generalization of a verbal response form in a speech-deficient child. *Journal of Applied Behaviour Analysis*, 3, 139–47.

Yoder, P. and Layton, T. (1988). Speech following sign language training in autistic children with minimal verbal language. *Journal of Autism and Developmental Disorders*, 18, 217–29.

Zigler, E. and Balla, D. (eds) (1982). *Mental Retardation: The Developmental-Difference Controversy*. Hillsdale, NJ: Erlbaum.

Chapter 18

Modifying challenging behaviour and planning positive supports

Brian McClean and Ian Grey

Individuals with intellectual disability and challenging behaviour are a vulnerable group. They are vulnerable in the sense that they are over-represented in large residential settings (Borthwick-Duffy, Eyeman and White, 1987), often without the most basic assessment and intervention services (Taggart and McConkey, 2001). The considerable variability in the treatment that such individuals receive is due, in part at least, to a lack of coherent policy in the field and to a frequent failure on the part of services and professionals to implement evidence-based interventions. In this chapter, we present a model of intervention, Positive Behavioural Support, that may help to ameliorate these outcomes. Excellent overviews of the emerging literature on the efficacy of positive behavioural support have been provided by Emerson (2001) and by Carr, Horner, Turnbull and Marquis (1999). Meta-analytic studies on treatment effectiveness (Didden, Duker and Korzilius, 1997), control group studies (e.g. Grey and McClean, 2004) and expert consensus each attest to the effectiveness of behavioural interventions for this group. The main purpose of this chapter is to provide practical examples of behavioural interventions and to offer guidelines on their implementation.

A case study

Sarah was referred for behavioural assessment when she was 22 years old. She had lived in a group home for four years. She had a history of behavioural outbursts dating back to when she was 18 months of age. These included self-injury, aggression towards staff, property destruction and throwing objects. On three occasions she caused injury when she threw boiling water from a kettle at support staff. At the time of referral, Sarah's behaviours had escalated in terms of frequency and severity. Two staff required lengthy sick leave as a result of her behaviour. Outbursts of physical aggression and property destruction were frequently sustained for intervals longer than two hours.

Comprehensive behavioural assessment consisted of cognitive, communicational, ecological, medical and psychiatric assessments as well as operational definitions of target behaviours, historical analysis, antecedent analysis for the occurrence and non-occurrence of behaviours, consequence analysis, motivational analysis, hypothesis development and systematic observation to test the hypotheses (Willis and LaVigna, 1996a; 1996b). The assessment operationally defined physical aggression as the target behaviour.

Results of the assessment indicated that Sarah was a visual learner and relied heavily on visual information; her abilities to deal with verbal information and abstract ideas such as concept of time were poor by comparison. A review of fifty-six incident analysis sheets indicated that almost two-thirds of incidents occurred in situations of noise or group activities. Frequently, Sarah requested of staff that she go for a walk during these activities and challenging behaviours escalated when she was asked to wait until a more appropriate time. Twenty percent of incidents happened at mealtimes. Consequence analysis indicated that response cost or punitive responses were also associated with escalation of behaviours. It was hypothesized that the function of the behaviour was

- To escape from noise and group situations
- To escape from refusal or delay of preferred activities
- To escape from changes in routine or irregular sequences of events.

A multi-element behaviour support plan was designed on the basis of these hypotheses at the time of initial referral (see Table 18.1).

Table 18.1 Sarah's behaviour support plan

Category	Intervention	Rationale
Environmental accommodation	Establishment of daily routines	Behavioural assessment indicates that behaviours are less likely when Sarah seems familiar with routines
Environmental accommodation	Picture sequencing book	(1) Pictures of Sarah's daily activities are rehearsed with her to increase her ability to predict her day; (2) a picture is taken from the book at the start of each new activity to assist her with transitions between activities; (3) if an activity cannot take place, the picture representing that activity is removed, and an alternative activity is negotiated with her using pictures

Environmental accommodation	Meals may be eaten on her own	Incident analysis indicated that group meals were associated with a higher likelihood of the behaviour
General skill	Using the telephone	General skills are designed to increase mastery over some feature of the environment. By learning to use the telephone, Sarah might increase her ability to contact family and increase her ability to predict family visits
Functionally equivalent skill	Escape training	By teaching Sarah to escape to her own room when confronted with noise, escape-motivated outbursts may be replaced
Functionally related skill	Visual problem solving	Picture stories representing problems that Sarah commonly faces (e.g. noise, crowds, change in routine) are rehearsed to give her visual examples of practical solutions
Coping skill	Relaxation training	Sarah moves to a location with preferred music, and this activity appears to relax her
Direct intervention	Differential reward of other behaviours	Sarah is rewarded for every half day in which she exhibits no target behaviours
Direct intervention	Respond to precursors	Staff respond to behavioural warning signs (e.g. facial grimaces) to avert incidents of challenging behaviour
Direct intervention	Antecedent control	Staff avoid refusals and requests to wait
Reactive strategies	Active listening; redirection to picture sequence book; facilitated relaxation	The goal of reactive strategies to respond to Sarah's outbursts in a way that minimizes the likelihood of escalation

Following initial assessment and implementation of the behaviour support plan, the frequency of the physically aggressive behaviour reduced to near-zero levels in subsequent months and consultation meetings were faded to one per month. However, nineteen months after initial referral, Sarah was referred for reoccurrence of target behaviours. Consultation with staff indicated that the behaviour support plan had not been implemented for the previous five months. A new functional assessment was conducted which

Table 18.2 History of assessment, implementation and staff training

Month 1	Initial assessment
Months 2–6	Weekly consultation meetings each lasting approximately one hour. These consisted of training staff in recommended interventions, revising the strategies in the light of feedback from staff, and providing staff with performance-based feedback
Month 7–11	Frequency of consultations were faded to one per month
Month 11	Termination report and maintenance plan were filed
Month 19	Sarah was re-referred for behavioural assessment. No behavioural records had been kept for 5 months. None of the recommended behaviour support plan was being implemented. She had moved to a different apartment as part of a service reorganization, and there had been a number of changes to the staff team working with her. Another comprehensive assessment of her behaviour was conducted by the first author in month 19, and hypothesized the same functions of behaviour as were identified in the initial behavioural assessment
Months 20–32	Minor changes were made to the previous intervention plan, including more explicit scheduling of daily routines, replacement of a Differential Reinforcement of Other behaviours (DRO) schedule of reinforcement with a variable schedule of reinforcement (Variable Interval (VI) = 1 day). Monthly meetings involved fidelity checks to ensure intervention and behavioural recording were being implemented consistently. The behaviour reduced to near-zero levels, and specialist consultation was withdrawn
Month 43	Sarah was referred for a third time in month 43 with aggressive outbursts. By this time, continuous staff turnover had resulted in an entirely new staff team working with Sarah. Behavioural recording had been discontinued for seven months. Aspects of Sarah's original support plan had persisted A member of her new staff team was trained in the design and implementation of multi-element behaviour support plans (Person-Focused Training). Her functional assessment suggested that Sarah's frequent requests for walks functioned as her way of escaping from over-stimulation in her group home
Months 44–84	Minor adjustments to the behaviour support plan included increasing the frequency with which walks were scheduled (stimulus satiation); providing access to walks when there is noise in the environment (antecedent control), and providing access to walks in response to precursor behaviours (chain interrupt). In addition, a protocol recommended that staff remain silent on walks unless Sarah initiated interaction. The intervention plan was organized as a weekly checklist of implementation (Periodic Service Review (PSR) LaVigna *et al.*, 1994)

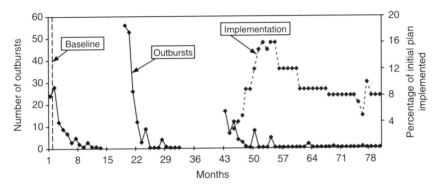

Figure 18.1 Graph of behavioural outbursts.

indicated the same functions as identified in the previous assessment. At forty-three months after initial referral, Sarah was again referred for aggressive behaviours. On this occasion, a staff member working with Sarah was selected to undergo training in positive behavioural support. Results of this third functional assessment indicated very similar functions to those identified in the previous assessments. The history of referral, assessments, support plans and progress of the intervention are presented in Table 18.2. There was no change to Sarah's regimen of medication over the seven-year period.

Figure 18.1 shows the graph of Sarah's behaviour over a seven-year period. The frequency of Sarah's behavioural outbursts and the percentage of interventions implemented each month are also presented. The graph suggests that the reduction in outbursts from month 44 is associated with an accumulation of implemented interventions. Sarah moved apartment twice during the two years from month 48 to month 72, and now lives with a different group of service-users and staff with no effect on her behaviour. Target behaviours have been largely absent for approximately forty months.

The case illustrates a number of features of positive behavioural support; first, that challenging behaviours tend to be persistent (Emerson *et al.*, 1996; Kiernan and Alborz, 1996; Murphy *et al.*, 1993). Second, it illustrates that long-term maintenance is possible, but is likely to require multi-element intervention, staff training and the construction of an 'ecology of support' (Lucyshyn, Olson and Horner, 1995) around the individual. These issues will be addressed later in the chapter.

DEFINITION OF CHALLENGING BEHAVIOUR

Challenging behaviour is most frequently defined as behaviour of such intensity, frequency or duration that the physical safety of the person or others is likely to be placed in serious jeopardy, or behaviour which is likely seriously to limit use of, or result in the person being denied access to, ordinary community facilities (Emerson and Bromley, 1995). Severe challenging behaviour often involves physical aggression or self-injurious behaviour, verbal aggression, shouting or screaming, and refusing to move or refusing to carry out a request may also be present. However, the first implication of the definition of challenging behaviour is that it is defined by its impact rather than by its topography. Challenging behaviour can take many forms, and may result from a variety of underlying social, psychological or biological processes. But behaviour qualifies as challenging not because of its frequency but because of its consequences. Individuals with challenging behaviour are often inappropriately placed (Borthwick-Duffy *et al.*, 1987; Emerson and Hatton, 1994), have a poorer quality of life (Mansell, 1994) and have high levels of long-term medication (Sternfert Kroese, Dewhurst and Holmes, 2001). Behaviours such as physical aggression, self-injury or property destruction can threaten an individual's residential placement (Bruininks, Hill and Morreau, 1988), interfere with opportunities for social interaction (Anderson, Lakin, Hill and Chen, 1992), and threaten vocational placement and community participation (Larson, 1991). The effects of challenging behaviours on care-giver stress and staff turnover are equally well documented (e.g. Russell and Harris, 1993). Challenging behaviour can have a negative impact on the health and well-being of the person, those who care for the person and those who live or work with the person (Emerson, 1998). Part of the rationale for positive behavioural support is the need to address the consequences of challenging behaviour – to improve the quality of life of the individual and to produce change that has social validity, as well as to reduce or eliminate behaviour.

A second implication of the definition of challenging behaviour is that the person who presents with the behaviour is challenged. Like other forms of impairment, severe challenging behaviour may present barriers to the person's participation in ordinary community living. In this sense, the person has a behavioural disability. A comparison may be made with physical disability. A person who has physical challenge may need a physical prosthesis, such as a wheelchair, to enjoy community access. Similarly, a person who has a behavioural challenge needs a behavioural prosthesis or behaviour support plan to gain control over behaviour and to enjoy full community presence and participation. And just as people with physical disabilities advocate the right to ramps and other environmental accommodations, so it is the right of the person with behavioural disabilities to have access to the appropriate behavioural support plan that promotes his or her social inclusion.

PREVALENCE

In an Irish survey of 1,447 people with intellectual disability, 28 percent were identified as having a challenging behaviour which met the definition provided by Emerson above, and 15 percent were identified as having a severe challenging behaviour (defined according to a tissue damage criterion; McClean and Walsh, 1995). This is consistent with other epidemiological studies conducted in the UK (e.g. Harris, 1993; Oliver, Murphy and Corbett, 1987). Generally, it is accepted that somewhere between 10 percent and 15 percent of people with intellectual disability present with serious challenging behaviour, where the safety of the person or others is compromised by the behaviour, or would be compromised in the absence of intervention. Additional survey information suggests that people with challenging behaviours represent an extremely vulnerable group. They are disproportionately represented in large residential centres, rather than in community settings. According to recent Irish figures, at least 494 people are inappropriately placed in long-stay psychiatric hospitals. In general, people with challenging behaviours are frequently placed in congregate settings that mitigate against the remediation of their behaviours. Serious challenging behaviours are more prevalent among men, and among the 15–35 age group (Emerson, 1998). They are more frequent among people with severe intellectual disabilities and among people who have other forms of disability, such as sensory impairment, autism or psychiatric illness (Deb, Thomas and Bright, 2001). In general, challenging behaviour is most likely to present when the ability to communicate effectively is persistently compromised.

BEHAVIOURAL APPROACHES

Considerable empirical evidence exists for the efficacy of the application of behavioural principles in bringing about changes in challenging behaviour (Emerson, 2001). However, criticism has frequently been expressed in relation to the nature of the historical application of these principles. Examples of such criticism include: (a) a narrow focus on deceasing problem behaviour rather than increasing adaptive behaviour; (b) the reliance on single intervention approaches; (c) the use of punishment as a technology of creating behaviour change; and (d) a reliance on modifying consequences to create behaviour change. As an example of the latter, the following is worth considering: 'behaviour modification . . . is limited mostly to hierarchical interactions in which powerful persons seek to modify the behaviour of the less powerful through the control of sanctions' (Kipnis, 1987). Such views about behavioural interventions are not uncommon and negative stereotypes continue to exist, fuelled in part by a degree of historical truth. A characteristic of behavioural interventions up until the late 1970s was the reliance on modifying the consequences of problem behaviour to bring about changes in behaviour without a consideration of function or purpose of that behaviour for the individual. Powerful contingencies of reinforcement and punishment were applied in an attempt to 'override' existing contingencies maintaining target behaviour. While applied behaviour analysis defines itself as a science and as a science it informs practitioners about how to change behaviour, what has been less explicit within the behavioural field is a statement of values about what is worth changing and perhaps how such change should take place (Carr, Robinson and Polumbo, 1990).

Though a behavioural model for challenging behaviour has been dominant in the field for approximately thirty years, one of the major developments has been the reintroduction of the concept of behavioural function and its implications for assessment and the development of interventions. This model considers challenging behaviour as essentially adaptive. The implication is that all behaviour, no matter how bizarre or self-defeating it seems to be, serves some function or conveys some meaning for the person. Once the meaning of the behaviour is understood, intervention usually aims to teach the person a more effective way of conveying the same meaning, and ensuring that the environment adapts to respond efficiently to this alternative behaviour. This is in contrast to the earlier approach of modifying consequences of challenging behaviour. In order to establish the meaning of behaviour, a detailed and comprehensive assessment of the person is usually required. This usually involves interpreting the meaning of behaviour within a wide range of contexts: the cognitive abilities of the person; the communication repertoire of the person; the historical context; the ecological context; the health and medical status of the person; and the environmental conditions that evoke the occurrence and non-occurrence of the behaviour and the social context of response to the behaviour. This kind of comprehensive assessment can be viewed as an act of empathy: a stepping inside the psychological skin of the person; seeing the world from the person's point of view; and a search for meaning and legitimacy of message underlying the person's behaviour, if not in the manner of the person's expression.

POSITIVE BEHAVIOUR SUPPORT

The 1990s witnessed the emergence of a discipline called 'Positive Behaviour Support' through the writings of several influential practitioner researchers such as LaVigna, Carr, Horner, Dunlap and Koegel. Its goals are 'applying behavioural principles in order to reduce problem behaviours and build appropriate behaviours that result in durable change and a rich lifestyle' (Carr *et al.*, 1999: 3). The achievement of these goals are brought about by a comprehensive set of procedures and support strategies that are selectively employed on the basis of the person's individual needs and characteristics, and in particular on the basis of an assessment of the function of the person's challenging behaviours. It aims to bring about such changes in quality of life and positive lifestyle change by altering deficient environmental conditions and/or deficient behaviour repertoires (Carr *et al.*, 1999). Positive behavioural support has its theoretical roots in the constructional approach to behaviour (Goldiamond, 1974; Schwartz and Goldiamond, 1975). This approach focuses on the alleviation of distress by the construction of behavioural repertoires. Rather than asking the question 'what is the problem to be eliminated' (a pathological approach), the constructional approach asks, 'what skill would achieve the same ends for the person as the current behaviour achieves'. The key elements of the constructional model are the identification of a target behaviour, the identification of relevant skills that the person already has, the teaching of new skills and the adaptation of the environment in order to maintain the new skills (Carr *et al.*, 1999).

Key characteristics of positive behaviour support

Positive Behavioural Support is defined in terms of three key elements: (1) selection of interventions on the basis of functional assessments; (2) the nature of the interventions themselves; and (3) the emphasis on social validation as further criterion for intervention selection.

1. Functional assessment

The most obvious characteristic of positive behavioural support is that the interventions for an individual are based, at least in part, upon the results of a functional assessment (e.g. Kemp and Carr, 1995; LaVigna and Willis, 1995; O'Neill, Horner, Albin, Storey and Sprague, 1997; Repp, 1994). At present there is no agreed protocol for conducting a functional assessment but underpinning the majority of approaches is the common goal of systematic-ally 'identifying problem behaviours and the events that (a) reliably predict occurrences and non-occurrence of those behaviours and (b) maintain the behaviours across time' (Sugai, Horner *et al.*, 2000: 137). Functional assessment methods include three broad classes: observation, interview and psychometric instruments. Another assessment method is that of analogue assessment which involves the experimental manipulation of variables across different conditions to demonstrate causality with respect to problem behaviour and aspects of the environment (Iwata, Dorsey, Slifer, Bauman and Richman, 1982; Iwata, Pace, Dorsey, Zarcone *et al.*, 1994). A distinction has subsequently emerged within the literature with analogue assessment methodology being referred to as functional analysis (Mace, 1994) and non-experimental methods such as observation and interview referred to as methods of functional assessment. Functional analysis is generally not considered to be a very practical method of assessment in ordinary clinical situations. One survey (Desrochers, Hile and Williams-Mosely, 1997) asked 300 practitioners to rank the degree of usefulness of a number of assessment procedures. ABC analysis and interviews were ranked first and second respectively whereas functional analysis was ranked fifth in terms of usefulness. A number of meta-reviews do suggest that analogue assessment is effective in identifying behavioural function in a number of cases and in developing intervention plans to reduce problem behaviour (Iwata *et al.*, 1994). However, the use of analogue assessment must be offset against a number of key considerations:

1   **Internal validity.** Possible sources of artefact in analogue assessment include multiple contingencies in single analogue conditions, adaptation to analogue conditions, carry-over effects, and new learning.
2   **Test – retest reliability.** Analogue assessments are no more objective in their interpretation of test results than descriptive assessments. Martin, Gaffan and Williams (1999) found agreement rates of 35 percent between analogue assessments conducted just sixteen weeks apart.
3   **Clinical utility.** Analogue assessment is only useful for high-rate behaviours. In an Irish sample, only 2 percent of the population of people with challenging behaviours have behaviours that are frequent enough to be subjected to 15-minute analogue assessment conditions (McClean and Walsh, 1995). Other total population surveys of the frequency of challenging behaviours support this finding (e.g. Harris, 1993; Oliver *et al.*, 1987).
4   **Ethical concerns.** Many services settings do not consider it ethical to set knowingly the occasion for higher rates of challenging behaviour for the purpose of behaviour assessment (Repp, 1994). In these settings naturalistic hypothesis-testing techniques rather than analogue assessments are required.

A number of manuals are available for the practitioner to draw on when conducting a functional assessment. Examples include O'Neill *et al.* (1997), and Nelson *et al.* (1998). A third example is Carr *et al.* (1994). Though the number of functional assessment instruments are increasing, there remains a lack of studies testifying to the validity of these methods in identifying function (Emerson, 2001). The authors use a format of functional assessment adapted from Willis and LaVigna (1996a; 1996b). This is illustrated in Table 18.3 and is an example of a comprehensive nature of functional assessment. Although adapted, the assessment format outlined in Table 18.3 is very similar to that of Wacker, Peck, Derby, Berg and Harding (1996), with the exception that the assessment model does not utilize analogue assessment.

2. The nature of the interventions

A second characteristic of Positive Behavioural Support is the range of specific interventions for supporting people with challenging behaviours which

Table 18.3 Analyses used in functional assessment

Method	Purpose
Phase 1: Informant assessment	
Interview with key social agents	Identify behavioural concerns, identify events associated with occurrence of behaviour
Cognitive assessment	Identify functional cognitive competencies (sensory, attention, memory, comprehension, matching, performance, problem solving)
Communication assessment	Identify functional communicational competencies
Medical assessment	Establish medical and psychiatric status; list medications used
Analysis of previous interventions	Identify resources and constraints in mediator system
Motivational assessment	Identify possible activities for environmental enrichment; identify potential reinforcers
Phase 2: Descriptive assessment	
Description of problem behaviour	Topography of target behaviour, precursor behaviours and aftermath behaviours; frequency recording of behaviour
Historical analysis	Identify historical factors associated with increase and decrease in response strength
Scatterplot§	Identify times of day associated with behaviour
Antecedent analysis	Identify naturally occurring events associated with occurrence and non-occurrence of behaviour
Consequence analysis	Identify naturally occurring maintaining events for behaviour
Ecological analysis	Evaluate goodness of fit of the environment with the needs and characteristics of the individual
Phase 3: Hypothesis testing	
Hypothesis development	Synthesise informant and descriptive data; identify common themes; identify contradictory evidence; distinguish setting events and triggers;
Incident analysis*	Prospective test of hypotheses

Notes: §From Touchette, MacDonald and Langer (1985). *From Repp, Felce and Barton (1988).

have received renewed emphasis since the development of functional assessment methodologies (e.g. Horner, Dunlap, Koegel, Carr *et al.*, 1990; Koegel, Koegel and Dunlap *et al.*, 1999; LaVigna and Donnellan, 1986). LaVigna and Willis (1995), for example, represent Positive Behavioural Support in terms of a multi-element behaviour support plan. Each behaviour support plan has at least four elements:

Environmental accommodation

Dietary adaptations, access to food and drink, leisure options, interactions and rapport, noise level, predictability of daily events, choice of activity, variety of activity, availability of augmentative communication systems and the quality of carer communication are all factors which may be incorporated in an overall plan to overcome challenging behaviour.

Functionally equivalent skills teaching

This focuses on identifying the function of behaviour through functional assessment and teaching the person more effective and more socially acceptable ways of achieving that function. The most frequent example of functionally equivalent skills teaching is functional communication training (Bird, Dores, Moniz and Robinson, 1989; Derby, Wacker, Berg, DeRaad *et al.*, 1997). In addition to functionally equivalent skills teaching, there is an emphasis on teaching the person skills for community participation, recreation or coping and tolerance.

Direct interventions

These interventions involve establishing rapid control over challenging behaviour using non-aversive strategies such as the removal or control of the antecedents to challenging behaviour, the non-contingent delivery of reinforcement on various schedules, or the reward of other behaviours (Jones, 1991).

Reactive strategies

Horner *et al.* (1990) propose a clear distinction between the proactive elements of the behaviour support plan and emergency procedures. Many challenging behaviours place the person, or carers, at severe social or physical risk. Frequently, the preferred response to dangerous behaviours is not to deliver a behavioural intervention designed to change behaviour, but to provide sufficient temporary control to prevent injury and to allow the person and others to survive with dignity.

Table 18.4 illustrates examples and a description of the interventions frequently used in Positive Behavioural Support. The table also represents a model of multi-element behavioural support. In LaVigna and Willis' (1995) formulation, behaviour support plans contain at least one element from each of the four components of the model. The first three components combine to make up a proactive plan, in that they are designed to reduce the likelihood of the challenging behaviour. The final component, the reactive strategy, is the recommended response after the behaviour has occurred.

Table 18.4 Examples of interventions used in Positive Behavioural Support, adapted from LaVigna and Willis (1995)

Proactive interventions			*Reactive strategies*
Environmental accommodations	*Skills teaching*	*Direct interventions*	
Activity sampling	Picture exchange communication	Differential reinforcement of other behaviour	Active listening
Community access			Feedback
Access to food and drink	Escape communication training	Differential reinforcement of low rates of behaviour	Redirection
			Limit setting
Access to relaxation	Discrimination skills training		Facilitated relaxation
Picture sequencing		Differential reinforcement of alternative behaviours	Facilitated communication
Adaptations to activity schedule	Relaxation training		
	Systematic desensitization		Facilitated problem solving
Adaptations to instructional style	Conversation skills	Instructional control	Interpositioning
Adaptations to duration and type of activities	Self-help skills	Stimulus satiation	Breakaway techniques
	Community living skills		Non-violent crisis intervention
Choice-making protocol	Leisure skills training		Debriefing
Transition protocol			
Adaptations to diet			

The link between functional assessment and intervention selection is critical and avoids a 'cookbook' approach to the selection of interventions. This link stresses that the selection or design of a behaviour support plan for an individual should ideally dovetail with the causal and maintaining factors underlying the persons challenging behaviour. Available evidence suggests that the likelihood of effective intervention outcome is increased if a pre-treatment functional assessment has been conducted (Kennedy and Carr, 2002).

3. Social validity

Most authors also propose as a third defining element of Positive Behavioural Support the use of social validation as a criterion for selecting an intervention (e.g. Horner *et al.*, 1990; LaVigna and Willis, 1996). On one hand, interventions should not be selected which compromise the dignity of the person. Horner *et al.* (1990), for example, recommend three criteria for including interventions within the rubric of positive behavioural support. These are:

(1) the intrusiveness, restrictiveness or aversiveness of an intervention; (2) the social acceptability of an intervention; and (3) ongoing monitoring of the intervention by a competent professional. On the other hand, the application of a social validity criterion to the selection of interventions involves an emphasis on lifestyle change. Challenging behaviour is perceived as a barrier to full community participation. Although elements of traditional therapy and treatment for challenging behaviour may be included in the plan, positive behavioural support also represents a kind of social prosthesis which allows people with behavioural disability to access and enjoy the community more freely. This is a different emphasis to the traditional conception of behavioural intervention as a treatment plan for a clinical problem. A social validity criterion requires interventions and systems of service delivery which produce durable, generalized changes in behaviour in order that the person may improve his or her access to the community, to relationships and to a range of activities (e.g. Dunlap and Fox, 1996).

THE DESIGN OF BEHAVIOUR SUPPORT PLANS

As mentioned above, behaviour support plans have four main components, environmental accommodations, skills teaching, direct interventions and reactive strategies. The purpose of the sections that follow is to offer some examples of the design of intervention protocols once the functional assessment has been conducted.

Environmental accommodations are central to the principle of challenging behaviour as disability. The person can overcome behavioural disability to the extent that the environment can adapt to meet the needs and character-istics of the person. A behavioural assessment must therefore identify com-prehensively the needs of the person, and the cognitive, communicational, motivational, health or psychiatric factors that predispose the person to chal-lenging behaviours. These factors may be understood as internal setting events which help explain why a person is motivated to obtain reinforcement in response to specific stimuli. In addition, a comprehensive assessment out-lines the external setting events (e.g. noise, schedule, transitions, predict-ability, variety of activity, choice) which may predispose the person to be motivated to exhibit challenging behaviour. Environmental accommoda-tions, then, may operate to remove or reduce external setting events or consist of environmental supports that reduce the impact of internal pre-disposing factors. Other environmental accommodations may also operate on setting events indirectly, by increasing the density and range of reinforcers so dramatically that reinforcement available from challenging behaviour wanes in its significance.

Activity sampling can be part of any behaviour support plan as a generic means of improving lifestyle and opportunity. It is especially important when functional analysis suggests that behaviours are more likely to occur when the person is bored or under-stimulated, or when motivational assessment fails to reveal a wide variety of activities of interest to the person. A typical activity sampling includes brainstorming, observing and recording (see Box 18.1).

Picture sequencing: some people with intellectual disability may have difficulties with concept of time, which can result in confusion about when preferred events can happen. Others may have more specific need for predictability, or certainty about the order of events in the day, or specific difficulties with transitions from one activity to another. Picture sequencing can be used to alert a person to upcoming changes in routine, as a means of negotiating the timing of preferred activity, and as a means of cueing a transition from one activity to another. A sample picture sequencing protocol is presented in Box 18.2.

Adaptation to interaction style is often necessary when impairment in

---

Box 18.1 Activity sampling protocol

1   Meet as a team for 15 minutes to brainstorm new activities. The rules of brainstorming are that no one is allowed to criticize any suggested activities. Generate a list of 20 activities.
2   Once the brainstorming is over, select four activities that Martina has never tried before, and plan how to introduce them to her.
3   For each new activity, record Martina's initial reaction, how long Martina participated, her reaction to the cessation of the activity and a 1–5 rating of her enjoyment.

Box 18.2 Sample picture sequencing protocol

1   Plan the sequence of Declan's day centre activities.
2   Arrange pictures corresponding to each activity in a one picture per page photo album.
3   Rehearse the full sequence with Declan first thing in the morning, early afternoon and late afternoon and at other times as necessary.
4   At the start of each activity, remove the corresponding picture and give it to Declan.
5   Guide Declan to the activity and prompt him to place the card beside the activity.

receptive communication is identified as an important predisposing factor for challenging behaviour. The sample protocol in Box 18.3 suggests several adaptations in carer communication style.

Skills teaching: teaching the person an alternative way of communicating the meaning of the challenging behaviour is at the heart of positive behavioural support. Typically behaviour support plans also feature general skills teaching, designed to teach skills for fun or mastery, and coping and tolerance skills. A number of principles can be applied.

Skills teaching involves error-free learning. This means using prompts to ensure the correct performance. Teaching involves gradually and system-

---

Box 18.3 Interaction style protocol

Joe sometimes becomes anxious and upset when he is asked to do things. He is very sensitive to losing face and asking for help is currently not within his repertoire of skills. A particular style of requests has been found to be helpful when asking Joe to do things.

Communication with Joe is less likely to be distressing if it is respectful and collaborative. Ask Joe questions like 'what do you think', and 'what can we do about this'.

Give choices. Joe is much more likely to carry out a request if it it is in the form of a two-way request: 'Joe, would you like to do a or b?'

Joe responds very well to praise and has often reacted badly to correction or what he perceives as criticism. Each day, there should be at least three times more incidents of praise than incidents of correction. The following are some examples of phrases he finds helpful: You are doing very well, That's a good point, Let me think about that, Thank you for doing . . ., Thank you for agreeing to . . .

Speak slowly and uses concrete language. Joe is not likely to indicate if he does not understand, and his confusion often adds to the pressure he is under. Pause after each sentence to allow him some time for processing.

Use a low-arousal approach. Try not to add unnecessary emotional content when communicating with Joe. Picture your speech as a table tennis ball that you want to land slowly and gently in the middle of the table for Joe.

atically fading the prompt until the person can complete more of the task independently. If the task is physical, such as handing an instructor an 'I want a break' card, the initial prompt may take the form of hand over hand help, which may then be systematically faded, for example, to hand over wrist, hand over elbow, hand over shoulder. If a task is verbal, for example asking an instructor 'give me time to think about that', then the prompt is given verbally.

Teaching is in context. Where possible, skills are taught in the conditions that best approximate those in which they will actually be used.

Communication skills training involves a co-trainer. Skills training is more effective with two trainers working in unison. One trainer is required to deliver the prompt to the learner and the second is needed to respond to the communication made. When only one trainer is involved, the learner may become confused with the same individual adopting different roles in a very short space of time.

Physical prompts are easier to fade. Prompts can be faded from hand over hand to hand over wrist, hand over elbow and hand over shoulder. Or prompts can be faded from full (hand over hand), to partial.

Teaching is silent. If the instructor speaks during the teaching trial, then in order for the learner to process the information, he or she needs to switch attention off the task, transfer attention onto the learner, switch processing to an auditory/verbal modality, process the verbal input, switch attention off the verbal input, switch attention back from auditory to visual modalities, transfer attention back onto the task and transfer processing from auditory to visual modalities. Many learners can still learn while an instructor is speaking. However, for some learners, whose ability to give attention may already be compromised, the process amounts to a form of attentional gymnastics! Box 18.4 and Box 18.5 provide examples of functionally equivalent skills teaching programmes.

Box 18.4 Informal skills teaching programme to teach appropriate greeting response

Tom sometimes greets by hugging his classmates and even wrestling them to the ground. His classroom assistant prompted him each day to give her a 'high five'. Once Joe had practised this with her, she prompted (hand over wrist) him to give high fives to his classmates once a day. She faded the prompt to a light touch on his elbow, until Joe started to do 'high fives' with classmates spontaneously. His classmates now greet him spontaneously instead of shying away from him.

Box 18.5 Skills teaching programme to teach appropriate refusal response

Sometimes Orla hits and scratches others when asked to go somewhere or to do something she is not sure about. The following procedure was put in place to teach Orla to communicate 'no' . . .

1   Ensure Orla is in good form before training commences
2   Provide Orla with a request of non-preferred activity
3   Co-trainer prompts Orla (hand over hand) to raise a red card or Orla says 'no'
4   Person making the request takes card, smiles, says 'no?' and walks away
5   After 10 consecutive successful trials, fade to hand over hand, then hand over shoulder.

At any other time when Orla says 'no' or lifts the red card, try to offer her a break, or an alternative activity. Similarly, when Orla first shows signs of anxiety, prompt her to lift a red card to communicate 'no'.

Behaviour support plans include other forms of skills teaching in addition to functionally equivalent skills teaching. General skills involve teaching a skill that will enhance the person's ability to exert control over an aspect of the environment or to increase a person's capacity for fun or enjoyment. For example, a person could learn to pour a drink of juice from the fridge, make a purchase from a shop or assist in the servicing of a car engine. Usually the emphasis is also on the strategic selection of a skill which will increase the standing of the person within the social system of significant others. There is little advantage to the person in learning to tie shoelaces, for example, if shoelace tying is not particularly valued by the person's family or group of friends. By contrast, learning to cook perfect spaghetti or to water flowers, for example, might be more likely to elicit the natural community of reinforcers when they are performed.

Another type of skills teaching typically included in a behaviour support plan involves teaching coping and tolerance skills. Noise, disappointment, criticism, refusal, waiting, transitions and non-preferred tasks frequently arise as events that people may be motivated to avoid. As well as adapting the environment to prevent or reduce these events, and teaching the person escape skills, a behaviour support plan may involve teaching a person a skill for coping with these events.

Direct interventions

The role of direct interventions is to bring about a rapid reduction in the rate or severity of the behaviour over time. The interventions are described as direct because they impact directly on the immediate antecedents or consequences of behaviour.

Antecedent control is an example of stimulus control and refers to the principle that in the presence of certain stimuli, behaviour is more likely to be reinforced and therefore more likely to occur. Stimulus control can be learned. For example, when children learn that undressing is done in private, or that toileting occurs in the bathroom, these behaviours may be said to be under the control of setting stimuli such as the bedroom or bathroom. Other behaviours, such as complaining or making unusual noises, may not be problem behaviours themselves, but present as problems because of the frequency with which they occur. In some of these cases, the need is to reduce the extent to which behaviours occur indiscriminately. This is accomplished by bringing the behaviour under the control of a stimulus, that is by reinforcing the behaviour every time it occurs in the presence of that stimulus and by withholding reinforcement when the behaviour occurs at other times.

Antecedent control, however, involves removing, reducing or altering some existing discriminative stimulus. For example, suppose a self-injurious behaviour is more likely to occur in response to a request to move. Antecedent control options include withdrawing requests to move, reducing the frequency of such requests, or modifying the ways in which such requests are made. (As an example of the latter, instead of saying, 'it's time to go to lunch', a carer might say, 'would you like to come to lunch now or would you like to stay here' (two-way choice format), or give the person a plate (object cue format).) When aggressive or self-injurious behaviours are dangerous, antecedent control is often the first choice of direct intervention. Examples include removing unnecessary demands, reducing the amount of speech or noise, making sequences of events highly predictable, eliminating provocative statements such as 'no' or 'wait' (e.g. instead of saying 'no', say 'yes, of course we will go swimming. Let's check the schedule and see when that will be . . .'). Box 18.6 contains an example of a detailed antecedent control procedure for an individual who frequently shows aggressive behaviour in response to a refusal.

Instructional control is another example of stimulus control where the behaviour occurs in response to an explicitly communicated request. The goal in teaching instructional control is to increase the frequency of request–response correspondence. It involves requesting a behaviour and rewarding the behaviour for occurring. In order to implement this intervention, some basic assessment of the reasons for non co-operation are required. For example, the requested skill must be within the learner's repertoire, the language (verbal or visual), used to request the skill must be comprehensible

Box 18.6 Sample antecedent control protocol

Interaction style: saying No to Sarah

Obtain Sarah's attention before talking to her.

Speak slowly.

Use clear, brief and simple language.

Use a warm friendly tone. Convey respect to Sarah as an adult. In particular, avoid using a bossy, authoritarian or demanding tone.

Spend time applying active listening. Put what Sarah is saying into her own words, in order to verify that you understand what she is saying. Say 'let me make sure I understand everything . . . is there anything I missed?' DO NOT evaluate, give an opinion, advise, analyse, or question what she is saying.

Wait for Sarah to give an indication that she feels she has been heard.

Keeping a warm friendly attitude, say, 'Sarah, I have listened to you, now will you listen to me? Can I tell you what I think?'

Try to get Sarah to go to a quieter or more private environment. If there is time, suggest you and she have a drink of juice and sit down and talk about it.

After gaining Sarah's acceptance, go to the quieter place, explain an advantage of the option that you suggest. Start with an I statement: 'I feel it would be better to . . . because. . . . Do you understand?'

If Sarah escalates, revert to active listening.

If Sarah remains calm, enter into a negotiation process, e.g. 'What do you think we should do to fix this situation, Sarah?'

Suggest some solutions . . . first this, then that, or postpone the scheduled activity, or schedule in Sarah's preference in her picture calendar, or this instead of that.

Box 18.7 Sample instructional control procedure

Instructional control: the five-second game

Patrick's teacher will set Patrick five requests in a day, which she has written down in advance. Patrick's challenge is to cooperate with four of the five requests. If he achieves this by the end of the day, he is given a 'well done' stamp to take home to show parents.

---

to the learner, the learner's attention must be obtained in advance, the style of the request must be acceptable to the learner, the nature of the task must be acceptable to the learner and the reinforcer must be one the learner is motivated to achieve at that time and place. Given these basic assumptions, an example of an instructional control protocol is presented in Box 18.7.

In our own clinical practice, the most frequently used direct intervention along with antecedent control is **stimulus satiation**. This procedure is in direct contrast to the traditional emphasis on identifying the reinforcing consequences for behaviour in order to withdraw them, thereby extinguishing the behaviour. Instead, stimulus satiation involves the continuous and non-contingent application of the reinforcer that has been identified as maintaining the target behaviour (Donnellan, LaVigna, Negri-Shoultz and Fassbender, 1988). One example was where a woman was performing severe self-injurious behaviour, which, it was hypothesized, was being reinforced by having access to a bath. (The form of self-injurious behaviour was often so severe as to necessitate bathing as a consequence.) The intervention involved a non-contingent schedule of four requests to take a bath each day. Requests were offered in a two-way choice format, using object cues, in order to ensure that there was no forced responding. She was also offered a bath when she appeared distressed. Incidents of self-injury reduced by 72 percent within one day. Another young man engaged in physical aggression and severe property destruction, which was hypothesized to be maintained by edible reinforcement. As part of a stimulus satiation procedure, fruit bowls were placed in his living room and other rooms in his house. These were replenished as often as necessary. He had free access to the fruit bowls, but was also reminded to use them, initially every 30 minutes. Prompting was required in order to ensure, for example, that he finished one fruit before starting another. Physical aggression and property destruction were eliminated on all occasions when fruit was available. Stimulus satiation interventions appear to work and are particularly recommended when the reinforcer maintaining the behaviour is attentional. For example, one young girl showed a high volume of aggressive behaviours towards siblings during the 60 minutes after arrival home from school. Her mother, instead of cooking the family meal that time, sat and gave her 10 minutes of non-contingent attention immediately after arrival home from school. Aggressive behaviours during this interval were eliminated.

Like all direct interventions, stimulus satiation is not a constructive intervention. Teach the person skills for relaxing, communicating or solving the problems that the environment sets. Perhaps for this reason, it is unlikely to bring about maintenance, in the sense that behavioural gains are unlikely to last after withdrawal of intervention. However, it works very well in combination with functionally equivalent skills teaching, and may be withdrawn once the appropriate functionally equivalent skill is established. It is not always possible or even advisable to recommend stimulus satiation. Some substances, such as alcohol or caffeine, may have an addictive quality and it may not be desirable to present them at an increased rate, as satiation may not be achieved at safe levels. Other reinforcers, such as some of those available from self-stimulatory behaviours, may be idiosyncratic or impossible to deliver reliably. On the other hand, when it is possible to provide reinforcing events continuously, or at least at an increased rate, then stimulus satiation is a powerful element in a multi-element behaviour support plan.

Another set of direct intervention strategies are the **differential reinforcement procedures**. The underlying principle is to provide reinforcement for the non-occurrence or reduced occurrence of target behaviours, or for the occurrence of alternative behaviours that compete with target behaviours. Generally these interventions make sense when the person has an alternative appropriate behaviour within his or her repertoire (and the issue is the individual's motivation to use the appropriate behaviour) or when it is used in combination with attempts to teach the person an alternative appropriate behaviour. There are three main variations of differential reinforcement procedures; Differential Reinforcement of Other behaviours (DRO), Differential Reinforcement of Low Rates of Responding (DRL) and Differential Reinforcement of Alternative Responses (Alt-R). Many of the principles of implementing a differential reinforcement programme may be illustrated by examining the Differential Reinforcement of Other behaviours schedule.

I Select and define a behaviour

Often a learner has a number of inappropriate behaviours. In such cases, it is usual to list these behaviours in order of priority and to select the highest priority behaviour or behaviours. These behaviours are then defined precisely. A precise definition includes a start criterion and a stop criterion. Take for example the behaviour of temper tantrums. The behaviour may start as a shout, and progress to a scream, then clenching of fists, then physical aggression. The start definition specifies the behavioural criterion that the person must perform in order for the behaviour to have commenced. It is important

---

Box 18.8 Example of behavioural definition

Mark presents with a number of problematic behaviours:

- Physical aggression (severe pinching or scratching, escalating to hitting, kicking or biting if the person does not withdraw)
- Throwing. Mark throws objects onto the ground. He also overturns furniture
- Lying on the ground.

In a meeting with Mark's support team it was decided to limit initial intervention to physically aggressive behaviours. For this reason the target behaviour was defined as any contact with another person which leaves a mark on the other person's skin.

---

that this definition is agreed with the people who are implementing the reinforcement programme, so that there is consistency between people as to what is being reinforced. An example is presented in Box 18.8.

2 Select a time interval

The key to a successful reinforcement programme is to set a target for the individual that is achievable. The optimal programme sets a target for the person that is realistic: typically where there is already a 50:50 chance of success. In order to calculate the period of time, it is necessary to calculate the interval response time (IRT) at baseline, that is the average length of time between behaviours. The probability that a behaviour will occur during half this time is probably 0.05, so the optimal period for the DRO programme is half the interval response time. For example, say the baseline of Billy's aggressive behaviours is 3.5 incidents per week. The average length of time between incidents is two days. The optimal period of time in a reward contract is two days.

3 Select the reinforcer

Reward contracts act as motivational systems, and so it is important that the person is motivated to receive the reinforcer when it becomes available. To avoid satiation effects, the maximum amount of the reward should be considerably less (no more than 60 percent) of what the person would choose if given free access. In general it is better to select reinforcers that do lend themselves as easily to satiation (e.g. money, social activities) if these are motivating for the person. It is also important that the reinforcer is available only when the person reaches the criterion specified in the DRO programme. If the reward is an opportunity to go to a football match, there must be no other access to going to a football match except if the reward is achieved. The corollary of this is that the only events that can be offered as reinforcers in reinforcement programmes are those events that can be withdrawn without an infringement of the rights of the individual and without a diminution in the individual's quality of life. Thus, attention should not be selected as the reward because (a) an individual should be in a state of deprivation relative to attention in order for attention to be motivating and (b) lack of access to attention may represent a significant impoverishment in the person's quality of life which (c) may set the occasion for the further occurrence or escalation of challenging behaviour. Similarly praise should not be the sole reinforcer in a reward contract if the withdrawal of access to praise has an aversive effect for the individual.

There are many ways of identifying potential reinforcers. These include asking the individual what he or she likes, asking parents or others who know the person very well, offering a range of potentially reinforcing events and carefully logging the person's response to the delivery and withdrawal of each one, presenting two-way samples of potential reinforcers and recording which one the person selects. If it is not possible to identify a viable reinforcer for the individual, then activity sampling (see above) is probably a better place to start in behavioural support than a differential reinforcement programme. An inventory of favourite things, such as the one presented in Figure 18.2, may be helpful in broadening the range of potential reinforcers prior to selecting one.

Select a mediating system for the programme. Many reinforcement pro-grammes can be enhanced by creative mediating systems that are based on the interests of the person. Consider, for example, a learner who is reinforced with a token representing a player from his or her favourite football team. Once the full team is collected the tokens are exchanged for a reward. Other examples include making progress on a game board (snakes and ladders without the snakes!); a workman making progress up a ladder, collecting vouchers along the way, or a jigsaw puzzle piece, which when assembled, depicts the rewarding event.

Other formats for reinforcement

When behaviours are very high frequency, the period of time required for a DRO programme may be so short that DRO is difficult to implement. There are a number of variations that are useful for high-rate behaviour, differential reinforcement of low rates of responding and DRO escalating schedule, DRO progressive schedule and differential reinforcement of alternative behaviour.

Inventory of favourite things

The items in this questionnaire refer to things that might give a person pleasure or satisfaction. Please rate how much the person enjoys each of the following by placing a number (1 to 5) in the appropriate space.

1 = Not at all,   2 = A little,   3 = A fair amount,   4 = Much,   5 = Very much.

Food		*Academic*		
Snacks	Table tennis	Reading	Feeding animals	
What kind?	Going to a match	Writing	Listening to stories	
a.	Visit to Old Trafford	Magazines	Compiling music tape	
b.	Painting	Being read to	Decorating own room	
	Pottery	Science	Choosing own bedtime	
Meals	Playing snooker	Social studies	Sleeping late	
What kind?	Playing pool	Physical education	Chairing a meeting	
a.	Card games	Maths	Magazine subscription	
b.	Other?	School	Being centre of attention	
	a.	Leave class early	Leave work early	
Drinks	b.	Free time	Choose type of work	
What kind?	c.	Doing responsible job		
a.		Video after class	*Tokens*	
b.	*Music*		Stars on chart	
	Playing an	*Domestic activities*	Special badges	
	instrument	Setting the table	Certificates	
Preparing food	Singing	Making the bed	Points	
	Dancing	Baking	Money	
Possessions	Buying CDs	Repairing	Note home	
Jewellery	Listening to music	Working outside		
Clothes		Going on messages		
Magazines	*Excursions*	Cooking	*Other*	
Computer games	Ride in a car	Washing car	a.	
Skate board	Visiting relatives	Sewing	b.	
Diary	Visiting friends	Shopping	c.	
Bicycle	Going to beach	Exempt from chores	d.	
Other possessions?	Having picnic		e.	
a.	Going out to dinner	*Personal appearance*		
b.	Going for a walk	Getting new clothes		
c.	Visiting the zoo	Putting on make-up		
d.	Shopping for clothes	Getting a haircut		
	Going to the library	Manicure		
	Going on the train	Massage		
Entertainment	Bus trip	Visit to beautician		
Watching TV	Other	Perfume or		
Cinema	a.	aftershave		
Pub	b.	Wearing jewellery		
Renting video	c.	Having picture taken		
Concert or show				
	Social interaction	*Other events*		
Sport	Playing with children	Staying past		
Playing soccer	Playing with adults	bedtime		
Playing hurling	Hugs, kisses	Earning money		
Playing football	Sleepovers	Free time		
Swimming	Coffee with others	Having a pet		
Riding a bike	Party with friends	Taking a bath		
Skating	Other	Jacuzzi		
Bowling	a.	Multi-sensory room		
Horse-riding	b.	Steam room		
Fishing	c.	Aromatherapy		

Figure 18.2 Example of reinforcement inventory.

Differential reinforcement of low rates of responding (DRL)

The average number of behaviours shown during a certain period of time is established. Reinforcement is delivered if the rate of behaviour is below this average rate of behaviour during the specified time. Once reinforcement has been delivered on a number of successive occasions, the criterion is gradually and systematically reduced until the behaviour is at an acceptable level or until the rate of the behaviour is low enough for a DRO programme to be feasible. DRL has a number of advantages for some learners. Typically, a visual mediating system is used for tracking progress in a DRL programme. For example, a token depicting the reward is placed on a chart for each behaviour at baseline. Each time the behaviour occurs, a token is moved to another location, and if at the end of the specified period of time there is at least one token left, reinforcement is delivered. It is not necessary that the learner has a concept of number in order to be able to understand a system such as this. Further, the visual mediating system allows an instructor opportunities to remind the learner of his or her progress. For learners who may associate an incident of behaviour in the middle of an interval with the non-delivery of reinforcement at the end of the interval, the DRL offers the possibility of moving the token immediately after an incident, helping the learner to observe the contingency. One caution using this system is the risk that the learner might interpret the removal of a token as an aversive event. To avoid this, it is important that the feedback to the person during the removal of the token is calm, encouraging and motivational. Further, the amount of reinforcement is not dependent on the number of tokens that are left at the end of an interval. Finally DRL is another helpful strategy when the problem is not the behaviour itself but the rate at which it occurs.

DRO escalating schedule

For very frequent behaviours, a DRO schedule can occur as a discrete trial. That is, rather than make reinforcement available after a number of consecutive intervals, it is possible to make a reinforcement available after a single interval, and, once the criterion is reached, the size of this interval is systematically increased. For example, at baseline, Sid pulled his teacher's hair on average 50 seconds after the onset of one-to-one instruction. The teacher gave Sid a piece of white chocolate (his favourite) 50 seconds after the start of each teaching session if no hairpulling occurred. Once Sid had achieved reinforcement on five successive occasions, the period of time was gradually increased until Sid was able to participate in a five-minute teaching session with no hairpulling.

DRO progressive schedule

Another powerful variation of differential reinforcement is a DRO Progressive (DROP) schedule. The amount of reinforcement increases for each consecutive successful interval up to a specified maximum. DROP is particularly usful for high-impact, low-frequency behaviours, where there can be a need to string several consecutive intervals together without incident. It also avoids

---

Box 18.9 Sample progressive schedule reward contract

Reward contract (DROP)

Each day is divided into three periods 9.30 to 11.30; 11.30 to 1.30 and 1.30 to 3.00.

For each section in which Jason does not hit or kick or push, he is given praise, and his grid is signed.

If he gets through one period without hitting, kicking or pushing behaviour he gets one signature, but if he completes two periods in a row without behaviour he gets two signatures after the second period. If he gets through a third consecutive period, he gets three more signatures; and so on up to a maximum of five more signatures after five consecutive periods (i.e. after a sixth consecutive period in a row, he still gets five signatures).

If he hits, kicks or pushes, no signature is given. At the end of the period, say, 'Hard luck, Jason, let's try again'. If the next period is clear, he again gets rewarded with one signature.

After 45 signatures, he can get the toy bailer (pictured on the 45th square of his grid). After 100 signatures, he can get to buy a model airplane, and after 150 signatures, he receives a trip to the airport.

---

the satiation effect that sometimes occurs immediately after delivery of reinforcement. An example of a DROP schedule is given in Box 18.9.

Differential reinforcement of alternative behaviour (Alt-R)

Perhaps the most important variation of differential reinforcement schedules is Alt-R. The alternative response selected for reinforcement may be physically incompatible with target behaviour, but this may lead to the reinforcement of redundant or non-functional behaviours. For example, an individual with face-slapping self-injurious behaviour may be reinforced for placing his hands in his pockets for five minutes' duration. It may be physically impossible to slap his face, but the incompatible behaviour is unlikely to be functional. However, if the alternative response is functionally equivalent to challenging behaviour, an Alt-R schedule would ensure effective reinforcement for this response. When used in combination with DRO, the plan ensures that the reinforcement available for the alternative response is more powerful than the reinforcement available for challenging behaviour. A functionally equivalent response may be selected from the person's repertoire, or is established as part of a skills teaching programme. These interventions (ALT-R, DRO, functionally equivalent skills teaching) are used in combination with environmental accommodations to provide the opportunity, the skill and the motivation for successful performance. This is the essential rationale of a multi-element proactive behaviour support plan.

Reactive strategies

The primary purpose of reactive strategies in multi-component interventions is to optimize the safety of all concerned. Assuming the situation is safe, the secondary objective is that the participants survive together with dignity. At the heart of reactive planning is the principle that the response to behaviour should be matched to the level of escalation of the individual. In assessment, then, it is important to know the person's behavioural indices of anxiety, the typical precursors or warning signs of challenging behaviour and a clear identification of the topography of challenging behaviour. The usefulness of this information is illustrated in Table 18.5, where responses are matched to the person's indices of anxiety and escalation.

Table 18.5 Sample reactive strategies

No anxiety	If Ciara makes reasonable requests . . .	Give her what she requests **Or** encourage her to help herself **Or** refer her to the schedule
Anxiety	If Ciara frowns, grimaces or changes facial expression to look upset . . .	Listen to her carefully Reflect back to her what you hear her say Allow her time to talk. Say, 'use your words'. Acknowledge her difficulty Ask her what she needs to do next Ask her what she needs staff to do
Precursor 1	If Ciara makes unreasonable requests . . .	Try to negotiate with her, using 'if . . . then . . .' statements; or by scheduling the requested activity where possible. Try to say yes instead of no: e.g. 'Yes you can . . . Yes, and first we will do this . . . Yes, let's look at the schedule and see when this is going to happen . . . Yes, let's make sure we put that into the schedule for tomorrow . . . Yes, that sounds like a good idea . . . Yes, what do you need to do for that to happen?' Try to refer Ciara to her schedule before saying wait If Ciara is unable or unwilling to negotiate, try to redirect her, and encourage her to take time to think

Precursor 2	If Ciara becomes uncooperative . . .	Present the problem to Ciara in terms of the choice she has to make Consider backing down with grace and dignity **Or** allow her time and space to make her choice Praise her for making a choice **Or** acknowledge that this must be difficult for her
Precursor 3	If Ciara screams . . .	Manage her arousal level Try to stay calm Try not to speak (to minimize the amount of information that Ciara has to contend with) Tag with another team member – every five minutes if necessary Wait until the screaming subsides before negotiating with her
Physical aggression	If Ciara hits, kicks, attempts to pull hair . . .	Stand back. Avoid personal injury If necessary, use beanbags or soft cushions to make the environment safer If necessary, remove furniture likely to cause injury Try to stay calm Use words sparingly to direct Ciara's behaviour Try not to negotiate until Ciara is calm Try to communicate with your non-verbal behaviour that the situation must be very difficult for Ciara, and that this will pass
Physical aggression	If Ciara continues to be aggressive . . .	Stand back. Avoid personal injury Refer to crisis intervention training; block and move to avoid strikes; use momentum and leverage to release from a hair pull Do not talk to her or be near her until she is calm, **except** . . . To offer her a choice every half hour to take part in the next activity on her timetable . . . .To offer her assistance to go to the toilet after four hours
Aftermath	When Ciara shows a reduction in tension . . .	First, try to facilitate relaxation. Once Ciara is calm, try to facilitate communication Once Ciara has named the problem, try to facilitate problem solving

In designing a reactive strategy for dangerous behaviour, one of the most important features is to create options for the participants. Many times people commence acting out behaviours when they are out of options, and staff exhibit aversive responses when they do not know what else to do. A good reactive plan should attempt to help all participants consider all the options at their disposal. Instructors may become stuck when there is an insistence (usually from psychology) that the immediate consequences of behaviour are not rewarding. For example, when it is established that a behaviour is reinforced by attention, the traditional response is to ignore behaviour. However, in practice, this response can become an establishing operation for escalation in aggressive or self-injurious responding. In the behaviour modification literature, the escalation in behaviour that typically occurred was known as an extinction spike. The effects of behavioural escalation, and the possibility that the person will replace existing topographies with more dangerous ones, was seldom reported in the literature. Moreover, when behaviour is dangerous, extinction may be impractical or unsafe. These concerns are reduced considerably in the context of a multi-element behaviour plan, which ensures that when behaviour is reinforced inadvertently in the course of a reactive strategy, there is more powerful differential reinforcement available for appropriate alternative behaviours. For example, one woman engaged in a pattern of verbally abusive behaviour, which would escalate to screaming and physical aggression. Throughout the incident, she would repeat demands for a cup of tea. If tea were offered, the behaviour would cease, strengthening the hypothesis that the behaviour was reinforced by tea. A multi-element plan was established, in which tea was offered as a capitulation to prevent physical aggression. However, the reinforcing properties of tea were weakened by the establishment of a regular, non-contingent schedule of cups of tea (stimulus satiation) which were signalled to her on a visual timetable (environmental accommodation).

EFFICACY OF POSITIVE BEHAVIOURAL SUPPORT (PBS)

The challenge for PBS is to demonstrate a three-fold goal: reductions in challenging behaviour; the teaching of replacement behaviours; and increases in quality of life. In a meta-review by Carr *et al.* (1999) involving 109 studies, over half of these presented data in respect of increasing positive behaviours. In these cases, modest to substantial increases were reported. Such data are important as they show a move away from the more traditional criterion of reduction in problem behaviour and a move towards the construction of new behavioural repertoires in individuals. In respect of problem behaviour, a reduction to zero rates of problem behaviour occurred in almost 27 percent of cases. In the context of a 90 percent reduction, this figure increased to 52 percent. With an 80 percent reduction criterion, this figure rose to 68 percent. However, in 9 percent of cases problem behaviour decreased only minimally (0–19 percent) or increased. In respect of quality-of-life outcomes, data regarding successful lifestyle change were only taken from 8 out of the total 230 participants in the study therefore making it difficult to draw valid conclusions about quality of life. There may be several reasons for such a low figure. Quality-of-life outcomes are by their very nature highly individualized and the challenge for researchers is to identify methods by which such outcomes can be tracked across the favoured single-case design. Furthermore, it is only relatively recently that quality of life has become a criterion by which studies are evaluated. Since that review, the number of individual case studies has grown, consolidating such outcomes.

DUAL DIAGNOSIS

Individuals with intellectual disability are reported as displaying higher rates of mental health problems than in the general population (Deb *et al.*, 2001). This is attributed in part to social factors (e.g. increased poverty), psychological (e.g. reduced problem-solving abilities) and biological processes. Aside from any other presenting difficulty such as challenging behaviour, identifying the presence of mental health problems is itself difficult owing to factors such as communication difficulties, atypical symptom presentation and diagnostic overshadowing. However, when challenging behaviour is present, the diagnostic puzzle facing professionals becomes even more complex. The relationship between challenging behaviour and mental health problems has been conceptualized in three ways: (a) the psychiatric illness may operate as a setting event for challenging behaviour; (b) that challenging behaviour be a manifestation of the core symptoms of a psychiatric illness; and (c) challenging behaviours may occur as secondary features of psychiatric disorders among people with severe intellectual disabilities (Emerson, Moss and Kiernan, 1999). Consequently, services are presented with the complex challenge of meeting their assessment and treatment effectively. Unfortunately, the complexity of this task is often consolidated by the difference in the philosophy of care and service models underpinning the approaches of the different professionals. These differences in turn can easily lead to disjointed and un-coordinated services for these individuals.

Few effective examples of collaborative working leading to effective team functioning and client outcomes are available within the literature. Those that do exist stress the existence of a shared model of assessment and intervention. One example is the bio-behavioural model of self-injury developed by Mace and colleagues (Mace, 1994; Mace, Blum, Sierp, Delaney and Mauk, 2001). This model effectively discriminates between operant-controlled self-injury and that maintained by biological processes and it leads to the creation of interventions matching identified maintaining factors; an outcome that is axiomatic to both medical and behavioural approaches. What allows such discrimination to take place is the essentially behavioural approach to operational definition and data collection within a single-case research design format (Kazin, Anisova, Galeev, Golenda *et al.*, 2001; Grey, McClean, Kulkarni and Hillary, 2003). An increasing number of case studies involve the use of single-case design to determine medication effects (Crosland, Zarcone, Lindauer, Valdovinos *et al.*, 2003, Northup and Gulley, 2001). Furthermore, recently published guidelines have recommended the inclusion of functional assessment within a mental health assessment (Deb *et al.*, 2001).

STAFF TRAINING

The individuals often charged with the day-to-day implementation of behavioural supports are front-line staff. It has been argued that staff competence in the application of positive behavioural supports is critical to an improvement of the quality of life of those with an intellectual disability (Jahr, 1998) and also in reducing the frequency of challenging behaviour (Emerson, 2001). Evaluations of training for staff working with intellectually disabled clients have typically reported mixed results. However, this appears to be primarily mediated by what the goals of training actually are. In respect of goals, two broad categories are evident: education and specific skill acquisition. The former is essentially concerned with the provision of information to bring about attribution change and reappraisal of some aspect of client behaviour with the implicit assumption that such cognitive change will bring about actual behaviour change. Identifying training that can achieve this end has proved somewhat difficult (Hastings, Remington and Hatton, 1995) as very few, if any, attribution or 'knowledge gain' studies investigate actual staff behaviour change. Those training programs that do include a measure of staff behaviour typically report no change in this domain despite positive changes in attitudes or attributions.

Even when the goal of training is explicitly increased knowledge surrounding treatment integrity, it appears that knowledge alone is insufficient. This also appears to be largely the case irrespective of teaching method as instructional procedures including lectures, discussions and written and/or verbal information alone are also noted to be largely ineffective in teaching staff proper applications of treatment (Jahr, 1998). For example, Jenkins, Rose and Jones (1998) noted that despite increases in staff knowledge about facilitating eating in clients with impairments in this area, no actual change in respect of practice was observed.

In contrast, staff training programs that explicitly target and measure overt staff behaviour directly have enjoyed more success. The majority of these studies are typically behaviour-analytic in design and reflect a focus on discrete staff behaviours in areas such as paired preference assessment (Lavie and Sturmey, 2002), embedding teaching within natural routines in school settings (Schepis, Reid, Ownbey and Parsons, 2001), client nutritional programs in community-based homes (Kneringer and Page, 1999), staff–client interactions (Hendrickson, Gardner, Kaiser and Riley, 1993), promoting generalization of teaching skills (Ducharme and Feldman, 1992) and choice availability (McKnight and Kearney, 2001). However, though staff training that explicitly targets overt behaviour has been successful, taken collectively, these studies have been largely confined to implementing interventions not directly related to challenging behaviour.

One model of staff training, Person Focused Training, that has been shown to bring about positive outcomes in the area of challenging behaviour has been developed and evaluated by McClean, Dench, Grey, Shanahan *et al.* (in press). The model is defined as training staff who work with service users displaying challenging behaviour to conduct a functional assessment, to design and to implement a multi-element behaviour support plan for a particular individual. An analysis of longitudinal data from 138 staff-developed behaviour support plans indicated that significant improvements were observed in 77 percent of cases (defined as a reduction to below 30 percent of baseline rates of behaviour) and that at an average follow-up of 22 months such improvements were maintained. In a control group study by Grey and McClean (2004) such improvements were observed in a target group of clients but not for a matched control group of clients over a six-month period, lending further support to a competency and case-based model of staff training.

Relatively few empirical studies identify critical components of successful training of staff within intellectual disability. This task of course is complicated by a definition of what constitutes successful training. Those factors critical to the success of training and which require logistical planning prior to onset of training include: (1) the attainment of some qualification for successful completion for staff; (2) the assignment of a mentor for the duration of the training to provide practical support; (3) support from immediate line management for participation in training and implementation of interventions; (4) examples of completed assignments; (5) access to key reading materials; (6) time to complete assignments.

TOWARDS AN ECOLOGY OF SUPPORT

Although placement in a Special Treatment Unit is often sought when there is a behavioural crisis, there is limited evidence for the efficacy of these units (Emerson, Toogood, Mansell, Barrett *et al.*, 1987). Special treatment units aim to develop a therapeutic environment capable of transferring individuals to mainstream services after a temporary stay. However, behaviour change is not guaranteed and there may even be behavioural deterioration after admission (Hoefkens and Allen, 1990). The main problem with residential treatment units is that any changes that do occur there are unlikely to be maintained after discharge (Hoefkens and Allen, 1990; Lowe, Felce and Blackman, 1996). The removal of the person from the mainstream service reduces the need for training and the development of competence within mainstream services, which can act as a barrier to discharge. As a consequence, silting up is a common experience.

Specialist teams provide assessments and recommend interventions in situ, and in so doing, increase the likelihood that improvements will be maintained after the specialist has withdrawn. It has been shown that these teams can bring about changes in severe challenging behaviours within the natural settings (Donnellan, LaVigna, Zambito and Thvedt, 1985; Hudson, Wilken, Jauernig and Radler, 1995) and that these changes can be maintained or improved upon at six-month follow-up. They have been found to require less intervention time than residential units (Maguire and Piersel, 1992), and to be more cost-effective than residential services (Allen and Lowe, 1995). The main disadvantage of this model is the problem of coverage. The specialists required to meet the needs of the population of people with challenging behaviours may not be available in sufficient number (Sprague, Flannery, O'Neill and Baker, 1996). In a survey of forty-six peripatetic teams, Emerson, Forrest, Cambridge and Mansell, 1996 found that 49 percent had caseloads of between one and six cases. The caseload range was between one and twenty-five. It was estimated that only 48 percent of people with severe challenging behaviours are on current team caseloads. Thus, like special treatment units, special teams may also be prone to the problem of silting up and hence fail to provide the level of specialist support services required.

It is important to draw a distinction between a specialist team and a team of specialists. Bringing about enduring behavioural improvement and efficient client throughput should not be assumed as following the designation of specialist resources such as members of different disciplines (Stancliffe, Hayden and Lakin, 1999). Lowe, Felce and Blackman (1996) evaluated the effectiveness of different specialist intervention teams and concluded that teams that lack a coherent and coordinated approach to assessment and intervention may not be effective despite the efforts of specialists. However, challenging behaviours can be overcome when teams operate from a sound basis in functional assessment.

People with challenging behaviours have the right to live in the community. In order to achieve this, families caring for people with challenging behaviours may need to access regular respite care, intensive behavioural support at home, outpatient psychiatric evaluation and monitoring, and access to acute psychiatric service or an alternative place of safety at times of acute crisis.

With these concerns in mind, we propose the following model of service provision for people with challenging behaviour or psychiatric illness which is individualized, flexible over time, supports community living and provides a place of safety when necessary (see Figure 18.3).

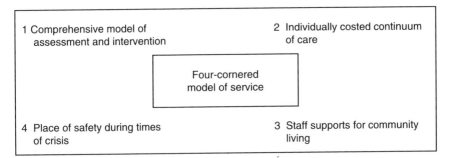

Figure 18.3 Four-cornered model of service provision for people with severe challenging behaviour.

I. Comprehensive model of assessment and intervention

People with challenging behaviour or dual diagnosis need a comprehensive assessment which includes both psychiatric evaluation and an assessment of the function of challenging behaviour. To date, the combination of psychiatric assessment and functional assessment has been primarily limited to the domain of self-injurious behaviour (Mace *et al.*, 2001) and although additional research is needed, results have been promising.

In the absence of accurate self-report, observation of the individual is critical and it is in this area that a strength of functional assessment lies. Central to functional assessment are clear operational definitions of challenging behaviours, appropriate methods of recording and identification of consequences of challenging behaviours. Information gathered is then analysed in the context of additional information collated from a cognitive and communication assessment. Such assessment can point to or exclude psychiatric illness as an aetiological factor of challenging behaviour (Grey *et al.*, 2003) and consequently increase the likelihood of correct treatment decisions.

2. Individually costed continuum of care

People with dual diagnosis represent a very diverse client group, with needs which vary greatly from individual to individual and from one time to another. The service response needs to be individualized and flexible over time. A typical individually costed continuum of care will include an estimate of per diem costs for:

- Residential staff
- Day support staff
- Intensive support workers for times of crisis
- Consultation with a consultant psychiatrist

- Consultation with a challenging behaviour specialist
- Transport costs
- Rental accommodation or social housing costs

The costing should be subject to mandatory review each quarter.

3. Staff supports for community living

The objective of service for people with dual diagnosis is to enhance well-being and quality of life in the community. To this end, people with dual diagnosis require residential support staff, present or on-call, job coaches for employment or training, present or on-call, and intensive support workers, present during period of crisis and on-call.

4. Place of safety during times of crisis

People with dual diagnosis can live with their families or with others for large parts of their lives if given the supports they need to do so. Crisis plans need to be established on a case-by-case basis, from a comprehensive range of service options, including:

- Acute psychiatric treatment in mainstream psychiatric hospitals for some individuals with mild intellectual disability or where challenging behaviour is not unduly disruptive
- Small community-based respite facilities, adapted for challenging behaviour, which receive outreach psychiatric support
- High-support homes in the community for people with chronic psychiatric difficulties and persistent challenging behaviour.

EXERCISE

Rod is a 12-year-old boy with mild to moderate intellectual disability. He attends a mainstream school, has classroom support and lives with his parents and two older siblings. He was referred because he has recently bitten two children in school. One episode occurred in class and the other in the playground.

Work in teams of four to plan an assessment; possible outcomes of the assessment; and potential interventions using the material in the chapter. Present your assessment plan, and possible outcomes and interventions, to the class.

FURTHER READING FOR CLINICIANS

Sprague, J.R., Flannery, B., O'Neill, R. and Baker, D.J. (1996). *Effective Behavioural Consultation: Supporting the Implementation of Positive Behaviour Support Plans for Persons with Severe Challenging Behaviours.* Eugene, OR: Specialised Training Program.

O'Neill, R.E., Horner, R.H., Albin, R.W., Sprague, J.R. and Newton, J.S. (1997). *Functional Assessment and Program Development for Problem Behaviour: A Practical Handbook* (2nd edn). Pacific Grove, CA: Brooks/Cole.

LaVigna, G.W. and Donnellan, A.M. (1986). *Alternatives to Punishment: Solving Behaviour Problems with Non-aversive Strategies.* New York: Irvington.

REFERENCES

Allen, D. and Lowe, K. (1995). Providing intensive community support to people with learning disabilities and challenging behaviour: A preliminary analysis of outcomes and costs. *Journal of Intellectual Disability Research*, 39, 67–82.

Anderson, D.J., Lakin, K.C., Hill B.K. and Chen, T. (1992). Social integration of older persons with mental retardation in residential facilities. *American Journal on Mental Retardation*, 96, 488–501.

Bird, F., Dores, P.A., Moniz, D. and Robinson, J. (1989). Reducing self-injurious behaviours with functional communication training. *American Journal on Mental Retardation*, 94, 37–48.

Borthwick-Duffy, S.A., Eyeman, R.K. and White, J.F. (1987). Client characteristics and residential placement patterns. *American Journal of Mental Deficiency*, 92, 24–30.

Bruininks, R., Hill, B.K. and Morreau, L.E. (1988). Prevalence and implications of maladaptive behaviours and dual diagnosis in residential settings. In J.A. Stark, F.J. Menolascino, M.H. Albarelli and V.C. Gray (eds), *Mental Retardation and Mental Health: Classification, Diagnosis, Treatment Services*. New York: Springer-Verlag.

Carr, E.G., Horner, R., Turnbull, A. and Marquis, J. (1999). *Positive Behaviour Support for People with Developmental Disabilities*. Washington, DC: AAMR.

Carr, E.G., Robinson, S. and Polumbo, L.W. (1990). The wrong issue: Aversive versus nonaversive treatment. The right issue: Functional versus nonfunctional treatment. In A. Repp and N. Singh (eds), *Aversive and Nonaversive Treatment: The Great Debate in Developmental Disabilities* (pp. 361–80). DeKalb, IL: Sycamore Press.

Crosland, K.A., Zarcone, J.R., Lindauer, S.E., Valdovinos, M.G., Zarcone, T.J., Hellings, J.A. and Schroeder, S.R. (2003). Use of functional analysis methodology in the evaluation of medication effects. *Journal of Autism and Developmental Disorders*, 3, 271–9.

Deb, S., Thomas, M. and Bright, C. (2001). Mental disorder in adults with intellectual disability. 1: Prevalence of functional psychiatric illness among a community-based population aged between 16 and 64 years. *Journal of Intellectual Disability Research*, 6, 495–505.

Derby, K.M., Wacker, D.P., Berg, W., DeRaad, A., Ulrich, S., Asmus, J., Harding, J., Prouty, A., Laffey, P. and Stoner, E.A. (1997). The long term effects of functional communication training in home settings. *Journal of Applied Behaviour Analysis*, 30, 507–31.

Desrochers, M.N., Hile M.G. and Williams-Mosely, T.L. (1997). Survey of functional assessment procedures used with individuals who display mental retardation and severe problem behaviours. *American Journal on Mental Retardation*, 101, 535–46.

Didden, R., Duker P.C. and Korzilius, H. (1997). Meta-analytic study on treatment effectiveness for problem behaviours with individuals who have mental retardation. *American Journal on Mental Retardation*, 10, 387–99.

Donnellan, A.M., LaVigna, G.W., Negri-Shoultz, N. and Fassbender, L.L. (1988). *Progress without Punishment*: New York: Teachers College Press.

Donnellan, A.M., LaVigna, G.W., Zambito, J. and Thvedt, J. (1985). A time limited intensive intervention programme model to support community placement for persons with severe behaviour problems. *Journal of the Association for Persons with Severe Handicaps*, 10, 123–31.

Ducharme, J.M. and Feldman, M.A. (1992). Comparison of staff training strategies to promote generalized teaching skills. *Journal of Applied Behaviour Analysis*, 1, 165–79.

Dunlap, G. and Fox, L. (1996). Early intervention for serious problem behaviours. In L.K., Koegel, R.L. Koegel, and G. Dunlap, (eds) (1999). *Positive Behavioural Support: Including People with Difficult Behaviour in the Community* (pp. 31–50). Baltimore: Paul Brookes Publishing.

Emerson, E. (1998). Working with people with challenging behaviour. In E. Emerson, C. Hatton, J. Bromley and A. Caine (eds), *Clinical Psychology and People with Intellectual Disabilities* (pp. 127–53). Chichester: Wiley.

Emerson, E. (2001). *Challenging Behaviour: Analysis and Intervention in People with Severe Intellectual Disabilities*. Cambridge: Cambridge University Press.

Emerson, E. and Bromley, J. (1995). The form and function of challenging behaviours. *Journal of Intellectual Disability Research*, 39, 388–98.

Emerson, E. and Hatton, C. (1994). *Moving Out: The Effect of the Move from Hospital to Community on the Quality of Life of People with Learning Disabilities*. London: HMSO.

Emerson, E., Forrest, J., Cambridge, P. and Mansell, J. (1996). Community support teams for people with learning disabilities and challenging behaviours: Results of a national survey. *Journal of Mental Health*, 5, 395–406.

Emerson, E., Moss, S. and Kiernan, C. (1999). The relationship between challenging behaviour and psychiatric disorder in people with severe developmental disabilities. In N. Bouras (ed.), *Psychiatric and Behavioural Disorders in Developmental Disabilities and Mental Retardation* (pp. 38–48). Cambridge: Cambridge University Press.

Emerson, E., Toogood, A., Mansell, J., Barrett, S., Bell, C., Cummings, R. and McCool, C. (1987). Challenging behaviours and community services: 1. Introduction and overview. *Mental Handicap*, 15, 166–9.

Goldiamond, I. (1974). Toward a constructional approach to social problems: Ethical and constitutional issues raised by behaviour analysis. *Behaviourism*, 2, 1–84.

Grey, I. and McClean, B. (2004). An evaluation of Person Focused Training. *Journal of Intellectual Disability Research*, 48, 4 and 5, 298.

Grey, I.M., McClean, B., Kulkarni, L. and Hillary, J. (2003). Combining psychiatric and psychological approaches in the inpatient assessment of aggression in a client with moderate intellectual disability. *Irish Journal of Psychology*, 20 (3), 91–5.

Harris, P. (1993). The nature and extent of aggressive behaviour amongst people with learning difficulties (mental handicap) in a single health district. *Journal of Intellectual Disability Research*, 37, 221–42.

Hastings, R. P., Remington, B. and Hatton, C. (1995). Future directions for research on staff performance in services for people with learning disabilities. *Mental Handicap Research*, 8, 333–9.

Hendrickson, J.M., Gardner, N., Kaiser, A. and Riley, A. (1993). Evaluation of a social interaction coaching program in an integrated day-care setting. *Journal of Applied Behaviour Analysis*, 2, 213–25.

Hoefkens, A. and Allen, D. (1990). Evaluation of a special unit for people with mental handicaps and challenging behaviour. *Journal of Mental Deficiency Research*, 34, 213–28.

Horner, R.H., Dunlap, G., Koegel, R.L., Carr, E.G., Sailor, W., Anderson, J., Albin, R.W. and O'Neill, R.E. (1990). Toward a technology of 'nonaversive' behavioural support. *Journal of the Association for Persons with Severe Handicaps*, 15, 125–32.

Hudson, A., Wilken, P., Jauernig, R. and Radler, G. (1995). Behavioural treatment of challenging behaviour: A cost benefit analysis of a service delivery model. *Behaviour Change*, 12, 216–26.

Iwata, B., Dorsey, M., Slifer, K., Bauman, K. and Richman, G. (1982). Toward a functional analysis of self-injury. *Analysis and Intervention in Developmental Disabilities*, 2, 3–20.

Iwata, B.A., Pace, G.M., Dorsey, M.F., Zarcone, J.R., Vollmer, T.R., Smith, R.G., Rodgers, T.D., Lerman, D.C., Shore, B.A., Mazaleski, J.L., Goh, H.L., Cowdrey, G.E., Kalsher, M.J., McCosh, K.C. and Willis, K.D. (1994). The functions of self injury: An experimental-epidemiological analysis. *Journal of Applied Behaviour Analysis*, 27, 215–41.

Jahr, E. (1998). Current issues in staff training. *Research in Developmental Disabilities*, 19, 1, 73–87.

Jenkins, R., Rose, J. and Jones, T. (1998). The Checklist of Challenging Behaviour and its relationship with the Psychopathology Inventory for Mentally Retarded Adults. *Journal of Intellectual Disability Research*, 4, 273–8.

Jones, R.S.P. (1991). Reducing inappropriate behaviours using nonaversive procedures: Evaluating differential reinforcement schedules. In B. Remington (ed.), *The Challenge of Severe Mental Handicap: A Behaviour Analytic Approach*. Chichester: Wiley.

Kazin, E.M., Anisova, E.A., Galeev, A.R., Golenda, I.L., Gol'dshmidt, E.S., Grishina, K.V., Drapezo, R.G., Ignisheva, L.N., Minin, V.V., Ovchinnikova, O.V. and Shabasheva, S.V. (2001). Complex approach to the functional state evaluation in humans. Communication I. Methodology of diagnostics of functional states. *Fiziola Cheloveka*, 2, 112–21.

Kemp, D.C. and Carr, E.G. (1995). Reduction of severe problem behaviour in community employment using an hypothesis-driven, multi-component intervention approach. *Journal of the Association of Persons with Severe Handicaps*, 20, 229–47.

Kennedy, B. and Carr, A. (2002). Chapter 7. Prevention of challenging behaviour in children with intellectual disabilities. In A. Carr (ed.), *Prevention: What Works with Children and Adolescents? A Critical Review of Psychological Prevention Programmes for Children, Adolescents and their Families* (pp. 129–53). London: Routledge.

Kiernan, C. and Alborz, A. (1996). Persistence and change in challenging and problem behaviours of young adults with intellectual disability living in the family home. *Journal of Applied Research in Intellectual Disabilities*, 9, 181–93.

Kipnis, D. (1987). Psychology and behavioural technology. *American Psychologist*, 42, 30–6.

Kneringer, M.J. and Page, T.J. (1999). Improving staff nutritional practices in community-based group homes: Evaluation, training, and management. *Journal of Applied Behaviour Analysis*, 2, 221–4.

Koegel, L.K., Koegel, R.L. and Dunlap, G. (1999). *Positive Behavioural Support: Including People with Difficult Behaviour in the Community*. Baltimore: Paul Brookes Publishing.

Larson, S. (1991). Quality of life for people with challenging behaviour living in community settings. *IMPACT*, 4 (1), 4–5.

Lavie, T. and Sturmey, P. (2002). Training staff to conduct a paired-stimulus preference assessment. *Applied Behaviour Analysis*, 2, 209–11.

LaVigna, G.W. and Donnellan, A.M. (1986). *Alternatives to Punishment: Solving Behaviour Problems with Non-aversive Strategies*. New York: Irvington.

LaVigna, G.W. and Willis, T.J. (1995). Challenging behaviour: A model for breaking the barriers to social and community integration, *Positive Practices*, 1 (1) 8–16.

LaVigna, G.W. and Willis, T.J. (1996). Behavioural technology in support of values. *Positive Practices*, 1 (4) 1–17.

LaVigna, G.W., Willis, T.J., Shaull, J.F., Abedi, M. and Sweitzer, M. (1994). *The Periodic Service Review: A Total Quality Assurance System for Human Services and Education*. Baltimore: Paul Brookes Publishing.

Lowe, K., Felce, D., and Blackman, D. (1996). Challenging behaviour the effectiveness of specialist support teams. *Journal of Intellectual Disability Research*, 40, 336–47.

Lucyshyn, J.M., Olson, D. and Horner, R.H. (1995). Building an ecology of support: A case study of one young woman with severe problem behaviours living in the community. *Journal of the Association for Persons with Severe Handicaps*, 20, 16–30.

Mace, F. C. (1994). The significance and future of functional analysis methodologies. *Journal of Applied Behaviour Analysis*, 27, 385–92.

Mace, F.C., Blum, N.J., Sierp, B.J., Delaney, B.A. and Mauk, J.E. (2001). Differential response of operant self-injury to pharmacological versus behavioural treatment. *Developmental and Behavioural Paediatrics*, 22, 85–91.

Maguire, K.B. and Piersel, W.C. (1992). Specialised treatment for behaviour problems of institutionalised persons with mental retardation. *Mental Retardation*, 30, 227–32.

Mansell, J. (1994). Specialised group homes for persons with severe or profound mental retardation and serious behaviour problems in England. *Research in Developmental Disabilities*, 15, 371–88.

Martin, N., Gaffan, E. and Williams, T. (1999). Experimental functional analysis for challenging behaviours: A study of validity and reliability. *Research in Developmental Disabilities*, 20, 125–46.

McClean, B. and Walsh, P. (1995). Positive programming – an organisational response to challenging behaviour. *Positive Practices*, 1, 3–8.

McClean, B., Dench, C., Grey, I., Shanahan, S., Fitzsimons, E., Hendler J. and Corrigan, M. (in press). Person focused training: A model for delivering positive behavioural supports to people with challenging behaviours. Manuscript accepted by *Journal of Intellectual Disability Research*.

McKnight, T. J. and Kearney, C. A. (2001). Staff training regarding choice availability for persons with mental retardation: A preliminary analysis. *Journal of Developmental and Physical Disabilities*, 13 (1), 1–10.

Murphy, G.H., Oliver, C., Corbett, J. *et al.* (1993). Epidemiology of self-injury, characteristics of people with severe self-injury and initial treatment outcome. In C. Kiernan (ed.), *Research to Practice? Implications of Research on the Challenging Behaviour of People with Learning Disabilities* (pp. 1–35). Kidderminister: BILD.

Nelson, J.R., Roberts, M.L. and Smith, D.J. (1998). *Conducting Functional Behavioral Assessments: A Practical Guide*. Longmont, CO: Sopris West.

Northup, J. and Gulley, V. (2001). Some contributions of functional analysis to the assessment of behaviours associated with attention deficit hyperactivity disorder and the effects of stimulant medication. *School Psychology Review*, 2, 227–38.

O'Neill, R.E., Horner, R.H., Albin, R.W., Storey, K. and Sprague, J.R. (1997). *Functional Assessment and Program Development for Problem Behaviour: A Practical Handbook* (2nd edn). Pacific Grove, CA: Brooks/Cole.

Oliver, C., Murphy, G. and Corbett, J.A. (1987). Self-injurious behaviour in people with mental handicap: A total population study. *Journal of Mental Deficiency Research*, 31, 147–62.

Repp, A.C. (1994). Comments on functional analysis procedures for school-based behaviour problems. *American Journal of Applied Behaviour Analysis*, 27, 409–12.

Repp, A.C., Felce, D. and Barton, L.E. (1988). Basing the treatment of stereotypic and self-injurious behaviours on hypotheses of their causes. *Journal of Applied Behaviour Analysis*, 21, 281–9.

Russell, O. and Harris, P. (1993). Assessing the prevalence of aggressive behaviour and the effectiveness of interventions. In C. Kiernan (ed.), *Research to Practice: Implications of Research on the Challenging Behaviours of People with Learning Disability* (pp. 60–73). Clevedon: BILD Publications.

Schepis, M.M., Reid, D.H., Ownbey, J. and Parsons, M.B. (2001). Training support staff to embed teaching within natural routines of young children with disabilities in an inclusive preschool. *Journal of Applied Behaviour Analysis*, 34, 313–27.

Schwartz, A. and Goldiamond, I. (1975). *Social Casework: A Behavioural Approach*. New York: Columbia University Press.

Sprague, J.R., Flannery, B., O'Neill, R. and Baker, D.J. (1996). *Effective Behavioural Consultation: Supporting the Implementation of Positive Behaviour Support Plans for Persons with Severe Challenging Behaviours*. Eugene, OR: Specialised Training Program.

Stancliffe, R.J., Hayden, M.F. and Lakin, K.C. (1999). Effectiveness of challenging behaviour IHP objectives in residential settings: A longitudinal study. *Mental Retardation*, 37, 483–93.

Sternfert Kroese, B., Dewhurst, D. and Holmes, G. (2001). Diagnosis and drugs: Help or hindrance when people with learning disabilities have psychological problems? *British Journal of Learning Disabilities*, 29, 26–34.

Sugai, G., Horner, R. H., Dunlap, G., Hieneman, M., Lewis, T. J., Nelson, C. M., *et al.*

(2000). Applying positive behaviour support and functional behavioural assessment in schools. *Journal of Positive Behaviour Interventions*, 2 (3), 131–43.

Taggart, L. and McConkey, R. (2001). Working practices employed within and across hospital and community service provision for adults with an intellectual disability and additional needs. *Journal of Learning Disabilities*, 5, (2), 175–90.

Touchette, P.E., MacDonald, R.F. and Langer, S.N. (1985). A scatter plot for identifying stimulus control of problem behaviour. *Journal of Applied Behaviour Analysis*, 18, 343–51.

Wacker, D.P. Peck, S., Derby, M.K., Berg, W. and Harding, J. (1996). Developing long-term reciprocal interactions between parents and their young children. In L.K. Koegel, R.L. Koegel and G. Dunlap, *Positive Behavioural Support: Including People with Difficult Behaviour in the Community* (pp. 47–67). Baltimore: Paul Brookes Publishing.

Willis, T.J. and LaVigna, G.W. (1996a). Behaviour assessment: An overview. *Positive Practices*, 1 (2), 1–16.

Willis, T.J. and LaVigna, G.W. (1996b). Behaviour assessment: An overview. Part 2. *Positive Practices*, 1 (3), 1–19.

Section 6

Adolescence

Chapter 19

Life skills training for adolescents with intellectual disabilities

Trevor R. Parmenter, Anthony D. Harman, Marie Yazbeck and Vivienne C. Riches

One of the most significant features of the contemporary literature on the study of intellectual disability has been the focus on quality of life. In a position paper developed by the Special Interest Research Group (SIRG) on quality of life for the International Association for the Scientific Study of Intellectual Disabilities (IASSID) (Schalock, Brown, Brown, Cummins *et al.*, 2002) the following issues were highlighted:

- Quality of life of people with a disability has been influenced by a shift in focus away from the belief that scientific, medical and technological advances, alone, would result in an understanding that personal, family, community, and societal well-being emerge from complex combinations of these advances, together with values, perceptions, and environmental conditions.
- Quality of life is the next logical step emerging from the normalization movement that stressed community-based services, to measuring outcomes from a person's life in the community.
- The rise of consumer empowerment and its emphasis on person-centred planning, personal outcomes, and self-determination has shifted the decision-making focus away from professionals and service agencies to the person with the disability, and where relevant, his or her family.

In his development of a model of quality of life Parmenter (1992) stressed the pivotal role that the development of an authentic identity by the person with a disability played in his or her perception of a satisfactory life of quality. Other components of the model embraced three domains that were seen as interacting to influence quality-of-life outcomes. These were competence in a variety of functional skills or behaviours; the influence of cognitive and affective behaviours; and environmental influences including community supports, acceptance and attitudes that impact upon the person.

Participation in community activities has been a central goal of the normalization movement. However, the implicit assumption is that people with an intellectual disability possess the necessary life skills to participate effectively and meaningfully. By definition, however, people with an intellectual disability have deficiencies in the area of adaptive behaviours that act as limitations to various activities (Schalock, 2004; World Health Organization, 2001). The World Health Organization (2001), *International Classification of Functioning, Disability and Health* (ICF), has emphasized that environments can also present barriers to the level of a person's participation.

This chapter will examine limitations and barriers that adolescents with an intellectual disability and those with additional autism spectrum disorders face in becoming an active participant in a community. It will especially address the important roles support staff have in assisting these people to acquire and apply life skills that will help them to be contributing members of their communities, and to enjoy a sense of satisfaction, well-being and contentment that is their inherent right as a citizen in their communities. Adolescence is a time when young people generally are developing an adult identity. However, for adolescents with an intellectual disability there is a double jeopardy. In addition to a developmental delay, they experience an environment that is extremely challenging from both psychological and social perspectives. A number of illustrative vignettes of adolescents with an intellectual disability will provide a context for the discussions.

CASE STUDY: A GIRL WITH MODERATE ID AND EPILEPSY

Margaret is 19-years-old, and has a moderate level of intellectual disability and photic epilepsy. She lives in the family home with both parents and an older brother who also has an intellectual disability. Margaret enjoys shopping, visiting discos, dancing, talking to friends, stamp collecting, writing letters, colouring in, swimming, and going out to dinner, the movies, and line dancing at the local RSL club.

Margaret attended a special school until she turned 18 years. She had several work experience placements during her final school years, including jobs at a hospital, a sheltered workshop, McDonalds and a childcare centre. She received employment training for three months and was then referred to a supported employment agency. She was placed and trained in a cleaning position in a hospital setting where she job-shares with two co-workers who also have a disability. Margaret walks to work but is very dependent for travel. Others claim she is able to be travel trained but her parents are resistant. She is caring of and keen to support co-workers and be supported by them, but frequent failure of one of her male co-workers to respond to her friendliness is usually interpreted as dislike or disinterest. This makes her very upset. She also gets upset when teased or 'bossed'. She is inclined to reject instructions at times, as she thinks others telling her what to do means they think she is stupid. When upset, typically Margaret cries and refuses to speak to others or she slams doors, bangs things, is disruptive or 'emotionally fragile'. Case records detailed twelve instances in which she had become disruptive at work over the past year. Margaret commonly complains of headaches and her mother reports she comes home very tired each day and often sleeps or rests after work. Margaret's parents stated she does not cope well with pressure, and work reports are that she becomes very anxious and panicky in response to change or provocation. Like many teenagers, Margaret wants more independence at home, and is in conflict with her parents over this. Her parents report that at home, Margaret throws major temper tantrums, is bossy and 'stands over' her parents, to the point that her mother is afraid for the future. While recognizing that Margaret has grown in social ability, they are also worried that Margaret is testing out control and pushing boundaries. They feel she has gained too much confidence and that she wants to order everyone around and tell them what to do, but will not take direction from others. Working in open employment has opened up significant social opportunities for Margaret, but she has difficulties in discriminating between appropriate and inappropriate behaviours in the workplace.

ADOLESCENCE AND THE PERSON WITH AN INTELLECTUAL DISABILITY

Adolescence is generally considered to be a time of preparation for the future, and as a transition time, enabling the young person to move smoothly from the dependency of childhood to greater independence and life as an adult citizen. This is when adolescents are expected to master a number of life skills. It is during this time that the adolescent begins to develop an adult identity. For a person with an intellectual disability this is problematic. Physically, they are following the same biological trajectory as other young people, but they are generally at a much younger psychological developmental stage. In addition, throughout their childhood and early adolescence they have been exposed to an environment that frequently reinforces an 'eternal child' identity. Parents and their wider networks, including school, can be overprotective leading to a phenomenon of 'learned helplessness'. In Margaret's case, this has manifested itself in the parents' failure to allow Margaret to be travel trained. This effectively keeps Margaret under their control, since she cannot go anywhere without their knowledge or approval.

Protection and isolation from the vicissitudes of community life was one of the drivers for the institutional era of care. From a eugenics perspective it was also driven by the perceived need to protect society from exposure to people deemed as a threat to the maintenance of sound genetic stock (Parmenter, 2001). Indeed, a recent study of community attitudes towards people with an intellectual disability confirms that vestiges of the eugenics era remain (Yazbeck, McVilley and Parmenter, 2004).

Life skills, suggested Brolin (1993), refer to a wide range of knowledge and skill interactions believed to be essential for adult independent living. Life skills can be defined as adaptive and positive behaviours that allow individuals to deal with the demands and challenges of everyday life. They also refer to skills that enhance psychological and social development such as decision making and problem solving, creative and critical thinking, communication and interpersonal relations, self-awareness, and coping with emotions and causes of stress. Development and exploration of life skills is a particularly important facet of adolescent reproductive health (Reproductive Health Outlook, 1997–2005).

Trzcinski and Brandell (2000–2001) pointed out that adolescence is a developmental phase characterized by rapid physical, intellectual, and socioemotional growth and change, frequently accompanied by turbulence, perplexity, and confusion. Adolescence as a developmental phase first received professional attention in the 1950s. Anna Freud (1969) referred to adolescence as a prolonged 'normative crisis', while the object relations theorist Winnicott recognized adolescents' engagement in vital developmental tasks (cited in Lanyado, 1999). One of the earliest explorations of adolescent development was Erikson's (1968) psychosocial epigenetic theory, which examined ego development across eight life-span stages. He theorized that healthy ego development was contingent upon the mastery of specific developmental tasks and normative crises in each stage of development (Brandell and Perlman, 1997). To Erikson (1968), adolescence is the stage of identity versus identity diffusion. This stage was developed by Erikson more extensively than any of the other seven stages and requires the integration of formative experiences that give the child the sense that he is a person with a history, a stability, and a continuity that is recognizable by others.

Adolescence usually occurs between the ages of 13 and 20 years. It is important to note that the presence of intellectual disability does not mean that a special 'psychology of disability' be invented. Young people with intellectual disabilities experience these developmental stages even though they may not correspond in the same chronological order and may be longer. For instance, for a person with intellectual disability the identity phase may last well into their twenties. Furthermore, a person with an intellectual disability in their teens may still be addressing Erikson's (1968) Industry phase (stage before adolescence) in learning the rules about relating to competition with peers. Some may not have mastered what Gold (1975) has referred to as Zero Order skills which are usually acquired in early childhood, e.g. knowing how to respond correctly to a simple hello or goodbye. When basic social skills are not acquired, it makes the person more dependent on others and may attract negative attention, disapproval, criticism and isolation. These skill deficits should be recognized early and appropriate teaching interventions put in place.

Eath and Walls (2005) suggested that adolescence is a time of transition from childhood to adulthood and a time of preparation for the adult responsibilities of employment and parenthood. The key issues in the psycho-social development of adolescence are still around identity formation, increasing independence and individuation from the family. The adolescent is separating from the attachments of a familiar social setting into the world with greater independence and individuality. Steinberg (2001) identified five sets of psychosocial concerns that are of greater significance in adolescence, although they are important throughout the entire life cycle of a person. These are identity or the sense of self; autonomy as in independence; intim-acy in having close caring relationships; sexuality in having physical contact with others and experiencing sexual feelings and achievement in becoming a successful competent member of society. Similarly Konopka (1973) and Pittman (1991) identified seven 'Keys for Kids' at this stage: Security: Youth feel physically and emotionally safe ('I feel safe'); Belonging: Youth experi-ence belonging and ownership ('I'm in'); Acceptance: Youth develop self-worth ('What I say and do counts'); Independence: Youth discover self ('I like to try new things'); Relationships: Youth develop quality relationships with peers and adults ('I care about others'); Values: Youth discuss conflicting values and form their own ('I believe . . .'); Achievement: Youth feel the pride and accountability that comes with mastery ('I can do it'). LoConto and Dodder (1997) asked people with developmental disabilities what they wanted from life and the response was that that they wanted the same things that all people want: material goods; a home of their own; emotional and intimate connections; vacations and leisure; and a way to feel useful. They pointed out that safety and physical health are often considered of greater importance to people with disability than a valued social role and the need for human connections.

Nevertheless, a young person with intellectual disability experiences ado-lescence not too differently from that of their peers without disability. Many of the issues of concern are common to both groups including those of identity, independence, friendship, sexuality and leisure activities. It is the friends and peers that provide the security for adolescents to individuate from families and to establish adult identities. Friends are pivotal for the enjoyment of leisure, which, in turn, leads to the expansion of their social circle. The lives of teenagers with intellectual disability may not be identical to the lives of teenagers without intellectual disability, but there should be equality in addressing these issues as much as possible. Eath and Walls (2005) pointed out that young people with an intellectual disability may experience the need for independence in the same way as their peers without disability. Increased autonomy for them is often more difficult to achieve because of their reliance on parents. This high level of parental involvement, which may continue into adulthood, may hinder the individuation process. In fact, there is often an increasing, rather than decreasing dependence on family, particularly on par-ents and siblings. Contrary to this, Buckley and Sacks (2001) noted the insightful comments made by parents on the progress many young people with Down syndrome made in their twenties after leaving home. Parents realized that the more independence and control their children had over their lives, the more self-esteem they had, and they had an increased ability to take on a more adult and confident identity.

Well-being of the adolescent is strongly related to the parent–child relationship. From a parent's point of view Peterson (2004) saw that the individuation process for the adolescent often indicates a time of turbulence and challenge to parents' authority. Emotional highs and lows are not far apart. Strong feelings are stirred up in both parents and their children. Adolescence is a period of awakening and discovery in relation to sexuality. The dawn of their emerging sexuality means that parents have to think about their authority relationship with their almost adult child. Teenagers can be disrespectful, testing, worrisome, and upsetting. Limit setting and guidance are still needed, but they must be based on the particular child's needs. The impending separation and accepting the child as a sexual being may introduce feelings of envy, fear, anger, pride, and regret. While this situation is common for adolescents without disability, parents of adolescents with an intellectual disability may also have to confront the reality of how far their child may be different from normal psychosocial development. They consequently may have special fears about their child being taken advantage of in the world.

Parents have a vision for their children's future for them to mature and move away to develop lives of their own (Hanley-Maxwell, Whitney-Thomas and Pogoloff, 1995). However, a child with a disability may distort this vision. DeMarie and LeRoux (2002) suggested that while families may be able to adapt, build resilience, and develop greater emotional growth and togetherness as they come to terms with the disability, they also may experience an ongoing stress as they move through their own life cycles as well as their child's.

Teenagers typically move through what Sugar (1968) called a 'period of normal adolescent mourning' that involves the recognition of imperfections in parents, the loss of childish ideas and fantasies, and the loss of the intimacy and dependency on family life. This new awareness may lead to associated anger, anxiety, helplessness and yearning for what is lost. Similarly, Ostrov and Offer (1978) and Rutter (1979) described the ordinary adolescent grief responses of depression, misery, unhappiness and loneliness as a natural part of the normal developmental process of growing up.

While adolescents cope with their own grief, loss and grief is a process experienced by parents when a child is born with, or acquires, a disability (Seligman and Darling, 1997). No matter what the disability, suggested DeMarie and LeRoux (2002), families find themselves in 'uncharted emotional territory with no guides to direct them toward ways to express their grief in a culturally acceptable format'. Parents may also experience chronic sorrow, which was first described by Olshansky (1962) as a natural and pervasive psychological reaction of the parent in response to living with a child with a disability. The defining characteristics of chronic sorrow now emerging from the literature include periodic, inescapable recurrences of pain and sadness, and roller coaster cycles of elation and depression fuelled by denial; as well as grief at the loss of the idealized 'normal' child. There are paradoxes and ambiguities, conflict and confusion. Rather than grief being a linear process, there can be varying intensities of grieving from time to time and from situation to situation; with the process of chronic sorrowing occurring in phases of denial, developing awareness and restitution with adaptive and/ or maladaptive coping (Bolst, 1990; Copley and Bodensteiner, 1987; Featherstone, 1980; Kearney and Griffin, 2001; Solnit and Stark, 1961; Winkler, Wasow and Hatfield, 1983; Young, 1977). Pivotal milestones such as graduation from high school can trigger stress, grief or fears that impede a vision of normal adulthood. Despite the fact that parents may be supported during the process of the child's development during adolescence, their fears may impact on the outcomes for the young person.

There must also be a greater concentration on transitional processes for teenagers with intellectual disabilities during the period of adolescence. Families need to be supported by holistic services to overcome the barriers their teenage children with an intellectual disability face as they move towards adulthood.

RELATIONAL COMPETENCE

Many students with intellectual disabilities will become adults who marry and raise families. It is crucial, therefore, that they learn how to manage a home, family, and finances as effectively as possible. However, the Australian Bureau of Statistics (2001), reported that in 1998, around one in five of those with a disability aged between 15 and 64 years needed help to make friends, interact with others, maintain relationships, cope with feelings or emotions, make decisions, or think through problems. This highlights a significant challenge often encountered within this population – that many of these critical life skills are not developed through incidental or experiential learning, but instead require systematic training and instruction.

Thus common challenges regarding individuals with both autism and intellectual disability, reported by Volkmar, Paul, Klin, and Cohen (2005a), can include the continued development or refinement of self-help skills, which can be problematic and continue to cause difficulties in adolescence and beyond. For others, relational competence takes prominence in adolescence.

The concept of relational competence acknowledges, and is based on the assumptions, that competence is a continuum and not a dichotomy, and that both appropriateness and effectiveness are important aspects of relationships (Spitzberg and Cupach, 1984). Each individual brings to encounters with others their own needs and longings; perceptions and cognitions; choices and goals that affect behaviour; along with emotional and personality variables, and biological and organic factors. And each person is continually challenged, shaped and influenced by interactions with others in the various environments in which they operate, that is the living environment, the school/work or daytime activity environment and the community environment as shown in Figure 19.1.

Typically, adolescents with and without disabilities value and strive to belong, to feel valued and respected by others who are important to them, and they strive to feel competent across a range of areas, but most especially in relationships and friendships. However, individuals with intellectual and associated developmental disabilities have often experienced difficulty with relationships and relational competence across these environments. This has often been attributed to difficulties in learning necessary prosocial and communication skills, in addition to lack of sensitivity and difficulties in abiding by social and cultural rules that are often implicit in relationships. Difficulties with social interaction skills have been one of the consistent marks of autism since its first description and social interaction deficits are invariably intertwined with the language problems and narrowness of interest that make up current definitions of autism (Volkmar, Paul, Klin and Cohen, 2005a). Practices such as segregation and restricted living and working opportunities can further narrow the possibilities for meaningful relationships.

Many adolescents with intellectual disabilities also experience low self-esteem and loneliness and many have, for various reasons, suffered from inadequate, insecure, alienated or separated bonds in key relationships. In other cases, disrespect or unacknowledged shame experienced in relation to others may be a particularly potent force, significantly affecting relational

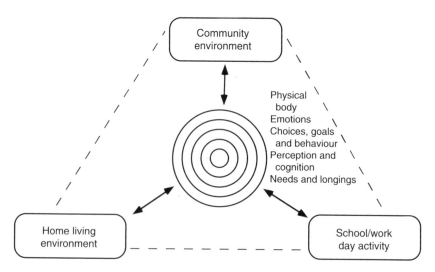

Figure 19.1 A model of relational competence across environments.

competence by influencing communication and cooperation and contributing to the degree of attunement or alienation experienced.

Individuals who feel overwhelmed by or alienated from others may experience heightened levels of anger and resentment or aggression (Riches, 1996b). Margaret (in the first case study), for example, would become angry and disruptive at work and at home when she felt rejected, teased or 'instructed' by others. Such interactions would trigger feelings of insecurity that were driven by beliefs that others thought she was 'stupid' or 'not good enough'.

Contemporary emphasis is now on comprehensive and individualized curriculum, with many programs treating social skills as the core. Recent research continues to provide evidence for the value of many elements of curriculum for social skills training, while cognitive behavioural techniques that address the thinking-feeling-behaviour triad provide further positive opportunities for increasing relational competence and quality of life (Kazdin and Wiesz, 2003).

Eath and Walls (2005) suggested that as a means of preparation for adulthood there needs to be a provision of experiences such as employment and training for potential parenthood for young people with intellectual disability. They suggested that there should be:

- A development of a greater understanding of the purpose and tasks of adolescence in their bridge to adulthood.
- The need to develop the necessary supports for leisure activities to remove the reliance on families, which will include:
  — Practical support, e.g. support workers / leisure coaches
  — Support for the development of community of interests
  — Developing community inclusion and community responsiveness

- The development of a model of transition to adulthood with adolescents to address the needs of:
  — Supports for friendship
  — Leisure and recreational activities
  — Development of community of interests

This is an important life stage for people with an intellectual disability, and skill development with a concentration on specific issues regarding the quality of life for young people is important. The teaching of these key life skills is necessary to compensate for deficits accumulated throughout the developmental life stages. They must be recognized and addressed in order to lay a foundation for early adulthood and beyond.

OVERVIEW OF EDUCATIONAL APPROACHES

In examining the development of life skills for adolescents with an intellectual disability, it is useful to trace the factors that have influenced curricular content and programming location for these people within the school context. In the 1960s the content was developmental in nature, with students being taught motor and cognitive skills that were seen as prerequisites to more advanced academic and functional skills, examples being fine motor manipulation of pegs in a pegboard (Westling and Fox, 2000) and information processing training (Parmenter, 1984). Students were educated in either a special school or special class setting. The following decades saw the focus shift to teaching functional behaviours that would be of use to students in their future environments, such as home living skills, personal care and appearance, job skills and functional academic skills (Horner, McDonnell and Bellamy, 1986; Snell and Brown, 2000). Here the emphasis was on a community-based curriculum, with skills being taught in settings where the skills were to be used. This approach was influenced by an emphasis on strategies that would assist maintenance and generalization of training, especially for those with very high support needs. More recently, with the emphasis upon inclusive schooling for students with disabilities generally, teachers are attempting to identify important student goals within the general curriculum followed in regular education (Ryndak and Alper, 1996). O'Neill and Heathfield (2004) have observed that there has been a decline in the overall frequency and proportion of research studies that have focused on curricular and instructional methods with a concomitant increase in studies targeting social interaction and integration skills. The difficulties in incorporating a more functional approach in regular school settings and the importance of social interactions for inclusive school settings has possibly influenced this trend. This may lead to a situation where the school graduate may lack those important life skills necessary for independence in the post-school environment.

Goodship (1990) stressed that the three major skill areas that need to be addressed are daily living, personal/social and occupational skills, while Clarke, Clarke, and Berg (1985) included the elimination of problem behaviour. A life skills curriculum approach therefore blends academic, daily living, personal/social, and occupational skills into integrated lessons designed to help students learn to function independently in society. When factors such as literacy, participation, and inclusion with others are added, it is seen that the task of education in this critical area becomes both complex and challenging.

TRANSITION

Leaving high school can be an exciting threshold for many youth, both with and without disabilities. It can occasion many changes, which when taken together can alter students' daily lives dramatically. The impression is that an individual should be more capable of making their own way in the world and normally a recommended 'skills for life' course has been suitably applied as part of the final transition to the workplace. The familiar schedule of early rising, classroom instruction until mid afternoon, often followed by school-sponsored extracurricular activities, and then homework in the evenings gives way to the more flexible structure, or the configuration, of a full or part-time job (SRI International, 2005). Some young adults remain in the family home, some live independently with little outside help, some select supported housing, while others live on campus as they pursue post-secondary education.

Successful support and management structures that facilitate academic progress, access to the curriculum, through to the workplace or further education must be transferable. In addition, particularly for students with autism spectrum disorders (ASD), central to the student's success must be the ability to match the transition program to the individual student in all aspects (South Australia Ministerial Advisory Committee: Students with Disabilities, 2000).

The USA National Longitudinal Transition Study (NLTS), which was begun in 1987, described the experiences and outcomes of young people with disabilities in the USA during the secondary school years and early adulthood (Wagner et al., 1993). It developed the first nationally representative database on students with disabilities, and provided a clear picture of the experiences of young people with disabilities while they were in secondary school and in the first years afterward (SRI Centre for Education and Human Services, 1993). A follow-up study (NLTS2: SRI International, 2005)) that included many of the same research questions, provided important information about the ways in which secondary education and post-school experiences have changed for youth with disabilities over the previous decade or more. On the positive side, improved employment experiences were recorded for youth with disabilities (SRI Centre for Education and Human Services, 2003).

However, the NLTS2 study also confirmed that the pattern of social interactions changed markedly once school had been left behind as adolescents no longer saw their friends every day in and between classes or during extracurricular activities. Perhaps the most dramatic changes occurred for those whose plans entailed leaving home, as this can precipitate them into environments that are fundamentally different from their previous experiences. These changes require one quickly to 'step up' to increased expectations for maturity and independence. These transitions can be difficult for any youth, but they can be particularly difficult for youth with disabilities who invariably encounter additional challenges in negotiating this transition to young adulthood.

The NLTS2 study (SRI International, 2005) reported that:

- When they had been out of secondary school for up to two years, about half of youth with a disability had been stopped by police for other than a traffic infringement, and 16 percent had spent a night in jail, both significant increases in a two-year period.
- Adolescents with intellectual disabilities or multiple disabilities are the categories most likely to be reported to have low functional cognitive skills and difficulty communicating. These are functional limitations that can affect all aspects of life and set them apart from other youth with disabilities.
- They are more likely to remain in high school until they reach age 21. Those who have left high school are among the least likely to have completed high school, and if completed, are among the least likely to have graduated with a regular diploma.
- Their rates of engagement in school, work, or preparation for work shortly after high school were the lowest of all disability categories, yet young people with intellectual disability are among the most likely to be living on their own and to be parenting. Few had the tools to support that independence.
- Independent of other differences in functioning between them, adolescents with multiple disabilities were 17 percent less likely to see friends frequently than were youth with specific intellectual disability, and when more functional domains are affected by their disabilities, the likelihood of frequent friendship interactions falls even lower.
- Youth with intellectual disabilities and those with multiple disabilities were also among the least likely to take part in organized community groups or volunteer activities up to two years after leaving high school.

Even allowing for those remaining in school until age 21, the probability is that many have still not grasped sufficient skills to maintain the substance of any 'normality' of life style.

Thus transition is a time when the following challenges detailed by Johnson, Stodden, Emanuel, Luecking, and Mack (2002), should be addressed:

- Ensure students with disabilities have access to the full range of general education, curricular options and learning experiences;
- Make school graduation decisions based on meaningful indicators of students learning and skills, and clarify the implications of different diploma options for students with disabilities;
- Ensure students access to, and full participation in, post-secondary education, employment, and independent living opportunities;
- Support student and family participation;
- Improve collaboration and system linkages at all levels.

SELF-DETERMINATION

Whitney-Thomas and Moloney (2001) explored the role of self-determination for people with cognitive disability. The self-determined individual has a strong sense of self, a clear vision for the future and a sense of control over the immediate environment and decisions. He or she is able to self-advocate, and obtain support to meet needs. Self-determination has its roots in childhood and these skills are taught usually by parents, teachers, and friends. However, issues of independence, autonomy, and self-determination are complicated for transition-aged youths with disabilities who have support and service needs (Hanley-Maxwell et al., 1995; Schulzinger, 1998). Indeed, many young people with intellectual disability fail to develop the necessary skills needed to become self-determined individuals (Geisthardt and Munsch, 1996; Swanson, Swartz, Estroff, Borum, Wagner and Hiday, 1998; Wehmeyer, Agran and Hughes, 1998).

This is partly attributable to the fact that during the secondary-school years where services are mandatory, needs are assessed and 'services' are planned and provided to and for individuals with disabilities, who in many cases are passive observers of the system (Stodden, Jones and Chang, 2002). It is the responsibility of the school to ensure individual education plans (IEP) are developed, coordinated and implemented. Apart from curriculum adaptations, services and special environments often include reduced class sizes, increased attention to students by teaching and support staff, and less demanding work schedules.

As youth with disabilities transition to post-school environments where individuals are responsible for identifying themselves, however, the focus changes from the provision of services to 'reasonable accommodations' and 'non-discrimination', and the level of support available also decreases significantly. Such accommodations often include priority enrolment, orientation, exam modifications, communication assistance, transcription services, access to adaptive technology, provision of note-takers, tutoring, lab and library assistance, counselling, advocacy, and housing assistance. In this environment, it is the student's responsibility to obtain the required educational assistance, manage and monitor their support provisions, and balance these with any related services and supports (such as transportation and health care) (Brinckerhoff, 1994; Izzo, Hertzfeld and Aaron, 2001; Stodden, Jones and Chang, 2002). It is now evident that many students with disabilities make this transition without the skills necessary to identify their own support needs and link their needs with desired outcomes (Grigal, Test, Beattie and Wood, 1997; National Centre for the Study of Postsecondary Educational Supports, 2000; Stodden et al., 2002).

While youth without disabilities increasingly learn self-determination skills, it appears the very processes instigated to support students with disabilities often shield them from learning and applying these important skills.

Indeed, it appears that to achieve post-secondary success, youth with disabilities need to be aware of the implications their disability has on their ability to function in this new environment, and the kinds of services and supports they are entitled to. They also need to possess the advocacy skills required to procure that assistance (Brinckerhoff, 1994; Izzo, Hertzfeld and Aaron, 2001; Stodden and Dowrick, 1999; Stodden *et al.*, 2002). Consequently, training opportunities for self-definition, and the provision of greater opportunities for independence need to be provided. This highlights the need for friendships and the inherent social skills required (Emerson and McVilly, 2004; McVilly, Stancliffe, Parmenter and Burton-Smith, 2006). Person-centred planning can also be useful to help them reach out to a network of support beyond the immediate family, while skills that enable them to identify their need for support are critical components of self-determination.

AUTISM SPECTRUM DISORDER

Autism Spectrum Disorder (ASD) is a lifelong neurodevelopmental disability that typically appears during the first three years of life and primarily affects an individual's abilities in the areas of communication and social interaction. Leo Kanner first described it in 1943 distinguishing it from childhood schizophrenia in his study of eleven boys. Cognitive impairment often co-occurs with autism and 70–75 percent of people with autism also have an intellectual disability with an IQ below 70. Half of all individuals with autism also fail to develop functional and communicative language (Perry and Condillac, 2003).

Criteria for diagnosis are arranged under three categories: social interaction; communication; and restricted, repetitive and stereotyped behaviours and interests. Autism occurs in 2–5 per 10,000 live births, and 3–4 times more often in boys than girls. It is the third most common developmental disability.

Case study: boy with autism

Rajinder is a 16-year-old, Grade 11 student diagnosed with autism spectrum disorders (ASD) after many years of being mislabelled 'emotionally disturbed with acting-out behaviour'. He has developed oral language, but his rapid speech without inflection is difficult to understand. He tends to use oral language without ensuring that anyone is listening. Raj takes some regular Grade 11 courses, and is supported by a teacher assistant who works with his classroom teachers. For part of each day, Raj works in the resource room on assignments. His receptive and expressive vocabularies are significantly below age level, but he can master concepts that are represented visually.

Raj often has difficulty completing assignments, because he is rigid about how they should look, insisting on starting his work over if he makes errors. He is interested in computers and this might be an area for possible training and employment in the future.

Raj has strengths as well as difficulties in social relationships. His poor judgement and inflexibility have had a disruptive effect on the lives of his parents and siblings. He follows family routines well as long as they are predictable. He has poor eye contact when talking to people outside his family, and does not follow social rules for personal space and touching. Raj loves to work independently on the computer and is a *Star Trek* fan, but he has poor group leisure skills. He is often excessively social with both familiar people and strangers, e.g. he touches inappropriately, sometimes attempting to kiss people. He has few friends at school because other students find his behaviour strange, even threatening. Raj has developed self-care skills but doesn't follow them regularly, so his hygiene and appearance contribute to poor peer acceptance. Raj has serious problems with social judgement, cannot handle money wisely (will give it to anyone who asks), and becomes anxious when routines at home or school are changed. When anxious, Raj pulls at his hair and recites dialogue from *Star Trek* rapidly. For example, when his normal bus route to school was changed, he refused to get off the bus and recited *Star Trek* dialogue until the principal came onto the bus and talked him into the school.

Raj's preoccupation with the computer and *Star Trek* can be problematic. He does not realize that other people might not be similarly interested. He often tries to start conversations in the middle of a story plot and does not understand when other people do not know the stories. Raj's parents have started to lock the door to his bedroom at night so he does not wander the house. He has been known to stay on *Star Trek* chatrooms on the Internet all night.

The exact cause of autism is unknown. Defined as a spectrum disorder, symptoms range from mild to severe, however, research suggests that it has a biological rather than a psychological cause (National Institute of Child Health and Human Development (NICHD), 2001). Whilst there are many strategies that assist an individual to learn important functional skills, there is no treatment or intervention strategy that cures autism (University of South Dakota, 2002).

The National Institute of Child Health and Human Development (NICHD, 2001) also indicates that autism generally lasts throughout a person's life; no two people with autism present exactly the same or respond to treatment in the same way.

In most cases, autism causes problems with:

- Communication, both verbal and non-verbal.
- Social interactions with other people, both physical (such as hugging or holding) and verbal (such as having a conversation).

- Routines or repetitive behaviours such as repeating words or actions over and over, obsessively following routines or schedules for their actions, or having very specific ways of arranging their belongings.

In Rajinder's case, some of these problems are indicated by his rapid speech without inflection, poor eye contact, inappropriate touching and attempting to kiss people, and his rigidity and inflexibility plus becoming anxious when routines are changed. The symptoms of the disorder cut off people with autism from the world around them. Children with autism may not want their mothers to hold them. Adults with autism may not look others in the eye and some never learn how to speak. These behaviours not only make life difficult for people who have ASD, particularly in relation to life skills development, but also make life hard for their families, their health care providers, their teachers, and anyone who comes in contact with them.

Volkmar *et al.* (2005a) pointed out that some individuals with autism at adolescence improve markedly, while others experience deterioration in functioning and many continue a stable maturational course. Common challenges concerning individuals with both autism and intellectual disability include the continued need for the development or refinement of self-help skills. In the majority of cases, independent self-help skills are problematic and continue to cause difficulties in adolescence and beyond.

Individuals within the spectrum have difficulty with both expressive and receptive communication, including non-verbal behaviours. Specifically, students with autism may demonstrate delay in, or lack of development of, spoken language without attempting to compensate through other modes of communication such as gesture. The Oregon Department of Education (2003) has suggested a comprehensive breakdown of how such problems may be manifested with possible resultant behaviours. These are as follows:

- Impairment in the ability to initiate/sustain conversation with others;
- Stereotyped/repetitive use of language or idiosyncratic language; and
- Lack of varied and spontaneous make-believe or social imitative play at the appropriate developmental level.

These may result in the following behaviours:

- Lack of attention and response to verbal instructions (lack of understanding);
- Does not respond to name;
- Frustration (tantrums, aggression, 'tuning out');
- Non-compliance and/or frustration;
- Difficulty with comprehension;
- Difficulty initiating conversation;
- Difficulty responding appropriately in conversation;

- Difficulty maintaining a topic interesting to a peer or other conversational partner;
- Inappropriate perseverance on a topic of interest;
- Difficulty with topic maintenance in conversation;
- Unusual vocal inflection or tone of voice;
- Uses and interprets language literally;
- Does not volunteer information to initiate conversation;
- Misunderstanding of or inattention to facial expressions in others;
- Misunderstanding and inappropriate response to figurative, metaphorical language and 'turns of phrase' used by others; and
- Repetition of sounds both immediate and delayed referred to as 'echolalia'.

Although autism characteristics vary, it is the social deficits that most notably compromise the individual's ability to engage with peers and the environment. These individuals typically have difficulty with social expression and understanding of other's behaviours, which manifests in lack of social motivation, whilst social appropriateness is frequently not a priority. Referring to the case study of Rajinder, one can see this in his use of oral language without first ensuring someone is listening, together with the rapidity of his utterances, recitation of dialogue, and the commencement of conversations in the middle of a story plot. Additionally, he is preoccupied, has poor eye contact, poor group leisure skills, and takes insufficient care of his hygiene and appearance; all of which contribute to negligible peer acceptance.

The Oregon Department of Education (2003) also listed some of the social challenges common to students with ASD:

- Difficulty with expression of non-verbal behaviours such as eye contact, facial expression, body postures and gestures to regulate social interaction;
- Failure to develop developmentally appropriate peer relationships;
- Lack of spontaneous seeking to share enjoyment, interests or achievements with other people; and
- Lack of social or emotional reciprocity.

These are issues that are highlighted in the case study of Rajinder.

Behavioural challenges bring attention to the fact that a student may have ASD. Although these behaviours can be disruptive and difficult to deal with, they are most often the result of a frustrated attempt at communication and should first be viewed from that perspective – as a form of communicating. Some of these may include:

- Preoccupation with stereotyped and restricted patterns of interest that is abnormal either in its intensity or focus;

- Inflexible adherence to mainly non-functional routines/rituals; and
- Repetitive and stereotyped motor mannerisms (such as hand flapping or object manipulation).

Alberta Learning (2003) indicated that social skills are often considered the primary deficit associated with autism spectrum disorders and it is therefore necessary to teach basic social awareness and interaction skills, such as tolerating others in environment, before addressing advanced skills, such as turn-taking or sharing. There are several social interaction skills that are critical for positive, long-term outcomes. These include: the ability to orient when others attempt to gain attention; eye contact; tolerating others in the physical space; imitation skills; parallel play; sharing and friendship behaviours. Before addressing higher-level social skills, such as friendship behaviours, prerequisite skills, such as making eye contact, may need to be taught (for some persons with ASD this may be counter-productive). Furthermore, access to models and opportunities to develop social skills is not usually sufficient; generally individuals with ASD need explicit teaching to develop social skills and understanding of social situations.

The kinds of instructional strategies used for communication and social skills can also be applied to instruction in the areas of self-care. Students with ASD, particularly those with intellectual disabilities, often need direct instruction in personal hygiene, grooming and dressing. Toileting can be an area requiring significant planning and instruction; again this can be seen in Rajinder's poor self-care skills. Additionally, planning meals, food preparation and even eating may be an appropriate part of students' programs. Household skills required for living independently, such as doing laundry, caring for clothing and cleaning, may also need to be taught.

In many instances, their areas of interest and their specific behavioural characteristics may not lead to feasible job options. However, in the case of Rajinder his interest in computers could be developed into a possible job opportunity. Capitalizing upon the person's interests is the best place to start from when planning for the future. In many cases, however, people are being prepared for a lifetime of dependency on social services or poorly matched jobs. During the school years, there are skills, which can be taught within the context of the school curriculum, to enhance the likelihood of future success. Competencies such as being organized, being prepared, completing assigned tasks, following directions, and interacting with others are important work skills, and not only for the person with ASD.

Adolescents with ASD need encouragement to participate in extracurricular activities, such as school clubs, and other social events with a view to building a network of support for the person to assist them in accessing employment and a satisfying life. However, given their natural tendency to avoid many social situations that other people with an intellectual disability enjoy, care must be taken to treat each individual according to their specific needs and wishes.

There are many occasions where a minor change can be made to the environment or workplace setting, thus alleviating a potential behaviour problem if one has a good understanding of the individual. Also, present information in a manner that is respectful of the individual and of his or her co-workers. With careful planning, people with ASD can be supported to have a life of success, despite the inherent struggles they will face (Pratt, 2002).

Social interaction deficits have been one of the consistent marks of autism since its first description and are invariably intertwined with the language problems and narrowness of interest that make up current definitions of autism. Although many programmes treat social skills as the core, research continues to provide evidence for including a range of elements in the curriculum (Volkmar, Paul, Klin and Cohen, 2005b).

PRE-VOCATIONAL TRAINING AND EMPLOYMENT

It is during the adolescent period when the acquisition of life skills is so important that the process of transition between school and the workplace occurs. It is essential that students with disabilities are given choices, and learning experiences, that allow them to build careers with adequate provision of support as required (Beach Centre on Families and Disability, 2000; Johnson, Stodden, Emanuel, Luecking, and Mack, 2002; Routledge, 2001).

Case study: boy with Down syndrome

Robert is an 18-year-old male with Down syndrome. He lives at home with his mother, father and younger brother and sister. Robert has a lively and likeable personality. He loves listening to music, going to the gym, swimming, and watching movies and TV with his family. He is sociable and kind-hearted but he has a strong desire to prove himself as tough, capable and competent. Like many adolescent males, he believes the best way to do this is through a 'macho image'.

Robert greatly admires muscles and an aggressive image. His role models are derived from video and TV watching, particularly John Travolta. He has learnt by heart every song and can mimic every movement Travolta made in the movie Grease. He has engaged in violent and hostile fantasy and thinking patterns, including destruction of property and beating others up in response to provocation. He is very keen to gain independence from his parents and enjoys disobeying them in little ways. He thinks this is 'cool' and 'manly'.

Robert attended an early intervention program in infancy, a support unit for students with disabilities during the primary years, and he completed his secondary years in a special school. He was involved in a work experience program during his transition from school to adulthood that involved several community job placements. He was referred directly to a supported employment program, and was quickly employed in a fast food restaurant, doing basic food preparation and some cleaning. Following travel training, Robert was able to travel to work independently using public transport. He worked 25–30 hours per week. After a number of months, problems developed at work such that his job was in jeopardy. Robert stated he did not like being 'bossed around', being watched at work by another person (his supervisor) and he hated to make mistakes. Storms, lightning, and thunder also agitated him. Robert was cranky with his support worker/supervisor because she did not help him complete job tasks which he thought she should. He was angry they were not treated as equals. He also became very angry with himself when he made a mistake, saying he 'felt bad' about himself.

Robert admitted that when upset at work, he would swear, and kick a box that was under his workbench. He would deliberately work slowly and occasionally he actively sabotaged the job. On one occasion, he told his supervisor/support worker that he was 'good on the inside and bad on the outside'. Several times Robert refused to wear gloves, and after one occasion when told to do so, he wrote with a marker pen over lids, and reported to his supervisor that this was to get her into trouble and to pay her back. Eventually Robert received a formal and final warning from his employer threatening job dismissal, due to deliberate disobedience, poor attitude and failure to comply with directions.

Robert participated in an anger management program and some social skills training. He did settle down at work, particularly when his worker/supervisor left. However, in conjunction with the employment agency, Robert decided to change jobs, which occurred successfully. He now works as a trolley boy in a supermarket chain, and has several other duties such as helping unload trucks and cleaning the floor. Robert appears considerably happier, and his anger levels have dropped significantly. He is very popular with staff and customers in his new workplace and he enjoys interacting with them and assisting customers and nearby shop owners. He is very much appreciated and has won several employee of the month awards.

Edgar (1988) pointed out that in the United States context several million individuals with learning problems were still denied the opportunity to engage in meaningful employment, while large numbers of students with disabilities, both high school graduates and dropouts, earned very low salaries with little potential for career advancement. The low participation rate of people with an intellectual disability in integrated employment remains a concern in other countries (Parmenter, 1999). These students do possess the potential to live and work in the community if they receive appropriate life skills instruction (Rusch and Phelps, 1987). However, without this preparation they often fail to obtain and hold jobs.

The crucial role that appropriate social interactions play in the workplace has long been recognized (Riches, 1993; 1996a) Moreover, the need for appropriate social interactions in the workplace has grown rather than diminished in recent years, with the steady increase in jobs in retail, health and community services, hospitality and personal and other services, in addition to the more traditional manufacturing sector (Anderson, 1999; Riches and Green, 2003). Lignugaris-Kraft, Salzberg, Rule, and Stowitschek (1988) found that successful workers were those who not only performed job-related skills but who also interacted socially and competently with supervisors, co-workers, and customers. This requires a combination of social behaviours that are classified as both task-related and non-task-related to be mastered. Many employers place a high priority on task-related social skills, and rate non-task-related interactions as less crucial for employment success (Rusch, Schutz and Agran, 1982; Salzberg, Agran and Lignugaris-Kraft, 1986). However, it has often been the non-task-related behaviours that have resulted in job loss (Chadsey-Rusch, 1992). Robert's story supports this finding.

Young people with intellectual disability have been found to be over-represented among the homeless and in the criminal justice population, in comparison to the prevalence of intellectual disability in the greater community (Price-Kelly and Hill, 1995). Hayes (2004) has highlighted the inadequate social skills of those people with an intellectual disability who come into contact with the criminal justice system, and who face intractable problems when seeking to enter the workforce upon release from prison. Appropriate interventions, such as those outlined in Robert's story, could ameliorate problems that often escalate into criminal offences being committed. Goodship (1990) suggested that the following are important life-skills experiences that lead to successful vocational outcomes:

- **Exhibiting Appropriate Work Habits and Behaviours** Following directions and observing regulations; recognizing the importance of attendance and punctuality; recognizing the importance of supervision; demonstrating knowledge of safety; work with others; meeting demands for high-quality work; and working at a satisfactory rate.
- **Seeking, Securing, and Maintaining Employment** Searching for a job; applying for a job, interviewing for a job; maintaining post-school occupational adjustment; demonstrating knowledge of competitive standards; knowing how to adjust to changes in employment.
- **Exhibiting Sufficient Physical and Manual Skills** Demonstrating stamina and endurance; demonstrating satisfactory balance and coordination; demonstrating manual dexterity; demonstrating sensory discrimination.
- **Obtaining Specific Occupational Skills** Attending pre-vocational learning stations or centres; taking advantage of in-school work experiences; taking advantage of volunteer experiences; serving in community rotations; taking advantage of work/study services; attending vocational

classrooms; obtaining special vocational education; obtaining on-the-job training.

In a follow-along study of the outcomes a pilot transitional system trialed in a state educational program, Riches, Parmenter and Robertson (1996) found that the best predictor for a vocational outcome was the presence of a work experience program in the final years of schooling.

ACTIVITY AND PARTICIPATION SKILLS

Doyle (2003) offered ten important 'Lifetime Goals' that all adolescents need to accomplish in order to pursue safe and productive lives:

- Using only safe behaviour such as moving away from danger or crossing the street;
- Taking complete care of his or her own body – independence in the bathroom, protection from abuse;
- Understanding appropriate touching, for example when to hug, touch or when being brushed off;
- Respectful use of property – treating things with respect and care;
- Knowing two different responses to give when people tell you Yes or No;
- Knowing who to ask for help and how and when;
- Learning to identify internal states and express them – the need to identify feelings, sensations or when ill; and
- Learning to express empathy, sympathy, and caring – to understand and share feelings;
- Giving negative feedback – how to choose the correct words to indicate dislike of what is happening, whilst maintaining respect and friendship; and
- Making Plan B – fixing situations and dealing with the unexpected, for example how to develop options to fix a problem.

An example of a program that includes both an assessment and a curriculum component for teaching life skills is the Functional Assessment and Curriculum for Teaching Everyday Routines (FACTER) (Arick, Nave, Hoffman and Krug, 2004). Life-skill instruction covers a broad category of activities, the majority of which may be performed in non-school environments. Because of the struggle to generalize information, especially common among those with cognitive disabilities, this instruction is best set in a 'real environment', which is why 'on-site' instruction is considered superior to in-class simulations or role-plays. Accordingly, work skills are taught in a business situation, life skills (e.g. housekeeping, personal care, cooking) in the home, and social skills in the community.

While most of us learn these life skills over a long period of time, from childhood into adult life, rarely are they taught in a systematic fashion. Rather, life-skill instruction is imitative. They are learnt over time in the context of their natural environments, as we mature and become members of the community. These environments are many and varied and might include: the workplace; independent or semi-independent living arrangements; and the endless number of community sites we must access daily, ranging from department store to public restroom to transportation systems.

By its nature, community-based instruction is time-consuming, as is the step-by-step guidance in daily living skills. This is why supporters of traditional life-skill instruction regard it as a priority of special education. They feel that without a compelling curriculum for life-skill instruction, it is unlikely that students with disabilities will acquire all the skills they need. Further, if they do not have a functional repertoire of life skills upon graduation from high school, their quest for an independent adult life style will be seriously compromised (Bastian and Kinney, 2004).

PERSONAL AND SOCIAL SKILLS

Personal and social skills are critical in keeping a job and maintaining friendships. Learning to get along with others is a challenge for everyone. Students with cognitive problems often do not learn by observing. Personal and social skills are an important part of the post-school adult living area. Critical to independent living is the mastery of tasks such as: selecting clothing; getting dressed; grooming and personal appearance; planning for social activities; home decorating and maintenance; shopping for self and household; and budgeting and financial planning. It is imperative that students receive support in these life skills as they make choices about and prepare for their futures. Social skills deficits may be related to impulsivity, both verbal and motor; poor visual perception of facial and body language cues; poor auditory perception of vocal cues; invasion of the personal space of others; inappropriate touching; untidiness; disorganization; mood swings; overreaction; and depression, all of which may cause social or vocational difficulties (Hayes, 1994/2005).

Brolin (1989) suggested that skill instruction in this area should include:

- Achieving self-awareness
- Acquiring self-confidence
- Achieving socially responsible behaviour
- Maintaining good interpersonal skills demonstrating
- Achieving independence
- Achieving problem-solving skills
- Communicating with others.

Each of these titles can be further itemized into specific skill areas defined by each heading, such as identifying interests and abilities or using appropriate methods to cope with stress under 'Achieving self-awareness', respect for others' rights and property and recognition of authority under 'Socially responsible behaviour'. It is well worth referring to Brolin's latest offering as detailed under suggested Further Reading.

DAILY LIVING SKILLS

Post-school adult living requires a variety of skills and knowledge that enable an individual to live as independently as possible. Every student needs to consider where he or she will live immediately after leaving high school and do the necessary planning to see it happen. Some young adults remain in the family home, some live independently with little outside help, some select supported housing, while others live on campus as they pursue post-secondary education. Many students with disabilities will marry and raise families. The majority will probably earn modest salaries; therefore, it is crucial that they learn how to manage a home, family, and finances as effectively as possible.

The following skills are some that have been identified as essential for independent adult living. Here again Brolin (1989) offers a wealth of detailed information with a breakdown of suggested items under each heading:

- Managing personal finances
- Selecting and managing a household
- Caring for personal needs
- Safety awareness
- Preparing and consuming food
- Buying and caring for clothing
- Exhibiting responsible citizenship
- Using recreational facilities and engaging in leisure activities
- Getting around the community.

COMMUNICATION SKILLS

Social communication skills are essential for the adolescent with an intellectual disability if they are to enter open employment. They are also important for the young adult in becoming more independent, e.g. using public transport, shopping. In all these social interactions non-verbal as well as verbal communication skills are required. A checklist for the main areas in social communication skills are:

- How does the person demonstrate they are listening, i.e. body posture, eye contact, hand movements, head nodding, facial expression?
- How does the person greet you/ farewell you?
- Is the person able to start a conversation?
- Does the person know how to finish a conversation?
- Does the person know how to interrupt you, i.e. if you are working on something?
- Does the person acknowledge and let you know if they understand what you are saying?
- Does the person let you know if they don't understand what you are saying?

All adolescents have a challenging time developing adult skills and interests whether there is intellectual disability present or not. However, those young adults with intellectual disability require more systematic rather than purely incidental learning experiences. However, it is essential that opportunities are provided for the young adult to participate in social settings and that they are not always being the loner or quiet one. Specific learning experiences may include:

- Encourage leisure activities which involve other people, e.g. movie/ shopping with friend, bush walking with group.
- Where applicable initiate some direct discussion and demonstration of skills. Take a photo of the person using different postures, facial expressions and talk about them in a positive and encouraging manner. Use mirrors to provide feedback.
- Provide opportunities for the person to stand up and be assertive. They need to be able to respond to disappointments and have the resilience and confidence to try again. Any improvement, however small, in social communication skills increases the independence of the person and encourages social participation.

ASSESSMENT INSTRUMENTS

Nollan, Wolf, Ansell, Burns *et al.* (2000) broadly separated self-sufficiency and life skills into tangible and intangible skills.

Tangible skills are needed for daily living, self-maintenance and obtaining and sustaining gainful employment. These are skills 'we know or do' and include skills such as money management, household management, transportation, finding and using resources for leisure and recreation, and vocational interests and aptitudes.

Intangible skills are those needed for interpersonal relationships and for maintaining employment. They include decision making, problem solving, planning, communication, self-esteem, anger and grief management, and social skills. Both tangible and intangible skills need to be assessed simultaneously to provide a complete picture of youth functioning.

Recommended instruments for measuring life skills are:

The Life Skills Inventory (Brigance, 1998), which assesses areas such as practical living skills, personal growth and management, social skills: speaking and listening; functional writing; common signs and warning labels; telephone skills; money and finance; food; clothing; health; travel and transportation.

The Independent Living Skills Assessment Tool (Children's Administration Division of Children and Family Services, 2000), which covers fifteen categories defining competence as basic, intermediate, advanced, and exceptional.

The Scales of Independent Behaviour-Revised (SIB-R; Bruininks, Woodcock, Weatherman and Hill, 2004) is a comprehensive, norm-referenced assessment of adaptive and maladaptive behaviour. It may be administered in a structured interview or by a checklist procedure. All items appear in each response booklet to facilitate either administration procedure.

The Vineland Adaptive Behaviour Scales, 2nd edn (Vineland-II; Sparrow, Cicchetti and Balla, 2005), a leading measure of personal and social skills needed for everyday living. Psychologists and other professionals continue to depend on it to identify individuals who have intellectual disability, developmental delays, autism spectrum disorders, and other impairments. It covers a number of categories including daily living skills, communication, and socialization.

Inventory for Client and Agency Planning (ICAP; Bruininks, Hill, Weatherman and Woodcock, 1986) is a short, easy-to-use, standardized assessment instrument that measures adaptive and maladaptive behaviour. Its strong psychometric properties make it a valuable tool for determining eligibility, planning services, evaluating, reporting progress, or for use in funding reports.

AAMR Adaptive Behaviour Scale-School edn (Lambert, Nihira and Leland, 1993) assesses the current functioning of children from 3 to 21 years of age being evaluated for evidence of intellectual disability. It has also been useful in evaluating adaptive behaviour characteristics of autistic children and differentiating behaviour-disordered children who require special education assistance from those with behaviour problems who can be educated in regular class programs.

The Adaptive Living Skills Curriculum (ALSC; Bruininks, Moreau, Gilman and Anderson, 2004) is a comprehensive curriculum designed to facilitate instruction of specific skills needed in everyday living, including those related to personal care, home living, and school, work, leisure, and community participation. Instructional activities for developing functional independence and adaptive behaviours span a broad range of difficulty levels that address the needs of learners of varying ages and skills and with all levels of disabilities. Each instructional unit facilitates learning by providing a general instructional framework and detailed strategies of specific, practical skills.

The Checklist of Adaptive Living Skills (CALS; Bruininks and Moreau, 2004) is a criterion-referenced, individually administered measure of adaptive living skills and an ideal tool for planning. As a measure of adaptive living skills, CALS may be used to determine the specific skills an individual has mastered or needs to master in important environments. As a tool for planning, CALS may be used to determine instructional needs, develop individual training objectives, and monitor progress of learners toward achieving instructional goals. It is intended to be used with a wide range of individuals, with and without disabilities, from infancy to mature adult. CALS may be used in a variety of educational, residential, day care, rehabilitation, work activity, employment training, and other human service settings. CALS can be used each time the individual's long-term goals are evaluated, each time the individual experiences a major change in environment, and each time there is a need to select new or different skills areas for evaluation and instruction.

The Ansell-Casey Life Skills Assessment (Casey Family Programs, 2000–2005), a sound instrument that assesses current levels of life skills knowledge and use of users in out-of-home care; used for both individual case planning and program development around self-sufficiency. It can be used both pre- and post-test.

Adolescent Autonomy Checklist (AAC; Youth in Transition Project, 1984–1987) was developed by the Youth in Transition Project at the University of Washington Division of Adolescent Medicine and is based on a model developed by the Children's Rehabilitation Centre at the University of Virginia. It can be used by youth, families and providers to measure progress towards developing the skills necessary for adult independence.

The above instruments, apart from the AAC, do not usually permit individuals, caregivers, or service providers to complete the same or similar measures independently. Most of the self-sufficiency measures do not directly capture the user's opinion regarding skill level. Furthermore the differences between users and caregivers can provide useful information to service providers and educators on the life skill areas in which individuals may need training and development as well as on skills users' self-identify as strengths and weaknesses.

Assessing life skills in young working adults involves using techniques and tools to help and assist a person to overcome self-defeating behavioural problems, to acquire and practise new abilities, to minimize weaknesses, and maximize one's potential (van der Wal and van der Wal, 2003). The assessment covers the development of personal skills such as self-confidence, creativity, listening and communication skills, handling of stress, conflict, and time management that are necessary to achieve success in one's work. Learning programs arising from such assessments can be divided into three categories:

1   Skills for being human – emphasis on the individual and the skills necessary to cope in modern society.
2   Social skills – examines the social skills and attitudes that will enable to the learners to undertake a variety of work roles amid rapid technological change and to be a responsible member of society.
3   Thinking skills – emphasis on effectiveness, due to need for flexible and creative thinking skills to cope with life in general.

Specific instructional strategies that can be used in learning programs are described in the next section.

INSTRUCTIONAL STRATEGIES

Goldstein (1988) described how the learning process is a central concern of psychology. In the 1950s, psychotherapists and researchers began to see psychotherapeutic treatment more in terms of learning. The growth of behaviour modification grew from a joint learning-clinical focus, shifting its emphasis from remediation, to an equal concern with prevention. This movement away from a medical, impairment-focused model, has formed the basis for a psychoeducational theoretical approach, which in turn has added a greater impetus to the skills training movement.

Bandura's Social Learning Theory has contributed significantly to the psychological skills training movement (Bandura, 1973). He based much of his work within this framework, particularly his use of modelling, behaviour rehearsal and social reinforcement. It is in this context that the role of psychologists needs to be considered. Consequently, guiding and teaching frontline staff becomes a central role of the psychologist in the provision of services for people with an intellectual disability.

Teaching people with an intellectual disability varies with the needs of the individual. The choice of instructional strategies will vary according to the needs and preferences of the learner. Riches (1996a) suggested that verbal instruction with prompts and ongoing error correction may be appropriate and effective for many learners. She also suggested that some learners do better with demonstrations that they can imitate, while others prefer a combination of visual and tactile modes. Self-instructional procedures have proved to be an advantage for some learners as they foster a greater independence. Verbal instruction can be very effective, but it is dependent upon the learner having good language ability. Riches (1996a) found that verbal instruction with correct modelling is more effective with learners with mild levels of intellectual disability, while Gold (1975), who popularized the 'Try Another Way' approach, discouraged the use of verbal instruction with learners with poorer communication skills.

It is important to adhere to good principles of instruction when teaching skills to people with intellectual disability. Riches (1996a) outlined a training procedure that included ten basic training steps, which can be modified, and adjusted to meet the needs and requirements of the learner:

1   Instruct the learner what to do;
2   Model the target behaviour with the learner observing;
3   Check that the learner knows exactly what to do;
4   Have the learner perform the skill or behaviour, possibly using a self-instructional strategy, and guide the learner where necessary;
5   Reward the learning attempts;
6   Record performance and use data for decision making;
7   Ensure plenty of practice with supervision occurs and in the desired environment;
8   Correct any errors immediately as they occur;
9   Teach discrimination training where necessary; and
10 Fade prompts and rewards as quickly as possible so the learner becomes independent in using the new skill.

The level and type of assistance required will vary depending on the difficulty of the task and the individual learner. It is important to identify the natural cues for each step of the skill or behaviour that will assist in determining if the individual responds without additional instruction. If the learner does not respond to the natural cue, you will need to pair the natural cue with an instructional strategy. Following training, your goal will be to fade the instructional strategy and reinforce the individual for responding to the natural cue. Instructional and support strategies must not compromise the rights and dignity of the worker. Carry out instruction as inconspicuously as possible in community sites or places with which the learner may be familiar and do not draw unnecessary attention to the learner or yourself.

There is an array of instructional strategies or tools available to choose from to meet the individual needs and learning style of the person. Various training strategies and techniques that can be used to teach skills and behaviours include: modelling; role-play; behaviour and verbal rehearsal; videotape; replay and feedback; simulation games; group games such as choices and trust games; behavioural and self-management techniques; real-life experience such as a restaurant visit; visits to community facilities; discussion; debate; contracting; backward chaining and matching to sample (Hauritz, Riches, Parmenter and Ward, 1980).

Most teaching situations include a dynamic use of a number of teaching techniques. It is important to understand the different phases or stages of the learning process when different strategies may need to be used. The following five stages: (a) Acquisition of skills; (b) Practice of skills (fluency); (c) Mastery of skills; (d) Maintenance; and (e) Generalization, can be equated to the scenario of learning to drive a car (see Figure 19. 2). At the acquisition level or phase the learner driver makes many errors and the instructor sensitively corrects and gives constant reinforcement for skills performed correctly. Next, after much practice the learner driver becomes more confident and fluent in his or her driving behaviour, makes fewer errors with the result of smoother and less hesitant driving. The instructor continues reinforcement and correction of errors. Further practice leads to the mastery level and the learner driver is ready to take the driving test. Upon achieving the provisional licence the driver maintains his or her skill by further driving practice, with feelings of competence acting as a self-reinforcer (not incurring demerit points can also act as a negative reinforcer). The final stage of generalization is reached when the driver can generalize the driving skills to other types of vehicles and to other conditions they may not have experienced in the learning phase. Maintenance and generalization do not automatically occur because a skill has been learned. It has to be facilitated systematically.

While the model portrays the role of consequences, it is important that antecedents that relate to specific teaching techniques are of equal importance. The following suggestions for each of the phases are relevant.

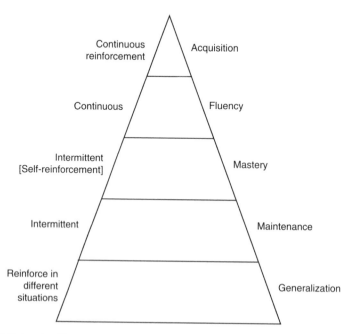

Figure 19.2 Levels of learning.

The acquisition phase

This is the stage where the learner is becoming familiar with the new task/ behaviour. The criterion of performance or standard is set. Individuals vary in the time required to master the skill. The trainer has the responsibility of structuring the skill in such a way as to assist learning. Select specific techniques and strategies most likely to be successful with the learner to aid learning and ensure the learner notices the right cues and does not get distracted. Accuracy is the prime consideration and the trainer should always try to prevent mistakes.

It is important to identify where a learner is and how best to assist him or her. Discuss the student's own experiences learning to do something new, such as learning to swim, driving a car, learning to use a computer or a new software program, playing the piano, etc. And these stages will make sense. In the acquisition stage, for example, having to think through each step, feeling like fingers or feet that don't coordinate may well be common.

Then there comes a time when you realize your fingers or feet are used to doing the right action at the right time without consciously having to direct them. A good swimmer does not have to remind themselves to keep kicking when they take a breath. An experienced driver will not need to think when or how far to push the accelerator or brake, or when to change gear, as well as how to steer. The competent musician will not have to worry about where to put their fingers when playing the piano.

Performance criterion

At the acquisition stage of learning, a criterion of performance is set. This criterion is the standard of how good the learning has to be to prove that the skill has been learnt. This is often set at 80 percent or above. Very high criteria may be set for some tasks, for example when skills have a safety element such as using a machine that would be physically unsafe with anything less than 100 percent accuracy. The trainer should also determine how often the criterion has to be met before being confident that the skills have been mastered to the level desired and the performance at the set standard was not due to chance. Frequently the criterion set is three out of three consecutive trials correct. When this is reached, the trainer is confident the learner has performed the steps correctly and consistently enough and it is not an accident. In some cases the criteria set may be 100 percent mastery on five consecutive trials correct (no errors). Once the criteria are set, the trainer then has the responsibility of structuring the skill in such a way as to assist learning.

Specific techniques and strategies most likely to be successful with the learner to aid learning are selected. When learning new knowledge or acquiring a new skill, the instructor must be constantly watching and helping, to ensure the learner does not make mistakes or become discouraged. Ensure that the learner notices the right cues and does not get distracted through all the steps of the task. Everything the learner does at this stage is part of what they learn. If they learn the wrong thing (an error) it is harder to learn the right thing, as they have to unlearn the error first.

Data collection

Assessment data are consistently collected during the stages of learning to assist the trainer in decision making. This should cover such things as:

- Speed or progress of learning, e.g. too slow or OK
- Projected time of reaching criterion given current program
- When program phase changes are required, such as a change in strategy, more or less assistance required, finer breakdowns of the skill required, changes to time target
- Determination of when the criterion set has been attained
- Task analysis data sheets are best used during acquisition – to graph the learning curve and to monitor what learning is taking place. It is important to choose the most relevant type of data collection for the appropriate stage of learning.

Fluency phase

At this stage, the skill has been acquired and quality control is being maintained. It will be noticed now that pressure for speed is a reasonable expectation. Occasional errors may be made requiring some monitoring, but note that assistance should be faded so the learner becomes more independent. It is ideal now to use checklists more often than task analyses for monitoring and evaluation purposes. Once the task is basically learnt, i.e. the criterion of performance is met, the learner can perform each of the steps correctly and in sequence. However, performance may still be slow and hesitant at times, although improving. In this stage, the instructor needs to be on guard against mistakes, but offer less and less help, so the learner is able to do the task on his or her own. Mistakes or errors can still occur at this stage, particularly after a long break (e.g. a weekend) but generally errors are not so serious. In fact, they can be useful, as the learner can see how the consequences differ from the expected results. The type of data collected often changes – from checking whether steps are performed correctly and how much assistance is required, to other measures focusing on speed. Consequently data collection forms often involve checklists of tasks completed, or graphs showing numbers produced, or time taken per unit.

Mastery

At this phase the individual performs the skills or behaviours required to a set standard of excellence, or mastery, and is not merely familiar with the skills or behaviours concerned. Once mastered, the learner is 'automatic' and may make personalized short cuts, but still meets quality control. Generalization to other skills or other environments may occur. Assessment data focus on production goals. Refresher training may be necessary if the skill/behaviour is left too long unused. Mastery learning assumes each individual can learn the skills or behaviours required to a set standard of excellence. That is, each person can be taught to master, not merely be familiar with the skills or behaviours concerned. The criterion set during the acquisition stage of learning has been met, and the person is now proficient at the task (accuracy) – not only are the steps mastered but speed is also at an acceptable level. The program is successfully completed when the set criterion is attained to the trainer's satisfaction. Once this criterion has been met, the trainer will assume that the learner has mastered the skills or behaviours and any subsequent errors are simply are due to carelessness or loss of concentration, etc. It is at this stage that the learner will be moved on to meet other goals. Appropriate data such as number completed, speed and accuracy data are then collected, often using charts and graphs.

Maintenance and generalization

These phases are often overlooked, especially for those people with higher support needs. As indicated above, intermittent practice is required to maintain skills and specific strategies need to be employed for generalization to occur. Training in the environment where the skill needs to be used assists the generalization processes. General case programming has been found to be an effective strategy for people with high support needs (Horner, Dunlap and Koegel, 1988).

Where should life-skills instruction occur?

Bastian and Kinney (2004) suggested that life-skill instruction covers a broad category of activities, of which the majority should be performed in natural community environments. Because of the necessity to generalize information, which is especially common among those with cognitive disabilities, it is preferable to deliver this instruction in real environments. This is why 'on-site' instruction is deemed superior to role-plays or simulations in a classroom environment. Correspondingly, work skills should be taught in the workplace, life skills (e.g. housekeeping, personal care, cooking) in the home, and social skills in the community.

While most of us learn these life skills over a considerable period of time, from childhood through into adult life, they are rarely taught in a methodical fashion. More accurately, life-skill instruction is imitative. We learn these skills over time in the context of their natural environments, as we mature and become members of the community. By definition these environments are many and varied and might include the workplace; independent or semi-independent living arrangements; and the endless number of community sites that we invariably access on a daily basis. These range from the department store to eating places, the public restroom and to transportation systems.

CONCLUSION

The recognition that adaptive behaviour is an integral defining characteristic of intellectual disability, in addition to measured intelligence (Heber, 1959), was a watershed in the development of policies that supported the notion that people with an intellectual disability could learn life skills given an appropriate learning environment. Contemporary philosophies, in many cases driven by a human rights perspective, have supported the view that people with an intellectual disability are citizens who have a right to participate as fully as possible in the life of their community. Limitations in their basic life skills, together with environmental barriers, will often limit their quality of life. The strategies outlined in this chapter provide a framework for professional support personnel to enhance the skills and behaviours of this population, in cooperation with families and other supports in the community.

FURTHER READING FOR CLIENTS

Hollins, S., Downer, J., Farquarson, L. and Raji, O. (2002). *Speaking up for Myself*. London: Gaskell Press and St George's Hospital Medical School.

Hollins, S., Flynn, M. and Russell, P. (2001). *George Gets Smart*. Books Beyond Words. London: Gaskell Press and St George's Hospital Medical School.

Hollins, S. and Sinason, V. (2001). *Susan's Growing Up*. Books Beyond Words. London: Gaskell Press and St George's Hospital Medical School.

Hollins, S., Avis, A. and Cheverton, S. (1998). *Going into Hospital*. Books Beyond Words. London: Gaskell Press and St George's Hospital Medical School.

Hollins, S. and Barnett, S. (1997). *Michelle Finds a Voice*. Books Beyond Words. London: Gaskell Press and St George's Hospital Medical School.

Hollins, S., Bernal, J. and Gregory, M. (1998). *Going to Outpatients*. Books Beyond Words. London: Gaskell Press and St George's Hospital Medical School.

Hollins, S., Bernal, J. and Gregory, M. (1996). *Going to the Doctor*. Books Beyond Words. London: Gaskell Press and St George's Hospital Medical School.

Hollins, S., Clare, I. and Murphy, G. (1996). *You're under Arrest*. Books Without Words. London: Gaskell Press and St George's Hospital Medical School.

FURTHER READING FOR CLINICIANS

Agran, M. and Wehmeyer, M. (1999). *Teaching Problem Solving to Students with Mental Retardation*. Washington, DC: American Association on Mental Retardation.

Bender, M. A. (1996). *A Functional Curriculum for Teaching Students with Disabilities: Volume I: Self-Care, Motor Skills, Household Management, and Living Skills* (vol. 1 of 3). Austin, TX: Pro-Ed.

Bradley, A. (2004). *Positive Approaches to Person Centred Planning*. Glasgow: BILD Publications.

Bradley, A. (2004). *Positive Approaches to Supporting People with Autistic Spectrum Disorders*. Glasgow: BILD Publications.

Brolin, D. E. (1989). *Life Centred Career Education: A Competency Based Approach* (3rd edn). Reston, VA: Council for Exceptional Children.

Brolin, D. E. (1997). *Life Centred Career Education: A Competency Based Approach* (5th edn). Reston, VA: Council for Exceptional Children.

Brolin, D. E., Kokaska, C. J., Davis, A. C. and Lopez, J. (1995). *Career Education: A Functional Life Skills Approach* (3rd edn). New York: Simon and Schuster.

Buros Institute of Mental Measurements (2005). *Behaviour Assessment*, 2005, from http://www.unl.edu/buros/bimm/html/index19.html

Casey Family Programs (2001). *Ready, Set, Fly! A Parent's Guide to Teaching Life Skills*. Tucson, AZ: Casey Family Programs.

Cattermole, M. and Blunden, R. (2002). *My Life: A Person-Centred Approach to Checking Outcomes for People with Learning Difficulties*. Glasgow: BILD Publications.

Cattermole, M., McGowan, C., Brunning, K. and Blunden, R. (2002). *Using My Life: A Guide to Conducting a Quality Network Review*. Glasgow: BILD Publications.

Council for Exceptional Children (CEC). (2004). *Life Centred Career Education (LCCE)*, 2005, from http:www.cec.sped.org/pd/lcce-what.html

Council for Exceptional Children (CEC). (2004, Jan 7 2005). *Journals, Books and Media*, 2005, from http://www.cec.sped.org/bk/

Dever, R. B. (1989). A taxonomy of community living skills. *Exceptional Children*, 55(ej387194), 395–404.

Edgar, G. (1990). Quality of life: Is it time to change our view of the world? *Beyond Behaviour*, 1(1), 9–13.

Elder, J. (1986). Transitional services needed to help disabled enter work forces. *Education of the Handicapped*, 12(19), 5.

Heal, L., Copher, J., Stefano, L. and Rusch, F. (1989). A comparison of successful and unsuccessful placements of secondary students with mental handicaps into competitive employment. *Career Development for Exceptional Individuals*, 12(2), 167–77.

Heslop, P., Mallett, R., Simons, K. and Ward, L. (2002). *Bridging the Divide at Transition: What Happens for Young People with Learning Difficulties and their Families*. Glasgow: BILD Publications.

Hill, B. (2004). *Adaptive and Maladaptive Behaviour Scales*, 2005, from http://www.cpinternet.com/~bhill/icap/compare.htm

Sands, D. and Doll, B. (2000). *Teaching Goal Setting and Decision Making to Students with Developmental Disabilities*. Washington, DC: American Association on Mental Retardation.

Wircenski, J. L. (1982). *Employability Skills for the Special Needs Learner*. Rockville, MD: Aspen.

REFERENCES

Alberta Learning (ed.) (2003). *Teaching Students with Autism Spectrum Disorders* (vol. 9). Alberta: Alberta Learning and Teaching Resources Branch.

Anderson, P. R. (1999). Open employment services for people with disabilities in Australia, 1995–1997. *Journal of Vocational Rehabilitation*, 13(2), 79–94.

Arick, J. R., Nave, G., Hoffman, T. and Krug, D. A. (2004). *FACTER: Functional Assessment and Curriculum for Teaching Everyday Routines*. Austin, TX: ProEd.

Australian Bureau of Statistics (2001). *Measuring Wellbeing: Frameworks for Australian Social Statistics. Chapter 8: Housing Social Issues*. Retrieved 15 October 2002.

Bandura, A. (1973). *Aggression: A Social Learning Analysis*. Englewood Cliffs, NJ: Prentice-Hall.

Bastian, D. and Kinney, T. (2004). *Life Skill Instruction in the Age of Inclusion*. Retrieved 20 January 2005, from http://www.attainmentcompany.com/news_edit5.html

Beach Centre on Families and Disability (2000). *Quality Indicators of Exemplary Transition Programs* (Fact Sheet). Kansas: The University of Kansas, Lawrence, Kansas.

Bolst, A. (1990). *Grief, loss and disability: Parent and student perceptions and experiences*. Paper presented at the Australian Association of Special Education Conference, Canberra.

Brandell, J. and Perlman, F. (1997). Psychoanalytic theory. In J. Brandell (ed.), *Theory and Practice in Clinical Social Work* (pp. 38–80). New York: Free Press/Simon and Schuster.

Brigance, A. (1998). *Life Skills Inventory*. Billerica, MA: Curriculum Associates, Inc.

Brinckerhoff, L. C. (1994). Developing effective self-advocacy skills in college-bound students with learning disabilities. *Intervention in School and Clinic*, 29(4), 229–37.

Brolin, D. E. (1989). *Life Centred Career Education: A Competency Based Approach* (3rd edn). Reston, VA: Council for Exceptional Children.

Brolin, D. E. (1993). Life centred career education. In Brolin, *Life Centred Education: A Competency Based Approach*. Reston, VA: The Council for Exceptional Children.

Bruininks, R. H., Hill, B. K., Weatherman, R. E. and Woodcock, R. W. (1986). *Inventory for Client and Agency Planning Response Booklet*. Chicago, IL: Riverside Publishing Company.

Bruininks, R. H. and Moreau, L. (2004). *Checklist of Adaptive Living Skills* (CALS). Chicago, IL: Riverside Publishing Company.

Bruininks, R. H., Moreau, L., Gilman, C. J. and Anderson, J. L. (2004). *Adaptive Living Skills Curriculum* (ALSC). Chicago, Il: Riverside Publishing Company.

Bruininks, R. H., Woodcock, R. W., Weatherman, R. E. and Hill, B. K. (2004). *Scales of Independent Behaviour-Revised* (SIB-R). Chicago, IL: Riverside Publishing Company.

Buckley, S. and Sacks, B. (2001). *From Adolescence to Adulthood*. Retrieved 10 July 2005, from http://down-syndrome.info/library/pdst-news

Casey Family Programs (2000–2005). *Ansell-Casey Life Skills Assessments (ACLSA)*, 2005, from http://www.casey.org/Home

Chadsey-Rusch, J. (1992). Toward defining and measuring social skills in employment settings. *American Journal on Mental Retardation*, 96(4), 405–18.

Children's Administration Division of Children and Family Services (2000). *Life Skills Inventory: The Independent Living Skills Assessment Tool*. Washington, DC: Department of Social and Health Services.

Clarke, A. M., Clarke, A. D. B. and Berg, J. M. (eds) (1985). *Mental Deficiency: The Changing Outlook* (4th edn). London: Methuen and Co. Ltd.

Copley, M. F. and Bodensteiner, J. B. (1987). Chronic sorrow in families of disabled children. *Journal of Child Neurology*, 2 (January), 67–70.

DeMarie, D. and LeRoux, P. (2002). *The Life Cycle and Disability: Experiences of Discontinuity in Child and Family Development*. Retrieved 28 July 2003, from http://www.discoveryifi.org

Doyle, B. T. (2003). *Teaching Ten Important Lifetime Goals to Children and Adults with Autism Spectrum Disorders*. Retrieved 30 May 2005, from http://www.newhorizons.org

Eath, M. D. and Walls, M. (2005). *Quality of Life of Young People with Intellectual Disability in Ireland*. Retrieved 10 July 2005, from http://www.nda.ie/CntMgmt.nsf/0/9642E314AEBD463880256FC100522E50?OpenDocument

Edgar, G. (1988). Employment as an outcome for mildly handicapped students: Current status and future direction. *Focus on Exceptional Children*, 21(1), 1–8.

Emerson, E. and McVilley, K. (2004). Friendship activities of adults with intellectual disabilities in supported accommodation in northern England. *Journal of Applied Research in Intellectual Disabilities*, 17, 191–7.

Erikson, E. (1968). *Identity, Youth and Crisis*. New York: Norton.

Featherstone, H. (1980). *A Difference in the Family: Living with a Disabled Child*. Middlesex: Penguin.

Freud, A. (1969). Adolescence as a developmental disturbance. In *The Writings of Anna Freud* (vol. VII, 1966–1970). New York: International Universities Press.

Geisthardt, C. and Munsch, J. (1996). Coping with school stress: A comparison of adolescents with and without learning disabilities. *Journal of Learning Disabilities*, 29, 287–96.

Gold, M. W. (1975). Vocational Training. In J. Wortis (ed.), *Mental Retardation and Developmental Disabilities: An Annual Review* (vol. 7). New York: Brunner Mazel.

Goldstein, A. P. (1988). *The Prepare Curriculum: Teaching Prosocial Competencies*. Champaign, IL: Research Press.

Goodship, J. M. (1990). Life skills mastery for students with special needs. *Eric Digest*, E469(ED321502), 11.

Grigal, M., Test, D., Beattie, J. and Wood, W. (1997). An evaluation of transition components of individualized education programs. *Exceptional Children*, 63(3), 357–72.

Hanley-Maxwell, C., Whitney-Thomas, J. and Pogoloff, S. (1995). The second shock: A qualitative study of parents' perspectives and needs during their child's transition from school to adult life. *Journal of the Association for Persons with Severe Handicaps*, 20, 3–15.

Hauritz, M., Riches, V., Parmenter, T. R. and Ward, J. (1980). Program development for the acquisition of work and social skills. *Australian Journal of Developmental Disabilities*, 6(1), 11–16.

Hayes, M. L. (1994/2005). *Social Skills: The Bottom Line for Adult LD Success.* Retrieved 22 June 2005, from http://www.ldonline.org/ld_indepth/social_skills/social-1.html

Hayes, S. (2004). Interaction with the criminal justice system. In E. Emerson, C. Hatton, T. Thompson and T. R. Parmenter (eds), *International Handbook of Applied Research in Intellectual Disabilities* (pp. 489–515). London: Wiley.

Heber, R. (1959). A manual on terminology and classification in mental retardation. *American Journal of Mental Deficiency*, 64 (Monograph Suppl).

Horner, R. H., Dunlap, G. and Koegel, R. L. (eds) (1988). *Generalization and Maintenance: Life Style Changes in Applied Settings.* Baltimore: Paul H Brookes.

Horner, R. H., McDonnell, J. S., and Bellamy, G. T. (1986). Teaching generalized skills: general care instruction in simulation and community settings. In R. H. Horner, L. H. Meyer and H. D. B. Fredericks (eds), *Education of Learners with Severe Handicaps: Exemplary Service Strategies* (pp. 289–314). Baltimore, MD: Paul H. Brookes.

Izzo, M. V., Hertzfeld, J. E. and Aaron, J. H. (2001). Raising the bar: Student self determination + good teaching = success. *Journal of Vocational Special Needs Educators*, 1–28.

Johnson, D. R., Stodden, R. A., Emanuel, E. J., Luecking, R. and Mack, M. (2002). Current challenges facing secondary education and transition services: What research tells us. *Exceptional Children*, 68(4), 519–31.

Kazdin, A. E. and Wiesz, J. R. (2003). Context and background of evidence-based psychotherapies for children and adults. In A. E. Kazdin and J. R. Wiesz (eds), *Evidence-Based Psychotherapy for Children and Adults* (pp. 3–20). New York: Guilford Press.

Kearney, P. and Griffin, T. (2001). Between joy and sorrow: Being a parent of a child with developmental disability. *Journal of Advanced Nursing*, 34(5), 582–92.

Konopka, G. (1973). Requirements for the healthy development of adolescent youth. *Adolescence*, 8(31), 2–25.

Lambert, N. M., Nihira, K., and Leland, H. (1993). *AAMR Adaptive Behaviour Scale-School*: 2nd edn (ABS-S:2). Lutz, Fl: PAR Psychological Assessment Resources Inc.

Lanyado, M. (1999). 'It's just an ordinary pain': Thoughts on joy and heartache in puberty and early adolescence. In D. Hindle and M. Smith (eds), *Personality Development: A Psychoanalytic Perspective*. London and New York: Routledge.

Lignugaris-Kraft, B., Salzberg, C. L., Rule, S. and Stowitschek, J. J. (1988). Social-vocational skills of workers with and without mental retardation in two community employment sites. *Mental Retardation*, 26(5), 297–305.

LoConto, D. and Dodder, R. (1997). The right to be human: Deinstitutionalization and the wishes of people with developmental disabilities. *Education and Training in Mental Retardation and Developmental Disabilities*, 32(2), 77–84.

McVilly, K. R., Stancliffe, R. J., Parmenter, T. R. and Burton-Smith, R. M. (2006). 'I get by with a little help from my friends': Adults with intellectual disability discuss loneliness. *Journal of Applied Research in Intellectual Disabilities*, 19(2), 191–203.

National Centre for the Study of Postsecondary Educational Supports (2000).

National Survey of Educational Support Provision to Students with Disabilities in Postsecondary Education Settings (Technical report). Honolulu, HI: National Centre for the Study of Postsecondary Educational Supports.

National Institute of Child Health and Human Development (NICHD) (2001). *Autism Facts* (Fact Sheet No. NIH Pub. 01–4962). Rockville, MD: US Department of Health and Human Services.

Nollan, K. A., Wolf, M., Ansell, D., Burns, J., Barr, L., Copeland, W. *et al.* (2000). Ready or not: Assessing youths' preparedness for independent living. *Child Welfare*, 79(2), 159–76.

Olshansky, S. (1962). Chronic sorrow: A response to having a mentally defective child. *Social Casework*, 43, 190–3.

O'Neill, R. E. and Heathfield, L. T. (2004). Educational supports. In E. Emerson, C. Hatton, T. Thompson and T. R. Parmenter (eds), *International Handbook of Applied Research in Intellectual Disabilities* (pp. 445–58). London: Wiley.

Oregon Department of Education (2003). *Strategies for Transition Planning for Students with Autism Spectrum Disorder* (ASD). Retrieved 20 September 2004, from www.ode.state.or.us/gradelevel/hs/transition/asd.pdf

Ostrov, E. and Offer, D. (1978). Loneliness and the adolescent. In S. C. Feinstein and P. L. Giovacchini (eds), *Developmental and Clinical Studies, Adolescent Psychiatry* (vol. 6). Chicago: University of Chicago.

Parmenter, T. R. (1984). A comparison of the effects of teaching direct and indirect strategies on the acquisition of reading skills by developmentally disabled adolescents. In S. M. Berg (ed.), *Perspectives and Progress in Mental Retardation* (vol. 1, pp. 293–301). Baltimore: University Park Press.

Parmenter, T. R. (1992). Quality of life of people with developmental disabilities. In N. W. Bray (ed.), *International Review of Research in Mental Retardation* (vol. 18, pp. 247–87). New York: Academic Press.

Parmenter, T. R. (1999). Effecting a system change in the delivery of employment services for people with disabilities: A view from Australia. *Journal of Vocational Rehabilitation*, 13, 117–29.

Parmenter, T. R. (2001). Intellectual Disabilities – quo vadis? In G. L. Albrecht, K. D. Seelman and M. Bury (eds), *Handbook of Disability Studies* (pp. 267–96). New York: Sage.

Perry, A. and Condillac, R. (2003). *Evidence-Based Practices for Children and Adolescents with Autism Spectrum Disorders: Review of the Literature and Practice Guide* (Review). Ontario: Children's Mental Health Ontario.

Peterson, K. (2004). Supporting the dynamic development of youth with disabilities during transition: A guide for families. *Information Brief* 3(2), www.ncset.org

Pittman, K. (1991). *Promoting Youth Development: Strengthening the Role of Youth Serving and Community Organizations*. Washington, DC: Academy for Educational Development, Centre for Youth Development and Policy Research.

Pratt, C. (2002). *Transition: Preparing for a Lifetime*. Retrieved 15 August 2004, from http://www.bbbautism.com

Price-Kelly, S. and Hill, J. (1995). *Homeless and fifteen: Young People with Intellectual Disability in Crisis*: Sydney: NSW Council for Intellectual Disability and the Opposition Youth Crisis Centre.

Reproductive Health Outlook (1997–2005). *Glossary*. Retrieved 31 May 2005, from http://www.rho.org/html/glossary.html

Riches, V. C. (1993). *Standards of Work Performance*. Sydney: Maclennan and Petty.

Riches, V. C. (1996a). *Everyday Social Interaction: A Program for People with Disabilities* (2nd edn). Sydney: Maclennan and Petty.

Riches, V. C. (1996b). A review of transition from school to community for students with disabilities in NSW, Australia. *Journal of Intellectual and Developmental Disability*, 21(1), 71–88.

Riches, V. C. and Green, V. A. (2003). Social Integration in the workplace for people with disabilities: An Australian perspective. *Journal of Vocational Rehabilitation*, 19(3), 127–42.

Riches, V. C., Parmenter, T. R. and Robertson, G. (1996). *Youth with Disabilities in Transition from School to Community. Report of a Follow-along of Students with Disabilities Involved in the New South Wales Transition Initiative 1989–1994*. Sydney: Unit for Community Integration Studies, Macquarie University.

Routledge, M. (2001). *Transition and Person Centred Planning*. London: Department of Health, www.valuingpeople.gov.uk/documents/pcpTransition1.doc

Rusch, F. and Phelps, L. A. (1987). Secondary special education and transition from school to work: A national priority. *Exceptional Children*, 53, 487–92.

Rusch, F., Schutz, R. P. and Agran, M. (1982). Validating entry-level survival skills for service occupations: Implications for curriculum development. *Journal of the Association for Persons with Severe Handicaps*, 7, 32–41.

Rutter, M. (1979). *Changing Youth in a Changing World*. London: Nuffield.

Ryndak, D. L. and Alper, S. (1996). *Curriculum Content for Students with Moderate and Severe Disabilities in Inclusive Settings*. Boston, MA: Allyn and Bacon.

Salzberg, C. L., Agran, M. and Lignugaris-Kraft, B. (1986). Behaviours that contribute to entry-level employment: A profile of five jobs. *Applied Research in Mental Retardation*, 7, 299–314.

Schalock, R. L. (2004). Adaptive behaviour: Its conceptualization and measurement. In E. Emerson, C. Hatton, T. Thompson and T. R. Parmenter (eds), *The International Handbook of Applied Research in Intellectual Disabilities* (pp. 369–84). London: Wiley.

Schalock, R. L., Brown, I., Brown, R., Cummins, R. A., Felce, D., Matikka, L. *et al.* (2002). Conceptualization, measurement, and application of quality of life for persons with intellectual disabilities: Report of an international panel of experts. *Mental Retardation*, 40(6), 457–70.

Schulzinger, R. (1998). *Key Transition Issues for Youth with Disabilities and Chronic Health Conditions* (Occasional policy brief). Gainesville, FL: Institute for Child Health Policy.

Seligman, M. and Darling, R. (1997). *Ordinary Families, Special Children: A System Approach to Childhood Disability* (2nd edn). New York: Guilford.

Snell, M. E. and Brown, F. (eds) (2000). *Instruction of Students with Severe Disabilities* (5th edn). Columbus, OH: Merrill.

Solnit, A. J. and Stark, M. H. (1961). Mourning the birth of a defective child. In A. J. Solnit (ed.), *An Anthology of the Psychoanalytic Study of the Child: Physical Illness and Handicap in Childhood* (1977 edn, pp. 181–94). Newhaven: Yale University Press.

South Australia Ministerial Advisory Committee: Students with Disabilities (2000). *Secondary Schooling for Students with Autism Spectrum Disorders* (Report). Adelaide: Task Group – Autism Spectrum Disorders.

Sparrow, S. S., Cicchetti, D. V. and Balla, D. A. (2005). *Vineland-II: Adaptive Behaviour Scales.* Circle Pines, MN: AGS Publishing.

Spitzberg, B. H. and Cupach, W. R. (1984). Interpersonal communication competence. In *Sage Series in Interpersonal Communication* (vol. 4). Beverley Hills, CA: Sage Publications.

SRI Centre for Education and Human Services (1993/2004). *The National Longitudinal Transition Study (NLTS).* Retrieved 28 November 2004, from http://www.sri.com/policy/cehs/publications/dispub/nlts/nltssum.html

SRI Centre for Education and Human Services (2003). *NLTS2 Update.* Retrieved 28 November 2004, from http://www.nlts2.org/gindex.html

SRI International (2005). *National Longitudinal Transition Study 2. After High School: A First Look at the Postschool Experiences of Youth with Disabilities* (prepared by Mary Wagner, Lynn Newman, Renée Cameto, Nicolle Garza, and Phyllis Levine for the Office of Special Education Programs US Department of Education). Menlo Park, CA: SRI International/US Office of Special Education Programs.

Steinberg, L. (2001). *Adolescence.* New York: McGraw-Hill Inc.

Stodden, R. A. and Dowrick, P. W. (1999). Postsecondary education and employment of adults with disabilities. *American Rehabilitation,* 25(3), 19–23.

Stodden, R. A., Jones, M. A. and Chang, K. (2002). *Services, supports and accommodations for individuals with disabilities: An analysis across secondary education, post secondary education and employment.* Unpublished manuscript, Centre for Disability Studies, University of Hawaii.

Sugar, M. (1968). Normal adolescent mourning. *American Journal of Psychotherapy,* 22, 258–69.

Swanson, J., Swartz, M., Estroff, S., Borum, R., Wagner, R. and Hiday, V. (1998). Psychiatric impairment, social contact, and violent behaviour: Evidence from a study of outpatient-committed persons with severe mental disorder. *Social Psychiatry and Psychiatric Epidemiology,* 33(1), 86–94.

University of South Dakota (2002). *Autism.* South Dakota: The University of South Dakota School of Medicine.

Trzcinski, E. and Brandell, J. (2000–2001). *Adolescent Outcomes, Poverty Status, and Welfare Reform: An Analysis Based on the Survey of Program Dynamics* (Research Development Grant, Final Report). Chicago: US Bureau of the Census U.S. Health and Human Service and Joint Centre for Poverty Research.

van der Wal, R. J. and van der Wal, R. (2003). Assessing life skills in young working adults – Part 1: the development of an alternative instrument. *Education and Training,* 45(3), 139–51.

Volkmar, F. R., Paul, R., Klin, A. and Cohen, D. J. (eds) (2005a). *Handbook of Autism and Pervasive Developmental Disorders* (3rd edn, vol. 1). New York: John Wiley and Sons, Inc.

Volkmar, F. R., Paul, R., Klin, A. and Cohen, D. J. (eds) (2005b). *Handbook of Autism and Pervasive Developmental Disorders* (3rd edn, vol. 2). New York: John Wiley and Sons, Inc.

Wagner, M., Blackorby, J., Cameto, R., Hebbeler, K. and Newman, L. (1993). *The Transition Experiences of Young People with Disabilities: A Summary of Findings from the National Longitudinal Transition Study of Special Education Students.* Menlo Park, CA: SRI International.

Wehmeyer, M. L., Agran, M. and Hughes, C. (1998). *Teaching Self-Determination to Students with Disabilities: Basic Skills for Successful Transition.* Baltimore: Paul H. Brookes.

Westling, D. L. and Fox, L. (2000). *Teaching Students with Severe Disabilities* (2nd edn). Columbus, OH: Merrill.

Whitney-Thomas, J. and Moloney, M. (2001). Who I am and what I want: Adolescents' self-definition and struggles. *Exceptional Children,* 67(3), 375–89.

Winkler, L., Wasow, M. and Hatfield, E. (1983). Seeking strength in families of developmentally disabled children. *Social Work,* 28, 313–15.

World Health Organization (2001). *International Classification of Functioning, Disability and Health: ICF* (Vol. short version). Geneva: WHO.

Yazbeck, M., McVilley, K. and Parmenter, T. R. (2004). Attitudes toward people with intellectual disability: An Australian perspective. *Journal of Disability Policy Studies,* 15, 97–111.

Young, R. K. (1977). Chronic sorrow: Parent's response to the birth of a child with a defect. *MCN,* 2, 38–42.

Youth in Transition Project (1984–1987). *Adolescent Autonomy Checklist* (developed by the Youth in Transition Project and based on a model developed by the Children's Rehabilitation Center at the University of Virginia). Washington, DC: University of Washington Division of Adolescent Medicine.

Chapter 20

Relationships and sexuality in adolescence and young adulthood

Denise Valenti-Hein and Coral Choinski

CASE STUDY

At a young age, Jenny was placed in protective services and parental rights terminated on her mother, a chronic alcoholic, and her father, who was sent to prison for sexual assault of children. Jenny had fetal alcohol syndrome, which affected her cognitive functioning. She was adopted by a couple who believed they could help her. Having had no issues with their own three naturally born children, they felt competent in their parenting abilities. Jenny did present unique challenges, however. She was frequently sexual and violent in play and her parents struggled to deal with these issues. Sometimes they would ignore it, sometimes they would punish it, at other times they tried to teach about better ways of acting. Like the approaches, the results were mixed. But the story does not end there . . .

INTRODUCTION

The acceptance of sexuality in individuals with developmental disabilities is still a difficult and sensitive issue. Reluctance of caregivers to teach the necessary skills that would allow an adolescent independently to manage the responsibilities of sexuality ignores the natural course of human development. In 1995 the Alan Guttmacher Institute found that by 15 years of age, 24 per cent of females and 27 per cent of males in the general population have had sexual intercourse. By the age of 16, this number has risen to 39 per cent of females and 45 per cent of males. Each year, 19 per cent of those who have had sexual intercourse will become pregnant and about one in four sexually experienced teens contract a sexually transmitted disease (AGI, 1999).

Clinicians and parents alike have questioned the similarity between the sexuality of adolescents with developmental disabilities and their intellectually average peers. Chamberlain, Rauh, Passer, McGrath, and Burket (1984) found that 34 per cent of adolescents attending their clinic with mild to severe intellectual disabilities had engaged in sexual intercourse at least once. Specifically, half of the adolescents with a mild disability, 30 per cent of those with a moderate disability, and 9 per cent with a severe disability had engaged in intercourse. Moreover, like their intellectually average peers, about one third of adolescents with a mild disability remained sexually active, and 15 per cent became pregnant. These findings suggest that the issue of relationships and sexuality in adolescents and young adults with intellectual disabilities cannot be ignored. Like Jenny and her parents, we need to find a way to approach this complex topic effectively.

DEVELOPMENT OF RELATIONSHIP AND SEXUALITY SKILLS ACROSS THE LIFESPAN

Case study continued

Unfortunately, Jenny's adoptive parents eventually divorced. Even in divorce the family was quite competent. They shared custody of the children, who went back and forth between the two homes in a rural area of the state. It soon became apparent that Jenny needed special education services that the area could only minimally accommodate. At 7, Jenny was put into a class that served both youth with cognitive disabilities and those with emotional disturbances. This not only branded her as 'different', but provided a forum where she could learn from more behaviourally disturbed peers.

Like all other competencies, relationship and sexuality skills are developed through a learning process that takes place over one's lifetime. This is perhaps even more the case for those with special needs. Clearly children are informally taught by a myriad of interactions, most notably with parents, which will create the basis of all future relationships. This includes how parents touch and express love, how consistently they meet their child's needs, and how they model extra-familial social interactions. At some point, however, formal education will be needed. However, knowing when to teach which skills can be difficult.

Development may progress at uniquely different rates for each person depending on factors such as age, severity of the disability, medical complications and experience. Nevertheless, Melberg-Schwier and Hingsburger (2000) note that all children will progress through four stages where their needs in relationships with their parents differ. They refer to these stages 'as pick me up', 'put me down', 'leave me alone' and 'let me go'. Parents and caregivers are advised to recognize and respect the child's lead into these stages, which will influence readiness for outside relationships.

Timelines have been developed to assist parents and caregivers in teaching different aspects of sexuality (Maksym, 1990) but some believe topics should only be introduced at the 'teachable moment'. For example, Mesibov (1985) states that an adolescent's interest in relationships and sexuality, motivation to learn, and need for knowledge must be evaluated before teaching can begin. But how do you know what a person desires to learn or whether they 'need the knowledge'?

Researchers have attempted to determine when someone with intellectual disabilities 'needs knowledge' by asking caregivers about the feelings and ideas of their charges. These studies invite caregivers to speculate about what individuals with intellectual disabilities want out of personal relationships with others. However, caregivers may believe, or even wish, that people with developmental disabilities do not crave closeness or intimacy and may interpret behaviours in accordance with these feelings. Elgar (1985), for example, stated that when a person with autism expresses interest in 'getting married', that statement is merely a reflection of what they see others engaging in. Hence, explicit sex education for most of them would be meaningless. It could confuse some and initiate socially unacceptable behaviour that would not easily be influenced by any subsequent set of rules for correction. Thus, in letting others speculate we may find out what caretakers want or believe, but not what individuals with intellectual disabilities want or believe. Parents may not want to put their child down, leave them alone, or let them go.

If you were to ask a teenager with an intellectual disability about his or her interests, you would find that many expect to be married and have children. They want to have intimate relationships, and list many of the same goals as intellectually average adolescents (Heshusius, 1982). If we know that this is the goal of most teens, with or without disabilities, why wait until adolescence or for the 'teachable moment' to begin the process of relationship and sexuality education? Waiting may be wrong for many reasons.

For an individual with average intelligence, adolescence is a time of adjustment and change. The adolescent is trying to individuate, making it harder for parents to communicate with their children. Concurrently, youth may be less interested in what their parents have to offer. This might also be true for adolescents with intellectual disabilities, and encourages the commencement of relationship and sexuality education before puberty begins (Siegel, 1974 as cited in Rowitz, 1988).

An adolescent's experiences are exacerbated by having an intellectual disability. Not informing a young person of normal events that will happen to them physically, emotionally, and socially can only further the difficulties they may encounter. Some adolescents with intellectual disabilities have been confused by puberty in ways that could have been avoided had they received some forewarning. Consequently, children might apologize for 'wetting the bed' when ejaculating during sleep, or express confusion and fright with erections, fearful that their penis is broken. Ruble and Dalrymple (1993) found that 50 per cent of parents reported that their daughters who had autism worried about menstruation or sensations in their sexual organs. Clearly, these normal developments are causing unwarranted stress that could be prevented by early education.

In addition to normal developmental changes, children with intellectual disabilities may have deterioration of functionality during adolescence. Gillberg (1984) reports that over one third of teens affected by autism worsen during adolescence. This is not to say that *only* adolescents with autism are affected by deterioration. Gillberg also notes that adolescents with any developmental disability which affects communication, socialization, and imagination are similarly at risk. Females, on average, may be more severely affected than boys by this deterioration.

Adolescence is a time when an individual's role in society is defined and feedback from others helps to validate that role. An adolescent with intellectual disabilities is also struggling with the roles they will assume. Zetlin and Turner (1985) note that there are conflicting role expectations for these young people due to the discrepancy between their physical maturation and cognitive development. Parents may encourage dependency and obedience, rather than individuation, causing stress by adopting inconsistent or conflicting parenting styles. Indeed, Zetlin and Turner found that teens with intellectual disabilities receiving the mixed drives of individuation and parental dependency were more likely to have acted out and adopted anti-social forms of behaviour. Starting formal relationship training early communicates the message that parents are seeking as much independence as possible for their child.

Furthermore, starting sexuality and relationship education early builds up appropriate skills that can help deflect later inappropriate learning. This is especially important when people with developmental disabilities are placed in behaviourally challenging circumstances. Like Jenny, children with intellectual disabilities will have more exposure to, and opportunities to learn, inappropriate behaviour. Teaching appropriate skills early on may be a form of stress inoculation. That is, exposing a person to appropriate behaviour may make them more resistant to developing problems later on. This is not to say that it is ever too late to start the process of relationship and sexuality education, or that it will ever be completely finished. Throughout life there will be many 'teachable moments', or times to review what has been learned in a new context.

SPECIFIC CONSIDERATIONS RELATED TO INTELLECTUAL DISABILITY

Case study continued

Jenny's psychological testing indicated strong verbal skills, but her social judgment was quite poor. Her intellectually average but more emotionally disturbed and delinquent classmates used sexual language that she quickly picked up. Not being educated as to the appropriate context for these statements combined with her lack of physical boundaries in dangerous ways. She had difficulty understanding how her behaviours had contributed to the social problems she was experiencing – especially in physical education which was mainstreamed. Moreover, she could not clearly discern the emotions of others – interpreting the attention male peers paid to her due to these actions as romantic interest.

Intellectually disabling conditions themselves may complicate the task of learning socio-sexual skills. Since sexuality is not just about sex, but rather about relationships, individuals who are affected by impairment in socialization, communication, and imaginative skills may find this learning to be particularly challenging.

Autism is defined, in part, by a disruption in socialization. This has led some to believe that individuals with autism are unable, or uninterested, in bonding with others. When a person with autism does demonstrate social behaviours, these actions may be minimized. For example, Lettick (1985: 218) states that social activities initiated by autistic individuals are only imitations of their peers, noting 'the appearance of love is not love'. Still, when asked, most individuals with autistic disorder report an interest in sexual activity, getting married, and having children (Haracopos and Pedersen, 1992; Konstantareas and Lunsky, 1997).

People with conditions associated with intellectual disability may also show deficits in socialization. Historically, these individuals were viewed as 'childlike' and thus uninterested in relationships or sex (Smith, D. C., Valenti-Hein, D. C. and Heller, T., 1985). However, interest in sexual issues has been documented for people with intellectual disabilities both by expressed interest, and by reported activity, in the United States of America, Japan, and Denmark (Haracopos and Pedersen, 1992; Ousley and Mesibov, 1991; Yamashita, 1990 cited in Haracopos and Pedersen, 1992). The presence of social deficits among those with intellectual disabilities emphasizes the need explicitly to teach the proper context for behaviours. Boundaries such as social distance are not maintained innately. Indeed, young children also violate such boundaries as interpersonal distance until they learn the rules of interaction.

Language barriers present problems in relationships well. As many as 50 per cent of people with autism will not develop functional speech (Gillberg, 1991). Haracopos and Pedersen (1992) found language to be a critical factor in forming relationships. Individuals with little or no spoken language were more likely to engage in self-destructive behaviours as a result of frustration at being unable to communicate. Additionally, when verbally limited individuals showed a genuine interest in someone, they tended to be aggressive towards the person of interest, leading to rejection. Thus, a continuous cycle occurs where attempts at contact are met with rejection, and frustration results in self-injury. People with moderate to severe forms of intellectual disability likewise show impaired communication.

An individual with communication deficits may also interpret the meaning of terms literally, or by the way they sound, creating misunderstanding. Konstantareas and Lunsky (1997) give some examples of these difficulties for individuals with mild autism. Terms such as 'homosexual' were interpreted as 'having sex at home'; while diaphragm was thought to mean the same as 'frying pan'. Individuals with intellectual disability may similarly have literal interpretations of sexuality related concepts (Garwick *et al.*, 1993). Similarly, individuals may be unable to adequately verbalize their wants or needs. Like Jenny, they may have difficulty understanding the full meaning of the words they use, even if they are able to point correctly to a picture representation of it (Konstantareas and Lunsky, 1997). Thus, communication skills must be carefully scrutinized for developmental language level and unique interpretations for assessing as well as teaching sexual issues.

Communication of non-verbal material may likewise be impaired. Chertkoff-Walz and Benson (1996) found that neither individuals with intellectual disability nor those with autism were able to identify pictures that reflected expressed emotion. This held true, despite the ability of these individuals to interpret the meaning of words of similar difficulty that were not emotionally laden. Expressed non-verbal communication also presents challenges. In describing youth with intellectual disability, Wood (1985) argues that some do not know when they are acting provocatively. Often, the individual feels comfortable touching a person they are talking to, which others could misconstrue. Wood further states that they may also be more passive when others touch them, which may lead to an unwanted sexual encounter. Thus, when the communication of emotions is at stake, people with intellectual disabilities have specific deficits and require instruction on how to interpret and express emotions.

Individuals with cognitive disabilities are often unable to use their imagination in conventional ways. This may lead to difficulties in expressing empathy for others as they are unable to project themselves into similar situations. This, coupled with trouble interpreting social cues such as facial expression during conversations, might also lead to rejection (Wood, 1985).

Unusual behaviours in expressing sexuality could be attributed to the lack of ability to fantasize – a form of imagination. Haracopos and Pedersen (1992) assert that the use of unusual objects during sexual expression are compensations for this lack of imagination. Thus a specific visual stimulus may be used in order to arouse and maintain sexual desire. Haracopos and Pedersen (1992) give an example of a man who was unable to masturbate without the ritual of putting on a pair of galoshes, and proceeded to search for another pair in the middle of the night when his parents took them away.

Limitations in imagination can result in an inability to acquire information when it is presented in a purely linguistic form. Consequently, an adolescent with autism, for example, may find it easier to learn material when familiar characters, such as those seen on TV or in movies, are included in instructional approaches – a concept known as 'power cards' (Gagnon, 2001). Thus, to teach social interactions such as demonstrating excitement, the trainer may say, 'Bob Barker on *The Price is Right* has just called a contestant's name – the person called is excited because he gets to play. He wants people to know so he jumps up and down and smiles and laughs.' Using this special area of interest as a model for excitement, the trainer can then help the person show excitement in a classroom, and in exciting places outside the classroom to generalize the skill. Being aware of how limitations might affect learning will help in the adaptation of educational material.

SPECIAL ISSUES IN RELATIONSHIPS, SEXUALITY, AND DISABILITY

Case study continued

Jenny was 15 years old when she entered the juvenile justice system for acting out. While she always had more challenging behaviours, many were dealt with appropriately in the educational system. After puberty this changed. She started bringing alcohol to school to appear 'normal and cool' and overcome her special education status. She was provocative with males in her class-room, which eventually led to her leaving school and having sex.

In addition to the multitude of issues that adolescence presents, teens with intellectual disabilities have the added issue of contending with the negative evaluations of others. At a time when the self-esteem of the healthiest teen is at risk, the teen with intellectual disabilities is particularly vulnerable. Rowitz (1988) notes that since other teens are the primary socialization agents during this time, the teen with intellectual disabilities becomes prey to the evaluations of others more than most. How does this affect the adolescent with developmental disabilities?

Society's labels rest heavily on those who are aware that they are different. Labelled as slow learners, young people with intellectual disabilities are often ostracized by their peers. One mode of response is to distance yourself from everything associated with disability. These individuals desperately want to establish social relationships but are unable to due to their disability (Gillberg, 1984). Rejected by intellectually average and successful peers, and rejecting each other as peers to avoid the disability status, teens with developmental disabilities might be particularly vulnerable to affiliating with intellectually average adolescents with problems. Many like Jenny, in a desire to fit in, experience depression and loneliness. They may become victimized by their own motive to avoid such victimization.

Substance abuse may be one avenue through which the identification with intellectually average peers with behavioural problems is acted out. Already more common in teens in the general population, studies suggest that the use of alcohol and other drugs is also significant among people with disabilities (Longo, 1997). Given that many teens with intellectual disabilities have medications to control various aspects of their disability (e.g. neuroleptics and mood stabilizers) poly-substance drug effects might be a particular risk for these teens (Rowitz, 1988). As with Jenny, the issue was not so much a desire to use, but a desire to be normal. Studies with 'normal' teens, however, suggest that they are particularly at risk of sexual victimization and failure to use contraception while drinking (Koss and Cook, 1998). Thus, the use of drugs might further the sexual problems of the already compromised intellectually disabled teen.

Teens with disabilities, when rejected by peers, turn to media surrogates for information. Individuals with intellectual disabilities look to fictional human interaction such as TV and movies in order to imitate 'normal' human social interactions (Walker-Hirsch, 1995). These sources, however, are inaccurate depictions of reality, a concept that is lost on teens with and without intellectual disabilities. In the USA in the year 2000, 84 per cent of television sitcom content dealt with sex, an increase from 56 per cent in 1998 (Kaiser Family Foundation, 2003) while the advertisement of means for appropriately responsible sexual behaviour is banned. This gives a message to teens that sexual behaviour is not just normal, but pervasive. It might also give the message that responsible sexuality is not. In an effort to 'be normal', a teen with a disability might act in ways consistent with the images gleaned from TV.

An increase in alcohol and drug abuse, and an increase in exposure to models of sexuality without an appropriate focus on responsible behaviour, increases the risk for HIV for this group. Kerr (1989) polled representatives at a national forum on HIV/AIDS prevention and found that most people at this conference agreed that individuals with intellectual disabilities were at an increased risk for HIV/AIDS. They listed many reasons for this, including the susceptibility to peer pressure, the increased risk of blood exposure due to self-injurious behaviours, and the greater risk from employment options such as janitorial work that would put the person in contact with biohazards. The risks of sexually transmitted infections should not be ignored or oversimplified and suggests the need for training on barrier-type methods of birth control. The choice of birth control, however, is often overshadowed by parent fears and beliefs. Studies of birth-control choice of the parents of those with intellectual disabilities suggest that their favoured methods are suppressant hormones or IUDs (Chamberlain, Rauh, Passer, McGrath and Burket, 1984). While these protect against pregnancy, they do not protect against STIs.

PRINCIPLES FOR SOCIAL SKILLS AND SEXUALITY TRAINING

Case study continued

Jenny's partner in sexual activity was a youth already convicted of sexually assaulting other girls. While she believed she was consenting to sexual activity, her parents knew that their age, the discrepancy in cognitive functioning between the two, as well as his history, suggested otherwise. Jenny thought it was love and resented her parents' protests, feeling that they just objected to her having a boyfriend. She did not seem to understand that it was not the sexual behaviour alone but the greater context that was at issue.

Society's expectations and rules do not change to fit people's needs; therefore what we teach individuals with intellectual disabilities cannot be different because of their limitations. Does this mean that we ignore individuality altogether? A model for educational design of sexuality programming suggested by Tyler (1949) recommends otherwise. Indeed, it states that a collective approach must be taken which considers: (1) societal expectations; (2) individual needs; and (3) expert opinion.

Societal expectations

Society's expectations, reflected by its rights, rules and laws, may at times conflict. Still, everyone has basic human rights that must be allowed while respecting society's laws and rules. It follows that people with disabilities should know their rights so that they are able to assert them. Several sources have suggested these rights include: (1) the right to be treated with respect and dignity, including recognition as a sexual being; (2) the right to have access to information; (3) the right to be involved in an honest sensitive and realistic way in decisions affecting him or her, including the right to be sexual and make and break relationships; and (4) the right to live within real limitations to his or her maximum potential in a dignified environment (Craft, 1987).

Sexuality education must convey the laws of the society. Without this, individuals with intellectual disabilities are unable to demonstrate their ability to conform to these laws (Abramson, Parker and Weisberg, 1988). Competency to give consent is defined as the ability to understand a sexual act and its possible consequences. At a minimum, an individual with disabilities must learn that exposure is illegal, that hurting someone is wrong, and that touching someone who does not want to be touched is also wrong. The ability to give consent is crucial to defining sexual abuse, and thus teaching this information is crucial.

'Society' may refer to not only the greater community but also the microcosms of work and living environment in which a person finds themselves.

Individuals with intellectual disabilities are a part of a number of different environments, each with its own set of rules, which are not always consistent. For example, holding hands or kissing may be acceptable in the living arrangement but not at work. Sexuality education must not teach behaviours that may put a person in violation of the rules of their supportive environment, thus discrimination skills must be taught as well. Individuals with disabilities must have the skills to make decisions in each separate environment, including weighing alternatives, making choices and putting these into practice.

Individual needs

How does one assess individual needs for sexuality and relationship education? One way is to assess the person for their level of social behaviour and knowledge regarding sexuality. Several tools exist for this. Measurements of adaptive behaviours assess social skills in a variety of contexts. Scores can be compared to an intellectually average teen of the same age to identify pockets of needs. Some tests specifically designed to assess socialization also exist (Matson, 1981). To assess sexual knowledge directly, many have used the *Socio-Sexual Knowledge and Attitude Test* (Wish, McCombs and Edmonson, 1980). Socio-sexual behaviours may be assessed in pretest role-plays, or other questioning techniques associated with specific programmes (Foxx and McMorrow, 1983; Valenti-Hein and Mueser, 1990). These general tests, however, do not reflect the entire array of socio-sexual skills. Aside from these formal techniques, an individual's behaviour may suggest what is needed. Clearly Jenny needed to learn skills to help her discriminate between good and bad relationships. She also needed to be affirmed in appropriate social contexts, as her behaviour stemmed from feeling isolated, different, and deprived.

Expert opinion

'Experts' have developed a myriad of programmes designed for ease of use. Pre-made programmes have several advantages. They may have been evaluated, have a body of literature that supports them, and save time. Several of these programmes are referenced at the end of this chapter. While those listed are primarily designed for individuals with intellectual disabilities, several programmes exist for intellectually average teens, which might also be appropriate when adapted for those with developmental disabilities. To merely 'choose and use', however, does a disservice to the learner. Indeed, as far as sexuality training goes, one size does not fit all. Most of these programmes do not address the first two issues in Tyler's (1949) model, that is, the specific society regulations and the unique needs and abilities of the individual. Thus, any programme must be adapted to include these two areas.

Garwick, Valenti-Hein and Jurkowski (1993) suggest how pre-set pro-grammes can be used under best-case and worst-case scenarios. They noted that programmes are really 'jumping-off' points for a fuller curriculum of sexuality training. The information they contain must be integrated into a person's environment, repeated often, and used as a means to increase staff motivation and interest in this area. If they are used as 'one shot thank God we are done with that' programmes, they are sure to fail. Using them as a panacea or an island of 'normalized thinking' in an environment that opposes self-expression is also dangerous. All too often, preset programmes are used to teach 'no-nos', primarily to those who have been sexually inappropriate, and thus may be viewed as punishment by the learner rather than as part of an education about being fully human.

Of special note is that pre-produced programmes often include the use of visual tools. These provide an additional avenue to help teach important concepts. Props such as anatomical dolls, drawings, models, have been sug-gested. The successful use of most of these tools require some degree of ability to perform the cognitive process of symbolic representation. That is, the individual must be able to understand that the prop represents a person, specifically, themselves. Some studies have found that this kind of symbolic thinking is difficult for individuals with more severe intellectual impairments (Lunsky and Benson, 2001; Valenti-Hein, 2003).

Furthermore, the nature of the representational tool used may inadvert-ently confuse the issue. For example a programme by Planned Parenthood of Wisconsin, developed specifically to aid people with intellectual disabilities to learn body parts (Maurer, 1992) uses nude pictures of two well-known dolls with internal and external sexual organs pictured simultaneously. In contrast, a book targeted at intellectually average preteens to help with the same discussion (Harris, 1996) used a series of drawings of nudes of all sizes, ages, colours, and abilities, with some people pictured in wheelchairs or on crutches. Internal sexual organs are not included in these drawings. Which is easier to understand? A picture of a doll that simultaneously reveals internal and external organs, or line drawings of more realistic people that conveys that we come in all varieties but still have the same body parts? A good rule of thumb is that if the picture is confusing to you, it will be confusing to an individual with an intellectual disability. Alternatively, simply using old magazines to cut out pictures of real people and label sexual anatomy over clothes is a low-cost way to individualize a programme on anatomy while reducing the symbolic representation issues, and increasing generalization.

We will now consider how pre-made programmes address the issue of explaining the social context of behaviour. One approach is illustrated by the Life Horizons programme which uses a picture of two people kissing on a bus to generate discussion (Kempton, 1988). The programme facilitator helps participants discuss whether this behaviour is okay, and the reasons for their choices. Other programmes use conceptual strategies to address the same topic. The Circles Program uses a series of concentric circles, with the participant's picture at the centre, to display whether a person is 'close enough' to engage in particular types of touch (Champagne and Walker-Hirsch, 1986). Using the participant's family and friends, they describe the degree of psychological distance that each relationship possesses. Role-plays and modelling can help people identify what might constitue a violation of rules. The Dating Skills Program uses a problem-solving strategy to generate more socially acceptable alternatives to the specific issues encountered by participants (Valenti-Hein and Mueser, 1990). A person's ability to think abstractly, take on roles, or discuss issues verbally must be considered before deciding which strategies are most appropriate.

COACHING IN SAFETY SKILLS AND SEXUAL ABUSE PREVENTION

Case study continued

The District Attorney's Office attempted to get involved but found Jenny a poor witness due to her reporting inconsistencies as well as her statement that this was a sexual act that she wanted to engage in. When her parents tried to force her to face her disabled status, she became very emotional and suicidal, resulting in several hospitalizations. Several attempts to return her to home and school failed. A year passed and things went from bad to worse. Jenny was very confused about who she was, but knew she wanted to be accepted and to fit in.

One area that needs specific address is that of abuse prevention. Individuals with intellectual disabilities are more likely to be abused than intellectually average peers (Sobsey, 1994). This suggests that adolescents, particularly females, will need specific coaching to stay safe. While several good programmes exist to address this issue, many of which are referenced in the final section of this chapter, some specific points can be made here. Good abuse prevention addresses issues related to: (1) self-esteem; (2) empowerment to make choices; and (3) assertiveness.

Without self-esteem, a person may not see him- or herself as important enough to express an opinion. The strong tendency for people with intellectual disabilities to be deferent may further contribute to difficulties in this area. Self-esteem does not develop by positive self-statements but by opportunities for success, and a vision based on abilities rather than disabilities. This does not happen in a 'class' on sexuality or abuse prevention, but rather in life. What can be shared in a 'class' forum, however, are some basic rights that everyone should be allowed to assert. These rights include:

(1) that no one should be allowed to touch sexual parts of your body with their body without your permission; (2) that private behaviours should be conducted privately; and (3) that interpersonal space should be respected. It is imperative that these principles are then applied in all aspects of daily living, including dressing, toileting, and bathing regimes. For example, hand-over-hand guidance in bathing, or use of sponges at all times, would respect these rights in everyday care interactions.

Choices are also important in letting people with an intellectual disability know that their opinions matter. While there are many things that we have no choice about, everyday practice in simple choices will make the big choices of when to stand up for your rights easier. Choice of clothes, meals, and how to spend free time are all examples of daily activities that can incorporate the views of people with intellectual disabilities. There may be times when there is disagreement about the choices made, but it is important for people to be able live with their choices and their consequences. There may be a temptation to make all choices for a person with an intellectual disability, to do all their grooming and dressing for them, and protect them with our 'good judgment'. Unfortunately, this actually removes the power of choice from an individual and serves only to increase their confusion or compliance, and these are characteristics on which an abuser may capitalize. Teaching about *why* you make the choices you do and finding out why people with intellectual disabilities make the choices they make, will go further to increase responsible and independent behaviour.

Assertiveness is the ability to defend your rights while not hurting others. Once a person knows their rights, and feels that they can make choices, assertiveness can be practised with very concrete everyday behaviours (Valenti-Hein, 1994). If a person with an intellectual disability has been sexually abused they need to feel that they can tell someone. If the person is able, having them identify a 'safe person' is a good way to do this. For those who are unable to understand this concept, vigilance of staff is a must. Indeed, some have suggested that seeing abuse prevention as something the person alone does is to blame the victim (Sobsey, 1994). Several 'lists' exist of behaviours that may indicate that a person with an intellectual disability has been subject to abuse; however, these are not 'proof' in and of themselves. Referral to a psychologist or other professional is an appropriate step if these behaviours emerge.

Adapting investigations of sexual abuse to the level of the individual with an intellectual disability is necessary to improve reporting consistency (Valenti-Hein and Schwartz, 1995). Staff must be aware of the need to call proper authorities before doing any questioning. The role of staff in this situation is to advise about the abilities of the individual involved so that the client gets the best chance of disclosing their experience.

To state that abuse prevention is a specific area of intervention, however, underestimates the importance of general learning of appropriate behaviour to the overall solution of this problem. One cannot know what is inappropriate if one does not know what is appropriate. Sometimes well-meaning staff and family make this distinction harder. Giving a person with an intellectual disability the kind of touch typically reserved for close relationships (such as hugging) can be confusing as it undermines their sense of a clear boundary that such touching is special. As a general rule, if it is something you would not do with an intellectually average teen, you certainly should not do it with a teen with disabilities. As noted earlier, training in understanding verbal and non-verbal cues, both given and received, is needed. When one can learn to distinguish feelings, by expressions, by internal sensations and by the situations that may engender them, feelings can be used to help guide behaviour. 'If you don't feel right about it don't do it' means nothing to the person who does not distinguish feelings. Just as socio-sexual behaviour needs integration in daily life, abuse prevention is also a daily activity reinforced by simple actions, options, and behaviours.

MANAGING INAPPROPRIATE SEXUAL EXPRESSION

Case study continued

In therapy, Jenny was asked what she wanted. She saw her hospitalizations as preventing her from completing school – making her all the more unusual. She wanted to complete high school as other students do. She talked about going to dances and taking her senior photos, things that were quite normal for a teenager. It was clear that she would only repeat problems at her past high school and that the rural area could not provide her with a programme tailored to her. As a result, it was decided that a group home placement in a larger school district nearby was best for her.

Sexual behaviour must be considered in context before a treatment programme is suggested. Sometimes behaviours that appear unusual are developmentally typical when considered with reference to a person's level of cognitive development. Developmental levels of individuals seem likewise to determine whom they direct their sexual attention towards. Pre-adolescent children with typical cognitive functioning may engage in sexual experimentation with both sexes (Masters, Johnson, and Kolodny, 1988). Experimental play at this age is common, and is mainly a means of gaining knowledge. When expressing sexuality towards others, 35 per cent of individuals with autism expressed interest in both sexes and, similar to young children, the individual with autism may encourage another to look at their genitals (Haracopos and Pedersen, 1992). Similarly, both groups may engage in masturbating with objects such as blankets or dolls. Understanding these as developmentally typical behaviours may help in determining how best to cope with them.

The intent of the person exhibiting the behaviours should also be considered when determining treatment. Individuals with autism may touch others just to experience their environment through their senses (Lettick, 1985). Misconceptions about these behaviours may lead to the counterfeit labelling of deviance – behaviours that are sexually inappropriate on the surface, but may be caused by other factors. Hingsburger, Griffiths and Quinsey (1991) give eleven causes of such behaviour, with corresponding implications for treatment. For example, one key cause is an environment that does not respect privacy and sexual expression. Inappropriate public behaviours may be a way to cope with sexual drive in a system that prevents privacy. Intervention in this case involves changing the environment. Over-reaction by caregivers is another example of a cause or maintaining factor for inappropriate sexual behaviours. That is, any reaction, good or bad, may be interpreted as attention, thus reinforcing and increasing the behaviour. The intervention in this case is that the caretaker must treat this educational process in much the same manner that we deal with table manners, or how to cross the street (Torisky and Torisky, 1985). Thus, it is important to understand the cause of the inappropriate sexual expression before instigating an intervention. Some behaviours that appear to be sexual may not be. In Jenny's case, her sexual acting out came from a drive to be 'normal'. For her, allowing experiences of 'normality' and building self-esteem were key.

If the behaviour is clearly sexually motivated, all parties must agree that an intervention is needed, and must agree on the appropriateness of that intervention. Managing this inappropriate behaviour is not just about suppressing the act, rather it is about teaching the appropriate place, time and context in which to do it (Elgar, 1985). For example, if a teen is self-injuring due to misguided attempts at masturbation, the decision may be to teach masturbation skills, including when and where to engage in this behaviour. There are many types of masturbation education programmes, some including videos and kits. Sample programmes are included in the resource list at the conclusion of this chapter. Agencies must have a policy as to when these are appropriate interventions, however, and the agreement of the guardian as well as the individual involved is critical. Additionally, age may be a factor for consideration. Haracopos and Pedersen (1992) note that by the penal laws of Denmark, children under the age of 15 may receive only verbal teaching and not formal 'sexual training'. Forcing explicit sexual education on someone who is too young, or who does not want to learn, may turn it into a type of sexual abuse.

STAFF AND SUPPORT TRAINING

Case study continued

Jenny's therapy involved educating the support systems around her. Her parents entered into regular therapy where they talked about their desires for Jenny's future. Consistency between homes, and between home and school was stressed. As time went on, Jenny entered her senior year. Her desire to go to prom prompted another encounter with inappropriate sexual behaviour. Staff were tempted to ignore the behaviour as Jenny did 'not know what she was doing'. It was explained that ignoring the behaviour removes not only her responsibility but the consequences from her behaviour – making it likely to continue or even increase. School policy clearly dictated no sexual behaviour should occur on the property of the school. This time the incident involved a younger boy and she had obtained the age of majority. She was surprised when the police were asked to join the session held with school staff to explain to her that she could be considered a perpetrator. When Jenny became aware of all the ramifications, the behaviour quickly ceased.

Frontline staff are in the position of having to actually carry out sexuality education and relationship training. How successful they are in promoting appropriate relationship and sexuality skills will depend on their own comfort with the topic as well as their own knowledge, time and resources. Perhaps even more importantly, caregivers need to know that their agency supports and encourages their efforts – that it is an expected part of their job. The role of the psychologist in this setting is as a support to these individuals by providing resources, experiences and encouragement to the frontline staff in their endeavours.

In the USA, *ASSECT* (American Association of Sex Educators, Counsellors and Therapists) is the organization that supports best practices in sexuality education. This agency has pointed to the need for educators, instructors and counsellors to know their own attitudes and feelings about sexual issues before attempting to work with others. To meet their certification standards, one must complete a 'Sexual Attitude Reassessment Seminar', in which a person's own beliefs about a number of areas of sexuality are thoroughly explored. While frontline staff cannot be expected to become certified relationship and sexuality educators, a workshop to 'psychologically prepare' caregivers is strongly recommended. Numerous resources exist that psychologists can use to facilitate such a workshop.

Since sexuality is usually not openly discussed, giving permission to discuss this topic is an important first step. Standard sexuality education activities like 'The Dirty Word Game' can be used as an icebreaker. In this activity, people are asked to list as many slang words as they can for the appropriate names of body parts and sexual activities. Attitude assessment is also important. A sexual myth test allows participants to assess their beliefs against real information. Such 'tests' consist of statements such as: 'If a person does not think he or she has been abused, then it wasn't abuse', to which the person answers as either 'True' or 'False'. The facilitator can lead a discussion about the veracity of these statements while allowing staff members privately to reassess their beliefs.

What a staff member believes is an appropriate expression of relationships or sexuality may change when discussing a person with a disability. Thus, any activities must include knowledge and attitude assessment that is specifically geared to assess unique attitude difference towards this population. For example, the individual may be asked in a paper and pencil attitude test whether they believe that 'The more disabled a person is, the less sexual drive he or she will have.' When differences are suggested for people with disabilities, the reason for believing these differences exist should be explored.

Support must be given in the form of access to materials, time to become familiar with them, and ongoing help in using them. (Several resources are listed in the final section of this chapter.) In all cases, the facilitator must be respectful of difficulties these issues may raise for staff and not judge them on their beliefs. Instead, the facilitator should remind the individual of the agency's position and suggest that the person ask for help with situations when their own views might prevent them from supporting the agency's position.

A single staff member should not be responsible for all socio-sexual education. Curricular integration is the key to success. If socio-sexual education remains in the classroom, it is not helpful (Kerr, 1989). Everyone must work together towards the same goals. This, of course, implies a clear agency stand in the form of written policies. In one study that investigated the nature of such policies, only three programmes out of twenty-six submitted formal written policies upon request (Van Bourgondien, Reichle and Palmer, 1997). Good policies define behaviours of concern (such as intercourse), the roles of everyone involved (staff, administration, student) and what is expected (the action to be taken).

Even when a staff member understands the issues and is supportive of the goals of a socio-sexuality programme, they may feel at odds with the family. A main concern of parents is that teaching individuals about sexuality may increase interest, thereby causing more problems. Studies do not support this concern. Ousley and Mesibov (1991) found that sexual knowledge does not correlate with either interest or experience. Information did not stimulate interest, but was an important way of helping already interested individuals. Indeed, Konstantareas and Lunksy (1997) found that those individuals with more knowledge about sex and sexuality actually engaged in fewer sexual behaviours.

At times parents becomes unable to separate what they need from what their child needs (Torisky and Torisky, 1985). Exercises in empathy training can help here. Asking parents to recall their own needs during adolescence, how they learnt about sex, and what they would have liked to have learnt, may improve their sensitivity to the need for relationship and sexuality education. Parents need to be engaged as partners in the process of such education, or efforts may result in cross-purposes, resulting in confusion for the adolescent, and problems with their emotional well-being. As with staff discomfort, parents should be subtly supported in discussing their feelings about sexuality and social issues, encouraged to express their concerns, and, if appropriate, encouraged in their own growth.

An exercise in working with both staff and parents might help. Ask them to brainstorm how they might alter their interactions in one day-to-day situation (such as brushing teeth), in order to emphasize socio-sexual skills training. They might say, 'Whew, no one would want to be around bad breath!' or maybe, 'Now I want to talk with you more, you smell so fresh' or even, 'Now you will be more kissable!' What about the activity of watching an episode of *Friends*? Any day-to-day activity can serve. This process suggests that socio-sexual issues are part of everyday life and that learning is going on anyway – the question is whether parents, carers, and professionals adopt a natural and influential role.

CONCLUSION

In the end, what is most important in a successful transition to adult life for a teen with intellectual disabilities is an active and informed participation in their own future. Not all teens with intellectual disabilities will be found to be competent to determine all the choices in their lives, but all should be allowed to express some opinion about their own future. Knowing as much as possible about the benefits, risks, and alternatives of choices in socio-sexual behaviour is the goal. As Zetlin and Turner (1985) pointed out, only as adolescents accumulate skills and knowledge will they assume a more adult-like pattern of behaviour.

Case study concluded

Jenny was transitioned from school to work in a sheltered employment programme. Her placement at the group home helped a healthy separation from her parents and increased her social competence and independent living skills, which in turn increased her self-esteem. She continued to find potential partners, having varied success in the appropriateness of her choices. At this point, however, she makes those choices informed as to the pros and cons. When she picks poor relationships, she knows the weaknesses and works to improve on them. She looks at the alternatives and is willing to explore these. Now Jenny can write the end for her own story.

RESOURCES FOR PEOPLE WITH INTELLECTUAL DISABILITIES

All of Us: Talking Together: Sex Education for People with Developmental Disabilities. Program Development Associates (1999). Syracuse, NY. This video presents views on sexuality from the child and parent's perspectives. Communication about sexuality issues, sexual abuse, STIs, and discussions with health care providers are included. (Also appropriate for parents and caregivers.)

Falling in Love. Hollins, S., Perez, W., and Abdelnoor, A. (1999). London: Gaskell Press and St. George's Hospital Medical School.

Finger Tips: A Guide for Teaching about Female Masturbation. Hingsburger, Dave and Haar, Sandra (2000). Ontario, Canada: Diverse City Press. This book and video set teaches women with intellectual disabilities about masturbation. Myths about female sexuality are addressed. The book includes step-by-step photographs.

Hand Made Love: A Guide for Teaching about Male Masturbation. Hingsburger, Dave (1996). Ontario, Canada: Diverse City Press. This book and video set discusses key issues with masturbation including privacy, pleasure, and shared living arrangements. Myths are discussed. Masturbation is presented as a self-exploration activity as well as a healthy outlet for pleasure.

I Have the Right to Know: A Course on Sexuality and Personal Relationships for People with Learning Disabilities. Atkinson, D., Gingell, A. and Martin, J. (1997). BILD. http://www.bild.org.uk/

Keeping Healthy Down Below. Hollins, S. and Downer, J. (2000). London: Gaskell Press and St. George's Hospital Medical School.

Looking after My Breasts. Hollins, S. and Perez, W. (2000). London: Gaskell Press and St. George's Hospital Medical School.

Making Connections. Carmody, Mary Ann and American Film and Video (1995). Syracuse, NY: Making Connections-Looking for Choices, Inc. This is a video about dating a cast made up primarily of persons with disabilities. Discussion guide included. (Also appropriate for parents.)

No! How!!! Co-written by Dave Hingsburger. Ontario, Canada: Diverse City Press. This video about abuse prevention includes people in all phases of production: acting, writing, producing and directing.

Under Cover Dick: A Guide for Teaching about Condom Use through Video and Understanding. Hingsburger, Dave (1996). Ontario, Canada: Diverse City Press. This book and video set provides clear direction in the use of condoms. Disease transmission is discussed. An illustrated book is included.

RESOURCES FOR PARENTS AND CAREGIVERS

Abuse of Children and Adults with Disabilities: A Risk Reduction and Intervention Guidebook for Parents and Other Advocates. Baladerian, Nora J., PhD (1999). Mental Health Consultants. This publication discusses increased vulnerability to abuse, how to recognize abuse and its consequences, and risk reduction strategies. (Also appropriate for professionals.)

An Easy Guide for Caring Parents: Sexuality and Socialization: A Book for Parents of

People with Mental Handicaps. McKee, Lynn and Blacklidge, Virginia, MD (1986). Concord, CA: Planned Parenthood Shasta-Diablo. This book addresses the social needs of children with intellectual disabilities, as well as parent roles and sexuality issues such as growing up, responsible sexual behaviour, masturbation, social life, sexual orientation, fertility and birth control, sexual abuse, and marriage.

Circle of Friends. Perske, Robert (1988). Nashville, TN: Abingdon Press. This book describes the importance of friendships in the lives of people with intellectual disabilities with multiple personal stories.

Couples with Intellectual Disabilities Talk about Living and Loving. Melberg Karen Schwier (1994). Woodbine House. A collection of stories of people with intellectual disabilities who are in intimate relationships. (Also appropriate for professionals.)

I Openers. Hingsburger, David (1993). Vancouver Family Support Institute Press. Parents ask questions about sexuality and their children with intellectual disabilities.

Person to Person. Carmody, Mary Ann and American Film and Video (1991). Syracuse, NY: Looking for Choices, Inc. This video addresses sexuality education. Discussion guide included.

Roots and Wings. Carmody, Mary Ann and American Film and Video (1995). Syracuse, NY: Looking for Choices, Inc. This video addresses the social-sexual development of adolescents with cognitive disabilities. (Also appropriate for professionals.) Discussion guide included.

Sexuality: Your Sons and Daughters with Intellectual Disabilities. Melberg Schwier, Karin and Hingsburger, David (2000). Baltimore, MD: Brookes Publishers. This guide addresses stages of development. It includes stories of families with a member who has an intellectual disability providing practical exercises. An annotated bibliography is also included.

Sexuality: Your Sons and Daughters with Intellectual Disability. Melberg-Schwier, K. and Hingsburger, D. (2000). Baltimore, MD: Brookes. (A parents' guide to sexuality and ID.)

The Sexuality and Sexual Rights of People with Learning Disabilities: Considerations for Staff and Carers. Cambridge, P. (1996). BILD. http://www.bild.org.uk/

Your Rights about Sex. McCarthy, M. and Cambridge, P. (1996). BILD. http://www.bild.org.uk/

FURTHER READING FOR CLINICIANS

Informed Consent, Sexuality, and People with Developmental Disabilities: Strategies for Professional Decision-Making. Griffin, Laura K. (1996). Milwaukee: ARC. This workbook is intended to increase knowledge about sexual consent and decision making for those working with people who have intellectual disabilities.

Just Say Know! Hingsburger, Dave (1995). Ontario, Canada: Diverse City Press. This book explores issues concerning the abuse of people with intellectual disabilities and provides information on self-protection and skills to reduce the risk of abuse.

Sexuality and Disabilities: A Guide for Human Service Practitioners. Mackelprang, Romel W. and Valentine, Deborah (eds) (1993). Binghamton, NY: The Haworth Press, Inc. A collection of articles on issues related to sexuality, intimacy, and disability.

Sexuality and People with Intellectual Disability (2nd edn). Fegan, Lydia, Rauch, Anne and McCarthy, Wendy (1993). Baltimore, MD: Brookes Publishers. This book addresses the attitudes towards sexuality of both individuals with intellectual disabilities and their caregivers. Case studies, sexual rights, and policy guidelines are included.

Social and Personal Relationships: Policy and Good Practice Guidelines for Staff Working with Adults with Learning Disabilities. BILD (2001). BILD and West Midlands Learning Disability Forum. http://www.bild.org.uk/

Socialization and Sexuality: A Comprehensive Training Guide for Professionals Helping People with Disabilities. Kempton, Winifred (1998). Syracuse, NY: Program Development Associates. Chapters include Understanding Sexuality, Attitudes, Counselling, Abuse and Informed Consent, Special Considerations Relating to Living Centres, Working with Parents and Families, Sexuality Programs, and Assessments.

Violence and Abuse in the Lives of People with Disabilities: The End of Silent Acceptance? Sobsey, Dick (1994). Baltimore, MD: Brookes Publishers. This book is a wonderful guide to understanding and preventing abuse. Practical strategies for abuse detection and prevention according to an integrated framework is presented. A thorough review of literature and an annotated list of individuals and organizations are included.

ASSESSMENT INSTRUMENTS

Forensic Assessment of Consent to Sex. Baladerian, Nora J., PhD (1998). Disability, Abuse and Personal Rights Project. This interviewing instrument assesses consent to sexual relations in adults with cognitive impairments.

Matson's Evaluation of Social Skills with Youngsters. Matson, John, PhD (1981). International Diagnostic Systems. A paper and pencil test with self-rating and teacher-forms to assess appropriate and inappropriate social skills.

Socio-Sexual Knowledge and Attitudes Test. Wish, J., McCombs, K. and Edmonson, B. (1980). Chicago: Stoelting. This verbally administered assessment tool helps evaluate the knowledge and attitudes of individuals with developmental disabilities using pictures and questions.

The Sexual Abuse Interview for Adults with Developmental Disabilities (SAIDD). Valenti-Hein, Denise, PhD and Schwartz, Linda, PhD (1996). Santa Barbara, CA: James Stanfield Publishing Co. This tool helps individuals conducting interviews regarding sexual abuse to use a developmentally appropriate phrasing in assessment to reduce inconsistency in reporting. Competency to testify, consent, developmental language abilities and assessing the incident are included. A background book and assessment pictures accompanies this programme.

CURRICULA

Changes in You: An Introduction to Sexuality Education through an Understanding of Puberty. Siegel, Peggy C., illust. Vivien Cohen (1991). Santa Barbara, CA: James Stanfield Publishing Co. Intended for students with cognitive disabilities in grades 4–9 to address the transition into puberty, this programme includes illustrations, student books for boys and girls, and a teacher's guide.

Child Sexual Abuse Curriculum for the Developmentally Disabled. Rappaport, Sol R. Burkhardt, Sandra A. and Rotatori, Anthony F. (1997). Springfield, IL: Charles C. Thomas Publishers, Ltd. This curriculum includes: understanding child sexual abuse, treatment, emotional and behavioural sequelae, factors that mediate the sequelae, and a prevention curriculum. Designed for children who are in the mild range of mental retardation, an appendix is included. (Also appropriate for caregivers.)

CIRCLES I: Intimacy and Relationships CIRCLES II: Stop Abuse CIRCLES III: AIDS: Safer Ways. Champagne, Marklyn and Walker-Hirsch, Leslie (1986; 1988; 1993). Santa Barbara, CA: James Stanfield Publishing Co. For people with mild to moderate intellectual disabilities, *Circles I* addresses social distance and relationship building; *Circles II* includes recognizing and reacting to sexual exploitation and learning protective behaviours; and *Circles III* focuses on communicable diseases. Each programme comes with videos, supplemental materials, and a teacher's guide.

Dating Skills Program. Valenti-Hein, Denise and Mueser, Kim (1990). Worthington, OH: International Diagnostic Systems. This programme uses problem solving as a model for addressing the issues that arise in social-sexual contexts, such as compromising, understanding emotions, and dealing with rejection. One of the few programmes supported by research outcome studies, with evaluation tools included. Available from the author.

FACTS: Positive Approaches: A Sexuality Guide for Teaching Developmentally Disabled Persons. Maurer, Lisa (1991). Wilmington, DE: Planned Parenthood of Delaware. This guide includes background information, exercises, fact sheets, and programmes relating to anatomy, physiology, contraception, relationships, pregnancy, and parenthood.

The Family Education Program. Simpson, Katherine (1990). Concord, CA: Planned Parenthood Shasta-Diablo. Curricula topics include teaching sexuality, self-esteem, and abuse prevention. Working with schools, setting up educational plans, working with parents, and dealing with teachers' concerns are also reviewed. Audiovisual instruction, reproducible teaching graphics, and pre- and post-test evaluations are also included.

Social Skills Activities for Special Children. Mannix, Darlene (1995). New York: Jossey-Bass. Inc. Publishers. This programme has ready-to-use lessons and worksheets to help children become proficient at basic social skills.

Stacking the Deck. Foxx, Richard and McMorrow, M.J. (1983). Champaign, IL: Research Press. These cards are used with a standard board game to present social skills situations to solve in three areas: general social skills, socio-sexual skills, and work-related skills. Situations are divided by giving *vs* receiving skills in four areas. Research-based results.

Special Education: Secondary FLASH (Family Life and Sexual Health): A Curriculum for Grades 7–12. Stangle, Jane (1991). Seattle, WA: Family Planning Publications. This programme is designed for adolescents and addresses the physical, emotional, and safety aspects of sexuality education; encourages family involvement; and includes a section on preparing community-based sexuality education programmes. Relationships, communication, abuse, anatomy, reproduction, and STDs are included in this curriculum. Guidelines for answering questions, audio-visuals, teacher preparation suggestions, transparencies, handouts and a resource guide are included.

The GYN Exam Handbook: An Illustrated Guide to the Gynecological Examination for Women with Special Needs. Taylor, Maria Olivia (1991). Santa Barbara, CA: James Stanfield Publishing Co. For females with mild to moderate intellectual disabilities, this curriculum takes participants through a gynaecological examination. It encourage taking care of sexual health needs. Two videos, a handbook, and teacher's guide are included.

Janet's Got Her Period. Gray, Judi and Jilich, Jitka (1990). Santa Barbara, CA: James Stanfield Publishing Co. For girls and young women with severe intellectual disabilities, this curriculum includes a video and illustrated storybook, telling the story of a girl who learns menstrual care. A teacher's guide is also included.

LIFEFACTS: Essential Information about Life for Persons with Special Needs 1990, AIDS; 1992, Sexuality; 1990, Sexual Abuse Prevention. Santa Barbara, CA: James Stanfield Company. Of the seven programmes available, three address sexuality: AIDS, Sexuality, and Sexual Abuse Prevention. They are designed to teach adolescents and adults with mild to moderate intellectual disabilities.

Life Horizons I* The Physiological and Emotional Aspects of Being Male and Female Life Horizons II* The Moral, Social and Legal Aspects of Sexuality. Kempton, Winifred (1999). Santa Barbara, CA: James Stanfield Publishing Co. Developed for people with mild to moderate intellectual disabilities, Life Horizons I addresses Parts of the Body, Sexual Life Cycle, Reproduction, Regulation of Fertility, and Sexually Transmitted Diseases; Life Horizons II covers Self-Esteem and Establishing Relationships, Moral, Legal and Social Aspects of Sexual Behaviour – Male, Dating Skills and Learning to Love, Marriage and Other Adult Lifestyles, Parenting, and Sexual Abuse. Teaching slides, a teacher's guide, and video are included.

Mind Your Manners. (1991). Santa Barbara, CA: James Stanfield Publishing. This videotaped series explores proper social behaviour including table manners, greetings, and conversations.

'No-Go-Tell'. Krents, Elisabeth, J. and Brenner, Shella A. (1991). Santa Barbara, CA: James Stanfield Publishing Co. Designed for children ages 3–7 to learn self-protection skills; concepts include: who are family, friends, familiar people and strangers; 'ok' and 'not ok' touch; private parts; and who and how to tell about an abusive incident. The curriculum includes illustrations, male and female anatomically detailed dolls, and a teacher's guide.

Preventing Sexual Abuse: Activities and Strategies for those Working with Children and Adolescents (2nd edn). Plummer, Carol A. (1997). Holmes Beach, FL: Learning Publications, Inc. This sexual abuse-prevention curriculum is divided into two sections. One is grades K through six, and the other is for grades seven through 12. Designed for intellectually average children they are adaptable for people with intellectual disabilities. Information on involving parents is included as well as guidelines for instructors and an appendix.

Sexuality Education for Persons with Severe Developmental Disabilities (rev edn). Brekke, Beverly (1988). Santa Barbara, CA: James Stanfield Publishing Co. This curriculum is for people with severe intellectual disabilities. Slide presentations and a teacher's guide address anatomy, appropriate social behaviour, menstruation, and medical examinations.

Social Skills and Sex Education: 'Sex Education and Self Care for the Forgotten Adult'. Steege, Mark and Steege, Syl (1998). Syracuse, NY: Program Development Associates. This teaching tool covers anatomy, sexual functioning, and appropriate *vs* inappropriate touch. It includes audio cassettes and picture books to be used while following along with the instruction manual.

WEBSITES

American Association of Sex Educators, Counselors, and Therapists (AASECT), PO Box 5488, Richmond, VA 23220–0488; 804/644–3288; http://www.aasect.org

Autism Society of America 7910 Woodmont Avenue, Ste. 300 Bethesday, MD 20814–3067; 301/657–0881; http://www.autism-society.org

The Arc. This national organization for people with mental retardation and their families provides support for sexuality education and referrals for those who have been sexually abused. 1010 Wayne Ave., Suite 650, Silver Spring, MD 20910; Phone: 301/565–3842 Fax: 301/565–5342; http://www.thearc.org

The National Information Centre for Children and Youth with Disabilities. An information and referral centre providing information on disability-related issues for professionals and families alike. PO Box 1492, Washington, DC 20013–1492, Phone: 202/884–8200; Voice and TTY 800/695–0285; Fax: 202/884–8444; http://www.nichcy.org

Parents Advocacy Coalition for Educational Rights. The PACER Centre is a parent training and information centre for families of children and youth with disabilities. A library of resources is available for families addressing sexuality and reproductive health. 8161 Normandale Boulevard, Minneapolis, MN 55437–1044; Phone: 952/838–9000; Fax: 952/838–0199; http://www.pacer.org

Planned Parenthood Federation of America. This organization addresses sexuality and reproductive health needs of all individuals. 810 7th Avenue; New York, NY 10019; Phone: 212/541–7800; 800/829–7732; Fax: 212/245–1845; http://www.plannedparenthood.org

L'Institut Roeher. This Canadian organization promotes self-determination of people with intellectual and other disabilities and provides public policy analysis, publications, training, education, and leadership development. Kinsmen Building; York University; 4700 Keele Street; Toronto, ON; Canada M3J 1P3; Phone: 800/856–2207; 416/661–9611; Fax: 416/661–5701; TYY: 416/661–2023; http://www.roeher.ca

Sexuality and Developmental Disability Network, Sex Information and Information Council of Canada. A national non-profit educational organization dedicated to informing and educating the public and professionals about all aspects of human sexuality. 850 Coxwell Avenue; East York, Ontario; Canada M4C 5R1; Phone: 416/466–5304; Fax: 416/778–0785; http://www.sieccan.org

Sexuality Information and Education Council of the United States. SIECUS develops, collects, and disseminates information, promotes education about sexuality, and advocates the right of individuals to make responsible sexual choices. 130 West 42nd Street, Suite 350, New York, NY 10036, Phone: 212/819–9770; Fax: 212/819–9776; http://www.siecus.org

Special Interest Group on Social and Sexual Concerns. American Association on Mental Retardation. This group of professionals is dedicated to improving information about sexuality issues for people with mental retardation. 444 North Capitol Street NW, Suite 846 Washington, DC 20001; Phone: 800/424–3688; 914/245–3384; http://www.aamr.org

Young Adult Institute YAI provides publications, conferences and resources specifically for youth with disabilities and those who work with them. 460 West 34th Street, New York, NY 10001–2382; 212/273–6517; http://www.yai.org

Xandria Collection. This company offers a catalog of adult sexual products for disabled people. P.O. Box 319005, San Francisco, CA 94131–9988, Phone: 800/242–2823 or 415/468–3812; Fax: 415/468–3912; http://www.xandria.com

REFERENCES

Abramson, P.R., Parker, T. and Weisberg, S.R. (1988). Sexual expression of mentally retarded people: Educational and legal implications. *American Journal on Mental Retardation*, 93(3), 328–34.

AGI (1999). Teen sex and pregnancy. Retrieved August 8, 2003 from http://www.agi-usa.org/pubs/fb_teen_sex.html

Chamberlain, A., Rauh, J., Passer, A., McGrath, M. and Burket, R. (1984). Issues in fertility control for mentally retarded female adolescents: 1. Sexual activity, sexual abuse and contraception. *Paediatrics*, 73(4), 445–50.

Champagne, M. and Walker-Hirsch, L. (1986). *Circles*. Santa Barbara, CA: Stanfield Publishers.

Chertkoff-Walz, N. and Benson, B.A. (1996). Labeling and discrimination of facial expressions by aggressive and nonaggressive men with mental retardation. *American Journal on Mental Retardation*, 101, 282–91.

Craft, A. (1987). *Mental Handicap and Sexuality: Issues and Perspectives*. Kent, England: Costello.

Elgar, S. (1985). Sex education and sexual awareness building for autistic children and youth: Some viewpoints and considerations. *Journal of Autism and Developmental Disorders*, 15, 214–16.

Foxx, R.M. and McMorrow, M.J. (1983). *Stacking the Deck*. Champaign, IL: Research Press.

Gagnon, E. (2001). *Power Cards: Using Special Interests to Motivate Children and Youth with Asperger Syndrome and Autism*. Autism Asperger Publishing Company.

Garwick, G., Valenti-Hein, D. and Jurkowski, E. (1993). *Integration of Research and Practice in Sexuality Training for Adults with Mental Retardation*. Workshop, May, American Association on Mental Retardation. Washington, DC.

Gillberg, C. (1991). Outcome in autism and autistic-like conditions. *Journal of the American Academy of Child and Adolescent Psychiatry*, 30, 375–82.

Gillberg, C. (1984). Autistic children growing up: Problems during puberty and adolescence. *Developmental Medicine and Child Neurology*, 26(1), 125–9.

Haracopos, D. and Pedersen, L. (1992). Sex education for people with autism matching programmes to levels of functioning: Danish report. *Society for the Autistically Handicapped*. Retrieved August 11, 2003, from http://www.autismuk.com/index9sub1.htm

Harris, Robie H. (1996). *It's Perfectly Normal: Changing Bodies, Growing Up, Sex and Sexual Health*. Cambridge, MA: Candlewick Press.

Heshusius, L. (1982). Research and perceptions of sexuality by persons labeled mentally retarded. In A. Craft (ed), *Mental Handicap and Sexuality: Issues and Perspectives*. Kent, England: Costello.

Hingsburger, D., Griffiths, D. and Quinsey, V. (1991). Detecting counterfeit deviance: Differentiating sexual deviance from sexual inappropriateness. *The Habilitative Mental Healthcare Newsletter*, 10(9), 51–6.

Kaiser Family Foundation. (2003). TV sex getting 'safer' Kaiser Family Foundation study finds. Retrieved November 12, 2003, from www.plannedparenthood.org/about/pr/030211_tvsafersex.html

Kempton, W. (1988). *Sex Education for Persons with Disabilities that Hinder Learning: A Teacher's Guide*. Santa Barbara, CA: James Stanfield.

Kerr, D.L. (1989). Forum addresses HIV education for children and youth with special educational needs. *Journal of School Health*, 59(3), 129.

Konstantareas, M.M. and Lunsky, Y.J. (1997). Sociosexual knowledge, experience, attitudes, and interests of individuals with autistic disorder and developmental delay. *Journal of Autism and Developmental Disorders*, 27(4), 397–413.

Koss, M. and Cook, S. (1998). Facing the facts: Date and acquaintance rape are significant problems for women. In R. Bergen (ed.), *Issues in Intimate Violence*. (pp. 147–56). Thousand Oaks, CA: Sage.

Lettick, A.L. (1985). Response to parents speak. *Journal of Autism and Developmental Disorders*, 15, 218–20.

Longo, L.P. (1997). Alcohol abuse in persons with developmental disabilities. *American Journal of Mental Retardation*, 16(4), 61–4.

Lunsky, Y. and Benson, B.A. (2001). Are anatomically detailed dolls and drawings appropriate tools for use with adults with developmental disabilities? A preliminary investigation. *Cognitive Therapy and Research*, 25(1), 77–90.

Maksym, D. (1990). *Shared Feelings: A Parent Guide to Sexuality Education for Children, Adolescents, and Adults who have a Mental Handicap*. Ontario, Canada: G. Allan Rocher Institute.

Masters, W., Johnson, V. and Kolodny, R. (1988). *Masters and Johnson on Sex and Human Loving*. Toronto, Canada: Little Brown.

Matson, J. (1981). *Matson Evaluation of Social Skills with Youngsters (Messy)*. Worthington, OH: IDS Publishing Corporation.

Matson, J.L., LeBlanc, L.A. and Weinheimer, B. (1999). Reliability of the Matson evaluation of social skills in individuals with severe retardation (MESSIER). *Behavior Modification*, 23, 647–61.

Maurer, Lisa (1992). *Positive Approaches: A Sexuality Guide for Teaching Developmentally Disabled Persons*. Planned Parenthood of Wisconsin.

Melberg-Schwier, K. and Hingsburger, D. (2000). *Sexuality: Your Sons and Daughters with Intellectual Disabilities*. Baltimore, MD: Paul H. Brooks Publishing.

Mesibov, G.B. (1985). Response to parents speak. *Journal of Autism and Developmental Disorders*, 15, 223–4.

Ousley, O.Y. and Mesibov, G.B. (1991). Sexual attitudes and knowledge of high-functioning adolescents and adults with autism. *Journal of Autism and Developmental Disorders*, 21(4), 471–81.

Rowitz, L. (1988). The forgotten ones: Adolescence and mental retardation. *Mental Retardation*, 26(3), 115–17.

Ruble, L.A. and Dalrymple, N.J. (1993). Social/sexual awareness of persons with autism: A parental persepective. *Archives of Sexual Behaviour*, 22(3), 229–40.

Smith, D.C., Valenti-Hein, D.C. and Heller, T. (1985). Interpersonal competence and community adjustment of mentally retarded adults. In M. Sigman (ed.), *Children with Emotional Disorders and Developmental Disabilities* (pp. 71–94). Orlando, FL: Grune and Stratton, Inc.

Sobsey, R. (1994). *Violence and Abuse in the Lives of People with Disabilities*. Baltimore, MD: Brookes.

Torisky, D. and Torisky, C. (1985). Sex education and sexual awareness building for autistic children and youth: Some viewpoints and considerations. *Journal of Autism and Developmental Disorders*, 15(2), 213–27.

Tyler, R.W. (1949). *Basic Principles of Curriculum and Instruction*. Chicago: University of Chicago Press.

Valenti-Hein, D.C. (June, 1994). *Taking Charge: A Group for Women who have Been Abused*. Boston, MA: *American Association on Mental Retardation*.

Valenti-Hein, D.C. (2003). Use of media to report sexual abuse for adults with mental retardation. *Mental Retardation*, 40, 297–303.

Valenti-Hein, D.C. and Mueser, K.T. (1990). *The Dating Skills Program*. Worthington, OH: International Diagnostic Systems.

Valenti-Hein, D.C. and Schwartz, L.D. (1995). *The Sexual Abuse Interview for Those with Developmental Disabilities*. Santa Barbara, CA: James Stanfield Company, Inc.

Van Bourgondien, M., Reichle, N.C. and Palmer, A. (1997). Sexual behaviour in adults with autism. *Journal of Autism and Developmental Disorders*, 27(2), 113–25.

Walker-Hirsch, L. (1995). Meeting the needs of people with developmental disabilities. *SIECUS Report*, 23, 9–13.

Wish, J., McCombs, K. and Edmonson, B. (1980). *The Socio-sexual Knowledge and Attitude Test*. Chicago: Stoelting.

Wood, M.H. (1985). Learning disabilities and human sexuality. *Academic Therapy*, 20(5), 543–7.

Zetlin, A.G. and Turner, J.L. (1985). Transition from adolescence to adulthood: Perspectives of mentally retarded individuals and their families. *American Journal of Mental Deficiency*, 89(6), 570–9.

ACKNOWLEDGEMENT

The Authors would like to thank Casey Hanson for helpful feedback on this chapter.

Section 7

Adulthood

Chapter 21

Living and working in the community

Patricia Noonan Walsh and Christine Linehan

> What are days for?
> Days are where we live.
> They come, they wake us
> Time and time over.
> They are to be happy in.
> Where can we live but days?
> > Philip Larkin

Today, people with intellectual disabilities may expect to live longer and to have a more visible presence in the communities where they live. These global trends will have a corresponding impact on the daily practice of clinical psychologists working with people who have intellectual disabilities, their families, support staff and other agents. Traditionally, meticulous assessment of performance was a priority so that clinicians might allocate adults with intellectual disabilities to niches within special day centres, workshops and residences. But today's practitioners are more likely to draw on constructs such as self-determination and quality of life to plan interventions on behalf of individuals in this group. Applying the American Association on Mental Retardation's definition and system of classification of intellectual disability means that practitioners must identify what supports individuals need and at what intensity so that they can strive to live satisfying, ordinary lives (AAMR, 2002).

Will collaborating with people to achieve their preferred life outcomes make clinical psychologists and their exemplary skills – such as assessment – redundant? On the contrary, support needs and personal competence are related but distinct constructs, and both need to be adequately assessed. Assessment serves the purpose of identifying an individual's needs for support at various levels of intensity and in different life domains. Put simply, clinical psychologists working within this framework must develop useful, supple ways to support adults with intellectual disabilities wherever they choose to live and work.

This chapter addresses two distinct but overlapping life domains of great importance for all adults, not least those with intellectual disabilities: living arrangements and employment. It addresses key research findings that may inform practice on the part of psychologists across their linked activities of assessment, formulation and intervention. Some ways to develop competence in supporting men and women in ordinary homes and employment are suggested. The chapter includes case studies to prompt reflection and identifies some ethical and professional issues to consider in shaping any interventions on behalf of adults with intellectual disabilities.

LIVING ARRANGEMENTS

Throughout the world, most people with intellectual disabilities rely on their families for support (Braddock and Parish, 2001). Poorer countries may have no history of building costly, separate residences for their citizens with intellectual disabilities. Elsewhere, evidence indicates that families are not merely the main carers, but the mainstay in providing a place to live. In 2003, almost two-thirds (61 per cent) of Irish people with intellectual disabilities at all ages lived in a 'home setting' with family or foster family. Nearly one third (30 per cent) of those aged over 35 years and 17 per cent of those aged 55 years or older lived with their families (Barron and Mulvany, 2004: Table 3.4). Irish government policy has applauded the role played by families as caregivers, and endorsed community living for adults with intellectual disabilities who have moved out of their family home or who have perhaps never lived at home (*Needs and Abilities*, 1991). Nonetheless, many hundreds of Irish adults are waiting to move from places that are not appropriate, such as family homes where elderly parents are long past the capacity to provide full-time primary care, or in purpose-built special residences rather than ordinary homes. And even now, it is likely that some Irish adults with intellectual disabilities will live out their lives in psychiatric hospital wards.

FAMILY LIFE

It has been estimated that more than half of adults with intellectual disabilities in the United Kingdom live with their families. A Government White Paper, *Valuing People* (2001), reported that in the previous thirty years, the numbers of people with intellectual disabilities living in NHS hospitals in the UK had declined steeply, and that very few children lived away from home. A similar pattern of family residence was apparent in a review of the evidence related to the living arrangements of people with intellectual disabilities in five countries – England, Wales, Australia, Canada and the USA (Braddock, Emerson, Felce and Stancliffe, 2001). However, these authors reported that as people aged they tended to move out of the family home.

Although family care is the dominant form of care for people with intellectual disabilities, relatively little research has documented the quality of life of adults living with their families rather than in publicly supported residential settings. In their extensive review of literature, Seltzer and Krauss (2001) observed that families follow a life course during which family members' relationships and roles change over time. But when a family member has intellectual disability, there may be altered stages of family life as adults may not depart from the family home as young adults, and their relationships with siblings may grow to reflect an expectation of providing care as all adult children reach middle and even older adulthood. Seltzer and Krauss concluded that family relationships have much to contribute to the quality of life of the individual with intellectual disability and that families are advised to make plans for the individual's future life.

Schalock and Verdugo (2002) have reviewed hundreds of publications related to quality of life and developed a set of *Caregiver Guidelines* related to the quality of life of families where a family member has an intellectual disability. As these authors note, 'A person's quality of life cannot be separated from the care provided or the people providing the care' (177). It is suggested that families may follow these guidelines – respect for privacy, opportunities for physical activity – in order to promote the quality of life of their family member (Schalock and Verdugo, 2002: Table 8.3). In practice, clinical psychologists may apply their skills to support families through any transitional stage in the family's life course – the death or illness of a parent, launch of a younger sibling and readjustment when other siblings marry and form their own households. They may also assist families in planning how best to support the family member with intellectual disability in the future, a process that make take some years. They can also help families avoid situations like those described in Box 21.1.

Box 21.1 Family care: another perspective

Family members are primary caregivers for most adults with intellectual disabilities. They may also act as the person's gatekeepers to the wider community. Lifelong habits of protecting the individual as a child and adolescent may fossilize and sometimes hinder the adult's exercise of decision-making. Too much care may halt self-determination – in matters related to health, for example. A woman living in the United Kingdom reported that 'I wanted some new false teeth but my brother wouldn't let me. He said it would make my face sore' (Keywood, Fovargue and Flynn, 1999: 2).

POLICY TRENDS

Policies in favour of community living surged from many sources to form a groundswell by the close of the twentieth century. Widespread social reform led the way in Norway and other Nordic countries (Tøssebro, Gustavsson and Dyrendahl, 1996). In the United States, decades of federal legislation mandated vast changes in living circumstances for people with intellectual disabilities. One after another, large 'training schools', hospitals and other institutions – some housing thousands of men and women in virtual towns – closed their doors (Braddock and Parish, 2001). Robert Perske recalls the residence for 200 children and adults in the Midwest of the United States where he served as chaplain in the 1960s:

> My institution contained wards of 40 persons. In each ward one found a large room with 40 beds in two or three long rows, a day room with many benches, and an aide station in the centre. At breakfast, lunch, and supper, the residents filled a large, noisy dining hall, very much like those Charles Dickens described in his novels. Also, the funerals of some of those I cared about took place with the undertaker at one end of the hole and me at the other. At that time it was deemed unprofessional for workers or other residents to attend the funerals of those they had cared for in life.

> (2004: 148)

In Ireland, congregate residential care for people with intellectual disabilities waxed until the middle of the last century. McCormack (2004) cites an eighteenth-century survey of some Dublin residents distinguished into two groups – fools and mad:

> In one early Dublin reference to individuals with specific disabilities, it was reported that in 1774 there were 'one mad woman, one foolish ditto, one ditto subject to fits and one boy fool' in James' Street Bridewell.

> (McCormack, 2004: 4)

Provision of care perhaps reached a nadir when people with intellectual disabilities were housed in the newly developed workhouses for paupers in the mid nineteenth century (Robins, 1986). While this solution was quickly deemed unsuitable, the workhouses nonetheless retained their role as shelters for some time, in spite of grave deficiencies in treatment for residents and the very low calibre of the often-unwilling assistants who worked there. Remnants of institutional living have persisted until the present, as this excerpt from the Report of the Inspector of Mental Hospitals in Ireland documented in 1988:

A [women's] dormitory with seven beds had no curtains. Many patients were in bed for the night at the time of our visit, 5:15 p.m. Another dormitory housed ten patients and was also without curtains . . . on the opposite wall a structure had been erected in which five patients were separately incarcerated. Each unit was roofed in the manner of a stall and each door was closed by three farmyard bolts. Mattresses were generally on the floor. These units did not have external windows or fresh air.

(McCormack, 2004: II)

Great strides towards community living, due in part to the initiatives of parents and friends associations as well as the ripple effect of normalization policies in other countries, contributed to the changing shape of residential supports in Ireland at the end of the twentieth century.

Has community living fulfilled its promise? Deinstitutionalization has been linked with positive outcomes for adults with intellectual disabilities in the United Kingdom. These included: increased user satisfaction; increased choice over day-to-day matters; increased participation in community-based activities; increased engagement in ongoing domestic and personal activities; and increased support from care staff (Emerson, 1994). Elsewhere, Emerson (2001) concluded that while deinstitutionalization has been associated with a range of benefits it had little impact on levels of challenging behaviour. These results are broadly comparable with those of North American and Australian studies investigating the process of deinstitutionalization (e.g. Kim, Larson and Lakin, 2001; Larson and Lakin, 1989; Young, Sigafoos, Suttie, Ashman and Grevell, 1998).

Regional policies also drove comprehensive service change. In the United Kingdom, the All Wales Strategy (http://www.wales.gov.uk/subisocialpolicy/content/mentalhealth/handicap/contents-e.htm; accessed 16 June 2006), for example, was launched in 1983 in order to secure a full life in the community for people with intellectual disabilities in Wales. The initiative was evaluated comprehensively over some years, with reports appearing in many publications. One achievement was radical reform of residential provision for people with intellectual disabilities, and Wales committed itself vigorously to the development of small, ordinary homes in the wake of hospital closures (Perry, Beyer, Felce and Todd, 1998).

In their account of the court-ordered closure of the Hissom Memorial Centre in Oklahoma, USA, Conroy, Spreat, Yuskauskas and Elks (2003) applied pre-post measures on many aspects of quality of life among 254 people moving to supported living in ordinary homes. They found significant improvements in individuals' adaptive and challenging behaviours, employment participation, hours of developmental service, integration in the community, contact with family and use of anti-psychotic medication. These authors commented that, while deinstitutionalization itself is part of a civil rights movement, any outcomes observed when residents move into ordinary homes in the community are properly the matter of scientific scrutiny. Their findings added to a growing body of evidence indicating that a move from congregate to community living is typically associated with heightened levels of adaptive behaviour on the part of residents.

OUTCOMES FOR RESIDENTS

Does place of residence make a difference in determining outcomes for individuals with intellectual disabilities? Emerson *et al.* summarized the findings of a large study of the quality and costs of adults with intellectual disabilities in a range of residential settings – large campus residences, village communities and dispersed housing schemes such as group homes. Data on the instruments applied in the study and the various outcomes are reported in detail elsewhere (Emerson, Robertson, Gregory, Hatton *et al.*, 2000a; 2001; Emerson, Robertson, Gregory, Kessissoglou *et al.*, 2000b; Emerson, Robertson, Hatton, Knapp and Walsh, 2005; Gregory, Robertson, Kessissoglou, Emerson and Hatton, 2001; Robertson, Emerson, Gregory, Hatton, *et al.*, 2001a; Robertson, Emerson, Hatton, Gregory *et al.*, 2001b; Walsh, Linehan, Hillery, Durkan *et al.*, 2001). Adults living in group homes or other **dispersed housing schemes** experienced relatively greater choice, more extensive social networks with people with intellectual disabilities, local people and overall, a more physically active life, fewer accidents in their home, and a greater number and variety of leisure activities.

On the other hand, residents in community-based settings such as group homes were also more likely to experience exposure to crime and verbal abuse, and a shorter 'working week'. Participants in **village communities** experienced relatively more extensive social networks overall, less exposure to crime and verbal abuse and a longer 'working week'. On the other hand, they could also expect to experience relatively less choice, and a reduced number and variety of leisure activities. Residents of larger, campus-type settings experienced relatively less choice, less extensive social networks, a less physically active life, more accidents in their home, a reduced number and variety of leisure activities, greater exposure to crime and verbal abuse and a shorter 'working week'.

PRACTICE IN RESIDENTIAL SETTINGS

In practice, psychologists may work throughout residential systems to support adults in residential settings – at individual, home unit and systems levels. Not so long ago, psychologists carried out their role in traditional service agencies by assessing individuals with a view to taking decisions about where they might live and what fine-tuning of adaptive skills they required to do so.

Typically, psychologists who work in residential settings assume the task of helping to assess and manage the challenging behaviours displayed by residents. Behaviours in this category may range from repetitive questions that staff find irritating, or stereotypy that hinders the individual's engagement in more productive, socially acceptable pursuits, to serious injury inflicted on oneself or others. Emerson (2001) suggests that key issues involved in assessment are: to identify what it is that the person does; to determine the impact of challenging behaviour upon the individual's quality of life; to try to understand the processes underlying such behaviour; and to propose possible alternatives to the behaviour. Assessment tools may include interviews, standardized scales, direct observation, functional analysis or some combination of these. Observational methods, some relying on technologies such as hand-held computers, have been applied in assessing behaviours in residential settings (Thompson, Felce and Symons, 2000: see Box 21.2).

Box 21.2 Skill development: observational assessment

Direct observation is an assessment strategy that is helpful in identifying factors that may contribute to an individual's behaviour in a group home setting, for example. It has advanced from the traditional pen and paper format to more sophisticated electronic recording (Thompson *et al.*, 2000). Hand-held computers – '*Psion Organizers*' – allow real-time recordings of multiple topographies of behaviour for the purpose of functional assessment and treatment planning (Emerson, Reeves and Felce, 2000; Emerson, Thompson, Reeves, Henderson and Robertson, 1995). Each category is assigned a button on the 'Organizer', which is pressed when the behaviour is observed. Categories may include behaviours such as 'Social Engagement', 'Challenging Behaviour toward Self or Other' and 'Collaborative Assistance by Staff'. Data may be downloaded using a DOS-based HARCLAG programme (Reeves, 1994a) and analysed for reliability using HARCREL (Reeves, 1994b) and statistically using SPSS.

Figure 21.1 is extracted from an observational study of twenty-six residents attending two forms of residential settings in Ireland, group homes and village campus settings (Walsh, Walsh, Linehan, Hillery *et al.*, 2000): details of measures and procedures, including steps to secure participants' informed consent, are available. It presents data from observational studies in graphic form. The figure presents the relationship between residents' level of ability and their engagement in stereotyped behaviours. The graph presents the duration of time residents were observed engaging in stereotyped behaviour on the Y axis. The residents are plotted on the X axis in ascending order of ability (as measured on the Adoptive Behavior Scale (ABS)). Figure 21.1 indicates that 69 per cent of the twenty-six residents observed engaged in stereotyped behaviour: those with higher ability scores were less likely to do so.

Figure 21.2 presents the frequency of behaviours (horizontal axis) classified under the category 'Interaction by Staff towards Resident' within the two residential models (Walsh *et al.*, 2000). The vertical axis displays the percentage of residents engaged in these behaviours. These data reveal that staff interaction with residents in village campus settings are characterized by 'negative restraint' (e.g. physically or verbally restraining a resident from engaging in a behaviour that may be harmful) and 'processing' (staff undertaking a task for a resident without encouraging the resident to participate in the task).

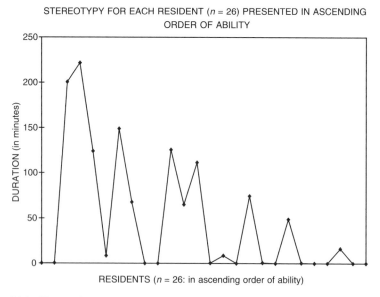

STEREOTYPY FOR EACH RESIDENT (*n* = 26) PRESENTED IN ASCENDING ORDER OF ABILITY

Figure 21.1 Observed stereotypy by residents' ability.

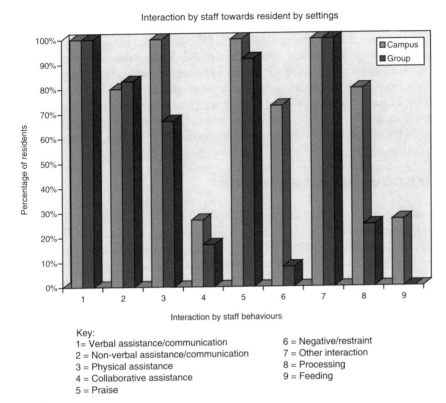

Interaction by staff towards resident by settings

Key:
1= Verbal assistance/communication
2 = Non-verbal assistance/communication
3 = Physical assistance
4 = Collaborative assistance
5 = Praise

6 = Negative/restraint
7 = Other interaction
8 = Processing
9 = Feeding

Figure 21.2 Staff Interactions by setting.

WORKING WITH SUPPORT STAFF

Typically, clinical psychologists may also assume the role of supporting and training frontline staff who provide direct care to residents with intellectual disabilities. Difficulties in recruiting and retaining staff may result in relatively high rates of staff turnover, and thus impede continuity of support to residents and development of skills. In the United States, Hewitt, Larson and Lakin (2000) cited reports of 30 per cent turnover rates for frontline supervisors in their study, which used job analysis and focus group techniques to develop a set of core competencies for supervisors in community services for people with intellectual disabilities. Competencies ranged widely, from 'maintaining homes, vehicles and property' to 'maintaining health and safety' (128). These authors suggested that further research is needed to determine whether heightened skills among frontline supervisors may be associated with better outcomes both for staff and residents.

When support staff in small group homes in the UK implemented 'active support', the outcomes for residents were significantly increased engagement in meaningful activity and adaptive behaviour; a comparison group home showed no significant change (Mansell, Elliott, Beadle-Brown, Ashman and Macdonald, 2002). Elsewhere Mansell, Beadle-Brown, Macdonald and Ashman (2003) investigated the effects of functional grouping of people with intellectual disabilities on care practices in small residential community-based homes. They found that higher adaptive behaviour of residents and mixed settings predicted better care practices on the Active Support Measure (ASM). Care practices varied only for people with challenging behaviour.

LIFE COURSE TRANSITIONS

As men and women with intellectual disabilities grow and change throughout their increasingly longer lives, they negotiate life transitions that are simply part of the human condition. They will encounter family worries, the pleasure of achievement, happy times with friends, new learning, travel or other adventures, a sense of loss as their companions and family members die and what their own aging means.

When 167 older women with intellectual disabilities in eighteen countries spoke about their life experiences and dreams for the future, many showed resilience honed during years of living in arduous circumstances and with great personal loneliness (Walsh and LeRoy, 2004). Most of the women appraised their living arrangements as adequate, and some were happy. Yet a recurring theme of the women's narratives was that they had to make efforts to cope day after day with irritating co-residents, bossy staff and disagreeable furnishings not of their choosing. It was clear that institutional practices – making residents wake up or take showers at the same time, for example – had seeped into many different types of residential settings, even smaller community homes. Some women dreamed that one day they might live just as they pleased with people for whom they cared. A lifelong sense of loss through removal from home and family as children, or because of the death of the women's mothers – even if this had taken place years ago – was threaded through these narratives. Others spoke of abiding fears: 'My mother – I am afraid when she dies. I am afraid I will be alone; (I) Worry about my family, how they cope, what will happen to my parents as they get older, and my brother and sisters' (Walsh and LeRoy, 2004: ch. 7).

Inevitably, psychologists working with individuals with intellectual disabilities and their direct support staff will confront death, dying and bereavement issues. Adults with intellectual disabilities may be expected to show culturally familiar responses to bereavement – being sad or anxious or angry – and to understand that death is irreversible (Harper and Wadsworth, 1993). Yet their family members or professional workers may not interpret these responses appropriately, especially if adults who have recently been bereaved may lack the eloquence or opportunities to relate their feelings and find comfort. In some cultures people with intellectual disabilities may even be excluded from funeral rites and rituals (Raji, Hollins and Drinnan, 2003), thus exacerbating a sense of loss and isolation. They may express their distress and loneliness in ways that demand sensitivity and perspicacity on the part of clinicians. MacHale and Carey (2002) found that a group of bereaved adults in Ireland differed from peers who had not been bereaved in measures of mental health and challenging behaviour. Support for staff may take the form of a training programme in bereavement issues.

Increased life expectancy for adults with intellectual disabilities may yield wider opportunities and richer experiences, but also a greater likelihood of age-related risks to health, such as dementia. Alzheimer's disease is the major cause of dementia, and is a significant risk factor for adults with Down syndrome. The onset of dementia – typically apparent in loss of memory and competence in activities of daily living – has a profound impact on all aspects of the individual's well-being and triggers important decisions for long-term support (Janicki, McCallion and Dalton, 2000). These authors list some questions for residential service managers: will the building in which the individual with dementia lives be modified easily? What funds are available for this purpose? Will others in the home be affected? Will staff require additional training? Does the service agency endorse *aging in place*, that is, readaptation of the existing home rather than abrupt removal of the individual, as a policy?

Psychologists working with older adults with dementia living in community settings may engage in decision-making from assessment to planning and monitoring long-term daily supports and ultimately how to support family members, friends and staff members as the individual nears the end of her/his life. There is a lack of appropriate residential and day services for people in this group – in the UK, for example (Turk, Dodd and Christmas, 2001).

Looking ahead, it is evident that developing best practice in identifying the needs of older men and women with intellectual disabilities and supporting them and their family members – particularly those who are vulnerable to dementia and other age-related disorders – is a priority for clinicians in a greying Europe.

Psychologists contribute to all aspects of the living arrangements for people with intellectual disabilities. They cite research evidence to shape practice, and indeed carry out research, provide staff development and training, and apply their skills to support individuals and their family members. Overall, diverse views on where men and women with intellectual disabilities should live have fuelled considerable debate, although the voices of people themselves have only lately emerged. In Northern Ireland, Smyth and McConkey (2003) explored what people think about where they live now and where they wish to live in the future. It was striking that so many participants named having their own key to the front door as a personal priority.

Research should inform policies to shape residential supports that are more likely to yield measurable benefits for men and women with intellectual disabilities. In practice, this means supporting individuals so that they may lead satisfying lives in a setting that resembles 'a good family home' (*Needs and Abilities*, 1991: 38). Psychologists may contribute to the strength and flexibility of the scaffolding set in place so that men and women may pursue this fundamental life goal.

EMPLOYMENT

Wherever they live, most adults seek daily occupation. Those with intellectual disabilities in developing countries may contribute to family income, for example – and thus to their own livelihood – by working in fields or shops (O'Toole and McConkey, 1995). In countries with developed market economies and systems of health and social care, options are rather different. Although recently promoted as a rightful opportunity for all people regardless of ability level (UN, 1994), ordinary paid employment remains elusive for people with intellectual disabilities. In Ireland, a minority of adults in this group are engaged in supported or other open forms of employment, and patterns of occupation are associated with level of ability. According to the National Intellectual Disability Database, most Irish adults with a mild level of intellectual disability who avail of any day services attend sheltered work centres (35 per cent), special vocational training (13 per cent), supported employment (13 per cent) or activation programmes (12 per cent). By contrast, adults with moderate, severe or profound levels are more likely to attend activation programmes (39 per cent), sheltered work (26 per cent), special vocational training (8 per cent), support services (8 per cent) or high support services (4 per cent) (Barron and Mulvany, 2004: 39). Most attend sheltered work or day activity programmes.

During the 1980s and 1990s, European-funded initiatives in favour of social and vocational integration paradoxically strengthened special vocational training or employment. In Ireland, for example, many adults worked at contract assembly or production jobs as long-term *trainees* for a token weekly wage. To fit such schemes, they underwent assessment to determine their suitability for special vocational and other day activity programmes.

Ordinary employment

Two paradoxes emerge when current patterns of daily occupation or employment for adults with intellectual disabilities are surveyed. First, in terms of practice, while supported employment was devised a generation ago specifically to enable people with more severe levels of disability to secure ordinary jobs, people in this population are most often excluded from these opportunities. And second, although sheltered workplaces dominate the landscape for adults with disabilities in many European countries and elsewhere, there is surprisingly little empirical evidence to support retention of this model of employment. Far more research findings have emerged about the quality and outcomes of supported and other forms of inclusive employment and their meaning for adults with intellectual disabilities.

Fundamentally, the question, 'who should work?' asks whether people with intellectual disabilities are equipped to seek employment. Adults may find that only sheltered work is available, or perhaps none at all. But the question triggers wider issues rooted in social values and policies: cultural assumptions play their part in shaping diverse interpretations of what 'community employment' means for people with disabilities (Walsh, Mank, Beyer, Macdonald and O'Bryan, 1999). Is competitive employment desirable? Should it be foisted on people with complex disabilities or older folk edging near what would be retirement age for their peers? Do sheltered forms of work provide greater stability and companionship? Or is ordinary employment, with or without support, the defining moment for all adults, regardless of their capacities?

Supported employment emerged during the past three decades, and may be defined as helping individuals to find, get and keep real jobs with a real income, with ongoing support as required. Gradually, the notion of ongoing supports to maintain employees in the workplace successfully extended to include 'natural supports' (Nisbet and Hagner, 1988). In their critical review, Wehman and Bricout (1999) concluded that co-workers are most frequently identified as natural supports for the employee with disabilities. Some authors extend this term to include families, friends and community workers, while others distinguish paid from unpaid supports.

By placing the individual in a likely job and providing tailor-made training and other supports on site, the approach was fundamentally different to traditional models in which people with intellectual disabilities spent many years in special training for jobs that might never be realized. Evidence suggests that individuals in supported employment stand to make widespread gains, apart from obvious increases in earned income and hours of community contact.

Satisfactory employment potentially yields personal and social benefits for employees. In their review of literature on social relationships in the workplace, Chadsey and Beyer (2001) observed that close relationships are associated with a number of positive outcomes for employees – happiness, less stress – and that these outcomes should be pursued on behalf of individuals with disabilities who are employed competitively. Psychologists working with adults with intellectual disabilities who enter ordinary employment may adopt strategies to change social behaviours and also to nurture natural supports already embedded in the workplace – by training co-workers without disabilities to involve themselves with employees with disabilities, for example (Mank, Cioffi and Yovanoff, 1999).

Evidence suggests that people with disabilities who live or work in community-based settings are more self-determined, have higher autonomy, have more choices and are more satisfied than their peers – matched for age and intelligence – living or working in congregate settings (Wehmeyer and Bolding, 1999). Elsewhere, significant differences in locus of control scores were observed between adults with cognitive and developmental disabilities who were employed competitively and those who were either unemployed or employed in sheltered settings (Wehmeyer, 1994).

Some job attributes predict better outcomes for employees with intellectual disabilities. More typical jobs – that is, jobs that more closely resembled typical jobs in a given sector – have been found to yield more positive benefits for supported employees (Mank, Cioffi and Yovanoff, 1997). Women with intellectual disabilities in ordinary employment have shown themselves at a disadvantage in terms of job type and income, and more likely to work in jobs traditionally stereotyped by gender. In a United States study, women with intellectual disabilities worked fewer hours and accordingly earned less money than men (Olsen, Cioffi, Yovanoff and Mank, 2000).

Evidence related to larger populations or regional studies suggests striking patterns in finding and keeping employment. Participants with intellectual disabilities in the United States who had good physical and emotional health, were male, were aged between 18 and 49 years, had an IQ between 50 and 75 and good adaptive skills were more likely to be employed (McDermott, Martin and Butkus, 1999). When they do find and keep paid jobs for three or more years, adults with intellectual disabilities may cluster in particular sectors such as food service or manufacturing (Pierce, McDermott and Butkus, 2003). In their analysis of population-based data in the United States, Yamaki and Fujiura (2002) concluded that most adults with developmental disabilities were unemployed and most – including those who had jobs – reported incomes near or below the poverty level.

Overall, the personal, social and economic benefits of ordinary employment have been documented, yet it remains a minority option for most adults with intellectual disabilities. It is likely that systemic factors such as local or regional funding mechanisms, staff development and training priorities and service agency traditions help to maintain current patterns (see Box 21.3). Accordingly, psychologists in countries with formal service systems, such as Ireland and the UK, will engage with individuals at different stages of employment. Some men and women may actively seek or have already found employment, others attend congregate work programmes such as sheltered workshops and still others wish to move from a sheltered to an ordinary job in the community. Many adults may prefer not to work or will never have a chance to do so. Options for these men and women currently range from high-quality, individualized support programmes (see Box 21.4) that offer adult education, volunteering, sport and leisure or other community experiences to traditional day rooms where anything might or might not happen.

Box 21.3 John Paul: a case study

Last week things came to breaking point in the workshop. Gerry, the manager, asked the psychologist for advice on how to manage John Paul's disruptive behaviour. Lately John Paul, aged 24, has been downing tools at the bench, distracting the other workers and talking back when the supervisor in his section instructs him. Observing John Paul in the workplace (see Box 21.2 on Skill Development) did not reveal any consistent pattern related to the particular task at hand or the time of day or what the supervisor said. But when Dr O'Brien – who recently joined the psychology team – interviewed him, John Paul said that he just doesn't like the noisy assembly bench, and reckons that the token payment he receives each Friday doesn't buy much – so why bother? Besides, his girlfriend, Sarah, has just got a job in the local hotel and he thinks it is not fair for him to be stuck in the workshop. He points out that one summer after he left the special school in the next town he helped out at his uncle's garage, and still talks about how well he can valet cars now. Besides, he really enjoyed the talk and the company of the other men there very much.

What is keeping John Paul from making a move? Parallel lines may meet in infinity – but rarely in day-to-day practice. Most adults in this traditional service organization travel each day to the timeworn sheltered workshop, while only a handful scatter to their part-time jobs in local restaurants and shops. Senior managers argue that there is a demand for maintaining both employment tracks, although the costs of doing so are considerable and do not leave any reserves for new ventures. Older parents fear that a move to a real job will result in their sons and daughters losing out on hours of supervised activity each week, whether in sheltered work or an adjoining day centre. Budget cutbacks hit hard last year and there are no easy ways to free-up more staff to support individuals like John Paul in ordinary jobs in ones or twos, and at the same time ensure that enough experienced staff are retained in the workshop to keep up production rates. Besides, the profits generated by the sale of workshop products return as discretionary income and this is disbursed with good intentions – funding annual holidays for some service users, for example. Dr O'Brien has been gathering evidence to make a case for closing the workshop and reallocating resources so that people may live and work where they wish. She believes that the team should support John Paul and other young adults who have expressed a preference for a real job in the course of their person-centred plans. But it seems that for the moment they will have to wait.

Box 21.4 Person-centred planning

Person-centred planning is a complex route to a simple destination: the individual's vision of how he or she wishes to lead a life. It refers to an array of models with a unifying principle, a focus on the individual so as to identify what he or she needs to achieve that vision.

> The essence of person-centred planning is to listen closely
> to the hearts of people with disabilities and to imagine with
> them a better world in which they can be valued members,
> contribute and belong.
>
> (Holburn and Vietze, 2002: xxi)

Friends, family members and professionals are invited to work collaboratively to build supports according to the individual's preferences. By contrast, a traditional approach might fit the person to the mould – for example asking if an individual might be 'suitable for' a particular residence or type of occupation.

Various models of person-centred planning are likely to become more widespread in interventions on behalf of people with intellectual disabilities, given a recent policy statement in England, *Valuing People* (2001) that endorsed person-centred planning as the lead approach in implementing policies. Currently – an evaluation process is under way in the UK to determine the impact of person-centred planning and other policy-driven initiatives (Walsh, 2003).

In Ireland, the NDA – National Disability Authority – has established a set of national standards to appraise services for people with intellectual and other disabilities. A pilot programme was under review at time of writing.

Practice with adults in day or employment settings

Not so long ago, assessment was the chief professional task carried out by psychologists. They carried their wares in a toolbox of standardized measures to assess individuals' suitability for vocational training or employment (Walsh, 2005a). Answering the query, 'Is this person employable?' was traditionally the reason for referral. By contrast functional models have supplanted traditional, structured models of assessment (Walsh, 2005b). A current approach is to ask: 'What will it take to obtain a job that maximally enhances the quality of his or her life?' (Pancsofar and Steere, 1997: 108):

these authors outline an assessment process coupling situational assessment with an individual profile.

Broadly, assessment may be defined as the process by which information is gathered in order 'to guide the design and implementation of constructional and socially valid intervention' (Emerson, 1998: 114). The findings of this process should inform other stages of practice. For example, Davies and Hastings (2003) have reviewed the potential uses of computer technology in clinical psychology services for people with intellectual disabilities, concluding that technologies can facilitate practitioners at each of three stages – assessment, formulation and intervention.

In the past, men and women with intellectual disabilities and others who lived for many years in hospitals or large congregate residential settings traditionally spent their days in home-grown activities – cleaning or working in gardens and laundries (Robins, 1986). Leisure pursuits were similarly confined to day rooms or group recreation within or outside the walls: special holiday camps and bus tours persist even today. As more adults moved to the community, other forms of day activity emerged: special day centres or ATCs – adult training centres (Race, 1995) offering a mix of craftwork, physical activation and independent skill training for several hours daily. Yet the research base underpinning the quality and outcomes for participants of day services – rather than supported employment – remains slender (McConkey, 2001).

In Ireland, the NDA (National Disability Authority) prepared a report on current patterns of occupation and recommended strategies to achieve best practice in further education, employment and training for people with disabilities (NDA, 2003). The report named an absence of basic data on how many Irish people with various disabilities are involved in these services, or how they may progress within the system, as a major information gap (2003: 84).

Adults with intellectual disabilities who already live in, or move to, homes in the community, may have varied options for daily occupation. Those served by large, *one-stop* service agencies – a long-standing tradition in Ireland, for example – may tap into an array of day activities, sheltered work or supported employment programmes. Opportunities for daily occupation varied by type of residence for UK participants in the large study summarized by Emerson *et al.* (2005). In the United Kingdom, residents in community settings such as group homes may or may not find local employment or adult education: if so it is typically provided by another, separately funded agency within the area. Trying to please all members of a group with diverse preferences at all ages has often resulted in very little satisfaction for anyone using omnibus day services – prompting questions about their utility, apart from the obvious purpose of providing a focal point for individuals and perhaps respite for their family carers. One response has been the growth of fresh approaches based on person-centred planning processes in which individuals are supported to identify and gain their own life goals – including daily occupation. Current options include involvement in volunteer work, further education and inclusive programmes in community development, sport and leisure.

Putting practice in context

In practice, some psychologists will address individual needs and preferences, and engage with family carers, perhaps over many years. Others work within service systems focused on residential or employment services, or some combination of these. Mastering a complex human service system means learning the rules of engagement with local custom and practice in the surrounding region. Consider St Jude's Centre, whose board has adopted a mission statement aiming at community inclusion for all the people whom it serves. Understandably, at St Jude's the staff pride themselves on offering real jobs with real wages to all adults using its day programmes as the default option for daily occupation.

Mere miles away, the ironclad statutory body coordinates all of its regional services through a central clinic housed in a now-defunct sanatorium. Residents therein are chiefly middle-aged and expect little more than lifelong rural seclusion. Although some men and women welcome employment to eke out their pocket money, it is chiefly contract work imported from neighbouring towns and carried out within the residence's grounds. And yet each provider may claim that its services deserve high marks for quality assurance and that the men and women who use these services experience community living. Each agency may attract thankful appraisals from parents and other relatives, illustrating the widespread finding that, in the main, relatives express satisfaction with the services provided to their family members, no matter how disparate their features (Walsh et al., 2001).

As people with intellectual disabilities become embedded in their communities, clinical psychologists and other professionals will increasingly practise in dispersed settings. Whatever the context of practice – rural or urban, congregate or local, residential or employment, traditional or cutting-edge – it seems that individualized supports for people with intellectual disabilities will potentially contribute to their enhanced quality of life and community engagement. But moving this worthy professional activity from theory to practice is a work still in progress, as illustrated by Box 21.3.

Work in progress

Private and public domains intersect at the point where an individual encounters support: personal intimacy, friendship, adult education, behavioural skills, instrumental assistance in carrying out daily tasks, income or other benefits in kind. As tools like person-centred planning are applied more widely within human and social service systems, it is likely that adults with intellectual disabilities will experience greater opportunities to direct the course of their lives (Holburn and Vietze, 2002: see Box 21.4 on person-centred planning).

Grounding practice in real-world settings entails dilemmas – both risks and benefits – such as how to manage risk, how to engage with the wider community and how to find evidence to buttress emerging, more complex interventions. How best might one support two adults who choose to live by themselves in an apartment with minimal support, for example?

Risk and autonomy

Life in prosperous, fast-changing twenty-first-century Europe is not without risk for any citizen. People with intellectual disabilities are at least as likely, perhaps more so, to encounter insecure employment, exposure to taunts or unscrupulous neighbours whom the individual meets in the community. They are also vulnerable to physical and sexual abuse. Perhaps the best option is to strive for a balance between exposure to risk and the underlying drive towards greater self-determination by promoting the individual's competence.

Building community skills

Fresh approaches to practice mean that clinical psychologists must develop competence extending beyond a toolkit, clinic, classroom or workshop. In the future, they will engage with diverse community agents – on the shop floor or in a local firm, in the realms of adult education, sport and leisure, public health, and local facilities such as the library or swimming pool. Individualized supports means that someone has to assemble a troupe of would-be supporters for a focus individual and group them so as to make realistic plans. This is an endeavour closer to choreography than engineering, and certainly far removed from administering a standardized checklist.

Joining up practice and research

In this aspect of clinical work, as in others in health and human services, research, policy, practice do not always triangulate. An agency's practices may diverge markedly from national or regional policy. Research evidence may be available on the shelf, but not underpin policy or practice in a service agency where traditional structures resist change. These disparities may provoke new ethical or professional quandaries (see Box 21.5).

Box 21.5 Ethical and professional issues: case study of Nancy

Is Nancy suitable? – in this case, for open employment. She is a fit, cheerful woman with intellectual disabilities nearing 40. Nancy has attended a sheltered workshop for nearly twenty years but now she would like to try a part-time job in a gift shop in a nearby town. She lives with her widowed mother, Sadie, aged 83. Sadie resists any change in daily arrangements for her daughter, as the two women have lived together and helped each other for many years in their modest house-hold. Just how long do parental wishes hold sway? Opinions among professionals in a service agency may vary a good deal.

Dr Murphy, recently qualified, is one of the clinicians who support employment and other day programmes in Nancy's service agency. He is eager to press ahead with individualized support planning for Nancy and other adults using services, given their undeniable human right to help determine the shape of their own lives. He has cited publications showing that successful open employment is likely to yield many benefits for Nancy and people like her – more opportunities to meet and befriend other people without disabilities in the wider community, more income and an enriched sense of personal control and confidence. Dr Murphy believes that the combined evidence drawn from several sources – Nancy's own preferences, global rights directives, EU disability policy and academic data about employment outcomes – will ultimately win the day. Perhaps he should keep telling everyone in Nancy's agency about the exceptionally good employment services in the agency abroad where he completed a placement just last year.

A separate clinic team is responsible for direct support to families such as Nancy's. For many years Nancy's mother has depended on home visits from Ms Barton, a social worker with considerable experience and authority who has become a family friend. Ms Barton points out that the agency endeavours to support families, mainly by providing them with a break when their sons or daughters have 6–7 hours of reliable, well-supervised occupation at a day centre or workshop five days weekly. After all, some elderly parents strive to care for their adult children in trying circumstances as the waitlist for residential care lengthens month by month. Some family members, such as Nancy's married brothers, fear that a move to open employment will mean a decline in benefits for the household and a more lonely life for their relative with intellectual disabilities. Nancy would only work part-time and the earnings would amount to not much more than pocket money to supplement a weekly allowance that helps the whole family. Besides, the workshop is a pivotal point for clinical services, companionship and recreation. Arguably, Nancy will be just as content, and her mother will be much more at ease, if things stay as they are.

SUMMARY

Demography, global and national policies and the weight of evidence about optimal supports for adults in community settings will drive the shape of clinical psychology practice with people who have intellectual disabilities. They will apply their skills with individuals, couples, families and the community so as to enhance the lives of people in this population. In addition, psychologists make valuable contributions at service system level by helping to plan and manage interventions and supports for people with intellectual disabilities. Often, psychologists are relied on to carry out evaluation studies and other forms of service-based research. Regionally and nationally, psychologists have a part to play in shaping policy.

Supporting people in pursuit of desired life outcomes is a long-term pursuit. Thus any other aspect of clinical practice – therapeutic work, applying behavioural analysis, appraising risk of abuse, working with family systems or managing challenging behaviour may be interwoven with efforts to support people with intellectual disabilities where they live and work now, and wherever they wish to live and work in the future.

FURTHER READING AND RESOURCES FOR FAMILIES AND CLIENTS

Further reading

Bray, A. (2003). *Work for Adults with an Intellectual Disability*. Wellington NZ: National Health Committee (http://www.nhc.govt.nz). Reviews the literature for the National Advisory Committee on Health and Disability to inform its project on services for adults with an intellectual disability.

Dixon, T. (2001). *Shared Ownership for People with Learning Disabilities*. BILD. http://www.bild.org.uk/.

Harker, M. and King, N. (2002). *Renting Your Own Home: Housing Options for People with Learning Disabilities*. BILD. http://www.bild.org.uk/.

Holburn, S. and Vietze, P. (eds) (2002). *Person-Centred Planning: Research, Practice and Future Directions*. Baltimore: Paul H. Brookes Publishing. Various models and recent evidence about the efficacy of person-centred planning are presented in this book.

Kroese, B. (1998). *Choosing Your New Home*. BILD. http://www.bild.org.uk/.

Resources

Face to Face – Respectful Coping with Dementia in Older People with Intellectual Disability (1995). Video and accompanying booklets available from Centre for Disability Studies, UCD. cds@ucd.ie.

The Foundation for People with Intellectual Disability (www.learningdisabilities.org.uk) in the UK publishes research summaries and guidelines of topics related to living and working conditions for people with intellectual disabilities.

Irish Union for Supported Employment promotes best practice in supported employment for people with disability. National Office, c/o Brothers of Charity Services, Failte House, John Paul Centre, Ballybane, Galway <michaelfleming@galway.brothersofcharity.ie>.

LABOR website available through website of European Association of Service Providers for People with Disabilities (EASPD) (www.easpd.org) includes abstracts of publications related to supported employment.

Living My Own Life, a film by Michael Loukinen (2000), is available from the Developmental Disabilities Institute, Wayne State University, 4809 Woodward Avenue, Suite 268, Detroit, Michigan, USA (fax +1–313–577–3770). This video gives an account of six men and women with disabilities who have moved into more independent lives in the community through person-centred planning initiatives.

namhi, 5 FitzWilliam Place, Dublin 2 (www.namhi.ie) is the national voluntary agency for advocacy and policy related to people with intellectual disabilities in Ireland.

FURTHER READING FOR CLINICIANS

Chadsey, J. and Beyer, S. (2001). Social Relationships in the Workplace. *Intellectual Disability and Developmental Disabilities Research Reviews*, 7(2), 128–33.

Davies, S. and Hastings, R. (2003). Computer Technology in Clinical Psychology Services for People with Intellectual Disability: A Review. *Education and Training in Intellectual Disability and Developmental Disabilities*, 38, 341–52.

Schalock, R.S. and Verdugo, M.-A. (2002). *Handbook on Quality of Life for Human Services Practitioners*. Washington DC: AAMR.

Turk, V., Dodd, K. and Christmas, M. (2001). *Down's Syndrome and Dementia – Briefing for Commissioners*. Briefing paper from the GOLD – Growing Older with Intellectual Disability – programme supported by the Foundation for People with Intellectual Disability, UK <www.learningdisabilities.org.uk>.

ASSESSMENT INSTRUMENTS

Bennett, George K. (1985). *Bennett Hand-Tool Dexterity Test* (H-TDT) (Psychology Corporation). Available from: Harcourt Assessment, 1 Procter Street, London WC1V 6EU UK.

Stancliffe, R. and Lakin, K. (eds) (In press). *Costs and Outcomes: Community Services for People with Intellectual Disabilities*. Baltimore: Brookes Publishing. Contains instruments and procedures widely used to measure the quality and costs of residential settings for people with intellectual disabilities.

Stromberg Dexterity Test measures the speed and accuracy of arm and hand coordination (Stromberg, 1985). A candidate sorts discs and inserts them into a form board as quickly as possible.

Transferable Skills Analysis is an assessment procedure applied in vocational rehabilitation in an attempt to quantify functional abilities (Dunn and Growick, 2000).

Valpar's products rely heavily on *criterion-referenced* testing, using an objective standard of achievement <http://www.valparint.com/>.

Walsh, P.N. (2005a). Outside the box: Assessment for life and work in the community. In: J. Hogg and A. Langa (eds), *Assessing Adults with Intellectual Disabilities: A Service Provider's Guide* (Part 1: Conceptual and contextual issues) (pp. 23–8). Oxford: Blackwell.

Walsh, P.N. (2005b). Assessment – Part 2: Assessment and employment of people with intellectual disabilities: assessment strategies. In J. Hogg and A. Langa (eds), *Assessing Adults with Intellectual Disabilities: A Service Provider's Guide* (Part 2: Assessment strategies and instruments) (pp. 138–51). Oxford: Blackwell. These two references by Walsh discuss employment-related approaches to assessment and the following measures of performance traditionally applied in vocational settings.

Work Ability Tables or WAT assessments aim to quantify an individual's work-related level of function. The tables generate a profile of nine core work abilities, including the ability to report for work regularly, to communicate with others and manipulate objects, among other tasks. A candidate's numerical score determines whether the individual is referred to a disability employment service (Sutherland and Kirby, 2000).

REFERENCES

AAMR (2002). *Mental Retardation: Definition, Classification, and Systems of Supports* (10th edn, AAMR 10). Washington, DC: American Association on Mental Retardation.

Barron, S. and Mulvany, F. (2004). *National Intellectual Disability Database Committee – Annual Report 2003*. Dublin: Health Research Board.

Bennett, George K. (1985). *Bennett Hand-Tool Dexterity Test* (H-TDT) Available from: Harcourt Assessment, 1 Procter Street, London WC1V 6EU UK.

Braddock, D., Emerson, E., Felce, D. and Stancliffe, R.J. (2001). Living circumstances of children and adults with mental retardation or developmental disabilities in the United States, Canada, England and Wales, and Australia. *Mental Retardation and Developmental Disabilities Research Reviews*, 7, 115–21.

Braddock, D. and Parish, S. (2001). Disability history from antiquity to the Americans with Disabilities Act. In G.L. Albrecht, K.D. Seelman and M. Bury (eds), *Handbook of Disability Studies* (pp. 11–68). Thousand Oaks, CA: Sage.

Chadsey, J. and Beyer, S. (2001). Social relationships in the workplace. *Mental Retardation and Developmental Disabilities Research Reviews*, 7(2), 128–33.

Conroy, J., Spreat, S., Yuskauskas, A. and Elks, M. (2003). The Hissom closure outcomes study: A report on six years of movement to supported living. *Mental Retardation*, 41(4), 263–75.

Davies, S. and Hastings, R. (2003). Computer technology in clinical psychology services for people with intellectual disability: A review. *Education and Training in Intellectual Disability and Developmental Disabilities*, 38, 341–52.

Dunn, P.L. and Growick, B.S. (2000). Transferable skills analysis in vocational rehabilitation: Historical foundations, current status, and future trends. *Journal of Vocational Rehabilitation*, 14, 79–87.

Emerson, E. (1994). Deinstitutionalisation in England. *Journal of Intellectual and Developmental Disability*, 29, 79–84.

Emerson, E. (1998). Assessment. In E. Emerson, C. Hatton, J. Bromley and A. Caine (eds), *Clinical Psychology and People with Intellectual Disabilities* (pp. 114–24). Chichester: John Wiley and Sons.

Emerson, E. (2001). *Challenging Behaviour: Analysis and Intervention in People with Intellectual Disabilities* (2nd edn). Cambridge: Cambridge University Press.

Emerson, E., Hatton, C., Bromley, J. and Caine, A. (eds) (1998). *Clinical Psychology and People with Intellectual Disabilities*. Chichester: John Wiley and Sons.

Emerson, E., Reeves, D. and Felce, D. (2000). Palm-top computer technologies for behavioural observation in research. In T. Thompson, D. Felce and F. Symons, *Behavioural Observation Technology and Applications in Developmental Disabilities*. Baltimore, MD: Paul H. Brooks.

Emerson, E., Robertson, J., Gregory, N., Hatton, C., Kessissoglou, S., Hallam, A. *et al.* (2001). Quality and costs of supported living residences and group homes in the United Kingdom. *American Journal on Mental Retardation*, 106(5), 401–15.

Emerson, E., Robertson, J., Gregory, N., Hatton, C., Kessissoglou, S., Hallam, A. *et al.* (2000a). Quality and costs of community-based residential supports, village communities, and residential campuses in the United Kingdom. *American Journal on Mental Retardation*, 105(2), 81–102.

Emerson, E., Robertson, J., Gregory, N., Kessissoglou, S., Hatton, C., Hallam, A. *et al.* (2000b). The quality and costs of community-based residential supports and residential campuses for people with severe and complex disabilities. *Journal of Intellectual and Developmental Disability*, 25(4), 263–79.

Emerson, E., Robertson, J., Hatton, C., Knapp, M. and Walsh, P.N. (2005). A comparison of costs and outcomes of supported accommodation in England. In R.J. Stancliffe and K.C. Lakin (eds), *Costs and Outcomes: Community Services for People with Intellectual Disabilities*. Baltimore: Brookes Publishing.

Emerson, E., Thompson, S., Reeves, D., Henderson, D. and Robertson, J. (1995). Descriptive analysis of multiple response topographies of challenging behaviour across two settings. *Research in Developmental Disabilities*, 16(4), 301–29.

Gregory, N., Robertson, J., Kessissoglou, S., Emerson, E. and Hatton, C. (2001). Factors associated with expressed satisfaction among people with intellectual disability receiving residential supports. *Journal of Intellectual Disability Research*, 45, 279–92.

Harper, D.C. and Wadsworth, J.S. (1993). Grief in adults with mental retardation: Preliminary findings. *Research in Developmental Disabilities*, 14, 313–30.

Hewitt, A., Larson, S.A. and Lakin, K.C. (2000). An independent evaluation of the quality of services and system performance of Minnesota's Medicaid Home and Community Based Services for persons with mental retardation and related conditions. Minneapolis: University of Minnesota, Research and Training Centre on Community Living. Available from Research and Training Center on Community Living, University of Minnesota http://rtc.umn.edu/publications/. Website accessed 16 June 2006.

Holburn, S. and Vietze, P. (eds) (2002). *Person-Centred Planning: Research, Practice and Future Directions*. Baltimore: Paul H. Brookes Publishing.

Janicki, M.P., McCallion, P. and Dalton, A.J. (2000). Supporting people with dementia in community settings. In M.P. Janicki and E.F. Ansello (eds), *Community Supports for Aging Adults with Lifelong Disabilities* (pp. 387–413). Baltimore MD: Paul H. Brookes Publishing.

Keywood, K., Fovargue, S. and Flynn, M. (1999). *Adults with Learning Difficulties' Involvement in Health Care Decision-Making*. York: Joseph Rowntree Foundation.

Kiernan, W.E. and Schalock, R.L. (eds) (1997). *Integrated Employment: Current Status and Future Directions*. Washington DC: AAMR.

Kim, S., Larson, S.A. and Lakin, K.C. (2001). Behavioural outcomes of deinstitutionalisation for people with intellectual disability: A review of US studies conducted between 1980 and 1999. *Journal of Intellectual and Developmental Disability: Special Issue: Part II: Community Living and People with Intellectual Disability*, 26(1), 35–50.

Larson, S.A. and Lakin, K.C. (1989). Deinstitutionalization of persons with mental retardation: Behavioural outcomes. *Journal of the Association for Persons with Severe Handicaps (JASH)*, 14(4), 324–32.

Mank, D., Cioffi, A. and Yovanoff, P. (1997). Analysis of the typicalness of supported employment jobs, natural supports, and wage and integration outcomes. *Mental Retardation*, 35, 185–97.

Mank, D., Cioffi, A. and Yovanoff, P. (1999). Impact of coworker involvement with supported employees on wage and integration outcomes. *Mental Retardation*, 37, 383–94.

Mansell, J., Beadle-Brown, J., Macdonald, S. and Ashman, B. (2003). Functional grouping in residential homes for people with intellectual disabilities. *Research in Developmental Disabilities*, 24, 170–82.

Mansell, J., Elliott, T., Beadle-Brown, J., Ashman, B. and Macdonald, Susan (2002). Engagement in meaningful activity and 'active support' of people with intellectual disabilities in residential care. *Research in Developmental Disabilities*, 23, 342–52.

McConkey, R. (2001). Community care and resettlement. *Current Opinion in Psychiatry*, 13, 491–5.

McCormack, B. (2004). In P.N. Walsh and H. Gash (eds), *Lives and Times: Practice, Policy and People with Disabilities* (pp. 7–29). Dublin: Rathdown Press.

McDermott, S., Martin, M. and Butkus, S. (1999). What individual, provider, and community characteristics predict employment of individuals with mental retardation? *American Journal on Mental Retardation*, 104, 346–55.

MacHale, R. and Carey, S. (2002). An investigation of the effects of bereavement on mental health and challenging behaviour in adults with learning disability. *British Journal of Learning Disabilities*, 30(3), 113–17.

National Disability Authority (NDA) (2003). *Requirements for a System of Independent Needs Assessment in Ireland*. Dublin: NDA.

Needs and Abilities (1991). *A Policy for the Intellectually Disabled*. Dublin: Government Printing Office.

Nisbet, J. and Hagner, D. (1988). Natural supports in the workplace: A reexamination of supported employment. *Journal of the Association for Persons with Severe Handicaps* (JASH), 13(4), 260–7.

O'Toole, B. and McConkey, R. (1995). *Innovations in Developing Countries for People With Disabilities*. New York: Paul Brookes.

Olsen, D., Cioffi, A., Yovanoff, P. and Mank, D. (2000). Gender differences in supported employment. *Mental Retardation*, 38, 89–96.

Pancsofar, E.L. and Steere, D.E. (1997). The C.A.P.A.B.L.E. process: Critical dimensions of community-based assessment. *Journal of Vocational Rehabilitation*, 8, 99–108.

Perry, J., Beyer, S., Felce, D. and Todd, S. (1998). Strategic service change: Development of core services in Wales, 1983–1995. *Journal of Applied Research in Intellectual Disabilities*, 11(1), 15–33.

Perske, R. (2004). Nirje's Eight Planks. *Mental Retardation*, 42, 147–50.

Pierce, K., McDermott, S. and Butkus, S. (2003). Predictors of job tenure for new hires with mental retardation. *Research in Developmental Disabilities*, 24, 369–80.

Race, D. (1995). Historical development of service provision. In N. Malin (ed.), *Services for People with Learning Disabilities* (pp. 46–78). London: Routledge.

Raji, O., Hollins, S. and Drinnan, A. (2003). How far are people with learning disabilities involved in funeral rites? *British Journal of Learning Disabilities*, 31, 42–5.

Reeves, D. (1994a). *HARCLAG: A Program for the Sequential Analysis of Observational Data*. Manchester, UK: Hester Adrian Research Centre, University of Manchester.

Reeves, D. (1994b). *Calculating Inter-Observation Agreement and Cohen's Kappa on Time-Based Observational Data Allowing for 'Natural' Measurement Error*. Manchester, UK: Hester Adrian Research Centre, University of Manchester.

Robertson, J., Emerson, E., Gregory, N., Hatton, C., Kessissoglou, S., Hallam, A. and Linehan, C. (2001a). Social networks of people with mental retardation in residential settings. *Mental Retardation*, 39(3), 201–14.

Robertson, J., Emerson, E., Hatton, C., Gregory, N., Kessissoglou, S., Hallam, A. and Walsh, P.N. (2001b). Environmental opportunities and supports for exercising self-determination in community-based residential settings. *Research in Developmental Disabilities*, 22(6), 489–502.

Robins, J. (1986). *Fools and Mad: A History of the Insane in Ireland*. Dublin: Institute of Public Administration.

Schalock, R.S. and Verdugo, M.A. (2002). *Handbook on Quality of Life for Human Services Practitioners*. Washington DC: AAMR.

Seltzer, M.M. and Krauss, M.W. (2001). Quality of life of adults with mental retardation/developmental disabilities who live with family. *Mental Retardation and Developmental Disabilities Research Reviews*, 7, 105–14.

Smyth, M. and McConkey, R. (2003). Future aspirations of parents and students with severe learning disabilities on leaving special schooling. *British Journal of Learning Disabilities*, 31, 54–9.

Stromberg, E.L. (1985). *Stromberg Dexterity Test*. Austin, TX: The Psychological Corporation.

Sutherland, M. and Kirby, N. (2000). *Intellectual Disability and Models of Employment*

– *The Australian Experience*. Adelaide, AU: Disability Research Unit, University of Adelaide, Australia. http://www.minds.org.sg/papers/mms22.htm.

Thompson, T., Felce, D. and Symons, F.J. (eds) (2000). *Behavioural Observation Technology and Applications in Developmental Disabilities*. Baltimore MD: Paul H. Brookes Publishing.

Tøssebro, J., Gustavsson, A. and Dyrendahl, G. (eds) (1996). *Intellectual Disabilities in the Nordic Welfare States*. Kristiansand S: Høyskoleforlaget AS – Norwegian Academic Press.

Turk, V., Dodd, K. and Christmas, M. (2001). *Down's Syndrome and Dementia – Briefing for Commissioners*. Briefing paper from the GOLD – Growing Older with Intellectual Disability – programme supported by the Foundation for People with Intellectual Disability, UK www.learningdisabilities.org.uk.

United Nations (1994). *Human Rights and the Environment: Draft Declaration*. Geneva: UN.

Valuing People: A New Strategy for Learning Disability for the 21st Century (2001). London: Stationery Office.

Walsh, M., Walsh, P.N., Linehan, C., Hillery, J., Durkan, J., Emerson, E., Robertson, J., Hatton, C., Gregory, N., Kessissoglou, S., Hallam, A., Knapp, M., Järbrink, K. and Netten, A. (2000). *The Quality and Outcomes of Residential Supports Provided for Irish Adults with Intellectual Disabilities: An Observational Study*. Dublin, Ireland: Centre for Disability Studies, University College Dublin.

Walsh, P.N. (2003). A courtly welcome: Observations on the research initiative. *British Journal of Learning Disabilities*, 31, 190–3.

Walsh, P.N. (2005a). Outside the box: Assessment for life and work in the community. Part 1: Conceptual and contextual issues. In J. Hogg and A. Langa (eds), *Assessing Adults with Intellectual Disabilities: A Service Provider's Guide* (pp. 23–38). Oxford: Blackwell.

Walsh, P.N. (2005b). Assessment – Part 2: Assessment and employment of people with intellectual disabilities: assessment strategies. Part 2: Assessment strategies and instruments. In J. Hogg and A. Langa (eds), *Assessing Adults with Intellectual Disabilities: A Service Provider's Guide* (pp. 138–51). Oxford: British Psychological Society and Blackwell.

Walsh, P.N. and LeRoy, B. (2004). *Women with Disabilities Aging Well: A Global View*. Baltimore, MD: Paul H. Brookes Publishing.

Walsh, P.N., Linehan, C., Hillery, J., Durkan, J., Emerson, E., Hatton, C. *et al.* (2001). Family views of the quality of residential supports. *Journal of Applied Research in Intellectual Disabilities*, 14(3), 292–309.

Walsh, P.N., Mank, D., Beyer, S., McDonald, R. and O'Bryan, A. (1999). Continuous quality improvement in supported employment: A European perspective. *Journal of Vocational Rehabilitation*, 12, 165–74.

Wehman, P. and Bricout, J. (1999). Supported employment and natural supports: A critique and analysis. In G. Revell, K. Inge, D. Mank and P. Wehman (eds), *The Impact of Supported Employment for People with Significant Disabilities: Preliminary Findings from the National Supported Employment Consortium* <http//www.vcu.edu/rrtcweb/sec/manual.html>.

Wehmeyer, M.L. (1994). Employment status and perceptions of control of adults with cognitive and developmental disabilities. *Research in Developmental Disabilities*, 15, 119–31.

Wehmeyer, M.L. and Bolding, N. (1999). Self-determination across living and working environments: A matched-samples study of adults with mental retardation. *Mental Retardation*, 37, 353–63.

Yamaki, K. and Fujiura, G.T. (2002). Employment and income status of adults with developmental disabilities living in the community. *Mental Retardation*, 40, 132–41.

Young, I., Sigafoos, J., Suttie, J., Ashman, A. and Grevell, P. (1998). 'Deinstitutionalisation of persons with intellectual disabilities: A review of Australian studies'. *Journal of Intellectual and Developmental Disabilities*, 23, 155–70.

ACKNOWLEDGEMENT

'Days' from COLLECTED POEMS by Philip Larkin. Copyright (c) 1988, 2003 by the Estate of Philip Larkin. Reprinted by permission of Farrar, Straus and Giroux, LLC.

Chapter 22

Managing mental health problems in people with intellectual disabilities

Shahid H. Zaman, Geraldine Holt and Nick Bouras

EPIDEMIOLOGY OF MENTAL HEALTH PROBLEMS

In people with intellectual disabilities (ID) mental illness is three to four times more common (Deb, Thomas and Bright, 2001) than in those without ID. Estimates of point prevalence vary from 10 to 39 per cent (Borthwick-Duffy, 1994; Borthwick-Duffy and Eyman, 1990; Bouras and Drummond, 1992; Cooper, 1997; Corbett, 1979; Deb *et al.*, 2001; Eaton and Menolascino, 1982; Göstason, 1985; Hagnell, Ojesjo, Otterbeck and Rorsman, 1994; Iverson and Fox, 1989; Jacobson, 1982; Lund, 1985; Reid, 1994; Reiss, 1990). The reasons for the differing estimates include the use of different samples (such as community versus institution-based samples) and diagnostic criteria. If conditions like personality disorders, autism, behavioural disorders, dementia and attention deficit hyperactivity disorders are excluded, then there is little difference between the ID and non-ID populations' prevalence rates (Deb *et al.*, 2001). There are also difficulties in diagnosing some mental disorders – the criteria that are often employed have been based on those who do not have an ID and may be even less valid for those with more severe ID. This may be one reason why not all studies agree that there may be a higher prevalence of schizophrenia in people with ID (Borthwick-Duffy and Eyman, 1990; Corbett, 1979; Göstason, 1985; Iverson and Fox, 1989; Jacobson, 1982; Lund, 1985; Reid, 1994). An increased vulnerability to mental health problems is likely to be due to an increased incidence of brain abnormalities including associated epilepsy, physical and sensory problems, and social and psychological adversities.

AETIOLOGY OF COMMON MENTAL HEALTH PROBLEMS IN PEOPLE WITH ID

A framework for understanding the aetiology of mental health problems is to divide the causes into biological, psychological and social categories as shown in Table 22.1. For example, an adult with depression may have a

Table 22.1 Examples of aetiological factors in the categories of biological, psychological and social to help to formulate a case of a person with a mental disorder and ID

Factor	Examples
BIOLOGICAL	Genetic vulnerability (family history); previous episodes or relapses; physical illness or disability (cerebral palsy, sensory impairment, epilepsy, hypothyroidism, encephalitis, stroke or other medical conditions), side-effects of medication, substance misuse
PSYCHOLOGICAL	Poor/limited coping mechanisms; abuse; separation; losses; negative learning experiences; significant personality traits; language/communication difficulties; impact of ID on self-esteem and development
SOCIAL	Difficult or lack of socio-economic circumstances or resources; access to education, leisure or employment; social isolation; dependence; negative social feedback; rejection, vulnerability, victimization, infantilization; stigmatization, unrealistic expectations; life cycle transitions or crises (bereavements, change of staff); response to impact on immediate family of disability in family member

biological vulnerability with a strong family history of depression suggesting a genetic component to this vulnerability. There may be other biological factors, such as alcohol misuse, which are known to alter mood. The person may have **psychological** predisposing factors such as difficulty in dealing with changes or a predisposition to anxiety. **Social** factors (which includes family factors) may also contribute, for example a change of support staff or lack of appropriate leisure opportunities. All these factors can act as 'predisposing', 'precipitating or trigger', and as 'perpetuating or maintaining' issues. Conceptualizing the aetiology helps to understand the person's difficulties and to address each problem in the most relevant manner.

Causes of schizophrenia

Evidence suggests that schizophrenia is a neurodevelopmental disorder (Sawa and Kamiya, 2003). Family studies support a genetic component and more than one gene is likely to be involved. Environmental factors including *in utero* exposure to putative viral agents, and adverse family situations such as those seen when there is high expressed emotion are also thought to affect clinical manifestation. As the dopamine receptor antagonistic drugs (especially those acting on the type-2 receptor) can successfully be used to treat the symptoms of schizophrenia, it is likely that dopamine plays an important role in the pathogenesis of this condition. The serotonin (or 5-hydroxytryptophan, 5-HT) type 2A and C receptor subtypes also appear to play a role as the newer drugs, the 'atypicals', seem to be more effective at controlling the negative symptoms of schizophrenia by presumably acting at these sites. Other receptors such as the glutamate and gamma-aminobutyric acid (GABA) receptors also play a role.

The most consistent brain imaging studies' findings show an increase in the volume of the lateral ventricles and a cortical volume decrease, but this is not useful diagnostically as it is not specific and is seen in other psychiatric conditions. These and other brain imaging findings correlate with the neuropsychological abnormalities that are seen in schizophrenia, such as in executive functioning (see Gelder, Lopez-Ibor and Andreasen, 2000: section 4.3, 567–649).

Causes of mood disorders

Twin and family studies reveal a genetic contribution to these conditions, particularly in bipolar affective disorder.

The amine hypothesis proposes that depression is due to an under-functioning of the noradrenergic and serotoninergic neurotransmitter pathways and, conversely, mania is caused by an over-functioning. Many endocrine changes are also seen in depression, such as an increase in the steroid cortisol from the adrenals and a suppression of thyroid function.

Psychodynamic theories view depression as aggression directed towards oneself. The notion of loss plays a central role. Mania is viewed as a psychological defence against depression, 'manic defence'. Bowlby (1988) proposed an innate need of children to seek closeness and attachment to the carer. If this relationship is of a poor quality and especially if there is abandonment, not only will this affect the development of the child, but it will also predispose to depression.

In depression, people often have characteristic cognitive changes or 'distortions' about how they view themselves, the world or the future (Beck, 1967). Behavioural theories of depression express the view that in an environment where efforts to avoid or prevent being exposed to undesirable situations or stimuli are thwarted for whatever reason, a state of 'learned helplessness' (after Seligman) can develop.

Brown and Harris (1978) identified social conditions associated with depression in women. These included unemployment, the lack of a confiding relationship and the loss of mother before the age of eleven years.

Causes of anxiety disorders

We react to an environmental threat or perceived danger with anxiety, i.e. the 'flight and fright' reaction. This is the result of increased activity of the sympathetic nervous system. Some parts of the brain have been identified from neuroimaging studies to be particularly involved in anxiety disorders, e.g. the amygdala (along with other areas of the brain – especially the limbic system) has a crucial role in fear conditioning. The GABAergic, noradrenergic and serotoninergic neurochemical systems are involved in anxiety (Nutt, 2001; Nutt and Malizia, 2001).

Genetic factors are important, for example a relative of a person with panic disorder has a twenty times greater chance of having an anxiety disorder. There is also a female preponderance for most anxiety disorders.

In psychodynamic theory, anxiety is the manifestation of unmet unconscious desires and drives. In order to survive such an unhappy situation the mind uses coping strategies or 'defence mechanisms', such as denial or projection, in order to reduce the inner conflict. The source of these conflicts can be traced to childhood psychological development, when the infant gradually learns to separate and live independently. During this process a problem can develop which depends on the quality of the relationship between parent and child, the degree of attachment, any prolonged periods of separation or any other traumas.

Learning theory also offers an explanation for certain neurotic disorders, especially obsessional or phobic disorders. By classical conditioning or vicarious learning, neutral stimuli or thoughts may be associated with anxiety. This results in avoidance behaviour or behaviour that will end the thought or stimulus. It is maintained and perpetuated by a reduction in anxiety that will result from such strategies.

GUIDELINES FOR CLINICAL PRACTICE IN ASSESSING AND TREATING COMMON MENTAL HEALTH PROBLEMS

Clinical assessment involves obtaining a detailed history, a mental state and physical examination, and special investigations including using diagnostic tools (such as questionnaires). Its aim is to make a diagnosis and to understand the problem in terms of factors that precipitated and are maintaining it. This will inform management, give an indication of prognosis and facilitate communication between practitioners.

Diagnoses are based on patterns of symptoms and signs which are defined in Box 22.1. The ICD-10 (WHO, 1992; 1996) and DSM-IV-TR (American Psychiatric Association, 2000) describe internationally agreed criteria for the diagnosis of psychiatric conditions. There are major problems with using these criteria in people with greater than mild degrees of ID. Poor communication skills, cognitive problems such as a poor working memory or the inability to abstract, and the tendency to acquiesce make it more difficult to access the person's internal world. Greater reliance is therefore placed on observations of changes in behaviour as the degree of ID increases. Additionally people with ID may present in atypical ways (compared to a person without an ID), e.g. a person with severe ID and depression may develop

> **Box 22.1 Symptoms and signs**
>
> **SYMPTOMS** are **reported** distresses and experiences, e.g. may feel sad or hear voices or have palpitations
>
> **SIGNS** are the **observable** manifestations of the condition, e.g. may look restless or perplexed or may have a fast heartbeat

aggression. The DC-LD (Royal College of Psychiatrists, 2001) is designed to be used in conjunction with the ICD-10 and specifically addresses these diagnostic problems.

Assessment begins before meeting the person concerned, with the gathering of background information. Often there will have been encounters with various services or agencies in the past such as school educational psychology departments, paediatric services or hospitals. Reports from these will help develop a picture of the person. It is necessary to get the consent of the person and/or carer to obtain certain reports to ensure confidentiality.

The time taken for the initial assessment is approximately one hour, but care is necessary not to frustrate or fatigue the client. The location may be an outpatient clinic, or another setting, e.g. home of the person concerned. The person may find a particular place more comfortable and less stressful, and so make their assessment easier and more valid. This will need to be balanced against the need to carry out certain procedures such as a physical examination, blood tests, etc., the risks presented and resources available.

The interview begins with the introduction of those present, their roles, and the reason for and process of assessment. Often the person will choose to be supported by a carer, but it is important to check whether they want the carer in the room with them or not, and whether they mind you seeking information from them. It is often helpful for two professionals to do the assessment to gain a wider perspective and to enable division of tasks, e.g. one person talking to the carer whilst the other clinician talks with the service user. It is important to try to ascertain the client's language skills if not already known. Talking about, for example, what he or she is planning for later that day or a chat about likes and dislikes will begin to give some measure of language ability and hopefully begin to initiate rapport and some sense of ease with the service user. The key to all clinical assessments is careful observation.

History taking involves gaining information from all possible sources for the sake of comprehensiveness and corroboration. Relying on just one source may mislead and result in an incorrect formulation of the problem. The most important person to talk to is the service user and if there are difficulties or idiosyncrasies in communication skills, a person best known to be able to interpret is essential to have present at the interview. History taking should provide the information listed in Table 22.2, although it may not be possible to gain all this at an initial interview.

Table 22.2 Layout of history taking and information required

Type of information needed	Comments
Personal details including GP details	
Who referred and when	
Reason for referral	
Persons present during assessment	
Place of assessment	
Presenting problem or complaint	Simple sentence describing difficulty and the length of time it's been present
History of presenting complaint	Details of how the problem evolved, its severity and periodicity; any ameliorating and exacerbating factors; effects of problem on person and carers and effects on everyday functioning; what is the view held as to the cause of the problem? Is there a specific event that may explain the start of symptoms, e.g. a carer leaving or bereavement? Importantly, what were the emotional repertoires, cognitive and functional skills and behaviours prior to now? Always ask for specific symptoms, e.g. hearing voices, paranoid ideation, stereotypical movements and other symptoms of depression, psychosis or neurosis that will help to support your final formulation
Past psychiatric history	To include any previous similar episodes or difficulties; any contact with psychiatric services previously. Any self-harm or aggression in the past
Past medical history	Any previous contacts with doctors and why; any hospital admissions; any other illnesses including head injuries. Ask about any hearing or visual disabilities
Epilepsy	As this is common, it is important to find out about this and have a low index of suspicion
Current medication and allergies	All medication including doses and the length of time of treatment; degree of response to medication; any side-effects

Alcohol and illicit substances	The type of alcoholic drink and amount (in units of alcohol); current and previous drug taking and any treatment programme or complications need to be known. Any cigarette smoking?
Functional assessment (includes physical and communication disability and visual and hearing impairments)	What activities of daily living is the person able to undertake? Include self-care, cooking, cleaning, leisure activities, shopping and dealing with finances. The degree of physical, communication, visual and hearing disability will be important determinants
Social history	What is a typical day for him/her; is he or she able to work? What accommodation and type of support does s/he have? Is the present accommodation fulfilling all needs adequately? What leisure and educational activities are available? Any problems with finance? Who are the carers and how extensive is the social network?
Family history	Names, ages, occupation, health (including mental health) and the quality of relationships of family members, including between mother, father, siblings and grandparents
Personal History **Birth** **Development** **Pre-school** **School** **College** **Abuse** **Psychosexual history** **Occupational history**	Place of birth; any complications during pregnancy (e.g. infections) and during labour (e.g. if prolonged or any obstetric complications); any problems as a neonate (e.g. was any hospitalization needed); any problems with developmental delay; ask about pre-school difficulties or behaviours; ask about difficulties at school such as bullying and any scholastic achievements; any childhood separations or physical, sexual or emotional abuse; the type of school and when and why; degree of success at school; first sexual and relationship experience; number of partners; degree of sexual knowledge; any pregnancies; any employment
Personality (include coping mechanisms, impulse control, self image, mood, etc.)	What is his/her enduring character normally? Note that by the late teens or early adulthood, it is assumed that personality traits become relatively stable. Enquire about how the person responds to stress, what is the pervading mood and any likes and dislikes
Forensic history	Any offences committed, the motivation or premeditation for it and details of any charges; detail any court proceedings

Risk assessment

This needs to be up to date as the risk a person poses to others, themselves and property changes with time and circumstances. It should be multidisciplinary and an agreed format is helpful. The aim is to identify and describe the degree and nature of the risky behaviour and to clarify factors that affect this. Previous behaviours tend to be repeated and so details of such behaviours needs to be sought. The presence of command hallucinations, access to weapons, expressed thoughts of harm to self or others and co-morbid illicit substance misuse are indicators of increased risk. Each factor identified should be evaluated and individually managed in order to reduce the risk. If the level of risk of aggression, self-harm or self-neglect cannot be safely managed in the community, then compulsory hospital assessment and treatment may be necessary using mental health legislation.

Mental state examination

This is the examination of the mental processes and behaviour by the assessor at the interview and the areas covered are set out in Table 22.3. It is divided into: 'appearance and behaviour', 'speech or talk', 'affect', 'mood', 'thoughts', 'perceptions', 'cognition' and 'insight'. The appearance and behaviour includes a description of the person's appearance, the type and state of their clothing and self-care, degree of eye contact, any abnormal movements including tics, mannerisms and stereotypies, and any evidence of injuries. When describing the speech, consider the rate of speech (how fast the words are produced), the volume (the amount of words per unit time), the degree of loudness of speech production and the prosody (the natural undulation and variation in tone and rhythm).

Physical examination

Some physical conditions may present as changes in behaviour or as mental illness (e.g. middle-ear infection, urinary tract infection or a stroke) in people with ID who may not be able to complain or seek health advice. Some physical conditions (e.g. thyroid disease) predispose to mental illness, as do certain medications (e.g. steroids or propanolol). A physical examination that especially focuses on the nervous system (including sensory impairment), endocrine system (especially thyroid status) and is dictated by the physical symptoms is crucial.

Investigations

Physical investigations may help to elucidate the aetiology of the ID. Blood tests are often undertaken as a health screen, to confirm the suspicion of an

Table 22.3 Mental state examination layout and findings

Feature	Examples of findings and their associations
Appearance and behaviour	Unkempt (may indicate e.g. depression, psychosis, or abuse) Typical feature of a genetic syndrome e.g. Down's or fragile X syndrome Expressionless 'unemotional' face (autistic spectrum disorders, negative symptoms of schizophrenia, parkinsonism, schizotypal personality disorder) Over-familiar or disinhibited (mania, dissocial personality disorder, intoxicated (alcohol or other drugs)) Restless or agitated (anxiety, depression, mania, substance misuse) Involuntary movements such as tics (Gilles de la Tourette's), akathisia (an involuntary inner restlessness that manifests as the inability to stay still; can be side-effect of antipsychotics) Psychomotor retardation (depression, hypothyroidism)
Speech or talk	Fast rate, high volume and loud and uninterruptible (mania or drugs) Monotonic and slow rate (depression) Concrete responses (autistic spectrum disorder)
Affect	Non-reactive, i.e. does not respond to appropriate cues to social communication Cheerful or sad or irritable, etc.
Mood	*Subjectively*: write a verbatim phrase on how the person feels now in their mood, e.g. 'I'm alright', then describe any biological symptoms namely: appetite and weight (>5%) decrease, early morning wakening, diurnal variation of mood, poor concentration (depression) *Objectively*, describe in your opinion given the evidence you have the mood, e.g. mild, moderate or severe depression, with or without psychotic symptoms, irritable, manic, incongruent mood (i.e. mood that does not match with the prevailing difficulties, e.g. laughing when talking about a recent parental bereavement as in schizophrenia and autistic spectrum disorders)
Thoughts	*The Contents* – including delusions, i.e. false beliefs: persecutory (paranoid as in depression or schizophrenia), grandiose (believing they can now travel by bus alone when they cannot as in mania or schizophrenia), nihilistic (often if psychotic depression, e.g. 'my inside is rotting') Ideas of self-reference (where chance observations are misinterpreted as having personal significance; schizophrenia) Passivity (delusion that one's own thoughts, actions, feelings, volition and impulses are controlled by an outside agency or force. There may be thought alienation (i.e. thought broadcast, insertion or withdrawal – or a loss of control of thoughts); schizophrenia Any ruminations or obsessions or compulsions (may occur in a number of conditions) Rituals

(Continued overleaf)

Table 22.3 Continued

Feature	Examples of findings and their associations
	Form (structure of thought, how it is constructed and conveyed to another, e.g. it may be very disorganized and hard to follow as it is jumbled as in schizophrenia, with e.g. loose associations) *Flow* (fast in mania, slow in depression)
Perceptions	Perceptual abnormalities in all modalities of perceptions including hallucinations (a false perception in the absence of an external stimulus. It can be in any sensory modality – auditory, visual, gustatory, olfactory or tactile. They are not distortions of real perceptions, but arise *de novo* and are experienced as a real perception in the objective space): if auditory and are in the second person (mood disorder), or if in the third person (schizophrenia); giving a running commentary on the person's thoughts or activities (schizophrenia); gustatory, visual (organic psychosis, schizophrenia); tactile (organic psychosis or schizophrenia Note that pseudo-hallucinations (perceptual experiences that lack the reality of a true perception and so are experienced in the inner subjective space and are like images), may be hard to differentiate from true hallucinations but are common in those who have experienced childhood abuse Illusions (A false perception of a real external stimulus)
Cognition	Degree of alertness (in confusional states attention is decreased), orientation, memory
Insight	Does the person think she/he is unwell? In psychoses insight is lost. Are the symptoms considered abnormal and why? Would the person consider treatment (and compliance)?

illness, or to monitor drug levels or side-effects. X-rays may be necessary. Structural imaging (with computerized tomographic head scan: CT scan or magnetic resonance imaging: MRI) is usually only necessary if clinically there are neurological signs or it is a first presentation especially and if there are atypical features in the psychiatric presentation. Functional imaging with functional MRI or single photon emission computerized tomography (SPECT) and positron emission topography (PET) scans can measure various aspects of brain dynamic function such as local blood flow or oxygen use which are proxy indicators of neuronal tissue activity.

An electroencephalogram (EEG) is not routinely requested unless epilepsy is suspected. Diagnostic tools are used to formalize and standardize the monitoring of symptoms or diagnostic procedure. There are many tools, based on questionnaires and/or observations available. See end of the chapter for a list.

Neuropsychological tests may have to be repeated to ascertain or confirm the ID. The involvement of other disciplines may be appropriate, e.g. an occupational therapy assessment of adaptive skills. Further assessment of social needs including housing, work, education, leisure and finances may also be required.

Diagnosis and formulation

When making a psychiatric diagnosis in people with ID, it is important to consider factors that may modify the presentation. Psychopathology is modified by developmental level, e.g. an adult with a profound ID will have adult drives and years of experience and learning but may have aspects that are relatively immature, for example phobias that are more commonly seen in children, a less developed social awareness or an 'imaginary friend'. Sovner (1986) describes intellectual distortion; psychosocial masking; cognitive disintegration; and baseline exaggeration as factors that should be taken into account when making a diagnosis in people with ID. Intellectual distortion is the difficulty someone has in describing his or her emotions or experiences because of impaired communication and, for example, concrete thinking. Psychosocial masking refers to unsophisticated presentation of significant symptoms that could be missed. The naïve presentation is due to the impoverished social skills and life experiences of the person. Cognitive disintegration is due to abnormalities of information processing that can present following exposure to a stressful situation as bizarre behaviour and psychotic symptoms and therefore be misdiagnosed as a mental health problem. This non-specific response to stress often quickly resolves when the stressor is removed. Baseline exaggeration is when pre-morbid functioning deteriorates and it can be difficult to assign this to a mental health problem alone. The 'behavioural equivalents' idea is based on the concept that most symptoms (psychopathology) that have been well characterized in the average population have an equivalent. This applies to symptoms such as worthlessness or guilt where the behavioural equivalent may be a reduction in self-care or social withdrawal. Diagnostic overshadowing may also occur where all attributes of behaviour and mental state are thought to be the direct consequence of the ID *per se*.

DC-LD adopts a hierarchical, multi-axial approach. On Axis I severity of the intellectual disability and whether it occurs with or without challenging behaviour is recorded. On Axis II the cause of ID and other medical conditions are noted. Psychiatric conditions are recorded on Axis III.

As previously noted, when assessing mental health, as the level of ID increases so does the reliance on changes in behaviour rather than access to the person's inner world (see Box 22.2). This may lead to diagnostic uncertainty. In such cases a hypothesis-testing approach is often taken. This involves making a presumptive diagnosis, making relevant and careful observations, instituting an intervention and evaluating the outcome. The assumption is that if the disorder improves with the intervention, then the diagnosis is supported (though not proven).

Box 22.2 Psychopathology and ID

Psychopathology is defined with respect to experiences of the average IQ population. When it is used in people with ID, language and communication are amongst the factors that skew and obscure access especially to the 'inner world'. In mild ID, this is not always a problem, but it often is in those with more severe ID. In such cases changes in behaviour are important in inferring psychopathology (such as thought disorder, hallucinations and delusions, guilt). Because of limited capacity to undertake some average ID population activities (such as spending sprees in mania), the baseline behaviour and functional capacity are important.

Treatment and management

A multidisciplinary and multi-agency approach is necessary and the key issues for case management listed in Box 22.3 should be considered.

Care programme approach (CPA)

The care programme approach (used in the UK) requires there to be a care co-ordinator to oversee the assessment and implementation of the care plan using a service-user centred process. There will be issues that need to be addressed urgently and others that will need greater attention once the person's clinical state improves. It is important to agree the priorities with the service user and multidisciplinary team. For example, the immediate safety of the person or carers and any unpleasant symptoms may need to be addressed urgently before tackling other parts of the care plan.

Box 22.3 Important aspects of case management

Community or inpatient?
Compulsory or informal treatment?
Risk assessment
Capacity to consent
Follow-up arrangements including comprehensive needs assessment
Referrals to other professionals (physicians, audiologists, etc.)
Documentation and communication with all concerned

Consent and capacity

When treating people with ID, capacity to consent for a treatment may be lacking and people are treated 'in their best interests'. One must be aware of the ethics involved, mental health legislation, capacity legislation and Human Rights Act. As a general guideline, a person is considered to have capacity to give consent for a given intervention if s/he: (1) understands the nature of the intervention and why it is being proposed; (2) understands the benefits and risks of the intervention and any possible alternatives that may be available; (3) understands the likely outcome if the intervention is not accepted; (4) is able to retain information long enough such that a decision can be made on the basis of this information; and (5) is able to communicate this. Consent is voluntary and can be withdrawn at any time. The presence of mental illness does not preclude capacity to consent and no one can give consent for another adult.

Sometimes by explaining in simple terms, using pictures and taking time, capacity can be developed. If capacity to consent for a treatment is lacking, interventions can be made 'in the person's best interests' following full discussion with the multidisciplinary team and advocates of the client. Mental health legislation can be used if it is necessary compulsorily to assess or treat someone's mental health problem in hospital.

CATEGORIES OF TREATMENTS, INTERVENTIONS AND SUPPORT

These are best divided into, *psychological, biological* and *social*. Such an approach will involve different professionals, support groups and voluntary organizations.

Psychological treatments

In the non-ID population many types of psychological therapies are used and have been evaluated for use in many psychiatric disorders (Department of Health, 2001). For example, in schizophrenia, family therapy is used to address high expressed emotions (excess criticism; over-involvement; ambivalence), individual cognitive behavioural therapy (CBT) to reduce positive symptoms, and motivational interviewing to improve compliance with medication. In depression, supportive psychotherapy, CBT, interpersonal therapy and psychodynamic psychotherapy, with or without the use of antidepressant medication has been shown to be valuable. CBT or graded exposure is used in some types of anxiety disorders, such as panic disorder, isolated phobias, agoraphobia, social phobia and generalized anxiety disorders. The situation in the ID population, however, is still evolving, as in the past it has been assumed that people with ID did not suffer emotional problems, stress or psychiatric disorders (Fletcher, 1993) and therefore were not considered to be suitable for psychotherapy. Behavioural approaches for behavioural problems (including for anger management) are more extensively researched and used in everyday practice. The evidence base available for psychological treatments for psychiatric illness in people with ID is based on a paucity of case-controlled clinical trials; most evidence-based practice is guided by case studies (Beail, 1989, 1994; Frankish, 1989; Kilchenstein, 1999; Sinason, 1992; Symington, 1981) and there is a need for more clinical trials to evaluate the effectiveness of outcomes (Nezu and Nezu, 1994; Prout and Nowak-Drabik, 2003). Some studies have shown the usefulness of CBT (Lindsay, Howells and Pitcaithly, 1993) in depression in people with ID when used alone or in conjunction with antidepressant medication (Burnand, Andreoli, Kolatte, Venturini and Rosset, 2002).

In people with ID, by the nature of their disability there are impairments in, for example, reasoning, abstraction, memory, judgement and planning that can lead to difficulties in assimilating complex ideas and information in 'thinking' and therefore understanding. This results in a limited capacity to process internal and external experiences and to adjust psychologically. There are often difficulties in communication (especially about the internal world; but using non-verbal processes and communication overcomes this in therapy to a degree) and there is also often a lack of independence because of poor adaptive skills, which can make them more vulnerable. Furthermore, the families of people with ID may experience much stress and emotional turmoil, which they have to come to terms with. This impacts on the emotional development of the person with ID.

A person with ID is unlikely to self-refer for treatment and so consent may be an issue. It is important that these issues are addressed before embarking on any course of therapy. Making an informed choice is not only vital for the success of the therapy, but is also an important ethical issue.

Making formal arrangements for attendance (transport and escorts, where necessary) is also important. Difficult feelings (such as envy or impatience) may be evoked in the carers during regular attendance at therapy sessions that relate to difficulties the carer may themselves have. A therapist needs to be aware of these, as the carer may attempt to jeopardize the process. When forming a therapeutic alliance with a service user who is undergoing therapy, one must also be aware that feelings of mistrust, of being disliked or rejected are possible because of their adverse early experiences and impairment. In some therapy sessions, looser boundaries are probably more acceptable, such as being more familiar and friendly, not being strict with the ending of session times or engaging appropriate physical contact. In some cases, however, this may lead to a situation where this safe containment may not result in the ventilation of or facing any negative thoughts or feelings.

As mentioned above, communication problems may be overcome by using non-verbal means; this can be extended to using formal art, drama and music therapy, but also pictorial means of communication. Getting attuned to the method of communication of the client can take time, but is an essential early step for therapy. The 'Books beyond Words' series (Royal College of Psychiatrists, http://www.rcpsych.ac.uk/), for example, have been used by therapists and cover subjects such as bereavement or relationships.

Confidentiality is also important. It is not always possible to maintain full confidentiality in all cases but a difficult judgement may have to be made as to what, and to what extent, information should be discussed with a carer, in the best interests of the service user. Cultural issues are often relevant too, and a therapist needs to be sensitive to the individual's cultural background and belief systems and intervene accordingly.

In practice most practitioners use a range of treatment models and options, with or without modifications sensitive to the person's disabilities. Both the cognitive and psychodynamic approaches have been used with varying degrees of success (Beail, 2003; Hollins and Sinason, 2000; Hollins, 2003). When cognitive approaches are used, procedures may have to be simplified or modified, such as the use of role-play, pictures/photographs or drawings, symbols or dolls. Often service users have difficulties in generalizing from the therapy setting to the real-life situation; this can be overcome with much repetition, practice and support after the sessions have formally ended.

Psychoanalytic studies with positive outcome measures are small in number (Beail and Warden, 1996; Bichard, Sinason and Usiskin, 1996; Frankish, 1989; Gaedt, 1995; Sigman, 1985). Examples of other approaches that have been employed are family (Black, 1987; Goldberg, Magrill, Hale, Damaskindou, Paul, and Tham, 1995; Shulman, 1988; Vetere, 1993) and group therapy (Gravestock and McGauley, 1994, Hollins and Evered, 1990). A flexible approach is crucial if there is to be success with using psychodynamic therapies (Hollins and Sinason, 2000). People with ID may use 'secondary handicap' as a psychological defence mechanism of exaggerating their handicap in order to cover up for the trauma of having to endure being handicapped and different, by, for example, being unusually compliant or adopting a 'smile of appeasement' (Sinason, 1992). If the secondary handicap is addressed during the first stage of therapy, a very vulnerable state where there is a realization of the handicap is acknowledged and feelings of loss and wasted years may be realized. With further therapy, these conflicts and feelings may be worked through with a final improvement in functioning. Hollins and Sinason (2000) describe three areas that commonly arise in psychodynamic therapy with people with ID; these are, their ID itself and their dependency requirements, sexuality, death and the fear of annihilation. These are sometimes too painful to discuss with family and friends and the therapist needs to be aware of these (Hollins, 2003).

Biological treatments: pharmacotherapy

Pharmacotherapy is usually only one aspect of intervention. The basic guideline for using medication is to prescribe low doses and increase slowly. Drugs may be used to treat a diagnosed condition, e.g. depression, or to ameliorate specific symptoms or challenging behaviour. For example, in a person hearing voices, the hallucination may be thought to be due to depression or schizophrenia. If it is not possible to clarify the diagnosis (for instance because of communication difficulties) it may be reasonable to commence an antipsychotic for symptom relief with careful and regular monitoring of the mental state. People with ID have a greater chance of suffering drug-induced adverse effects. Vigilance is mandatory, especially as the patient may not volunteer the problems. Prescribing at a lower dose and increasing the dose slowly with careful monitoring alleviates the problem to some degree. The question as to what agent to use for a given mental health condition will depend on, the condition being treated, any evidence of previous response or non-response, any contra-indications for using the drug for that particular person (e.g. drug interaction with other prescribed drugs, or a medical condition may preclude use), consent to treatment (see above), the tolerability expected and the cost of treatment. The main classes of drugs used in the psychiatry of people with ID are now described (for further details see, Einfeld, 2001; Matson, Bamburg, Mayville, Pinkston, *et al.* 2000; Santosh and Baird, 1999).

Antipsychotics

Antipsychotics (neuroleptics or 'major tranquillizers') are used in schizophrenia, related psychoses, bipolar affective disorder, and depression with psychotic features and sometimes as part of the management of behaviour disturbances, especially if there is aggression. They can be taken orally, intramuscularly or as a depot injection (which achieves a steady plasma drug level over a period of 1–4 weeks per intramuscular injection).

There are two groups of antipsychotics: the 'typicals' and the newer 'atypicals'. The former are being used less and less because of their undesirable movement disorder side-effects. Examples of typicals include haloperidol, chlorpromazine and trifluoperazine. Antipsychotics differ in their receptor binding profiles; knowing these helps to understand the side-effects and the likely mode of action. For example, the blockade of the dopamine-type 2 receptors leads to the control of positive symptoms of schizophrenia, but also the movement or 'extra-pyramidal' side-effects if the binding is not predominantly in the striatal as opposed to the meso-limbic dopaminergic neurones. A block of the tuberohypohyseal dopaminergic neurones can cause increased prolactin levels, which manifests as a disruption of menstruation and secretion of breast milk (galactorrhea) and contributes to sexual side-effects. When the drug blocks acetyl choline (muscarinic subtype) receptors, there are likely to be anticholinergic (or antimuscarinic) side-effects, e.g. dry mouth, blurred vision, constipation and urinary retention. If the drug has antihistamine action, sedation often occurs. Some drugs by blocking the alpha2-adrenergic receptors lead to dizziness because of postural hypotension; sexual side-effects include poor erection and inability to ejaculate. A rare side-effect is malignant neuroleptic syndrome. This presents with increased muscle tone, high temperature (pyrexia), labile blood pressure and pulse due to autonomic nervous system instability and sweating. It can lead to coma and be fatal if not treated intensively in hospital. It occurs rarely with the atypicals.

Most atypicals have a much lower dopamine-type 2 antagonistic activity and the reasons for their more favourable effects on the negative symptoms (whilst still ameliorating the positive symptoms) and lower incidence of motor side-effects may be related to their different spectrum of receptor binding profile including the blocking to the 5HT2a/c receptors. Commonly used agents are risperidone, olanzapine and clozapine (Bokszanska, Martin, Vanstraelen, Holt, Bouras and Taylor, 2003). Quetiapine and amisulpiride are also used. The atypicals are not without their problems, including weight gain (olanzapine more than risperidone) and the associated physical health problems, especially diabetes mellitus (Taylor, Paton and Kerwin, 2003). Clozapine is the only drug licensed in the UK for use in 'treatment-resistant' schizophrenia (see p. 807 below). It needs careful blood monitoring of white cell count to prevent a dangerous but reversible agranuolcytosis (lowering of the white cells). There are other side-effects, such as sedation, weight gain, hypotension, hypertension, cardiac problems and constipation.

Antidepressants

The main classes of antidepressants are the tricyclics (e.g. amitryptylline and clomipramine) now less commonly used, the selective-serotonin re-uptake inhibitors (SSRIs, e.g. fluoxetine, paroxetine), the selective noradrenergic and serotonin re-uptake inhibitors (venlafaxine), the monoamine oxidase inhibitors (phenelzine, meclobomide) and others (reboxitine, mirtazepine). The onset of antidepressant effect takes seven to fourteen days usually. Approximately 70 per cent of people with depressive disorders will respond. A minority who fail to respond will require a review of the diagnosis, an assessment of compliance (a common problem with all medication) and factors that could be maintaining the problem or co-morbidity (such as alcoholism or hypothyroidism). Another class of antidepressant can then be tried. Obsessive-compulsive disorders can be treated with antidepressants; examples are clomipramine and the SSRIs.

Anxiolytics

Anxiolytics reduce many features of anxiety. The benzodiazepines, which act on the GABA-type A receptors, are widely used. Examples are diazepam, lorazepam, clonazepam, temazepam and chlordiazepoxide. Benzodiazepines act quickly, within minutes (up to 30 minutes following an oral dose) but cause tolerance (i.e. greater doses are required to attain the same effect), dependence and withdrawal effects (if doses are terminated too suddenly, after a period of three to four weeks of chronic dosing).

The SSRIs and other antidepressants (including venlafaxine and the tricyclic antidepressants) also have anxiolytic properties, but also take at least seven or more days to show any benefit.

Buspirone acts on the 5-hydorxytryptine (5HT=serotonin) type 1A receptors. It takes about two weeks to show benefit. It is less commonly used and has been used to benefit anxiety disorders over a relatively short period.

Mood stabilizers

These reduce the swings in mood that characterize bipolar affective disorders and some personality disorders. They include lithium (which is well established in the acute treatment and prophylaxis of mania), and some anticonvulsants, e.g. carbamazepine, semi-sodium valproate and sodium valproate (see Table 22.4). Lamotrigine is considered to provide relapse protection against depressive episodes in patients with bipolar affective disorder. The mode of action is not known.

COMMON PSYCHIATRIC CONDITIONS: DIAGNOSIS AND MANAGEMENT

In the next two sections the diagnosis and management of schizophreneia and psychoses and bipolar disorder will be considered. In later sections other mood disorders, anxiety disorders, somatoform disorders, organic disorders and personality disorders will be covered.

SCHIZOPHRENIA AND RELATED PSYCHOSES

The ICD-10 (WHO, 1992) and the DSM-IV (American Psychiatric Association, 1994) have broadly similar criteria for categorizing schizophrenia and the related psychoses. The schizophrenia subtypes elaborated in these classification systems (such as 'paranoid', 'hebephrenic' or 'catatonic' schizophrenia) are not easily applied to people with ID, as discussed in DC-LD (Royal College of Psychiatrists, 2001). It is difficult to elaborate such sub-categories

Table 22.4 Mood stabilizers and their side-effects

Medication	Adverse effects
Lithium	At therapeutic doses: fine tremor; metallic taste; dry mouth, mild polyuria; nausea, weight gain; hypothyroidism and renal impairment (needs regular monitoring) Higher doses: coarse tremor; agitation; twitching; thirst; polyuria; renal failure; seizures: coma
Carbamazepine	Dizziness; diplopia (double vision); skin rash; cognitive impairment; nausea and vomiting; hypothyroidism; anaemia and leucopoenia (low white cell count); hyponatraemia (low plasma sodium concentration); photosensitivity; teratogenicity
Sodium valproate	Tremor; weight gain; confusion; gastric intolerance; hair loss; polycystic ovaries; sedation
Lamotrigine	Rash; fever; malaise; drowsiness, nausea; dizziness; ataxia (unsteadiness); headache; diplopia; insomnia; hepatic dysfunction; blood disorders

because of the reliance of eliciting psychopathology from verbal accounts of a person's experiences and thoughts (as discussed above). When this is the case the DC-LD manual can be used which classifies the schizophrenia and related psychoses to the 'non-affective psychotic disorders', and further subdivides them into schizophrenic/delusional disorders, schizoaffective disorders and other non-affective psychotic disorders (Melville, 2003). Hallucinations, delusions and passivity phenomena (see Table 22.3 above) are important symptoms seen in schizophreniform illness. The operational criteria required for a diagnosis of schizophrenia are outlined in the ICD-10 and include the following features:

- Thought echo (hearing thoughts being spoken out loud), thought insertion or withdrawal and thought broadcasting (the latter three are passivity phenomena where the thoughts are put in the person's mind, are taken away from him/her or are more widely known by others, respectively)
- Delusions of control, influence or passivity; delusional perception (a primary perception giving rise to a highly significant apparently unconnected meaning or realization)
- Hallucinatory voices
- Persistent delusions
- Persistent hallucinations in any modality when accompanied by either fleeting or half-formed delusions without clear affect content or by persistent over-valued ideas

- Disordered or disorganized thought (formal thought disorder)
- Catatonic behaviour, such as excitement, posturing (maintenance of manneristic postures), or waxy flexibility, negativism (a motiveless resistance to movement), mutism (a loss of speech, but not unconscious), and stupor (extreme motor retardation and mutism)
- 'Negative' symptoms such as marked apathy, paucity of speech, and blunting or incongruity of emotional responses
- A significant and consistent change in the overall quality of some aspects of personal behaviour, manifest as loss of interest, aimlessness, idleness, a self-absorbed attitude, and social withdrawal.

It is a requirement that organic brain disease is excluded including substance misuse and that the criteria for pervasive developmental disorders are not present.

A person with ID presenting with these psychoses may have become withdrawn or be behaving in an uncharacteristic manner. There may be indications that they are responding to auditory or visual hallucinations, e.g. talking to themselves or looking into space and pointing. The content of delusions is usually related to the developmental stage of the person. For example, there may be delusions of grandeur of being a wizard or monster. The auditory hallucinations are often simple statements, commands or accusations pertaining to an earlier developmental stage, e.g. being accused of naughtiness. Passivity phenomena, thought alienation, thought echo, auditory hallucinations giving a running commentary and delusional perception are not easily elicited in people with ID.

Negative symptoms may also be due to autistic features or a personality trait. The point prevalence of schizophrenia is estimated to be approximately 0.4 per cent in the general population (Meltzer, Gill, Petticrew and Hinds, 1995) and a range of 1.3 per cent to 3.7 per cent in people with ID (Deb *et al.*, 2001). As the degree of ID increases, the diagnosis relies more on observable features (change of behaviour or movement problems as in catatonia) and a detailed longitudinal history with comparison of a reliable pre-morbid state or baseline.

Differential diagnosis

Other psychiatric conditions (such as mania, schizoaffective disorder and depression), drugs of abuse and medication, organic conditions (which include, temporal lobe epilepsy or tumour, Wilson's disease, Huntington's Chorea, multiple sclerosis, systemic lupus erythematosis or encephalitis) need to be excluded. Note that mania will present with elation, grandiosity, disinhibition, irritability, overactivity, lability of mood and mood-*congruent* hallucinations and delusions, whereas in schizophrenia there tends to be mood-*incongruent* hallucinations and delusions and persecutory delusions, suspiciousness or perplexity. Depression can present with mood congruent nihilistic delusions (e.g. 'my insides are rotting').

Investigations

In order to make the diagnosis it is usually necessary to exclude drug-induced states and organic causes using standard blood tests; to exclude drugs of abuse a urine test for drugs will help. Brain imaging with CT or MRI, and an EEG may also be relevant depending on the clinical picture.

Management

As mentioned above, this must be undertaken within a team setting and where medical, psychological and social needs are explicitly identified and actions to intervene planned for. In the UK, this is formalized as the care programme approach, which is not only multidisciplinary and multi-agency but also client-centred. The immediate safety of the person or the carers and any agitation or unpleasant symptoms need to be addressed as a priority.

Pharmacotherapy

Pharmacology is the mainstay of treatment. Acute cases may require rapid tranquillization for the safety of the person. In the short, intermediate and longer term, most practitioners would use an atypical antipsychotic (see earlier, p. 802). If after maximum tolerable doses there is no response, the possible reason should be sought. It may be due to non-compliance with medication (checked by counting tablets or measuring drug levels in the blood), the diagnosis may be incorrect and so a detailed review of the assessment with current information is important, or there may still be maintaining factors; these include adverse home situation or continuation of substance misuse. If a second antipsychotic agent fails to show response after six weeks of a maximum and tolerable dose and the above factors have been ruled out, then the patient has a 'treatment-resistant' form of schizophrenia. It is important that clozapine be considered urgently in these situations.

Psychological treatments

CBT (for auditory hallucinations), family therapy (reduce high expressed emotion) and psycho-education are useful; see 'Categories of Treatments' above.

Social interventions

Addressing housing, leisure, educational, finance and accommodation needs are important components of the care package.

BIPOLAR AFFECTIVE DISORDER (BAD)

These are a heterogeneous group of disorders that include acute mania, acute hypomania, and bipolar affective disorder (at least one manic/hypomanic and one or more depressive episodes). In rapid cycling bipolar illness there are more than four episodes of hypomania or mania per year (Vanstraelen and Tyrer, 1999). If there are features of depression and elation at the same time it is termed a 'mixed state'.

Hypomania disrupts social functioning. In ICD-10 the core features of hypomania are (possible behavioural equivalents and examples are in square brackets, after DC-LD):

• An elevated mood or irritability that is sustained [increased verbal/physical aggression; a reduced level of tolerance]
• Increased activity or restlessness [increased verbal/physical aggression; a reduced level of tolerance]
• Increased talkativeness [or vocalization]
• Difficulty in concentration or distractibility
• Decreased need for sleep
• Increased sexual energy [e.g. masturbating in public; touching others in a sexual way]
• Overspending or other reckless or irresponsible behaviour [e.g. spending sprees, giving away belongings, placing oneself in danger]
• Increased sociability or over-familiarity.

In mania, there is a *greater degree of disruption* of personal functioning and more severe symptoms, e.g. the mood must be predominantly elevated, expansive or irritable for at least a week or the behaviour is foolhardy or reckless, e.g. spending sprees, reckless driving or sexual indiscretions. Other features must also be present:

• Increased activity or physical restlessness
• Increased talkativeness [pressure of speech]
• Flight of ideas or the subjective experience of thoughts racing
• Loss of normal social inhibitions resulting in behaviour that is inappropriate to the circumstances [e.g. talking to strangers; over-familiarity; intrusiveness]

- Inflated self-esteem or grandiosity [e.g. claiming to have skills not present pre-morbidly].

Mania can present with psychotic symptoms such as grandiose delusions that may have an erotic or persecutory content and auditory hallucinations not usually in the third person. The flight of ideas may be so extreme that it may manifest as disorganized thought. The hallucinations may be either mood-congruent (e.g. grandiose delusions and voices saying that the subject has superpowers), or mood-incongruent, where the voice says neutral or negative and disturbing things. It can be difficult to differentiate between mania and schizophrenia.

Differential diagnosis

This includes schizophrenia, schizoaffective disorders and recurrent depressive disorders. Frontal lobe syndromes are associated with poor judgement, lack of inhibition, disorganized chaotic behaviour, labile mood and irritability and can appear to be like mania. Causes include tumours, infections (e.g. HIV or syphilis or encephalitis due to other causes), neurodegenerative diseases (e.g. Picks, Alzheimer's disease) or head injury. Other organic conditions that should be included in the differential diagnosis are, for example, temporal lobe epilepsy, hyperthyroidism, Wilson's disease and drugs (such as amphetamines, cocaine, steroids and hallucinogens). If it is a first presentation of mania, it is possible that it will not occur again, especially if there is no family history of bipolar affective disorder.

Investigations

Investigations to exclude physical causes including blood tests, MRI and EEG if first presentation would be reasonable undertakings.

Management

Again the same principles of making an accurate assessment of the diagnosis, risk and co-morbidity are important. Admission to hospital may be necessary if there are psychotic symptoms, or a high risk to the person or others.

Pharmacotherapy

Acute treatment

This depends on whether there is an acute manic relapse whilst on treatment previously or if this is a first presentation. If previously on treatment, consider compliance with medication by noting the history and taking a blood sample for assay; consider any precipitating factors such as life events or illicit substance misuse. A mood stabilizer may have to be increased or recommenced. Agitated and restless patients may benefit from a short course of a benzodiazepine (Goodwin, 2003) with or without an antipsychotic.

Prophylaxis

After an acute episode, prevention is the most important part of management using both psycho-education and medication. Lithium is the most commonly used first-line mood stabilizer, but it needs to be regularly monitored by blood tests to ensure that the concentration in the blood does not reach toxic levels. Abruptly stopping lithium can lead to a greater chance of relapse and it should only be prescribed to people who are likely to take the medication. Semi-sodium valproate and sodium valproate are also widely used; neither is licensed for prevention but sodium valproate is a commonly used prophylactic agent. The former is licensed for use in acute mania (for details of side-effects see the British National Formulary and prescribing guidelines (Taylor *et al.*, 2003). Side-effects of mood stabilizers are presented in Table 22.4 above.

Depressive episodes in bipolar affective disorder (BAD)

These are difficult to treat in the context of BAD as antidepressants can initiate a manic relapse, especially the tricyclic antidepressants. The main principle is to make sure that the patient is covered with a mood stabilizer or an antipsychotic when using any antidepressant (Goodwin, 2003).

Psychological treatment

Psycho-education helps the service user and his or her carers to understand the nature of the illness and help to manage it better. A life chart depicting previous relapses and indicating life events and medication may help someone with a mild degree of ID. It is very helpful to identify the earliest signs of relapse such as sleep (relapse signature) disturbance so that appropriate action is taken early.

Social interventions

Appropriate housing, financial help, etc. contribute to the person's mental well-being.

MOOD, ANXIETY, AND SOMATOFORM DISORDERS AND ADJUSTMENT REACTIONS

In this section a description of major episodic depression; persistent mood disorders; anxiety disorders; somatoform disorders will be given first, followed by a consideration of the differential diagnosis of mood and anxiety disorders and their management.

Depression

Depression can present as a depressive episode or as a recurrent depressive disorder with relapses and remissions. A depressive episode may be mild, moderate or severe and either with or without psychotic features. The core features of depression (ICD-10) include at least two out of the following three:

- A persistent lowering of mood
- A reduction in energy or activity levels; or fatigability
- A lack of enjoyment or pleasure from activities that are usually pleasurable (anhedonia).

The following are associated features of depression:

- A loss of confidence or self-esteem
- Feelings of excessive or inappropriate guilt and self-reproach
- Recurrent thoughts of death, suicide or suicidal behaviour
- Poor concentration
- Agitation or retardation (either subjective or objective)
- Sleep disturbance
- A decrease or an increase in appetite with a corresponding change in weight.

Such features may not be seen in people with moderate or more severe ID. It has been noted that irritability is more likely than a depressed mood and the DC-LD considers this as the core symptom. Other features more likely are regressive behaviour, such as pica or rocking, reassurance-seeking behaviour, an increase in aggressive behaviour, social withdrawal, lessening of communication, self-injury, screaming, tearfulness and somatic/hypochondriacal complaints (McBrien, 2003; Smiley and Cooper, 2003). Less common symptoms are feelings of guilt or worthlessness and recurrent thoughts of suicide. Suicidal behaviour is uncommon in this group even in the presence of a depressive disorder (Walters, 1990).

Persistent mood disorders: dysthymia and cyclothymia

Persistent mood disorders differ from major depression and bipolar disorder in degree of severity and duration of symptoms. In cyclothymia, there are mood instabilities over a period of at least two years ranging from mild elation to low mood (not worse than mild depression), but not to the same degree as in bipolar affective disorders or recurrent depressive disorders. There is little information published on this category in people with ID.

In dysthymia, there is at least a two-year period of constant mild but not more severe depressive symptoms. There are no periods of elation or hypomania. This is probably under-diagnosed in people with ID (Jancar and Gunaratne, 1994).

Anxiety disorders

People with ID may not be able to describe feelings of anxiety but may present with changes in behaviour such as agitation, aggression, self-injurious behaviour, oppositional behaviour, frequent urination, smearing of faeces, screaming, crying, withdrawal, freezing or regressive clingy behaviour (Bailey and Andrews, 2003). Signs and symptoms of anxiety are given in Table 22.5.

Table 22.5 Signs and symptoms of anxiety

	Symptoms or signs	*Comments*
Autonomic arousal	Palpitations; fast heart rate Sweating Trembling or shaking Dry mouth	A dry mouth may result in the person asking for more drinks than usual
Symptoms involving chest and abdomen	Breathing difficulty Feeling of choking Chest discomfort or pain Nausea or abdominal distress	Hyperventilation; abdominal symptoms may be like 'the stomach turning over' or 'butterflies'
Symptoms involving mental state	Feeling dizzy, unsteady, faint or light-headed Feeling that objects are unreal (derealization), or that the self is distant or 'not really here' (depersonalization) Fear of losing control, 'going crazy' or passing out Fear of dying	Irritability and restlessness
General symptoms	Hot flushes or cold chills Numbness or tingling sensations	Irritability or restlessness

Phobic anxiety disorders

In these, anxiety is evoked only in certain well-defined situations. As a consequence, these situations are avoided or are endured with great dread. Depressive symptoms often co-exist with anxiety symptoms. The feared situation must not be delusional and be external to the subject (i.e. not fear of disease or a misshapen body-part; this is classed under 'hypochondriacal disorder').

Agoraphobia

Consistent marked fear or avoidance of at least two of the following situations: (1) crowds; (2) public places; (3) travelling alone (using public transport); or (4) living away from home.

This may exist with panic attacks (see below p 813–814).

Social phobia

Fear of situations where there is perceived to be scrutiny by other people, e.g. parties or eating in public. There can be fear of criticism and low-self esteem. It can lead to a panic attack. In addition to the symptoms listed in Table 22.5 above, there should be at least one of the following symptoms: (1) blushing or shaking; (2) vomiting, retching or the fear of vomiting; or (3) urgency of urination or defecation, or incontinence.

Specific (isolated) phobias

Phobia related to very specific situations such as animals (e.g. snakes or spiders), heights, flying, small enclosed spaces, sight of blood, hospitals and injections. The situation or object, when avoided, causes no symptoms, but there may be anticipatory fear and avoidance behaviour. They can result in a panic attack.

Other anxiety disorders

Whereas the above anxiety disorders evoke anxiety in predictable or limited scenarios, the disorders described below are not situation-dependent. Depressive or obsessional symptoms may also be present as a secondary feature.

Panic disorder

A typical panic attack does not last more than a few minutes and certainly not longer than 30 minutes. They are recurrent, unpredictable and not limited to a particular situation. The symptoms experienced are of severe anxiety (described in Table 22.5 above) starting as a crescendo followed by a decline to previous functioning. Physical disorders such as hyperthyroidism, drugs, cardiac conditions and epilepsy and other psychiatric conditions, e.g. depression, should be excluded.

Generalized anxiety disorder

Anxiety is not restricted to any specific situation, but is present most of the time, a 'free floating anxiety'. There is at least a six-month period of feelings of nervousness, prominent tension, worry, and apprehension about everyday events. There may also be an exaggerated response to minor surprises or being startled, difficulty in concentrating, the mind 'going blank' because of worrying or anxiety, persistent irritability and difficulty in getting to sleep because of worries.

Mixed anxiety and depressive disorder

When both symptoms of anxiety and depression are present and roughly equally prominent, then this category is used.

Obsessive-compulsive disorder

The ICD-10 criteria that define the essential features of obsessions and compulsions are shown in Box 22.4. Only when they cause distress and interfere

---

Box 22.4 Features of obsessions and compulsions

OBSESSIONS are thoughts, ideas, impulses to act or mental images (such as indecisiveness or repugnant thoughts)

COMPULSIONS are stereotypical *acts* (such as cleaning, washing, checking, orderliness, tidiness, hoarding, touching, arranging, grooming) whose function is to prevent objectively unlikely events, often harmful, that might occur otherwise

NECESSARY FEATURES OF OBSESSIONS AND COMPULSIONS

The sufferer believes they emanate from his/her own mind and not from an outside influence or agency
They are repetitive and excessive

> They are not inherently enjoyable, but are unpleasant and purposeless (there may be a temporary relief of tension if not resisted; this is not considered as pleasurable)
>
> The person may try to resist them, but in chronic cases this may not be so
>
> Interfering with the person's compulsions may cause him or her distress and may result in aggression

with the person's functioning are they considered a disorder. They must not be a direct result of another psychiatric disorder (including a pervasive developmental disorder), drugs or a physical disorder. People with ID may not be able to explain their obsessions. Self-injurious behaviour may be due to compulsions (King, 1993). It may be difficult to judge compulsions as excessive or unreasonable, but if it provides temporary comfort, interferes with daily activities, or there is resistance to change, then it is viewed as a disorder. Compulsions need to be distinguished from 'stereotypies', which are repetitive, purposeless, often rhythmic movements (Bodfish, Crawford, Powell, Parker, *et al.*, 1995) and tics, which are sudden, involuntary, rapid, recurrent, non-rhythmic motor movements or vocalizations.

Post-traumatic stress disorder and acute stress reaction

Acute stress reaction occurs within about seventy-two hours of a severely stressful event (such as assault, rape, car accident, natural disaster); anxiety symptoms (that should start within one hour) usually start to resolve.

Post-traumatic stress disorder, according to the ICD-10, may occur after a delay of a few weeks or months following a stressful situation that was extremely threatening or catastrophic. There are the following symptoms:

- A persistent remembering or 'reliving' of the event in the form of intrusive memories ('flashbacks'), recurring dreams or nightmares or experiencing distress when exposed to circumstances resembling or associated with the event
- Actual or preferred avoidance of circumstances resembling or associated with the event which was not present before
- An inability to recall, either partially or completely, some important aspects of the event, or
- Persistent symptoms of increased psychological sensitivity and arousal shown by any two of the following: (a) difficulty in falling or staying asleep; (b) irritability or outbursts of anger; (c) difficulty in concentrating; (d) hypervigilance; and (e) an exaggerated startle response.

Adjustment disorders

Significant life changes or stressful events can lead to distress and emotional disturbance, which can significantly affect social and personal functioning. There may be individual vulnerability. The manifestations are varied and include anxiety symptoms, depressive symptoms, a disturbance of behaviour, and an inability to cope or perform usual routines. The response may be in the following categories (ICD-10):

- A brief depressive reaction not lasting more than a month
- A prolonged depressive reaction (lasting less than two years)
- A mixed anxiety and depressive reaction
- A predominant disturbance of other emotions (including anxiety, depression, worry, tension or anger)
- A predominant disturbance of conduct (e.g. aggression)
- A mixed disturbance of emotions and conduct.

Except in the prolonged depressive subtype, the symptoms do not last longer than six months.

Somatoform disorders

These are subdivided depending on whether the person frequently complains of changing physical symptoms (aches and pains) despite extensive medical investigations to no avail (somatization disorder), or expresses the conviction that there is an underlying physical illness (hypochondriacal disorder) that has been missed by the medical practitioners. It also may manifest as an over-valued idea (as opposed to a delusion) that there is a body dysmorphology (such as a big nose).

Differential diagnosis for depressive disorders

It is rare for depression to exist in the complete absence of anxiety symptoms and so other psychiatric conditions such as obsessive-compulsive disorder, generalized anxiety disorder, post-traumatic stress disorder, and mixed anxiety and depressive disorder must be considered. Schizophrenia can present like depression and complications of schizophrenia include depression. Depression may present similarly to dementia ('psuedodementia'). Certain prescribed drugs (such as propanolol and steroids) and alcohol are associated with mood problems. Viral infections, tumours such as pancreatic and brain tumours, head injuries, malnutrition and endocrine causes (including hypothyroidism, hyperparathyroidism and Cushing's disease) can also contribute to depressive symptoms.

Investigations of depressive disorders

These should exclude possible physical causes of depression as suspected in a given person.

Management of depressive disorders

Acute treatment has different priorities to longer-term therapy. The safety of the sufferer is paramount. Consideration should be given for admission to hospital, if there is evidence of significant suicidality, psychotic symptoms or if the person has stopped eating and drinking.

Most practitioners prescribe an SSRI or less commonly tricyclic anti-depressants as a first line in drug treatment. The SSRIs are relatively safe in overdose when compared with the tricyclics. Furthermore, the tricyclics have more anti-cholinergic (antimuscarinic) and cardiac side-effects. Advice should be given to the patient that the medication can take ten to fourteen days to show any benefit, and they should not stop it suddenly because of the possibility of discontinuation symptoms. For the SSRIs, these include, 'flu-like symptoms, dizziness exacerbated by movement, insomnia, irritability, crying spells and movement problems. They can be avoided by reducing the medication gradually.

If after four weeks of maximum tolerable doses of an antidepressant there is no improvement in the person's symptoms, a second-line treatment must be considered. This is with the precondition that there are no compliance, diag-nostic or ongoing maintaining factors. Most practitioners would switch to a different class of antidepressant, such as mirtazepine. If a full trial of the second-line antidepressant has failed, augmentation treatment with lithium and/or tri-odothyronine may be tried or combination antidepressants, but advice should be sought from specialist centres (Anderson, Nutt and Deakin, 2000; Taylor et al., 2003).

A first episode of depression needs to be successfully treated for about six to nine months before considering stopping. Many cases will relapse and a close follow-up is necessary. If there is a relapse, this increases the chances of even more relapses and so prophylaxis with a medication regimen that worked before needs to be considered. In some people regular adjunctive ECT may be necessary and it has been shown to be of value in people with ID (Aziz, Maixner, DeQuardo, Aldridge and Tandon, 2001; Cutajar and Wilson, 1999; Thuppal and Fink, 1999).

Many studies have shown the value of CBT in the treatment of depression. High expressed emotion in the family environment can have a detrimental effect on many mental heath parameters including depression and may need to be addressed in the form of family therapy. Exploration of the social contribution to the condition should be made and addressed.

Differential diagnosis of anxiety disorders

This will include other psychiatric conditions, medical conditions (e.g. thyroid disease) and alcohol withdrawal. In depression there are usually some anxiety symptoms; if the depressive symptoms are more prominent then they should be diagnosed as a depressive disorder.

Investigations of anxiety disorders

To exclude possible medical causes as indicated by the history and physical findings, a routine blood screen is usually undertaken, including a test for thyroid function.

Management of anxiety disorders

The anxiolytic benzodiazepines are used in the short term, as are the SSRIs in higher doses, for some conditions such as obsessive-compulsive disorder. The monoamine oxidase inhibitors can also be used in certain anxiety disorders (see Taylor *et al.*, 2003). Psychological treatments and social interventions are the main interventions for many of these disorders.

PERSONALITY DISORDERS

A personality disorder (PD) is diagnosed when the traits or behaviours associated with the person's personality cause significant distress and impairment to the individual or to those that they interact with. There are many difficulties associated with diagnosing these in people with ID (Alexander and Cooray, 2003; Flynn, Matthews and Hollins, 2002; Torr, 2003). In the DC-LD, people with PDs are described as having the following:

- Markedly disharmonious attitudes and behaviour with those which are culturally expected and accepted; involving: affectivity; emotional control; arousal; impulse-control; outlook; interpreting and thinking; and a style of relating to others
- These are not a direct consequence of severity of ID, pervasive developmental disorder, other psychiatric disorder, drugs or physical disorders
- These should be chronic, pervasive and maladaptive across a broad range of personal and social situations and cause personal distress to the individual and/or to others causing significant problems in occupational and/or social functioning
- The diagnosis should not be made for anyone under the age of 21 years old, nor in those with severe or profound ID.

Management of personality disorders involves using medication, psychological therapies and social interventions; see Torr (2003) for a discussion.

ORGANIC SYNDROMES

In delirium or an 'acute confusional state', there is disorientation in time, place and person. The person has poor attention and is distractible. The presentation fluctuates with patches of full alertness and orientation. At night the confusion may be worse. There is often fearfulness and suspiciousness. There are a plethora of causes ranging from infections of the brain (such as meningitis or encephalitis) or of other tissues (such as urinary tract infection or a chest infection), malignancies, acute head trauma, metabolic and endocrine causes, drugs and toxins.

The most important aspect of management is to treat the underlying medical condition. This may require urgent admission to hospital. The person may require sedation if agitated and lorazepam or diazepam can be used as well as haloperidol as a short-term measure.

STAFF TRAINING

It is important for people who are employed to care for people with ID to have the relevant knowledge. Otherwise not only are the people they are meant to serve put at a risk, but staff themselves are likely to suffer 'burn-out' from stress (Hatton, 1999; Holt and Oliver, 2000). Clinical psychologists have a role to play in staff training to recognize behaviours and symptoms that may be the manifestation of a mental illness and require further investigation. Staff should understand the importance of 'baseline' functioning, idiosyncrasies in abilities to communicate and that some apparently mental health problems will have a physical or medical cause. The importance of being able to monitor target behaviours or symptoms so that the effectiveness of an intervention may be judged and any evidence of a relapse of an illness can be picked up early are skills staff can be trained in. The clinical psychologist, as a part of the multidisciplinary team, will be able to advise on steps to promote positive mental health in people with IDs and their carers. Training packs are now available which aid training of staff highlighting the issues mentioned here (Holt and Bouras, 1997).

EXERCISE

This exercise is to help developing competencies in treating depression and anxiety in people with ID. Read the case example in Box 22.5 and then work in groups of four to answer the following questions:

What are the possible diagnoses and why?

What are the possible predisposing, precipitating and perpetuating factors? Speculate on the biological, psychological and social causes for each factor.

What other information and further investigations would you consider to support your diagnosis?

How would you manage this man? Use the biopsychosocial framework.

Box 22.5 Depression, anxiety, persistent delusional or adjustment disorder?

A 36-year-old man (Mr B) with a mild ID, and living in supported accommodation was referred because of a change in his behaviour over a period of one year. He was seen in an outpatient clinic. He had become obsessed with a female resident who was not reciprocating his advances. He had been undergoing counselling, but there was some worry whether he had a psychiatric illness or not. A history was obtained from his father and care staff. He had been a 'quiet and happy person' until his present problems. He became emotionally involved with another female resident. He felt dragged in, but she rejected him. Over the months he gradually became more withdrawn, refusing to have meals in the company of others or getting involved with other residents. He would often state that no one liked him and he was expressing a wish to leave. He even expressed a thought that his parents did not love him. At times he had shouted and hit furniture. His moods had become more labile and he generally appeared more stressed. In the last three weeks he was described as having 'panic attacks' occurring approximately once a week. He also claimed that people had been talking about him behind his back, but this only occurred when he was at his normal residence and not outside, for example at his regular club outings. He felt angry and aggressive and recently he threw a glass at a resident because he thought that people were talking about him. The key worker expressed the thought that the safety of the female resident may be now an issue. Mr B's appetite and weight had remained steady and he apparently was sleeping. Although he was isolating himself, he still engaged in his daily leisure activities. He claimed he had no sadness, no suicidal thoughts or thoughts of harming others. His father said that Mr B felt rejected and volatile because of 'boredom' and that his son has recently been rejected for work experience. His father claimed that for the last 12–18 months his son had definitely become changed in himself and 'depressed'. Prior to that he was a happy person and if he was to score 10 out of 10 before, now he scored 1 out of 10.

Medical history. Visual impairment; mild intellectual disability; five years ago, left cataract extraction; four years ago, right cataract extraction; Lawrence-Moon-Biedl Syndrome; asthma.

Psychiatric and forensic history. Nil

Family history. His father is 75 years old and is a commissionaire for a security firm. His mother is 67, a housewife and lives with her husband. She has Alzheimer's disease. The couple never had their own children and adopted Mr B when he was 6 weeks old. There is no information available on early pregnancy and birth, but it was noted that he was overweight and started to walk at the age of 18 months and to say short sentences at the age of 2 years. He developed asthma at the age of 2 years and was described as a happy child, but a poor sleeper and this often caused difficulties with his adoptive parents. He started school at the age of 7 years for the first time. This was a special school and then between 10 and 16 years he went to a school for the 'educationally sub-normal'. During ages 16–17 he went to a college, but attained no qualifications. He remained with his parents until the age of 31 until they were not able to cope. There is no family history of psychiatric illnesses apparent.

Present circumstances. He lives in residential accommodation and he has no major financial problems. He was fully integrated until his recent problems.

Alcohol, drugs and tobacco. He drinks 1–2 pints of beer a week and takes no illicit drugs and does not smoke.

Pre-morbid personality (from father). He is described as being bright with a good sense of humour, being secretive and not having many friends. He enjoys bowling, horse riding, watching videos and music. Mr B said that he did not believe in God, nor did he go to church.

Provisional functional assessment. As Mr B is partially sighted he uses a white stick and he is able to see only outlines of windows and colours. His hearing is normal. He was able to read when he was very young, but at a very low standard. He did not learn Braille. In terms of communication he could not elaborate complicated sentences, but could understand basic English. He did not seem to be good at expressing his emotions in words. He has a good memory for dates. His self-care is adequate and he is able to dress himself, but he needed help with cooking and shopping. If he goes shopping he has to go to a shop that he is familiar with as he tends to get help from the shopkeepers.

Provisional risk assessment. Risk to self – nil. Risk to others – he has thrown a glass at another resident once recently. Risk to property – as above.

Mental state examination. *Appearance and behaviour:* Overweight, partially sighted man with a white stick. There was no evidence of psychomotor disturbances or movement problems. He was tidy. He answered questions with short replies. *Speech –* soft, normal in rate and prosody. *Affect:* this was flat with little reactivity. There was no perplexity. *Mood: subjectively,* he said, 'I am OK'. He had no biological/somatic symptoms of sleep disturbance, appetite or weight loss, no diurnal variation of mood. *Objectively,* mildly depressed. *Thoughts:* he thought that people talked behind his back, but only at his residence and not anywhere else. This belief was held with great conviction despite no obvious evidence for it. His rate of thoughts was normal and there was no formal thought disorder or delusions. *Perceptions:* nil, abnormal. *Cognition:* he was alert and orientated in time, place and person. His attention and short-term memory were intact. *Insight:* he felt he was not depressed and he did not want any medication, but was happy to continue with psychotherapy.

Physical examination. He had no physical signs to suggest an acute physical illness including any evidence of thyroid dysfunction and autonomic arousal.

FURTHER READING FOR CARERS

Hollins, S. and Curran, J. (1996). *Understanding Depression in People with Learning Disabilities.* Books without Words Series. London: Pavilion Publishing.
Holt, G., Gratsa, A. and Bouras, N. (2004). *A Guide to Mental Health for Families and Carers of People with Intellectual Disabilities.* London: Jessica Kingsley.

FURTHER READING FOR CLINICIANS

Bouras, N. (1999). *Psychiatric and Behavioural Disorders in Developmental Disabilities and Mental Retardation*. Cambridge: Cambridge University Press.

Deb, S., Matthews, T., Holt, G. and Bouras, N. (2001). *Practice Guidelines for the Assessment and Diagnosis of Mental Health Problems in Adults with Intellectual Disability*. Brighton: Pavilion.

Dosen, A. and Day, K. (2001). *Treating Mental Illness and Behaviour Problems in Children and Adults with Mental Retardation*. Washington, DC: American Psychiatric Publishing.

Einfield, S. L. (2001). Systematic management approach to pharmacotherapy for people with learning disabilities. *Advances in Psychiatric Treatment*, 7, 43–9.

Fraser, W. and Kerr, M. (2003). *Seminars in the Psychiatry of Learning Disabilities*. London: Gaskell, Royal College of Psychiatrists.

Gelder, M., Lopez-Ibor, J. and Andreasen, N. (2000). *New Oxford Textbook of Psychiatry*. Oxford: Oxford University Press.

Gelder, M. and Mayou, R. (2001). *Shorter Oxford Textbook of Psychiatry*. Oxford: Oxford University Press.

Holt, G. and Bouras, N. (1997). *Mental Health in Learning Disabilities: A Training Pack for Staff Working with People who have a Dual Diagnosis of Mental Health Needs and Learning Disabilities*. Brighton: Pavilion.

Jacobson, J. and Mulick, J. (1996). *Manual of Diagnosis and Professional Practice in Mental Retardation*. Washington, DC: American Psychological Association.

Matson, J. L. and Bamburg, J. W. (2000). Psychopharmacology and mental retardation: A 10 year review (1990–1999). *Research in Developmental Disabilities*, 21, 263–96.

Reiss, S. and Aman, M. (1998). *Psychotropic Medications and Developmental Disabilities: The International Consensus Handbook*. Baltimore, MD: Brookes.

Royal College of Psychiatrists (2001). *DC-LD. Diagnostic Criteria for Psychiatric Disorders for Use with Adults with Learning Disabilities/Mental Retardation*. London: Gaskell.

Rush, J. and Frances, A. (2000). Treatment of psychiatric and behavioural problems in mental retardation. Special issue of the *American Journal on Mental Retardation*. Washington, DC: American Association on Mental Retardation.

Taylor, D. and Paton, C. (2003). *The Maudsley Prescribing Guidelines*. London and New York: Martin Dunitz.

ASSESSMENT INSTRUMENTS

Affective Rating Scale. Wieseler, N., Campbell, C. and Sonis, W. (1988). Ongoing use of an affective rating scale in the treatment of a mentally retarded individual with a rapid-cycling bipolar affective disorder. *Research in Developmental Disabilities*, 9(1), 47–53.

Assessment of Dual Diagnosis (ADD). Matson, J. and Bamburg, J. (1998). Reliability of the Assessment of Dual Diagnosis (ADD). *Research in Developmental Disabilities*, 20, 89–95.

Beck Depression Inventory (BDI). Kazdin, A., Matson, J. and Senatore, V. (1983). Assessment of depression in mentally retarded adults. *American Journal of Psychiatry,* 140(8), 1040–3.

Beck, A. T., Ward, C., Mendelsohn, M., Mock, J. and Erbaugh, J. (1961). An inventory for measuring depression. *Archives of General Psychiatry,* 4, 561–71.

CANDID. Xenitidis, K., Thornicroft, G., Leese, M., Slade, M., Fotiadou, M., Philip, H., Sayer, J., Harris, E., McGee, D. and Murphy, D. (2000). Reliability and validity of the CANDID – a needs assessment instrument for adults with learning disabilities and mental health problems. *British Journal of Psychiatry,* 176, 473–8.

Clinical Interview Schedule (CIS) – Mental Handicap Version. Ballinger, B., Armstrong, J., Presly, A. and Reid, A. (1975). Use of a standardized psychiatric interview in mentally handicapped patients. *British Journal of Psychiatry,* 127, 540–4.

Diagnostic Assessment of the Severely Handicapped (DASH) Scale. Matson, J., Gardner, W., Coe, D. and Sovner, R. (1991). A scale for evaluating emotional disorders in severely and profoundly mentally retarded persons. Development of the Diagnostic Assessment for the Severely Handicapped (DASH) scale. *British Journal of Psychiatry,* 159, 404–9.

Diagnostic Assessment of the Severely Handicapped (DASH) II Scale. Matson, J., Rush, K., Hamilton, M., Anderson, S., Bbaglio, C., Williams, D. and Kirkpatrick-Sanchez, S. (1999). Characteristics of depression as assessed by the Diagnostic Assessment for the Severely Handicapped-II (DASH-II). *Research in Developmental Disabilities,* 20(4), 305–13.

Diagnostic Criteria for Research – 10th Version (DCR-10) (modified). Clarke, D. and Gomez, G. (1999). Utility of modified DCR-10 criteria in the diagnosis of depression associated with intellectual disability. *Journal of Intellectual Disabilities Research,* 43(5), 413–20.

Hamilton Depression Scale-Mental Handicap Version. Sireling, L. (1986). Depression in mentally handicapped patients: Diagnostic and neuroendocrine evaluation. *British Journal of Psychiatry,* 149, 274–8.

Hamilton Rating Scale for Depression. Hamilton, M. (1960). A rating scale for depression. *Journal of Neurology, Neurosurgery and Psychiatry,* 23, 56–62.

Health of the Nation Outcome Scales for People with Learning Disabilities. Roy, A., Matthews, H., Clifford, P., Fowler, V. and Martin, D. (2002). Health of the Nation Outcome Scales for People with Learning Disabilities (HoNOS-LD). *British Journal of Psychiatry,* 180, 61–6.

Roy, A., Matthews, H., Clifford, P., Fowler, V. and Martin, D. (2002) Health of the Nation Outcome Scales for People with Learning Disabilities (HoNOS-LD). Glossary for HoNOS-LD score sheet. *British Journal of Psychiatry,* 180, 67–70. http://www.rcpsych.ac.uk/cru/honoscales/honosld/index.htm.

Learning Disability version of the Cardinal Needs Schedule (LDCNS). Marshall, M., Hogg, L., Gath, D. and Lockwood, A. (1995). The Cardinal Needs Schedule – a modified version of the MRC Needs for Care Assessment Schedule. *Psychological Medicine,* 25(3), 605–17.

Mental Retardation Depression Scale. Meins, W. (1996). A new depression scale designed for use with adults with mental retardation. *Journal of Intellectual Disabilities Research,* 40(3), 222–6.

Mini PAS-ADD. Prosser, H., Moss, S., Costello, H., Simpson, N., Patel, P. and

Rowe, S. (1998). Reliability and validity of the Mini PAS-ADD for assessing psychiatric disorders in adults with intellectual disability. *Journal of Intellectual Disabilities Research*, 42(4), 264–72.

Minnesosta Multiphasic Personality Inventory (MMPI–168L). McDaniel, W. and Harris, D. (1999). Mental health outcomes in dually diagnosed individuals with mental retardation assessed with the MMPI–168(L): case studies. *Journal of Clinical Psychology*, 55(4), 487–96.

Present Psychiatric State-Learning Disability (PPS-LD). Cooper, S. (1997). Psychiatry of elderly compared to younger adults with intellectual disabilities. *Journal of Applied Research in Intellectual Disabilities*, 10, 303–11.

Psychiatric Assessment Schedule for Adults with Developmental Disabilities (PAS-ADD). Moss, S., Patel, P., Prosser, H., Goldberg, D., Simpson, N., Rowe, S. and Lucchino, R. (1993). Psychiatric morbidity in older people with moderate and severe learning disability. I: Development and reliability of the patient interview (PAS-ADD). *British Journal of Psychiatry*, 163, 471–80.

PAS-ADD Checklist. Moss, S., Prosser, H., Costello, H., Simpson, N. and Patel, P. (1998). Reliability and validity of the PAS-ADD Checklist for detecting psychiatric disorders in adults with intellectual disability. *Journal of Intellectual Disabilities Research*, 42(2), 173–83.

Psychopathology Instrument for Mentally Retarded Adults (PIMRA). Matson, J. (1988). The *PIMRA Manual*. Orlando Park, IL: International Diagnostic Systems Inc. Matson, J., Kazdin, A. and Senatore, V. (1991). Psychometric properties of the Psychopathology Instrument for Mentally Retarded Adults. *Applied Research in Mental Retardation*, 5, 81–90.

Self-Report Depression Questionnaire (SRDQ). Reynolds, W. and Baker, J. (1988). Assessment of depression in persons with mental retardation. *American Journal of Mental Retardation*, 93(1), 93–103.

Standardised Assessment of Personality (SAP). Reid, A. and Ballinger, B. (1987). Personality disorder in mental handicap. *Psychological Medicine*, 17(4), 983–7.

Khan, A., Cowan, C. and Roy, A. (1997). Personality disorders in people with learning disabilities: a community survey. *Journal of Intellectual Disabilities Research*, 41(4), 324–30.

Yale-Brown Obsessive Compulsive Scale (Y-BOCS). Feurer, I., Dimitropoulos, A. and Stone, W. (1998). The latent variable structure of the Compulsive Behaviour Checklist in people with Prader-Willi syndrome. *Journal of Intellectual Disabilities Research*, 42 (Pt 6): 472–80.

Goodman, W. K., Price, L. H., Rasmussen, S., Mazure, C., Fleischmann, R., Hill, C., Heninger, G. and Charney, D. (1989). The Yale-Brown Obsessive Compulsive Scale. I. Development, use, and reliability. *Archives of General Psychiatry*, 46(11), 1006–11.

Zung Anxiety Rating Scale: Adults Mental Handicap Version. Lindsay, W. and Michie, A. (1988). Adaptation of the Zung self-rating anxiety scale for people with a mental handicap. *Journal of Mental Deficiency Research*, 32(6), 485–90.

Zung, W. (1971). A rating instrument for anxiety disorders. *Psychosomatics*, 12(6), 371–9.

Zung Self-Rating Depression Inventory: Mental Handicap Version. Helsel, W. and Matson, J. (1988). The relationship of depression to social skills and intellectual functioning in mentally retarded adults. *Journal of Mental Deficiency Research*, 32(5), 411–18.

Zung, W. (1965). A Self-Rating Depression Scale. *Archives of General Psychiatry*, 12, 63–70.

REFERENCES

Alexander, R. and Cooray, S. (2003). Diagnosis of personality disorders in learning disability. *British Journal of Psychiatry Supplement*, 44, S28–31.

American Psychiatric Association (1994). *Diagnostic and Statistical Manual of Mental Disorders* (4th edn). Washington, DC: APA.

American Psychiatric Association (2000). *Diagnostic and Statistical Manual of the Mental Disorders (Fourth Edition-Text Revision, DSM –IV-TR)*. Washington, DC: APA.

Anderson, I., Nutt, D. and Deakin, J. (2000). Evidence-based guidelines for treating depressive disorders with antidepressants: A revision of the 1993 British Association for Psychopharmacology guidelines. British Association for Psychopharmacology. *Journal of Psychopharmacology*, 14(1), 3–20.

Aziz, M., Maixner, D., DeQuardo, J., Aldridge, A. and Tandon, R. (2001). ECT and mental retardation: A review and case reports. *Journal of ECT*, 17(2), 149–52.

Bailey, N. and Andrews, T. (2003). Diagnostic criteria for psychiatric disorders for use with adults with learning disabilities/mental retardation (DC-LD) and the diagnosis of anxiety disorders: A review. *Journal of Intellectual Disability Research*, 47 Suppl. 1, 50–61.

Beail, N. (1989). Understanding emotions. In D. Brandon (ed.), *Mutual Respect: Therapeutic Approaches in Working with People who have Learning Difficulties* (pp. 27–45). Surbiton: Good Impressions.

Beail, N. (1994). Fire, coffins and skeletons. In V. Sinason (ed.), *Treating Survivors of Satanic Abuse* (pp. 153–8). London: Routledge.

Beail, N. (2003). What works for people with mental retardation? Critical commentary on cognitive-behavioural and psychodynamic psychotherapy research. *Mental Retardation*, 41(6), 468–72.

Beail, N. and Warden, S. (1996). Evaluation of a psychodynamic psychotherapy service for adults with intellectual disabilities: Rational, design and preliminary outcome data. *Journal of Applied Research in Intellectual Disabilities*, 71, 223–8.

Beck, A. (1967). *Depression: Clinical, Theoretical and Experimental Aspects*. Philadelphia, PA: University of Pennsylvania.

Bichard, S., Sinason, V. and Usiskin, J. (1996). Measuring change in mentally retarded clients in long term psychoanalytical psychotherapy. *The National Association for Dual Diagnosis*, 13, 6–11.

Black, D. (1987). Handicap and family therapy. In A. Bentovim, G. Gorell Barnes and A. Cooklin (eds), *Family Therapy: Complementary Frameworks of Theory and Practice* (2nd edn, pp. 117–39). London: Academic Press.

Bodfish, J., Crawford, T., Powell, S., Parker, D., Golden, R. and Lewis, M. (1995). Compulsions in adults with mental retardation: prevalence, phenomenology, and comorbidity with stereotypy and self-injury. *American Journal of Mental Retardation*, 100(2), 183–92.

Bokszanska, A., Martin, G., Vanstraelen M., Holt, G., Bouras, N. and Taylor, D.

(2003). Risperidone and olanzapine in adults with intellectual disability: A clinical naturalistic study. *International Clinical Psychopharmacology*, 18(5), 285–91.

Borthwick-Duffy, S. (1994). Epidemiology and prevalence of psychopathology in people with mental retardation. *Journal of Consulting and Clinical Psychology*, 62(1), 17–27.

Borthwick-Duffy, S. and Eyman, R. (1990). Who are the dually diagnosed? *American Journal of Mental Retardation*, 94(6), 586–95.

Bouras, N. and Drummond, C. (1992). Behaviour and psychiatric disorders of people with mental handicaps living in the community. *Journal of Intellectual Disability Research*, 36(4), 349–57.

Bowlby, J. (1988). *A Secure Base: Clinical Applications of Attachment Theory*. London: Routledge.

Brown, G. and Harris, T. (1978). *The Social Origins of Depression*. London: Tavistock.

Burnand, Y., Andreoli, A., Kolatte, E., Venturini, A. and Rosset, N. (2002). Psychodynamic psychotherapy and clomipramine in the treatment of major depression. *Psychiatric Services*, 53(5), 585–90.

Cooper, S. A. (1997). Epidemiology of psychiatric disorders in elderly compared with younger adults with learning disabilities. *British Journal of Psychiatry*, 170, 375–80.

Corbett, J. A. (1979). *Psychiatric Morbidity and Mental Retardation*. London: Gaskell Press.

Cutajar, P. and Wilson, D. (1999). The use of ECT in intellectual disability. *Journal of Intellectual Disability Research*, 43(5), 421–7.

Deb, S., Thomas, M. and Bright, C. (2001). Mental disorder in adults with intellectual disability. 1: Prevalence of functional psychiatric illness among a community-based population aged between 16 and 64 years. *Journal of Intellectual Disability Research*, 45(6), 495–505.

Department of Health (2001). *Treatment Choice in Psychological Therapies and Counselling: Evidence Based Clinical Practice Guidelines*. London: Stationery Office.

Eaton, L. and Menolascino, J. (1982). Psychiatric disorders in the mentally retarded: Types, problems, and challenges. *American Journal of Psychiatry*, 139(10), 1297–1303.

Einfeld, S. (2001). Systematic management approach to pharmacotherapy for people with learning disabilities. *Advances in Psychiatric Treatment*, 7, 43–9.

Fletcher, R. (1993). Mental Health Aspects of Mental Retardation. In R. Fletcher and A. Dosen (eds), *Individual Psychotherapy for Persons with Mental Retardation* (pp. 327–49). New York: Lexington Books.

Flynn, A., Matthews, H. and Hollins, S. (2002). Validity of the diagnosis of personality disorder in adults with learning disability and severe behavioural problems. Preliminary study. *British Journal of Psychiatry*, 180, 543–6.

Frankish, P. (1989). Meeting the emotional needs of handicapped people: A psychodynamic approach. *Journal of Mental Deficiency Research*, 33, 407–14.

Gaedt, C. (1995). Psychotherapeutic approaches in the treatment of mental illness and behavioural disorders in mentally retarded people: The significance of a psychoanalytic perspective. *Journal of Intellectual Disability Research*, 39(3), 233–9.

Gelder, M., Lopez-Ibor, J. and Andreasen, N. (2000). *New Oxford Textbook of Psychiatry*. Oxford: Oxford University Press.

Goldberg, D., Magrill, L., Hale, J., Damaskindou, K., Paul, J. and Tham, S. (1995).

Protection and loss: Working with learning disabled adults and their families. *Journal of Family Therapy*, 17, 263–80.

Goodwin, G. M. (2003). Evidence-based guidelines for treating bipolar disorder: Recommendations from the British Association for Psychopharmacology. *Journal of Psychopharmacology*, 17(2), 149–73.

Göstason, R. (1985). Psychiatric illness among the mentally retarded: A Swedish population study. *Acta Psychiatrica Scandinavia Supplement*, 318, 1–117.

Gravestock, S. and McGauley, G. (1994). Connecting confusions with painful realities: Group analytic psychotherapy for adults with learning disabilities. *Psychoanalytic Psychotherapy*, 8, 153–67.

Hagnell, O., Ojesjo, L., Otterbeck, L. and Rorsman, B. (1994). Prevalence of mental disorders, personality traits and mental complaints in the Lundby Study: A point prevalence study of the 1957 Lundby cohort of 2,612 inhabitants of a geographically defined area who were re-examined in 1972 regardless of domicile. *Scandinavian Journal of Social Medicine Supplement*, 50, 1–77.

Hatton, C. (1999). Staff Stress. In N. Bouras (ed.), *Psychiatric and Behavioural Disorders in Developmental Disabilities and Mental Retardation* (pp. 427–38). Cambridge: Cambridge University Press.

Hollins, S. (2003). Counselling and psychotherapy. In W. Fraser and M. Kerr (eds), *Seminars in the Psychiatry of Learning Disabilities* (pp. 186–200). London: Gaskell.

Hollins, S. and Evered, C. (1990). Group content and process: The challenge of mental handicap. *Group Analysis*, 23, 55–67.

Hollins, S. and Sinason, V. (2000). Psychotherapy, learning disabilities and trauma: New perspectives. *British Journal of Psychiatry*, 176, 32–6.

Holt, G. and Bouras, N. (1997). *Mental Health in Learning Disabilities: A Training Pack for Staff Working with People who have a Dual Diagnosis of Mental Health Needs and Learning Disabilities*. Brighton: Pavilion Publishing.

Holt, G. and Oliver, B. (2000). Training direct care staff about the mental health needs and related issues of people with developmental disabilities. *Mental Health Aspects of Developmental Disabilities*, 3, 132–9.

Iverson, J. and Fox, R. (1989). Prevalence of psychopathology among mentally retarded adults. *Research on Developmental Disabilities*, 10(1), 77–83.

Jacobson, J. W. (1982). Problem behaviour and psychiatric impairment within a developmentally disabled population I: Behaviour frequency. *Applied Research in Mental Retardation*, 3(2), 121–39.

Jancar, J. and Gunaratne, I. (1994). Dysthymia and mental handicap. *British Journal of Psychiatry*, 164(5), 691–3.

Kilchenstein, M. W. (1999). The psychoanalytic psychotherapy of a mentally retarded man. *International Journal of Psychoanalysis*, 80(4), 739–53.

King, B. H. (1993). Self-injury by people with mental retardation: A compulsive behaviour hypothesis. *American Journal of Mental Retardation*, 98(1), 93–112.

Lindsay, W., Howells, L. and Pitcaithly, D. (1993). Cognitive therapy for depression with individuals with intellectual disabilities. *British Journal of Medical Psychology*, 66(2), 135–41.

Lund, J. (1985). The prevalence of psychiatric morbidity in mentally retarded adults. *Acta Psychiatrica Scandinavia*, 72(6), 563–70.

Matson, J., Bamburg, J., Mayville, E., Pinkston, J., Bielecki, J., Kuhn, D., Smalls,

Y. and Logan, J. (2000). Psychopharmacology and mental retardation: A 10 year review (1990–1999). *Research on Developmental Disabilities*, 21(4), 263–96.

McBrien, J. A. (2003). Assessment and diagnosis of depression in people with intellectual disability. *Journal of Intellectual Disability Research*, 47(1), 1–13.

Meltzer, H., Gill, B., Petticrew, M. and Hinds, K. (1995). *The Prevalence of Psychiatric Morbidity among Adults Living in Private Households: OPCS Survey of Psychiatric Morbidity in Great Britain*. London: HMSO.

Melville, C. (2003). A critique of the DC-LD chapter on non-affective psychotic disorders. *Journal of Intellectual Disability Research*, 47(51), 16–25.

Nezu, C. and Nezu, A. (1994). Outpatient psychotherapy for adults with mental retardation and concomitant psychopathology: Research and clinical imperatives. *Journal of Consulting and Clinical Psychology*, 62(1), 34–42.

Nutt, D. (2001). Neurobiological mechanisms in generalized anxiety disorder. *Journal of Clinical Psychiatry*, 62 (Supplement 11), 22–7.

Nutt, D. and Malizia, A. (2001). New insights into the role of the GABA(A)-benzodiazepine receptor in psychiatric disorder. *British Journal of Psychiatry*, 179, 390–6.

Prout, H. and Nowak-Drabik, K. (2003). Psychotherapy with persons who have mental retardation: An evaluation of effectiveness. *American Journal of Mental Retardation*, 108(2), 82–93.

Reid, A. H. (1994). Psychiatry and learning disability. *British Journal of Psychiatry*, 164(5), 613–18.

Reiss, S. (1990). Prevalence of dual diagnosis in community-based day programs in the Chicago metropolitan area. *American Journal of Mental Retardation*, 94(6), 578–85.

Royal College of Psychiatrists (2001). *DC-LD (Diagnostic Criteria for Psychiatric Disorders for Use with Adults with Learning Disabilities/Mental Retardation)*. London: Gaskell.

Santosh, P. and Baird, G. (1999). Psychopharmacotherapy in children and adults with intellectual disability. *Lancet*, 354(9174), 233–42.

Sawa, A. and Kamiya, A. (2003). Elucidating the pathogenesis of schizophrenia. *British Medical Journal*, 327(7416), 632–3.

Shulman, S. (1988). The family of the severely handicapped child: The sibling perspective. *Journal of Family Therapy*, 10, 125–34.

Sigman, M. (1985). Individual and group psychotherapy with mentally retarded adolescents. In M. Sigman (ed.), *Children with Emotional Disorders and Developmental Disabilities: Assessment and Treatment* (pp. 259–77). Orlando, FL: Grune and Stratton.

Sinason, V. (1992). *Mental Handicap and the Human Condition: New Approaches from the Tavistock*. London: Free Association Books.

Smiley, E. and Cooper, S. (2003). Intellectual disabilities, depressive episode, diagnostic criteria and Diagnostic Criteria for Psychiatric Disorders for Use with Adults with Learning Disabilities/Mental Retardation (DC-LD). *Journal of Intellectual Disability Research*, 47, Supplement, 62–71.

Sovner, R. (1986). Limiting factors in the use of DSM-III criteria with mentally ill/mentally retarded persons. *Psychopharmacology Bulletin*, 22(4), 1055–9.

Symington, N. (1981). The psychotherapy of a subnormal patient. *British Journal of Medical Psychology*, 54, 187–99.

Taylor, D., Paton, D. and Kerwin, R. (2003). *The Maudsley Prescribing Guidelines*. London and New York: Martin Dunitz.

Thuppal, M. and Fink, M. (1999). Electroconvulsive therapy and mental retardation. *Journal of ECT*, 15(2), 140–9.

Torr, J. (2003). Personality disorder in intellectual disability. *Current Opinion in Psychiatry*, 16, 517–21.

Vanstraelen, M. and Tyrer, S. (1999). Rapid cycling bipolar affective disorder in people with intellectual disability: A systematic review. *Journal of Intellectual Disability Research*, 43(5), 349–59.

Vetere, A. (1993). Using family therapy for people with learning disabilities. In J. Carpenter and A. Treacher (eds), *Using Family Therapy in the 90s*. Oxford: Blackwell.

Walters, R. M. (1990). Suicidal behaviour in severely mentally handicapped patients. *British Journal of Psychiatry*, 157, 444–6.

World Health Organization (WHO) (1992). *ICD-10 Classification of Mental and Behavioural Disorders: Clinical Descriptions and Diagnostic Guidelines*. Geneva: World Health Organization.

World Health Organization (1996). *ICD-10 Guide for Mental Retardation*. Geneva: World Health Organization.

Chapter 23

Intellectual disability, sexual abuse, and sexual offending

Glynis Murphy

Attitudes to the sexuality of people with intellectual disabilities have changed considerably over the years (Kempton and Kahn, 1991; McCarthy, 1999). At the turn of the twentieth century, during the eugenics era, the general population seemed to think that people with intellectual disabilities were either asexual eternal children (despite their physical development) or risky over-sexed individuals who were liable to reproduce to excess, commit crimes and be a risk to the rest of society. Thus, as McCarthy (1999: 53) says, two contradictory beliefs were held: that society needed protection from the sexuality of people with ID and that people with ID needed protection from sex in society.

Attitudes have changed over the last half-century, however, so that people with ID are now more accepted, and are usually seen as individuals with rights and responsibilities, including sexual rights, like other citizens. At the same time, though, it has become clear that sexual abuse is alarmingly prevalent in society and people with ID may be especially vulnerable to sexual abuse, for a number of reasons. In addition, it seems that people with ID may at times perpetrate sexually abusive behaviour, often following sexually abusive behaviour perpetrated against them in earlier years. It is thus not uncommon for clinical psychologists working with people with ID to be asked to assess possible victims of sexual abuse and alleged perpetrators of sexual abuse, for court or for clinical reasons. Both victims and alleged perpetrators may also be referred for treatment following incidents of abuse. In this chapter, the definitions and prevalence of sexual abuse will be discussed, followed by a consideration of people with ID as victims and survivors of abuse, and finally an examination of people with ID as perpetrators of abuse.

DEFINITIONS OF SEXUAL ABUSE

There are a variety of definitions of sexual abuse. The basis for the definitions may be criminological, sociological or clinical but they all share the idea of sexual behaviour perpetrated either without the victim's consent or with a victim who is defined as not able to consent (for example, a child). Definitions of child sexual abuse often include the idea of an age differential between the people engaged in sexual behaviour, as an indication of the abusive nature of the act, although as Salter has commented this could result in the exclusion of forced assaults by peers (Salter, 1988). Most definitions include the idea of unwanted sexual fondling, rape and attempted rape (whether vaginal or anal). Some definitions also include non-contact abuse (see below), such as exhibitionism.

The British Crime Survey of 2000 (Myhill and Allen, 2002), for example, asked women and men the following question about sexual victimization: 'Since the age of 16, has someone, either a stranger or someone you know, used violence, threats or intimidation to force you to do sexual things against your will?' Further questions went on to ask victims about attempted rape and actual rape.

Baker and Duncan (1985), in their survey of over 2,000 people, used the following definition of child sexual abuse: 'A child (anyone under 16 years) is sexually abused when another person, who is sexually mature, involves the child in any activity which the other person expects to lead to their sexual arousal. This might involve intercourse, touching, exposure of the sexual organs, showing pornographic material or talking about sexual things in an erotic way.'

In contrast, Turk and Brown's (1993) definition, used in their work with people with intellectual disabilities, is probably one of the most comprehensive:

> Sexual abuse occurs when a perpetrator exposes his/her genitals or looks at or touches certain parts of a victim's body (breasts, buttocks, thighs, mouth, genital or anal areas) or requires the victim to perform sexual acts, for the purpose of gratifying or satisfying the needs of the first person and when one or more of the following apply:
>
> 1. The second person withholds their consent
> 2. The second person is unable to give their consent because the severity or nature of their intellectual disability severely affects their understanding of the basic elements of sexual behaviour
> 3. Some other barrier to consent is present for the victim, which means that they are unduly pressured in this particular situation (including the presence of a parental, familial, caretaking or other authority relationship between the persons involved; the use of force, a weapon or the threat of injury or punishment by the first person; the abuse of a power relationship which precludes consent by the weaker person).

One of the most important distinctions between definitions of sexual abuse relates to whether physical contact was made with the victim. Non-contact sexual abuse includes sexual behaviours where the perpetrator makes no physical contact with the victim, such as voyeurism and exhibitionism. Contact abuse involves physical contact between the perpetrator and victim and includes sexual assaults (such as touching genitalia), frottage, non-consensual oral sex, vaginal rape and anal rape. Most prevalence studies refer to contact abuse.

EPIDEMIOLOGY

In this section epidemiology of sexual abuse in people with and without ID will be considered.

Prevalence of sexual abuse against people without ID

Sexual abuse is a crime that often takes place in conditions of secrecy (Salter, 1988) and it is thought that very many victims do not report what happened to them. Thus, according to Finkelhor (1994), only 50 per cent of victims of child sexual abuse ever tell *anyone* about what happened to them. Where they do tell someone, they are likely to tell friends or family members, rather than professionals or the police (McGee, Garavan, de Barra, Byrne et al., 2002). In a recent study in Ireland only 6 per cent of victims of adult sexual abuse told the police (McGee et al., 2002). Similarly, according to recent British Crime Survey data, only about 20 per cent of sexual crimes against adult women became known to the police in the UK and only half of these (i.e. 10 per cent of the total) were reported by the victim herself (Myhill and Allen, 2002). Similarly, Torrey (1991) estimated that no more than 10 per cent of the sexual crimes that take place in the UK, US and Canada are reported to the police.

Sexual abuse is thus known to be grossly under-reported to the police in most Western countries, probably partly because the victims fear (McElvaney, 2001):

* insensitive questioning by the police
* attitudes of scepticism or disbelief amongst family, friends and authorities
* anxiety about testifying in court, especially about hostile cross-examination by defence lawyers
* fear of what actions the alleged perpetrator may take.

In addition, victims often feel that they themselves were partly to blame for what happened and they therefore feel too ashamed to report the abuse, especially when it happened in childhood (McGee et al., 2002). Prevalence rates derived from police statistics are therefore gross underestimates of the true rate and most researchers agree that the best estimates of prevalence come from victim surveys.

Figures for sexual abuse derived from victim surveys vary with the definition of sexual abuse employed and the age period asked about (see, for example, Salter, 1988: 18). It seems that sexual offences may be more common in some countries than in others (though Finkelhor (1994) points out that this is difficult to establish because of methodological differences between studies) and it is clear from victim surveys that some types of offence are more common than others. Exhibitionism is probably the most prevalent sexual offence: around 50 per cent of women report having been victims of this crime (Di Vasto, Kaufman, Jackson, Christy, et al., 1984). Very serious contact offences such as rape (or attempted rape) are less common.

In a large study of child sexual abuse, Badgley (1984) conducted a random survey of over 1,000 men and women in Canada and found that 22 per cent of female respondents and 9 per cent of male respondents had suffered unwanted sexual touching, or attempted rape or actual rape by the age of 18 years. Figures from a recent study in Ireland are very similar for women but higher for men: McGee et al. (2002) reported that following a telephone interview of over 3,000 people, 20 per cent of women and 16 per cent of men reported (contact) sexual abuse before 17 years. Russell (1984) reported even higher figures: in her random survey of 930 women in the USA, she found 38 per cent had experienced unwanted sexual touching or attempted rape/ actual rape by the age of 18 years. Baker and Duncan (1985) in a UK survey of child sexual abuse in over 2,000 individuals reported that 12 per cent of females and 8 per cent of males had been sexually abused, including both contact and non-contact offences (before the age of 16 years). Finkelhor (1994) has commented that the difference in rates between Russell's study and Baker and Duncan's is likely to be due to the careful and sensitive questioning in the former, as compared to more superficial questioning in the latter.

For adults, figures from the 1998 and 2000 British Crime Surveys, each of over 6,000 women over 16 years, suggested that about 10 per cent of women had experienced some form of sexual victimization (including rape) during their adult years and 5 per cent had been raped (Myhill and Allen, 2002). The US National Center for Victims of Crime and Crime Victims Research and Treatment Center (1992) reported that one in eight women (12.5 per cent) in America had been raped. The *lifetime* prevalence figures of sexual victimization in the 2001 British Crime Survey of over 22,000 men and women, showed that 24 per cent of women and 5 per cent of men had been sexually victimized, with 5 per cent of women and 1 per cent of men having been raped, at some time in their lives (Walby and Allen, 2004). The lifetime prevalence figures from the recent study in Ireland reported that 21 per cent of women and 18 per cent of men had experienced contact abuse, with 10 per cent of women and 3 per cent of men experiencing rape.

Most often, for both child and adult sexual victimization, the perpetrators have been found to be male (over 90 per cent of cases in all known studies). Most studies have reported that the perpetrators were usually known to the victims, though the exact levels of sexual abuse by strangers varies from study to study (for example, the perpetrators were strangers in only 8 per cent of cases in the British Crime Surveys of 1998 and 2000, according to Myhill and Allen (2002), but strangers were responsible for over 20 per cent of child sexual abuse and over 30 per cent of adult sexual abuse in the Irish study, according to McGee *et al.* (2002). Sexual abuse is often of long duration, particularly where it is familial. Moreover, being a victim of sexual abuse once appears to increase the risk of being re-victimized by a different perpetrator. In the Irish study, for example, 28 per cent of the women and 20 per cent of the men who disclosed abuse were victims of more than one perpetrator (McGee *et al.*, 2002). For both men and women in the Irish study, penetrative sexual abuse during childhood led to a sixteen-fold increase in the risk of penetrative abuse in adulthood.

Prevalence of sexual abuse against people with intellectual disabilities

People with ID are not included or identified in many victim surveys (for example, neither in the UK nor in the USA) and therefore the figures derived from these studies do not apply directly to people with ID. Nevertheless, people with ID are often the victims of sexual abuse and they have been said to be particularly vulnerable to it, compared with other care groups (Tharinger, Horton and Millea, 1990), though it is difficult to get hard evidence of this, apart from a very small number of studies (Brown and Stein, 1998). The methodology of the surveys of people with ID, particularly the period of time covered and the type of sample, have a major impact on the findings, much as in surveys of abuse against non-disabled people. Some studies, for example, ask whether sexual abuse has ever occurred (prevalence), such as McCarthy and Thompson (1997), whereas others ask about only new cases (incidence), such as Brown, Stein and Turk (1995) and Brown and Stein (1998). Incidence figures are clearly likely to be lower. Moreover, surveys that take place in clinics (Chamberlain, Rauh, Passer, McGrath and Burket, 1984; McCarthy and Thompson, 1997) tend to produce high prevalence rates because the participants have been selected as distressed or in need of help by their presence at the clinic. In contrast, service-level surveys, which examine the number of incidents of sexual abuse reported to social services departments by carers or by day or residential services, tend to produce lower rates than do those which involve the direct interviewing of staff and carers of those with ID (especially as the former often examine incidence and not prevalence). The studies producing the highest rates, however, are those which ask the people with ID themselves about their lifetime experience of abuse. Table 23.1 gives the figures from

Table 23.1 Selected surveys of people with ID

Authors	Definitions	Method	Rates
Chamberlain et al., 1984	Completed or attempted intercourse (penetration)	Case notes study only of the clinic notes on 87 female adolescents with intellectual disability, attending an adolescent clinic	25% had been sexually abused (clinic-based but case notes only)
Hard and Plumb, 1987, quoted in Turk and Brown, 1993	Not known	Face-to-face interviews with 65 people with ID attending a day centre	58% reported having been sexually abused
Sobsey and Varnhagen, 1989	Not known	A survey of national agencies that support children and adults with disabilities in Canada	88 victims traced, 67% had intellectual disability. Prevalence rates not given
Buchanan and Wilkins, 1991	Proven or strongly suspected 'sexual exploitation'	Survey of 37 day and residential workers in one county in UK, regarding cases of known sexual abuse of people with ID	25 cases of sexual abuse identified. Prevalence rate 8%
Turk and Brown, 1993 and Brown et al., 1995	See text	In 1st survey: all statutory providers in one health region in England asked to provide data on all new incidents of sexual abuse of adults with ID over a 2-year period. 2nd survey: similar	1st survey: 60 new cases/year in general pop. of 3.6 million. 2nd survey: Similar. Estimated 1400 new cases of sexual abuse per year in England
McCarthy and Thompson, 1997	Sexual abuse as defined in law and other (see article)	185 people referred to a sex education team; all individuals interviewed face to face	61% of women and 25% of men had been sexually abused
Brown and Stein, 1998	New cases of poss. abuse reported to and recorded by Social Services	Abuse alerts (physical, sexual, financial, etc.) across all care groups in Social Services depts in two counties in England	14–26 alerts per 100,000 general population; 34% of alerts for people with ID; one third of these sexual abuse

a selection of studies of sexual abuse of people with ID, to illustrate these points.

Victims of sexual abuse in the non-disabled general population are thought to be overwhelmingly female, while the perpetrators are overwhelmingly male, usually known to the victim (see above). Studies of people with ID have suggested considerable similarities:

- Many victims are female, though male victimization may be somewhat more common than in the general population. Thus, in surveys of adults with ID, women have made up between 50 per cent and 85 per cent of victims, and men the remainder of victims (Brown *et al.*, 1995; Buchanan and Wilkins, 1991; Hard and Plumb, 1987; Sobsey, 1994; Turk and Brown, 1993).
- Perpetrators are again largely male (all surveys have reported that perpetrators of sexual abuse against people with ID are 90 per cent male – see Brown *et al.*, 1995; Buchanan and Wilkins, 1991; McCarthy and Thompson, 1997; Turk and Brown, 1993).
- Victims with ID usually know the alleged perpetrators: in all, familiar adults were involved in perpetrating 95 per cent of cases in the survey by Turk and Brown, 1993.

Perpetrators of abuse against people with ID include staff, family members, local shopkeepers, volunteers, other service users. Most studies have found that around one quarter to one fifth of alleged perpetrators are staff and similar proportions are family members (28 per cent staff and 19 per cent family members in Sobsey and Doe (1991); 14 per cent staff and 18 per cent family members in Turk and Brown (1993); 20 per cent staff and 8 per cent family members in Brown *et al.* (1995)) but a sizable proportion of alleged perpetrators are other service users with ID (44 per cent in Sobsey and Doe (1991); 42 per cent in Turk and Brown (1993); 53 per cent in Brown *et al.* (1995)). The most likely settings for abuse, according to many studies, are day and residential services, rather than family homes: for example, in Turk and Brown (1993), only 31 per cent of the victims were abused in the family home and in Brown *et al.* (1995), this figure was 25 per cent. Some caution is necessary in interpreting these figures, however, since abuse by family members may be less likely to be reported to anyone (Brown *et al.*, 1995).

Most studies have reported that the majority of the victims have mild or moderate ID but it may well be that this is simply because most abuse comes to light through the victim's disclosure (Brown *et al.*, 1995; Buchanan and Wilkins, 1991; Turk and Brown, 1993; so that those cases of sexual abuse perpetrated against people with severe disabilities (i.e. people with very limited communication skills) may simply not be being recognized. The type of abuse reported in most studies is serious: over 50 per cent of abuse in Brown *et al.* (1995) and McCarthy and Thompson (1997), involved vaginal or anal penetration. Multiple abuse has been reported as common in most studies (for example, 47 per cent of reported abuse in Brown *et al.* (1995) involved multiple incidents). Of course, with under-reporting it is likely that the more serious incidents and the more frequent incidents get reported, so that it may be that one-off incidents of non-contact abuse are underestimated.

VICTIMS AND SURVIVORS WITH ID

In this section the process of court attendance following abuse, the consequeces of sexual abuse for people with and without ID and the treatment of psychologoical sequelae of abuse will be considered.

Being a witness in court

Sexually abusive behaviour in the general population is known to be very under-reported (see above) and, even once reported to the police, convictions for sexual offences are known to be difficult to obtain in court. Difficulties with evidence often mean that convictions for less serious crimes than were originally contemplated have to be accepted (Grubin, 1998).

In many countries, the police are concerned about under-reporting of sexual crimes in the general population and have been at pains to improve services for victims, so as to encourage people to report sexual crimes. In Ireland, for example, reported sexual offences have increased from 18 per cent of indictable crimes against the person in 1988, to 56 per cent in 1997 (McElvaney, 2001). Similarly, the total number of offences recorded as rape by the police in England and Wales was 1,842 in 1985 but 7,809 by 1999 (Myhill and Allen, 2002). In the same period, however, the percentage of offenders found guilty of rape fell from 24 per cent in 1985 to 8 per cent in 1999 (Myhill and Allen, 2002). Nevertheless, as many researchers have commented, whether this increase in recorded sexual crimes reflects an increased rate of sexual crimes or improved reporting is unclear.

A number of studies of victims of sexual crimes in the general population have shown that the majority of victims do not themselves report the crimes (see under 'Prevalence' above). This is even more likely with people with ID, since they may lack the communication skills and the ability to find the police station without support. Most often, they will tell staff or carers and usually they will need staff or carers' support to inform the police. Thus, reports to the police that people with ID have been victims of crimes are frequently made on their behalf, by staff or family carers or by professionals, such as social workers. The police may then interview the victim later.

In a number of jurisdictions, there has been considerable concern that few of these alleged crimes against people with ID, however reported, reach court (Kebbell and Hatton, 1999; Luckasson, 1992). For example, in Brown *et al.*'s

(1995) study of victims of sexual abuse with ID, the police were called in under half of all recorded cases and only 14 per cent of the alleged incidents of abuse were investigated with a view to prosecution. It is known that part of the problem here is the extent to which staff report crimes to the police when the alleged perpetrator is another person with ID. Lyall, Holland and Collins, (1995) found that 60 per cent of the staff in day and residential services in one area of England said they would not necessarily report to the police a major assault by a service user with ID against another service user with ID. More-over, 10 per cent said they would not necessarily report a rape. A later study by McBrien and Murphy (2006) confirmed the relative reluctance of staff to report such incidents to the police and found that carers tended to think the person (the alleged perpetrator) needed help, rather than the intervention of the law. Carers were also concerned that, if they reported incidents to the police, they risked criticism themselves, suggesting that the ethos in services was that this was not an appropriate action to take. Only 50 per cent of staff said their services had policies in place to guide them in reporting incidents to the police (McBrien and Murphy, 2006).

The low rate of prosecution of crimes of abuse against people with ID may also be attributed to inaction by the police (see the examples in Luckasson, 1992). McBrien and Murphy's study suggested that police assert that they will take alleged suspects with ID to court if they can (McBrien and Murphy, 2006) but the evidence from studies of abuse (e.g. Brown et al., 1995) is that they tend not to. It may be that in many cases where the victim of a sexual crime has ID, the police are reluctant to proceed because they think the person with ID will be an 'unsafe' witness. For example, in England, the advice to the police in the Codes of Practice (Home Office, 1995), associated with the Police and Criminal Evidence Act 1984, which dictates how they should proceed to collect evidence about alleged crimes, is: 'although . . . mentally handicapped people [sic] are often capable of providing reliable evidence, they may without knowing or wishing to do so, be particularly prone in certain circumstances to provide information which is unreliable, misleading or self-incriminating' (p. 78).

The more recent version of the Codes of Practice (Home Office, 2003) reiterated this advice, widening the caveat to 'people who are mentally dis-ordered or otherwise mentally vulnerable' (p. 85). Nevertheless, in a survey of twenty-four police forces in England, Wales and Northern Ireland, Bailey and Barr (2000) reported that fewer than 30 per cent of forces had written policies for investigating crimes where the victim was a person with ID and very few had had training in interviewing people with ID.

The difficulties that people with ID have in communication and memory (Murphy and Clare, 2003) mean that some of the fears about their testimony in the police station when being interviewed as witnesses may be justified. Studies have shown that people with ID sometimes have more difficulty pro-viding eye-witness accounts than non-disabled people (Milne, Clare and Bull,

1999; Perlman, Ericson, Esses and Isaacs, 1994) and they have, on average, a higher rate of acquiescence and suggestibility on questioning than non-disabled people (Clare and Gudjonsson, 1993; Finlay and Lyons, 2002; Heal and Sigelman, 1995). Nevertheless, with the use of careful forms of questioning, avoiding suggestion and leading questions, people with ID may be perfectly good witnesses (Perlman *et al.*, 1994).

However, neither the police nor lawyers may be relied on to use such careful forms of questioning. Witness studies by Kebbell, Hatton and colleagues (Kebbell, Hatton, Johnson and O'Kelly, 2001; Kebbell, Hatton and Johnson 2004) found that witnesses with ID were questioned by lawyers in court in just the same way as other witnesses (i.e. no allowance was made for their ID). Moreover, witnesses with ID were more likely than other witnesses to be led by leading questions, especially in cross-examination, compared to witnesses without disabilities (Kebbell *et al.*, 2004), suggesting that people with ID do have a harder time surviving cross-examination than do non-disabled people. Moreover, in some jurisdictions, the judge may be required to decide before a court case begins whether a person with ID is able to give evidence. In England, until recently, for example, the judge had to decide whether a witness was 'capable of giving rational evidence', whether he or she was able to take the oath and whether he or she had understood the special obligation to tell the truth in court (Gudjonsson, 1999). Gudjonnson, Murphy and Clare, (2000) demonstrated that the reliance on the oath was preventing some people with ID who could give evidence from appearing as witnesses in court.

There has been concern in several countries that the end result of all these difficulties was that people with ID were not getting equal access to justice (Luckasson, 1992; Sanders, Creaton, Bird and Weber, 1997). This led, in England, to a campaign for changes to the law (VOICE UK, 1998; Mencap, 1997), as a result of which the Youth Justice and Criminal Evidence Act 1999 was passed. This Act allowed the use of special measures to assist 'vulnerable witnesses' (such as those with ID) to give evidence in court. The special measures included being able to give evidence unsworn, to give evidence by video link, the use of an intermediary and of communication aids in court (Cooke and Davies, 2001). The Guidance associated with the Act, gave suggestions as to how the police should identify people with ID (in order to set up assessments of the need for special measures) and also gave guidance on how to interview people with ID in order to get the best evidence (Home Office, 2000). One study completed since the implementation of the new law has suggested that vulnerable witnesses in general have found it an improvement on the previous arrangements (Hamlyn, Phelps, Turtle and Sattar, 2004) but it is too early to tell whether people with ID have found it helpful.

Psychological consequences: victims without ID

The seriousness of the psychological consequences of abuse have been reported for years (Beitchman, Zucker, Hood, DaCosta and Akman, 1991; Finkelhor, 1986; Kendall-Tackett, Williams and Finkelhor, 1993) and there are now many well-controlled studies, both for non-disabled adults and children (see, for example, Ferguson and Mullen, 1999; Kendler, Bulik, Silberg, Hettema *et al.*, 2000; McLeer, Deblinger, Henry and Orvaschel, 1992). Early reports suggested that symptoms included anxiety, sleep problems, eating problems, fears, phobias, depression, guilt, shame, disruptive behaviour, sexualized behaviour, anger, hostility, lack of trust in others, difficulties with social and sexual intimacy and poor self-esteem (Beitchman *et al.*, 1991; Finkelhor, 1986). Later studies commented on the similarity of symptoms to those of Post-Traumatic Stress Disorder (PTSD) as well (see Table 23.2 for the main features of the DSM-IV criteria for PTSD, according to the American Psychiatric Association, 1994). Thus the list of sequelae of sexual

Table 23.2 The main features of PTSD, according to DSM-IV

Section	Features
A Traumatic event (both features present)	1 Event(s) involved actual or threatened death or serious injury, or threat to physical integrity of self or others 2 Response involved intense fear, helplessness or horror
B Traumatic event consistently re-experienced (at least one feature present)	1 Recurrent distressing recollections of the event 2 Recurrent distressing dreams of the event 3 Acting or feeling as if event recurring 4 Intense psychological distress to internal or external cues associated with the event 5 Physiological reactions to these cues
C Persistent avoidance of stimuli associated with the traumatic event and numbing of responsiveness (at least three features present)	1 Efforts to avoid thoughts feelings or conversations associated with the trauma 2 Efforts to avoid activities, places or people that arouse recollections of the trauma 3 Inability to recall important aspects of trauma 4 Markedly diminished interest or participation in activities 5 Feelings of detachment or estrangement from others 6 Restricted range of affect (unable to have loving feelings) 7 Sense of a foreshortened future
D Persistent symptoms of increased arousal (at least two features present)	1 Difficulty falling or staying asleep 2 Irritability or outbursts of anger 3 Difficulty concentrating 4 Hypervigilance 5 Exaggerated startle response

E Duration of disturbance of symptoms in B, C, D at least one month

F Disturbance causes clinically significant distress or impairment in social, occupational or other important areas of functioning abuse expanded to include intrusive thoughts, recollections and 'flashbacks', exaggerated startle response, feelings of self-blame, detachment, estrangement, withdrawal, difficulty concentrating, self-harm and a sense of a fore-shortened future. Frequently, victims and survivors of sexual abuse, when being assessed for symptoms, have been interviewed using standardized psychiatric interview schedules or have been asked to report their symptoms using self-report measures (Wilson and Keane, 1997), such as the *Revised Impact of Events Scale* (Horowitz, Wilner and Alvarez, 1979; Sundin and Horowitz, 2002). The common association of PTSD with depression and anxiety means that measures of these psychological sequelae have often also been employed.

The proportion of the survivors of sexual abuse who suffer serious consequences seems to be very high. For example, in the recent Irish study, 30 per cent of women and 20 per cent of men who reported abuse said that the abuse had had a major effect on their lives, with 25 per cent of abused women and 16 per cent of abused men reporting symptoms consistent with a diagnosis of PTSD. Moreover, serious abuse appeared to result in worse sequelae. Thus people who had suffered penetrative sexual abuse were eight times more likely to have been psychiatric in-patients at some time in their lives than those who had not been abused (McGee *et al.*, 2002). Other studies have reported very similar findings and it seems that violent abuse, long-term abuse and abuse by close family members have more deleterious effects than other forms of sexual abuse (Beitchman *et al.*, 1991; Bulik, Prescott and Kendler, 2001), and although Grubin (1998) asserts that some of these findings may be the result of dysfunctional family life rather than abuse *per se*, well-controlled studies (Kendler *et al.*, 2000) show that it is a real effect that cannot be attributed to a generally disturbed family life. Many studies also find that the psychological effects of sexual abuse are very long-term. For example, in Kilpatrick's research, 17 per cent of women who were sexually assaulted still had the symptoms of PTSD (see below) 17 years later (Kilpatrick, Saunders, Veronen, Best and Von, 1987).

Psychological consequences: victims with ID

Surprisingly few studies of the psychological symptoms of abuse have been conducted in people with ID, although a number of studies have commented anecdotally on the sequelae of sexual abuse or have analysed case notes retrospectively (see Sequeira and Hollins, 2003, for a review). Buchanan and Wilkins (1991), for example, commented that the indicators of sexual abuse included physical symptoms (e.g. vaginal bruising), behavioural symptoms (changes in mood and behaviour, such as sudden withdrawal and depression, or a sudden upsurge in aggression, self-injury, soiling or sexually inappropriate behaviour) and social symptoms (such as poor parental relationships, in cases of incest). Sobsey and Doe (1991) reported similar findings from a large but uncontrolled study, using questionnaires with people with ID and their advocates. In one of the few systematic studies employing standardized measures, albeit of a single case, Davison, Clare, Georgiades, Divall and Holland (1994) described the assessment and treatment of a man with ID who had symptoms of PTSD following an alleged rape, perpetrated against him when he was in prison.

There have also been two recent systematic studies of larger numbers of people with ID. In one, O'Callaghan, Murphy and Clare (2003) traced eighteen people with severe ID who had been abused (outside the family) and whose cases had been reported to the police. The participants' parents/carers were interviewed about the person's symptoms following the abuse, using a method similar to that of Howlin and Clements (1995) (participants themselves could not be interviewed due to their degree of disability and lack of expressive language). Parents/carers were asked to recall the person's skills and disabilities at three time points: before the abuse began, just after the abuse and in the three months before the research interview. Symptoms of PTSD were also considered and a standardized measure of skills and behaviour was completed. It was found that, despite the fact that the abuse had sometimes taken place years before the interviews, very significant changes in people's skills (apparent loss of skills) and challenging behaviours (worsening of behaviours) had occurred following the abuse, with only some recovery in the subsequent years. Symptoms of PTSD were extremely common after the abuse, with 58 per cent having severe sleeping problems, 50 per cent of people experiencing frequent dreams and flashbacks, 68 per cent showing extreme distress at cues, 76 per cent showing loss of interest in activities. Again there was only some recovery by the time of the interviews. Relatively few people with ID seemed to have been offered consistent treatment. Most families felt extremely traumatized by what had happened and blamed the services for not protecting their son or daughter.

In the second systematic study, Sequeira, Howlin and Hollins (2003) compared fifty-four people with ID who had experienced sexual abuse with fifty-four people with ID who had not been abused, matching the groups for age, gender, degree of disability and communication skills. Behavioural difficulties, mental health needs and symptoms of PTSD were investigated using standardized measures and it was found that the abused group was showing significantly more challenging behaviour (including self-injury and sexualized behaviour), significantly more mental health symptoms and significantly more PTSD symptoms than the comparison group. As in O'Callaghan *et al.* (2003), much of the abuse had been long-term and relatively few people (39 per cent) had received treatment from qualified professionals after the abuse.

Treatment following sexual abuse

Considerable advances have been made recently in the provision of treatment for people in the general population who have been sexually abused and who have developed post-traumatic stress disorder or other symptoms, including both group and individual forms of treatment (Hembree and Foa, 2003; Trowell, Kolvin, Weermanthri, Sadowski *et al.*, 2002) and even self-help manuals (Herbert and Wetmore, 1999). Treatment packages for non-disabled survivors of sexual abuse often include psycho-education (i.e. information about the type of trauma and likely effects), as well as a variety of anxiety management techniques (such as relaxation training) and systematic desensitization or graded exposure or flooding, and cognitive techniques, such as cognitive restructuring (Hembree and Foa, 2003; Yule, 1999). Some of these methods, such as graded exposure, would be widely applicable and suitable for many people with ID, while some (e.g. psycho-educational materials, relaxation training) would need to be carefully tailored, and others (such as cognitive restructuring) would be more difficult to apply, especially for people with severely limited communication skills. So far only a few single-case studies have appeared that have evaluated aspects of cognitive-behavioural treatment for people with ID (Davison *et al.*, 1994). They have demonstrated that exposure, relaxation training and sex education can help alleviate the symptoms of PTSD following sexual abuse in people with ID.

PREVENTION OF SEXUAL ABUSE

The high prevalence and the severe consequences of sexual abuse have led to a variety of initiatives intended to prevent sexual abuse against people with ID. These initiatives have normally taken one of two approaches: the provision of training and information for people with ID (to enhance their self-protection or to increase the likelihood that they will seek help and inform the police if they are abused) and the development of policies and procedures at a service level.

Sex education and self-protection

There is considerable evidence that people with ID have lower levels of sexual knowledge and poorer self-protection skills than people from the general population (Edmonson and Wish, 1973; Konstantareas and Lunsky, 1997; McCabe, 1999; McCarthy, 1999; Murphy and O'Callaghan, 2004; Ousley and Mesibov, 1991; Tang and Lee, 1999; Timmers, Du Charme and Jacob, 1981). Sex education, whilst widely available to children in the general population has not always been part of the curriculum for children with ID and thus many services for adults with ID now provide sex education and 'keeping safe' programmes for service users, often in day service settings. There are a number of sex education packages available, including slide packages (such as Kempton, 1988), pictorial packs (such as Cambridge, 1997; McCarthy and Thompson, 1992) and videos (for example, Family Planning Association of New South Wales, 1993; South East London Health Promotion Services, 1992). Most programmes also include teaching of 'keeping safe' procedures (recognizing abuse, the right to say 'No' and how to report abuse to staff and/ or police). However, relatively few sex education/'keeping safe' packs have been evaluated, so it is uncertain how effective they are, although Lindsay, Bellshaw, Culross, Staires and Michie (1992) and Caspar and Glidden (2001) showed that people with ID made gains in knowledge and attitudes following sex education and Murphy and O'Callaghan (2004) reported that those adults in their study who had had sex education had significantly better sexual knowledge and understanding of abuse than those who had not.

A number of recent studies have argued that improved sexual knowledge does not necessarily generalize and translate into better self-protection skills (Lumley and Miltenberger, 1997), with the implication that programmes often need to employ behavioural training methods, rather than just didactic instruction, and programme evaluations need to include role play of likely scenarios (Haseltine and Miltenberger, 1990; Lumley, Miltenberger, Long, Rapp and Roberts, 1998; Miltenberger, Roberts, Ellingson, Galensky et al., 1999). A few studies have hypothesized that one of the crucial skills in abuse self-protection is people's decision-making abilities (Khemka and Hickson, 2000) and some investigation into how to improve decision-making skills in abuse situations has begun (Khemkha, 2000). Finally, some books have also been developed to assist witnesses with ID to understand the criminal justice system process, so as to support them if they go to the police and to court as witnesses (Hollins, Sinason, Boniface and Webb, 1994).

Whilst it is undoubtedly important to provide sex education, 'keeping safe' programmes and decision-making training, nevertheless some people, particularly those with severe ID, may never know enough about sexuality in general and sexual abuse in particular to be able to keep themselves safe and they may be deemed not to have the capacity to consent to sexual relationships (Murphy and O'Callaghan, 2004; Niederbuhl and Morris, 1993; Sundram and Stavis, 1994). For these individuals policies and procedures adopted at service levels are particularly crucial.

Policies and procedures

McCarthy (1999) has argued that one of the first necessary steps in improving services for people with intellectual disabilities, from the point of view of the prevention of sexual abuse, is the closure of hospital provision, because of the high likelihood of predatory men there (with and without ID) and the relative lack of close supervision (as well as the opportunities provided by large grounds and numerous buildings). Similar points can be made about large residential provision of any kind (McCarthy and Thompson, 1996).

Some researchers and professionals have asked whether mixed services should be provided at all, given that so many perpetrators are men (McCarthy and Thompson, 1996). Yet to cloister all women with intellectual disabilities in all-female-staffed services would be an extreme step, which in any case would not protect men with ID from abuse. Nevertheless, many large service organizations are ensuring that at least some of their services are single-sex and most services are becoming more aware of abuse issues in the design of services, frequently considering the mix of people in each house and adopting gender-sensitive policies for personal and intimate care. Staff in many organizations are being more carefully vetted prior to employment and in many countries (including the UK and the US) all staff are supposed to be checked by the police for criminal records prior to employment (Gust, Wang, Grot, Ransom and Levine, 2003).

It has also been argued that staff in services need considerable support and training in order to be able to prevent and deal with sexual abuse. A recent US survey has suggested that most staff do now get at least one-off training in sexual abuse recognition and reporting (88 per cent of organizations provided this) but far fewer organizations provided more frequent training (Gust *et al.*, 2003). Most services also now have sexuality policies (61 per cent of organizations in Gust *et al.* (2003), have these, compared with only 23 per cent in Mulhern's 1975 survey). Some service policies provide guidance to staff just with respect to the recognition and reporting of sexual abuse but, in order to be more than just reactive, the best ones contain broad advice in relation to how to support service users in their relationships more generally (including in friendships, physical contact, courting, personal hygiene, marriage and cohabitation, parenting, birth control, and sexual relationships issues such as consent and abuse).

PERPETRATORS WITH ID: PREVALENCE OF CRIMINAL OFFENDING

During the eugenics era, it used to be thought that men with ID were particularly likely to commit crimes (the implication was that they were more likely to do this than men without disabilities). The following extract illustrates the thinking of the time: 'There is no investigator who denies the fearful role played by mental deficiency in the production of crime, vice and delinquency . . . not all criminals are feeble-minded but all feeble-minded are at least potential criminals' (Terman, 1916, quoted by Craft, 1984).

Some studies of people with ID did appear to show that they were over-represented in the criminal justice system but in many cases the methodology of the studies was flawed and the interpretation of the results questionable.

Early studies of prison populations, for example, tended to show over-representation of men with ID in prisons (e.g. Brown and Courtless (1971), claimed 10 per cent of the men in prison in the USA had 'intellectual disability'). Later studies, using better methodology (such as assessing all men, with a full, individually administered, standardized IQ test) demonstrated that men with ID were not over-represented in prisons, at least in the US (Denkowski and Denkowski, 1985; MacEachron, 1979; Noble and Conley, 1992) and the UK (Birmingham, Mason and Grubin, 1996; Brooke, Taylor, Gunn and Maden, 1996; Gunn, Maden and Swinton, 1991; Murphy, Harnett and Holland, 1995). Nevertheless, it did seem that men with intellectually disabilities were over-represented at the police station (Lyall *et al.*, 1995) and on probation in the UK (Mason and Murphy, 2002) but whether this was a result of the vulnerabilities of people with ID (for example, being more easy to trace, recognize and detain) rather than a raised prevalence of criminal offending was uncertain. In some jurisdictions, such as Australia, studies have consistently demonstrated over-representation of people with ID at all stages in the criminal justice system (Hayes, 1996), and a recent study in Ireland has suggested that people with ID are over-represented in prison populations there too (Murphy, Harrold, Carey and Mulrooney, 2000). It is likely that the numbers of people in the criminal justice system in any one jurisdiction is the complex outcome of a series of filters (Murphy and Mason, 1999), such as the extent to which:

- People with ID are visible in the community (and can be arrested)
- People with ID are adequately supported in the community
- People with ID, if arrested, understand and can exercise their rights (such as the right to legal representation)
- Police and prosecution services proceed against people with ID
- Methods of diversion for people with ID out of the criminal justice system are available, either through fitness to plead/capacity to stand trial legislation or through diversion into hospital or other settings under mental health legislation.

Interestingly, neither Ireland nor Australia has possible means to divert offenders with ID into hospitals or other settings (their mentally disordered offender legislation covers only people with mental health needs) so that prevalence rates of people with ID in prison in these jurisdictions may be relatively high as a result.

Relatively few research studies of offending and ID have commented directly on the prevalence of *sexual* offending by men with ID, though where they do, they often assert a high prevalence (Hawk, Rosenfeld and Warren, 1993; Murphy, Coleman and Haynes, 1983; Nezu, Nezu and Dudek, 1998). One of the early influential studies was that of Walker and McCabe (1973), who investigated a 90 per cent sample of all the men with mental disorders detained in hospital, following conviction for offences, under the mental health legislation in England. Of the 960 men so detained, about one third had intellectual disabilities and two-thirds had mental health needs and/or personality disorder. It transpired that, of the total number of sexual crimes committed by the cohort, two-thirds were committed by the one third of the cohort that had ID. This has sometimes been interpreted as meaning that men with ID are particularly likely to commit sexual offences. In fact, of course, it means nothing of the kind. For example, it is known that only about 10 per cent of sexual crimes are reported to the police (see above) and even fewer end in convictions, so that very little is known about the perpetrators of the 'invisible' sexual crimes, with or without disabilities. Moreover, numerous selective filters operate between a crime being notified to the police and the offender being convicted and sent to hospital under mental health legislation (including the police decision about proceeding, the prosecution decision about proceeding, the availability of evidence, the competence of the lawyers, the availability of psychiatric opinions regarding disability for the court, the availability of hospital beds, and so on). It has to be concluded that Walker and McCabe's data cannot be interpreted to mean that men with ID are particularly prone to commit sexual crimes.

Other studies have also drawn conclusions about the prevalence of sexual offending by men with ID from samples that were highly selected, such as those in hospital or those referred for special pre-trial evaluation (Hawk *et al.*, 1993) and while many assert that large numbers of men with ID commit sexual offences, there are also studies that suggest they are only as likely as other men to do so. Hayes (1991), for example, showed men with disabilities in prison in Australia are as likely to be there due to conviction following a sexual offence as are men without intellectual disabilities (4 per cent of both groups had committed sexual offences). In the absence of good total population studies it has to be concluded that the prevalence of sexual offending in men with ID is unknown.

Characteristics of non-disabled men with sexually abusive behaviour

General population studies have shown that sexually abusive behaviour is overwhelmingly committed by men who are known to their victims and this also seems to be true for sexual abuse of people with ID (see under 'Prevalence of sexual abuse' above).

A considerable amount is known about non-disabled convicted men who commit sexual offences, as a result of decades of research. Non-disabled sex offenders often come from dysfunctional families where violence is common, the parents have a poor relationship and fathers are frequently rejecting (Langevin, Bain, Ben-Aron, Coulthard, Day *et al.*, 1984a; Rada, 1978; Williams and Finkelhor, 1990). The sex offenders may have been abused themselves as children (Groth and Burgess, 1979; Langevin *et al.*, 1984a) and frequently have abnormal sexual interests as adolescents (Abel and Rouleau, 1990). They are commonly reported to have low self-esteem, to be socially isolated, emotionally lonely and/or lacking in the social skills required for intimate relationships (Awad and Saunders, 1991; Fisher, Beech and Browne, 1999; Garlick, Marshall and Thornton, 1996; Knight, Prentky, Schneider and Rosenberg, 1983; Seidman, Marshall, Hudson and Robertson, 1994). Sex offenders have been found to show reduced empathy for their victims, though they do not normally show reduced empathy generally (Beckett, Beech, Fisher and Fordham, 1994; Fernandez, Marshall, Lightbody and O'Sullivan 1999; Fisher *et al.*, 1999; Scully, 1988) and to be susceptible to cognitive distortions that deny and minimize their offences and blame their victims (Abel, Becker and Cunningham-Rathner, 1984; Happel and Auffrey, 1995; Murphy, 1990). Some sex offenders may have very large numbers of victims, target more than one age group and have multiple paraphilias (Abel and Rouleau, 1990). Frequently sex offenders spend a great deal of time grooming their victims prior to offences; often this may involve elaborate planning and preparation.

Characteristics of men with intellectual disabilities and sexually abusive behaviour

Far less is known about the characteristics of men with ID who engage in sexually abusive behaviour and there are, as yet, no good large-scale studies. Evidence from smaller studies, many of which involve men detained or living informally in clinical settings (who may be a biased sample of all such men) and few of which include comparison groups, suggest that men with ID and sexually abusive behaviour are similar in many respects to non-disabled sex offenders, although relatively few of them are ever convicted of sexual offences in the courts (Thompson, 1997). They tend to come from chaotic, violent and neglectful families who often have criminal histories themselves (Day, 1994; Gilby, Wolf and Goldberg, 1989), they frequently show other challenging behaviours, such as aggression and may have other non-sexual convictions (Day, 1994; Gilby *et al.*, 1989; Lindsay, Smith, Law, Quinn, Anderson *et al.*, 2002) and often have a history of mental health problems (Day, 1994; Lindsay *et al.*, 2002). They have an increased likelihood of a history of sexual abuse as victims themselves (Gilby *et al.*, 1989; Lindsay, Law, Quinn, Smart and Smith, 2001) and they commit the full range of sexual offences (Day, 1994; Lindsay *et al.*, 2002; Thompson, 1997), usually knowing their victims (Gilby *et al.*, 1989) and frequently reoffending (Day, 1994; Gilby *et al.*, 1989; Klimecki, Jenkinson and Wilson, 1994). There is some evidence that men with ID who engage in sexually abusive behaviour also show cognitive distortions (Lindsay, Carson and Whitefield, 2000; Lindsay, Marshall, Neilson, Quinn and Smith, 1998b; Lindsay, Neilson, Morrison and Smith, 1998a;

Lindsay, Olley, Jack, Morrison and Smith, 1998c) and have little empathy for their victims. Where they differ from non-disabled sex offenders is that the men with ID more often have adult victims (usually other people with ID) and more frequently target male victims (Gilby *et al.*, 1989; Murrey, Briggs and Davis, 1992). There is some suggestion that they may be less likely to be violent during their sexual offences than non-disabled men and less likely to commit penetrative offences (Murrey *et al.*, 1992). Men with ID and sexually abusive behaviour are rarely reported to the police, especially if the victim is another person with ID: Thompson (1997), for example, found over 70 per cent of offences against children but only 11 per cent of offences against another person with ID were reported to the police. The men are very rarely convicted, even after being reported to the police (for the reasons discussed in the sections on victims, above) and the consequences of their behaviour are often minimal (Thompson, 1997). According to some reports, men with ID and sexually abusive behaviour have less specific victim patterns than non-disabled sex offenders (i.e. may have some male victims, some female, some children) but this has sometimes been disputed, especially since the data from Abel and Rouleau's (1990) study on non-disabled men's sexual preferences and victim types.

TREATMENT FOR ALLEGED PERPETRATORS

Treatment of non-disabled perpetrators

Researchers have tried to develop theories of sexual offending to account for the characteristics of sex offenders and to allow treatment programmes to be developed to reduce the likelihood of reoffending. All of the theories have been based on what is known about convicted non-disabled male sex offenders. Early theories tended to be based on the idea that abnormal sexual arousal underlay deviant sexual responding, as a result of early conditioning. Paedophiles were reported to be more aroused to images of children than adults (Quinsey and Chaplin, 1988) and rapists more aroused to violent sexual scenes than to consenting sex (Quinsey, Chaplin and Varney, 1981). Treatment programmes at the time were either medicinal (involving anti-androgens, such as in Bancroft, Tennant and Loucas (1974) and Cooper (1981)) or were behavioural. Behavioural programmes focused on correcting abnormal arousal either by punishment, such as in aversive conditioning (Quinsey, Chaplin and Carrigan, 1980) and covert sensitization (Maletsky, 1980) or by reinforcement, such as in orgasmic reconditioning (Marquis, 1970). However, it gradually became clear that sexual preferences, especially as measured by phallometry, were not good predictors of sexual offending and many of the related treatments proved unsatisfactory when properly designed evaluations of their effectiveness were undertaken (see Marshall,

Anderson and Fernandez (1999: ch. 8) for a review of the evidence). Moreover, Marshall *et al.* (1999) argued that many of these behavioural treatment programmes were unethical, as they provided treatment for sexual behaviours that were not illegal (such as homosexuality, fetishism and transvestism) and were frequently punitive.

During the 1980s and the next few decades, a number of very influential theories appeared, which attempted to explain the sexual offending of non-disabled men, in terms of cognitive and emotional precursors and components. Three of the most successful have been those of Wolf (1988), Finkelhor (1984; 1986), and Marshall *et al.* (1999). Wolf (1988) proposed a model of the cycle of offending that attempted to explain how sex offenders came to repeat their offences. His hypothesis was that sexual offenders began with poor self-esteem and personal problems, which, when the problems worsened, led to a retreat into self-reinforcing fantasies, including sexual fantasies. These then led the offender on to targeting a victim, getting to know him/her and planning how to offend. At this stage it was hypothesized that the offender would begin to engage in cognitive distortions (such as 'it is only a bit of fun'), so as to excuse himself from his actions. The offence itself would follow, with a brief period of sexual satisfaction, but quickly guilt and further lowering of self-esteem would ensue, only for the offender to repeat the whole cycle when further events threatened his well-being.

Finkelhor's theories (1984; 1986) reinforced Wolf's model and expanded on some aspects of the behaviour of sex offenders. Finklehor proposed that in order to commit child sexual abuse, four preconditions had to be present:

- the sexual offender had to be motivated to offend
- he must overcome his internal inhibitions to offend (through cognitive distortions, such as denial of harm, minimization of intended actions and victim blaming)
- he must overcome external obstacles (through planning how to make contact with victims)
- he must overcome the victim's resistance (through grooming and befriending the victims).

There is considerable evidence of cognitive distortions and of planning, grooming and befriending of victims from numerous studies (Abel *et al.*, 1984; Murphy, 1990).

Finally, Marshall and colleagues' model attempted to explain the social isolation and loneliness in sex offenders, the presence of attachment deficits, and the role of empathy (Marshall, 1996; Marshall *et al.*, 1999). They proposed that sex offenders had insecure attachments to their parents as young boys, leading to either fearful or avoidant attitudes to social intimacy with peers (according to whether parents had been inconsistent or detached/unresponsive, respectively), and thus loneliness followed. Marshall and colleagues proposed that during puberty, because of their social relationships difficulties, boys with insecure attachments began to seek intimate experiences through sexual acts, particularly when transitory personal factors (such as anger, depression, resentment) or situational factors (such as alcohol) were operating (Marshall and Barbaree, 1990; Marshall *et al.*, 1999: 27–31). The proposed intimacy deficits and the increased loneliness of sex offenders were confirmed by Seidman *et al.* (1994) and Bumby and Hansen (1997).

Hudson and Ward later attempted to extend Marshall's theory, using Bartholomew and Horowitz's (1991, cited in Hudson and Ward, 1997) four-category model of social attachment. Bartholomew and Horowitz proposed that there were really four attachment styles: secure (in which a person's view of him/herself and others was positive); preoccupied (in which a person viewed others positively but him/herself negatively); fearful (in which a person viewed both him/herself and others negatively); and dismissing (in which a person viewed him/herself positively but others negatively). Ward, Hudson and Marshall (1996) predicted that child molesters would have a preoccupied or fearful attachment style, while rapists would be more likely to have a dismissing style, and their data supported this prediction. Nevertheless, there was no clear differentiation between offender types in a later study, suggesting that the relationship between attachment style and offender type is not clear-cut (Hudson and Ward, 1997).

In line with these more sophisticated theories of sexual offending, treatment for non-disabled men who had committed sex offences became better targeted at the cognitive and affective reasons for sexual offending (Marshall, 1996). Increasingly cognitive behaviour therapy (CBT) became the treatment of choice and recent large meta-analyses have demonstrated that such treatment approximately halves reoffending rates, the reconviction rate for untreated men averaging 17 per cent while treated men average 10 per cent over about a four-year period (Hanson, Gordon, Harris, Marques, *et al.*, 2002). These days, CBT is usually provided to groups of sex offenders, partly to allow some support to be offered by the men to other men within the group but also partly to enhance the challenging of cognitive distortions by group members. The content of CBT programmes, which are usually run by one male and one female therapist, vary somewhat, but most programmes last about one year and include modules on:

- Enhancing self-esteem
- Improving social skills, usually focused on relationship skills
- Enhancing victim empathy
- The role of fantasy and sexual preferences
- The cognitive model and challenging of cognitive distortions
- Relapse prevention.

Increasingly such programmes are mandatory for men convicted of sexual offences, whether they are serving sentences in prison or in the community (Beckett *et al.*, 1994; Beech, Fisher and Beckett, 1998).

Treatment of men with intellectual disabilities who have sexually abused others

While there has been considerable debate and enormous research effort put into discovering the causes of sexual offending amongst non-disabled men, research into the causes of sexual offending amongst men with intellectual disabilities is only just beginning. Some evidence suggests that there are many similarities between men without disabilities who commit sexual offences and men with intellectual disabilities who engage in similar behaviours (see above, under 'Characteristics'). Treatment for men with ID has usually followed that developed for non-disabled men. In the early years, therefore, treatment tended to be medicinal, with anti-libidinal drugs (Clarke, 1989; Cooper, 1995) or to focus on behavioural methods (Foxx, Bittle, Bechtel and Livesay, 1986; Murphy *et al.*, 1983), often with sex education and social skills training components (Charman and Clare, 1992; Griffiths, Quinsey and Hingsburger, 1989; Haaven, Little and Petre-Miller, 1990; Lund, 1992; O'Connor, 1996; Swanson and Garwick, 1990). Latterly, group CBT has become more likely to be the treatment of choice and there are now some treatment manuals and training courses available for therapists: for example, the ASOTP programme used in a number of prisons and hospital settings in the UK for men with ID (Rogers and Fairbanks, 2003) and the UK Sex Offender Treatment Services Collaborative (SOTSEC-ID) model (Sinclair, Booth and Murphy, 2002). Frequently these programmes are similar to, but simplified versions of, the kind of group CBT for non-disabled sex offenders. They almost always include an additional component on sex education, however, as men with ID tend to have lower sexual knowledge than non-disabled men (Murphy and O'Callaghan, 2004), though it is not known for certain whether this has any real link to sexually abusive behaviour.

The feasibility of CBT generally for people with ID (Stenfert Kroese, Dagnan and Loumidis, 1997) and its effectiveness for men with ID and sexually abusive behaviour, in particular, is only just beginning to be established. While there are a few controlled studies of CBT (Willner, Jones, Tams and Green, 2002), none of these as yet are for men with sexually abusive behaviour. Nevertheless, in an uncontrolled study, Rose, Jenkins, O'Connor, Jones and Felce (2002) demonstrated that a closed group intervention lasting sixteen weeks (for two hours per week), for a group of five men, focusing on sex education, identifying feelings and enhancing empathy, sexual fantasies, offending cycles and planning how not to reoffend, had some (non-significant) effect in improving empathy and cognitive distortions, in some men. A similar programme lasting a year also showed significant improvements in sexual knowledge and empathy (Murphy and O'Callaghan, 2004). Moreover, Lindsay and colleagues, in a series of studies, have shown that group CBT, involving some victim empathy work, challenging of cognitive distortions about responsibility, intent, harm done to the victim, and relapse prevention did reduce cognitive distortions in treated men (Lindsay et al., 1998a; 1998b; 1998c) and those receiving two years of treatment did better than those with one year of treatment (Lindsay and Smith, 1998).

PREVENTION OF SEXUAL OFFENDING

Non-disabled men

For men without disabilities, relapse prevention is an important part of cognitive-behavioural treatment programmes (Eccles and Marshall, 1999; Pithers, 1990). The method chosen to promote relapse prevention for sex offenders came originally from Marlatt's work with people who had addictive behaviours (Marlatt, 1982). The model proposes that there is a chain of events from seemingly unimportant decisions (or SUDs, such as to walk to the shops past the school, at a time when children are in the playground), to lapses (such as engaging in deviant fantasies), to full-blown relapses, as a result of an abstinence violation effect (AVE). During treatment, non-disabled sex offenders are taught to recognize the stages that lead to relapse and to avoid the slide from SUDs to lapse, to AVE, to full relapse. Recent reviews have suggested that relatively few non-disabled men reoffend following treatment (10 per cent approximately, according to Hanson et al., 2002). Nevertheless, this is too many and so increasingly, in addition to treatment and risk prevention for non-disabled men, both of which rely on self-control, standardized measures of risk are used to predict who will reoffend (Hanson and Thornton, 2000) and increased supervision is provided for high-risk men, in order to reduce the risks.

Men with ID

CBT programmes for men with intellectual disabilities also include relapse prevention components, though the importance of this part of the programme has yet to be ascertained. It seems likely that the baseline relapse rate for men with ID who commit sexual offences may be higher than that for men without disabilities: Klimecki et al. (1994), for example, found a recidivism rate of 31 per cent amongst men with ID who had not had treatment and who had been convicted of sexual offences in one part of Australia. Results from Lindsay and Smith (1998) suggested that treatment reduces this rate considerably but nevertheless reoffending does sometimes occur.

Of course, many men with ID who have sexually abusive behaviours are not yet being offered treatment. In the majority of cases, their behaviours are managed through clinical risk assessment and risk management: a recent survey in the US of 240 service providers indicated that 74 per cent of services managed sexually abusive men through close supervision (Ward, Trigler and Pfeiffer, 2001). This has advantages but also disadvantages for the men themselves. Many men are reluctant to go through a treatment programme for a whole year that will force them to confront their attitudes and behaviour; on the other hand, if they are simply closely supervised, there is no logical reason to stop such supervision, when the risks they pose unsupervised have not necessarily lessened. Standardized risk assessment measures are only just beginning to be used for men with ID (Johnston, 2002) and it is, as yet, too early to tell whether such measures will help to contribute to reductions in risk through targeted increased supervision.

Providing treatment and risk management for men who have been sexually abusive is only one form of prevention, of course. It would be preferable to prevent men from offending in the first place. We are as yet a very long way from knowing how to do this. Feminists argue that one important issue is the way that society generally (and men in particular) tolerate attitudes and behaviours associated with sexual offending, as indicated by the widespread availability of pornography, of use of prostitutes and of hostile attitudes to women (McCarthy, 1999: 35–40). Furthermore, the social inequalities inherent in most societies make it more likely that some families will struggle to create harmonious and nurturing family relationships, thus creating some of the insecure attachment and other preconditions thought to be important in the development of sexually abusive behaviour. In addition, in services for people with intellectual disabilities there is often an unjustified toleration of inappropriate sexual behaviour, with insufficient notification to the police and a tendency simply to move men who sexually abuse to another residential setting. The criminal justice system, when involved, also frequently fails the victim with intellectual disabilities, making it more likely that perpetrators will reoffend.

EXERCISE

Work in groups of four. Imagine you have been asked to set up a project to treat adolescents with intellectual disabilities who have persistently behaved in a sexually inappropriate way. What practical steps would you take to organize the project? What key elements would you include in the programme? How would you network the programme in with other important services and relationships in clients' lives? When you have reached a decision on each of these questions, summarize these and read them to the class.

FURTHER READING FOR CLINICIANS

Churchill, J., Craft, A., Holding, A. and Horrocks, C. (eds) (1996). *It Could Never Happen Here: The Prevention and Treatment of Sexual Abuse of Adults with Learning Disabilities in Residential Settings*, rev. edn. Chesterfield: ARC and NAPSAC.

Marshall, W.L., Anderson, D. and Fernandez, Y. (1999). *Cognitive-Behavioural Treatment of Sex Offenders*. Chichester: Wiley.

O'Callaghan, A.C., Murphy, G.H. and Clare, I.C.H. (2003). *Symptoms of Abuse in Adults with Severe Learning Disabilities*. Final Report to the Dept of Health (obtainable from g.h.murphy@lancaster.ac.uk).

O' Reilly, G., Marshall, W., Beckett, R. and Carr, A. (eds) (2004). *The Handbook of Clinical Intervention with Young People Who Sexually Abuse*. London: Brunner-Routledge.

Sinclair, N., Booth, S.J. and Murphy, G.H. (2002). *Cognitive-Behavioural Treatment for Men with Intellectual Disabilities Who Are at Risk of Sexual Offending: A Treatment Manual*. Unpublished manuscript (obtainable from g.h.murphy@lancaster.ac.uk).

REFERENCES

Abel, G.C. and Rouleau, J.L. (1990). The nature and extent of sexual assault. In W.L. Marshall, D.R. Laws and H.E. Barbaree (eds), *Handbook of Sexual Assault: Issues, Theory and Treatment of the Offender* (pp. 9–21). New York: Plenum Press.

Abel, G.C., Becker J.V. and Cunningham-Rathner, J. (1984). Complications, consent and cognitions in sex between children and adults. *International Journal of Law and Psychiatry*, 7, 89–103.

American Psychiatric Association (1994). *Diagnostic and Statistical Manual of Mental Disorders*, 4th edn. Washington, DC: American Psychiatric Press.

Awad, G.A. and Saunders, E.B. (1991). Male adolescent sexual assaulters: Clinical observations. *Journal of Interpersonal Violence*, 6, 446–60.

Badgely, R. (1984). *Sexual Offences against Children: Report of the Committee on Sexual Offences against Children and Youth*. Ottawa: Government of Canada.

Bailey, A. and Barr, O. (2000). Police policies on the investigation of sexual crimes committed against adults who have a learning disability. *Journal of Learning Disabilities*, 4, 129–39.

Baker, A.W. and Duncan, S.P. (1985). Child sexual abuse: A study of prevalence in Great Britain. *Child Abuse and Neglect*, 9, 457–67.

Bancroft, J., Tennant, G. and Loucas, K. (1974). The control of deviant sexual behaviour by drugs. *British Journal of Psychiatry*, 125, 310–15.

Bartholomew, K. and Horowitz, L.M. (1991). Attachment styles among young adults: A test of a four-category model. *Journal of Personality and Social Psychology*, 61(2), 226–44.

Beckett, R., Beech, A., Fisher, D. and Fordham, A.S. (1994). *Community-Based Treatment for Sex Offenders: An Evaluation of Seven Treatment Programmes*. London: Home Office.

Beech, A., Fisher, D. and Beckett, R. (1998). *An Evaluation of the Prison Sex Offender Treatment Programme*. London: Home Office.

Beitchman, J.H., Zucker, K.J., Hood, J.E., DaCosta, G.A. and Akman, D. (1991). A review of the short-term effects of child sexual abuse. *Child Abuse and Neglect*, 15, 537–56.

Birmingham, L., Mason, D. and Grubin, D. (1996). Prevalence of mental disorder in remand prisoners: Consecutive case study. *British Medical Journal*, 313, 1521–4.

Brooke, D., Taylor, C., Gunn, J. and Maden, A. (1996). Point prevalence of mental disorder in unconvicted male prisoners in England and Wales. *British Medical Journal*, 313, 1524–7.

Brown, B.S. and Courtless, T.F. (1971). *The Mentally Retarded Offender*. Washington, DC: US Government Printing Office.

Brown, H. and Stein, J. (1998). Implementing Adult Protection policies in Kent and East Sussex. *Journal of Social Policy*, 27, 371–96.

Brown, H., Stein, J. and Turk, V. (1995). The sexual abuse of adults with learning disabilities: A second incidence study. *Mental Handicap Research*, 8, 3–24.

Buchanan, A.H. and Wilkins, R. (1991). Sexual abuse of the mentally handicapped: Difficulties in establishing prevalence. *Psychiatric Bulletin*, 15, 601–5.

Bulik, C.M., Prescott, C.A. and Kendler, K.S. (2001). Features of childhood sexual abuse and the development of psychiatric and substance abuse disorders. *British Journal of Psychiatry*, 179, 444–9.

Bumby, K.M. and Hansen, D.J. (1997). Intimacy deficits, fear of intimacy and loneliness among sexual offenders. *Criminal Justice and Behaviour*, 24, 315–31.

Cambridge, P. (1997). *HIV, Sex and Learning Disability*. Brighton: Pavilion Publishing.

Caspar, L.A. and Glidden, L.M. (2001). Sexuality education for adults with developmental disabilities. *Education and Training in Mental Retardation and Developmental Disabilities*, 36, 172–7.

Chamberlain, A., Rauh, J., Passer, A., McGrath, M. and Burket, R. (1984). Issues in fertility control for mentally retarded female adolescents: 1. Sexual activity, sexual abuse and contraception. *Pediatrics*, 73, 445–50.

Charman, T. and Clare, I.C.H. (1992). Education about the laws and social rules relating to sexual behaviour. *Mental Handicap*, 20, 74–80.

Clare, I.C.H. and Gudjonsson, G.H. (1993). Interrogative suggestibility, confabulation, and acquiescence in people with mild learning disabilities (mental handicap): Implications for reliability during police interview. *British Journal of Clinical Psychology*, 32, 295–301.

Clarke, D.J. (1989). Anti-libidinal drugs and mental retardation: A review. *Medicine, Science and the Law*, 29, 136–48.

Cooke, P. and Davies, G. (2001). Achieving best evidence from witnesses with learning disabilities: New guidance. *British Journal of Learning Disabilities*, 29, 84–7.

Cooper, A.J. (1981). A placebo-controlled trial of the anti-androgen cyproterone acetate in deviant hypersexuality. *Comprehensive Psychiatry*, 22, 458–66.

Cooper, A.J. (1995). Review of the role of two anti-libidinal drugs in the treatment of sex offenders with mental retardation. *Mental Retardation*, 33, 42–8.

Craft, M. (1984). Low intelligence, mental handicap and criminality. In M. Craft and A. Craft (eds), *Mentally Abnormal Offenders* (pp. 35–52). London: Balliere-Tindall.

Davison, F., Clare, I.C.H., Georgiades, S., Divall, J. and Holland, A.J. (1994).

Treatment of a man with a mild learning disability who was sexually assaulted whilst in prison. *Medicine, Science and the Law*, 34(4), 346–53.

Day, K. (1994). Male mentally handicapped sex offenders. *British Journal of Psychiatry*, 165, 630–9.

Denkowski, G.C. and Denkowski, K.M. (1985). The mentally retarded offender in the state prison system: Indentification, prevalence, adjustment and rehabilitation. *Criminal Justice and Behaviour*, 12, 53–70.

Di Vasto, P.V., Kaufman, L.R., Jackson, R., Christy, J., Pearson, S. and Burgett, T. (1984). The prevalence of sexually stressful events among females in the general population. *Archives of Sexual Behaviour*, 13, 59–67.

Eccles, A. and Marshall, W.L. (1999). Relapse prevention. In W.L. Marshall, D. Anderson and Y. Fernandez (eds), *Cognitive-Behavioural Treatment of Sex Offenders* (pp. 127–46). Chichester: Wiley.

Edmonson, B. and Wish, J. (1973). Sex knowledge and attitudes of moderately retarded males. *American Journal of Mental Deficiency*, 84, 11–18.

Family Planning Association of New South Wales (1993). *Feeling Sexy, Feeling Safe.* A sex education video for people with intellectual disabilities.

Ferguson, D.M. and Mullen, P.E. (1999). *Childhood Sexual Abuse: An Evidence Based Perspective*. Thousand Oaks, CA: Sage.

Fernandez, Y.M., Marshall, W.L., Lightbody, S. and O'Sullivan, C. (1999). The child molester empathy measure. *Sexual Abuse: A Journal of Research and Treatment*, 11, 17–32.

Finklehor, D. (1984). *Child Sexual Abuse: New Theory and Research*. New York: Free Press.

Finkelhor, D. (1986). *A Sourcebook on Child Sexual Abuse*. Beverly Hills, CA: Sage Publications.

Finklehor, D. (1994). The international epidemiology of child sexual abuse. *Child Abuse and Neglect*, 18, 409–17.

Finlay, W.M.L. and Lyons, E. (2002). Acquiescence in interviews with people who have mental retardation. *Mental Retardation*, 40, 14–29.

Fisher, D. Beech, A. and Browne, K. (1999). Comparison of sex offenders to non-offenders on selected psychological measures. *International Journal of Offender Therapy and Comparative Criminology*, 43, 473–91.

Foxx, R.M., Bittle, R.G., Bechtel, D.R. and Livesay, J.R. (1986). Behavioural treatment of the sexually deviant behaviour of mentally retarded individuals. In N.R. Ellis and N.W. Bray (eds), *International Review of Research in Mental Retardation* (vol. 14, pp. 291–317). New York: Academic Press.

Garlick, Y., Marshall, W.L. and Thornton, D. (1996). Intimacy deficits and attribution of blame among sex offenders. *Legal and Criminological Psychology*, 1, 251–8.

Gilby, R., Wolf, L. and Goldberg, B. (1989). Mentally retarded adolescent sex offenders: A survey and pilot study. *Canadian Journal of Psychiatry*, 34, 542–8.

Griffiths, S.D.M., Quinsey, V.L. and Hingsburger, D. (1989). *Changing Inappropriate Sexual Behaviour: A Community Based Approach for Persons with Developmental Disabilities*. Baltimore, MD: Paul H. Brookes.

Groth, N. A. and Burgess, A. (1979). Sexual trauma in the life histories of rapists and child molesters. *Victimology: An International Journal*, 4, 10–16.

Grubin, D. (1998). *Sex Offending against Children: Understanding the Risk*. Police

Research Series paper 99. London: Home Office Research Development and Statistics Directorate.

Gudjonsson, G.H. (1999). Testimony from persons with mental disorders. In A. Heaton-Armstrong, E. Shepherd and D. Wolchover (eds), *Analysing Witness Testimony: A Guide for Legal Practitioners and Other Professionals* (pp. 62–75). London: Blackstone Press.

Gudjonsson, G.H., Murphy, G.H. and Clare, I.C.H. (2000). Assessing the capacity of people with intellectual disabilities to be witnesses in court. *Psychological Medicine*, 30, 307–14.

Gunn, J., Maden, A. and Swinton, M. (1991). Treatment needs of prisoners with psychiatric disorders. *British Medical Journal*, 303, 338–41.

Gust, D.A., Wang, S.A., Grot, J., Ransom, R. and Levine, W.C. (2003). National survey of sexual behaviour and sexual behaviour policies in facilities for individuals with mental retardation/developmental disabilities. *Mental Retardation*, 41, 365–73.

Haaven, J., Little, R. and Petre-Miller, D. (1990). *Treating Intellectually Disabled Sex Offenders: A Model Residential Programme*. Orwell, VT: Safer Society Press.

Hamlyn, B., Phelps, A., Turtle, J. and Sattar, G. (2004). *Are Special Measures Working? Evidence from Surveys of Vulnerable and Intimated Witnesses*. London: Home Office Research Report, Study 283.

Hanson, R.K. and Thornton, D. (2000). Improving risk assessments for sex offenders: A comparison of three actuarial scales. *Law and Human Behaviour*, 24, 119–36.

Hanson, R.K., Gordon, A., Harris, A.J.R., Marques, J.K., Murphy, W., Quinsey, V.L. and Seto, M.C. (2002). First report of the collaborative outcome data project on the effectiveness of psychological treatment for sex offenders. *Sexual Abuse: A Journal of Research and Treatment*, 14, 169–94.

Happel, R.M. and Auffrey, J.J. (1995). Sex offender assessment: Interrupting the dance of denial. *American Journal of Forensic Psychiatry*, 13, 5–22.

Hard, S. and Plumb, W. (1987). *Sexual Abuse of Persons with Developmental Disabilities. A Case Study*. Unpublished manuscript.

Haseltine, B. and Miltenberger, R. (1990). Teaching self-protection skills to persons with mental retardation. *American Journal on Mental Retardation*, 95, 188–97.

Hawk, G.L., Rosenfeld, B.D. and Warren, J.I. (1993). Prevalence of sexual offences among mentally retarded criminal defendants. *Hospital and Community Psychiatry*, 44, 784–6.

Hayes, S. (1991). Sex offenders. *Australia and New Zealand Journal of Developmental Disabilities*, 17, 220–7.

Hayes, S. (1996). Recent research on offenders with learning disabilities. *Tizard Learning Disability Review*, 1, 7–15.

Heal, L.W. and Sigelman, C.K. (1995). Response biases in interviews of individuals with limited mental ability. *Journal of Intellectual Disability Research*, 39, 331–40.

Hembree, E.A. and Foa, E.B. (2003). Promoting cognitive change in posttraumatic stress disorder. In M.A. Reinecke and D.A. Clark (eds), *Cognitive Therapy across the Lifespan: Evidence and Practice* (pp. 231–57). Cambridge: Cambridge University Press.

Herbert, C. and Wetmore, A. (1999). *Overcoming Traumatic Stress: A Self-Help Guide Using Cognitive-Behavioural Techniques*. London: Robinson Publishing Ltd.

Hollins, S., Sinason, V., Boniface, J. and Webb, B. (1994). *Going to Court*. London: St George's Mental Health Library.

Home Office (1995). *Police and Criminal Evidence Act 1984: Codes of Practice*, rev. edn. London: HMSO.

Home Office (2000). *Consultation Paper: Achieving Best Evidence in Criminal Proceedings: Guidance for Vulnerable or Intimidated Witnesses, Including Children*. London: HMSO.

Home Office (2003). *Police and Criminal Evidence Act 1984. Codes of Practice*. Rev. edn. London: HMSO.

Horowitz, M., Wilner, N. and Alvarez, W. (1979). Impact of Events Scale: A measure of subjective stress. *Psychosomatic Medicine*, 41, 209–18.

Howlin, P. and Clements, J. (1995). Is it possible to assess the impact of abuse on children with pervasive developmental disorders? *Journal of Autism and Developmental Disabilities*, 25, 337–54.

Hudson, S.M. and Ward, T. (1997). Intimacy, loneliness and attachment style in sexual offenders. *Journal of Interpersonal Violence*, 12, 323–39.

Johnston, S.J. (2002). Risk assessment in offenders with intellectual disability: The evidence base. *Journal of Intellectual Disability Research*, 46, 47–56.

Kebbell, M.R. and Hatton, C. (1999). People with mental retardation as witnesses in court: a review. *Mental Retardation*, 37, 179–87.

Kebbell, M.R., Hatton, C. and Johnson, S.D. (2004). Witnesses with intellectual disabilities in court: What questions are asked and what influence do they have? *Legal and Criminological Psychology*, 9, 23–5.

Kebbell, M.R., Hatton, C., Johnson, S.D. and O'Kelly, C.M.E. (2001). People with learning disabilities as witnesses in court: What questions should lawyers ask? *British Journal of Learning Disabilities*, 29, 98–102.

Kempton, W. (1988). *Life Horizons I and II*. Santa Monica: James Stanfield and Co.

Kempton, W. and Kahn, E. (1991). Sexuality and people with intellectual disabilities: A historical perspective. *Sexuality and Disability*, 9, 93–111.

Kendall-Tackett, K.A., Williams, L.M. and Finkelhor, D. (1993). Impact of sexual abuse on children: A review and synthesis of recent empirical studies. *Psychological Bulletin*, 113, 164–80.

Kendler, K.S., Bulik, C.M., Silberg, J., Hettema, J.M., Myers, J. and Prescott, C.A. (2000). Childhood sexual abuse and adult psychiatric and substance abuse disorders in women: An epidemiological and co-twin control analysis. *Archives of General Psychiatry*, 57, 953–9.

Khemkha, I. (2000). Increasing independent decision-making skills of women with mental retardation in simulated interpersonal situations of abuse. *American Journal on Mental Retardation*, 105, 387–401.

Khemkha, I. and Hickson, L. (2000). Decision-making by adults with mental retardation in simulated situations of abuse. *Mental Retardation*, 38, 15–26.

Kilpatrick, D.G., Saunders, B.E., Veronen, L.J., Best, C.L. and Von, J.M. (1987). Criminal victimisation: Lifetime prevalence reporting to police and psychological impact. *Crime and Delinquency*, 33, 479–89.

Klimecki, M.R., Jenkinson, J. and Wilson, L. (1994). A study of recidivism among offenders with intellectual disability. *Australia and New Zealand Journal of Developmental Disabilities*, 19, 209–19.

Knight, R., Prentky, R., Schneider, B. and Rosenberg, R. (1983). Linear causal modelling of adaptation and criminal history in sex offenders. In K. Van Dusen and S. Mednick (eds), *Prospective Studies of Crime and Delinquency* (pp. 303–41). Boston: Kluwer-Nijhoff.

Konstantereas, M.M. and Lunsky, Y.J. (1997). Sociosexual knowledge, experience, attitudes and interests of individuals with autistic disorder and developmental delay. *Journal of Autism and Developmental Disorders*, 27, 397–413.

Langevin, R., Bain, J., Ben-Aron, M., Coulthard, R., Day, D., Handy L., Heasman, G., Hucker, S., Pudins, J., Roper, V., Ruson, A., Webster, C. and Wortzman, G. (1984a). Sexual aggression: Constructing a predictive equation. A controlled pilot study. In R. Langevin (ed.), *Erotic Preference, Gender Identity and Aggression in Men: New Research Studies* (pp. 39–76). Hillside, NJ: Lawrence Erlbaum.

Langevin, R., Handy, L., Hook, H., Day, D. and Russon, A. (1984b). Are incestuous fathers paedophilic and aggressive? In R. Langevin (ed.), *Erotic Preference, Gender Identity and Aggression in Men: New Research Studies* (pp. 155–76). Hillside, NJ: Lawrence Erlbaum.

Lindsay, W.R. and Smith, A.H.W. (1998). Responses to treatment for sex offenders with intellectual disability: A comparison of men with one and two year probation sentences. *Journal of Intellectual Disability Research*, 42, 346–53.

Lindsay, W.R., Bellshaw, E., Culross, G., Staines, C. and Michie, A. (1992). Increases in knowledge following a sex education course for people with intellectual disability. *Journal of Intellectual Disability Research*, 36, 531–9.

Lindsay, W.R., Carson, D. and Whitefield, E. (2000). Development of a questionnaire on attitudes consistent with sex offending for men with intellectual disabilities. *Journal of Intellectual Disability Research*, 44, 368–78.

Lindsay, W.R., Law, J., Quinn, K., Smart, N. and Smith, A.H.W. (2001). A comparison of physical and sexual abuse histories: Sexual and non-sexual offenders with intellectual disability. *Child Abuse and Neglect*, 25, 989–95.

Lindsay, W.R., Marshall, L., Neilson, C., Quinn, K. and Smith, A.H.W. (1998b). The treatment of men with a learning disability convicted of exhibitionism. *Research in Developmental Disabilities*, 19, 295–316.

Lindsay, W.R., Neilson, C., Morrison, F. and Smith, A.H.W. (1998a). The treatment of six men with a learning disability convicted of sex offences with children. *British Journal of Clinical Psychology*, 37, 83–98.

Lindsay, W.R., Olley, S., Jack, C., Morrison, F. and Smith, A.H.W. (1998c). The treatment of two stalkers with intellectual disabilities using a cognitive approach. *Journal of Applied Research in Intellectual Disabilities*, 11, 333–44.

Lindsay, W.R., Smith, A.H.W., Law, J., Quinn, K., Anderson, A., Smith, A., Overend, T. and Allan, R. (2002). A treatment service for sex offenders and abusers with intellectual disability: Characteristics of referrals and evaluation. *Journal of Applied Research in Intellectual Disabilities*, 15, 166–74.

Luckasson, R. (1992). People with mental retardation as victims of crime. In R.W. Conley, R. Luckasson and G.N. Bouthilet (eds), *The Criminal Justice System and Mental Retardation*. London: Paul Brookes Publishing Company.

Lumley, V.A. and Miltenberger, R.G. (1997). Sexual abuse prevention for persons with mental retardation. *American Journal on Mental Retardation*, 101, 459–72.

Lumley, V.A., Miltenberger, R.G., Long, E.S., Rapp, J. and Roberts, J.A. (1998). Evaluation of a sexual abuse prevention program for adults with mental retardation. *Journal of Applied Behaviour Analysis*, 31, 91–101.

Lund, C.A. (1992). Long-term treatment of sexual behaviour problems in adolescent and adult developmentally disabled persons. *Annals of Sex Research*, 5, 5–31.

Lyall, I., Holland, A.J. and Collins, S. (1995). Offending by adults with learning disabilities and the attitudes of staff to offending behaviour: Implications for service development. *Journal of Intellectual Disability Research*, 39, 501–8.

MacEachron, A.E. (1979). Mentally retarded offenders prevalence and characteristics. *American Journal of Mental Deficiency*, 84, 165–76.

Maletsky, B.M. (1980). Self-referred vs court-referred sexually deviant patients: Success with assisted covert sensitisation. *Behaviour Therapy*, 11, 306–14.

Marlatt, G.A. (1982). Relapse prevention: A self-control programme for the treatment of addictive behaviours. In R.B. Stuart (ed.), *Adherence, Compliance and Generalisation in Behavioural Medicine* (pp. 329–78). New York: Brunner-Mazel.

Marquis, J.N. (1970). Orgasmic reconditioning: Changing sexual object choice through controlling masturbation fantasies. *Journal of Behaviour Therapy and Experimental Psychiatry*, 1, 263–71.

Marshall, W.L. (1996). Assessment, treatment and theorising about sex offenders: Developments during the past twenty years and future directions. *Criminal Justice and Behaviour*, 23, 162–99.

Marshall, W.L. and Barbaree, H.E. (1990). An integrated theory of the aetiology of sexual offending. In W.L. Marshall, D.R. Laws and H.E. Barbaree (eds), *Handbook of Sexual Assault: Issues, Theories and Treatment of the Offender* (pp. 257–71). New York: Plenum.

Marshall, W.L., Anderson, D. and Fernandez, Y. (1999). *Cognitive-Behavioural Treatment of Sex Offenders*. Chichester: Wiley.

Mason, J. and Murphy, G. (2002). Intellectual disability amongst people on probation: Prevalence and outcome. *Journal of Intellectual Disability Research*, 46, 230–8.

McBrien, J. and Murphy, G. (2006). Police and carers' beliefs about intellectually disabled offenders. *Psychology, Crime and Law*, 12, 127–44.

McCabe, M.P. (1999). Sexual knowledge, experience and feelings among people with disability. *Sexuality and Disability*, 17, 157–70.

McCarthy, M. (1999). *Sexuality and Women with Learning Disabilities*. London: Jessica Kingsley.

McCarthy, M. and Thompson, D. (1992). *Sex and the 3Rs: Rights, Responsibilities and Risks*. Brighton: Pavilion Publishing.

McCarthy, M. and Thompson, D. (1996). Sexual abuse by design: An examination of the issues in learning disability services. *Disability and Society*, 11, 205–17.

McCarthy, M. and Thompson, D. (1997). A prevalence study of sexual abuse of adults with intellectual disabilities referred for sex education. *Journal of Applied Research in Intellectual Disabilities*, 10, 105–24.

McElvaney, R. (2001). Delays in reporting childhood sexual abuse and implications for legal proceedings. In D. P. Farrington, C. R. Hollin and M. McMurran (eds), *Sex and Violence: The Psychology of Crime and Risk Assessment* (pp. 138–52). London: Routledge.

McGee, H., Garavan, R., de Barra, M., Byrne, J. and Conroy, R. (2002). *The SAVI Report : Sexual Abuse and Violence in Ireland*. Dublin: Liffey Press.

McLeer, S.V., Deblinger, E., Henry, D. and Orvaschel, H. (1992). Sexually abused children at high risk for Post Traumatic Stress Disorder. *Journal of the American Academy of Child and Adolescent Psychiatry*, 31, 875–9.

Mencap (1997). *Barriers to Justice*. London: Mencap.

Milne, R., Clare, I.C.H. and Bull, R. (1999). Using the cognitive interview with adults with mild learning disabilities. *Psychology, Crime and Law*, 5, 81–101.

Miltenberger, R.G., Roberts, J.A., Ellingson, S., Galensky, T., Rapp, J.T., Long, E.S. and Lumley, V.A. (1999). Training and generalisation of sexual abuse prevention skills for women with mental retardation. *Journal of Applied Behaviour Analysis*, 32, 385–8.

Mulhern, T.J. (1975). Survey of reported sexual behaviour and policies characterising residential facilities for retarded citizens. *American Journal of Mental Deficiency*, 75, 670–3.

Murphy, G.H. (2000). Justice denied. *Mental Health Care*, 31, 256–7.

Murphy, G.H. and Clare, I.C.H. (2003). Adults' capacity to make legal decisions. In Carson, D. and Bull, R. (eds), *Handbook of Psychology in Legal Contexts* (2nd edn, pp. 31–66). Chichester: Wiley.

Murphy, G.H. and Mason, J. (1999). People with developmental disabilities who offend. In N. Bouras (ed.), *Psychiatric and Behavioural Disorders in Developmental Disabilities and Mental Retardation* (pp. 226–46). Cambridge: Cambridge University Press.

Murphy, G.H. and O'Callaghan, A. (2004). Capacity of adults with intellectual disabilities to consent to sexual relationships. *Psychological Medicine*, 34, 1347–57.

Murphy, G.H., Harnett, H. and Holland, A.J. (1995). A survey of intellectual disabilities amongst men on remand in prison. *Mental Handicap Research*, 8, 81–98.

Murphy, M., Harrold, M., Carey, S. and Mulrooney, M. (2000). *A Survey of the Level of Learning Disability among the Prison Population in Ireland*. Unpublished final report.

Murphy, W.D. (1990). Assessment and modification of cognitive distortions in sex offenders. In W.L. Marshall, D.R. Laws and H.E. Barbaree (eds), *Handbook of Sexual Assault: Issues, Theories and Treatment of the Offender* (pp. 331–42). New York: Plenum.

Murphy, W.D., Coleman, E.M. and Haynes, M.R. (1983). Treatment and evaluation issues with the mentally retarded sex offender. In J.D. Greer and I.R. Stuart (eds), *The Sexual Aggressor: Current Perspectives on Treatment* (pp. 21–41). New York: Nostrand-Rheinhold.

Murrey, G.H., Briggs, D. and Davis, C. (1992). Psychopathically disordered, mentally ill and mentally handicapped sex offenders: A comparative study. *Medicine, Science and the Law*, 32, 331–6.

Myhill, A. and Allen, J. (2002). *Rape and Sexual Assault of Women: The Extent and Nature of the Problem*. Home Office Research Study 237. London: Home Office Research, Development and Statistics Directorate.

Nezu, C.M., Nezu, A.M., Dudek, J.A. (1998). A cognitive-behavioural model of assessment and treatment for intellectually disabled sex offenders. *Cognitive and Behavioural Practice*, 5, 25–64.

Niederbuhl, J.M. and Morris, C.D. (1993). Sexual knowledge and the capability of persons with dual diagnoses to consent to sexual contact. *Sexuality and Disability*, 11, 295–307.

Noble, J.H. and Conley, R.W. (1992). Toward an epidemiology of relevant attributes. In Conley, R.W., Luckasson, R. and Bouthilet, G.N. (eds), *The Criminal Justice*

System and Mental Retardation: Defendants and Victims (pp. 17–53). Baltimore, MD: Paul H. Brookes Publishing Co.

O'Callaghan, A.C., Murphy, G.H. and Clare, I.C.H. (2003). *Symptoms of Abuse in Adults with Severe Learning Disabilities*. Final Report to the Dept of Health (obtainable from g.h.murphy@lancaster.ac.uk).

O'Connor, H. (1996). A problem-solving intervention for sex offenders with an intellectual disability. *Journal of Intellectual and Developmental Disability*, 21, 219–35.

Ousley, O. and Mesibov, G. (1991). Sexual attitudes and knowledge of high functioning adolescents and adults with autism. *Journal of Autism and Developmental Disorders*, 21, 471–81.

Perlman, N.B., Ericson, K.I., Esses, V.M., and Isaacs, B.J. (1994). The developmentally handicapped witness. *Law and Human Behaviour*, 18, 171–87.

Pithers, W.D. (1990). Relapse prevention with sexual aggressors. In W.L. Marshall, D.R. Laws and H.E. Barbaree (eds), *Handbook of Sexual Assault: Issues, Theories and Treatment of the Offender* (pp. 343–61). New York: Plenum.

Quinsey, V.L. and Chaplin, T.C. (1988). Penile responses of child molesters and normals to descriptions of encounters with children involving sex and violence. *Journal of Interpersonal Violence*, 3, 259–74.

Quinsey, V.L., Chaplin, T.C. and Carrigan, W.F. (1980). Biofeedback and signalled punishment in the modification of inappropriate sexual age preferences. *Behaviour Therapy*, 11, 567–76.

Quinsey, V.L. Chaplin, T.C. and Varney, G. (1981). A comparison of rapists' and non-sex offenders' sexual preferences for mutually consenting sex, rape and physical abuse of women. *Behavioural Assessment*, 3, 127–35.

Rada, R.T. (1978). *Clinical Aspects of the Rapist*. New York: Grune and Stratton.

Rogers, J. and Fairbanks, A. (2003). ASOTP Applying the adapted sex offender treatment programme for patients with cognitive deficits. *Forensic Update*, 74, 6–11.

Rose, J., Jenkins, R., O'Connor, C., Jones, C. and Felce, D. (2002). A group treatment for men with intellectual disabilities who sexually offend or abuse. *Journal of Applied Research in Intellectual Disabilities*, 15, 138–50.

Russell, D. (1984). *Sexual Exploitation: Rape, Child Sexual Abuse and Workplace Harassment*. Beverly Hills, CA: Sage.

Salter, A. (1988). *Treating Child Sex Offenders and Victims: A Practical Guide*. Newbury Park, California: Sage Publications.

Sanders, A., Creaton, J., Bird, S. and Weber, L. (1997). *Victims with Learning Disabilities: Negotiating the Criminal Justice System*. Occasional paper no. 17, Centre for Criminological Research, University of Oxford.

Scully, D. (1988). Convicted rapist perceptions of self and victim: Role-taking and emotions. *Gender and Society*, 2, 200–13.

Seidman, B.T., Marshall, W.L., Hudson, S.M. and Robertson, P.J. (1994). An examination of intimacy and loneliness in sex offenders. *Journal of Interpersonal Violence*, 9, 518–34.

Sequeira, H. and Hollins, S. (2003). Clinical effects of sexual abuse on people with learning disability. *British Journal of Psychiatry*, 182, 13–19.

Sequeira, H., Howlin, P. and Hollins, S. (2003). Psychological disturbance associated with sexual abuse in people with learning disabilities. *British Journal of Psychiatry*, 183, 451–6.

Sinclair, N., Booth, S.J. and Murphy, G.H. (2002). *Cognitive-Behavioural Treatment for Men with Intellectual Disabilities Who Are at Risk of Sexual Offending: A Treatment Manual.* Unpublished manuscript.

Sobsey, D. (1994). *Violence and Abuse in the Lives of People with Disabilities: The End of Silent Acceptance?* Baltimore: Paul H. Brookes.

Sobsey, D. and Doe, T. (1991). Patterns of sexual abuse and assault. *Sexuality and Disability*, 9, 243–59.

Sobsey, D. and Varnhagen, C. (1989). Sexual abuse and exploitation of people with disabilities: Toward prevention and treatment. In M. Caspo and L. Gougen (eds), *Special Education across Canada: Challenges for the 90s* (pp. 199–218). Vancouver: Vancouver Centre for Human Developmental and Research.

South East London Health Promotion Services (1992). *My Choice, My Own Choice.* A sex education video for people with learning disabilities.

Stenfert Kroese, B., Dagnan, D. and Loumidis, K. (1997). *Cognitive-Behaviour Therapy for People with Learning Disabilities.* London: Routledge.

Sundin, E.C. and Horowitz, M.J. (2002). Impact of Events Scale: psychometric properties. *British Journal of Psychiatry*, 180, 205–9.

Sundram, C. J. and Stavis, P.F. (1994). Sexuality and mental retardation: Unmet challenges. *Mental Retardation*, 32, 255–64.

Swanson, C.K. and Garwick, G.B. (1990). Treatment for low functioning sex offenders: group therapy and interagency coordination. *Mental Retardation*, 28, 155–61.

Tang, C.S.K. and Lee, Y.K.S. (1999). Knowledge on sexual abuse and self-protection skills: A study on female Chinese adolescents with mild mental retardation. *Child Abuse and Neglect*, 23, 269–79.

Tharinger, D., Horton, C.B. and Millea, S. (1990). Sexual abuse and exploitation of children and adults with mental retardation and other handicaps. *Child Abuse and Neglect*, 14, 301–12.

Thompson, D. (1997). Profiling the sexually abusive behaviour of men with intellectual disabilities. *Journal of Applied Research in Intellectual Disabilities*, 10, 125–39.

Timmers, R.L., Du Charme, P. and Jacob, G. (1981). Sexual knowledge, attitudes and behaviour of developmentally disabled adults living in a normalised apartment setting. *Sexuality and Disability*, 4, 27–39.

Torrey, M. (1991). When will we be believed? Rape myths and the idea of a fair trial in rape prosecutions. *David Law Review*, 24, 1013.

Trowell, J., Kolvin, I., Weermanthri, T., Sadowski, H., Berelowitz, M., Glasser, D. and Leitch, I. (2002). Psychotherapy for sexually abused girls: Psychopathological outcome findings and patterns of change. *British Journal of Psychiatry*, 180, 234–47.

Turk, V. and Brown, H. (1993). The sexual abuse of adults with learning disabilities: Results of a two-year incidence survey. *Mental Handicap Research*, 6, 193–216.

US National Center for Victims of Crime and Crime Victims Research and Treatment Center (1992). *Rape in America: A Report to the Nation.* Arlington, VA: National Center for Victims of Crime and Crime Victims Research and Treatment Center.

Voice UK (1998). *Competent to Tell the Truth.* Derby: Voice UK.

Walby, S. and Allen, J. (2004). *Domestic Violence, Sexual Assault and Stalking: Findings from the British Crime Survey.* Home Office Research Study 276. London: Home Office Research Development and Statistics Directorate.

Walker, N. and McCabe, S. (1973). *Crime and Insanity in England*. Edinburgh: Edinburgh University Press.

Ward, K.M., Trigler, J.S. and Pfeiffer, K.T. (2001). Community services, issues, and service gaps for individuals with developmental disabilities who exhibit inappropriate sexual behaviours. *Mental Retardation*, 39, 11–19.

Ward, T., Hudson, S.M. and Marshall, W.L. (1996). Attachment style in sex offenders: a preliminary study. *Journal of Sex Research*, 33, 17–26.

Ward, T., Hudson, S.M., Johnston, L. and Marshall, W.L. (1997). Cognitive distortions in sex offenders: An integrative review. *Clinical Psychology Review*, 17, 479–507.

Williams, L.M. and Finklehor, D. (1990). The characteristics of incestuous fathers: a review of recent studies. In W.L. Marshall, D.R. Laws and H.E. Barbaree (eds), *Handbook of Sexual Assault: Issues, Theories and Treatment of the Offender* (pp. 231–56). New York: Plenum.

Willner, P., Jones, J. Tams, R. and Green, G. (2002). A randomized controlled trial of the efficacy of a cognitive-behavioural anger management group for clients with learning disabilities. *Journal of Applied Research in Intellectual Disabilities*, 15, 224–35.

Wilson, J.P. and Keane, T.M. (1997). *Assessing Psychological Trauma and PTSD*. New York: Guilford Press.

Wolf, S.C. (1988). A model of sexual aggression/addiction. (Special issue: The sexually unusual: Guide to understanding and helping). *Journal of Social Work and Human Sexuality*, 7, 131–48.

Yule, W. (1999). *Post-Traumatic Stress Disorders: Concepts and Therapy*. Chichester: Wiley.

Chapter 24

Supporting families with ageing members who have intellectual disabilities

Mary McCarron and Philip McCallion

This chapter must begin by noting both the success that ageing of persons with intellectual disabilities (ID) represents and the challenge it means for families and the services providers who must provide new forms of care. The ageing of persons with ID requires all of us to renew our perspectives, tools and approaches. Of all the stages in life it most demands that we respect the individuality and achievements of the person with ID and of her/his family. The increasing complexity of life history and experiences, health needs and life transitions also require that a holistic and multidisciplinary perspective be embraced. In the spirit of such a holistic and multidisciplinary approach it seems appropriate then to draw in perspectives from nursing, social work and other disciplines as well as from psychology and to offer a perspective that challenges psychologists to play roles perhaps beyond their discipline's traditions. Drawing upon the related research and practice literatures, the chapter will outline key demographic, health and life transitions issues for persons with ID and their families as they age, and offer suggestions for their assessment and management.

THE DEMOGRAPHICS OF AGEING

Adults with ID are experiencing increased longevity, and concerns have been raised that this means increased needs for carers including family caregivers and a demand for services and special attention that many jurisdictions are ill-prepared to address (Braddock, 1999; Seltzer and Krauss, 1994). When persons with ID were not expected to live into old age there was a reasonable expectation that parents would outlive their offspring and offer a lifetime of care. The reality then that most care was provided in the home also meant that no services for old age were developed or provided (Ludlow, 1999). For the first time we have sizeable groups of individuals with ID ageing and needing related services. Ageing persons also represent a greater number of those either using or in need of out-of-home care, more directly impacting professional service delivery in provider agencies. Yet, providing services for ageing persons with ID and supporting their families are areas where psychologists, social workers, nurses and other professionals have received little training (McCallion, 1993).

Estimates of the ageing population

In nations with national databases such as Ireland changes in life expectancy can be dramatically illustrated. From 1974 through 2002 the number of persons in the Irish database aged 35–54 increased 132 per cent and those over 55 by 70 per cent (Barron and Mulvany, 2005). Certainly concerns can be raised about whether everyone is being included in such databases or conversely, if some of the increase is due to better case finding over time. In the US, it is acknowledged there are no mechanisms for complete counts and there is greater reliance on estimates. Here, similarly dramatic changes are reported. Life expectancy for persons with ID has increased from an average 18.5 years in 1930 to 59.1 years in 1970 to an estimated 66.2 years in 1993 (Braddock, 1999). Based upon analyses of New York State data, Janicki and colleagues go further, projecting continued growth to match life expectancy of the general population (Janicki, Dalton, Henderson, and Davidson, 1999); by 2020 the number of persons with ID aged over 65 is expected to have doubled (Janicki and Dalton, 2000). There are reports of similar growth in the UK, other European countries and Australia (Hogg, Lucchino, Wang and Janicki, 2001). It has become obvious that services and particularly residential care, i.e. the prime service locations for psychologists and other professionals, are already and increasingly about care for an ageing population. Given these dramatic increases and demographic shifts in ageing of persons with ID, psychologists and other professionals should ask for agency-specific demographic data and trends in order to better understand the implications of these global trends for the consumers they serve and to guide a proactive reorientation of their professions and a redesign of programmes at a local level.

THE CHALLENGES OF LATER LIFE

As much as the ageing of persons with ID is a credit to the sustained efforts of families, providers, communities and professionals to improve their lives, ageing also presents its own challenges. Looking at UK trends, Holland speculates that the survivors into old age were probably healthier and hardier than those who did not, but expresses concern about their potential to develop additional ageing-related disabilities and the lack of preparedness of service networks to address this (Holland, 2000), a concern echoed by Cooper (1999). For all of us ageing is a time of transitions, it may be compromised by ill health, and its success is sustained by a different set of services and experiences than was true in our younger years. This is also true for people with ID.

Transitions

The ID services network has devoted considerable resources to developing work and day programme placements and community-based living arrangements. A philosophy of care has emerged which is prevalent in most developed countries (Schalock, Brown, Brown, Cummins, et al., 2002). Optimum living plans for persons with ID assume that the individual will live in the community, control to the extent possible their life, have a vital and supportive network of friends and relationships and experience more independence this year as compared to last (McCallion and McCarron, in press). These ideas have been enshrined (Schalock et al., 2002) in a consensus set of quality-of-life principles. The usefulness and relevance of these otherwise important principles has been particularly challenged when one ages and one experiences age-associated health concerns such as dementia (McCallion and McCarron, in press). Ageing for persons with ID may be a time, as it is for many other ageing persons, when work experiences end, and decrements rather than expansions in ability and independence occur. Different expectations may be critical to quality of life.

Old age may also be a time of losses. When persons with ID did not live to old age it was possible for parents to outlive their offspring (McCallion and Tobin, 1995). Today, it is more likely that there will be multiple losses in one's lifetime of parents, other valued friends and neighbours and many transitions in key staff in day programmes (from transfer and promotion more than death) with whom the person comes in contact (McCallion and Toseland, 1993). Addressing these transitions and supporting persons with ID are important tasks for professionals. Such losses may also presage other important transitions in the person's life, e.g. movement from the family home to an out-of-home placement and related separation from well-established and valued social networks and neighbourhoods (Bigby, 1996; McCallion and Tobin, 1995).

Ill health

In his consideration of fundamental principles underpinning the concept of successful ageing, Kahn (2002) argues for the importance of an absence of illness and of illness-related disability. However, he acknowledges the argument by Baltes and Baltes (1990) that successful ageing may also require a willingness to accept age-determined, health-related decrements to independence and Riley and Riley's (1990) belief that such decrements mean that successful ageing will also require the application of compensatory external resources. The maintenance of good health and the application of additional external resources when ill health does occur are likely to be of particular concern for persons with ID, given that when combined with existing disabilities, relatively small additional health concerns can have major implications for independence.

A different set of service expectations and outcomes

Given the life transitions and potential for ageing-related health concerns experienced, the needs of both families and persons with an intellectual disability are likely to change. Services continue to be based upon and assume fixed needs for persons with ID, at levels usually established in their younger years. Those needs will change with ageing and so must the services (McCallion and McCarron, 2003). Regarding day-to-day care there is a need for retirement planning, ageing-focused day programming, attention to and support of health needs, and new attention to adaptations in the home and programme sites to maintain personal independence, given new or increased impairments (McCarron and Griffiths, 2003). Planning for transitions in living situations whether with other family members or in out-of-home care and support of individuals as they experience bereavements will also be more prominent.

LIVING PATTERNS FOR AGEING PERSONS WITH INTELLECTUAL DISABILITIES

The greatest focus of service providers is usually upon children with ID. In school and in care in different jurisdictions there are mandates, legal or implied, for a basic level of services, for example for special education services (McCallion, 1993). For adults with ID mandates are less defined and attention is paid most to those in out-of-home placements. Those living at home who are attending work or day programmes may also receive professional services. In many jurisdictions, however, adults living at home are less likely to receive professional services and may indeed need few such services while they are in their young and middle adult years (McCallion and Kolomer, 2003). Therefore it is often a surprise to professionals to realize how many persons with ID and their families have minimal or no contact with services and first or sustained contacts may only be in the older years (McCallion and Tobin, 1995).

For all the attention paid to out-of-home care, the majority of people with ID are cared for at home. For example, the Irish national database (Barron and Mulvaney, 2005) indicates that 61 per cent of persons known to the database live at home, over half with families and about 23 per cent are in out-of-home care. Again, those living at home with minimal or no contact with providers are less likely to be counted in this database so that their numbers may be even higher. Estimates from the United States for family caregiving are similar at 61 per cent but only 10 per cent there live in out-of-home placements. Instead 14 per cent live in their own households and 15 per cent live with a spouse (Braddock, Emerson, Felce and Stanliffe, 2001; Fujiura, 1998). As can be seen in Figure 24.1, the US estimates offer additional insights. Already over 26 per cent of family caregivers are themselves over age 60. There is every expectation that the majority of those with ID being cared for by older caregivers will themselves be over 60 by 2020, likely cared for by the same but much older caregiver, and that those currently being cared for by individuals in their 40s and 50s will by 2020 still be cared for by these individuals, who will then be in their 60s and 70s. Therefore, the growth of the ageing population for this group of individuals has double the implications. There are ageing needs for both the person with ID and for their caregiver, and a likelihood that greater and rapidly growing demands will be placed on limited out-of-home services when caregivers are no longer able or available to provide care (Braddock, 1999).

REWARDS, STRESSES AND COPING APPROACHES OF FAMILY CAREGIVERS

Effective work with family caregivers of ageing adults with ID requires an understanding of the experiences of those families. For psychologists and other professionals there is a danger of only seeing caregiving families and ageing in terms of needs and deficits (McCallion and Toseland, 1993). Often

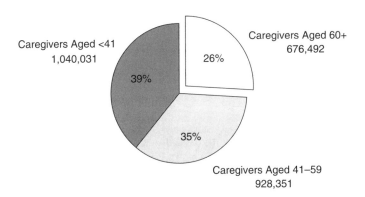

Caregivers Aged <41
1,040,031

26%

Caregivers Aged 60+
676,492

39%

35%

Caregivers Aged 41–59
928,351

Total Estimated Population of Persons with a
Developmental Disability Living with Family Caregivers: 2,644,874

Figure 24.1 Distribution of individuals with a developmental disability living with family caregivers in the United States in 2000.

Source: Adapted from Braddock *et al.* (2001) and Fujiura (1998)

this occurs because provider-based services may have limited contact with families and professional staff are only brought in when problems are being experienced. It is important for professionals to recognize that despite or maybe because of the demands of caring for an adult with ID, there are also rewards associated with being a caregiver. For example, older mothers caring for adults with intellectual disability have been reported as having high morale and as rating their health as good or excellent (Seltzer, Greenberg, Krauss and Hong, 1997). Also, in contrast to mothers caring for an adult child with a mental illness, mothers caring for an adult child with ID reported more social support, less subjective burden, and more effective coping strategies (Greenberg, Seltzer, Krauss and Kim, 1997; Seltzer, Greenberg and Krauss, 1995; Seltzer *et al.*, 1997). It appears that a history of addressing ID-related concerns builds strengths and confidence in many families (Seltzer *et al.*, 1997). One way for psychologists and other professionals to anchor their work with families with an understanding of caregiving strengths is to measure the extent to which families feel in control of their caregiving situation. Useful standardized measures are the Caregiving Mastery Scale (originally developed by Pearlin and Schooler, 1978 and used with family caregivers of persons with ID by Pruchno, Patrick and Burant, 1997 and McCallion, Janicki, Grant-Griffin and Kolomer, 2000) and the Family Empowerment Scale (Koren, DeChillo and Freisen, 1992). However, ID-related concerns may also be experienced as stresses.

Caregiving stress

Families with members with ID are reported to endure stresses that other families do not experience. In a review of the available research and clinical literatures, McCallion and Toseland (1993) found that these stresses result from or are expressed in: (1) emotional strain; (2) marital discord; (3) sibling conflicts; (4) difficult developmental transitions; (5) unresponsive service delivery systems; and (6) permanency planning concerns.

Emotional strain

The reality of birthing a child with disabilities was often difficult to reconcile with a family's ideal image and the family often grieved the loss of its 'ideal' and experienced shock, denial, sadness, and anger. While parents generally work through these feelings to a stage of adaptation and reorganization, for different members of the family this grieving can reoccur, especially when particular events, e.g. increased infirmity and loss of previously learned independence in older age, remind family members of the individual's disability and the changes and sacrifices they have had to make.

Marital discord

Not all children with ID are born into traditional two-parent households. When they are, similar to the general population, their parents experience various levels of marital satisfaction. The presence of a child with ID, however, has been found to exacerbate conflicts and joys and can place great stress on a marriage, often a major reason for parents requesting out-of-home placement. Their own old age may be a time of retirement for one or both of the parents, i.e. a time anticipated to be one of reduced responsibilities. This expected scenario may not be the case when there is an adult with ID in the home, increasing the potential for discord.

Sibling conflict

The presence of a child with ID may have been a joy but may also have caused problems for other children in the family. The needs of the person with ID may have monopolized the family's resources, limiting the attention that could be paid to other family members. Siblings may have resented the expectation that they should spend large amounts of time caring for a sibling with a disability. Parents rarely tolerated the expression of these or other negative feelings thus encouraging guilt and anxiety and creating internal conflict. These feelings and concerns may be revisited as increasing age of the parents requires that decisions be made as to whether a sibling will now assume caregiving responsibilities.

Difficult developmental transitions

Transitions in the lifecycle of the person with ID cause stress for the entire family. These include being surpassed by younger siblings, onset of puberty, sex and dating issues, and emancipation into adulthood. Job loss, career changes, divorce, retirement, birth of other siblings, ageing, relocation, deaths, and similar transitions in the family's lifecycle can also be particularly stressful when a member with ID is present. In addition, if parents found that the people (including psychologists) they turned to for help when their child with ID was born (or experienced other transitions) were unsupportive and they had to work things through alone, they are more likely both to rely on their own resources during later transitions and to revisit earlier stresses.

Unresponsive service delivery systems

Families of persons with ID often experienced service delivery systems as unresponsive, fragmented, and dehumanizing. They were 'referred around' or were told that they 'fall through the cracks', i.e. no services meet the needs of their child. This is a particular concern for psychologists as families may experience their unique roles and services as disconnected from what they 'need' and as likely to lead to denial as to connection with services. From a family's perspective much attention is paid to deficits, and little or no attention is paid to the person's assets. Also, professionals in consultant roles are seen as partializing the person with ID or the family, not spending enough time to understand the entire caregiving situation. This contributes to a frequent report by parents that service systems and the professionals within them made them feel just as labelled and stigmatized as their child (McNett, 1980). Yet, it is widely thought that active participation of families in the planning and delivery of needed services will result in more appropriate services and greater functional achievement by the family member with ID (McCallion and Kolomer, 2003). However, professionals are not always sensitive to the 'barriers' that obstruct family involvement in treatment planning. The findings of Moxley, Raider and Cohen (1989) are no less relevant today. They argued that barriers for families include: (1) resource barriers such as the time, financial means, and other supports to be able to get involved; (2) training and skill barriers such as the knowledge and skills needed to participate effectively in planning discussions; and (3) communication barriers such as the failure of families and professionals to understand each other's subjective experience and expectations of the process. When parents faced these difficulties in obtaining needed information and services, their relationships with professionals became an additional source of stress. That stress will be revisited when, in the older years of the family, they must re-engage with professionals.

Permanency planning

Traditionally, permanency planning has focused on maintaining children with ID in their own homes, reunifying families, facilitating adoptions, and finding permanent foster homes (McCallion and Toseland, 1993). However, the increasing longevity of people with ID has raised the new issue of permanency, futures or long-term planning for persons with ID who outlive parents, and even siblings. Reviews of studies of the self-identified needs of families of persons with ID report that fears about future care were the highest rated need (Bradley, 1991; McCallion and Kolomer, 2003). There is a growing need to help ageing parents plan for the needs of their adult children with disabilities (Bigby, 1996; Smith and Tobin, 1989).

Regardless of their source, psychologists and other professionals will be best prepared to offer assistance with stress if they understand the course and history of the stresses experienced. A review of any records available, interviews with family members and use of standardized measures such as the Caregiving Appraisal Scale (Lawton, Kleban, Moss, Rovine and Glicksman, 1989) are all useful tools in achieving these purposes for psychologists and other professionals.

Coping approaches

Psychologists and other professionals planning to work with caregiving families need an understanding of the coping approaches used by families if they are to build upon strengths and increase the likelihood that their interventions will be successful.

Coping can be defined as the different ways in which people respond to stressful events (Essex, Seltzer and Krauss, 1999). The available research has particularly focused upon coping by mothers. Mothers have been found to use a variety of coping strategies as they provide care for their adult child with ID. Adaptive coping strategies include acceptance, positive reinterpretation and growth, turning to religion, and planning (Hayden and Heller, 1997). Problem-focused coping, i.e. cognitive and behavioural problem-solving efforts, was also found and mothers were significantly more likely than fathers to use problem-focused coping strategies (Essex et al., 1999).

The coping strategies of older caregivers have also been found to differ from younger caregivers. For example, Hayden and Heller (1997) found that older caregivers sought spiritual support more often than younger counter-parts and the younger caregivers experienced a greater sense of personal burden. Seltzer and Krauss (1994) have previously posed the possibility that what we are looking at here is greater adaptation to the caregiving situation by older caregivers. Hayden and Heller (1997) suggest that the differences also reflect greater expectations by younger caregivers of assistance from the formal service system and other family members.

Regardless, no caregiving parent's coping should be assumed to follow stereotypes of gender or age. Reviews of available records, interviews with family members and the use of standardized instruments such as the Ways of Coping Scale (Vitaliano, Russo, Carr, Maiuro and Becker, 1985) will help establish past coping practices. Interventions are more likely to be successful if they are preferred and previously useful coping approaches are employed (McCallion and Toseland, 1995). Some situations, however, will require helping the caregiver to modify coping approaches which are not successful.

ILLNESSES AND CONDITIONS THAT COMPROMISE INDEPENDENT LIVING

The experience of chronic illness among people with ID and the similarities and dissimilarities with experiences of the general population of persons who are ageing has been the subject of a number of investigations.

Physical health

A recently completed systematic study of the health needs of persons with ID aged 40 and over, living in group homes in two catchment areas of New York State, found them to be similar to other adults of the same age in terms of overall health status (outside expected disability-related conditions). For example, psychiatric and behavioural disorders tended to decline in frequency with increasing age while cardiovascular diseases and sensory impairments increased with age (Janicki, Davidson, Henderson, McCallion et al., 2002). However, low rates of exercise and high rates of diet-related conditions were evident. Over half the cohort was classified as obese according to their Body Mass Index (BMI) (Flegal, 1999). However, physicians did not often note obesity as a concern among these individuals. Other researchers have also observed such under-recognition and under-reporting, and these discrepancies raise concerns that health practitioners may be accepting obesity as normal among adults with ID and are not aggressively addressing the health consequences. Similarly, cardiovascular and respiratory diseases and cancers have been reported to be as prevalent as causes of death among these individuals as they are among the general population, and may occur more frequently for people with ID (Evenhuis, 1997; Kapell, Nightingale, Rodriguez, Lee et al., 1998), yet there were few reports of these diseases in the two catchment areas. This may be due to the relatively younger age of this group of adults (their mean age was 54), but given the risk status of this population for these diseases due to high BMIs, and their infrequent exercise, these results were considered surprising and may reflect under-recognition of health conditions (Janicki et al., 2002). Similar concerns about under-recognition of health-related symptoms and conditions are echoed in other studies (see for example, Kapell et al., 1998) and in many countries (see, for example, Beange, McElduff and Baker, 1995). The usefulness of most studies is limited by the selective nature of their samples – usually people in out-of-home placements or individuals who access specialist clinics. An advantage of the Kapell et al. study (1998) is that the National Health Interview Survey includes data from individuals cared for at home as well as in out-of-home care. Many of the reports rely on records reviews and caregiver reports. Studies that included independent assessment (e.g. Criscione, Kastner, O'Brian and Nathanson, 1994), although their samples are small and selective, appear to confirm under-diagnosis of conditions such as thyroid dysfunction, cardiac disorders, epilepsy and medication side-effects.

Findings of less than quality health-care assessment and delivery fuel an ongoing concern within the ID field about the mortality of persons with ID and its relationship to health care provided (for a review, see Hayden, 1998). Some argue that those receiving institutional as opposed to community-based care actually have greater longevity, and that this may be because of greater ability to access specialized and consistent health care (Strauss and Kastner, 1996). Yet, there is a need to ensure that community-based care is pursued as the preferred option for persons ageing with ID (Hayden, 1998). While they are not directly involved in the assessment of and response to physical health concerns, the preservation of independent community living requires that psychologists as members of multidisciplinary teams ensure that these health concerns be addressed as part of comprehensive care plans.

Psychosocial health

Health concerns include psychosocial health. Although limitations have been noted for reported estimates of mental and behavioural disorders, a recent summation of available studies suggests that total rates range from 20 per cent to 40 per cent of assessed older persons with ID. Several studies suggest that psychiatric disorders including dementia increase as persons with ID age (for a review see Tyrrell and Dodd, 2003). Other reviews argue that it is more complex; the occurrence of most mental health concerns appears to decline with age except for dementia, which increases with age (Jacobson, 2003). Regardless, mental health issues are of concern and six factors are posited to place ageing persons with ID at particular risk: their life experiences; behavioural phenotypes (particularly for dementia); side-effects of medications which they may metabolize differently from others; higher rates of sensory impairments which increase communication difficulties; ageing-specific disorders such as Alzheimer's, cardiovascular disease and cancer which may predispose to depression and anxiety; and life events such as bereavements and abuse (Tyrrell and Dodd, 2003). Disorders to be identified and treated include anxiety, depression, dementia, mania and schizophrenia. From a day-to-day care perspective the report (Jacobson, 2003) that as many as 50 per cent of cases include behavioural problems is another reason why attention to psychosocial health is of concern for psychologists and other professionals. For the purposes of this chapter it should be noted that behavioural concerns have been previously reported as a predictor of residential placement and of siblings not choosing to assume care (Heller and Factor, 1991; Krauss, Seltzer, Gordon and Friedman, 1996).

Dementia

The experience of dementia symptoms is the subject of another chapter in this text and has been briefly noted above under 'Psychosocial Health'. However, a consideration of illnesses and conditions that compromise independent living for persons with ID as they age would be incomplete without specifically addressing dementia. Alzheimer's dementia (AD) in persons with Down syndrome (DS) exceeds that of the general population. One study reported a prevalence of 2 per cent in persons aged 30–39 years, 9.4 per cent in persons aged 40–49 years, 36.1 per cent in persons aged 50–59 years and 54.5 per cent in persons aged 60–69 years (Prasher, 1995). These rates are considerably higher than prevalence rates reported for the general population of between 4.3 per cent and 10 per cent in persons aged 65 years and over (see, for example, Hofman, Brayne, Breleler, *et al.*, 1991). Reports of prevalence for other persons with ID are more equivocal, with some finding that rates are similar to the general population (Janicki and Dalton, 2000) and others that it is also higher (Cooper, 1997a). Regardless, recent studies have indicated that people with DS often experience with dementia an early and precipitous decline in cognitive functions and skills (Prasher, Chung and Haque, 1998), pose behavioural and care concerns, such as wandering, sleep disturbance and incontinence, and may present with auditory and visual hallucinations (Cooper and Prasher, 1998; Cosgrave, Tyrrell, McCarron, Gill and Lawlor, 1999; Holland, Hon, Huppert and Stevens, 2000; Tyrrell, Cosgrave, McCarron, McPherson, *et al.*, 2001). In addition, symptoms of depression and other mental health concerns may be mistaken for symptoms of dementia and may also co-occur with dementia, further impairing functioning and compromising behaviour (McCarron and Griffiths, 2003). Also a recent study confirmed earlier reports of increased incidence of other health conditions when dementia symptoms were present. These included hearing, vision and mobility impairments and increased incidence of depression, epilepsy and lung disease (McCarron, Gill, McCallion and Begley, 2005).

There is often lack of awareness on the part of the family caregiver of the significance of cognitive and functional decline. These changes may be ascribed to old age and/or underlying intellectual disability and not investigated. This, together with the anticipated increase in the numbers of people with ID and dementia, poses new and additional challenges for psychologists and other multidisciplinary professionals. A mobile regional dementia clinic model has been proposed to support persons with ID and their caregivers (McCarron and Lawlor, 2003).

ASSESSING AND MANAGING ILLNESS ISSUES

The attention to dementia issues for ageing persons with ID serves to highlight comorbidity concerns for psychologists and other professionals. A multidisciplinary focus is clearly needed to assess and manage health concerns. A useful framework is drawn from work by McCallion and McCarron (in press) on key issues in quality of life for persons with ID (see Table 24.1), in particular the four principles: (1) absence of pain; (2) maintenance of health; (3) psychosocial well-being; and (4) absence of and supportive responses to problem behaviours.

Table 24.1 Quality of life for ageing persons with ID

- Absence of pain
- Maintenance of health
- Psychosocial well-being
- Skills maintenance and support
- Absence of and supportive responses to problem behaviours
- Leisure and community participation
- Family and friends
- Dementia and ageing focused programming
- Supportive environments
- Alleviation of caregiver burden

Note: Adapted from McCallion and McCarron, 2003.

Absence of pain

The diseases of old age tend to be chronic rather than acute, i.e. efforts must be allocated towards the relief of symptoms as well as towards increasingly unlikely cure. Many of those diseases such as arthritis are accompanied by pain, yet persons with ID are often unable or unaware of the need to complain about that pain in order for it to be treated (McCallion and McCarron, in press; McCallion, 2003). Psychologists in their investigations of the causes of behaviour problems and other symptoms should be sensitive to identifying pain issues and, when identified, should encourage appropriate responses. Medications may be appropriate and may be prescribed by the attending physician but multidisciplinary input should be encouraged to identify other strategies including positioning, complementary therapies, and proactive addressing of comfort needs. It is acknowledged that identifying pain in persons with ID, particularly those with multiple and profound disabilities, is complex (Bromley, Emerson and Caine, 1998). The consequences of ageing and comorbid health conditions add to both the complexity and the urgency for assessment tools and pain responses. Given the extensive training psychologists receive in assessment, use of standardized instruments and instrument construction, they are uniquely positioned on the multidisciplinary team to work with physicians and nurses to identify and develop instruments to assess persons with ID for pain. Examples of pain instruments used in the generic population include the Verbal Rating Scale (Melzack, 1995), the Facial Rating Scale (Bieri, Reeve, Champion and Addicott, 1990), the Box Scale (Jensen, Miller and Fisher, 1998) and descriptor scales for pain intensity and unpleasantness (Gracely and Kwilosz, 1988). However, as is often true for people with ID in other areas, available pain assessment tools may not be sensitive or useful and psychologists can contribute to creative efforts to identify and monitor pain experiences.

Maintenance of health

Study findings reported earlier of the under-diagnosis of medical conditions in ageing persons with ID point out the first recommendations and tasks for psychologists. As multidisciplinary team members, psychologists should be aware of recommended ageing and intellectual disability-related routine health screenings and should advocate for their completion. They should also question which preventive and supportive health strategies are part of service delivery and not encourage beliefs that decline is just something to be 'expected'. Modification of diet and exercise patterns have been shown to be effective for improved health for persons with ID similar to the general population but are not yet part of routine programming (Heller, Hsieh and Rimmer, 2002). It will take multidisciplinary advocacy and support for this to be achieved. Next, when referrals are received for assessment of behavioural concerns, psychologists should request documentation that physical causes/ explanations of the concerns have been assessed and ruled out. Finally, in making recommendations for programming and programme modification, psychologists should also bear in mind how health issues and concerns for the individual will be supported.

Psychosocial well-being

Psychosocial well-being is not only about treating psychosocial concerns but also preventing their occurrence (Lawton, 1983). Proactive, appropriate and sensitive programmes and services, early identification of symptoms and their causes, and effectively delivered responses will all contribute to such well-being. A challenge in care of the ageing person with ID is finding appropriate assessment instruments. The range of instruments designed for direct assessment of psychosocial concerns for persons with ID or for use with informants has grown (Tyrrell and Dodd, 2003). They include the Diagnostic Assessment of the Severely Handicapped that measures frequency, duration and severity of psychiatric disorders (Matson, Gardner, Coe and Sovner, 1991); the Psychiatric Assessment Schedule for Adults with a Developmental Disability, a semi-structured interview schedule for use with both people with ID and informers (Moss, Patel, Prosser, Goldberg, et al., 1993); the Psychopathology Inventory for Mentally Retarded Adults assessing seven specific disorders (Matson, 1988) and the Present Psychiatric State for Adults with Intellectual Disability which integrates data from carers and subjects leading to an ICD-10 diagnosis (Cooper, 1997b).

Consideration of dementia symptoms among persons with ID has led to a consensus document (Burt and Alyward, 2000) on instruments to be used to assess those symptoms, out-rule other causes and establish a diagnosis. One instrument is specifically recommended by its author for use by psychologists, the Dementia Scale for Down Syndrome (Geyde, 1995). However, no one scale is seen as sufficient and psychologists should view the assessment process as multi-phase and multidisciplinary.

For all psychosocial concerns including dementia symptoms their identification requires the capture of sometimes subtle changes from previous functioning. As well as the use of appropriate instruments, timely diagnosis and treatment will be aided by routine reassessment and by the completion of documentation in ways that permit comparison with previous reports of functioning. It is being suggested that annual assessments of physical and psychosocial functioning with a recommended battery of instruments be initiated for people with DS over 35 and other people with ID over age 50. It is important that psychologists familiarize themselves with these recommendations (see Burt and Alyward, 2000; McCarron and Lawlor, 2003; Wilkinson and Janicki, 2002) and play a role in their implementation.

Absence of and supportive responses to problem behaviours

The traditional behavioural model used in addressing problem behaviours, the ABC model assumes that there are (A)ntecedents, a series of behaviours and events prior to a behaviour, there is the (B)ehaviour itself, and then there are (C)onsequences, all the things that happen subsequent to the behaviour. Responses to problem behaviours have tended to target the antecedents and the consequences for change opportunities. Indeed there are beliefs that behaviour modification is most effective and better sustained when the consequences are successfully targeted (Reid, 2003). Successful consequence manipulation requires learning and remembering on the part of the person targeted. In ageing for persons with ID and particularly when symptoms of dementia are present, learning and remembering will be impaired and consequence manipulation less likely to be successful. Particularly when dementia is present what is seen as challenging is instead often purposeful and meaningful for the person, and is often an effort to communicate needs and concerns. Professional staff including psychologists have a critical role in helping families to understand the behaviour from the perspective of the person with ID and in the context of her/his experience of dementia and to equip them with strategies to respond to these needs. A more humanistic approach will often result in changes in the environment, programme expectations and the actions and attitudes of caregivers around the person with ID that are more likely to be successful and sustainable (McCallion and McCarron, 2003). This is not simply a manipulation of antecedents; this may also include a redefinition of the behaviour as no longer a problem! For example, rather than seeking ways to stop an individual with dementia from wandering outside the home, the intervention may be to question why wandering is a 'problem', recognizing and addressing instead that the area outside the home must be made safer so the individual may wander more freely because it is something he or she seems to enjoy. The emphasis is on ways of avoiding confrontations and being supportive of the person with ID rather than on changing behaviours.

LIFE CHANGE AND BEREAVEMENT ISSUES

Life/future planning

Addressing long-term, future or permanency planning needs of ageing persons with ID and their families has to begin with an understanding of family caregiving and with the reasons why such planning is difficult. Parents are often averse to creating detailed future care plans for their adult children with ID and many do not involve the person with ID themselves in such planning (Heller and Factor, 1991; McCallion and Tobin, 1995). Stress, concerns for safety, and anxiety all contribute to parents being reluctant to make concrete plans and concern about how the person with ID will feel, and their ability to understand is used to justify not involving the person with ID in any planning that does occur (Bigby, 1996; 1997; Freedman, Krauss and Seltzer, 1997). For example Heller and Factor (1991) found almost 75 per cent of family care providers for persons over 30 years of age with ID did not make future living arrangements for their family member. Often, too, there was a reluctance to speak of future living arrangements with other family members. Therefore the expectations of other family members assuming care responsibilities were often implied rather than formally documented (Bigby, 1996). This is the reality then in which psychologists and other professionals must address future planning.

Responsibility for the care of an ageing person with an ID is rarely shared equally by all family members. It is primarily, but not exclusively a female responsibility, usually the mother, and generally there is one primary caregiver. The identification of a primary caregiver has led many psychologists and other service providers to focus attention solely on this family member. However, there is increasing evidence of the importance of the additional support provided by fathers (McCallion and Kolomer, 2003), siblings (Connidis, 1997), including sons (Archer and MacLean, 1993; Harris, 1998), and by adolescent grandchildren (Beach, 1997). When a mother or father is no longer able or available to provide care, persons with ID generally do not have either spouses or children to assume care, as do many other ageing persons, so the responsibility falls to siblings or to out-of-home placements.

Most literature identifies a positive connection between persons with ID and their siblings. However, there are limited data on sibling relationships in later life. Research to date suggests that support by siblings is expressed in a variety of ways. Most often siblings provide emotional, affective support, for example through telephone calls and visits to an adult with ID (Seltzer,

Begun, Seltzer and Krauss, 1991). Siblings are less likely to provide hands-on or instrumental care. Indeed, parents are reported to be more likely to expect their other children to take on the role of overseer rather than as the hands-on care provider to their sibling (Seltzer, Begun, Magan and Luchterhand, 1993). Psychologists and professionals must therefore be careful not to assume that siblings will simply continue the traditional family care. Where one sibling is unmarried and childless there is a greater likelihood of instrumental support to the adult with ID as the siblings age (Bigby 1997). In addition, siblings who identify themselves as the future care providers of their adult brother or sister are reported to be more likely to be older than the person with ID, and more likely to be sisters rather than brothers. Persons with ID with fewer behaviour problems have been found to be more likely to live with a sibling (Krauss *et al.*, 1996; Seltzer *et al.*, 1991). Again, without stereotyping families and siblings, this is important information for psychologists and other professionals to consider when helping families of older persons with ID to plan for the future.

However, traditional transitions in caregiving responsibility are being affected by other important trends: the dramatic increase in single-parent families and lowered birth rates, reducing the size of caregiving networks; greater participation by women in the workforce increasing the potential for conflict between work and caregiving responsibilities (Doty, Jackson and Crown, 1998); and delayed childbearing by siblings and increased age of parents increasing the likelihood of multiple coincident caregiving demands on siblings. Traditional divisions of caregiving roles by gender are being eroded, caregiving demands are being placed on all available family members, and family caregivers are increasingly likely to be stressed by their multiple responsibilities (Kaye and Applegate, 1990; Sanborn and Bould, 1991; Toseland, Smith and McCallion, 1995).

For psychologists called upon to assist in the planning for future care of the adult with ID, out-of-home care may seem the easier and more preferable approach, but that assumes that 'a bed' is available and that this transition is the desire of the person with ID and the family. Instead, planning really needs to begin with an assessment of the desires of the individual and the family (family may need to be 'helped', not told to include the person with ID), an understanding of the available social network and past patterns of care, and consideration of possible improvements in informal support and then the addition of formal services. Even if the chosen future plan is out-of-home placement, in the short term attention will still need to be paid to the other steps.

Grief and bereavement

There is both a long-standing belief that persons with ID do not experience the range of emotions of others, including feelings of grief at the loss of family members and close friends/neighbours, and conversely concerns that they will not be able to 'handle' the associated feelings (Yanok and Beifus, 1993). These beliefs and concerns are often used by family members to justify not informing persons with ID of the death of parents and for not involving them in funerals and other death and mourning rituals. It is not just a 'family' problem. Todd (2002) points out that staff too have difficulties with the issue of death and family desires become a convenient explanation for a lack of advocacy for death experiences and education for persons with ID. Yet people with ID as they age are likely to experience losses through death; the implications of the losses may be greater for the individuals with ID as the loss may also mean they will have to move to a sibling's home or to an out-of-home placement (McHale and Carey, 2002) and, not having experienced death and mourning, they will poorly understand death and not be prepared for their own deaths (Clegg and Lansdall-Welfare, 2003).

While death and bereavement are a poorly researched area (Todd, 2002), there is evidence that people with ID do indeed understand the finality of death and have often formed bonds with family members and others such that they feel personal loss and grief. What they do not often have experience in is how to express that grief (Yanok and Beifus, 1993). Being shielded from funerals, even the announcement of death means they do not know how to grieve or have the opportunity of doing so.

Yet that grief does surface. Symptoms of normal grief as defined by ICD-10 occur within one month of the bereavement and do not exceed six months' duration. For persons with ID, later onset and longer duration of grief symptoms are more likely. Also, as well as through increased levels of depression, anxiety and distress, grief reactions in persons with ID are often manifested in behavioural difficulties. These are more likely to be viewed by family members and professionals assisting them as psychosocial concerns than as the expression of grief (Hollins and Esterhuyzen, 1997; McHale and Carey, 2002).

ASSESSING AND MANAGING LIFE CHANGES AND BEREAVEMENT

Assessing and managing life changes

Permanency, long-term or futures planning in the ID services field is related to the management of life transitions in later stages of life, for both the family member with ID and the parents, and refers to establishing future life arrangements for the person with ID, generally outside the parent–child household, in the areas of residential living, legal protection and financial well-being (Smith and Tobin, 1989). Examples of residential living permanency planning would be consideration of independent living, of shared households with siblings, other relatives or family friends, and of transitions into supervised apartment, adult foster care, and group home programmes. Legal protection issues include consideration of legal guardianship, trusteeship, and conservatorship of person and property issues, including the drafting of wills and other documents. Financial issues include the development of financial arrangements that will ensure continued financial eligibility for needed services for the person with ID, while providing for a safety net of resources if those services are not available or are insufficient (McCallion, 1993). The development of the future plan will require effort and collaboration by many disciplines including psychology, not least because each must ensure that their recommendations for care are cognizant of the need for a plan, merge in a joint rather than discipline specific approach and engage and support families and the person with ID in a process they will find difficult.

In a qualitative study of sixty-two adults with ID, Bigby (1996) identified four types of planning by parents. The first two are explicit and implicit key person succession plans which transfer the responsibility of overseeing care of the adult with ID to an appointed person. Key person succession plans ranged from formal documented plans (explicit) to open-ended and vague plans (implicit). Family members who had been designated as the implicit key person were usually aware of their designation, and were unsure of the exact expectations that accompanied the role. Psychologists and other professionals must encourage plans that are explicit and where key people are aware of their roles. The next type of plan is a financial plan. These are decisions about income and monies for the future care of an adult with ID. Often well-intentioned plans have been found to have unintended consequences as families do not understand the implications of their financial arrangements for future eligibility for services or in creating opportunities for the financial exploitation of the person by others. Again, even if not qualified to provide this advice themselves, psychologists can play key roles in ensuring that such information is provided. The final type is residential plans. These plans concern where the person with ID will reside following the parent's death or inability to continue to provide care. Again these may be marked by unrealistic expectations of what other family members or the service system can provide and under what timeframes, or they may be informed by outdated information. Bigby (1996) found residential care plans were least likely to be the plans families had discussed or put into place. Indeed, Bigby found that parents who designated a key person for succession of care often then felt relieved of the responsibility to make emotionally charged decisions, such as future residential planning.

The planning role for psychologists and other professionals, once they have engaged families in future planning, is to ensure that adequate and up-to-date information is available and that this final step of planning for residential transitions is not missed. In the absence of such residential planning, illness or death of a caregiver requires a crisis response (McCallion and

Tobin, 1995). This often precludes choosing the best living options for the person with ID and exacerbates the sense of loss the individual will feel (McCallion and Kolomer, 2003). Families who successfully utilize respite and other services have been found to be more likely to consider residential placement (Caldwell and Heller, 2003); therefore, a role for psychologists and other professionals may be to encourage and facilitate such related service use. Effective advocacy requires that psychologists be aware of and able to refer families to those services. Key services to be familiar with include: in-home respite, out-of-home respite or holiday programmes, home help services, transportation assistance, and day and recreation/leisure programmes.

There are several manualized approaches to future planning available which psychologists may want to access for more information and as a basis for developing formal programmes. The Family Futures Planning Project offered a ten-session curriculum addressing housing options, estate planning, home- and community-based services and caregivers' emotional, physical and recreational health. A facilitator is equipped to assist families with developing a plan and building a support network. A unique feature of this approach is that the focus is on the family's not just the individual's needs.

The Planned Lifetime Advocacy Network (PLAN) is a family operated non-profit organization that charges a membership fee. A six-step approach guides the development of a personal future plan: clarifying the vision; building relationships; controlling the home environment; preparing for decision-making; developing wills and estate plans; and deciding steps to secure the plan. PLAN provides many levels of support and services including workshops, technical assistance, mentor families, and paid facilitators.

The Family-to-Family Project was a response to the waiting lists for residential services in one US state. Eight Family-to-Family Support Centres were developed. The centres offered presentations on financial arrangements and wills, home ownership and consumer-controlled housing, and circles of support. A resource manual is available with information concerning funding sources, housing options, and legal issues (translated into several different languages) and suggestions on outreach to hard-to-reach families.

The RRTC Family Future Planning Project uses paid facilitators and mentor families to provide information on available supports to both the family caregivers and the person with ID so that they can make informed choices. Families are encouraged to think about their dreams for the future of their relative with ID and to get involved in advocacy activities that can lead to systems change, develop long-term financial plans for their relative with ID and facilitate more involvement by the people with ID in self-advocacy groups.

Although the programmes described here are tailored to the jurisdictions in which they were offered, they also contain many more universal ideas and approaches. Information on all these programmes including references and contact information are summarized in Heller (2000). A particular challenge for psychologists and other professionals is to locate and develop materials and approaches that explain the complex issues involved in future planning in ways that support and facilitate genuine participation by people with ID in planning which will ultimately affect their lives.

Assessing and managing grief and bereavement

Some authors argue that families have been in a perpetual state of bereavement since the birth of an individual with ID (Todd, 2002). There is research, however, that suggests that as the person with ID ages, many families gain strength and are well adjusted (Seltzer *et al.*, 1997). It may be, however, that family members revisit past senses of loss at major life transitions such as the death of the primary caregivers (McCallion and Toseland, 1993). Regardless, in work with families psychologists and other professionals must recognize the sensitivities and grief of family members when they resist informing the persons with ID. In many ways too, the loss of the primary caregiver or another significant family member is a late point to be addressing issues of death and bereavement. Yanok and Beifus (1993) argue that understanding death and appropriate expression of grief by people with ID requires prior education to encompass visits to funeral homes, cemeteries and churches, an understanding of community standards and acceptance for the expression of grief in public places, knowledge that death is inevitable and irreversible, and pertinent vocabulary words. Fauri and Grimes (1994) argue for, where possible, preparing for rather than reacting to death. Finally, families and professionals must develop an openness to dealing with grief and bereavement issues after a time when they and society have decided grief should be over.

At the very least in their data gathering around problem behaviour referrals psychologists should be sensitive to recent losses the individual with ID may have experienced and their implications for the reported behaviours. They should also be available to explain to families the contribution of unresolved grief to later behaviour problems in persons with ID and to support informing the person with ID of losses. Also, as part of multidisciplinary teams, psychologists may advocate for and provide grief and bereavement education and supports. There are a number of reported formal programmes that offer suggested approaches and resource materials (see, for example, Blackman, 2002; Botsford, 2000; Cathcart, 1995; James, 1995). Also, the Scottish Down Syndrome Society has booklets on explaining death and on dementia for persons with ID (downloads at http://www.dsscotland.org.uk/publications.htm).

ROLE FOR PSYCHOLOGISTS IN TRAINING

As has already been said, effective delivery of services to ageing persons with ID and their family caregivers requires a comprehensive reorientation of services and a multidisciplinary approach. Psychologists must be willing to be the recipients of training in these approaches as well as to play a role in their delivery. More specifically looking at issues of long-term planning, differential diagnosis, treatment of dementia and other ageing-related health concerns and responses to bereavement, psychologists and other professionals must play education roles in:

1   Helping all staff understand the general ageing processes of persons with ID and their family caregivers and how to assess the unique experiences of families who present for assistance;
2   Implementing systematic and sensitive approaches to helping families engage in long-term planning;
3   Developing and delivering training and developing mechanisms to support self-advocacy and decision-making for persons with ID;
4   Designing and implementing documentation, screening and routine assessment processes designed to monitor change in persons with ID and offer critical information to inform differential diagnosis;
5   Developing and teaching holistic approaches to presenting problem behaviours that help understanding of causes of those behaviours, how behaviours may be avoided, and the delivery of appropriate, effective responses;
6   Supporting the expression of grief and bereavement by persons with ID;
7   Demonstrating where psychologists' unique skills and experiences fit within multidisciplinary service delivery.

Delivery of such training will involve daily modelling of these values and skills as much as formal teaching and in-service.

SUMMARY

This chapter has sought to outline critical issues involved in working with ageing people with ID and their families, with particular emphasis upon those most likely to affect and involve psychologists working in the ID field. The size of the ageing population of persons with ID is only expected to grow further and, as the age distribution of the population of people with ID changes, many psychologists who thought they would be working with children or with young adults will increasingly find themselves working with elderly people. For many psychologists (and other professionals) this will be a cultural shift and may require renewal of training to be effective. Family caregivers will also likely be older and family care may involve multiple supporters more than the traditional primary caregiver approach, challenging preset notions about caregiving support. Dementia will be of increased concern as will other chronic illness, losses and life transitions will be common and there is the potential for new issues not discussed here for professionals to address. Increased old age, just like the other stages of life, should also be about the enjoyment of community living. An emphasis on deficits for people with ID will be no less inadequate when people age than in earlier years. For needs to be addressed and goals and dreams to be achieved, all professional groups including psychologists have been challenged to reorient and re-evaluate their priorities in service delivery and recognize the multidisciplinary nature of interventions now required. Therefore, a multidisciplinary perspective has informed all recommendations offered here, specific suggestions on assessment instruments and model programmes have been offered where appropriate and, as will be true for all professional groups, psychologists have been challenged to look at new roles particularly with families and to accept advocacy as well as service delivery responsibilities.

EXERCISE

Work in groups of four. Read the case study of Robert in Box 24.1. As a team discuss the following questions, and share your team's view with the class.

What are the most pressing problems to be addressed?

What immediate steps would the psychologist recommend to address the crisis in care concerns?

Robert doesn't want to move into care and it is not what his mother would have wanted for him. What supports might be offered to maintain Robert with his sister?

What types of data from earlier records and family interviews and what types of assessment would be recommended to understand Robert's physical and psychosocial health concerns?

What end-of-life issues and bereavement issues have occurred in Robert's life and how have they been handled?

What additional issues should the multidisciplinary team address?

What roles could and should psychologists play in all of the above activities?

Box 24.1 Case study of Robert

Robert is a 74-year-old individual with moderate intellectual disability who lived at home with his parents and then his widowed mother most of his life. Upon the death of his mother three years ago Robert moved in with his sister. Robert was very independent while living with his parents, holding a job at the local supermarket, taking the bus to work and frequenting local shops. Robert retired from his job at 65. As his mother became more infirm herself, Robert assumed more and more responsibility for laundry, cleaning, and dishwashing and even cooking simple dishes for the two of them while his mother supervised and supported his completion of these activities, managed the household and ensured that Robert received the programmes and financial supports to which he was entitled. Neighbours and other family talked about how well they supported each other, but the ageing of both reportedly was taxing their ability to manage.

When his mother suffered a stroke, Robert wanted to care for her post-hospitalization but it was determined that she needed nursing home care and she died there some months later. Robert's sister was very concerned about Robert and how he would handle the death and chose not to tell him until after the funeral. She herself was very distraught, was unable to visit her mother's grave for some time and felt it was in Robert's interest to be saved from this experience. Robert had continued living in the family home with support from his sister and her husband while his mother was in the hospital and in the nursing home, but this had strained their abilities to support him. His mother deceased, his sister decided that maintaining him in the home was beyond her ability and she had Robert move in with her. She felt it was going to be hard for Robert to cope with all these changes and told him at first that staying with her was a 'holiday'. Meantime she arranged for the family home to be sold and, as specified in her mother's will, set the money up in a trust fund for Robert. Only when all of this was arranged did she tell Robert.

The move to his sister's home has not been very successful but for three years she has tried to make it work. There have been several incidents of Robert leaving his sister's house late at night and trying to return to his home. In one recent incident Robert was struck by a car as he crossed a busy road but fortunately he was not seriously injured. Robert has become increasingly uncooperative, less interested in things he previously enjoyed, his sleep has been disturbed and for the first time he has experienced seizures. He is also less willing to do things like dressing himself and helping around the house (that he had done previously). His sister has described these behaviours as almost as though he can no longer do some of these things or remember the steps involved but she also feels at times that the behaviour is purposeful and punishing. Robert's sister is increasingly concerned about leaving Robert alone in the home (both she and her husband work) and about the amount of time caring for him is requiring and although she had promised her mother to care for Robert she felt that the time had come for out-of-home placement.

Robert's sister has approached the intellectual disabilities services system about the situation and is concerned not to upset him. She wants all paperwork completed without Robert being involved in the planning. Staff at the service agency have stated they are concerned about how strained the sister appears. This is a crisis situation that requires intervention before a future plan can be created and implemented. A referral has been made to the psychology department for assessment and preliminary intervention prior to the development of a plan for care.

FURTHER READING FOR FAMILIES AND CARERS

Cathcart, F. (1994). *Understanding Death and Dying. Book 1: Your Feelings* (illustrated), *Book 2: A Guide for Families and Friends, Book 3: A Guide for Carers and Others*. Kidderminster, UK: BILD.

Debrine, E., Caldwell, J., Factor, A. and Heller, T. (2003). *The Future is Now: A Future Planning Training Curriculum for Families and their Adult Relatives with Developmental Disabilities*. Chicago, IL: RRTC-UIC.

Down Syndrome Scotland Booklets. *Let's Talk about Getting Older. Let's Talk about Death. What is Dementia*. Down Syndrome Scotland, 158/160 Balgreen Road, Edinburgh, Scotland EH11 3AU.

Kerr, D. and Wilson, W. (2001). *Learning Disability and Dementia*. Stirling: University of Stirling Dementia Services Development Centre. (A workbook for frontline staff.)

McCallion, P. and Janicki, M.P. (2002). *Intellectual disabilities and Dementia: A Two CD-Rom Self-Instructional Training Package*. Albany, NY: NYS Developmental Disabilities Planning Council.

McCarron, M. (2003). *Alzheimer's Dementia in Persons with Intellectual Disability: Common Questions and Concerns*. Dublin, Ireland: The National Association for the Mentally Handicapped in Ireland (NAMHI).

Sterns, H.L., Kennedy, E.A. and Sed, C.M. (2000). *Person-Centred Planning for Later Life: Death and Dying – A Curriculum for Adults with Mental Retardation*. Chicago, IL: RRTC-UIC.

Todd, K., Turk, V. and Christmas, M. (2002). *Resource Pack for Carers of Adults with Down Syndrome and Dementia*. BILD. http://www.bild.org.uk/

FURTHER READING FOR CLINICIANS ON ID AND AGEING

Bigby, C. (2000). *Moving on Without Parents: Planning, Transitions and Sources of Support for Middle-Aged and Older Adults with Intellectual Disability*. Maryland, MD: Brookes.

Blackman, N. (2002). Grief and intellectual disability: A systemic approach. *Journal of Gerontological Social Work*, 38(1/2), 253–63.

Bouras, N. (2000). *Psychiatric and Behavioural Disorders in Mental Retardation*. Cambridge: Cambridge University Press.

Burt, D.B., and Aylward, E.H. *et al.* (2000). Test battery for the diagnosis of dementia in individuals with intellectual disability. *Journal of Intellectual Disability Research*, 44, 175–80.

Cathcart, C. (1995). Death and people with learning disabilities: Interventions to support clients and carers. *British Journal of Clinical Psychology*, 34(2), 165–75.

Cooper, S. (1997). Epidemiology of psychiatric disorders in elderly compared with younger adults with learning disabilities. *British Journal of Psychiatry*, 170: 375–80.

Davidson, P.W. Prasher, V.P. and Janicki, M.P. (eds) (2003). *Mental Health, Intellectual Disabilities, and the Aging Process*. London: Blackwell Press.

Herr, S.S. and Weber, G. (eds) (1999). *Aging, Rights and Quality of Life*. Baltimore: Paul Brookes Publishing.

Hogg, J., Lucchino, R., Wang, K. and Janicki, M. P. (2001). Healthy ageing-adults with intellectual disabilities: Ageing and social policy. *Journal of Applied Research in Intellectual Disabilities*, 14(3), 229–25.

Holland, A., Hon, J., Huppert, F. and Stevens, F. (2000). Incidence and course of dementia in people with Down's Syndrome: Findings from a population based study. *Journal of Intellectual Disability Research*, 44, 138–46.

Hollins, S. and Sireling, L. (1999). *Understanding Grief: Working with Grief and People Who Have Learning Disabilities*. London: Pavilion.

Hubert, J. and Hollins, S. (2000). Working with elderly carers of people with learning disabilities and planning for the future. *Advances in Psychiatric Treatment*, 6, 41–8.

Janicki, M. and Ansello, E. (eds) (2000). *Community Supports for Aging Adults with Lifelong Disabilities*. Baltimore: Paul Brookes Publishing.

Janicki, M. and Dalton, A. (1999). *Dementia, Aging, and Intellectual Disabilities: A Handbook*. Philadelphia, PA: Brunner-Mazel.

Janicki, M., Heller, T., Seltzer, G. *et al.* (1996). Practice guidelines for the clinical assessment and care management of Alzheimer's disease and other dementias among adults with intellectual disabilities. *Journal of Intellectual Disability Research*, 40(4), 374–82.

Janicki, M.P. and Dalton, A.J. (eds) (1999). *Dementia, Aging, and Intellectual Disabilities: A Handbook*. Philadelphia: Brunner-Mazel.

McCallion, P. and Janicki, M.P. (2002). *Intellectual Disabilities and Dementia. A Two CD-Rom Self-Instructional Training Package*. Albany, NY: NYS Developmental Disabilities Planning Council.

McCallion, P. and Kolomer, S.R. (2003). Aging persons with developmental disabilities and their aging caregivers. In B. Berkman and L. Harootyan (eds), *Social Work and Health Care in an Aging World* (pp. 201–25). New York: Springer.

McCarron, M. and Lawlor, B.A. (2003). Responding to the challenges of ageing and dementia in intellectual disability in Ireland. *Ageing and Mental Health*, 7(6), 413–17.

Prasher, V.P. and Janicki, M.P. (2002). *Physical Health of Adults with Intellectual Disabilities*. London: Blackwell Press.

Roberto, K.A. (ed.) (1993). *The Elderly Caregiver*. Newbury Park, CA: Sage.

Thorpe, L., Davidson, P.W. and Janicki, M.P. (2000). Healthy aging: Adults with intellectual disabilities: Biobehavioural issues. *Journal of Applied Research in Intellectual Disabilities*, 14(3), 218–28.

Walsh, P.N. and Heller, T. (2002). *Health of Women with Intellectual Disabilities*. London: Blackwell Press.

WEBSITES

Alzheimer's and Down Syndrome Research Group, Trinity College Dublin. http://www.tcd.ie/Psychiatry/Neuropsychiatry/downsyndrome1.htm

British Institute on Learning Disabilities. http://www.bild.org.uk/index.htm

Down Syndrome Scotland. http://www.dsscotland.org.uk/publications.htm

Website devoted to dementia and disability. http://www.alz.org/ResourceCentre/Resources/rtrldowns.htm

Website on End of Life Care Issues maintained by the University at Albany. http://www.albany.edu/aging/endoflife.html

Website on Intellectual Disabilities and Aging maintained by University of Illinois at Chicago. http://www.uic.edu/orgs/rrtcamr/

Website on Intellectual Disabilities, Aging and Dementia maintained by the University at Albany. http://www.albany.edu/ssw/aging

REFERENCES

Archer, C. and MacLean, M. (1993). Husbands and sons as caregivers of chronically ill women. *Journal of Gerontological Social Work*, 21(1/2), 5–23.

Baltes, P.B. and Baltes, M.M. (1990). Pyschological perspectives on successful aging. In P.B. Baltes and M.M. Baltes (eds). *Successful Aging: Perspectives from the Behavioural Sciences* (pp. 1–34). Cambridge: Cambridge University Press.

Barron, S. and Mulvany, F. (2005). *National Intellectual Disability Database. Annual Report 2005*. Dublin: Health Research Board.

Beach, D. (1997). Family caregiving: The positive impact on adolescent relationships. *The Gerontologist*, 37, 233–8.

Beange, H., McElduff, A. and Baker, W. (1995). Medical disorders of adults with mental retardation: A population study. *Journal on Mental Retardation*, 99, 595–604.

Bieri, D., Reeve, R.A., Champion, C.D. and Addicott, L. (1990). The FACES Pain Scale for the self-assessment of the severity of pain experienced by children. *Pain*, 41(2), 139–50.

Bigby, C. (1996). Transferring responsibility: The nature and effectiveness of parental planning for the future of adults with intellectual disability who remain at home until mid-life. *Australian Society for the Study of Intellectual Disability*, 21(4), 295–312.

Bigby, C. (1997). Parental substitutes? The role of siblings in the lives of older people with intellectual disability. *Journal of Gerontological Social Work*, 29(1), 3–21.

Blackman, N. (2002). Grief and intellectual disability: A systemic approach. *Journal of Gerontological Social Work*, 38(1/2), 253–63.

Botsford, A. (2000). Integrating end of life care into services for people with an intellectual disability. *Social Work in Health Care*, 31(1), 35–48.

Braddock, D. (1999). Aging and developmental disabilities: Demographic and policy issues affecting American families. *Mental Retardation*, 37, 155–61.

Braddock, D., Emerson, E., Felce, D. and Stanliffe, R.J. (2001). Living with circumstances of children and adults with mental retardation and developmental disabilities in the United States, Canada, England and Wales. *Mental Retardation and Developmental Disabilities Research Reviews*, 7(2), 115–21.

Bradley, V. (1991). AAMR testifies on family support. *AAMR News and Notes*, 4(4), 1,5.

Bromley, J., Emerson, E. and Caine, A. (1998). The development of a self report measure to assess the location and intensity of pain in people with learning disabilities. *Journal of Intellectual Disability Research*, 42, 72–80.

Burt, D.B. and Aylward, E.H. *et al.* (2000). Test battery for the diagnosis of dementia in persons with intellectual disability. *Journal of Intellectual Disability Research*, 44, 175–80.

Caldwell, J. and Heller, T. (2003). Management of respite and personal assistance services in a consumer-directed family support programme. *Journal of Intellectual Disability Research*, 47(4–5), 352–67.

Cathcart, C. (1995). Death and people with learning disabilities: Interventions to support clients and carers. *British Journal of Clinical Psychology*, 34(2), 165–75.

Clegg, J. and Lansdall-Welfare, R. (2003). Death, disability and dogma. *Philosophy, Psychiatry and Psychology*, 10(1), 67–79.

Connidis, I. (1997). Sibling support in older age. *Journals of Gerontology*, 49(6), S309–317.

Cooper, S.A. (1997a). Epidemiology of psychiatric disorders in elderly compared to younger adults with learning disabilities. *British Journal of Psychiatry*, 170, 375–80.

Cooper, S.A. (1997b). Psychiatry of elderly compared to younger adults with intellectual disability. *Journal of Applied Research in Intellectual Disability*, 10, 303–11.

Cooper, S.A. (1999). The relationship between psychiatric and physical health in elderly people with intellectual disability. *Journal of Intellectual Disability Research*, 43, 54–60.

Cooper, S.A. and Prasher, V.P. (1998). Maladaptive behaviours and symptoms of dementia in adults with Down's syndrome compared to adults with intellectual disability from other aetiologies. *Journal of Intellectual Disability Research*, 42(4), 293–300.

Cosgrave, M.P., Tyrrell, J., McCarron, M., Gill, M. and Lawlor, B.A. (1999). Age at onset of dementia and age of menopause in women. *Journal of Intellectual Disability Research*, 43(6) 461–5.

Criscione, T., Kastner, T.A., O'Brian, D. and Nathanson, R. (1994). Replication of a managed health care initiative for people with mental retardation living in the community. *Mental Retardation*, 32, 53–9.

Doty, P., Jackson, M. and Crown, W. (1998). The impact of female caregivers' employment status on patterns of formal and informal elder care. *The Gerontologist*, 38(3), 331–5.

Essex, E.L., Seltzer, M.M. and Krauss, M.W. (1999). Differences in coping effectiveness and well-being among aging mothers and fathers of adults with mental retardation. *American Journal on Mental Retardation*, 104(6), 545–63.

Evenhuis, H.M. (1997). Medical aspects of ageing in a population with intellectual disabilities: III. Mobility, internal conditions and cancer. *Journal of Intellectual Disability Research*, 41, 8–18.

Fauri, D.P. and Grimes, D.R. (1994). Bereavement services for families and peers of deceased residents of psychiatric institutions. *Social Work*, 39(2), 185–90.

Flegal, K. (1999). The obesity epidemic in children and adults: current evidence and research issues. *Medicine and Science in Sports and Exercise, Supplement*, S509–S514.

Freedman, R.I., Krauss, M.W. and Seltzer, M.M. (1997). Aging parents, residential plans for adult children with mental retardation. *Mental Retardation*, 35(2), 114–23.

Fujiura, G.T. (1998). Demography of family households. *American Journal of Mental Retardation*, 103, 225–35.

Geyde, A. (1995). *Dementia Scale for Down Syndrome Manual*. Vancouver: Geyde Research and Consulting.

Gracely, R.H. and Kwilosz, D.M. (1988). The Descriptor Differential Scale: Applying psychophysical principles to clinical pain assessment. *Pain*, 35, 279–88.

Greenberg, J.S., Seltzer, M.M., Krauss, M.W. and Kim, H. (1997). The differential effects of social support on the psychological well-being of aging mothers of adults with mental illness or mental retardation. *Family Relations*, 46, 383–94.

Harris, P.B. (1998). Listening to caregiving sons: Misunderstood realities. *The Gerontologist*, 38(3), 342–52.

Hayden, M.F. (1998). Mortality among people with mental retardation living in the United States: Research review and policy application. *Mental Retardation*, 36, 345–59.

Hayden, M.F. and Heller, T. (1997). Support, problem-solving/coping ability, and personal burden of younger and older caregivers of adults with mental retardation. *Mental Retardation*, 35(5), 364–72.

Heller, T. (2000). Assisting older family caregivers of adults with intellectual disabilities. Paper presented at the 12th IASSID Aging and Intellectual Disabilities Roundtable, Japan.

Heller, T. and Factor, A. (1991). Permanency planning for adults with mental retardation living with family caregivers. *American Journal on Mental Retardation*, 96, 163–76.

Heller, T., Hsieh, K. and Rimmer, J. (2002). Barriers and supports for exercise participation among adults with Down syndrome. *Journal of Gerontological Social Work*,
38(1/2), 161–78.

Hofman, A., Brayne, C., Breleler, M.M. *et al.* (1991). The prevalence of dementia
in Europe: A collaborative study of 1890–1990 findings, *International Journal of
Epidemiology*, 20, 736–48.

Hogg, J., Lucchino, R., Wang, K. and Janicki, M. P. (2001). Healthy ageing-adults
with intellectual disabilities: Ageing and social policy. *Journal of Applied Research
in Intellectual Disabilities*, 14(3), 229–25.

Holland, A.J. (2000). Ageing and learning disability. *British Journal of Psychiatry*,
176, 26–31.

Holland, A. J., Hon, J., Huppert, F.A. and Stevens, F. (2000). Incidence and course of
dementia in people with Down's syndrome: Findings from a population-based
study. *Journal of Intellectual Disability Research*, 44(2), 138–46.

Hollins, S. and Esterhuyzen, A. (1997). Bereavement and grief in adults with learning
disabilities. *British Journal of Psychiatry*, 170, 497–501.

Jacobson, J. (2003). Prevalence of mental and behavioural disorders. In P.W. Davidson,
V.P. Prasher and M.P. Janicki (eds), *Mental Health, Intellectual Disabilities and the
Aging Process* (pp. 9–21). Oxford: Blackwell Publishing.

James, I.A. (1995). Helping people with learning disability to cope with bereavement.
Mental Handicap, 23, 74–8.

Janicki, M.P. and Dalton, A.J. (2000). Prevalence of dementia and impact on
intellectual disability services. *Mental Retardation*, 38, 277–89.

Janicki, M.P., Dalton, A.J., Henderson, C.M. and Davidson, P.W. (1999). Mortality
and morbidity among older adults with intellectual disability: Health services
considerations. *Disability and Rehabilitation*, 21(5/6), 284–94.

Janicki, M.P., Davidson, P.W., Henderson, C.M., McCallion, P., Taets, J.D., Force,
L.T., Sulkes, S.B., Frangenberg, E. and Ladrigan, P.M. (2002). Health characteristics and health services utilization in older adults with intellectual disability
living in community residences. *Journal of Intellectual Disability Research*, 46(4),
287–98.

Jensen, M.P., Miller, L. and Fisher, L.D. (1998) Assessment of pain during medical
procedures: A comparison of three scales. *Pain*, 14(4): 343–9.

Kahn, R.L. (2002). Guest editorial on 'Successful aging and well-being'. *The
Gerontologist*, 42, 725–6.

Kapell, D., Nightingale, B., Rodriguez, A., Lee, H.J., Zigman, B.W. and Schupf, N.
(1998). Prevalence of chronic medical problems with adults with mental retardation:
Comparison with the general population. *Mental Retardation*, 36, 269–79.

Kaye, L.W. and Applegate, J.S. (1990). Men as elder caregivers: A response to
changing families. *American Journal of Orthopsychiatry*, 60, 86–95.

Koren, P.E., DeChillo, N. and Freisen, B.J. (1992). Measuring empowerment
in families whose children have emotional disabilities: A brief questionnaire.
Rehabilitation Psychology, 37(4), 305–21.

Krauss, M.W., Seltzer, M.M., Gordon, R. and Friedman, D.H. (1996). Binding ties:
The roles of adult siblings of persons with mental retardation. *Mental Retardation*,
34, 83–93.

Lawton, M.P. (1983). The dimensions of well-being. *Experimental Aging Research*,
9(2), 65–72.

Lawton, M.P., Kleban, M.H., Moss, M., Rovine, M. and Glicksman, A. (1989). Measuring caregiving appraisal. *Journal of Gerontology*, 44, 61–71.

Ludlow, B.L. (1999). Life after loss: Legal, ethical and practical issues. In S.S. Herr and G. Weber (eds), *Aging, Rights and Quality of Life* (pp.189–222). Baltimore: Brookes.

Matson, J. (1988). *The PIMRA Manual*. Orland Park, Il: International Diagnostics Systems.

Matson, J., Gardner, W., Coe, D. and Sovner, R. (1991). A scale for evaluating emotional disorders in severely and profoundly mentally retarded persons: Development of the DASH. *British Journal of Psychiatry*, 159, 404–9.

McCallion, P. (1993). *Social worker orientations to permanency planning with older parents caring at home for family members with developmental disabilities*. Unpublished dissertation, University at Albany.

McCallion, P. (2003). *Promoting Positive Behaviours*. Albany, NY: NYS Dept of Health. A CD-Rom training package.

McCallion, P. and Kolomer, S.R. (2003). Aging persons with developmental disabilities and their aging caregivers. In B. Berkman and L. Harootyan (eds), *Social Work and Health Care in an Aging World* (pp. 201–25). New York: Springer.

McCallion, P. and McCarron, M. (2003). Behavioural programming. In P. McCallion, *Promoting Positive Behaviours*. Albany, NY: NYS Dept of Health. A CD-Rom training package.

McCallion, P. and McCarron, M. (in press). A perspective on quality of life in dementia care. *Mental Retardation*.

McCallion, P. and Tobin, S. (1995). Social worker orientations to permanency planning by older parents caring at home for sons and daughters with developmental disabilities. *Mental Retardation*, 33(3), 153–62.

McCallion, P. and Toseland, R.W. (1993). An empowered model for social work services to families of adolescents and adults with developmental disabilities. *Families in Society*, 74, 579–89.

McCallion, P. and Toseland, R.W. (1995). Supportive group interventions with caregivers of frail older adults. *Social Work with Groups*, 18(1), 11–25.

McCallion, P., Janicki, M.P., Grant-Griffin, L. and Kolomer, S.R. (2000). Grandparent caregivers II: Service needs and service provision issues. *Journal of Gerontological Social Work*, 33(3), 63–90.

McCarron M. and Griffiths, C. (2003). Nurses Roles in Supporting Aging Persons with Intellectual Disability and Mental Health Problems: Challenges and Opportunities for Care. In P. Davidson, V. Prasher, and M.P. Janicki (eds), *Mental Health, Intellectual Disabilities and the Aging Process* (pp. 223–37). London: Blackwell.

McCarron M. and Lawlor B.A. (2003). Responding to the challenges of ageing and dementia in intellectual disability in Ireland. *Ageing and Mental Health*, 7(6), 413–17.

McCarron, M., Gill, M., McCallion, P. and Begley, C. (2005). Health co-morbidities in ageing persons with Down syndrome and Alzheimer's dementia. *JIDR*, 49(7), 560–6.

McHale, R. and Carey, S. (2002). An investigation of the effects of bereavement on mental health and challenging behaviour in adults with learning disability. *British Journal of Learning Disabilities*, 30, 113–17.

McNett, J. (1980). Part II: Mental health services for the handicapped fall between agencies. *APA Monitor*, 11, 15.

Melzack R. (1995). The McGill Pain Questionnaire: Major properties and scoring methods. *Pain*, 1, 277–99.

Moss, S., Patel, P., Prosser, H., Goldberg, D.P., Simpson, N., Rowe, S. and Lucchino, R. (1993). Psychiatric morbidity in older people with moderate and severe learning disability. *British Journal of Psychiatry*, 163, 471–80.

Moxley, D.P., Raider M.D. and Cohen, S.N. (1989). Specifying and facilitating family involvement in services to persons with developmental disabilities. *Child and Adolescent Social Work*, 6, 301–13.

Pearlin L.I. and Schooler, C. (1978). The structure of coping. *Journal of Health and Social Behaviour*, 19, 2–21.

Prasher, V.P. (1995). End-stage dementia in adults with Down syndrome. *International Journal of Geriatric Psychiatry*, 10, 1067–9.

Prasher, V.P., Chung, M.C. and Haque, M.S. (1998). Longitudinal changes in adaptive behaviour in adults with Down syndrome: Interim finding from a longitudinal study. *American Journal on Mental Retardation*, 130(1), 40–6.

Pruchno, R., Patrick, J.H. and Burant, C.J. (1997). African American and white mothers of adults with chronic disabilities: Caregiving burden and satisfaction. *Family Relations*, 46, 335–46.

Reid, T. (2003). The ABC Model. In P. McCallion (ed.), *Promoting Positive Behaviours*. Albany, NY: NYS Dept of Health. A CD-Rom training package.

Riley, M.W. and Riley, J.W. (1990). Structural lag: Past and future. In M.W. Riley, R.L. Kahn and A. Foner (eds), *Age and Structural Lag* (pp. 15–36). New York: Wiley.

Sanborn, B. and Bould, S. (1991). Intergenerational caregivers of the oldest old. In S.K. Pfiefer and M.B. Sussman (eds), *Families: Intergenerational and Generational Connections* (pp.125–42). Binghamton, NY: Haworth.

Schalock, R., Brown, I., Brown, R., Cummins, R.A., Felce, D., Matikka, L., Keith, K.D. and Parmenter, T. (2002). Conceptualization, measurement, and application of quality of life for persons with intellectual disabilities: report of an international panel of experts. *Mental Retardation*, 40(6), 457–70.

Seltzer, G., Begun, A., Magan, R. and Luchterhand, C. (1993). Social supports and expectations of family involvement after out-of-home placement. In E. Hutton, T. Heller, A. Factor, B. Seltzer and G. Hawkins (eds), *Older Adults with Developmental Disabilities* (pp. 123–40). Baltimore: Paul H. Brookes.

Seltzer, G., Begun, A., Seltzer, M.M. and Krauss, M.W. (1991). The impacts of siblings on adults with mental retardation and their aging mothers. *Family Relations*, 40, 310–17.

Seltzer, M.M. and Krauss, M.W. (1994). Aging parents with coresident adult children: The impact of lifelong caregiving. In M.M. Seltzer, M.W. Krauss and M.P. Janicki (eds), *Lifecourse Perspectives on Adulthood and Old Age* (pp. 3–18). Washington, DC: American Association on Mental Retardation.

Seltzer, M.M., Greenberg, J.S. and Krauss, M.W. (1995). A comparison of coping strategies of aging mothers of adults with mental illness or mental retardation. *Psychology and Aging*, 10, 64–75.

Seltzer, M.M., Greenberg, J.S., Krauss, M.W. and Hong, J. (1997). Predictors and outcomes of the end of co-resident caregiving in aging families of adults with mental retardation or mental illness. *Family Relations*, 46, 13–22.

Smith, G.C. and Tobin, S.S. (1989). Permanency planning among older parents of adults with lifelong disabilities. *Journal of Gerontological Social Work*, 14, 35–9.

Strauss, D. and Kastner, T.A. (1996). Comparative mortality of people with developmental disabilities in institutions and the community. *American Journal on Mental Retardation*, 101, 269–81.

Todd, S. (2002). Death does not become us: The absence of death and dying in intellectual disability research. *Journal of Gerontological Social Work*, 38(1/2), 225–40.

Toseland, R., Smith, G. and McCallion, P. (1995). Supporting the family in elder care. In G. Smith, S. Tobin, E. Robertson-Tchabo and P. Power (eds), *Strengthening Aging Families: Diversity in Practice and Policy* (pp. 3–24). Newbury Park, CA: Sage.

Tyrrell, J. and Dodd, P. (2003). Psychopathology in older age. In P.W. Davidson, V.P. Prasher and M.P. Janicki (eds), *Mental Health, Intellectual Disabilities and the Aging Process* (pp. 22–37). Oxford: Blackwell Publishing.

Tyrrell, J., Cosgrave, M., McCarron, M., McPherson, J., Calvert, J., Kelly, A., McLaughlin, M., Gill, M. and Lawlor, B.A. (2001). Dementia in people with Down syndrome. *International Journal of Geriatric Psychiatry*, 16(12), 1168–74.

Vitaliano, P., Russo, J., Carr, J.E., Maiuro, R.D. and Becker, J. (1985). The Ways of Coping Checklist: Revision and psychometric properties. *Multivariate-Behavioural-Research*, 20(1), 3–26.

Wilkinson, H. and Janicki, M.P. (2002). The Edinburgh Principles with accompanying guidelines and recommendations. *Journal of Intellectual Disabilities Research*, 46, 279–84.

Yanok, J. and Beifus, J.A. (1993). Communicating about loss and mourning: Death education for individuals with mental retardation. *Mental Retardation*, 31(3), 144–7.

Chapter 25

The macro-system and professional issues

Brian McGuire and John McEvoy

The field of intellectual disabilities presents a number of unique challenges to the work of the clinical psychologist. The broad cultural, social and professional environment, or 'macro-system', in which the person with an intellectual disability exists has many individual and interrelated components within multiple layers of complexity. Even taking the relatively straightforward context of a person with an intellectual disability who lives with his or her family, there are a range of systemic and professional issues with which the psychologist should be familiar and which must be taken into account in arriving at clinical decisions. This chapter will orientate the reader to some of these systemic variables and provide guidance on consultation and other models for working within complex systems, whilst maintaining the client or service user at the centre of the decision-making process.

Following our review of the macro-system, the reader's attention will be drawn to a range of clinically relevant issues around policy development. Through the recognition of the clinical relevance of policy, it is envisaged that the reader will identify that an important role exists for clinical psychologists in shaping the future of service ideology and policy.

This chapter will also highlight a universal range of legal and professional issues of relevance to clinical psychologists working in intellectual disability services. Underpinning and overarching many professional issues for psychologists in this area of practice is the uncertainty arising from the law and its application to people with intellectual disabilities. Some of these issues include the rights and responsibilities of people with intellectual disabilities who are chronologically of adult status, but are restricted in their opportunities to be autonomous by virtue of their intellectual disability. These contradictory positions become most evident around issues of capacity and consent, which will also be explored in this chapter.

SECTION I – THE MACRO-SYSTEM

In order to work effectively in intellectual disability services, the psychologist should have a broad appreciation of the range of social, cultural, legal and professional variables that may influence the shape of service delivery. The relative contribution of each of these influences will vary from one service to another, but an awareness that these influences exist is the first step to negotiating one's way successfully through the system. In this context, success can be thought of as a positive outcome for the service user whilst taking account of the socio-cultural milieu and the views of relevant stakeholders.

Borrowing from Bronfenbrenner's 'Ecological Systems' model (1979; 1989) Figure 25.1 provides a diagrammatic representation of some of the key structures and agencies that are influential in the life of a person with an intellectual disability. Bronfenbrenner's multi-system perspective emphasizes the reciprocal relations among the variety of systems influencing a person's behaviour. The diagram places the person with an intellectual disability at the centre of the model, with three surrounding layers of influence. The inner layer contains the people and agencies likely to be most influential in the person's life on a day-to-day basis. These include parents and family members, caregivers (who frequently are not family members, but paid staff), legal guardians (who, depending on the local service structure and legal system, may either be family members or an almost anonymous person appointed by the state), and life partners (unfortunately a rarity). Depending on the ability

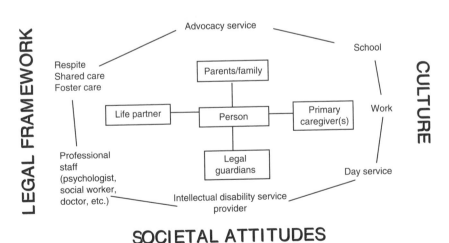

Figure 25.1 Key structures and agencies that are influential in the life of a person with an intellectual disability.

and autonomy of the individual, the agencies in the inner layer may have a more distant role at an advisory or supportive level, or conversely may be responsible for the most 'basic' of decisions in the person's life, including what they eat, how they dress, and who they live with.

The middle layer contains people and agencies that have a moderate level of influence in the person's life, including school, workplace or day service; an intellectual disability service provider; professional staff such as psychologists, social workers, case managers, doctors and therapists; respite services, shared care families, or short-term foster carers; and advocacy services which are not statutorily empowered, i.e. are not legal guardians. These various individuals and agencies, which include psychologists, have the potential to be quite influential in the life of a person with an intellectual disability. Focusing on the potential influence of psychologists, they may make important decisions about the content of a person's skills development programme, the school or day service a service user will attend, how 'challenging behaviour' is responded to, and whether the individual has the capacity to make their own decisions in certain aspects of their life.

The outer layer reflects the broad socio-cultural and legal frameworks applicable to all individuals in a society. These influences can shape the broad parameters within which an individual functions, can determine the broad range of opportunities and restrictions confronting the person, and can have (arguably excessive) influence on the decision making of people and individuals in the middle and inner layers, who in turn are highly influential in the lives of persons with an intellectual disability. Examples of this influence might include the impact of social or religious attitudes towards sexual expression in people with an intellectual disability, or a decision made by a professional which 'errs on the side of caution' when the legal ramifications of a decision are unclear – often in order to protect the professional although it may deny the service user an opportunity for greater autonomy.

It should be noted that the relative influence of each of these variables does not depend solely on the prevailing social and legal systems, nor solely on the local service models and arrangements, but also on the individual service users themselves. The components of an individual's macro-system are largely dependent on how the individual is assessed by others to require the support of the various agencies, how well the individual can self-advocate for support and, even more so, how well s/he can advocate *not* to be supported in order to be autonomous. Also, it is important to note that the configuration of a person's macro-system is not static, but in fact is quite fluid, reflecting changes in the individual's status (e.g. age, competency) and changes in components of the system (service models and ideologies evolve, staff come and go). Variations at any point in the system can produce significant changes in the systemic picture. For example, a change in the legal framework or social attitudes can have a ripple effect through the rest of the system. Even small changes at the individual level, for example development of the ability to catch a bus independently, can result in changes in the model of support, supervision, and service provision.

In clinical situations, psychologists frequently find themselves with a dilemma – they may believe that a particular course of action is in the best interest of a service user, but they also experience pressure from other influential sources such as parents, care staff, service managers or social and legal pressures. Some stakeholders can be vociferous in expressing their views and the clinician should be careful not to give undue weight to a particular viewpoint simply because it has been expressed assertively or with particular eloquence. Due regard must be given to the views of stakeholders, and inevitably there will be differences in the weight a particular view carries or the importance of a particular socio-cultural or legal variable. In such situations, the clinician must try to answer the questions outlined in the decision-making framework (Box 25.1).

Box 25.1 A decision-making framework

- Who is the 'client' or in whose best interest is the clinical decision?
- Who are the inner-layer 'stakeholders' in the decision outcome?
- Who are the middle-layer 'stakeholders' in the decision outcome?
- How can you ensure that the views of all stakeholders have been heard and considered in the decision making, whilst keeping the best interests of the 'client' at the core of the decision making?
- What relevant influences from the outer layer have a bearing on the decision?
- Are there 'best practice' guidelines to help you to reach a decision?
- If necessary, have you consulted with a supervisor or colleague for a second opinion?
- Have you documented your decision-making process and can you justify your decision-making rationale in an adversarial context?

CONSULTATION AND INTERDISCIPLINARY TEAMWORK

Most intellectual disability services provide input from a range of professions such as psychology, education, social work, physiotherapy, occupational therapy, speech therapy and vocational services. Usually, these services are delivered within a teamwork model, although the extent to which they truly function as a team may vary greatly. These clinical teams fulfil a range of pivotal roles, outlined in Box 25.2.

The specific work of the psychologist can encompass many, or all, of

---

Box 25.2 Roles of clinical teams

- Assessment and diagnosis
- Treatment and intervention
- Case management
- Service planning
- Service coordination
- Family support
- Public information

---

the roles outlined above. In addition to the requirement for working across professional disciplines, psychologists in intellectual disability services will also typically be required to work with direct care staff, teachers or vocational instructors, and family members. These parties will have varying degrees of knowledge in terms of theory and techniques in working with people with an intellectual disability. Consequently, the psychologist must be skilled both in communicating assessment findings to a broad audience and in delivering interventions through others. Working with a range of disciplines requires special skills in order both to maintain one's own discipline-specific expertise and to work effectively as part of a cross-disciplinary team. A report of the British Psychological Society (BPS) Division of Clinical Psychology (2001) cites the distinction drawn by Opie (1997) regarding different models of cross-disciplinary teamwork, as follows:

- **interdisciplinary teams** – members operate from within their particular disciplinary orientations but undertake some joint collaborative work.
- **multidisciplinary teams** – members, operating out of their disciplinary bases, work parallel to each other, their primary objective being that of coordination of service.
- **transdisciplinary teams** – aim for a significantly higher level of work integration where professional values and terminology are scrutinized and the team is able to develop a common language.

Using these definitions as the basis for distinguishing between team formats, Table 25.1 provides a detailed comparison of these different approaches to cross-disciplinary teamwork.

Some of the typical barriers to effective interdisciplinary work include 'territoriality' by professions, lack of role clarity and discipline elitism (Hanley, 2000). A practical guide to the typical organizational difficulties confronting the psychologist working in intellectual disability services has been provided by McBrien and Candy (1998). They highlight the fact that

Table 25.1 Models of cross-disciplinary teamwork

Interdisciplinary teams	Multidisciplinary teams	Transdisciplinary teams
A group of practitioners from different disciplines that meets occasionally, or on a case-by-case basis, or on a needs basis.	A group of practitioners from different disciplines that meets regularly.	A group of practitioners from different disciplines that meets frequently and works closely as a team.
Team members apply discipline-specific skills whilst allocating some time to the pursuit of the team's objectives.	Team members allocate a significant portion of their available time to the pursuit of the team's objectives.	Team members are highly integrated and work primarily in the pursuit of the team's objectives.
Team objectives may not be agreed, or may not be specific or explicit.	Team objectives are agreed and explicit.	Team objectives are agreed and explicit, highly valued and actively pursued by the team.
Team structure may reflect clusters of disciplines, not necessarily pursuing an explicit common objective.	Team structure and operation is determined by explicit objectives and identified in policy documents.	Team structure is highly specific to the team's objectives.
Coordination of the work of individual disciplines with possibly some overarching coordination.	Coordination of the work of the team both administratively and clinically, although not necessarily by the same person on all occasions.	Clinical and administrative coordination of the team by an identified person.
High level of skill differentiation and application of expertise in day-to-day practice.	Differentiation of those skills and roles that are specific or unique to individual members and those that may be common or shared.	Low level of skill differentiation in day-to-day practice although individual expertise is recognized.

Note: An adaptation and extension of British Psychological Society, 2001 and Opie, 1997.

most individuals with intellectual disability are enmeshed within a complex array of service providers and support agencies and that the majority of interventions are carried out via third parties – usually parents and care staff. They make the very valid, and oft-forgotten point, that carrying out an assessment and identifying an appropriate intervention is perhaps the easiest part – the challenge is to have a plan for implementing the treatment. In the context of working through third parties, this means having a plan to 'increase advice compliance' (1998: 267). McBrien and Candy have suggested the following strategies for increasing the likelihood that the psychologist's advice will be accepted and implemented:

- Provide a rationale for the plan (preferably based on information or data provided by the third party)
- Ensure all those involved in implementing the plan have clear instructions about their role in implementation
- Provide a written, easy-to-follow plan
- Follow up regularly, reviewing data and progress, providing feedback, and modifying the plan as required.

It is not uncommon for treatments or interventions to be only partially successful, or not successful at all. This may arise out of difficulties attributable to the nature of the clinical problem itself. More often, however, it will reflect a lack of commitment to the intervention plan due to problems arising from the psychologist's contribution or because of difficulties with the implementers (parents or care staff) (McBrien and Candy, 1998). Common problems associated with the psychologist and the implementers are listed below.

Problems with the psychologist

- Inadequate information about the specific clinical problem or setting
- Not hearing the viewpoints of important stakeholders
- An overly theoretical approach
- An overly complex intervention
- Failure to monitor and follow up on intervention.

Problems with implementers

- Poor communication among team members
- Lack of staff and other resources
- Disaffected staff and poor morale
- Lack of knowledge/experience
- Conflicting attitudes or beliefs.

The report on teamwork produced by the British Psychological Society, Division of Clinical Psychology (2001) outlines, in a very practical and accessible way, some of the core requirements for effective interdisciplinary teamwork. These requirements span the ideological, structural and procedural aspects of team functioning. Some of those requirements are outlined in Box 25.3.

Box 25.3 Guidelines for effective interdisciplinary teamwork

- Outline the purpose and function of the team.
- Have a clear statement of the aims and objectives of the team and the core values on which these aims are based.
- Ensure that values and aims translate into realistic, achievable and measurable objectives.
- Develop a description of the ways in which the various members of the team support the achievement of these objectives in the form of unambiguous statements of their responsibilities and accountability relationships. This will include:

  - core responsibilities that will be shared by other members of the team;
  - responsibilities that are specific to either the discipline or the individual health care practitioner.

- Have an operational policy for the team.
- Identify where the team fits within an organizational plan or service strategy.
- Identify a team leader.
- Address issues arising from cross-disciplinary supervision.
- Where discipline-specific supervision is in place external to the team, be aware that this may impact on team functioning and team dynamics.
- Identify the person(s) responsible to coordinate client care or case management.
- Have clear lines of reporting.
- Have a mechanism for resolving disagreements and conflicts among team members.

Note: Adapted from British Psychological Society, 2001.

SECTION 2 – POLICY ISSUES IN CLINICAL PRACTICE

The importance of policy development and the subsequent delivery of health services at a strategic level is often poorly appreciated, if not actively ignored, by clinicians. Particularly at the earlier stages of their career, clinical psychologists are often poorly represented at the level of health policy formulation and this absence at national level is often mirrored even at the organizational level.

This tendency of clinicians to be poorly informed about policy issues may reflect some combination of the demands of day-to-day clinical work as well as a belief that individuals are unlikely to be able to influence developments at the 'macro' level. However, this perception is not necessarily accurate. Policy formulators often rely a great deal on the advice and guidance of people 'on the ground' in arriving at policy decisions. This is especially so for managers of intellectual disability services who are regularly faced with difficult issues impacting on both service philosophy and policy. Because these issues often arise in the context of a range of clinical variables, managers and policy formulators will often seek advice from clinicians and this advice is frequently utilized in addressing the policy difficulty. Furthermore, there are opportunities for influencing policy 'from the ground up' (rather than top-down), by being aware of current issues affecting policy and practice and finding a way of expressing one's views.

In the intellectual disability sector, voluntary organizations founded by parents and friends were often the driving force behind service development. These organizations continue to influence policy development at all levels. Indeed, recent legislative changes regarding the right to educational provision has resulted from lobbying and legal action by individual parents as well as carer associations.

In addition to policies in existence in individual legal jurisdictions, a certain degree of policy formation and development of service ideology has arisen from the work of international advocacy and scientific organizations. In terms of health-related policies, for example, the World Health Organization is highly influential. Disability-specific organizations such as the American Association on Intellectual disability (AAMR) and the International Association for the Scientific Study of Intellectual Disability (IASSID) have also played an important role in developing policy statements and guidelines for best practice.

An important new IASSID journal, the *Journal of Policy and Practice in Intellectual Disabilities*, now provides an invaluable forum for dissemination of position papers, ideological views and policy guidelines. A review of the early issues of the journal reveals several important policy and position papers. For example, Schalock and Luckasson (2004) carried out an analysis of one of the most clinically relevant documents in the field of intellectual disability – the American Association on Intellectual Disability's 2002 system for diagnosing, classifying and describing intellectual disability/intellectual disability. In their review, Schalock and Luckasson examined the utility and relevance of the AAMR classification system in light of five significant international trends in ideology and practice in the field of intellectual disability. They described those trends as: (a) the evolution of an ecological perspective; (b) a view of disablement as a limitation in functioning; (c) the multi-dimensionality of intellectual disability; (d) the linking of assessment to intervention; and (e) the importance of clinical judgment in diagnosing and classifying. The utility of the AAMR model was examined in light of these trends. The authors concluded that the new model is helping to achieve a greater universal employment of a multidimensional classification system; a better understanding of the unique interaction between person and environment; and a better alignment of the process of assessment to some obvious, tangible outcome for the individual.

Meijer, Carpenter and Scholte (2004), in another important paper, reported on the development of a 'European Manifesto on basic standards of health care for people with intellectual disabilities', which outlines the core elements of adequate health care required by people with an intellectual disability. Broadly, these basic standards include availability and access to mainstream health services, that personnel in mainstream services have a better understanding of people with an intellectual disability, a right to specialist care, the availability of a multidisciplinary team, and a proactive approach to health care.

In an important position paper, Dalton and McVilly (2004) presented IASSID's *Ethics Guidelines for Multicenter Research*. This paper provides internationally agreed recommendations on the format and protocol for ethics applications, the ethics review process, research design considerations, consent processes and the general conduct of research involving people with an intellectual disability. Clearly, such guidelines will have considerable relevance for psychologists in clinical roles and will provide an invaluable framework for those engaged in, or considering, research with people with intellectual disabilities.

The papers described here provide a sense of the breadth of policy areas that have direct relevance for clinicians. Importantly, all were developed taking account of the views of clinicians and other stakeholders. Practising psychologists should endeavour to stay abreast of changes in both service ideology and policy, and where opportunities arise, to make their views heard. This will often require a deliberate act such as joining a professional society, writing to influential decision makers, or expressing views in the public domain.

SECTION 3 – LEGAL AND FORENSIC ISSUES

The laws relating to people with an intellectual disability vary from one jurisdiction to another. There are, nevertheless, a range of issues at the interface of law and clinical practice which appear to be universally controversial and about which there is no clear consensus. Of importance and relevance to clinical psychologists is the complex issue of capacity to consent and capacity to make decisions. Other forensic issues include the reliability of people with an intellectual disability as witnesses, and their capacity to understand and participate in the legal process from initial contact with the police through to the court process and the correctional system. These areas will be discussed further below.

Capacity to consent

The laws of most western countries explicitly make the assumption that a person of adult age has the capacity to make informed, autonomous decisions. However, when a person is not capable of making such decisions, various legal constraints, designed to protect the 'vulnerable adult', may actually serve to deny the individual the opportunity for self-direction and self-determination.

In considering a person's capacity to give informed consent, the most widely accepted legal criteria are knowledge, understanding and voluntariness (Stavis, 1991). These concepts can be defined as follows:

Knowledge of the important aspects of a behaviour and its risks and attendant benefits. Knowledge means information. Adequate information is necessary to make appropriate decisions. Persons with intellectual disabilities may need more information than others about a specific decision. We must not confuse a person's informational poverty with his or her decisional capacity. We must seek out ways to enhance the person's knowledge base, to help them to make an informed decision (Dinerstein, Herr and O'Sullivan, 1998).

Understanding, intelligence, reason or rationality which shows that the knowledge is comprehended and applied in a manner consistent with a person's values or beliefs.

Voluntariness – the person is not subjected to coercion and understands that there is a choice and that s/he has the ability to say 'yes' or 'no' (Sundram and Stavis, 1994).

As the importance of the decision increases, the need for more formal determinations of capacity to consent increases. For example, if the proposed action or decision would expose the person to significant physical or psychological risk, there should be greater assurance that the person's consent is valid (Campbell, 1997).

Despite the importance of accurately assessing capacity, few instruments exist to assist clinicians in reaching a decision. A helpful framework or protocol designed specifically to assess capacity to make decisions in people with an intellectual disability has been published (Lyden and Peters, 2004). Based on the core elements of knowledge, understanding and voluntariness, the protocol provides a helpful and systematic framework for assessing capacity.

Sexuality and consent

One topical and contentious area where the issue of capacity has been debated is in relation to sexual expression and the establishment of sexual relationships. Kennedy (1999) argues that psychologists and mental health providers have a responsibility to promote patients' rights to sexual expression, but also to protect patients when impairments interfere with the ability to make informed decisions.

A recent review of the current issues in intellectual disability practice showed that there is a growing interest in providing relevant knowledge and information about sexuality (Garwood and McCabe, 2000; McCabe and Cummins, 1996), but that the views of service users about their own relationships and sexuality have rarely been explored (Halstead, 2002). In addressing this deficit, a study by Evans, Healy and McGuire (2002) sought the views of service users through a series of focus groups. They also surveyed the views of parents and staff. They found that service users were clearly able to express their sense of entitlement to have a range of relationships, including sexual relationships, and were vociferous in expressing their frustration at the many obstacles preventing them from having 'normal' relationships. In a survey of parents and staff, the same authors showed that parents tended to be more conservative than staff members in their views about the sexuality of service users. There was evidence of an ongoing 'paternalistic' view among many respondents in both the parent and staff groups and many respondents highlighted their uncertainty about service users' rights and responsibilities under the law.

Assessment of capacity to consent is complex because people may have the capacity to consent to some, but not all, sexual activities. Sexual contacts can be categorized in at least three ways, depending on the level of intimacy of the sexual contact (see the American Association on Mental Retardation's (1999) book on 'Consent' for further guidance), and each category has implications from both the legal and clinical approach to assessing consent (Stavis and Walker-Hirsch, 1999). On the basis of 'levels of intimacy', decision-making pathways (based on DSM-IV decision trees model) for arriving at clinical decisions in relation to capacity for sexual relationships have been proposed by McGuire and Healy (2003).

There is an urgent need for objective, scientifically established empirical information about the capacity of individuals in the intellectual disability population to give consent on a range of sexuality-related matters. Several researchers have demonstrated that sex education programmes produce a measurable post-intervention change in knowledge about sexuality, but this knowledge-gain has rarely been applied to the issue of capacity to consent (Chivers and Mathieson, 2000). However, a recent single-case series study has examined the relationship between education and knowledge and changes in capacity, demonstrating that sex education led to significant increases on a measure of capacity to make decisions on sexual matters and that such changes were maintained at six-month follow-up (Dukes and McGuire, 2004).

The only published specialized instrument for the evaluation of competency to consent to sexual activity in the cognitively impaired population is the Sexual Consent and Education Assessment (SCEA; Kennedy, 1993), developed in Maryland, USA. It has not as yet been widely used in services, but the SCEA appears to be a useful tool for assessing two important aspects of the capacity to consent in sexual interactions, namely Knowledge of Sexuality and Safety Practices. When competence criteria are set, the SCEA has acceptably high predictive power, correlating with decisions of clinical teams in over 90 per cent of cases (Kennedy, 1993) and demonstrating sensitivity to change in capacity following intervention (Dukes and McGuire, 2004).

Other areas of decision making are also relevant in considering capacity and consent. For example, capacity to make medical decisions is an issue that arises on practically a daily basis in our hospitals (Cea and Fisher, 2003; Hart, 1999; Iacono and Murray, 2003). The process by which medical personnel arrive at decisions about treating or not treating is not at all clear, and psychologists are frequently asked to provide an assessment of the person's ability to give informed consent for non-emergency procedures. Holland (2003) has outlined the variables to be assessed in reaching a decision about capacity to make a medical decision:

- to be able to understand and retain information about the nature and purpose of the treatment,
- the risks of having and not having the treatment,
- alternative treatment options,
- the capacity to balance the information in order to arrive at a choice,
- the ability to communicate the decision.

Other topical and contentious areas relate to financial decisions, the capacity to make a will and decisions about living arrangements. A recent Irish publication (NAMHI, 2003) provides an excellent overview of these issues and provides invaluable guidance on the current legal situation regarding such decisions. Recently introduced legislation in Scotland, the Adults with Incapacity Act 2000, also provides a model for a client-centred but practical legal framework for reaching decisions about capacity in people with cognitive impairment. Some of the factors to be considered by clinicians in assessing the capacity of people with an intellectual disability are outlined in Box 25.4.

In the context of a tension between a protective or paternalistic stance on the one hand whereby the presence of mental disability automatically precludes the capacity to make decisions, and on the other hand a stance of self-determination at any cost, Holland (2003) argues that the solution to this tension lies in the legal concept of decision-making capacity and its valid and reliable assessment. Clinical psychologists have the potential to make an immense contribution to this assessment process (see also Chapter 26 in this volume).

Box 25.4 Factors in assessing capacity to make decisions

- Individual's age
- Individual's level of intellectual ability
- Individual's history and experience of decision making
- Level of seriousness of the specific issue/decision
- History of education about issue
- Current information and knowledge regarding the specific issue
- Ability to consider the consequences or implications, both positive and negative, of a particular decision
- Ability to communicate decision
- Process of assessing capacity should be clear, transparent, accessible and non-intimidating

Note: Adapted from AAMR, 1999; McGuire and Healy, 2003; NAMHI, 2003.

Forensic issues

There is a growing interest in the specialist field of practice spanning both the forensic and intellectual disability domains. Much of the research literature has focused on the assessment and treatment of sex offenders (Lindsay *et al.*, 2004a; 2004b) and on risk assessment as outlined in Chapter 26 of this volume. A review of the main published topic areas in the field of intellectual disability in 2000 (Halstead, 2002) highlights that several forensic issues were evident in the literature, including:

- the increased risk of engaging in misdemeanours following deinstitutionalization,
- the increased prevalence of people with an intellectual disability in the correctional system,
- the high rate of crime victimization among people with an intellectual disability and the significant barriers to accessing the justice system,
- fitness to stand trial,
- capacity to give evidence in court,
- the vulnerability of people with intellectual disability during police interrogation (interrogative suggestibility) and their vulnerability during cross-examination,
- the high rate of execution of intellectually disabled offenders in the USA,
- programmes aimed at prevention and court diversion schemes.

In addition to the areas outlined above, an important forensic area that warrants particular mention is the applicability of mental health legislation to people with an intellectual disability. Specific laws vary between jurisdictions but suffice it to say that people with an intellectual disability are often affected by such legislation. Psychologists should be familiar with the client groups subsumed under their local legislation and should also be clear about the role of the psychologist within that framework. In Ireland, for example, the Mental Health Act 2001 is due to be implemented in the near future. Reen and McGuire (2003) have highlighted some of the implications for psychologists in intellectual disability services. For example, the revised definition of 'mental disorder' specifically includes significant intellectual disability as one form of mental disorder that may lead to involuntary detention in a mental health facility. Most importantly, it appears that challenging behaviour in a person with significant intellectual disability may be interpreted as reasonable grounds for involuntary admission. An important 'entitlement' to mental health services is implicit in the Act, but it remains to be seen whether access to mental health services for people with an intellectual disability will be made easier by the Act. The Act also emphasizes the importance of consent to treatment whenever this is achievable, and as we saw earlier, this is an area in which psychologists can play an important role.

In the UK, the draft Mental Health Act 2000 applies to all persons, including children and those with intellectual disabilities. The new law proposes sweeping changes for a sub-population of the most dangerous offenders (those with 'Dangerous Severe Personality Disorder') as well as much greater responsibilities for psychologists both in admitting persons to hospital and in clinical responsibility for the person's treatment plan. An outline of the implications for psychologists is provided by Cooke, Harper and Kinderman (2001). A useful overview of clinically relevant legislation in the UK is provided by Johnston (2003).

While acts or behaviours which breach the law can be perpetrated by people with all levels of intellectual disability, Clare and Murphy (1998) rightly make the point that people with mild intellectual disabilities are most likely both to fulfil the legal criteria for a crime and to be meaningfully involved in criminal justice procedures. Thus, the majority of people with intellectual disabilities who come in contact with the law are likely to be people with a mild intellectual disability and behavioural difficulties. As indicated earlier, they are also likely to be more vulnerable at each stage of the judicial process, from police interview (and probably even from the stage of commission of a crime) through to incarceration. In their review of this sub-population, Clare and Murphy (1998) concluded that offenders with intellectual disabilities are overwhelmingly likely to be young, male and to have had behavioural difficulties from childhood. They are more likely to have had a childhood characterized by instability, loss, financial disadvantage and frequent extra-familial placements. In addition, they are likely to have had difficulty maintaining friendships and other sources of support and are at increased risk for mental ill health.

In conducting a thorough and comprehensive forensic psychological assessment of a person with an intellectual disability, one should assess the usual range of historical and current issues addressed during a clinical assessment and should also assess a number of offence-specific variables (see Box 25.5).

Box 25.5 Forensic psychological assessment of a person with an intellectual disability

Assessment of intellectual ability, communication skills (receptive and expressive), problem-solving skills, coping strategies, functional/adaptive skills, literacy.

History of the offending behaviour.

- when and how it developed
- evidence of incremental severity of offending behaviour
- influences on offending behaviour such as substance use, lack of occupation, peer group pressure, financial necessity
- intrapsychic variables (mood, anxiety, tension, obsessions and compulsions, beliefs and attitudes, cognitive distortions) and their relative contribution (if any) to the offence

Offender's perspective on offending behaviour.

- when and how it developed
- knowledge of legal and social acceptance of behaviour
- awareness of impact on others

Summary conceptualization of role of intellectual disability in the subject offence (state in terms of vulnerability, capacity to reason, awareness of consequences and so on).

Capacity to engage in treatment.

- motivation to change
- co-morbid psychopathology
- attitude towards victim
- attitude towards authority
- current risk factors
- ameliorating factors

CONCLUSION

This brief review of legal and forensic issues has explored some (but not all) of the complexities and controversies which exist in this area and has highlighted the important contribution of clinical psychologists in addressing these issues. While the complexities and dilemmas at the interface of law and psychology are particularly intriguing, progress in these areas is reliant on a sound working knowledge and understanding of the micro- and macro-systems influencing the behaviour of all stakeholders. Similarly, a commitment to teamwork and a motivation to contribute to local and national policy in the area of intellectual disability presents the clinical psychologist with a formidable challenge but also exciting opportunities. Finally, the single most important challenge facing the busy practitioner lies in ensuring that persons with intellectual disabilities remain at the heart of the decision-making process at all levels of the macro-system (Walsh, 2003).

EXERCISES

1   Systems: in groups of three, discuss a specific client known to one of the group. Map out the levels of intervention pertaining to that client (see Figure 25.1). Identify where the psychologist fits in the map, how the psychologist influences and is influenced by the other actors. Discuss whether the client is truly at the centre of this map, where 'centre' implies importance rather than simply as a passive recipient of a range of influences.
2   Capacity: what factors might you consider in determining the capacity of a client to:

   a.   consent to a non-emergency surgical procedure, e.g. removal of gallstones.
   b.   make a will.

   What questions would you ask and what tests (if any) would you consider using?
3   Policy: in small groups, identify and discuss the following:

   a.   an example in the area of intellectual disability where clinical practice has led to a significant policy development.
   b.   an example in the area of intellectual disability where a policy development has had a significant impact on clinical psychological practice.

FURTHER READING FOR CLINICIANS

American Association on Mental Retardation (1999). *A Guide to Consent.* Washington, DC: AAMR. Although set in the context of existing legislative frameworks in the USA, this is a helpful exploration of the issue of consent across a range of important decisions such as finance, making a will, and sexuality.

British Psychological Society. (2001). *Working in Teams: A Report of the Division of Clinical Psychology, British Psychological Society.* Leicester: British Psychological Society. A useful overview of the different models of teamwork in which psychologists might work within the health services.

Keywood, K, Fovargue, S. and Flynn, M. (1999). *Best Practice? Healthcare Decision-Making by, with and for Adults with Learning Disabilities.* Manchester: NDT.

Lord Chancellor's Department (1999). *Making Decisions: The Government's Proposals for Making Decisions on Behalf of Mentally Incapacitated Adults.* London: The Stationery Office.

Lord Chancellor's Department (2003). *Making Decisions: Helping People Who Have Difficulty Deciding for Themselves: A Guide for Legal Practitioners.* London: The Stationery Office.

Lord Chancellor's Department (2003). *Making Decisions: Helping People Who Have Difficulty Deciding for Themselves: A Guide for Social Care Professionals.* London: The Stationery Office.

Lord Chancellor's Department (2003). *Making Decisions: Helping People Who Have Difficulty Deciding for Themselves. A Guide for Healthcare Professionals.* London: The Stationery Office.

Lord Chancellor's Department (2003). *Making Decisions: Helping People Who Have Difficulty Deciding for Themselves. A Guide for Family and Friends.* London: The Stationery Office.

Lord Chancellor's Department (2003). *Making Decisions: Helping People Who Have Difficulty Deciding for Themselves. Planning Ahead: A Guide for People Who Wish to Plan for Possible Future Incapacity.* London: The Stationery Office.

Lord Chancellor's Department (2003). *Making Decisions: Helping People Who Have Difficulty Deciding for Themselves. A Guide for People with Learning Difficulties.* London: The Stationery Office.

NAMHI (2003). *Who Decides and How? People with Intellectual Disabilities – Legal Capacity and Decision Making.* Dublin: NAMHI. An excellent reference book that not only clarifies the law as it stands in relation to capacity and consent, but also highlights a range of philosophical and ethical issues, and makes recommendations for legal reform.

REFERENCES

American Association on Mental Retardation (AAMR) (1999). *A Guide to Consent.* Washington, DC: AAMR.

British Psychological Society (2001). *Working in Teams: A Report of the Division of Clinical Psychology, British Psychological Society.* Leicester: British Psychological Society.

Bronfenbrenner, U. (1979). *The Ecology of Human Development: Experiments by Nature and Design*. Cambridge, MA: Harvard University Press.

Bronfenbrenner, U. (1989). Ecological systems theory. In R. Vasta (ed.), *Annals of Child Development* (vol. 6, pp. 187–251). Greenwich, CT: JAI.

Campbell, J. (1997). Growing pains' disability politics: The journey explained and described by Jane Campbell. In L. Barton and M. Oliver (eds), *Disability Studies: Past Present and Future* (pp. 78–90). Leeds: Disability Press.

Cea, C.D. and Fisher, C.B. (2003). Health care decision-making by adults with mental retardation. *Mental Retardation*, 41, 78–87.

Chivers, J. and Mathieson, S. (2000). Training in sexuality and relationships: An Australian model. *Sexuality and Disability*, 18, 73–80.

Clare, I.C.H. and Murphy, G.H. (1998). Working with offenders or alleged offenders with intellectual disabilities. In E. Emerson, C. Hatton, J. Bromley and A. Caine (eds), *Clinical Psychology and People with Intellectual Disabilities* (pp. 154–76). Chichester: Wiley.

Cooke, A., Harper, D. and Kinderman, P. (2001). Reform of the Mental Health Act: Implications for clinical psychologists. *Clinical Psychology*, 1, 48–52.

Dalton, A.J. and McVilly, K.R. (2004). Ethics guidelines for international, multicenter research involving people with intellectual disabilities. *Journal of Policy and Practice in Intellectual Disabilities*, 1, 57–70.

Dinerstein, R., Herr, S. and O'Sullivan, J. (1998). *A Guide to Consent*. Washington, DC: APA.

Dukes, E. and McGuire, B. (2004). *Capacity to consent to sexual relationships in people with an intellectual disability following a sex education intervention*. Poster presented at the Annual Conference of the Psychological Society of Ireland, Cork, November.

Evans, D., Healy, E. and McGuire, B.E. (2002). *Sexuality and Interpersonal Relationships in Learning Disability*. Paper presented at the National Disability Authority Annual Conference, Dublin, December.

Garwood, M. and McCabe, M. (2000). Impact of sex education programs on sexual knowledge and feelings of men with a mild intellectual disability. *Education and Training in Mental Retardation and Developmental Disabilities*, 35, 269–83.

Halstead, S. (2002). Service-user and professional issues. *Journal of Intellectual Disability Research*, 46, 31–46.

Hanley, B. (2000). Barriers to interdisciplinary teaming across multiple settings [abstract]. *Journal of Intellectual Disability Research*, 44 (Suppl. 1), 307–8.

Hart, S.L. (1999). Meaningful choices: Consent to treatment in general health care settings for people with learning disabilities. *Journal of Learning Disabilities for Nursing, Health and Social Care*, 3, 20–6.

Holland, A. (2003). Consent and decision-making capacity. In W. Fraser and M. Kerr (eds), *Seminars in the Psychiatry of Intellectual Disability* (2nd edn, pp. 307–18). London: Gaskell.

Iacono, T. and Murray, V. (2003). Issues of informed consent in conducting medical research involving people with intellectual disability. *Journal of Applied Research in Intellectual Disabilities*, 16, 41–51.

Johnston, S. (2003). Forensic psychiatry and learning disability. In W. Fraser and M. Kerr (eds), *Seminars in the Psychiatry of Intellectual Disability* (2nd edn pp. 287–306). London: Gaskell.

Kennedy, C.H. (1993). *Sexual Consent and Education Assessment*. Philadelphia: Drexel University.

Kennedy, C.H. (1999). Assessing capacity to consent to sexual activity in the cognitively impaired population. *Journal of Forensic Neuropsychology*, 1, 17–33.

Lindsay, W.R., Elliot, S.F. and Astell, A. (2004a). Predictors of sexual offences recidivism in offenders with intellectual disabilities. *Journal of Applied Research in Intellectual Disabilities*, 17, 299–305.

Lindsay, W.R., Taylor, J.L. and Sturmey, P. (2004b). *Offenders with Developmental Disabilities*. Chichester, UK: Wiley.

Lyden, M. and Peters, M. (2004). Assessing capacity for informed consent: A rationale and framework. *Mental Health Aspects of Developmental Disabilities*, 7(3), 97–106.

McBrien, J. and Candy, S. (1998). Working with organisations or: Why won't they follow my advice? In E. Emerson, C. Hatton, J. Bromley and A. Caine (eds), *Clinical Psychology and People with Intellectual Disabilities* (pp. 265–79). Chichester: Wiley.

McCabe, M. and Cummins, R. (1996). The sexual knowledge, experience, feelings and needs of people with mild intellectual disability, *Education and Training in Mental Retardation and Developmental Disabilities*, (March), 13–21.

McGuire, B.E. and Healy, E. (2003). *Sexuality and Consent: Decision-making pathways*. Paper presented at the Annual Conference of the Psychological Society of Ireland Learning Disability Group, Galway, Ireland, April.

Meijer, M.M., Carpenter, S. and Scholte, F.A. (2004). European Manifesto on basic standards of health care for people with intellectual disabilities. *Journal of Policy and Practice in Intellectual Disabilities*, 1, 10–16.

NAMHI (2003). *Who Decides and How? People with Intellectual Disabilities – Legal Capacity and Decision Making*. Dublin: NAMHI.

Opie, A. (1997). Thinking teams, thinking clients: A discourse and representation in the work of health care teams. *Sociology of Health and Illness*, 19, 259–80.

Reen, M. and McGuire, B.E. (2003). *The new Mental Health Act: Implications for Learning Disability services*. Paper presented at the Annual Conference of the Psychological Society of Ireland Learning Disability Group, Galway, Ireland, April.

Schalock, R.L. and Luckasson, R. (2004). American Association on Mental Retardation's *Definition, Classification and System of Supports* and its relation to international trends and issues in the field of intellectual disabilities. *Journal of Policy and Practice*, 1, 147–54.

Stavis, P.F. (1991). Harmonizing the right to sexual expression and the right to protection from harm for persons with mental disability. *Sexuality and Disability. Special Issue: Sexuality and Developmental Disability*, 9(2), 131–41.

Stavis, P.F. and Walker-Hirsch, L.W. (1999). Consent to sexual activity. In R.D. Dinerstein, S.S. Herr and J.L. O'Sullivan (eds), *A Guide to Consent* (pp. 57–67). Washington, DC: American Association on Mental Retardation.

Sundram, C.J. and Stavis, P.F. (1994). Sexuality and mental retardation: Unmet challenges. *Mental Retardation*, 32(4), 255–64.

Walsh, P.N. (2003). Human rights, development and disability. *British Journal of Learning Disabilities*, 31, 110–12.

Chapter 26

Risk assessment

John McEvoy and Brian McGuire

Throughout history people with intellectual disabilities have been viewed either as a source of risk or in need of protection (Alaszewski, Parker and Alaszewski, 1999). More recently, the expansion of community care has highlighted the vulnerability of people with intellectual disabilities, bringing the assessment and management of risk to the forefront of service delivery (Hickson and Khemka, 1999; Sellars, 2002; Sykes, 2005).

The drive within agencies to manage or eliminate potentially risky situations raises a number of challenges and dilemmas for the practitioner including: deciding what is or is not a risk; balancing individual rights and safety; maintaining objectivity while conducting risk assessments; and ensuring that risk assessment does not become an obstacle to self-determination. However, despite the long-standing link between risk and people with intellectual disabilities and increasing pressure on care agencies to manage risk, advice on the topic is sparse and research on risk management within the intellectual disability sector minimal.

This chapter focuses on risk assessment in people with intellectual disabilities with a view to encouraging responsible risk taking and avoiding harm. The chapter provides a general overview of the issues and factors relating to taking and curtailing risks. The focus is mainly on the principles and characteristics associated with everyday risk, the attitudes of families and service agencies to risk taking and some of the legal issues associated with risk. A brief analysis of how harmful events occur and the influence of bias in decision making is also included. The chapter concludes with some generic principles and suggestions for identifying, analysing and assessing risk in individuals with intellectual disabilities.

RISK AND PEOPLE WITH INTELLECTUAL DISABILITIES

Self-determination

Self-determination refers to the right of individuals to direct and control their own personal growth and development. According to Wehmeyer (2001) self-determination consists of a variety of aptitudes and behaviours including: setting personal goals and understanding what is entailed in achieving them; and the ability to evaluate one's own performance.

Wehmeyer, Abery, Mithaug and Stancliffe (2003) make the key observation that while problem solving and the capability to act are essential, environmental influences are also crucial in facilitating self-determination. The natural tendency of humans towards personal growth can only be achieved within an environment which affords personal challenges and learning opportunities. Self-determination can only be developed by direct engagement with the 'real world' which involves taking risks, being allowed to make mistakes, and learning from those mistakes. This does not mean that individuals should be encouraged to 'go it alone' or act irresponsibly or that sensible boundaries and constraint should be removed (Wehmeyer, 1998). Rather, the challenge is to provide opportunities, along with requisite supports, which encourage people to make meaningful decisions about their lives and their future. Regrettably, people with intellectual disabilities are frequently steered away from situations and experiences where there is potential for failure and subsequent learning. And while concentrating on positive experiences is laudable, every individual needs the freedom to make some mistakes, as mistakes are often the catalyst for new goals, resolutions and achievements. Unfortunately, self-determination can be hampered or seriously 'knocked off course' by environmental barriers such as over-protective individuals and institutions (Wehmeyer, 1992; Wehmeyer, Kelchner and Richards, 1996).

Attitudes of families and carers to risk taking

For people with intellectual disabilities, getting the balance between risk and safety is less heavily influenced by their own personal decision-making capacity than by cultural and societal factors, in particular the views of their family, carers and service agencies. Carers are frequently unsure about their relative's capacity to cope with risks and how they might react in hazardous situations. A number of studies report widespread parental control, even for the most basic of lifestyle choices, and families expressing fears that increased independence for their son or daughter may result in serious risks (Heyman and Huckle, 1993; Redmond, 1996; Shepperdson, 2000; Smyth and McConkey, 2003). This resultant protectiveness can create a tension between risk taking and the opportunity to learn, ultimately resulting in a 'vicious circle' of over-protectiveness and restrictive lifestyle (Alaszewski and Alaszewski, 2002; Heyman and Huckle, 1993; Shepperdson, 2000).

While, the ability to take risks is often equated with level of disability and parental authority used as a way of protecting individuals, not all families are equally over-protective (Heyman and Huckle, 1993). Some families (both carers and adult relative), view risk as too much trouble to cope with and to be avoided at all costs. Others continually evaluate the level of risk against constantly changing circumstances in an effort to balance the need for learning opportunities with a need to protect the adult. A third approach frequently leads to family conflict, with carers advocating that risk situations should be avoided and their adult relatives more prepared to accept certain risks in order to enhance their autonomy (Heyman and Huckle, 1993).

Professionals and formal carers too, can mirror the family's reluctance to provide new opportunities and experiences for people with intellectual disabilities (Alaszewski et al., 1999; Alaszewski and Alaszewski, 2002). Most professionals and service agencies take a restrictive approach to risk. The main emphasis is on health and safety issues, with only a minority acknowledging the need for their agency to promote personal development and support participation in decision making (Alaszewski et al., 1999; Alaszewski and Alaszewski, 2002). Even where decisions concerning lifestyle are made on the basis of 'good practice' this is frequently for the convenience or self-interest of service providers (West and Parent, 1992), with individuals allowed only minor choices within a predetermined social context (Jenkinson, 1993; Tyne, 1994). Finally, although many service agencies acknowledge the importance of managing risk, only a minority have developed policies and guidelines to deal with risk issues (Alaszewski and Manthorpe, 1991; Turner, 2000).

RISK AND RISK MANAGEMENT

As we can see from the above, perceptions of risk are highly subjective with one person's acceptable level of risk seen as another's reckless behaviour (Gale, Woodward, Hawley, Hayes et al., 2002; Sellars, 2002; Sykes, 2005). This makes defining risk a difficult, probably impossible, proposition (Adams, 1995; Pidgeon, Hood, Jones, Turner and Gibson, 1992; Slovic, 1996). Despite the subjective nature of risk, most people would agree risk is associated with: (1) exposure to an event; (2) making predictions about the occurrence of certain outcomes, usually in terms of probabilities or chance; and (3) forecasting the possible impact of those outcomes.

Prins (1995; 1999) distinguishes between risk as prediction: how likely is it that things will go wrong? And risk as outcome: what can go wrong and what are the consequences? Thus, central to the notion of risk is making predictions about the future under conditions of uncertainty. Conditions of uncertainty arise from insufficient information about an event or a lack of quantifiable knowledge about the probability of potential harm. Thus, when forecasting the likelihood of a risk occurring, rather than guessing, one can reduce the level of uncertainty by basing predictions on data.

Risk typically involves making judgements on the impact or consequences of taking the risk. These judgements are made usually in terms of trade-offs along the good/bad; loss/gain continuum with the decision maker basing their assessment of whether taking the risk (the cost) is worth it (the benefit) (Sellars, 2002; Teigen and Brun, 1997).

Of course the process of judging outcomes is further complicated by the possibility of unintended or unexpected outcomes (Wharton, 1992), and an additional influencing factor is the degree of control one can exercise over the situation to reduce potentially negative effects (Brun, 1994; McKenna, 1993). Hence, a rational, simple cost–benefit model of risk taking may be inadequate in explaining risk management within social and care situations. Slovic (1987) identified three subjective factors influencing perceptions of risk: 'dread' the degree to which the risk evokes a feeling of fear, which is dependent on perceived control and the severity of the consequences; 'unknown' reflecting the degree of knowledge of and familiarity with the hazard; and the 'extent of risk' or the numbers of people affected by the risk. The greater people's fearfulness and lack of familiarity with a situation the more serious the perceptions of risk and the greater the effort taken to reduce negative consequences (Slovic, 1992).

Risk management is a term used in different ways by different professional groupings and ranges from concerns for health and safety to avoiding malpractice suits. Essentially risk management describes the process of methodically focusing on the risks attached to an activity with the goal of identifying and treating risks, so as to achieve sustained benefits (Halstead, 1997). Obviously all risks cannot be eliminated. However, risk management may help to control the risk either by reducing the likelihood of its occurrence or by minimizing the impact of potentially negative consequences (Calder, 2002; Crighton, 2005; Walshe, 2001).

A critical part of any risk-management process is risk assessment. Risk assessment is a form of problem solving and entails describing an event, predicting the probability of risk associated with that event and forecasting consequences in an attempt to control outcomes. Potential risk events are closely analysed in order to generate alternative courses of action with a view to achieving a goal. The most suitable of the alternatives is chosen based on probability judgements as to potential losses and benefits. The risk-assessment process has a number of important objectives: (1) the collection and analysis of information to identify 'risk-heightening' factors; (2) the identification of the likelihood of future harm; (3) the identification of risk-reduction factors; (4) deciding on what is an acceptable level of risk; and

(5) the implementation of a reliable risk-management strategy (Calder, 2002; Crighton, 2005).

In summary, risky behaviour can bring both predicted and unintended benefits and harm. How one views risk is to a large extent subjective, and may be influenced by perceptions of control over the outcomes, making definition of risk difficult. Risk management is the attempt to plan for the unexpected so as to avoid harm, while achieving one's goals and gaining benefits. Risk assessment is the process of evaluating key information in order to generate alternative course of actions and strategies to manage specific risk situations.

COLLECTING INFORMATION AND IDENTIFYING RISK FACTORS

Prior to the identification of potential risk factors and collecting of information, agreement must be reached as to the nature of the risk. This can be a difficult and complex process with two potentially contentious areas for disagreement: (1) conceptual issues around the nature and likelihood of outcomes; and (2) decisions on an agreed assessment format.

Deciding on the nature of risk

Not all decision making around risk is of the same magnitude and many potentially risky situations do not require a risk assessment. For instance, the consequences of choosing whether to have tea or coffee are obviously of a different type compared with deciding to move house or supporting an offender in the community. Risk is very much part of daily living, though we ignore most potential risks in order to go about our daily lives with confidence (Manthorpe, Walsh, Alaszewski and Harrison, 1997). Occasionally unintended outcomes may emerge from a particular course of action, bringing harmful or beneficial consequences. Such outcomes have been described as 'fateful moments'; turning points in our lives, which cannot be reversed (Giddens, 1991; Manthorpe et al., 1997). Difficulties can arise in identifying or understanding the nature of these 'fateful moments' when planning daily activities. And it is the prospect of these 'fateful moments' which becomes the focus of considerable disagreement between care staff, individuals and their families as to the benefits or otherwise of certain outcomes or courses of action.

Even where there is agreement about the risk, as in the case of potential sexual offending or violence, agreement around probability of occurrence can be a significant source of disagreement. Use of words such as 'low', 'medium' and 'high' to describe the level of risk leaves open the dangers of individual interpretation. Typically then, discussion around risk in service settings is often characterized by ill-structured problem definition, poorly defined or competing goals and differing opinions as to the likelihood and value of outcomes (Schon, 1991).

Collecting information and identifying risk factors

Having decided that a risk assessment is necessary, the next stage is to agree on what information is required and how best to collect it. Historically two methods of predicting risk have been prevalent within psychology: actuarial and clinical decision making. Actuarial decision making is a formal, data-based process, generally viewed as rational as it employs an explicit step-by-step approach known as 'analytic reasoning'. Clinical decision making utilizes 'intuitive reasoning' and is largely impressionistic or subjective with decisions based on a 'hunch'. Traditionally, actuarial decision making based on the statistical prediction of risk has been viewed as more reliable than predictions relying solely on clinical judgement (Crighton, 2005; Dawes, Faust and Meehl, 1989; Meehl, 1954; Sawyer, 1966), although actuarial methods may have poor predictive value for individual cases (Crighton, 2005), and where behaviour base rates are low (Szmulker, 2003). Moreover, actuarial methods generally focus on the risks, providing little guidance for risk management (Crighton, 2005) and ignore potentially protective factors (Rogers, 2000). Within the field of intellectual disability the application of actuarial methods to life decisions may be too simplistic as too many unknown variables are at play. On the other hand, relying solely on clinical judgement, particularly when assessing intellectually disabled individuals for potential violence or sexual offending, is seriously disadvantageous, as clinical judgements may be overly subjective and lack validity and reliability (Crighton, 2005; Lindsay and Beail, 2004).

Although both approaches have their drawbacks, this assessment dilemma can be resolved somewhat if statistical – actuarial and intuitive – clinical approaches are treated as extreme ends of the decision-making continuum (Hammond, 1996). Frequently, risk decisions within service agencies fall somewhere in the middle of this continuum and therefore require both the collection and analysis of empirical data and sound clinical judgement, a process known as structured professional judgement.

Structured professional judgement assesses risk by combining the use of empirically supported risk factors with clinical decision making (Johnston, 2002). The amalgamation of sound clinical judgement and the use of empirical data is best exemplified by recent developments in forensic services which shows that the risk evaluation process is still dependent on the use of professional discretion but with the level of risk measured against empirically supported predictive risk factors (Harris and Tough, 2004; Lindsay, Murphy, Smith, Murphy et al., 2004; McMillan, Hastings and Coldwell, 2004; Smith and Willner, 2004).

Risk assessment materials

Within intellectual disability services assessment of risk is usually focused on the tasks of daily living, parenting ability and the risks associated with mental disorders, violence and sexual offending (Sellars, 2002). However, risk assessment within the field of intellectual disability is still in its infancy (Halstead, 1997) and unfortunately there is a paucity of evidence-based measures to assist practitioners in predicting risk and developing appropriate management strategies for this population.

Several strategies have been suggested to aid decision making during risk assessment (Worthley, 1999). Checklists offer a simple flexible method of keeping track during complicated discussions and the use of guiding questions and principles agreed upon in advance aids focus, helps to ground the decision-making process and encourages transparency. Consequence tables are simple matrices of the 'pros' and 'cons' associated with each of the alternatives, which are then sorted according to likelihood of occurrence. It may be helpful in some instances to rate the level of risk using a simple matrix or grid system, as illustrated in Figure 26.1. Each of the vulnerabilities is considered in turn and an estimate of the potential frequency of occurrence and the severity of the outcome calculated. Using the grid, a score can be assigned indicating the level of threat.

A decision tree is a device for keeping track of alternatives and for comparing vulnerabilities and threats. The format for developing a decision tree follows a simple convention (Watts, 1995): (1) a branching tree is drawn on its side; (2) key events are shown left to right across the page in the order in which they are expected to occur; (3) squares are used to indicate each point at which a choice is made between two or more alternatives for action; (4) circles are used to indicate points at which at least two possible consequences of action will become known; (5) lines branching from these choices and chance

Frequency severity	Very likely (4)	Likely (3)	Less likely (2)	Unlikely (1)
Very serious (4)	16	12	8	4
Serious (3)	12	9	6	3
Less serious (2)	8	6	4	2
Not serious (1)	4	3	2	1

Interpretation of total risk scores: 16–12 = unacceptable risk; 6–9 = very high risk; 3–4 = Significant risk; 1–2 = low risk

Figure 26.1 Simple matrix for assessing the level of risk.

Source: adapted from Secker-Walker and Taylor-Adams, 2001

points carry short labels describing the option to be considered and consequences that may be seen. Decision trees are useful in identifying possible alternatives and in 'teasing out' the impact of decisions and outcomes.

Actuarial and other clinical data-based measures can be used where appropriate. The reader is referred to Lindsay (2002) for an excellent overview of the clinical and methodological issues facing practitioners assessing offenders and to Lindsay, Taylor and Sturmey (2004), for an extensive review of the topic. Also, Ward and Bosek (2002) and Boer, Tough and Haven (2004) provide particularly useful advice for the ongoing assessment and management of sex offenders with intellectual disabilities.

Similarly, a variety of assessment materials have been developed specifically for use with parents with intellectual disabilities concentrating on personal information, parenting skills and experiences of and attitudes to parenting and home safety (Tymchuk, 1990; Tymchuk, Andron and Bavolek, 1990; Tymchuk, Hamada, Andron and Anderson 1990). A reading recognition scale, with good reliability and validity, designed to assess parental ability to read labels on household products, brochures and general household information is also available (Tymchuk, Groen and Dolyniuk, 2000). In addition, McGaw and Sturmey (1994) provide a multi-component assessment tool specifically designed to assess parenting ability in parents with intellectual disabilities. The 'Parent Assessment Manual' (McGaw, Beckley, Connolly and Ball, 1998) includes questionnaires, checklists, vignettes and rating scales for developing child and parent profiles. The assessment is scored but currently norms are unavailable.

The risk of violence to staff supporting people with challenging behaviours is an area of frequent concern to service providers (Allen, 2000; Emerson, Robertson, Gregory, Hatton *et al.*, 2000; Harris, 1996; Murphy, Kelly-Pike and McGill, 2001). While a number of risk factors associated with challenging behaviours have been identified (Emerson, 2001; McClintock, Hall and Oliver, 2003), carers are often unclear on how to manage the risk of physical assault (Heyman, Swain and Gillman, 1998; Jenkins, Rose and Lovell, 1997) and lack training in emergency management techniques (Allen, 2001). Advice on coping with potentially violent situations can be found in McDonnell, McEvoy and Dearden (1994) and McDonnell, Waters, and Jones (2002), Harris (1996) and Harris, Allen, Cornick, Jefferson and Mills (1996); information on developing appropriate reactive strategies and a template for managing risk as a response to challenging behaviour has been made available in Allen (2002; 2004).

IDENTIFYING THE LIKELIHOOD OF FUTURE HARM

The relevant information having been gathered, the next phase of the risk-assessment process focuses on pulling together all the information in order to make a decision as to the advantages and disadvantages of engaging in the proposed course of action. However, as already mentioned above, risk decisions are not simply a matter of cost–benefit trade-off: perceptions of risk are highly subjective and there can be 'hidden' psychosocial factors affecting our judgement of risk.

Bias in judgement and decision making

One might assume that estimating the probability of risk is a logical, rational process; a careful and systematic weighing of evidence aimed at maximizing benefit (Von Neumann and Morgenstern, 1944). However, Newell and Simon (1972) argue that even if we had access to all the relevant information we would still be unable to carry out the necessary calculations because of our limited cognitive ability. Human reason is limited or 'rationally bounded'. Consequently, when faced with complex decisions, individuals 'satisfice' or choose the first option that meets their needs (Simon, 1957). 'Satisficing' is an example of heuristic reasoning: a 'cognitive shortcut' or simple rule of thumb used to make a 'good enough' decision. Unfortunately 'satisficing' encourages belief in the correctness of the decision in situations where we have the least knowledge. Such overconfidence and a belief in one's own infallibility can lead to an underestimation of risk (Fischoff, Slovic and Lichtenstein, 1977).

Research suggests that risk decisions are influenced by our past experiences (Fischoff, Lichtenstein, Slovic, Derby and Keeney, 1981; Teigen and Brun, 1997) which leaves us open to further cognitive bias or 'heuristic errors' including: 'representativeness' – ignoring base rates and perceiving a risk as more likely to the extent that characteristics of the risk situation resemble previously familiar risk situations; availability – judging vivid, more easily remembered events as more likely to happen; and anchoring – preferring to maintain the status quo, despite the presentation of new or contrary information (Kahneman, Slovic and Tversky, 1982; Slovic, Fischoff and Lichtenstein, 1982; Tversky and Kahneman, 1974). Therefore, it is worth bearing in mind that when conducting a risk assessment our choice of what to assess and expectations of what we might find will be influenced by past experience. In addition, cognitive bias leaves us open to overestimating or underestimating the likelihood of an event happening and pursuing risks that don't really exist or perhaps a reluctance to change our minds despite the availability of relevant information.

How one describes the risk situation can influence risk judgement. Differing descriptions of the same event, or 'framing', can give rise to different perceptions of risk. For example, describing the same problem in terms of gains or losses produces different appraisals of risk leading to different risk-taking behaviour (Kahneman and Tversky, 1984; Mellers, Schwartz and Cooke, 1998). Similarly, breaking down an event into descriptive components increases the plausibility and perceived likelihood of the event happening (Brenner and Koehler, 1999; Rottenstreich and Tversky, 1997; Tversky and Koehler, 1994), and negative information, which is 'automatically alerting', is given more credence (Skowronski and Carlston, 1989). Familiarity and habit may engender 'unrealistic optimism': the more familiar the task, the higher our perception of control and the less concerned are we about risk (Barnett and Breakwell, 2001; Teigen and Brun, 1997).

There are also motivational and social explanations for bias in risk judgements (Joffe, 2003). Emotions and mood frequently guide decision making (Damasio, 1994; Isen, 1993; Lowenstein, Weber, Hsee and Welch, 2001; Mellers and McGraw, 2001) and motivational issues, such as personal agendas and maintaining self-esteem (Higgins and Bargh, 1987) frequently influence judgement of risk. Janis and Mann's (1977) 'conflict model' of decision making suggests that the ambiguity inherent in everyday decisions results in 'decisional conflict' or psychological distress, which influences the decision maker's choice of response. In general, individuals consciously opt for alternatives which minimize the chance that they will experience later regret (Mellers, Schwartz and Ritov, 1999). As the conflict between various options increases, the decision to avoid making a decision increases (Tversky and Shafir, 1992), with those who opt for the status quo or choose not to make a decision reporting less distress than people who choose other options (Luce, Bettman and Payne, 1997). Tetlock's (2002) social functionalist approach emphasizes the importance of social context, personal values and the individual's understanding of 'reality' on judgement of risk, and how often when making decisions we are conscious of 'doing the right thing' and of how the decision might look to others.

Decision making within service providers is rarely the prerogative of one individual and typically occurs in groups or team meetings. Indeed, where risk assessment is the responsibility of one individual they can feel alone and isolated (Raven and Rix, 1999; Watts, Bindman, Slade, Holloway, et al., 2004). While decision making in groups is seen to be more 'efficient' and fair, offering a greater pool of knowledge, experience and a variety of perspectives (Kreitner, 1998; Tindale, Kameda and Hinsz, 2003), group decision making can also bring disadvantages. When people share the same set of values and are working towards the same goal they can engage in 'groupthink' and ignore new information which may lead to viable alternatives. Groups can be biased towards consensus and the maintenance of teamwork and collaboration may take priority over the needs of service users (Janis, 1982; Tindale et al., 2003; West and Parent, 1992). Also, the status of a group member or the 'vocal few' can exert considerable influence on the decision making process even when presenting a minority viewpoint (Kameda, Ohtsubo and Takezawa, 1997; Kreitner, 1998).

Group bias may be counteracted by appointing a group member as 'critical evaluator' to take the opposing point of view and generate reasons why the decision arrived at might be incorrect (Koriat, Lichtenstein and Fischoff, 1980; Plous, 1993). Presenting the risk situation as a problem to be solved and encouraging group members to think critically rather than simply to reach a consensus leads to enhanced information sharing and decision making (Stasser and Stewart, 1992). Similarly, having groups rank order alternative solutions rather than opting for one solution increases information sharing (Postmes, Spears and Cihangir, 2001). Finally, where resources allow, different groups might be used to explore the same issue (Janis, 1982).

In summary, risk is both a cognitive and emotional response to perceived potential loss. Risk decisions are also influenced by the social and cultural contexts in which they are taken and the social pressure of being seen not to fail. The limitations of cognitive processing means that people rarely consider 'all the evidence' and tend to rely on past experience for a solution. The complexities and ambiguities of the situation can encourage 'groupthink' and leave the individual open to the influence of others. Deciding to take a risk is stressful, though this can be attenuated by increasing levels of benefit. Risk decisions, rather than being 'irrational', are often guided by emotional concerns such as the fear of the unknown and the dread associated with the consequences should things go wrong.

Decision making and intellectual disability

Within the context of a growing requirement for people with intellectual disabilities to make their own decisions it is acknowledged that many have limited competence as a result of cognitive and motivational difficulties and require training and support (Hickson and Khemkha, 1999; Short and Evans, 1990; Tymchuk, Yokota and Rahbar, 1990). Among the difficulties that may be encountered are: (1) a tendency to rely on a limited number of past solutions; (2) a lack of systematic decision-making processes; (3) an impulsive or over-reactive response style; and (4) constantly looking to others for help and guidance rather than acting on the information given (Hickson and Khemkha, 1999).

Despite these drawbacks several effective methods have been developed to assist individuals with problem solving and decision making (Hickson and Khemkha, 1999; Hughes and Rusch, 1989; Sigelman and Budd, 1986; Tymchuk, Yokota and Rahbar, 1990). Attending to behavioural cues that indicate preference (Shevin and Klein, 1984), allowing individuals to proceed at their own pace (Mount, Ducharme and Beeman, 1991), using photographs (March, 1992) and teaching decision making as a sequence of cognitive steps (Powers, Wilson, Matuszewski, Phillips et al., 1996) have been found to improve judgement in adults with intellectual disabilities. Individualized training packages incorporating simulated risk situations along with corrective feedback have been found to be effective in developing coping skills (Loumidis and Hill, 1997; McAfee, 1998). Considerable success has been achieved using personal safety training initiatives (Harper, Hopkinson and McAfee, 2002; Mazzuchelli, 2001), such as training individuals to call for assistance when lost in the community by answering a mobile phone and providing the caller with information about their whereabouts (Taber, Alberto, Hughes and Seltzer, 2002; Taber, Alberto, Seltzer and Hughes, 2003). While it is acknowledged that people with intellectual disabilities have difficulties in decision making, it should be remembered from our discussion above that mainstream judgement of risk is frequently subjective and biased. Moreover, where appropriate training is provided and information adapted to avoid contextual constraints, many of the assumed obstacles to individuals with intellectual disabilities making their own decisions can be overcome.

UNDERSTANDING AND PREVENTING HARM

Understanding how things can go wrong; the complexities and multiple factors contributing to serious incidents, aids proactive decision making and provides for a greater degree of control in managing risk. Reason (1990; 2001) presents a useful framework for discussing the human and systems factors that can contribute to accidents and misfortune. According to Reason adverse events can be classified into three categories: (a) errors and mistakes, usually the result of difficulties in cognitive and decision-making processes; (b) violations, resulting from motivational and morale difficulties; and (c) 'active' and 'latent' failures which are attributable to decisions made higher up the organization.

Information, planning and communication

According to Reason (1990; 2001) errors occur because of either poor planning or the misapplication, or non-application, of planned actions. Thus, even though a risk-management plan may be adequate, risks can occur because the plan was incorrectly executed. Similarly, a good plan may fail as a result of faulty judgement, or the inflexible use of good practice such as a carer blindly following instructions. Problems may also arise from a lack of knowledge or training on the part of the carer, particularly where the person is faced with a novel situation requiring 'on-the-spot' problem solving (Reason, 2001). While many direct care staff working in services for people with intellectual disabilities are unqualified (Hatton, Emerson, Rivers, Mason et al., 1999; 2001), many of these problems could be solved by training staff to support people with intellectual disabilities to take appropriate risks, and by specialized training in the prevention of risk with high-risk groups (Bell and Espie, 2002; Gentry, Iceton and Milne, 2001; Hastings and Brown, 2002; Hill and Dagnan, 2002; Taylor, Keddie and Lee, 2003; Wanless and Jahoda, 2002).

A common source of harm results from the implementation of inadequate plans. A proposed course of action proceeds as planned but fails to achieve the intended outcome because the planned action was based on incorrect or inadequate information in the first place (Reason, 2001). This may be as a result of incorrect assessment or insufficient knowledge of the individual or situation. Information and communication failures are frequently cited as significant contributory factors to accidents and catastrophic events (Edmondson, 1996; Turner and Pidgeon, 1997).

Teamwork

Motivational problems and difficulties in interpersonal relations within staff teams provide a second source of risk (Reason, 2001). Unnecessary risks may be taken where there is poor accountability, and inadequate or insufficient supervision or where staff morale is low (Reason, 2001). Low morale and high stress levels (Allen, Pahl and Quine, 1990; Hatton and Emerson, 1993; Hatton, Brown, Caine and Emerson, 1995) can lead to poor adherence to risk-management plans and inhibit the development of a responsible risk-taking culture within service agencies.

Operational difficulties, such as high rates of staff turnover and recruitment difficulties resulting in poor staffing ratios and inadequate skill mix, influence staff morale and ultimately affect service delivery, particularly for high-risk service users who may have complex needs (Taggart and McConkey, 2001). An overly hierarchical management style, lack of participation in decision making, and a feeling of alienation from the service (possibly as a result of role ambiguity and role conflict) have all been implicated in staff stress, low morale and performance (Allen *et al.*, 1990; Bersani and Heifetz, 1985; Browner, Ellis, Ford, Silsby *et al.*, 1987; Hatton and Emerson, 1993; Hatton *et al.*, 1995; Rose, 1993), and may prompt carers to deviate from safe practices and protocols.

Organizational culture and decision making

In describing the third source of risk, Reason (1990; 2001) makes a distinction between 'active' and 'latent' failures. Active errors tend to happen at the 'sharp end' of service delivery and describe actions which have immediately adverse consequences. Latent errors, on the other hand, occur higher up the organizational chain, usually at senior management level, and can take a long time to surface. On occasion the damaging impact of such decisions (often related to policy or funding constraints) may lie dormant for some time yet set the agenda for the delivery of services at the operational end. Reason (2001) contends that eventually the negative consequences of management decisions create the conditions for unsafe acts. Frequently these unsafe practices go undetected either because the outcomes are insufficiently serious to be brought to the attention of senior staff or because service processes are insufficiently sensitive or robust to pick them up. Reason (1990; 2001) concludes that latent errors pose the greatest threat to safety because they often go unrecognized and have the capacity to result in multiple types of hazard and risk. Similarly, Turner and Pidgeon (1997) attribute accidents to a lack of foresight and insufficient knowledge and information amongst teams, and they point out that mishaps occur as a result of the accumulation of 'trigger events', which are ignored or are at odds with existing beliefs about levels of risk.

In sum, accident and misfortune results from poor information handling and communication, errors in decision making, poor motivation, interpersonal difficulties, and organizational decisions which lie dormant and act as precursors for subsequent mishaps. The implications of Reason's (2001) analysis for the practitioner are that people rarely intend to cause accidents and accidents are rarely caused by a single event. Rather, accidents are the culmination of a series of smaller factors some of which may be latent or go unnoticed for some time. Accidents and 'near misses' are best viewed as a symptom of underlying problems and risk assessment as a process whereby service delivery can be improved and developed.

DECIDING ON AN ACCEPTABLE LEVEL OF RISK

Duty of care

Many of the anxieties associated with risk taking emanate from the tension between allowing individuals with intellectual disability personal autonomy and control over their lives and at the same time taking responsible measures to ensure their safety and the safety of others (Alaszewski *et al.*, 1999). This tension between autonomy and safety is highlighted in 'duty of care'. 'Duty of care' is a key element of the legal concept of negligence (Alaszewski *et al.*, 1999; Carson, 1996; Raven and Rix, 1999; Sellars, 2002). Negligence refers to accountability for decision making. Therefore an important consideration is whether allowing the person to take the risk will increase the likelihood and magnitude of potentially adverse consequences (Carson, 1996).

A duty of care is owed in situations where one can foresee or ought to foresee that taking or failing to take a particular course of action might cause harm (Carson, 1996). Thus one is negligent if one fails to intervene to prevent risk. Should an intellectually disabled individual suffer harm because of a risky decision, then the decision maker(s) may be held negligent and required to compensate the individual for the damage suffered (Carson, 1996). A key issue is whether the decision maker(s) acted in a manner comparable with how others would have acted. Carson (1996) advises that in the course of decision making it is helpful to predict: (1) how your decision might be perceived by others; (2) whether your decision would stand up to analysis in a court of law; and (3) whether the information or value system on which the decision is based is reliable and transparent.

Capacity to consent

A central characteristic of adulthood is being able to give consent on matters that have a direct bearing on one's life. Unfortunately, the argument that people with intellectual disabilities are incapable of giving consent frequently denies them the opportunity to make important life decisions (Lindsey, 1996; Wong, Clare, Gunn and Holland, 1999).

Consent is an important legal concept incorporating three constituent elements: (1) 'capacity': which assumes the ability to make decisions; (2) 'information': which assumes that the person has been fully informed; and (3) 'voluntariness': which implies a person is free to make a decision without coercion (Meisel, Roth and Lidz, 1977; Murphy and Clare, 2003). Until recently capacity to consent was viewed as a general ability to make relevant life decisions based on an assumption about an individual's intellectual ability (Murphy and Clare, 2003). However, as intellectual ability is a poor predictor of capacity to consent, this rather static, global view of capacity has been challenged in favour of a 'functional' approach, which focuses on decision making in relation to specific tasks or situations (Murphy and Clare, 2003). This more fluid concept of consent views capacity as varying within each individual and from situation to situation (Grisso, 1986). Following this approach, capacity to consent should be measured on an individualized basis and according to the extent to which a person understands the risks and benefits associated with specific situations (Dinerstein, Herr and O'Sullivan, 1999).

Where it is assumed that the person with an intellectual disability is incapable of making decisions for themselves, 'proxy' or 'surrogate decision making' is common, with family members and staff making decisions on their behalf. Making decisions on the basis of 'best interest' involves weighing the impact of the risks and benefits in order to minimize harm and maximize potential benefits (Freedman, 2001; Lindsey, 1996; Wong *et al.*, 1999). Among the drawbacks with this approach are misinterpretation, ignoring the individual's wishes, insufficient knowledge or familiarity with the individual, or making decisions on the basis of one's own personal preferences (Freedman, 2001; Muncie, Magaziner, Hebel and Warren, 1997; Warren, Sobal, Tenney, Hoopes, Damron *et al.*, 1986).

It would appear from the research that people with intellectual disabilities are able to understand simplified information and procedures but struggle somewhat in their understanding of the risks and benefits associated with certain courses of action. However, levels of understanding are highly dependent on the manner in which the information is presented, how people are questioned and the nature of the task which individuals are asked to consent to (Arscott, Dagnan and Stenfert Kroese, 1998; Wong, Clare, Holland, Watson and Gunn 2000). The interested reader is referred to Ball, Bush and Emerson (2004), Murphy and Clare (2003) and Dinerstein *et al.* (1999) for an in-depth review of these issues.

IMPLEMENTING A RELIABLE RISK-MANAGEMENT STRATEGY

Principles of risk assessment

1. Promote personal development and safety

Individuals with intellectual disabilities cannot be expected to make decisions and cope with risk if they have not had the learning experiences and opportunity to practise these skills in the first place. Emphasizing what individuals should not do rather than teaching them the adaptive skills necessary to cope with life denies individuals the 'dignity of risk' (Perske, 1972). Self-determination implies 'learning from one's mistakes' and therefore adults with intellectual disabilities should be encouraged to take 'responsible' risks (Wehmeyer, Agran and Hughes, 1998). It is important that individuals are not put at risk from the risk-assessment process itself and that risk-management plans do not become a form of 'policing' but respect the dignity of the individual and adhere to 'least restrictive practice'. Indeed, levels of risk taking and how risk taking is managed within service agencies should be regarded as an indicator of quality of life (Manthorpe *et al.* 1997).

2. Take a long-term view of risk

An important goal of risk assessment is to focus on obtaining better outcomes for individuals and improved quality of life. The extent to which this is achieved will vary depending on whether the purpose of the risk assessment is to minimize risk or encourage risk taking (Turner, 2000). It is important therefore to clarify the impact that 'taking a risk' may have on the individual's future actions or decisions and long-term quality of life. It is advisable continually to question and review the purpose of the risk assessment on a regular basis.

3. Conduct a thorough and detailed assessment

Practitioners should obtain detailed and accurate accounts of the person's developmental history and in particular details of previous risk incidents or problematic situations, using as many sources as possible to obtain quality information (Blumenthal and Lavender, 2000; Kemshall, 2001; Monahan, 1993). Be mindful of contextual factors and possible 'triggers' for risk behaviours.

4. Systematically record and communicate findings

While it is important to guard against risk assessment becoming a form-filling exercise, clearly recording information supporting a decision to take or not take a risk and a lucid enunciation of the reasoning and conclusions behind the decision are strongly advised (Blumenthal and Lavender, 2000; Kemshall, 2001; Monahan, 1993).

5. Work as part of a risk-assessment team

Risk assessment is not the sole responsibility of one profession or individual but should be conducted by teams. A prerequisite is high-quality team-work (Raven and Rix, 1999). An agreed vision of what must be achieved and coordination of effort and resources is an important element of the risk-management approach. Moreover, inter- and intra-agency liaison and cooperation is crucial to successful risk management.

6. Involve service users at each stage of the assessment process

It is imperative that service users are involved at each stage of the assessment process and are communicated with on a regular and consistent basis. Encourage service users to keep in contact with their service agency and/or statutory authorities, particularly where individuals have additional needs or are deemed to be high-risk (Blumenthal and Lavender, 2000; Kemshall, 2001; Monahan, 1993).

7. Involve relatives and family members in the assessment process

The involvement of stakeholders – such as family members and carers – is critical to implementing sound, informed decisions and is a crucial element in managing risk. Families and staff cannot be expected to comply with plans unless they fully understand and are involved in the process; therefore it is advisable, early on in the process, to establish how communication will be handled, so that stakeholders' views about the risks as they see them can be constantly checked and monitored.

8. *Continually assess and reassess what could go wrong*

Risk management should be proactive, ideally integrated into daily activities and person-centred planning (Sellars, 2002; Turner, 2000). Limiting risk assessment as a response to 'critical incidents' results in a minimization approach to risk and ultimately to restrictive practices (Davis, 1995; Turner, 2000). Also, risk management should be a dynamic process. Situations can change rapidly and new information or different perspectives emerge during any stage of the risk-management process. Tracking and monitoring these changes is vital. Therefore, each stage of the process should be constantly revisited, particularly in the light of new findings. In this way the risk-management process can be recursive and sensitive to changing circumstances (Sellars, 2002).

9. *Ensure that sufficient resources are available to manage the risk*

It is important to ensure that sufficient resources are available for managing the identified risks. In some instances resources may be needed to develop service-user coping skills. Similarly, considerable resources should be concentrated on staff training and support, in particular training to assess and manage risks (Blumenthal and Lavender, 2000).

10. *Encourage a responsible risk-taking culture*

A responsible risk-taking culture is open-minded about possibilities, aware of potential bias, carefully assesses and acts upon information, complies with the statutory regulations and communicates emergent dangers.

Risk-management guidelines

Kaplan and Garrick (1981) state that the goal of a risk assessment is to answer the following questions: 'What can go wrong?' 'How likely is it to happen?' 'And if it does happen what are the consequences?' This section provides general guidelines for risk management with people with intellectual disabilities and borrows from the work of Allen (2002), Sellars (2002) and Calder (2002). While an attempt has been made to cover all aspects of the risk continuum, the guidelines are offered as a starting point; general advice which may be adapted to suit a variety of risk situations.

Haimes (1998) suggests that fundamentally risk assessment is a form of systems analysis and lays out the following steps in the systems approach:

1 Identify the problem
2 Determine the objectives and goals of the analysis

3 Become familiar with the total problem environment
4 Analyse the associated risks
5 Identify feasible solutions
6 Evaluate the cost and benefits of the solutions
7 Communicate the solutions to clients and stakeholders
8 Make decisions about the adequacy of the options and preferred options
9 Implement the selected solution
10 Conduct an evaluation of the risk-management plan
11 Implement the revised plan.

Step 1: identify the problem

Kinsella (2000) stresses the importance of gaining clarity around the perceived risk(s) (what's happening, why it might be happening, and the consequences), so that everyone agrees on the issues. Defining risk entails capturing the context of the risk: the what, when, where, and how, and ensuring that all the routines and actions typically associated with the risk situation are considered (Allen, 2002; Sellars, 2002). Also, consideration should be given not only to risks to the individual but also to the potential risks they may pose to others (Sellars, 2002). Record and consider each issue separately defining each problem in one short simple sentence. This helps improve focus and aids understanding of the problem (see Box 26.1).

Box 26.1 Identifying the risks

- What can happen?
- How can it happen?
- Where might it happen?
- When might it happen?
- Who is at risk?
- Are there any historical or current antecedents?
- Are there any risk triggers?

Step 2: determine the objectives of the risk assessment

Risk assessment can have a variety of purposes including: the development of action plans to prevent harm; teaching an individual additional coping skills to deal with a risk situation; or reviewing the adequacy of current risk management strategies. Therefore it is important to determine the purpose and scope of the assessment and to agree on how the assessment will be conducted. In addition, it is helpful at this stage to identify the main stakeholders; establish the risk-management team; describe procedures for how the assessment will be conducted; and to define the context in which the risk assessment is to take place. Key questions to be addressed at this stage are given in Box 26.2.

Box 26.2 Establishing the goals

- What does the risk assessment hope to achieve?
- What are the main objectives of the assessment process?
- What outcomes are expected and how will we know when we have achieved them?
- Who are the key stakeholders?
- Who will attend risk-management team meetings?
- Are there any additional formal assessments to be included in the overall risk assessment (e.g. psychological or actuarial, medical, speech and language, occupational therapy assessments etc.)?

Step 3: familiarize yourself with the total problem environment

Conduct an audit of the service agency, care team, family and situational factors that may contribute to vulnerability and risk. Each domain to be assessed is outlined in Box 26.3.

A contextual analysis of the risk also involves an assessment of benefits as in the exposure to factors which will enhance personal development and life skills. An examination of benefits acknowledges that some exposure to risk is necessary for personal development and avoids focusing exclusively on hazards and dangers. Make a list of the potential benefits the person

---

Box 26.3 Assessing situational factors

- Service agency factors (e.g. policy, resources, management attitudes and values, poor accountability and supervisory systems, resource deficits)
- Individual staff and team factors (e.g. inexperienced or untrained staff, attitudes, morale and motivation, poor communication, poor record-keeping)
- Environmental and situational factors (e.g. carers' attitudes, supportive relationships and neighbourhood support, domestic circumstances, geographical location)

---

would gain from participating in the activity, for example enhancement of quality of life and self-esteem, enjoyment and pleasure, less time spent engaging in behaviours which challenge, skills development, and so forth (Sellars, 2002). Key questions to be addressed in assessing benefits are given in Box 26.4.

Box 26.4 Assessing potential benefits

- What will the person gain from the experience that requires the risk to be taken?
- How likely is it that this experience will be useful or pleasurable to the person?
- What would be the consequences for the person if the proposed course of action was not taken?
- What would be the effects on their overall quality of life and emotional well-being?
- What consequences would it have for the person's behaviour and sense of control over their own life?
- Does the likelihood of harm outweigh the benefit?
- What would you choose for yourself, or for members of your family?
- What do colleagues feel they would choose?

Step 4: analyse the risks

A central purpose of risk assessment is to identify the key risk factors: the existence of threats and degree of vulnerability. As mentioned in step 3, vulnerabilities are individual weaknesses that could be exploited or result in harm. Threat refers to any external indication of imminent harm.

Develop an in-depth profile of the person by compiling a list of strengths, weaknesses, preferences, communication methods and personality characteristics. A variety of methods can be used, such as reviewing written records; conducting structured interviews; and observing the individual's behaviour. Where at all possible, the use of formal or actuarial assessment measures should be employed as the measurement of risk factors enhances accuracy in forecasting the likelihood of risk (Crighton, 2005). Carefully examine the individual's current and past behaviour in terms of both potential risks to themselves and risks to others. Note that the absence of information does not mean an absence of risk (Sellars, 2002). Box 26.5 contains a list of important questions to be addressed in assessing personal risk factors.

Having identified the factors that contribute to a potential risk, including personal characteristics, human errors and external events, the professional's

---

Box 26.5 Assessing personal risk factors

- Are there any particular attributes or personal needs which make the individual particularly vulnerable? (e.g. skills and abilities, communication, behavioural history)
- What are the past and current events indicating risk vulnerability?
- Are there any personal attributes or strengths which make the individual potentially able to cope?
- Are there actuarial measures or formal assessments that can be used to provide a baseline risk appraisal?
- To what degree is the individual themselves aware of the likely risks and outcomes? Can the individual weigh up the costs and benefits of this particular risk?

---

next step is to estimate the level of threat or how likely the risk is to occur. Determining whether a situation is low, moderate, or high risk is a complex decision-making process which requires predicting the likelihood or probability of the risk occurring. Such predictions are based on a consideration of the vulnerabilities and threats associated with the proposed activity or situation and consideration of the potential impact of the outcomes, including the amount and type of harm and/or benefits.

Threat refers to the level of probability associated with the occurrence of harm. The level of threat is assessed by addressing each potential weakness in turn and estimating the probability that it could be exploited and assessing the impact or the severity of outcomes should harm occur. While each vulnerability and associated level of threat are assessed and ranked independently of each other, the overall risk of harm is frequently the result of the interaction of all the factors present. For some risks, though the probability of occurrence may be low, exposure to the risk could have devastating effects. Similarly, although some risks may initially have only a small-scale impact they can have major effects in the long term, and the presence of several factors in the moderate risk range might, together, result in a high-risk situation for the individual. Mitigating factors should also be considered as the presence of one strong mitigating or safety factor may reduce a high risk to a low-risk situation. Identifying and making explicit those positive behaviours, which complement the more harmful, high-risk behaviours, guards against simply equating risk with danger and helps focus on the relevant safety factors that can be strengthened to mitigate risk.

Step 5: identify feasible solutions for addressing the risks

Examination of the options for addressing the risks focuses on determining the level and type of support needed in order for the person to participate safely in the targeted activity. Tasks at this stage of the process include determining the risk-management strategy and developing detailed action plans (see Box 26.6).

Box 26.6 Developing risk-management options

- Can any action be taken to reduce the impact of the outcome if problems do occur?
  - Environmental precautions: when will be the best time to do it?
  - Person's mood: does risk vary with the person's mood? If so how can things be arranged to suit them and ensure success?
- What can support staff do? How can staff keep the person calm? How can potential 'triggers' be avoided?
- Is there any equipment or materials that would help distract or relax the person or make the situation safer should they become upset?
- How can staff seek help quickly if they need to?
- Person's physical health/abilities: do any physical problems need to be tackled to reduce the risks associated with the activity?
- What will be the response should an incident occur? Try to cover all reasonable probabilities and consider the following: what will support staff do? If appropriate how would you remove the person from the dangerous situation? How would you deal with members of the public and whose responsibility would it be to do so?
- How will you respond later? You may need to take into consideration: would you need to speak to the individual following an incident? Would you need to have any further contact with the public following the incident? How would you inform other stakeholders about what has happened?

Step 6: evaluate the costs and benefits of the plan

This stage of the assessment process is important as it involves deciding on the acceptability of risk and whether the impact of possible negative outcomes can be sufficiently curtailed to allow the benefits of risk taking to accrue. Potential barriers to successful implementation such as human error and the impact of policy or management decisions on the proposed course of action will also need to be carefully reconsidered at this stage of the assessment. It would be important to ascertain if there are any further environmental or attitudinal constraints that may interfere with the realization of the targeted goal and to discuss with the team how these can be minimized. It may be necessary to develop further contingency plans to deal with these secondary problems. Also at this stage it is advisable to identify any residual or unmanaged risk, as all risks cannot be eliminated and no risk-management plan can cover all eventualities (Allen, 2002).

Step 7: communicate the solutions to the client and stakeholders

Communication is a crucial element in the risk-assessment process. It is essential that information around risk be communicated consistently and on a regular basis to all stakeholders. Relevant information needs to be sifted from the mass of data and opinion and 'warnings' or triggers for behaviour acted upon.

Good record-keeping is a prerequisite for any risk-assessment process and a system for documentation and tracking risk decisions should be implemented (Raven and Rix, 1999). Documentation should include as a minimum: descriptions of the risk, including the contributory factors and contingency plans to support the person; the consequences should an undesired event occur with an estimate of the likelihood of occurrence; information about the effectiveness of any implemented plans and actions; the measures to prevent or mitigate the risk and a clear statement regarding the acceptability or unacceptability of the risk with a supporting rationale for the decision. In addition, the risk-management documentation should clearly identify who is responsible for what, and specify dates for the implementation of action plans and a date for review. (see Box 26.7).

In addition, before proceeding with the plan, agreement must be reached on assigning and delegating responsibility for tasks, and arrangements put in

---

Box 26.7 Transparent decision making

- How would this decision appear to other practitioners, and would they reach a similar consensus?
- Has the decision been made on the basis of an appropriate risk assessment?
- Is the reasoning process and decision framework explicit?
- Can the decisions be justified and backed up by evidence?
- Have all stages of the decision-making process been carefully recorded?

place for all necessary supports to be made available in the most appropriate and unobtrusive way.

Step 8: decide on the manageability of the risk

When considering whether to proceed with risk taking, three alternatives for action are available: one can proceed with the proposed course of action and implement the risk-management plan; delay action to review the situation and evaluate matters further; or simply do nothing (Watts, 1995). Whether one proceeds with risk taking depends on the acceptability of the risk, the degree of support built into the risk-management plan and the robustness of contingency plans.

Kinsella (2000) suggests that priority should be given to risk-management decisions which maximize the safety and the happiness of the person based on the following criteria: (a) where the prospect for happiness is high and safety high, always proceed with the proposed course of action; (b) where happiness is high but safety low – proceed only if the person and all stake-holders agree the risk is worth taking and danger is minimal; (c) where the prospect for happiness is low and safety high, proceed only if the person or others are in real danger; (d) finally, obviously one should not proceed in situations where happiness is predicted to be low and safety low.

Step 9: implement the plan

The plan should be implemented as agreed with attention to key elements, responsibilities of key participants, communication among involved parties and for a specified period of time.

Step 10: evaluate the effectiveness of risk-management plan

The impact of taking the risk and the effectiveness of the risk-management strategy is evaluated to determine whether the risk-management plans supported the individual in achieving their goals and in particular whether the agreed course of action had a noticeable effect on the person's quality of life (see Box 26.8).

It is at this stage of the process that critical or untoward incidents are reported and the risk-assessment process reactivated from step 4 onwards. Should an incident occur it is important to establish with those members of the team directly involved, what happened, how it happened and why the incident happened. When investigating incidents, Reason's (2001) multiple causation model of how accidents take place can be used as a framework for analysis and discussion (Vincent and Taylor-Adams, 2001). In addition, there are a number of general contributory factors which are regarded as being responsible for poor risk-management implementation (Blumenthal

Box 26.8 Evaluating risk-management plans

- How many times did the activity take place?
- What benefits did the person gain?
- Did any of the potential risks occur? If so describe what happened.
- Was it possible to apply the agreed measures to minimize the risk?
- How well did they work? Did the measures significantly affect the benefits of the activity?
- Are there any changes, which need to be made to the approach taken? If so, what are they?
- Is the person going to continue with the activity in the future?
- When will risk levels associated with the activity be next evaluated?

Box 26.9 Possible contributory factors to poor risk management

- Failing to acknowledge bias
- Basing judgements on too little information
- Failing to obtain historical records
- Poor communication
- Failing to take 'trigger' and warning signs seriously
- Failing to set aside sufficient time for discussion and planning
- Poor problem formulation
- Failing to investigate discrepancies in observations and information
- Poor teamwork and low morale
- Failing to revise and re-evaluate actions and contingencies in the light of new information
- Poor staff training
- Failing to keep accurate records
- Poor staff supervision and accountability
- Devoting insufficient time to the process

and Lavender, 2000; Lipsedge 2001; Munro, 1999; Reed, 1997; Snowden, 1997; Watts *et al.*, 2004). These are outlined in Box 26.9.

Step 11: reactivate the revised risk-management plan

Risk management is a recursive process. Where further episodes of risky behaviour occur, the process described above may be repeated with revised risk-management plan which takes into account new information gained during the implementation of the original risk-management plan.

SUMMARY AND CONCLUSION

The majority of daily events carry the potential for some kind of danger or risk. This uncertainty prompts us to try to understand and manage risk. However, many of these attempts are guesswork. For if we knew for certain we would not be dealing with risk (Adams, 1995). Risk is a subjective construct influenced by a variety of personal, group and societal factors. Similarly, decisions around risk taking with people with intellectual disabilities are not developed in a vacuum but are bound up with societal and cultural factors, such as the views of the media, political policy and service culture, all of which influence carers' judgements of risk (Joffe, 2003; Slovic, 1996).

According to Joffe (2003) groups develop their own consensual understanding of risk on the basis of shared historical knowledge and current experiences. Perceptions of risk are not simply cognitive phenomena but incorporate social, emotional and symbolic factors. Social representations and perceptions of risk evolve from the social interactions between individuals, groups and society as a whole. People do not simply process information, but seek meaning through questions and answers about their experiences and the events which happen to them. Thus risk should be regarded as a way of making sense of difficult emotionally laden situations and resistance to risk taking viewed as a means of coping with ambiguity and socially sensitive issues (Joffe, 2003).

Two major factors help explain our perceptions and tolerance for risk: dread and novelty (Slovic, 1992). It would appear that for the majority of people with intellectual disabilities the challenge to practitioners is one of encouraging individuals to take more control over their lives (Wehmeyer, 1998). In the main this control is in the hands of others who are naturally fearful of 'letting go' or feel constrained by legal considerations. It may be that this reluctance to take risks is related more to the severity of the consequences and the novelty of risk taking rather than to 'risk' *per se*. For instance, because of the severe penalties imposed, modern health and social care services are becoming increasingly preoccupied with managing dangers and hazards (Allen, 2002; Walshe, 2001). Unfortunately, overemphasizing risk may raise professional and service-based anxieties to such an extent that risk avoidance becomes a central organizing principle of service providers (Sykes, 2005). Where risk is strongly associated with danger and harmful outcomes, risk management is driven by concerns to protect individuals and organizations from threats and misfortune (Calder, 2002; Douglas, 1992; Green, 1997; Kettles, 2004; Sykes, 2005; Walshe, 2001). The result is increased organizational defensiveness and a preference for the legally defensible rather than the right decision, stymieing opportunities for personal development (Kemshall, Parton, Walsh and Waterson, 1997). Within such a culture, risk is seen as something intrinsic to people with intellectual disabilities that must be managed or minimized. Thus, a major challenge to practitioners is to avoid risk assessment becoming yet another means of controlling the lives of people with intellectual disabilities.

Undoubtedly, intellectually disabled individuals (like us all) are prone to bad decision making and engage in risky behaviours which should be avoided. However, because risk has to be controlled it does not mean that a culture of control should dominate over a culture of opportunity (Manthorpe *et al.*, 1997). Sykes (2005) has alluded to the rigid responses of services to needs and a culture of risk overriding individuals' rights. Accident and misfortune are an inevitable part of life and tolerance for an acceptable and responsible level of risk taking is an important and healthy element of service culture. A totally rational approach to risk management in which all negative incidents are predictable and can be eliminated or controlled is not possible (Raven and Rix, 1999). Sykes (2005) suggests that acknowledging that risk is an inherent part of human development best offsets this creeping encroachment of control. Proper management of the tension between risk and rights requires an acceptance that service delivery is a risky business and that carers need to be trained to support service users in risk taking in conjunction with quality risk assessment, which are best achieved through building relationships with service users and employing reflective practice (Sykes, 2005). Therefore of central concern to practitioners should be the extent to which service agencies are creating the right environment for responsible risk taking.

While risk means different things to different people, taking risks is essential for personal development and learning. Risk is as much about gaining benefits and opening up opportunities as about hazards and loss; taking action for the purpose of gaining benefits during which harmful or unintended consequences may occur (Alaszewki and Manthorpe, 1991; Calder, 2002; Fischoff *et al.*, 1981; Heason, Stracey and Rey, 2001; Sellars, 2002; Teigen and Brun, 1997; Wharton, 1992). Therefore, rather than concentrating solely on what might go wrong, considerable weight should be placed on identifying the necessary interventions and training required by the individual and their carers and the resources necessary to achieve goals safely and responsibly. Risk should not be seen as integral to disability but to the likelihood and level of outcome, and the purpose of risk assessment should be to support choice and self-determination. Indeed, how one defines risk determines how one assesses and manages risk (Sykes, 2005).

In addition to balancing the tension between autonomy and control, a further challenge to practitioners is gaining agreement around the nature of risk and how best to assess risk levels. It must be acknowledged that a sizeable minority of individuals with intellectual disabilities engage in seriously problematic behaviour and present as a significant threat both to themselves and to the wider community. In analysing the probability of risk, obviously the characteristics of the service user must be taken into account. In addition, familiarity with individuals and situations and an overestimate of levels of control may lead to complacency and a lack of vigilance. There is an urgent need to develop evidence-based measures to assist practitioners in predicting risk and developing appropriate management strategies for this population. In the meantime, it is hoped that we can move away from reactive approaches to risk towards more structured and transparent decision-making processes (Carson, 1996; Turner, 2000).

A further consideration for the practitioner is the importance of teamwork and communication in risk-management initiatives. A number of authors have highlighted the importance of good planning and communication in avoiding risks and have emphasized that accidents and harm rarely occur in isolation. Negative outcomes are the product of an accumulation of multiple factors including 'trigger' incidents that go unnoticed, underlying problems and decisions which are disregarded as having implications for safety, poor teamwork and accountability, and breakdowns in communication (Reason, 1999; 2001; Turner and Pidgeon, 1997). In addition, policy implementation and the operational and strategic decisions of management will have a direct bearing on how care teams operate and families relate to the service agency, with agencies affected by government policy and the availability of economic resources (Vincent and Taylor-Adams, 2001).

Finally, risk assessment is limited to reducing not eliminating uncertainties (Green, 1997) and risk-assessment guidelines are simply helpful in maintaining a structured and transparent approach to decision making. Unfortunately there is always the danger of creating a false air of validity, or of using risk assessments in a mechanistic or purely administrative manner (Sellars, 2002). One must guard against the danger that guidelines can contribute to an illusion of a single answer for a complex problem and the practitioner should remember that risk-management guidelines can never cover all the decisions that practitioners have to make in the course of professional practice (Berg, 1997; Schon, 1991). When managing risk one must avoid narrow approaches which concentrate solely on just one aspect of the risk situation. Risk-management approaches which simply concentrate on risk assessment, while failing to empower people with intellectual disabilities, or on implementing policy and guidelines in the absence of staff training are doomed to failure.

EXERCISES

Training goal

To develop an awareness of how risk is perceived in organizations and service agencies.

Exercises

1   Attend a person-centered planning meeting. Identify potential areas of risk. What is the nature of these risks? Is the perception of risk influenced by the person's level of vulnerability; the motivation and capability of staff; parental or carer attitude or the potential legal consequences of a hazard for the service agency?
2   Talk to colleagues, people with intellectual disabilities, care staff and parents about their perceptions of risk.
3   Contact local health, social and service agencies. Engage in discussion around risk policy, risk management and how their organization deals with emergencies. Are there differences between agencies?

Training goal

To develop an awareness of how decisions are arrived at within organizations.

Exercises

1   Attend a planning or team meeting. Observe the quality of information and how the information is presented to the group. Look for sources of bias. What are your own biases and blind-spots?
2   Review local risk-management policies. Put yourself in the shoes of a member of the care staff. How 'user friendly' and informative is the documentation? How relevant is it to the lives of service users? What steps have been taken within the documentation to balance empowerment and protection?
3   Observe how risk is assessed. Does the assessment process inform the risk-management process?

Training goal

To develop an awareness of the risk-assessment and risk-management process.

Exercise

1   In small groups brainstorm potential areas of risk for people with intellectual disabilities. Develop case studies. Group members should identify goals and strategies for risk management systematically working through each of the eleven steps outlined in the managing-risk guidelines outlined above.

FURTHER READING

Alaszewski, H., Parker, A. and Alaszewski, A. (1999). *Empowerment and Protection*. Glagow: The Mental Health Foundation.
The British Institute of Learning Disabilities (2001). *Code of Practice for Trainers in Physical Interventions*. Kidderminster: BILD.
Carson, D. and Bull R. (2003). *Handbook of Psychology in Legal Contexts* (2nd edn). Chichester: John Wiley and Sons.
Mikkelsen, E.J. and Spelk, W.J. (1999). *Criminal Offenders with Mental Retardation: Risk Assessment and the Continuum of Community-Based Treatment Programs*. Kingston, New York: NADD Press.
Royal College of Psychiatrists (1998). *Management of Imminent Violence – Clinical Practice Guidelines: Quick Reference Guide*. London: Royal College of Psychiatrists.
Sellars, C. (2002). *Risk Assessment in People with Learning Disabilities*. Oxford: Blackwell Publishing.
Thompson, D. and Brown, H. (1998). *Responsibility: Helping Services to Work with Men with Learning Disabilities Who Have Unacceptable or Abusive Sexual Behaviours*. Brighton: Pavilion Publishing.

REFERENCES

Adams, J. (1995). *Risk*. London: UCL Press.
Alaszewski, A. and Alaszewski, H. (2002). Towards the creative management of risk: perceptions, practices and policies. *British Journal of Learning Disabilities*, 30, 56–62.
Alaszewski, A. and Manthorpe, J. (1991). Welfare agencies and risk: The missing link? *Health and Social Care in the Community*, 6, 4–15.
Alaszewski, H., Parker, A. and Alaszewski, A. (1999). *Empowerment and Protection*. London: Mental Health Foundation.
Allen, D. (2000). Recent research on physical aggression in persons with intellectual disability: An overview. *Journal of Intellectual and Developmental Disability*, 25, 41–57.
Allen, D. (2001). Success and failure in community placements for people with learning disabilities and challenging behaviour: An analysis of key variables. *Journal of Intellectual and Developmental Disability*, 26, 243–56.
Allen, D. (2002). Devising individualised risk management plans. In David Allen (ed.), *Ethical Approaches to Physical Interventions: Responding to Challenging Behaviour in People with Intellectual Disability* (pp. 71–88). Kidderminster: BILD.
Allen, D. (2004). Ethical approaches to physical interventions: Responding to challenging behaviour in people with intellectual disabilities. *Journal of Applied Research in Intellectual Disabilities*, 17, 227–8.
Allen, P., Pahl, J. and Quine, L. (1990). *Care Staff in Transition*. London: HMSO.
Arscott, K., Dagnan, D. and Stenfert Kroese, B. (1998). Consent to psychological research by people with an intellectual disability. *Journal of Applied Research in Intellectual Disabilities*, 11, 77–83.
Ball, T., Bush, A. and Emerson, E. (2004). *Challenging Behaviours: Psychological*

Interventions for Severely Challenging Behaviours Shown by People with Learning Disabilities: Clinical Practice Guidelines. Leicester: The British Psychological Society. (Also available at http://www.bps.org.uk/sub-syst/dcp/publications.cfm)

Barnett, J. and Breakwell, G.M. (2001). Risk perception and experience: Hazard personality profiles and individual differences. *Risk Analysis*, 21, 171–7.

Bell, D. and Espie, C. (2002). A preliminary investigation into job satisfaction, and staff emotions and attitudes in a unit for men with learning disabilities and serious challenging behaviour. *British Journal of Learning Disabilities*, 30, 19–27.

Berg, M. (1997). Problems and promises of the protocol. *Social Science and Medicine*, 44, 1081–8.

Bersani, H.A. and Heifetz, L.J. (1985). Perceived stress and satisfaction of direct-care staff members in community residences for mentally retarded adults. *American Journal of Mental Deficiency*, 90, 289–95.

Blumenthal, S. and Lavender, T. (2000). *Violence and Mental Disorder: A Critical Aid to Assessment and Management of Risk.* London: Jessica Kingsley Publishers.

Boer, D.P., Tough, S. and Haven, J. (2004). Assessment of risk manageability of intellectually disabled sex offenders. *Journal of Applied Research in Intellectual Disabilities*, 17, 275–83.

Brenner, L.A. and Koehler, D.J. (1999). Subjective probability of disjunctive hypotheses: Local-weight models for decomposition of evidential support. *Cognitive Psychology*, 38, 16–47.

Browner, C.H., Ellis, K.A., Ford, T., Silsby, J., Tampoya, J. and Yee, C. (1987). Stress, social support, and health of psychiatric technicians in a state facility. *Mental Retardation*, 25, 31–8.

Brun, W. (1994). Risk perception: Main issues, approaches and findings. In G. Wright, and P. Ayton (eds), *Subjective Probability* (pp. 295–320). Chichester: Wiley.

Calder, M. (2002). A framework for conducting risk assessment. *Child Care in Practice*, 8, 7–18.

Carson, D. (1996). Risking legal repercussions. In H. Kemshall and J. Pritchard (eds), *Good Practice in Risk Assessment and Risk Management* (vol. 1, pp. 3–12). London: Jessica Kingsley Publishers.

Crighton, D. (2005). Risk assessment. In David Crighton and Graham Towl (eds), *Psychology in Probation Services* (pp. 52–66). Oxford: BPS-Blackwell.

Damasio, A.R. (1994). *Descartes' Error: Emotion Reason and the Human Brain.* New York: Grosset-Putnam.

Davis, A. (1995). Risk work and mental health. In H. Kemshall and J. Pritchard (eds), *Good Practice in Risk Assessment and Risk Management* (pp. 109–20). London: Jessica Kingsley.

Dawes, R. M., Faust, D. and Meehl, P. E. (1989). Clinical versus actuarial judgment. *Science*, 243, 1668–74.

Dinerstein, R.D., Herr, S.S. and O'Sullivan, J.L. (1999). *A Guide to Consent.* Washington, DC: AAMR.

Douglas, M. (1992). *Risk and Blame.* London: Routledge.

Edmondson, A.C. (1996). Learning from mistakes is easier said than done: Group and organisational influences on the detection and correction of human error. *Journal of Applied Behavioural Science*, 32, 5–28.

Emerson, E. (2001). *Challenging Behaviour: Analysis and Intervention in People with Intellectual Disabilities* (2nd edn). Cambridge: Cambridge University Press.

Emerson, E., Robertson, J., Gregory, N., Hatton, C., Kessissoglou, S., Hallam, A. and Hillery, J. (2000). Treatment and management of challenging behaviours in residential settings. *Journal of Applied Research in Intellectual Disabilities*, 13, 197–215.

Fischoff, B., Lichtenstein, S., Slovic, P., Derby, S.L. and Keeney, R.L. (1981). *Acceptable Risk*. New York: Cambridge University Press.

Fischoff, B., Slovic, P. and Lichtenstein, S. (1977). Knowing with certainty: The appropriateness of extreme confidence. *Journal of Experimental Psychology: Human Perception and Performance*, 3, 552–64.

Freedman, R.I. (2001). Ethical challenges in the conduct of research involving persons with mental retardation. *Mental Retardation*, 39, 130–41.

Gale, T.M., Woodward, A., Hawley, C.J., Hayes, J., Sivakumaran, T. and Hansen, G. (2002). Risk assessment for people with mental health problems: A pilot study of reliability in working practice. *International Journal of Psychiatry in Clinical Practice*, 6, 73–81.

Gentry, M., Iceton, J. and Milne, D. (2001). Managing challenging behaviour in the community: Methods and results of interactive staff training. *Health and Social Care in the Community*, 9, 143–50.

Giddens, A. (1991). *Modernity and Self Identity: Self and Society in the Late Modern Age*. Cambridge: Polity Press.

Green, J. (1997). *Risk and Misfortune*. London: UCL Press.

Grisso, T. (1986). *Evaluating Competencies: Forensic Assessments and Instruments*. New York: Plenum Press.

Haimes, Y.Y. (1998). *Risk Modelling, Assessment and Management*. New York: Wiley.

Halstead, S. (1997). Risk assessment and management in psychiatric practice: Inferring predictors of risk. A view from learning disability. *International Review of Psychiatry*, 9, 217–24.

Hammond, K. (1996). *Human Judgement and Social Policy*. Oxford: Oxford University Press.

Harper, G., Hopkinson, P. and McAfee, J.G. (2002). Protective behaviours: A useful approach in working with people with learning disabilities. *British Journal of Learning Disabilities*, 30, 149–52.

Harris, A.J.R. and Tough, S. (2004). Should actuarial risk assessments be used with sex offenders who are intellectually disabled? *Journal of Applied Research in Intellectual Disabilities*, 17, 235–41.

Harris, J. (1996). Physical restraint procedures for managing challenging behaviour presented by mentally retarded adults and children. *Research in Developmental Disabilities*, 17, 99–134.

Harris, J. (2003). Time to make up your mind: Why choosing is difficult. *British Journal of Learning Disabilities*, 31, 3–8.

Harris, J., Allen, D., Cornick, M., Jefferson, A. and Mills, R. (1996). *Physical Interventions: A Policy Framework*. Kidderminster: BILD Publications.

Hastings, R. and Brown, T. (2002). Behavioural knowledge, causal beliefs and self efficacy as predictors of special educators' emotional reactions to challenging behaviours. *Journal of Intellectual Disability Research*, 46, 144–50.

Hatton, C. and Emerson, E. (1993). Organizational predictors of staff stress, satisfaction, and intended turnover in a service for people with multiple disabilities. *Mental Retardation*, 31, 388–95.

Hatton, C., Brown, R., Caine, A. and Emerson, E. (1995). Stressors, coping strategies and stress related outcomes among direct care staff in staffed houses for people with learning disabilities. *Mental Handicap Research*, 8, 252–71.

Hatton, C., Emerson, E., Rivers, M., Mason, H., Mason, L. *et al.* (1999). Factors associated with staff stress and work satisfaction in services for people with intellectual disability. *Journal of Intellectual Disability Research*, 43, 253–67.

Hatton, C., Emerson, E., Rivers, M., Mason, H., Swarbrick, R. *et al.* (2001). Factors associated with intended staff turnover and job search behaviour in services for people with intellectual disability. *Journal of Intellectual Disability Research*, 45, 258–70.

Heason, C., Stracey, L. and Rey, D. (2001). Valued occupation for people who have a learning disability. In J. Thompson and S. Pickering (eds), *Meeting the Health Needs of People who have a Learning Disability* (pp.195–210). London: Balliere-Tindall.

Heyman, B. and Huckle S. (1993). Normal life in a hazardous world: How adults with moderate learning difficulties and their carers cope with risks and dangers. *Disability, Handicap and Society*, 8, 143–60.

Heyman, B., Swain, J. and Gillman, M. (1998). A risk management dilemma: How day centre staff understand challenging behaviour. *Disability and Society*, 13, 163–82.

Hickson, L. and Khemkha, I. (1999). Decision-making and mental retardation. *International Review of Research in Mental Retardation*, 22, 227–65.

Higgins, E.T. and Bargh, J.A. (1987). Social cognition and social perception. *Annual Review of Psychology*, 38, 369–425.

Hill, C. and Dagnan, D. (2002). Helping attributions, emotions and coping styles in response to people with learning disabilities and challenging behaviour. *Journal of Learning Disabilities*, 6, 363–72.

Hughes, C. and Rusch, R. (1989). Teaching supported employees with severe mental retardation to solve problems. *Journal of Applied Behaviour Analysis*, 22, 365–72.

Isen, A.M. (1993). Positive affect and decision-making In M. Lewis and J.M. Haviland (eds), *Handbook of Emotions* (pp. 261–77). New York: Guilford.

Janis, I.L. (1982). *Groupthink: Psychological Studies of Policy Decisions and Fiascos.* Boston, MA: Houghton Mifflin.

Janis, I.L. and Mann, L. (1977). *Decision Making: A Psychological Analysis of Conflict, Choice and Commitment.* New York: The Free Press.

Jenkins, R., Rose, J. and Lovell, C. (1997). Psychological well-being of staff working with people who have challenging behaviour. *Journal of Intellectual Disability Research*, 41, 502–11.

Jenkinson, J. (1993). Who shall decide? The relevance of theory and research to decision-making by people with an intellectual disability. *Disability, Handicap and Society*, 8, 361–74.

Joffe, H. (2003). Risk: From perception to social representation. *British Journal of Psychology*, 42(1), 55–73.

Johnston, S.J. (2002). Risk Assessment in offenders with intellectual disability: The evidence base. *Journal of Intellectual Disability Research*, 46, 47–56.

Kahneman, D. and Tversky, A. (1984). Choices, values and frames. *American Psychologist*, 39, 341–50.

Kahneman, D., Slovic, P. and Tversky, A. (1982). *Judgment under Uncertainty: Heuristics and Biases*. Cambridge: Cambridge University Press.

Kameda, T., Ohtsubo, Y. and Takezawa, M. (1997). Centrality in socio-cognitive network and social influence: An illustration in a group decision making context. *Journal of Personality and Social Psychology*, 73, 296–309.

Kaplan, S. and Garrick, B.J. (1981). On the quantitative definition of risk. *Risk Analysis*, 1, 11–27.

Kemshall, H. (2001). *Risk Assessment and Management of Known Sexual and Violent Offenders: A Review of Current Issues*. London: Policing and Reducing Crime Unit: Police Research Series, Paper 140.

Kemshall, H., Parton, N., Walsh, M. and Waterson, J. (1997). Concepts of risk in relation to organisational structure and functioning within the personal social services and probation. *Social Policy and Administration*, 31, 213–32.

Kettles, A.M. (2004). A concept of forensic risk. *Journal of Psychiatric and Mental Health Nursing*, 11, 484–93.

Kinsella, P. (2000). *Person Centred Risk Assessment*. Oxford: Paradigm.

Koriat, A., Lichenstein, S. and Fischoff, B. (1980). Reasons for confidence. *Journal of Experimental Psychology: Human Learning and Memory*, 6, 107–18.

Kreitner, R. (1998). *Management* (7th edn). Boston, MA: Houghton Mifflin.

Lindsay, W.R. (2002). Research and literature on sex offenders with intellectual and developmental disabilities. *Journal of Intellectual Disability Research*, 46, 74–85.

Lindsay, W.R. and Beail, N. (2004). Assessment: Actuarial prediction and clinical judgement of offending incidents and behaviour for intellectual disability services. *Journal of Applied Research in Intellectual Disabilities*, 17, 229–34.

Lindsay, W.R., Murphy, L., Smith, G., Murphy, D., Edwards, Z., Chittock, C., Grieve, A. and Young, S.J. (2004). The dynamic risk assessment and management system: An assessment of immediate risk of violence for individuals with offending and challenging behaviour. *Journal of Applied Research in Intellectual Disabilities*, 17, 267–74.

Lindsay, W.R., Taylor, J.L. and Sturmey, P. (2004). *Offenders with Developmental Disabilities*. Chichester, UK: Wiley.

Lindsey, P. (1996). The right to choose: Informed consent in the lives of adults with mental retardation and developmental disabilities. *Education and Training in Mental Retardation and Developmental Disabilities*, 30, 171–6.

Lipsedge, M. (2001). Risk management in psychiatry. In Charles Vincent (ed.), *Clinical Risk Management: Enhancing Patient Safety* (2nd edn, pp. 219–40). London: BMJ Books.

Loumidis, K. and Hill, A.B. (1997). Training in groups with intellectual disabilities in social problem solving skills to reduce maladaptive behaviour: The influence of individual difference factors. *Journal of Applied Research in Intellectual Disabilities*, 10, 3, 217–38.

Lowenstein, G.F., Weber, E.U., Hsee, C.K. and Welch, N. (2001). Risk as feelings. *Psychological Bulletin*, 127, 267–86.

Luce, M.F., Bettman, J.R. and Payne, J.W. (1997). Choice processing in emotionally difficult decisions. *Journal of Experimental Psychology: Learning, Memory, and Cognition*, 23, 384–405.

Manthorpe, J., Walsh, M., Alaszewski, A. and Harrison, L. (1997). Issues of risk practice and welfare in learning disability services *Disability and Society*, 12, 69–82.

March, P. (1992). Do photographs help adults with severe mental handicaps make choices? *British Journal of Mental Subnormality*, 38, 122–8.

Mazzucchelli, T.G. (2001). Feel Safe: A pilot study of a protective behaviours programme for people with intellectual disability. *Journal of Intellectual and Developmental Disability*, 26, 115–26.

McAfee, J.K. (1998). Individuals with significant disabilities who are victims of crime. *TASH Newsletter*, 24, 21–4, 30.

McClintock, K., Hall, S. and Oliver, C. (2003). Risk markers associated with challenging behaviours in people with intellectual disabilities: A meta-analytic study. *Journal of Intellectual Disability Research*, 47, 405–16.

McDonnell, A., McEvoy, J. and Dearden, R.L. (1994). Coping with violent situations in the caring environment. In T. Wykes (ed.), *Violence and Health Care Professionals* (pp. 189–206). London: Chapman and Hall.

McDonnell, A.A., Waters, T. and Jones, D. (2002). Low arousal approaches in the management of challenging behaviour. In D. Allen (2001), *Training Carers in Physical Interventions: Research towards Evidence-Based Practice* (pp. 104–13). Kidderminster: BILD.

McGaw, S. and Sturmey, P. (1994). Assessing parents with learning disabilities: The parental skills model. *Child Abuse Review*, 3, 36–51.

McGaw, S., Beckley, K., Connolly, N. and Ball, K. (1998). *Parent Assessment Manual*. Truro: Trecare NHS Trust.

McKenna, F.P. (1993). It won't happen to me: Unrealistic optimism or illusion of control? *British Journal of Psychology*, 84, 39–50.

McMillan, D., Hastings, R.P. and Coldwell, J. (2004). Clinical and actuarial prediction of physical violence in a forensic intellectual disability hospital: A longitudinal study. *Journal of Applied Research in Intellectual Disabilities*, 17, 255–65.

Meehl, P.E. (1954). *Clinical Versus Statistical Prediction*. Minneapolis, MN: University of Minnesota Press.

Meisel, J.D., Roth, L.H. and Lidz, C.W. (1977). Toward a model of the legal doctrine of informed consent. *American Journal of Psychiatry*, 134, 285–89.

Mellers, B. and McGraw, A.P. (2001). Anticipated emotions as guides to choices. *Current Direction in Psychological Science*, 10, 210–14.

Mellers, B.A., Schwartz, A. and Cooke, A.D.J. (1998). Judgment and decision making. *Annual Review of Psychology*, 49, 447–77.

Mellers, B.A., Schwartz, A. and Ritov, I. (1999). Emotion-based choice. *Journal of Experimental Psychology: General*, 128, 1–14.

Monahan, J. (1993). Limiting therapist exposure to Tarasoff liability: Guidelines for risk containment. *American Psychologist*, 48, 242–50.

Mount, B., Ducharme, G. and Beeman, P. (1991). *Person-Centred Development: A Journey in Learning to Listen to People with Disabilities*. Manchester, CT: Comunitas.

Muncie, H.L., Magaziner, J., Hebel, R. and Warren, J.W. (1997). Proxies' decisions about clinical research participation for their charges. *Journal of the American Geriatrics Society*, 45, 929–33.

Munro, E. (1999). Common errors of reasoning in child protection work. *Child Abuse and Neglect*, 23, 745–58.

Murphy, G., Kelly-Pike, A. and McGill, P. (2001). Physical interventions for people with intellectual disabilities: Initial survey of training and evaluation of a policy framework. *Journal of Applied Research in Intellectual Disabilities*, 14, 401–11.

Murphy, G.H. and Clare, I.C.H. (2003). Adult's capacity to make legal decisions. In D. Carson and R. Bull (eds), *Handbook of Psychology in Legal Contexts* (2nd edn, pp. 31–66). London: John Wiley and Sons.

Newell, A. and Simon. H, (1972). *Human Problem Solving*, Englewood Cliffs, NJ: Prentice-Hall.

Perske, R. (1972). The dignity of risk and the mentally retarded. *Mental Retardation*, 10, 24–7.

Pidgeon, N., Hood, C., Jones, C.D., Turner, B.A. and Gibson, R. (1992). *Risk: Analysis, Perception and Management* (pp. 89–134). Royal Society Study Group, London: The Royal Society.

Plous, S. (1993). *The Psychology of Judgment and Decision Making*. New York: McGraw-Hill.

Postmes, T., Spears, R. and Cihangir, S. (2001). Quality of decision making and group norms. *Journal of Personality and Social Psychology*, 80, 918–30.

Powers, L., Wilson, R., Matuszewski, J., Phillips, A., Rein, C., Schumacher, D. and Gensert, J. (1996). Facilitating adolescent self-determination: What does it take? In D.J. Sands and M.L. Wehmeyer (eds), *Self-Determination across the Life Span: Independence and Choice for People with Disabilities* (pp. 257–84). Baltimore, MD: Paul H. Brookes.

Prins, H. (1995). *Offenders, Deviants or Patients* (2nd edn). London: Routledge.

Prins, H. (1999). *Will They Do it Again? Risk Assessment and Management*. London: Routledge.

Raven, J. and Rix, P. (1999). Managing the unmanageable: Risk assessment and risk management in contemporary professional practice. *Journal of Nursing Management*, 7, 201–6.

Reason, J. (1990). *Human Error*. New York: Cambridge University Press.

Reason, J.T. (2001). Understanding adverse events: The human factor. In Charles Vincent (ed.), *Clinical Risk Management: Enhancing Patient Safety* (2nd edn, pp. 9–30). London: BMJ Books.

Redmond, B. (1996). *Listening to Parents*. Dublin: The Family Studies Centre, University College Dublin.

Reed, J. (1997). Risk assessment and clinical management: The lessons from recent inquiries. *British Journal of Psychiatry*, 170, 4–7.

Rogers, R. (2000). The uncritical acceptance of risk assessment in forensic practice. *Law and Human Behaviour*, 24, 595–605.

Rose, J. (1993). Stress and staff in residential settings: The move from hospital to the community. *Mental Handicap Research*, 6, 312–32.

Rottenstreich, Y. and Tversky, A. (1997). Unpacking, repacking, and anchoring: Advances in support theory. *Psychological Review*, 104, 406–15.

Sawyer, J. (1966). Measurement and prediction, clinical and statistical. *Psychological Bulletin*, 66, 178–200.

Schon, D. (1991). *The Reflective Practitioner* (2nd edn). New York: Basic Books.

Secker-Walker, J. and Taylor-Adams, S. (2001). Clinical incident reporting. In Charles Vincent (ed.), *Clinical Risk Management: Enhancing Patient Safety* (2nd edn, pp. 419–38). London: BMJ Books.

Sellars, C. (2002). *Risk Assessment in People with Learning Disabilities*. Oxford: Blackwell Publishing.

Shepperdson, B. (2000). Negotiating adolescence. In D. May (ed.), *Transition and Change in the Lives of People with Intellectual Disabilities* (pp. 55–74). London: Jessica Kingsley Publishers

Shevin, M. and Klein, N. (1984). The importance of choice-making skills for students with severe disabilities. *Journal of the Association for Persons with Severe Handicaps*, 9, 159–66.

Short, E.J. and Evans, S.W. (1990). Individual differences in cognitive and social problem solving and planning. In N.W. Bray (ed.), *International Review of Research in Mental Retardation* (vol. 16, pp. 89–123). San Diego, CA: Academic Press.

Sigelman, C. and Budd, E. (1986). Pictures as an aid in questioning mentally retarded persons. *Rehabilitation Counselling Bulletin*, 29, 173–81.

Simon, H.A. (1957). *Models of Man, Social and Rational: Mathematical Essays on Rational Human Behaviour in Social Settings*. New York: Wiley.

Skowronski, J.J. and Carlston, D.E. (1989). Negativity and extremity biases in impression formation: A review of explanations. *Psychological Bulletin*, 105, 131–42.

Slovic, P. (1987). Perception of risk. *Science*, 236, 280–5.

Slovic, P. (1992). Perception of risk: Reflections on the psychometric paradigm. In S. Krimsky, and D. Golding (eds), *Social Theories of Risk* (pp.117–52). Westport, CT: Praeger.

Slovic, P. (1996). Trust, emotion, sex, politics and science: Surveying the risk assessment battlefield. In M. Bazerman, D. Messick, A. Tenbrunsel and K. Wade-Benzoni (eds), *Psychological Perspectives to Environment and Ethics in Management* (pp. 277–313). San Francisco: Jossey-Bass.

Slovic, P., Fischoff, B. and Lichtenstein, S. (1982). Facts versus fears: Understanding perceived risk. In D. Kahneman, P. Slovic and A. Tversky (eds), *Judgment under Uncertainty: Heuristics and Biases* (pp. 463–89). Cambridge: Cambridge University Press.

Smith, M. and Willner, P. (2004). Psychological factors in risk assessment and management of inappropriate sexual behaviour by men with intellectual disabilities. *Journal of Applied Research in Intellectual Disabilities*, 17, 285–97.

Smyth, M. and McConkey, R. (2003). Future aspirations of students with severe learning disabilities and of their parents on leaving special schooling. *British Journal of Learning Disabilities*, 31, 54–9.

Snowden, P. (1997). Practical aspects of clinical risk assessment and management. *British Journal of Psychiatry*, 170, 32–4.

Stasser, G. and Stewart, D. (1992). Discovery of hidden profiles by decision-making groups: Solving a problem versus making a judgment, *Journal of Personality and Social Psychology*, 31, 244–65.

Sykes, D. (2005). Risks and rights: The need to redress the imbalance. *Journal of Intellectual and Developmental Disability*, 30, 185–8.

Szmulker, G. (2003). Risk assessment: Numbers and 'values'. *Psychiatric Bulletin*, 27, 205–7.

Taber, T.A. Alberto, P.A., Hughes, M. and Seltzer, A. (2002). A strategy for students with moderate disabilities when lost in the community. *Research and Practice for People with Severe Disabilities*, 27, 141–52.

Taber, T.A., Alberto, P.A., Seltzer, A. and Hughes, M. (2003). Obtaining assistance when lost in the community using cell phones. *Research and Practice for People with Severe Disabilities*, 28, 105–16.

Taggart, L. and McConkey, R. (2001). Working practices employed within and across hospital services and community service provision for adults with an intellectual disability and additional needs. *Journal of Learning Disabilities*, 5, 175–90.

Taylor, J., Keddie, T. and Lee, S. (2003). Working with sex offenders with intellectual disability: Evaluation of an introductory workshop for direct care staff. *Journal of Intellectual Disability Research*, 47, 203–9.

Teigen, K.H. and Brun, W. (1997). Anticipating the future: Appraising risk and uncertainty. In R. Ranyard, W.R. Crozier and O. Svenson (eds), *Decision Making: Cognitive Models and Explanations* (pp. 113–27). London: Routledge.

Tetlock, P.E. (2002). Social functionalist frameworks for judgment and choice: Intuitive politicians, theologians, and prosecutors. *Psychological Review*, 109, 451–71.

Tindale, R.S., Kameda, T. and Hinsz, V.B. (2003). Group decision making. In Michael, A. Hogg and Joel Cooper (eds), *The Sage Book of Social Psychology* (pp. 381–403). London: Sage.

Turner, B.A. and Pidgeon, N.F. (1997). *Man Made Disasters* (2nd edn). Oxford: Butterworth-Heinemann.

Turner, S. (2000). Forensic risk assessment in intellectual disabilities: The evidence base and current practice in one English region. *Journal of Applied Research in Intellectual Disabilities*, 13, 239–55.

Tversky, A. and Koehler, D.J. (1994). Support theory: A nonextensional representation of subjective probability. *Psychological Review*, 101, 547–67.

Tversky, A. and Kahneman, D. (1974). Judgement in uncertainty: Heuristics and biases. *Science*, 185, 1124–31.

Tversky, A. and Shafir, E. (1992). Choice under conflict: The dynamics of deferred decision. *Psychological Science*, 3, 358–61.

Tymchuk, A. (1990). *Parents with Mental Retardation: A National Strategy*. Los Angeles, SHARE/UCLA Parenting Project, Department of Psychiatry, School of Medicine, CA: UCLA.

Tymchuk, A.J., Andron, L. and Bavolek, S.J. (1990). *Parenting Skills: Assessment and Interview*. Family Park City, UT: Development Resources, Inc.

Tymchuk A.J., Groen A. and Dolyniuk C.A. (2000). Health, safety, and well-being reading recognition abilities of young parents with functional disabilities: Construction and preliminary validation of a prescriptive assessment instrument. *Journal of Developmental and Physical Disabilities*, 12, 349–66.

Tymchuk, A.J., Hamada, D., Andron, L. and Anderson, S. (1990). Home safety training with mothers who are mentally retarded. *Education and Training of the Mentally Retarded* (June), 142–9.

Tymchuk, A., Yokota, A. and Rahbar, B. (1990). Decision-making abilities of mothers with mental retardation. *Research on Developmental Disabilities*, 11, 97–109.

Tyne, A. (1994). Taking responsibility and giving power. *Disability and Society*, 9, 249–54.

Vincent, C. and Taylor-Adams, S. (2001). The investigation and analysis of clinical incidents. In Charles Vincent (ed.), *Clinical Risk Management: Enhancing Patient Safety* (2nd edn, pp. 439–60). London: BMJ Books.

Von Neumann, J. and Morgenstern, O. (1944). *Theory of Games and Economic Behaviour*. Princeton, NJ: Princeton University Press.

Walshe, K. (2001). The development of clinical risk management. In Charles Vincent (ed.), *Clinical Risk Management: Enhancing Patient Safety* (2nd edn, pp. 45–60). London: BMJ Books.

Wanless, L. and Jahoda, A. (2002). Responses of staff towards people with mild to moderate intellectual disability who behave aggressively: A cognitive emotional analysis. *Journal of Intellectual Disability Research*, 46, 507–16.

Ward, K.M. and Bosek, R.L. (2002). Behavioural risk management: Supporting individuals with developmental disabilities who exhibit inappropriate sexual behaviours. *Research and Practice for Persons with Severe Disabilities*, 27, 2–42.

Warren, J.W., Sobal, J., Tenney, J.H., Hoopes, J.M., Damron, D., Levenson, S., DeForges, B.R. and Muncie, H.L. (1986). Informed consent by proxy: An issue in research with elderly patients. *New England Journal of Medicine*, 315, 1124–8.

Watts, D., Bindman, J., Slade, M., Holloway, F., Rosen, A. and Thornicroft, G. (2004). Clinical assessment of risk decision support (CARDS): The development and evaluation of a feasible violence risk assessment for routine psychiatric practice. *Journal of Mental Health*, 13, 569–81.

Watts, N.T. (1995). Teaching the components of clinical decision analysis in the classroom and clinic. In Joy Higgs and Mark Jones (eds), *Clinical Reasoning in the Health Professions* (pp. 204–12). Oxford: Butterworth-Heinman.

Wehmeyer, M.L. (1992). Self-determination and the education of students with mental retardation. *Education and Training in Mental Retardation*, 27, 302–14.

Wehmeyer, M.L. (1998). Self-determination and individuals with significant disabilities: Examining meanings and misinterpretations. *Journal of the Association for Persons with Severe Handicaps*, 23, 5–16.

Wehmeyer, M.L. (2001). Self-determination and mental retardation. In L.M. Glidden (ed.), *International Review of Research Mental Retardation* (vol. 24, pp. 1–48). Englewood Cliffs, NJ: Academic Press.

Wehmeyer, M.L. and Garner, N.W. (2003). The impact of personal characteristics of people with intellectual and developmental disability on self-determination and autonomous functioning. *Journal of Applied Research in Intellectual Disabilities*, 16, 255–65.

Wehmeyer, M.L., Abery, B., Mithaug, D.E and Stancliffe, R. (2003). *Self-Determination: Theoretical Foundations for Education*. Springfield, IL: Charles C. Thomas.

Wehmeyer, M.L., Agran, M. and Hughes, C. (1998). *Teaching Self-Determination to Students with Disabilities: Basic Skills for Successful Transition*. Baltimore: MD: Paul H. Brookes Publishing Co.

Wehmeyer, M.L., Kelchner, K. and Richards, S. (1996). Essential characteristics of self-determined behaviour in individuals with mental retardation. *American Journal on Mental Retardation*, 100, 632–42.

West, M.M. and Parent, W. (1992). Consumer choice and empowerment in supported employment services: Issues and strategies. *Journal of the American Association for Persons with Severe Handicaps*, 17, 47–52.

Wharton, F. (1992). Risk management: Basic concepts and general principles. In J. Ansell and F. Wharton (eds), *Risk: Analysis, Assessment and Management* (pp. 1–14). Chichester: John Wiley.

Wong, J.G., Clare, I.C.H., Gunn, M.J. and Holland, A.J. (1999). Capacity to make health care decisions: Its importance in clinical practice. *Psychological Medicine*, 29, 437–46.

Wong, J.G., Clare, I.C.H., Holland, A.J., Watson, P.C. and Gunn, M. (2000). The capacity of people with a 'mental disability' to make a health care decision. *Psychological Medicine*, 30, 295–306.

Worthley, J.A. (1999). The ethical dimension of ordinary professional life. *Healthcare Executive* (Sep/Oct), 6–10.

Index